THE U.S. ATLAS

OF NUCLEAR FALLOUT

VOLUME III

COUNTY COMPARISONS

THE U.S. ATLAS

OF NUCLEAR FALLOUT

VOLUME III

COUNTY COMPARISONS

RICHARD L. MILLER

LEGIS BOOKS

Div of LEGIS CORP

THE WOODLANDS, TEXAS

LEGIS BOOKS
Division of LEGIS CORP.
P.O. Box 7888
The Woodlands, Texas 77387-7888

Printed in the United States of America

Printing number

1 2 3 4 5 6 7 8 9 10

Library of Congress Cataloging-in-Publication Data

Miller, Richard L. (Richard Lee)
The U.S. Atlas of Nuclear Fallout: Volume III: County Comparisons
1. Nuclear weapons–Testing.
2. Radioactive fallout–United States.
3. United States–History.
4. United States–Geography.
5. Science Reference.

ISBN: I-881043-10X (Hardcover Edition)

ISBN I-881043-126 (Softcover Edition)

For Chrissy McHenry

THE U.S ATLAS OF NUCLEAR FALLOUT
1951-1962

VOLUMES IN THE SERIES

Volume I: Total Fallout (Technical Edition) ISBN 1881043-11-8

Volume II: Total Fallout (Abridged General Reader Edition)

ISBN 1881043-13-4

Volume II: Radionuclides   ISBN 1881043-15-0

Volume III: County Comparisons   ISBN 1881043-12-6

Volume IV: Trajectories   ISBN 1881043-07-X

Volume V: Calculations   ISBN 1881043-19-3

CONTENTS

ACKNOWLEDGEMENTS

The volumes in this series would have been impossible without the dedication and commitment of the scientists of the National Cancer Institute, who produced the original I-131 deposition data. Theirs was the most difficult task of all, and they have my deepest appreciation and respect.

I would also like to thank the following software companies for donating or providing discounted software to support my research: Palisades Corporation (@Risk and Risk Optimizer); Attar Software (Xpert Rule); Decisioneering (Crystal Ball Predictor); Spotfire (Spotfire Pro); MapInfo (MapInfo Pro); Golden Software (Didger); Cytel Software (EGRET); Salford Systems (CART and MARS); and SPSS (Systat). And, of course, a tip of the hat to Microsoft, maker of the only software that should be classified as heavy equipment: Excel 97. Additionally, I would like to express thanks to the makers of Spreadsheet Assistant™ for Excel 97 and 2000. Without it, the work would have taken four times as long to complete.

Thanks to Lynn Anspaugh of the University of Utah for his help and suggestions regarding the Hicks Tables, and to Owen Hoffman of SENES, Oak Ridge, Tennessee, for his assistance, suggestions and patience regarding geometric means, geometric standard deviations, arithmetic means of log normal distributions, and Monte Carlo simulations.

It should be noted that Cliff Honicker performed the original investigations on rainouts in both South Dakota and Minnesota, and also kindly provided me with the AEC reports of investigations. The device specs were provided by the indefatigable nuke researcher Chuck Hansen.

Special thanks to Leah Stratmann, for her excellent work transcribing the 1983-4 NCI Cancer Atlas for the 513 Midwestern counties, and to the fine technical writers Roy Constible and Mary Constible for the many hours spent transcribing the Hicks Tables to Excel. Thirty radionukes and not a single mistake. Also a tip of the hat to my friends Brian Thorne, Walter Hirsch and Wally Cummins for their unflagging encouragement and optimism.

And now a pause for the legal stuff: The map that appears on the cover of Volume I and the city lists of fallout trajectories are reprinted with the publisher's permission from *Under the Cloud: The Decades of Nuclear Testing* by Richard L. Miller, copyright © 1991 by Richard L. Miller (Two-Sixty Press, 1999).

Finally, I would like to thank my mother, Ruth E. Miller and my wife, Kim and daughter Trace for their continued interest and encouragement and support throughout the long days and nights working on this project. This book belongs to them.

PREFACE TO THE SERIES

The era of aboveground nuclear testing at the Nevada Test Site began on January 27, 1951 with the detonation of Ranger ABLE. For over ten years millions of Curies of radioactive isotopes were deposited across the country, making their way into the food chain and exposing several generations of Americans to radiation. While the Atomic Energy Commission was aware that a thunderstorm could theoretically scavenge an entire nuclear cloud within an hour, there was no effort to evaluate hot spots and rainouts downwind of the Test Site. Similarly, there were relatively few attempts to evaluate potential links between nuclear fallout and disease rates.

In 1981 Harry G. Hicks published tables that allowed researchers to theoretically determine deposition rates of over a hundred radionuclides. Using the Hicks Tables, and fallout data from the 1950s and early 1960s, any researcher with a computer could determine deposition values for any of over a hundred radioisotopes.. Despite this, no research project was ever launched.

In 1997, after 15 years of work, the National Cancer Institute published fallout data for every county in the continental United States. Yet, the values were for only one radionuclide, the relatively short-lived I-131, a radioisotope that accounts for approximately 2 percent of the total fallout deposited across the country.

Currently (July, 2001) there are indications of further research by the NCI and other government agencies regarding analysis of possible links between radionuclides in fallout and cancer.

Hopefully, this series of books will contribute to that process.

PREFACE TO VOLUME III:
COUNTY COMPARISONS

The first volume of this series, **Total Fallout**, provided an overview of the calculation processes used to obtain the data   And, as the name suggests, the primary focus of the first volume involved the overall total fallout patterns both from each aboveground test, but from the entire group of tests.

Volume II, **Radionuclides** discussed the fallout in terms of selected radionuclides, derived from ratios found in the Hicks Tables.

This book, Volume III **County Comparisons**, continues the effort by identifying *specific instances of fallout deposition* by date, shot and county. Like the earlier books, a brief statistical analysis is included evaluating the data against published cancer rates in the area.

As before, the cancer data was obtained from three sources, the National Cancer Institute's 1983 survey, the National Cancer Institute's 2000 Atlas and the Centers for Disease Control's WONDER site.   Fallout deposition information was derived from the National Cancer Institute's 1997 I-131 study.

In statistics, multiple comparisons can result in high correlations simply due to chance.   Thus, the statistics appearing in this series were analyzed using a procedure called the *Bonferroni correction*, which divides the alpha significance level (for 95% confidence interval, the alpha is 0.05) by the number of comparisons made per variable.   For example, a single pairwise comparison of variables, in order to reach significance at the 0.05 probability level may require a test statistic (Z score) of 1.96.   Applying the Bonferroni correction, the probability level is first divided by the number of comparisons and then the Z score is calculated.   Ten pairwise comparisons, to attain a significance level of $p<0.05$ (95% probability that the result is not due to chance) would require a Z score associated with [0.05/10 = 0.005], or approximately 2.80.   To a attain a $p<0.05$ level (95% confidence that the association was not due to chance alone.) or *five hundred* pairwise comparisons would require a Z score of 3.88.

Due to low background population values, many of the county rates listed in the Centers for Disease Control's WONDER data are considered unstable, or are theoretically subject to fluctuation based upon changes in the raw incidence values. That said, the numbers still suggest clear patterns of association between fallout events and cancer rates. Further work should help determine if there is indeed a causative link between intense fallout events and certain cancers in a particular population.

INTRODUCTION TO THE SERIES

In January 1983, the 97th Congress directed the National Institute of Health to evaluate the extent and effects of Iodine-131 (I-131) fallout resulting from the Nevada nuclear tests conducted in the 1950s and early 1960s[1][2]

The task was finally completed and published in 1997. The report consisted of I-131 fallout deposition rates from nearly 60 above-ground and subsurface nuclear tests—for each of more than 3000 counties. The finished product included data for up to 20 fallout days subsequent to the nuclear test. All together, the report was equivalent to more than 120,000 pages of data.

Officials at the National Cancer Institute decided that publication of such a mass of data would be feasible only over the Internet. Interested citizens could download data for their own home counties and learn just how much I-131 was deposited from each test, and when. Not only that, they could enter their birth date and estimated milk consumption and read an estimate of the radiation exposure to their thyroid.

There were some problems, however. The uncertainty involved in the original sampling procedures and analysis resulted in data with a wide range. So, instead of presenting the information as minimums and maximums over a certain confidence interval, the information was given in terms of the Geometric Mean (GM) and Geometric Standard Deviation (GSD). Statistically, the geometric mean represents the average estimate of the log normal distribution, and the geometric standard deviation refers to the uncertainty in the estimate. In practical terms, the Geometric Mean refers to the average estimated fallout while the Geometric Standard Deviation refers to the uncertainty around that average.

While these statistical procedures were certainly appropriate for the subject, it was unclear how the data should be interpreted. Simply dividing the GM by the GSD results in a minimum value (lower bound), while multiplying the GM by this same GSD value will result in a *maximum* value (upper bound) with a confidence interval of 67%. Squaring the GSD before performing the same mathematical operations results in a wider range—lower minimums and higher maximums—but with a 97% confidence interval. In essence, each pair of NCI fallout data—the GM and GSD combination— represent *ranges* of values.

This presented an obvious problem: Should the reader assume that the county in question received the amount represented by the Geometric Mean? Even if the reader took the time to make the calculations for each particular shot-day, should she assume the maximum value, or the minimum value—and at which confidence interval?

The natural inclination would be to simply take the difference between the maximum and minimum and divide by two to obtain an average. But this procedure would work only if the distribution were normally distributed—as in a bell-shaped curve. And fallout is *not* normally-distributed. Given the NCI's calculations, fallout is *lognormally* distributed. To average the fallout using the standard procedures would result in an overestimation the Geometric Means of the fallout by 4.7 times. As a compromise I chose to evaluate the data based upon a special form of average: the **arithmetic mean of the lognormal distribution**. The formula is expressed as:

$$\mathbf{AM} = GM\left(\exp\left(\frac{\left(\ln GSD\right)^2}{2}\right)\right)$$

Where AM =Arithmetic Mean of the Lognormal Distribution;

GM = Geometric mean of the lognormal distribution

GSD = Geometric standard deviation of the lognormal distribution

exp = exponent e = 2.7183

ln = natural logarithm

Using the total fallout values from shot Tumbler-Snapper George (TS-7) as an example, the arithmetic means of the lognormal distribution values are typically equal to one-third (32.8%) of the simple means-between-bounds (97% confidence interval) values and twice (1.97 times) the raw geometric mean values.

I-131 AND TOTAL FALLOUT

The published NCI data included values for only a single radioactive component of fallout—one of the radioactive isotopes of the element iodine. This particular radioactive isotope, I-131, makes up approximately 2 percent of the initial radionuclide output. In theory, one can determine total fallout simply by multiplying the I-131 activity values by 50 to arrive at the total fallout values. In practice, however, it is considerably more complicated.

For one thing, different nuclear tests produce different groups of radionuclides as well as varying amounts of I-131. To make matters more complicated, each radionuclide has its own particular chemical and physical composition and decay scheme. Thus, the ratio of I-131 to total fallout for a particular test will vary depending on which day post-shot it is evaluated. The ratio between the activity level of I-131 and the activity level of total fallout on the day after the nuclear test will be significantly different than the ratio between the I-131 activity and total fallout activity on the second day after the test. In short, the ratio varies not only by the nuclear test, but also according to how many days have elapsed since detonation.

All these assumptions were theoretical. It would take experimentation and hard work to determine the actual ratios between I-131 and total fallout (as well as the other radionuclides).

Fortunately, that work had been done —and published— by Livermore physicist Harry G. Hicks in 1981. Through experimentation and long hours on a mainframe computer, Hicks calculated ratios for more than 100 radionuclides produced by every aboveground test ever detonated at the Nevada Test Site.

The work came to be called the Hicks Tables and, importantly, I-131 was among the radionuclides listed. After some interval analysis to recover the missing days (the Hicks Tables included only days 1, 2, 5 and 10), ratios were calculated that could be used to determine total fallout from I-131 activity values. From this point, relative total fallout activities could be determined, by nuclear test and by shot day, for every county in the United States.

The subject of total fallout formed the basis for the first volume. Volume II characterized the radionuclide deposition pattern. This book, Volume III discusses individual fallout events on a county-by-county basis.

Hopefully, this series will provide a new perspective on an important part of our history and will stimulate further research in the field.

ORGANIZATION OF VOLUME III

Volume III of the **U.S. ATLAS OF NUCLEAR FALLOUT** is a continuation of the U.S. Atlas of Nuclear Fallout Volumes I and II. This volume is divided into the following main sections:

- Sections 1, **INDIVIDUAL FALLOUT EVENTS BY U.S. COUNTY** is a listing of individual fallout events for each county in the United States, ranked from highest to lowest amount of deposition.

- Section 2, **U.S. COUNTY RANKS FOR SIGNIFICANT FALLOUT EVENTS** consists of a table listing the times a U.S. county appeared among the top ten counties for highest deposition of fallout. Also included are the date of the fallout event and the number of times that county has appeared in the top ten nationally for highest levels of fallout.

- Section 3, **TOP 500 SHOT DAYS: HIGHEST AVERAGE TOTAL FALLOUT BY DATE** ranks the highest 500 fallout event dates or "shot days."

- Section 4, **COUNTIES RANKED BY AMOUNT OF NUCLEAR FALLOUT DEPOSITED ON SINGLE FALLOUT DAY** lists the shot, the date, and the five counties receiving the most fallout nationally for those dates.

- Section 5, **COUNTIES RECEIVING MOST FALLOUT NATIONWIDE FOR A SINGLE FALLOUT DAY** lists the number one fallout counties and the number of times these counties have been number one during the aboveground nuclear testing period.

- Section 6 **INDIVIDUAL FALLOUT EVENTS ASSOCIATED WITH CANCER RATES**, includes statistical analyses of shot days against cancer rates for the all United States counties as well as for the counties in the states of Iowa, Illinois, Kansas, Missouri, and Nebraska.

All information regarding fallout is derived from the data published in the 1997 National Cancer Institute I-131 study.

ADDITIONAL INFORMATION

2-D MAPS

Two-dimensional maps are presented showing areas of fallout by county. Among the volumes in this series, the information is organized in two different ways: first by **equal intervals** of data and then by **equal numbers** of counties. The equal interval maps and the equal number maps both represent the same total fallout values (arithmetic mean of lognormal distributions of fallout) but the data is categorized differently. Equal interval maps divide the fallout **values** into four equivalent categories, and then shade counties according to the fallout category.

Equal-umber maps divide the counties into four equally- numbered groups and assign shading based upon relative amounts of fallout among the groups.

Maps organized by equal number of counties typically show greater fallout coverage, while the maps organized by equal intervals show only the counties with the *highest* fallout amounts.

3-D MAPS: RELATIVE AVERAGE TOTAL FALLOUT

Three-dimensional prism maps of the United States represent relative total fallout for each NCI-evaluated nuclear test. County borders are projected into the third dimension (z axis) in proportion to their deposition of fallout *relative to the entire United States* and is based on the **equal interval map** (see above). Thus, only the counties with the highest relative amount of fallout will ascend above the plane of the map. Some shots may include several 3-D prism maps with close-ups of hot spots or fallout paths.

NAMING CONVENTIONS

In this series, the nuclear tests are generally referred to first by the series, then by the specific name, as in Upshot-Knothole HARRY. Abbreviated, the shot may be listed as UK9 (shot HARRY was the ninth listed by the National Cancer Institute's I-131 survey in the Upshot-Knothole Series), followed by the number of the fallout day. For example, UK9-3 refers to the third day of fallout resulting from the ninth shot in the Upshot-Knothole Series, as listed by the National Cancer Institute.

Where space permits, shots are listed by the series name or abbreviation, followed by the shot name. Some nuclear tests were not included in the NCI study. Others, such as Teapot BEE and Teapot ESS were combined. Also, some tests, such as Ranger-FOX (R-3) and Plumbbob STOKES (PB-7), which were associated with minimal fallout, were excluded from some lists and maps. A complete list of abbreviations used in the book is found at the end of this section.

SHOT DAYS

The term "shot day" refers to a particular day after detonation. For example, TS1-1 refers to the day of detonation of the first shot in the Tumbler-Snapper series, that is, Tumbler-Snapper ABLE. In this case, that day would be April 1, 1952. The term TS1-2 refers to the first day after detonation of Tumbler-Snapper 1, or April 2, 1952. TS1-3 refers to the *second* day after the detonation. In this case, since TS1 refers to shot Tumbler-Snapper ABLE, and since that detonation occurred on April 1, 1952 (see above), TS1-3 refers to April 3, 1952.

CURIES AND NANOCURIES

Radioactive forms of elements are called radioactive isotopes or *radionuclides.* These radionuclides are found in great quantity in nuclear fallout. Depending upon their internal nuclear makeup, the individual atoms will change from a state of higher energy but less stability, to a state of lower energy but greater stability. As these transformations occur, radiation is given off from the nucleus of the atom. While the type of radiation depends on the radionuclide, the transformation itself can be thought of as the central radioactive "event." That is, a single unit of radiation from a radioactive material such as fallout is direct result of the transformation of a single atom from a state of higher energy to a state of lower energy. The energy difference is, in effect, the radiation itself.

Scientists term such transformation *disintegration.* A radionuclide is said to disintegrate or decay from a state of relative instability to a state of greater stability. All things being equal, the faster the rate of decay or transformation of these radioactive atoms the more radiation is emitted. A substance that decays rapidly, emitting more units of radiation per second is said to have a higher activity than a substance that decays slowly, emitting fewer units of radiation per second.

This rate of decay, or *activity*, can be measured in units called *Curies.* One Curie of activity is defined as producing 3.7×10^{10} disintegrations per second.

As an illustration, suppose someone somehow traveled to ground zero and scooped up a vial containing a mixture of very hot nuclear fallout. If a perfectly calibrated Geiger counter placed near the vial recorded 37,000,000,000 clicks per second, the vial could be said to have an activity equal to *one Curie.*

An aboveground nuclear test such as occurred in the 1950s, released fallout into the atmosphere that was equal to *millions* of Curies of activity.

Dispersion of a 1000-ft diameter nuclear cloud over thousands of cubic miles of air will decrease the overall activity considerably. As a consequence, the radioactivity of the fallout, when it finally fell to earth, was measured not in Curies, but in millionths and billionths of a Curie.

In Section 8, the fallout values for counties with the highest levels of fallout are expressed in terms of microCuries. you will see microCurie represented by the symbol μCi. *One microCurie is defined as radiological decay equal to 37,000 disintegrations per second.* (37,000,000,000 divided by 1,000,000).

The fallout values used for the maps in Sections 1-7 and for the Table in Section 9 are given in *nanoCuries*. A nanoCurie represents an activity level equal to one thousandth of a microCurie. NanoCuries, are represented in this book by the symbol nCi, and represent an activity equal to 37 disintegrations per second.

The 1997 National Cancer Institute study gave fallout levels in terms of nanocuries per square meter (nCi/sq meter). A square meter is equal to 10.76 square feet, or an area 3 ft. 3 inches on a side. Thus, if you read that fallout from a particular shot produced an average of 1 nCi/sq meter on a given county on a particular day, you may reasonably conclude that for each square plot of land 3.3 ft on a side, the fallout produced 37 units of radiation. Similarly, since there are 2,589,988.1 square meters in a square mile, you can conclude that, on average, 1 nCi/square meter is equivalent to 95,829,559.7 units of radiation produced per square mile. ($37 \times 2,589,988.1$)

RELATIVE FALLOUT VALUES

A primary purpose of this series is to show *relative* fallout levels for each county from each nuclear test. To do that, arithmetic means were calculated from the geometric means and geometric standard deviations given in the NCI tables. These arithmetic means were then used as central values to evaluate relative fallout levels. Where tables or maps refer to Averages, the term specifically refers to the *Arithmetic mean of the log-normal distribution.* The data represents not only estimated fallout levels, but also uncertainties associated with measurement. Thus, the numbers found in the tables should be interpreted carefully. Hopefully, they are starting points for further research.

	SHOT/SERIES NAME	DETONATION DATE	INCLUDED IN NCI STUDY?
R	Ranger Series	Jan 27-Feb 6 1951	Yes
BJ	Buster-Jangle Series	22 Oct-29 Nov 1951	Yes
TS	Tumbler-Snapper Series	15 Apr Jun 1952	Yes
UK	Upshot-Knothole Series	17 Mar-4 Jun 1953	Yes
TP	Teapot Series	18 Feb-15 May 1955	Yes
PB	Plumbbob Series	28 May-7 Oct 1957	Yes
S	Shot SEDAN	6 Jul 1962	Yes
(Ranger ABLE)	Ranger ABLE	27 Jan 1951	No
R1	Ranger BAKER	28 Jan 1951	Yes
(Ranger EASY)	Ranger EASY	1 Feb 1951	No
R2	Ranger BAKER-2	2 Feb 1951	Yes
R3	Ranger-FOX	6 Feb 51	Yes
(Buster-Jangle ABLE)	Buster-Jangle ABLE	22 Oct 1951	No
BJ1	Buster-Jangle BAKER	28 Oct 1951	Yes
BJ2	Buster-Jangle CHARLIE	30 Oct 1951	Yes
BJ3	Buster-Jangle DOG	1 Nov 1951	Yes
BJ4	Buster-Jangle EASY	5 Nov 1951	Yes
BJ5	Buster-Jangle SUGAR	19 Nov 1951	Yes
BJ6	Buster-Jangle UNCLE	29 Nov 1951	Yes
TS1	Tumbler-Snapper ABLE	1 Apr 1952	Yes
TS2	Tumbler-Snapper BAKER	15 Apr 1952	Yes
TS3	Tumbler-Snapper CHARLIE	22 Apr 1952	Yes
TS4	Tumbler-Snapper DOG	1 May 1952	Yes

ABBREVIATION	SHOT/SERIES NAME	DETONATION DATE	INCLUDED IN NCI STUDY?
	DOG		
TS5	Tumbler-Snapper EASY	7 May 1952	Yes
TS6	Tumbler-Snapper FOX	25 May 1952	Yes
TS7	Tumbler-Snapper GEORGE	1 Jun 1952	Yes
TS8	Tumbler-Snapper HOW	5 Jun 1952	Yes
UK1	Upshot-Knothole ANNIE	17 Mar 1953	Yes
UK2	Upshot-Knothole NANCY	24 Mar 1953	Yes
UK3	Upshot-Knothole RUTH	31 Mar 1953	Yes
UK4	Upshot-Knothole DIXIE	6 Apr 1953	Yes
UK5	Upshot-Knothole RAY	11 Apr 1953	Yes
UK6	Upshot-Knothole BADGER	18 Apr 1953	Yes
UK7	Upshot-Knothole SIMON	25 Apr 1953	Yes
UK8	Upshot-Knothole ENCORE	8 May 1953	Yes
UK9	Upshot-Knothole HARRY	19 May 1953	Yes
UK10	Upshot-Knothole GRABLE	25 May 1953	Yes
UK11	Upshot-Knothole CLIMAX	4 Jun 1953	Yes
TP1	Teapot WASP	18 Feb 1955	Yes
TP2	Teapot MOTH	22 Feb 1955	Yes
TP3	Teapot TESLA	1 Mar 1955	Yes
TP4	Teapot TURK	7 Mar 1955	Yes
TP5	Teapot HORNET	12 Mar 1955	Yes
TP6	Teapot BEE	22 Mar 1955	Combined with Teapot ESS

	SHOT/SERIES NAME	DETONATION DATE	INCLUDED IN NCI STUDY?
TP6	Teapot ESS	23 Mar 1955	Combined with Teapot BEE
TP7	Teapot APPLE-1	29 Mar 1955	Yes
(Teapot WASP PRIME)	Teapot WASP PRIME	29 Mar 1955	No
(Teapot HA)	Teapot High Altitude	6 Apr 1955	No
TP8	Teapot POST	9 Apr 1955	Yes
TP9	Teapot MET	15 Apr 1955	Yes
TP10	Teapot APPLE-2	5 May 1955	Yes
TP11	Teapot ZUCCHINI	15 May 1955	Yes
PB1	Plumbbob BOLTZMANN	28 May 1957	Combined with Plumbbob FRANKLIN
PB1	Plumbbob FRANKLIN	2 Jun 1957	Combined with Plumbbob BOLTZMANN
PB2	Plumbbob WILSON	18 Jun 1957	Yes
PB3	Plumbbob PRISCILLA	24 Jun 1957	Yes
PB4	Plumbbob HOOD	5 Jul 1957	Yes
PB5	Plumbbob DIABLO	15 Jul 1957	Yes
(Plumbbob JOHN)	Plumbbob JOHN	19 Jul 1957	No
PB6	Plumbbob KEPLER	24 Jul, 1957	Combined with Plumbbob OWENS
PB6	Plumbbob OWENS	25 Jul 1957	Combined with Plumbbob KEPLER
PB7	Plumbbob STOKES	7 Aug 1957	Yes (but not fallout listed)
PB8	Plumbbob SHASTA	18 Aug 1957	Yes

ABBREVIATION	SHOT/SERIES NAME	DETONATION DATE	INCLUDED IN NCI STUDY?
PB9	Plumbbob DOPPLER	23 Aug 1957	Yes
PB10	Plumbbob FRANKLIN PRIME	30 Aug 1957	Yes (but no fallout listed)
PB11	Plumbbob SMOKY	31 Aug 1957	Yes
PB12	Plumbbob GALILEO	2 Sep 1957	Yes
PB13	Plumbbob WHEELER	6 Sep 1957	Combined with Plumbbob COULOMB B and Plumbbob LA PLACE
PB13	Plumbbob COULOMB B	6 Sep 1957	Combined with Plumbbob WHEELER and Plumbbob LA PLACE
PB13	Plumbbob LA PLACE	8 Sep 1957	Combined with Plumbbob WHEELER and Plumbbob COULOMB B
PB14	Plumbbob FIZEAU	14 Sep 1957	Yes
PB15	Plumbbob NEWTON	16 Sep 1957	Yes
PB 16	Plumbbob WHITNEY	23 Sep 1957	Yes
PB 17	Plumbbob CHARLESTON	28 Sep 1957	Yes
PB18	Plumbbob MORGAN	7 Oct 1957	Yes
S or SEDAN	Storax SEDAN	6 Jul 1962	Yes

	SHOT/SERIES NAME	DETONATION DATE	INCLUDED IN NCI STUDY?

NOTES

1 Eisler, Peter and Steve Sternberg. "Fallout: Did It Harm? Study shows contaminants fell far from Nevada test site." USA Today. 26 Jul 1997.

1 Section 7(a) of Public Law 97-414 directs the Secretary of Health and Human Services to "(1) conduct scientific research and prepare analysis necessary to develop valid and credible assessments of the risks of thyroid cancer that are associated with thyroid doses of Iodine 131; (2) conduct scientific research and prepare analysis necessary to develop valid and credible methods to estimate the thyroid doses of Iodine 131 that are received by individuals from nuclear bomb fallout; and (3) conduct scientific research and prepare analysis necessary to develop valid and credible assessments of the exposure to Iodine 131 that the American people received from the Nevada atmospheric nuclear bomb tests"

SECTION 1

INDIVIDUAL FALLOUT EVENTS
BY U.S. COUNTY

1951-1962

U.S. FALLOUT ATLAS : COUNTY COMPARISIONS

INDIVIDUAL FALLOUT DAYS
ALABAMA

COUNTY	SHOT	DATE	µCi/SQ METER	INDEX	COUNTY	SHOT	DATE	µCi/SQ METER	INDEX
AUTAUGA	TP6-5	26-Mar-55	3.54	2	CALHOUN	TS5-1	07-May-52	5.54	3
AUTAUGA	TS5-1	07-May-52	4.36	2	CALHOUN	BJ3-5	05-Nov-51	7.66	3
AUTAUGA	PB16-5	27-Sep-57	5.14	3	CALHOUN	PB16-5	27-Sep-57	9.37	3
AUTAUGA	TS3-3	24-Apr-52	8.89	3	CHAMBERS	TS5-1	07-May-52	3.90	2
BALDWIN	TP6-5	26-Mar-55	3.54	2	CHAMBERS	BJ2-3	01-Nov-51	3.97	2
BALDWIN	TS3-3	24-Apr-52	8.89	3	CHAMBERS	PB16-5	27-Sep-57	9.87	3
BALDWIN	PB12-6	07-Sep-57	9.67	3	CHAMBERS	TS3-3	24-Apr-52	17.78	4
BALDWIN	UK2-3	26-Mar-53	10.75	4	CHEROKEE	PB17-3	30-Sep-57	3.96	2
BALDWIN	PB3-3	26-Jun-57	22.97	4	CHEROKEE	PB16-5	27-Sep-57	7.47	3
BARBOUR	BJ2-4	02-Nov-51	3.76	2	CHEROKEE	BJ3-6	06-Nov-51	8.10	3
BARBOUR	PB17-6	03-Oct-57	4.37	2	CHILTON	PB16-5	27-Sep-57	4.86	2
BARBOUR	TS5-2	08-May-52	5.29	3	CHILTON	TS5-2	08-May-52	5.15	3
BARBOUR	PB17-3	30-Sep-57	5.99	3	CHILTON	TS3-3	24-Apr-52	8.89	3
BARBOUR	TS3-3	24-Apr-52	8.89	3	CHOCTAW	TP6-5	26-Mar-55	3.54	2
BARBOUR	PB16-5	27-Sep-57	11.07	4	CHOCTAW	TP6-3	24-Mar-55	5.55	3
BIBB	TP6-5	26-Mar-55	3.54	2	CHOCTAW	PB3-3	26-Jun-57	11.44	4
BIBB	PB17-3	30-Sep-57	3.96	2	CLARKE	TP6-5	26-Mar-55	3.54	2
BIBB	TP11-6	20-May-55	4.21	2	CLARKE	PB12-6	07-Sep-57	5.21	3
BIBB	TS7-8	08-Jun-52	4.83	2	CLARKE	TP6-3	24-Mar-55	5.55	3
BIBB	TS3-3	24-Apr-52	8.89	3	CLARKE	PB3-3	26-Jun-57	11.44	4
BLOUNT	TP6-4	25-Mar-55	3.99	2	CLARKE	TS3-3	24-Apr-52	17.78	4
BLOUNT	PB16-5	27-Sep-57	4.43	2	CLAY	TS5-2	08-May-52	4.57	2
BLOUNT	TS3-3	24-Apr-52	4.45	2	CLAY	TS3-3	24-Apr-52	8.89	3
BLOUNT	TS5-2	08-May-52	8.97	3	CLAY	PB16-5	27-Sep-57	14.75	4
BULLOCK	TS3-3	24-Apr-52	4.45	2	CLEBURNE	TS5-2	08-May-52	3.94	2
BULLOCK	TS5-2	08-May-52	5.09	3	CLEBURNE	PB17-3	30-Sep-57	3.96	2
BULLOCK	PB17-3	30-Sep-57	5.99	3	CLEBURNE	TS5-1	07-May-52	9.34	3
BULLOCK	BJ2-4	02-Nov-51	6.48	3	CLEBURNE	PB16-5	27-Sep-57	10.93	4
BULLOCK	PB16-5	27-Sep-57	7.24	3	COFFEE	TP6-5	26-Mar-55	3.54	2
BUTLER	TP6-5	26-Mar-55	3.54	2	COFFEE	PB17-3	30-Sep-57	3.96	2
BUTLER	PB16-5	27-Sep-57	4.23	2	COFFEE	TS5-2	08-May-52	4.10	2
BUTLER	TS3-3	24-Apr-52	4.45	2	COFFEE	PB16-5	27-Sep-57	6.09	3
BUTLER	TS5-2	08-May-52	7.44	3	COFFEE	TS3-3	24-Apr-52	8.89	3

INDIVIDUAL FALLOUT DAYS
ALABAMA

COUNTY	SHOT	DATE	µCi/SQ METER	INDEX	COUNTY	SHOT	DATE	µCi/SQ METER	INDEX
COFFEE	BJ2-4	02-Nov-51	9.52	3	DE KALB	PB17-6	03-Oct-57	3.96	2
COLBERT	UK1-3	19-Mar-53	3.68	2	DE KALB	BJ3-6	06-Nov-51	4.86	2
COLBERT	UK9-3	21-May-53	4.61	2	DE KALB	PB17-3	30-Sep-57	5.99	3
COLBERT	TS5-1	07-May-52	4.65	2	ELMORE	TS5-2	08-May-52	7.29	3
COLBERT	TP11-6	20-May-55	4.68	2	ELMORE	PB16-5	27-Sep-57	8.07	3
COLBERT	UK7-4	28-Apr-53	9.05	3	ELMORE	TS3-3	24-Apr-52	8.89	3
CONECUH	TP6-5	26-Mar-55	3.54	2	ESCAMBIA	TP6-5	26-Mar-55	3.54	2
CONECUH	TP6-3	24-Mar-55	5.55	3	ESCAMBIA	UK2-3	26-Mar-53	3.69	2
CONECUH	TS3-3	24-Apr-52	26.68	5	ESCAMBIA	PB12-6	07-Sep-57	6.43	3
CONECUH	PB3-3	26-Jun-57	45.85	5	ESCAMBIA	TS3-3	24-Apr-52	8.89	3
COOSA	TS5-2	08-May-52	4.98	2	ESCAMBIA	PB3-3	26-Jun-57	22.97	4
COOSA	PB16-5	27-Sep-57	7.55	3	ETOWAH	TP6-4	25-Mar-55	3.99	2
COOSA	TS3-3	24-Apr-52	8.89	3	ETOWAH	PB17-6	03-Oct-57	3.99	2
COVINGTON	TP6-5	26-Mar-55	3.54	2	ETOWAH	TS5-2	08-May-52	4.28	2
COVINGTON	BJ2-4	02-Nov-51	10.27	4	ETOWAH	PB17-3	30-Sep-57	5.99	3
COVINGTON	TS3-3	24-Apr-52	17.78	4	ETOWAH	PB16-5	27-Sep-57	6.76	3
CRENSHAW	TP6-5	26-Mar-55	3.54	2	ETOWAH	BJ3-6	06-Nov-51	8.10	3
CRENSHAW	PB16-5	27-Sep-57	4.03	2	FAYETTE	TS3-3	24-Apr-52	4.45	2
CRENSHAW	TS5-2	08-May-52	4.05	2	FAYETTE	PB17-5	02-Oct-57	4.46	2
CRENSHAW	TS3-3	24-Apr-52	4.45	2	FRANKLIN	UK9-3	21-May-53	4.55	2
CULLMAN	PB17-3	30-Sep-57	3.96	2	FRANKLIN	TS5-1	07-May-52	4.80	2
CULLMAN	BJ3-6	06-Nov-51	4.86	2	FRANKLIN	TP11-6	20-May-55	4.86	2
CULLMAN	TS5-1	07-May-52	6.14	3	GENEVA	TP6-5	26-Mar-55	3.54	2
CULLMAN	TS3-3	24-Apr-52	8.89	3	GENEVA	PB17-3	30-Sep-57	3.96	2
DALE	TP6-5	26-Mar-55	3.54	2	GENEVA	PB16-5	27-Sep-57	5.73	3
DALE	PB17-3	30-Sep-57	3.96	2	GENEVA	BJ2-4	02-Nov-51	17.03	4
DALE	PB16-5	27-Sep-57	7.83	3	GENEVA	TS3-3	24-Apr-52	26.68	5
DALE	BJ2-4	02-Nov-51	8.35	3	GREENE	TP6-5	26-Mar-55	3.54	2
DALE	TS3-3	24-Apr-52	17.78	4	GREENE	TP6-4	25-Mar-55	3.99	2
DALLAS	TP6-5	26-Mar-55	3.54	2	GREENE	BJ2-4	02-Nov-51	4.98	2
DALLAS	UK2-3	26-Mar-53	5.25	3	GREENE	TP6-3	24-Mar-55	5.55	3
DALLAS	TS3-3	24-Apr-52	17.78	4	GREENE	TS3-3	24-Apr-52	26.68	5
DE KALB	PB16-5	27-Sep-57	3.72	2	HALE	TP6-5	26-Mar-55	3.54	2

INDIVIDUAL FALLOUT DAYS
ALABAMA

COUNTY	SHOT	DATE	µCi/SQ METER	INDEX	COUNTY	SHOT	DATE	µCi/SQ METER	INDEX
HALE	TS5-2	08-May-52	3.76	2	LIMESTONE	PB17-3	30-Sep-57	3.96	2
HALE	TP11-6	20-May-55	3.94	2	LOWNDES	TP6-5	26-Mar-55	3.54	2
HALE	TP6-4	25-Mar-55	3.99	2	LOWNDES	PB12-6	07-Sep-57	4.41	2
HALE	TP6-3	24-Mar-55	5.55	3	LOWNDES	PB16-5	27-Sep-57	4.82	2
HALE	TS3-3	24-Apr-52	17.78	4	LOWNDES	TS3-3	24-Apr-52	26.68	5
HENRY	PB17-3	30-Sep-57	3.96	2	MACON	TS5-2	08-May-52	3.53	2
HENRY	TS3-3	24-Apr-52	4.45	2	MACON	PB17-3	30-Sep-57	3.96	2
HENRY	PB16-5	27-Sep-57	9.96	3	MACON	PB16-5	27-Sep-57	8.15	3
HOUSTON	PB17-3	30-Sep-57	5.99	3	MACON	TS3-3	24-Apr-52	8.89	3
HOUSTON	TS3-7	28-Apr-52	6.40	3	MADISON	TP6-4	25-Mar-55	3.99	2
HOUSTON	BJ2-4	02-Nov-51	7.10	3	MADISON	BJ3-6	06-Nov-51	4.86	2
HOUSTON	PB16-5	27-Sep-57	7.87	3	MADISON	PB17-3	30-Sep-57	5.99	3
JACKSON	TP6-4	25-Mar-55	3.99	2	MARENGO	TP6-5	26-Mar-55	3.54	2
JACKSON	BJ3-6	06-Nov-51	4.86	2	MARENGO	PB12-6	07-Sep-57	4.84	2
JACKSON	PB17-3	30-Sep-57	5.99	3	MARENGO	TP6-3	24-Mar-55	5.55	3
JEFFERSON	PB16-5	27-Sep-57	3.84	2	MARENGO	UK2-3	26-Mar-53	5.67	3
JEFFERSON	TS3-3	24-Apr-52	8.89	3	MARENGO	TP6-4	25-Mar-55	5.98	3
LAMAR	TS3-3	24-Apr-52	4.45	2	MARENGO	TS3-3	24-Apr-52	17.78	4
LAMAR	PB2-4	21-Jun-57	4.55	2	MARENGO	PB3-3	26-Jun-57	68.82	6
LAMAR	PB17-5	02-Oct-57	5.11	3	MARION	UK9-3	21-May-53	4.18	2
LAUDERDALE	UK1-3	19-Mar-53	4.08	2	MARION	PB2-5	22-Jun-57	4.64	2
LAUDERDALE	UK9-3	21-May-53	4.31	2	MARION	PB17-5	02-Oct-57	4.88	2
LAUDERDALE	TP11-6	20-May-55	4.45	2	MARSHALL	TP11-6	20-May-55	4.07	2
LAUDERDALE	PB12-6	07-Sep-57	4.71	2	MARSHALL	PB17-3	30-Sep-57	5.99	3
LAUDERDALE	UK7-4	28-Apr-53	5.61	3	MARSHALL	BJ3-6	06-Nov-51	8.10	3
LAWRENCE	UK9-3	21-May-53	3.88	2	MOBILE	UK2-3	26-Mar-53	7.26	3
LAWRENCE	TP11-6	20-May-55	4.65	2	MOBILE	UK6-2	19-Apr-53	37.36	5
LEE	BJ2-3	01-Nov-51	3.65	2	MOBILE	PB3-3	26-Jun-57	68.82	6
LEE	PB17-3	30-Sep-57	3.96	2	MONROE	TP6-5	26-Mar-55	3.54	2
LEE	PB17-6	03-Oct-57	4.73	2	MONROE	PB12-6	07-Sep-57	3.95	2
LEE	TS5-2	08-May-52	5.79	3	MONROE	TS3-3	24-Apr-52	4.45	2
LEE	TS3-3	24-Apr-52	8.89	3	MONROE	TP6-3	24-Mar-55	5.55	3
LEE	PB16-5	27-Sep-57	11.27	4	MONROE	PB3-3	26-Jun-57	45.85	5

INDIVIDUAL FALLOUT DAYS
ALABAMA

COUNTY	SHOT	DATE	μCi/SQ METER	INDEX	COUNTY	SHOT	DATE	μCi/SQ METER	INDEX
MONTGOMERY	TS3-3	24-Apr-52	3.69	2	ST CLAIR	PB16-5	27-Sep-57	6.13	3
MONTGOMERY	PB16-5	27-Sep-57	5.14	3	ST CLAIR	TS3-3	24-Apr-52	8.89	3
MORGAN	PB17-3	30-Sep-57	3.96	2	SUMTER	TP6-5	26-Mar-55	3.54	2
MORGAN	BJ3-6	06-Nov-51	4.86	2	SUMTER	PB2-5	22-Jun-57	4.64	2
MORGAN	TS5-1	07-May-52	5.69	3	SUMTER	TP6-3	24-Mar-55	5.55	3
PERRY	PB12-6	07-Sep-57	3.53	2	SUMTER	TS3-3	24-Apr-52	17.78	4
PERRY	TP6-5	26-Mar-55	3.54	2	TALLADEGA	TS5-2	08-May-52	5.21	3
PERRY	TP11-6	20-May-55	3.94	2	TALLADEGA	TS5-1	07-May-52	5.84	3
PERRY	TS7-8	08-Jun-52	4.83	2	TALLADEGA	PB16-5	27-Sep-57	7.79	3
PERRY	TP6-3	24-Mar-55	5.55	3	TALLADEGA	TS3-3	24-Apr-52	8.89	3
PERRY	TS3-3	24-Apr-52	8.89	3	TALLAPOOSA	PB17-3	30-Sep-57	3.96	2
PICKENS	TP6-4	25-Mar-55	3.99	2	TALLAPOOSA	TS3-3	24-Apr-52	8.89	3
PICKENS	TS3-3	24-Apr-52	4.45	2	TALLAPOOSA	PB16-5	27-Sep-57	11.39	4
PICKENS	PB17-5	02-Oct-57	4.92	2	TUSCALOOSA	TP6-5	26-Mar-55	3.54	2
PICKENS	TP6-3	24-Mar-55	5.55	3	TUSCALOOSA	TS3-3	24-Apr-52	4.45	2
PICKENS	UK9-4	22-May-53	5.77	3	TUSCALOOSA	PB17-5	02-Oct-57	4.70	2
PICKENS	UK7-4	28-Apr-53	10.20	4	TUSCALOOSA	UK7-4	28-Apr-53	8.42	3
PIKE	TP6-5	26-Mar-55	3.54	2	TUSCALOOSA	TP6-3	24-Mar-55	11.09	4
PIKE	BJ2-4	02-Nov-51	3.90	2	WALKER	PB12-6	07-Sep-57	3.62	2
PIKE	PB17-3	30-Sep-57	3.96	2	WALKER	TS3-3	24-Apr-52	4.45	2
PIKE	PB16-5	27-Sep-57	5.46	3	WALKER	UK9-3	21-May-53	3.51	1
PIKE	TS3-3	24-Apr-52	17.78	4	WASHINGTON	TP6-5	26-Mar-55	3.54	2
RANDOLPH	PB17-3	30-Sep-57	5.99	3	WASHINGTON	UK2-3	26-Mar-53	3.84	2
RANDOLPH	TS5-2	08-May-52	6.54	3	WASHINGTON	TP6-3	24-Mar-55	5.55	3
RANDOLPH	PB16-5	27-Sep-57	13.06	4	WASHINGTON	TS3-3	24-Apr-52	8.89	3
RUSSELL	PB17-3	30-Sep-57	3.96	2	WASHINGTON	PB3-3	26-Jun-57	22.97	4
RUSSELL	TS3-3	24-Apr-52	8.89	3	WILCOX	TP6-5	26-Mar-55	3.54	2
RUSSELL	PB16-5	27-Sep-57	11.07	4	WILCOX	PB12-6	07-Sep-57	3.70	2
SHELBY	BJ2-3	01-Nov-51	3.65	2	WILCOX	TP6-3	24-Mar-55	5.55	3
SHELBY	PB17-3	30-Sep-57	3.96	2	WILCOX	PB3-3	26-Jun-57	22.97	4
SHELBY	TS3-3	24-Apr-52	4.45	2	WILCOX	TS3-3	24-Apr-52	26.68	5
SHELBY	PB16-5	27-Sep-57	4.94	2	WINSTON	UK9-3	21-May-53	3.81	2
ST CLAIR	TP11-6	20-May-55	4.02	2	WINSTON	TS3-3	24-Apr-52	4.45	2

INDIVIDUAL FALLOUT DAYS
ARKANSAS

COUNTY	SHOT	DATE	µCi/SQ METER	INDEX	COUNTY	SHOT	DATE	µCi/SQ METER	INDEX
ARKANSAS	UK3-6	05-Apr-53	3.67	2	BENTON	TP11-6	20-May-55	3.53	2
ARKANSAS	UK1-2	18-Mar-53	3.71	2	BENTON	TP10-5	09-May-55	3.81	2
ARKANSAS	PB8-3	20-Aug-57	4.00	2	BENTON	PB8-3	20-Aug-57	4.00	2
ARKANSAS	UK7-3	27-Apr-53	4.26	2	BENTON	PB13-6	11-Sep-57	4.42	2
ARKANSAS	UK2-3	26-Mar-53	4.45	2	BENTON	TS7-6	06-Jun-52	4.99	2
ARKANSAS	PB9-2	24-Aug-57	5.46	3	BENTON	UK3-5	04-Apr-53	6.83	3
ARKANSAS	UK8-3	10-May-53	6.18	3	BENTON	UK1-1	17-Mar-53	7.40	3
ARKANSAS	TP11-6	20-May-55	6.35	3	BENTON	TP11-5	19-May-55	9.19	3
ARKANSAS	TS1-3	03-Apr-52	9.02	3	BENTON	PB4-5	09-Jul-57	10.65	4
ARKANSAS	UK2-7	30-Mar-53	12.19	4	BENTON	PB12-4	05-Sep-57	15.20	4
ARKANSAS	UK2-8	31-Mar-53	14.03	4	BENTON	TP10-3	07-May-55	23.94	4
ARKANSAS	UK7-4	28-Apr-53	18.07	4	BENTON	TS1-3	03-Apr-52	24.86	4
ARKANSAS	TP10-3	07-May-55	27.50	5	BENTON	TS7-5	05-Jun-52	29.87	5
ASHLEY	UK7-3	27-Apr-53	5.22	3	BOONE	UK2-3	26-Mar-53	3.87	2
ASHLEY	TP6-3	24-Mar-55	5.55	3	BOONE	PB8-3	20-Aug-57	4.00	2
ASHLEY	TS6-4	28-May-52	7.71	3	BOONE	UK3-5	04-Apr-53	4.10	2
ASHLEY	PB12-6	07-Sep-57	8.58	3	BOONE	UK7-3	27-Apr-53	4.19	2
ASHLEY	UK7-4	28-Apr-53	25.13	5	BOONE	TP11-5	19-May-55	5.97	3
BAXTER	TP11-5	19-May-55	3.70	2	BOONE	TS6-4	28-May-52	6.75	3
BAXTER	PB12-4	05-Sep-57	3.80	2	BOONE	UK7-4	28-Apr-53	8.18	3
BAXTER	TP11-6	20-May-55	3.89	2	BOONE	PB12-4	05-Sep-57	11.89	4
BAXTER	PB8-3	20-Aug-57	4.00	2	BOONE	TS1-3	03-Apr-52	24.86	4
BAXTER	UK3-5	04-Apr-53	4.10	2	BOONE	TP10-3	07-May-55	36.97	5
BAXTER	TS7-5	05-Jun-52	4.27	2	BRADLEY	UK5-4	14-Apr-53	3.91	2
BAXTER	UK7-3	27-Apr-53	4.40	2	BRADLEY	BJ3-5	05-Nov-51	4.02	2
BAXTER	UK2-3	26-Mar-53	5.18	3	BRADLEY	UK7-3	27-Apr-53	4.33	2
BAXTER	PB9-2	24-Aug-57	5.46	3	BRADLEY	TP6-3	24-Mar-55	5.55	3
BAXTER	PB4-5	09-Jul-57	7.08	3	BRADLEY	PB12-6	07-Sep-57	7.44	3
BAXTER	UK1-1	17-Mar-53	7.40	3	BRADLEY	TS6-4	28-May-52	13.50	4
BAXTER	UK7-4	28-Apr-53	12.43	4	BRADLEY	UK7-4	28-Apr-53	18.92	4
BAXTER	UK2-7	30-Mar-53	18.26	4	CALHOUN	UK7-3	27-Apr-53	3.71	2
BAXTER	TS1-3	03-Apr-52	24.86	4	CALHOUN	UK5-4	14-Apr-53	3.91	2
BAXTER	TP10-3	07-May-55	34.57	5	CALHOUN	PB11-2	01-Sep-57	4.26	2

INDIVIDUAL FALLOUT DAYS
ARKANSAS

COUNTY	SHOT	DATE	µCi/SQ METER	INDEX	COUNTY	SHOT	DATE	µCi/SQ METER	INDEX
CALHOUN	TP6-3	24-Mar-55	5.55	3	CLAY	PB9-2	24-Aug-57	5.46	3
CALHOUN	UK7-4	28-Apr-53	14.33	4	CLAY	UK7-4	28-Apr-53	6.29	3
CARROLL	UK7-3	27-Apr-53	3.92	2	CLAY	UK2-8	31-Mar-53	7.04	3
CARROLL	PB8-3	20-Aug-57	4.00	2	CLAY	TS1-3	03-Apr-52	9.02	3
CARROLL	UK3-5	04-Apr-53	4.10	2	CLAY	UK2-7	30-Mar-53	12.19	4
CARROLL	UK7-4	28-Apr-53	4.65	2	CLAY	PB9-3	25-Aug-57	13.72	4
CARROLL	PB12-5	06-Sep-57	5.78	3	CLAY	TP10-3	07-May-55	29.31	5
CARROLL	TS7-5	05-Jun-52	6.25	3	CLEBURNE	PB12-5	06-Sep-57	3.60	2
CARROLL	TP11-5	19-May-55	7.86	3	CLEBURNE	UK3-6	05-Apr-53	3.67	2
CARROLL	TP11-6	20-May-55	7.87	3	CLEBURNE	TS7-6	06-Jun-52	3.97	2
CARROLL	UK1-1	17-Mar-53	12.33	4	CLEBURNE	UK7-3	27-Apr-53	3.99	2
CARROLL	PB12-4	05-Sep-57	13.58	4	CLEBURNE	PB8-3	20-Aug-57	4.00	2
CARROLL	TP10-3	07-May-55	14.30	4	CLEBURNE	PB11-2	01-Sep-57	4.26	2
CARROLL	TS1-3	03-Apr-52	24.86	4	CLEBURNE	UK8-3	10-May-53	6.18	3
CHICOT	PB12-6	07-Sep-57	4.38	2	CLEBURNE	TP11-6	20-May-55	7.63	3
CHICOT	TP6-3	24-Mar-55	5.55	3	CLEBURNE	PB9-2	24-Aug-57	8.19	3
CHICOT	UK7-3	27-Apr-53	5.71	3	CLEBURNE	TS1-3	03-Apr-52	9.02	3
CHICOT	UK7-4	28-Apr-53	28.17	5	CLEBURNE	UK2-7	30-Mar-53	12.19	4
CLARK	UK1-2	18-Mar-53	3.52	2	CLEBURNE	UK7-4	28-Apr-53	14.41	4
CLARK	UK5-4	14-Apr-53	3.91	2	CLEBURNE	UK2-8	31-Mar-53	21.07	4
CLARK	PB8-3	20-Aug-57	4.00	2	CLEBURNE	TP10-3	07-May-55	41.26	5
CLARK	BJ3-5	05-Nov-51	4.02	2	CLEVELAND	UK5-4	14-Apr-53	3.91	2
CLARK	TP11-5	19-May-55	4.51	2	CLEVELAND	UK7-3	27-Apr-53	3.99	2
CLARK	TP11-6	20-May-55	5.44	3	CLEVELAND	TP11-6	20-May-55	7.22	3
CLARK	UK7-4	28-Apr-53	6.68	3	CLEVELAND	PB12-6	07-Sep-57	7.27	3
CLARK	PB12-6	07-Sep-57	9.04	3	CLEVELAND	TS1-3	03-Apr-52	9.02	3
CLARK	TS6-4	28-May-52	13.50	4	CLEVELAND	UK7-4	28-Apr-53	16.25	4
CLARK	TS1-3	03-Apr-52	24.86	4	CLEVELAND	TP10-3	07-May-55	20.97	4
CLARK	TP10-3	07-May-55	27.05	5	COLUMBIA	UK5-4	14-Apr-53	3.91	2
CLAY	UK8-3	10-May-53	3.68	2	COLUMBIA	BJ3-5	05-Nov-51	4.02	2
CLAY	PB8-3	20-Aug-57	4.00	2	COLUMBIA	PB12-6	07-Sep-57	4.92	2
CLAY	TP11-6	20-May-55	4.56	2	COLUMBIA	TP6-3	24-Mar-55	5.55	3
CLAY	UK2-3	26-Mar-53	4.77	2	COLUMBIA	UK7-4	28-Apr-53	9.37	3

INDIVIDUAL FALLOUT DAYS
ARKANSAS

COUNTY	SHOT	DATE	µCi/SQ METER	INDEX	COUNTY	SHOT	DATE	µCi/SQ METER	INDEX
COLUMBIA	TS6-4	28-May-52	11.57	4	CRAWFORD	TS1-3	03-Apr-52	24.86	4
COLUMBIA	TP10-3	07-May-55	17.28	4	CRAWFORD	TS7-5	05-Jun-52	28.44	5
COLUMBIA	TS1-3	03-Apr-52	24.86	4	CRITTENDEN	UK9-3	21-May-53	3.64	2
CONWAY	PB8-3	20-Aug-57	4.00	2	CRITTENDEN	UK3-6	05-Apr-53	3.67	2
CONWAY	BJ3-5	05-Nov-51	4.02	2	CRITTENDEN	PB8-3	20-Aug-57	4.00	2
CONWAY	TP11-6	20-May-55	5.26	3	CRITTENDEN	TP11-6	20-May-55	4.70	2
CONWAY	UK2-3	26-Mar-53	5.94	3	CRITTENDEN	UK1-2	18-Mar-53	5.26	3
CONWAY	UK7-4	28-Apr-53	6.90	3	CRITTENDEN	TS1-3	03-Apr-52	6.02	3
CONWAY	UK1-1	17-Mar-53	12.33	4	CRITTENDEN	UK8-3	10-May-53	6.18	3
CONWAY	TS1-3	03-Apr-52	24.86	4	CRITTENDEN	UK2-7	30-Mar-53	12.19	4
CONWAY	TP10-3	07-May-55	43.29	5	CRITTENDEN	UK2-3	26-Mar-53	12.28	4
CRAIGHEAD	PB8-3	20-Aug-57	4.00	2	CRITTENDEN	UK7-4	28-Apr-53	12.73	4
CRAIGHEAD	TP11-6	20-May-55	4.50	2	CRITTENDEN	UK2-8	31-Mar-53	21.07	4
CRAIGHEAD	UK1-2	18-Mar-53	4.56	2	CROSS	PB8-3	20-Aug-57	4.00	2
CRAIGHEAD	PB2-5	22-Jun-57	4.64	2	CROSS	UK2-8	31-Mar-53	3.50	1
CRAIGHEAD	PB9-2	24-Aug-57	5.46	3	CROSS	UK1-2	18-Mar-53	5.33	3
CRAIGHEAD	UK8-3	10-May-53	6.18	3	CROSS	TP10-3	07-May-55	5.83	3
CRAIGHEAD	TS1-3	03-Apr-52	9.02	3	CROSS	UK8-3	10-May-53	6.18	3
CRAIGHEAD	UK7-4	28-Apr-53	9.10	3	CROSS	TS1-3	03-Apr-52	9.02	3
CRAIGHEAD	PB9-3	25-Aug-57	13.72	4	CROSS	UK2-3	26-Mar-53	12.51	4
CRAIGHEAD	TP10-3	07-May-55	15.82	4	CROSS	UK2-7	30-Mar-53	18.26	4
CRAIGHEAD	UK2-3	26-Mar-53	17.42	4	CROSS	UK7-4	28-Apr-53	26.41	5
CRAIGHEAD	UK2-7	30-Mar-53	18.26	4	DALLAS	UK5-4	14-Apr-53	3.91	2
CRAIGHEAD	UK2-8	31-Mar-53	21.07	4	DALLAS	PB8-3	20-Aug-57	4.00	2
CRAWFORD	PB8-3	20-Aug-57	4.00	2	DALLAS	BJ3-5	05-Nov-51	4.02	2
CRAWFORD	UK3-5	04-Apr-53	4.10	2	DALLAS	PB12-6	07-Sep-57	6.14	3
CRAWFORD	PB13-9	14-Sep-57	4.15	2	DALLAS	TP10-3	07-May-55	8.19	3
CRAWFORD	PB13-6	11-Sep-57	4.17	2	DALLAS	UK7-4	28-Apr-53	10.96	4
CRAWFORD	UK2-3	26-Mar-53	4.29	2	DALLAS	TS6-4	28-May-52	24.11	4
CRAWFORD	TP11-5	19-May-55	7.38	3	DALLAS	TS1-3	03-Apr-52	24.86	4
CRAWFORD	TP11-6	20-May-55	8.66	3	DESHA	UK3-6	05-Apr-53	3.67	2
CRAWFORD	PB12-4	05-Sep-57	14.26	4	DESHA	UK8-3	10-May-53	3.68	2
CRAWFORD	TP10-3	07-May-55	15.31	4	DESHA	PB12-6	07-Sep-57	4.28	2

INDIVIDUAL FALLOUT DAYS
ARKANSAS

COUNTY	SHOT	DATE	µCi/SQ METER	INDEX	COUNTY	SHOT	DATE	µCi/SQ METER	INDEX
DESHA	UK7-3	27-Apr-53	4.74	2	FRANKLIN	TP11-6	20-May-55	10.03	4
DESHA	TP11-6	20-May-55	5.94	3	FRANKLIN	UK1-1	17-Mar-53	12.33	4
DESHA	UK2-8	31-Mar-53	7.04	3	FRANKLIN	TS7-5	05-Jun-52	15.36	4
DESHA	TP10-3	07-May-55	7.18	3	FRANKLIN	TP10-3	07-May-55	27.18	5
DESHA	TS6-4	28-May-52	8.68	3	FRANKLIN	TS1-3	03-Apr-52	41.51	5
DESHA	TS1-3	03-Apr-52	9.02	3	FULTON	PB12-5	06-Sep-57	3.69	2
DESHA	UK2-7	30-Mar-53	12.19	4	FULTON	PB8-3	20-Aug-57	4.00	2
DESHA	UK7-4	28-Apr-53	30.16	5	FULTON	UK7-3	27-Apr-53	4.33	2
DREW	TP10-3	07-May-55	3.59	2	FULTON	TS7-5	05-Jun-52	5.27	3
DREW	UK7-3	27-Apr-53	4.81	2	FULTON	PB9-2	24-Aug-57	5.46	3
DREW	TP6-3	24-Mar-55	5.55	3	FULTON	PB9-3	25-Aug-57	13.72	4
DREW	TP11-6	20-May-55	6.17	3	FULTON	UK2-8	31-Mar-53	14.03	4
DREW	TS6-4	28-May-52	14.46	4	FULTON	TS1-3	03-Apr-52	15.04	4
DREW	UK7-4	28-Apr-53	35.20	5	FULTON	UK7-4	28-Apr-53	15.94	4
FAULKNER	PB6-6	29-Jul-57	3.54	2	FULTON	UK2-7	30-Mar-53	18.26	4
FAULKNER	PB12-4	05-Sep-57	3.63	2	FULTON	UK2-3	26-Mar-53	24.65	4
FAULKNER	UK7-3	27-Apr-53	3.71	2	FULTON	TP10-3	07-May-55	31.41	5
FAULKNER	PB8-3	20-Aug-57	4.00	2	GARLAND	UK5-4	14-Apr-53	3.91	2
FAULKNER	UK3-5	04-Apr-53	4.10	2	GARLAND	PB8-3	20-Aug-57	4.00	2
FAULKNER	TS7-5	05-Jun-52	4.85	2	GARLAND	UK1-2	18-Mar-53	4.02	2
FAULKNER	TP11-6	20-May-55	4.86	2	GARLAND	BJ3-5	05-Nov-51	4.02	2
FAULKNER	UK2-3	26-Mar-53	6.51	3	GARLAND	PB12-5	06-Sep-57	5.77	3
FAULKNER	UK1-1	17-Mar-53	12.33	4	GARLAND	TP11-6	20-May-55	5.79	3
FAULKNER	UK7-4	28-Apr-53	14.41	4	GARLAND	UK7-4	28-Apr-53	5.93	3
FAULKNER	UK2-7	30-Mar-53	18.26	4	GARLAND	TS6-4	28-May-52	7.71	3
FAULKNER	TS1-3	03-Apr-52	24.86	4	GARLAND	TP10-3	07-May-55	23.30	4
FAULKNER	TP10-3	07-May-55	40.81	5	GARLAND	TS1-3	03-Apr-52	24.86	4
FRANKLIN	PB12-5	06-Sep-57	3.60	2	GRANT	UK5-4	14-Apr-53	3.91	2
FRANKLIN	PB13-6	11-Sep-57	3.76	2	GRANT	PB8-3	20-Aug-57	4.00	2
FRANKLIN	PB8-3	20-Aug-57	4.00	2	GRANT	UK7-3	27-Apr-53	3.51	1
FRANKLIN	UK3-5	04-Apr-53	4.10	2	GRANT	UK7-4	28-Apr-53	12.24	4
FRANKLIN	PB12-4	05-Sep-57	4.25	2	GRANT	TS6-4	28-May-52	13.50	4
FRANKLIN	TP11-5	19-May-55	5.46	3	GRANT	TS1-3	03-Apr-52	24.86	4

INDIVIDUAL FALLOUT DAYS
ARKANSAS

COUNTY	SHOT	DATE	µCi/SQ METER	INDEX	COUNTY	SHOT	DATE	µCi/SQ METER	INDEX
GRANT	TP10-3	07-May-55	33.74	5	HOWARD	UK5-4	14-Apr-53	3.91	2
GREENE	TS7-5	05-Jun-52	3.61	2	HOWARD	PB8-3	20-Aug-57	4.00	2
GREENE	UK8-3	10-May-53	3.68	2	HOWARD	BJ3-5	05-Nov-51	4.02	2
GREENE	PB8-3	20-Aug-57	4.00	2	HOWARD	TP11-5	19-May-55	4.15	2
GREENE	TP11-6	20-May-55	4.16	2	HOWARD	TS7-6	06-Jun-52	4.60	2
GREENE	UK1-2	18-Mar-53	4.33	2	HOWARD	UK1-2	18-Mar-53	4.94	2
GREENE	UK2-8	31-Mar-53	3.50	1	HOWARD	PB12-6	07-Sep-57	6.60	3
GREENE	UK2-3	26-Mar-53	7.78	3	HOWARD	TS6-4	28-May-52	7.71	3
GREENE	TS1-3	03-Apr-52	9.02	3	HOWARD	TP10-3	07-May-55	9.77	3
GREENE	PB9-3	25-Aug-57	13.72	4	HOWARD	TP6-2	23-Mar-55	13.77	4
GREENE	UK7-4	28-Apr-53	16.89	4	HOWARD	TS1-3	03-Apr-52	24.86	4
GREENE	UK2-7	30-Mar-53	18.26	4	INDEPENDENCE	UK1-2	18-Mar-53	3.71	2
GREENE	TP10-3	07-May-55	28.56	5	INDEPENDENCE	UK7-3	27-Apr-53	3.92	2
HEMPSTEAD	UK5-4	14-Apr-53	3.91	2	INDEPENDENCE	TS7-6	06-Jun-52	3.97	2
HEMPSTEAD	UK1-2	18-Mar-53	3.94	2	INDEPENDENCE	PB8-3	20-Aug-57	4.00	2
HEMPSTEAD	PB8-3	20-Aug-57	4.00	2	INDEPENDENCE	UK8-3	10-May-53	6.18	3
HEMPSTEAD	TP11-5	19-May-55	5.59	3	INDEPENDENCE	TP11-6	20-May-55	6.55	3
HEMPSTEAD	TP6-2	23-Mar-55	13.77	4	INDEPENDENCE	PB9-2	24-Aug-57	8.19	3
HEMPSTEAD	TP10-3	07-May-55	20.82	4	INDEPENDENCE	TS1-3	03-Apr-52	9.02	3
HEMPSTEAD	TS1-3	03-Apr-52	24.86	4	INDEPENDENCE	UK7-4	28-Apr-53	11.87	4
HOT SPRING	UK1-2	18-Mar-53	3.61	2	INDEPENDENCE	PB9-3	25-Aug-57	13.72	4
HOT SPRING	UK5-4	14-Apr-53	3.91	2	INDEPENDENCE	UK2-8	31-Mar-53	14.03	4
HOT SPRING	PB8-3	20-Aug-57	4.00	2	INDEPENDENCE	UK2-7	30-Mar-53	18.26	4
HOT SPRING	BJ3-5	05-Nov-51	4.02	2	INDEPENDENCE	TP10-3	07-May-55	25.93	5
HOT SPRING	PB11-2	01-Sep-57	4.26	2	IZARD	PB12-5	06-Sep-57	3.65	2
HOT SPRING	UK7-4	28-Apr-53	7.59	3	IZARD	UK8-3	10-May-53	3.68	2
HOT SPRING	TS6-4	28-May-52	7.71	3	IZARD	PB8-3	20-Aug-57	4.00	2
HOT SPRING	PB12-4	05-Sep-57	13.51	4	IZARD	UK7-3	27-Apr-53	4.26	2
HOT SPRING	TP10-3	07-May-55	22.02	4	IZARD	TS7-6	06-Jun-52	4.33	2
HOT SPRING	TS1-3	03-Apr-52	24.86	4	IZARD	TP11-6	20-May-55	6.70	3
HOWARD	TP11-6	20-May-55	3.54	2	IZARD	PB9-2	24-Aug-57	8.19	3
HOWARD	PB12-4	05-Sep-57	3.63	2	IZARD	TS1-3	03-Apr-52	9.02	3
HOWARD	PB5-4	18-Jul-57	3.80	2	IZARD	UK7-4	28-Apr-53	12.05	4

INDIVIDUAL FALLOUT DAYS
ARKANSAS

COUNTY	SHOT	DATE	μCi/SQ METER	INDEX	COUNTY	SHOT	DATE	μCi/SQ METER	INDEX
IZARD	UK2-7	30-Mar-53	12.19	4	JOHNSON	TP11-6	20-May-55	4.99	2
IZARD	PB9-3	25-Aug-57	13.72	4	JOHNSON	TS7-6	06-Jun-52	5.46	3
IZARD	UK2-8	31-Mar-53	14.03	4	JOHNSON	TP11-5	19-May-55	8.04	3
IZARD	TP10-3	07-May-55	43.89	5	JOHNSON	UK1-1	17-Mar-53	12.33	4
JACKSON	UK7-3	27-Apr-53	3.64	2	JOHNSON	PB12-4	05-Sep-57	12.64	4
JACKSON	UK3-6	05-Apr-53	3.67	2	JOHNSON	TP10-3	07-May-55	36.80	5
JACKSON	PB8-3	20-Aug-57	4.00	2	JOHNSON	TS1-3	03-Apr-52	41.51	5
JACKSON	UK1-2	18-Mar-53	4.64	2	LAFAYETTE	TP11-5	19-May-55	3.70	2
JACKSON	PB9-2	24-Aug-57	5.46	3	LAFAYETTE	UK5-4	14-Apr-53	3.91	2
JACKSON	UK8-3	10-May-53	6.18	3	LAFAYETTE	BJ3-5	05-Nov-51	4.02	2
JACKSON	TP11-6	20-May-55	6.23	3	LAFAYETTE	PB12-6	07-Sep-57	4.08	2
JACKSON	TS1-3	03-Apr-52	9.02	3	LAFAYETTE	TP11-6	20-May-55	4.68	2
JACKSON	TS7-5	05-Jun-52	9.35	3	LAFAYETTE	UK7-4	28-Apr-53	4.99	2
JACKSON	UK7-4	28-Apr-53	13.31	4	LAFAYETTE	TS6-4	28-May-52	11.57	4
JACKSON	UK2-3	26-Mar-53	13.35	4	LAFAYETTE	TP6-2	23-Mar-55	13.77	4
JACKSON	PB9-3	25-Aug-57	13.72	4	LAFAYETTE	TP10-3	07-May-55	23.97	4
JACKSON	UK2-8	31-Mar-53	14.03	4	LAFAYETTE	TS1-3	03-Apr-52	24.86	4
JACKSON	UK2-7	30-Mar-53	18.26	4	LAWRENCE	UK7-3	27-Apr-53	3.57	2
JACKSON	TP10-3	07-May-55	22.17	4	LAWRENCE	UK1-2	18-Mar-53	3.81	2
JEFFERSON	PB12-6	07-Sep-57	3.54	2	LAWRENCE	PB8-3	20-Aug-57	4.00	2
JEFFERSON	UK3-6	05-Apr-53	3.67	2	LAWRENCE	PB9-2	24-Aug-57	5.46	3
JEFFERSON	PB8-3	20-Aug-57	4.00	2	LAWRENCE	TP11-6	20-May-55	5.64	3
JEFFERSON	UK8-3	10-May-53	6.18	3	LAWRENCE	UK8-3	10-May-53	6.18	3
JEFFERSON	UK2-8	31-Mar-53	7.04	3	LAWRENCE	UK2-3	26-Mar-53	7.60	3
JEFFERSON	TP11-6	20-May-55	7.19	3	LAWRENCE	TS1-3	03-Apr-52	9.02	3
JEFFERSON	TS6-4	28-May-52	7.71	3	LAWRENCE	PB9-3	25-Aug-57	13.72	4
JEFFERSON	TS1-3	03-Apr-52	9.02	3	LAWRENCE	UK2-8	31-Mar-53	14.03	4
JEFFERSON	UK2-7	30-Mar-53	12.19	4	LAWRENCE	UK7-4	28-Apr-53	15.93	4
JEFFERSON	UK7-3	27-Apr-53	17.79	4	LAWRENCE	UK2-7	30-Mar-53	18.26	4
JEFFERSON	UK7-4	28-Apr-53	21.42	4	LAWRENCE	TP10-3	07-May-55	34.19	5
JEFFERSON	TP10-3	07-May-55	22.39	4	LEE	UK3-6	05-Apr-53	3.67	2
JOHNSON	PB12-5	06-Sep-57	3.73	2	LEE	PB8-3	20-Aug-57	4.00	2
JOHNSON	PB8-3	20-Aug-57	4.00	2	LEE	PB11-2	01-Sep-57	4.26	2

INDIVIDUAL FALLOUT DAYS
ARKANSAS

COUNTY	SHOT	DATE	µCi/SQ METER	INDEX	COUNTY	SHOT	DATE	µCi/SQ METER	INDEX
LEE	UK1-2	18-Mar-53	4.30	2	LOGAN	TP11-5	19-May-55	10.38	4
LEE	UK8-3	10-May-53	6.18	3	LOGAN	UK1-1	17-Mar-53	12.33	4
LEE	TS1-3	03-Apr-52	9.02	3	LOGAN	TP10-3	07-May-55	17.92	4
LEE	UK2-7	30-Mar-53	12.19	4	LOGAN	TS1-3	03-Apr-52	24.86	4
LEE	UK2-8	31-Mar-53	21.07	4	LONOKE	UK3-6	05-Apr-53	3.67	2
LEE	UK7-4	28-Apr-53	22.19	4	LONOKE	UK7-3	27-Apr-53	3.99	2
LINCOLN	UK3-6	05-Apr-53	3.67	2	LONOKE	PB8-3	20-Aug-57	4.00	2
LINCOLN	UK8-3	10-May-53	3.68	2	LONOKE	UK2-8	31-Mar-53	3.50	1
LINCOLN	UK7-3	27-Apr-53	4.47	2	LONOKE	UK2-3	26-Mar-53	5.61	3
LINCOLN	UK2-8	31-Mar-53	3.50	1	LONOKE	UK8-3	10-May-53	6.18	3
LINCOLN	UK2-7	30-Mar-53	6.07	3	LONOKE	TS6-4	28-May-52	6.75	3
LINCOLN	TP11-6	20-May-55	6.55	3	LONOKE	TS1-3	03-Apr-52	9.02	3
LINCOLN	TS6-4	28-May-52	7.71	3	LONOKE	UK2-7	30-Mar-53	18.26	4
LINCOLN	TS1-3	03-Apr-52	9.02	3	LONOKE	UK7-4	28-Apr-53	20.59	4
LINCOLN	TP10-3	07-May-55	20.14	4	LONOKE	TP10-3	07-May-55	35.02	5
LINCOLN	UK7-4	28-Apr-53	25.44	5	MADISON	PB13-6	11-Sep-57	3.68	2
LITTLE RIVER	UK5-4	14-Apr-53	3.91	2	MADISON	PB8-3	20-Aug-57	4.00	2
LITTLE RIVER	PB8-3	20-Aug-57	4.00	2	MADISON	TP11-6	20-May-55	4.36	2
LITTLE RIVER	UK1-2	18-Mar-53	4.30	2	MADISON	TS7-6	06-Jun-52	5.46	3
LITTLE RIVER	TP11-5	19-May-55	4.58	2	MADISON	UK3-5	04-Apr-53	6.83	3
LITTLE RIVER	TS7-6	06-Jun-52	4.76	2	MADISON	UK1-1	17-Mar-53	7.40	3
LITTLE RIVER	PB12-4	05-Sep-57	4.82	2	MADISON	TP11-5	19-May-55	8.68	3
LITTLE RIVER	TS6-4	28-May-52	11.28	4	MADISON	UK7-3	27-Apr-53	11.48	4
LITTLE RIVER	TP6-2	23-Mar-55	13.77	4	MADISON	PB12-4	05-Sep-57	13.78	4
LITTLE RIVER	TS1-3	03-Apr-52	24.86	4	MADISON	TS1-3	03-Apr-52	24.86	4
LITTLE RIVER	TP10-3	07-May-55	30.74	5	MADISON	TS7-5	05-Jun-52	25.51	5
LOGAN	PB12-5	06-Sep-57	3.82	2	MADISON	TP10-3	07-May-55	26.72	5
LOGAN	PB8-3	20-Aug-57	4.00	2	MARION	PB12-5	06-Sep-57	3.78	2
LOGAN	UK3-5	04-Apr-53	4.10	2	MARION	UK3-5	04-Apr-53	4.10	2
LOGAN	UK1-2	18-Mar-53	5.16	3	MARION	UK7-3	27-Apr-53	4.33	2
LOGAN	TS7-5	05-Jun-52	5.87	3	MARION	TP11-5	19-May-55	4.62	2
LOGAN	PB12-4	05-Sep-57	9.26	3	MARION	TP11-6	20-May-55	7.19	3
LOGAN	TP11-6	20-May-55	10.27	4	MARION	PB12-4	05-Sep-57	7.36	3

INDIVIDUAL FALLOUT DAYS
ARKANSAS

COUNTY	SHOT	DATE	µCi/SQ METER	INDEX	COUNTY	SHOT	DATE	µCi/SQ METER	INDEX
MARION	UK1-1	17-Mar-53	7.40	3	MONROE	TS1-3	03-Apr-52	9.02	3
MARION	PB8-3	20-Aug-57	7.99	3	MONROE	UK2-7	30-Mar-53	18.26	4
MARION	UK7-4	28-Apr-53	9.95	3	MONROE	UK7-4	28-Apr-53	18.76	4
MARION	UK2-7	30-Mar-53	18.26	4	MONROE	UK2-8	31-Mar-53	21.07	4
MARION	TS1-3	03-Apr-52	24.86	4	MONTGOMERY	PB5-4	18-Jul-57	3.80	2
MARION	TP10-3	07-May-55	36.22	5	MONTGOMERY	UK5-4	14-Apr-53	3.91	2
MILLER	PB5-4	18-Jul-57	3.80	2	MONTGOMERY	PB8-3	20-Aug-57	4.00	2
MILLER	TP11-6	20-May-55	4.80	2	MONTGOMERY	BJ3-5	05-Nov-51	4.02	2
MILLER	TS7-4	04-Jun-52	4.95	2	MONTGOMERY	TP11-5	19-May-55	4.08	2
MILLER	UK7-3	27-Apr-53	8.20	3	MONTGOMERY	PB11-1	31-Aug-57	4.09	2
MILLER	TS6-4	28-May-52	10.48	4	MONTGOMERY	UK1-2	18-Mar-53	4.73	2
MILLER	TP6-2	23-Mar-55	13.77	4	MONTGOMERY	TS7-6	06-Jun-52	5.19	3
MILLER	TP10-3	07-May-55	17.36	4	MONTGOMERY	TS6-4	28-May-52	7.71	3
MILLER	TS1-3	03-Apr-52	24.86	4	MONTGOMERY	TP11-6	20-May-55	9.83	3
MISSISSIPPI	UK1-3	19-Mar-53	3.69	2	MONTGOMERY	TP10-3	07-May-55	9.88	3
MISSISSIPPI	PB8-3	20-Aug-57	4.00	2	MONTGOMERY	TP6-2	23-Mar-55	13.77	4
MISSISSIPPI	TP10-3	07-May-55	4.20	2	MONTGOMERY	TS1-3	03-Apr-52	41.51	5
MISSISSIPPI	TS7-5	05-Jun-52	4.62	2	NEVADA	UK1-2	18-Mar-53	3.61	2
MISSISSIPPI	UK1-2	18-Mar-53	5.29	3	NEVADA	UK5-4	14-Apr-53	3.91	2
MISSISSIPPI	UK8-3	10-May-53	6.18	3	NEVADA	TP11-5	19-May-55	3.93	2
MISSISSIPPI	UK2-3	26-Mar-53	6.67	3	NEVADA	BJ3-5	05-Nov-51	4.02	2
MISSISSIPPI	TS1-3	03-Apr-52	9.02	3	NEVADA	PB12-6	07-Sep-57	4.67	2
MISSISSIPPI	UK2-7	30-Mar-53	12.19	4	NEVADA	PB12-5	06-Sep-57	5.30	3
MISSISSIPPI	UK2-8	31-Mar-53	14.03	4	NEVADA	TP6-3	24-Mar-55	5.55	3
MISSISSIPPI	UK7-4	28-Apr-53	16.06	4	NEVADA	UK7-4	28-Apr-53	5.66	3
MONROE	UK3-6	05-Apr-53	3.67	2	NEVADA	TS6-4	28-May-52	6.75	3
MONROE	UK1-2	18-Mar-53	3.92	2	NEVADA	TP10-3	07-May-55	21.49	4
MONROE	UK7-3	27-Apr-53	3.92	2	NEVADA	TS1-3	03-Apr-52	24.86	4
MONROE	PB8-3	20-Aug-57	4.00	2	NEWTON	TS7-6	06-Jun-52	3.55	2
MONROE	UK2-3	26-Mar-53	5.44	3	NEWTON	UK7-3	27-Apr-53	3.57	2
MONROE	PB9-2	24-Aug-57	5.46	3	NEWTON	PB12-5	06-Sep-57	3.69	2
MONROE	UK8-3	10-May-53	6.18	3	NEWTON	PB12-4	05-Sep-57	3.80	2
MONROE	TP11-6	20-May-55	6.35	3	NEWTON	PB8-3	20-Aug-57	4.00	2

INDIVIDUAL FALLOUT DAYS
ARKANSAS

COUNTY	SHOT	DATE	µCi/SQ METER	INDEX	COUNTY	SHOT	DATE	µCi/SQ METER	INDEX
NEWTON	BJ3-5	05-Nov-51	4.02	2	PHILLIPS	TS6-4	28-May-52	14.46	4
NEWTON	UK7-4	28-Apr-53	6.63	3	PHILLIPS	UK2-7	30-May-53	18.26	4
NEWTON	TP11-5	19-May-55	7.32	3	PHILLIPS	UK7-4	28-Apr-53	21.22	4
NEWTON	TP11-6	20-May-55	9.10	3	PIKE	UK7-4	28-Apr-53	3.52	2
NEWTON	UK1-1	17-Mar-53	12.33	4	PIKE	UK5-4	14-Apr-53	3.91	2
NEWTON	TP10-3	07-May-55	34.27	5	PIKE	PB8-3	20-Aug-57	4.00	2
NEWTON	TS1-3	03-Apr-52	41.51	5	PIKE	BJ3-5	05-Nov-51	4.02	2
OUACHITA	PB1-6	02-Jun-57	3.52	2	PIKE	UK1-2	18-Mar-53	4.90	2
OUACHITA	PB12-4	05-Sep-57	3.74	2	PIKE	TP11-5	19-May-55	6.17	3
OUACHITA	BJ3-5	05-Nov-51	4.02	2	PIKE	TP10-3	07-May-55	6.99	3
OUACHITA	TP11-6	20-May-55	4.59	2	PIKE	TP11-6	20-May-55	10.73	4
OUACHITA	TP6-3	24-Mar-55	5.55	3	PIKE	TP6-2	23-Mar-55	13.77	4
OUACHITA	UK7-4	28-Apr-53	10.26	4	PIKE	TS1-3	03-Apr-52	24.86	4
OUACHITA	PB12-6	07-Sep-57	10.30	4	POINSETT	UK7-4	28-Apr-53	3.82	2
OUACHITA	TS6-4	28-May-52	12.54	4	POINSETT	PB8-3	20-Aug-57	4.00	2
OUACHITA	TS1-3	03-Apr-52	24.86	4	POINSETT	UK1-2	18-Mar-53	5.24	3
PERRY	UK2-3	26-Mar-53	3.71	2	POINSETT	PB9-2	24-Aug-57	5.46	3
PERRY	PB8-3	20-Aug-57	4.00	2	POINSETT	TS1-3	03-Apr-52	6.02	3
PERRY	UK1-2	18-Mar-53	3.50	1	POINSETT	UK2-7	30-May-53	6.07	3
PERRY	TP11-6	20-May-55	5.62	3	POINSETT	UK8-3	10-May-53	6.18	3
PERRY	UK7-4	28-Apr-53	6.90	3	POINSETT	TP10-3	07-May-55	8.62	3
PERRY	PB12-4	05-Sep-57	7.50	3	POINSETT	UK2-3	26-Mar-53	15.90	4
PERRY	UK1-1	17-Mar-53	12.33	4	POINSETT	UK2-8	31-Mar-53	21.07	4
PERRY	TS1-3	03-Apr-52	41.51	5	POLK	PB8-3	20-Aug-57	4.00	2
PERRY	TP10-3	07-May-55	57.34	6	POLK	BJ3-5	05-Nov-51	4.02	2
PHILLIPS	UK3-6	05-Apr-53	3.67	2	POLK	TS7-6	06-Jun-52	5.42	3
PHILLIPS	PB8-3	20-Aug-57	4.00	2	POLK	UK1-2	18-Mar-53	5.72	3
PHILLIPS	TP11-6	20-May-55	4.92	2	POLK	PB11-1	31-Aug-57	6.14	3
PHILLIPS	UK1-2	18-Mar-53	3.50	1	POLK	PB12-4	05-Sep-57	8.99	3
PHILLIPS	PB9-2	24-Aug-57	5.46	3	POLK	TP11-5	19-May-55	11.92	4
PHILLIPS	TS1-3	03-Apr-52	6.02	3	POLK	UK1-1	17-Mar-53	12.33	4
PHILLIPS	UK8-3	10-May-53	6.18	3	POLK	TP6-2	23-Mar-55	13.77	4
PHILLIPS	UK2-8	31-Mar-53	7.04	3	POLK	TP10-3	07-May-55	16.57	4

INDIVIDUAL FALLOUT DAYS
ARKANSAS

COUNTY	SHOT	DATE	µCi/SQ METER	INDEX	COUNTY	SHOT	DATE	µCi/SQ METER	INDEX
POLK	TS1-3	03-Apr-52	24.86	4	PULASKI	TP10-3	07-May-55	37.72	5
POPE	PB12-5	06-Sep-57	3.86	2	RANDOLPH	UK8-3	10-May-53	3.68	2
POPE	PB8-3	20-Aug-57	4.00	2	RANDOLPH	PB8-3	20-Aug-57	4.00	2
POPE	BJ3-5	05-Nov-51	4.02	2	RANDOLPH	PB11-2	01-Sep-57	4.26	2
POPE	TP11-6	20-May-55	5.41	3	RANDOLPH	TP10-3	07-May-55	4.79	2
POPE	TP11-5	19-May-55	6.43	3	RANDOLPH	UK7-3	27-Apr-53	3.51	1
POPE	UK7-4	28-Apr-53	6.79	3	RANDOLPH	TP11-6	20-May-55	5.18	3
POPE	PB12-4	05-Sep-57	11.08	4	RANDOLPH	TS7-5	05-Jun-52	7.71	3
POPE	UK1-1	17-Mar-53	12.33	4	RANDOLPH	PB9-2	24-Aug-57	8.19	3
POPE	TS1-3	03-Apr-52	41.51	5	RANDOLPH	UK2-3	26-Mar-53	8.92	3
POPE	TP10-3	07-May-55	45.24	5	RANDOLPH	TS1-3	03-Apr-52	9.02	3
PRAIRIE	UK3-6	05-Apr-53	3.67	2	RANDOLPH	PB9-3	25-Aug-57	13.72	4
PRAIRIE	UK1-2	18-Mar-53	3.81	2	RANDOLPH	UK2-8	31-Mar-53	14.03	4
PRAIRIE	UK7-3	27-Apr-53	3.99	2	RANDOLPH	UK7-4	28-Apr-53	15.13	4
PRAIRIE	PB8-3	20-Aug-57	4.00	2	RANDOLPH	UK2-7	30-Mar-53	18.26	4
PRAIRIE	PB11-2	01-Sep-57	4.26	2	SALINE	UK5-4	14-Apr-53	3.91	2
PRAIRIE	PB6-6	29-Jul-57	4.47	2	SALINE	PB8-3	20-Aug-57	4.00	2
PRAIRIE	UK8-3	10-May-53	6.18	3	SALINE	BJ3-5	05-Nov-51	4.02	2
PRAIRIE	TP11-6	20-May-55	6.84	3	SALINE	PB11-2	01-Sep-57	4.26	2
PRAIRIE	TS1-3	03-Apr-52	9.02	3	SALINE	TP11-6	20-May-55	5.35	3
PRAIRIE	UK2-7	30-Mar-53	12.19	4	SALINE	UK7-4	28-Apr-53	9.14	3
PRAIRIE	PB9-2	24-Aug-57	13.65	4	SALINE	TS1-3	03-Apr-52	24.86	4
PRAIRIE	UK7-4	28-Apr-53	16.14	4	SALINE	TP10-3	07-May-55	53.43	6
PRAIRIE	TP10-3	07-May-55	31.56	5	SCOTT	PB5-4	18-Jul-57	3.80	2
PRAIRIE	UK2-8	31-Mar-53	35.10	5	SCOTT	PB8-3	20-Aug-57	4.00	2
PULASKI	UK1-4	20-Mar-53	3.55	2	SCOTT	PB13-9	14-Sep-57	4.15	2
PULASKI	UK5-4	14-Apr-53	3.91	2	SCOTT	UK1-2	18-Mar-53	4.15	2
PULASKI	PB8-3	20-Aug-57	4.00	2	SCOTT	PB12-4	05-Sep-57	5.61	3
PULASKI	UK2-3	26-Mar-53	4.37	2	SCOTT	TP11-5	19-May-55	5.83	3
PULASKI	TP11-6	20-May-55	4.80	2	SCOTT	PB11-1	31-Aug-57	6.14	3
PULASKI	UK7-4	28-Apr-53	14.79	4	SCOTT	TP10-3	07-May-55	6.17	3
PULASKI	UK7-3	27-Apr-53	15.91	4	SCOTT	TP11-6	20-May-55	6.21	3
PULASKI	TS1-3	03-Apr-52	16.64	4	SCOTT	UK1-1	17-Mar-53	12.33	4

INDIVIDUAL FALLOUT DAYS
ARKANSAS

COUNTY	SHOT	DATE	µCi/SQ METER	INDEX	COUNTY	SHOT	DATE	µCi/SQ METER	INDEX
SCOTT	TP6-2	23-Mar-55	13.77	4	SEVIER	TS1-3	03-Apr-52	24.86	4
SCOTT	TS1-3	03-Apr-52	24.86	4	SEVIER	TP10-3	07-May-55	34.79	5
SEARCY	PB12-5	06-Sep-57	3.78	2	SHARP	PB12-4	05-Sep-57	3.58	2
SEARCY	PB8-3	20-Aug-57	4.00	2	SHARP	UK7-3	27-Apr-53	3.99	2
SEARCY	BJ3-5	05-Nov-51	4.02	2	SHARP	PB8-3	20-Aug-57	4.00	2
SEARCY	UK7-3	27-Apr-53	4.06	2	SHARP	PB9-2	24-Aug-57	5.46	3
SEARCY	TP11-5	19-May-55	4.85	2	SHARP	UK8-3	10-May-53	6.18	3
SEARCY	UK7-4	28-Apr-53	7.75	3	SHARP	UK2-3	26-Mar-53	6.84	3
SEARCY	TP11-6	20-May-55	8.04	3	SHARP	TS7-6	06-Jun-52	6.90	3
SEARCY	PB9-2	24-Aug-57	8.19	3	SHARP	TS1-3	03-Apr-52	9.02	3
SEARCY	UK1-1	17-Mar-53	12.33	4	SHARP	TP11-6	20-May-55	10.68	4
SEARCY	TS1-3	03-Apr-52	24.86	4	SHARP	UK7-4	28-Apr-53	13.64	4
SEARCY	TP10-3	07-May-55	34.19	5	SHARP	PB9-3	25-Aug-57	13.72	4
SEBASTIAN	PB13-6	11-Sep-57	3.88	2	SHARP	UK2-8	31-Mar-53	14.03	4
SEBASTIAN	PB8-3	20-Aug-57	4.00	2	SHARP	UK2-7	30-Mar-53	18.26	4
SEBASTIAN	TS7-6	06-Jun-52	4.07	2	SHARP	TP10-3	07-May-55	39.98	5
SEBASTIAN	PB13-9	14-Sep-57	4.15	2	ST FRANCIS	UK3-6	05-Apr-53	3.67	2
SEBASTIAN	UK7-3	27-Apr-53	5.68	3	ST FRANCIS	PB8-3	20-Aug-57	4.00	2
SEBASTIAN	TP11-5	19-May-55	8.16	3	ST FRANCIS	UK2-3	26-Mar-53	4.15	2
SEBASTIAN	TP11-6	20-May-55	9.80	3	ST FRANCIS	UK1-2	18-Mar-53	4.99	2
SEBASTIAN	PB12-4	05-Sep-57	13.72	4	ST FRANCIS	UK8-3	10-May-53	6.18	3
SEBASTIAN	TP6-2	23-Mar-55	13.77	4	ST FRANCIS	TP10-3	07-May-55	7.94	3
SEBASTIAN	TP10-3	07-May-55	14.17	4	ST FRANCIS	TS1-3	03-Apr-52	9.02	3
SEBASTIAN	TS1-3	03-Apr-52	17.24	4	ST FRANCIS	UK2-7	30-Mar-53	12.19	4
SEBASTIAN	TS7-5	05-Jun-52	17.88	4	ST FRANCIS	UK2-8	31-Mar-53	21.07	4
SEVIER	UK5-4	14-Apr-53	3.91	2	ST FRANCIS	UK7-4	28-Apr-53	28.01	5
SEVIER	PB8-3	20-Aug-57	4.00	2	STONE	UK8-3	10-May-53	3.68	2
SEVIER	BJ3-5	05-Nov-51	4.02	2	STONE	PB12-5	06-Sep-57	3.69	2
SEVIER	TP11-5	19-May-55	4.69	2	STONE	UK2-3	26-Mar-53	3.94	2
SEVIER	TS7-6	06-Jun-52	4.74	2	STONE	PB8-3	20-Aug-57	4.00	2
SEVIER	UK1-2	18-Mar-53	5.37	3	STONE	UK7-3	27-Apr-53	4.12	2
SEVIER	TP11-6	20-May-55	6.32	3	STONE	PB9-2	24-Aug-57	5.46	3
SEVIER	TP6-2	23-Mar-55	13.77	4	STONE	TS7-6	06-Jun-52	6.90	3

INDIVIDUAL FALLOUT DAYS
ARKANSAS

COUNTY	SHOT	DATE	µCi/SQ METER	INDEX	COUNTY	SHOT	DATE	µCi/SQ METER	INDEX
STONE	TP11-6	20-May-55	7.55	3	WASHINGTON	PB12-4	05-Sep-57	14.73	4
STONE	UK2-7	30-Mar-53	12.19	4	WASHINGTON	TP10-3	07-May-55	19.50	4
STONE	UK7-4	28-Apr-53	13.45	4	WASHINGTON	TS1-3	03-Apr-52	24.86	4
STONE	UK2-8	31-Mar-53	14.03	4	WASHINGTON	TS7-5	05-Jun-52	26.20	5
STONE	TS1-3	03-Apr-52	15.04	4	WHITE	UK3-6	05-Apr-53	3.67	2
STONE	TP10-3	07-May-55	18.02	4	WHITE	UK1-2	18-Mar-53	3.81	2
UNION	TP11-6	20-May-55	3.77	2	WHITE	UK7-3	27-Apr-53	3.92	2
UNION	TP10-3	07-May-55	4.03	2	WHITE	PB8-3	20-Aug-57	4.00	2
UNION	TP6-3	24-Mar-55	5.55	3	WHITE	PB6-6	29-Jul-57	4.41	2
UNION	PB12-6	07-Sep-57	6.43	3	WHITE	PB9-2	24-Aug-57	5.46	3
UNION	TS6-4	28-May-52	12.54	4	WHITE	UK8-3	10-May-53	6.18	3
UNION	UK7-4	28-Apr-53	15.18	4	WHITE	TP11-6	20-May-55	7.19	3
UNION	UK7-3	27-Apr-53	22.55	4	WHITE	TS1-3	03-Apr-52	9.02	3
VAN BUREN	PB12-5	06-Sep-57	3.82	2	WHITE	UK2-7	30-Mar-53	12.19	4
VAN BUREN	UK7-3	27-Apr-53	3.85	2	WHITE	UK7-4	28-Apr-53	14.54	4
VAN BUREN	PB8-3	20-Aug-57	4.00	2	WHITE	UK2-8	31-Mar-53	21.07	4
VAN BUREN	UK3-5	04-Apr-53	4.10	2	WHITE	TP10-3	07-May-55	36.15	5
VAN BUREN	PB11-2	01-Sep-57	4.26	2	WOODRUFF	UK3-6	05-Apr-53	3.67	2
VAN BUREN	UK7-4	28-Apr-53	6.52	3	WOODRUFF	UK7-3	27-Apr-53	3.71	2
VAN BUREN	PB9-2	24-Aug-57	8.19	3	WOODRUFF	PB8-3	20-Aug-57	4.00	2
VAN BUREN	TP11-6	20-May-55	8.69	3	WOODRUFF	UK1-2	18-Mar-53	4.74	2
VAN BUREN	UK2-7	30-Mar-53	12.19	4	WOODRUFF	UK8-3	10-May-53	6.18	3
VAN BUREN	UK1-1	17-Mar-53	12.33	4	WOODRUFF	TS1-3	03-Apr-52	9.02	3
VAN BUREN	TS1-3	03-Apr-52	24.86	4	WOODRUFF	TP11-6	20-May-55	11.55	4
VAN BUREN	TP10-3	07-May-55	45.62	5	WOODRUFF	PB9-3	25-Aug-57	13.72	4
WASHINGTON	PB8-3	20-Aug-57	4.00	2	WOODRUFF	UK7-4	28-Apr-53	17.91	4
WASHINGTON	PB13-6	11-Sep-57	4.30	2	WOODRUFF	UK2-8	31-Mar-53	21.07	4
WASHINGTON	TP11-6	20-May-55	4.50	2	WOODRUFF	TP10-3	07-May-55	29.68	5
WASHINGTON	TS7-6	06-Jun-52	4.95	2	YELL	UK1-2	18-Mar-53	3.70	2
WASHINGTON	UK3-5	04-Apr-53	6.83	3	YELL	TP11-5	19-May-55	3.89	2
WASHINGTON	UK1-1	17-Mar-53	7.40	3	YELL	PB12-5	06-Sep-57	3.95	2
WASHINGTON	UK7-3	27-Apr-53	8.26	3	YELL	PB8-3	20-Aug-57	4.00	2
WASHINGTON	TP11-5	19-May-55	12.09	4	YELL	UK7-4	28-Apr-53	4.38	2

INDIVIDUAL FALLOUT DAYS
ARKANSAS

COUNTY	SHOT	DATE	µCi/SQ METER	INDEX	COUNTY	SHOT	DATE	µCi/SQ METER	INDEX
YELL	PB12-4	05-Sep-57	8.51	3	YELL	TP10-3	07-May-55	21.67	4
YELL	TP11-6	20-May-55	9.52	3	YELL	TS1-3	03-Apr-52	41.51	5
YELL	UK1-1	17-Mar-53	12.33	4					

INDIVIDUAL FALLOUT DAYS
ARIZONA

COUNTY	SHOT	DATE	µCi/SQ METER	INDEX	COUNTY	SHOT	DATE	µCi/SQ METER	INDEX
APACHE	UK3-1	31-Mar-53	3.56	2	COCONINO1	UK3-1	31-Mar-53	5.12	3
APACHE	TS4-1	01-May-52	4.43	2	COCONINO1	TS3-1	22-Apr-52	8.12	3
APACHE	PB17-1	28-Sep-57	8.20	3	COCONINO1	PB17-1	28-Sep-57	8.20	3
APACHE	PB13-3	08-Sep-57	9.40	3	COCONINO1	TP11-1	15-May-55	8.30	3
APACHE	PB18-1	10-Jul-57	9.94	3	COCONINO1	TS2-1	15-Apr-52	9.41	3
APACHE	PB1-1	28-May-57	10.25	4	COCONINO1	PB1-1	28-May-57	10.25	4
APACHE	TP11-1	15-May-55	12.11	4	COCONINO1	PB3-1	24-Jun-57	11.31	4
APACHE	TS3-1	22-Apr-52	12.35	4	COCONINO1	PB11-1	31-Aug-57	12.32	4
APACHE	TP4-1	07-Mar-55	15.77	4	COCONINO1	TS7-1	01-Jun-52	17.80	4
APACHE	TP7-1	29-Mar-55	16.89	4	COCONINO1	UK6-1	18-Apr-53	21.65	4
APACHE	TP5-1	12-Mar-55	26.01	5	COCONINO1	TP3-1	01-Mar-55	29.68	5
APACHE	UK1-1	17-Mar-53	27.92	5	COCONINO1	TP7-1	29-Mar-55	32.62	5
APACHE	PB3-1	24-Jun-57	32.07	5	COCONINO1	TP6-1	22-Mar-55	42.35	5
APACHE	UK11-1	04-Jun-53	33.12	5	COCONINO1	TP5-1	12-Mar-55	42.85	5
APACHE	TS6-1	25-May-52	44.42	5	COCONINO1	UK11-1	04-Jun-53	44.82	5
APACHE	TS7-1	01-Jun-52	44.50	5	COCONINO1	TS6-1	25-May-52	46.41	5
APACHE	UK9-1	19-May-53	281.09	8	COCONINO1	UK7-1	25-Apr-53	155.03	7
APACHE	UK6-1	18-Apr-53	319.19	8	COCONINO1	UK9-1	19-May-53	1522.26	10
APACHE	UK7-1	25-Apr-53	537.54	9	COCONINO2	TP11-1	15-May-55	4.10	2
COCHISE	UK3-1	31-Mar-53	4.41	2	COCONINO2	UK5-1	11-Apr-53	4.90	2
COCHISE	TS2-1	15-Apr-52	6.26	3	COCONINO2	TS2-1	15-Apr-52	5.33	3
COCHISE	TP6-1	22-Mar-55	6.74	3	COCONINO2	PB18-1	10-Jul-57	5.43	3
COCHISE	PB17-1	28-Sep-57	8.20	3	COCONINO2	TS4-1	01-May-52	5.86	3
COCHISE	PB1-1	28-May-57	10.25	4	COCONINO2	PB17-1	28-Sep-57	8.20	3
COCHISE	PB3-1	24-Jun-57	17.47	4	COCONINO2	UK3-1	31-Mar-53	10.24	4
COCHISE	TS6-1	25-May-52	29.06	5	COCONINO2	PB1-1	28-May-57	10.25	4
COCHISE	PB4-1	05-Jul-57	32.72	5	COCONINO2	TS3-1	22-Apr-52	14.11	4
COCHISE	TS7-1	01-Jun-52	35.60	5	COCONINO2	TP6-1	22-Mar-55	14.27	4
COCONINO1	TP8-1	09-Apr-55	4.43	2	COCONINO2	TP7-1	29-Mar-55	16.31	4
COCONINO1	UK1-1	17-Mar-53	4.67	2	COCONINO2	TS7-1	01-Jun-52	17.80	4
COCONINO1	TS4-1	01-May-52	4.86	2	COCONINO2	PB13-3	08-Sep-57	25.64	5
COCONINO1	UK5-1	11-Apr-53	5.05	3	COCONINO2	TP5-1	12-Mar-55	43.96	5
COCONINO1	PB18-1	10-Jul-57	5.09	3	COCONINO2	TS6-1	25-May-52	45.09	5

INDIVIDUAL FALLOUT DAYS
ARIZONA

COUNTY	SHOT	DATE	µCi/SQ METER	INDEX	COUNTY	SHOT	DATE	µCi/SQ METER	INDEX
COCONINO2	UK9-1	19-May-53	47.53	5	GRAHAM	UK3-1	31-Mar-53	9.10	3
COCONINO2	UK11-1	04-Jun-53	115.24	7	GRAHAM	TP6-1	22-Mar-55	9.57	3
COCONINO2	UK6-1	18-Apr-53	328.54	8	GRAHAM	PB1-1	28-May-57	10.25	4
COCONINO2	UK7-1	25-Apr-53	912.14	10	GRAHAM	PB3-1	24-Jun-57	17.47	4
COCONINO3	TS4-1	01-May-52	4.31	2	GRAHAM	TS6-1	25-May-52	32.38	5
COCONINO3	UK5-1	11-Apr-53	5.12	3	GRAHAM	PB4-1	05-Jul-57	32.72	5
COCONINO3	PB18-1	10-Jul-57	5.43	3	GRAHAM	TS7-1	01-Jun-52	35.60	5
COCONINO3	TS2-1	15-Apr-52	5.91	3	GREENLEE	TS3-1	22-Apr-52	3.71	2
COCONINO3	TP7-1	29-Mar-55	7.64	3	GREENLEE	UK3-1	31-Mar-53	4.41	2
COCONINO3	PB17-1	28-Sep-57	8.20	3	GREENLEE	TS2-1	15-Apr-52	6.26	3
COCONINO3	TP6-1	22-Mar-55	9.32	3	GREENLEE	TP6-1	22-Mar-55	6.74	3
COCONINO3	UK3-1	31-Mar-53	9.52	3	GREENLEE	PB17-1	28-Sep-57	8.20	3
COCONINO3	PB1-1	28-May-57	10.25	4	GREENLEE	PB1-1	28-May-57	10.25	4
COCONINO3	UK11-1	04-Jun-53	13.39	4	GREENLEE	PB3-1	24-Jun-57	18.04	4
COCONINO3	TS7-1	01-Jun-52	17.80	4	GREENLEE	PB4-1	05-Jul-57	25.11	5
COCONINO3	TS3-1	22-Apr-52	19.47	4	GREENLEE	TS6-1	25-May-52	32.38	5
COCONINO3	PB13-3	08-Sep-57	25.64	5	GREENLEE	TS7-1	01-Jun-52	35.60	5
COCONINO3	TP5-1	12-Mar-55	41.27	5	MARICOPA	PB3-1	24-Jun-57	3.73	2
COCONINO3	TS6-1	25-May-52	42.52	5	MARICOPA	PB17-1	28-Sep-57	8.20	3
COCONINO3	UK7-1	25-Apr-53	172.07	7	MARICOPA	PB1-1	28-May-57	10.54	4
GILA	TP7-1	29-Mar-55	3.96	2	MARICOPA	TS2-1	15-Apr-52	14.38	4
GILA	TS2-1	15-Apr-52	6.26	3	MARICOPA	TP6-1	22-Mar-55	15.68	4
GILA	TS3-1	22-Apr-52	6.70	3	MARICOPA	TS6-1	25-May-52	16.80	4
GILA	PB17-1	28-Sep-57	8.20	3	MARICOPA	UK3-1	31-Mar-53	25.62	5
GILA	PB3-1	24-Jun-57	8.66	3	MARICOPA	TS7-1	01-Jun-52	26.70	5
GILA	PB1-1	28-May-57	10.25	4	MARICOPA	PB4-1	05-Jul-57	41.34	5
GILA	TP6-1	22-Mar-55	13.96	4	MOHAVE1	TP8-1	09-Apr-55	4.43	2
GILA	UK3-1	31-Mar-53	18.78	4	MOHAVE1	UK5-1	11-Apr-53	4.73	2
GILA	TS7-1	01-Jun-52	26.70	5	MOHAVE1	PB18-1	10-Jul-57	5.09	3
GILA	TS6-1	25-May-52	32.38	5	MOHAVE1	UK3-1	31-Mar-53	5.26	3
GILA	PB4-1	05-Jul-57	32.72	5	MOHAVE1	TS4-1	01-May-52	6.26	3
GRAHAM	TS2-1	15-Apr-52	6.26	3	MOHAVE1	TS3-1	22-Apr-52	8.12	3
GRAHAM	PB17-1	28-Sep-57	8.20	3	MOHAVE1	PB17-1	28-Sep-57	8.20	3

INDIVIDUAL FALLOUT DAYS
ARIZONA

COUNTY	SHOT	DATE	µCi/SQ METER	INDEX	COUNTY	SHOT	DATE	µCi/SQ METER	INDEX
MOHAVE1	TP11-1	15-May-55	8.30	3	MOHAVE2	TP6-1	22-Mar-55	102.51	7
MOHAVE1	TS2-1	15-Apr-52	9.41	3	MOHAVE2	UK7-1	25-Apr-53	139.35	7
MOHAVE1	UK1-1	17-Mar-53	9.45	3	MOHAVE2	TP11-1	15-May-55	207.52	8
MOHAVE1	PB1-1	28-May-57	10.25	4	MOHAVE2	PB11-1	31-Aug-57	230.98	8
MOHAVE1	PB3-1	24-Jun-57	11.31	4	MOHAVE2	UK9-1	19-May-53	1986.84	10
MOHAVE1	PB11-1	31-Aug-57	16.52	4	MOHAVE3	TP7-1	29-Mar-55	4.33	2
MOHAVE1	UK6-1	18-Apr-53	22.04	4	MOHAVE3	TP8-1	09-Apr-55	4.43	2
MOHAVE1	UK11-1	04-Jun-53	22.83	4	MOHAVE3	TS4-1	01-May-52	6.41	3
MOHAVE1	TS7-1	01-Jun-52	26.70	5	MOHAVE3	PB13-3	08-Sep-57	6.48	3
MOHAVE1	TP3-1	01-Mar-55	29.87	5	MOHAVE3	TS3-1	22-Apr-52	8.12	3
MOHAVE1	TP7-1	29-Mar-55	32.62	5	MOHAVE3	PB17-1	28-Sep-57	8.20	3
MOHAVE1	TP5-1	12-Mar-55	43.35	5	MOHAVE3	UK5-1	11-Apr-53	10.24	4
MOHAVE1	TS6-1	25-May-52	46.41	5	MOHAVE3	UK3-1	31-Mar-53	11.23	4
MOHAVE1	TP6-1	22-Mar-55	56.78	6	MOHAVE3	TS6-1	25-May-52	18.57	4
MOHAVE1	UK7-1	25-Apr-53	156.16	7	MOHAVE3	TP6-1	22-Mar-55	19.08	4
MOHAVE1	UK9-1	19-May-53	1045.83	10	MOHAVE3	UK11-1	04-Jun-53	22.41	4
MOHAVE2	UK5-1	11-Apr-53	5.05	3	MOHAVE3	UK6-1	18-Apr-53	25.98	5
MOHAVE2	PB18-1	10-Jul-57	5.09	3	MOHAVE3	TS7-1	01-Jun-52	26.70	5
MOHAVE2	TS4-1	01-May-52	6.26	3	MOHAVE3	TP11-1	15-May-55	88.60	6
MOHAVE2	PB13-3	08-Sep-57	6.48	3	MOHAVE3	UK7-1	25-Apr-53	146.09	7
MOHAVE2	PB17-1	28-Sep-57	8.20	3	MOHAVE3	TS2-1	15-Apr-52	193.08	7
MOHAVE2	TS2-1	15-Apr-52	9.41	3	MOHAVE4	TP7-1	29-Mar-55	4.33	2
MOHAVE2	PB3-1	24-Jun-57	11.44	4	MOHAVE4	TP8-1	09-Apr-55	4.43	2
MOHAVE2	UK3-1	31-Mar-53	15.93	4	MOHAVE4	TS4-1	01-May-52	6.41	3
MOHAVE2	UK1-1	17-Mar-53	17.83	4	MOHAVE4	PB13-3	08-Sep-57	6.48	3
MOHAVE2	UK6-1	18-Apr-53	22.04	4	MOHAVE4	TS3-1	22-Apr-52	8.12	3
MOHAVE2	TS3-1	22-Apr-52	23.11	4	MOHAVE4	PB17-1	28-Sep-57	8.20	3
MOHAVE2	TP5-1	12-Mar-55	23.87	4	MOHAVE4	UK5-1	11-Apr-53	10.24	4
MOHAVE2	TP7-1	29-Mar-55	24.61	4	MOHAVE4	UK3-1	31-Mar-53	11.23	4
MOHAVE2	TS7-1	01-Jun-52	26.70	5	MOHAVE4	TS6-1	25-May-52	18.57	4
MOHAVE2	TP3-1	01-Mar-55	30.06	5	MOHAVE4	TP6-1	22-Mar-55	19.08	4
MOHAVE2	UK11-1	04-Jun-53	34.93	5	MOHAVE4	UK11-1	04-Jun-53	22.41	4
MOHAVE2	TS6-1	25-May-52	46.41	5	MOHAVE4	UK6-1	18-Apr-53	25.98	5

INDIVIDUAL FALLOUT DAYS
ARIZONA

COUNTY	SHOT	DATE	µCi/SQ METER	INDEX	COUNTY	SHOT	DATE	µCi/SQ METER	INDEX
MOHAVE4	TS7-1	01-Jun-52	26.70	5	PINAL	PB1-1	28-May-57	10.25	4
MOHAVE4	TP11-1	15-May-55	88.60	6	PINAL	TP6-1	22-Mar-55	13.96	4
MOHAVE4	UK7-1	25-Apr-53	146.09	7	PINAL	UK3-1	31-Mar-53	14.08	4
MOHAVE4	TS2-1	15-Apr-52	193.08	7	PINAL	TS2-1	15-Apr-52	14.38	4
NAVAJO	UK5-1	11-Apr-53	3.62	2	PINAL	TS7-1	01-Jun-52	26.70	5
NAVAJO	TS4-1	01-May-52	4.57	2	PINAL	TS6-1	25-May-52	31.27	5
NAVAJO	UK3-1	31-Mar-53	5.40	3	PINAL	PB4-1	05-Jul-57	41.34	5
NAVAJO	TP4-1	07-Mar-55	7.89	3	SANTA CRUZ	PB17-1	28-Sep-57	8.20	3
NAVAJO	TP11-1	15-May-55	8.11	3	SANTA CRUZ	TP6-1	22-Mar-55	9.57	3
NAVAJO	PB17-1	28-Sep-57	8.20	3	SANTA CRUZ	PB1-1	28-May-57	10.25	4
NAVAJO	TP7-1	29-Mar-55	8.55	3	SANTA CRUZ	TS2-1	15-Apr-52	15.31	4
NAVAJO	UK1-1	17-Mar-53	9.34	3	SANTA CRUZ	PB3-1	24-Jun-57	17.47	4
NAVAJO	PB18-1	10-Jul-57	9.94	3	SANTA CRUZ	TS7-1	01-Jun-52	26.70	5
NAVAJO	PB1-1	28-May-57	10.25	4	SANTA CRUZ	TS6-1	25-May-52	29.06	5
NAVAJO	TS3-1	22-Apr-52	12.53	4	SANTA CRUZ	PB4-1	05-Jul-57	98.28	6
NAVAJO	PB13-3	08-Sep-57	12.68	4	YAVAPAI	TS4-1	01-May-52	3.57	2
NAVAJO	PB3-1	24-Jun-57	22.22	4	YAVAPAI	TP7-1	29-Mar-55	4.05	2
NAVAJO	TS7-1	01-Jun-52	26.70	5	YAVAPAI	PB1-1	28-May-57	5.17	3
NAVAJO	TP5-1	12-Mar-55	34.78	5	YAVAPAI	UK5-1	11-Apr-53	5.56	3
NAVAJO	UK11-1	04-Jun-53	38.55	5	YAVAPAI	PB17-1	28-Sep-57	8.20	3
NAVAJO	TS6-1	25-May-52	44.76	5	YAVAPAI	PB4-1	05-Jul-57	8.50	3
NAVAJO	UK6-1	18-Apr-53	321.49	8	YAVAPAI	TS3-1	22-Apr-52	12.70	4
NAVAJO	UK7-1	25-Apr-53	363.55	8	YAVAPAI	UK3-1	31-Mar-53	14.51	4
PIMA	PB17-1	28-Sep-57	4.83	2	YAVAPAI	TP6-1	22-Mar-55	21.33	4
PIMA	PB1-1	28-May-57	7.69	3	YAVAPAI	TS6-1	25-May-52	26.08	5
PIMA	TP6-1	22-Mar-55	9.17	3	YAVAPAI	TS7-1	01-Jun-52	26.70	5
PIMA	PB3-1	24-Jun-57	13.68	4	YAVAPAI	TS2-1	15-Apr-52	75.75	6
PIMA	TS2-1	15-Apr-52	14.44	4	YUMA	PB17-1	28-Sep-57	8.20	3
PIMA	TS6-1	25-May-52	26.05	5	YUMA	PB4-1	05-Jul-57	8.37	3
PIMA	TS7-1	01-Jun-52	31.46	5	YUMA	TS2-1	15-Apr-52	13.56	4
PIMA	PB4-1	05-Jul-57	148.41	7	YUMA	UK5-1	11-Apr-53	46.04	5
PINAL	PB17-1	28-Sep-57	8.20	3	YUMA	TP1-1	18-Feb-55	68.08	6
PINAL	PB3-1	24-Jun-57	8.66	3					

INDIVIDUAL FALLOUT DAYS
CALIFORNIA

COUNTY	SHOT	DATE	µCi/SQ METER	INDEX	COUNTY	SHOT	DATE	µCi/SQ METER	INDEX
ALAMEDA	TS7-1	01-Jun-52	4.48	2	COLUSA	TS8-1	05-Jun-52	66.47	6
ALAMEDA	TS5-1	07-May-52	5.21	3	CONTRA COSTA	TS7-1	01-Jun-52	4.48	2
ALAMEDA	TS6-1	25-May-52	5.27	3	CONTRA COSTA	TS5-1	07-May-52	4.67	2
ALAMEDA	TS8-1	05-Jun-52	13.29	4	CONTRA COSTA	TS6-1	25-May-52	5.27	3
ALPINE	TS7-5	05-Jun-52	3.87	2	CONTRA COSTA	TS8-1	05-Jun-52	26.59	5
ALPINE	TS7-1	01-Jun-52	5.73	3	DEL NORTE	TS3-4	25-Apr-52	6.13	3
ALPINE	TS8-2	06-Jun-52	6.74	3	EL DORADO	TS7-1	01-Jun-52	4.48	2
ALPINE	TS6-2	26-May-52	8.91	3	EL DORADO	TS6-1	25-May-52	5.27	3
ALPINE	TS6-1	25-May-52	10.54	4	EL DORADO	TS3-3	24-Apr-52	6.67	3
ALPINE	UK6-2	19-Apr-53	14.01	4	EL DORADO	TS6-2	26-May-52	7.41	3
ALPINE	TS5-1	07-May-52	16.03	4	EL DORADO	TS5-1	07-May-52	16.33	4
ALPINE	TS3-3	24-Apr-52	20.01	4	EL DORADO	TS8-1	05-Jun-52	146.23	7
ALPINE	TS8-1	05-Jun-52	1169.86	10	FRESNO	TS5-1	07-May-52	5.52	3
AMADOR	TS7-1	01-Jun-52	4.48	2	FRESNO	BJ1-1	28-Oct-51	12.11	4
AMADOR	TS6-1	25-May-52	5.27	3	FRESNO	TS8-1	05-Jun-52	15.42	4
AMADOR	TS6-2	26-May-52	6.44	3	GLENN	TS7-6	06-Jun-52	4.41	2
AMADOR	TS5-1	07-May-52	19.94	4	GLENN	TS7-1	01-Jun-52	4.48	2
AMADOR	TS3-3	24-Apr-52	20.01	4	GLENN	TS6-1	25-May-52	5.27	3
AMADOR	TS8-1	05-Jun-52	239.29	8	GLENN	TS3-4	25-Apr-52	36.81	5
BUTTE	TS7-1	01-Jun-52	4.48	2	GLENN	TS8-1	05-Jun-52	190.26	7
BUTTE	TS5-1	07-May-52	5.21	3	HUMBOLDT	TS8-1	05-Jun-52	9.23	3
BUTTE	TS6-1	25-May-52	5.27	3	IMPERIAL	TS2-5	19-Apr-52	10.84	4
BUTTE	TS3-3	24-Apr-52	20.01	4	IMPERIAL	TS8-1	05-Jun-52	13.29	4
BUTTE	TS8-1	05-Jun-52	53.18	6	INYO1	TP11-1	15-May-55	3.52	2
CALAVERAS	TS7-1	01-Jun-52	4.48	2	INYO1	TS2-1	15-Apr-52	5.10	3
CALAVERAS	TS6-1	25-May-52	5.27	3	INYO1	PB1-1	28-May-57	7.53	3
CALAVERAS	TS5-1	07-May-52	6.11	3	INYO1	TS8-2	06-Jun-52	10.81	4
CALAVERAS	TS6-2	26-May-52	6.12	3	INYO1	TS3-1	22-Apr-52	14.64	4
CALAVERAS	TS3-3	24-Apr-52	20.01	4	INYO1	TS7-1	01-Jun-52	20.14	4
CALAVERAS	TS8-1	05-Jun-52	66.47	6	INYO1	PB16-1	23-Sep-57	29.60	5
COLUSA	TS7-1	01-Jun-52	4.48	2	INYO1	PB2-1	18-Jun-57	31.32	5
COLUSA	TS6-1	25-May-52	5.27	3	INYO1	TP10-1	05-May-55	40.59	5
COLUSA	TS3-3	24-Apr-52	13.34	4	INYO1	PB6-1	24-Jul-57	88.07	6

INDIVIDUAL FALLOUT DAYS
CALIFORNIA

COUNTY	SHOT	DATE	µCi/SQ METER	INDEX	COUNTY	SHOT	DATE	µCi/SQ METER	INDEX
INYO1	TS8-1	05-Jun-52	1878.24	10	KINGS	TS6-1	25-May-52	6.02	3
INYO2	TP11-1	15-May-55	3.52	2	KINGS	TS8-1	05-Jun-52	11.09	4
INYO2	TS2-1	15-Apr-52	5.10	3	KINGS	BJ1-1	28-Oct-51	12.11	4
INYO2	PB1-1	28-May-57	7.53	3	LAKE	TS5-1	07-May-52	4.07	2
INYO2	TS8-2	06-Jun-52	10.81	4	LAKE	TS7-1	01-Jun-52	4.48	2
INYO2	TS3-1	22-Apr-52	14.64	4	LAKE	TS6-1	25-May-52	5.27	3
INYO2	TS7-1	01-Jun-52	20.14	4	LAKE	TS3-4	25-Apr-52	12.27	4
INYO2	PB16-1	23-Sep-57	29.60	5	LAKE	TS8-1	05-Jun-52	39.88	5
INYO2	PB2-1	18-Jun-57	31.32	5	LASSEN	TS7-1	01-Jun-52	5.73	3
INYO2	TP10-1	05-May-55	40.59	5	LASSEN	TS3-3	24-Apr-52	6.67	3
INYO2	PB6-1	24-Jul-57	88.07	6	LASSEN	TS6-1	25-May-52	10.54	4
INYO2	TS8-1	05-Jun-52	1878.24	10	LASSEN	TS8-1	05-Jun-52	319.05	8
INYO3	TP11-1	15-May-55	3.52	2	LOS ANGELES	TP11-1	15-May-55	4.51	2
INYO3	UK6-1	18-Apr-53	5.25	3	LOS ANGELES	TS3-1	22-Apr-52	4.83	2
INYO3	UK5-1	11-Apr-53	5.42	3	LOS ANGELES	TS2-1	15-Apr-52	24.28	4
INYO3	PB1-1	28-May-57	7.07	3	LOS ANGELES	BJ2-1	30-Oct-51	71.77	6
INYO3	TS8-2	06-Jun-52	10.81	4	MADERA	TS5-1	07-May-52	5.11	3
INYO3	TS3-1	22-Apr-52	14.64	4	MADERA	TS6-1	25-May-52	6.02	3
INYO3	TP10-1	05-May-55	16.31	4	MADERA	TS8-1	05-Jun-52	66.54	6
INYO3	TP8-1	09-Apr-55	18.27	4	MARIN	TS7-1	01-Jun-52	4.48	2
INYO3	UK7-1	25-Apr-53	28.30	5	MARIN	TS6-1	25-May-52	5.27	3
INYO3	BJ2-1	30-Oct-51	72.80	6	MARIN	TS3-4	25-Apr-52	12.27	4
INYO3	TS7-1	01-Jun-52	100.72	7	MARIN	TS8-1	05-Jun-52	13.29	4
INYO3	TS2-1	15-Apr-52	193.83	7	MARIPOSA	TS6-2	26-May-52	4.94	2
INYO3	TP4-1	07-Mar-55	341.80	8	MARIPOSA	TS6-1	25-May-52	6.02	3
INYO3	PB11-1	31-Aug-57	898.04	10	MARIPOSA	TS5-1	07-May-52	9.10	3
INYO3	TS8-1	05-Jun-52	1878.24	10	MARIPOSA	TS8-1	05-Jun-52	132.94	7
KERN	TS5-1	07-May-52	4.31	2	MENDOCINO	TS3-4	25-Apr-52	9.26	3
KERN	TS2-4	18-Apr-52	5.11	3	MENDOCINO	TS8-1	05-Jun-52	26.59	5
KERN	TS2-2	16-Apr-52	8.04	3	MERCED	TS6-1	25-May-52	6.02	3
KERN	TS3-2	23-Apr-52	9.73	3	MERCED	TS8-1	05-Jun-52	13.29	4
KERN	BJ1-1	28-Oct-51	12.11	4	MODOC	TS7-3	03-Jun-52	4.45	2
KERN	TS8-1	05-Jun-52	13.29	4	MODOC	TS8-2	06-Jun-52	4.75	2

INDIVIDUAL FALLOUT DAYS
CALIFORNIA

COUNTY	SHOT	DATE	µCi/SQ METER	INDEX	COUNTY	SHOT	DATE	µCi/SQ METER	INDEX
MODOC	TS3-3	24-Apr-52	10.00	4	PLACER	TS7-1	01-Jun-52	4.48	2
MODOC	TS8-1	05-Jun-52	824.47	10	PLACER	TS6-1	25-May-52	5.27	3
MONO	TP11-1	15-May-55	3.52	2	PLACER	TS6-2	26-May-52	6.44	3
MONO	TS6-1	25-May-52	3.66	2	PLACER	TS5-1	07-May-52	12.59	4
MONO	UK6-1	18-Apr-53	5.13	3	PLACER	TS3-3	24-Apr-52	13.34	4
MONO	PB13-1	06-Sep-57	9.07	3	PLACER	TS8-1	05-Jun-52	146.23	7
MONO	PB2-1	18-Jun-57	10.01	4	PLUMAS	TS5-1	07-May-52	5.24	3
MONO	TS3-1	22-Apr-52	14.64	4	PLUMAS	TS7-1	01-Jun-52	5.73	3
MONO	TS7-1	01-Jun-52	18.04	4	PLUMAS	TS3-3	24-Apr-52	6.67	3
MONO	TS8-2	06-Jun-52	21.47	4	PLUMAS	TS6-1	25-May-52	10.54	4
MONO	PB14-1	14-Sep-57	23.62	4	PLUMAS	TS8-1	05-Jun-52	438.70	9
MONO	TP10-1	05-May-55	24.18	4	RIVERSIDE	TS2-5	19-Apr-52	5.42	3
MONO	PB6-1	24-Jul-57	46.65	5	RIVERSIDE	TS8-1	05-Jun-52	26.59	5
MONO	PB16-1	23-Sep-57	48.97	5	SACRAMENTO	TS6-1	25-May-52	4.27	2
MONO	TS8-1	05-Jun-52	3728.54	10	SACRAMENTO	TS3-3	24-Apr-52	13.34	4
MONTEREY	TS6-1	25-May-52	6.02	3	SACRAMENTO	TS8-1	05-Jun-52	39.88	5
MONTEREY	TS5-1	07-May-52	7.72	3	SAN BENITO	TS6-1	25-May-52	6.02	3
MONTEREY	BJ1-1	28-Oct-51	12.11	4	SAN BENITO	BJ1-1	28-Oct-51	12.11	4
MONTEREY	TS8-1	05-Jun-52	13.29	4	SAN BENITO	TS8-1	05-Jun-52	13.29	4
NAPA	TS7-6	06-Jun-52	3.93	2	SAN BERNADIN	TP11-1	15-May-55	3.52	2
NAPA	TS7-1	01-Jun-52	4.48	2	SAN BERNADIN	PB1-1	28-May-57	3.54	2
NAPA	TS6-1	25-May-52	5.27	3	SAN BERNADIN	UK6-1	18-Apr-53	10.76	4
NAPA	TS8-1	05-Jun-52	93.06	6	SAN BERNADIN	TS3-1	22-Apr-52	11.12	4
NEVADA	TS7-1	01-Jun-52	5.73	3	SAN BERNADIN	UK3-1	31-Mar-53	11.23	4
NEVADA	TS6-2	26-May-52	5.80	3	SAN BERNADIN	UK5-1	11-Apr-53	22.71	4
NEVADA	UK6-2	19-Apr-53	9.34	3	SAN BERNADIN	PB11-1	31-Aug-57	44.25	5
NEVADA	TS6-1	25-May-52	10.54	4	SAN BERNADIN	TS2-1	15-Apr-52	91.14	6
NEVADA	TS5-1	07-May-52	10.64	4	SAN BERNADIN	TP1-1	18-Feb-55	107.56	7
NEVADA	TS3-3	24-Apr-52	20.01	4	SAN DIEGO	TS2-4	18-Apr-52	6.76	3
NEVADA	TS8-1	05-Jun-52	159.53	7	SAN DIEGO	TS2-2	16-Apr-52	8.04	3
ORANGE	TS2-4	18-Apr-52	6.76	3	SAN DIEGO	TS3-2	23-Apr-52	12.97	4
ORANGE	TS2-2	16-Apr-52	8.04	3	SAN DIEGO	TS8-1	05-Jun-52	26.59	5
ORANGE	TS3-2	23-Apr-52	9.73	3	SAN FRANCISC	TS7-1	01-Jun-52	4.48	2

INDIVIDUAL FALLOUT DAYS
CALIFORNIA

COUNTY	SHOT	DATE	µCi/SQ METER	INDEX	COUNTY	SHOT	DATE	µCi/SQ METER	INDEX
SAN FRANCISC	TS6-1	25-May-52	5.27	3	SIERRA	TS3-3	24-Apr-52	6.67	3
SAN FRANCISC	TS8-1	05-Jun-52	26.59	5	SIERRA	TS6-1	25-May-52	10.54	4
SAN JOAQUIN	TS6-2	26-May-52	3.86	2	SIERRA	TS5-1	07-May-52	10.79	4
SAN JOAQUIN	TS7-1	01-Jun-52	4.48	2	SIERRA	UK6-2	19-Apr-53	14.01	4
SAN JOAQUIN	TS6-1	25-May-52	5.27	3	SIERRA	TS8-1	05-Jun-52	279.17	8
SAN JOAQUIN	TS8-1	05-Jun-52	26.59	5	SISKIYOU	TS7-6	06-Jun-52	5.59	3
SAN LUIS OBI	TS5-1	07-May-52	5.93	3	SISKIYOU	TS8-1	05-Jun-52	39.88	5
SAN LUIS OBI	TS6-1	25-May-52	6.02	3	SOLANO	TS7-1	01-Jun-52	4.48	2
SAN LUIS OBI	BJ1-1	28-Oct-51	12.11	4	SOLANO	TS6-1	25-May-52	5.27	3
SAN LUIS OBI	TS8-1	05-Jun-52	26.59	5	SOLANO	TS8-1	05-Jun-52	26.59	5
SAN MATEO	TS7-6	06-Jun-52	3.93	2	SONOMA	TS7-1	01-Jun-52	4.48	2
SAN MATEO	TS7-1	01-Jun-52	4.48	2	SONOMA	TS6-1	25-May-52	5.27	3
SAN MATEO	TS6-1	25-May-52	5.27	3	SONOMA	TS5-1	07-May-52	5.36	3
SAN MATEO	TS8-1	05-Jun-52	39.88	5	SONOMA	TS8-1	05-Jun-52	13.29	4
SANTA BARBAR	TS6-1	25-May-52	4.01	2	SONOMA	TS3-4	25-Apr-52	24.54	4
SANTA BARBAR	TS7-1	01-Jun-52	4.48	2	STANISLAUS	TS6-2	26-May-52	3.54	2
SANTA BARBAR	BJ1-1	28-Oct-51	5.03	3	STANISLAUS	TS5-1	07-May-52	4.05	2
SANTA BARBAR	TS3-2	23-Apr-52	6.49	3	STANISLAUS	TS7-1	01-Jun-52	4.48	2
SANTA BARBAR	TS2-2	16-Apr-52	8.04	3	STANISLAUS	TS6-1	25-May-52	5.27	3
SANTA BARBAR	TS8-1	05-Jun-52	26.59	5	STANISLAUS	TS8-1	05-Jun-52	26.59	5
SANTA CLARA	TS7-1	01-Jun-52	4.48	2	SUTTER	TS7-1	01-Jun-52	4.48	2
SANTA CLARA	TP10-2	06-May-55	4.60	2	SUTTER	TS6-1	25-May-52	5.27	3
SANTA CLARA	TS6-1	25-May-52	5.27	3	SUTTER	TS3-3	24-Apr-52	6.67	3
SANTA CLARA	TS5-1	07-May-52	6.11	3	SUTTER	TS8-1	05-Jun-52	39.88	5
SANTA CLARA	TS8-1	05-Jun-52	13.29	4	TEHAMA	TS7-1	01-Jun-52	4.48	2
SANTA CRUZ	TS7-6	06-Jun-52	4.37	2	TEHAMA	TS6-1	25-May-52	5.27	3
SANTA CRUZ	TS7-1	01-Jun-52	4.48	2	TEHAMA	TS3-4	25-Apr-52	24.54	4
SANTA CRUZ	TS6-1	25-May-52	10.29	4	TEHAMA	TS8-1	05-Jun-52	53.18	6
SANTA CRUZ	TS5-1	07-May-52	10.71	4	TRINITY	TS3-4	25-Apr-52	6.13	3
SANTA CRUZ	TS8-1	05-Jun-52	39.88	5	TRINITY	TS6-4	28-May-52	19.29	4
SHASTA	TS8-1	05-Jun-52	79.76	6	TULARE	TS6-1	25-May-52	4.01	2
SIERRA	TS7-1	01-Jun-52	5.73	3	TULARE	TS5-1	07-May-52	4.20	2
SIERRA	TS6-2	26-May-52	6.33	3	TULARE	TS7-1	01-Jun-52	4.48	2

INDIVIDUAL FALLOUT DAYS
CALIFORNIA

COUNTY	SHOT	DATE	µCi/SQ METER	INDEX	COUNTY	SHOT	DATE	µCi/SQ METER	INDEX
TULARE	BJ1-1	28-Oct-51	12.11	4	VENTURA	TS8-1	05-Jun-52	26.59	5
TULARE	TS8-1	05-Jun-52	26.59	5	YOLO	TS7-1	01-Jun-52	4.48	2
TUOLUMNE	TS6-1	25-May-52	6.02	3	YOLO	TS6-1	25-May-52	5.27	3
TUOLUMNE	TS6-2	26-May-52	6.55	3	YOLO	TS3-3	24-Apr-52	6.67	3
TUOLUMNE	TS5-1	07-May-52	16.18	4	YOLO	TS8-1	05-Jun-52	26.59	5
TUOLUMNE	TS8-1	05-Jun-52	159.53	7	YUBA	TS6-2	26-May-52	3.65	2
VENTURA	TS6-1	25-May-52	4.01	2	YUBA	TS7-1	01-Jun-52	4.48	2
VENTURA	TS7-1	01-Jun-52	4.48	2	YUBA	TS6-1	25-May-52	5.27	3
VENTURA	TS3-2	23-Apr-52	6.49	3	YUBA	TS5-1	07-May-52	8.26	3
VENTURA	TS2-4	18-Apr-52	6.76	3	YUBA	TS3-3	24-Apr-52	20.01	4
VENTURA	TS2-2	16-Apr-52	8.04	3	YUBA	TS8-1	05-Jun-52	66.47	6
VENTURA	BJ1-1	28-Oct-51	12.11	4					

INDIVIDUAL FALLOUT DAYS
COLORADO

COUNTY	SHOT	DATE	µCi/SQ METER	INDEX	COUNTY	SHOT	DATE	µCi/SQ METER	INDEX
ADAMS	PB11-2	01-Sep-57	4.79	2	ALAMOSA	TS6-4	28-May-52	35.46	5
ADAMS	PB8-4	21-Aug-57	4.92	2	ALAMOSA	TP10-2	06-May-55	61.79	6
ADAMS	PB18-2	11-Jul-57	3.51	1	ALAMOSA	UK9-1	19-May-53	441.46	9
ADAMS	TP7-2	30-Mar-55	5.00	3	ARAPAHOE	UK7-4	28-Apr-53	3.88	2
ADAMS	PB12-4	05-Sep-57	5.07	3	ARAPAHOE	TP3-3	03-Mar-55	4.45	2
ADAMS	TS6-3	27-May-52	5.35	3	ARAPAHOE	TP9-2	15-Apr-55	4.49	2
ADAMS	TP10-3	07-May-55	5.64	3	ARAPAHOE	PB18-2	11-Jul-57	4.60	2
ADAMS	TP7-1	29-Mar-55	5.70	3	ARAPAHOE	PB11-2	01-Sep-57	4.79	2
ADAMS	TP9-2	15-Apr-55	6.34	3	ARAPAHOE	UK7-3	27-Apr-53	5.15	3
ADAMS	TS6-2	26-May-52	6.76	3	ARAPAHOE	TS6-2	26-May-52	6.87	3
ADAMS	TP11-2	16-May-55	7.98	3	ARAPAHOE	TP11-2	16-May-55	7.98	3
ADAMS	TP3-3	03-Mar-55	8.91	3	ARAPAHOE	TS1-2	02-Apr-52	8.70	3
ADAMS	UK7-3	27-Apr-53	9.12	3	ARAPAHOE	PB8-4	21-Aug-57	9.77	3
ADAMS	TP11-3	17-May-55	10.79	4	ARAPAHOE	TP11-3	17-May-55	11.17	4
ADAMS	TS1-2	02-Apr-52	17.73	4	ARAPAHOE	TS6-3	27-May-52	11.33	4
ADAMS	PB12-3	04-Sep-57	17.86	4	ARAPAHOE	PB12-3	04-Sep-57	17.43	4
ADAMS	TP3-2	02-Mar-55	40.29	5	ARAPAHOE	TP3-2	02-Mar-55	40.29	5
ADAMS	TP10-2	06-May-55	54.88	6	ARAPAHOE	TP10-2	06-May-55	54.88	6
ADAMS	TP4-2	08-Mar-55	155.94	7	ARAPAHOE	TP4-2	08-Mar-55	155.94	7
ALAMOSA	TS7-4	04-Jun-52	3.83	2	ARCHULETA	TP7-2	30-Mar-55	4.02	2
ALAMOSA	TP3-2	02-Mar-55	4.00	2	ARCHULETA	R1-2	29-Jan-51	4.08	2
ALAMOSA	UK7-2	26-Apr-53	4.16	2	ARCHULETA	TS7-4	04-Jun-52	4.49	2
ALAMOSA	TP11-2	16-May-55	4.44	2	ARCHULETA	TS6-3	27-May-52	4.70	2
ALAMOSA	UK9-2	20-May-53	4.81	2	ARCHULETA	TP9-2	15-Apr-55	7.37	3
ALAMOSA	UK9-3	21-May-53	4.81	2	ARCHULETA	UK9-3	21-May-53	8.80	3
ALAMOSA	PB8-4	21-Aug-57	4.92	2	ARCHULETA	PB13-4	09-Sep-57	9.99	3
ALAMOSA	UK1-2	18-Mar-53	5.26	3	ARCHULETA	PB3-2	25-Jun-57	11.19	4
ALAMOSA	TS6-3	27-May-52	9.12	3	ARCHULETA	TS8-1	05-Jun-52	13.29	4
ALAMOSA	TP11-3	17-May-55	13.12	4	ARCHULETA	TP7-1	29-Mar-55	16.00	4
ALAMOSA	UK7-3	27-Apr-53	13.13	4	ARCHULETA	TS6-2	26-May-52	18.14	4
ALAMOSA	TS8-1	05-Jun-52	13.29	4	ARCHULETA	UK6-2	19-Apr-53	20.14	4
ALAMOSA	TS6-2	26-May-52	15.67	4	ARCHULETA	R1-1	28-Jan-51	20.32	4
ALAMOSA	TP4-2	08-Mar-55	23.67	4	ARCHULETA	UK7-2	26-Apr-53	24.68	4

INDIVIDUAL FALLOUT DAYS
COLORADO

COUNTY	SHOT	DATE	µCi/SQ METER	INDEX	COUNTY	SHOT	DATE	µCi/SQ METER	INDEX
ARCHULETA	TS7-3	03-Jun-52	30.50	5	BENT	UK9-2	20-May-53	13.46	4
ARCHULETA	UK7-3	27-Apr-53	63.05	6	BENT	UK7-3	27-Apr-53	14.51	4
ARCHULETA	UK6-1	18-Apr-53	193.20	7	BENT	TP4-2	08-Mar-55	23.67	4
ARCHULETA	TS6-4	28-May-52	230.59	8	BENT	UK9-1	19-May-53	46.32	5
ARCHULETA	UK9-1	19-May-53	910.28	10	BENT	TP10-2	06-May-55	61.79	6
BACA	TP11-3	17-May-55	3.94	2	BOULDER	UK9-3	21-May-53	3.76	2
BACA	PB13-5	10-Sep-57	3.98	2	BOULDER	TP10-3	07-May-55	3.81	2
BACA	PB18-2	11-Jul-57	4.60	2	BOULDER	TS7-3	03-Jun-52	4.30	2
BACA	PB18-3	12-Jul-57	4.73	2	BOULDER	TP3-3	03-Mar-55	4.45	2
BACA	PB11-2	01-Sep-57	4.79	2	BOULDER	PB18-2	11-Jul-57	4.60	2
BACA	PB2-3	20-Jun-57	5.03	3	BOULDER	PB11-2	01-Sep-57	4.79	2
BACA	TS1-2	02-Apr-52	5.16	3	BOULDER	PB12-4	05-Sep-57	4.88	2
BACA	TS6-4	28-May-52	6.45	3	BOULDER	PB8-4	21-Aug-57	4.92	2
BACA	TP10-3	07-May-55	6.93	3	BOULDER	TP11-4	18-May-55	5.03	3
BACA	TP3-2	02-Mar-55	7.78	3	BOULDER	UK11-2	05-Jun-53	5.48	3
BACA	TP7-2	30-Mar-55	8.26	3	BOULDER	UK7-3	27-Apr-53	5.73	3
BACA	UK1-1	17-Mar-53	14.31	4	BOULDER	TS5-2	08-May-52	6.75	3
BACA	UK9-2	20-May-53	16.62	4	BOULDER	TS1-2	02-Apr-52	8.70	3
BACA	UK6-2	19-Apr-53	20.14	4	BOULDER	TS6-3	27-May-52	10.59	4
BACA	UK7-3	27-Apr-53	20.14	4	BOULDER	TS6-2	26-May-52	11.82	4
BACA	TS8-1	05-Jun-52	26.59	5	BOULDER	TP9-2	15-Apr-55	12.94	4
BACA	TP10-2	06-May-55	33.30	5	BOULDER	TP11-3	17-May-55	14.70	4
BACA	TP4-2	08-Mar-55	51.16	6	BOULDER	PB12-3	04-Sep-57	15.14	4
BACA	UK9-1	19-May-53	55.16	6	BOULDER	TP11-2	16-May-55	15.86	4
BENT	TP3-2	02-Mar-55	4.00	2	BOULDER	TP3-2	02-Mar-55	40.29	5
BENT	TP10-3	07-May-55	4.42	2	BOULDER	TP10-2	06-May-55	54.88	6
BENT	PB11-2	01-Sep-57	4.79	2	BOULDER	TP4-2	08-Mar-55	155.94	7
BENT	TS1-2	02-Apr-52	5.16	3	CHAFFEE	UK11-2	05-Jun-53	3.63	2
BENT	PB13-5	10-Sep-57	5.27	3	CHAFFEE	PB12-4	05-Sep-57	3.69	2
BENT	TS6-4	28-May-52	5.64	3	CHAFFEE	TS1-2	02-Apr-52	4.19	2
BENT	PB12-3	04-Sep-57	7.68	3	CHAFFEE	PB11-2	01-Sep-57	4.79	2
BENT	TS6-3	27-May-52	8.05	3	CHAFFEE	TP3-2	02-Mar-55	4.94	2
BENT	TS8-1	05-Jun-52	13.29	4	CHAFFEE	PB2-3	20-Jun-57	5.03	3

INDIVIDUAL FALLOUT DAYS
COLORADO

COUNTY	SHOT	DATE	μCi/SQ METER	INDEX	COUNTY	SHOT	DATE	μCi/SQ METER	INDEX
CHAFFEE	TP4-3	09-Mar-55	6.28	3	CLEAR CREEK	TS7-3	03-Jun-52	3.83	2
CHAFFEE	TS7-3	03-Jun-52	6.99	3	CLEAR CREEK	TS6-4	28-May-52	4.03	2
CHAFFEE	TS6-4	28-May-52	7.25	3	CLEAR CREEK	PB9-3	25-Aug-57	4.31	2
CHAFFEE	TP10-1	05-May-55	8.16	3	CLEAR CREEK	TP11-4	18-May-55	4.40	2
CHAFFEE	UK9-3	21-May-53	8.50	3	CLEAR CREEK	TP3-3	03-Mar-55	4.45	2
CHAFFEE	UK7-3	27-Apr-53	10.32	4	CLEAR CREEK	PB5-4	18-Jul-57	4.56	2
CHAFFEE	TP11-3	17-May-55	12.05	4	CLEAR CREEK	PB11-2	01-Sep-57	4.79	2
CHAFFEE	TS6-3	27-May-52	12.76	4	CLEAR CREEK	PB8-4	21-Aug-57	4.92	2
CHAFFEE	TS6-2	26-May-52	17.18	4	CLEAR CREEK	UK11-2	05-Jun-53	5.17	3
CHAFFEE	TP10-2	06-May-55	40.42	5	CLEAR CREEK	UK9-1	19-May-53	5.82	3
CHAFFEE	TP4-2	08-Mar-55	44.36	5	CLEAR CREEK	UK9-3	21-May-53	6.55	3
CHAFFEE	UK9-1	19-May-53	141.77	7	CLEAR CREEK	TP9-2	15-Apr-55	7.99	3
CHEYENNE	UK11-2	05-Jun-53	3.60	2	CLEAR CREEK	TS1-2	02-Apr-52	8.70	3
CHEYENNE	TP11-2	16-May-55	3.64	2	CLEAR CREEK	PB2-3	20-Jun-57	10.05	4
CHEYENNE	TS7-4	04-Jun-52	3.65	2	CLEAR CREEK	TP11-3	17-May-55	10.33	4
CHEYENNE	TP10-3	07-May-55	3.78	2	CLEAR CREEK	PB12-3	04-Sep-57	11.86	4
CHEYENNE	PB18-3	12-Jul-57	4.73	2	CLEAR CREEK	TP10-3	07-May-55	14.30	4
CHEYENNE	PB11-2	01-Sep-57	4.79	2	CLEAR CREEK	TS6-2	26-May-52	14.49	4
CHEYENNE	TS6-4	28-May-52	4.83	2	CLEAR CREEK	TP11-2	16-May-55	15.86	4
CHEYENNE	PB18-2	11-Jul-57	3.51	1	CLEAR CREEK	UK7-3	27-Apr-53	27.35	5
CHEYENNE	TS1-2	02-Apr-52	5.16	3	CLEAR CREEK	TP3-2	02-Mar-55	40.29	5
CHEYENNE	TP3-2	02-Mar-55	7.78	3	CLEAR CREEK	TP10-2	06-May-55	54.88	6
CHEYENNE	UK7-3	27-Apr-53	10.78	4	CLEAR CREEK	TP4-2	08-Mar-55	155.94	7
CHEYENNE	PB12-4	05-Sep-57	12.23	4	CONEJOS	UK1-2	18-Mar-53	3.61	2
CHEYENNE	UK9-2	20-May-53	12.25	4	CONEJOS	TS7-3	03-Jun-52	3.96	2
CHEYENNE	TS8-1	05-Jun-52	13.29	4	CONEJOS	TP3-2	02-Mar-55	4.00	2
CHEYENNE	UK9-1	19-May-53	15.94	4	CONEJOS	R1-2	29-Jan-51	4.08	2
CHEYENNE	TS6-3	27-May-52	18.08	4	CONEJOS	UK9-2	20-May-53	5.15	3
CHEYENNE	TP10-2	06-May-55	33.30	5	CONEJOS	UK9-3	21-May-53	6.03	3
CHEYENNE	TP4-2	08-Mar-55	51.16	6	CONEJOS	TS3-4	25-Apr-52	7.32	3
CLEAR CREEK	UK7-4	28-Apr-53	3.66	2	CONEJOS	TP11-3	17-May-55	8.02	3
CLEAR CREEK	TS6-3	27-May-52	3.75	2	CONEJOS	TS6-3	27-May-52	8.41	3
CLEAR CREEK	TP4-3	09-Mar-55	3.78	2	CONEJOS	TP11-2	16-May-55	8.89	3

INDIVIDUAL FALLOUT DAYS
COLORADO

COUNTY	SHOT	DATE	µCi/SQ METER	INDEX	COUNTY	SHOT	DATE	µCi/SQ METER	INDEX
CONEJOS	PB13-4	09-Sep-57	9.99	3	CROWLEY	TP3-2	02-Mar-55	4.00	2
CONEJOS	PB3-2	25-Jun-57	11.19	4	CROWLEY	PB11-2	01-Sep-57	4.79	2
CONEJOS	TS8-1	05-Jun-52	13.29	4	CROWLEY	TS6-4	28-May-52	4.83	2
CONEJOS	UK7-2	26-Apr-53	13.61	4	CROWLEY	TS1-2	02-Apr-52	5.16	3
CONEJOS	TS6-2	26-May-52	13.85	4	CROWLEY	TS6-2	26-May-52	6.01	3
CONEJOS	UK6-2	19-Apr-53	20.14	4	CROWLEY	UK7-3	27-Apr-53	8.78	3
CONEJOS	R1-1	28-Jan-51	20.32	4	CROWLEY	UK9-2	20-May-53	9.25	3
CONEJOS	UK1-1	17-Mar-53	21.46	4	CROWLEY	TS8-1	05-Jun-52	13.29	4
CONEJOS	UK7-3	27-Apr-53	25.16	5	CROWLEY	PB12-4	05-Sep-57	13.38	4
CONEJOS	TP4-2	08-Mar-55	35.51	5	CROWLEY	TS6-3	27-May-52	14.87	4
CONEJOS	TS6-4	28-May-52	44.32	5	CROWLEY	TP4-2	08-Mar-55	23.67	4
CONEJOS	TP10-2	06-May-55	92.68	6	CROWLEY	UK9-1	19-May-53	39.00	5
CONEJOS	UK9-1	19-May-53	1437.92	10	CROWLEY	TP10-2	06-May-55	61.79	6
COSTILLA	TP3-2	02-Mar-55	4.00	2	CUSTER	TP3-2	02-Mar-55	4.00	2
COSTILLA	PB4-5	09-Jul-57	4.60	2	CUSTER	TS6-3	27-May-52	4.04	2
COSTILLA	TP11-3	17-May-55	4.62	2	CUSTER	PB15-1	16-Sep-57	4.06	2
COSTILLA	UK7-2	26-Apr-53	4.88	2	CUSTER	PB18-2	11-Jul-57	4.60	2
COSTILLA	R1-2	29-Jan-51	5.57	3	CUSTER	PB11-2	01-Sep-57	4.79	2
COSTILLA	TS6-3	27-May-52	5.83	3	CUSTER	UK9-2	20-May-53	5.04	3
COSTILLA	UK1-2	18-Mar-53	6.10	3	CUSTER	UK1-2	18-Mar-53	5.24	3
COSTILLA	UK7-3	27-Apr-53	6.54	3	CUSTER	PB12-3	04-Sep-57	5.35	3
COSTILLA	UK9-2	20-May-53	6.92	3	CUSTER	UK9-3	21-May-53	5.48	3
COSTILLA	TP11-2	16-May-55	8.89	3	CUSTER	TS6-4	28-May-52	8.06	3
COSTILLA	PB13-4	09-Sep-57	9.99	3	CUSTER	UK7-3	27-Apr-53	10.31	4
COSTILLA	TS6-4	28-May-52	10.48	4	CUSTER	TS8-1	05-Jun-52	13.29	4
COSTILLA	PB3-2	25-Jun-57	11.19	4	CUSTER	PB12-4	05-Sep-57	15.61	4
COSTILLA	TS8-1	05-Jun-52	13.29	4	CUSTER	TS6-2	26-May-52	16.42	4
COSTILLA	UK1-1	17-Mar-53	14.31	4	CUSTER	TP11-3	17-May-55	19.44	4
COSTILLA	TS6-2	26-May-52	14.60	4	CUSTER	TP4-2	08-Mar-55	23.67	4
COSTILLA	UK6-2	19-Apr-53	20.14	4	CUSTER	TP10-2	06-May-55	61.79	6
COSTILLA	TP4-2	08-Mar-55	23.67	4	CUSTER	UK9-1	19-May-53	151.03	7
COSTILLA	TP10-2	06-May-55	123.57	7	DELTA	PB13-1	06-Sep-57	3.70	2
COSTILLA	UK9-1	19-May-53	363.68	8	DELTA	TS1-1	01-Apr-52	5.00	2

INDIGIDUAL FALLOUT DAYS
COLORADO

COUNTY	SHOT	DATE	µCi/SQ METER	INDEX	COUNTY	SHOT	DATE	µCi/SQ METER	INDEX
DELTA	PB1-1	28-May-57	6.17	3	DENVER	TP4-2	08-Mar-55	64.77	6
DELTA	PB17-1	28-Sep-57	7.68	3	DOLORES	PB13-1	06-Sep-57	3.70	2
DELTA	PB5-1	15-Jul-57	7.73	3	DOLORES	UK6-1	18-Apr-53	3.97	2
DELTA	TP3-1	01-Mar-55	8.63	3	DOLORES	UK10-1	25-May-53	4.13	2
DELTA	TP8-1	09-Apr-55	11.96	4	DOLORES	PB12-1	02-Sep-57	4.40	2
DELTA	PB12-1	02-Sep-57	12.48	4	DOLORES	PB3-1	24-Jun-57	4.92	2
DELTA	PB4-1	05-Jul-57	20.16	4	DOLORES	PB1-1	28-May-57	6.17	3
DELTA	UK11-1	04-Jun-53	21.71	4	DOLORES	PB18-1	10-Jul-57	7.57	3
DELTA	TP11-1	15-May-55	24.12	4	DOLORES	PB17-1	28-Sep-57	7.68	3
DELTA	UK10-1	25-May-53	32.92	5	DOLORES	TP7-1	29-Mar-55	8.24	3
DELTA	TP4-1	07-Mar-55	43.87	5	DOLORES	TP8-1	09-Apr-55	8.51	3
DELTA	TS6-1	25-May-52	63.65	6	DOLORES	TP5-1	12-Mar-55	8.67	3
DELTA	TS7-1	01-Jun-52	66.82	6	DOLORES	UK1-1	17-Mar-53	9.86	3
DELTA	UK7-1	25-Apr-53	83.38	6	DOLORES	TP3-1	01-Mar-55	18.43	4
DELTA	TP9-1	15-Apr-55	322.85	8	DOLORES	UK11-1	04-Jun-53	21.71	4
DELTA	UK9-1	19-May-53	323.30	8	DOLORES	TP4-1	07-Mar-55	21.80	4
DENVER	TS5-2	08-May-52	3.67	2	DOLORES	TP11-1	15-May-55	24.12	4
DENVER	UK9-3	21-May-53	3.73	2	DOLORES	TS7-1	01-Jun-52	44.50	5
DENVER	PB12-4	05-Sep-57	3.79	2	DOLORES	TS6-1	25-May-52	45.42	5
DENVER	PB18-2	11-Jul-57	3.82	2	DOLORES	UK7-1	25-Apr-53	165.53	7
DENVER	TS6-2	26-May-52	5.26	3	DOLORES	UK9-1	19-May-53	466.90	9
DENVER	TP9-1	15-Apr-55	5.57	3	DOUGLAS	PB12-4	05-Sep-57	3.65	2
DENVER	TP10-3	07-May-55	5.77	3	DOUGLAS	UK7-4	28-Apr-53	4.31	2
DENVER	PB8-4	21-Aug-57	6.10	3	DOUGLAS	UK11-2	05-Jun-53	4.31	2
DENVER	TP11-4	18-May-55	6.18	3	DOUGLAS	TP3-3	03-Mar-55	4.45	2
DENVER	TP11-3	17-May-55	10.17	4	DOUGLAS	PB11-2	01-Sep-57	4.79	2
DENVER	UK7-3	27-Apr-53	10.18	4	DOUGLAS	PB8-4	21-Aug-57	4.92	2
DENVER	TP9-2	15-Apr-55	13.10	4	DOUGLAS	TP7-2	30-Mar-55	5.00	3
DENVER	TP11-2	16-May-55	13.17	4	DOUGLAS	UK9-3	21-May-53	5.18	3
DENVER	TP3-2	02-Mar-55	16.73	4	DOUGLAS	TP10-3	07-May-55	5.96	3
DENVER	TS1-2	02-Apr-52	17.73	4	DOUGLAS	UK9-1	19-May-53	6.03	3
DENVER	PB12-3	04-Sep-57	21.92	4	DOUGLAS	TP11-2	16-May-55	7.98	3
DENVER	TP10-2	06-May-55	22.79	4	DOUGLAS	TS1-2	02-Apr-52	8.70	3

INDIVIDUAL FALLOUT DAYS
COLORADO

COUNTY	SHOT	DATE	µCi/SQ METER	INDEX	COUNTY	SHOT	DATE	µCi/SQ METER	INDEX
DOUGLAS	UK7-3	27-Apr-53	8.73	3	EL PASO	TP10-3	07-May-55	3.66	2
DOUGLAS	TS6-2	26-May-52	9.40	3	EL PASO	TS7-4	04-Jun-52	3.94	2
DOUGLAS	TP11-3	17-May-55	13.19	4	EL PASO	TS5-2	08-May-52	4.09	2
DOUGLAS	TS6-4	28-May-52	14.50	4	EL PASO	UK9-3	21-May-53	4.49	2
DOUGLAS	PB12-3	04-Sep-57	18.16	4	EL PASO	PB18-3	12-Jul-57	4.73	2
DOUGLAS	TS6-3	27-May-52	27.07	5	EL PASO	PB11-2	01-Sep-57	4.79	2
DOUGLAS	TP3-2	02-Mar-55	40.29	5	EL PASO	PB8-4	21-Aug-57	4.92	2
DOUGLAS	TP10-2	06-May-55	54.88	6	EL PASO	PB2-3	20-Jun-57	5.03	3
DOUGLAS	TP4-2	08-Mar-55	155.94	7	EL PASO	TS1-2	02-Apr-52	5.16	3
EAGLE	TS6-4	28-May-52	4.03	2	EL PASO	UK9-2	20-May-53	5.78	3
EAGLE	PB9-3	25-Aug-57	4.31	2	EL PASO	PB18-2	11-Jul-57	9.19	3
EAGLE	PB15-4	19-Sep-57	4.43	2	EL PASO	PB12-4	05-Sep-57	9.88	3
EAGLE	TP3-3	03-Mar-55	4.45	2	EL PASO	TS6-2	26-May-52	10.09	4
EAGLE	PB4-2	06-Jul-57	4.73	2	EL PASO	TP11-3	17-May-55	10.91	4
EAGLE	PB11-2	01-Sep-57	4.79	2	EL PASO	UK7-3	27-Apr-53	13.20	4
EAGLE	PB8-4	21-Aug-57	4.92	2	EL PASO	TS8-1	05-Jun-52	13.29	4
EAGLE	PB2-3	20-Jun-57	5.03	3	EL PASO	TS6-3	27-May-52	15.22	4
EAGLE	UK11-2	05-Jun-53	5.29	3	EL PASO	TS6-4	28-May-52	16.12	4
EAGLE	TP7-1	29-Mar-55	5.70	3	EL PASO	TP10-2	06-May-55	16.79	4
EAGLE	TP10-3	07-May-55	6.61	3	EL PASO	TP4-2	08-Mar-55	18.43	4
EAGLE	TP9-2	15-Apr-55	7.23	3	EL PASO	PB12-3	04-Sep-57	19.16	4
EAGLE	TS7-4	04-Jun-52	7.51	3	EL PASO	UK9-1	19-May-53	25.85	5
EAGLE	TS1-2	02-Apr-52	8.06	3	ELBERT	UK7-4	28-Apr-53	3.75	2
EAGLE	UK9-3	21-May-53	9.27	3	ELBERT	UK9-2	20-May-53	3.83	2
EAGLE	TS6-3	27-May-52	12.76	4	ELBERT	TS6-4	28-May-52	4.03	2
EAGLE	TS6-2	26-May-52	13.74	4	ELBERT	PB12-4	05-Sep-57	4.13	2
EAGLE	TS7-3	03-Jun-52	15.76	4	ELBERT	PB11-2	01-Sep-57	4.79	2
EAGLE	TP11-2	16-May-55	15.86	4	ELBERT	TP3-2	02-Mar-55	4.94	2
EAGLE	UK7-3	27-Apr-53	34.02	5	ELBERT	TS1-2	02-Apr-52	5.16	3
EAGLE	TP3-2	02-Mar-55	40.29	5	ELBERT	TS6-2	26-May-52	5.90	3
EAGLE	TP10-2	06-May-55	54.88	6	ELBERT	TP11-3	17-May-55	6.00	3
EAGLE	TP4-2	08-Mar-55	155.94	7	ELBERT	UK7-3	27-Apr-53	6.20	3
EAGLE	UK9-1	19-May-53	225.10	8	ELBERT	TP10-1	05-May-55	8.16	3

INDIVIDUAL FALLOUT DAYS
COLORADO

COUNTY	SHOT	DATE	µCi/SQ METER	INDEX	COUNTY	SHOT	DATE	µCi/SQ METER	INDEX
ELBERT	PB12-3	04-Sep-57	9.69	3	GARFIELD	TS1-1	01-Apr-52	5.00	2
ELBERT	UK9-1	19-May-53	9.70	3	GARFIELD	PB15-1	16-Sep-57	5.37	3
ELBERT	PB8-4	21-Aug-57	9.77	3	GARFIELD	PB1-1	28-May-57	6.17	3
ELBERT	TS8-1	05-Jun-52	13.29	4	GARFIELD	PB17-1	28-Sep-57	7.68	3
ELBERT	TS6-3	27-May-52	18.41	4	GARFIELD	PB9-1	23-Aug-57	9.95	3
ELBERT	TP10-2	06-May-55	40.42	5	GARFIELD	PB12-1	02-Sep-57	12.48	4
ELBERT	TP4-2	08-Mar-55	44.36	5	GARFIELD	PB5-1	15-Jul-57	15.57	4
FREMONT	PB12-3	04-Sep-57	3.76	2	GARFIELD	TP8-1	09-Apr-55	15.79	4
FREMONT	TS1-2	02-Apr-52	4.19	2	GARFIELD	UK11-1	04-Jun-53	21.71	4
FREMONT	UK9-2	20-May-53	4.21	2	GARFIELD	UK10-1	25-May-53	22.23	4
FREMONT	PB18-2	11-Jul-57	4.60	2	GARFIELD	TP11-1	15-May-55	24.12	4
FREMONT	PB11-2	01-Sep-57	4.79	2	GARFIELD	TS7-1	01-Jun-52	42.35	5
FREMONT	TP3-2	02-Mar-55	4.94	2	GARFIELD	UK7-1	25-Apr-53	58.33	6
FREMONT	TS7-3	03-Jun-52	4.97	2	GARFIELD	TP4-1	07-Mar-55	66.12	6
FREMONT	PB2-3	20-Jun-57	5.03	3	GARFIELD	TS6-1	25-May-52	72.49	6
FREMONT	PB4-10	14-Jul-57	5.20	3	GARFIELD	TP10-1	05-May-55	77.19	6
FREMONT	R1-2	29-Jan-51	5.57	3	GARFIELD	PB4-1	05-Jul-57	81.66	6
FREMONT	UK7-3	27-Apr-53	5.58	3	GARFIELD	TS8-1	05-Jun-52	111.72	7
FREMONT	UK9-3	21-May-53	6.96	3	GARFIELD	UK9-1	19-May-53	278.15	8
FREMONT	TS6-4	28-May-52	7.25	3	GARFIELD	TP9-1	15-Apr-55	322.85	8
FREMONT	TP10-1	05-May-55	8.16	3	GILPIN	TS6-3	27-May-52	3.57	2
FREMONT	TS6-3	27-May-52	9.40	3	GILPIN	TP4-3	09-Mar-55	3.86	2
FREMONT	TS8-1	05-Jun-52	13.29	4	GILPIN	TP3-3	03-Mar-55	4.45	2
FREMONT	TP11-3	17-May-55	15.03	4	GILPIN	PB5-4	18-Jul-57	4.56	2
FREMONT	TS6-2	26-May-52	15.89	4	GILPIN	PB11-2	01-Sep-57	4.79	2
FREMONT	TP10-2	06-May-55	40.42	5	GILPIN	UK9-3	21-May-53	4.79	2
FREMONT	TP4-2	08-Mar-55	44.36	5	GILPIN	TP11-4	18-May-55	4.93	2
FREMONT	UK9-1	19-May-53	103.63	7	GILPIN	UK9-1	19-May-53	6.03	3
GARFIELD	PB13-1	06-Sep-57	3.70	2	GILPIN	TP11-3	17-May-55	9.49	3
GARFIELD	PB8-1	18-Aug-57	3.91	2	GILPIN	TP9-2	15-Apr-55	10.57	4
GARFIELD	TP3-1	01-Mar-55	4.27	2	GILPIN	TS6-2	26-May-52	11.91	4
GARFIELD	TP7-1	29-Mar-55	4.63	2	GILPIN	TP10-3	07-May-55	13.14	4
GARFIELD	PB2-1	18-Jun-57	4.77	2	GILPIN	PB12-3	04-Sep-57	15.26	4

INDIVIDUAL FALLOUT DAYS
COLORADO

COUNTY	SHOT	DATE	µCi/SQ METER	INDEX	COUNTY	SHOT	DATE	µCi/SQ METER	INDEX
GILPIN	TP11-2	16-May-55	15.86	4	GUNNISON	TP3-1	01-Mar-55	3.92	2
GILPIN	UK7-3	27-Apr-53	16.13	4	GUNNISON	TP3-2	02-Mar-55	4.00	2
GILPIN	TS1-2	02-Apr-52	17.73	4	GUNNISON	TP6-3	24-Mar-55	4.11	2
GILPIN	TP3-2	02-Mar-55	40.29	5	GUNNISON	UK11-2	05-Jun-53	4.35	2
GILPIN	TP10-2	06-May-55	54.88	6	GUNNISON	TS7-4	04-Jun-52	6.19	3
GILPIN	TP4-2	08-Mar-55	155.94	7	GUNNISON	TP4-3	09-Mar-55	6.69	3
GRAND	PB12-3	04-Sep-57	4.27	2	GUNNISON	UK7-2	26-Apr-53	7.11	3
GRAND	TP7-1	29-Mar-55	4.38	2	GUNNISON	TS6-4	28-May-52	7.25	3
GRAND	TP3-3	03-Mar-55	4.45	2	GUNNISON	TS1-2	02-Apr-52	8.06	3
GRAND	PB5-4	18-Jul-57	4.56	2	GUNNISON	PB5-3	17-Jul-57	10.34	4
GRAND	PB11-2	01-Sep-57	4.79	2	GUNNISON	UK9-3	21-May-53	11.26	4
GRAND	TS7-5	05-Jun-52	5.04	3	GUNNISON	TP11-3	17-May-55	11.50	4
GRAND	UK9-3	21-May-53	6.30	3	GUNNISON	TS6-3	27-May-52	14.26	4
GRAND	TP4-3	09-Mar-55	6.57	3	GUNNISON	TP4-1	07-Mar-55	15.12	4
GRAND	TS7-4	04-Jun-52	6.99	3	GUNNISON	UK7-3	27-Apr-53	16.69	4
GRAND	UK7-3	27-Apr-53	7.46	3	GUNNISON	TP9-2	15-Apr-55	20.74	4
GRAND	UK11-2	05-Jun-53	7.88	3	GUNNISON	TS7-3	03-Jun-52	24.10	4
GRAND	TS1-2	02-Apr-52	8.06	3	GUNNISON	TS6-2	26-May-52	24.69	4
GRAND	TP9-2	15-Apr-55	8.41	3	GUNNISON	TP11-1	15-May-55	29.49	5
GRAND	TP10-3	07-May-55	9.77	3	GUNNISON	TP4-2	08-Mar-55	66.80	6
GRAND	PB8-4	21-Aug-57	9.77	3	GUNNISON	UK9-1	19-May-53	1570.05	10
GRAND	PB2-3	20-Jun-57	10.05	4	HINSDALE	UK11-2	05-Jun-53	3.63	2
GRAND	TS7-3	03-Jun-52	12.43	4	HINSDALE	TP3-1	01-Mar-55	3.92	2
GRAND	TS8-1	05-Jun-52	13.29	4	HINSDALE	TP3-2	02-Mar-55	4.00	2
GRAND	TS6-2	26-May-52	13.63	4	HINSDALE	R1-2	29-Jan-51	4.08	2
GRAND	TS6-3	27-May-52	19.21	4	HINSDALE	TS1-2	02-Apr-52	8.06	3
GRAND	TP11-2	16-May-55	31.71	5	HINSDALE	UK7-3	27-Apr-53	8.52	3
GRAND	TP3-2	02-Mar-55	40.29	5	HINSDALE	PB4-5	09-Jul-57	11.39	4
GRAND	UK9-1	19-May-53	51.39	6	HINSDALE	TS6-4	28-May-52	12.09	4
GRAND	TP10-2	06-May-55	54.88	6	HINSDALE	UK9-3	21-May-53	12.12	4
GRAND	TP4-2	08-Mar-55	155.94	7	HINSDALE	TS8-1	05-Jun-52	13.29	4
GUNNISON	UK10-2	26-May-53	3.66	2	HINSDALE	TS7-3	03-Jun-52	14.24	4
GUNNISON	PB4-5	09-Jul-57	3.80	2	HINSDALE	TP4-1	07-Mar-55	15.12	4

INDIVIDUAL FALLOUT DAYS
COLORADO

COUNTY	SHOT	DATE	µCi/SQ METER	INDEX	COUNTY	SHOT	DATE	µCi/SQ METER	INDEX
HINSDALE	TP11-3	17-May-55	17.31	4	JACKSON	TP8-2	10-Apr-55	5.36	3
HINSDALE	UK7-2	26-Apr-53	19.30	4	JACKSON	TP11-2	16-May-55	5.76	3
HINSDALE	TP11-1	15-May-55	29.49	5	JACKSON	TP9-2	15-Apr-55	6.56	3
HINSDALE	TS6-2	26-May-52	30.27	5	JACKSON	PB2-2	19-Jun-57	7.29	3
HINSDALE	TP4-2	08-Mar-55	66.80	6	JACKSON	UK9-4	22-May-53	7.78	3
HINSDALE	TS6-3	27-May-52	67.76	6	JACKSON	TS6-2	26-May-52	9.23	3
HINSDALE	UK9-1	19-May-53	747.40	9	JACKSON	UK11-2	05-Jun-53	10.78	4
HUERFANO	TS3-4	25-Apr-52	3.66	2	JACKSON	UK7-3	27-Apr-53	13.02	4
HUERFANO	TP3-2	02-Mar-55	4.00	2	JACKSON	TS7-3	03-Jun-52	16.09	4
HUERFANO	R1-2	29-Jan-51	4.08	2	JACKSON	UK9-1	19-May-53	19.02	4
HUERFANO	PB5-4	18-Jul-57	4.56	2	JACKSON	TP10-2	06-May-55	25.63	5
HUERFANO	PB18-2	11-Jul-57	4.60	2	JACKSON	TP10-1	05-May-55	84.89	6
HUERFANO	PB11-2	01-Sep-57	4.79	2	JEFFERSON	PB12-4	05-Sep-57	3.68	2
HUERFANO	UK7-3	27-Apr-53	5.15	3	JEFFERSON	TP3-3	03-Mar-55	4.45	2
HUERFANO	UK9-2	20-May-53	6.22	3	JEFFERSON	PB11-2	01-Sep-57	4.79	2
HUERFANO	UK1-2	18-Mar-53	6.58	3	JEFFERSON	PB8-4	21-Aug-57	4.92	2
HUERFANO	TP11-3	17-May-55	6.93	3	JEFFERSON	PB18-2	11-Jul-57	3.51	1
HUERFANO	TS6-2	26-May-52	17.60	4	JEFFERSON	TP7-2	30-Mar-55	5.00	3
HUERFANO	TS6-3	27-May-52	20.24	4	JEFFERSON	UK9-3	21-May-53	5.26	3
HUERFANO	TP4-2	08-Mar-55	23.67	4	JEFFERSON	TP11-4	18-May-55	5.29	3
HUERFANO	TS6-4	28-May-52	25.79	5	JEFFERSON	TP10-3	07-May-55	5.56	3
HUERFANO	TS8-1	05-Jun-52	39.88	5	JEFFERSON	UK11-2	05-Jun-53	6.73	3
HUERFANO	TP10-2	06-May-55	61.79	6	JEFFERSON	TP11-2	16-May-55	7.98	3
HUERFANO	UK9-1	19-May-53	127.55	7	JEFFERSON	TP9-2	15-Apr-55	8.22	3
JACKSON	PB11-2	01-Sep-57	3.83	2	JEFFERSON	TS1-2	02-Apr-52	8.70	3
JACKSON	TS5-2	08-May-52	3.84	2	JEFFERSON	TS6-2	26-May-52	8.72	3
JACKSON	PB9-3	25-Aug-57	3.88	2	JEFFERSON	UK7-3	27-Apr-53	9.21	3
JACKSON	TS1-2	02-Apr-52	4.19	2	JEFFERSON	TS6-4	28-May-52	11.01	4
JACKSON	PB2-3	20-Jun-57	4.36	2	JEFFERSON	TP11-3	17-May-55	15.12	4
JACKSON	PB12-4	05-Sep-57	4.82	2	JEFFERSON	PB12-3	04-Sep-57	17.52	4
JACKSON	TP4-2	08-Mar-55	4.84	2	JEFFERSON	TS6-3	27-May-52	22.27	4
JACKSON	UK9-3	21-May-53	4.91	2	JEFFERSON	TP3-2	02-Mar-55	40.29	5
JACKSON	TS7-4	04-Jun-52	5.03	3	JEFFERSON	TP10-2	06-May-55	54.88	6

INDIVIDUAL FALLOUT DAYS
COLORADO

COUNTY	SHOT	DATE	µCi/SQ METER	INDEX	COUNTY	SHOT	DATE	µCi/SQ METER	INDEX
JEFFERSON	TP4-2	08-Mar-55	155.94	7	KIT CARSON	TP4-2	08-Mar-55	51.16	6
KIOWA	TP11-2	16-May-55	3.64	2	LA PLATA	TS4-1	01-May-52	3.57	2
KIOWA	TP10-3	07-May-55	4.31	2	LA PLATA	PB13-1	06-Sep-57	3.70	2
KIOWA	PB11-2	01-Sep-57	4.79	2	LA PLATA	TP8-1	09-Apr-55	4.26	2
KIOWA	TS1-2	02-Apr-52	5.16	3	LA PLATA	TP5-1	12-Mar-55	4.34	2
KIOWA	TS6-4	28-May-52	5.64	3	LA PLATA	UK6-1	18-Apr-53	5.00	2
KIOWA	TP3-2	02-Mar-55	7.78	3	LA PLATA	PB17-1	28-Sep-57	7.68	3
KIOWA	PB2-3	20-Jun-57	10.05	4	LA PLATA	TP3-1	01-Mar-55	9.21	3
KIOWA	PB12-4	05-Sep-57	11.76	4	LA PLATA	PB18-1	10-Jul-57	10.06	4
KIOWA	TS8-1	05-Jun-52	13.29	4	LA PLATA	R1-2	29-Jan-51	10.15	4
KIOWA	UK9-2	20-May-53	13.46	4	LA PLATA	PB3-1	24-Jun-57	10.78	4
KIOWA	TS6-3	27-May-52	17.11	4	LA PLATA	PB1-1	28-May-57	12.24	4
KIOWA	UK9-1	19-May-53	25.85	5	LA PLATA	TP4-1	07-Mar-55	14.50	4
KIOWA	TP10-2	06-May-55	33.30	5	LA PLATA	TP7-1	29-Mar-55	16.58	4
KIOWA	TP4-2	08-Mar-55	51.16	6	LA PLATA	UK11-1	04-Jun-53	21.57	4
KIOWA	UK7-3	27-Apr-53	67.31	6	LA PLATA	TP11-1	15-May-55	23.93	4
KIT CARSON	TS7-5	05-Jun-52	3.69	2	LA PLATA	TS6-1	25-May-52	45.42	5
KIT CARSON	TS6-4	28-May-52	4.03	2	LA PLATA	UK1-1	17-Mar-53	46.06	5
KIT CARSON	PB12-3	04-Sep-57	4.19	2	LA PLATA	TS7-1	01-Jun-52	89.12	6
KIT CARSON	PB18-3	12-Jul-57	4.73	2	LA PLATA	UK7-1	25-Apr-53	124.23	7
KIT CARSON	PB18-2	11-Jul-57	3.51	1	LA PLATA	R1-1	28-Jan-51	179.46	7
KIT CARSON	PB2-3	20-Jun-57	5.03	3	LA PLATA	UK9-1	19-May-53	466.90	9
KIT CARSON	TS1-2	02-Apr-52	5.16	3	LAKE	TP11-3	17-May-55	3.82	2
KIT CARSON	TP11-2	16-May-55	5.45	3	LAKE	TP3-3	03-Mar-55	4.45	2
KIT CARSON	TP7-2	30-Mar-55	5.54	3	LAKE	PB11-2	01-Sep-57	4.79	2
KIT CARSON	TP3-2	02-Mar-55	7.78	3	LAKE	TS6-4	28-May-52	4.83	2
KIT CARSON	UK7-3	27-Apr-53	8.49	3	LAKE	PB8-4	21-Aug-57	4.92	2
KIT CARSON	UK9-2	20-May-53	8.72	3	LAKE	TS7-4	04-Jun-52	4.93	2
KIT CARSON	UK9-1	19-May-53	9.26	3	LAKE	TP7-2	30-Mar-55	5.00	3
KIT CARSON	PB11-2	01-Sep-57	9.58	3	LAKE	PB2-3	20-Jun-57	5.03	3
KIT CARSON	TS8-1	05-Jun-52	13.29	4	LAKE	UK11-2	05-Jun-53	5.29	3
KIT CARSON	TS6-3	27-May-52	22.00	4	LAKE	TP9-2	15-Apr-55	5.33	3
KIT CARSON	TP10-2	06-May-55	33.30	5	LAKE	TP10-3	07-May-55	7.67	3

INDIVIDUAL FALLOUT DAYS
COLORADO

COUNTY	SHOT	DATE	µCi/SQ METER	INDEX	COUNTY	SHOT	DATE	µCi/SQ METER	INDEX
LAKE	UK9-3	21-May-53	8.86	3	LAS ANIMAS	TP3-2	02-Mar-55	4.00	2
LAKE	TP4-3	09-Mar-55	10.18	4	LAS ANIMAS	UK8-2	09-May-53	4.04	2
LAKE	TS6-3	27-May-52	11.19	4	LAS ANIMAS	PB5-4	18-Jul-57	4.56	2
LAKE	TP11-2	16-May-55	15.86	4	LAS ANIMAS	PB8-4	21-Aug-57	4.92	2
LAKE	TS6-2	26-May-52	15.99	4	LAS ANIMAS	TP11-3	17-May-55	5.29	3
LAKE	TS1-2	02-Apr-52	16.44	4	LAS ANIMAS	TS6-3	27-May-52	5.54	3
LAKE	UK7-3	27-Apr-53	19.21	4	LAS ANIMAS	TS6-4	28-May-52	6.45	3
LAKE	TP3-2	02-Mar-55	40.29	5	LAS ANIMAS	PB12-4	05-Sep-57	7.30	3
LAKE	TP10-2	06-May-55	54.88	6	LAS ANIMAS	TP7-2	30-Mar-55	7.50	3
LAKE	TP4-2	08-Mar-55	155.94	7	LAS ANIMAS	UK1-2	18-Mar-53	7.58	3
LAKE	UK9-1	19-May-53	341.50	8	LAS ANIMAS	TP11-2	16-May-55	8.89	3
LARIMER	TP4-3	09-Mar-55	3.56	2	LAS ANIMAS	UK7-3	27-Apr-53	9.69	3
LARIMER	PB9-4	26-Aug-57	3.68	2	LAS ANIMAS	UK9-2	20-May-53	10.68	4
LARIMER	UK9-3	21-May-53	3.69	2	LAS ANIMAS	TS6-2	26-May-52	12.34	4
LARIMER	TS6-3	27-May-52	3.92	2	LAS ANIMAS	TS8-1	05-Jun-52	13.29	4
LARIMER	UK7-2	26-Apr-53	3.96	2	LAS ANIMAS	UK1-1	17-Mar-53	14.31	4
LARIMER	PB2-3	20-Jun-57	4.36	2	LAS ANIMAS	UK6-2	19-Apr-53	20.14	4
LARIMER	PB8-3	20-Aug-57	4.57	2	LAS ANIMAS	TP4-2	08-Mar-55	23.67	4
LARIMER	TS5-2	08-May-52	4.67	2	LAS ANIMAS	TP10-2	06-May-55	61.79	6
LARIMER	TP4-2	08-Mar-55	4.84	2	LAS ANIMAS	UK9-1	19-May-53	94.15	6
LARIMER	PB2-2	19-Jun-57	7.29	3	LINCOLN	PB18-3	12-Jul-57	3.55	2
LARIMER	TP9-2	15-Apr-55	7.40	3	LINCOLN	TP10-3	07-May-55	3.57	2
LARIMER	PB9-3	25-Aug-57	7.76	3	LINCOLN	TP3-2	02-Mar-55	4.00	2
LARIMER	TP11-3	17-May-55	9.11	3	LINCOLN	PB5-4	18-Jul-57	4.56	2
LARIMER	UK11-2	05-Jun-53	9.64	3	LINCOLN	PB18-2	11-Jul-57	4.60	2
LARIMER	UK7-3	27-Apr-53	10.59	4	LINCOLN	PB11-2	01-Sep-57	4.79	2
LARIMER	TS6-2	26-May-52	15.35	4	LINCOLN	PB12-3	04-Sep-57	4.99	2
LARIMER	PB12-3	04-Sep-57	17.35	4	LINCOLN	TP7-2	30-Mar-55	5.00	3
LARIMER	TS1-2	02-Apr-52	17.73	4	LINCOLN	PB2-3	20-Jun-57	5.03	3
LARIMER	TS5-1	07-May-52	17.78	4	LINCOLN	PB12-4	05-Sep-57	6.51	3
LARIMER	TP11-2	16-May-55	23.13	4	LINCOLN	UK9-2	20-May-53	6.77	3
LARIMER	TP10-2	06-May-55	25.63	5	LINCOLN	TS1-2	02-Apr-52	7.42	3
LARIMER	TP10-1	05-May-55	84.89	6	LINCOLN	TP11-2	16-May-55	8.89	3

INDIVIDUAL FALLOUT DAYS
COLORADO

COUNTY	SHOT	DATE	µCi/SQ METER	INDEX	COUNTY	SHOT	DATE	µCi/SQ METER	INDEX
LINCOLN	PB8-4	21-Aug-57	9.77	3	MESA	PB12-1	02-Sep-57	11.77	4
LINCOLN	UK7-3	27-Apr-53	10.15	4	MESA	TP8-1	09-Apr-55	14.97	4
LINCOLN	TS6-3	27-May-52	13.08	4	MESA	PB4-1	05-Jul-57	19.13	4
LINCOLN	TS8-1	05-Jun-52	13.29	4	MESA	UK11-1	04-Jun-53	20.61	4
LINCOLN	TS6-4	28-May-52	13.70	4	MESA	TP11-1	15-May-55	22.75	4
LINCOLN	UK9-1	19-May-53	19.61	4	MESA	UK10-1	25-May-53	28.89	5
LINCOLN	TP4-2	08-Mar-55	23.67	4	MESA	TS6-1	25-May-52	68.58	6
LINCOLN	TP10-2	06-May-55	61.79	6	MESA	TP4-1	07-Mar-55	69.50	6
LOGAN	TP11-3	17-May-55	3.61	2	MESA	TS7-1	01-Jun-52	71.92	6
LOGAN	PB9-4	26-Aug-57	3.68	2	MESA	UK7-1	25-Apr-53	102.26	7
LOGAN	TP9-2	15-Apr-55	3.97	2	MESA	TS8-1	05-Jun-52	105.36	7
LOGAN	TP3-2	02-Mar-55	4.00	2	MESA	UK9-1	19-May-53	365.84	8
LOGAN	UK7-4	28-Apr-53	4.70	2	MESA	TP9-1	15-Apr-55	382.05	8
LOGAN	PB18-3	12-Jul-57	4.73	2	MINERAL	TP9-2	15-Apr-55	3.52	2
LOGAN	UK11-2	05-Jun-53	5.09	3	MINERAL	TS7-4	04-Jun-52	3.72	2
LOGAN	TP4-2	08-Mar-55	5.97	3	MINERAL	PB4-5	09-Jul-57	3.80	2
LOGAN	PB5-2	16-Jul-57	6.07	3	MINERAL	PB17-5	02-Oct-57	3.81	2
LOGAN	PB5-3	17-Jul-57	6.78	3	MINERAL	TP3-1	01-Mar-55	3.92	2
LOGAN	PB2-3	20-Jun-57	7.04	3	MINERAL	TP3-2	02-Mar-55	4.00	2
LOGAN	PB9-3	25-Aug-57	7.76	3	MINERAL	TS1-2	02-Apr-52	4.19	2
LOGAN	UK2-7	30-Mar-53	9.91	3	MINERAL	TS6-3	27-May-52	5.42	3
LOGAN	TS5-1	07-May-52	11.24	4	MINERAL	TP11-3	17-May-55	8.02	3
LOGAN	TS8-1	05-Jun-52	13.29	4	MINERAL	UK9-3	21-May-53	9.66	3
LOGAN	TP11-2	16-May-55	14.24	4	MINERAL	R1-2	29-Jan-51	10.15	4
LOGAN	TS1-2	02-Apr-52	17.73	4	MINERAL	TS8-1	05-Jun-52	13.29	4
LOGAN	TS6-3	27-May-52	54.39	6	MINERAL	UK7-2	26-Apr-53	14.42	4
MESA	TP7-1	29-Mar-55	3.64	2	MINERAL	TP4-1	07-Mar-55	15.12	4
MESA	PB1-1	28-May-57	4.33	2	MINERAL	TS6-4	28-May-52	24.17	4
MESA	TS1-1	01-Apr-52	4.71	2	MINERAL	TS6-2	26-May-52	24.26	4
MESA	PB15-1	16-Sep-57	5.06	3	MINERAL	TP11-1	15-May-55	29.49	5
MESA	TP3-1	01-Mar-55	6.51	3	MINERAL	UK7-3	27-Apr-53	40.34	5
MESA	PB17-1	28-Sep-57	7.68	3	MINERAL	TS7-3	03-Jun-52	62.35	6
MESA	PB5-1	15-Jul-57	11.04	4	MINERAL	TP4-2	08-Mar-55	66.80	6

INDIVIDUAL FALLOUT DAYS
COLORADO

COUNTY	SHOT	DATE	µCi/SQ METER	INDEX	COUNTY	SHOT	DATE	µCi/SQ METER	INDEX
MINERAL	UK9-1	19-May-53	755.80	9	MONTEZUMA	PB1-1	28-May-57	12.24	4
MOFFAT	TS1-1	01-Apr-52	5.00	2	MONTEZUMA	TP7-1	29-Mar-55	16.58	4
MOFFAT	PB15-1	16-Sep-57	5.37	3	MONTEZUMA	UK11-1	04-Jun-53	21.13	4
MOFFAT	PB1-1	28-May-57	6.17	3	MONTEZUMA	TP4-1	07-Mar-55	21.98	4
MOFFAT	PB17-1	28-Sep-57	7.68	3	MONTEZUMA	TP11-1	15-May-55	24.12	4
MOFFAT	PB11-1	31-Aug-57	7.71	3	MONTEZUMA	TS7-1	01-Jun-52	44.50	5
MOFFAT	TP9-1	15-Apr-55	8.39	3	MONTEZUMA	TS6-1	25-May-52	45.42	5
MOFFAT	PB2-1	18-Jun-57	9.20	3	MONTEZUMA	UK1-1	17-Mar-53	47.94	5
MOFFAT	UK11-1	04-Jun-53	11.13	4	MONTEZUMA	UK7-1	25-Apr-53	125.13	7
MOFFAT	UK7-1	25-Apr-53	16.59	4	MONTEZUMA	UK9-1	19-May-53	374.79	8
MOFFAT	TS7-1	01-Jun-52	17.33	4	MONTROSE	PB13-1	06-Sep-57	3.70	2
MOFFAT	PB12-1	02-Sep-57	17.72	4	MONTROSE	TS1-1	01-Apr-52	3.81	2
MOFFAT	PB4-1	05-Jul-57	19.91	4	MONTROSE	UK6-1	18-Apr-53	3.84	2
MOFFAT	UK10-1	25-May-53	21.94	4	MONTROSE	PB2-1	18-Jun-57	4.77	2
MOFFAT	TP11-1	15-May-55	23.14	4	MONTROSE	PB1-1	28-May-57	6.17	3
MOFFAT	PB5-1	15-Jul-57	24.35	4	MONTROSE	TP7-1	29-Mar-55	7.42	3
MOFFAT	TP8-1	09-Apr-55	24.92	4	MONTROSE	PB17-1	28-Sep-57	7.68	3
MOFFAT	UK9-1	19-May-53	36.55	5	MONTROSE	PB5-1	15-Jul-57	7.73	3
MOFFAT	PB9-1	23-Aug-57	41.31	5	MONTROSE	TP3-1	01-Mar-55	8.72	3
MOFFAT	TP4-1	07-Mar-55	51.44	6	MONTROSE	PB4-1	05-Jul-57	10.40	4
MOFFAT	TS6-1	25-May-52	62.88	6	MONTROSE	PB12-1	02-Sep-57	13.32	4
MOFFAT	TS8-1	05-Jun-52	230.42	8	MONTROSE	TP8-1	09-Apr-55	16.94	4
MOFFAT	TP10-1	05-May-55	233.13	8	MONTROSE	UK11-1	04-Jun-53	21.71	4
MONTEZUMA	TS4-1	01-May-52	3.57	2	MONTROSE	UK10-1	25-May-53	22.23	4
MONTEZUMA	PB13-1	06-Sep-57	3.70	2	MONTROSE	TP11-1	15-May-55	24.12	4
MONTEZUMA	TP8-1	09-Apr-55	4.26	2	MONTROSE	TP4-1	07-Mar-55	43.87	5
MONTEZUMA	UK6-1	18-Apr-53	6.02	3	MONTROSE	TS6-1	25-May-52	54.48	6
MONTEZUMA	PB17-1	28-Sep-57	7.68	3	MONTROSE	UK7-1	25-Apr-53	83.38	6
MONTEZUMA	TP5-1	12-Mar-55	8.67	3	MONTROSE	TP9-1	15-Apr-55	85.85	6
MONTEZUMA	TP3-1	01-Mar-55	9.21	3	MONTROSE	TS7-1	01-Jun-52	133.62	7
MONTEZUMA	PB18-1	10-Jul-57	10.06	4	MONTROSE	UK9-1	19-May-53	463.51	9
MONTEZUMA	PB3-1	24-Jun-57	10.91	4	MORGAN	UK9-1	19-May-53	3.88	2
					MORGAN	TP3-3	03-Mar-55	4.45	2

INDIVIDUAL FALLOUT DAYS
COLORADO

COUNTY	SHOT	DATE	µCi/SQ METER	INDEX	COUNTY	SHOT	DATE	µCi/SQ METER	INDEX
MORGAN	UK7-3	27-Apr-53	4.47	2	OURAY	PB2-1	18-Jun-57	4.77	2
MORGAN	PB5-4	18-Jul-57	4.56	2	OURAY	PB4-1	05-Jul-57	4.82	2
MORGAN	UK11-2	05-Jun-53	4.77	2	OURAY	UK10-1	25-May-53	5.70	3
MORGAN	PB11-2	01-Sep-57	4.79	2	OURAY	PB1-1	28-May-57	6.17	3
MORGAN	TP9-2	15-Apr-55	5.24	3	OURAY	PB17-1	28-Sep-57	7.68	3
MORGAN	TS5-1	07-May-52	5.74	3	OURAY	PB12-1	02-Sep-57	8.81	3
MORGAN	PB12-3	04-Sep-57	7.09	3	OURAY	TP8-1	09-Apr-55	12.77	4
MORGAN	TS1-2	02-Apr-52	8.70	3	OURAY	TP3-1	01-Mar-55	18.43	4
MORGAN	TS6-3	27-May-52	20.10	4	OURAY	UK11-1	04-Jun-53	21.57	4
MORGAN	PB8-4	21-Aug-57	24.46	4	OURAY	TP4-1	07-Mar-55	21.80	4
MORGAN	TP3-2	02-Mar-55	40.29	5	OURAY	TP11-1	15-May-55	24.02	4
MORGAN	TP11-2	16-May-55	47.57	5	OURAY	TS7-1	01-Jun-52	44.50	5
MORGAN	TP10-2	06-May-55	54.88	6	OURAY	TS6-1	25-May-52	45.42	5
MORGAN	TP4-2	08-Mar-55	155.94	7	OURAY	UK7-1	25-Apr-53	83.38	6
OTERO	TP10-3	07-May-55	3.57	2	OURAY	UK9-1	19-May-53	466.90	9
OTERO	TP3-2	02-Mar-55	4.00	2	PARK	PB15-1	16-Sep-57	4.06	2
OTERO	TP11-2	16-May-55	4.44	2	PARK	TS1-2	02-Apr-52	4.19	2
OTERO	UK1-2	18-Mar-53	4.56	2	PARK	TS6-3	27-May-52	4.52	2
OTERO	PB12-4	05-Sep-57	4.70	2	PARK	PB11-2	01-Sep-57	4.79	2
OTERO	PB11-2	01-Sep-57	4.79	2	PARK	TP3-2	02-Mar-55	4.94	2
OTERO	TS1-2	02-Apr-52	5.16	3	PARK	PB2-3	20-Jun-57	5.03	3
OTERO	TS6-4	28-May-52	5.64	3	PARK	UK9-3	21-May-53	7.99	3
OTERO	TS6-2	26-May-52	6.76	3	PARK	TP10-1	05-May-55	8.16	3
OTERO	TS6-3	27-May-52	6.96	3	PARK	PB12-3	04-Sep-57	10.27	4
OTERO	UK7-3	27-Apr-53	11.01	4	PARK	TP11-3	17-May-55	11.29	4
OTERO	UK9-2	20-May-53	11.35	4	PARK	TS6-2	26-May-52	15.35	4
OTERO	TS8-1	05-Jun-52	13.29	4	PARK	UK7-3	27-Apr-53	19.73	4
OTERO	TP4-2	08-Mar-55	23.67	4	PARK	TS6-4	28-May-52	30.62	5
OTERO	UK9-1	19-May-53	56.66	6	PARK	UK9-1	19-May-53	32.53	5
OTERO	TP10-2	06-May-55	61.79	6	PARK	TP10-2	06-May-55	40.42	5
OURAY	PB13-1	06-Sep-57	3.70	2	PARK	TP4-2	08-Mar-55	44.36	5
OURAY	PB18-1	10-Jul-57	4.14	2	PHILLIPS	PB2-3	20-Jun-57	3.52	2
OURAY	R1-2	29-Jan-51	4.30	2	PHILLIPS	UK7-3	27-Apr-53	3.84	2

INDIVIDUAL FALLOUT DAYS
COLORADO

COUNTY	SHOT	DATE	µCi/SQ METER	INDEX	COUNTY	SHOT	DATE	µCi/SQ METER	INDEX
PHILLIPS	PB18-3	12-Jul-57	4.73	2	PITKIN	TS6-2	26-May-52	17.71	4
PHILLIPS	PB12-4	05-Sep-57	5.16	3	PITKIN	TP11-3	17-May-55	20.63	4
PHILLIPS	UK7-4	28-Apr-53	5.35	3	PITKIN	TS1-2	02-Apr-52	24.50	4
PHILLIPS	TS5-1	07-May-52	5.39	3	PITKIN	TP11-1	15-May-55	29.49	5
PHILLIPS	TP11-2	16-May-55	5.45	3	PITKIN	UK7-3	27-Apr-53	44.44	5
PHILLIPS	TP9-2	15-Apr-55	5.71	3	PITKIN	TP4-2	08-Mar-55	66.80	6
PHILLIPS	UK11-2	05-Jun-53	5.93	3	PITKIN	UK9-1	19-May-53	611.57	9
PHILLIPS	TP3-2	02-Mar-55	7.78	3	PROWERS	PB11-2	01-Sep-57	4.79	2
PHILLIPS	TS1-2	02-Apr-52	9.99	3	PROWERS	PB2-3	20-Jun-57	5.03	3
PHILLIPS	PB9-4	26-Aug-57	11.05	4	PROWERS	TS1-2	02-Apr-52	5.16	3
PHILLIPS	TS8-1	05-Jun-52	13.29	4	PROWERS	TP10-3	07-May-55	5.20	3
PHILLIPS	PB9-3	25-Aug-57	23.29	4	PROWERS	TP11-2	16-May-55	5.45	3
PHILLIPS	TP10-2	06-May-55	33.30	5	PROWERS	TS6-4	28-May-52	6.45	3
PHILLIPS	TP4-2	08-Mar-55	51.16	6	PROWERS	TP3-2	02-Mar-55	7.78	3
PHILLIPS	TS6-3	27-May-52	98.45	6	PROWERS	PB12-4	05-Sep-57	9.93	3
PITKIN	TP8-2	10-Apr-55	3.86	2	PROWERS	UK7-3	27-Apr-53	14.80	4
PITKIN	TP3-1	01-Mar-55	3.92	2	PROWERS	UK9-2	20-May-53	18.97	4
PITKIN	TP3-2	02-Mar-55	4.00	2	PROWERS	TS8-1	05-Jun-52	26.59	5
PITKIN	TP6-3	24-Mar-55	4.11	2	PROWERS	UK9-1	19-May-53	30.38	5
PITKIN	UK7-2	26-Apr-53	4.37	2	PROWERS	TP10-2	06-May-55	33.30	5
PITKIN	PB15-4	19-Sep-57	4.43	2	PROWERS	TP4-2	08-Mar-55	51.16	6
PITKIN	TS6-3	27-May-52	4.49	2	PUEBLO	PB18-3	12-Jul-57	3.55	2
PITKIN	TS6-4	28-May-52	4.83	2	PUEBLO	PB12-3	04-Sep-57	4.41	2
PITKIN	UK11-2	05-Jun-53	4.87	2	PUEBLO	UK9-2	20-May-53	4.45	2
PITKIN	TP9-2	15-Apr-55	5.99	3	PUEBLO	PB18-2	11-Jul-57	4.60	2
PITKIN	TP10-3	07-May-55	6.61	3	PUEBLO	UK1-2	18-Mar-53	4.60	2
PITKIN	UK10-2	26-May-53	7.76	3	PUEBLO	PB11-2	01-Sep-57	4.79	2
PITKIN	TP4-3	09-Mar-55	8.05	3	PUEBLO	TP11-3	17-May-55	5.09	3
PITKIN	TP7-2	30-Mar-55	9.57	3	PUEBLO	TS1-2	02-Apr-52	5.16	3
PITKIN	UK9-3	21-May-53	10.85	4	PUEBLO	UK11-2	05-Jun-53	5.35	3
PITKIN	TS7-4	04-Jun-52	13.64	4	PUEBLO	R1-2	29-Jan-51	5.57	3
PITKIN	TP4-1	07-Mar-55	15.12	4	PUEBLO	UK7-3	27-Apr-53	6.98	3
PITKIN	TS7-3	03-Jun-52	16.11	4	PUEBLO	TP4-2	08-Mar-55	9.83	3

INDIVIDUAL FALLOUT DAYS
COLORADO

COUNTY	SHOT	DATE	µCi/SQ METER	INDEX	COUNTY	SHOT	DATE	µCi/SQ METER	INDEX
PUEBLO	PB12-4	05-Sep-57	13.11	4	RIO GRANDE	UK9-2	20-May-53	3.70	2
PUEBLO	TS6-2	26-May-52	13.20	4	RIO GRANDE	TP3-2	02-Mar-55	4.00	2
PUEBLO	TS8-1	05-Jun-52	13.29	4	RIO GRANDE	UK9-3	21-May-53	7.57	3
PUEBLO	TP10-2	06-May-55	25.66	5	RIO GRANDE	UK7-3	27-Apr-53	9.35	3
PUEBLO	TS6-3	27-May-52	27.66	5	RIO GRANDE	UK7-2	26-Apr-53	9.45	3
PUEBLO	UK9-1	19-May-53	28.12	5	RIO GRANDE	PB13-4	09-Sep-57	9.99	3
PUEBLO	TS6-4	28-May-52	35.46	5	RIO GRANDE	TP11-3	17-May-55	10.29	4
RIO BLANCO	PB13-1	06-Sep-57	3.70	2	RIO GRANDE	TS7-3	03-Jun-52	10.53	4
RIO BLANCO	TP7-1	29-Mar-55	4.12	2	RIO GRANDE	TS6-3	27-May-52	10.83	4
RIO BLANCO	TS1-1	01-Apr-52	5.00	2	RIO GRANDE	PB3-2	25-Jun-57	11.19	4
RIO BLANCO	PB15-1	16-Sep-57	5.37	3	RIO GRANDE	TS6-4	28-May-52	12.89	4
RIO BLANCO	PB1-1	28-May-57	6.17	3	RIO GRANDE	TS8-1	05-Jun-52	13.29	4
RIO BLANCO	PB17-1	28-Sep-57	7.68	3	RIO GRANDE	TS6-2	26-May-52	18.03	4
RIO BLANCO	PB8-1	18-Aug-57	7.82	3	RIO GRANDE	TP4-2	08-Mar-55	23.67	4
RIO BLANCO	PB2-1	18-Jun-57	7.92	3	RIO GRANDE	TP10-2	06-May-55	61.79	6
RIO BLANCO	PB5-1	15-Jul-57	15.57	4	RIO GRANDE	UK9-1	19-May-53	643.77	9
RIO BLANCO	UK11-1	04-Jun-53	16.42	4	ROUTT	PB2-3	20-Jun-57	3.69	2
RIO BLANCO	PB12-1	02-Sep-57	17.72	4	ROUTT	UK7-2	26-Apr-53	3.76	2
RIO BLANCO	PB9-1	23-Aug-57	20.53	4	ROUTT	PB4-5	09-Jul-57	3.80	2
RIO BLANCO	UK10-1	25-May-53	22.09	4	ROUTT	TP3-1	01-Mar-55	3.92	2
RIO BLANCO	PB11-1	31-Aug-57	23.33	4	ROUTT	TP3-2	02-Mar-55	4.00	2
RIO BLANCO	TP11-1	15-May-55	23.73	4	ROUTT	PB15-1	16-Sep-57	4.06	2
RIO BLANCO	TP8-1	09-Apr-55	25.10	5	ROUTT	PB15-4	19-Sep-57	4.43	2
RIO BLANCO	TS7-1	01-Jun-52	26.70	5	ROUTT	TP11-2	16-May-55	4.44	2
RIO BLANCO	UK9-1	19-May-53	46.17	5	ROUTT	TP10-3	07-May-55	6.24	3
RIO BLANCO	UK7-1	25-Apr-53	58.00	6	ROUTT	TS7-4	04-Jun-52	6.40	3
RIO BLANCO	TP4-1	07-Mar-55	58.74	6	ROUTT	TP7-2	30-Mar-55	6.41	3
RIO BLANCO	TS6-1	25-May-52	63.43	6	ROUTT	TS6-2	26-May-52	6.44	3
RIO BLANCO	PB4-1	05-Jul-57	81.28	6	ROUTT	PB5-3	17-Jul-57	6.86	3
RIO BLANCO	TP9-1	15-Apr-55	159.66	7	ROUTT	TS1-2	02-Apr-52	8.06	3
RIO BLANCO	TS8-1	05-Jun-52	167.57	7	ROUTT	UK9-3	21-May-53	9.10	3
RIO BLANCO	TP10-1	05-May-55	232.25	8	ROUTT	TS7-3	03-Jun-52	12.39	4
RIO GRANDE	TS3-4	25-Apr-52	3.66	2	ROUTT	TP9-2	15-Apr-55	14.74	4

INDIVIDUAL FALLOUT DAYS
COLORADO

COUNTY	SHOT	DATE	µCi/SQ METER	INDEX	COUNTY	SHOT	DATE	µCi/SQ METER	INDEX
ROUTT	TP4-1	07-Mar-55	15.12	4	SAN JUAN	PB18-1	10-Jul-57	7.57	3
ROUTT	UK11-2	05-Jun-53	17.89	4	SAN JUAN	PB17-1	28-Sep-57	7.68	3
ROUTT	TP11-1	15-May-55	29.49	5	SAN JUAN	TP8-1	09-Apr-55	8.51	3
ROUTT	UK7-3	27-Apr-53	38.04	5	SAN JUAN	TP3-1	01-Mar-55	18.43	4
ROUTT	TP4-2	08-Mar-55	66.80	6	SAN JUAN	UK11-1	04-Jun-53	21.57	4
ROUTT	UK9-1	19-May-53	87.88	6	SAN JUAN	TP4-1	07-Mar-55	21.80	4
SAGUACHE	UK7-2	26-Apr-53	3.96	2	SAN JUAN	TP11-1	15-May-55	24.02	4
SAGUACHE	R1-2	29-Jan-51	4.30	2	SAN JUAN	TS7-1	01-Jun-52	44.50	5
SAGUACHE	PB4-2	06-Jul-57	4.73	2	SAN JUAN	TS6-1	25-May-52	45.42	5
SAGUACHE	PB11-2	01-Sep-57	4.79	2	SAN JUAN	UK7-1	25-Apr-53	83.38	6
SAGUACHE	TP3-2	02-Mar-55	4.94	2	SAN JUAN	UK9-1	19-May-53	466.90	9
SAGUACHE	PB2-3	20-Jun-57	5.03	3	SAN MIGUEL	PB13-1	06-Sep-57	3.70	2
SAGUACHE	TS1-2	02-Apr-52	6.13	3	SAN MIGUEL	TP7-1	29-Mar-55	4.12	2
SAGUACHE	UK9-3	21-May-53	7.32	3	SAN MIGUEL	PB4-1	05-Jul-57	4.69	2
SAGUACHE	TP10-1	05-May-55	8.16	3	SAN MIGUEL	PB2-1	18-Jun-57	4.77	2
SAGUACHE	TS7-3	03-Jun-52	8.93	3	SAN MIGUEL	PB18-1	10-Jul-57	5.09	3
SAGUACHE	PB8-4	21-Aug-57	9.77	3	SAN MIGUEL	PB1-1	28-May-57	6.17	3
SAGUACHE	TS6-4	28-May-52	10.48	4	SAN MIGUEL	PB17-1	28-Sep-57	7.68	3
SAGUACHE	TS7-4	04-Jun-52	11.82	4	SAN MIGUEL	TP8-1	09-Apr-55	8.51	3
SAGUACHE	TP11-3	17-May-55	11.96	4	SAN MIGUEL	PB12-1	02-Sep-57	8.81	3
SAGUACHE	TS8-1	05-Jun-52	13.29	4	SAN MIGUEL	TP3-1	01-Mar-55	18.52	4
SAGUACHE	UK7-3	27-Apr-53	14.51	4	SAN MIGUEL	UK11-1	04-Jun-53	21.71	4
SAGUACHE	TS6-2	26-May-52	19.00	4	SAN MIGUEL	TP4-1	07-Mar-55	21.89	4
SAGUACHE	TS6-3	27-May-52	35.45	5	SAN MIGUEL	TP11-1	15-May-55	24.12	4
SAGUACHE	TP10-2	06-May-55	40.42	5	SAN MIGUEL	TS6-1	25-May-52	45.42	5
SAGUACHE	TP4-2	08-Mar-55	44.36	5	SAN MIGUEL	TS7-1	01-Jun-52	53.52	6
SAGUACHE	UK9-1	19-May-53	391.91	8	SAN MIGUEL	UK7-1	25-Apr-53	83.38	6
SAN JUAN	PB13-1	06-Sep-57	3.70	2	SAN MIGUEL	UK9-1	19-May-53	466.90	9
SAN JUAN	R1-2	29-Jan-51	4.08	2	SEDGWICK	TP3-2	02-Mar-55	4.00	2
SAN JUAN	TP5-1	12-Mar-55	4.23	2	SEDGWICK	PB18-3	12-Jul-57	4.73	2
SAN JUAN	PB12-1	02-Sep-57	4.40	2	SEDGWICK	PB5-4	18-Jul-57	4.87	2
SAN JUAN	PB3-1	24-Jun-57	4.92	2	SEDGWICK	UK11-2	05-Jun-53	5.19	3
SAN JUAN	PB1-1	28-May-57	6.17	3	SEDGWICK	TP9-2	15-Apr-55	5.23	3

INDIVIDUAL FALLOUT DAYS
COLORADO

COUNTY	SHOT	DATE	μCi/SQ METER	INDEX	COUNTY	SHOT	DATE	μCi/SQ METER	INDEX
SEDGWICK	TP11-3	17-May-55	5.60	3	SUMMIT	TP3-2	02-Mar-55	40.29	5
SEDGWICK	TP4-2	08-Mar-55	5.97	3	SUMMIT	TP10-2	06-May-55	54.88	6
SEDGWICK	TS5-1	07-May-52	6.89	3	SUMMIT	UK9-1	19-May-53	139.79	7
SEDGWICK	UK7-4	28-Apr-53	6.90	3	SUMMIT	TP4-2	08-Mar-55	155.94	7
SEDGWICK	TP11-2	16-May-55	8.58	3	TELLER	TS7-4	04-Jun-52	3.91	2
SEDGWICK	PB9-4	26-Aug-57	11.05	4	TELLER	UK9-2	20-May-53	4.02	2
SEDGWICK	TS8-1	05-Jun-52	13.29	4	TELLER	PB15-1	16-Sep-57	4.06	2
SEDGWICK	PB2-3	20-Jun-57	14.08	4	TELLER	TS6-3	27-May-52	4.65	2
SEDGWICK	UK2-7	30-Mar-53	14.85	4	TELLER	PB11-2	01-Sep-57	4.79	2
SEDGWICK	UK7-3	27-Apr-53	16.73	4	TELLER	TP3-2	02-Mar-55	4.94	2
SEDGWICK	TS1-2	02-Apr-52	17.73	4	TELLER	PB2-3	20-Jun-57	5.03	3
SEDGWICK	PB9-3	25-Aug-57	23.29	4	TELLER	UK9-3	21-May-53	6.42	3
SEDGWICK	TS6-3	27-May-52	35.88	5	TELLER	TP10-1	05-May-55	8.16	3
SUMMIT	TP11-3	17-May-55	3.54	2	TELLER	TS1-2	02-Apr-52	8.70	3
SUMMIT	TS6-4	28-May-52	4.03	2	TELLER	TP11-3	17-May-55	9.12	3
SUMMIT	PB15-1	16-Sep-57	4.06	2	TELLER	UK7-3	27-Apr-53	12.24	4
SUMMIT	PB12-3	04-Sep-57	4.34	2	TELLER	TS8-1	05-Jun-52	13.29	4
SUMMIT	TP3-3	03-Mar-55	4.45	2	TELLER	TS6-2	26-May-52	13.95	4
SUMMIT	PB11-2	01-Sep-57	4.79	2	TELLER	PB12-3	04-Sep-57	14.10	4
SUMMIT	PB8-4	21-Aug-57	4.92	2	TELLER	TS6-4	28-May-52	31.43	5
SUMMIT	TP7-2	30-Mar-55	5.00	3	TELLER	UK9-1	19-May-53	39.64	5
SUMMIT	TS7-4	04-Jun-52	5.04	3	TELLER	TP10-2	06-May-55	40.42	5
SUMMIT	TP10-3	07-May-55	5.36	3	TELLER	TP4-2	08-Mar-55	44.36	5
SUMMIT	UK11-2	05-Jun-53	5.70	3	WASHINGTON	TP11-3	17-May-55	3.86	2
SUMMIT	TP9-2	15-Apr-55	6.98	3	WASHINGTON	TP10-3	07-May-55	4.15	2
SUMMIT	UK9-3	21-May-53	7.63	3	WASHINGTON	PB18-2	11-Jul-57	4.60	2
SUMMIT	TS6-3	27-May-52	7.79	3	WASHINGTON	PB4-2	06-Jul-57	4.73	2
SUMMIT	TP4-3	09-Mar-55	7.88	3	WASHINGTON	PB11-2	01-Sep-57	4.79	2
SUMMIT	TS1-2	02-Apr-52	8.06	3	WASHINGTON	UK11-2	05-Jun-53	4.97	2
SUMMIT	PB2-3	20-Jun-57	10.05	4	WASHINGTON	UK7-4	28-Apr-53	5.13	3
SUMMIT	TS6-2	26-May-52	14.92	4	WASHINGTON	TP11-2	16-May-55	5.45	3
SUMMIT	TP11-2	16-May-55	15.86	4	WASHINGTON	UK7-3	27-Apr-53	5.51	3
SUMMIT	UK7-3	27-Apr-53	32.79	5	WASHINGTON	TP7-2	30-Mar-55	5.54	3

INDIVIDUAL FALLOUT DAYS
COLORADO

COUNTY	SHOT	DATE	µCi/SQ METER	INDEX	COUNTY	SHOT	DATE	µCi/SQ METER	INDEX
WASHINGTON	UK9-1	19-May-53	6.25	3	WELD	TP10-1	05-May-55	84.89	6
WASHINGTON	TP3-2	02-Mar-55	7.78	3	YUMA	UK9-1	19-May-53	3.88	2
WASHINGTON	PB8-4	21-Aug-57	9.77	3	YUMA	PB9-3	25-Aug-57	4.31	2
WASHINGTON	TS1-2	02-Apr-52	9.99	3	YUMA	UK9-2	20-May-53	4.44	2
WASHINGTON	TS8-1	05-Jun-52	13.29	4	YUMA	PB12-4	05-Sep-57	4.48	2
WASHINGTON	TS6-3	27-May-52	22.54	4	YUMA	UK7-4	28-Apr-53	4.50	2
WASHINGTON	TP10-2	06-May-55	33.30	5	YUMA	PB18-3	12-Jul-57	4.73	2
WASHINGTON	TP4-2	08-Mar-55	51.16	6	YUMA	TP9-2	15-Apr-55	4.84	2
WELD	PB9-4	26-Aug-57	3.68	2	YUMA	PB5-4	18-Jul-57	4.87	2
WELD	PB9-3	25-Aug-57	3.88	2	YUMA	PB18-2	11-Jul-57	3.51	1
WELD	PB8-3	20-Aug-57	4.57	2	YUMA	TS1-2	02-Apr-52	5.16	3
WELD	TP4-2	08-Mar-55	4.84	2	YUMA	TS5-1	07-May-52	5.39	3
WELD	TS5-1	07-May-52	5.24	3	YUMA	TP11-2	16-May-55	5.45	3
WELD	TS6-2	26-May-52	5.82	3	YUMA	UK7-3	27-Apr-53	5.68	3
WELD	TP11-3	17-May-55	6.13	3	YUMA	UK11-2	05-Jun-53	5.78	3
WELD	TP9-2	15-Apr-55	6.74	3	YUMA	PB2-3	20-Jun-57	7.04	3
WELD	TS1-2	02-Apr-52	8.70	3	YUMA	TP3-2	02-Mar-55	7.78	3
WELD	TP11-2	16-May-55	11.61	4	YUMA	TS8-1	05-Jun-52	13.29	4
WELD	PB2-2	19-Jun-57	14.59	4	YUMA	TP10-2	06-May-55	33.30	5
WELD	PB12-3	04-Sep-57	15.91	4	YUMA	TS6-3	27-May-52	41.63	5
WELD	TP10-2	06-May-55	25.63	5	YUMA	TP4-2	08-Mar-55	51.16	6
WELD	TS6-3	27-May-52	28.09	5					

INDIVIDUAL FALLOUT DAYS
CONNECTICUTT

COUNTY	SHOT	DATE	µCi/SQ METER	INDEX	COUNTY	SHOT	DATE	µCi/SQ METER	INDEX
FAIRFIELD	BJ2-3	01-Nov-51	5.01	3	MIDDLESEX	BJ2-4	02-Nov-51	8.75	3
FAIRFIELD	TS8-3	07-Jun-52	6.34	3	MIDDLESEX	PB5-8	22-Jul-57	8.96	3
FAIRFIELD	BJ2-4	02-Nov-51	8.78	3	MIDDLESEX	R1-2	29-Jan-51	9.14	3
FAIRFIELD	TS7-5	05-Jun-52	8.94	3	MIDDLESEX	UK1-2	18-Mar-53	10.40	4
FAIRFIELD	R1-2	29-Jan-51	9.14	3	MIDDLESEX	TS1-4	04-Apr-52	10.77	4
FAIRFIELD	UK4-2	07-Apr-53	10.02	4	MIDDLESEX	TS8-3	07-Jun-52	10.80	4
FAIRFIELD	BJ3-7	07-Nov-51	11.62	4	MIDDLESEX	UK4-2	07-Apr-53	93.66	6
FAIRFIELD	TS1-4	04-Apr-52	19.67	4	NEW HAVEN	TP11-9	23-May-55	3.55	2
FAIRFIELD	UK1-2	18-Mar-53	28.46	5	NEW HAVEN	BJ2-3	01-Nov-51	5.91	3
HARTFORD	BJ2-3	01-Nov-51	4.17	2	NEW HAVEN	PB5-8	22-Jul-57	5.97	3
HARTFORD	PB5-8	22-Jul-57	5.97	3	NEW HAVEN	TS7-5	05-Jun-52	7.59	3
HARTFORD	TS7-5	05-Jun-52	6.26	3	NEW HAVEN	BJ2-4	02-Nov-51	8.17	3
HARTFORD	PB11-5	04-Sep-57	6.43	3	NEW HAVEN	TS8-3	07-Jun-52	9.05	3
HARTFORD	UK1-2	18-Mar-53	7.48	3	NEW HAVEN	R1-2	29-Jan-51	9.14	3
HARTFORD	BJ2-4	02-Nov-51	8.77	3	NEW HAVEN	TS1-4	04-Apr-52	11.87	4
HARTFORD	TS1-4	04-Apr-52	10.77	4	NEW HAVEN	UK1-2	18-Mar-53	15.10	4
HARTFORD	R1-2	29-Jan-51	11.65	4	NEW HAVEN	UK4-2	07-Apr-53	54.65	6
HARTFORD	TS8-3	07-Jun-52	11.76	4	NEW LONDON	UK1-2	18-Mar-53	4.73	2
HARTFORD	UK4-2	07-Apr-53	28.38	5	NEW LONDON	R1-2	29-Jan-51	3.50	1
LITCHFIELD	BJ2-3	01-Nov-51	5.10	3	NEW LONDON	PB5-8	22-Jul-57	5.97	3
LITCHFIELD	PB5-8	22-Jul-57	5.97	3	NEW LONDON	TS7-5	05-Jun-52	6.80	3
LITCHFIELD	UK7-2	26-Apr-53	6.30	3	NEW LONDON	BJ2-3	01-Nov-51	6.86	3
LITCHFIELD	PB11-5	04-Sep-57	6.43	3	NEW LONDON	TS1-4	04-Apr-52	7.18	3
LITCHFIELD	TS7-5	05-Jun-52	8.05	3	NEW LONDON	TS8-3	07-Jun-52	9.06	3
LITCHFIELD	UK4-2	07-Apr-53	8.18	3	NEW LONDON	BJ2-4	02-Nov-51	10.52	4
LITCHFIELD	TS8-3	07-Jun-52	9.88	3	NEW LONDON	UK4-2	07-Apr-53	58.76	6
LITCHFIELD	BJ2-4	02-Nov-51	11.42	4	TOLLAND	UK1-2	18-Mar-53	4.13	2
LITCHFIELD	UK1-2	18-Mar-53	11.61	4	TOLLAND	BJ2-3	01-Nov-51	5.19	3
LITCHFIELD	TS1-4	04-Apr-52	17.17	4	TOLLAND	TS7-5	05-Jun-52	6.51	3
LITCHFIELD	R1-2	29-Jan-51	28.94	5	TOLLAND	BJ2-4	02-Nov-51	10.20	4
MIDDLESEX	BJ2-3	01-Nov-51	5.06	3	TOLLAND	TS8-3	07-Jun-52	13.00	4
MIDDLESEX	TS7-5	05-Jun-52	7.80	3	TOLLAND	TS1-4	04-Apr-52	17.95	4

INDIVIDUAL FALLOUT DAYS
CONNECTICUTT

COUNTY	SHOT	DATE	µCi/SQ METER	INDEX	COUNTY	SHOT	DATE	µCi/SQ METER	INDEX
TOLLAND	R1-2	29-Jan-51	28.94	5	WINDHAM	TS1-4	04-Apr-52	10.77	4
TOLLAND	UK4-2	07-Apr-53	42.74	5	WINDHAM	BJ2-4	02-Nov-51	13.27	4
WINDHAM	R1-2	29-Jan-51	3.50	1	WINDHAM	TS8-3	07-Jun-52	13.92	4
WINDHAM	BJ2-3	01-Nov-51	6.86	3	WINDHAM	UK4-2	07-Apr-53	54.92	6

INDIVIDUAL FALLOUT DAYS
WASHINGTON D.C.

	COUNTY	SHOT	DATE	µCi/SQ METER	INDEX
DC	WASHINGTON	TS3-5	26-Apr-52	3.86	2
DC	WASHINGTON	TS3-4	25-Apr-52	3.87	2
DC	WASHINGTON	UK10-2	26-May-53	5.23	3
DC	WASHINGTON	PB5-8	22-Jul-57	5.97	3
DC	WASHINGTON	UK1-2	18-Mar-53	6.10	3
DC	WASHINGTON	BJ2-4	2-Nov-51	8.09	3
DC	WASHINGTON	BJ2-3	1-Nov-51	19.54	4

INDIVIDUAL FALLOUT DAYS
DELAWARE

COUNTY	SHOT	DATE	µCi/SQ METER	INDEX	COUNTY	SHOT	DATE	µCi/SQ METER	INDEX
KENT	PB12-6	7-Sep-57	4.47	2	NEW CASTLE	UK9-7	25-May-53	10.18	4
KENT	BJ2-4	2-Nov-51	7.10	3	NEW CASTLE	UK1-2	18-Mar-53	17.45	4
KENT	BJ2-3	1-Nov-51	9.55	3	SUSSEX	BJ2-4	2-Nov-51	4.34	2
KENT	UK9-7	25-May-53	10.18	4	SUSSEX	PB5-8	22-Jul-57	5.97	3
KENT	UK1-2	18-Mar-53	18.45	4	SUSSEX	UK9-7	25-May-53	6.11	3
NEW CASTLE	BJ2-4	2-Nov-51	6.48	3	SUSSEX	BJ2-3	1-Nov-51	9.22	3
NEW CASTLE	BJ2-3	1-Nov-51	7.51	3	SUSSEX	UK1-2	18-Mar-53	20.16	4
NEW CASTLE	PB5-8	22-Jul-57	8.96	3					

INDIVIDUAL FALLOUT DAYS
FLORIDA

COUNTY	SHOT	DATE	µCi/SQ METER	INDEX	COUNTY	SHOT	DATE	µCi/SQ METER	INDEX
ALACHUA	UK4-3	8-Apr-53	3.89	2	CITRUS	TS3-8	29-Apr-52	5.73	3
ALACHUA	TS3-8	29-Apr-52	5.73	3	CITRUS	PB11-4	3-Sep-57	11.66	4
ALACHUA	PB11-4	3-Sep-57	11.66	4	CLAY	UK4-3	8-Apr-53	3.89	2
BAKER	UK4-3	8-Apr-53	3.89	2	CLAY	TS3-8	29-Apr-52	5.73	3
BAKER	TS3-8	29-Apr-52	5.73	3	COLLIER	PB8-5	22-Aug-57	3.61	2
BAKER	PB11-4	3-Sep-57	11.66	4	COLLIER	TS3-8	29-Apr-52	5.73	3
BAY	TP6-5	26-Mar-55	3.54	2	COLLIER	UK2-3	26-Mar-53	6.29	3
BAY	PB12-6	7-Sep-57	3.76	2	COLUMBIA	UK4-3	8-Apr-53	3.89	2
BAY	PB17-3	30-Sep-57	3.96	2	COLUMBIA	TS3-8	29-Apr-52	5.73	3
BAY	PB16-5	27-Sep-57	4.93	2	COLUMBIA	PB11-4	3-Sep-57	11.66	4
BAY	TS3-7	28-Apr-52	6.40	3	DADE	TS3-8	29-Apr-52	5.73	3
BAY	BJ2-4	2-Nov-51	6.87	3	DADE	UK2-3	26-Mar-53	6.29	3
BRADFORD	UK4-3	8-Apr-53	3.89	2	DE SOTO	UK2-3	26-Mar-53	4.35	2
BRADFORD	TS3-8	29-Apr-52	5.73	3	DE SOTO	TS3-8	29-Apr-52	5.73	3
BREVARD	UK2-3	26-Mar-53	3.52	2	DIXIE	TS3-7	28-Apr-52	6.40	3
BREVARD	PB8-5	22-Aug-57	3.61	2	DIXIE	UK4-3	8-Apr-53	7.78	3
BREVARD	UK4-3	8-Apr-53	3.89	2	DIXIE	PB11-4	3-Sep-57	11.66	4
BREVARD	TS3-8	29-Apr-52	5.73	3	ESCAMBIA	TP6-5	26-Mar-55	3.54	2
BREVARD	PB11-4	3-Sep-57	19.43	4	ESCAMBIA	UK2-3	26-Mar-53	4.41	2
BROWARD	UK2-3	26-Mar-53	5.57	3	ESCAMBIA	PB12-6	7-Sep-57	7.74	3
BROWARD	TS3-8	29-Apr-52	5.73	3	ESCAMBIA	TS3-3	24-Apr-52	8.89	3
CALHOUN	TP6-5	26-Mar-55	3.54	2	ESCAMBIA	PB3-3	26-Jun-57	22.97	4
CALHOUN	PB12-6	7-Sep-57	5.87	3	FLAGLER	UK4-3	8-Apr-53	3.89	2
CALHOUN	PB17-3	30-Sep-57	5.99	3	FLAGLER	TS3-8	29-Apr-52	5.73	3
CALHOUN	PB16-5	27-Sep-57	6.35	3	FLAGLER	PB11-4	3-Sep-57	19.43	4
CALHOUN	TS3-7	28-Apr-52	6.40	3	FRANKLIN	PB12-7	8-Sep-57	4.15	2
CALHOUN	BJ2-4	2-Nov-51	10.02	4	FRANKLIN	PB16-5	27-Sep-57	5.31	3
CHARLOTTE	PB8-5	22-Aug-57	3.61	2	FRANKLIN	TS3-7	28-Apr-52	6.40	3
CHARLOTTE	UK2-3	26-Mar-53	4.56	2	FRANKLIN	PB11-4	3-Sep-57	11.66	4
CHARLOTTE	TS3-8	29-Apr-52	5.73	3	GADSDEN	BJ2-4	2-Nov-51	5.85	3
CITRUS	UK4-3	8-Apr-53	3.89	2	GADSDEN	TS3-7	28-Apr-52	6.40	3
					GADSDEN	PB16-5	27-Sep-57	7.28	3
					GILCHRIST	PB16-5	27-Sep-57	3.60	2

INDIVIDUAL FALLOUT DAYS
FLORIDA

COUNTY	SHOT	DATE	µCi/SQ METER	INDEX	COUNTY	SHOT	DATE	µCi/SQ METER	INDEX
GILCHRIST	TS3-8	29-Apr-52	5.73	3	HOLMES	PB17-3	30-Sep-57	3.96	2
GILCHRIST	UK4-3	8-Apr-53	7.78	3	HOLMES	PB16-5	27-Sep-57	6.21	3
GILCHRIST	PB11-4	3-Sep-57	11.66	4	HOLMES	BJ2-4	2-Nov-51	15.86	4
GLADES	PB8-5	22-Aug-57	3.61	2	HOLMES	TS3-3	24-Apr-52	26.68	5
GLADES	UK2-3	26-Mar-53	5.18	3	INDIAN RIVER	UK2-3	26-Mar-53	4.15	2
GLADES	TS3-8	29-Apr-52	5.73	3	INDIAN RIVER	TS3-8	29-Apr-52	5.73	3
GULF	TP6-5	26-Mar-55	3.54	2	JACKSON	TP6-5	26-Mar-55	3.54	2
GULF	PB11-4	3-Sep-57	3.89	2	JACKSON	TS3-7	28-Apr-52	6.40	3
GULF	PB12-7	8-Sep-57	4.15	2	JACKSON	PB16-5	27-Sep-57	6.68	3
GULF	PB16-5	27-Sep-57	4.69	2	JEFFERSON	UK4-3	8-Apr-53	3.89	2
GULF	PB12-6	7-Sep-57	6.27	3	JEFFERSON	PB12-6	7-Sep-57	4.11	2
GULF	TS3-7	28-Apr-52	6.40	3	JEFFERSON	TS3-7	28-Apr-52	6.40	3
HAMILTON	TS3-8	29-Apr-52	5.73	3	JEFFERSON	PB16-5	27-Sep-57	10.68	4
HAMILTON	UK4-3	8-Apr-53	7.78	3	LAFAYETTE	UK4-3	8-Apr-53	3.89	2
HAMILTON	PB16-5	27-Sep-57	8.22	3	LAFAYETTE	PB16-5	27-Sep-57	6.01	3
HARDEE	UK2-3	26-Mar-53	4.15	2	LAFAYETTE	TS3-7	28-Apr-52	6.40	3
HARDEE	TS3-8	29-Apr-52	5.73	3	LAKE	PB8-5	22-Aug-57	3.61	2
HENDRY	TS3-8	29-Apr-52	5.73	3	LAKE	UK4-3	8-Apr-53	3.89	2
HENDRY	UK2-3	26-Mar-53	5.87	3	LAKE	TS3-8	29-Apr-52	5.73	3
HERNANDO	UK4-3	8-Apr-53	3.89	2	LAKE	UK9-4	22-May-53	12.72	4
HERNANDO	TS3-8	29-Apr-52	5.73	3	LAKE	PB11-4	3-Sep-57	19.43	4
HERNANDO	PB11-4	3-Sep-57	19.43	4	LEE	PB8-5	22-Aug-57	3.61	2
HIGHLANDS	UK2-3	26-Mar-53	4.56	2	LEE	UK2-3	26-Mar-53	4.98	2
HIGHLANDS	TS3-8	29-Apr-52	5.73	3	LEE	TS3-8	29-Apr-52	5.73	3
HILLSBOROUGH	UK4-3	8-Apr-53	3.89	2	LEON	PB12-7	8-Sep-57	4.15	2
HILLSBOROUGH	PB11-4	3-Sep-57	7.77	3	LEON	PB11-4	3-Sep-57	7.77	3
HILLSBOROUGH	TS3-8	29-Apr-52	22.91	4	LEON	PB16-5	27-Sep-57	12.13	4
HOLMES	TP6-5	26-Mar-55	3.54	2	LEON	UK4-3	8-Apr-53	15.57	4
HOLMES	PB12-6	7-Sep-57	3.76	2	LEVY	UK4-3	8-Apr-53	3.89	2

INDIVIDUAL FALLOUT DAYS
FLORIDA

COUNTY	SHOT	DATE	µCi/SQ METER	INDEX	COUNTY	SHOT	DATE	µCi/SQ METER	INDEX
LEVY	TS3-8	29-Apr-52	5.73	3	A				
LIBERTY	TP6-5	26-Mar-55	3.54	2	OKEECHOBEE	UK2-3	26-Mar-53	4.56	2
LIBERTY	PB12-6	7-Sep-57	5.42	3	OKEECHOBEE	TS3-8	29-Apr-52	5.73	3
LIBERTY	TS3-7	28-Apr-52	6.40	3	ORANGE	PB8-5	22-Aug-57	3.61	2
LIBERTY	PB16-5	27-Sep-57	6.45	3	ORANGE	UK4-3	8-Apr-53	3.89	2
LIBERTY	BJ2-4	2-Nov-51	6.48	3	ORANGE	TS3-8	29-Apr-52	5.73	3
MADISON	TS3-7	28-Apr-52	6.40	3	ORANGE	PB11-4	3-Sep-57	11.66	4
MADISON	PB11-4	3-Sep-57	7.77	3	OSCEOLA	UK2-3	26-Mar-53	3.80	2
MADISON	UK4-3	8-Apr-53	7.78	3	OSCEOLA	PB11-4	3-Sep-57	3.89	2
MADISON	PB16-5	27-Sep-57	8.03	3	OSCEOLA	UK4-3	8-Apr-53	3.89	2
MANATEE	UK2-3	26-Mar-53	3.80	2	OSCEOLA	PB2-4	21-Jun-57	4.55	2
MANATEE	PB2-4	21-Jun-57	4.55	2	OSCEOLA	TS3-8	29-Apr-52	5.73	3
MANATEE	TS3-8	29-Apr-52	5.73	3	PALM BEACH	UK2-3	26-Mar-53	5.19	3
MARION	UK4-3	8-Apr-53	3.89	2	PALM BEACH	TS3-8	29-Apr-52	5.73	3
MARION	TS3-8	29-Apr-52	5.73	3	PASCO	PB11-4	3-Sep-57	3.89	2
MARION	PB11-4	3-Sep-57	7.77	3	PASCO	UK4-3	8-Apr-53	3.89	2
MARTIN	UK2-3	26-Mar-53	5.25	3	PASCO	TS3-8	29-Apr-52	5.73	3
MARTIN	TS3-8	29-Apr-52	5.73	3	PINELLAS	UK4-3	8-Apr-53	3.89	2
MONROE	TS3-8	29-Apr-52	5.73	3	PINELLAS	TS3-8	29-Apr-52	5.73	3
MONROE	UK2-3	26-Mar-53	7.88	3	PINELLAS	PB11-4	3-Sep-57	11.66	4
NASSAU	UK4-3	8-Apr-53	3.89	2	POLK	UK2-3	26-Mar-53	3.80	2
NASSAU	PB16-5	27-Sep-57	4.28	2	POLK	UK4-3	8-Apr-53	3.89	2
NASSAU	TP10-3	7-May-55	4.89	2	POLK	TS3-8	29-Apr-52	5.73	3
NASSAU	TS3-8	29-Apr-52	5.73	3	POLK	PB11-4	3-Sep-57	11.66	4
NASSAU	PB11-4	3-Sep-57	11.66	4	PUTNAM	UK4-3	8-Apr-53	3.89	2
OKALOOSA	TP6-5	26-Mar-55	3.54	2	PUTNAM	TS3-8	29-Apr-52	5.73	3
OKALOOSA	PB16-5	27-Sep-57	3.55	2	PUTNAM	PB11-4	3-Sep-57	11.66	4
OKALOOSA	UK2-3	26-Mar-53	3.87	2	SANTA ROSA	TP6-5	26-Mar-55	3.54	2
OKALOOSA	PB12-6	7-Sep-57	5.57	3	SANTA ROSA	PB12-6	7-Sep-57	7.27	3
OKALOOSA	TS3-3	24-Apr-52	17.78	4	SANTA ROSA	UK2-3	26-Mar-53	8.42	3
OKALOOS	PB3-3	26-Jun-57	68.82	6					

INDIVIDUAL FALLOUT DAYS
FLORIDA

COUNTY	SHOT	DATE	µCi/SQ METER	INDEX	COUNTY	SHOT	DATE	µCi/SQ METER	INDEX
SANTA ROSA	TS3-3	24-Apr-52	8.89	3	TAYLOR	UK4-3	8-Apr-53	3.89	2
SANTA ROSA	PB3-3	26-Jun-57	22.97	4	TAYLOR	PB12-6	7-Sep-57	4.01	2
SARASOTA	TS3-8	29-Apr-52	5.73	3	TAYLOR	TS3-7	28-Apr-52	6.40	3
SARASOTA	UK2-3	26-Mar-53	7.88	3	UNION	UK4-3	8-Apr-53	3.89	2
SEMINOLE	PB8-5	22-Aug-57	3.61	2	UNION	TS3-8	29-Apr-52	5.73	3
SEMINOLE	UK4-3	8-Apr-53	3.89	2	UNION	PB11-4	3-Sep-57	11.66	4
SEMINOLE	TS3-8	29-Apr-52	5.73	3	VOLUSIA	UK4-3	8-Apr-53	3.89	2
SEMINOLE	TP10-6	10-May-55	5.84	3	VOLUSIA	TS3-8	29-Apr-52	5.73	3
SEMINOLE	PB11-4	3-Sep-57	11.66	4	VOLUSIA	PB11-4	3-Sep-57	19.43	4
ST JOHNS	UK4-3	8-Apr-53	3.89	2	WAKULLA	PB11-4	3-Sep-57	3.89	2
ST JOHNS	PB5-9	23-Jul-57	4.71	2	WAKULLA	UK4-3	8-Apr-53	3.89	2
ST JOHNS	TS3-8	29-Apr-52	5.73	3	WAKULLA	PB12-7	8-Sep-57	4.15	2
ST JOHNS	PB11-4	3-Sep-57	19.43	4	WAKULLA	PB12-6	7-Sep-57	4.76	2
ST LUCIE	TS3-8	29-Apr-52	5.73	3	WAKULLA	TS3-7	28-Apr-52	6.40	3
ST LUCIE	UK2-3	26-Mar-53	9.33	3	WAKULLA	PB16-5	27-Sep-57	9.76	3
SUMTER	UK4-3	8-Apr-53	3.89	2	WALTON	TP6-5	26-Mar-55	3.54	2
SUMTER	TS3-8	29-Apr-52	5.73	3	WALTON	TS3-3	24-Apr-52	4.45	2
SUMTER	UK2-3	26-Mar-53	20.86	4	WALTON	PB16-5	27-Sep-57	4.55	2
SUWANNEE	PB11-4	3-Sep-57	3.89	2	WALTON	PB12-6	7-Sep-57	4.56	2
SUWANNEE	UK4-3	8-Apr-53	3.89	2	WASHINGTON	TP6-5	26-Mar-55	3.54	2
SUWANNEE	TS3-8	29-Apr-52	5.73	3	WASHINGTON	PB16-5	27-Sep-57	5.83	3
SUWANNEE	PB16-5	27-Sep-57	6.88	3	WASHINGTON	TS3-7	28-Apr-52	6.40	3
TAYLOR	PB11-4	3-Sep-57	3.89	2	WASHINGTON	BJ2-4	2-Nov-51	8.26	3

INDIVIDUAL FALLOUT DAYS
GEORGIA

COUNTY	SHOT	DATE	µCi/SQ METER	INDEX	COUNTY	SHOT	DATE	µCi/SQ METER	INDEX
APPLING	UK4-3	8-Apr-53	3.89	2	BEN HILL	BJ2-4	2-Nov-51	3.88	2
APPLING	UK9-4	22-May-53	3.99	2	BEN HILL	UK4-3	8-Apr-53	3.89	2
APPLING	TS3-4	25-Apr-52	8.50	3	BEN HILL	TS3-7	28-Apr-52	6.40	3
APPLING	PB16-5	27-Sep-57	11.51	4	BEN HILL	PB16-5	27-Sep-57	11.31	4
ATKINSON	PB11-4	3-Sep-57	3.89	2	BERRIEN	UK4-3	8-Apr-53	3.89	2
ATKINSON	UK4-3	8-Apr-53	3.89	2	BERRIEN	BJ2-4	2-Nov-51	6.37	3
ATKINSON	BJ2-4	2-Nov-51	5.58	3	BERRIEN	TS3-7	28-Apr-52	6.40	3
ATKINSON	TS3-8	29-Apr-52	5.73	3	BERRIEN	PB16-5	27-Sep-57	12.61	4
ATKINSON	PB16-5	27-Sep-57	7.24	3	BIBB	TS5-1	7-May-52	3.59	2
BACON	UK9-4	22-May-53	3.56	2	BIBB	PB17-3	30-Sep-57	3.96	2
BACON	PB16-5	27-Sep-57	7.04	3	BIBB	PB16-5	27-Sep-57	21.09	4
BACON	PB11-4	3-Sep-57	7.77	3	BLECKLEY	PB17-3	30-Sep-57	3.96	2
BACON	UK4-3	8-Apr-53	7.78	3	BLECKLEY	UK9-4	22-May-53	4.04	2
BACON	TS3-4	25-Apr-52	8.50	3	BLECKLEY	BJ2-4	2-Nov-51	4.28	2
BAKER	TS5-2	8-May-52	3.99	2	BLECKLEY	PB16-5	27-Sep-57	16.72	4
BAKER	PB17-3	30-Sep-57	5.99	3	BRANTLEY	PB11-4	3-Sep-57	3.89	2
BAKER	TS3-7	28-Apr-52	6.40	3	BRANTLEY	UK4-3	8-Apr-53	3.89	2
BAKER	BJ2-4	2-Nov-51	9.77	3	BRANTLEY	BJ2-4	2-Nov-51	4.28	2
BAKER	PB16-5	27-Sep-57	11.90	4	BRANTLEY	PB16-5	27-Sep-57	5.40	3
BALDWIN	UK9-4	22-May-53	5.00	3	BRANTLEY	TS3-8	29-Apr-52	5.73	3
BALDWIN	PB17-3	30-Sep-57	5.99	3	BROOKS	UK4-3	8-Apr-53	3.89	2
BALDWIN	TS5-2	8-May-52	7.93	3	BROOKS	BJ2-4	2-Nov-51	5.18	3
BALDWIN	PB16-5	27-Sep-57	9.08	3	BROOKS	TS3-7	28-Apr-52	6.40	3
BANKS	BJ2-3	1-Nov-51	3.54	2	BROOKS	PB16-5	27-Sep-57	10.16	4
BANKS	UK1-2	18-Mar-53	4.02	2	BRYAN	BJ2-3	1-Nov-51	4.35	2
BANKS	UK9-4	22-May-53	4.32	2	BRYAN	UK9-4	22-May-53	4.57	2
BANKS	PB16-5	27-Sep-57	5.17	3	BRYAN	PB16-5	27-Sep-57	5.65	3
BANKS	PB17-3	30-Sep-57	5.99	3	BRYAN	BJ2-4	2-Nov-51	6.67	3
BARROW	UK9-4	22-May-53	4.24	2	BRYAN	TS5-1	7-May-52	6.98	3
BARROW	PB17-3	30-Sep-57	5.99	3	BRYAN	TS3-4	25-Apr-52	12.70	4
BARROW	PB16-5	27-Sep-57	12.34	4	BULLOCH	BJ2-3	1-Nov-51	4.09	2
BARTOW	PB17-3	30-Sep-57	3.96	2	BULLOCH	UK9-4	22-May-53	5.24	3
BARTOW	PB16-5	27-Sep-57	13.23	4	BULLOCH	PB16-5	27-Sep-57	6.72	3

INDIVIDUAL FALLOUT DAYS
GEORGIA

COUNTY	SHOT	DATE	µCi/SQ METER	INDEX	COUNTY	SHOT	DATE	µCi/SQ METER	INDEX
BULLOCH	BJ2-4	2-Nov-51	7.77	3	CHATHAM	UK9-4	22-May-53	3.64	2
BULLOCH	TS3-4	25-Apr-52	12.70	4	CHATHAM	PB16-5	27-Sep-57	4.63	2
BURKE	BJ2-3	1-Nov-51	5.12	3	CHATHAM	BJ2-3	1-Nov-51	4.86	2
BURKE	UK9-4	22-May-53	5.92	3	CHATHAM	TS3-4	25-Apr-52	5.27	3
BURKE	PB16-5	27-Sep-57	6.92	3	CHATHAM	BJ2-4	2-Nov-51	6.87	3
BURKE	TS3-4	25-Apr-52	8.50	3	CHATHAM	TS5-1	7-May-52	10.10	4
BURKE	BJ2-4	2-Nov-51	8.56	3	CHATTAHOOCHE	TS5-1	7-May-52	4.31	2
BUTTS	UK9-4	22-May-53	3.72	2	CHATTAHOOCHE	PB17-6	3-Oct-57	4.62	2
BUTTS	PB17-3	30-Sep-57	5.99	3	CHATTAHOOCHE	PB17-3	30-Sep-57	5.99	3
BUTTS	PB16-5	27-Sep-57	18.76	4	CHATTAHOOCHE	PB16-5	27-Sep-57	13.96	4
CALHOUN	TS5-2	8-May-52	4.80	2	CHATTOOGA	TP6-4	25-Mar-55	3.99	2
CALHOUN	PB17-3	30-Sep-57	5.99	3	CHATTOOGA	PB16-5	27-Sep-57	5.17	3
CALHOUN	TS3-7	28-Apr-52	6.40	3	CHATTOOGA	PB17-3	30-Sep-57	5.99	3
CALHOUN	BJ2-4	2-Nov-51	10.94	4	CHATTOOGA	BJ3-6	6-Nov-51	8.10	3
CALHOUN	PB16-5	27-Sep-57	12.81	4	CHEROKEE	PB17-3	30-Sep-57	5.99	3
CAMDEN	UK4-3	8-Apr-53	3.89	2	CHEROKEE	PB16-5	27-Sep-57	11.58	4
CAMDEN	TS3-8	29-Apr-52	5.73	3	CLARKE	UK9-4	22-May-53	4.56	2
CAMDEN	PB16-5	27-Sep-57	6.15	3	CLARKE	PB16-5	27-Sep-57	9.81	3
CAMDEN	PB11-4	3-Sep-57	11.66	4	CLARKE	PB17-3	30-Sep-57	9.96	3
CANDLER	UK4-3	8-Apr-53	3.89	2	CLAY	PB17-6	3-Oct-57	4.07	2
CANDLER	UK9-4	22-May-53	5.19	3	CLAY	TS3-7	28-Apr-52	6.40	3
CANDLER	BJ2-4	2-Nov-51	7.57	3	CLAY	PB17-3	30-Sep-57	9.96	3
CANDLER	PB16-5	27-Sep-57	11.27	4	CLAY	PB16-5	27-Sep-57	11.90	4
CARROLL	PB17-3	30-Sep-57	3.96	2	CLAY	BJ2-4	2-Nov-51	12.61	4
CARROLL	TS5-1	7-May-52	11.85	4	CLAYTON	TS5-1	7-May-52	5.03	3
CARROLL	PB16-5	27-Sep-57	17.74	4	CLAYTON	PB17-6	3-Oct-57	5.58	3
CATOOSA	PB16-5	27-Sep-57	3.55	2	CLAYTON	PB17-3	30-Sep-57	5.99	3
CATOOSA	UK1-2	18-Mar-53	4.23	2	CLAYTON	PB16-5	27-Sep-57	26.92	5
CATOOSA	PB17-3	30-Sep-57	5.99	3	CLINCH	UK4-3	8-Apr-53	3.89	2
CATOOSA	BJ3-6	6-Nov-51	8.10	3	CLINCH	BJ2-4	2-Nov-51	4.18	2
CHARLTON	UK4-3	8-Apr-53	3.89	2	CLINCH	TS3-8	29-Apr-52	5.73	3
CHARLTON	TS3-8	29-Apr-52	5.73	3					
CHARLTON	PB11-4	3-Sep-57	11.66	4					

INDIVIDUAL FALLOUT DAYS
GEORGIA

COUNTY	SHOT	DATE	μCi/SQ METER	INDEX	COUNTY	SHOT	DATE	μCi/SQ METER	INDEX
CLINCH	PB11-4	3-Sep-57	7.77	3	DADE	PB17-3	30-Sep-57	3.96	2
CLINCH	PB16-5	27-Sep-57	9.89	3	DADE	TP6-4	25-Mar-55	3.99	2
COBB	PB17-3	30-Sep-57	3.96	2	DADE	BJ3-6	6-Nov-51	4.86	2
COBB	PB16-5	27-Sep-57	19.61	4	DAWSON	TP6-4	25-Mar-55	3.99	2
COFFEE	UK4-3	8-Apr-53	3.89	2	DAWSON	TS7-6	6-Jun-52	4.15	2
COFFEE	PB12-7	8-Sep-57	4.15	2	DAWSON	PB17-3	30-Sep-57	5.99	3
COFFEE	TS5-2	8-May-52	5.29	3	DAWSON	PB16-5	27-Sep-57	6.02	3
COFFEE	TS3-8	29-Apr-52	5.73	3	DE KALB	PB17-3	30-Sep-57	3.96	2
COFFEE	PB11-4	3-Sep-57	7.77	3	DE KALB	PB16-5	27-Sep-57	25.90	5
COLQUITT	UK4-3	8-Apr-53	3.89	2	DECATUR	UK4-3	8-Apr-53	3.89	2
COLQUITT	TS3-7	28-Apr-52	6.40	3	DECATUR	BJ2-4	2-Nov-51	6.27	3
COLQUITT	PB11-4	3-Sep-57	11.66	4	DECATUR	TS3-7	28-Apr-52	6.40	3
COLQUITT	PB16-5	27-Sep-57	12.22	4	DECATUR	PB16-5	27-Sep-57	9.73	3
COLUMBIA	BJ2-3	1-Nov-51	4.29	2	DODGE	UK9-4	22-May-53	3.85	2
COLUMBIA	PB16-5	27-Sep-57	5.66	3	DODGE	PB17-3	30-Sep-57	3.96	2
COLUMBIA	UK9-4	22-May-53	6.06	3	DODGE	BJ2-4	2-Nov-51	4.08	2
COLUMBUS	TS5-1	7-May-52	4.85	2	DODGE	PB16-5	27-Sep-57	17.64	4
COLUMBUS	PB16-5	27-Sep-57	20.01	4	DOOLY	BJ2-4	2-Nov-51	9.46	3
COOK	UK4-3	8-Apr-53	3.89	2	DOOLY	PB16-5	27-Sep-57	20.17	4
COOK	BJ2-4	2-Nov-51	5.51	3	DOUGHERTY	TS3-7	28-Apr-52	6.40	3
COOK	TS3-7	28-Apr-52	6.40	3	DOUGHERTY	BJ2-4	2-Nov-51	9.10	3
COOK	PB16-5	27-Sep-57	12.10	4	DOUGHERTY	PB17-3	30-Sep-57	9.96	3
COWETA	TS5-1	7-May-52	5.93	3	DOUGHERTY	PB16-5	27-Sep-57	14.16	4
COWETA	PB17-3	30-Sep-57	5.99	3	DOUGLAS	PB17-3	30-Sep-57	5.99	3
COWETA	PB16-5	27-Sep-57	17.51	4	DOUGLAS	PB17-6	3-Oct-57	6.15	3
CRAWFORD	BJ2-4	2-Nov-51	3.51	1	DOUGLAS	PB16-5	27-Sep-57	23.79	4
CRAWFORD	PB17-6	3-Oct-57	5.12	3	EARLY	PB12-7	8-Sep-57	4.15	2
CRAWFORD	PB17-3	30-Sep-57	9.96	3	EARLY	TS3-7	28-Apr-52	6.40	3
CRAWFORD	PB16-5	27-Sep-57	22.11	4	EARLY	PB16-5	27-Sep-57	10.32	4
CRISP	TS5-2	8-May-52	5.70	3	ECHOLS	UK4-3	8-Apr-53	3.89	2
CRISP	TS3-7	28-Apr-52	6.40	3	ECHOLS	TS3-8	29-Apr-52	5.73	3
CRISP	BJ2-4	2-Nov-51	9.46	3	ECHOLS	PB16-5	27-Sep-57	9.21	3
CRISP	PB16-5	27-Sep-57	18.03	4	EFFINGHAM	TS5-2	8-May-52	4.05	2

INDIVIDUAL FALLOUT DAYS
GEORGIA

COUNTY	SHOT	DATE	µCi/SQ METER	INDEX	COUNTY	SHOT	DATE	µCi/SQ METER	INDEX
EFFINGHAM	BJ2-3	1-Nov-51	4.86	2	FLOYD	BJ3-5	5-Nov-51	4.59	2
EFFINGHAM	UK9-4	22-May-53	5.10	3	FLOYD	BJ3-6	6-Nov-51	4.86	2
EFFINGHAM	PB16-5	27-Sep-57	7.24	3	FLOYD	PB16-5	27-Sep-57	9.74	3
EFFINGHAM	BJ2-4	2-Nov-51	7.97	3	FORSYTH	PB17-3	30-Sep-57	5.99	3
EFFINGHAM	TS3-4	25-Apr-52	12.70	4	FORSYTH	PB16-5	27-Sep-57	11.78	4
ELBERT	BJ2-3	1-Nov-51	4.08	2	FRANKLIN	PB16-5	27-Sep-57	4.28	2
ELBERT	UK9-4	22-May-53	5.82	3	FRANKLIN	UK9-4	22-May-53	4.52	2
ELBERT	PB16-5	27-Sep-57	5.92	3	FRANKLIN	PB5-8	22-Jul-57	5.97	3
ELBERT	PB17-3	30-Sep-57	5.99	3	FRANKLIN	PB17-3	30-Sep-57	5.99	3
EMANUEL	UK9-4	22-May-53	5.34	3	FULTON	PB16-5	27-Sep-57	26.01	5
EMANUEL	PB17-3	30-Sep-57	5.99	3	GILMER	PB17-3	30-Sep-57	3.96	2
EMANUEL	BJ2-4	2-Nov-51	7.97	3	GILMER	TP6-4	25-Mar-55	3.99	2
EMANUEL	PB16-5	27-Sep-57	12.69	4	GILMER	UK1-2	18-Mar-53	5.67	3
EVANS	BJ2-4	2-Nov-51	3.58	2	GILMER	PB16-5	27-Sep-57	5.89	3
EVANS	TS5-2	8-May-52	3.71	2	GLASCOCK	BJ2-3	1-Nov-51	3.84	2
EVANS	PB11-4	3-Sep-57	3.89	2	GLASCOCK	BJ2-4	2-Nov-51	3.98	2
EVANS	UK4-3	8-Apr-53	3.89	2	GLASCOCK	UK9-4	22-May-53	5.77	3
EVANS	BJ2-3	1-Nov-51	3.97	2	GLASCOCK	PB16-5	27-Sep-57	5.92	3
EVANS	UK9-4	22-May-53	4.86	2	GLASCOCK	PB17-3	30-Sep-57	9.96	3
EVANS	PB16-5	27-Sep-57	7.28	3	GLYNN	UK4-3	8-Apr-53	3.89	2
EVANS	TS3-4	25-Apr-52	8.50	3	GLYNN	TS3-8	29-Apr-52	5.73	3
FANNIN	TS7-6	6-Jun-52	3.82	2	GLYNN	PB16-5	27-Sep-57	6.29	3
FANNIN	PB17-3	30-Sep-57	3.96	2	GLYNN	PB11-4	3-Sep-57	11.66	4
FANNIN	TP6-4	25-Mar-55	3.99	2	GORDON	UK1-2	18-Mar-53	3.81	2
FANNIN	PB16-5	27-Sep-57	4.44	2	GORDON	PB17-3	30-Sep-57	3.96	2
FANNIN	BJ3-6	6-Nov-51	4.86	2	GORDON	BJ3-6	6-Nov-51	8.10	3
FANNIN	TP10-8	12-May-55	3.50	1	GORDON	PB16-5	27-Sep-57	9.18	3
FANNIN	UK1-2	18-Mar-53	9.28	3	GRADY	TS5-2	8-May-52	3.82	2
FAYETTE	TS5-1	7-May-52	5.21	3	GRADY	TS3-7	28-Apr-52	6.40	3
FAYETTE	PB17-3	30-Sep-57	5.99	3	GRADY	PB16-5	27-Sep-57	9.57	3
FAYETTE	PB17-6	3-Oct-57	6.27	3	GREENE	PB17-6	3-Oct-57	3.50	1
FAYETTE	PB16-5	27-Sep-57	29.19	5	GREENE	UK9-4	22-May-53	5.58	3
FLOYD	PB17-3	30-Sep-57	3.96	2	GREENE	PB17-3	30-Sep-57	5.99	3

INDIVIDUAL FALLOUT DAYS
GEORGIA

COUNTY	SHOT	DATE	µCi/SQ METER	INDEX	COUNTY	SHOT	DATE	µCi/SQ METER	INDEX
GREENE	BJ2-4	2-Nov-51	7.07	3	IRWIN	TS3-7	28-Apr-52	6.40	3
GREENE	PB16-5	27-Sep-57	10.53	4	IRWIN	PB16-5	27-Sep-57	10.72	4
GWINNETT	PB17-3	30-Sep-57	5.99	3	JACKSON	TS7-6	6-Jun-52	3.98	2
GWINNETT	PB16-5	27-Sep-57	22.38	4	JACKSON	PB17-6	3-Oct-57	4.08	2
HABERSHAM	PB16-5	27-Sep-57	3.69	2	JACKSON	UK9-4	22-May-53	4.36	2
HABERSHAM	UK9-4	22-May-53	4.12	2	JACKSON	PB17-3	30-Sep-57	5.99	3
HABERSHAM	PB17-3	30-Sep-57	5.99	3	JACKSON	PB16-5	27-Sep-57	9.61	3
HABERSHAM	UK1-2	18-Mar-53	6.39	3	JASPER	UK9-4	22-May-53	4.00	2
HALL	UK9-4	22-May-53	3.96	2	JASPER	PB17-3	30-Sep-57	9.96	3
HALL	PB17-3	30-Sep-57	5.99	3	JASPER	PB16-5	27-Sep-57	16.12	4
HALL	PB16-5	27-Sep-57	9.15	3	JEFF DAVIS	UK9-4	22-May-53	3.85	2
HANCOCK	UK9-4	22-May-53	5.53	3	JEFF DAVIS	PB11-4	3-Sep-57	7.77	3
HANCOCK	PB17-3	30-Sep-57	5.99	3	JEFF DAVIS	UK4-3	8-Apr-53	7.78	3
HANCOCK	PB16-5	27-Sep-57	10.40	4	JEFF DAVIS	PB16-5	27-Sep-57	8.00	3
HARALSON	UK9-3	21-May-53	5.60	3	JEFF DAVIS	TS3-4	25-Apr-52	8.50	3
HARALSON	PB17-3	30-Sep-57	5.99	3	JEFFERSON	BJ2-3	1-Nov-51	4.73	2
HARALSON	PB16-5	27-Sep-57	14.05	4	JEFFERSON	UK9-4	22-May-53	5.77	3
HARRIS	TS5-1	7-May-52	5.39	3	JEFFERSON	PB5-8	22-Jul-57	5.97	3
HARRIS	PB16-5	27-Sep-57	18.17	4	JEFFERSON	PB17-3	30-Sep-57	5.99	3
HART	UK1-2	18-Mar-53	3.69	2	JEFFERSON	PB16-5	27-Sep-57	7.57	3
HART	BJ2-3	1-Nov-51	4.73	2	JEFFERSON	TS3-4	25-Apr-52	8.50	3
HART	UK9-4	22-May-53	5.63	3	JENKINS	BJ2-3	1-Nov-51	3.97	2
HART	PB17-3	30-Sep-57	5.99	3	JENKINS	UK9-4	22-May-53	5.72	3
HEARD	TS5-2	8-May-52	5.85	3	JENKINS	BJ2-4	2-Nov-51	8.46	3
HEARD	PB17-3	30-Sep-57	5.99	3	JENKINS	TS3-4	25-Apr-52	8.50	3
HENRY	PB17-3	30-Sep-57	5.99	3	JENKINS	PB16-5	27-Sep-57	10.08	4
HENRY	PB16-5	27-Sep-57	17.90	4	JOHNSON	BJ2-3	1-Nov-51	3.71	2
HOUSTON	UK9-4	22-May-53	3.70	2	JOHNSON	UK9-4	22-May-53	5.19	3
HOUSTON	PB17-3	30-Sep-57	3.96	2	JOHNSON	PB5-8	22-Jul-57	5.97	3
HOUSTON	BJ2-4	2-Nov-51	4.48	2	JOHNSON	PB17-3	30-Sep-57	5.99	3
HOUSTON	PB16-5	27-Sep-57	18.69	4	JOHNSON	TS3-4	25-Apr-52	8.50	3
IRWIN	BJ2-4	2-Nov-51	3.78	2	JOHNSON	PB16-5	27-Sep-57	9.28	3
IRWIN	UK4-3	8-Apr-53	3.89	2	JONES	UK9-4	22-May-53	3.84	2

INDIVIDUAL FALLOUT DAYS
GEORGIA

COUNTY	SHOT	DATE	µCi/SQ METER	INDEX	COUNTY	SHOT	DATE	µCi/SQ METER	INDEX
JONES	PB17-3	30-Sep-57	3.96	2	LONG	TS3-4	25-Apr-52	12.70	4
JONES	PB16-5	27-Sep-57	20.53	4	LONG	PB11-4	3-Sep-57	19.43	4
LAMAR	PB17-3	30-Sep-57	5.99	3	LOWNDES	UK4-3	8-Apr-53	3.89	2
LAMAR	PB16-5	27-Sep-57	18.86	4	LOWNDES	TS3-7	28-Apr-52	6.40	3
LANIER	UK4-3	8-Apr-53	3.89	2	LOWNDES	PB11-4	3-Sep-57	7.77	3
LANIER	BJ2-4	2-Nov-51	5.08	3	LOWNDES	PB16-5	27-Sep-57	10.12	4
LANIER	TS3-7	28-Apr-52	6.40	3	LUMPKIN	UK9-4	22-May-53	3.52	2
LANIER	PB11-4	3-Sep-57	7.77	3	LUMPKIN	UK1-2	18-Mar-53	3.87	2
LANIER	PB16-5	27-Sep-57	10.95	4	LUMPKIN	PB16-5	27-Sep-57	4.87	2
LAURENS	TS3-4	25-Apr-52	4.20	2	LUMPKIN	PB17-3	30-Sep-57	5.99	3
LAURENS	UK9-4	22-May-53	4.52	2	MACON	BJ2-4	2-Nov-51	4.09	2
LAURENS	PB16-5	27-Sep-57	10.40	4	MACON	PB16-5	27-Sep-57	18.69	4
LEE	TS5-2	8-May-52	5.29	3	MADISON	BJ2-3	1-Nov-51	3.65	2
LEE	TS3-7	28-Apr-52	6.40	3	MADISON	UK9-4	22-May-53	4.64	2
LEE	BJ2-4	2-Nov-51	9.02	3	MADISON	PB17-3	30-Sep-57	5.99	3
LEE	PB16-5	27-Sep-57	16.49	4	MADISON	PB16-5	27-Sep-57	7.50	3
LIBERTY	UK9-4	22-May-53	3.52	2	MARION	BJ2-4	2-Nov-51	4.59	2
LIBERTY	PB8-5	22-Aug-57	3.61	2	MARION	PB16-5	27-Sep-57	12.70	4
LIBERTY	BJ2-3	1-Nov-51	3.84	2	MCDUFFIE	BJ2-3	1-Nov-51	4.61	2
LIBERTY	UK4-3	8-Apr-53	3.89	2	MCDUFFIE	UK9-4	22-May-53	5.96	3
LIBERTY	BJ2-4	2-Nov-51	6.07	3	MCDUFFIE	PB16-5	27-Sep-57	6.78	3
LIBERTY	PB16-5	27-Sep-57	7.91	3	MCDUFFIE	PB17-3	30-Sep-57	9.96	3
LIBERTY	TS3-4	25-Apr-52	12.70	4	MCINTOSH	BJ2-2	31-Oct-51	3.89	2
LIBERTY	PB11-4	3-Sep-57	19.43	4	MCINTOSH	UK4-3	8-Apr-53	3.89	2
LINCOLN	BJ2-5	3-Nov-51	3.73	2	MCINTOSH	BJ2-4	2-Nov-51	4.98	2
LINCOLN	BJ2-3	1-Nov-51	4.29	2	MCINTOSH	PB16-5	27-Sep-57	7.28	3
LINCOLN	PB16-5	27-Sep-57	5.66	3	MCINTOSH	TS3-4	25-Apr-52	12.70	4
LINCOLN	UK9-4	22-May-53	6.01	3	MERIWETHER	PB17-3	30-Sep-57	5.99	3
LONG	PB8-5	22-Aug-57	3.61	2	MERIWETHER	PB16-5	27-Sep-57	16.82	4
LONG	UK4-3	8-Apr-53	3.89	2	MILLER	TS3-7	28-Apr-52	6.40	3
LONG	UK9-4	22-May-53	4.14	2	MILLER	PB16-5	27-Sep-57	7.24	3
LONG	BJ2-4	2-Nov-51	5.77	3	MITCHELL	TS3-7	28-Apr-52	6.40	3
LONG	PB16-5	27-Sep-57	9.06	3	MITCHELL	BJ2-4	2-Nov-51	7.03	3

INDIVIDUAL FALLOUT DAYS
GEORGIA

COUNTY	SHOT	DATE	µCi/SQ METER	INDEX	COUNTY	SHOT	DATE	µCi/SQ METER	INDEX
MITCHELL	PB17-3	30-Sep-57	9.96	3	PAULDING	PB16-5	27-Sep-57	18.33	4
MITCHELL	PB16-5	27-Sep-57	11.86	4	PEACH	BJ2-4	2-Nov-51	3.67	2
MONROE	TS5-1	7-May-52	3.77	2	PEACH	UK9-4	22-May-53	3.70	2
MONROE	PB17-3	30-Sep-57	3.96	2	PEACH	TS5-2	8-May-52	3.76	2
MONROE	PB16-5	27-Sep-57	24.06	4	PEACH	PB17-6	3-Oct-57	4.55	2
MONTGOMERY	UK4-3	8-Apr-53	3.89	2	PEACH	PB17-3	30-Sep-57	9.96	3
MONTGOMERY	UK9-4	22-May-53	4.52	2	PEACH	PB16-5	27-Sep-57	20.17	4
MONTGOMERY	BJ2-4	2-Nov-51	7.27	3	PICKENS	TP6-4	25-Mar-55	3.99	2
MONTGOMERY	PB16-5	27-Sep-57	8.33	3	PICKENS	PB17-3	30-Sep-57	5.99	3
MONTGOMERY	TS3-4	25-Apr-52	21.20	4	PICKENS	PB16-5	27-Sep-57	8.29	3
MORGAN	PB17-6	3-Oct-57	4.29	2	PIERCE	TS5-2	8-May-52	3.65	2
MORGAN	UK9-4	22-May-53	4.40	2	PIERCE	UK4-3	8-Apr-53	3.89	2
MORGAN	BJ2-4	2-Nov-51	5.68	3	PIERCE	BJ2-4	2-Nov-51	4.88	2
MORGAN	PB17-3	30-Sep-57	5.99	3	PIERCE	TS3-8	29-Apr-52	5.73	3
MORGAN	PB16-5	27-Sep-57	13.36	4	PIERCE	PB16-5	27-Sep-57	6.15	3
MURRAY	PB17-3	30-Sep-57	3.96	2	PIKE	PB17-3	30-Sep-57	5.99	3
MURRAY	TP6-4	25-Mar-55	3.99	2	PIKE	PB16-5	27-Sep-57	19.02	4
MURRAY	UK1-2	18-Mar-53	5.57	3	POLK	PB16-5	27-Sep-57	12.50	4
MURRAY	BJ3-6	6-Nov-51	8.10	3	PULASKI	UK9-4	22-May-53	3.61	2
NEWTON	UK9-4	22-May-53	4.04	2	PULASKI	BJ2-4	2-Nov-51	8.76	3
NEWTON	PB17-3	30-Sep-57	5.99	3	PULASKI	PB17-3	30-Sep-57	9.96	3
NEWTON	PB16-5	27-Sep-57	17.67	4	PULASKI	PB16-5	27-Sep-57	19.73	4
OCONEE	PB17-3	30-Sep-57	3.96	2	PUTNAM	UK9-4	22-May-53	4.32	2
OCONEE	PB17-6	3-Oct-57	4.08	2	PUTNAM	PB17-3	30-Sep-57	9.96	3
OCONEE	UK9-4	22-May-53	4.52	2	PUTNAM	PB16-5	27-Sep-57	13.13	4
OCONEE	PB16-5	27-Sep-57	11.32	4	QUITMAN	PB17-6	3-Oct-57	3.71	2
OGLETHORPE	BJ2-3	1-Nov-51	3.54	2	QUITMAN	TS3-3	24-Apr-52	4.45	2
OGLETHORPE	UK9-4	22-May-53	5.72	3	QUITMAN	PB17-3	30-Sep-57	9.96	3
OGLETHORPE	PB17-3	30-Sep-57	5.99	3	QUITMAN	BJ2-4	2-Nov-51	12.44	4
OGLETHORPE	PB17-6	3-Oct-57	6.73	3	QUITMAN	PB16-5	27-Sep-57	13.33	4
OGLETHORPE	PB16-5	27-Sep-57	8.42	3	RABUN	TP10-2	6-May-55	3.62	2
PAULDING	PB17-6	3-Oct-57	5.63	3	RABUN	TP10-8	12-May-55	3.82	2
PAULDING	PB17-3	30-Sep-57	5.99	3	RABUN	BJ2-3	1-Nov-51	3.84	2

INDIVIDUAL FALLOUT DAYS
GEORGIA

COUNTY	SHOT	DATE	µCi/SQ METER	INDEX	COUNTY	SHOT	DATE	µCi/SQ METER	INDEX
RABUN	UK9-4	22-May-53	4.08	2	STEPHENS	UK1-2	18-Mar-53	6.15	3
RABUN	TP6-4	25-Mar-55	4.32	2	STEWART	PB17-6	3-Oct-57	4.10	2
RABUN	UK1-2	18-Mar-53	4.53	2	STEWART	TS3-3	24-Apr-52	4.45	2
RABUN	PB5-8	22-Jul-57	5.97	3	STEWART	PB17-3	30-Sep-57	5.99	3
RABUN	PB2-5	22-Jun-57	6.96	3	STEWART	BJ2-4	2-Nov-51	11.10	4
RABUN	PB17-3	30-Sep-57	14.98	4	STEWART	PB16-5	27-Sep-57	11.74	4
RANDOLPH	PB17-6	3-Oct-57	3.57	2	SUMTER	TS3-7	28-Apr-52	6.40	3
RANDOLPH	UK2-3	26-Mar-53	3.63	2	SUMTER	BJ2-4	2-Nov-51	9.02	3
RANDOLPH	PB12-7	8-Sep-57	4.15	2	SUMTER	PB16-5	27-Sep-57	18.94	4
RANDOLPH	TS3-7	28-Apr-52	6.40	3	TALBOT	BJ2-4	2-Nov-51	3.84	2
RANDOLPH	TS5-2	8-May-52	8.35	3	TALBOT	PB16-5	27-Sep-57	15.30	4
RANDOLPH	PB16-5	27-Sep-57	14.08	4	TALIAFERRO	PB17-6	3-Oct-57	3.61	2
RICHMOND	BJ2-3	1-Nov-51	4.83	2	TALIAFERRO	UK9-4	22-May-53	5.77	3
RICHMOND	PB16-5	27-Sep-57	5.40	3	TALIAFERRO	PB16-5	27-Sep-57	8.62	3
RICHMOND	UK9-4	22-May-53	6.06	3	TALIAFERRO	PB17-3	30-Sep-57	9.96	3
ROCKDALE	PB17-3	30-Sep-57	5.99	3	TATTNALL	PB11-4	3-Sep-57	3.89	2
ROCKDALE	PB16-5	27-Sep-57	16.64	4	TATTNALL	UK4-3	8-Apr-53	3.89	2
SCHLEY	PB17-6	3-Oct-57	4.38	2	TATTNALL	UK9-4	22-May-53	4.62	2
SCHLEY	PB17-3	30-Sep-57	5.99	3	TATTNALL	PB16-5	27-Sep-57	6.58	3
SCHLEY	BJ2-4	2-Nov-51	8.93	3	TATTNALL	TS3-4	25-Apr-52	8.50	3
SCHLEY	PB16-5	27-Sep-57	20.96	4	TAYLOR	BJ2-4	2-Nov-51	4.01	2
SCREVEN	BJ2-3	1-Nov-51	5.25	3	TAYLOR	PB17-3	30-Sep-57	5.99	3
SCREVEN	UK9-4	22-May-53	5.68	3	TAYLOR	PB16-5	27-Sep-57	14.97	4
SCREVEN	PB16-5	27-Sep-57	5.89	3	TELFAIR	UK9-4	22-May-53	3.75	2
SCREVEN	BJ2-4	2-Nov-51	8.76	3	TELFAIR	UK4-3	8-Apr-53	3.89	2
SCREVEN	TS3-4	25-Apr-52	12.70	4	TELFAIR	TS3-4	25-Apr-52	4.20	2
SEMINOLE	TS3-7	28-Apr-52	6.40	3	TELFAIR	BJ2-4	2-Nov-51	7.27	3
SEMINOLE	PB16-5	27-Sep-57	8.34	3	TELFAIR	PB16-5	27-Sep-57	11.03	4
SPALDING	PB17-3	30-Sep-57	5.99	3	TERRELL	TS5-2	8-May-52	5.15	3
SPALDING	PB16-5	27-Sep-57	20.63	4	TERRELL	TS3-7	28-Apr-52	6.40	3
STEPHENS	PB16-5	27-Sep-57	3.59	2	TERRELL	PB17-3	30-Sep-57	9.96	3
STEPHENS	UK9-4	22-May-53	4.36	2	TERRELL	BJ2-4	2-Nov-51	10.10	4
STEPHENS	PB17-3	30-Sep-57	5.99	3	TERRELL	PB16-5	27-Sep-57	15.62	4

INDIVIDUAL FALLOUT DAYS
GEORGIA

COUNTY	SHOT	DATE	µCi/SQ METER	INDEX	COUNTY	SHOT	DATE	µCi/SQ METER	INDEX
THOMAS	TS5-2	8-May-52	3.82	2	TWIGGS	UK9-4	22-May-53	4.28	2
THOMAS	UK4-3	8-Apr-53	3.89	2	TWIGGS	PB16-5	27-Sep-57	18.40	4
THOMAS	BJ2-4	2-Nov-51	5.36	3	UNION	TP10-8	12-May-55	3.69	2
THOMAS	TS3-7	28-Apr-52	6.40	3	UNION	TS5-2	8-May-52	3.88	2
THOMAS	PB16-5	27-Sep-57	10.00	4	UNION	PB17-3	30-Sep-57	3.96	2
TIFT	UK4-3	8-Apr-53	3.89	2	UNION	TP6-4	25-Mar-55	3.99	2
TIFT	TS3-7	28-Apr-52	6.40	3	UNION	PB16-5	27-Sep-57	4.41	2
TIFT	BJ2-4	2-Nov-51	7.77	3	UNION	UK1-2	18-Mar-53	9.69	3
TIFT	PB16-5	27-Sep-57	10.28	4	UPSON	TS5-1	7-May-52	4.31	2
TOOMBS	PB11-4	3-Sep-57	3.89	2	UPSON	PB16-5	27-Sep-57	17.51	4
TOOMBS	UK4-3	8-Apr-53	3.89	2	WALKER	PB16-5	27-Sep-57	4.05	2
TOOMBS	UK9-4	22-May-53	4.57	2	WALKER	PB17-3	30-Sep-57	5.99	3
TOOMBS	BJ2-4	2-Nov-51	6.97	3	WALKER	BJ3-6	6-Nov-51	8.10	3
TOOMBS	PB16-5	27-Sep-57	7.57	3	WALTON	UK9-4	22-May-53	4.24	2
TOOMBS	TS3-4	25-Apr-52	8.50	3	WALTON	PB17-3	30-Sep-57	5.99	3
TOWNS	TP10-2	6-May-55	3.62	2	WALTON	PB16-5	27-Sep-57	14.81	4
TOWNS	PB16-5	27-Sep-57	3.65	2	WARE	UK4-3	8-Apr-53	3.89	2
TOWNS	UK9-4	22-May-53	3.72	2	WARE	BJ2-4	2-Nov-51	4.18	2
TOWNS	TP6-4	25-Mar-55	4.32	2	WARE	PB16-5	27-Sep-57	4.31	2
TOWNS	UK1-2	18-Mar-53	9.58	3	WARE	TS3-8	29-Apr-52	5.73	3
TOWNS	PB17-3	30-Sep-57	14.98	4	WARREN	BJ2-3	1-Nov-51	4.09	2
TREUTLEN	TS3-4	25-Apr-52	4.20	2	WARREN	UK9-4	22-May-53	5.87	3
TREUTLEN	UK9-4	22-May-53	4.81	2	WARREN	PB16-5	27-Sep-57	8.00	3
TREUTLEN	PB16-5	27-Sep-57	8.72	3	WARREN	PB17-3	30-Sep-57	9.96	3
TROUP	TS5-1	7-May-52	3.95	2	WASHINGTON	BJ2-3	1-Nov-51	4.09	2
TROUP	PB17-3	30-Sep-57	5.99	3	WASHINGTON	UK9-4	22-May-53	5.39	3
TROUP	PB16-5	27-Sep-57	13.49	4	WASHINGTON	PB5-8	22-Jul-57	5.97	3
TURNER	TS5-2	8-May-52	5.64	3	WASHINGTON	PB17-3	30-Sep-57	5.99	3
TURNER	TS3-7	28-Apr-52	6.40	3	WASHINGTON	PB16-5	27-Sep-57	9.77	3
TURNER	BJ2-4	2-Nov-51	8.66	3	WAYNE	TS5-2	8-May-52	3.88	2
TURNER	PB16-5	27-Sep-57	11.74	4	WAYNE	UK4-3	8-Apr-53	3.89	2
TWIGGS	PB17-3	30-Sep-57	3.96	2	WAYNE	BJ2-4	2-Nov-51	5.28	3
TWIGGS	BJ2-4	2-Nov-51	4.18	2	WAYNE	PB16-5	27-Sep-57	5.69	3

INDIVIDUAL FALLOUT DAYS
GEORGIA

COUNTY	SHOT	DATE	µCi/SQ METER	INDEX	COUNTY	SHOT	DATE	µCi/SQ METER	INDEX
WAYNE	TS3-4	25-Apr-52	12.70	4	WHITFIELD	PB16-5	27-Sep-57	4.28	2
WAYNE	PB11-4	3-Sep-57	19.43	4	WHITFIELD	TS7-4	4-Jun-52	7.12	3
WEBSTER	PB17-3	30-Sep-57	5.99	3	WHITFIELD	BJ3-6	6-Nov-51	8.10	3
WEBSTER	TS3-7	28-Apr-52	6.40	3	WILCOX	PB17-3	30-Sep-57	5.99	3
WEBSTER	BJ2-4	2-Nov-51	10.10	4	WILCOX	TS3-7	28-Apr-52	6.40	3
WEBSTER	PB16-5	27-Sep-57	17.64	4	WILCOX	BJ2-4	2-Nov-51	8.46	3
WHEELER	UK4-3	8-Apr-53	3.89	2	WILCOX	PB16-5	27-Sep-57	12.81	4
WHEELER	UK9-4	22-May-53	4.23	2	WILKES	BJ2-3	1-Nov-51	5.88	3
WHEELER	BJ2-4	2-Nov-51	7.37	3	WILKES	UK9-4	22-May-53	5.92	3
WHEELER	PB16-5	27-Sep-57	8.92	3	WILKES	PB17-3	30-Sep-57	5.99	3
WHEELER	TS3-4	25-Apr-52	21.20	4	WILKES	PB16-5	27-Sep-57	7.01	3
WHITE	PB17-6	3-Oct-57	3.62	2	WILKINSON	BJ2-4	2-Nov-51	3.98	2
WHITE	UK9-4	22-May-53	3.88	2	WILKINSON	UK9-4	22-May-53	4.71	2
WHITE	PB16-5	27-Sep-57	3.95	2	WILKINSON	PB17-3	30-Sep-57	5.99	3
WHITE	TS5-2	8-May-52	4.34	2	WILKINSON	TS5-2	8-May-52	7.51	3
WHITE	PB17-3	30-Sep-57	5.99	3	WILKINSON	PB16-5	27-Sep-57	8.79	3
WHITE	UK1-2	18-Mar-53	6.90	3	WORTH	BJ2-4	2-Nov-51	3.92	2
WHITFIELD	UK1-2	18-Mar-53	3.52	2	WORTH	PB17-3	30-Sep-57	5.99	3
WHITFIELD	PB17-3	30-Sep-57	3.96	2	WORTH	TS3-7	28-Apr-52	6.40	3
WHITFIELD	TP6-4	25-Mar-55	3.99	2	WORTH	PB16-5	27-Sep-57	10.83	4

INDIVIDUAL FALLOUT DAYS
IOWA

COUNTY	SHOT	DATE	µCi/SQ METER	INDEX	COUNTY	SHOT	DATE	µCi/SQ METER	INDEX
ADAIR	UK7-4	28-Apr-53	4.06	2	APPANOOSE	TS7-4	4-Jun-52	5.71	3
ADAIR	PB13-5	10-Sep-57	4.21	2	APPANOOSE	TS6-4	28-May-52	5.79	3
ADAIR	TP4-2	8-Mar-55	5.25	3	APPANOOSE	PB12-4	5-Sep-57	6.80	3
ADAIR	PB12-4	5-Sep-57	8.04	3	APPANOOSE	PB9-4	26-Aug-57	8.37	3
ADAIR	TS6-4	28-May-52	8.68	3	APPANOOSE	PB8-3	20-Aug-57	15.90	4
ADAIR	PB8-3	20-Aug-57	15.90	4	APPANOOSE	UK9-2	20-May-53	27.64	5
ADAIR	UK9-2	20-May-53	24.48	4	APPANOOSE	TS7-3	3-Jun-52	177.61	7
ADAIR	TS7-4	4-Jun-52	35.85	5	APPANOOSE	SE3	8-Jul-62	345.56	8
ADAIR	PB9-4	26-Aug-57	83.35	6	AUDUBON	PB13-5	10-Sep-57	3.69	2
ADAIR	SE3	8-Jul-62	345.56	8	AUDUBON	UK7-5	29-Apr-53	4.61	2
ADAMS	UK7-4	28-Apr-53	4.01	2	AUDUBON	TP4-2	8-Mar-55	5.25	3
ADAMS	TP4-2	8-Mar-55	5.25	3	AUDUBON	UK9-5	23-May-53	5.67	3
ADAMS	PB13-5	10-Sep-57	8.05	3	AUDUBON	UK7-4	28-Apr-53	5.88	3
ADAMS	PB12-4	5-Sep-57	8.67	3	AUDUBON	TS7-4	4-Jun-52	7.12	3
ADAMS	UK9-2	20-May-53	19.96	4	AUDUBON	TS6-3	27-May-52	8.50	3
ADAMS	PB8-3	20-Aug-57	23.89	4	AUDUBON	PB12-4	5-Sep-57	10.61	4
ADAMS	PB9-4	26-Aug-57	50.01	6	AUDUBON	UK2-3	26-Mar-53	13.52	4
ADAMS	TS7-4	4-Jun-52	57.00	6	AUDUBON	UK9-2	20-May-53	29.34	5
ADAMS	SE3	8-Jul-62	345.56	8	AUDUBON	PB9-4	26-Aug-57	83.35	6
ALLAMAKEE	UK9-3	21-May-53	3.61	2	AUDUBON	SE3	8-Jul-62	345.56	8
ALLAMAKEE	PB18-8	17-Jul-57	3.98	2	BENTON	UK9-3	21-May-53	3.54	2
ALLAMAKEE	UK7-4	28-Apr-53	5.99	3	BENTON	TS5-1	7-May-52	3.90	2
ALLAMAKEE	PB9-4	26-Aug-57	8.37	3	BENTON	PB18-8	17-Jul-57	3.98	2
ALLAMAKEE	PB9-3	25-Aug-57	13.72	4	BENTON	TP4-2	8-Mar-55	5.25	3
ALLAMAKEE	TP10-2	6-May-55	14.02	4	BENTON	TS6-4	28-May-52	8.68	3
ALLAMAKEE	TS7-5	5-Jun-52	14.81	4	BENTON	TS7-3	3-Jun-52	9.86	3
ALLAMAKEE	TS6-4	28-May-52	15.43	4	BENTON	TS7-4	4-Jun-52	17.50	4
ALLAMAKEE	UK9-2	20-May-53	56.84	6	BENTON	PB9-3	25-Aug-57	27.43	5
ALLAMAKEE	SE3	8-Jul-62	139.44	7	BENTON	PB9-4	26-Aug-57	50.01	6
APPANOOSE	TP10-2	6-May-55	3.62	2	BENTON	UK9-2	20-May-53	57.28	6
APPANOOSE	PB13-5	10-Sep-57	3.50	1	BENTON	SE3	8-Jul-62	527.44	9
APPANOOSE	TP10-3	7-May-55	5.15	3	BLACK HAWK	PB18-8	17-Jul-57	3.98	2
APPANOOSE	TP4-2	8-Mar-55	5.25	3	BLACK HAWK	TS7-5	5-Jun-52	5.18	3

INDISPENSABLE FALLOUT DAYS
IOWA

COUNTY	SHOT	DATE	µCi/SQ METER	INDEX	COUNTY	SHOT	DATE	µCi/SQ METER	INDEX
BLACK HAWK	TP4-2	8-Mar-55	5.25	3	BUENA VISTA	TS6-3	27-May-52	14.88	4
BLACK HAWK	TS7-4	4-Jun-52	7.72	3	BUENA VISTA	UK9-2	20-May-53	19.81	4
BLACK HAWK	TS6-4	28-May-52	16.39	4	BUENA VISTA	TS7-4	4-Jun-52	37.93	5
BLACK HAWK	PB9-3	25-Aug-57	27.43	5	BUENA VISTA	SE3	8-Jul-62	527.44	9
BLACK HAWK	UK9-2	20-May-53	48.72	5	BUTLER	TS6-4	28-May-52	4.03	2
BLACK HAWK	PB9-4	26-Aug-57	50.01	6	BUTLER	TP4-2	8-Mar-55	5.25	3
BLACK HAWK	SE3	8-Jul-62	252.68	8	BUTLER	TS7-5	5-Jun-52	9.29	3
BOONE	TS6-3	27-May-52	4.70	2	BUTLER	TS7-4	4-Jun-52	13.74	4
BOONE	TP4-2	8-Mar-55	5.25	3	BUTLER	PB9-4	26-Aug-57	16.67	4
BOONE	TS7-4	4-Jun-52	26.53	5	BUTLER	UK9-2	20-May-53	61.50	6
BOONE	UK9-2	20-May-53	47.15	5	BUTLER	SE3	8-Jul-62	208.70	8
BOONE	PB9-4	26-Aug-57	83.35	6	CALHOUN	PB12-4	5-Sep-57	4.14	2
BOONE	SE3	8-Jul-62	527.44	9	CALHOUN	TP4-2	8-Mar-55	5.25	3
BREMER	TS6-3	27-May-52	3.56	2	CALHOUN	UK7-5	29-Apr-53	5.64	3
BREMER	TP4-2	8-Mar-55	5.25	3	CALHOUN	TS6-3	27-May-52	11.05	4
BREMER	TP10-2	6-May-55	5.48	3	CALHOUN	TS7-4	4-Jun-52	28.73	5
BREMER	TS7-4	4-Jun-52	10.35	4	CALHOUN	UK9-2	20-May-53	34.43	5
BREMER	PB9-3	25-Aug-57	27.43	5	CALHOUN	SE3	8-Jul-62	527.44	9
BREMER	PB9-4	26-Aug-57	50.01	6	CARROLL	UK9-5	23-May-53	3.87	2
BREMER	UK9-2	20-May-53	58.25	6	CARROLL	UK7-4	28-Apr-53	4.97	2
BREMER	SE3	8-Jul-62	220.22	8	CARROLL	PB12-4	5-Sep-57	5.21	3
BUCHANAN	PB18-8	17-Jul-57	3.98	2	CARROLL	TP4-2	8-Mar-55	5.25	3
BUCHANAN	TP4-2	8-Mar-55	5.25	3	CARROLL	UK7-5	29-Apr-53	5.39	3
BUCHANAN	TS7-4	4-Jun-52	6.35	3	CARROLL	TS6-3	27-May-52	10.12	4
BUCHANAN	PB9-3	25-Aug-57	13.72	4	CARROLL	UK9-2	20-May-53	26.20	5
BUCHANAN	PB9-4	26-Aug-57	50.01	6	CARROLL	TS7-4	4-Jun-52	51.05	6
BUCHANAN	UK9-2	20-May-53	50.67	6	CARROLL	PB9-4	26-Aug-57	83.35	6
BUCHANAN	SE3	8-Jul-62	220.22	8	CARROLL	SE3	8-Jul-62	527.44	9
BUENA VISTA	PB12-4	5-Sep-57	3.85	2	CASS	UK7-5	29-Apr-53	3.82	2
BUENA VISTA	PB5-5	19-Jul-57	4.02	2	CASS	PB13-5	10-Sep-57	4.17	2
BUENA VISTA	TP4-2	8-Mar-55	5.25	3	CASS	UK7-4	28-Apr-53	4.22	2
BUENA VISTA	UK7-5	29-Apr-53	6.51	3	CASS	TP4-2	8-Mar-55	5.25	3
BUENA VISTA	UK7-4	28-Apr-53	7.14	3	CASS	TS6-3	27-May-52	6.80	3

INDIVIDUAL FALLOUT DAYS
IOWA

COUNTY	SHOT	DATE	µCi/SQ METER	INDEX	COUNTY	SHOT	DATE	µCi/SQ METER	INDEX
CASS	PB8-3	20-Aug-57	7.99	3	CHEROKEE	SE3	8-Jul-62	527.44	9
CASS	PB12-4	5-Sep-57	12.50	4	CHICKASAW	UK9-3	21-May-53	3.69	2
CASS	UK9-2	20-May-53	27.61	5	CHICKASAW	PB18-8	17-Jul-57	3.98	2
CASS	TS7-4	4-Jun-52	57.52	6	CHICKASAW	UK7-4	28-Apr-53	4.06	2
CASS	PB9-4	26-Aug-57	83.35	6	CHICKASAW	TS6-3	27-May-52	4.63	2
CASS	SE3	8-Jul-62	345.56	8	CHICKASAW	TP4-2	8-Mar-55	5.25	3
CEDAR	UK9-3	21-May-53	3.54	2	CHICKASAW	TS7-4	4-Jun-52	7.66	3
CEDAR	TS5-1	7-May-52	4.49	2	CHICKASAW	PB9-3	25-Aug-57	13.72	4
CEDAR	UK7-4	28-Apr-53	4.86	2	CHICKASAW	TS7-5	5-Jun-52	16.55	4
CEDAR	TP4-2	8-Mar-55	5.25	3	CHICKASAW	PB9-4	26-Aug-57	16.67	4
CEDAR	PB18-8	17-Jul-57	6.63	3	CHICKASAW	UK9-2	20-May-53	59.34	6
CEDAR	PB9-3	25-Aug-57	13.72	4	CLARKE	PB13-5	10-Sep-57	3.66	2
CEDAR	TS7-3	3-Jun-52	14.32	4	CLARKE	TP10-3	7-May-55	3.94	2
CEDAR	PB9-4	26-Aug-57	33.34	5	CLARKE	UK7-4	28-Apr-53	4.15	2
CEDAR	UK9-2	20-May-53	41.07	5	CLARKE	TP4-2	8-Mar-55	5.25	3
CEDAR	SE3	8-Jul-62	146.81	7	CLARKE	PB8-3	20-Aug-57	15.90	4
CERRO GORDO	UK9-3	21-May-53	3.54	2	CLARKE	UK9-2	20-May-53	24.81	4
CERRO GORDO	TS7-5	5-Jun-52	3.73	2	CLARKE	PB9-4	26-Aug-57	50.01	6
CERRO GORDO	UK7-5	29-Apr-53	4.18	2	CLARKE	TS7-4	4-Jun-52	53.02	6
CERRO GORDO	TP4-2	8-Mar-55	5.25	3	CLARKE	SE3	8-Jul-62	345.56	8
CERRO GORDO	TS6-3	27-May-52	5.27	3	CLAY	TP4-2	8-Mar-55	5.25	3
CERRO GORDO	UK7-4	28-Apr-53	5.45	3	CLAY	PB2-3	20-Jun-57	5.36	3
CERRO GORDO	PB5-5	19-Jul-57	6.09	3	CLAY	UK7-5	29-Apr-53	6.76	3
CERRO GORDO	TS7-4	4-Jun-52	14.78	4	CLAY	UK7-4	28-Apr-53	9.76	3
CERRO GORDO	UK9-2	20-May-53	49.70	5	CLAY	UK9-2	20-May-53	9.96	3
CERRO GORDO	SE3	8-Jul-62	208.70	8	CLAY	TS6-3	27-May-52	10.29	4
CHEROKEE	TP4-2	8-Mar-55	5.25	3	CLAY	TS7-4	4-Jun-52	29.77	5
CHEROKEE	PB12-4	5-Sep-57	5.47	3	CLAY	SE3	8-Jul-62	527.44	9
CHEROKEE	UK7-5	29-Apr-53	6.12	3	CLAYTON	TP10-2	6-May-55	3.62	2
CHEROKEE	UK7-4	28-Apr-53	7.27	3	CLAYTON	TS5-2	8-May-52	3.62	2
CHEROKEE	UK9-2	20-May-53	14.29	4	CLAYTON	PB18-8	17-Jul-57	3.98	2
CHEROKEE	TS6-3	27-May-52	16.32	4	CLAYTON	TS5-1	7-May-52	4.35	2
CHEROKEE	TS7-4	4-Jun-52	31.27	5	CLAYTON	TP4-2	8-Mar-55	5.25	3

INDIVIDUAL FALLOUT DAYS
IOWA

COUNTY	SHOT	DATE	µCi/SQ METER	INDEX	COUNTY	SHOT	DATE	µCi/SQ METER	INDEX
CLAYTON	TS6-4	28-May-52	5.64	3	DALLAS	SE3	8-Jul-62	139.13	7
CLAYTON	TS7-5	5-Jun-52	13.07	4	DAVIS	TP10-2	6-May-55	3.62	2
CLAYTON	PB9-3	25-Aug-57	13.72	4	DAVIS	PB18-8	17-Jul-57	3.98	2
CLAYTON	PB9-4	26-Aug-57	33.34	5	DAVIS	TP4-2	8-Mar-55	5.25	3
CLAYTON	UK9-2	20-May-53	51.54	6	DAVIS	TS7-4	4-Jun-52	5.36	3
CLAYTON	SE3	8-Jul-62	139.13	7	DAVIS	TP10-3	7-May-55	5.67	3
CLINTON	UK9-3	21-May-53	3.54	2	DAVIS	PB8-3	20-Aug-57	7.99	3
CLINTON	PB18-8	17-Jul-57	3.98	2	DAVIS	PB12-4	5-Sep-57	8.45	3
CLINTON	TS5-1	7-May-52	4.05	2	DAVIS	PB9-3	25-Aug-57	13.72	4
CLINTON	TP5-3	14-Mar-55	4.65	2	DAVIS	UK9-2	20-May-53	29.23	5
CLINTON	UK7-4	28-Apr-53	8.80	3	DAVIS	TS7-3	3-Jun-52	71.70	6
CLINTON	PB9-3	25-Aug-57	13.72	4	DAVIS	PB9-4	26-Aug-57	83.35	6
CLINTON	PB9-4	26-Aug-57	16.67	4	DAVIS	SE3	8-Jul-62	345.56	8
CLINTON	UK9-2	20-May-53	25.88	5	DECATUR	PB5-7	21-Jul-57	4.15	2
CLINTON	TS7-3	3-Jun-52	28.73	5	DECATUR	UK11-3	6-Jun-53	4.50	2
CLINTON	SE3	8-Jul-62	172.89	7	DECATUR	PB13-5	10-Sep-57	4.51	2
CRAWFORD	UK9-3	21-May-53	3.54	2	DECATUR	TP10-3	7-May-55	4.94	2
CRAWFORD	TP4-2	8-Mar-55	5.25	3	DECATUR	UK7-4	28-Apr-53	5.13	3
CRAWFORD	UK7-5	29-Apr-53	5.58	3	DECATUR	TP4-2	8-Mar-55	5.25	3
CRAWFORD	PB12-4	5-Sep-57	6.01	3	DECATUR	PB12-4	5-Sep-57	8.08	3
CRAWFORD	PB5-5	19-Jul-57	6.09	3	DECATUR	UK9-2	20-May-53	10.90	4
CRAWFORD	TS7-4	4-Jun-52	6.95	3	DECATUR	PB9-4	26-Aug-57	33.34	5
CRAWFORD	UK7-4	28-Apr-53	7.91	3	DECATUR	TS7-4	4-Jun-52	38.48	5
CRAWFORD	TS6-3	27-May-52	13.09	4	DECATUR	PB8-3	20-Aug-57	39.79	5
CRAWFORD	UK9-2	20-May-53	19.38	4	DECATUR	SE3	8-Jul-62	345.56	8
CRAWFORD	SE3	8-Jul-62	527.44	9	DELAWARE	PB18-8	17-Jul-57	3.98	2
DALLAS	TP10-2	6-May-55	3.62	2	DELAWARE	TP4-2	8-Mar-55	5.25	3
DALLAS	UK9-5	23-May-53	3.76	2	DELAWARE	TS5-1	7-May-52	5.57	3
DALLAS	TP4-2	8-Mar-55	5.25	3	DELAWARE	TS6-4	28-May-52	11.57	4
DALLAS	UK2-3	26-Mar-53	11.01	4	DELAWARE	PB9-3	25-Aug-57	13.72	4
DALLAS	UK9-2	20-May-53	30.37	5	DELAWARE	PB9-4	26-Aug-57	50.01	6
DALLAS	TS7-4	4-Jun-52	32.47	5	DELAWARE	UK9-2	20-May-53	64.44	6
DALLAS	PB9-4	26-Aug-57	83.35	6	DELAWARE	SE3	8-Jul-62	345.56	8

INDIVIDUAL FALLOUT DAYS
IOWA

COUNTY	SHOT	DATE	µCi/SQ METER	INDEX	COUNTY	SHOT	DATE	µCi/SQ METER	INDEX
DES MOINES	TP10-3	7-May-55	3.84	2	FAYETTE	TP10-2	6-May-55	3.62	2
DES MOINES	PB18-8	17-Jul-57	3.98	2	FAYETTE	PB18-8	17-Jul-57	3.98	2
DES MOINES	PB5-7	21-Jul-57	4.15	2	FAYETTE	TS5-1	7-May-52	4.35	2
DES MOINES	TS7-4	4-Jun-52	5.09	3	FAYETTE	TS7-4	4-Jun-52	4.71	2
DES MOINES	PB9-3	25-Aug-57	13.72	4	FAYETTE	TP4-2	8-Mar-55	5.25	3
DES MOINES	UK9-2	20-May-53	19.71	4	FAYETTE	TS7-5	5-Jun-52	5.80	3
DES MOINES	PB9-4	26-Aug-57	33.34	5	FAYETTE	PB9-3	25-Aug-57	13.72	4
DES MOINES	SE3	8-Jul-62	139.13	7	FAYETTE	TS6-4	28-May-52	21.21	4
DICKINSON	TP4-2	8-Mar-55	5.25	3	FAYETTE	UK9-2	20-May-53	47.10	5
DICKINSON	UK7-5	29-Apr-53	6.88	3	FAYETTE	PB9-4	26-Aug-57	50.01	6
DICKINSON	UK7-4	28-Apr-53	7.78	3	FAYETTE	SE3	8-Jul-62	208.70	8
DICKINSON	TS6-3	27-May-52	10.71	4	FLOYD	TP10-2	6-May-55	3.62	2
DICKINSON	UK9-2	20-May-53	19.49	4	FLOYD	UK9-3	21-May-53	3.69	2
DICKINSON	TS7-4	4-Jun-52	23.18	4	FLOYD	TP4-2	8-Mar-55	5.25	3
DICKINSON	SE3	8-Jul-62	527.44	9	FLOYD	UK7-4	28-Apr-53	5.29	3
DUBUQUE	TS5-1	7-May-52	3.59	2	FLOYD	TS6-3	27-May-52	6.42	3
DUBUQUE	UK7-4	28-Apr-53	3.74	2	FLOYD	PB9-4	26-Aug-57	8.37	3
DUBUQUE	PB18-8	17-Jul-57	3.98	2	FLOYD	TS7-4	4-Jun-52	13.79	4
DUBUQUE	TP4-2	8-Mar-55	5.25	3	FLOYD	TS7-5	5-Jun-52	15.47	4
DUBUQUE	PB9-3	25-Aug-57	13.72	4	FLOYD	UK9-2	20-May-53	28.80	5
DUBUQUE	PB9-4	26-Aug-57	33.34	5	FLOYD	SE3	8-Jul-62	527.44	9
DUBUQUE	UK9-2	20-May-53	50.23	6	FRANKLIN	UK7-5	29-Apr-53	3.82	2
DUBUQUE	SE3	8-Jul-62	172.89	7	FRANKLIN	TS6-3	27-May-52	4.06	2
EMMET	UK7-4	28-Apr-53	4.97	2	FRANKLIN	TP4-2	8-Mar-55	5.25	3
EMMET	TP4-2	8-Mar-55	5.25	3	FRANKLIN	TS7-4	4-Jun-52	22.44	4
EMMET	UK7-5	29-Apr-53	6.42	3	FRANKLIN	UK9-2	20-May-53	50.67	6
EMMET	TS5-1	7-May-52	7.54	3	FRANKLIN	PB9-4	26-Aug-57	83.35	6
EMMET	TS6-3	27-May-52	10.63	4	FRANKLIN	SE3	8-Jul-62	208.70	8
EMMET	TS7-5	5-Jun-52	16.11	4	FREMONT	PB8-3	20-Aug-57	4.00	2
EMMET	UK9-2	20-May-53	27.61	5	FREMONT	TS6-3	27-May-52	4.00	2
EMMET	SE3	8-Jul-62	527.44	9	FREMONT	UK7-4	28-Apr-53	4.01	2
FAYETTE	UK9-3	21-May-53	3.54	2	FREMONT	TP4-2	8-Mar-55	5.25	3
FAYETTE	TS5-2	8-May-52	3.55	2	FREMONT	PB13-5	10-Sep-57	6.36	3

INDIVIDUAL FALLOUT DAYS
IOWA

COUNTY	SHOT	DATE	µCi/SQ METER	INDEX	COUNTY	SHOT	DATE	µCi/SQ METER	INDEX
FREMONT	TS7-4	4-Jun-52	6.51	3	GUTHRIE	SE3	8-Jul-62	345.56	8
FREMONT	PB12-4	5-Sep-57	10.20	4	HAMILTON	TP4-2	8-Mar-55	5.25	3
FREMONT	UK9-2	20-May-53	17.54	4	HAMILTON	TS7-5	5-Jun-52	6.97	3
FREMONT	SE3	8-Jul-62	76.52	6	HAMILTON	TS6-4	28-May-52	7.71	3
FREMONT	TS7-3	3-Jun-52	106.58	7	HAMILTON	TS7-4	4-Jun-52	9.04	3
GREENE	TP10-2	6-May-55	3.62	2	HAMILTON	TP10-3	7-May-55	11.03	4
GREENE	UK7-5	29-Apr-53	4.55	2	HAMILTON	UK9-2	20-May-53	49.59	5
GREENE	TP4-2	8-Mar-55	5.25	3	HAMILTON	PB9-4	26-Aug-57	50.01	6
GREENE	PB12-4	5-Sep-57	5.44	3	HAMILTON	SE3	8-Jul-62	527.44	9
GREENE	TS6-3	27-May-52	6.99	3	HANCOCK	UK7-5	29-Apr-53	4.94	2
GREENE	TS7-4	4-Jun-52	16.71	4	HANCOCK	TS5-1	7-May-52	5.09	3
GREENE	UK9-2	20-May-53	29.54	5	HANCOCK	TP4-2	8-Mar-55	5.25	3
GREENE	PB9-4	26-Aug-57	50.01	6	HANCOCK	TS7-4	4-Jun-52	6.12	3
GREENE	SE3	8-Jul-62	527.44	9	HANCOCK	TS6-4	28-May-52	10.61	4
GRUNDY	TS7-4	4-Jun-52	3.52	2	HANCOCK	TS6-3	27-May-52	11.65	4
GRUNDY	TP10-2	6-May-55	3.62	2	HANCOCK	TS7-5	5-Jun-52	12.40	4
GRUNDY	PB5-7	21-Jul-57	4.15	2	HANCOCK	UK9-2	20-May-53	49.81	5
GRUNDY	TP4-2	8-Mar-55	5.25	3	HANCOCK	SE3	8-Jul-62	527.44	9
GRUNDY	TS7-3	3-Jun-52	6.57	3	HARDIN	TP4-2	8-Mar-55	5.25	3
GRUNDY	TS7-5	5-Jun-52	8.01	3	HARDIN	TS7-5	5-Jun-52	7.18	3
GRUNDY	TS6-4	28-May-52	14.46	4	HARDIN	TS7-4	4-Jun-52	12.92	4
GRUNDY	PB9-4	26-Aug-57	33.34	5	HARDIN	TS6-4	28-May-52	13.50	4
GRUNDY	UK9-2	20-May-53	51.58	6	HARDIN	PB9-4	26-Aug-57	50.01	6
GUTHRIE	UK7-5	29-Apr-53	3.97	2	HARDIN	UK9-2	20-May-53	53.29	6
GUTHRIE	UK7-4	28-Apr-53	4.38	2	HARDIN	SE3	8-Jul-62	208.70	8
GUTHRIE	UK9-5	23-May-53	4.73	2	HARRISON	UK10-2	26-May-53	3.58	2
GUTHRIE	TP4-2	8-Mar-55	5.25	3	HARRISON	UK9-5	23-May-53	4.02	2
GUTHRIE	TS6-3	27-May-52	5.85	3	HARRISON	PB5-5	19-Jul-57	4.02	2
GUTHRIE	TS7-4	4-Jun-52	6.12	3	HARRISON	UK7-5	29-Apr-53	4.70	2
GUTHRIE	PB13-5	10-Sep-57	6.66	3	HARRISON	PB12-4	5-Sep-57	5.00	2
GUTHRIE	PB12-4	5-Sep-57	6.74	3	HARRISON	TP4-2	8-Mar-55	5.25	3
GUTHRIE	UK9-2	20-May-53	30.53	5	HARRISON	UK7-4	28-Apr-53	5.99	3
GUTHRIE	PB9-4	26-Aug-57	50.01	6	HARRISON	TS6-3	27-May-52	13.35	4

INDIVIDUAL FALLOUT DAYS
IOWA

COUNTY	SHOT	DATE	µCi/SQ METER	INDEX	COUNTY	SHOT	DATE	µCi/SQ METER	INDEX
HARRISON	UK9-2	20-May-53	16.24	4	IDA	PB12-4	5-Sep-57	4.86	2
HARRISON	TS7-4	4-Jun-52	41.00	5	IDA	TP4-2	8-Mar-55	5.25	3
HARRISON	SE3	8-Jul-62	139.13	7	IDA	UK7-5	29-Apr-53	5.97	3
HENRY	TP10-2	6-May-55	3.62	2	IDA	UK7-4	28-Apr-53	6.69	3
HENRY	TP10-3	7-May-55	4.10	2	IDA	TS6-3	27-May-52	15.30	4
HENRY	PB5-7	21-Jul-57	4.15	2	IDA	UK9-2	20-May-53	19.60	4
HENRY	TP4-2	8-Mar-55	5.25	3	IDA	SE4	9-Jul-62	21.28	4
HENRY	PB18-8	17-Jul-57	6.63	3	IDA	TS7-4	4-Jun-52	35.25	5
HENRY	UK9-2	20-May-53	12.78	4	IDA	SE3	8-Jul-62	527.44	9
HENRY	PB9-3	25-Aug-57	13.72	4	IOWA	TS7-4	4-Jun-52	3.94	2
HENRY	PB9-4	26-Aug-57	50.01	6	IOWA	PB18-8	17-Jul-57	3.98	2
HENRY	SE3	8-Jul-62	345.56	8	IOWA	TS7-5	5-Jun-52	4.21	2
HOWARD	PB18-8	17-Jul-57	3.98	2	IOWA	TP4-2	8-Mar-55	5.25	3
HOWARD	UK9-3	21-May-53	3.98	2	IOWA	TS6-4	28-May-52	6.75	3
HOWARD	TS6-3	27-May-52	5.11	3	IOWA	PB9-3	25-Aug-57	13.72	4
HOWARD	UK7-4	28-Apr-53	6.44	3	IOWA	PB9-4	26-Aug-57	33.34	5
HOWARD	TS7-4	4-Jun-52	6.80	3	IOWA	UK9-2	20-May-53	44.18	5
HOWARD	TP10-2	6-May-55	7.01	3	IOWA	SE3	8-Jul-62	527.44	9
HOWARD	PB9-4	26-Aug-57	8.37	3	JACKSON	TS7-5	5-Jun-52	3.83	2
HOWARD	TS7-5	5-Jun-52	10.53	4	JACKSON	TS5-1	7-May-52	3.95	2
HOWARD	PB9-3	25-Aug-57	13.72	4	JACKSON	PB18-8	17-Jul-57	3.98	2
HOWARD	UK9-2	20-May-53	59.98	6	JACKSON	UK7-4	28-Apr-53	4.22	2
HOWARD	SE3	8-Jul-62	950.00	10	JACKSON	TS6-4	28-May-52	5.64	3
HUMBOLDT	TP4-2	8-Mar-55	5.25	3	JACKSON	PB9-3	25-Aug-57	13.72	4
HUMBOLDT	UK7-5	29-Apr-53	5.33	3	JACKSON	UK9-2	20-May-53	40.55	5
HUMBOLDT	UK7-4	28-Apr-53	5.35	3	JACKSON	PB9-4	26-Aug-57	50.01	6
HUMBOLDT	PB5-5	19-Jul-57	6.09	3	JACKSON	SE3	8-Jul-62	172.89	7
HUMBOLDT	TS6-3	27-May-52	11.82	4	JASPER	PB4-9	13-Jul-57	3.64	2
HUMBOLDT	TS7-4	4-Jun-52	28.66	5	JASPER	PB9-3	25-Aug-57	4.14	2
HUMBOLDT	UK9-2	20-May-53	51.00	6	JASPER	TP4-2	8-Mar-55	5.25	3
HUMBOLDT	SE3	8-Jul-62	527.44	9	JASPER	PB8-3	20-Aug-57	7.99	3
IDA	UK9-5	23-May-53	3.51	2	JASPER	TS7-4	4-Jun-52	31.92	5
IDA	TS7-5	5-Jun-52	4.69	2	JASPER	UK9-2	20-May-53	37.66	5

INDIVIDUAL FALLOUT DAYS
IOWA

COUNTY	SHOT	DATE	µCi/SQ METER	INDEX	COUNTY	SHOT	DATE	µCi/SQ METER	INDEX
JASPER	PB9-4	26-Aug-57	83.35	6	KEOKUK	TP4-2	8-Mar-55	5.25	3
JASPER	SE3	8-Jul-62	527.44	9	KEOKUK	TP10-2	6-May-55	5.48	3
JEFFERSON	PB18-8	17-Jul-57	3.98	2	KEOKUK	PB8-3	20-Aug-57	7.99	3
JEFFERSON	PB8-3	20-Aug-57	4.00	2	KEOKUK	PB9-3	25-Aug-57	13.72	4
JEFFERSON	TS7-4	4-Jun-52	4.11	2	KEOKUK	UK9-2	20-May-53	40.60	5
JEFFERSON	TP10-3	7-May-55	4.47	2	KEOKUK	PB9-4	26-Aug-57	50.01	6
JEFFERSON	TP4-2	8-Mar-55	5.25	3	KEOKUK	SE3	8-Jul-62	345.56	8
JEFFERSON	TP10-2	6-May-55	5.48	3	KOSSUTH	UK7-4	28-Apr-53	3.92	2
JEFFERSON	PB9-4	26-Aug-57	8.37	3	KOSSUTH	TP4-2	8-Mar-55	5.25	3
JEFFERSON	PB9-3	25-Aug-57	13.72	4	KOSSUTH	UK7-5	29-Apr-53	5.64	3
JEFFERSON	UK9-2	20-May-53	27.83	5	KOSSUTH	TS7-5	5-Jun-52	8.59	3
JEFFERSON	SE3	8-Jul-62	621.15	9	KOSSUTH	TS7-4	4-Jun-52	12.93	4
JOHNSON	TS5-2	8-May-52	3.55	2	KOSSUTH	TS6-3	27-May-52	14.28	4
JOHNSON	TP4-2	8-Mar-55	5.25	3	KOSSUTH	UK9-2	20-May-53	38.55	5
JOHNSON	TS7-4	4-Jun-52	5.75	3	KOSSUTH	SE3	8-Jul-62	527.44	9
JOHNSON	UK7-4	28-Apr-53	6.57	3	LEE	PB5-7	21-Jul-57	4.15	2
JOHNSON	PB9-4	26-Aug-57	6.92	3	LEE	UK7-4	28-Apr-53	4.81	2
JOHNSON	PB9-3	25-Aug-57	11.39	4	LEE	TS1-3	3-Apr-52	5.01	3
JOHNSON	UK9-2	20-May-53	31.83	5	LEE	TP4-2	8-Mar-55	5.25	3
JOHNSON	SE3	8-Jul-62	345.56	8	LEE	TP10-2	6-May-55	5.48	3
JONES	UK9-3	21-May-53	3.69	2	LEE	TS7-5	5-Jun-52	6.14	3
JONES	PB18-8	17-Jul-57	3.98	2	LEE	PB18-8	17-Jul-57	6.63	3
JONES	TP4-2	8-Mar-55	5.25	3	LEE	TS6-4	28-May-52	6.75	3
JONES	TS7-3	3-Jun-52	11.12	4	LEE	TP10-3	7-May-55	7.12	3
JONES	PB9-3	25-Aug-57	13.72	4	LEE	PB9-3	25-Aug-57	13.72	4
JONES	PB9-4	26-Aug-57	16.67	4	LEE	PB9-4	26-Aug-57	16.67	4
JONES	UK9-2	20-May-53	39.74	5	LEE	UK9-2	20-May-53	22.09	4
JONES	SE3	8-Jul-62	139.13	7	LEE	TS7-3	3-Jun-52	24.66	4
KEOKUK	TP10-3	7-May-55	3.84	2	LEE	SE3	8-Jul-62	621.15	9
KEOKUK	TS7-5	5-Jun-52	3.87	2	LINN	PB18-8	17-Jul-57	3.98	2
KEOKUK	PB18-8	17-Jul-57	3.98	2	LINN	TS6-4	28-May-52	4.03	2
KEOKUK	TS7-4	4-Jun-52	4.71	2	LINN	UK7-4	28-Apr-53	4.28	2
KEOKUK	TS5-1	7-May-52	4.85	2	LINN	TP4-2	8-Mar-55	5.25	3

INDIVIDUAL FALLOUT DAYS
IOWA

COUNTY	SHOT	DATE	µCi/SQ METER	INDEX	COUNTY	SHOT	DATE	µCi/SQ METER	INDEX
LINN	TS5-1	7-May-52	5.75	3	LYON	UK9-2	20-May-53	7.04	3
LINN	PB9-3	25-Aug-57	13.72	4	LYON	PB2-3	20-Jun-57	8.04	3
LINN	TS7-4	4-Jun-52	17.37	4	LYON	TS6-3	27-May-52	8.76	3
LINN	UK9-2	20-May-53	42.99	5	LYON	TS7-4	4-Jun-52	39.43	5
LINN	PB9-4	26-Aug-57	50.01	6	LYON	SE3	8-Jul-62	527.44	9
LINN	SE4	9-Jul-62	68.45	6	MADISON	PB13-5	10-Sep-57	3.54	2
LINN	SE3	8-Jul-62	139.13	7	MADISON	TP4-2	8-Mar-55	5.25	3
LOUISA	TP10-2	6-May-55	3.62	2	MADISON	PB12-4	5-Sep-57	7.23	3
LOUISA	UK7-4	28-Apr-53	3.69	2	MADISON	UK9-2	20-May-53	14.73	4
LOUISA	TS6-4	28-May-52	4.03	2	MADISON	UK2-3	26-Mar-53	14.82	4
LOUISA	PB5-7	21-Jul-57	4.15	2	MADISON	PB8-3	20-Aug-57	23.89	4
LOUISA	TP4-2	8-Mar-55	5.25	3	MADISON	TS7-4	4-Jun-52	35.62	5
LOUISA	PB18-8	17-Jul-57	6.63	3	MADISON	PB9-4	26-Aug-57	83.35	6
LOUISA	TS5-1	7-May-52	9.16	3	MADISON	SE3	8-Jul-62	345.56	8
LOUISA	PB9-3	25-Aug-57	13.72	4	MAHASKA	PB9-3	25-Aug-57	4.14	2
LOUISA	PB9-4	26-Aug-57	16.67	4	MAHASKA	TP4-2	8-Mar-55	5.25	3
LOUISA	UK9-2	20-May-53	16.89	4	MAHASKA	TP10-3	7-May-55	5.36	3
LOUISA	SE3	8-Jul-62	345.56	8	MAHASKA	TP10-2	6-May-55	5.48	3
LUCAS	TP10-2	6-May-55	3.62	2	MAHASKA	TS7-4	4-Jun-52	8.04	3
LUCAS	TP10-3	7-May-55	4.20	2	MAHASKA	PB8-3	20-Aug-57	15.90	4
LUCAS	PB5-3	17-Jul-57	4.85	2	MAHASKA	PB9-4	26-Aug-57	33.34	5
LUCAS	TP4-2	8-Mar-55	5.25	3	MAHASKA	UK9-2	20-May-53	40.65	5
LUCAS	PB13-5	10-Sep-57	5.92	3	MAHASKA	TS7-3	3-Jun-52	42.03	5
LUCAS	TS7-4	4-Jun-52	6.69	3	MAHASKA	SE3	8-Jul-62	345.56	8
LUCAS	PB8-3	20-Aug-57	23.89	4	MARION	TP10-2	6-May-55	3.62	2
LUCAS	UK9-2	20-May-53	33.96	5	MARION	TP10-3	7-May-55	3.63	2
LUCAS	PB9-4	26-Aug-57	50.01	6	MARION	PB9-3	25-Aug-57	4.14	2
LYON	UK2-2	25-Mar-53	3.97	2	MARION	TP4-2	8-Mar-55	5.25	3
LYON	TS7-5	5-Jun-52	5.21	3	MARION	PB12-4	5-Sep-57	5.44	3
LYON	UK7-5	29-Apr-53	5.33	3	MARION	PB8-3	20-Aug-57	15.90	4
LYON	TS5-1	7-May-52	5.57	3	MARION	TS7-4	4-Jun-52	19.95	4
LYON	UK7-4	28-Apr-53	5.61	3	MARION	UK9-2	20-May-53	34.05	5
LYON	PB5-5	19-Jul-57	6.09	3	MARION	TS7-3	3-Jun-52	44.08	5

INDIVIDUAL FALLOUT DAYS
IOWA

COUNTY	SHOT	DATE	µCi/SQ METER	INDEX	COUNTY	SHOT	DATE	µCi/SQ METER	INDEX
MARION	PB9-4	26-Aug-57	50.01	6	MONONA	UK9-5	23-May-53	3.77	2
MARION	SE3	8-Jul-62	345.56	8	MONONA	PB5-5	19-Jul-57	4.02	2
MARSHALL	TP10-2	6-May-55	3.62	2	MONONA	UK9-3	21-May-53	4.20	2
MARSHALL	PB5-7	21-Jul-57	4.15	2	MONONA	UK7-5	29-Apr-53	5.03	3
MARSHALL	TP4-2	8-Mar-55	5.25	3	MONONA	TP4-2	8-Mar-55	5.25	3
MARSHALL	TS6-4	28-May-52	6.75	3	MONONA	PB12-4	5-Sep-57	5.81	3
MARSHALL	TS7-3	3-Jun-52	11.52	4	MONONA	UK7-4	28-Apr-53	6.63	3
MARSHALL	TS7-4	4-Jun-52	29.72	5	MONONA	UK9-2	20-May-53	10.03	4
MARSHALL	PB9-4	26-Aug-57	50.01	6	MONONA	TS6-3	27-May-52	16.32	4
MARSHALL	UK9-2	20-May-53	61.87	6	MONONA	TS7-4	4-Jun-52	41.98	5
MARSHALL	SE3	8-Jul-62	527.44	9	MONONA	SE3	8-Jul-62	527.44	9
MILLS	TS7-3	3-Jun-52	3.53	2	MONROE	TP10-3	7-May-55	4.68	2
MILLS	UK7-5	29-Apr-53	3.64	2	MONROE	TP4-2	8-Mar-55	5.25	3
MILLS	UK7-4	28-Apr-53	4.22	2	MONROE	TP10-2	6-May-55	5.48	3
MILLS	UK2-3	26-Mar-53	4.78	2	MONROE	TS7-4	4-Jun-52	6.30	3
MILLS	TP4-2	8-Mar-55	5.25	3	MONROE	PB8-3	20-Aug-57	15.90	4
MILLS	PB13-5	10-Sep-57	5.77	3	MONROE	PB9-4	26-Aug-57	16.67	4
MILLS	TS6-4	28-May-52	6.45	3	MONROE	UK9-2	20-May-53	38.30	5
MILLS	TS6-3	27-May-52	7.91	3	MONROE	TS7-3	3-Jun-52	151.83	7
MILLS	PB12-4	5-Sep-57	9.26	3	MONROE	SE3	8-Jul-62	345.56	8
MILLS	TS7-4	4-Jun-52	14.89	4	MONTGOMERY	PB8-3	20-Aug-57	4.00	2
MILLS	UK9-2	20-May-53	20.90	4	MONTGOMERY	TS6-3	27-May-52	4.00	2
MILLS	PB8-3	20-Aug-57	23.89	4	MONTGOMERY	PB13-5	10-Sep-57	4.66	2
MILLS	SE3	8-Jul-62	172.89	7	MONTGOMERY	UK7-4	28-Apr-53	5.24	3
MITCHELL	UK7-5	29-Apr-53	3.70	2	MONTGOMERY	TP4-2	8-Mar-55	5.25	3
MITCHELL	UK9-3	21-May-53	3.98	2	MONTGOMERY	PB12-4	5-Sep-57	5.95	3
MITCHELL	TP10-2	6-May-55	3.51	1	MONTGOMERY	UK9-2	20-May-53	20.57	4
MITCHELL	UK7-4	28-Apr-53	5.67	3	MONTGOMERY	TS7-4	4-Jun-52	37.02	5
MITCHELL	TS5-1	7-May-52	7.19	3	MONTGOMERY	PB9-4	26-Aug-57	83.35	6
MITCHELL	TS7-5	5-Jun-52	17.13	4	MONTGOMERY	SE3	8-Jul-62	172.89	7
MITCHELL	TS6-4	28-May-52	24.11	4	MUSCATINE	PB18-8	17-Jul-57	3.98	2
MITCHELL	UK9-2	20-May-53	69.62	6	MUSCATINE	TS6-4	28-May-52	4.03	2
MITCHELL	SE3	8-Jul-62	950.00	10	MUSCATINE	UK7-4	28-Apr-53	4.97	2

INDIVIDUAL FALLOUT DAYS
IOWA

COUNTY	SHOT	DATE	µCi/SQ METER	INDEX	COUNTY	SHOT	DATE	µCi/SQ METER	INDEX
MUSCATINE	TP4-2	8-Mar-55	5.25	3	PAGE	SE3	8-Jul-62	200.06	8
MUSCATINE	TP10-2	6-May-55	5.48	3	PALO ALTO	TP4-2	8-Mar-55	5.25	3
MUSCATINE	TS5-1	7-May-52	8.44	3	PALO ALTO	UK7-5	29-Apr-53	6.30	3
MUSCATINE	PB9-3	25-Aug-57	13.72	4	PALO ALTO	UK7-4	28-Apr-53	9.31	3
MUSCATINE	PB9-4	26-Aug-57	16.67	4	PALO ALTO	TS6-3	27-May-52	15.05	4
MUSCATINE	UK9-2	20-May-53	18.52	4	PALO ALTO	TS7-4	4-Jun-52	24.87	4
MUSCATINE	SE3	8-Jul-62	139.13	7	PALO ALTO	UK9-2	20-May-53	26.09	5
O BRIEN	TP4-2	8-Mar-55	5.25	3	PALO ALTO	SE3	8-Jul-62	527.44	9
O BRIEN	PB2-3	20-Jun-57	5.36	3	PLYMOUTH	UK9-3	21-May-53	3.61	2
O BRIEN	UK7-5	29-Apr-53	6.36	3	PLYMOUTH	UK2-2	25-Mar-53	3.97	2
O BRIEN	UK7-4	28-Apr-53	7.71	3	PLYMOUTH	PB5-5	19-Jul-57	4.02	2
O BRIEN	TS7-5	5-Jun-52	13.82	4	PLYMOUTH	TS5-1	7-May-52	4.05	2
O BRIEN	UK9-2	20-May-53	14.73	4	PLYMOUTH	PB12-4	5-Sep-57	4.19	2
O BRIEN	TS6-3	27-May-52	16.24	4	PLYMOUTH	UK7-5	29-Apr-53	6.08	3
O BRIEN	TS7-4	4-Jun-52	36.82	5	PLYMOUTH	UK9-2	20-May-53	6.86	3
O BRIEN	SE3	8-Jul-62	527.44	9	PLYMOUTH	UK7-4	28-Apr-53	7.71	3
OSCEOLA	UK8-2	9-May-53	4.04	2	PLYMOUTH	TS6-3	27-May-52	17.17	4
OSCEOLA	TP4-2	8-Mar-55	5.25	3	PLYMOUTH	TS7-4	4-Jun-52	22.01	4
OSCEOLA	PB2-3	20-Jun-57	5.36	3	PLYMOUTH	SE4	9-Jul-62	25.88	5
OSCEOLA	TS6-3	27-May-52	5.56	3	PLYMOUTH	SE3	8-Jul-62	527.44	9
OSCEOLA	UK7-5	29-Apr-53	6.51	3	POCAHONTAS	PB12-4	5-Sep-57	3.72	2
OSCEOLA	UK7-4	28-Apr-53	7.91	3	POCAHONTAS	TS7-5	5-Jun-52	5.14	3
OSCEOLA	UK9-2	20-May-53	13.10	4	POCAHONTAS	TP4-2	8-Mar-55	5.25	3
OSCEOLA	SE4	9-Jul-62	24.53	4	POCAHONTAS	UK7-4	28-Apr-53	5.61	3
OSCEOLA	TS7-4	4-Jun-52	29.44	5	POCAHONTAS	UK7-5	29-Apr-53	6.09	3
OSCEOLA	SE3	8-Jul-62	527.44	9	POCAHONTAS	TS6-3	27-May-52	13.18	4
PAGE	UK7-4	28-Apr-53	3.85	2	POCAHONTAS	UK9-2	20-May-53	32.48	5
PAGE	TP4-2	8-Mar-55	5.25	3	POCAHONTAS	TS7-4	4-Jun-52	32.90	5
PAGE	PB13-5	10-Sep-57	10.68	4	POCAHONTAS	SE3	8-Jul-62	527.44	9
PAGE	UK9-2	20-May-53	11.83	4	POLK	TP10-3	7-May-55	4.96	2
PAGE	TS7-4	4-Jun-52	13.19	4	POLK	TS7-3	3-Jun-52	5.42	3
PAGE	PB12-4	5-Sep-57	14.93	4	POLK	UK9-2	20-May-53	18.91	4
PAGE	PB8-3	20-Aug-57	23.89	4	POLK	TS7-4	4-Jun-52	27.34	5

INDIVIDUAL FALLOUT DAYS
IOWA

COUNTY	SHOT	DATE	µCi/SQ METER	INDEX	COUNTY	SHOT	DATE	µCi/SQ METER	INDEX
POLK	PB9-4	26-Aug-57	83.35	6	RINGGOLD	TS7-4	4-Jun-52	86.57	6
POLK	SE3	8-Jul-62	139.13	7	RINGGOLD	SE3	8-Jul-62	345.56	8
POTTAWATTAMI	UK7-5	29-Apr-53	4.15	2	SAC	UK9-5	23-May-53	3.56	2
POTTAWATTAMI	UK9-5	23-May-53	4.17	2	SAC	PB12-4	5-Sep-57	4.86	2
POTTAWATTAMI	UK7-4	28-Apr-53	4.49	2	SAC	TP4-2	8-Mar-55	5.25	3
POTTAWATTAMI	PB13-5	10-Sep-57	5.14	3	SAC	UK7-5	29-Apr-53	6.18	3
POTTAWATTAMI	TP4-2	8-Mar-55	5.25	3	SAC	UK7-4	28-Apr-53	6.50	3
POTTAWATTAMI	PB12-4	5-Sep-57	6.01	3	SAC	TS6-3	27-May-52	13.26	4
POTTAWATTAMI	TS6-3	27-May-52	9.61	3	SAC	UK9-2	20-May-53	21.76	4
POTTAWATTAMI	TS7-4	4-Jun-52	15.33	4	SAC	TS7-4	4-Jun-52	31.08	5
POTTAWATTAMI	UK9-2	20-May-53	25.12	5	SAC	SE3	8-Jul-62	527.44	9
POTTAWATTAMI	PB9-4	26-Aug-57	83.35	6	SCOTT	UK9-3	21-May-53	3.54	2
POTTAWATTAMI	SE3	8-Jul-62	146.81	7	SCOTT	TS5-1	7-May-52	4.65	2
POWESHIEK	TS7-5	5-Jun-52	3.76	2	SCOTT	TS6-4	28-May-52	4.83	2
POWESHIEK	PB18-8	17-Jul-57	3.98	2	SCOTT	TS7-3	3-Jun-52	4.95	2
POWESHIEK	TS7-3	3-Jun-52	4.83	2	SCOTT	PB9-3	25-Aug-57	13.72	4
POWESHIEK	TP4-2	8-Mar-55	5.25	3	SCOTT	PB9-4	26-Aug-57	16.67	4
POWESHIEK	TS6-4	28-May-52	6.75	3	SCOTT	UK9-2	20-May-53	17.16	4
POWESHIEK	PB8-3	20-Aug-57	7.99	3	SCOTT	SE3	8-Jul-62	139.13	7
POWESHIEK	PB9-4	26-Aug-57	16.67	4	SHELBY	PB13-5	10-Sep-57	4.42	2
POWESHIEK	TS7-4	4-Jun-52	25.95	5	SHELBY	UK7-5	29-Apr-53	4.85	2
POWESHIEK	UK9-2	20-May-53	43.72	5	SHELBY	TP4-2	8-Mar-55	5.25	3
POWESHIEK	PB9-3	25-Aug-57	54.87	6	SHELBY	UK9-5	23-May-53	5.67	3
POWESHIEK	SE3	8-Jul-62	208.70	8	SHELBY	UK7-4	28-Apr-53	7.20	3
RINGGOLD	TP10-3	7-May-55	3.94	2	SHELBY	PB12-4	5-Sep-57	7.30	3
RINGGOLD	UK7-4	28-Apr-53	5.03	3	SHELBY	TS6-3	27-May-52	10.71	4
RINGGOLD	TP4-2	8-Mar-55	5.25	3	SHELBY	UK9-2	20-May-53	24.04	4
RINGGOLD	TP10-2	6-May-55	5.48	3	SHELBY	TS7-4	4-Jun-52	57.91	6
RINGGOLD	PB12-4	5-Sep-57	6.97	3	SHELBY	PB9-4	26-Aug-57	83.35	6
RINGGOLD	PB13-5	10-Sep-57	8.42	3	SHELBY	SE3	8-Jul-62	345.56	8
RINGGOLD	UK9-2	20-May-53	12.48	4	SIOUX	UK2-2	25-Mar-53	3.97	2
RINGGOLD	PB9-4	26-Aug-57	33.34	5	SIOUX	PB12-4	5-Sep-57	4.86	2
RINGGOLD	PB8-3	20-Aug-57	39.79	5	SIOUX	UK7-5	29-Apr-53	5.30	3

INDIVIDUAL FALLOUT DAYS
IOWA

COUNTY	SHOT	DATE	µCi/SQ METER	INDEX	COUNTY	SHOT	DATE	µCi/SQ METER	INDEX
SIOUX	TS5-1	7-May-52	5.39	3	TAYLOR	TP10-2	6-May-55	5.48	3
SIOUX	TS7-5	5-Jun-52	7.94	3	TAYLOR	PB12-4	5-Sep-57	15.54	4
SIOUX	PB2-3	20-Jun-57	8.04	3	TAYLOR	UK9-2	20-May-53	17.70	4
SIOUX	UK9-2	20-May-53	9.74	3	TAYLOR	TS7-4	4-Jun-52	20.42	4
SIOUX	UK7-4	28-Apr-53	10.52	4	TAYLOR	PB9-4	26-Aug-57	33.34	5
SIOUX	TS6-3	27-May-52	15.30	4	TAYLOR	PB8-3	20-Aug-57	39.79	5
SIOUX	TS7-4	4-Jun-52	31.79	5	TAYLOR	SE3	8-Jul-62	200.06	8
SIOUX	SE3	8-Jul-62	527.44	9	UNION	TP10-3	7-May-55	3.63	2
STORY	TP10-2	6-May-55	3.62	2	UNION	PB13-5	10-Sep-57	4.55	2
STORY	PB5-7	21-Jul-57	4.15	2	UNION	TP4-2	8-Mar-55	5.25	3
STORY	TP4-2	8-Mar-55	5.25	3	UNION	PB12-4	5-Sep-57	7.61	3
STORY	TS6-4	28-May-52	5.79	3	UNION	PB8-3	20-Aug-57	23.89	4
STORY	TS7-3	3-Jun-52	13.08	4	UNION	UK9-2	20-May-53	27.73	5
STORY	TS7-4	4-Jun-52	27.77	5	UNION	PB9-4	26-Aug-57	50.01	6
STORY	PB9-4	26-Aug-57	50.01	6	UNION	TS7-4	4-Jun-52	54.79	6
STORY	UK9-2	20-May-53	53.97	6	UNION	SE3	8-Jul-62	345.56	8
STORY	SE3	8-Jul-62	527.44	9	VAN BUREN	TP10-2	6-May-55	3.62	2
TAMA	TP10-2	6-May-55	3.62	2	VAN BUREN	PB8-3	20-Aug-57	4.00	2
TAMA	PB18-8	17-Jul-57	3.98	2	VAN BUREN	TS7-4	4-Jun-52	4.05	2
TAMA	TS7-5	5-Jun-52	4.25	2	VAN BUREN	UK7-4	28-Apr-53	4.12	2
TAMA	TP4-2	8-Mar-55	5.25	3	VAN BUREN	PB12-4	5-Sep-57	4.53	2
TAMA	TS6-4	28-May-52	13.50	4	VAN BUREN	TS5-1	7-May-52	4.85	2
TAMA	TS7-4	4-Jun-52	21.29	4	VAN BUREN	TP10-3	7-May-55	5.17	3
TAMA	PB9-4	26-Aug-57	33.34	5	VAN BUREN	TP4-2	8-Mar-55	5.25	3
TAMA	TS7-3	3-Jun-52	47.52	5	VAN BUREN	PB18-8	17-Jul-57	6.63	3
TAMA	PB9-3	25-Aug-57	54.87	6	VAN BUREN	TS7-3	3-Jun-52	8.78	3
TAMA	UK9-2	20-May-53	56.84	6	VAN BUREN	UK9-2	20-May-53	24.36	4
TAMA	SE3	8-Jul-62	208.70	8	VAN BUREN	PB9-3	25-Aug-57	27.43	5
TAYLOR	TP10-3	7-May-55	3.91	2	VAN BUREN	PB9-4	26-Aug-57	33.34	5
TAYLOR	PB13-5	10-Sep-57	4.85	2	VAN BUREN	SE3	8-Jul-62	621.15	9
TAYLOR	UK7-4	28-Apr-53	5.03	3	WAPELLO	TP10-2	6-May-55	3.62	2
TAYLOR	TP4-2	8-Mar-55	5.25	3	WAPELLO	TS5-1	7-May-52	3.75	2
TAYLOR	PB2-3	20-Jun-57	5.36	3	WAPELLO	PB18-8	17-Jul-57	3.98	2

INDIVIDUAL FALLOUT DAYS
IOWA

COUNTY	SHOT	DATE	µCi/SQ METER	INDEX	COUNTY	SHOT	DATE	µCi/SQ METER	INDEX
WAPELLO	TS7-4	4-Jun-52	4.66	2	WAYNE	PB8-3	20-Aug-57	15.90	4
WAPELLO	TP10-3	7-May-55	4.98	2	WAYNE	PB9-4	26-Aug-57	16.67	4
WAPELLO	TP4-2	8-Mar-55	5.25	3	WAYNE	UK9-2	20-May-53	27.19	5
WAPELLO	PB8-3	20-Aug-57	7.99	3	WAYNE	TS7-3	3-Jun-52	79.90	6
WAPELLO	TS7-3	3-Jun-52	22.47	4	WAYNE	SE3	8-Jul-62	345.56	8
WAPELLO	UK9-2	20-May-53	38.98	5	WEBSTER	TS7-5	5-Jun-52	4.28	2
WAPELLO	PB9-4	26-Aug-57	50.01	6	WEBSTER	UK7-5	29-Apr-53	4.88	2
WAPELLO	PB9-3	25-Aug-57	54.87	6	WEBSTER	TS6-3	27-May-52	5.20	3
WAPELLO	SE3	8-Jul-62	345.56	8	WEBSTER	TP4-2	8-Mar-55	5.25	3
WARREN	TP4-2	8-Mar-55	5.25	3	WEBSTER	PB5-5	19-Jul-57	6.09	3
WARREN	TP10-2	6-May-55	5.48	3	WEBSTER	TS6-4	28-May-52	8.68	3
WARREN	PB12-4	5-Sep-57	6.02	3	WEBSTER	TS7-4	4-Jun-52	12.74	4
WARREN	TS7-4	4-Jun-52	19.75	4	WEBSTER	UK9-2	20-May-53	33.96	5
WARREN	PB8-3	20-Aug-57	23.89	4	WEBSTER	SE3	8-Jul-62	208.70	8
WARREN	UK9-2	20-May-53	39.92	5	WINNEBAGO	TS7-4	4-Jun-52	4.43	2
WARREN	PB9-4	26-Aug-57	50.01	6	WINNEBAGO	TP10-2	6-May-55	3.51	1
WARREN	SE3	8-Jul-62	139.13	7	WINNEBAGO	UK7-5	29-Apr-53	5.18	3
WASHINGTON	TP10-2	6-May-55	3.62	2	WINNEBAGO	UK7-4	28-Apr-53	8.13	3
WASHINGTON	PB18-8	17-Jul-57	3.98	2	WINNEBAGO	TS7-5	5-Jun-52	13.02	4
WASHINGTON	TP4-2	8-Mar-55	5.25	3	WINNEBAGO	TS6-3	27-May-52	13.69	4
WASHINGTON	TS7-3	3-Jun-52	5.89	3	WINNEBAGO	UK9-2	20-May-53	46.45	5
WASHINGTON	TS5-1	7-May-52	6.83	3	WINNEBAGO	SE3	8-Jul-62	527.44	9
WASHINGTON	PB9-4	26-Aug-57	8.37	3	WINNESHIEK	UK9-3	21-May-53	3.76	2
WASHINGTON	PB9-3	25-Aug-57	13.72	4	WINNESHIEK	PB18-8	17-Jul-57	3.98	2
WASHINGTON	UK9-2	20-May-53	29.13	5	WINNESHIEK	UK7-4	28-Apr-53	6.18	3
WASHINGTON	SE3	8-Jul-62	621.15	9	WINNESHIEK	TP10-2	6-May-55	7.01	3
WAYNE	PB13-5	10-Sep-57	4.06	2	WINNESHIEK	TS5-1	7-May-52	7.79	3
WAYNE	TP5-3	14-Mar-55	4.85	2	WINNESHIEK	PB9-4	26-Aug-57	8.37	3
WAYNE	PB12-4	5-Sep-57	5.25	3	WINNESHIEK	PB9-3	25-Aug-57	13.72	4
WAYNE	TP4-2	8-Mar-55	5.25	3	WINNESHIEK	TS7-5	5-Jun-52	16.92	4
WAYNE	TP10-3	7-May-55	5.31	3	WINNESHIEK	TS6-4	28-May-52	25.07	5
WAYNE	TP10-2	6-May-55	5.48	3	WINNESHIEK	UK9-2	20-May-53	50.46	6
WAYNE	TS7-4	4-Jun-52	7.12	3	WINNESHIEK	SE3	8-Jul-62	527.44	9

INDIVIDUAL FALLOUT DAYS
IOWA

COUNTY	SHOT	DATE	µCi/SQ METER	INDEX	COUNTY	SHOT	DATE	µCi/SQ METER	INDEX
WOODBURY	PB12-4	5-Sep-57	3.51	2	WORTH	UK7-5	29-Apr-53	4.51	2
WOODBURY	UK9-3	21-May-53	3.98	2	WORTH	UK7-4	28-Apr-53	7.75	3
WOODBURY	PB5-5	19-Jul-57	4.02	2	WORTH	TS6-3	27-May-52	10.05	4
WOODBURY	TP4-2	8-Mar-55	5.25	3	WORTH	TS7-4	4-Jun-52	10.29	4
WOODBURY	PB2-3	20-Jun-57	5.36	3	WORTH	TP10-2	6-May-55	14.02	4
WOODBURY	TS7-3	3-Jun-52	6.15	3	WORTH	UK9-2	20-May-53	55.33	6
WOODBURY	UK7-5	29-Apr-53	6.23	3	WORTH	SE3	8-Jul-62	950.00	10
WOODBURY	UK9-2	20-May-53	7.50	3	WRIGHT	UK7-5	29-Apr-53	4.55	2
WOODBURY	UK7-4	28-Apr-53	9.18	3	WRIGHT	TP4-2	8-Mar-55	5.25	3
WOODBURY	TS6-3	27-May-52	17.60	4	WRIGHT	TS6-3	27-May-52	7.98	3
WOODBURY	TS7-4	4-Jun-52	40.74	5	WRIGHT	TS7-5	5-Jun-52	11.41	4
WOODBURY	SE2	7-Jul-62	138.24	7	WRIGHT	UK9-2	20-May-53	45.16	5
WOODBURY	SE3	8-Jul-62	527.44	9	WRIGHT	SE3	8-Jul-62	208.70	8
WORTH	UK9-3	21-May-53	3.83	2					

INDIVIDUAL FALLOUT DAYS
IDAHO

COUNTY	SHOT	DATE	µCi/SQ METER	INDEX	COUNTY	SHOT	DATE	µCi/SQ METER	INDEX
ADA	PB15-1	16-Sep-57	5.38	3	BANNOCK	PB12-1	2-Sep-57	5.31	3
ADA	PB1-1	28-May-57	7.29	3	BANNOCK	PB9-1	23-Aug-57	5.87	3
ADA	TS2-1	15-Apr-52	9.41	3	BANNOCK	UK10-1	25-May-53	6.72	3
ADA	TP9-1	15-Apr-55	9.51	3	BANNOCK	PB15-1	16-Sep-57	7.27	3
ADA	UK10-1	25-May-53	9.94	3	BANNOCK	PB8-1	18-Aug-57	7.93	3
ADA	PB17-1	28-Sep-57	13.00	4	BANNOCK	PB16-1	23-Sep-57	8.07	3
ADA	PB16-1	23-Sep-57	13.27	4	BANNOCK	PB5-1	15-Jul-57	8.26	3
ADA	PB6-2	25-Jul-57	13.87	4	BANNOCK	PB6-2	25-Jul-57	11.04	4
ADA	TS7-1	1-Jun-52	15.73	4	BANNOCK	TS8-2	6-Jun-52	16.30	4
ADA	TP11-1	15-May-55	20.91	4	BANNOCK	UK2-1	24-Mar-53	43.88	5
ADA	BJ5 1	19-Nov-51	59.69	6	BANNOCK	TS7-1	1-Jun-52	51.32	6
ADA	TS8-2	6-Jun-52	99.56	6	BANNOCK	TS8-1	5-Jun-52	2831.55	10
ADA	TS8-1	5-Jun-52	17292.21	10	BEAR LAKE	UK6-1	18-Apr-53	3.59	2
ADAMS	TP9-2	15-Apr-55	3.63	2	BEAR LAKE	TP4-1	7-Mar-55	3.74	2
ADAMS	TP8-1	9-Apr-55	3.77	2	BEAR LAKE	TS6-1	25-May-52	3.87	2
ADAMS	PB17-5	2-Oct-57	3.88	2	BEAR LAKE	TP9-1	15-Apr-55	4.03	2
ADAMS	TS8-5	9-Jun-52	4.23	2	BEAR LAKE	TS1-1	1-Apr-52	4.28	2
ADAMS	UK10-2	26-May-53	4.60	2	BEAR LAKE	TP10-1	5-May-55	4.66	2
ADAMS	TP11-1	15-May-55	4.66	2	BEAR LAKE	UK10-1	25-May-53	10.26	4
ADAMS	TS2-4	18-Apr-52	5.26	3	BEAR LAKE	PB6-2	25-Jul-57	11.04	4
ADAMS	TP11-2	16-May-55	7.37	3	BEAR LAKE	PB8-1	18-Aug-57	15.96	4
ADAMS	PB16-3	25-Sep-57	7.58	3	BEAR LAKE	PB17-1	28-Sep-57	17.32	4
ADAMS	TS8-3	7-Jun-52	8.60	3	BEAR LAKE	PB12-1	2-Sep-57	17.72	4
ADAMS	TS5-1	7-May-52	9.34	3	BEAR LAKE	PB9-1	23-Aug-57	21.17	4
ADAMS	BJ5-3	21-Nov-51	9.82	3	BEAR LAKE	UK7-1	25-Apr-53	3.50	1
ADAMS	PB6-2	25-Jul-57	10.55	4	BEAR LAKE	TS8-2	6-Jun-52	6.87	3
ADAMS	PB6-3	26-Jul-57	12.28	4	BEAR LAKE	TP11-1	15-May-55	6.93	3
ADAMS	TS8-2	6-Jun-52	23.88	4	BEAR LAKE	PB15-1	16-Sep-57	7.27	3
ADAMS	BJ5-2	20-Nov-51	29.59	5	BEAR LAKE	PB16-1	23-Sep-57	8.07	3
ADAMS	TS8-1	5-Jun-52	4147.68	10					
BANNOCK	TP10-1	5-May-55	3.88	2					
BANNOCK	TP9-1	15-Apr-55	4.03	2					
BANNOCK	PB17-1	28-Sep-57	17.32	4					

INDIVIDUAL FALLOUT DAYS
IDAHO

COUNTY	SHOT	DATE	µCi/SQ METER	INDEX	COUNTY	SHOT	DATE	µCi/SQ METER	INDEX
BEAR LAKE	PB5-1	15-Jul-57	8.26	3	BLAINE	PB6-3	26-Jul-57	12.28	4
BEAR LAKE	UK9-1	19-May-53	8.49	3	BLAINE	PB16-3	25-Sep-57	7.58	3
BEAR LAKE	TS7-1	1-Jun-52	63.97	6	BLAINE	UK2-1	24-Mar-53	8.38	3
BEAR LAKE	UK2-1	24-Mar-53	443.88	9	BLAINE	TS8-3	7-Jun-52	9.83	3
BEAR LAKE	TS8-1	5-Jun-52	1193.97	10	BLAINE	TS5-1	7-May-52	35.56	5
BENEWAH	PB6-2	25-Jul-57	10.55	4	BLAINE	TS8-2	6-Jun-52	348.46	8
BENEWAH	PB6-3	26-Jul-57	12.28	4	BLAINE	TS8-1	5-Jun-52	60519.41	10
BENEWAH	TS8-2	6-Jun-52	24.74	4	BOISE	TP8-1	9-Apr-55	3.77	2
BENEWAH	PB17-3	30-Sep-57	6.34	3	BOISE	TP11-1	15-May-55	4.66	2
BENEWAH	UK10-2	26-May-53	7.48	3	BOISE	PB6-2	25-Jul-57	10.55	4
BENEWAH	PB16-3	25-Sep-57	7.58	3	BOISE	TS5-1	7-May-52	11.54	4
BENEWAH	TS8-1	5-Jun-52	4296.77	10	BOISE	PB6-3	26-Jul-57	12.28	4
BINGHAM	PB8-1	18-Aug-57	4.02	2	BOISE	BJ5-3	21-Nov-51	14.77	4
BINGHAM	TP9-1	15-Apr-55	4.03	2	BOISE	BJ5-2	20-Nov-51	19.72	4
BINGHAM	PB9-1	23-Aug-57	4.08	2	BOISE	TS2-4	18-Apr-52	5.26	3
BINGHAM	TP7-1	29-Mar-55	4.73	2	BOISE	TS8-3	7-Jun-52	6.77	3
BINGHAM	TS8-2	6-Jun-52	13.75	4	BOISE	TP11-2	16-May-55	7.37	3
BINGHAM	PB17-1	28-Sep-57	17.32	4	BOISE	PB16-3	25-Sep-57	7.58	3
BINGHAM	PB5-1	15-Jul-57	6.48	3	BOISE	TS8-2	6-Jun-52	129.43	7
BINGHAM	PB16-1	23-Sep-57	6.50	3	BOISE	TS8-1	5-Jun-52	22479.97	10
BINGHAM	UK10-1	25-May-53	7.12	3	BONNER	PB6-3	26-Jul-57	12.28	4
BINGHAM	PB15-1	16-Sep-57	7.27	3	BONNER	PB6-2	25-Jul-57	15.78	4
BINGHAM	PB6-2	25-Jul-57	7.33	3	BONNER	UK10-2	26-May-53	19.66	4
BINGHAM	TS7-1	1-Jun-52	45.31	5	BONNER	TS6-4	28-May-52	5.79	3
BINGHAM	TS8-1	5-Jun-52	2387.94	10	BONNER	TS8-2	6-Jun-52	6.20	3
BLAINE	TS7-3	3-Jun-52	4.24	2	BONNER	PB16-3	25-Sep-57	7.58	3
BLAINE	TS7-4	4-Jun-52	4.54	2	BONNER	TS8-1	5-Jun-52	1076.80	10
BLAINE	TS6-4	28-May-52	4.83	2	BONNEVILLE	PB8-1	18-Aug-57	4.02	2
BLAINE	PB6-2	25-Jul-57	10.55	4	BONNEVILLE	PB9-1	23-Aug-57	4.97	2
BLAINE	PB17-5	2-Oct-57	10.80	4	BONNEVILLE	TS8-2	6-Jun-52	13.75	4
					BONNEVILLE	PB17-1	28-Sep-57	17.32	4
					BONNEVI	PB5-1	15-Jul-57	6.48	3

INDIVIDUAL FALLOUT DAYS
IDAHO

COUNTY	SHOT	DATE	µCi/SQ METER	INDEX	COUNTY	SHOT	DATE	µCi/SQ METER	INDEX
LLE					CAMAS	TS8-3	7-Jun-52	11.07	4
BONNEVILLE	PB15-1	16-Sep-57	6.49	3	CAMAS	PB6-3	26-Jul-57	12.28	4
BONNEVILLE	PB16-1	23-Sep-57	6.50	3	CAMAS	TS5-1	7-May-52	14.98	4
BONNEVILLE	UK10-1	25-May-53	7.12	3	CAMAS	TP11-1	15-May-55	7.10	3
BONNEVILLE	PB6-2	25-Jul-57	7.33	3	CAMAS	PB16-3	25-Sep-57	7.58	3
BONNEVILLE	UK2-1	24-Mar-53	43.78	5	CAMAS	BJ5-3	21-Nov-51	9.82	3
BONNEVILLE	TS7-1	1-Jun-52	45.20	5	CAMAS	BJ5-2	20-Nov-51	9.86	3
BONNEVILLE	TS8-1	5-Jun-52	2387.94	10	CAMAS	TS8-2	6-Jun-52	150.48	7
BOUNDARY	TS8-2	6-Jun-52	3.52	2	CAMAS	TS8-1	5-Jun-52	26135.69	10
BOUNDARY	PB6-2	25-Jul-57	10.55	4	CANYON	TP9-1	15-Apr-55	3.53	2
BOUNDARY	PB6-3	26-Jul-57	12.28	4	CANYON	PB15-1	16-Sep-57	4.03	2
BOUNDARY	UK10-2	26-May-53	12.65	4	CANYON	PB6-2	25-Jul-57	11.04	4
BOUNDARY	PB16-3	25-Sep-57	7.58	3	CANYON	PB16-1	23-Sep-57	15.64	4
BOUNDARY	TS8-1	5-Jun-52	611.52	9	CANYON	TP11-1	15-May-55	22.17	4
BUTTE	TS7-3	3-Jun-52	4.30	2	CANYON	PB1-1	28-May-57	6.20	3
BUTTE	PB6-2	25-Jul-57	10.55	4	CANYON	UK10-1	25-May-53	7.27	3
BUTTE	TS5-1	7-May-52	11.35	4	CANYON	TS7-1	1-Jun-52	8.34	3
BUTTE	PB6-3	26-Jul-57	12.28	4	CANYON	PB17-1	28-Sep-57	8.66	3
BUTTE	TS7-4	4-Jun-52	5.04	3	CANYON	TS2-1	15-Apr-52	8.81	3
BUTTE	PB17-5	2-Oct-57	6.96	3	CANYON	TS8-2	6-Jun-52	35.06	5
BUTTE	PB16-3	25-Sep-57	7.58	3	CANYON	BJ5 1	19-Nov-51	45.24	5
BUTTE	TS8-3	7-Jun-52	8.22	3	CANYON	TS8-1	5-Jun-52	6088.55	10
BUTTE	UK2-1	24-Mar-53	8.38	3	CARIBOU	TP9-1	15-Apr-55	4.03	2
BUTTE	TS8-2	6-Jun-52	94.45	6	CARIBOU	UK9-1	19-May-53	4.19	2
BUTTE	TS8-1	5-Jun-52	16404.60	10	CARIBOU	TS1-1	1-Apr-52	4.28	2
CAMAS	TP11-2	16-May-55	3.64	2	CARIBOU	PB12-1	2-Sep-57	4.40	2
CAMAS	TS7-4	4-Jun-52	3.83	2	CARIBOU	UK10-1	25-May-53	10.26	4
CAMAS	PB17-5	2-Oct-57	4.23	2	CARIBOU	TS8-2	6-Jun-52	13.75	4
CAMAS	TS6-4	28-May-52	4.83	2	CARIBOU	PB17-1	28-Sep-57	17.32	4
CAMAS	PB6-2	25-Jul-57	10.55	4	CARIBOU	PB15-1	16-Sep-57	7.27	3
					CARIBOU	PB6-2	25-Jul-57	7.33	3
					CARIBOU	PB8-1	18-Aug-57	7.93	3
					CARIBOU	PB16-1	23-Sep-57	8.07	3

INDIVIDUAL FALLOUT DAYS
IDAHO

COUNTY	SHOT	DATE	µCi/SQ METER	INDEX	COUNTY	SHOT	DATE	µCi/SQ METER	INDEX
CARIBOU	PB5-1	15-Jul-57	8.26	3	CLARK	PB4-1	5-Jul-57	7.20	3
CARIBOU	PB9-1	23-Aug-57	8.29	3	CLARK	PB15-1	16-Sep-57	7.62	3
CARIBOU	TS7-1	1-Jun-52	54.64	6	CLARK	UK2-1	24-Mar-53	8.38	3
CARIBOU	UK2-1	24-Mar-53	176.27	7	CLARK	TS8-3	7-Jun-52	9.28	3
CARIBOU	TS8-1	5-Jun-52	2387.94	10	CLARK	PB8-2	19-Aug-57	29.82	5
CASSIA	TP9-1	15-Apr-55	4.03	2	CLARK	TS8-1	5-Jun-52	3017.70	10
CASSIA	PB1-1	28-May-57	4.67	2	CLEARWATER	UK10-2	26-May-53	4.81	2
CASSIA	UK10-1	25-May-53	10.54	4	CLEARWATER	BJ5-2	20-Nov-51	5.00	2
CASSIA	PB6-2	25-Jul-57	11.04	4	CLEARWATER	PB6-2	25-Jul-57	10.55	4
CASSIA	TS2-1	15-Apr-52	13.22	4	CLEARWATER	PB6-3	26-Jul-57	12.28	4
CASSIA	PB17-1	28-Sep-57	17.32	4	CLEARWATER	TS5-1	7-May-52	5.36	3
CASSIA	PB8-1	18-Aug-57	23.89	4	CLEARWATER	PB16-3	25-Sep-57	7.58	3
CASSIA	UK2-1	24-Mar-53	5.80	3	CLEARWATER	BJ5-3	21-Nov-51	39.28	5
CASSIA	PB9-1	23-Aug-57	5.87	3	CLEARWATER	TS8-2	6-Jun-52	76.68	6
CASSIA	PB15-1	16-Sep-57	6.49	3	CLEARWATER	TS8-1	5-Jun-52	13318.39	10
CASSIA	PB5-1	15-Jul-57	6.58	3	CUSTER	TP11-2	16-May-55	3.64	2
CASSIA	TP11-1	15-May-55	7.03	3	CUSTER	TP11-1	15-May-55	4.66	2
CASSIA	PB16-1	23-Sep-57	8.18	3	CUSTER	TS6-4	28-May-52	4.83	2
CASSIA	TS6-1	25-May-52	8.51	3	CUSTER	TS7-3	3-Jun-52	11.73	4
CASSIA	BJ5 1	19-Nov-51	8.62	3	CUSTER	TS5-1	7-May-52	12.03	4
CASSIA	TS8-2	6-Jun-52	69.87	6	CUSTER	PB6-3	26-Jul-57	12.28	4
CASSIA	TS7-1	1-Jun-52	92.60	6	CUSTER	TS8-3	7-Jun-52	12.77	4
CASSIA	TS8-1	5-Jun-52	12135.21	10	CUSTER	BJ5-3	21-Nov-51	14.77	4
CLARK	PB2-2	19-Jun-57	3.59	2	CUSTER	PB6-2	25-Jul-57	21.00	4
CLARK	TS7-4	4-Jun-52	4.60	2	CUSTER	PB16-3	25-Sep-57	7.58	3
CLARK	TP7-1	29-Mar-55	10.52	4	CUSTER	BJ5-2	20-Nov-51	9.86	3
CLARK	PB6-2	25-Jul-57	10.55	4	CUSTER	TS8-2	6-Jun-52	367.63	8
CLARK	PB9-2	24-Aug-57	11.17	4	CUSTER	TS8-1	5-Jun-52	63849.00	10
CLARK	PB5-2	16-Jul-57	12.01	4	ELMORE	TP9-1	15-Apr-55	3.53	2
CLARK	TS8-2	6-Jun-52	17.38	4	ELMORE	TS6-1	25-May-52	3.87	2
CLARK	TS7-3	3-Jun-52	17.87	4					
CLARK	PB5-1	15-Jul-57	20.41	4					
CLARK	TS5-1	7-May-52	24.97	4					

INDITIONAL FALLOUT DAYS
IDAHO

COUNTY	SHOT	DATE	µCi/SQ METER	INDEX	COUNTY	SHOT	DATE	µCi/SQ METER	INDEX
ELMORE	UK10-1	25-May-53	10.54	4	FREMONT	PB17-5	2-Oct-57	17.28	4
ELMORE	PB16-1	23-Sep-57	11.76	4	FREMONT	TS8-2	6-Jun-52	23.42	4
ELMORE	PB6-2	25-Jul-57	14.71	4	FREMONT	UK2-1	24-Mar-53	8.38	3
ELMORE	PB17-1	28-Sep-57	17.32	4	FREMONT	TS8-3	7-Jun-52	9.37	3
ELMORE	TS7-1	1-Jun-52	17.88	4	FREMONT	PB8-2	19-Aug-57	29.82	5
ELMORE	TP11-1	15-May-55	22.17	4	FREMONT	TS5-1	7-May-52	33.95	5
ELMORE	PB15-1	16-Sep-57	5.70	3	FREMONT	TS8-1	5-Jun-52	4067.92	10
ELMORE	PB1-1	28-May-57	6.20	3	GEM	TP11-2	16-May-55	3.64	2
ELMORE	TS2-1	15-Apr-52	9.97	3	GEM	TP8-1	9-Apr-55	3.77	2
ELMORE	BJ5 1	19-Nov-51	45.35	5	GEM	TS8-3	7-Jun-52	4.25	2
ELMORE	TS8-2	6-Jun-52	104.81	7	GEM	PB17-5	2-Oct-57	4.38	2
ELMORE	TS8-1	5-Jun-52	18202.82	10	GEM	PB6-2	25-Jul-57	10.55	4
FRANKLIN	TP4-1	7-Mar-55	3.74	2	GEM	PB6-3	26-Jul-57	12.28	4
FRANKLIN	TS6-1	25-May-52	3.87	2	GEM	TS8-1	5-Jun-52	67162.75	
FRANKLIN	TP9-1	15-Apr-55	4.03	2	GEM	TS5-1	7-May-52	6.24	3
FRANKLIN	TP10-1	5-May-55	4.66	2	GEM	TP11-1	15-May-55	7.10	3
FRANKLIN	UK10-1	25-May-53	10.26	4	GEM	PB16-3	25-Sep-57	7.58	3
FRANKLIN	TS8-2	6-Jun-52	10.37	4	GEM	BJ5-3	21-Nov-51	9.82	3
FRANKLIN	PB6-2	25-Jul-57	11.04	4	GEM	BJ5-2	20-Nov-51	29.59	5
FRANKLIN	PB5-1	15-Jul-57	12.44	4	GEM	TS8-2	6-Jun-52	386.71	8
FRANKLIN	PB17-1	28-Sep-57	17.32	4	GOODING	TS6-1	25-May-52	4.64	2
FRANKLIN	PB12-1	2-Sep-57	17.72	4	GOODING	UK10-1	25-May-53	10.54	4
FRANKLIN	PB9-1	23-Aug-57	21.17	4	GOODING	TS2-1	15-Apr-52	10.90	4
FRANKLIN	PB8-1	18-Aug-57	7.93	3	GOODING	PB6-2	25-Jul-57	11.04	4
FRANKLIN	PB16-1	23-Sep-57	8.07	3	GOODING	TP11-1	15-May-55	14.75	4
FRANKLIN	UK9-1	19-May-53	8.49	3	GOODING	PB17-1	28-Sep-57	17.32	4
FRANKLIN	PB15-1	16-Sep-57	9.73	3	GOODING	BJ5 1	19-Nov-51	18.16	4
FRANKLIN	TS7-1	1-Jun-52	72.85	6	GOODING	PB1-1	28-May-57	5.44	3
FRANKLIN	UK2-1	24-Mar-53	263.50	8	GOODING	PB15-1	16-Sep-57	5.70	3
FRANKLIN	TS8-1	5-Jun-52	1801.43	10	GOODING	PB16-1	23-Sep-57	8.29	3
FREMONT	TS7-4	4-Jun-52	3.83	2	GOODING	TS7-1	1-Jun-52	27.10	5
FREMONT	TP7-1	29-Mar-55	15.78	4	GOODING	TS8-2	6-Jun-52	139.74	7
FREMONT	PB6-2	25-Jul-57	15.87	4	GOODING	TS8-1	5-Jun-52	24270.43	10

INDIVIDUAL FALLOUT DAYS
IDAHO

COUNTY	SHOT	DATE	µCi/SQ METER	INDEX	COUNTY	SHOT	DATE	µCi/SQ METER	INDEX
IDAHO	UK10-2	26-May-53	3.76	2	JEROME	TS2-1	15-Apr-52	10.20	4
IDAHO	PB17-5	2-Oct-57	4.70	2	JEROME	UK10-1	25-May-53	10.40	4
IDAHO	TS2-4	18-Apr-52	10.37	4	JEROME	PB6-2	25-Jul-57	11.04	4
IDAHO	PB6-3	26-Jul-57	12.28	4	JEROME	TP11-1	15-May-55	13.96	4
IDAHO	PB6-2	25-Jul-57	15.78	4	JEROME	PB17-1	28-Sep-57	17.32	4
IDAHO	BJ5-3	21-Nov-51	19.64	4	JEROME	PB15-1	16-Sep-57	5.70	3
IDAHO	BJ5-2	20-Nov-51	19.72	4	JEROME	TS6-1	25-May-52	5.75	3
IDAHO	TP8-1	9-Apr-55	5.66	3	JEROME	PB8-1	18-Aug-57	7.93	3
IDAHO	TS5-1	7-May-52	6.11	3	JEROME	PB16-1	23-Sep-57	8.18	3
IDAHO	TP11-2	16-May-55	7.37	3	JEROME	BJ5 1	19-Nov-51	9.03	3
IDAHO	PB16-3	25-Sep-57	7.58	3	JEROME	TS7-1	1-Jun-52	54.97	6
IDAHO	TS8-2	6-Jun-52	153.28	7	JEROME	TS8-2	6-Jun-52	69.87	6
IDAHO	TS8-1	5-Jun-52	26620.93	10	JEROME	TS8-1	5-Jun-52	12135.21	10
JEFFERSON	TS7-3	3-Jun-52	3.54	2	KOOTENAI	PB6-2	25-Jul-57	10.55	4
JEFFERSON	TS7-4	4-Jun-52	4.25	2	KOOTENAI	PB6-3	26-Jul-57	12.28	4
JEFFERSON	TS8-3	7-Jun-52	4.85	2	KOOTENAI	UK10-2	26-May-53	13.48	4
JEFFERSON	PB6-2	25-Jul-57	10.55	4	KOOTENAI	PB16-3	25-Sep-57	7.58	3
JEFFERSON	PB9-2	24-Aug-57	11.17	4	KOOTENAI	TS8-2	6-Jun-52	8.42	3
JEFFERSON	PB5-2	16-Jul-57	12.01	4	KOOTENAI	TS8-1	5-Jun-52	1462.32	10
JEFFERSON	PB5-1	15-Jul-57	20.41	4	LATAH	PB6-3	26-Jul-57	12.28	4
JEFFERSON	TP7-1	29-Mar-55	5.26	3	LATAH	UK10-2	26-May-53	13.02	4
JEFFERSON	PB4-1	5-Jul-57	7.20	3	LATAH	PB6-2	25-Jul-57	21.00	4
JEFFERSON	PB15-1	16-Sep-57	7.62	3	LATAH	PB16-3	25-Sep-57	7.58	3
JEFFERSON	UK2-1	24-Mar-53	8.38	3	LATAH	PB17-3	30-Sep-57	9.52	3
JEFFERSON	TS5-1	7-May-52	28.32	5	LATAH	TS8-2	6-Jun-52	32.96	5
JEFFERSON	PB8-2	19-Aug-57	29.82	5	LATAH	TS8-1	5-Jun-52	5723.74	10
JEFFERSON	TS8-2	6-Jun-52	81.89	6	LEMHI	PB1-6	2-Jun-57	3.61	2
JEFFERSON	TS8-1	5-Jun-52	14222.14	10	LEMHI	UK8-2	9-May-53	3.64	2
JEROME	PB1-1	28-May-57	4.67	2	LEMHI	PB17-5	2-Oct-57	4.28	2
					LEMHI	TS8-3	7-Jun-52	10.35	4
					LEMHI	PB6-3	26-Jul-57	12.28	4

INDIVIDUAL FALLOUT DAYS
IDAHO

COUNTY	SHOT	DATE	µCi/SQ METER	INDEX	COUNTY	SHOT	DATE	µCi/SQ METER	INDEX
LEMHI	TS5-1	7-May-52	13.83	4	MADISON	PB5-1	15-Jul-57	20.41	4
LEMHI	PB6-2	25-Jul-57	21.00	4	MADISON	TS8-3	7-Jun-52	5.60	3
LEMHI	PB15-3	18-Sep-57	5.34	3	MADISON	PB4-1	5-Jul-57	7.20	3
LEMHI	PB16-3	25-Sep-57	7.58	3	MADISON	PB15-1	16-Sep-57	7.62	3
LEMHI	TS8-2	6-Jun-52	250.04	8	MADISON	PB6-2	25-Jul-57	7.94	3
LEMHI	TS8-1	5-Jun-52	43427.47	10	MADISON	UK2-1	24-Mar-53	8.38	3
LEWIS	PB6-2	25-Jul-57	10.55	4	MADISON	PB8-2	19-Aug-57	29.82	5
LEWIS	PB6-3	26-Jul-57	12.28	4	MADISON	TS8-2	6-Jun-52	43.00	5
LEWIS	UK10-2	26-May-53	5.12	3	MADISON	TS8-1	5-Jun-52	7467.81	10
LEWIS	TS5-1	7-May-52	6.11	3	MINIDOKA	TS6-1	25-May-52	4.09	2
LEWIS	PB16-3	25-Sep-57	7.58	3	MINIDOKA	PB5-1	15-Jul-57	4.18	2
LEWIS	TS8-2	6-Jun-52	110.37	7	MINIDOKA	PB1-1	28-May-57	4.67	2
LEWIS	TS8-1	5-Jun-52	19168.97	10	MINIDOKA	UK10-1	25-May-53	10.40	4
LINCOLN	PB8-1	18-Aug-57	4.02	2	MINIDOKA	PB6-2	25-Jul-57	11.04	4
LINCOLN	TS6-1	25-May-52	4.09	2	MINIDOKA	PB17-1	28-Sep-57	17.32	4
LINCOLN	PB1-1	28-May-57	4.59	2	MINIDOKA	PB15-1	16-Sep-57	6.49	3
LINCOLN	UK10-1	25-May-53	10.40	4	MINIDOKA	TS2-1	15-Apr-52	6.49	3
LINCOLN	PB6-2	25-Jul-57	11.04	4	MINIDOKA	TP11-1	15-May-55	7.03	3
LINCOLN	TP11-1	15-May-55	13.87	4	MINIDOKA	PB8-1	18-Aug-57	7.93	3
LINCOLN	PB17-1	28-Sep-57	17.32	4	MINIDOKA	PB16-1	23-Sep-57	8.18	3
LINCOLN	PB15-1	16-Sep-57	6.49	3	MINIDOKA	BJ5 1	19-Nov-51	9.14	3
LINCOLN	PB16-1	23-Sep-57	8.18	3	MINIDOKA	TS7-1	1-Jun-52	46.19	5
LINCOLN	BJ5 1	19-Nov-51	9.14	3	MINIDOKA	TS8-2	6-Jun-52	69.87	6
LINCOLN	TS2-1	15-Apr-52	9.28	3	MINIDOKA	TS8-1	5-Jun-52	12135.21	10
LINCOLN	TS7-1	1-Jun-52	27.43	5	NEZ PERCE	UK10-2	26-May-53	4.18	2
LINCOLN	TS8-2	6-Jun-52	104.81	7	NEZ PERCE	PB6-2	25-Jul-57	10.55	4
LINCOLN	TS8-1	5-Jun-52	18202.82	10	NEZ PERCE	PB6-3	26-Jul-57	12.28	4
MADISON	PB2-3	20-Jun-57	3.60	2	NEZ PERCE	PB16-4	26-Sep-57	5.16	3
MADISON	TS7-4	4-Jun-52	4.11	2	NEZ PERCE	PB17-3	30-Sep-57	6.34	3
MADISON	TP7-1	29-Mar-55	10.52	4	NEZ PERCE	PB16-3	25-Sep-57	7.58	3
MADISON	PB9-2	24-Aug-57	11.17	4	NEZ PERCE	TS8-2	6-Jun-52	49.21	5
MADISON	PB5-2	16-Jul-57	12.01	4					
MADISON	TS5-1	7-May-52	19.08	4					

INDIVIDUAL FALLOUT DAYS
IDAHO

COUNTY	SHOT	DATE	µCi/SQ METER	INDEX	COUNTY	SHOT	DATE	µCi/SQ METER	INDEX
NEZ PERCE	TS8-1	5-Jun-52	8545.97	10	PAYETTE	TS5-1	7-May-52	3.75	2
ONEIDA	TP10-1	5-May-55	3.88	2	PAYETTE	TP8-1	9-Apr-55	3.77	2
ONEIDA	TP9-1	15-Apr-55	4.03	2	PAYETTE	TP11-1	15-May-55	4.66	2
ONEIDA	PB1-1	28-May-57	4.67	2	PAYETTE	TS8-6	10-Jun-52	4.75	2
ONEIDA	PB9-1	23-Aug-57	10.07	4	PAYETTE	PB6-2	25-Jul-57	10.55	4
ONEIDA	UK10-1	25-May-53	10.40	4	PAYETTE	PB6-3	26-Jul-57	12.28	4
ONEIDA	PB6-2	25-Jul-57	11.04	4	PAYETTE	BJ5-2	20-Nov-51	19.72	4
ONEIDA	TS8-2	6-Jun-52	13.87	4	PAYETTE	PB16-3	25-Sep-57	7.58	3
ONEIDA	PB8-1	18-Aug-57	15.96	4	PAYETTE	TS8-3	7-Jun-52	7.67	3
ONEIDA	PB17-1	28-Sep-57	17.32	4	PAYETTE	PB17-3	30-Sep-57	9.52	3
ONEIDA	TP11-1	15-May-55	6.93	3	PAYETTE	BJ5-3	21-Nov-51	9.82	3
ONEIDA	PB16-1	23-Sep-57	8.07	3	PAYETTE	TS8-2	6-Jun-52	77.71	6
ONEIDA	TS6-1	25-May-52	8.18	3	PAYETTE	TS8-1	5-Jun-52	13496.85	10
ONEIDA	PB5-1	15-Jul-57	8.26	3	POWER	PB1-1	28-May-57	3.91	2
ONEIDA	PB12-1	2-Sep-57	8.81	3	POWER	TP9-1	15-Apr-55	4.03	2
ONEIDA	PB15-1	16-Sep-57	9.73	3	POWER	PB12-1	2-Sep-57	4.40	2
ONEIDA	UK2-1	24-Mar-53	87.55	6	POWER	UK2-1	24-Mar-53	4.96	2
ONEIDA	TS7-1	1-Jun-52	91.94	6	POWER	UK10-1	25-May-53	10.40	4
ONEIDA	TS8-1	5-Jun-52	2408.89	10	POWER	PB6-2	25-Jul-57	11.04	4
OWYHEE	UK10-1	25-May-53	10.54	4	POWER	PB17-1	28-Sep-57	17.32	4
OWYHEE	TS2-1	15-Apr-52	13.92	4	POWER	TS8-2	6-Jun-52	24.28	4
OWYHEE	PB6-2	25-Jul-57	14.71	4	POWER	PB9-1	23-Aug-57	5.10	3
OWYHEE	TS7-1	1-Jun-52	16.57	4	POWER	PB8-1	18-Aug-57	7.93	3
OWYHEE	PB16-1	23-Sep-57	16.70	4	POWER	PB16-1	23-Sep-57	8.07	3
OWYHEE	PB17-1	28-Sep-57	17.32	4	POWER	PB5-1	15-Jul-57	8.26	3
OWYHEE	TP11-1	15-May-55	22.36	4	POWER	PB15-1	16-Sep-57	9.73	3
OWYHEE	TS6-1	25-May-52	5.53	3	POWER	TS7-1	1-Jun-52	54.97	6
OWYHEE	PB1-1	28-May-57	7.73	3	POWER	TS8-1	5-Jun-52	4217.30	10
OWYHEE	BJ5 1	19-Nov-51	91.04	6	SHOSHONE	PB6-2	25-Jul-57	10.55	4
OWYHEE	TS8-2	6-Jun-52	104.81	7	SHOSHONE	PB6-3	26-Jul-57	12.28	4
OWYHEE	TS8-1	5-Jun-52	18202.82	10	SHOSHONE	UK10-2	26-May-53	5.33	3
PAYETTE	TP11-2	16-May-55	3.64	2	SHOSHONE	PB16-3	25-Sep-57	7.58	3

INDIVIDUAL FALLOUT DAYS
IDAHO

COUNTY	SHOT	DATE	µCi/SQ METER	INDEX	COUNTY	SHOT	DATE	µCi/SQ METER	INDEX
SHOSHONE	TS8-2	6-Jun-52	66.37	6	TWIN FALLS	TS7-1	1-Jun-52	91.29	6
SHOSHONE	TS8-1	5-Jun-52	11526.75	10	TWIN FALLS	TS8-1	5-Jun-52	12135.21	10
TETON	PB2-3	20-Jun-57	3.60	2	VALLEY	TS7-4	4-Jun-52	3.61	2
TETON	PB9-2	24-Aug-57	11.17	4	VALLEY	UK10-2	26-May-53	3.86	2
TETON	PB6-2	25-Jul-57	15.87	4	VALLEY	TP11-1	15-May-55	4.66	2
TETON	PB5-1	15-Jul-57	20.41	4	VALLEY	PB6-3	26-Jul-57	12.28	4
TETON	PB5-2	16-Jul-57	23.91	4	VALLEY	BJ5-3	21-Nov-51	19.64	4
TETON	TP7-1	29-Mar-55	5.26	3	VALLEY	BJ5-2	20-Nov-51	19.72	4
TETON	TS8-3	7-Jun-52	5.47	3	VALLEY	PB6-2	25-Jul-57	21.00	4
TETON	PB4-1	5-Jul-57	7.20	3	VALLEY	TS2-4	18-Apr-52	5.26	3
TETON	PB15-1	16-Sep-57	7.62	3	VALLEY	PB15-3	18-Sep-57	5.34	3
TETON	UK2-1	24-Mar-53	8.38	3	VALLEY	PB17-5	2-Oct-57	5.46	3
TETON	TS8-2	6-Jun-52	8.96	3	VALLEY	TP8-1	9-Apr-55	5.66	3
TETON	PB8-2	19-Aug-57	29.82	5	VALLEY	TP11-2	16-May-55	7.37	3
TETON	TS5-1	7-May-52	52.63	6	VALLEY	PB16-3	25-Sep-57	7.58	3
TETON	TS8-1	5-Jun-52	1555.38	10	VALLEY	TS8-3	7-Jun-52	7.81	3
TWIN FALLS	PB8-1	18-Aug-57	4.02	2	VALLEY	TS6-4	28-May-52	8.06	3
TWIN FALLS	PB15-1	16-Sep-57	4.03	2	VALLEY	TS5-1	7-May-52	9.34	3
TWIN FALLS	UK2-1	24-Mar-53	4.11	2	VALLEY	TS8-2	6-Jun-52	168.62	7
TWIN FALLS	PB1-1	28-May-57	4.67	2	VALLEY	TS8-1	5-Jun-52	29286.33	10
TWIN FALLS	UK10-1	25-May-53	10.54	4	WASHINGTON	TP11-2	16-May-55	3.64	2
TWIN FALLS	TS2-1	15-Apr-52	13.92	4	WASHINGTON	TP8-1	9-Apr-55	3.77	2
TWIN FALLS	PB6-2	25-Jul-57	14.71	4	WASHINGTON	TP9-2	15-Apr-55	3.97	2
TWIN FALLS	TP11-1	15-May-55	14.75	4	WASHINGTON	BJ5-7	25-Nov-51	4.05	2
TWIN FALLS	PB17-1	28-Sep-57	17.32	4	WASHINGTON	TP11-1	15-May-55	4.66	2
TWIN FALLS	BJ5 1	19-Nov-51	18.16	4	WASHINGTON	PB6-2	25-Jul-57	10.55	4
TWIN FALLS	PB16-1	23-Sep-57	8.29	3	WASHINGTON	PB6-3	26-Jul-57	12.28	4
TWIN FALLS	TS6-1	25-May-52	8.95	3	WASHINGTON	PB17-3	30-Sep-57	6.34	3
TWIN FALLS	TS8-2	6-Jun-52	69.87	6	WASHINGTON	PB16-3	25-Sep-57	7.58	3
					WASHINGTON	BJ5-3	21-Nov-51	9.82	3

INDIVIDUAL FALLOUT DAYS
IDAHO

COUNTY	SHOT	DATE	µCi/SQ METER	INDEX	COUNTY	SHOT	DATE	µCi/SQ METER	INDEX
WASHINGTON	BJ5-2	20-Nov-51	9.86	3	WASHINGTON	TS8-1	5-Jun-52	19741.35	10
WASHINGTON	TS8-2	6-Jun-52	113.67	7					

INDICIDUAL FALLOUT DAYS
ILLINOIS

COUNTY	SHOT	DATE	µCi/SQ METER	INDEX	COUNTY	SHOT	DATE	µCi/SQ METER	INDEX
ADAMS	PB6-4	27-Jul-57	3.82	2	BOONE	TS6-4	28-May-52	8.86	3
ADAMS	TP10-2	6-May-55	3.94	2	BOONE	SE3	8-Jul-62	146.81	7
ADAMS	TS7-4	4-Jun-52	4.20	2	BROWN	TP10-2	6-May-55	3.94	2
ADAMS	UK7-4	28-Apr-53	4.77	2	BROWN	UK9-2	20-May-53	4.52	2
ADAMS	PB9-3	25-Aug-57	13.72	4	BROWN	PB9-3	25-Aug-57	13.72	4
ADAMS	PB9-4	26-Aug-57	16.67	4	BROWN	TP10-3	7-May-55	5.42	3
ADAMS	TS5-2	8-May-52	5.08	3	BROWN	TS6-4	28-May-52	6.75	3
ADAMS	TS1-2	2-Apr-52	6.13	3	BROWN	TS7-5	5-Jun-52	7.30	3
ADAMS	UK9-2	20-May-53	6.23	3	BROWN	TS1-3	3-Apr-52	7.62	3
ADAMS	TS6-4	28-May-52	6.75	3	BROWN	PB9-4	26-Aug-57	33.34	5
ADAMS	TS7-5	5-Jun-52	8.17	3	BROWN	SE3	8-Jul-62	200.06	8
ADAMS	TP10-3	7-May-55	8.70	3	BUREAU	UK9-3	21-May-53	3.54	2
ADAMS	TS7-3	3-Jun-52	96.56	6	BUREAU	TS7-3	3-Jun-52	11.49	4
ADAMS	SE3	8-Jul-62	200.06	8	BUREAU	UK9-2	20-May-53	13.32	4
ALEXANDER	UK9-4	22-May-53	3.57	2	BUREAU	PB9-3	25-Aug-57	13.72	4
ALEXANDER	TP10-3	7-May-55	3.65	2	BUREAU	UK7-4	28-Apr-53	7.75	3
ALEXANDER	PB6-3	26-Jul-57	4.63	2	BUREAU	PB9-4	26-Aug-57	8.37	3
ALEXANDER	TS7-5	5-Jun-52	4.67	2	CALHOUN	UK2-3	26-Mar-53	3.65	2
ALEXANDER	UK7-4	28-Apr-53	12.94	4	CALHOUN	TP10-3	7-May-55	4.33	2
ALEXANDER	TS1-3	3-Apr-52	15.04	4	CALHOUN	PB6-4	27-Jul-57	4.35	2
BOND	TP10-3	7-May-55	3.94	2	CALHOUN	UK7-4	28-Apr-53	4.57	2
BOND	TS5-1	7-May-52	10.24	4	CALHOUN	TS1-2	2-Apr-52	11.93	4
BOND	UK7-4	28-Apr-53	11.33	4	CALHOUN	PB9-3	25-Aug-57	13.72	4
BOND	TS1-3	3-Apr-52	12.63	4	CALHOUN	TS5-1	7-May-52	14.55	4
BOND	TS6-4	28-May-52	7.71	3	CALHOUN	TS7-5	5-Jun-52	7.30	3
BOND	SE3	8-Jul-62	90.94	6	CALHOUN	PB9-4	26-Aug-57	8.37	3
BOONE	PB9-5	27-Aug-57	3.55	2	CALHOUN	SE3	8-Jul-62	90.94	6
BOONE	TS5-1	7-May-52	3.60	2	CARROLL	TS5-1	7-May-52	3.60	2
BOONE	PB9-3	25-Aug-57	13.72	4	CARROLL	PB5-7	21-Jul-57	4.15	2
BOONE	UK9-2	20-May-53	15.08	4	CARROLL	PB9-3	25-Aug-57	13.72	4
BOONE	PB9-4	26-Aug-57	16.67	4	CARROLL	PB9-4	26-Aug-57	8.37	3
BOONE	UK7-4	28-Apr-53	6.24	3	CARROLL	UK9-2	20-May-53	35.38	5
BOONE	TS7-5	5-Jun-52	7.13	3	CASS	UK9-2	20-May-53	3.70	2

INDIVIDUAL FALLOUT DAYS
ILLINOIS

COUNTY	SHOT	DATE	µCi/SQ METER	INDEX	COUNTY	SHOT	DATE	µCi/SQ METER	INDEX
CASS	TP10-2	6-May-55	3.94	2	CLARK	TS5-1	7-May-52	5.61	3
CASS	TP4-3	9-Mar-55	4.20	2	CLARK	TS6-4	28-May-52	5.64	3
CASS	TS7-5	5-Jun-52	4.40	2	CLARK	PB3-4	27-Jun-57	6.27	3
CASS	TS7-3	3-Jun-52	10.55	4	CLARK	UK9-3	21-May-53	7.96	3
CASS	PB9-3	25-Aug-57	13.72	4	CLARK	TS1-3	3-Apr-52	9.42	3
CASS	TS6-4	28-May-52	14.46	4	CLARK	SE3	8-Jul-62	99.74	6
CASS	PB9-4	26-Aug-57	16.67	4	CLAY	UK7-4	28-Apr-53	4.73	2
CASS	TS1-3	3-Apr-52	7.62	3	CLAY	PB5-3	17-Jul-57	4.85	2
CASS	TP10-3	7-May-55	25.02	5	CLAY	TP10-3	7-May-55	12.35	4
CASS	SE3	8-Jul-62	200.06	8	CLAY	UK9-4	22-May-53	6.53	3
CHAMPAIGN	UK9-3	21-May-53	3.91	2	CLAY	TS5-1	7-May-52	7.64	3
CHAMPAIGN	TS6-4	28-May-52	14.46	4	CLAY	TS6-4	28-May-52	7.71	3
CHAMPAIGN	TS1-3	3-Apr-52	5.61	3	CLAY	TS1-3	3-Apr-52	9.42	3
CHAMPAIGN	UK7-4	28-Apr-53	7.00	3	CLAY	SE3	8-Jul-62	35.48	5
CHAMPAIGN	TP10-3	7-May-55	8.63	3	CLAY	TS7-3	3-Jun-52	39.14	5
CHAMPAIGN	TS7-3	3-Jun-52	49.56	5	CLAY	SE4	9-Jul-62	57.04	6
CHAMPAIGN	SE3	8-Jul-62	99.74	6	CLINTON	TP10-3	7-May-55	3.89	2
CHRISTIAN	TP10-3	7-May-55	3.63	2	CLINTON	PB5-3	17-Jul-57	4.85	2
CHRISTIAN	UK9-3	21-May-53	3.83	2	CLINTON	TS1-3	3-Apr-52	12.63	4
CHRISTIAN	TP4-3	9-Mar-55	4.25	2	CLINTON	TS5-1	7-May-52	5.93	3
CHRISTIAN	PB9-3	25-Aug-57	13.72	4	CLINTON	UK7-4	28-Apr-53	7.31	3
CHRISTIAN	TS5-1	7-May-52	6.29	3	CLINTON	TS6-4	28-May-52	7.71	3
CHRISTIAN	TS1-3	3-Apr-52	7.62	3	COLES	TP10-3	7-May-55	4.22	2
CHRISTIAN	TS6-4	28-May-52	7.71	3	COLES	TS5-1	7-May-52	4.35	2
CHRISTIAN	PB9-4	26-Aug-57	8.37	3	COLES	PB3-4	27-Jun-57	4.78	2
CHRISTIAN	UK7-4	28-Apr-53	9.14	3	COLES	UK7-4	28-Apr-53	12.88	4
CHRISTIAN	SE3	8-Jul-62	76.52	6	COLES	UK9-3	21-May-53	5.53	3
CHRISTIAN	TS7-3	3-Jun-52	111.90	7	COLES	TS6-4	28-May-52	6.75	3
CLARK	UK7-4	28-Apr-53	4.28	2	COLES	TS1-3	3-Apr-52	9.42	3
CLARK	TP10-3	7-May-55	4.41	2	COLES	TS7-3	3-Jun-52	45.32	5
CLARK	PB9-5	27-Aug-57	4.52	2	COLES	SE3	8-Jul-62	200.06	8
CLARK	TS7-3	3-Jun-52	18.15	4	COOK	UK7-4	28-Apr-53	3.57	2
CLARK	TP5-3	14-Mar-55	5.00	3	COOK	TS7-3	3-Jun-52	4.42	2

INDIVIDUAL FALLOUT DAYS
ILLINOIS

COUNTY	SHOT	DATE	µCi/SQ METER	INDEX	COUNTY	SHOT	DATE	µCi/SQ METER	INDEX
COOK	PB9-5	27-Aug-57	4.52	2	DE WITT	TP10-3	7-May-55	3.78	2
COOK	TS6-4	28-May-52	13.50	4	DE WITT	TP4-3	9-Mar-55	4.00	2
COOK	TP5-3	14-Mar-55	5.11	3	DE WITT	TS6-4	28-May-52	16.39	4
COOK	UK9-2	20-May-53	5.97	3	DE WITT	TS1-3	3-Apr-52	7.62	3
CRAWFORD	TS5-1	7-May-52	3.62	2	DE WITT	TS7-3	3-Jun-52	39.66	5
CRAWFORD	PB3-4	27-Jun-57	4.25	2	DE WITT	SE3	8-Jul-62	139.13	7
CRAWFORD	PB9-5	27-Aug-57	4.52	2	DOUGLAS	UK7-4	28-Apr-53	4.01	2
CRAWFORD	TP5-3	14-Mar-55	4.85	2	DOUGLAS	TP10-3	7-May-55	4.22	2
CRAWFORD	TP10-3	7-May-55	22.62	4	DOUGLAS	PB4-4	8-Jul-57	4.29	2
CRAWFORD	TS1-3	3-Apr-52	5.61	3	DOUGLAS	TP5-3	14-Mar-55	4.39	2
CRAWFORD	UK9-3	21-May-53	6.41	3	DOUGLAS	PB3-4	27-Jun-57	4.51	2
CRAWFORD	TS6-4	28-May-52	6.75	3	DOUGLAS	TS6-4	28-May-52	13.50	4
CRAWFORD	UK7-4	28-Apr-53	8.87	3	DOUGLAS	TP4-3	9-Mar-55	5.14	3
CRAWFORD	TS7-3	3-Jun-52	39.07	5	DOUGLAS	UK9-3	21-May-53	6.12	3
CUMBERLAND	UK7-4	28-Apr-53	3.80	2	DOUGLAS	TS1-3	3-Apr-52	9.42	3
CUMBERLAND	TP5-3	14-Mar-55	3.98	2	DOUGLAS	SE3	8-Jul-62	80.75	6
CUMBERLAND	TP10-3	7-May-55	4.22	2	DOUGLAS	TS7-3	3-Jun-52	104.67	7
CUMBERLAND	PB3-4	27-Jun-57	4.95	2	DU PAGE	TS7-3	3-Jun-52	21.90	4
CUMBERLAND	TP4-3	9-Mar-55	10.88	4	DU PAGE	TP5-3	14-Mar-55	5.99	3
CUMBERLAND	UK9-3	21-May-53	5.01	3	DU PAGE	UK9-2	20-May-53	7.37	3
CUMBERLAND	UK9-4	22-May-53	5.36	3	DU PAGE	TS6-4	28-May-52	25.07	5
CUMBERLAND	TS1-3	3-Apr-52	9.42	3	EDGAR	PB4-4	8-Jul-57	3.72	2
CUMBERLAND	SE3	8-Jul-62	80.75	6	EDGAR	TP10-3	7-May-55	4.41	2
DE KALB	UK7-4	28-Apr-53	3.80	2	EDGAR	UK7-4	28-Apr-53	4.44	2
DE KALB	PB6-5	28-Jul-57	3.87	2	EDGAR	TS7-3	3-Jun-52	20.89	4
DE KALB	TS6-4	28-May-52	4.03	2	EDGAR	TS5-1	7-May-52	5.36	3
DE KALB	UK9-2	20-May-53	12.37	4	EDGAR	TS1-3	3-Apr-52	5.61	3
DE KALB	PB9-3	25-Aug-57	13.72	4	EDGAR	PB3-4	27-Jun-57	6.05	3
DE KALB	TS7-3	3-Jun-52	14.84	4	EDGAR	UK9-3	21-May-53	7.15	3
DE KALB	TP5-3	14-Mar-55	5.97	3	EDGAR	SE3	8-Jul-62	80.75	6
DE KALB	PB9-4	26-Aug-57	33.34	5	EDWARDS	TP10-3	7-May-55	3.84	2
DE WITT	TP5-3	14-Mar-55	3.52	2	EDWARDS	PB3-4	27-Jun-57	4.53	2
DE WITT	UK7-4	28-Apr-53	3.74	2	EDWARDS	TS7-3	3-Jun-52	13.71	4

INDIVIDUAL FALLOUT DAYS
ILLINOIS

COUNTY	SHOT	DATE	µCi/SQ METER	INDEX	COUNTY	SHOT	DATE	µCi/SQ METER	INDEX
EDWARDS	UK7-4	28-Apr-53	6.47	3	FULTON	UK7-4	28-Apr-53	10.71	4
EDWARDS	UK9-3	21-May-53	6.64	3	FULTON	PB9-3	25-Aug-57	13.72	4
EDWARDS	TP5-3	14-Mar-55	6.64	3	FULTON	PB9-4	26-Aug-57	16.67	4
EDWARDS	TS7-6	6-Jun-52	6.98	3	FULTON	UK9-2	20-May-53	6.59	3
EDWARDS	TS5-1	7-May-52	7.34	3	FULTON	TS1-3	3-Apr-52	7.62	3
EDWARDS	TS1-3	3-Apr-52	9.42	3	FULTON	TP4-3	9-Mar-55	7.76	3
EFFINGHAM	TP10-3	7-May-55	4.16	2	FULTON	TS6-4	28-May-52	9.64	3
EFFINGHAM	PB3-4	27-Jun-57	4.29	2	FULTON	SE3	8-Jul-62	345.56	8
EFFINGHAM	PB6-4	27-Jul-57	4.45	2	GALLATIN	TS1-4	4-Apr-52	4.22	2
EFFINGHAM	TS5-1	7-May-52	4.80	2	GALLATIN	TS1-3	3-Apr-52	5.61	3
EFFINGHAM	UK9-3	21-May-53	5.31	3	GALLATIN	TS7-6	6-Jun-52	6.34	3
EFFINGHAM	PB5-3	17-Jul-57	7.27	3	GALLATIN	PB5-3	17-Jul-57	7.27	3
EFFINGHAM	TS6-4	28-May-52	7.71	3	GREENE	TP4-3	9-Mar-55	3.86	2
EFFINGHAM	TS1-3	3-Apr-52	9.42	3	GREENE	TP10-3	7-May-55	3.98	2
EFFINGHAM	SE3	8-Jul-62	80.75	6	GREENE	UK7-4	28-Apr-53	4.64	2
EFFINGHAM	TS7-3	3-Jun-52	98.20	6	GREENE	TS6-4	28-May-52	13.50	4
FAYETTE	TP10-3	7-May-55	3.68	2	GREENE	PB9-3	25-Aug-57	13.72	4
FAYETTE	UK7-4	28-Apr-53	11.28	4	GREENE	PB4-4	8-Jul-57	15.17	4
FAYETTE	TS5-1	7-May-52	7.94	3	GREENE	TS7-5	5-Jun-52	6.68	3
FAYETTE	TS1-3	3-Apr-52	9.42	3	GREENE	TS1-3	3-Apr-52	7.62	3
FAYETTE	SE3	8-Jul-62	90.94	6	GREENE	TS5-1	7-May-52	7.64	3
FORD	UK9-3	21-May-53	3.98	2	GREENE	PB9-4	26-Aug-57	8.37	3
FORD	UK7-4	28-Apr-53	4.38	2	GREENE	SE3	8-Jul-62	200.06	8
FORD	TS6-4	28-May-52	15.43	4	GRUNDY	TP10-3	7-May-55	4.94	2
FORD	UK9-2	20-May-53	5.41	3	GRUNDY	UK7-4	28-Apr-53	13.45	4
FORD	TS1-3	3-Apr-52	5.61	3	GRUNDY	TS6-4	28-May-52	21.21	4
FORD	TS7-3	3-Jun-52	123.56	7	GRUNDY	UK9-2	20-May-53	7.95	3
FRANKLIN	TP10-3	7-May-55	3.91	2	GRUNDY	TS7-3	3-Jun-52	46.48	5
FRANKLIN	PB9-2	24-Aug-57	8.19	3	HAMILTON	TP10-3	7-May-55	3.72	2
FRANKLIN	TS1-3	3-Apr-52	9.42	3	HAMILTON	PB3-4	27-Jun-57	3.84	2
FULTON	TS5-1	7-May-52	3.65	2	HAMILTON	UK9-4	22-May-53	3.92	2
FULTON	TS8-5	9-Jun-52	3.82	2	HAMILTON	UK7-4	28-Apr-53	5.89	3
FULTON	TP10-3	7-May-55	3.84	2	HAMILTON	TS1-3	3-Apr-52	9.42	3

INDIVIDUAL FALLOUT DAYS
ILLINOIS

COUNTY	SHOT	DATE	µCi/SQ METER	INDEX	COUNTY	SHOT	DATE	µCi/SQ METER	INDEX
HANCOCK	TS5-1	7-May-52	3.74	2	IROQUOIS	UK9-2	20-May-53	5.31	3
HANCOCK	TP10-2	6-May-55	3.94	2	IROQUOIS	TS1-3	3-Apr-52	5.61	3
HANCOCK	UK7-4	28-Apr-53	4.28	2	IROQUOIS	TS7-3	3-Jun-52	65.63	6
HANCOCK	PB9-3	25-Aug-57	13.72	4	JACKSON	TP10-3	7-May-55	3.52	2
HANCOCK	UK9-2	20-May-53	20.27	4	JACKSON	PB9-2	24-Aug-57	5.46	3
HANCOCK	TP10-3	7-May-55	5.10	3	JACKSON	TS1-3	3-Apr-52	5.61	3
HANCOCK	TS5-2	8-May-52	5.29	3	JACKSON	UK7-4	28-Apr-53	9.36	3
HANCOCK	TS7-5	5-Jun-52	5.68	3	JASPER	TP5-3	14-Mar-55	3.98	2
HANCOCK	PB18-8	17-Jul-57	6.63	3	JASPER	TS5-1	7-May-52	4.65	2
HANCOCK	TS1-3	3-Apr-52	7.62	3	JASPER	PB5-3	17-Jul-57	4.85	2
HANCOCK	PB9-4	26-Aug-57	33.34	5	JASPER	TP10-3	7-May-55	12.66	4
HANCOCK	SE3	8-Jul-62	621.15	9	JASPER	UK7-4	28-Apr-53	6.31	3
HARDIN	UK7-4	28-Apr-53	4.46	2	JASPER	TS6-4	28-May-52	6.75	3
HARDIN	TS1-3	3-Apr-52	9.42	3	JASPER	TS1-3	3-Apr-52	9.42	3
HENDERSON	TP10-3	7-May-55	3.78	2	JASPER	TS7-3	3-Jun-52	97.35	6
HENDERSON	TP10-2	6-May-55	3.94	2	JASPER	SE3	8-Jul-62	99.74	6
HENDERSON	PB18-8	17-Jul-57	3.98	2	JEFFERSON	TP10-3	7-May-55	4.10	2
HENDERSON	TS5-1	7-May-52	10.64	4	JEFFERSON	TS6-4	28-May-52	13.50	4
HENDERSON	UK9-2	20-May-53	12.37	4	JEFFERSON	TS5-1	7-May-52	5.57	3
HENDERSON	PB9-3	25-Aug-57	13.72	4	JEFFERSON	UK9-4	22-May-53	6.75	3
HENDERSON	PB9-4	26-Aug-57	16.67	4	JEFFERSON	UK7-4	28-Apr-53	8.82	3
HENDERSON	TS7-3	3-Jun-52	21.90	4	JEFFERSON	TS1-3	3-Apr-52	9.42	3
HENDERSON	TS6-4	28-May-52	7.71	3	JEFFERSON	SE4	9-Jul-62	37.08	5
HENDERSON	UK7-4	28-Apr-53	8.42	3	JERSEY	UK2-3	26-Mar-53	3.65	2
HENDERSON	SE3	8-Jul-62	139.13	7	JERSEY	TP10-3	7-May-55	4.02	2
HENRY	PB18-8	17-Jul-57	3.98	2	JERSEY	TS7-5	5-Jun-52	4.60	2
HENRY	PB9-3	25-Aug-57	13.72	4	JERSEY	PB6-4	27-Jul-57	4.79	2
HENRY	PB9-4	26-Aug-57	16.67	4	JERSEY	TS1-3	3-Apr-52	12.63	4
HENRY	UK9-2	20-May-53	16.89	4	JERSEY	TS5-1	7-May-52	13.65	4
HENRY	SE3	8-Jul-62	139.13	7	JERSEY	PB9-3	25-Aug-57	13.72	4
IROQUOIS	TP5-3	14-Mar-55	3.57	2	JERSEY	R1-2	29-Jan-51	15.59	4
IROQUOIS	UK7-4	28-Apr-53	4.81	2	JERSEY	TS7-3	3-Jun-52	6.25	3
IROQUOIS	TS6-4	28-May-52	14.46	4	JERSEY	TS6-4	28-May-52	7.71	3

INDIVIDUAL FALLOUT DAYS
ILLINOIS

COUNTY	SHOT	DATE	µCi/SQ METER	INDEX	COUNTY	SHOT	DATE	µCi/SQ METER	INDEX
JERSEY	PB9-4	26-Aug-57	8.37	3	KNOX	TS1-3	3-Apr-52	5.01	3
JERSEY	SE3	8-Jul-62	90.94	6	KNOX	TS7-3	3-Jun-52	5.64	3
JO DAVIESS	TS5-1	7-May-52	3.59	2	KNOX	TP10-3	7-May-55	5.99	3
JO DAVIESS	PB18-8	17-Jul-57	3.98	2	KNOX	UK7-4	28-Apr-53	6.84	3
JO DAVIESS	PB5-7	21-Jul-57	4.15	2	KNOX	PB9-4	26-Aug-57	8.37	3
JO DAVIESS	UK7-4	28-Apr-53	11.22	4	KNOX	UK9-2	20-May-53	10.03	4
JO DAVIESS	TS7-5	5-Jun-52	6.51	3	KNOX	TS6-4	28-May-52	10.61	4
JO DAVIESS	UK9-2	20-May-53	31.94	5	KNOX	PB9-3	25-Aug-57	13.72	4
JOHNSON	TS5-2	8-May-52	3.69	2	KNOX	SE3	8-Jul-62	139.13	7
JOHNSON	UK7-4	28-Apr-53	9.25	3	LA SALLE	TS5-1	7-May-52	4.35	2
JOHNSON	PB9-3	25-Aug-57	13.72	4	LA SALLE	TS1-3	3-Apr-52	5.01	3
JOHNSON	TS1-3	3-Apr-52	5.61	3	LA SALLE	UK7-4	28-Apr-53	8.50	3
JOHNSON	PB5-3	17-Jul-57	7.27	3	LA SALLE	UK9-2	20-May-53	9.96	3
JOHNSON	PB9-4	26-Aug-57	33.34	5	LA SALLE	PB9-3	25-Aug-57	13.72	4
KANE	TP5-3	14-Mar-55	5.65	3	LA SALLE	PB9-4	26-Aug-57	16.67	4
KANE	UK9-2	20-May-53	9.94	3	LA SALLE	TS6-4	28-May-52	23.14	4
KANE	PB9-3	25-Aug-57	13.72	4	LA SALLE	TS7-3	3-Jun-52	31.06	5
KANE	TS6-4	28-May-52	15.43	4	LAKE	TS7-5	5-Jun-52	4.44	2
KANE	PB9-4	26-Aug-57	16.67	4	LAKE	TP5-3	14-Mar-55	6.20	3
KANE	TS7-3	3-Jun-52	17.45	4	LAKE	UK7-4	28-Apr-53	9.19	3
KANKAKEE	TS1-3	3-Apr-52	3.81	2	LAKE	UK9-2	20-May-53	10.37	4
KANKAKEE	UK7-4	28-Apr-53	4.60	2	LAKE	TS7-3	3-Jun-52	15.68	4
KANKAKEE	UK9-2	20-May-53	5.15	3	LAKE	TS6-4	28-May-52	32.79	5
KANKAKEE	TP5-3	14-Mar-55	5.35	3	LAWRENCE	UK7-4	28-Apr-53	4.01	2
KANKAKEE	TP10-3	7-May-55	5.56	3	LAWRENCE	TP10-3	7-May-55	4.22	2
KANKAKEE	TS6-4	28-May-52	17.36	4	LAWRENCE	TP5-3	14-Mar-55	4.80	2
KANKAKEE	TS7-3	3-Jun-52	61.46	6	LAWRENCE	TS1-3	3-Apr-52	9.42	3
KENDALL	UK7-4	28-Apr-53	3.96	2	LAWRENCE	TS7-3	3-Jun-52	82.37	6
KENDALL	TP5-3	14-Mar-55	5.27	3	LEE	UK7-4	28-Apr-53	3.58	2
KENDALL	UK9-2	20-May-53	5.94	3	LEE	TS5-1	7-May-52	3.90	2
KENDALL	TS6-4	28-May-52	13.50	4	LEE	TP5-3	14-Mar-55	4.49	2
KENDALL	TS7-3	3-Jun-52	19.64	4	LEE	PB9-4	26-Aug-57	8.37	3
KNOX	PB9-5	27-Aug-57	3.55	2	LEE	PB9-3	25-Aug-57	13.72	4

INDIVIDUAL FALLOUT DAYS
ILLINOIS

COUNTY	SHOT	DATE	µCi/SQ METER	INDEX	COUNTY	SHOT	DATE	µCi/SQ METER	INDEX
LEE	UK9-2	20-May-53	14.40	4	MACOUPIN	TS1-3	3-Apr-52	12.63	4
LEE	TS6-4	28-May-52	14.46	4	MACOUPIN	TS5-1	7-May-52	13.29	4
LEE	TS7-3	3-Jun-52	27.41	5	MACOUPIN	PB9-3	25-Aug-57	13.72	4
LIVINGSTON	UK9-2	20-May-53	4.06	2	MACOUPIN	SE3	8-Jul-62	200.06	8
LIVINGSTON	TP10-3	7-May-55	8.20	3	MADISON	TS1-3	3-Apr-52	7.62	3
LIVINGSTON	UK7-4	28-Apr-53	13.77	4	MADISON	PB9-4	26-Aug-57	8.37	3
LIVINGSTON	TS6-4	28-May-52	19.29	4	MADISON	TS5-1	7-May-52	11.50	4
LIVINGSTON	TP4-3	9-Mar-55	3.51	1	MADISON	PB9-3	25-Aug-57	13.72	4
LIVINGSTON	TS8-5	9-Jun-52	3.51	1	MARION	UK9-4	22-May-53	3.86	2
LIVINGSTON	TS7-3	3-Jun-52	39.19	5	MARION	TP10-3	7-May-55	4.28	2
LOGAN	UK9-2	20-May-53	3.52	2	MARION	TS5-1	7-May-52	5.75	3
LOGAN	TP4-3	9-Mar-55	4.40	2	MARION	TS6-4	28-May-52	7.71	3
LOGAN	TS1-3	3-Apr-52	7.62	3	MARION	UK7-4	28-Apr-53	8.77	3
LOGAN	TP10-3	7-May-55	11.72	4	MARION	TS1-3	3-Apr-52	9.42	3
LOGAN	UK7-4	28-Apr-53	11.99	4	MARSHALL	TS1-3	3-Apr-52	5.01	3
LOGAN	PB9-3	25-Aug-57	13.72	4	MARSHALL	UK7-4	28-Apr-53	8.34	3
LOGAN	TS6-4	28-May-52	16.39	4	MARSHALL	UK9-2	20-May-53	11.69	4
LOGAN	TS7-3	3-Jun-52	17.33	4	MARSHALL	PB9-3	25-Aug-57	13.72	4
LOGAN	PB9-4	26-Aug-57	33.34	5	MARSHALL	PB9-4	26-Aug-57	16.67	4
LOGAN	SE3	8-Jul-62	76.52	6	MARSHALL	SE3	8-Jul-62	172.89	7
MACON	UK9-3	21-May-53	3.98	2	MASON	TP4-3	9-Mar-55	4.10	2
MACON	TP4-3	9-Mar-55	4.00	2	MASON	UK9-2	20-May-53	5.06	3
MACON	TP10-3	7-May-55	4.03	2	MASON	TS7-3	3-Jun-52	6.92	3
MACON	PB4-4	8-Jul-57	6.80	3	MASON	TS1-3	3-Apr-52	7.62	3
MACON	TS1-3	3-Apr-52	7.62	3	MASON	UK7-4	28-Apr-53	11.22	4
MACON	UK7-4	28-Apr-53	11.67	4	MASON	TP10-3	7-May-55	12.22	4
MACON	TS6-4	28-May-52	15.43	4	MASON	PB9-3	25-Aug-57	13.72	4
MACON	SE3	8-Jul-62	76.52	6	MASON	TS6-4	28-May-52	16.39	4
MACON	TS7-3	3-Jun-52	106.89	7	MASON	PB9-4	26-Aug-57	16.67	4
MACOUPIN	TP10-3	7-May-55	3.59	2	MASON	SE3	8-Jul-62	139.13	7
MACOUPIN	TP4-3	9-Mar-55	4.19	2	MASSAC	TS7-6	6-Jun-52	4.45	2
MACOUPIN	UK7-4	28-Apr-53	7.45	3	MASSAC	PB5-3	17-Jul-57	7.27	3
MACOUPIN	PB9-4	26-Aug-57	8.37	3	MASSAC	TS1-3	3-Apr-52	9.02	3

INDIVIDUAL FALLOUT DAYS
ILLINOIS

COUNTY	SHOT	DATE	µCi/SQ METER	INDEX	COUNTY	SHOT	DATE	µCi/SQ METER	INDEX
MCDONOUGH	TS5-2	8-May-52	4.17	2	MENARD	PB9-3	25-Aug-57	13.72	4
MCDONOUGH	TP10-3	7-May-55	4.35	2	MENARD	TS6-4	28-May-52	16.39	4
MCDONOUGH	UK7-4	28-Apr-53	4.76	2	MENARD	SE3	8-Jul-62	76.52	6
MCDONOUGH	TS1-3	3-Apr-52	7.62	3	MERCER	PB18-8	17-Jul-57	3.98	2
MCDONOUGH	TS6-4	28-May-52	7.71	3	MERCER	TS6-4	28-May-52	4.03	2
MCDONOUGH	UK9-2	20-May-53	12.78	4	MERCER	UK7-4	28-Apr-53	4.33	2
MCDONOUGH	PB9-3	25-Aug-57	13.72	4	MERCER	TS5-1	7-May-52	5.84	3
MCDONOUGH	PB9-4	26-Aug-57	33.34	5	MERCER	PB9-3	25-Aug-57	13.72	4
MCDONOUGH	SE3	8-Jul-62	345.56	8	MERCER	UK9-2	20-May-53	14.36	4
MCHENRY	TS7-3	3-Jun-52	4.61	2	MERCER	PB9-4	26-Aug-57	16.67	4
MCHENRY	TP5-3	14-Mar-55	5.91	3	MERCER	SE3	8-Jul-62	139.13	7
MCHENRY	UK7-4	28-Apr-53	6.60	3	MONROE	PB6-4	27-Jul-57	3.71	2
MCHENRY	TS6-4	28-May-52	8.86	3	MONROE	TS1-3	3-Apr-52	4.01	2
MCHENRY	UK9-2	20-May-53	13.64	4	MONROE	UK2-3	26-Mar-53	4.56	2
MCHENRY	PB9-3	25-Aug-57	13.72	4	MONROE	TS6-4	28-May-52	6.75	3
MCHENRY	PB9-4	26-Aug-57	16.67	4	MONROE	PB9-3	25-Aug-57	13.72	4
MCLEAN	UK9-3	21-May-53	3.69	2	MONROE	TP10-3	7-May-55	19.92	4
MCLEAN	TP4-3	9-Mar-55	3.85	2	MONTGOMERY	TP10-3	7-May-55	3.89	2
MCLEAN	TP5-3	14-Mar-55	3.88	2	MONTGOMERY	TP4-3	9-Mar-55	4.25	2
MCLEAN	UK9-2	20-May-53	4.06	2	MONTGOMERY	TS5-1	7-May-52	6.14	3
MCLEAN	TS8-5	9-Jun-52	4.18	2	MONTGOMERY	TS6-4	28-May-52	7.71	3
MCLEAN	UK7-4	28-Apr-53	6.63	3	MONTGOMERY	PB9-4	26-Aug-57	8.37	3
MCLEAN	TS1-3	3-Apr-52	7.62	3	MONTGOMERY	UK7-4	28-Apr-53	8.93	3
MCLEAN	TS7-3	3-Jun-52	17.33	4	MONTGOMERY	TS1-3	3-Apr-52	12.63	4
MCLEAN	TS6-4	28-May-52	17.36	4	MONTGOMERY	PB9-3	25-Aug-57	13.72	4
MCLEAN	SE3	8-Jul-62	146.81	7	MONTGOMERY	SE3	8-Jul-62	200.06	8
MENARD	TP10-2	6-May-55	3.94	2	MORGAN	TS5-2	8-May-52	4.04	2
MENARD	TP10-3	7-May-55	4.28	2	MORGAN	PB6-4	27-Jul-57	4.08	2
MENARD	TP4-3	9-Mar-55	4.54	2	MORGAN	TP10-3	7-May-55	4.26	2
MENARD	TS7-3	3-Jun-52	7.31	3	MORGAN	TP4-3	9-Mar-55	4.59	2
MENARD	TS1-3	3-Apr-52	7.62	3	MORGAN	TS7-5	5-Jun-52	6.31	3
MENARD	PB9-4	26-Aug-57	8.37	3	MORGAN	TS1-3	3-Apr-52	7.62	3
MENARD	UK7-4	28-Apr-53	9.36	3	MORGAN	TS5-1	7-May-52	7.94	3

INDIGENOUS FALLOUT DAYS
ILLINOIS

COUNTY	SHOT	DATE	µCi/SQ METER	INDEX	COUNTY	SHOT	DATE	µCi/SQ METER	INDEX
MORGAN	UK7-4	28-Apr-53	8.82	3	PIATT	UK7-4	28-Apr-53	3.85	2
MORGAN	PB9-3	25-Aug-57	13.72	4	PIATT	TP10-3	7-May-55	3.97	2
MORGAN	PB9-4	26-Aug-57	33.34	5	PIATT	TS1-3	3-Apr-52	7.62	3
MORGAN	SE3	8-Jul-62	76.52	6	PIATT	TS6-4	28-May-52	14.46	4
MOULTRIE	UK7-4	28-Apr-53	3.64	2	PIATT	TP4-3	9-Mar-55	3.51	1
MOULTRIE	PB3-4	27-Jun-57	3.72	2	PIATT	SE3	8-Jul-62	80.75	6
MOULTRIE	TP10-3	7-May-55	4.16	2	PIATT	TS7-3	3-Jun-52	114.52	7
MOULTRIE	TS5-1	7-May-52	4.80	2	PIKE	UK2-3	26-Mar-53	3.52	2
MOULTRIE	UK9-3	21-May-53	5.46	3	PIKE	PB6-4	27-Jul-57	3.86	2
MOULTRIE	TS1-3	3-Apr-52	9.42	3	PIKE	TS1-2	2-Apr-52	6.13	3
MOULTRIE	TS7-3	3-Jun-52	113.03	7	PIKE	TS6-4	28-May-52	6.75	3
MOULTRIE	SE3	8-Jul-62	200.06	8	PIKE	TS7-5	5-Jun-52	7.59	3
OGLE	TS7-3	3-Jun-52	4.13	2	PIKE	UK7-4	28-Apr-53	7.97	3
OGLE	TP5-3	14-Mar-55	4.75	2	PIKE	TS5-1	7-May-52	8.09	3
OGLE	TS5-1	7-May-52	5.09	3	PIKE	TP10-3	7-May-55	10.78	4
OGLE	UK7-4	28-Apr-53	5.67	3	PIKE	PB9-4	26-Aug-57	16.67	4
OGLE	PB9-3	25-Aug-57	13.72	4	PIKE	PB9-3	25-Aug-57	27.43	5
OGLE	TS6-4	28-May-52	15.43	4	PIKE	TS7-3	3-Jun-52	40.27	5
OGLE	UK9-2	20-May-53	16.46	4	PIKE	SE3	8-Jul-62	200.06	8
OGLE	PB9-4	26-Aug-57	33.34	5	POPE	TS1-3	3-Apr-52	5.61	3
PEORIA	TP10-3	7-May-55	6.05	3	POPE	TS7-5	5-Jun-52	6.86	3
PEORIA	TP4-3	9-Mar-55	7.28	3	POPE	PB5-3	17-Jul-57	7.27	3
PEORIA	UK7-4	28-Apr-53	7.81	3	POPE	UK7-4	28-Apr-53	13.77	4
PEORIA	TS6-4	28-May-52	9.67	3	PULASKI	PB5-3	17-Jul-57	4.85	2
PEORIA	UK9-2	20-May-53	10.61	4	PULASKI	TS7-5	5-Jun-52	6.66	3
PEORIA	TS7-3	3-Jun-52	11.28	4	PULASKI	TS1-3	3-Apr-52	9.02	3
PEORIA	PB9-3	25-Aug-57	13.72	4	PULASKI	UK7-4	28-Apr-53	19.19	4
PEORIA	PB9-4	26-Aug-57	16.67	4	PUTNAM	UK7-4	28-Apr-53	3.85	2
PEORIA	SE3	8-Jul-62	146.81	7	PUTNAM	TS1-3	3-Apr-52	5.01	3
PERRY	TP10-3	7-May-55	3.68	2	PUTNAM	PB9-4	26-Aug-57	8.37	3
PERRY	TS1-3	3-Apr-52	9.42	3	PUTNAM	UK9-2	20-May-53	10.83	4
PERRY	UK7-4	28-Apr-53	11.60	4	PUTNAM	TS6-4	28-May-52	12.54	4
PIATT	UK9-3	21-May-53	3.69	2	PUTNAM	PB9-3	25-Aug-57	13.72	4

INDIVIDUAL FALLOUT DAYS
ILLINOIS

COUNTY	SHOT	DATE	µCi/SQ METER	INDEX	COUNTY	SHOT	DATE	µCi/SQ METER	INDEX
PUTNAM	TS7-3	3-Jun-52	27.76	5	SANGAMON	PB9-4	26-Aug-57	16.67	4
RANDOLPH	UK2-3	26-Mar-53	3.75	2	SANGAMON	SE3	8-Jul-62	200.06	8
RANDOLPH	TS1-3	3-Apr-52	4.01	2	SCHUYLER	UK9-2	20-May-53	4.79	2
RANDOLPH	PB9-2	24-Aug-57	5.46	3	SCHUYLER	TP10-3	7-May-55	4.85	2
RANDOLPH	R1-2	29-Jan-51	10.09	4	SCHUYLER	TS7-5	5-Jun-52	4.85	2
RANDOLPH	UK7-4	28-Apr-53	10.30	4	SCHUYLER	TP10-2	6-May-55	6.57	3
RANDOLPH	TP10-3	7-May-55	12.30	4	SCHUYLER	TS1-3	3-Apr-52	7.62	3
RANDOLPH	PB9-3	25-Aug-57	13.72	4	SCHUYLER	TS6-4	28-May-52	7.71	3
RICHLAND	UK7-4	28-Apr-53	3.74	2	SCHUYLER	PB9-4	26-Aug-57	8.37	3
RICHLAND	TP10-3	7-May-55	4.10	2	SCHUYLER	PB9-3	25-Aug-57	13.72	4
RICHLAND	PB3-4	27-Jun-57	4.42	2	SCHUYLER	SE3	8-Jul-62	200.06	8
RICHLAND	TS5-1	7-May-52	7.49	3	SCOTT	TP4-3	9-Mar-55	4.15	2
RICHLAND	TS1-3	3-Apr-52	9.42	3	SCOTT	UK7-4	28-Apr-53	5.49	3
RICHLAND	SE3	8-Jul-62	35.48	5	SCOTT	TS7-5	5-Jun-52	6.80	3
RICHLAND	TS7-3	3-Jun-52	81.67	6	SCOTT	TS1-3	3-Apr-52	7.62	3
ROCK ISLAND	PB18-8	17-Jul-57	3.98	2	SCOTT	TS6-4	28-May-52	13.50	4
ROCK ISLAND	PB5-7	21-Jul-57	4.15	2	SCOTT	PB9-3	25-Aug-57	13.72	4
ROCK ISLAND	UK7-4	28-Apr-53	4.49	2	SCOTT	TP10-3	7-May-55	13.98	4
ROCK ISLAND	TS5-1	7-May-52	8.24	3	SCOTT	TS5-1	7-May-52	24.43	4
ROCK ISLAND	PB9-3	25-Aug-57	13.72	4	SCOTT	PB9-4	26-Aug-57	33.34	5
ROCK ISLAND	PB9-4	26-Aug-57	16.67	4	SCOTT	SE3	8-Jul-62	76.52	6
ROCK ISLAND	UK9-2	20-May-53	21.55	4	SHELBY	PB3-4	27-Jun-57	3.55	2
ROCK ISLAND	SE3	8-Jul-62	139.13	7	SHELBY	TP10-3	7-May-55	4.22	2
SALINE	PB5-3	17-Jul-57	4.85	2	SHELBY	TS5-1	7-May-52	4.94	2
SALINE	TS1-3	3-Apr-52	5.61	3	SHELBY	UK9-3	21-May-53	5.38	3
SALINE	UK7-4	28-Apr-53	9.03	3	SHELBY	TS1-3	3-Apr-52	9.42	3
SANGAMON	TP10-3	7-May-55	3.73	2	SHELBY	TS7-3	3-Jun-52	107.95	7
SANGAMON	TS7-3	3-Jun-52	4.24	2	SHELBY	SE3	8-Jul-62	200.06	8
SANGAMON	UK7-4	28-Apr-53	6.02	3	ST CLAIR	UK2-3	26-Mar-53	3.74	2
SANGAMON	TS5-1	7-May-52	7.49	3	ST CLAIR	PB6-4	27-Jul-57	3.78	2
SANGAMON	TS1-3	3-Apr-52	7.62	3	ST CLAIR	UK9-4	22-May-53	4.28	2
SANGAMON	TP4-3	9-Mar-55	9.53	3	ST CLAIR	PB6-3	26-Jul-57	4.63	2
SANGAMON	PB9-3	25-Aug-57	13.72	4	ST CLAIR	TS5-1	7-May-52	6.47	3

INDIVIDUAL FALLOUT DAYS
ILLINOIS

COUNTY	SHOT	DATE	µCi/SQ METER	INDEX	COUNTY	SHOT	DATE	µCi/SQ METER	INDEX
ST CLAIR	TS6-4	28-May-52	6.75	3	VERMILION	PB9-5	27-Aug-57	4.52	2
ST CLAIR	UK7-4	28-Apr-53	9.81	3	VERMILION	UK9-3	21-May-53	4.94	2
ST CLAIR	TS1-3	3-Apr-52	12.63	4	VERMILION	TS1-3	3-Apr-52	5.61	3
ST CLAIR	PB9-3	25-Aug-57	13.72	4	VERMILION	TP10-3	7-May-55	6.17	3
STARK	PB5-7	21-Jul-57	4.15	2	VERMILION	UK7-4	28-Apr-53	10.16	4
STARK	TS1-3	3-Apr-52	5.01	3	VERMILION	TS6-4	28-May-52	12.54	4
STARK	UK7-4	28-Apr-53	7.54	3	VERMILION	TS7-3	3-Jun-52	26.58	5
STARK	PB9-3	25-Aug-57	13.72	4	VERMILION	SE3	8-Jul-62	99.74	6
STARK	UK9-2	20-May-53	14.83	4	WABASH	TS1-4	4-Apr-52	4.22	2
STARK	PB9-4	26-Aug-57	16.67	4	WABASH	PB3-4	27-Jun-57	4.95	2
STARK	SE3	8-Jul-62	139.13	7	WABASH	TS1-3	3-Apr-52	5.61	3
STEPHENSON	PB18-8	17-Jul-57	3.98	2	WABASH	TS7-6	6-Jun-52	5.96	3
STEPHENSON	TS6-4	28-May-52	4.03	2	WABASH	TS5-1	7-May-52	7.19	3
STEPHENSON	TS5-1	7-May-52	4.50	2	WABASH	TP5-3	14-Mar-55	7.40	3
STEPHENSON	TP10-2	6-May-55	5.04	3	WABASH	UK9-3	21-May-53	8.33	3
STEPHENSON	UK7-4	28-Apr-53	5.08	3	WABASH	TP10-3	7-May-55	11.97	4
STEPHENSON	TS7-5	5-Jun-52	6.22	3	WABASH	TS7-3	3-Jun-52	13.85	4
STEPHENSON	PB9-3	25-Aug-57	13.72	4	WABASH	UK7-4	28-Apr-53	15.94	4
STEPHENSON	PB9-4	26-Aug-57	16.67	4	WARREN	TS7-3	3-Jun-52	3.60	2
STEPHENSON	UK9-2	20-May-53	25.12	5	WARREN	PB18-8	17-Jul-57	3.98	2
TAZEWELL	UK9-2	20-May-53	7.90	3	WARREN	UK7-4	28-Apr-53	9.18	3
TAZEWELL	UK7-4	28-Apr-53	8.13	3	WARREN	PB9-3	25-Aug-57	13.72	4
TAZEWELL	PB9-4	26-Aug-57	8.37	3	WARREN	UK9-2	20-May-53	15.70	4
TAZEWELL	PB9-3	25-Aug-57	13.72	4	WARREN	PB9-4	26-Aug-57	33.34	5
TAZEWELL	TS6-4	28-May-52	16.12	4	WARREN	SE3	8-Jul-62	345.56	8
TAZEWELL	TP4-3	9-Mar-55	21.82	4	WASHINGTON	UK9-4	22-May-53	3.80	2
TAZEWELL	SE3	8-Jul-62	139.13	7	WASHINGTON	TP10-3	7-May-55	3.84	2
UNION	TP10-3	7-May-55	3.78	2	WASHINGTON	TS6-4	28-May-52	7.71	3
UNION	TS7-5	5-Jun-52	4.62	2	WASHINGTON	TS1-3	3-Apr-52	9.42	3
UNION	PB6-3	26-Jul-57	4.63	2	WASHINGTON	UK7-4	28-Apr-53	11.44	4
UNION	UK7-4	28-Apr-53	12.30	4	WAYNE	PB3-4	27-Jun-57	3.90	2
UNION	TS1-3	3-Apr-52	15.04	4	WAYNE	TP10-3	7-May-55	3.91	2
VERMILION	TP4-3	9-Mar-55	4.30	2	WAYNE	UK7-4	28-Apr-53	4.68	2

INDIVIDUAL FALLOUT DAYS
ILLINOIS

COUNTY	SHOT	DATE	µCi/SQ METER	INDEX	COUNTY	SHOT	DATE	µCi/SQ METER	INDEX
WAYNE	PB5-3	17-Jul-57	4.85	2	WILL	TS6-4	28-May-52	20.25	4
WAYNE	TS7-3	3-Jun-52	5.66	3	WILL	TS7-3	3-Jun-52	55.24	6
WAYNE	UK9-4	22-May-53	6.95	3	WILLIAMSON	TP10-3	7-May-55	3.72	2
WAYNE	TS5-1	7-May-52	9.16	3	WILLIAMSON	UK7-4	28-Apr-53	9.09	3
WAYNE	TS1-3	3-Apr-52	9.42	3	WILLIAMSON	TS1-3	3-Apr-52	9.42	3
WHITE	TP5-3	14-Mar-55	3.57	2	WINNEBAGO	TS5-1	7-May-52	3.90	2
WHITE	TP10-3	7-May-55	3.59	2	WINNEBAGO	UK7-4	28-Apr-53	5.93	3
WHITE	PB3-4	27-Jun-57	4.32	2	WINNEBAGO	TS7-5	5-Jun-52	6.55	3
WHITE	TS5-1	7-May-52	4.65	2	WINNEBAGO	TS6-4	28-May-52	8.06	3
WHITE	TS7-5	5-Jun-52	4.67	2	WINNEBAGO	PB9-3	25-Aug-57	13.72	4
WHITE	UK7-4	28-Apr-53	6.07	3	WINNEBAGO	PB9-4	26-Aug-57	16.67	4
WHITE	UK9-4	22-May-53	6.88	3	WINNEBAGO	UK9-2	20-May-53	20.25	4
WHITE	TS1-3	3-Apr-52	9.42	3	WINNEBAGO	SE3	8-Jul-62	146.81	7
WHITESIDE	PB18-8	17-Jul-57	3.98	2	WOODFORD	PB9-5	27-Aug-57	3.55	2
WHITESIDE	TS5-1	7-May-52	4.35	2	WOODFORD	UK7-4	28-Apr-53	4.01	2
WHITESIDE	UK7-4	28-Apr-53	6.79	3	WOODFORD	TS8-5	9-Jun-52	4.23	2
WHITESIDE	PB9-3	25-Aug-57	13.72	4	WOODFORD	TS1-3	3-Apr-52	5.01	3
WHITESIDE	PB9-4	26-Aug-57	16.67	4	WOODFORD	UK9-2	20-May-53	5.87	3
WHITESIDE	UK9-2	20-May-53	18.95	4	WOODFORD	PB9-3	25-Aug-57	13.72	4
WHITESIDE	TS7-3	3-Jun-52	25.50	5	WOODFORD	PB9-4	26-Aug-57	16.67	4
WILL	TP10-3	7-May-55	5.03	3	WOODFORD	TS6-4	28-May-52	20.25	4
WILL	UK9-2	20-May-53	5.56	3	WOODFORD	SE3	8-Jul-62	172.89	7
WILL	UK7-4	28-Apr-53	7.67	3					

INDIVIDUAL FALLOUT DAYS
INDIANA

COUNTY	SHOT	DATE	µCi/SQ METER	INDEX	COUNTY	SHOT	DATE	µCi/SQ METER	INDEX
ADAMS	UK9-3	21-May-53	3.61	2	BOONE	TS1-3	3-Apr-52	5.61	3
ADAMS	PB6-3	26-Jul-57	3.96	2	BOONE	UK7-4	28-Apr-53	6.36	3
ADAMS	UK7-4	28-Apr-53	11.92	4	BOONE	UK9-3	21-May-53	6.64	3
ADAMS	SE3	8-Jul-62	35.48	5	BOONE	PB3-4	27-Jun-57	10.82	4
ADAMS	SE4	9-Jul-62	85.56	6	BOONE	TS7-3	3-Jun-52	32.83	5
ALLEN	PB6-3	26-Jul-57	3.96	2	BROWN	TP10-3	7-May-55	3.52	2
ALLEN	TS5-1	7-May-52	4.27	2	BROWN	TS5-1	7-May-52	3.60	2
ALLEN	TP4-4	10-Mar-55	4.91	2	BROWN	UK9-3	21-May-53	6.52	3
ALLEN	UK7-4	28-Apr-53	11.48	4	BROWN	TP5-3	14-Mar-55	6.64	3
ALLEN	SE3	8-Jul-62	99.74	6	BROWN	PB3-4	27-Jun-57	7.58	3
ALLEN	SE4	9-Jul-62	208.78	8	BROWN	TS1-3	3-Apr-52	8.02	3
BARTHOLOMEW	PB3-4	27-Jun-57	4.47	2	BROWN	UK7-4	28-Apr-53	16.95	4
BARTHOLOMEW	UK7-4	28-Apr-53	5.17	3	BROWN	TS7-3	3-Jun-52	20.10	4
BARTHOLOMEW	TS5-1	7-May-52	5.84	3	CARROLL	TS4-5	5-May-52	3.70	2
BARTHOLOMEW	UK9-3	21-May-53	7.38	3	CARROLL	PB3-4	27-Jun-57	4.69	2
BARTHOLOMEW	PB9-5	27-Aug-57	7.53	3	CARROLL	UK9-3	21-May-53	4.79	2
BARTHOLOMEW	TS7-3	3-Jun-52	7.75	3	CARROLL	TS6-4	28-May-52	4.82	2
BARTHOLOMEW	TP10-3	7-May-55	15.88	4	CARROLL	TP5-3	14-Mar-55	5.26	3
BARTHOLOMEW	SE4	9-Jul-62	85.56	6	CARROLL	UK7-4	28-Apr-53	6.09	3
BENTON	TP5-3	14-Mar-55	3.57	2	CARROLL	TS1-3	3-Apr-52	9.42	3
BENTON	UK9-3	21-May-53	4.13	2	CARROLL	TS7-3	3-Jun-52	46.98	5
BENTON	UK7-4	28-Apr-53	5.56	3	CARROLL	SE3	8-Jul-62	80.75	6
BENTON	TS1-3	3-Apr-52	5.61	3	CASS	PB6-3	26-Jul-57	3.96	2
BENTON	TS6-4	28-May-52	11.57	4	CASS	PB3-4	27-Jun-57	4.21	2
BENTON	TS7-3	3-Jun-52	36.81	5	CASS	TP10-3	7-May-55	6.80	3
BLACKFORD	TP5-3	14-Mar-55	3.78	2	CASS	TS6-4	28-May-52	7.71	3
BLACKFORD	PB3-4	27-Jun-57	3.94	2	CASS	UK7-4	28-Apr-53	19.19	4
BLACKFORD	PB6-3	26-Jul-57	3.96	2	CASS	TS7-3	3-Jun-52	52.28	6
BLACKFORD	PB8-6	23-Aug-57	4.03	2	CASS	SE4	9-Jul-62	103.59	7
BLACKFORD	UK9-3	21-May-53	4.87	2	CLARK	TS1-3	3-Apr-52	4.81	2
BLACKFORD	UK7-4	28-Apr-53	5.03	3	CLARK	TP10-3	7-May-55	5.45	3
BOONE	TS6-4	28-May-52	3.86	2	CLARK	TP5-3	14-Mar-55	9.09	3
BOONE	PB9-5	27-Aug-57	4.52	2	CLARK	SE3	8-Jul-62	35.48	5

INDIVIDUAL FALLOUT DAYS
INDIANA

COUNTY	SHOT	DATE	µCi/SQ METER	INDEX	COUNTY	SHOT	DATE	µCi/SQ METER	INDEX
CLARK	SE4	9-Jul-62	73.06	6	DE KALB	UK7-4	28-Apr-53	8.34	3
CLAY	TS1-3	3-Apr-52	5.61	3	DEARBORN	TS1-3	3-Apr-52	3.61	2
CLAY	PB3-4	27-Jun-57	5.83	3	DEARBORN	UK7-4	28-Apr-53	4.06	2
CLAY	TP5-3	14-Mar-55	6.23	3	DEARBORN	TP5-3	14-Mar-55	4.24	2
CLAY	UK9-3	21-May-53	7.82	3	DEARBORN	UK9-3	21-May-53	8.48	3
CLAY	UK7-4	28-Apr-53	8.66	3	DEARBORN	PB6-3	26-Jul-57	39.25	5
CLAY	TP10-3	7-May-55	14.24	4	DECATUR	PB9-5	27-Aug-57	4.52	2
CLAY	TS7-3	3-Jun-52	20.35	4	DECATUR	TS1-3	3-Apr-52	4.81	2
CLINTON	TS4-5	5-May-52	3.70	2	DECATUR	UK7-4	28-Apr-53	4.99	2
CLINTON	TS6-4	28-May-52	3.86	2	DECATUR	TP5-3	14-Mar-55	5.26	3
CLINTON	PB8-6	23-Aug-57	4.03	2	DECATUR	PB3-4	27-Jun-57	5.52	3
CLINTON	UK9-3	21-May-53	4.79	2	DECATUR	UK9-3	21-May-53	9.22	3
CLINTON	TP5-3	14-Mar-55	5.46	3	DECATUR	PB6-3	26-Jul-57	23.55	4
CLINTON	PB3-4	27-Jun-57	5.87	3	DECATUR	SE3	8-Jul-62	35.48	5
CLINTON	UK7-4	28-Apr-53	6.31	3	DELAWARE	UK9-4	22-May-53	3.81	2
CLINTON	TS1-3	3-Apr-52	9.42	3	DELAWARE	PB6-3	26-Jul-57	3.96	2
CLINTON	TS7-3	3-Jun-52	13.93	4	DELAWARE	PB3-4	27-Jun-57	4.56	2
CLINTON	SE3	8-Jul-62	99.74	6	DELAWARE	UK9-3	21-May-53	5.60	3
CRAWFORD	UK7-4	28-Apr-53	3.64	2	DELAWARE	R1-2	29-Jan-51	9.31	3
CRAWFORD	UK9-3	21-May-53	3.94	2	DELAWARE	UK7-4	28-Apr-53	11.71	4
CRAWFORD	TP5-3	14-Mar-55	5.65	3	DELAWARE	SE3	8-Jul-62	76.52	6
CRAWFORD	TP10-3	7-May-55	17.92	4	DELAWARE	SE4	9-Jul-62	85.56	6
CRAWFORD	SE3	8-Jul-62	157.12	7	DUBOIS	TS5-1	7-May-52	3.75	2
DAVIESS	UK9-3	21-May-53	3.69	2	DUBOIS	UK7-4	28-Apr-53	3.92	2
DAVIESS	TS5-1	7-May-52	4.05	2	DUBOIS	TP5-3	14-Mar-55	10.57	4
DAVIESS	PB3-4	27-Jun-57	5.61	3	DUBOIS	TP10-3	7-May-55	36.07	5
DAVIESS	TS1-3	3-Apr-52	5.61	3	DUBOIS	SE3	8-Jul-62	37.44	5
DAVIESS	UK7-4	28-Apr-53	6.56	3	DUBOIS	TS7-3	3-Jun-52	52.70	6
DAVIESS	TP5-3	14-Mar-55	10.36	4	ELKHART	PB6-3	26-Jul-57	3.96	2
DAVIESS	TP10-3	7-May-55	25.25	5	ELKHART	UK7-4	28-Apr-53	7.05	3
DAVIESS	TS7-3	3-Jun-52	29.70	5	ELKHART	TS6-4	28-May-52	7.71	3
DE KALB	PB6-3	26-Jul-57	3.96	2	ELKHART	TS7-3	3-Jun-52	17.22	4
DE KALB	UK9-2	20-May-53	4.66	2	FAYETTE	TS1-3	3-Apr-52	3.61	2

INDIVIDUAL FALLOUT DAYS
INDIANA

COUNTY	SHOT	DATE	µCi/SQ METER	INDEX	COUNTY	SHOT	DATE	µCi/SQ METER	INDEX
FAYETTE	PB3-4	27-Jun-57	4.29	2	GIBSON	TS1-3	3-Apr-52	9.42	3
FAYETTE	UK7-4	28-Apr-53	4.46	2	GIBSON	TS7-3	3-Jun-52	12.01	4
FAYETTE	UK9-3	21-May-53	6.27	3	GRANT	PB6-3	26-Jul-57	3.96	2
FAYETTE	PB6-3	26-Jul-57	7.85	3	GRANT	PB3-4	27-Jun-57	4.47	2
FLOYD	TP5-3	14-Mar-55	4.90	2	GRANT	R1-2	29-Jan-51	9.31	3
FLOYD	TP10-3	7-May-55	15.49	4	GRANT	UK7-4	28-Apr-53	18.30	4
FLOYD	SE3	8-Jul-62	35.48	5	GRANT	SE4	9-Jul-62	208.78	8
FLOYD	SE4	9-Jul-62	73.06	6	GREENE	PB3-4	27-Jun-57	3.99	2
FOUNTAIN	TP5-3	14-Mar-55	3.57	2	GREENE	TS1-4	4-Apr-52	4.22	2
FOUNTAIN	TP10-3	7-May-55	4.22	2	GREENE	UK7-4	28-Apr-53	4.37	2
FOUNTAIN	PB9-5	27-Aug-57	4.52	2	GREENE	UK9-3	21-May-53	4.80	2
FOUNTAIN	PB3-4	27-Jun-57	4.56	2	GREENE	TS1-3	3-Apr-52	5.61	3
FOUNTAIN	UK9-3	21-May-53	5.31	3	GREENE	TP5-3	14-Mar-55	6.43	3
FOUNTAIN	TS1-3	3-Apr-52	5.61	3	GREENE	TS6-4	28-May-52	6.75	3
FOUNTAIN	TS6-4	28-May-52	10.61	4	GREENE	R1-2	29-Jan-51	14.48	4
FOUNTAIN	UK7-4	28-Apr-53	18.11	4	GREENE	TP10-3	7-May-55	36.90	5
FOUNTAIN	TS7-3	3-Jun-52	30.23	5	GREENE	TS7-3	3-Jun-52	39.78	5
FRANKLIN	PB9-5	27-Aug-57	4.52	2	GREENE	SE3	8-Jul-62	76.52	6
FRANKLIN	UK9-3	21-May-53	6.71	3	HAMILTON	TS6-4	28-May-52	3.86	2
FRANKLIN	UK7-4	28-Apr-53	7.05	3	HAMILTON	PB6-3	26-Jul-57	3.96	2
FRANKLIN	TP10-3	7-May-55	9.99	3	HAMILTON	PB9-5	27-Aug-57	4.52	2
FRANKLIN	R1-2	29-Jan-51	19.06	4	HAMILTON	UK9-3	21-May-53	5.46	3
FRANKLIN	PB6-3	26-Jul-57	23.55	4	HAMILTON	TS7-3	3-Jun-52	7.48	3
FRANKLIN	SE4	9-Jul-62	90.29	6	HAMILTON	PB3-4	27-Jun-57	9.19	3
FULTON	PB6-3	26-Jul-57	3.96	2	HAMILTON	UK7-4	28-Apr-53	13.58	4
FULTON	TS6-4	28-May-52	7.71	3	HAMILTON	SE4	9-Jul-62	208.78	8
FULTON	TP10-3	7-May-55	9.09	3	HANCOCK	TS5-1	7-May-52	3.90	2
FULTON	UK7-4	28-Apr-53	17.34	4	HANCOCK	PB6-3	26-Jul-57	3.96	2
FULTON	SE4	9-Jul-62	103.59	7	HANCOCK	PB3-4	27-Jun-57	5.71	3
GIBSON	TP10-3	7-May-55	4.03	2	HANCOCK	UK9-3	21-May-53	6.19	3
GIBSON	TS5-1	7-May-52	4.35	2	HANCOCK	UK7-4	28-Apr-53	6.25	3
GIBSON	PB3-4	27-Jun-57	5.37	3	HANCOCK	PB9-5	27-Aug-57	7.53	3
GIBSON	TP5-3	14-Mar-55	8.22	3	HANCOCK	TS7-3	3-Jun-52	12.11	4

INDIVIDUAL FALLOUT DAYS
INDIANA

COUNTY	SHOT	DATE	µCi/SQ METER	INDEX	COUNTY	SHOT	DATE	µCi/SQ METER	INDEX
HARRISON	UK9-3	21-May-53	3.55	2	HUNTINGTON	PB6-3	26-Jul-57	3.96	2
HARRISON	TP5-3	14-Mar-55	5.78	3	HUNTINGTON	UK7-4	28-Apr-53	15.43	4
HARRISON	TP10-3	7-May-55	15.09	4	HUNTINGTON	PB3-4	27-Jun-57	3.51	1
HARRISON	SE3	8-Jul-62	35.48	5	HUNTINGTON	SE3	8-Jul-62	76.52	6
HARRISON	SE4	9-Jul-62	60.19	6	JACKSON	UK7-4	28-Apr-53	4.27	2
HENDRICKS	TS1-4	4-Apr-52	4.22	2	JACKSON	TS7-3	3-Jun-52	5.98	3
HENDRICKS	PB9-5	27-Aug-57	4.52	2	JACKSON	PB3-4	27-Jun-57	6.70	3
HENDRICKS	TS6-4	28-May-52	4.82	2	JACKSON	TP5-3	14-Mar-55	9.35	3
HENDRICKS	TP5-3	14-Mar-55	6.18	3	JACKSON	TP10-3	7-May-55	19.03	4
HENDRICKS	UK9-3	21-May-53	7.82	3	JACKSON	SE3	8-Jul-62	76.52	6
HENDRICKS	PB3-4	27-Jun-57	10.18	4	JACKSON	SE4	9-Jul-62	90.29	6
HENDRICKS	UK7-4	28-Apr-53	13.31	4	JASPER	UK9-2	20-May-53	3.79	2
HENDRICKS	TP10-3	7-May-55	20.21	4	JASPER	TS6-4	28-May-52	12.54	4
HENDRICKS	SE3	8-Jul-62	69.52	6	JASPER	TP10-3	7-May-55	14.24	4
HENDRICKS	SE4	9-Jul-62	72.20	6	JASPER	UK7-4	28-Apr-53	17.85	4
HENRY	TS5-1	7-May-52	3.90	2	JASPER	TS7-3	3-Jun-52	40.55	5
HENRY	PB6-3	26-Jul-57	3.96	2	JAY	PB6-3	26-Jul-57	3.96	2
HENRY	PB3-4	27-Jun-57	5.00	2	JAY	UK9-3	21-May-53	4.20	2
HENRY	TS7-3	3-Jun-52	6.23	3	JAY	PB3-4	27-Jun-57	5.21	3
HENRY	UK9-3	21-May-53	6.64	3	JAY	UK9-4	22-May-53	7.63	3
HENRY	PB9-5	27-Aug-57	7.53	3	JAY	UK7-4	28-Apr-53	8.98	3
HENRY	TP10-3	7-May-55	13.68	4	JAY	R1-2	29-Jan-51	11.06	4
HENRY	UK7-4	28-Apr-53	18.81	4	JEFFERSON	UK7-4	28-Apr-53	3.97	2
HENRY	SE3	8-Jul-62	35.48	5	JEFFERSON	TP10-3	7-May-55	6.91	3
HENRY	SE4	9-Jul-62	90.29	6	JEFFERSON	TP5-3	14-Mar-55	7.73	3
HOWARD	TS6-4	28-May-52	3.86	2	JEFFERSON	SE3	8-Jul-62	157.12	7
HOWARD	PB6-3	26-Jul-57	3.96	2	JENNINGS	UK7-4	28-Apr-53	4.19	2
HOWARD	UK9-3	21-May-53	4.28	2	JENNINGS	TS1-3	3-Apr-52	4.81	2
HOWARD	PB3-4	27-Jun-57	5.21	3	JENNINGS	PB3-4	27-Jun-57	5.70	3
HOWARD	TP10-3	7-May-55	6.68	3	JENNINGS	TS7-3	3-Jun-52	6.38	3
HOWARD	UK7-4	28-Apr-53	13.04	4	JENNINGS	TP5-3	14-Mar-55	8.16	3
HOWARD	SE4	9-Jul-62	208.78	8	JOHNSON	TP10-3	7-May-55	3.59	2
HUNTINGTON	UK9-3	21-May-53	3.91	2	JOHNSON	TP5-3	14-Mar-55	3.62	2

INDIVIDUAL FALLOUT DAYS
INDIANA

COUNTY	SHOT	DATE	µCi/SQ METER	INDEX	COUNTY	SHOT	DATE	µCi/SQ METER	INDEX
JOHNSON	TS5-1	7-May-52	3.75	2	LAGRANGE	UK9-2	20-May-53	5.41	3
JOHNSON	TS1-3	3-Apr-52	4.81	2	LAGRANGE	TS7-3	3-Jun-52	17.95	4
JOHNSON	TS6-4	28-May-52	4.82	2	LAKE	PB9-5	27-Aug-57	4.52	2
JOHNSON	UK7-4	28-Apr-53	5.26	3	LAKE	TP5-3	14-Mar-55	5.14	3
JOHNSON	PB3-4	27-Jun-57	6.92	3	LAKE	UK9-2	20-May-53	6.59	3
JOHNSON	UK9-3	21-May-53	7.74	3	LAKE	UK7-4	28-Apr-53	13.47	4
JOHNSON	TS7-3	3-Jun-52	9.51	3	LAKE	TS6-4	28-May-52	16.39	4
JOHNSON	R1-2	29-Jan-51	15.59	4	LAKE	TS7-3	3-Jun-52	34.69	5
KNOX	TS1-4	4-Apr-52	4.22	2	LAWRENCE	UK7-4	28-Apr-53	4.77	2
KNOX	TS5-1	7-May-52	4.35	2	LAWRENCE	TS1-3	3-Apr-52	4.81	2
KNOX	TP5-3	14-Mar-55	5.46	3	LAWRENCE	PB3-4	27-Jun-57	6.75	3
KNOX	TS1-3	3-Apr-52	5.61	3	LAWRENCE	TP5-3	14-Mar-55	11.69	4
KNOX	UK7-4	28-Apr-53	5.93	3	LAWRENCE	TP10-3	7-May-55	12.41	4
KNOX	TS6-4	28-May-52	6.75	3	LAWRENCE	R1-2	29-Jan-51	14.48	4
KNOX	R1-2	29-Jan-51	10.09	4	LAWRENCE	TS7-3	3-Jun-52	31.53	5
KNOX	TP10-3	7-May-55	13.61	4	LAWRENCE	SE3	8-Jul-62	99.74	6
KNOX	TS7-3	3-Jun-52	80.18	6	LAWRENCE	SE4	9-Jul-62	103.59	7
KOSCIUSKO	UK9-4	22-May-53	3.63	2	MADISON	PB6-3	26-Jul-57	3.96	2
KOSCIUSKO	PB6-3	26-Jul-57	3.96	2	MADISON	PB9-5	27-Aug-57	4.52	2
KOSCIUSKO	TS5-1	7-May-52	4.35	2	MADISON	UK9-3	21-May-53	5.97	3
KOSCIUSKO	TP10-3	7-May-55	5.41	3	MADISON	PB3-4	27-Jun-57	8.85	3
KOSCIUSKO	UK7-4	28-Apr-53	14.86	4	MADISON	TP10-3	7-May-55	10.45	4
KOSCIUSKO	TS7-3	3-Jun-52	18.49	4	MADISON	UK7-4	28-Apr-53	12.88	4
LA PORTE	PB6-3	26-Jul-57	3.96	2	MADISON	R1-2	29-Jan-51	13.36	4
LA PORTE	PB9-5	27-Aug-57	4.52	2	MADISON	SE4	9-Jul-62	90.29	6
LA PORTE	TP5-3	14-Mar-55	4.54	2	MARION	TS6-4	28-May-52	3.86	2
LA PORTE	UK9-2	20-May-53	5.06	3	MARION	TS1-3	3-Apr-52	5.61	3
LA PORTE	UK7-4	28-Apr-53	8.38	3	MARION	PB3-4	27-Jun-57	7.65	3
LA PORTE	TS7-3	3-Jun-52	17.21	4	MARION	UK9-3	21-May-53	7.67	3
LA PORTE	TS6-4	28-May-52	23.14	4	MARION	TS7-3	3-Jun-52	11.38	4
LAGRANGE	PB6-3	26-Jul-57	3.96	2	MARION	UK7-4	28-Apr-53	21.04	4
LAGRANGE	PB4-4	8-Jul-57	4.01	2	MARION	TP10-3	7-May-55	24.12	4
LAGRANGE	UK7-4	28-Apr-53	4.68	2	MARION	SE3	8-Jul-62	69.52	6

INDIVIDUAL FALLOUT DAYS
INDIANA

COUNTY	SHOT	DATE	µCi/SQ METER	INDEX	COUNTY	SHOT	DATE	µCi/SQ METER	INDEX
MARION	SE4	9-Jul-62	72.20	6	MONTGOMERY	TS7-3	3-Jun-52	30.94	5
MARSHALL	PB6-3	26-Jul-57	3.96	2	MORGAN	TP5-3	14-Mar-55	3.88	2
MARSHALL	TS6-4	28-May-52	4.82	2	MORGAN	TS1-4	4-Apr-52	4.22	2
MARSHALL	UK7-4	28-Apr-53	7.97	3	MORGAN	PB9-5	27-Aug-57	4.52	2
MARSHALL	TS7-3	3-Jun-52	20.80	4	MORGAN	TS6-4	28-May-52	4.82	2
MARTIN	TS5-1	7-May-52	3.75	2	MORGAN	UK7-4	28-Apr-53	5.08	3
MARTIN	UK7-4	28-Apr-53	4.33	2	MORGAN	TS5-1	7-May-52	6.14	3
MARTIN	TS1-3	3-Apr-52	5.61	3	MORGAN	PB4-4	8-Jul-57	6.54	3
MARTIN	PB3-4	27-Jun-57	6.13	3	MORGAN	PB3-4	27-Jun-57	6.77	3
MARTIN	TP5-3	14-Mar-55	11.13	4	MORGAN	UK9-3	21-May-53	9.29	3
MARTIN	R1-2	29-Jan-51	11.68	4	MORGAN	TS7-3	3-Jun-52	9.32	3
MARTIN	TP10-3	7-May-55	21.86	4	MORGAN	TP10-3	7-May-55	21.72	4
MARTIN	TS7-3	3-Jun-52	28.58	5	NEWTON	PB9-5	27-Aug-57	4.52	2
MARTIN	SE3	8-Jul-62	76.52	6	NEWTON	TS1-3	3-Apr-52	5.61	3
MIAMI	PB6-3	26-Jul-57	3.96	2	NEWTON	TS6-4	28-May-52	13.50	4
MIAMI	PB3-4	27-Jun-57	4.16	2	NEWTON	UK7-4	28-Apr-53	17.41	4
MIAMI	UK7-4	28-Apr-53	18.49	4	NEWTON	TS7-3	3-Jun-52	35.89	5
MIAMI	SE3	8-Jul-62	76.52	6	NOBLE	PB6-3	26-Jul-57	3.96	2
MONROE	UK7-4	28-Apr-53	4.91	2	NOBLE	TS7-3	3-Jun-52	7.21	3
MONROE	TS1-3	3-Apr-52	5.61	3	NOBLE	UK7-4	28-Apr-53	10.26	4
MONROE	TS5-1	7-May-52	5.99	3	OHIO	UK7-4	28-Apr-53	4.06	2
MONROE	TP5-3	14-Mar-55	6.84	3	OHIO	TP5-3	14-Mar-55	4.34	2
MONROE	PB3-4	27-Jun-57	7.32	3	OHIO	TS1-3	3-Apr-52	4.81	2
MONROE	UK9-3	21-May-53	7.96	3	OHIO	PB6-3	26-Jul-57	23.55	4
MONROE	TS7-3	3-Jun-52	19.27	4	ORANGE	UK9-3	21-May-53	3.74	2
MONROE	TP10-3	7-May-55	20.35	4	ORANGE	UK7-4	28-Apr-53	3.79	2
MONROE	SE3	8-Jul-62	99.74	6	ORANGE	TP5-3	14-Mar-55	9.64	3
MONTGOMERY	TP10-3	7-May-55	4.03	2	ORANGE	TP10-3	7-May-55	21.99	4
MONTGOMERY	TS6-4	28-May-52	4.82	2	ORANGE	TS7-3	3-Jun-52	23.22	4
MONTGOMERY	TS1-3	3-Apr-52	5.61	3	ORANGE	SE3	8-Jul-62	35.48	5
MONTGOMERY	UK9-3	21-May-53	6.64	3	ORANGE	SE4	9-Jul-62	60.19	6
MONTGOMERY	PB3-4	27-Jun-57	8.85	3	OWEN	TS1-3	3-Apr-52	3.81	2
MONTGOMERY	UK7-4	28-Apr-53	19.64	4	OWEN	TS1-4	4-Apr-52	4.22	2

INDIVIDUAL FALLOUT DAYS
INDIANA

COUNTY	SHOT	DATE	µCi/SQ METER	INDEX	COUNTY	SHOT	DATE	µCi/SQ METER	INDEX
OWEN	PB9-5	27-Aug-57	4.52	2	PORTER	UK7-4	28-Apr-53	13.53	4
OWEN	UK7-4	28-Apr-53	4.64	2	PORTER	TS6-4	28-May-52	14.46	4
OWEN	TS5-1	7-May-52	5.11	3	PORTER	TS7-3	3-Jun-52	39.63	5
OWEN	TS6-4	28-May-52	5.79	3	POSEY	TP10-3	7-May-55	3.53	2
OWEN	TP5-3	14-Mar-55	6.54	3	POSEY	TP5-3	14-Mar-55	4.19	2
OWEN	PB3-4	27-Jun-57	6.75	3	POSEY	TS5-1	7-May-52	4.50	2
OWEN	UK9-3	21-May-53	8.41	3	POSEY	TS1-3	3-Apr-52	5.61	3
OWEN	TS7-3	3-Jun-52	22.28	4	POSEY	TS7-6	6-Jun-52	6.54	3
OWEN	TP10-3	7-May-55	24.57	4	POSEY	PB5-3	17-Jul-57	7.27	3
OWEN	SE4	9-Jul-62	103.59	7	POSEY	SE4	9-Jul-62	39.12	5
PARKE	PB4-4	8-Jul-57	3.65	2	PULASKI	PB6-3	26-Jul-57	3.96	2
PARKE	TP10-3	7-May-55	4.47	2	PULASKI	UK9-2	20-May-53	4.11	2
PARKE	TS6-4	28-May-52	4.83	2	PULASKI	TS6-4	28-May-52	9.64	3
PARKE	UK9-3	21-May-53	7.52	3	PULASKI	TP10-3	7-May-55	12.78	4
PARKE	PB3-4	27-Jun-57	8.11	3	PULASKI	UK7-4	28-Apr-53	17.79	4
PARKE	UK7-4	28-Apr-53	8.82	3	PULASKI	TS7-3	3-Jun-52	48.60	5
PARKE	TS1-3	3-Apr-52	9.42	3	PUTNAM	TS1-4	4-Apr-52	4.22	2
PARKE	TS7-3	3-Jun-52	23.89	4	PUTNAM	PB9-5	27-Aug-57	4.52	2
PERRY	UK9-3	21-May-53	3.74	2	PUTNAM	TS6-4	28-May-52	4.82	2
PERRY	TP5-3	14-Mar-55	5.27	3	PUTNAM	TP5-3	14-Mar-55	6.38	3
PERRY	SE4	9-Jul-62	39.12	5	PUTNAM	UK9-3	21-May-53	8.18	3
PERRY	TP10-3	7-May-55	49.52	5	PUTNAM	PB3-4	27-Jun-57	10.25	4
PIKE	UK7-4	28-Apr-53	3.52	2	PUTNAM	UK7-4	28-Apr-53	12.35	4
PIKE	UK9-3	21-May-53	3.69	2	PUTNAM	TP10-3	7-May-55	22.92	4
PIKE	TS5-1	7-May-52	4.20	2	RANDOLPH	PB3-4	27-Jun-57	3.64	2
PIKE	TS7-6	6-Jun-52	4.32	2	RANDOLPH	PB6-3	26-Jul-57	3.96	2
PIKE	TP10-3	7-May-55	4.54	2	RANDOLPH	UK9-4	22-May-53	4.38	2
PIKE	TS1-3	3-Apr-52	5.61	3	RANDOLPH	UK9-3	21-May-53	5.68	3
PIKE	TP5-3	14-Mar-55	9.55	3	RANDOLPH	TP10-3	7-May-55	9.02	3
PIKE	TS7-3	3-Jun-52	10.25	4	RANDOLPH	UK7-4	28-Apr-53	9.73	3
PORTER	PB6-3	26-Jul-57	3.96	2	RANDOLPH	SE4	9-Jul-62	85.56	6
PORTER	TP5-3	14-Mar-55	4.50	2	RIPLEY	PB3-4	27-Jun-57	4.47	2
PORTER	UK9-2	20-May-53	5.24	3	RIPLEY	UK7-4	28-Apr-53	4.64	2

INDIVIDUAL FALLOUT DAYS
INDIANA

COUNTY	SHOT	DATE	µCi/SQ METER	INDEX	COUNTY	SHOT	DATE	µCi/SQ METER	INDEX
RIPLEY	TS1-3	3-Apr-52	4.81	2	ST JOSEPH	TP5-3	14-Mar-55	3.52	2
RIPLEY	TP5-3	14-Mar-55	4.90	2	ST JOSEPH	UK7-4	28-Apr-53	3.61	2
RIPLEY	UK9-3	21-May-53	9.51	3	ST JOSEPH	PB6-3	26-Jul-57	3.96	2
RIPLEY	PB6-3	26-Jul-57	39.25	5	ST JOSEPH	PB9-5	27-Aug-57	7.53	3
RUSH	TS5-1	7-May-52	3.90	2	ST JOSEPH	TS6-4	28-May-52	10.61	4
RUSH	PB6-3	26-Jul-57	3.96	2	ST JOSEPH	TS7-3	3-Jun-52	19.27	4
RUSH	PB9-5	27-Aug-57	4.52	2	ST JOSEPH	SE3	8-Jul-62	99.74	6
RUSH	UK9-4	22-May-53	4.61	2	STARKE	PB6-3	26-Jul-57	3.96	2
RUSH	TS7-3	3-Jun-52	5.00	3	STARKE	TS6-4	28-May-52	5.79	3
RUSH	PB3-4	27-Jun-57	5.43	3	STARKE	UK7-4	28-Apr-53	8.39	3
RUSH	PB4-4	8-Jul-57	5.51	3	STARKE	TS7-3	3-Jun-52	18.86	4
RUSH	UK9-3	21-May-53	6.64	3	STEUBEN	PB4-4	8-Jul-57	3.58	2
RUSH	UK7-4	28-Apr-53	16.36	4	STEUBEN	PB6-3	26-Jul-57	3.96	2
RUSH	TP10-3	7-May-55	17.13	4	STEUBEN	UK9-2	20-May-53	4.06	2
SCOTT	PB3-4	27-Jun-57	3.68	2	STEUBEN	UK7-4	28-Apr-53	7.59	3
SCOTT	TS7-3	3-Jun-52	3.98	2	STEUBEN	TS7-3	3-Jun-52	19.47	4
SCOTT	UK7-4	28-Apr-53	4.19	2	SULLIVAN	PB9-5	27-Aug-57	4.52	2
SCOTT	TP5-3	14-Mar-55	8.92	3	SULLIVAN	PB4-4	8-Jul-57	5.65	3
SCOTT	SE4	9-Jul-62	85.56	6	SULLIVAN	PB3-4	27-Jun-57	7.76	3
SHELBY	TS5-1	7-May-52	3.75	2	SULLIVAN	UK9-3	21-May-53	8.18	3
SHELBY	PB9-5	27-Aug-57	4.52	2	SULLIVAN	TS1-3	3-Apr-52	9.42	3
SHELBY	TS1-3	3-Apr-52	4.81	2	SULLIVAN	UK7-4	28-Apr-53	14.92	4
SHELBY	UK7-4	28-Apr-53	5.22	3	SULLIVAN	TS7-3	3-Jun-52	16.68	4
SHELBY	TP5-3	14-Mar-55	5.57	3	SULLIVAN	TP10-3	7-May-55	34.64	5
SHELBY	PB3-4	27-Jun-57	7.01	3	SWITZERLAND	PB6-3	26-Jul-57	3.96	2
SHELBY	UK9-3	21-May-53	7.30	3	SWITZERLAND	UK7-4	28-Apr-53	4.15	2
SHELBY	R1-2	29-Jan-51	15.59	4	SWITZERLAND	TP5-3	14-Mar-55	4.49	2
SHELBY	SE4	9-Jul-62	90.29	6	SWITZERLAND	TP10-3	7-May-55	6.04	3
SPENCER	TS5-1	7-May-52	3.90	2	SWITZERLAND	R1-2	29-Jan-51	15.23	4
SPENCER	TS7-4	4-Jun-52	5.04	3	SWITZERLAND	SE3	8-Jul-62	157.12	7
SPENCER	TP5-3	14-Mar-55	5.72	3	TIPPECANOE	TS4-5	5-May-52	3.70	2
SPENCER	SE4	9-Jul-62	39.12	5	TIPPECANOE	PB9-5	27-Aug-57	4.52	2
SPENCER	TP10-3	7-May-55	46.14	5	TIPPECANOE	PB3-4	27-Jun-57	4.78	2

INDIVIDUAL FALLOUT DAYS
INDIANA

COUNTY	SHOT	DATE	µCi/SQ METER	INDEX	COUNTY	SHOT	DATE	µCi/SQ METER	INDEX
TIPPECANOE	UK9-3	21-May-53	5.38	3	VERMILLION	UK9-3	21-May-53	7.00	3
TIPPECANOE	TS1-3	3-Apr-52	5.61	3	VERMILLION	UK7-4	28-Apr-53	8.18	3
TIPPECANOE	TS6-4	28-May-52	9.64	3	VERMILLION	TS1-3	3-Apr-52	9.42	3
TIPPECANOE	UK7-4	28-Apr-53	12.88	4	VERMILLION	TS7-3	3-Jun-52	23.49	4
TIPPECANOE	R1-2	29-Jan-51	13.36	4	VERMILLION	SE3	8-Jul-62	76.52	6
TIPPECANOE	TP10-3	7-May-55	19.01	4	VIGO	PB9-5	27-Aug-57	4.52	2
TIPPECANOE	TS7-3	3-Jun-52	33.65	5	VIGO	PB4-4	8-Jul-57	6.23	3
TIPTON	PB6-3	26-Jul-57	3.96	2	VIGO	UK9-3	21-May-53	7.30	3
TIPTON	PB8-6	23-Aug-57	4.03	2	VIGO	PB3-4	27-Jun-57	7.71	3
TIPTON	UK9-3	21-May-53	5.60	3	VIGO	UK7-4	28-Apr-53	15.75	4
TIPTON	PB3-4	27-Jun-57	5.87	3	VIGO	TS7-3	3-Jun-52	18.40	4
TIPTON	UK7-4	28-Apr-53	8.02	3	VIGO	TP10-3	7-May-55	34.57	5
TIPTON	TS7-3	3-Jun-52	8.37	3	WABASH	PB3-4	27-Jun-57	3.77	2
TIPTON	SE4	9-Jul-62	208.78	8	WABASH	PB6-3	26-Jul-57	3.96	2
UNION	TS1-3	3-Apr-52	3.61	2	WABASH	R1-2	29-Jan-51	11.06	4
UNION	PB4-4	8-Jul-57	3.86	2	WABASH	UK7-4	28-Apr-53	17.02	4
UNION	UK7-4	28-Apr-53	4.65	2	WABASH	SE3	8-Jul-62	76.52	6
UNION	UK9-3	21-May-53	5.97	3	WARREN	TP5-3	14-Mar-55	3.57	2
UNION	PB6-3	26-Jul-57	7.85	3	WARREN	TS1-3	3-Apr-52	3.81	2
UNION	PB3-4	27-Jun-57	3.51	1	WARREN	PB3-4	27-Jun-57	3.86	2
UNION	SE3	8-Jul-62	37.44	5	WARREN	TP10-3	7-May-55	4.16	2
UNION	SE4	9-Jul-62	85.56	6	WARREN	PB9-5	27-Aug-57	4.52	2
VANDERBURGH	TS5-1	7-May-52	4.35	2	WARREN	UK9-3	21-May-53	4.65	2
VANDERBURGH	TP5-3	14-Mar-55	4.70	2	WARREN	TS6-4	28-May-52	11.57	4
VANDERBURGH	TS1-3	3-Apr-52	5.61	3	WARREN	UK7-4	28-Apr-53	17.79	4
VANDERBURGH	TP10-3	7-May-55	7.75	3	WARREN	TS7-3	3-Jun-52	65.01	6
VANDERBURGH	UK9-3	21-May-53	8.04	3	WARRICK	TS5-1	7-May-52	4.20	2
VANDERBURGH	UK7-4	28-Apr-53	9.89	3	WARRICK	TP5-3	14-Mar-55	5.36	3
VANDERBURGH	SE4	9-Jul-62	45.80	5	WARRICK	PB4-5	9-Jul-57	5.58	3
VERMILLION	TP10-3	7-May-55	4.41	2	WARRICK	TS1-3	3-Apr-52	5.61	3
VERMILLION	TS6-4	28-May-52	5.64	3	WARRICK	UK9-3	21-May-53	8.70	3
VERMILLION	TP4-3	9-Mar-55	6.69	3	WARRICK	TS7-3	3-Jun-52	9.04	3
VERMILLION	PB3-4	27-Jun-57	6.79	3	WARRICK	TP10-3	7-May-55	31.04	5

INDIVIDUAL FALLOUT DAYS
INDIANA

COUNTY	SHOT	DATE	µCi/SQ METER	INDEX	COUNTY	SHOT	DATE	µCi/SQ METER	INDEX
WARRICK	SE4	9-Jul-62	39.12	5	WELLS	UK9-3	21-May-53	3.54	2
WASHINGTON	UK7-4	28-Apr-53	4.16	2	WELLS	PB6-3	26-Jul-57	3.96	2
WASHINGTON	PB3-4	27-Jun-57	6.27	3	WELLS	R1-2	29-Jan-51	9.31	3
WASHINGTON	TS1-3	3-Apr-52	8.02	3	WELLS	UK7-4	28-Apr-53	14.28	4
WASHINGTON	TP5-3	14-Mar-55	9.81	3	WELLS	SE4	9-Jul-62	208.78	8
WASHINGTON	TP10-3	7-May-55	10.24	4	WHITE	TS1-3	3-Apr-52	3.81	2
WASHINGTON	TS7-3	3-Jun-52	11.49	4	WHITE	PB3-4	27-Jun-57	3.81	2
WASHINGTON	SE3	8-Jul-62	76.52	6	WHITE	TP10-3	7-May-55	9.58	3
WAYNE	PB3-4	27-Jun-57	3.72	2	WHITE	TS6-4	28-May-52	9.64	3
WAYNE	PB6-3	26-Jul-57	3.96	2	WHITE	UK7-4	28-Apr-53	19.26	4
WAYNE	UK9-3	21-May-53	5.53	3	WHITE	TS7-3	3-Jun-52	43.80	5
WAYNE	TP10-3	7-May-55	7.44	3	WHITLEY	PB6-3	26-Jul-57	3.96	2
WAYNE	UK7-4	28-Apr-53	10.16	4	WHITLEY	TS5-1	7-May-52	4.36	2
WAYNE	SE3	8-Jul-62	90.94	6	WHITLEY	UK7-4	28-Apr-53	7.00	3
WAYNE	SE4	9-Jul-62	208.78	8					

INDIVIDUAL FALLOUT DAYS
KANSAS

COUNTY	SHOT	DATE	µCi/SQ METER	INDEX	COUNTY	SHOT	DATE	µCi/SQ METER	INDEX
ALLEN	PB13-6	11-Sep-57	3.59	2	ATCHISON	TS6-4	28-May-52	14.46	4
ALLEN	PB8-3	20-Aug-57	4.00	2	ATCHISON	PB12-4	5-Sep-57	19.46	4
ALLEN	PB14-7	20-Sep-57	4.04	2	BARBER	PB12-4	5-Sep-57	3.63	2
ALLEN	UK11-2	5-Jun-53	4.35	2	BARBER	PB3-2	25-Jun-57	3.78	2
ALLEN	UK9-2	20-May-53	4.44	2	BARBER	TS6-7	31-May-52	3.87	2
ALLEN	TP10-3	7-May-55	4.66	2	BARBER	PB8-3	20-Aug-57	4.00	2
ALLEN	TS6-4	28-May-52	5.64	3	BARBER	TP10-3	7-May-55	5.04	3
ALLEN	BJ2-2	31-Oct-51	5.84	3	BARBER	TS1-2	2-Apr-52	5.16	3
ALLEN	UK7-3	27-Apr-53	6.14	3	BARBER	PB13-5	10-Sep-57	6.24	3
ALLEN	TS1-2	2-Apr-52	10.32	4	BARBER	TP9-2	15-Apr-55	9.23	3
ALLEN	PB12-4	5-Sep-57	16.69	4	BARBER	UK7-3	27-Apr-53	9.97	3
ALLEN	TS7-5	5-Jun-52	36.84	5	BARBER	PB12-3	4-Sep-57	10.44	4
ANDERSON	PB8-3	20-Aug-57	4.00	2	BARBER	TS7-5	5-Jun-52	13.56	4
ANDERSON	PB14-7	20-Sep-57	4.04	2	BARBER	UK9-2	20-May-53	16.62	4
ANDERSON	PB12-3	4-Sep-57	4.14	2	BARBER	TS8-1	5-Jun-52	39.88	5
ANDERSON	UK9-2	20-May-53	4.28	2	BARTON	PB13-4	9-Sep-57	3.55	2
ANDERSON	TP10-3	7-May-55	4.73	2	BARTON	TS6-7	31-May-52	3.78	2
ANDERSON	PB13-5	10-Sep-57	4.78	2	BARTON	TP10-3	7-May-55	3.78	2
ANDERSON	UK7-3	27-Apr-53	5.85	3	BARTON	UK7-4	28-Apr-53	3.80	2
ANDERSON	UK11-2	5-Jun-53	6.96	3	BARTON	TS1-2	2-Apr-52	5.16	3
ANDERSON	TS6-4	28-May-52	12.54	4	BARTON	UK7-3	27-Apr-53	8.49	3
ANDERSON	PB12-4	5-Sep-57	16.42	4	BARTON	PB12-3	4-Sep-57	9.14	3
ANDERSON	TS7-5	5-Jun-52	24.02	4	BARTON	TS7-5	5-Jun-52	11.05	4
ATCHISON	PB8-3	20-Aug-57	4.00	2	BARTON	TP4-2	8-Mar-55	12.66	4
ATCHISON	PB5-7	21-Jul-57	4.15	2	BARTON	UK9-2	20-May-53	14.28	4
ATCHISON	TP10-3	7-May-55	4.41	2	BARTON	TP9-2	15-Apr-55	17.98	4
ATCHISON	TS1-3	3-Apr-52	4.81	2	BARTON	PB8-3	20-Aug-57	19.73	4
ATCHISON	UK11-2	5-Jun-53	5.70	3	BARTON	PB13-5	10-Sep-57	26.73	5
ATCHISON	UK9-2	20-May-53	6.46	3	BARTON	TS8-1	5-Jun-52	39.88	5
ATCHISON	TP10-2	6-May-55	8.76	3	BOURBON	UK9-2	20-May-53	3.61	2
ATCHISON	TS7-5	5-Jun-52	10.78	4	BOURBON	PB13-6	11-Sep-57	3.64	2
ATCHISON	TP4-2	8-Mar-55	12.66	4	BOURBON	PB8-3	20-Aug-57	4.00	2
ATCHISON	PB13-5	10-Sep-57	14.34	4	BOURBON	PB14-7	20-Sep-57	4.04	2

INDIVIDUAL FALLOUT DAYS
KANSAS

COUNTY	SHOT	DATE	µCi/SQ METER	INDEX	COUNTY	SHOT	DATE	µCi/SQ METER	INDEX
BOURBON	TS6-4	28-May-52	4.83	2	CHASE	TP9-2	15-Apr-55	4.76	2
BOURBON	TP10-3	7-May-55	4.85	2	CHASE	UK7-3	27-Apr-53	7.74	3
BOURBON	BJ2-2	31-Oct-51	5.84	3	CHASE	UK9-2	20-May-53	8.57	3
BOURBON	UK11-2	5-Jun-53	5.84	3	CHASE	TS1-2	2-Apr-52	10.32	4
BOURBON	UK7-3	27-Apr-53	6.25	3	CHASE	PB12-3	4-Sep-57	10.61	4
BOURBON	TS1-2	2-Apr-52	10.32	4	CHASE	PB12-4	5-Sep-57	11.58	4
BOURBON	PB12-4	5-Sep-57	11.76	4	CHASE	PB13-5	10-Sep-57	13.76	4
BOURBON	TS7-5	5-Jun-52	21.93	4	CHASE	TS6-4	28-May-52	20.25	4
BROWN	TS7-4	4-Jun-52	3.72	2	CHASE	TS7-5	5-Jun-52	59.28	6
BROWN	TS7-5	5-Jun-52	3.73	2	CHAUTAUQUA	PB13-6	11-Sep-57	3.72	2
BROWN	TS7-3	3-Jun-52	3.81	2	CHAUTAUQUA	UK11-2	5-Jun-53	3.73	2
BROWN	TP10-3	7-May-55	4.10	2	CHAUTAUQUA	PB8-3	20-Aug-57	4.00	2
BROWN	TS1-3	3-Apr-52	4.81	2	CHAUTAUQUA	TS1-2	2-Apr-52	5.16	3
BROWN	TP10-2	6-May-55	5.81	3	CHAUTAUQUA	UK9-2	20-May-53	7.67	3
BROWN	TS6-4	28-May-52	6.45	3	CHAUTAUQUA	UK7-3	27-Apr-53	8.26	3
BROWN	UK9-2	20-May-53	7.59	3	CHAUTAUQUA	PB13-5	10-Sep-57	8.65	3
BROWN	PB8-3	20-Aug-57	7.99	3	CHAUTAUQUA	BJ2-2	31-Oct-51	8.76	3
BROWN	TP4-2	8-Mar-55	12.66	4	CHAUTAUQUA	PB12-4	5-Sep-57	10.03	4
BROWN	PB13-5	10-Sep-57	14.56	4	CHAUTAUQUA	TP10-3	7-May-55	24.42	4
BROWN	PB12-4	5-Sep-57	18.11	4	CHAUTAUQUA	TS7-5	5-Jun-52	53.68	6
BUTLER	PB8-3	20-Aug-57	4.00	2	CHEROKEE	PB8-3	20-Aug-57	4.00	2
BUTLER	PB14-7	20-Sep-57	4.04	2	CHEROKEE	UK9-2	20-May-53	4.70	2
BUTLER	TS1-2	2-Apr-52	5.16	3	CHEROKEE	UK7-3	27-Apr-53	5.98	3
BUTLER	TP9-2	15-Apr-55	5.68	3	CHEROKEE	PB13-6	11-Sep-57	5.99	3
BUTLER	BJ2-2	31-Oct-51	5.84	3	CHEROKEE	UK1-1	17-Mar-53	7.40	3
BUTLER	UK9-2	20-May-53	8.79	3	CHEROKEE	BJ2-2	31-Oct-51	8.76	3
BUTLER	UK7-3	27-Apr-53	9.54	3	CHEROKEE	TP10-3	7-May-55	10.08	4
BUTLER	PB12-4	5-Sep-57	10.15	4	CHEROKEE	PB12-4	5-Sep-57	16.42	4
BUTLER	PB13-5	10-Sep-57	13.30	4	CHEROKEE	TS6-4	28-May-52	23.18	4
BUTLER	PB12-3	4-Sep-57	15.44	4	CHEROKEE	TS7-5	5-Jun-52	24.81	4
BUTLER	TS7-5	5-Jun-52	49.74	5	CHEROKEE	TS1-3	3-Apr-52	24.86	4
CHASE	PB8-3	20-Aug-57	4.00	2	CHEYENNE	PB2-3	20-Jun-57	3.52	2
CHASE	PB14-7	20-Sep-57	4.04	2	CHEYENNE	PB12-4	5-Sep-57	4.42	2

INDIVIDUAL FALLOUT DAYS
KANSAS

COUNTY	SHOT	DATE	µCi/SQ METER	INDEX	COUNTY	SHOT	DATE	µCi/SQ METER	INDEX
CHEYENNE	PB12-3	4-Sep-57	4.48	2	CLAY	PB12-4	5-Sep-57	12.36	4
CHEYENNE	UK11-2	5-Jun-53	4.59	2	CLAY	TP4-2	8-Mar-55	12.66	4
CHEYENNE	PB18-2	11-Jul-57	4.60	2	CLAY	PB13-5	10-Sep-57	24.70	4
CHEYENNE	UK7-4	28-Apr-53	4.86	2	CLOUD	PB12-4	5-Sep-57	3.51	2
CHEYENNE	TS7-5	5-Jun-52	4.97	2	CLOUD	TS7-5	5-Jun-52	3.69	2
CHEYENNE	TS1-2	2-Apr-52	5.16	3	CLOUD	PB8-3	20-Aug-57	4.00	2
CHEYENNE	TP11-2	16-May-55	5.45	3	CLOUD	UK9-3	21-May-53	4.02	2
CHEYENNE	UK7-3	27-Apr-53	5.73	3	CLOUD	TP4-2	8-Mar-55	5.26	3
CHEYENNE	TP9-2	15-Apr-55	6.67	3	CLOUD	PB13-4	9-Sep-57	5.36	3
CHEYENNE	TP3-2	2-Mar-55	7.78	3	CLOUD	TS7-3	3-Jun-52	5.39	3
CHEYENNE	UK9-2	20-May-53	8.10	3	CLOUD	TP9-2	15-Apr-55	5.52	3
CHEYENNE	TS8-1	5-Jun-52	13.29	4	CLOUD	UK10-2	26-May-53	6.90	3
CHEYENNE	TP10-2	6-May-55	33.30	5	CLOUD	TS7-4	4-Jun-52	8.51	3
CHEYENNE	TS6-3	27-May-52	51.08	6	CLOUD	UK9-2	20-May-53	9.86	3
CHEYENNE	TP4-2	8-Mar-55	51.16	6	CLOUD	PB13-5	10-Sep-57	23.98	4
CLARK	TP9-2	15-Apr-55	4.09	2	COFFEY	PB8-3	20-Aug-57	4.00	2
CLARK	TS7-5	5-Jun-52	6.10	3	COFFEY	PB14-7	20-Sep-57	4.04	2
CLARK	TP10-3	7-May-55	7.69	3	COFFEY	TP10-3	7-May-55	4.73	2
CLARK	PB12-4	5-Sep-57	8.38	3	COFFEY	TS1-2	2-Apr-52	5.16	3
CLARK	UK9-2	20-May-53	13.37	4	COFFEY	UK7-3	27-Apr-53	5.51	3
CLARK	UK7-3	27-Apr-53	20.21	4	COFFEY	PB12-3	4-Sep-57	5.69	3
CLARK	PB13-5	10-Sep-57	21.67	4	COFFEY	UK9-2	20-May-53	6.24	3
CLARK	TS6-4	28-May-52	26.59	5	COFFEY	PB13-5	10-Sep-57	8.80	3
CLARK	TS8-1	5-Jun-52	39.88	5	COFFEY	PB12-4	5-Sep-57	16.69	4
CLAY	TS7-4	4-Jun-52	3.72	2	COFFEY	TS7-5	5-Jun-52	33.27	5
CLAY	UK11-2	5-Jun-53	3.73	2	COMANCHE	PB12-3	4-Sep-57	4.31	2
CLAY	TS6-7	31-May-52	3.88	2	COMANCHE	UK9-5	23-May-53	4.43	2
CLAY	TS7-3	3-Jun-52	3.92	2	COMANCHE	TS6-7	31-May-52	4.70	2
CLAY	PB8-3	20-Aug-57	4.00	2	COMANCHE	PB13-5	10-Sep-57	6.49	3
CLAY	TP9-2	15-Apr-55	4.62	2	COMANCHE	TP10-3	7-May-55	6.62	3
CLAY	UK10-2	26-May-53	7.21	3	COMANCHE	TP9-2	15-Apr-55	7.23	3
CLAY	UK9-2	20-May-53	8.29	3	COMANCHE	PB12-4	5-Sep-57	8.24	3
CLAY	TS7-5	5-Jun-52	9.09	3	COMANCHE	UK7-3	27-Apr-53	9.62	3

INDIVIDUAL FALLOUT DAYS
KANSAS

COUNTY	SHOT	DATE	µCi/SQ METER	INDEX	COUNTY	SHOT	DATE	µCi/SQ METER	INDEX
COMANCHE	UK9-2	20-May-53	13.82	4	DECATUR	UK9-2	20-May-53	10.93	4
COMANCHE	TS8-1	5-Jun-52	39.88	5	DECATUR	TS8-1	5-Jun-52	26.59	5
COWLEY	BJ5-6	24-Nov-51	3.70	2	DECATUR	TS6-3	27-May-52	29.16	5
COWLEY	PB8-3	20-Aug-57	4.00	2	DECATUR	TP10-2	6-May-55	33.30	5
COWLEY	PB14-7	20-Sep-57	4.04	2	DECATUR	TP4-2	8-Mar-55	51.16	6
COWLEY	TP9-2	15-Apr-55	4.36	2	DICKINSON	UK11-2	5-Jun-53	3.83	2
COWLEY	PB13-6	11-Sep-57	4.51	2	DICKINSON	PB8-3	20-Aug-57	4.00	2
COWLEY	UK7-3	27-Apr-53	9.07	3	DICKINSON	UK10-2	26-May-53	4.39	2
COWLEY	PB13-5	10-Sep-57	10.11	4	DICKINSON	UK7-3	27-Apr-53	4.53	2
COWLEY	UK9-2	20-May-53	10.45	4	DICKINSON	TS1-2	2-Apr-52	5.16	3
COWLEY	PB12-4	5-Sep-57	11.48	4	DICKINSON	TS6-4	28-May-52	6.45	3
COWLEY	PB12-3	4-Sep-57	12.94	4	DICKINSON	TP9-2	15-Apr-55	7.54	3
COWLEY	TS7-5	5-Jun-52	63.62	6	DICKINSON	UK9-2	20-May-53	10.67	4
CRAWFORD	PB8-3	20-Aug-57	4.00	2	DICKINSON	PB12-4	5-Sep-57	11.67	4
CRAWFORD	PB13-6	11-Sep-57	4.05	2	DICKINSON	TP4-2	8-Mar-55	12.66	4
CRAWFORD	UK11-2	5-Jun-53	4.10	2	DICKINSON	PB12-3	4-Sep-57	13.45	4
CRAWFORD	UK9-2	20-May-53	4.52	2	DICKINSON	PB13-5	10-Sep-57	24.86	4
CRAWFORD	TP10-3	7-May-55	4.85	2	DICKINSON	TS7-5	5-Jun-52	34.00	5
CRAWFORD	PB13-5	10-Sep-57	6.04	3	DONIPHAN	UK7-4	28-Apr-53	3.52	2
CRAWFORD	BJ2-2	31-Oct-51	8.76	3	DONIPHAN	PB8-3	20-Aug-57	4.00	2
CRAWFORD	UK7-3	27-Apr-53	11.01	4	DONIPHAN	TP10-3	7-May-55	4.35	2
CRAWFORD	PB12-4	5-Sep-57	22.84	4	DONIPHAN	UK11-3	6-Jun-53	4.86	2
CRAWFORD	TS7-5	5-Jun-52	34.01	5	DONIPHAN	TP4-2	8-Mar-55	5.25	3
CRAWFORD	TS1-3	3-Apr-52	41.51	5	DONIPHAN	TP10-2	6-May-55	5.48	3
DECATUR	TP11-2	16-May-55	3.64	2	DONIPHAN	TS7-5	5-Jun-52	6.60	3
DECATUR	UK7-4	28-Apr-53	4.65	2	DONIPHAN	PB13-5	10-Sep-57	7.44	3
DECATUR	PB8-4	21-Aug-57	4.92	2	DONIPHAN	UK9-2	20-May-53	7.97	3
DECATUR	TS1-2	2-Apr-52	5.16	3	DONIPHAN	PB12-4	5-Sep-57	13.38	4
DECATUR	PB13-4	9-Sep-57	5.36	3	DOUGLAS	TS7-6	6-Jun-52	3.69	2
DECATUR	PB12-4	5-Sep-57	5.44	3	DOUGLAS	UK7-3	27-Apr-53	3.77	2
DECATUR	UK7-3	27-Apr-53	6.60	3	DOUGLAS	PB8-3	20-Aug-57	4.00	2
DECATUR	TP3-2	2-Mar-55	7.78	3	DOUGLAS	PB14-7	20-Sep-57	4.04	2
DECATUR	TP9-2	15-Apr-55	8.85	3	DOUGLAS	UK9-2	20-May-53	4.21	2

INDIVIDUAL FALLOUT DAYS
KANSAS

COUNTY	SHOT	DATE	μCi/SQ METER	INDEX	COUNTY	SHOT	DATE	μCi/SQ METER	INDEX
DOUGLAS	UK11-2	5-Jun-53	6.11	3	ELLIS	PB12-4	5-Sep-57	9.12	3
DOUGLAS	PB13-5	10-Sep-57	8.61	3	ELLIS	UK7-3	27-Apr-53	9.28	3
DOUGLAS	TS7-5	5-Jun-52	12.20	4	ELLIS	TP4-2	8-Mar-55	12.66	4
DOUGLAS	PB12-4	5-Sep-57	15.41	4	ELLIS	TP9-2	15-Apr-55	13.22	4
DOUGLAS	TP10-3	7-May-55	24.27	4	ELLIS	UK9-2	20-May-53	14.27	4
DOUGLAS	TS6-4	28-May-52	28.97	5	ELLIS	PB8-3	20-Aug-57	19.73	4
EDWARDS	PB3-2	25-Jun-57	3.78	2	ELLIS	PB13-5	10-Sep-57	21.19	4
EDWARDS	TS6-7	31-May-52	3.81	2	ELLIS	TS8-1	5-Jun-52	39.88	5
EDWARDS	TS6-4	28-May-52	4.03	2	ELLSWORTH	UK7-4	28-Apr-53	3.57	2
EDWARDS	TP10-3	7-May-55	6.11	3	ELLSWORTH	PB12-4	5-Sep-57	3.85	2
EDWARDS	PB12-3	4-Sep-57	6.90	3	ELLSWORTH	PB8-3	20-Aug-57	4.00	2
EDWARDS	TS1-2	2-Apr-52	10.32	4	ELLSWORTH	UK10-2	26-May-53	4.49	2
EDWARDS	UK7-3	27-Apr-53	11.14	4	ELLSWORTH	UK11-2	5-Jun-53	4.72	2
EDWARDS	TP9-2	15-Apr-55	11.42	4	ELLSWORTH	TS1-2	2-Apr-52	5.16	3
EDWARDS	PB12-4	5-Sep-57	12.64	4	ELLSWORTH	UK7-3	27-Apr-53	7.46	3
EDWARDS	UK9-2	20-May-53	15.45	4	ELLSWORTH	PB12-3	4-Sep-57	11.73	4
EDWARDS	PB13-5	10-Sep-57	22.72	4	ELLSWORTH	TP4-2	8-Mar-55	12.66	4
EDWARDS	TS8-1	5-Jun-52	39.88	5	ELLSWORTH	TP9-2	15-Apr-55	14.84	4
ELK	TP10-3	7-May-55	3.84	2	ELLSWORTH	UK9-2	20-May-53	14.96	4
ELK	PB8-3	20-Aug-57	4.00	2	ELLSWORTH	TS7-5	5-Jun-52	24.06	4
ELK	PB14-7	20-Sep-57	4.04	2	ELLSWORTH	PB13-5	10-Sep-57	24.93	4
ELK	BJ2-2	31-Oct-51	5.84	3	FINNEY	TP9-2	15-Apr-55	3.52	2
ELK	UK9-2	20-May-53	7.52	3	FINNEY	UK9-1	19-May-53	3.88	2
ELK	UK7-3	27-Apr-53	8.26	3	FINNEY	UK7-4	28-Apr-53	3.95	2
ELK	PB13-5	10-Sep-57	9.89	3	FINNEY	TP11-3	17-May-55	4.69	2
ELK	PB12-4	5-Sep-57	14.33	4	FINNEY	TS1-2	2-Apr-52	5.16	3
ELK	TS7-5	5-Jun-52	55.50	6	FINNEY	TS6-4	28-May-52	5.64	3
ELLIS	TP7-3	31-Mar-55	3.77	2	FINNEY	TP3-2	2-Mar-55	7.78	3
ELLIS	UK9-3	21-May-53	4.06	2	FINNEY	TP7-2	30-Mar-55	8.26	3
ELLIS	TP10-3	7-May-55	4.66	2	FINNEY	TP11-2	16-May-55	9.09	3
ELLIS	TS6-3	27-May-52	4.76	2	FINNEY	PB13-5	10-Sep-57	9.89	3
ELLIS	PB12-3	4-Sep-57	5.35	3	FINNEY	UK7-3	27-Apr-53	13.34	4
ELLIS	PB8-4	21-Aug-57	5.37	3	FINNEY	UK9-2	20-May-53	18.52	4

INDIVIDUAL FALLOUT DAYS
KANSAS

COUNTY	SHOT	DATE	µCi/SQ METER	INDEX	COUNTY	SHOT	DATE	µCi/SQ METER	INDEX
FINNEY	TP10-3	7-May-55	21.04	4	GEARY	PB13-4	9-Sep-57	3.55	2
FINNEY	TP10-2	6-May-55	33.30	5	GEARY	UK11-2	5-Jun-53	3.94	2
FINNEY	TS8-1	5-Jun-52	39.88	5	GEARY	PB8-3	20-Aug-57	4.00	2
FINNEY	TP4-2	8-Mar-55	51.16	6	GEARY	TP9-2	15-Apr-55	4.36	2
FORD	PB13-4	9-Sep-57	3.55	2	GEARY	UK7-3	27-Apr-53	4.42	2
FORD	TP11-3	17-May-55	3.68	2	GEARY	PB12-4	5-Sep-57	5.20	3
FORD	PB12-3	4-Sep-57	4.57	2	GEARY	PB12-3	4-Sep-57	7.16	3
FORD	PB18-2	11-Jul-57	4.60	2	GEARY	UK9-2	20-May-53	8.49	3
FORD	TS7-5	5-Jun-52	4.69	2	GEARY	TS6-4	28-May-52	10.48	4
FORD	TS6-4	28-May-52	4.83	2	GEARY	TP4-2	8-Mar-55	12.66	4
FORD	TP9-2	15-Apr-55	5.33	3	GEARY	PB13-5	10-Sep-57	21.62	4
FORD	TP11-2	16-May-55	5.45	3	GEARY	TS7-5	5-Jun-52	39.37	5
FORD	TP10-3	7-May-55	7.31	3	GOVE	UK7-4	28-Apr-53	3.80	2
FORD	TP3-2	2-Mar-55	7.78	3	GOVE	TS6-4	28-May-52	4.03	2
FORD	R1-2	29-Jan-51	7.80	3	GOVE	TP11-3	17-May-55	4.04	2
FORD	PB12-4	5-Sep-57	9.05	3	GOVE	TP10-3	7-May-55	4.21	2
FORD	TS1-2	2-Apr-52	9.99	3	GOVE	TS1-2	2-Apr-52	5.16	3
FORD	UK7-3	27-Apr-53	11.62	4	GOVE	TP3-2	2-Mar-55	7.78	3
FORD	UK9-2	20-May-53	15.08	4	GOVE	TP9-2	15-Apr-55	7.99	3
FORD	PB13-5	10-Sep-57	22.53	4	GOVE	PB13-5	10-Sep-57	9.84	3
FORD	TP10-2	6-May-55	33.30	5	GOVE	PB12-4	5-Sep-57	9.86	3
FORD	TS8-1	5-Jun-52	39.88	5	GOVE	UK7-3	27-Apr-53	10.52	4
FORD	TP4-2	8-Mar-55	51.16	6	GOVE	UK9-2	20-May-53	16.98	4
FRANKLIN	PB8-3	20-Aug-57	4.00	2	GOVE	TS6-3	27-May-52	20.74	4
FRANKLIN	PB14-7	20-Sep-57	4.04	2	GOVE	TP10-2	6-May-55	33.30	5
FRANKLIN	UK9-2	20-May-53	4.13	2	GOVE	TS8-1	5-Jun-52	39.88	5
FRANKLIN	TS1-2	2-Apr-52	5.16	3	GOVE	TP4-2	8-Mar-55	51.16	6
FRANKLIN	UK7-3	27-Apr-53	5.22	3	GRAHAM	TP11-2	16-May-55	3.64	2
FRANKLIN	PB13-5	10-Sep-57	8.57	3	GRAHAM	UK9-3	21-May-53	3.81	2
FRANKLIN	TS7-5	5-Jun-52	8.88	3	GRAHAM	TP10-3	7-May-55	4.22	2
FRANKLIN	TP10-3	7-May-55	14.24	4	GRAHAM	PB13-5	10-Sep-57	5.23	3
FRANKLIN	PB12-4	5-Sep-57	15.95	4	GRAHAM	TS6-3	27-May-52	5.56	3
FRANKLIN	R1-2	29-Jan-51	17.85	4	GRAHAM	UK7-4	28-Apr-53	5.88	3

INDIVIDUAL FALLOUT DAYS
KANSAS

COUNTY	SHOT	DATE	µCi/SQ METER	INDEX	COUNTY	SHOT	DATE	µCi/SQ METER	INDEX
GRAHAM	TS1-2	2-Apr-52	7.42	3	GRAY	UK9-2	20-May-53	16.08	4
GRAHAM	TP3-2	2-Mar-55	7.78	3	GRAY	TP10-2	6-May-55	33.30	5
GRAHAM	UK7-3	27-Apr-53	7.84	3	GRAY	TS8-1	5-Jun-52	39.88	5
GRAHAM	TP9-2	15-Apr-55	9.70	3	GRAY	TP4-2	8-Mar-55	51.16	6
GRAHAM	UK9-2	20-May-53	12.83	4	GREELEY	TP11-2	16-May-55	3.64	2
GRAHAM	PB8-3	20-Aug-57	19.73	4	GREELEY	TP10-3	7-May-55	4.57	2
GRAHAM	TP10-2	6-May-55	33.30	5	GREELEY	TS1-2	2-Apr-52	5.16	3
GRAHAM	TS8-1	5-Jun-52	39.88	5	GREELEY	TS6-4	28-May-52	5.64	3
GRAHAM	TP4-2	8-Mar-55	51.16	6	GREELEY	PB12-4	5-Sep-57	6.40	3
GRANT	TS6-4	28-May-52	6.45	3	GREELEY	PB13-5	10-Sep-57	6.67	3
GRANT	TP3-2	2-Mar-55	7.78	3	GREELEY	TP3-2	2-Mar-55	7.78	3
GRANT	TP10-3	7-May-55	8.07	3	GREELEY	PB11-2	1-Sep-57	9.58	3
GRANT	PB12-4	5-Sep-57	8.78	3	GREELEY	UK9-1	19-May-53	10.13	4
GRANT	TP11-2	16-May-55	9.09	3	GREELEY	UK7-3	27-Apr-53	12.04	4
GRANT	UK9-1	19-May-53	10.34	4	GREELEY	TS6-3	27-May-52	12.07	4
GRANT	UK7-3	27-Apr-53	15.40	4	GREELEY	UK9-2	20-May-53	18.27	4
GRANT	PB13-5	10-Sep-57	15.54	4	GREELEY	TS8-1	5-Jun-52	26.59	5
GRANT	UK9-2	20-May-53	18.43	4	GREELEY	TP10-2	6-May-55	33.30	5
GRANT	TS1-2	2-Apr-52	19.99	4	GREELEY	TP4-2	8-Mar-55	51.16	6
GRANT	TP10-2	6-May-55	33.30	5	GREENWOOD	TP10-3	7-May-55	3.73	2
GRANT	TS8-1	5-Jun-52	39.88	5	GREENWOOD	PB8-3	20-Aug-57	4.00	2
GRANT	TP4-2	8-Mar-55	51.16	6	GREENWOOD	PB14-7	20-Sep-57	4.04	2
GRAY	TP11-3	17-May-55	4.34	2	GREENWOOD	TP5-3	14-Mar-55	4.24	2
GRAY	PB18-2	11-Jul-57	4.60	2	GREENWOOD	TS1-2	2-Apr-52	5.16	3
GRAY	TS1-2	2-Apr-52	5.16	3	GREENWOOD	UK9-2	20-May-53	7.22	3
GRAY	TP7-2	30-Mar-55	5.54	3	GREENWOOD	UK7-3	27-Apr-53	7.57	3
GRAY	TS6-4	28-May-52	5.64	3	GREENWOOD	PB12-3	4-Sep-57	9.14	3
GRAY	TS6-3	27-May-52	5.70	3	GREENWOOD	PB13-5	10-Sep-57	11.09	4
GRAY	TP10-3	7-May-55	7.56	3	GREENWOOD	PB12-4	5-Sep-57	14.45	4
GRAY	TP3-2	2-Mar-55	7.78	3	GREENWOOD	TS6-4	28-May-52	16.39	4
GRAY	TP11-2	16-May-55	9.09	3	GREENWOOD	TS7-5	5-Jun-52	56.41	6
GRAY	PB13-5	10-Sep-57	10.97	4	HAMILTON	PB5-4	18-Jul-57	4.56	2
GRAY	UK7-3	27-Apr-53	12.51	4	HAMILTON	PB11-2	1-Sep-57	4.79	2

INDIVIDUAL FALLOUT DAYS
KANSAS

COUNTY	SHOT	DATE	µCi/SQ METER	INDEX	COUNTY	SHOT	DATE	µCi/SQ METER	INDEX
HAMILTON	TS1-2	2-Apr-52	5.16	3	HASKELL	TS1-2	2-Apr-52	5.16	3
HAMILTON	TP10-3	7-May-55	5.57	3	HASKELL	TS7-4	4-Jun-52	5.22	3
HAMILTON	TS7-5	5-Jun-52	6.06	3	HASKELL	UK9-1	19-May-53	5.82	3
HAMILTON	TS6-4	28-May-52	6.45	3	HASKELL	TS6-4	28-May-52	6.45	3
HAMILTON	PB13-5	10-Sep-57	7.31	3	HASKELL	TP3-2	2-Mar-55	7.78	3
HAMILTON	TP3-2	2-Mar-55	7.78	3	HASKELL	TP10-3	7-May-55	8.07	3
HAMILTON	UK9-1	19-May-53	14.65	4	HASKELL	UK7-3	27-Apr-53	13.95	4
HAMILTON	UK7-3	27-Apr-53	15.74	4	HASKELL	UK9-2	20-May-53	16.71	4
HAMILTON	UK9-2	20-May-53	20.96	4	HASKELL	PB13-5	10-Sep-57	17.31	4
HAMILTON	TS8-1	5-Jun-52	26.59	5	HASKELL	TP10-2	6-May-55	33.30	5
HAMILTON	TP10-2	6-May-55	33.30	5	HASKELL	TS8-1	5-Jun-52	39.88	5
HAMILTON	TP4-2	8-Mar-55	51.16	6	HASKELL	TP4-2	8-Mar-55	51.16	6
HARPER	PB8-3	20-Aug-57	4.00	2	HODGEMAN	TP11-3	17-May-55	3.63	2
HARPER	PB13-9	14-Sep-57	4.15	2	HODGEMAN	TS6-4	28-May-52	4.83	2
HARPER	PB12-4	5-Sep-57	4.49	2	HODGEMAN	TP7-2	30-Mar-55	5.54	3
HARPER	PB13-5	10-Sep-57	5.88	3	HODGEMAN	PB12-4	5-Sep-57	5.67	3
HARPER	UK7-3	27-Apr-53	9.18	3	HODGEMAN	TP10-3	7-May-55	6.74	3
HARPER	TP9-2	15-Apr-55	9.42	3	HODGEMAN	PB12-3	4-Sep-57	6.81	3
HARPER	UK9-2	20-May-53	14.66	4	HODGEMAN	TP9-2	15-Apr-55	6.85	3
HARPER	PB12-3	4-Sep-57	16.30	4	HODGEMAN	TP3-2	2-Mar-55	7.78	3
HARPER	TS7-5	5-Jun-52	34.89	5	HODGEMAN	PB13-5	10-Sep-57	10.77	4
HARVEY	TS8-4	8-Jun-52	3.52	2	HODGEMAN	UK7-3	27-Apr-53	11.62	4
HARVEY	PB8-3	20-Aug-57	4.00	2	HODGEMAN	UK9-2	20-May-53	15.99	4
HARVEY	UK7-4	28-Apr-53	4.75	2	HODGEMAN	TS1-2	2-Apr-52	19.99	4
HARVEY	TS1-2	2-Apr-52	5.16	3	HODGEMAN	TP10-2	6-May-55	33.30	5
HARVEY	UK7-3	27-Apr-53	8.30	3	HODGEMAN	TS8-1	5-Jun-52	39.88	5
HARVEY	PB12-4	5-Sep-57	9.24	3	HODGEMAN	TP4-2	8-Mar-55	51.16	6
HARVEY	TP9-2	15-Apr-55	9.71	3	JACKSON	PB12-3	4-Sep-57	3.54	2
HARVEY	UK9-2	20-May-53	11.24	4	JACKSON	TP10-3	7-May-55	4.22	2
HARVEY	PB12-3	4-Sep-57	14.75	4	JACKSON	TS1-3	3-Apr-52	4.81	2
HARVEY	PB13-5	10-Sep-57	16.49	4	JACKSON	PB8-3	20-Aug-57	5.95	3
HARVEY	TS7-5	5-Jun-52	49.05	5	JACKSON	UK9-2	20-May-53	8.72	3
HASKELL	TP11-3	17-May-55	5.05	3	JACKSON	TS7-5	5-Jun-52	11.39	4

INDIVIDUAL FALLOUT DAYS
KANSAS

COUNTY	SHOT	DATE	µCi/SQ METER	INDEX	COUNTY	SHOT	DATE	µCi/SQ METER	INDEX
JACKSON	TP4-2	8-Mar-55	12.66	4	JOHNSON	PB13-5	10-Sep-57	4.06	2
JACKSON	PB12-4	5-Sep-57	14.05	4	JOHNSON	UK2-3	26-Mar-53	4.89	2
JACKSON	TS6-4	28-May-52	15.43	4	JOHNSON	PB18-8	17-Jul-57	5.26	3
JACKSON	PB13-5	10-Sep-57	17.09	4	JOHNSON	PB8-3	20-Aug-57	7.99	3
JEFFERSON	PB13-4	9-Sep-57	3.55	2	JOHNSON	TS6-4	28-May-52	12.54	4
JEFFERSON	UK7-3	27-Apr-53	3.61	2	JOHNSON	PB12-4	5-Sep-57	15.14	4
JEFFERSON	TS7-5	5-Jun-52	3.82	2	JOHNSON	PB4-5	9-Jul-57	17.72	4
JEFFERSON	PB8-3	20-Aug-57	4.00	2	JOHNSON	TP10-3	7-May-55	25.40	5
JEFFERSON	TP10-3	7-May-55	4.54	2	KEARNY	PB13-4	9-Sep-57	3.55	2
JEFFERSON	UK9-2	20-May-53	4.59	2	KEARNY	TS7-4	4-Jun-52	3.78	2
JEFFERSON	TS1-3	3-Apr-52	4.81	2	KEARNY	PB5-4	18-Jul-57	4.56	2
JEFFERSON	UK11-2	5-Jun-53	6.74	3	KEARNY	TS6-3	27-May-52	4.85	2
JEFFERSON	TP10-2	6-May-55	8.76	3	KEARNY	TP7-2	30-Mar-55	5.54	3
JEFFERSON	TP4-2	8-Mar-55	12.66	4	KEARNY	TS6-4	28-May-52	6.45	3
JEFFERSON	TS6-4	28-May-52	14.46	4	KEARNY	TP10-3	7-May-55	6.99	3
JEFFERSON	PB13-5	10-Sep-57	15.24	4	KEARNY	TP3-2	2-Mar-55	7.78	3
JEFFERSON	PB12-4	5-Sep-57	20.34	4	KEARNY	UK9-1	19-May-53	8.19	3
JEWELL	UK7-4	28-Apr-53	3.79	2	KEARNY	PB13-5	10-Sep-57	8.39	3
JEWELL	TS7-3	3-Jun-52	3.87	2	KEARNY	TS1-2	2-Apr-52	9.99	3
JEWELL	TS7-5	5-Jun-52	3.89	2	KEARNY	PB12-4	5-Sep-57	13.38	4
JEWELL	UK9-3	21-May-53	4.86	2	KEARNY	UK7-3	27-Apr-53	14.92	4
JEWELL	UK10-2	26-May-53	5.43	3	KEARNY	UK9-2	20-May-53	20.78	4
JEWELL	TS7-4	4-Jun-52	5.70	3	KEARNY	TP10-2	6-May-55	33.30	5
JEWELL	PB13-5	10-Sep-57	6.49	3	KEARNY	TS8-1	5-Jun-52	39.88	5
JEWELL	TP9-2	15-Apr-55	7.46	3	KEARNY	TP4-2	8-Mar-55	51.16	6
JEWELL	PB12-4	5-Sep-57	10.61	4	KINGMAN	PB3-2	25-Jun-57	3.78	2
JEWELL	UK9-2	20-May-53	10.98	4	KINGMAN	PB8-3	20-Aug-57	4.00	2
JEWELL	TP4-2	8-Mar-55	12.66	4	KINGMAN	PB13-9	14-Sep-57	4.15	2
JEWELL	PB8-3	20-Aug-57	19.73	4	KINGMAN	UK7-4	28-Apr-53	4.33	2
JOHNSON	UK7-3	27-Apr-53	3.63	2	KINGMAN	TS1-2	2-Apr-52	5.16	3
JOHNSON	PB12-3	4-Sep-57	3.97	2	KINGMAN	PB13-5	10-Sep-57	6.92	3
JOHNSON	TS1-3	3-Apr-52	4.01	2	KINGMAN	PB12-4	5-Sep-57	9.03	3
JOHNSON	PB14-7	20-Sep-57	4.04	2	KINGMAN	TP10-3	7-May-55	9.62	3

INDIVIDUAL FALLOUT DAYS
KANSAS

COUNTY	SHOT	DATE	µCi/SQ METER	INDEX	COUNTY	SHOT	DATE	µCi/SQ METER	INDEX
KINGMAN	UK7-3	27-Apr-53	10.21	4	LANE	TP9-2	15-Apr-55	6.18	3
KINGMAN	TP9-2	15-Apr-55	11.43	4	LANE	TP3-2	2-Mar-55	7.78	3
KINGMAN	UK9-2	20-May-53	15.41	4	LANE	UK7-3	27-Apr-53	11.82	4
KINGMAN	PB12-3	4-Sep-57	17.59	4	LANE	TS6-3	27-May-52	15.30	4
KINGMAN	TS7-5	5-Jun-52	40.07	5	LANE	UK9-2	20-May-53	17.98	4
KIOWA	PB3-2	25-Jun-57	3.78	2	LANE	PB13-5	10-Sep-57	18.55	4
KIOWA	PB12-4	5-Sep-57	3.80	2	LANE	TP10-2	6-May-55	33.30	5
KIOWA	TS6-4	28-May-52	4.03	2	LANE	TS8-1	5-Jun-52	39.88	5
KIOWA	TP10-3	7-May-55	6.43	3	LANE	TP4-2	8-Mar-55	51.16	6
KIOWA	TP9-2	15-Apr-55	9.51	3	LEAVENWORTH	PB13-4	9-Sep-57	3.55	2
KIOWA	PB12-3	4-Sep-57	10.69	4	LEAVENWORTH	UK2-3	26-Mar-53	3.93	2
KIOWA	PB13-5	10-Sep-57	12.40	4	LEAVENWORTH	PB5-7	21-Jul-57	4.15	2
KIOWA	UK9-2	20-May-53	14.90	4	LEAVENWORTH	UK11-3	6-Jun-53	4.58	2
KIOWA	UK7-3	27-Apr-53	28.12	5	LEAVENWORTH	TS1-3	3-Apr-52	4.81	2
KIOWA	TS8-1	5-Jun-52	132.94	7	LEAVENWORTH	UK9-2	20-May-53	6.01	3
LABETTE	PB13-5	10-Sep-57	3.79	2	LEAVENWORTH	PB13-3	8-Sep-57	6.38	3
LABETTE	PB8-3	20-Aug-57	4.00	2	LEAVENWORTH	PB13-5	10-Sep-57	7.66	3
LABETTE	PB13-6	11-Sep-57	4.46	2	LEAVENWORTH	PB8-3	20-Aug-57	7.99	3
LABETTE	PB13-4	9-Sep-57	5.36	3	LEAVENWORTH	TP10-2	6-May-55	8.76	3
LABETTE	UK9-2	20-May-53	5.69	3	LEAVENWORTH	TS1-2	2-Apr-52	10.32	4
LABETTE	BJ2-2	31-Oct-51	5.84	3	LEAVENWORTH	TP4-2	8-Mar-55	12.66	4
LABETTE	PB13-3	8-Sep-57	6.38	3	LEAVENWORTH	TS6-4	28-May-52	13.50	4
LABETTE	PB12-3	4-Sep-57	6.38	3	LEAVENWORTH	PB12-4	5-Sep-57	20.41	4
LABETTE	UK7-3	27-Apr-53	6.53	3	LEAVENWORTH	TP10-3	7-May-55	24.27	4
LABETTE	TP10-3	7-May-55	13.99	4	LINCOLN	TP7-3	31-Mar-55	3.60	2
LABETTE	PB12-4	5-Sep-57	16.69	4	LINCOLN	UK9-3	21-May-53	3.84	2
LABETTE	TS7-5	5-Jun-52	22.77	4	LINCOLN	UK10-2	26-May-53	5.01	3
LABETTE	TS1-3	3-Apr-52	24.86	4	LINCOLN	UK7-3	27-Apr-53	5.11	3
LANE	TP11-3	17-May-55	4.14	2	LINCOLN	PB12-3	4-Sep-57	9.40	3
LANE	PB12-4	5-Sep-57	4.31	2	LINCOLN	PB12-4	5-Sep-57	11.82	4
LANE	TS6-4	28-May-52	4.83	2	LINCOLN	TP4-2	8-Mar-55	12.66	4
LANE	TS1-2	2-Apr-52	5.16	3	LINCOLN	TP9-2	15-Apr-55	13.01	4
LANE	TP10-3	7-May-55	6.05	3	LINCOLN	UK9-2	20-May-53	14.06	4

INDIVIDUAL FALLOUT DAYS
KANSAS

COUNTY	SHOT	DATE	µCi/SQ METER	INDEX	COUNTY	SHOT	DATE	µCi/SQ METER	INDEX
LINCOLN	TS6-4	28-May-52	16.12	4	LOGAN	TP4-2	8-Mar-55	51.16	6
LINCOLN	PB8-3	20-Aug-57	19.73	4	LYON	PB13-4	9-Sep-57	3.55	2
LINCOLN	TS7-5	5-Jun-52	20.64	4	LYON	PB8-3	20-Aug-57	4.00	2
LINCOLN	PB13-5	10-Sep-57	26.87	5	LYON	PB14-7	20-Sep-57	4.04	2
LINN	TP5-3	14-Mar-55	3.61	2	LYON	TS7-4	4-Jun-52	5.68	3
LINN	PB13-5	10-Sep-57	3.88	2	LYON	UK9-2	20-May-53	6.62	3
LINN	UK2-3	26-Mar-53	3.92	2	LYON	UK7-3	27-Apr-53	7.86	3
LINN	PB8-3	20-Aug-57	4.00	2	LYON	PB13-5	10-Sep-57	10.87	4
LINN	PB14-7	20-Sep-57	4.04	2	LYON	PB12-3	4-Sep-57	11.13	4
LINN	UK9-4	22-May-53	5.25	3	LYON	TP10-3	7-May-55	13.36	4
LINN	UK11-2	5-Jun-53	5.60	3	LYON	PB12-4	5-Sep-57	13.71	4
LINN	UK7-3	27-Apr-53	6.42	3	LYON	TS1-2	2-Apr-52	15.48	4
LINN	TS7-5	5-Jun-52	8.09	3	LYON	TS7-5	5-Jun-52	36.71	5
LINN	TP10-3	7-May-55	10.21	4	MARION	PB13-4	9-Sep-57	3.55	2
LINN	TS1-2	2-Apr-52	10.32	4	MARION	TS6-7	31-May-52	3.91	2
LINN	TS6-4	28-May-52	11.57	4	MARION	PB8-3	20-Aug-57	4.00	2
LINN	PB12-4	5-Sep-57	16.01	4	MARION	TS1-2	2-Apr-52	5.16	3
LOGAN	UK9-1	19-May-53	3.66	2	MARION	PB13-3	8-Sep-57	6.38	3
LOGAN	UK7-4	28-Apr-53	3.84	2	MARION	UK7-3	27-Apr-53	7.11	3
LOGAN	TS6-4	28-May-52	4.03	2	MARION	TP9-2	15-Apr-55	7.66	3
LOGAN	PB13-5	10-Sep-57	4.41	2	MARION	UK9-2	20-May-53	9.42	3
LOGAN	PB12-4	5-Sep-57	4.48	2	MARION	PB12-4	5-Sep-57	11.06	4
LOGAN	PB8-4	21-Aug-57	4.92	2	MARION	PB12-3	4-Sep-57	13.20	4
LOGAN	TS1-2	2-Apr-52	5.16	3	MARION	PB13-5	10-Sep-57	13.96	4
LOGAN	TP11-2	16-May-55	5.45	3	MARION	TP10-3	7-May-55	14.74	4
LOGAN	TP9-2	15-Apr-55	5.87	3	MARION	TS7-5	5-Jun-52	50.36	6
LOGAN	PB2-3	20-Jun-57	7.04	3	MARSHALL	PB13-4	9-Sep-57	3.55	2
LOGAN	TP3-2	2-Mar-55	7.78	3	MARSHALL	UK11-2	5-Jun-53	3.73	2
LOGAN	UK7-3	27-Apr-53	8.45	3	MARSHALL	PB8-3	20-Aug-57	4.00	2
LOGAN	UK9-2	20-May-53	17.36	4	MARSHALL	UK10-2	26-May-53	4.28	2
LOGAN	TS6-3	27-May-52	20.96	4	MARSHALL	TS7-5	5-Jun-52	4.38	2
LOGAN	TS8-1	5-Jun-52	26.59	5	MARSHALL	TS7-4	4-Jun-52	4.57	2
LOGAN	TP10-2	6-May-55	33.30	5	MARSHALL	TS7-3	3-Jun-52	4.83	2

INDIVIDUAL FALLOUT DAYS
KANSAS

COUNTY	SHOT	DATE	µCi/SQ METER	INDEX	COUNTY	SHOT	DATE	µCi/SQ METER	INDEX
MARSHALL	UK7-4	28-Apr-53	4.86	2	MIAMI	PB14-7	20-Sep-57	4.04	2
MARSHALL	TS1-2	2-Apr-52	5.16	3	MIAMI	UK2-3	26-Mar-53	4.51	2
MARSHALL	UK9-2	20-May-53	8.12	3	MIAMI	UK7-3	27-Apr-53	4.96	2
MARSHALL	PB12-4	5-Sep-57	12.09	4	MIAMI	TS7-5	5-Jun-52	7.55	3
MARSHALL	TP4-2	8-Mar-55	12.66	4	MIAMI	UK11-2	5-Jun-53	7.67	3
MARSHALL	PB13-5	10-Sep-57	18.75	4	MIAMI	TS6-4	28-May-52	12.54	4
MCPHERSON	TS7-4	4-Jun-52	3.89	2	MIAMI	PB12-4	5-Sep-57	15.61	4
MCPHERSON	PB8-3	20-Aug-57	4.00	2	MIAMI	TP10-3	7-May-55	36.75	5
MCPHERSON	TS6-4	28-May-52	4.03	2	MITCHELL	UK9-3	21-May-53	3.81	2
MCPHERSON	TS1-2	2-Apr-52	5.16	3	MITCHELL	TS7-4	4-Jun-52	3.84	2
MCPHERSON	UK7-3	27-Apr-53	7.40	3	MITCHELL	TS7-5	5-Jun-52	3.92	2
MCPHERSON	PB12-4	5-Sep-57	9.74	3	MITCHELL	UK7-3	27-Apr-53	4.06	2
MCPHERSON	TP9-2	15-Apr-55	11.56	4	MITCHELL	UK10-2	26-May-53	5.54	3
MCPHERSON	UK9-2	20-May-53	11.56	4	MITCHELL	PB12-4	5-Sep-57	8.11	3
MCPHERSON	PB12-3	4-Sep-57	19.06	4	MITCHELL	TP9-2	15-Apr-55	8.78	3
MCPHERSON	PB13-5	10-Sep-57	30.39	5	MITCHELL	TP4-2	8-Mar-55	12.66	4
MCPHERSON	TS7-5	5-Jun-52	32.48	5	MITCHELL	PB13-3	8-Sep-57	12.75	4
MEADE	UK6-3	20-Apr-53	4.23	2	MITCHELL	PB8-3	20-Aug-57	19.73	4
MEADE	TP11-3	17-May-55	4.29	2	MITCHELL	PB13-5	10-Sep-57	23.76	4
MEADE	PB18-2	11-Jul-57	4.60	2	MITCHELL	UK9-2	20-May-53	28.09	5
MEADE	UK3-5	4-Apr-53	5.46	3	MONTGOMERY	UK11-2	5-Jun-53	3.73	2
MEADE	TS6-4	28-May-52	5.64	3	MONTGOMERY	PB8-3	20-Aug-57	4.00	2
MEADE	TP10-3	7-May-55	8.25	3	MONTGOMERY	PB13-6	11-Sep-57	4.46	2
MEADE	PB12-4	5-Sep-57	8.38	3	MONTGOMERY	TS1-2	2-Apr-52	5.16	3
MEADE	UK7-3	27-Apr-53	11.89	4	MONTGOMERY	BJ2-2	31-Oct-51	5.84	3
MEADE	UK9-2	20-May-53	13.37	4	MONTGOMERY	PB13-5	10-Sep-57	6.92	3
MEADE	PB13-5	10-Sep-57	19.36	4	MONTGOMERY	UK9-2	20-May-53	7.05	3
MEADE	TP7-2	30-Mar-55	26.42	5	MONTGOMERY	UK7-3	27-Apr-53	7.84	3
MEADE	TP10-2	6-May-55	32.43	5	MONTGOMERY	TP10-3	7-May-55	10.14	4
MEADE	TS8-1	5-Jun-52	39.88	5	MONTGOMERY	PB12-4	5-Sep-57	16.76	4
MIAMI	PB8-3	20-Aug-57	4.00	2	MONTGOMERY	TS7-5	5-Jun-52	35.84	5
MIAMI	TS1-3	3-Apr-52	4.01	2	MORRIS	UK11-2	5-Jun-53	3.94	2
MIAMI	PB13-5	10-Sep-57	4.01	2	MORRIS	PB8-3	20-Aug-57	4.00	2

U.S. FALLOUT ATLAS: COUNTY COMPARISONS

INDIVIDUAL FALLOUT DAYS
KANSAS

COUNTY	SHOT	DATE	µCi/SQ METER	INDEX	COUNTY	SHOT	DATE	µCi/SQ METER	INDEX
MORRIS	PB14-7	20-Sep-57	4.04	2	NEMAHA	TP10-2	6-May-55	5.81	3
MORRIS	TP9-2	15-Apr-55	4.52	2	NEMAHA	UK9-2	20-May-53	7.41	3
MORRIS	TS1-2	2-Apr-52	5.16	3	NEMAHA	TS6-4	28-May-52	8.06	3
MORRIS	UK7-3	27-Apr-53	5.85	3	NEMAHA	PB13-5	10-Sep-57	9.42	3
MORRIS	UK9-2	20-May-53	8.42	3	NEMAHA	TP4-2	8-Mar-55	12.66	4
MORRIS	PB12-4	5-Sep-57	12.92	4	NEMAHA	PB12-4	5-Sep-57	17.70	4
MORRIS	PB13-5	10-Sep-57	12.97	4	NEOSHO	PB8-3	20-Aug-57	4.00	2
MORRIS	PB12-3	4-Sep-57	13.11	4	NEOSHO	UK11-2	5-Jun-53	4.10	2
MORRIS	TS6-4	28-May-52	37.61	5	NEOSHO	TP10-3	7-May-55	4.66	2
MORRIS	TS7-5	5-Jun-52	39.82	5	NEOSHO	UK9-2	20-May-53	5.51	3
MORTON	UK6-3	20-Apr-53	4.23	2	NEOSHO	BJ2-2	31-Oct-51	5.84	3
MORTON	PB18-2	11-Jul-57	4.60	2	NEOSHO	PB13-5	10-Sep-57	7.53	3
MORTON	PB11-2	1-Sep-57	4.79	2	NEOSHO	TS1-2	2-Apr-52	15.48	4
MORTON	PB13-8	13-Sep-57	5.51	3	NEOSHO	UK7-3	27-Apr-53	15.89	4
MORTON	TP11-3	17-May-55	6.36	3	NEOSHO	PB12-4	5-Sep-57	16.76	4
MORTON	TS6-4	28-May-52	7.25	3	NEOSHO	TS7-5	5-Jun-52	38.44	5
MORTON	PB13-5	10-Sep-57	8.23	3	NESS	TP11-3	17-May-55	3.53	2
MORTON	TP10-3	7-May-55	8.63	3	NESS	TP11-2	16-May-55	3.64	2
MORTON	UK9-2	20-May-53	16.35	4	NESS	TP7-3	31-Mar-55	3.90	2
MORTON	UK7-3	27-Apr-53	17.80	4	NESS	TS6-4	28-May-52	4.03	2
MORTON	UK9-1	19-May-53	25.21	5	NESS	PB12-3	4-Sep-57	4.14	2
MORTON	TP7-2	30-Mar-55	26.42	5	NESS	TS7-5	5-Jun-52	4.59	2
MORTON	TP10-2	6-May-55	32.43	5	NESS	TP10-3	7-May-55	6.05	3
MORTON	TS8-1	5-Jun-52	39.88	5	NESS	TP3-2	2-Mar-55	7.78	3
NEMAHA	PB13-4	9-Sep-57	3.55	2	NESS	TP9-2	15-Apr-55	8.28	3
NEMAHA	UK7-4	28-Apr-53	3.64	2	NESS	TS6-3	27-May-52	9.18	3
NEMAHA	TS7-3	3-Jun-52	3.71	2	NESS	TS1-2	2-Apr-52	9.99	3
NEMAHA	TP10-3	7-May-55	3.72	2	NESS	UK7-3	27-Apr-53	11.07	4
NEMAHA	PB8-3	20-Aug-57	4.00	2	NESS	PB12-4	5-Sep-57	13.31	4
NEMAHA	TS7-4	4-Jun-52	4.05	2	NESS	UK9-2	20-May-53	16.08	4
NEMAHA	UK10-2	26-May-53	4.26	2	NESS	PB13-5	10-Sep-57	22.31	4
NEMAHA	TS7-5	5-Jun-52	4.56	2	NESS	TP10-2	6-May-55	33.30	5
NEMAHA	TS1-3	3-Apr-52	4.81	2	NESS	TS8-1	5-Jun-52	39.88	5

INDIVIDUAL FALLOUT DAYS
KANSAS

COUNTY	SHOT	DATE	µCi/SQ METER	INDEX	COUNTY	SHOT	DATE	µCi/SQ METER	INDEX
NESS	TP4-2	8-Mar-55	51.16	6	OSBORNE	UK7-3	27-Apr-53	5.62	3
NORTON	PB13-4	9-Sep-57	3.55	2	OSBORNE	PB12-3	4-Sep-57	5.95	3
NORTON	TP11-2	16-May-55	3.64	2	OSBORNE	PB12-4	5-Sep-57	8.38	3
NORTON	UK9-3	21-May-53	4.00	2	OSBORNE	UK9-2	20-May-53	11.73	4
NORTON	TS7-5	5-Jun-52	5.07	3	OSBORNE	TP4-2	8-Mar-55	12.66	4
NORTON	TS1-2	2-Apr-52	5.16	3	OSBORNE	TP9-2	15-Apr-55	13.89	4
NORTON	PB12-4	5-Sep-57	5.21	3	OSBORNE	PB8-3	20-Aug-57	19.73	4
NORTON	UK7-3	27-Apr-53	5.91	3	OSBORNE	TS7-5	5-Jun-52	21.40	4
NORTON	PB13-3	8-Sep-57	6.38	3	OSBORNE	PB13-5	10-Sep-57	21.86	4
NORTON	TS6-3	27-May-52	6.99	3	OSBORNE	TS8-1	5-Jun-52	39.88	5
NORTON	TP3-2	2-Mar-55	7.78	3	OTTAWA	PB8-3	20-Aug-57	4.00	2
NORTON	TS7-4	4-Jun-52	8.27	3	OTTAWA	UK7-3	27-Apr-53	4.20	2
NORTON	PB13-5	10-Sep-57	9.89	3	OTTAWA	TS6-7	31-May-52	4.24	2
NORTON	UK9-2	20-May-53	10.21	4	OTTAWA	UK11-2	5-Jun-53	4.56	2
NORTON	TP9-2	15-Apr-55	14.65	4	OTTAWA	TS1-2	2-Apr-52	5.16	3
NORTON	PB8-3	20-Aug-57	19.73	4	OTTAWA	UK10-2	26-May-53	6.87	3
NORTON	TP10-2	6-May-55	33.30	5	OTTAWA	TP9-2	15-Apr-55	8.19	3
NORTON	TS8-1	5-Jun-52	39.88	5	OTTAWA	PB12-4	5-Sep-57	10.08	4
NORTON	TP4-2	8-Mar-55	51.16	6	OTTAWA	UK9-2	20-May-53	10.43	4
OSAGE	PB8-3	20-Aug-57	4.00	2	OTTAWA	PB12-3	4-Sep-57	10.61	4
OSAGE	PB14-7	20-Sep-57	4.04	2	OTTAWA	TP4-2	8-Mar-55	12.66	4
OSAGE	UK7-3	27-Apr-53	4.65	2	OTTAWA	TS7-5	5-Jun-52	22.92	4
OSAGE	PB12-3	4-Sep-57	5.00	3	OTTAWA	PB13-5	10-Sep-57	27.63	5
OSAGE	TS1-2	2-Apr-52	5.16	3	PAWNEE	UK11-2	5-Jun-53	3.85	2
OSAGE	UK9-2	20-May-53	5.26	3	PAWNEE	TS6-4	28-May-52	4.03	2
OSAGE	TS6-4	28-May-52	7.25	3	PAWNEE	TS1-2	2-Apr-52	5.16	3
OSAGE	TP10-3	7-May-55	9.70	3	PAWNEE	PB13-4	9-Sep-57	5.36	3
OSAGE	PB13-5	10-Sep-57	10.55	4	PAWNEE	TP10-3	7-May-55	5.67	3
OSAGE	PB12-4	5-Sep-57	15.95	4	PAWNEE	PB12-3	4-Sep-57	6.99	3
OSAGE	TS7-5	5-Jun-52	21.78	4	PAWNEE	UK7-3	27-Apr-53	11.00	4
OSBORNE	TP7-3	31-Mar-55	3.73	2	PAWNEE	PB12-4	5-Sep-57	12.84	4
OSBORNE	TS1-2	2-Apr-52	3.87	2	PAWNEE	TP9-2	15-Apr-55	13.70	4
OSBORNE	UK9-3	21-May-53	4.04	2	PAWNEE	UK9-2	20-May-53	15.63	4

INDIVIDUAL FALLOUT DAYS
KANSAS

COUNTY	SHOT	DATE	µCi/SQ METER	INDEX	COUNTY	SHOT	DATE	µCi/SQ METER	INDEX
PAWNEE	PB13-5	10-Sep-57	23.44	4	PRATT	PB13-5	10-Sep-57	12.30	4
PAWNEE	TS8-1	5-Jun-52	39.88	5	PRATT	TP9-2	15-Apr-55	13.13	4
PHILLIPS	PB8-5	22-Aug-57	3.78	2	PRATT	UK9-2	20-May-53	17.34	4
PHILLIPS	TS6-3	27-May-52	4.35	2	PRATT	TS7-5	5-Jun-52	22.86	4
PHILLIPS	TS7-4	4-Jun-52	4.38	2	PRATT	TS8-1	5-Jun-52	39.88	5
PHILLIPS	UK9-3	21-May-53	4.74	2	RAWLINS	UK11-2	5-Jun-53	3.56	2
PHILLIPS	UK7-3	27-Apr-53	5.36	3	RAWLINS	TS7-5	5-Jun-52	4.14	2
PHILLIPS	PB13-4	9-Sep-57	5.36	3	RAWLINS	PB12-4	5-Sep-57	4.19	2
PHILLIPS	PB13-3	8-Sep-57	6.38	3	RAWLINS	UK7-4	28-Apr-53	4.86	2
PHILLIPS	TP9-2	15-Apr-55	9.04	3	RAWLINS	TS1-2	2-Apr-52	5.16	3
PHILLIPS	UK9-2	20-May-53	10.30	4	RAWLINS	TP11-2	16-May-55	5.45	3
PHILLIPS	PB12-4	5-Sep-57	11.42	4	RAWLINS	UK7-3	27-Apr-53	6.31	3
PHILLIPS	TP4-2	8-Mar-55	12.66	4	RAWLINS	PB2-3	20-Jun-57	7.04	3
PHILLIPS	PB8-3	20-Aug-57	19.73	4	RAWLINS	TP3-2	2-Mar-55	7.78	3
PHILLIPS	TS8-1	5-Jun-52	39.88	5	RAWLINS	TP9-2	15-Apr-55	8.09	3
POTTAWATOMIE	UK7-4	28-Apr-53	3.58	2	RAWLINS	UK9-2	20-May-53	10.22	4
POTTAWATOMIE	TS1-2	2-Apr-52	3.87	2	RAWLINS	TS6-3	27-May-52	25.02	5
POTTAWATOMIE	PB8-3	20-Aug-57	4.00	2	RAWLINS	TS8-1	5-Jun-52	26.59	5
POTTAWATOMIE	UK10-2	26-May-53	4.13	2	RAWLINS	TP10-2	6-May-55	33.30	5
POTTAWATOMIE	UK11-2	5-Jun-53	4.60	2	RAWLINS	TP4-2	8-Mar-55	51.16	6
POTTAWATOMIE	TS1-3	3-Apr-52	4.81	2	RENO	TS5-1	7-May-52	3.90	2
POTTAWATOMIE	TS6-4	28-May-52	8.86	3	RENO	PB8-3	20-Aug-57	4.00	2
POTTAWATOMIE	UK9-2	20-May-53	9.17	3	RENO	TS1-2	2-Apr-52	5.16	3
POTTAWATOMIE	TP4-2	8-Mar-55	12.66	4	RENO	TS7-5	5-Jun-52	5.97	3
POTTAWATOMIE	TS7-5	5-Jun-52	13.53	4	RENO	PB12-4	5-Sep-57	6.71	3
POTTAWATOMIE	PB12-4	5-Sep-57	13.65	4	RENO	TP9-2	15-Apr-55	14.68	4
POTTAWATOMIE	PB13-5	10-Sep-57	20.51	4	RENO	UK9-2	20-May-53	15.64	4
PRATT	PB3-2	25-Jun-57	3.78	2	RENO	PB13-5	10-Sep-57	16.28	4
PRATT	TP10-3	7-May-55	5.04	3	RENO	PB12-3	4-Sep-57	18.20	4
PRATT	TS1-2	2-Apr-52	5.16	3	RENO	UK7-3	27-Apr-53	45.30	5
PRATT	PB12-4	5-Sep-57	10.37	4	REPUBLIC	TP9-2	15-Apr-55	3.86	2
PRATT	PB12-3	4-Sep-57	10.78	4	REPUBLIC	UK7-4	28-Apr-53	3.90	2
PRATT	UK7-3	27-Apr-53	10.93	4	REPUBLIC	TS7-5	5-Jun-52	4.18	2

INDIVIDUAL FALLOUT DAYS
KANSAS

COUNTY	SHOT	DATE	µCi/SQ METER	INDEX	COUNTY	SHOT	DATE	µCi/SQ METER	INDEX
REPUBLIC	PB12-4	5-Sep-57	4.53	2	ROOKS	PB12-4	5-Sep-57	8.72	3
REPUBLIC	UK9-3	21-May-53	4.53	2	ROOKS	PB13-5	10-Sep-57	10.86	4
REPUBLIC	TS1-2	2-Apr-52	5.16	3	ROOKS	TP9-2	15-Apr-55	11.51	4
REPUBLIC	UK10-2	26-May-53	5.91	3	ROOKS	TP4-2	8-Mar-55	12.66	4
REPUBLIC	TS7-3	3-Jun-52	7.21	3	ROOKS	UK7-3	27-Apr-53	14.02	4
REPUBLIC	UK9-2	20-May-53	8.67	3	ROOKS	UK9-2	20-May-53	14.45	4
REPUBLIC	PB13-5	10-Sep-57	11.68	4	ROOKS	PB8-3	20-Aug-57	19.73	4
REPUBLIC	TP4-2	8-Mar-55	12.66	4	ROOKS	TS8-1	5-Jun-52	39.88	5
REPUBLIC	TS7-4	4-Jun-52	23.75	4	RUSH	UK9-3	21-May-53	3.57	2
REPUBLIC	PB8-3	20-Aug-57	39.46	5	RUSH	TP7-3	31-Mar-55	3.69	2
RICE	PB8-3	20-Aug-57	4.00	2	RUSH	TS6-4	28-May-52	4.03	2
RICE	TS7-5	5-Jun-52	4.28	2	RUSH	TS1-2	2-Apr-52	5.16	3
RICE	TS1-2	2-Apr-52	5.16	3	RUSH	TP10-3	7-May-55	5.29	3
RICE	PB12-3	4-Sep-57	14.32	4	RUSH	TS7-5	5-Jun-52	6.11	3
RICE	UK9-2	20-May-53	15.56	4	RUSH	PB12-3	4-Sep-57	6.12	3
RICE	TP9-2	15-Apr-55	15.63	4	RUSH	UK7-3	27-Apr-53	10.45	4
RICE	PB13-5	10-Sep-57	26.93	5	RUSH	TP4-2	8-Mar-55	12.66	4
RICE	UK7-3	27-Apr-53	38.84	5	RUSH	PB12-4	5-Sep-57	12.91	4
RILEY	TP9-2	15-Apr-55	3.57	2	RUSH	TP9-2	15-Apr-55	13.60	4
RILEY	UK11-2	5-Jun-53	3.73	2	RUSH	UK9-2	20-May-53	15.27	4
RILEY	TS1-2	2-Apr-52	5.16	3	RUSH	PB13-5	10-Sep-57	22.49	4
RILEY	UK10-2	26-May-53	5.22	3	RUSH	TS8-1	5-Jun-52	39.88	5
RILEY	TS6-4	28-May-52	5.64	3	RUSSELL	PB13-4	9-Sep-57	3.55	2
RILEY	PB8-3	20-Aug-57	5.95	3	RUSSELL	PB12-4	5-Sep-57	3.85	2
RILEY	UK9-2	20-May-53	8.12	3	RUSSELL	UK7-4	28-Apr-53	4.17	2
RILEY	TP4-2	8-Mar-55	12.66	4	RUSSELL	TS7-4	4-Jun-52	4.76	2
RILEY	PB12-4	5-Sep-57	13.31	4	RUSSELL	TS1-2	2-Apr-52	5.16	3
RILEY	PB13-5	10-Sep-57	23.35	4	RUSSELL	PB12-3	4-Sep-57	7.50	3
RILEY	TS7-5	5-Jun-52	26.26	5	RUSSELL	TP4-2	8-Mar-55	12.66	4
ROOKS	PB12-3	4-Sep-57	4.48	2	RUSSELL	UK9-2	20-May-53	13.23	4
ROOKS	UK9-3	21-May-53	4.49	2	RUSSELL	TP9-2	15-Apr-55	17.12	4
ROOKS	TS6-3	27-May-52	6.38	3	RUSSELL	PB8-3	20-Aug-57	19.73	4
ROOKS	TP10-3	7-May-55	8.25	3	RUSSELL	UK7-3	27-Apr-53	22.82	4

INDIVIDUAL FALLOUT DAYS
KANSAS

COUNTY	SHOT	DATE	µCi/SQ METER	INDEX	COUNTY	SHOT	DATE	µCi/SQ METER	INDEX
RUSSELL	PB13-5	10-Sep-57	24.61	4	SCOTT	TS8-1	5-Jun-52	39.88	5
RUSSELL	TS7-5	5-Jun-52	29.87	5	SCOTT	TP4-2	8-Mar-55	51.16	6
RUSSELL	TS8-1	5-Jun-52	39.88	5	SEDGWICK	UK7-4	28-Apr-53	3.79	2
SALINE	UK11-2	5-Jun-53	3.52	2	SEDGWICK	PB8-3	20-Aug-57	4.00	2
SALINE	PB13-4	9-Sep-57	3.55	2	SEDGWICK	TS8-4	8-Jun-52	4.45	2
SALINE	TS6-7	31-May-52	3.63	2	SEDGWICK	TP9-2	15-Apr-55	9.60	3
SALINE	UK7-4	28-Apr-53	3.66	2	SEDGWICK	UK9-2	20-May-53	9.92	3
SALINE	PB8-3	20-Aug-57	4.00	2	SEDGWICK	UK7-3	27-Apr-53	10.05	4
SALINE	UK10-2	26-May-53	5.33	3	SEDGWICK	PB12-4	5-Sep-57	13.18	4
SALINE	UK7-3	27-Apr-53	5.49	3	SEDGWICK	PB13-5	10-Sep-57	14.17	4
SALINE	TP9-2	15-Apr-55	9.84	3	SEDGWICK	PB12-3	4-Sep-57	22.14	4
SALINE	TS1-2	2-Apr-52	10.32	4	SEDGWICK	TS7-5	5-Jun-52	26.83	5
SALINE	PB12-4	5-Sep-57	10.82	4	SEWARD	PB12-4	5-Sep-57	3.57	2
SALINE	TP4-2	8-Mar-55	12.66	4	SEWARD	UK6-3	20-Apr-53	4.23	2
SALINE	UK9-2	20-May-53	13.15	4	SEWARD	TP11-3	17-May-55	5.10	3
SALINE	TS7-4	4-Jun-52	13.79	4	SEWARD	UK3-5	4-Apr-53	5.46	3
SALINE	PB12-3	4-Sep-57	13.97	4	SEWARD	PB13-5	10-Sep-57	5.59	3
SALINE	PB13-5	10-Sep-57	26.36	5	SEWARD	TS6-4	28-May-52	6.45	3
SALINE	TS7-5	5-Jun-52	32.97	5	SEWARD	UK9-1	19-May-53	6.46	3
SCOTT	UK9-1	19-May-53	3.66	2	SEWARD	TP10-3	7-May-55	8.76	3
SCOTT	PB12-4	5-Sep-57	4.36	2	SEWARD	UK7-3	27-Apr-53	13.89	4
SCOTT	TS6-4	28-May-52	4.83	2	SEWARD	UK9-2	20-May-53	14.36	4
SCOTT	PB8-4	21-Aug-57	4.92	2	SEWARD	TP7-2	30-Mar-55	26.42	5
SCOTT	TP10-3	7-May-55	4.94	2	SEWARD	TP10-2	6-May-55	32.43	5
SCOTT	TP9-2	15-Apr-55	4.95	2	SEWARD	TS8-1	5-Jun-52	39.88	5
SCOTT	TS1-2	2-Apr-52	5.16	3	SHAWNEE	PB13-4	9-Sep-57	3.55	2
SCOTT	PB13-8	13-Sep-57	5.51	3	SHAWNEE	UK7-3	27-Apr-53	3.84	2
SCOTT	TP3-2	2-Mar-55	7.78	3	SHAWNEE	PB8-3	20-Aug-57	4.00	2
SCOTT	UK7-3	27-Apr-53	10.90	4	SHAWNEE	PB12-3	4-Sep-57	4.23	2
SCOTT	PB13-5	10-Sep-57	15.97	4	SHAWNEE	TS7-4	4-Jun-52	8.75	3
SCOTT	UK9-2	20-May-53	16.91	4	SHAWNEE	TP10-3	7-May-55	9.39	3
SCOTT	TS6-3	27-May-52	23.38	4	SHAWNEE	UK9-2	20-May-53	11.65	4
SCOTT	TP10-2	6-May-55	33.30	5	SHAWNEE	TP4-2	8-Mar-55	12.66	4

INDIVIDUAL FALLOUT DAYS
KANSAS

COUNTY	SHOT	DATE	µCi/SQ METER	INDEX	COUNTY	SHOT	DATE	µCi/SQ METER	INDEX
SHAWNEE	TS7-5	5-Jun-52	14.35	4	SMITH	UK9-3	21-May-53	4.35	2
SHAWNEE	TS6-4	28-May-52	15.43	4	SMITH	TS7-4	4-Jun-52	4.61	2
SHAWNEE	TS1-2	2-Apr-52	15.48	4	SMITH	UK7-4	28-Apr-53	4.70	2
SHAWNEE	PB13-5	10-Sep-57	18.08	4	SMITH	TP4-3	9-Mar-55	5.51	3
SHAWNEE	PB12-4	5-Sep-57	20.88	4	SMITH	PB13-5	10-Sep-57	6.00	3
SHERIDAN	TP11-2	16-May-55	3.64	2	SMITH	UK7-3	27-Apr-53	7.68	3
SHERIDAN	TP11-3	17-May-55	3.78	2	SMITH	TS7-5	5-Jun-52	8.49	3
SHERIDAN	PB12-4	5-Sep-57	4.14	2	SMITH	TP9-2	15-Apr-55	9.80	3
SHERIDAN	PB5-4	18-Jul-57	4.87	2	SMITH	UK9-2	20-May-53	9.85	3
SHERIDAN	TS1-2	2-Apr-52	5.16	3	SMITH	TP4-2	8-Mar-55	12.66	4
SHERIDAN	UK7-4	28-Apr-53	5.51	3	SMITH	PB8-3	20-Aug-57	19.73	4
SHERIDAN	TP3-2	2-Mar-55	7.78	3	SMITH	TS8-1	5-Jun-52	39.88	5
SHERIDAN	UK7-3	27-Apr-53	8.59	3	STAFFORD	TP10-3	7-May-55	3.99	2
SHERIDAN	TP9-2	15-Apr-55	9.13	3	STAFFORD	TS6-7	31-May-52	4.30	2
SHERIDAN	UK9-2	20-May-53	11.88	4	STAFFORD	TS1-2	2-Apr-52	5.16	3
SHERIDAN	TS6-3	27-May-52	16.15	4	STAFFORD	PB12-4	5-Sep-57	10.71	4
SHERIDAN	TP10-2	6-May-55	33.30	5	STAFFORD	PB12-3	4-Sep-57	10.78	4
SHERIDAN	TS8-1	5-Jun-52	39.88	5	STAFFORD	UK7-3	27-Apr-53	11.07	4
SHERIDAN	TP4-2	8-Mar-55	51.16	6	STAFFORD	TP9-2	15-Apr-55	16.46	4
SHERMAN	TS1-2	2-Apr-52	4.15	2	STAFFORD	UK9-2	20-May-53	17.79	4
SHERMAN	PB18-2	11-Jul-57	4.60	2	STAFFORD	PB13-5	10-Sep-57	27.63	5
SHERMAN	PB12-4	5-Sep-57	4.65	2	STAFFORD	TS8-1	5-Jun-52	39.88	5
SHERMAN	TS7-4	4-Jun-52	4.67	2	STANTON	TP11-3	17-May-55	3.58	2
SHERMAN	TP9-2	15-Apr-55	5.28	3	STANTON	PB11-2	1-Sep-57	4.79	2
SHERMAN	UK7-3	27-Apr-53	5.41	3	STANTON	TS1-2	2-Apr-52	5.16	3
SHERMAN	TS6-3	27-May-52	8.72	3	STANTON	TP11-2	16-May-55	5.45	3
SHERMAN	UK9-2	20-May-53	12.34	4	STANTON	TS6-4	28-May-52	7.25	3
SHERMAN	TP10-2	6-May-55	13.83	4	STANTON	TP10-3	7-May-55	7.75	3
SHERMAN	PB2-3	20-Jun-57	14.08	4	STANTON	TP3-2	2-Mar-55	7.78	3
SHERMAN	TP4-2	8-Mar-55	21.25	4	STANTON	PB12-4	5-Sep-57	8.72	3
SHERMAN	TS8-1	5-Jun-52	26.59	5	STANTON	PB13-5	10-Sep-57	13.87	4
SMITH	PB13-4	9-Sep-57	3.55	2	STANTON	PB2-3	20-Jun-57	15.08	4
SMITH	PB8-5	22-Aug-57	3.78	2	STANTON	UK7-3	27-Apr-53	16.77	4

INDIVIDUAL FALLOUT DAYS
KANSAS

COUNTY	SHOT	DATE	µCi/SQ METER	INDEX	COUNTY	SHOT	DATE	µCi/SQ METER	INDEX
STANTON	UK9-2	20-May-53	18.79	4	THOMAS	TP11-2	16-May-55	5.45	3
STANTON	UK9-1	19-May-53	19.61	4	THOMAS	UK7-3	27-Apr-53	6.87	3
STANTON	TP10-2	6-May-55	33.30	5	THOMAS	TP3-2	2-Mar-55	7.78	3
STANTON	TS8-1	5-Jun-52	39.88	5	THOMAS	TP9-2	15-Apr-55	7.86	3
STANTON	TP4-2	8-Mar-55	51.16	6	THOMAS	UK9-2	20-May-53	14.28	4
STEVENS	UK6-3	20-Apr-53	4.23	2	THOMAS	TS6-3	27-May-52	23.17	4
STEVENS	PB13-5	10-Sep-57	5.05	3	THOMAS	TS8-1	5-Jun-52	26.59	5
STEVENS	PB13-4	9-Sep-57	5.36	3	THOMAS	TP10-2	6-May-55	33.30	5
STEVENS	PB13-3	8-Sep-57	6.38	3	THOMAS	TP4-2	8-Mar-55	51.16	6
STEVENS	TS6-4	28-May-52	6.45	3	TREGO	UK9-3	21-May-53	3.57	2
STEVENS	TP11-3	17-May-55	9.99	3	TREGO	PB12-3	4-Sep-57	3.88	2
STEVENS	UK9-1	19-May-53	12.71	4	TREGO	TS6-4	28-May-52	4.03	2
STEVENS	UK7-3	27-Apr-53	15.81	4	TREGO	UK7-4	28-Apr-53	4.06	2
STEVENS	UK9-2	20-May-53	15.90	4	TREGO	TS1-2	2-Apr-52	5.16	3
STEVENS	TP10-2	6-May-55	32.43	5	TREGO	TP3-2	2-Mar-55	7.78	3
STEVENS	TS8-1	5-Jun-52	39.88	5	TREGO	TS6-3	27-May-52	7.82	3
STEVENS	TP10-3	7-May-55	46.59	5	TREGO	UK7-3	27-Apr-53	9.69	3
STEVENS	TP7-2	30-Mar-55	158.51	7	TREGO	TP9-2	15-Apr-55	9.70	3
SUMNER	BJ5-6	24-Nov-51	3.70	2	TREGO	TP10-3	7-May-55	10.71	4
SUMNER	PB8-3	20-Aug-57	4.00	2	TREGO	PB12-4	5-Sep-57	13.11	4
SUMNER	PB13-9	14-Sep-57	4.15	2	TREGO	UK9-2	20-May-53	14.99	4
SUMNER	TP9-2	15-Apr-55	6.41	3	TREGO	PB13-5	10-Sep-57	21.40	4
SUMNER	TP10-3	7-May-55	6.87	3	TREGO	TP10-2	6-May-55	33.30	5
SUMNER	UK7-3	27-Apr-53	9.59	3	TREGO	TS8-1	5-Jun-52	39.88	5
SUMNER	PB12-4	5-Sep-57	10.30	4	TREGO	TP4-2	8-Mar-55	51.16	6
SUMNER	UK9-2	20-May-53	11.06	4	WABAUNSEE	TP10-3	7-May-55	3.52	2
SUMNER	PB13-5	10-Sep-57	11.92	4	WABAUNSEE	PB13-4	9-Sep-57	3.55	2
SUMNER	PB12-3	4-Sep-57	22.94	4	WABAUNSEE	UK7-3	27-Apr-53	4.19	2
SUMNER	TS7-5	5-Jun-52	38.01	5	WABAUNSEE	TS1-3	3-Apr-52	4.81	2
THOMAS	PB2-3	20-Jun-57	3.52	2	WABAUNSEE	PB12-3	4-Sep-57	5.78	3
THOMAS	PB12-4	5-Sep-57	4.36	2	WABAUNSEE	TP10-2	6-May-55	5.81	3
THOMAS	UK7-4	28-Apr-53	4.42	2	WABAUNSEE	PB8-3	20-Aug-57	5.95	3
THOMAS	TS1-2	2-Apr-52	5.16	3	WABAUNSEE	UK9-2	20-May-53	7.59	3

INDIVIDUAL FALLOUT DAYS
KANSAS

COUNTY	SHOT	DATE	µCi/SQ METER	INDEX	COUNTY	SHOT	DATE	µCi/SQ METER	INDEX
WABAUNSEE	TS1-2	2-Apr-52	10.32	4	WASHINGTON	UK9-2	20-May-53	11.65	4
WABAUNSEE	PB12-4	5-Sep-57	12.63	4	WASHINGTON	TP4-2	8-Mar-55	12.66	4
WABAUNSEE	TP4-2	8-Mar-55	12.66	4	WASHINGTON	PB13-5	10-Sep-57	20.47	4
WABAUNSEE	TS6-4	28-May-52	17.36	4	WICHITA	TP10-3	7-May-55	4.73	2
WABAUNSEE	PB13-5	10-Sep-57	21.91	4	WICHITA	PB11-2	1-Sep-57	4.79	2
WABAUNSEE	TS7-5	5-Jun-52	34.97	5	WICHITA	TS6-4	28-May-52	4.83	2
WALLACE	TP11-2	16-May-55	3.64	2	WICHITA	PB8-4	21-Aug-57	4.92	2
WALLACE	TP9-2	15-Apr-55	3.83	2	WICHITA	TS1-2	2-Apr-52	5.16	3
WALLACE	TS6-4	28-May-52	4.13	2	WICHITA	TP11-2	16-May-55	5.45	3
WALLACE	PB11-2	1-Sep-57	4.79	2	WICHITA	UK9-1	19-May-53	6.25	3
WALLACE	PB2-3	20-Jun-57	5.03	3	WICHITA	TS7-5	5-Jun-52	6.26	3
WALLACE	TS1-2	2-Apr-52	5.16	3	WICHITA	TP3-2	2-Mar-55	7.78	3
WALLACE	PB4-5	9-Jul-57	5.18	3	WICHITA	PB13-5	10-Sep-57	7.80	3
WALLACE	PB12-4	5-Sep-57	6.57	3	WICHITA	TS6-3	27-May-52	9.57	3
WALLACE	TS7-5	5-Jun-52	6.87	3	WICHITA	UK7-3	27-Apr-53	11.76	4
WALLACE	UK9-1	19-May-53	6.89	3	WICHITA	UK9-2	20-May-53	18.49	4
WALLACE	TP3-2	2-Mar-55	7.78	3	WICHITA	TS8-1	5-Jun-52	26.59	5
WALLACE	TS7-4	4-Jun-52	8.86	3	WICHITA	TP10-2	6-May-55	33.30	5
WALLACE	UK7-3	27-Apr-53	8.88	3	WICHITA	TP4-2	8-Mar-55	51.16	6
WALLACE	UK9-2	20-May-53	15.33	4	WILSON	PB13-6	11-Sep-57	3.97	2
WALLACE	PB18-2	11-Jul-57	3.51	1	WILSON	PB8-3	20-Aug-57	4.00	2
WALLACE	TS6-3	27-May-52	26.34	5	WILSON	PB14-7	20-Sep-57	4.04	2
WALLACE	TS8-1	5-Jun-52	26.59	5	WILSON	PB13-5	10-Sep-57	4.44	2
WALLACE	TP10-2	6-May-55	33.30	5	WILSON	TP10-3	7-May-55	4.79	2
WALLACE	TP4-2	8-Mar-55	51.16	6	WILSON	UK9-2	20-May-53	5.71	3
WASHINGTON	TS7-5	5-Jun-52	4.12	2	WILSON	UK7-3	27-Apr-53	6.65	3
WASHINGTON	TS1-2	2-Apr-52	5.16	3	WILSON	BJ2-2	31-Oct-51	8.76	3
WASHINGTON	UK10-2	26-May-53	5.64	3	WILSON	PB12-4	5-Sep-57	23.58	4
WASHINGTON	TS7-3	3-Jun-52	6.08	3	WILSON	TS7-5	5-Jun-52	51.44	6
WASHINGTON	TS7-4	4-Jun-52	6.12	3	WOODSON	PB13-6	11-Sep-57	3.51	2
WASHINGTON	PB12-3	4-Sep-57	6.47	3	WOODSON	PB8-3	20-Aug-57	4.00	2
WASHINGTON	PB8-3	20-Aug-57	7.99	3	WOODSON	PB14-7	20-Sep-57	4.04	2
WASHINGTON	PB12-4	5-Sep-57	11.22	4	WOODSON	UK11-2	5-Jun-53	4.22	2

INDIVIDUAL FALLOUT DAYS
KANSAS

COUNTY	SHOT	DATE	µCi/SQ METER	INDEX	COUNTY	SHOT	DATE	µCi/SQ METER	INDEX
WOODSON	TP10-3	7-May-55	4.79	2	WYANDOTTE	PB18-8	17-Jul-57	5.26	3
WOODSON	UK9-2	20-May-53	5.56	3	WYANDOTTE	TP10-2	6-May-55	5.48	3
WOODSON	BJ2-2	31-Oct-51	5.84	3	WYANDOTTE	UK2-3	26-Mar-53	5.57	3
WOODSON	UK7-3	27-Apr-53	6.25	3	WYANDOTTE	UK9-2	20-May-53	5.86	3
WOODSON	PB13-5	10-Sep-57	8.46	3	WYANDOTTE	UK7-3	27-Apr-53	5.94	3
WOODSON	TS1-2	2-Apr-52	10.32	4	WYANDOTTE	UK11-2	5-Jun-53	6.38	3
WOODSON	PB12-4	5-Sep-57	14.22	4	WYANDOTTE	PB13-5	10-Sep-57	7.08	3
WOODSON	TS7-5	5-Jun-52	34.47	5	WYANDOTTE	PB8-3	20-Aug-57	7.99	3
WYANDOTTE	PB12-3	4-Sep-57	3.62	2	WYANDOTTE	PB4-5	9-Jul-57	10.65	4
WYANDOTTE	UK11-3	6-Jun-53	3.86	2	WYANDOTTE	PB12-4	5-Sep-57	14.73	4
WYANDOTTE	TP10-3	7-May-55	4.91	2	WYANDOTTE	TS1-2	2-Apr-52	18.05	4
WYANDOTTE	TP4-2	8-Mar-55	5.25	3					

INDIVIDUAL FALLOUT DAYS
KENTUCKY

COUNTY	SHOT	DATE	µCi/SQ METER	INDEX	COUNTY	SHOT	DATE	µCi/SQ METER	INDEX
ADAIR	TP5-3	14-Mar-55	3.93	2	BOONE	PB6-3	26-Jul-57	15.70	4
ADAIR	PB4-5	9-Jul-57	16.75	4	BOONE	SE4	9-Jul-62	90.29	6
ALLEN	TP10-3	7-May-55	9.09	3	BOURBON	PB6-3	26-Jul-57	3.96	2
ANDERSON	TP5-3	14-Mar-55	3.61	2	BOURBON	R1-2	29-Jan-51	5.83	3
ANDERSON	UK7-4	28-Apr-53	11.39	4	BOURBON	BJ2-4	2-Nov-51	12.81	4
ANDERSON	BJ2-4	2-Nov-51	11.91	4	BOURBON	SE3	8-Jul-62	90.94	6
ANDERSON	SE3	8-Jul-62	157.12	7	BOYD	TP10-2	6-May-55	3.62	2
BALLARD	UK1-3	19-Mar-53	3.97	2	BOYD	BJ2-4	2-Nov-51	4.48	2
BALLARD	PB5-3	17-Jul-57	4.85	2	BOYD	PB6-3	26-Jul-57	23.55	4
BALLARD	TS7-5	5-Jun-52	6.61	3	BOYD	SE4	9-Jul-62	208.78	8
BALLARD	TS1-3	3-Apr-52	9.02	3	BOYLE	TP5-3	14-Mar-55	3.73	2
BALLARD	UK7-4	28-Apr-53	19.06	4	BOYLE	TP10-3	7-May-55	4.68	2
BALLARD	UK9-3	21-May-53	3.51	1	BOYLE	BJ2-4	2-Nov-51	10.66	4
BARREN	TP10-3	7-May-55	4.10	2	BOYLE	PB4-5	9-Jul-57	16.75	4
BARREN	PB4-5	9-Jul-57	5.58	3	BOYLE	SE4	9-Jul-62	39.12	5
BARREN	SE4	9-Jul-62	17.11	4	BRACKEN	PB6-3	26-Jul-57	3.96	2
BATH	TP5-3	14-Mar-55	3.57	2	BRACKEN	PB6-4	27-Jul-57	4.32	2
BATH	PB6-3	26-Jul-57	3.96	2	BRACKEN	BJ2-4	2-Nov-51	4.46	2
BATH	TS5-1	7-May-52	4.20	2	BRACKEN	R1-2	29-Jan-51	15.23	4
BATH	SE3	8-Jul-62	35.48	5	BRACKEN	SE3	8-Jul-62	37.44	5
BATH	SE4	9-Jul-62	208.78	8	BRACKEN	SE4	9-Jul-62	85.56	6
BELL	TP10-2	6-May-55	3.62	2	BREATHITT	TP10-2	6-May-55	3.62	2
BELL	BJ2-4	2-Nov-51	3.68	2	BREATHITT	UK1-2	18-Mar-53	5.15	3
BELL	PB17-3	30-Sep-57	3.79	2	BREATHITT	PB17-3	30-Sep-57	5.64	3
BELL	PB6-3	26-Jul-57	3.96	2	BREATHITT	PB5-8	22-Jul-57	5.97	3
BELL	PB2-5	22-Jun-57	4.18	2	BREATHITT	PB4-5	9-Jul-57	7.83	3
BELL	TP6-4	25-Mar-55	4.32	2	BREATHITT	BJ2-4	2-Nov-51	11.15	4
BELL	PB4-5	9-Jul-57	5.24	3	BREATHITT	UK9-4	22-May-53	14.70	4
BELL	UK1-2	18-Mar-53	11.69	4	BREATHITT	PB6-3	26-Jul-57	23.55	4
BELL	SE4	9-Jul-62	43.75	5	BREATHITT	SE4	9-Jul-62	164.78	7
BOONE	TP5-3	14-Mar-55	3.83	2	BRECKINRIDGE	UK9-3	21-May-53	3.69	2
BOONE	TP10-3	7-May-55	9.54	3	BRECKINRIDGE	TP5-3	14-Mar-55	5.01	3
BOONE	R1-2	29-Jan-51	15.23	4	BRECKINRIDGE	TP10-3	7-May-55	25.08	5

INDIVIDUAL FALLOUT DAYS
KENTUCKY

COUNTY	SHOT	DATE	µCi/SQ METER	INDEX	COUNTY	SHOT	DATE	µCi/SQ METER	INDEX
BULLITT	TP5-3	14-Mar-55	5.14	3	CARTER	BJ2-4	2-Nov-51	5.38	3
BULLITT	UK7-4	28-Apr-53	15.30	4	CARTER	PB5-8	22-Jul-57	8.96	3
BULLITT	SE4	9-Jul-62	39.12	5	CARTER	SE4	9-Jul-62	208.78	8
BUTLER	SE4	9-Jul-62	17.11	4	CASEY	BJ2-4	2-Nov-51	3.55	2
BUTLER	TP10-3	7-May-55	29.46	5	CASEY	TP5-3	14-Mar-55	3.57	2
CALDWELL	TS1-3	3-Apr-52	4.81	2	CASEY	TP10-3	7-May-55	4.91	2
CALDWELL	UK7-4	28-Apr-53	5.26	3	CASEY	UK9-4	22-May-53	6.45	3
CALDWELL	PB4-5	9-Jul-57	5.58	3	CASEY	PB4-5	9-Jul-57	11.16	4
CALDWELL	PB5-3	17-Jul-57	7.27	3	CASEY	SE4	9-Jul-62	18.06	4
CALLOWAY	PB3-4	27-Jun-57	3.90	2	CHRISTIAN	UK1-3	19-Mar-53	4.37	2
CALLOWAY	UK1-3	19-Mar-53	6.26	3	CHRISTIAN	TP10-3	7-May-55	16.53	4
CALLOWAY	TS1-3	3-Apr-52	9.02	3	CHRISTIAN	PB4-5	9-Jul-57	16.75	4
CALLOWAY	UK7-4	28-Apr-53	10.53	4	CLARK	PB6-3	26-Jul-57	3.96	2
CAMPBELL	TP10-3	7-May-55	7.59	3	CLARK	TP5-3	14-Mar-55	4.44	2
CAMPBELL	R1-2	29-Jan-51	7.80	3	CLARK	TS5-1	7-May-52	4.65	2
CAMPBELL	PB6-3	26-Jul-57	7.85	3	CLARK	R1-2	29-Jan-51	15.23	4
CAMPBELL	PB6-4	27-Jul-57	9.38	3	CLARK	SE3	8-Jul-62	90.94	6
CAMPBELL	SE3	8-Jul-62	90.94	6	CLARK	SE4	9-Jul-62	149.13	7
CAMPBELL	SE4	9-Jul-62	208.78	8	CLAY	TP10-2	6-May-55	3.62	2
CARLISLE	UK8-3	10-May-53	3.68	2	CLAY	PB17-3	30-Sep-57	3.79	2
CARLISLE	UK9-3	21-May-53	3.88	2	CLAY	PB6-3	26-Jul-57	3.96	2
CARLISLE	UK1-3	19-Mar-53	5.24	3	CLAY	TP6-4	25-Mar-55	4.32	2
CARLISLE	UK2-7	30-Mar-53	12.19	4	CLAY	UK1-2	18-Mar-53	6.49	3
CARLISLE	UK2-8	31-Mar-53	3.50	1	CLAY	PB4-5	9-Jul-57	7.83	3
CARROLL	UK7-4	28-Apr-53	3.56	2	CLAY	BJ2-4	2-Nov-51	8.68	3
CARROLL	BJ2-4	2-Nov-51	3.76	2	CLAY	SE4	9-Jul-62	43.75	5
CARROLL	TP5-3	14-Mar-55	3.95	2	CLINTON	TP10-2	6-May-55	3.62	2
CARROLL	R1-2	29-Jan-51	4.06	2	CLINTON	PB17-3	30-Sep-57	3.79	2
CARROLL	TP10-3	7-May-55	6.78	3	CLINTON	PB2-5	22-Jun-57	4.18	2
CARROLL	SE3	8-Jul-62	90.94	6	CLINTON	UK1-2	18-Mar-53	4.33	2
CARROLL	SE4	9-Jul-62	208.78	8	CLINTON	PB4-5	9-Jul-57	7.83	3
CARTER	TP10-2	6-May-55	3.62	2	CRITTENDEN	TP5-3	14-Mar-55	3.52	2
CARTER	PB6-3	26-Jul-57	3.96	2	CRITTENDEN	UK7-4	28-Apr-53	4.33	2

INDIVIDUAL FALLOUT DAYS
KENTUCKY

COUNTY	SHOT	DATE	µCi/SQ METER	INDEX	COUNTY	SHOT	DATE	µCi/SQ METER	INDEX
CRITTENDEN	TS1-3	3-Apr-52	9.42	3	FLOYD	TP10-2	6-May-55	3.62	2
CUMBERLAND	TP5-3	14-Mar-55	3.83	2	FLOYD	PB6-3	26-Jul-57	3.96	2
CUMBERLAND	TS7-4	4-Jun-52	3.83	2	FLOYD	PB2-5	22-Jun-57	6.96	3
CUMBERLAND	PB4-5	9-Jul-57	27.91	5	FLOYD	BJ2-4	2-Nov-51	8.96	3
CUMBERLAND	SE4	9-Jul-62	43.75	5	FLOYD	PB17-3	30-Sep-57	14.98	4
DAVIESS	TS7-6	6-Jun-52	3.78	2	FLOYD	UK9-4	22-May-53	19.39	4
DAVIESS	PB4-5	9-Jul-57	4.20	2	FLOYD	SE4	9-Jul-62	149.13	7
DAVIESS	TP5-3	14-Mar-55	5.26	3	FRANKLIN	TP10-3	7-May-55	3.89	2
DAVIESS	TP10-3	7-May-55	27.88	5	FRANKLIN	BJ2-4	2-Nov-51	10.55	4
DAVIESS	SE4	9-Jul-62	31.92	5	FRANKLIN	SE3	8-Jul-62	90.94	6
EDMONSON	TP10-3	7-May-55	4.52	2	FRANKLIN	SE4	9-Jul-62	149.13	7
EDMONSON	TP5-3	14-Mar-55	5.00	3	FULTON	UK8-3	10-May-53	3.68	2
EDMONSON	SE4	9-Jul-62	17.11	4	FULTON	UK9-3	21-May-53	4.24	2
EDMONSON	TS7-4	4-Jun-52	3.50	1	FULTON	UK1-3	19-Mar-53	5.49	3
ELLIOTT	TP10-2	6-May-55	3.62	2	FULTON	TS7-6	6-Jun-52	5.94	3
ELLIOTT	PB6-3	26-Jul-57	3.96	2	FULTON	TS1-3	3-Apr-52	9.02	3
ELLIOTT	UK1-2	18-Mar-53	4.42	2	FULTON	TP10-3	7-May-55	14.28	4
ELLIOTT	BJ2-4	2-Nov-51	5.68	3	FULTON	UK2-7	30-Mar-53	18.26	4
ELLIOTT	SE4	9-Jul-62	208.78	8	FULTON	UK2-8	31-Mar-53	21.07	4
ESTILL	TP10-2	6-May-55	3.62	2	GALLATIN	UK7-4	28-Apr-53	3.75	2
ESTILL	BJ2-4	2-Nov-51	11.98	4	GALLATIN	BJ2-4	2-Nov-51	3.83	2
ESTILL	PB6-3	26-Jul-57	23.55	4	GALLATIN	PB6-3	26-Jul-57	3.96	2
ESTILL	SE4	9-Jul-62	94.45	6	GALLATIN	TP5-3	14-Mar-55	4.14	2
FAYETTE	UK9-4	22-May-53	3.94	2	GALLATIN	TP10-3	7-May-55	5.36	3
FAYETTE	PB6-3	26-Jul-57	3.96	2	GALLATIN	R1-2	29-Jan-51	6.15	3
FAYETTE	TS1-3	3-Apr-52	4.81	2	GALLATIN	SE4	9-Jul-62	208.78	8
FAYETTE	TP5-3	14-Mar-55	5.36	3	GARRARD	TS1-3	3-Apr-52	4.81	2
FAYETTE	SE3	8-Jul-62	90.94	6	GARRARD	BJ2-4	2-Nov-51	5.68	3
FLEMING	PB6-3	26-Jul-57	3.96	2	GARRARD	PB4-5	9-Jul-57	16.75	4
FLEMING	TS5-1	7-May-52	4.05	2	GARRARD	SE4	9-Jul-62	37.08	5
FLEMING	R1-2	29-Jan-51	5.83	3	GRANT	PB6-3	26-Jul-57	3.96	2
FLEMING	BJ2-4	2-Nov-51	6.18	3	GRANT	PB6-4	27-Jul-57	4.65	2
FLEMING	SE4	9-Jul-62	208.78	8	GRANT	TP5-3	14-Mar-55	6.08	3

INDIVIDUAL FALLOUT DAYS
KENTUCKY

COUNTY	SHOT	DATE	μCi/SQ METER	INDEX	COUNTY	SHOT	DATE	μCi/SQ METER	INDEX
GRANT	BJ2-4	2-Nov-51	7.59	3	HARLAN	TP6-4	25-Mar-55	4.32	2
GRANT	R1-2	29-Jan-51	15.23	4	HARLAN	UK9-4	22-May-53	6.78	3
GRANT	SE4	9-Jul-62	85.56	6	HARLAN	UK1-2	18-Mar-53	7.63	3
GRANT	SE3	8-Jul-62	90.94	6	HARLAN	BJ2-4	2-Nov-51	7.77	3
GRAVES	TS7-6	6-Jun-52	4.09	2	HARLAN	SE4	9-Jul-62	77.90	6
GRAVES	UK9-3	21-May-53	5.66	3	HARRISON	PB6-3	26-Jul-57	3.96	2
GRAVES	UK1-3	19-Mar-53	6.30	3	HARRISON	TP5-3	14-Mar-55	5.16	3
GRAVES	TS1-3	3-Apr-52	9.02	3	HARRISON	PB6-4	27-Jul-57	5.93	3
GRAVES	UK7-4	28-Apr-53	9.03	3	HARRISON	BJ2-4	2-Nov-51	10.43	4
GRAVES	SE4	9-Jul-62	43.75	5	HARRISON	R1-2	29-Jan-51	15.23	4
GRAYSON	TP5-3	14-Mar-55	4.55	2	HARRISON	SE3	8-Jul-62	37.44	5
GRAYSON	TP10-3	7-May-55	5.57	3	HARRISON	SE4	9-Jul-62	208.78	8
GREEN	TP5-3	14-Mar-55	3.82	2	HART	BJ2-4	2-Nov-51	3.92	2
GREEN	PB4-5	9-Jul-57	5.58	3	HART	TP5-3	14-Mar-55	4.16	2
GREEN	TP10-3	7-May-55	9.64	3	HART	TP10-3	7-May-55	6.47	3
GREENUP	TP10-2	6-May-55	3.62	2	HENDERSON	TP5-3	14-Mar-55	4.60	2
GREENUP	PB6-3	26-Jul-57	3.96	2	HENDERSON	UK7-4	28-Apr-53	4.73	2
GREENUP	TP6-4	25-Mar-55	4.32	2	HENDERSON	PB5-3	17-Jul-57	7.27	3
GREENUP	PB6-4	27-Jul-57	4.45	2	HENDERSON	TS1-3	3-Apr-52	9.42	3
GREENUP	BJ2-4	2-Nov-51	9.66	3	HENDERSON	TS7-3	3-Jun-52	16.11	4
GREENUP	R1-2	29-Jan-51	15.23	4	HENDERSON	UK9-3	21-May-53	3.51	1
GREENUP	SE4	9-Jul-62	359.52	8	HENRY	TP5-3	14-Mar-55	3.99	2
HANCOCK	R1-2	29-Jan-51	4.06	2	HENRY	TP10-3	7-May-55	4.02	2
HANCOCK	TP5-3	14-Mar-55	5.82	3	HENRY	BJ2-4	2-Nov-51	4.53	2
HANCOCK	BJ2-4	2-Nov-51	6.57	3	HENRY	SE3	8-Jul-62	35.48	5
HANCOCK	SE4	9-Jul-62	31.92	5	HENRY	SE4	9-Jul-62	208.78	8
HANCOCK	TP10-3	7-May-55	44.04	5	HICKMAN	UK8-3	10-May-53	3.68	2
HARDIN	TP5-3	14-Mar-55	4.93	2	HICKMAN	UK9-3	21-May-53	4.18	2
HARDIN	TP10-3	7-May-55	13.25	4	HICKMAN	UK1-3	19-Mar-53	6.30	3
HARLAN	TP10-2	6-May-55	3.62	2	HICKMAN	TS7-6	6-Jun-52	6.34	3
HARLAN	PB17-3	30-Sep-57	3.79	2	HICKMAN	TS1-3	3-Apr-52	9.02	3
HARLAN	PB6-3	26-Jul-57	3.96	2	HICKMAN	TP10-3	7-May-55	13.75	4
HARLAN	PB2-5	22-Jun-57	4.18	2	HICKMAN	UK2-7	30-Mar-53	18.26	4

INDITIVIDUAL FALLOUT DAYS
KENTUCKY

COUNTY	SHOT	DATE	µCi/SQ METER	INDEX	COUNTY	SHOT	DATE	µCi/SQ METER	INDEX
HICKMAN	UK2-8	31-Mar-53	21.07	4	KNOTT	UK1-2	18-Mar-53	3.71	2
HOPKINS	PB5-3	17-Jul-57	4.85	2	KNOTT	PB17-3	30-Sep-57	3.79	2
HOPKINS	TP10-3	7-May-55	8.32	3	KNOTT	PB2-5	22-Jun-57	4.18	2
JACKSON	TP10-2	6-May-55	3.62	2	KNOTT	TP6-4	25-Mar-55	4.32	2
JACKSON	PB17-3	30-Sep-57	3.79	2	KNOTT	PB4-5	9-Jul-57	5.24	3
JACKSON	PB6-3	26-Jul-57	3.96	2	KNOTT	TS3-6	27-Apr-52	5.50	3
JACKSON	TP6-4	25-Mar-55	4.32	2	KNOTT	PB6-3	26-Jul-57	7.85	3
JACKSON	UK1-2	18-Mar-53	6.49	3	KNOTT	UK9-4	22-May-53	8.99	3
JACKSON	BJ2-4	2-Nov-51	11.77	4	KNOTT	BJ2-4	2-Nov-51	9.16	3
JACKSON	SE4	9-Jul-62	164.78	7	KNOTT	SE4	9-Jul-62	94.45	6
JEFFERSON	PB3-4	27-Jun-57	4.95	2	KNOX	BJ2-4	2-Nov-51	3.59	2
JEFFERSON	TP5-3	14-Mar-55	7.53	3	KNOX	TP10-2	6-May-55	3.62	2
JEFFERSON	SE3	8-Jul-62	37.44	5	KNOX	PB17-3	30-Sep-57	3.79	2
JESSAMINE	TP5-3	14-Mar-55	5.62	3	KNOX	PB2-5	22-Jun-57	4.18	2
JESSAMINE	UK7-4	28-Apr-53	10.48	4	KNOX	TP6-4	25-Mar-55	4.32	2
JESSAMINE	UK9-4	22-May-53	12.63	4	KNOX	UK1-2	18-Mar-53	7.14	3
JESSAMINE	BJ2-4	2-Nov-51	14.72	4	KNOX	SE4	9-Jul-62	43.75	5
JESSAMINE	SE3	8-Jul-62	90.94	6	LARUE	TP5-3	14-Mar-55	4.42	2
JOHNSON	TP10-2	6-May-55	3.62	2	LARUE	TP10-3	7-May-55	18.52	4
JOHNSON	PB6-3	26-Jul-57	3.96	2	LAUREL	TP10-2	6-May-55	3.62	2
JOHNSON	TP6-4	25-Mar-55	4.32	2	LAUREL	PB17-3	30-Sep-57	3.79	2
JOHNSON	UK9-4	22-May-53	7.17	3	LAUREL	PB2-5	22-Jun-57	6.96	3
JOHNSON	BJ2-4	2-Nov-51	9.66	3	LAUREL	BJ2-4	2-Nov-51	8.77	3
JOHNSON	SE3	8-Jul-62	35.48	5	LAUREL	UK1-2	18-Mar-53	8.97	3
JOHNSON	SE4	9-Jul-62	149.13	7	LAWRENCE	UK1-2	18-Mar-53	3.56	2
KENTON	UK7-4	28-Apr-53	3.92	2	LAWRENCE	TP10-2	6-May-55	3.62	2
KENTON	TP10-3	7-May-55	4.91	2	LAWRENCE	PB6-3	26-Jul-57	3.96	2
KENTON	R1-2	29-Jan-51	5.83	3	LAWRENCE	BJ2-4	2-Nov-51	9.26	3
KENTON	PB6-4	27-Jul-57	6.39	3	LAWRENCE	SE4	9-Jul-62	359.52	8
KENTON	PB6-3	26-Jul-57	23.55	4	LEE	TP10-2	6-May-55	3.62	2
KENTON	SE3	8-Jul-62	35.48	5	LEE	PB17-3	30-Sep-57	3.79	2
KENTON	SE4	9-Jul-62	208.78	8	LEE	UK1-2	18-Mar-53	3.81	2
KNOTT	TP10-2	6-May-55	3.62	2	LEE	BJ2-4	2-Nov-51	6.01	3

INDIVIDUAL FALLOUT DAYS
KENTUCKY

COUNTY	SHOT	DATE	µCi/SQ METER	INDEX	COUNTY	SHOT	DATE	µCi/SQ METER	INDEX
LEE	UK9-4	22-May-53	6.45	3	LIVINGSTON	UK7-4	28-Apr-53	13.33	4
LEE	PB4-5	9-Jul-57	7.83	3	LOGAN	PB4-5	9-Jul-57	5.58	3
LEE	PB6-3	26-Jul-57	7.85	3	LOGAN	TP10-3	7-May-55	11.05	4
LESLIE	TP10-2	6-May-55	3.62	2	LYON	UK1-3	19-Mar-53	3.66	2
LESLIE	TP10-8	12-May-55	3.65	2	LYON	TS1-3	3-Apr-52	5.61	3
LESLIE	PB17-3	30-Sep-57	3.79	2	LYON	PB4-5	9-Jul-57	11.16	4
LESLIE	PB6-3	26-Jul-57	3.96	2	MADISON	BJ2-4	2-Nov-51	6.20	3
LESLIE	PB2-5	22-Jun-57	4.18	2	MADISON	PB6-3	26-Jul-57	15.70	4
LESLIE	TP6-4	25-Mar-55	4.32	2	MADISON	SE4	9-Jul-62	94.45	6
LESLIE	UK1-2	18-Mar-53	6.49	3	MAGOFFIN	TP10-2	6-May-55	3.62	2
LESLIE	BJ2-4	2-Nov-51	9.16	3	MAGOFFIN	PB17-3	30-Sep-57	3.79	2
LESLIE	PB5-8	22-Jul-57	14.93	4	MAGOFFIN	PB6-3	26-Jul-57	3.96	2
LESLIE	SE5	10-Jul-62	47.25	5	MAGOFFIN	PB2-5	22-Jun-57	4.18	2
LESLIE	SE4	9-Jul-62	77.90	6	MAGOFFIN	UK1-2	18-Mar-53	4.23	2
LETCHER	TP10-2	6-May-55	3.62	2	MAGOFFIN	TP6-4	25-Mar-55	4.32	2
LETCHER	PB17-3	30-Sep-57	3.79	2	MAGOFFIN	UK9-4	22-May-53	4.57	2
LETCHER	PB2-5	22-Jun-57	4.18	2	MAGOFFIN	PB5-8	22-Jul-57	8.96	3
LETCHER	BJ2-4	2-Nov-51	4.18	2	MAGOFFIN	BJ2-4	2-Nov-51	10.45	4
LETCHER	UK1-2	18-Mar-53	4.23	2	MAGOFFIN	SE3	8-Jul-62	35.48	5
LETCHER	TP6-4	25-Mar-55	4.32	2	MAGOFFIN	SE4	9-Jul-62	149.13	7
LETCHER	PB4-5	9-Jul-57	5.24	3	MARION	TP5-3	14-Mar-55	3.74	2
LETCHER	PB6-3	26-Jul-57	7.85	3	MARION	TS1-3	3-Apr-52	4.81	2
LETCHER	UK9-4	22-May-53	10.29	4	MARION	TP10-3	7-May-55	10.21	4
LETCHER	SE4	9-Jul-62	94.45	6	MARSHALL	UK9-3	21-May-53	3.69	2
LEWIS	PB6-3	26-Jul-57	3.96	2	MARSHALL	UK1-3	19-Mar-53	5.31	3
LEWIS	BJ2-4	2-Nov-51	5.01	3	MARSHALL	TS1-3	3-Apr-52	9.02	3
LEWIS	R1-2	29-Jan-51	5.83	3	MARSHALL	SE4	9-Jul-62	43.75	5
LEWIS	SE4	9-Jul-62	359.52	8	MARTIN	TP10-2	6-May-55	3.62	2
LINCOLN	PB4-5	9-Jul-57	16.75	4	MARTIN	PB17-3	30-Sep-57	3.79	2
LINCOLN	SE4	9-Jul-62	37.08	5	MARTIN	PB6-3	26-Jul-57	3.96	2
LIVINGSTON	TS1-3	3-Apr-52	5.61	3	MARTIN	PB2-5	22-Jun-57	4.18	2
LIVINGSTON	TS7-5	5-Jun-52	7.11	3	MARTIN	BJ2-4	2-Nov-51	4.28	2
LIVINGSTON	PB5-3	17-Jul-57	7.27	3	MARTIN	TP6-4	25-Mar-55	4.32	2

INDIVIDUAL FALLOUT DAYS
KENTUCKY

COUNTY	SHOT	DATE	µCi/SQ METER	INDEX	COUNTY	SHOT	DATE	µCi/SQ METER	INDEX
MARTIN	PB5-8	22-Jul-57	14.93	4	MERCER	TP10-3	7-May-55	5.10	3
MARTIN	SE4	9-Jul-62	57.04	6	MERCER	BJ2-4	2-Nov-51	6.41	3
MASON	PB6-3	26-Jul-57	3.96	2	MERCER	PB4-5	9-Jul-57	16.75	4
MASON	PB6-4	27-Jul-57	4.43	2	MERCER	SE4	9-Jul-62	37.08	5
MASON	BJ2-4	2-Nov-51	4.67	2	METCALFE	TP10-3	7-May-55	3.78	2
MASON	R1-2	29-Jan-51	5.83	3	METCALFE	TS7-6	6-Jun-52	7.56	3
MASON	SE4	9-Jul-62	208.78	8	METCALFE	PB4-5	9-Jul-57	11.16	4
MCCRACKEN	UK9-3	21-May-53	3.63	2	MONROE	TS7-6	6-Jun-52	7.20	3
MCCRACKEN	UK1-3	19-Mar-53	4.11	2	MONROE	PB4-5	9-Jul-57	16.75	4
MCCRACKEN	TS7-6	6-Jun-52	4.33	2	MONROE	SE4	9-Jul-62	17.11	4
MCCRACKEN	PB5-3	17-Jul-57	7.27	3	MONTGOMERY	TP5-3	14-Mar-55	3.88	2
MCCRACKEN	TS1-3	3-Apr-52	9.02	3	MONTGOMERY	PB6-3	26-Jul-57	3.96	2
MCCRACKEN	UK7-4	28-Apr-53	14.03	4	MONTGOMERY	TS5-1	7-May-52	4.35	2
MCCREARY	TP10-2	6-May-55	3.62	2	MONTGOMERY	SE3	8-Jul-62	157.12	7
MCCREARY	PB17-3	30-Sep-57	3.79	2	MORGAN	TP10-2	6-May-55	3.62	2
MCCREARY	TP6-4	25-Mar-55	4.32	2	MORGAN	PB6-3	26-Jul-57	3.96	2
MCCREARY	BJ2-4	2-Nov-51	5.68	3	MORGAN	UK1-2	18-Mar-53	5.90	3
MCCREARY	UK1-2	18-Mar-53	6.79	3	MORGAN	BJ2-4	2-Nov-51	6.07	3
MCCREARY	SE4	9-Jul-62	17.11	4	MORGAN	SE3	8-Jul-62	35.48	5
MCLEAN	TP5-3	14-Mar-55	4.80	2	MORGAN	SE4	9-Jul-62	149.13	7
MCLEAN	PB5-3	17-Jul-57	7.27	3	MUHLENBERG	TP5-3	14-Mar-55	4.54	2
MCLEAN	TP10-3	7-May-55	16.98	4	MUHLENBERG	TS1-3	3-Apr-52	4.81	2
MEADE	TS1-3	3-Apr-52	4.81	2	MUHLENBERG	TP10-3	7-May-55	14.28	4
MEADE	PB3-4	27-Jun-57	5.13	3	NELSON	BJ2-4	2-Nov-51	4.09	2
MEADE	TP5-3	14-Mar-55	5.44	3	NELSON	TS7-3	3-Jun-52	5.01	3
MEADE	TS7-3	3-Jun-52	12.79	4	NICHOLAS	PB6-3	26-Jul-57	3.96	2
MENIFEE	TP10-2	6-May-55	3.62	2	NICHOLAS	BJ2-4	2-Nov-51	12.26	4
MENIFEE	UK1-2	18-Mar-53	3.92	2	NICHOLAS	R1-2	29-Jan-51	15.23	4
MENIFEE	UK9-4	22-May-53	11.01	4	NICHOLAS	SE3	8-Jul-62	37.44	5
MENIFEE	BJ2-4	2-Nov-51	12.44	4	NICHOLAS	SE4	9-Jul-62	208.78	8
MENIFEE	SE3	8-Jul-62	35.48	5	OHIO	TP5-3	14-Mar-55	5.16	3
MENIFEE	PB6-3	26-Jul-57	39.25	5	OHIO	SE4	9-Jul-62	18.06	4
MENIFEE	SE4	9-Jul-62	149.13	7	OHIO	TP10-3	7-May-55	24.65	4

INDIVIDUAL FALLOUT DAYS
KENTUCKY

COUNTY	SHOT	DATE	µCi/SQ METER	INDEX	COUNTY	SHOT	DATE	µCi/SQ METER	INDEX
OLDHAM	R1-2	29-Jan-51	4.06	2	PIKE	TP10-2	6-May-55	3.62	2
OLDHAM	TP5-3	14-Mar-55	8.07	3	PIKE	PB6-3	26-Jul-57	3.96	2
OLDHAM	SE3	8-Jul-62	157.12	7	PIKE	BJ2-4	2-Nov-51	3.98	2
OWEN	UK7-4	28-Apr-53	3.57	2	PIKE	PB4-5	9-Jul-57	5.24	3
OWEN	PB6-3	26-Jul-57	3.96	2	PIKE	UK9-4	22-May-53	5.63	3
OWEN	TP5-3	14-Mar-55	4.08	2	PIKE	PB17-3	30-Sep-57	7.49	3
OWEN	BJ2-4	2-Nov-51	4.29	2	PIKE	PB5-8	22-Jul-57	8.96	3
OWEN	UK9-4	22-May-53	5.48	3	PIKE	SE4	9-Jul-62	149.13	7
OWEN	R1-2	29-Jan-51	15.23	4	POWELL	TP10-2	6-May-55	3.62	2
OWEN	SE3	8-Jul-62	90.94	6	POWELL	BJ2-4	2-Nov-51	11.77	4
OWEN	SE4	9-Jul-62	208.78	8	POWELL	PB6-3	26-Jul-57	23.55	4
OWSLEY	TP10-2	6-May-55	3.62	2	POWELL	SE3	8-Jul-62	90.94	6
OWSLEY	PB17-3	30-Sep-57	3.79	2	POWELL	SE4	9-Jul-62	263.65	8
OWSLEY	UK1-2	18-Mar-53	4.74	2	PULASKI	TP10-2	6-May-55	3.62	2
OWSLEY	BJ2-4	2-Nov-51	5.26	3	PULASKI	PB17-3	30-Sep-57	3.79	2
OWSLEY	UK9-4	22-May-53	7.17	3	PULASKI	UK1-2	18-Mar-53	4.81	2
OWSLEY	PB4-5	9-Jul-57	7.83	3	PULASKI	BJ2-4	2-Nov-51	8.26	3
OWSLEY	PB6-3	26-Jul-57	7.85	3	PULASKI	SE4	9-Jul-62	43.75	5
OWSLEY	SE4	9-Jul-62	164.78	7	ROBERTSON	PB6-4	27-Jul-57	3.66	2
PENDLETON	PB6-3	26-Jul-57	3.96	2	ROBERTSON	PB6-3	26-Jul-57	3.96	2
PENDLETON	TP5-3	14-Mar-55	5.26	3	ROBERTSON	BJ2-4	2-Nov-51	5.36	3
PENDLETON	BJ2-4	2-Nov-51	7.30	3	ROBERTSON	R1-2	29-Jan-51	15.23	4
PENDLETON	PB6-4	27-Jul-57	7.98	3	ROBERTSON	SE4	9-Jul-62	208.78	8
PENDLETON	R1-2	29-Jan-51	15.23	4	ROCKCASTLE	TP10-2	6-May-55	3.62	2
PENDLETON	SE3	8-Jul-62	37.44	5	ROCKCASTLE	PB17-3	30-Sep-57	3.79	2
PENDLETON	SE4	9-Jul-62	85.56	6	ROCKCASTLE	TP6-4	25-Mar-55	4.32	2
PERRY	TP10-2	6-May-55	3.62	2	ROCKCASTLE	UK1-2	18-Mar-53	5.67	3
PERRY	PB17-3	30-Sep-57	3.79	2	ROCKCASTLE	BJ2-4	2-Nov-51	9.82	3
PERRY	UK1-2	18-Mar-53	5.05	3	ROCKCASTLE	SE4	9-Jul-62	94.45	6
PERRY	PB6-3	26-Jul-57	7.85	3	ROWAN	TP10-2	6-May-55	3.62	2
PERRY	BJ2-4	2-Nov-51	9.56	3	ROWAN	TP6-4	25-Mar-55	4.32	2
PERRY	UK9-4	22-May-53	17.35	4	ROWAN	BJ2-4	2-Nov-51	5.68	3
PERRY	SE4	9-Jul-62	94.45	6	ROWAN	PB6-3	26-Jul-57	15.70	4

INDIVIDUAL FALLOUT DAYS
KENTUCKY

COUNTY	SHOT	DATE	µCi/SQ METER	INDEX	COUNTY	SHOT	DATE	µCi/SQ METER	INDEX
ROWAN	SE3	8-Jul-62	90.94	6	TRIGG	UK7-4	28-Apr-53	4.99	2
ROWAN	SE4	9-Jul-62	208.78	8	TRIGG	UK1-3	19-Mar-53	5.14	3
RUSSELL	TP5-3	14-Mar-55	3.52	2	TRIGG	PB4-5	9-Jul-57	5.58	3
RUSSELL	UK1-2	18-Mar-53	5.36	3	TRIMBLE	UK7-4	28-Apr-53	3.82	2
RUSSELL	PB4-5	9-Jul-57	16.75	4	TRIMBLE	R1-2	29-Jan-51	4.06	2
RUSSELL	SE4	9-Jul-62	43.75	5	TRIMBLE	TP10-3	7-May-55	6.82	3
SCOTT	TP5-3	14-Mar-55	3.52	2	TRIMBLE	TP5-3	14-Mar-55	7.52	3
SCOTT	PB6-3	26-Jul-57	3.96	2	TRIMBLE	SE4	9-Jul-62	359.52	8
SCOTT	BJ2-4	2-Nov-51	6.49	3	UNION	TS7-6	6-Jun-52	3.69	2
SCOTT	R1-2	29-Jan-51	15.23	4	UNION	TP5-3	14-Mar-55	3.88	2
SCOTT	SE3	8-Jul-62	90.94	6	UNION	TS1-4	4-Apr-52	4.22	2
SCOTT	SE4	9-Jul-62	149.13	7	UNION	PB4-5	9-Jul-57	5.58	3
SHELBY	TP10-3	7-May-55	4.24	2	UNION	TS1-3	3-Apr-52	5.61	3
SHELBY	BJ2-4	2-Nov-51	4.74	2	UNION	PB5-3	17-Jul-57	7.27	3
SHELBY	TP5-3	14-Mar-55	6.93	3	UNION	TP10-3	7-May-55	16.23	4
SHELBY	SE3	8-Jul-62	35.48	5	UNION	SE4	9-Jul-62	21.81	4
SHELBY	SE4	9-Jul-62	149.13	7	WARREN	TP5-3	14-Mar-55	4.65	2
SIMPSON	TP10-3	7-May-55	9.69	3	WARREN	TS7-5	5-Jun-52	5.02	3
SIMPSON	PB4-5	9-Jul-57	16.75	4	WARREN	TS7-6	6-Jun-52	6.43	3
SPENCER	BJ2-4	2-Nov-51	4.25	2	WARREN	UK7-4	28-Apr-53	7.05	3
SPENCER	TP5-3	14-Mar-55	4.29	2	WARREN	TP10-3	7-May-55	11.65	4
SPENCER	SE4	9-Jul-62	37.08	5	WASHINGTON	BJ2-4	2-Nov-51	4.53	2
SPENCER	SE3	8-Jul-62	90.94	6	WASHINGTON	TP5-3	14-Mar-55	6.33	3
TAYLOR	TP5-3	14-Mar-55	3.61	2	WASHINGTON	SE4	9-Jul-62	37.08	5
TAYLOR	TS1-3	3-Apr-52	4.81	2	WAYNE	TP10-2	6-May-55	3.62	2
TAYLOR	TP10-3	7-May-55	9.20	3	WAYNE	PB17-3	30-Sep-57	3.79	2
TODD	UK1-3	19-Mar-53	3.79	2	WAYNE	UK1-2	18-Mar-53	4.64	2
TODD	TP10-3	7-May-55	16.08	4	WAYNE	PB4-5	9-Jul-57	13.06	4
TODD	PB4-5	9-Jul-57	16.75	4	WAYNE	SE4	9-Jul-62	17.11	4
TODD	SE4	9-Jul-62	21.81	4	WEBSTER	TP5-3	14-Mar-55	4.19	2
TRIGG	PB3-4	27-Jun-57	4.00	2	WEBSTER	TS1-3	3-Apr-52	5.61	3
TRIGG	TS1-3	3-Apr-52	4.81	2	WEBSTER	TS7-5	5-Jun-52	7.41	3
TRIGG	TS7-4	4-Jun-52	4.90	2	WEBSTER	TP10-3	7-May-55	9.01	3

INDIVIDUAL FALLOUT DAYS
KENTUCKY

COUNTY	SHOT	DATE	µCi/SQ METER	INDEX	COUNTY	SHOT	DATE	µCi/SQ METER	INDEX
WHITLEY	TP10-2	6-May-55	3.62	2	WOLFE	UK9-4	22-May-53	12.57	4
WHITLEY	PB17-3	30-Sep-57	3.79	2	WOLFE	PB6-3	26-Jul-57	23.55	4
WHITLEY	TP6-4	25-Mar-55	4.32	2	WOLFE	SE3	8-Jul-62	35.48	5
WHITLEY	UK9-4	22-May-53	4.32	2	WOLFE	SE4	9-Jul-62	149.13	7
WHITLEY	BJ2-4	2-Nov-51	6.26	3	WOODFORD	TP5-3	14-Mar-55	3.78	2
WHITLEY	UK1-2	18-Mar-53	8.00	3	WOODFORD	PB4-5	9-Jul-57	5.58	3
WHITLEY	SE4	9-Jul-62	17.11	4	WOODFORD	BJ2-4	2-Nov-51	13.33	4
WOLFE	TP10-2	6-May-55	3.62	2	WOODFORD	SE3	8-Jul-62	90.94	6
WOLFE	UK1-2	18-Mar-53	4.23	2	WOODFORD	SE4	9-Jul-62	149.13	7
WOLFE	BJ2-4	2-Nov-51	11.02	4					

INDICUAL FALLOUT DAYS
LOUISIANA

COUNTY	SHOT	DATE	µCi/SQ METER	INDEX	COUNTY	SHOT	DATE	µCi/SQ METER	INDEX
ACADIA	UK7-3	27-Apr-53	3.71	2	BIENVILLE	TP10-3	7-May-55	4.35	2
ACADIA	TS6-4	28-May-52	3.86	2	BIENVILLE	TP11-2	16-May-55	4.75	2
ACADIA	TP6-3	24-Mar-55	8.63	3	BIENVILLE	TP6-3	24-Mar-55	8.63	3
ACADIA	UK6-2	19-Apr-53	77.35	6	BIENVILLE	UK7-4	28-Apr-53	17.59	4
ACADIA	PB3-3	26-Jun-57	114.67	7	BOSSIER	UK5-4	14-Apr-53	3.91	2
ALLEN	TP6-3	24-Mar-55	8.63	3	BOSSIER	BJ3-5	5-Nov-51	4.02	2
ALLEN	UK7-4	28-Apr-53	9.30	3	BOSSIER	TS6-4	28-May-52	5.79	3
ALLEN	TP11-2	16-May-55	11.92	4	BOSSIER	TP6-3	24-Mar-55	8.63	3
ALLEN	PB3-3	26-Jun-57	68.82	6	BOSSIER	UK7-4	28-Apr-53	9.89	3
ALLEN	UK6-2	19-Apr-53	77.35	6	BOSSIER	TS1-3	3-Apr-52	24.86	4
ASCENSION	PB17-5	2-Oct-57	5.34	3	CADDO	PB12-4	5-Sep-57	3.68	2
ASCENSION	UK7-3	27-Apr-53	6.65	3	CADDO	PB11-1	31-Aug-57	4.09	2
ASCENSION	UK7-4	28-Apr-53	20.21	4	CADDO	UK7-4	28-Apr-53	5.13	3
ASCENSION	UK6-2	19-Apr-53	37.36	5	CADDO	TP6-3	24-Mar-55	8.63	3
ASCENSION	PB3-3	26-Jun-57	68.82	6	CADDO	TS6-4	28-May-52	17.36	4
ASSUMPTION	UK7-4	28-Apr-53	4.15	2	CADDO	UK7-3	27-Apr-53	18.78	4
ASSUMPTION	UK7-3	27-Apr-53	5.96	3	CALCASIEU	TS6-4	28-May-52	3.86	2
ASSUMPTION	UK6-2	19-Apr-53	37.36	5	CALCASIEU	TP11-2	16-May-55	4.75	2
ASSUMPTION	PB3-3	26-Jun-57	114.67	7	CALCASIEU	UK7-4	28-Apr-53	6.29	3
AVOYELLES	TS1-3	3-Apr-52	4.01	2	CALCASIEU	TP6-3	24-Mar-55	8.63	3
AVOYELLES	UK7-3	27-Apr-53	5.43	3	CALCASIEU	UK6-2	19-Apr-53	77.35	6
AVOYELLES	TP6-3	24-Mar-55	5.55	3	CALCASIEU	PB3-3	26-Jun-57	114.67	7
AVOYELLES	UK7-4	28-Apr-53	9.37	3	CALDWELL	UK7-3	27-Apr-53	5.50	3
AVOYELLES	PB3-3	26-Jun-57	114.67	7	CALDWELL	TP6-3	24-Mar-55	5.55	3
BEAUREGARD	TP11-2	16-May-55	7.17	3	CALDWELL	UK7-4	28-Apr-53	31.18	5
BEAUREGARD	UK7-4	28-Apr-53	8.39	3	CAMERON	TS6-4	28-May-52	3.86	2
BEAUREGARD	TP6-3	24-Mar-55	8.63	3	CAMERON	TP11-2	16-May-55	4.75	2
BEAUREGARD	TS6-4	28-May-52	8.68	3	CAMERON	TP6-3	24-Mar-55	8.63	3
BEAUREGARD	UK7-3	27-Apr-53	13.86	4	CAMERON	UK6-2	19-Apr-53	77.35	6
BEAUREGARD	UK6-2	19-Apr-53	77.35	6	CAMERON	PB3-3	26-Jun-57	114.67	7
BEAUREGARD	PB3-3	26-Jun-57	114.67	7	CATAHOULA	TS1-3	3-Apr-52	4.01	2
BIENVILLE	BJ3-5	5-Nov-51	4.02	2	CATAHOULA	TP6-3	24-Mar-55	5.55	3
BIENVILLE	PB11-1	31-Aug-57	4.09	2	CATAHOULA	UK7-3	27-Apr-53	6.39	3

INDIVIDUAL FALLOUT DAYS
LOUISIANA

COUNTY	SHOT	DATE	µCi/SQ METER	INDEX	COUNTY	SHOT	DATE	µCi/SQ METER	INDEX
CATAHOULA	UK7-4	28-Apr-53	33.41	5	EVANGELINE	PB3-3	26-Jun-57	114.67	7
CATAHOULA	PB3-3	26-Jun-57	68.82	6	FRANKLIN	PB9-2	24-Aug-57	5.46	3
CLAIBORNE	TP11-6	20-May-55	3.74	2	FRANKLIN	TP6-3	24-Mar-55	5.55	3
CLAIBORNE	TP6-3	24-Mar-55	5.55	3	FRANKLIN	UK7-3	27-Apr-53	6.74	3
CLAIBORNE	TS6-4	28-May-52	5.79	3	FRANKLIN	UK7-4	28-Apr-53	30.10	5
CLAIBORNE	UK7-4	28-Apr-53	15.93	4	GRANT	TS6-4	28-May-52	4.82	2
CONCORDIA	TS1-3	3-Apr-52	4.01	2	GRANT	TP11-2	16-May-55	7.17	3
CONCORDIA	TP6-3	24-Mar-55	5.55	3	GRANT	UK7-3	27-Apr-53	8.39	3
CONCORDIA	UK7-3	27-Apr-53	6.87	3	GRANT	TP6-3	24-Mar-55	8.63	3
CONCORDIA	UK7-4	28-Apr-53	34.43	5	GRANT	UK7-4	28-Apr-53	32.45	5
CONCORDIA	PB3-3	26-Jun-57	68.82	6	GRANT	UK6-2	19-Apr-53	77.35	6
DE SOTO	BJ3-5	5-Nov-51	4.02	2	GRANT	PB3-3	26-Jun-57	114.67	7
DE SOTO	PB11-1	31-Aug-57	6.14	3	IBERIA	TS6-4	28-May-52	4.82	2
DE SOTO	TP11-2	16-May-55	7.17	3	IBERIA	UK7-3	27-Apr-53	5.29	3
DE SOTO	TS6-4	28-May-52	7.71	3	IBERIA	UK7-4	28-Apr-53	17.66	4
DE SOTO	TP6-3	24-Mar-55	8.63	3	IBERIA	UK6-2	19-Apr-53	37.36	5
DE SOTO	UK7-4	28-Apr-53	10.48	4	IBERIA	PB3-3	26-Jun-57	114.67	7
EAST BATON R	UK7-4	28-Apr-53	4.95	2	IBERVILLE	UK7-4	28-Apr-53	4.28	2
EAST BATON R	UK7-3	27-Apr-53	6.37	3	IBERVILLE	UK7-3	27-Apr-53	5.56	3
EAST BATON R	UK6-2	19-Apr-53	37.36	5	IBERVILLE	UK6-2	19-Apr-53	37.36	5
EAST BATON R	PB3-3	26-Jun-57	114.67	7	IBERVILLE	PB3-3	26-Jun-57	114.67	7
EAST CARROLL	TP6-3	24-Mar-55	5.55	3	JACKSON	UK7-3	27-Apr-53	4.33	2
EAST CARROLL	UK7-3	27-Apr-53	5.68	3	JACKSON	TP6-3	24-Mar-55	5.55	3
EAST CARROLL	UK7-4	28-Apr-53	32.08	5	JACKSON	PB12-6	7-Sep-57	6.94	3
EAST FELICIA	PB12-6	7-Sep-57	6.42	3	JACKSON	UK7-4	28-Apr-53	30.54	5
EAST FELICIA	UK7-3	27-Apr-53	6.48	3	JEFFERSON	UK7-3	27-Apr-53	4.67	2
EAST FELICIA	UK7-4	28-Apr-53	22.77	4	JEFFERSON	UK7-4	28-Apr-53	5.52	3
EAST FELICIA	UK6-2	19-Apr-53	37.36	5	JEFFERSON	TS6-4	28-May-52	14.46	4
EAST FELICIA	PB3-3	26-Jun-57	68.82	6	JEFFERSON	PB3-3	26-Jun-57	22.97	4
EVANGELINE	UK7-3	27-Apr-53	3.99	2	JEFFERSON	UK6-2	19-Apr-53	37.36	5
EVANGELINE	TP11-2	16-May-55	7.17	3	JEFFERSON DA	UK7-4	28-Apr-53	8.23	3
EVANGELINE	TP6-3	24-Mar-55	8.63	3	JEFFERSON DA	TP6-3	24-Mar-55	8.63	3
EVANGELINE	UK6-2	19-Apr-53	77.35	6	JEFFERSON DA	TP11-2	16-May-55	11.92	4

INDIVIDUAL FALLOUT DAYS
LOUISIANA

COUNTY	SHOT	DATE	µCi/SQ METER	INDEX	COUNTY	SHOT	DATE	µCi/SQ METER	INDEX
JEFFERSON DA	PB3-3	26-Jun-57	68.82	6	MADISON	PB12-6	7-Sep-57	10.55	4
JEFFERSON DA	UK6-2	19-Apr-53	77.35	6	MADISON	UK7-4	28-Apr-53	43.14	5
LA SALLE	BJ3-5	5-Nov-51	4.02	2	MOREHOUSE	TP6-3	24-Mar-55	5.55	3
LA SALLE	UK7-3	27-Apr-53	5.43	3	MOREHOUSE	UK7-3	27-Apr-53	5.64	3
LA SALLE	TP6-3	24-Mar-55	5.55	3	MOREHOUSE	PB12-6	7-Sep-57	8.75	3
LA SALLE	TP5-2	13-Mar-55	5.89	3	MOREHOUSE	UK7-4	28-Apr-53	26.84	5
LA SALLE	TS6-4	28-May-52	9.64	3	NATCHITOCHES	UK7-3	27-Apr-53	6.32	3
LA SALLE	UK7-4	28-Apr-53	38.96	5	NATCHITOCHES	TS6-4	28-May-52	7.71	3
LA SALLE	PB3-3	26-Jun-57	114.67	7	NATCHITOCHES	TP6-3	24-Mar-55	8.63	3
LAFAYETTE	UK7-3	27-Apr-53	4.47	2	NATCHITOCHES	TP11-2	16-May-55	11.92	4
LAFAYETTE	TP6-3	24-Mar-55	8.63	3	NATCHITOCHES	UK7-4	28-Apr-53	22.44	4
LAFAYETTE	TS6-4	28-May-52	14.46	4	ORLEANS	UK7-3	27-Apr-53	4.55	2
LAFAYETTE	UK7-4	28-Apr-53	21.81	4	ORLEANS	UK7-4	28-Apr-53	7.75	3
LAFAYETTE	UK6-2	19-Apr-53	77.35	6	ORLEANS	UK6-2	19-Apr-53	15.52	4
LAFAYETTE	PB3-3	26-Jun-57	114.67	7	ORLEANS	PB3-3	26-Jun-57	19.04	4
LAFOURCHE	UK7-4	28-Apr-53	3.64	2	OUACHITA	TP10-3	7-May-55	4.79	2
LAFOURCHE	UK7-3	27-Apr-53	5.49	3	OUACHITA	UK7-3	27-Apr-53	5.16	3
LAFOURCHE	UK6-2	19-Apr-53	37.36	5	OUACHITA	PB9-2	24-Aug-57	5.46	3
LAFOURCHE	PB3-3	26-Jun-57	45.85	5	OUACHITA	TP6-3	24-Mar-55	5.55	3
LAFOURCHE	PB12-6	7-Sep-57	55.67	6	OUACHITA	PB12-6	7-Sep-57	8.03	3
LINCOLN	UK5-4	14-Apr-53	3.91	2	OUACHITA	UK7-4	28-Apr-53	29.33	5
LINCOLN	UK7-3	27-Apr-53	3.92	2	PLAQUEMINES	PB12-3	4-Sep-57	3.62	2
LINCOLN	TP6-3	24-Mar-55	5.55	3	PLAQUEMINES	UK7-4	28-Apr-53	4.68	2
LINCOLN	PB12-6	7-Sep-57	6.52	3	PLAQUEMINES	UK6-2	19-Apr-53	37.36	5
LINCOLN	UK7-4	28-Apr-53	22.19	4	PLAQUEMINES	PB3-3	26-Jun-57	68.82	6
LIVINGSTON	PB17-5	2-Oct-57	5.27	3	POINTE COUPE	UK7-4	28-Apr-53	4.55	2
LIVINGSTON	UK7-3	27-Apr-53	6.94	3	POINTE COUPE	UK7-3	27-Apr-53	6.26	3
LIVINGSTON	UK7-4	28-Apr-53	22.08	4	POINTE COUPE	UK6-2	19-Apr-53	37.36	5
LIVINGSTON	UK6-2	19-Apr-53	37.36	5	POINTE COUPE	PB3-3	26-Jun-57	114.67	7
LIVINGSTON	PB3-3	26-Jun-57	68.82	6	RAPIDES	UK7-3	27-Apr-53	4.12	2
MADISON	TP6-3	24-Mar-55	5.55	3	RAPIDES	TP11-6	20-May-55	4.21	2
MADISON	UK7-3	27-Apr-53	6.19	3	RAPIDES	TP11-2	16-May-55	7.17	3
MADISON	TS6-4	28-May-52	8.68	3	RAPIDES	TP6-3	24-Mar-55	8.63	3

INDIVIDUAL FALLOUT DAYS
LOUISIANA

COUNTY	SHOT	DATE	µCi/SQ METER	INDEX	COUNTY	SHOT	DATE	µCi/SQ METER	INDEX
RAPIDES	UK7-4	28-Apr-53	31.43	5	ST JAMES	UK7-3	27-Apr-53	6.82	3
RAPIDES	UK6-2	19-Apr-53	77.35	6	ST JAMES	UK7-4	28-Apr-53	12.84	4
RAPIDES	PB3-3	26-Jun-57	114.67	7	ST JAMES	UK6-2	19-Apr-53	37.36	5
RED RIVER	BJ3-5	5-Nov-51	4.02	2	ST JAMES	PB3-3	26-Jun-57	45.85	5
RED RIVER	TP11-2	16-May-55	4.75	2	ST JOHN THE	PB12-3	4-Sep-57	3.71	2
RED RIVER	TP6-3	24-Mar-55	8.63	3	ST JOHN THE	UK7-3	27-Apr-53	6.20	3
RED RIVER	TS6-4	28-May-52	8.68	3	ST JOHN THE	UK7-4	28-Apr-53	13.96	4
RED RIVER	UK7-4	28-Apr-53	14.70	4	ST JOHN THE	UK6-2	19-Apr-53	37.36	5
RICHLAND	PB9-2	24-Aug-57	5.46	3	ST JOHN THE	PB3-3	26-Jun-57	45.85	5
RICHLAND	TP6-3	24-Mar-55	5.55	3	ST LANDRY	UK7-4	28-Apr-53	3.88	2
RICHLAND	TS6-4	28-May-52	13.50	4	ST LANDRY	UK7-3	27-Apr-53	4.95	2
RICHLAND	TP10-3	7-May-55	13.53	4	ST LANDRY	UK6-2	19-Apr-53	37.36	5
RICHLAND	UK7-3	27-Apr-53	16.43	4	ST LANDRY	PB3-3	26-Jun-57	68.82	6
RICHLAND	UK7-4	28-Apr-53	28.71	5	ST MARTIN	UK7-4	28-Apr-53	3.88	2
SABINE	PB11-1	31-Aug-57	6.14	3	ST MARTIN	UK7-3	27-Apr-53	5.39	3
SABINE	TS6-4	28-May-52	6.75	3	ST MARTIN	UK6-2	19-Apr-53	37.36	5
SABINE	TP6-3	24-Mar-55	8.63	3	ST MARTIN	PB3-3	26-Jun-57	114.67	7
SABINE	TP11-2	16-May-55	11.92	4	ST MARY	UK7-3	27-Apr-53	5.84	3
SABINE	UK7-4	28-Apr-53	12.99	4	ST MARY	UK6-2	19-Apr-53	37.36	5
SABINE	UK6-2	19-Apr-53	77.35	6	ST MARY	PB3-3	26-Jun-57	114.67	7
ST BERNARD	UK7-4	28-Apr-53	5.12	3	ST TAMMANY	UK7-3	27-Apr-53	3.91	2
ST BERNARD	UK6-2	19-Apr-53	37.36	5	ST TAMMANY	UK6-2	19-Apr-53	37.36	5
ST BERNARD	PB3-3	26-Jun-57	68.82	6	ST TAMMANY	PB3-3	26-Jun-57	68.82	6
ST CHARLES	UK7-4	28-Apr-53	3.57	2	TANGIPAHOA	UK7-3	27-Apr-53	5.20	3
ST CHARLES	UK7-3	27-Apr-53	5.42	3	TANGIPAHOA	UK7-4	28-Apr-53	29.56	5
ST CHARLES	UK6-2	19-Apr-53	37.36	5	TANGIPAHOA	UK6-2	19-Apr-53	37.36	5
ST CHARLES	PB3-3	26-Jun-57	45.85	5	TANGIPAHOA	PB3-3	26-Jun-57	114.67	7
ST CHARLES	PB12-6	7-Sep-57	52.55	6	TENSAS	PB12-6	7-Sep-57	4.95	2
ST HELENA	UK7-3	27-Apr-53	6.54	3	TENSAS	TP6-3	24-Mar-55	5.55	3
ST HELENA	UK7-4	28-Apr-53	30.26	5	TENSAS	UK7-3	27-Apr-53	6.42	3
ST HELENA	UK6-2	19-Apr-53	37.36	5	TENSAS	TS6-4	28-May-52	7.71	3
ST HELENA	PB3-3	26-Jun-57	114.67	7	TENSAS	UK7-4	28-Apr-53	42.50	5
ST JAMES	PB12-3	4-Sep-57	3.54	2	TENSAS	PB3-3	26-Jun-57	114.67	7

INDIVIDUAL FALLOUT DAYS
LOUISIANA

COUNTY	SHOT	DATE	µCi/SQ METER	INDEX	COUNTY	SHOT	DATE	µCi/SQ METER	INDEX
TERREBONNE	UK7-3	27-Apr-53	5.91	3	WASHINGTON	UK6-2	19-Apr-53	37.36	5
TERREBONNE	UK7-4	28-Apr-53	8.07	3	WASHINGTON	PB3-3	26-Jun-57	68.82	6
TERREBONNE	UK6-2	19-Apr-53	37.36	5	WEBSTER	UK5-4	14-Apr-53	3.91	2
TERREBONNE	PB3-3	26-Jun-57	114.67	7	WEBSTER	TP11-6	20-May-55	3.92	2
UNION	UK5-4	14-Apr-53	3.91	2	WEBSTER	TS6-4	28-May-52	5.79	3
UNION	UK7-3	27-Apr-53	4.40	2	WEBSTER	TP6-3	24-Mar-55	8.63	3
UNION	TP6-3	24-Mar-55	5.55	3	WEBSTER	UK7-4	28-Apr-53	12.35	4
UNION	PB12-6	7-Sep-57	7.19	3	WEBSTER	TS1-3	3-Apr-52	24.86	4
UNION	UK7-4	28-Apr-53	30.48	5	WEST BATON R	UK7-4	28-Apr-53	4.59	2
VERMILION	UK7-3	27-Apr-53	3.71	2	WEST BATON R	UK7-3	27-Apr-53	5.79	3
VERMILION	TS6-4	28-May-52	3.86	2	WEST BATON R	UK6-2	19-Apr-53	37.36	5
VERMILION	PB17-5	2-Oct-57	6.82	3	WEST BATON R	PB3-3	26-Jun-57	114.67	7
VERMILION	TP11-2	16-May-55	7.17	3	WEST CARROLL	UK7-3	27-Apr-53	5.33	3
VERMILION	TP6-3	24-Mar-55	8.63	3	WEST CARROLL	TP6-3	24-Mar-55	5.55	3
VERMILION	PB3-3	26-Jun-57	68.82	6	WEST CARROLL	UK7-4	28-Apr-53	29.99	5
VERMILION	UK6-2	19-Apr-53	77.35	6	WEST FELICIA	UK7-4	28-Apr-53	4.99	2
VERNON	TP11-2	16-May-55	7.17	3	WEST FELICIA	UK7-3	27-Apr-53	6.94	3
VERNON	TP6-3	24-Mar-55	8.63	3	WEST FELICIA	UK6-2	19-Apr-53	37.36	5
VERNON	PB3-3	26-Jun-57	11.44	4	WEST FELICIA	PB3-3	26-Jun-57	114.67	7
VERNON	UK7-4	28-Apr-53	20.28	4	WINN	UK7-3	27-Apr-53	4.19	2
VERNON	UK6-2	19-Apr-53	77.35	6	WINN	TP6-3	24-Mar-55	8.63	3
WASHINGTON	UK7-3	27-Apr-53	3.53	2	WINN	UK7-4	28-Apr-53	30.54	5
WASHINGTON	UK7-4	28-Apr-53	4.19	2					

INDIVIDUAL FALLOUT DAYS
MASSACHUSETTS

COUNTY	SHOT	DATE	µCi/SQ METER	INDEX	COUNTY	SHOT	DATE	µCi/SQ METER	INDEX
BARNSABLE	UK4-3	8-Apr-53	3.56	2	DUKES	UK4-2	7-Apr-53	92.32	6
BARNSABLE	BJ2-3	1-Nov-51	4.22	2	ESSEX	UK4-4	9-Apr-53	3.98	2
BARNSABLE	R1-2	29-Jan-51	6.41	3	ESSEX	TS8-4	8-Jun-52	4.07	2
BARNSABLE	TS8-3	7-Jun-52	7.72	3	ESSEX	UK4-3	8-Apr-53	4.67	2
BARNSABLE	BJ2-4	2-Nov-51	7.77	3	ESSEX	TS8-3	7-Jun-52	5.49	3
BARNSABLE	TS7-5	5-Jun-52	8.59	3	ESSEX	BJ2-3	1-Nov-51	5.76	3
BARNSABLE	UK4-2	7-Apr-53	87.65	6	ESSEX	BJ2-4	2-Nov-51	8.76	3
BERKSHIRE	BJ2-3	1-Nov-51	4.38	2	ESSEX	R1-2	29-Jan-51	36.05	5
BERKSHIRE	UK8-3	10-May-53	5.26	3	ESSEX	UK4-2	7-Apr-53	84.14	6
BERKSHIRE	UK1-2	18-Mar-53	5.59	3	FRANKLIN	PB11-5	4-Sep-57	3.55	2
BERKSHIRE	PB5-8	22-Jul-57	5.97	3	FRANKLIN	BJ3-7	7-Nov-51	3.71	2
BERKSHIRE	PB11-5	4-Sep-57	6.43	3	FRANKLIN	TS7-5	5-Jun-52	3.77	2
BERKSHIRE	TS1-4	4-Apr-52	10.30	4	FRANKLIN	BJ2-3	1-Nov-51	6.11	3
BERKSHIRE	R1-2	29-Jan-51	11.65	4	FRANKLIN	TS1-4	4-Apr-52	10.30	4
BERKSHIRE	BJ2-4	2-Nov-51	13.02	4	FRANKLIN	TS8-3	7-Jun-52	10.47	4
BERKSHIRE	TS8-3	7-Jun-52	14.61	4	FRANKLIN	UK7-2	26-Apr-53	10.78	4
BERKSHIRE	UK7-2	26-Apr-53	37.31	5	FRANKLIN	UK4-2	7-Apr-53	11.35	4
BRISTOL	PB5-8	22-Jul-57	5.97	3	FRANKLIN	R1-2	29-Jan-51	11.65	4
BRISTOL	TS8-3	7-Jun-52	6.23	3	FRANKLIN	BJ2-4	2-Nov-51	12.74	4
BRISTOL	BJ2-3	1-Nov-51	6.27	3	HAMPDEN	BJ3-7	7-Nov-51	3.71	2
BRISTOL	R1-2	29-Jan-51	6.41	3	HAMPDEN	TS6-4	28-May-52	4.03	2
BRISTOL	TS7-5	5-Jun-52	6.77	3	HAMPDEN	UK1-2	18-Mar-53	4.21	2
BRISTOL	TS1-4	4-Apr-52	7.18	3	HAMPDEN	UK7-2	26-Apr-53	4.72	2
BRISTOL	BJ2-4	2-Nov-51	9.56	3	HAMPDEN	BJ2-3	1-Nov-51	4.92	2
BRISTOL	UK4-2	7-Apr-53	153.92	7	HAMPDEN	PB11-5	4-Sep-57	6.43	3
DUKES	BJ3-7	7-Nov-51	3.71	2	HAMPDEN	TS7-5	5-Jun-52	7.47	3
DUKES	TS7-5	5-Jun-52	3.73	2	HAMPDEN	BJ2-4	2-Nov-51	10.66	4
DUKES	UK4-3	8-Apr-53	3.89	2	HAMPDEN	TS1-4	4-Apr-52	10.77	4
DUKES	BJ2-4	2-Nov-51	4.08	2	HAMPDEN	TS8-3	7-Jun-52	13.41	4
DUKES	BJ2-3	1-Nov-51	5.88	3	HAMPDEN	UK4-2	7-Apr-53	19.70	4
DUKES	PB5-8	22-Jul-57	5.97	3	HAMPDEN	R1-2	29-Jan-51	28.94	5
DUKES	TS8-3	7-Jun-52	6.57	3	HAMPSHIRE	TS7-5	5-Jun-52	4.44	2
DUKES	R1-2	29-Jan-51	6.76	3	HAMPSHIRE	BJ2-3	1-Nov-51	5.28	3

INDIVIDUAL FALLOUT DAYS
MASSACHUSETTS

COUNTY	SHOT	DATE	µCi/SQ METER	INDEX	COUNTY	SHOT	DATE	µCi/SQ METER	INDEX
HAMPSHIRE	TS1-4	4-Apr-52	6.87	3	NORFOLK	PB5-8	22-Jul-57	5.97	3
HAMPSHIRE	UK7-2	26-Apr-53	7.87	3	NORFOLK	BJ2-3	1-Nov-51	6.52	3
HAMPSHIRE	PB5-8	22-Jul-57	8.96	3	NORFOLK	BJ2-4	2-Nov-51	10.06	4
HAMPSHIRE	TS8-3	7-Jun-52	10.28	4	NORFOLK	R1-2	29-Jan-51	36.05	5
HAMPSHIRE	R1-2	29-Jan-51	11.65	4	NORFOLK	UK4-2	7-Apr-53	181.58	7
HAMPSHIRE	BJ2-4	2-Nov-51	12.88	4	PLYMOUTH	UK4-3	8-Apr-53	3.56	2
HAMPSHIRE	UK4-2	7-Apr-53	13.69	4	PLYMOUTH	TS8-3	7-Jun-52	5.28	3
HAMPSHIRE	PB11-5	4-Sep-57	19.28	4	PLYMOUTH	BJ2-3	1-Nov-51	5.76	3
MIDDLESEX	UK4-3	8-Apr-53	3.56	2	PLYMOUTH	PB5-8	22-Jul-57	5.97	3
MIDDLESEX	BJ3-7	7-Nov-51	3.71	2	PLYMOUTH	TS7-5	5-Jun-52	6.11	3
MIDDLESEX	TS7-5	5-Jun-52	3.90	2	PLYMOUTH	R1-2	29-Jan-51	6.41	3
MIDDLESEX	TS8-3	7-Jun-52	6.48	3	PLYMOUTH	BJ2-4	2-Nov-51	8.46	3
MIDDLESEX	BJ2-3	1-Nov-51	6.65	3	PLYMOUTH	UK4-2	7-Apr-53	205.84	8
MIDDLESEX	UK4-4	9-Apr-53	7.95	3	SUFFOLK	TS7-5	5-Jun-52	3.69	2
MIDDLESEX	BJ2-4	2-Nov-51	10.55	4	SUFFOLK	TS8-3	7-Jun-52	3.95	2
MIDDLESEX	R1-2	29-Jan-51	36.05	5	SUFFOLK	BJ2-3	1-Nov-51	6.14	3
MIDDLESEX	UK4-2	7-Apr-53	122.70	7	SUFFOLK	BJ2-4	2-Nov-51	9.36	3
NANTUCKET	BJ2-4	2-Nov-51	3.78	2	SUFFOLK	R1-2	29-Jan-51	36.05	5
NANTUCKET	BJ2-3	1-Nov-51	3.84	2	SUFFOLK	UK4-2	7-Apr-53	123.51	7
NANTUCKET	R1-2	29-Jan-51	6.41	3	WORCESTER	TS7-5	5-Jun-52	4.11	2
NANTUCKET	TS8-3	7-Jun-52	6.83	3	WORCESTER	PB5-8	22-Jul-57	5.97	3
NANTUCKET	UK4-4	9-Apr-53	7.95	3	WORCESTER	BJ2-3	1-Nov-51	6.54	3
NANTUCKET	TS7-5	5-Jun-52	12.08	4	WORCESTER	TS1-4	4-Apr-52	7.18	3
NANTUCKET	UK4-2	7-Apr-53	37.40	5	WORCESTER	TS8-3	7-Jun-52	8.52	3
NORFOLK	UK4-4	9-Apr-53	3.98	2	WORCESTER	BJ2-4	2-Nov-51	12.19	4
NORFOLK	TS7-5	5-Jun-52	4.30	2	WORCESTER	R1-2	29-Jan-51	18.06	4
NORFOLK	UK4-3	8-Apr-53	4.67	2	WORCESTER	UK4-2	7-Apr-53	50.58	6
NORFOLK	TS8-3	7-Jun-52	5.21	3					

INDIVIDUAL FALLOUT DAYS
MARYLAND

COUNTY	SHOT	DATE	µCi/SQ METER	INDEX	COUNTY	SHOT	DATE	µCi/SQ METER	INDEX
ALLEGANY	PB5-8	22-Jul-57	8.96	3	CECIL	UK1-2	18-Mar-53	12.29	4
ALLEGANY	SE4	9-Jul-62	57.04	6	CHARLES	TS3-4	25-Apr-52	3.87	2
ANNE ARUNDEL	BJ2-4	2-Nov-51	3.59	2	CHARLES	BJ2-4	2-Nov-51	4.06	2
ANNE ARUNDEL	TS3-4	25-Apr-52	3.87	2	CHARLES	UK1-2	18-Mar-53	7.57	3
ANNE ARUNDEL	TS3-5	26-Apr-52	4.02	2	CHARLES	BJ2-3	1-Nov-51	20.31	4
ANNE ARUNDEL	UK1-2	18-Mar-53	7.58	3	DORCHESTER	PB5-8	22-Jul-57	5.97	3
ANNE ARUNDEL	PB5-8	22-Jul-57	8.96	3	DORCHESTER	BJ2-4	2-Nov-51	7.24	3
ANNE ARUNDEL	BJ2-3	1-Nov-51	14.82	4	DORCHESTER	UK1-2	18-Mar-53	10.51	4
BALTIMORE	BJ2-4	2-Nov-51	5.08	3	DORCHESTER	BJ2-3	1-Nov-51	11.80	4
BALTIMORE	UK1-2	18-Mar-53	6.44	3	FREDERICK	UK9-3	21-May-53	4.18	2
BALTIMORE	BJ2-3	1-Nov-51	8.95	3	FREDERICK	UK1-2	18-Mar-53	4.56	2
BALTIMORE	PB5-8	22-Jul-57	8.96	3	FREDERICK	BJ2-4	2-Nov-51	4.67	2
BALTIMORE	TS3-5	26-Apr-52	3.50	1	FREDERICK	BJ2-3	1-Nov-51	7.70	3
BALTIMORE	SE4	9-Jul-62	73.06	6	FREDERICK	PB5-8	22-Jul-57	8.96	3
CALVERT	TS3-5	26-Apr-52	3.86	2	GARRETT	PB5-8	22-Jul-57	8.96	3
CALVERT	TS3-4	25-Apr-52	3.87	2	GARRETT	SE4	9-Jul-62	103.59	7
CALVERT	BJ2-4	2-Nov-51	4.46	2	HARFORD	BJ3-6	6-Nov-51	4.63	2
CALVERT	UK1-2	18-Mar-53	6.65	3	HARFORD	BJ2-4	2-Nov-51	4.94	2
CALVERT	PB5-8	22-Jul-57	8.96	3	HARFORD	UK10-6	30-May-53	6.63	3
CALVERT	BJ2-3	1-Nov-51	14.59	4	HARFORD	BJ2-3	1-Nov-51	8.14	3
CAROLINE	PB5-8	22-Jul-57	5.97	3	HARFORD	UK1-2	18-Mar-53	8.77	3
CAROLINE	BJ2-4	2-Nov-51	7.10	3	HARFORD	PB5-8	22-Jul-57	8.96	3
CAROLINE	BJ2-3	1-Nov-51	8.41	3	HARFORD	SE4	9-Jul-62	60.19	6
CAROLINE	UK1-2	18-Mar-53	10.66	4	HOWARD	BJ2-4	2-Nov-51	5.85	3
CARROLL	BJ2-4	2-Nov-51	3.54	2	HOWARD	UK1-2	18-Mar-53	6.87	3
CARROLL	PB4-4	8-Jul-57	3.72	2	HOWARD	PB5-8	22-Jul-57	8.96	3
CARROLL	UK1-2	18-Mar-53	6.02	3	HOWARD	BJ2-3	1-Nov-51	11.91	4
CARROLL	BJ2-3	1-Nov-51	6.11	3	KENT	TS3-5	26-Apr-52	3.52	2
CECIL	TS3-4	25-Apr-52	3.87	2	KENT	BJ2-4	2-Nov-51	6.41	3
CECIL	BJ3-6	6-Nov-51	4.63	2	KENT	PB5-8	22-Jul-57	8.96	3
CECIL	BJ2-4	2-Nov-51	5.71	3	KENT	BJ2-3	1-Nov-51	10.02	4
CECIL	BJ2-3	1-Nov-51	8.04	3	KENT	UK1-2	18-Mar-53	12.55	4
CECIL	PB5-8	22-Jul-57	8.96	3	MONTGOMERY	TS3-4	25-Apr-52	3.87	2

INDIVIDUAL FALLOUT DAYS
MARYLAND

COUNTY	SHOT	DATE	µCi/SQ METER	INDEX	COUNTY	SHOT	DATE	µCi/SQ METER	INDEX
MONTGOMERY	UK1-2	18-Mar-53	5.51	3	ST MARYS	UK1-2	18-Mar-53	11.34	4
MONTGOMERY	BJ2-4	2-Nov-51	6.32	3	ST MARYS	BJ2-3	1-Nov-51	12.26	4
MONTGOMERY	PB5-8	22-Jul-57	8.96	3	TALBOT	TS3-5	26-Apr-52	4.05	2
MONTGOMERY	BJ2-3	1-Nov-51	12.88	4	TALBOT	BJ2-4	2-Nov-51	7.38	3
PRINCE GEORG	UK10-2	26-May-53	3.63	2	TALBOT	PB5-8	22-Jul-57	8.96	3
PRINCE GEORG	TS3-4	25-Apr-52	3.87	2	TALBOT	BJ2-3	1-Nov-51	9.75	3
PRINCE GEORG	TS3-5	26-Apr-52	4.21	2	TALBOT	UK1-2	18-Mar-53	12.78	4
PRINCE GEORG	UK1-2	18-Mar-53	7.66	3	WASHINGTON	UK1-2	18-Mar-53	3.92	2
PRINCE GEORG	BJ2-4	2-Nov-51	8.93	3	WASHINGTON	UK9-3	21-May-53	4.37	2
PRINCE GEORG	BJ2-3	1-Nov-51	18.02	4	WASHINGTON	BJ2-3	1-Nov-51	5.55	3
QUEEN ANNES	BJ2-4	2-Nov-51	6.83	3	WASHINGTON	TS3-4	25-Apr-52	6.03	3
QUEEN ANNES	UK1-2	18-Mar-53	11.52	4	WASHINGTON	PB5-8	22-Jul-57	8.96	3
QUEEN ANNES	BJ2-3	1-Nov-51	11.58	4	WICOMICO	BJ2-4	2-Nov-51	8.26	3
SOMERSET	BJ2-4	2-Nov-51	8.18	3	WICOMICO	PB5-8	22-Jul-57	8.96	3
SOMERSET	BJ2-3	1-Nov-51	8.90	3	WICOMICO	BJ2-3	1-Nov-51	9.44	3
SOMERSET	PB5-8	22-Jul-57	8.96	3	WICOMICO	UK1-2	18-Mar-53	15.49	4
SOMERSET	BJ3-6	6-Nov-51	11.57	4	WORCESTER	UK10-2	26-May-53	4.93	2
SOMERSET	UK1-2	18-Mar-53	12.78	4	WORCESTER	BJ2-3	1-Nov-51	7.94	3
ST MARYS	TS3-4	25-Apr-52	3.87	2	WORCESTER	BJ2-4	2-Nov-51	8.26	3
ST MARYS	TS3-5	26-Apr-52	4.05	2	WORCESTER	PB5-8	22-Jul-57	14.93	4
ST MARYS	BJ2-4	2-Nov-51	8.22	3	WORCESTER	UK1-2	18-Mar-53	15.61	4
ST MARYS	PB5-8	22-Jul-57	8.96	3					

INDIVIDUAL FALLOUT DAYS
MAINE

COUNTY	SHOT	DATE	µCi/SQ METER	INDEX	COUNTY	SHOT	DATE	µCi/SQ METER	INDEX
ANDROSCOGGIN	UK7-3	27-Apr-53	3.53	2	KENNEBEC	BJ2-3	1-Nov-51	4.22	2
ANDROSCOGGIN	UK4-4	9-Apr-53	3.98	2	KENNEBEC	UK7-3	27-Apr-53	4.35	2
ANDROSCOGGIN	R1-2	29-Jan-51	6.76	3	KENNEBEC	PB12-6	7-Sep-57	5.30	3
ANDROSCOGGIN	TS8-3	7-Jun-52	10.77	4	KENNEBEC	R1-2	29-Jan-51	6.41	3
ANDROSCOGGIN	BJ2-4	2-Nov-51	16.73	4	KENNEBEC	TS8-3	7-Jun-52	9.33	3
AROOSTOOK	PB11-5	4-Sep-57	3.55	2	KENNEBEC	BJ2-4	2-Nov-51	20.31	4
AROOSTOOK	TS8-3	7-Jun-52	3.58	2	KNOX	UK2-4	27-Mar-53	3.74	2
AROOSTOOK	TS7-5	5-Jun-52	4.66	2	KNOX	UK7-3	27-Apr-53	4.10	2
AROOSTOOK	TS7-4	4-Jun-52	7.67	3	KNOX	BJ2-3	1-Nov-51	4.61	2
AROOSTOOK	PB5-8	22-Jul-57	8.96	3	KNOX	PB12-6	7-Sep-57	4.96	2
AROOSTOOK	UK7-3	27-Apr-53	15.43	4	KNOX	TS7-5	5-Jun-52	5.92	3
AROOSTOOK	UK2-4	27-Mar-53	24.09	4	KNOX	PB5-8	22-Jul-57	5.97	3
AROOSTOOK	BJ2-4	2-Nov-51	85.07	6	KNOX	TS8-3	7-Jun-52	9.00	3
CUMBERLAND	BJ2-3	1-Nov-51	3.97	2	KNOX	R1-2	29-Jan-51	16.75	4
CUMBERLAND	UK4-4	9-Apr-53	3.98	2	KNOX	BJ2-4	2-Nov-51	19.91	4
CUMBERLAND	R1-2	29-Jan-51	6.41	3	LINCOLN	TS7-5	5-Jun-52	3.98	2
CUMBERLAND	TS8-3	7-Jun-52	12.02	4	LINCOLN	UK7-3	27-Apr-53	5.08	3
CUMBERLAND	BJ2-2	31-Oct-51	12.07	4	LINCOLN	PB12-6	7-Sep-57	5.13	3
CUMBERLAND	BJ2-4	2-Nov-51	13.84	4	LINCOLN	TS8-3	7-Jun-52	9.65	3
FRANKLIN	UK2-4	27-Mar-53	5.36	3	LINCOLN	R1-2	29-Jan-51	16.75	4
FRANKLIN	TS7-4	4-Jun-52	5.42	3	LINCOLN	BJ2-4	2-Nov-51	18.52	4
FRANKLIN	TS8-3	7-Jun-52	6.66	3	OXFORD	UK4-4	9-Apr-53	3.98	2
FRANKLIN	BJ2-2	31-Oct-51	7.98	3	OXFORD	UK7-3	27-Apr-53	4.02	2
FRANKLIN	BJ2-4	2-Nov-51	19.32	4	OXFORD	TS7-4	4-Jun-52	6.46	3
HANCOCK	PB11-5	4-Sep-57	3.55	2	OXFORD	TS8-3	7-Jun-52	11.30	4
HANCOCK	PB12-6	7-Sep-57	5.37	3	OXFORD	BJ2-2	31-Oct-51	12.07	4
HANCOCK	TS7-5	5-Jun-52	5.42	3	OXFORD	BJ2-4	2-Nov-51	15.23	4
HANCOCK	BJ2-3	1-Nov-51	6.14	3	PENOBSCOT	PB12-6	7-Sep-57	5.47	3
HANCOCK	UK7-3	27-Apr-53	6.31	3	PENOBSCOT	TS8-3	7-Jun-52	5.56	3
HANCOCK	R1-2	29-Jan-51	6.41	3	PENOBSCOT	TS7-5	5-Jun-52	6.22	3
HANCOCK	TS8-3	7-Jun-52	6.94	3	PENOBSCOT	R1-2	29-Jan-51	6.41	3
HANCOCK	UK2-4	27-Mar-53	14.03	4	PENOBSCOT	BJ2-3	1-Nov-51	6.65	3
HANCOCK	BJ2-4	2-Nov-51	29.47	5	PENOBSCOT	UK7-3	27-Apr-53	8.94	3

INDIVIDUAL FALLOUT DAYS
MAINE

COUNTY	SHOT	DATE	µCi/SQ METER	INDEX	COUNTY	SHOT	DATE	µCi/SQ METER	INDEX
PENOBSCOT	UK2-4	27-Mar-53	17.23	4	WALDO	UK7-3	27-Apr-53	5.08	3
PENOBSCOT	BJ2-4	2-Nov-51	45.80	5	WALDO	TS7-5	5-Jun-52	5.92	3
PISCATAQUIS	TS7-5	5-Jun-52	5.02	3	WALDO	PB12-6	7-Sep-57	5.92	3
PISCATAQUIS	BJ2-3	1-Nov-51	5.50	3	WALDO	PB5-8	22-Jul-57	5.97	3
PISCATAQUIS	TS7-4	4-Jun-52	6.40	3	WALDO	R1-2	29-Jan-51	6.41	3
PISCATAQUIS	TS8-3	7-Jun-52	6.90	3	WALDO	TS8-3	7-Jun-52	8.27	3
PISCATAQUIS	UK7-3	27-Apr-53	9.67	3	WALDO	BJ2-4	2-Nov-51	23.80	4
PISCATAQUIS	UK2-4	27-Mar-53	14.25	4	WASHINGTON	PB12-6	7-Sep-57	4.51	2
PISCATAQUIS	BJ2-4	2-Nov-51	44.31	5	WASHINGTON	TS8-3	7-Jun-52	4.82	2
SAGADAHOC	UK4-4	9-Apr-53	3.98	2	WASHINGTON	UK7-3	27-Apr-53	5.79	3
SAGADAHOC	R1-2	29-Jan-51	6.41	3	WASHINGTON	R1-2	29-Jan-51	6.41	3
SAGADAHOC	TS8-3	7-Jun-52	11.82	4	WASHINGTON	TS7-5	5-Jun-52	7.01	3
SAGADAHOC	BJ2-2	31-Oct-51	12.07	4	WASHINGTON	BJ2-3	1-Nov-51	7.68	3
SAGADAHOC	BJ2-4	2-Nov-51	17.03	4	WASHINGTON	UK2-4	27-Mar-53	21.42	4
SOMERSET	BJ2-3	1-Nov-51	4.73	2	WASHINGTON	BJ2-4	2-Nov-51	37.84	5
SOMERSET	TS8-3	7-Jun-52	7.68	3	YORK	TS7-5	5-Jun-52	4.11	2
SOMERSET	UK2-4	27-Mar-53	9.56	3	YORK	TS8-3	7-Jun-52	5.65	3
SOMERSET	UK7-3	27-Apr-53	9.92	3	YORK	TS6-4	28-May-52	7.71	3
SOMERSET	BJ2-4	2-Nov-51	13.94	4	YORK	UK4-2	7-Apr-53	9.24	3
WALDO	UK2-4	27-Mar-53	4.93	2	YORK	R1-2	29-Jan-51	14.56	4
WALDO	BJ2-3	1-Nov-51	4.99	2	YORK	BJ2-4	2-Nov-51	21.21	4

INDIVIDUAL FALLOUT DAYS
MICHIGAN

COUNTY	SHOT	DATE	µCi/SQ METER	INDEX	COUNTY	SHOT	DATE	µCi/SQ METER	INDEX
ALCONA	TP10-2	6-May-55	3.83	2	BARRY	TS6-4	28-May-52	10.48	4
ALCONA	TS6-4	28-May-52	5.64	3	BARRY	TS7-3	3-Jun-52	56.75	6
ALCONA	PB11-4	3-Sep-57	6.71	3	BAY	TP9-2	15-Apr-55	4.05	2
ALCONA	TS7-3	3-Jun-52	8.31	3	BAY	TS6-4	28-May-52	12.54	4
ALCONA	UK9-2	20-May-53	14.72	4	BAY	UK9-2	20-May-53	13.10	4
ALGER	TP10-2	6-May-55	4.16	2	BAY	TS7-3	3-Jun-52	17.24	4
ALGER	TS6-4	28-May-52	8.86	3	BENZIE	PB9-5	27-Aug-57	4.52	2
ALGER	UK9-2	20-May-53	41.91	5	BENZIE	UK9-2	20-May-53	12.83	4
ALLEGAN	PB6-3	26-Jul-57	3.96	2	BENZIE	TS6-4	28-May-52	19.29	4
ALLEGAN	UK9-2	20-May-53	4.21	2	BERRIEN	PB6-3	26-Jul-57	3.96	2
ALLEGAN	TS6-4	28-May-52	8.06	3	BERRIEN	PB8-6	23-Aug-57	4.03	2
ALLEGAN	UK7-4	28-Apr-53	3.50	1	BERRIEN	UK9-2	20-May-53	5.87	3
ALLEGAN	TS7-3	3-Jun-52	41.84	5	BERRIEN	UK7-4	28-Apr-53	10.75	4
ALPENA	PB11-4	3-Sep-57	4.47	2	BERRIEN	TS6-4	28-May-52	13.50	4
ALPENA	UK9-2	20-May-53	6.09	3	BERRIEN	TS7-3	3-Jun-52	16.21	4
ANTRIM	TS7-3	3-Jun-52	3.53	2	BRANCH	PB6-3	26-Jul-57	3.96	2
ANTRIM	TP10-2	6-May-55	3.83	2	BRANCH	PB9-5	27-Aug-57	4.52	2
ANTRIM	PB11-4	3-Sep-57	6.71	3	BRANCH	UK9-2	20-May-53	5.51	3
ANTRIM	UK9-2	20-May-53	14.72	4	BRANCH	UK7-4	28-Apr-53	7.06	3
ANTRIM	TS6-4	28-May-52	30.86	5	BRANCH	TS7-3	3-Jun-52	45.03	5
ARENAC	PB11-4	3-Sep-57	4.47	2	CALHOUN	PB6-3	26-Jul-57	3.96	2
ARENAC	TS6-4	28-May-52	12.54	4	CALHOUN	UK9-2	20-May-53	6.68	3
ARENAC	TS7-3	3-Jun-52	13.28	4	CALHOUN	TS6-4	28-May-52	7.71	3
ARENAC	UK9-2	20-May-53	13.82	4	CALHOUN	TS7-3	3-Jun-52	81.15	6
BARAGA	TS6-3	27-May-52	7.40	3	CASS	PB6-3	26-Jul-57	3.96	2
BARAGA	TS6-4	28-May-52	8.06	3	CASS	PB8-6	23-Aug-57	4.03	2
BARAGA	TP10-2	6-May-55	8.33	3	CASS	PB9-5	27-Aug-57	4.52	2
BARAGA	UK9-2	20-May-53	44.17	5	CASS	TS7-3	3-Jun-52	8.13	3
BARRY	PB6-3	26-Jul-57	3.96	2	CASS	UK7-4	28-Apr-53	10.05	4
BARRY	PB11-4	3-Sep-57	4.47	2	CASS	TS6-4	28-May-52	10.61	4
BARRY	PB9-5	27-Aug-57	4.52	2	CHARLEVOIX	TP10-2	6-May-55	3.83	2
BARRY	UK7-4	28-Apr-53	5.04	3	CHARLEVOIX	PB11-4	3-Sep-57	6.71	3
BARRY	UK9-2	20-May-53	6.09	3	CHARLEVOIX	UK9-2	20-May-53	18.34	4

INDIVIDUAL FALLOUT DAYS
MICHIGAN

COUNTY	SHOT	DATE	µCi/SQ METER	INDEX	COUNTY	SHOT	DATE	µCi/SQ METER	INDEX
CHARLEVOIX	TS6-4	28-May-52	32.79	5	EATON	PB11-4	3-Sep-57	4.47	2
CHEBOYGAN	TP5-3	14-Mar-55	3.78	2	EATON	UK9-2	20-May-53	5.04	3
CHEBOYGAN	TP10-2	6-May-55	3.83	2	EATON	TS6-4	28-May-52	5.79	3
CHEBOYGAN	PB11-4	3-Sep-57	6.71	3	EATON	TP9-2	15-Apr-55	37.10	5
CHEBOYGAN	UK9-2	20-May-53	13.46	4	EATON	TS7-3	3-Jun-52	65.24	6
CHEBOYGAN	TS6-4	28-May-52	29.89	5	EATON	SE4	9-Jul-62	68.45	6
CHIPPEWA	TP10-2	6-May-55	3.83	2	EMMET	TS6-4	28-May-52	4.83	2
CHIPPEWA	TS8-4	8-Jun-52	4.46	2	EMMET	PB11-4	3-Sep-57	6.71	3
CHIPPEWA	PB11-4	3-Sep-57	4.47	2	EMMET	UK9-2	20-May-53	12.65	4
CHIPPEWA	UK9-2	20-May-53	20.23	4	GENESEE	UK2-8	31-Mar-53	4.23	2
CHIPPEWA	TS6-4	28-May-52	45.13	5	GENESEE	PB9-5	27-Aug-57	4.52	2
CLARE	PB11-4	3-Sep-57	4.47	2	GENESEE	TS6-4	28-May-52	4.82	2
CLARE	TS6-4	28-May-52	4.83	2	GENESEE	UK9-2	20-May-53	12.01	4
CLARE	TS7-3	3-Jun-52	10.74	4	GENESEE	TP9-2	15-Apr-55	27.70	5
CLARE	UK9-2	20-May-53	15.81	4	GENESEE	TS7-3	3-Jun-52	71.87	6
CLINTON	PB9-5	27-Aug-57	4.52	2	GLADWIN	TS6-4	28-May-52	4.03	2
CLINTON	UK9-2	20-May-53	7.22	3	GLADWIN	UK9-2	20-May-53	10.07	4
CLINTON	TS6-4	28-May-52	10.61	4	GLADWIN	TS7-3	3-Jun-52	12.43	4
CLINTON	TP9-2	15-Apr-55	18.17	4	GOGEBIC	PB11-3	2-Sep-57	3.98	2
CLINTON	TS7-3	3-Jun-52	62.80	6	GOGEBIC	TS6-3	27-May-52	5.95	3
CRAWFORD	TP10-2	6-May-55	3.83	2	GOGEBIC	PB5-5	19-Jul-57	6.09	3
CRAWFORD	TS7-3	3-Jun-52	6.15	3	GOGEBIC	TP10-2	6-May-55	8.33	3
CRAWFORD	PB11-4	3-Sep-57	6.71	3	GOGEBIC	TS6-4	28-May-52	26.65	5
CRAWFORD	TS6-4	28-May-52	11.57	4	GOGEBIC	UK9-2	20-May-53	48.43	5
CRAWFORD	UK9-2	20-May-53	12.55	4	GRAND TRAVER	TS7-3	3-Jun-52	4.03	2
DELTA	TS6-4	28-May-52	4.13	2	GRAND TRAVER	PB11-4	3-Sep-57	4.47	2
DELTA	TP10-2	6-May-55	4.16	2	GRAND TRAVER	UK9-2	20-May-53	13.01	4
DELTA	UK9-2	20-May-53	36.76	5	GRAND TRAVER	TS6-4	28-May-52	17.36	4
DICKINSON	TP5-3	14-Mar-55	4.12	2	GRATIOT	PB11-4	3-Sep-57	4.47	2
DICKINSON	TP10-2	6-May-55	4.16	2	GRATIOT	TS6-4	28-May-52	6.75	3
DICKINSON	PB5-5	19-Jul-57	6.09	3	GRATIOT	UK9-2	20-May-53	11.20	4
DICKINSON	UK9-2	20-May-53	36.13	5	GRATIOT	TS7-3	3-Jun-52	47.12	5
EATON	UK7-4	28-Apr-53	3.52	2	HILLSDALE	TP9-2	15-Apr-55	3.61	2

INDIVIDUAL FALLOUT DAYS
MICHIGAN

COUNTY	SHOT	DATE	µCi/SQ METER	INDEX	COUNTY	SHOT	DATE	µCi/SQ METER	INDEX
HILLSDALE	PB6-3	26-Jul-57	3.96	2	IRON	TP10-2	6-May-55	8.33	3
HILLSDALE	UK9-2	20-May-53	4.21	2	IRON	UK9-2	20-May-53	39.65	5
HILLSDALE	SE3	8-Jul-62	35.48	5	ISABELLA	PB11-4	3-Sep-57	4.47	2
HILLSDALE	TS7-3	3-Jun-52	50.86	6	ISABELLA	UK9-2	20-May-53	12.01	4
HOUGHTON	PB11-3	2-Sep-57	3.98	2	ISABELLA	TS7-3	3-Jun-52	14.76	4
HOUGHTON	PB5-5	19-Jul-57	6.09	3	ISABELLA	TS6-4	28-May-52	16.39	4
HOUGHTON	TP10-2	6-May-55	8.33	3	JACKSON	UK9-2	20-May-53	3.53	2
HOUGHTON	TS6-3	27-May-52	9.52	3	JACKSON	TS6-4	28-May-52	3.86	2
HOUGHTON	TS6-4	28-May-52	18.32	4	JACKSON	TP9-2	15-Apr-55	4.29	2
HOUGHTON	UK9-2	20-May-53	49.81	5	JACKSON	UK2-8	31-Mar-53	6.34	3
HURON	TS6-4	28-May-52	4.82	2	JACKSON	TS7-3	3-Jun-52	42.43	5
HURON	UK9-2	20-May-53	7.37	3	KALAMAZOO	PB6-3	26-Jul-57	3.96	2
HURON	TS7-3	3-Jun-52	15.26	4	KALAMAZOO	UK7-4	28-Apr-53	4.16	2
HURON	TP9-2	15-Apr-55	41.76	5	KALAMAZOO	UK9-2	20-May-53	4.44	2
INGHAM	PB11-4	3-Sep-57	4.47	2	KALAMAZOO	TP9-2	15-Apr-55	6.75	3
INGHAM	TS6-4	28-May-52	4.82	2	KALAMAZOO	TS6-4	28-May-52	10.61	4
INGHAM	TP9-2	15-Apr-55	4.84	2	KALAMAZOO	TS7-3	3-Jun-52	72.02	6
INGHAM	UK2-8	31-Mar-53	6.34	3	KALKASKA	TP10-2	6-May-55	3.83	2
INGHAM	UK9-2	20-May-53	9.30	3	KALKASKA	PB11-4	3-Sep-57	4.47	2
INGHAM	SE4	9-Jul-62	68.45	6	KALKASKA	UK9-2	20-May-53	9.76	3
INGHAM	TS7-3	3-Jun-52	85.98	6	KENT	UK7-4	28-Apr-53	3.82	2
IONIA	PB9-5	27-Aug-57	4.52	2	KENT	PB6-3	26-Jul-57	3.96	2
IONIA	UK9-2	20-May-53	5.28	3	KENT	PB9-5	27-Aug-57	4.52	2
IONIA	TS7-3	3-Jun-52	7.99	3	KENT	UK9-2	20-May-53	6.53	3
IONIA	TS6-4	28-May-52	14.46	4	KENT	TS6-4	28-May-52	9.67	3
IOSCO	PB11-4	3-Sep-57	6.71	3	KENT	SE4	9-Jul-62	57.79	6
IOSCO	TP9-2	15-Apr-55	7.22	3	KENT	TS7-3	3-Jun-52	28.99	5
IOSCO	TS7-3	3-Jun-52	9.78	3	KEWEENAW	PB5-5	19-Jul-57	6.09	3
IOSCO	TS6-4	28-May-52	11.57	4	KEWEENAW	TP10-2	6-May-55	8.33	3
IOSCO	UK9-2	20-May-53	13.91	4	KEWEENAW	TS6-3	27-May-52	11.05	4
IRON	TS6-4	28-May-52	4.83	2	KEWEENAW	UK9-2	20-May-53	56.63	6
IRON	TS6-3	27-May-52	5.36	3	LAKE	PB11-4	3-Sep-57	4.24	2
IRON	PB5-5	19-Jul-57	6.09	3	LAKE	TS7-3	3-Jun-52	7.49	3

INDIVIDUAL FALLOUT DAYS
MICHIGAN

COUNTY	SHOT	DATE	µCi/SQ METER	INDEX	COUNTY	SHOT	DATE	µCi/SQ METER	INDEX
LAKE	UK9-2	20-May-53	13.10	4	MACOMB	UK9-2	20-May-53	6.22	3
LAKE	TS6-4	28-May-52	16.39	4	MACOMB	BJ3-5	5-Nov-51	6.32	3
LAPEER	TP5-3	14-Mar-55	3.57	2	MACOMB	TS7-3	3-Jun-52	8.96	3
LAPEER	TS6-4	28-May-52	3.86	2	MACOMB	TP9-2	15-Apr-55	55.74	6
LAPEER	BJ3-5	5-Nov-51	4.21	2	MANISTEE	TS7-3	3-Jun-52	4.73	2
LAPEER	PB11-4	3-Sep-57	4.47	2	MANISTEE	UK9-2	20-May-53	15.27	4
LAPEER	UK2-8	31-Mar-53	6.34	3	MARQUETTE	PB5-5	19-Jul-57	4.02	2
LAPEER	TP9-2	15-Apr-55	14.36	4	MARQUETTE	UK9-2	20-May-53	37.06	5
LAPEER	UK9-2	20-May-53	15.92	4	MASON	PB6-3	26-Jul-57	3.96	2
LAPEER	TS7-3	3-Jun-52	59.23	6	MASON	TS7-3	3-Jun-52	6.36	3
LEELANAU	UK9-2	20-May-53	16.80	4	MASON	UK9-2	20-May-53	8.19	3
LEELANAU	TS6-4	28-May-52	19.29	4	MASON	TS6-4	28-May-52	34.72	5
LENAWEE	PB9-5	27-Aug-57	4.52	2	MECOSTA	TS7-3	3-Jun-52	10.31	4
LENAWEE	TP9-2	15-Apr-55	5.56	3	MECOSTA	UK9-2	20-May-53	11.29	4
LENAWEE	UK2-8	31-Mar-53	6.34	3	MECOSTA	TS6-4	28-May-52	11.57	4
LENAWEE	TS7-3	3-Jun-52	9.66	3	MENOMINEE	UK10-4	28-May-53	3.55	2
LENAWEE	SE3	8-Jul-62	90.94	6	MENOMINEE	TP10-2	6-May-55	8.33	3
LIVINGSTON	TS6-4	28-May-52	3.86	2	MENOMINEE	PB9-4	26-Aug-57	8.37	3
LIVINGSTON	UK2-8	31-Mar-53	6.34	3	MENOMINEE	PB9-3	25-Aug-57	13.72	4
LIVINGSTON	UK9-2	20-May-53	6.46	3	MENOMINEE	UK9-2	20-May-53	30.53	5
LIVINGSTON	TP9-2	15-Apr-55	8.65	3	MIDLAND	TS6-4	28-May-52	7.71	3
LIVINGSTON	TS7-3	3-Jun-52	85.90	6	MIDLAND	UK9-2	20-May-53	12.83	4
LUCE	TP10-2	6-May-55	4.16	2	MIDLAND	TS7-3	3-Jun-52	36.88	5
LUCE	TS8-4	8-Jun-52	4.38	2	MISSAUKEE	PB11-4	3-Sep-57	6.71	3
LUCE	TS6-4	28-May-52	25.07	5	MISSAUKEE	TS7-3	3-Jun-52	6.99	3
LUCE	UK9-2	20-May-53	38.22	5	MISSAUKEE	UK9-2	20-May-53	11.05	4
MACKINAC	TP10-2	6-May-55	3.83	2	MISSAUKEE	TS6-4	28-May-52	13.50	4
MACKINAC	TS8-4	8-Jun-52	4.27	2	MONROE	TS7-4	4-Jun-52	3.84	2
MACKINAC	PB11-4	3-Sep-57	4.47	2	MONROE	UK2-8	31-Mar-53	6.34	3
MACKINAC	UK9-2	20-May-53	20.69	4	MONROE	TP9-2	15-Apr-55	9.18	3
MACKINAC	TS6-4	28-May-52	46.29	5	MONROE	SE4	9-Jul-62	85.56	6
MACOMB	UK2-8	31-Mar-53	4.23	2	MONROE	UK9-3	21-May-53	3.51	1
MACOMB	TP4-4	10-Mar-55	4.63	2	MONTCALM	TS6-4	28-May-52	9.64	3

INDIVIDUAL FALLOUT DAYS
MICHIGAN

COUNTY	SHOT	DATE	µCi/SQ METER	INDEX	COUNTY	SHOT	DATE	µCi/SQ METER	INDEX
MONTCALM	UK9-2	20-May-53	11.65	4	OSCEOLA	UK9-2	20-May-53	13.19	4
MONTCALM	TS7-3	3-Jun-52	32.30	5	OSCEOLA	TS6-4	28-May-52	13.50	4
MONTMORENCY	TP10-2	6-May-55	5.81	3	OSCODA	TP10-2	6-May-55	3.83	2
MONTMORENCY	UK9-2	20-May-53	8.34	3	OSCODA	TS6-4	28-May-52	9.64	3
MONTMORENCY	TS6-4	28-May-52	10.61	4	OSCODA	UK9-2	20-May-53	10.30	4
MUSKEGON	UK7-4	28-Apr-53	3.70	2	OTSEGO	TP10-2	6-May-55	3.83	2
MUSKEGON	PB6-3	26-Jul-57	3.96	2	OTSEGO	PB11-4	3-Sep-57	6.71	3
MUSKEGON	UK9-2	20-May-53	8.04	3	OTSEGO	UK9-2	20-May-53	10.66	4
MUSKEGON	TS6-4	28-May-52	15.43	4	OTSEGO	TS6-4	28-May-52	13.50	4
MUSKEGON	TS7-3	3-Jun-52	25.11	5	OTTAWA	PB6-3	26-Jul-57	3.96	2
NEWAYGO	PB6-3	26-Jul-57	3.96	2	OTTAWA	UK7-4	28-Apr-53	4.42	2
NEWAYGO	TS6-4	28-May-52	6.45	3	OTTAWA	PB9-5	27-Aug-57	4.52	2
NEWAYGO	UK9-2	20-May-53	12.28	4	OTTAWA	UK9-2	20-May-53	7.89	3
NEWAYGO	TS7-3	3-Jun-52	20.92	4	OTTAWA	TS6-4	28-May-52	10.48	4
OAKLAND	TP4-4	10-Mar-55	3.77	2	OTTAWA	TS7-3	3-Jun-52	62.73	6
OAKLAND	TS6-4	28-May-52	3.86	2	PRESQUE ISLE	TP10-2	6-May-55	3.83	2
OAKLAND	UK9-2	20-May-53	7.22	3	PRESQUE ISLE	PB11-4	3-Sep-57	6.71	3
OAKLAND	TP9-2	15-Apr-55	14.33	4	PRESQUE ISLE	UK9-2	20-May-53	8.42	3
OAKLAND	SE4	9-Jul-62	68.45	6	PRESQUE ISLE	TS6-4	28-May-52	8.86	3
OAKLAND	TS7-3	3-Jun-52	31.72	5	ROSCOMMON	PB11-4	3-Sep-57	6.71	3
OCEANA	PB6-3	26-Jul-57	3.96	2	ROSCOMMON	TS7-3	3-Jun-52	8.48	3
OCEANA	UK9-2	20-May-53	11.47	4	ROSCOMMON	UK9-2	20-May-53	15.63	4
OCEANA	TS7-3	3-Jun-52	17.09	4	SAGINAW	UK2-8	31-Mar-53	4.23	2
OCEANA	TS6-4	28-May-52	17.36	4	SAGINAW	TP9-2	15-Apr-55	5.24	3
OGEMAW	PB11-4	3-Sep-57	4.47	2	SAGINAW	UK9-2	20-May-53	8.80	3
OGEMAW	TS6-4	28-May-52	8.68	3	SAGINAW	TS6-4	28-May-52	10.61	4
OGEMAW	UK9-2	20-May-53	10.90	4	SAGINAW	TS7-3	3-Jun-52	49.38	5
ONTONAGON	PB11-3	2-Sep-57	3.98	2	SANILAC	TS6-4	28-May-52	3.86	2
ONTONAGON	TP10-2	6-May-55	4.16	2	SANILAC	UK2-8	31-Mar-53	6.34	3
ONTONAGON	TS6-4	28-May-52	6.75	3	SANILAC	UK9-2	20-May-53	12.56	4
ONTONAGON	TS6-3	27-May-52	9.78	3	SANILAC	TS7-3	3-Jun-52	20.05	4
ONTONAGON	UK9-2	20-May-53	50.88	6	SANILAC	TP9-2	15-Apr-55	34.60	5
OSCEOLA	TS7-3	3-Jun-52	8.90	3	SCHOOLCRAFT	TS8-4	8-Jun-52	3.66	2

INDIVIDUAL FALLOUT DAYS
MICHIGAN

COUNTY	SHOT	DATE	µCi/SQ METER	INDEX	COUNTY	SHOT	DATE	µCi/SQ METER	INDEX
SCHOOLCRAFT	TP10-2	6-May-55	8.33	3	TUSCOLA	TP5-3	14-Mar-55	4.70	2
SCHOOLCRAFT	TS6-4	28-May-52	40.50	5	TUSCOLA	TS6-4	28-May-52	4.82	2
SCHOOLCRAFT	UK9-2	20-May-53	44.93	5	TUSCOLA	UK2-8	31-Mar-53	6.34	3
SHIAWASSEE	UK2-8	31-Mar-53	4.23	2	TUSCOLA	TP9-2	15-Apr-55	8.49	3
SHIAWASSEE	TS6-4	28-May-52	4.82	2	TUSCOLA	UK9-2	20-May-53	16.57	4
SHIAWASSEE	TP9-2	15-Apr-55	5.95	3	TUSCOLA	TS7-3	3-Jun-52	19.57	4
SHIAWASSEE	UK9-2	20-May-53	6.84	3	VAN BUREN	PB6-3	26-Jul-57	3.96	2
SHIAWASSEE	SE4	9-Jul-62	21.68	4	VAN BUREN	UK9-2	20-May-53	6.32	3
SHIAWASSEE	TS7-3	3-Jun-52	66.41	6	VAN BUREN	UK7-4	28-Apr-53	7.45	3
ST CLAIR	TS6-4	28-May-52	3.86	2	VAN BUREN	TS6-4	28-May-52	13.50	4
ST CLAIR	BJ3-5	5-Nov-51	4.21	2	VAN BUREN	TS7-3	3-Jun-52	67.01	6
ST CLAIR	UK2-8	31-Mar-53	4.23	2	WASHTENAW	TP4-4	10-Mar-55	3.83	2
ST CLAIR	PB11-4	3-Sep-57	4.47	2	WASHTENAW	UK9-2	20-May-53	5.49	3
ST CLAIR	UK9-3	21-May-53	5.47	3	WASHTENAW	UK2-8	31-Mar-53	6.34	3
ST CLAIR	UK9-2	20-May-53	8.31	3	WASHTENAW	TP9-2	15-Apr-55	9.13	3
ST CLAIR	TS7-3	3-Jun-52	8.34	3	WASHTENAW	TS7-3	3-Jun-52	16.23	4
ST CLAIR	TP9-2	15-Apr-55	18.89	4	WAYNE	TS7-3	3-Jun-52	5.49	3
ST JOSEPH	UK9-2	20-May-53	3.83	2	WAYNE	BJ3-5	5-Nov-51	6.32	3
ST JOSEPH	PB6-3	26-Jul-57	3.96	2	WAYNE	UK9-2	20-May-53	6.53	3
ST JOSEPH	PB8-6	23-Aug-57	4.03	2	WAYNE	TP9-2	15-Apr-55	84.20	6
ST JOSEPH	TS6-4	28-May-52	7.71	3	WEXFORD	TS6-4	28-May-52	4.03	2
ST JOSEPH	UK7-4	28-Apr-53	8.71	3	WEXFORD	TS7-3	3-Jun-52	5.72	3
ST JOSEPH	TS7-3	3-Jun-52	15.79	4	WEXFORD	UK9-2	20-May-53	15.18	4
TUSCOLA	PB11-4	3-Sep-57	4.47	2					

INDIVIDUAL FALLOUT DAYS
MINNESOTA

COUNTY	SHOT	DATE	µCi/SQ METER	INDEX	COUNTY	SHOT	DATE	µCi/SQ METER	INDEX
AITKIN	PB11-3	2-Sep-57	3.98	2	BLUE EARTH	UK7-5	29-Apr-53	5.85	3
AITKIN	PB15-2	17-Sep-57	4.11	2	BLUE EARTH	PB5-5	19-Jul-57	6.09	3
AITKIN	PB5-5	19-Jul-57	10.11	4	BLUE EARTH	UK7-4	28-Apr-53	9.41	3
AITKIN	UK9-2	20-May-53	16.24	4	BLUE EARTH	TS6-3	27-May-52	12.33	4
AITKIN	TP10-2	6-May-55	3.51	1	BLUE EARTH	TP10-2	6-May-55	3.51	1
AITKIN	TS6-3	27-May-52	25.25	5	BLUE EARTH	UK9-2	20-May-53	27.39	5
ANOKA	UK7-5	29-Apr-53	3.95	2	BLUE EARTH	SE3	8-Jul-62	325.19	8
ANOKA	PB11-3	2-Sep-57	3.98	2	BROWN	PB5-5	19-Jul-57	6.09	3
ANOKA	UK9-1	19-May-53	4.37	2	BROWN	UK7-5	29-Apr-53	6.48	3
ANOKA	TS6-4	28-May-52	8.06	3	BROWN	TS6-3	27-May-52	6.70	3
ANOKA	PB5-5	19-Jul-57	10.11	4	BROWN	TS7-4	4-Jun-52	7.31	3
ANOKA	TS6-3	27-May-52	13.97	4	BROWN	UK7-4	28-Apr-53	10.52	4
ANOKA	TP10-2	6-May-55	3.51	1	BROWN	UK9-2	20-May-53	17.76	4
ANOKA	UK9-2	20-May-53	25.78	5	BROWN	TP10-2	6-May-55	3.51	1
BECKER	UK7-5	29-Apr-53	3.51	2	BROWN	SE3	8-Jul-62	325.19	8
BECKER	PB11-3	2-Sep-57	3.98	2	CARLTON	PB15-2	17-Sep-57	4.11	2
BECKER	TP9-3	16-Apr-55	4.08	2	CARLTON	PB11-3	2-Sep-57	6.62	3
BECKER	PB5-5	19-Jul-57	6.09	3	CARLTON	PB5-5	19-Jul-57	10.11	4
BECKER	TS6-3	27-May-52	20.06	4	CARLTON	TP11-5	19-May-55	11.44	4
BELTRAMI	PB15-2	17-Sep-57	4.11	2	CARLTON	TS6-3	27-May-52	23.04	4
BELTRAMI	PB5-5	19-Jul-57	6.09	3	CARLTON	TP10-2	6-May-55	3.51	1
BELTRAMI	TS6-3	27-May-52	13.52	4	CARLTON	UK9-2	20-May-53	33.58	5
BENTON	PB11-3	2-Sep-57	3.98	2	CARVER	PB6-9	1-Aug-57	4.05	2
BENTON	UK7-5	29-Apr-53	4.24	2	CARVER	UK7-5	29-Apr-53	4.66	2
BENTON	PB5-5	19-Jul-57	10.11	4	CARVER	UK7-4	28-Apr-53	7.05	3
BENTON	UK9-2	20-May-53	19.60	4	CARVER	PB5-5	19-Jul-57	10.11	4
BENTON	TP10-2	6-May-55	3.51	1	CARVER	TS6-3	27-May-52	20.67	4
BENTON	TS6-3	27-May-52	28.51	5	CARVER	UK9-2	20-May-53	21.32	4
BIG STONE	UK7-4	28-Apr-53	3.96	2	CARVER	TP10-2	6-May-55	3.51	1
BIG STONE	TS6-3	27-May-52	4.42	2	CASS	TS6-4	28-May-52	4.03	2
BIG STONE	TS7-4	4-Jun-52	4.43	2	CASS	PB15-2	17-Sep-57	4.11	2
BIG STONE	UK7-5	29-Apr-53	4.94	2	CASS	PB5-5	19-Jul-57	6.09	3
BLUE EARTH	TS5-1	7-May-52	3.75	2	CASS	UK9-2	20-May-53	7.75	3

INDIVIDUAL FALLOUT DAYS
MINNESOTA

COUNTY	SHOT	DATE	µCi/SQ METER	INDEX	COUNTY	SHOT	DATE	µCi/SQ METER	INDEX
CASS	TS6-3	27-May-52	21.42	4	CROW WING	UK9-2	20-May-53	10.07	4
CASS	TP10-2	6-May-55	3.51	1	CROW WING	TP10-2	6-May-55	3.51	1
CHIPPEWA	PB6-9	1-Aug-57	4.05	2	CROW WING	TS6-3	27-May-52	25.76	5
CHIPPEWA	UK9-2	20-May-53	4.98	2	DAKOTA	UK9-3	21-May-53	3.58	2
CHIPPEWA	UK7-5	29-Apr-53	5.94	3	DAKOTA	PB11-3	2-Sep-57	3.98	2
CHIPPEWA	UK7-4	28-Apr-53	8.03	3	DAKOTA	UK7-5	29-Apr-53	4.15	2
CHIPPEWA	TS6-3	27-May-52	14.20	4	DAKOTA	UK7-4	28-Apr-53	5.60	3
CHISAGO	PB5-5	19-Jul-57	4.02	2	DAKOTA	PB5-5	19-Jul-57	10.11	4
CHISAGO	UK9-1	19-May-53	4.63	2	DAKOTA	TS6-3	27-May-52	17.82	4
CHISAGO	TS6-4	28-May-52	8.06	3	DAKOTA	TP10-2	6-May-55	3.51	1
CHISAGO	TS6-3	27-May-52	15.64	4	DAKOTA	UK9-2	20-May-53	35.86	5
CHISAGO	TP10-2	6-May-55	3.51	1	DODGE	UK7-5	29-Apr-53	4.27	2
CHISAGO	UK9-2	20-May-53	31.89	5	DODGE	TS5-1	7-May-52	4.49	2
CLAY	PB11-3	2-Sep-57	3.98	2	DODGE	TS3-8	29-Apr-52	5.92	3
CLAY	TP9-3	16-Apr-55	4.21	2	DODGE	TP10-2	6-May-55	7.01	3
CLEARWATER	PB15-2	17-Sep-57	4.11	2	DODGE	UK7-4	28-Apr-53	8.29	3
CLEARWATER	TS6-3	27-May-52	8.42	3	DODGE	TS7-5	5-Jun-52	10.05	4
COOK	PB5-5	19-Jul-57	4.02	2	DODGE	TS6-3	27-May-52	11.66	4
COOK	TP10-2	6-May-55	4.16	2	DODGE	TS6-4	28-May-52	18.32	4
COOK	TS6-3	27-May-52	11.39	4	DODGE	UK9-2	20-May-53	47.69	5
COOK	UK9-2	20-May-53	35.51	5	DODGE	SE3	8-Jul-62	181.88	7
COTTONWOOD	PB5-5	19-Jul-57	4.02	2	DOUGLAS	PB6-9	1-Aug-57	4.05	2
COTTONWOOD	UK7-5	29-Apr-53	6.94	3	DOUGLAS	UK7-5	29-Apr-53	4.73	2
COTTONWOOD	UK7-4	28-Apr-53	10.07	4	DOUGLAS	PB15-2	17-Sep-57	6.81	3
COTTONWOOD	TS7-4	4-Jun-52	12.54	4	FARIBAULT	TS5-1	7-May-52	3.75	2
COTTONWOOD	UK9-2	20-May-53	14.08	4	FARIBAULT	UK7-5	29-Apr-53	5.61	3
COTTONWOOD	TS6-3	27-May-52	17.26	4	FARIBAULT	PB5-5	19-Jul-57	6.09	3
COTTONWOOD	TP10-2	6-May-55	3.51	1	FARIBAULT	TS7-4	4-Jun-52	7.12	3
COTTONWOOD	SE3	8-Jul-62	132.13	7	FARIBAULT	UK7-4	28-Apr-53	8.82	3
CROW WING	UK7-5	29-Apr-53	3.90	2	FARIBAULT	TS7-5	5-Jun-52	8.84	3
CROW WING	PB11-3	2-Sep-57	3.98	2	FARIBAULT	TS6-3	27-May-52	16.49	4
CROW WING	PB15-2	17-Sep-57	4.11	2	FARIBAULT	TP10-2	6-May-55	3.51	1
CROW WING	PB5-5	19-Jul-57	6.09	3	FARIBAULT	UK9-2	20-May-53	38.55	5

INDIVIDUAL FALLOUT DAYS
MINNESOTA

COUNTY	SHOT	DATE	µCi/SQ METER	INDEX	COUNTY	SHOT	DATE	µCi/SQ METER	INDEX
FARIBAULT	SE3	8-Jul-62	584.61	9	HOUSTON	PB18-8	17-Jul-57	3.98	2
FILLMORE	UK9-3	21-May-53	4.13	2	HOUSTON	PB5-7	21-Jul-57	4.15	2
FILLMORE	TS7-4	4-Jun-52	4.43	2	HOUSTON	TS5-1	7-May-52	4.65	2
FILLMORE	TS5-2	8-May-52	4.46	2	HOUSTON	UK7-4	28-Apr-53	6.89	3
FILLMORE	TS6-3	27-May-52	5.77	3	HOUSTON	TP10-2	6-May-55	7.01	3
FILLMORE	TP10-2	6-May-55	7.01	3	HOUSTON	TS7-5	5-Jun-52	11.53	4
FILLMORE	UK7-4	28-Apr-53	10.20	4	HOUSTON	PB9-3	25-Aug-57	13.72	4
FILLMORE	TS7-5	5-Jun-52	11.43	4	HOUSTON	TS6-4	28-May-52	16.39	4
FILLMORE	UK9-2	20-May-53	60.85	6	HOUSTON	PB9-4	26-Aug-57	16.67	4
FILLMORE	SE3	8-Jul-62	327.38	8	HOUSTON	UK9-2	20-May-53	51.86	6
FREEBORN	UK7-5	29-Apr-53	4.85	2	HOUSTON	SE3	8-Jul-62	139.44	7
FREEBORN	TS7-4	4-Jun-52	7.39	3	HUBBARD	UK7-5	29-Apr-53	3.53	2
FREEBORN	UK7-4	28-Apr-53	8.55	3	HUBBARD	PB11-3	2-Sep-57	3.98	2
FREEBORN	PB5-5	19-Jul-57	10.11	4	HUBBARD	UK9-2	20-May-53	4.26	2
FREEBORN	TS6-3	27-May-52	12.47	4	HUBBARD	PB5-5	19-Jul-57	6.09	3
FREEBORN	UK9-2	20-May-53	24.47	4	HUBBARD	TS6-4	28-May-52	6.45	3
FREEBORN	TP10-2	6-May-55	3.51	1	HUBBARD	TS6-3	27-May-52	17.34	4
GOODHUE	TS7-5	5-Jun-52	5.25	3	ISANTI	PB5-5	19-Jul-57	4.02	2
GOODHUE	TP10-2	6-May-55	7.01	3	ISANTI	UK9-1	19-May-53	4.37	2
GOODHUE	UK7-4	28-Apr-53	8.29	3	ISANTI	TS6-4	28-May-52	8.06	3
GOODHUE	TS6-4	28-May-52	9.67	3	ISANTI	TS6-3	27-May-52	14.76	4
GOODHUE	PB5-5	19-Jul-57	10.11	4	ISANTI	UK9-2	20-May-53	24.30	4
GOODHUE	TS6-3	27-May-52	12.90	4	ISANTI	TP10-2	6-May-55	3.51	1
GOODHUE	UK9-2	20-May-53	47.60	5	ITASCA	PB15-2	17-Sep-57	4.11	2
GOODHUE	SE3	8-Jul-62	181.88	7	ITASCA	TP10-2	6-May-55	5.26	3
GRANT	PB11-3	2-Sep-57	3.98	2	ITASCA	TS6-4	28-May-52	5.79	3
GRANT	PB15-2	17-Sep-57	4.11	2	ITASCA	UK9-2	20-May-53	9.56	3
GRANT	UK7-5	29-Apr-53	4.88	2	ITASCA	PB5-5	19-Jul-57	10.11	4
HENNEPIN	UK7-5	29-Apr-53	3.89	2	ITASCA	TS6-3	27-May-52	13.09	4
HENNEPIN	UK7-4	28-Apr-53	4.12	2	JACKSON	UK7-5	29-Apr-53	6.97	3
HENNEPIN	PB5-5	19-Jul-57	4.20	2	JACKSON	UK7-4	28-Apr-53	7.91	3
HENNEPIN	TS6-3	27-May-52	21.03	4	JACKSON	TS6-3	27-May-52	11.05	4
HENNEPIN	UK9-2	20-May-53	22.18	4	JACKSON	UK9-2	20-May-53	17.22	4

INDIVIDUAL FALLOUT DAYS
MINNESOTA

COUNTY	SHOT	DATE	µCi/SQ METER	INDEX	COUNTY	SHOT	DATE	µCi/SQ METER	INDEX
JACKSON	TS7-4	4-Jun-52	17.43	4	LAKE	TS6-3	27-May-52	11.48	4
JACKSON	TP10-2	6-May-55	3.51	1	LAKE	TP10-2	6-May-55	3.51	1
JACKSON	SE3	8-Jul-62	173.92	7	LAKE	UK9-2	20-May-53	34.35	5
KANABEC	PB5-5	19-Jul-57	6.09	3	LAKE OF THE	PB15-2	17-Sep-57	4.11	2
KANABEC	UK9-2	20-May-53	21.77	4	LAKE OF THE	TP9-3	16-Apr-55	4.66	2
KANABEC	TS6-3	27-May-52	22.88	4	LAKE OF THE	TS6-3	27-May-52	6.97	3
KANABEC	TP10-2	6-May-55	3.51	1	LE SUEUR	UK9-1	19-May-53	3.60	2
KANDIYOHI	PB11-3	2-Sep-57	3.98	2	LE SUEUR	UK7-5	29-Apr-53	4.74	2
KANDIYOHI	UK7-5	29-Apr-53	5.70	3	LE SUEUR	TS7-5	5-Jun-52	8.34	3
KANDIYOHI	PB5-5	19-Jul-57	6.09	3	LE SUEUR	PB5-5	19-Jul-57	10.11	4
KANDIYOHI	UK9-2	20-May-53	7.36	3	LE SUEUR	UK7-4	28-Apr-53	10.48	4
KANDIYOHI	UK7-4	28-Apr-53	8.48	3	LE SUEUR	TS6-3	27-May-52	17.75	4
KANDIYOHI	TS6-3	27-May-52	16.25	4	LE SUEUR	TP10-2	6-May-55	3.51	1
KANDIYOHI	TP10-2	6-May-55	3.51	1	LE SUEUR	UK9-2	20-May-53	30.53	5
KITTSON	TS7-3	3-Jun-52	3.79	2	LE SUEUR	SE3	8-Jul-62	325.19	8
KITTSON	TS6-4	28-May-52	3.86	2	LINCOLN	UK2-2	25-Mar-53	3.97	2
KITTSON	PB11-3	2-Sep-57	3.98	2	LINCOLN	TP9-3	16-Apr-55	4.37	2
KITTSON	TS7-5	5-Jun-52	5.22	3	LINCOLN	UK9-2	20-May-53	4.66	2
KITTSON	TP9-3	16-Apr-55	10.96	4	LINCOLN	UK7-5	29-Apr-53	5.51	3
KOOCHICHING	UK9-2	20-May-53	4.11	2	LINCOLN	PB5-5	19-Jul-57	6.09	3
KOOCHICHING	TS7-5	5-Jun-52	5.81	3	LINCOLN	UK7-4	28-Apr-53	9.12	3
KOOCHICHING	PB5-5	19-Jul-57	6.09	3	LINCOLN	TS6-3	27-May-52	9.27	3
KOOCHICHING	PB15-2	17-Sep-57	6.81	3	LINCOLN	TS7-4	4-Jun-52	19.32	4
KOOCHICHING	TP10-2	6-May-55	7.01	3	LINCOLN	SE3	8-Jul-62	181.88	7
KOOCHICHING	TS6-3	27-May-52	10.71	4	LYON	UK2-2	25-Mar-53	3.97	2
LAC QUI PARL	TS7-5	5-Jun-52	3.97	2	LYON	UK9-2	20-May-53	5.85	3
LAC QUI PARL	UK7-5	29-Apr-53	5.48	3	LYON	UK7-5	29-Apr-53	6.15	3
LAC QUI PARL	PB5-5	19-Jul-57	6.09	3	LYON	UK7-4	28-Apr-53	9.25	3
LAC QUI PARL	UK7-4	28-Apr-53	7.65	3	LYON	PB5-5	19-Jul-57	10.11	4
LAC QUI PARL	TS6-3	27-May-52	8.84	3	LYON	TS6-3	27-May-52	12.67	4
LAKE	PB5-5	19-Jul-57	6.09	3	LYON	TS7-4	4-Jun-52	14.82	4
LAKE	PB11-3	2-Sep-57	6.62	3	LYON	SE3	8-Jul-62	181.88	7
LAKE	TS6-4	28-May-52	7.71	3	MAHNOMEN	PB5-5	19-Jul-57	4.02	2

INDIVIDUAL FALLOUT DAYS
MINNESOTA

COUNTY	SHOT	DATE	µCi/SQ METER	INDEX	COUNTY	SHOT	DATE	µCi/SQ METER	INDEX
MAHNOMEN	UK9-1	19-May-53	4.37	2	MORRISON	PB11-3	2-Sep-57	3.98	2
MAHNOMEN	PB11-3	2-Sep-57	6.62	3	MORRISON	UK7-5	29-Apr-53	4.00	2
MARSHALL	PB15-2	17-Sep-57	4.11	2	MORRISON	PB5-5	19-Jul-57	10.11	4
MARSHALL	TS6-3	27-May-52	4.51	2	MORRISON	UK9-2	20-May-53	11.04	4
MARSHALL	TP9-3	16-Apr-55	6.52	3	MORRISON	TS6-3	27-May-52	19.68	4
MARTIN	UK7-5	29-Apr-53	6.30	3	MORRISON	TP10-2	6-May-55	3.51	1
MARTIN	PB5-5	19-Jul-57	10.11	4	MOWER	TS7-4	4-Jun-52	3.61	2
MARTIN	UK7-4	28-Apr-53	10.33	4	MOWER	UK9-3	21-May-53	3.69	2
MARTIN	TS6-3	27-May-52	11.22	4	MOWER	UK7-5	29-Apr-53	3.88	2
MARTIN	TS7-4	4-Jun-52	12.99	4	MOWER	TS5-1	7-May-52	4.49	2
MARTIN	UK9-2	20-May-53	22.63	4	MOWER	TS3-8	29-Apr-52	5.92	3
MARTIN	TP10-2	6-May-55	3.51	1	MOWER	TP10-2	6-May-55	7.01	3
MARTIN	SE3	8-Jul-62	327.38	8	MOWER	UK7-4	28-Apr-53	7.64	3
MCLEOD	UK7-5	29-Apr-53	5.67	3	MOWER	TS6-3	27-May-52	8.92	3
MCLEOD	TS7-5	5-Jun-52	7.55	3	MOWER	TS7-5	5-Jun-52	10.56	4
MCLEOD	UK7-4	28-Apr-53	9.46	3	MOWER	TS6-4	28-May-52	15.43	4
MCLEOD	UK9-2	20-May-53	18.79	4	MOWER	UK9-2	20-May-53	59.23	6
MCLEOD	TS6-3	27-May-52	20.10	4	MOWER	SE3	8-Jul-62	584.61	9
MCLEOD	TP10-2	6-May-55	3.51	1	MURRAY	UK2-2	25-Mar-53	3.97	2
MEEKER	UK9-1	19-May-53	3.85	2	MURRAY	PB5-5	19-Jul-57	4.02	2
MEEKER	PB11-3	2-Sep-57	3.98	2	MURRAY	UK7-5	29-Apr-53	6.33	3
MEEKER	UK7-5	29-Apr-53	5.51	3	MURRAY	TS5-1	7-May-52	6.65	3
MEEKER	PB5-5	19-Jul-57	6.09	3	MURRAY	TS7-5	5-Jun-52	7.26	3
MEEKER	UK7-4	28-Apr-53	6.31	3	MURRAY	UK9-2	20-May-53	7.58	3
MEEKER	UK9-2	20-May-53	15.27	4	MURRAY	TS6-3	27-May-52	9.01	3
MEEKER	TS6-3	27-May-52	17.01	4	MURRAY	UK7-4	28-Apr-53	9.82	3
MEEKER	TP10-2	6-May-55	3.51	1	MURRAY	TS7-4	4-Jun-52	19.06	4
MILLE LACS	UK7-5	29-Apr-53	3.67	2	MURRAY	SE3	8-Jul-62	327.38	8
MILLE LACS	PB11-3	2-Sep-57	3.98	2	NICOLLET	UK9-1	19-May-53	3.60	2
MILLE LACS	PB5-5	19-Jul-57	6.09	3	NICOLLET	TS7-4	4-Jun-52	5.03	3
MILLE LACS	UK9-2	20-May-53	16.71	4	NICOLLET	UK7-5	29-Apr-53	5.94	3
MILLE LACS	TS6-3	27-May-52	24.45	4	NICOLLET	PB5-5	19-Jul-57	6.09	3
MILLE LACS	TP10-2	6-May-55	3.51	1	NICOLLET	UK7-4	28-Apr-53	9.57	3

INDIVIDUAL FALLOUT DAYS
MINNESOTA

COUNTY	SHOT	DATE	µCi/SQ METER	INDEX	COUNTY	SHOT	DATE	µCi/SQ METER	INDEX
NICOLLET	TS6-3	27-May-52	17.61	4	PINE	UK9-2	20-May-53	33.89	5
NICOLLET	UK9-2	20-May-53	20.59	4	PIPESTONE	UK2-2	25-Mar-53	3.97	2
NICOLLET	TP10-2	6-May-55	3.51	1	PIPESTONE	UK9-2	20-May-53	4.87	2
NICOLLET	SE3	8-Jul-62	325.19	8	PIPESTONE	UK7-5	29-Apr-53	5.55	3
NOBLES	UK2-2	25-Mar-53	3.97	2	PIPESTONE	TS6-3	27-May-52	6.72	3
NOBLES	PB5-5	19-Jul-57	4.02	2	PIPESTONE	TS7-5	5-Jun-52	6.87	3
NOBLES	UK7-5	29-Apr-53	6.36	3	PIPESTONE	UK7-4	28-Apr-53	7.97	3
NOBLES	TS5-1	7-May-52	7.18	3	PIPESTONE	TS5-1	7-May-52	8.26	3
NOBLES	TS7-5	5-Jun-52	7.63	3	PIPESTONE	PB5-5	19-Jul-57	10.11	4
NOBLES	UK9-2	20-May-53	8.88	3	PIPESTONE	TS7-4	4-Jun-52	26.05	5
NOBLES	TS6-3	27-May-52	9.52	3	PIPESTONE	SE3	8-Jul-62	327.38	8
NOBLES	UK7-4	28-Apr-53	10.14	4	POLK	PB11-3	2-Sep-57	3.98	2
NOBLES	TS7-4	4-Jun-52	25.53	5	POLK	PB15-2	17-Sep-57	4.11	2
NOBLES	SE3	8-Jul-62	208.70	8	POLK	TS7-5	5-Jun-52	4.98	2
NORMAN	TP9-3	16-Apr-55	3.94	2	POLK	TS6-3	27-May-52	5.19	3
NORMAN	PB11-3	2-Sep-57	3.98	2	POLK	TP9-3	16-Apr-55	5.82	3
OLMSTED	UK9-3	21-May-53	3.91	2	POPE	UK9-2	20-May-53	4.55	2
OLMSTED	PB5-5	19-Jul-57	6.09	3	POPE	UK7-4	28-Apr-53	4.85	2
OLMSTED	UK7-4	28-Apr-53	7.11	3	POPE	UK7-5	29-Apr-53	5.21	3
OLMSTED	TS6-3	27-May-52	7.28	3	POPE	TS6-3	27-May-52	8.05	3
OLMSTED	UK9-2	20-May-53	51.76	6	RAMSEY	UK7-5	29-Apr-53	3.57	2
OLMSTED	TP10-2	6-May-55	3.51	1	RAMSEY	PB11-3	2-Sep-57	3.98	2
OTTER TAIL	PB11-3	2-Sep-57	3.98	2	RAMSEY	PB5-5	19-Jul-57	10.11	4
OTTER TAIL	PB15-2	17-Sep-57	4.11	2	RAMSEY	TP10-2	6-May-55	14.02	4
OTTER TAIL	UK7-5	29-Apr-53	4.21	2	RAMSEY	TS6-3	27-May-52	19.67	4
OTTER TAIL	TS6-3	27-May-52	13.01	4	RAMSEY	UK9-2	20-May-53	28.49	5
PENNINGTON	PB15-2	17-Sep-57	4.11	2	RED LAKE	PB11-3	2-Sep-57	3.98	2
PENNINGTON	TS6-3	27-May-52	5.70	3	RED LAKE	PB15-2	17-Sep-57	4.11	2
PENNINGTON	TP9-3	16-Apr-55	6.00	3	RED LAKE	TP9-3	16-Apr-55	6.19	3
PINE	PB11-3	2-Sep-57	3.98	2	REDWOOD	PB5-5	19-Jul-57	4.02	2
PINE	PB5-5	19-Jul-57	10.11	4	REDWOOD	UK9-2	20-May-53	5.69	3
PINE	TS6-3	27-May-52	23.63	4	REDWOOD	UK7-5	29-Apr-53	6.67	3
PINE	TP10-2	6-May-55	3.51	1	REDWOOD	TS7-4	4-Jun-52	8.94	3

INDIVIDUAL FALLOUT DAYS
MINNESOTA

COUNTY	SHOT	DATE	µCi/SQ METER	INDEX	COUNTY	SHOT	DATE	µCi/SQ METER	INDEX
REDWOOD	UK7-4	28-Apr-53	9.76	3	ROSEAU	TP9-3	16-Apr-55	8.47	3
REDWOOD	TS6-3	27-May-52	10.88	4	SCOTT	PB11-3	2-Sep-57	3.98	2
REDWOOD	SE3	8-Jul-62	73.41	6	SCOTT	UK7-5	29-Apr-53	4.66	2
REDWOOD	TP10-2	6-May-55	3.51	1	SCOTT	UK7-4	28-Apr-53	7.36	3
RENVILLE	PB5-5	19-Jul-57	6.09	3	SCOTT	PB5-5	19-Jul-57	10.11	4
RENVILLE	UK7-5	29-Apr-53	6.21	3	SCOTT	TS6-3	27-May-52	19.10	4
RENVILLE	UK7-4	28-Apr-53	9.69	3	SCOTT	UK9-2	20-May-53	23.68	4
RENVILLE	UK9-2	20-May-53	11.48	4	SCOTT	TP10-2	6-May-55	3.51	1
RENVILLE	TS6-3	27-May-52	19.21	4	SHERBURNE	UK7-5	29-Apr-53	3.87	2
RENVILLE	TP10-2	6-May-55	3.51	1	SHERBURNE	PB11-3	2-Sep-57	3.98	2
RICE	UK9-3	21-May-53	3.69	2	SHERBURNE	PB5-5	19-Jul-57	10.11	4
RICE	UK9-1	19-May-53	3.85	2	SHERBURNE	UK9-2	20-May-53	23.76	4
RICE	PB11-3	2-Sep-57	3.98	2	SHERBURNE	TP10-2	6-May-55	3.51	1
RICE	UK7-5	29-Apr-53	4.36	2	SHERBURNE	TS6-3	27-May-52	32.41	5
RICE	UK7-4	28-Apr-53	8.56	3	SIBLEY	UK7-5	29-Apr-53	5.82	3
RICE	PB5-5	19-Jul-57	10.11	4	SIBLEY	UK7-4	28-Apr-53	7.54	3
RICE	TS6-3	27-May-52	16.97	4	SIBLEY	PB5-5	19-Jul-57	10.11	4
RICE	TP10-2	6-May-55	3.51	1	SIBLEY	UK9-2	20-May-53	16.35	4
RICE	UK9-2	20-May-53	40.20	5	SIBLEY	TS6-3	27-May-52	18.82	4
RICE	SE3	8-Jul-62	325.19	8	SIBLEY	TP10-2	6-May-55	3.51	1
ROCK	UK2-2	25-Mar-53	3.97	2	SIBLEY	SE3	8-Jul-62	181.88	7
ROCK	UK7-5	29-Apr-53	5.42	3	ST LOUIS	TS6-4	28-May-52	3.86	2
ROCK	UK9-2	20-May-53	5.96	3	ST LOUIS	TS7-5	5-Jun-52	3.91	2
ROCK	TS7-5	5-Jun-52	7.28	3	ST LOUIS	PB11-3	2-Sep-57	3.98	2
ROCK	TS6-3	27-May-52	7.65	3	ST LOUIS	TP10-2	6-May-55	7.01	3
ROCK	UK7-4	28-Apr-53	8.61	3	ST LOUIS	PB5-5	19-Jul-57	10.11	4
ROCK	TS5-1	7-May-52	9.16	3	ST LOUIS	TS6-3	27-May-52	12.92	4
ROCK	PB5-5	19-Jul-57	10.11	4	ST LOUIS	UK9-2	20-May-53	24.67	4
ROCK	TS7-4	4-Jun-52	33.10	5	STEARNS	PB11-3	2-Sep-57	3.98	2
ROCK	SE3	8-Jul-62	527.44	9	STEARNS	PB15-2	17-Sep-57	4.11	2
ROSEAU	PB15-2	17-Sep-57	4.11	2	STEARNS	UK7-5	29-Apr-53	4.94	2
ROSEAU	TS7-5	5-Jun-52	4.74	2	STEARNS	UK7-4	28-Apr-53	4.97	2
ROSEAU	TS6-3	27-May-52	5.10	3	STEARNS	UK9-2	20-May-53	9.42	3

INDIVIDUAL FALLOUT DAYS
MINNESOTA

COUNTY	SHOT	DATE	µCi/SQ METER	INDEX	COUNTY	SHOT	DATE	µCi/SQ METER	INDEX
STEARNS	TS6-3	27-May-52	17.42	4	WABASHA	TS6-4	28-May-52	8.26	3
STEARNS	TP10-2	6-May-55	3.51	1	WABASHA	TS6-3	27-May-52	9.69	3
STEELE	UK9-1	19-May-53	3.60	2	WABASHA	UK9-2	20-May-53	60.85	6
STEELE	PB11-3	2-Sep-57	3.98	2	WABASHA	SE3	8-Jul-62	325.19	8
STEELE	UK7-5	29-Apr-53	4.91	2	WADENA	UK7-5	29-Apr-53	3.61	2
STEELE	UK7-4	28-Apr-53	9.14	3	WADENA	UK9-2	20-May-53	4.33	2
STEELE	PB5-5	19-Jul-57	10.11	4	WADENA	PB11-3	2-Sep-57	6.62	3
STEELE	TS6-3	27-May-52	14.68	4	WADENA	TS6-4	28-May-52	7.25	3
STEELE	TP10-2	6-May-55	3.51	1	WADENA	PB5-5	19-Jul-57	10.11	4
STEELE	UK9-2	20-May-53	43.09	5	WADENA	TS6-3	27-May-52	18.87	4
STEELE	SE3	8-Jul-62	181.88	7	WASECA	UK9-1	19-May-53	3.60	2
STEVENS	UK7-4	28-Apr-53	3.85	2	WASECA	TS7-4	4-Jun-52	5.36	3
STEVENS	PB11-3	2-Sep-57	3.98	2	WASECA	UK7-5	29-Apr-53	5.39	3
STEVENS	UK7-5	29-Apr-53	5.24	3	WASECA	UK7-4	28-Apr-53	9.68	3
STEVENS	TS6-3	27-May-52	6.38	3	WASECA	PB5-5	19-Jul-57	10.11	4
SWIFT	UK7-4	28-Apr-53	5.55	3	WASECA	TS6-3	27-May-52	15.40	4
SWIFT	UK7-5	29-Apr-53	5.67	3	WASECA	TP10-2	6-May-55	3.51	1
SWIFT	TS7-5	5-Jun-52	8.75	3	WASECA	UK9-2	20-May-53	36.22	5
SWIFT	TS6-3	27-May-52	13.01	4	WASECA	SE3	8-Jul-62	325.19	8
TODD	UK7-5	29-Apr-53	4.27	2	WASHINGTON	UK7-5	29-Apr-53	3.67	2
TODD	UK9-2	20-May-53	6.17	3	WASHINGTON	PB11-3	2-Sep-57	3.98	2
TODD	PB11-3	2-Sep-57	6.62	3	WASHINGTON	PB5-5	19-Jul-57	10.11	4
TODD	PB5-5	19-Jul-57	10.11	4	WASHINGTON	TP10-2	6-May-55	14.02	4
TODD	TS6-3	27-May-52	17.54	4	WASHINGTON	TS6-3	27-May-52	18.68	4
TODD	TP10-2	6-May-55	3.51	1	WASHINGTON	UK9-2	20-May-53	34.50	5
TRAVERSE	PB11-3	2-Sep-57	3.98	2	WATONWAN	UK7-5	29-Apr-53	6.42	3
TRAVERSE	UK7-5	29-Apr-53	4.55	2	WATONWAN	TS7-4	4-Jun-52	9.34	3
TRAVERSE	TS7-4	4-Jun-52	8.87	3	WATONWAN	PB5-5	19-Jul-57	10.11	4
WABASHA	PB5-5	19-Jul-57	4.02	2	WATONWAN	UK7-4	28-Apr-53	10.52	4
WABASHA	TS5-1	7-May-52	4.86	2	WATONWAN	TS6-3	27-May-52	18.53	4
WABASHA	UK7-4	28-Apr-53	5.03	3	WATONWAN	UK9-2	20-May-53	21.98	4
WABASHA	TS7-5	5-Jun-52	6.46	3	WATONWAN	TP10-2	6-May-55	3.51	1
WABASHA	TP10-2	6-May-55	7.01	3	WATONWAN	SE3	8-Jul-62	584.61	9

INDIVIDUAL FALLOUT DAYS
MINNESOTA

COUNTY	SHOT	DATE	µCi/SQ METER	INDEX	COUNTY	SHOT	DATE	µCi/SQ METER	INDEX
WILKIN	PB11-3	2-Sep-57	3.98	2	WRIGHT	UK7-5	29-Apr-53	4.30	2
WILKIN	PB5-5	19-Jul-57	4.02	2	WRIGHT	PB5-5	19-Jul-57	10.11	4
WILKIN	TS6-3	27-May-52	6.20	3	WRIGHT	UK9-2	20-May-53	17.79	4
WINONA	TS6-3	27-May-52	4.21	2	WRIGHT	TS6-3	27-May-52	19.51	4
WINONA	TS5-1	7-May-52	5.24	3	WRIGHT	TP10-2	6-May-55	3.51	1
WINONA	TS7-5	5-Jun-52	6.32	3	YELLOW MEDIC	UK9-2	20-May-53	4.76	2
WINONA	UK7-4	28-Apr-53	6.82	3	YELLOW MEDIC	UK7-5	29-Apr-53	5.97	3
WINONA	TP10-2	6-May-55	14.02	4	YELLOW MEDIC	PB5-5	19-Jul-57	6.09	3
WINONA	TS6-4	28-May-52	18.32	4	YELLOW MEDIC	TS7-4	4-Jun-52	8.29	3
WINONA	UK9-2	20-May-53	61.39	6	YELLOW MEDIC	UK7-4	28-Apr-53	8.61	3
WINONA	SE3	8-Jul-62	181.88	7	YELLOW MEDIC	TS6-3	27-May-52	11.73	4
WRIGHT	UK7-4	28-Apr-53	3.93	2					

INDIVIDUAL FALLOUT DAYS
MISSOURI

COUNTY	SHOT	DATE	μCi/SQ METER	INDEX	COUNTY	SHOT	DATE	μCi/SQ METER	INDEX
ADAIR	PB6-3	26-Jul-57	4.63	2	ATCHISON	PB12-4	5-Sep-57	11.35	4
ADAIR	UK7-4	28-Apr-53	5.13	3	ATCHISON	PB13-5	10-Sep-57	12.08	4
ADAIR	TP4-2	8-Mar-55	5.25	3	ATCHISON	UK9-2	20-May-53	17.00	4
ADAIR	TP10-2	6-May-55	5.48	3	ATCHISON	SE3	8-Jul-62	99.74	6
ADAIR	TP10-3	7-May-55	6.93	3	AUDRAIN	PB6-4	27-Jul-57	4.50	2
ADAIR	PB12-4	5-Sep-57	7.84	3	AUDRAIN	PB6-3	26-Jul-57	4.63	2
ADAIR	PB8-3	20-Aug-57	7.99	3	AUDRAIN	UK9-2	20-May-53	4.70	2
ADAIR	PB18-8	17-Jul-57	8.80	3	AUDRAIN	PB18-8	17-Jul-57	5.26	3
ADAIR	TS1-2	2-Apr-52	11.93	4	AUDRAIN	UK2-3	26-Mar-53	5.32	3
ADAIR	UK9-2	20-May-53	15.81	4	AUDRAIN	TP10-3	7-May-55	7.75	3
ADAIR	PB9-4	26-Aug-57	16.67	4	AUDRAIN	PB9-4	26-Aug-57	8.37	3
ADAIR	SE3	8-Jul-62	76.52	6	AUDRAIN	TS7-5	5-Jun-52	10.63	4
ADAIR	TS7-4	4-Jun-52	31.97	5	AUDRAIN	TS6-4	28-May-52	11.57	4
ADAIR	TS7-3	3-Jun-52	39.42	5	AUDRAIN	PB9-3	25-Aug-57	13.72	4
ANDREW	UK2-3	26-Mar-53	3.63	2	AUDRAIN	PB8-3	20-Aug-57	15.90	4
ANDREW	UK7-4	28-Apr-53	3.70	2	AUDRAIN	SE3	8-Jul-62	35.48	5
ANDREW	UK11-3	6-Jun-53	3.79	2	AUDRAIN	R1-2	29-Jan-51	37.86	5
ANDREW	PB8-3	20-Aug-57	4.00	2	AUDRAIN	TS7-3	3-Jun-52	128.50	7
ANDREW	TS7-4	4-Jun-52	4.05	2	BARRY	PB13-4	9-Sep-57	3.55	2
ANDREW	TP10-3	7-May-55	4.47	2	BARRY	PB13-6	11-Sep-57	3.84	2
ANDREW	TP4-2	8-Mar-55	5.25	3	BARRY	TS7-6	6-Jun-52	3.93	2
ANDREW	UK9-2	20-May-53	5.41	3	BARRY	PB8-3	20-Aug-57	4.00	2
ANDREW	TS7-5	5-Jun-52	5.56	3	BARRY	UK3-5	4-Apr-53	4.10	2
ANDREW	TS6-4	28-May-52	5.64	3	BARRY	UK7-4	28-Apr-53	4.49	2
ANDREW	PB13-5	10-Sep-57	6.72	3	BARRY	PB12-6	7-Sep-57	4.54	2
ANDREW	PB12-4	5-Sep-57	13.04	4	BARRY	UK7-3	27-Apr-53	4.61	2
ATCHISON	TP10-3	7-May-55	3.53	2	BARRY	PB18-8	17-Jul-57	5.26	3
ATCHISON	UK7-4	28-Apr-53	3.74	2	BARRY	TP11-6	20-May-55	6.41	3
ATCHISON	TS7-3	3-Jun-52	3.96	2	BARRY	TP11-5	19-May-55	7.28	3
ATCHISON	PB8-3	20-Aug-57	4.00	2	BARRY	UK1-1	17-Mar-53	7.40	3
ATCHISON	TP4-2	8-Mar-55	5.25	3	BARRY	TS6-4	28-May-52	7.71	3
ATCHISON	TS7-5	5-Jun-52	5.52	3	BARRY	TS7-5	5-Jun-52	7.96	3
ATCHISON	TS7-4	4-Jun-52	5.53	3	BARRY	BJ2-2	31-Oct-51	8.76	3

INDIVIDUAL FALLOUT DAYS
MISSOURI

COUNTY	SHOT	DATE	µCi/SQ METER	INDEX	COUNTY	SHOT	DATE	µCi/SQ METER	INDEX
BARRY	TP10-3	7-May-55	9.64	3	BENTON	TS6-4	28-May-52	7.71	3
BARRY	PB12-4	5-Sep-57	14.73	4	BENTON	UK2-3	26-Mar-53	7.81	3
BARRY	TS1-3	3-Apr-52	41.51	5	BENTON	PB9-4	26-Aug-57	8.37	3
BARTON	PB18-8	17-Jul-57	3.53	2	BENTON	PB12-4	5-Sep-57	9.46	3
BARTON	UK2-3	26-Mar-53	3.59	2	BENTON	PB4-5	9-Jul-57	10.65	4
BARTON	UK9-2	20-May-53	3.61	2	BENTON	PB8-3	20-Aug-57	23.89	4
BARTON	TS7-6	6-Jun-52	3.69	2	BENTON	R1-2	29-Jan-51	28.72	5
BARTON	PB13-6	11-Sep-57	3.84	2	BENTON	TP10-3	7-May-55	41.11	5
BARTON	PB8-3	20-Aug-57	4.00	2	BOLLINGER	PB8-3	20-Aug-57	4.00	2
BARTON	TP10-3	7-May-55	5.67	3	BOLLINGER	UK2-3	26-Mar-53	4.56	2
BARTON	UK7-3	27-Apr-53	6.74	3	BOLLINGER	PB9-2	24-Aug-57	5.46	3
BARTON	BJ2-2	31-Oct-51	8.76	3	BOLLINGER	TP10-3	7-May-55	7.83	3
BARTON	TS6-4	28-May-52	9.64	3	BOLLINGER	TS1-3	3-Apr-52	9.02	3
BARTON	PB12-4	5-Sep-57	15.95	4	BOONE	PB4-4	8-Jul-57	4.44	2
BARTON	TS1-3	3-Apr-52	24.86	4	BOONE	UK9-2	20-May-53	4.52	2
BARTON	TS7-5	5-Jun-52	29.73	5	BOONE	TS5-1	7-May-52	4.59	2
BATES	UK7-4	28-Apr-53	3.52	2	BOONE	UK7-4	28-Apr-53	4.77	2
BATES	UK11-2	5-Jun-53	3.83	2	BOONE	TS6-4	28-May-52	4.83	2
BATES	TS7-5	5-Jun-52	4.73	2	BOONE	PB18-8	17-Jul-57	5.26	3
BATES	UK9-4	22-May-53	4.79	2	BOONE	UK2-3	26-Mar-53	6.36	3
BATES	PB18-8	17-Jul-57	5.26	3	BOONE	PB6-3	26-Jul-57	7.72	3
BATES	UK2-3	26-Mar-53	6.17	3	BOONE	TP10-3	7-May-55	8.07	3
BATES	PB12-4	5-Sep-57	6.68	3	BOONE	PB9-4	26-Aug-57	8.37	3
BATES	PB8-3	20-Aug-57	7.99	3	BOONE	TS7-5	5-Jun-52	8.48	3
BATES	TP10-3	7-May-55	8.38	3	BOONE	TS7-4	4-Jun-52	10.41	4
BATES	UK7-3	27-Apr-53	11.58	4	BOONE	PB9-3	25-Aug-57	13.72	4
BATES	PB4-5	9-Jul-57	17.72	4	BOONE	PB8-3	20-Aug-57	15.90	4
BATES	TS1-2	2-Apr-52	18.05	4	BUCHANAN	PB8-3	20-Aug-57	4.00	2
BENTON	PB4-4	8-Jul-57	3.65	2	BUCHANAN	UK2-3	26-Mar-53	4.03	2
BENTON	TS1-3	3-Apr-52	4.01	2	BUCHANAN	UK7-4	28-Apr-53	4.42	2
BENTON	UK7-3	27-Apr-53	4.67	2	BUCHANAN	UK9-2	20-May-53	4.44	2
BENTON	PB18-8	17-Jul-57	5.26	3	BUCHANAN	TP10-3	7-May-55	4.66	2
BENTON	UK7-4	28-Apr-53	7.59	3	BUCHANAN	TP4-2	8-Mar-55	5.25	3

INDIVIDUAL FALLOUT DAYS
MISSOURI

COUNTY	SHOT	DATE	µCi/SQ METER	INDEX	COUNTY	SHOT	DATE	µCi/SQ METER	INDEX
BUCHANAN	UK11-3	6-Jun-53	5.43	3	CALLAWAY	TS1-2	2-Apr-52	6.13	3
BUCHANAN	TS7-5	5-Jun-52	5.97	3	CALLAWAY	UK2-3	26-Mar-53	6.29	3
BUCHANAN	PB13-5	10-Sep-57	6.94	3	CALLAWAY	PB9-4	26-Aug-57	8.37	3
BUCHANAN	PB12-4	5-Sep-57	9.86	3	CALLAWAY	TS7-5	5-Jun-52	10.91	4
BUTLER	UK7-4	28-Apr-53	3.57	2	CALLAWAY	PB9-3	25-Aug-57	13.72	4
BUTLER	UK8-3	10-May-53	3.68	2	CALLAWAY	PB8-3	20-Aug-57	15.90	4
BUTLER	TS7-6	6-Jun-52	3.69	2	CALLAWAY	PB4-4	8-Jul-57	16.56	4
BUTLER	PB8-3	20-Aug-57	4.00	2	CALLAWAY	R1-2	29-Jan-51	26.39	5
BUTLER	UK2-3	26-Mar-53	4.91	2	CALLAWAY	TP10-3	7-May-55	41.41	5
BUTLER	UK2-7	30-Mar-53	6.07	3	CAMDEN	PB12-5	6-Sep-57	3.56	2
BUTLER	PB9-2	24-Aug-57	8.19	3	CAMDEN	PB11-2	1-Sep-57	3.73	2
BUTLER	TS1-3	3-Apr-52	9.02	3	CAMDEN	TS1-3	3-Apr-52	4.01	2
BUTLER	PB9-3	25-Aug-57	13.72	4	CAMDEN	UK7-3	27-Apr-53	4.33	2
BUTLER	TP10-3	7-May-55	22.32	4	CAMDEN	UK2-3	26-Mar-53	6.64	3
BUTLER	UK2-8	31-Mar-53	3.50	1	CAMDEN	TS6-4	28-May-52	7.71	3
CALDWELL	TS7-4	4-Jun-52	3.78	2	CAMDEN	PB9-4	26-Aug-57	8.37	3
CALDWELL	TS1-3	3-Apr-52	4.01	2	CAMDEN	PB4-4	8-Jul-57	9.38	3
CALDWELL	PB5-7	21-Jul-57	4.15	2	CAMDEN	PB4-5	9-Jul-57	10.65	4
CALDWELL	TP4-2	8-Mar-55	5.25	3	CAMDEN	PB12-4	5-Sep-57	10.74	4
CALDWELL	PB13-5	10-Sep-57	5.82	3	CAMDEN	UK7-4	28-Apr-53	11.35	4
CALDWELL	TP10-3	7-May-55	6.30	3	CAMDEN	TS1-2	2-Apr-52	11.93	4
CALDWELL	UK2-3	26-Mar-53	6.80	3	CAMDEN	TS7-5	5-Jun-52	12.32	4
CALDWELL	PB9-4	26-Aug-57	8.37	3	CAMDEN	PB8-3	20-Aug-57	23.89	4
CALDWELL	UK9-2	20-May-53	9.85	3	CAMDEN	TP10-3	7-May-55	61.10	6
CALDWELL	TS6-4	28-May-52	10.61	4	CAPE GIRARDE	UK2-3	26-Mar-53	3.52	2
CALDWELL	PB12-4	5-Sep-57	13.18	4	CAPE GIRARDE	TS7-6	6-Jun-52	4.01	2
CALDWELL	SE3	8-Jul-62	90.94	6	CAPE GIRARDE	TS7-3	3-Jun-52	8.34	3
CALDWELL	PB8-3	20-Aug-57	39.79	5	CAPE GIRARDE	TS1-3	3-Apr-52	9.02	3
CALLAWAY	UK9-2	20-May-53	3.88	2	CAPE GIRARDE	UK7-4	28-Apr-53	13.53	4
CALLAWAY	PB6-4	27-Jul-57	4.14	2	CARROLL	PB5-7	21-Jul-57	4.15	2
CALLAWAY	PB6-3	26-Jul-57	4.63	2	CARROLL	UK9-2	20-May-53	4.21	2
CALLAWAY	PB18-8	17-Jul-57	5.26	3	CARROLL	PB6-3	26-Jul-57	4.63	2
CALLAWAY	TS6-4	28-May-52	5.79	3	CARROLL	TP4-2	8-Mar-55	5.25	3

INDIVIDUAL FALLOUT DAYS
MISSOURI

COUNTY	SHOT	DATE	µCi/SQ METER	INDEX	COUNTY	SHOT	DATE	µCi/SQ METER	INDEX
CARROLL	UK2-3	26-Mar-53	6.80	3	CEDAR	UK2-3	26-Mar-53	5.32	3
CARROLL	TP10-3	7-May-55	7.18	3	CEDAR	TP10-3	7-May-55	7.06	3
CARROLL	PB9-4	26-Aug-57	8.37	3	CEDAR	PB8-3	20-Aug-57	7.99	3
CARROLL	PB18-8	17-Jul-57	8.80	3	CEDAR	TS6-4	28-May-52	8.68	3
CARROLL	TS7-5	5-Jun-52	11.32	4	CEDAR	PB4-5	9-Jul-57	10.65	4
CARROLL	PB8-3	20-Aug-57	23.89	4	CEDAR	UK7-3	27-Apr-53	16.29	4
CARROLL	SE3	8-Jul-62	35.48	5	CEDAR	TS7-5	5-Jun-52	16.46	4
CARTER	PB8-3	20-Aug-57	4.00	2	CEDAR	TS1-2	2-Apr-52	18.05	4
CARTER	TS7-6	6-Jun-52	4.01	2	CEDAR	PB12-4	5-Sep-57	20.95	4
CARTER	TP11-6	20-May-55	4.36	2	CHARITON	UK7-4	28-Apr-53	3.66	2
CARTER	UK2-3	26-Mar-53	5.46	3	CHARITON	PB6-3	26-Jul-57	4.63	2
CARTER	UK7-4	28-Apr-53	5.49	3	CHARITON	TP4-2	8-Mar-55	5.25	3
CARTER	PB5-3	17-Jul-57	7.27	3	CHARITON	PB18-8	17-Jul-57	5.26	3
CARTER	TS1-3	3-Apr-52	9.02	3	CHARITON	TS1-2	2-Apr-52	6.13	3
CARTER	PB9-3	25-Aug-57	13.72	4	CHARITON	UK9-2	20-May-53	6.14	3
CARTER	UK7-3	27-Apr-53	15.58	4	CHARITON	UK2-3	26-Mar-53	6.22	3
CARTER	TP10-3	7-May-55	16.32	4	CHARITON	TS6-4	28-May-52	6.75	3
CASS	PB18-8	17-Jul-57	3.53	2	CHARITON	TP10-3	7-May-55	7.62	3
CASS	TP10-2	6-May-55	3.62	2	CHARITON	PB12-4	5-Sep-57	7.77	3
CASS	TS1-3	3-Apr-52	4.01	2	CHARITON	PB9-4	26-Aug-57	8.37	3
CASS	UK11-2	5-Jun-53	4.66	2	CHARITON	TS7-5	5-Jun-52	13.77	4
CASS	UK7-3	27-Apr-53	4.72	2	CHARITON	R1-2	29-Jan-51	17.85	4
CASS	TP4-2	8-Mar-55	5.25	3	CHARITON	PB8-3	20-Aug-57	23.89	4
CASS	UK2-3	26-Mar-53	7.29	3	CHARITON	SE3	8-Jul-62	90.94	6
CASS	TS7-5	5-Jun-52	9.17	3	CHRISTIAN	PB18-8	17-Jul-57	3.53	2
CASS	TS6-4	28-May-52	10.61	4	CHRISTIAN	UK7-3	27-Apr-53	4.88	2
CASS	PB4-5	9-Jul-57	10.65	4	CHRISTIAN	BJ2-2	31-Oct-51	5.84	3
CASS	PB12-4	5-Sep-57	14.93	4	CHRISTIAN	UK1-1	17-Mar-53	7.40	3
CASS	PB8-3	20-Aug-57	15.90	4	CHRISTIAN	TP10-3	7-May-55	7.69	3
CASS	TP10-3	7-May-55	42.91	5	CHRISTIAN	UK7-4	28-Apr-53	8.42	3
CEDAR	PB18-8	17-Jul-57	3.53	2	CHRISTIAN	TS7-5	5-Jun-52	8.84	3
CEDAR	TP5-3	14-Mar-55	3.79	2	CHRISTIAN	PB12-4	5-Sep-57	17.57	4
CEDAR	UK7-4	28-Apr-53	4.28	2	CHRISTIAN	PB8-3	20-Aug-57	23.89	4

INDIVIDUAL FALLOUT DAYS
MISSOURI

COUNTY	SHOT	DATE	µCi/SQ METER	INDEX	COUNTY	SHOT	DATE	µCi/SQ METER	INDEX
CHRISTIAN	TS1-3	3-Apr-52	41.51	5	CLINTON	TP4-2	8-Mar-55	5.25	3
CLARK	UK7-4	28-Apr-53	3.69	2	CLINTON	PB2-3	20-Jun-57	5.36	3
CLARK	PB8-3	20-Aug-57	4.00	2	CLINTON	TP10-2	6-May-55	5.48	3
CLARK	TS5-2	8-May-52	4.80	2	CLINTON	UK2-3	26-Mar-53	5.81	3
CLARK	TP4-2	8-Mar-55	5.25	3	CLINTON	PB13-5	10-Sep-57	6.45	3
CLARK	TS6-4	28-May-52	5.79	3	CLINTON	PB12-4	5-Sep-57	13.65	4
CLARK	TS7-5	5-Jun-52	6.18	3	CLINTON	TS7-4	4-Jun-52	17.37	4
CLARK	PB18-8	17-Jul-57	6.63	3	CLINTON	SE3	8-Jul-62	35.48	5
CLARK	PB9-4	26-Aug-57	8.37	3	COLE	PB18-8	17-Jul-57	3.65	2
CLARK	TP10-3	7-May-55	17.45	4	COLE	TS7-5	5-Jun-52	5.52	3
CLARK	UK9-2	20-May-53	18.52	4	COLE	PB12-4	5-Sep-57	5.68	3
CLARK	PB9-3	25-Aug-57	54.87	6	COLE	PB8-3	20-Aug-57	6.60	3
CLARK	TS7-3	3-Jun-52	29.04	5	COLE	UK2-3	26-Mar-53	6.84	3
CLARK	SE3	8-Jul-62	358.08	8	COLE	PB9-4	26-Aug-57	8.37	3
CLAY	PB18-8	17-Jul-57	3.53	2	COLE	PB9-3	25-Aug-57	13.72	4
CLAY	UK7-4	28-Apr-53	3.60	2	COLE	PB4-4	8-Jul-57	30.54	5
CLAY	PB8-3	20-Aug-57	4.00	2	COLE	TP10-3	7-May-55	42.31	5
CLAY	TS5-1	7-May-52	5.21	3	COOPER	PB4-5	9-Jul-57	3.57	2
CLAY	TP4-2	8-Mar-55	5.25	3	COOPER	TS1-3	3-Apr-52	4.01	2
CLAY	TP10-3	7-May-55	5.36	3	COOPER	UK9-2	20-May-53	4.16	2
CLAY	TP10-2	6-May-55	5.48	3	COOPER	PB6-3	26-Jul-57	4.63	2
CLAY	PB13-5	10-Sep-57	6.49	3	COOPER	PB12-4	5-Sep-57	4.65	2
CLAY	UK2-3	26-Mar-53	6.50	3	COOPER	PB18-8	17-Jul-57	5.26	3
CLAY	UK9-2	20-May-53	8.49	3	COOPER	UK2-3	26-Mar-53	7.40	3
CLAY	PB4-5	9-Jul-57	10.65	4	COOPER	PB9-4	26-Aug-57	8.37	3
CLAY	PB12-4	5-Sep-57	14.12	4	COOPER	PB4-4	8-Jul-57	11.95	4
CLAY	PB4-4	8-Jul-57	3.51	1	COOPER	TS7-5	5-Jun-52	12.08	4
CLAY	TS1-2	2-Apr-52	29.98	5	COOPER	TS6-4	28-May-52	12.54	4
CLINTON	UK7-4	28-Apr-53	3.61	2	COOPER	PB8-3	20-Aug-57	15.90	4
CLINTON	PB8-3	20-Aug-57	4.00	2	COOPER	TP10-3	7-May-55	41.93	5
CLINTON	PB5-7	21-Jul-57	4.15	2	CRAWFORD	PB12-5	6-Sep-57	3.82	2
CLINTON	UK9-2	20-May-53	4.65	2	CRAWFORD	TS1-3	3-Apr-52	4.01	2
CLINTON	TP10-3	7-May-55	5.23	3	CRAWFORD	UK7-4	28-Apr-53	4.64	2

INDIVIDUAL FALLOUT DAYS
MISSOURI

COUNTY	SHOT	DATE	µCi/SQ METER	INDEX	COUNTY	SHOT	DATE	µCi/SQ METER	INDEX
CRAWFORD	PB18-8	17-Jul-57	5.26	3	DAVIESS	TS7-4	4-Jun-52	4.87	2
CRAWFORD	TS7-5	5-Jun-52	6.72	3	DAVIESS	UK2-3	26-Mar-53	5.19	3
CRAWFORD	PB4-5	9-Jul-57	7.08	3	DAVIESS	TP4-2	8-Mar-55	5.25	3
CRAWFORD	UK2-3	26-Mar-53	7.12	3	DAVIESS	TP10-3	7-May-55	6.11	3
CRAWFORD	PB4-4	8-Jul-57	7.16	3	DAVIESS	PB9-4	26-Aug-57	8.37	3
CRAWFORD	TS6-4	28-May-52	7.71	3	DAVIESS	TS6-4	28-May-52	9.64	3
CRAWFORD	PB8-3	20-Aug-57	7.99	3	DAVIESS	UK9-2	20-May-53	12.37	4
CRAWFORD	R1-2	29-Jan-51	12.25	4	DAVIESS	PB12-4	5-Sep-57	12.77	4
CRAWFORD	PB9-3	25-Aug-57	13.72	4	DAVIESS	PB8-3	20-Aug-57	39.79	5
CRAWFORD	TP10-3	7-May-55	21.49	4	DAVIESS	SE3	8-Jul-62	200.06	8
CRAWFORD	UK7-3	27-Apr-53	3.51	1	DE KALB	TS7-4	4-Jun-52	4.11	2
DADE	PB18-8	17-Jul-57	3.53	2	DE KALB	UK2-3	26-Mar-53	5.19	3
DADE	PB13-6	11-Sep-57	3.64	2	DE KALB	TP4-2	8-Mar-55	5.25	3
DADE	PB8-3	20-Aug-57	4.00	2	DE KALB	UK9-2	20-May-53	6.84	3
DADE	UK2-3	26-Mar-53	4.15	2	DE KALB	PB9-4	26-Aug-57	8.37	3
DADE	UK7-3	27-Apr-53	5.91	3	DE KALB	TS7-5	5-Jun-52	10.04	4
DADE	TS7-6	6-Jun-52	6.70	3	DE KALB	PB13-5	10-Sep-57	11.22	4
DADE	TP10-3	7-May-55	6.99	3	DE KALB	TS6-4	28-May-52	11.57	4
DADE	BJ2-2	31-Oct-51	8.76	3	DE KALB	PB12-4	5-Sep-57	13.18	4
DADE	TS6-4	28-May-52	18.54	4	DE KALB	TP10-3	7-May-55	26.45	5
DADE	TS7-5	5-Jun-52	25.51	5	DE KALB	SE3	8-Jul-62	35.48	5
DADE	TS1-3	3-Apr-52	41.51	5	DE KALB	PB8-3	20-Aug-57	39.79	5
DALLAS	PB18-8	17-Jul-57	3.53	2	DENT	UK7-3	27-Apr-53	3.99	2
DALLAS	UK7-3	27-Apr-53	4.88	2	DENT	TS1-3	3-Apr-52	4.01	2
DALLAS	UK2-3	26-Mar-53	5.67	3	DENT	PB12-5	6-Sep-57	4.04	2
DALLAS	TS6-4	28-May-52	7.71	3	DENT	PB18-8	17-Jul-57	5.26	3
DALLAS	PB8-3	20-Aug-57	7.99	3	DENT	UK2-3	26-Mar-53	6.43	3
DALLAS	UK7-4	28-Apr-53	10.01	4	DENT	PB4-5	9-Jul-57	7.08	3
DALLAS	PB12-4	5-Sep-57	12.03	4	DENT	PB8-3	20-Aug-57	7.99	3
DALLAS	PB4-5	9-Jul-57	17.72	4	DENT	PB9-2	24-Aug-57	8.19	3
DALLAS	TP10-3	7-May-55	42.01	5	DENT	TS6-4	28-May-52	13.50	4
DAVIESS	PB5-7	21-Jul-57	4.15	2	DENT	PB9-3	25-Aug-57	13.72	4
DAVIESS	PB13-5	10-Sep-57	4.85	2	DENT	R1-2	29-Jan-51	23.97	4

INDIVIDUAL FALLOUT DAYS
MISSOURI

COUNTY	SHOT	DATE	µCi/SQ METER	INDEX	COUNTY	SHOT	DATE	µCi/SQ METER	INDEX
DENT	TP10-3	7-May-55	36.67	5	FRANKLIN	R1-2	29-Jan-51	10.09	4
DOUGLAS	PB12-5	6-Sep-57	3.86	2	FRANKLIN	PB9-3	25-Aug-57	13.72	4
DOUGLAS	TS1-3	3-Apr-52	4.01	2	FRANKLIN	TP10-3	7-May-55	17.56	4
DOUGLAS	TP11-5	19-May-55	4.41	2	FRANKLIN	TS7-3	3-Jun-52	55.44	6
DOUGLAS	UK7-3	27-Apr-53	4.67	2	GASCONADE	PB3-5	28-Jun-57	3.91	2
DOUGLAS	PB18-8	17-Jul-57	5.26	3	GASCONADE	PB8-3	20-Aug-57	4.00	2
DOUGLAS	TP11-6	20-May-55	5.56	3	GASCONADE	PB6-4	27-Jul-57	4.76	2
DOUGLAS	UK2-3	26-Mar-53	7.67	3	GASCONADE	PB18-8	17-Jul-57	5.26	3
DOUGLAS	PB8-3	20-Aug-57	7.99	3	GASCONADE	TS6-4	28-May-52	6.75	3
DOUGLAS	UK7-4	28-Apr-53	11.92	4	GASCONADE	UK2-3	26-Mar-53	6.98	3
DOUGLAS	UK1-1	17-Mar-53	12.33	4	GASCONADE	PB9-4	26-Aug-57	8.37	3
DOUGLAS	TP10-3	7-May-55	55.53	6	GASCONADE	PB4-4	8-Jul-57	12.52	4
DUNKLIN	UK8-3	10-May-53	3.68	2	GASCONADE	PB9-3	25-Aug-57	13.72	4
DUNKLIN	UK2-3	26-Mar-53	3.75	2	GASCONADE	TP10-3	7-May-55	23.00	4
DUNKLIN	UK1-2	18-Mar-53	3.81	2	GASCONADE	R1-2	29-Jan-51	31.35	5
DUNKLIN	UK1-3	19-Mar-53	3.84	2	GENTRY	UK2-3	26-Mar-53	3.81	2
DUNKLIN	PB8-3	20-Aug-57	4.00	2	GENTRY	UK7-4	28-Apr-53	4.76	2
DUNKLIN	UK1-4	20-Mar-53	5.09	3	GENTRY	TP10-3	7-May-55	4.85	2
DUNKLIN	TS7-5	5-Jun-52	7.71	3	GENTRY	PB13-5	10-Sep-57	5.15	3
DUNKLIN	TS1-3	3-Apr-52	9.02	3	GENTRY	TP4-2	8-Mar-55	5.25	3
DUNKLIN	UK2-7	30-Mar-53	12.19	4	GENTRY	TS7-4	4-Jun-52	5.26	3
DUNKLIN	TP10-3	7-May-55	17.96	4	GENTRY	TS7-5	5-Jun-52	5.35	3
DUNKLIN	UK7-4	28-Apr-53	21.22	4	GENTRY	UK9-2	20-May-53	6.31	3
DUNKLIN	UK2-8	31-Mar-53	3.50	1	GENTRY	PB12-4	5-Sep-57	7.59	3
FRANKLIN	TS1-3	3-Apr-52	4.01	2	GENTRY	PB9-4	26-Aug-57	16.67	4
FRANKLIN	PB3-6	29-Jun-57	4.17	2	GENTRY	PB8-3	20-Aug-57	39.79	5
FRANKLIN	TS1-2	2-Apr-52	4.51	2	GREENE	PB18-8	17-Jul-57	3.53	2
FRANKLIN	PB6-4	27-Jul-57	5.38	3	GREENE	PB4-5	9-Jul-57	3.57	2
FRANKLIN	UK2-3	26-Mar-53	6.17	3	GREENE	UK2-3	26-Mar-53	4.08	2
FRANKLIN	TS6-4	28-May-52	6.75	3	GREENE	TP11-5	19-May-55	4.58	2
FRANKLIN	PB8-3	20-Aug-57	7.99	3	GREENE	BJ2-2	31-Oct-51	5.84	3
FRANKLIN	PB4-4	8-Jul-57	8.16	3	GREENE	UK7-4	28-Apr-53	8.22	3
FRANKLIN	PB9-4	26-Aug-57	8.37	3	GREENE	TP10-3	7-May-55	16.19	4

INDIVIDUAL FALLOUT DAYS
MISSOURI

COUNTY	SHOT	DATE	µCi/SQ METER	INDEX	COUNTY	SHOT	DATE	µCi/SQ METER	INDEX
GREENE	TS1-2	2-Apr-52	18.05	4	HENRY	PB18-8	17-Jul-57	5.26	3
GREENE	PB12-4	5-Sep-57	18.51	4	HENRY	UK2-3	26-Mar-53	7.32	3
GREENE	UK7-3	27-Apr-53	22.55	4	HENRY	PB4-4	8-Jul-57	8.37	3
GREENE	PB8-3	20-Aug-57	23.89	4	HENRY	TS6-4	28-May-52	9.64	3
GRUNDY	TP10-2	6-May-55	3.62	2	HENRY	PB12-4	5-Sep-57	10.47	4
GRUNDY	UK2-3	26-Mar-53	4.21	2	HENRY	PB4-5	9-Jul-57	10.65	4
GRUNDY	TP4-2	8-Mar-55	5.25	3	HENRY	TS7-5	5-Jun-52	11.28	4
GRUNDY	TS7-4	4-Jun-52	5.97	3	HENRY	TP10-3	7-May-55	53.81	6
GRUNDY	TP10-3	7-May-55	6.68	3	HENRY	PB8-3	20-Aug-57	39.79	5
GRUNDY	TS7-5	5-Jun-52	6.76	3	HICKORY	TS1-3	3-Apr-52	4.01	2
GRUNDY	PB13-5	10-Sep-57	7.63	3	HICKORY	UK7-3	27-Apr-53	5.09	3
GRUNDY	TS6-4	28-May-52	7.71	3	HICKORY	PB18-8	17-Jul-57	5.26	3
GRUNDY	PB12-4	5-Sep-57	10.03	4	HICKORY	UK7-4	28-Apr-53	5.77	3
GRUNDY	PB9-4	26-Aug-57	16.67	4	HICKORY	BJ2-2	31-Oct-51	5.84	3
GRUNDY	UK9-2	20-May-53	21.22	4	HICKORY	UK2-3	26-Mar-53	6.64	3
GRUNDY	SE3	8-Jul-62	76.52	6	HICKORY	TS6-4	28-May-52	7.71	3
GRUNDY	PB8-3	20-Aug-57	39.79	5	HICKORY	TP10-3	7-May-55	7.94	3
HARRISON	UK2-3	26-Mar-53	3.57	2	HICKORY	PB12-4	5-Sep-57	9.59	3
HARRISON	PB13-5	10-Sep-57	4.78	2	HICKORY	PB4-5	9-Jul-57	10.65	4
HARRISON	TP4-2	8-Mar-55	5.25	3	HICKORY	PB8-3	20-Aug-57	23.89	4
HARRISON	TP10-3	7-May-55	5.80	3	HOLT	TS7-3	3-Jun-52	3.60	2
HARRISON	TS7-4	4-Jun-52	6.51	3	HOLT	PB8-3	20-Aug-57	4.00	2
HARRISON	TS7-5	5-Jun-52	7.43	3	HOLT	TP10-3	7-May-55	4.10	2
HARRISON	TS6-4	28-May-52	8.68	3	HOLT	TS7-4	4-Jun-52	4.32	2
HARRISON	PB12-4	5-Sep-57	10.25	4	HOLT	TP4-2	8-Mar-55	5.25	3
HARRISON	UK9-2	20-May-53	10.30	4	HOLT	TS7-5	5-Jun-52	6.39	3
HARRISON	PB9-4	26-Aug-57	16.67	4	HOLT	UK9-2	20-May-53	6.96	3
HARRISON	SE3	8-Jul-62	80.75	6	HOLT	PB12-4	5-Sep-57	12.57	4
HARRISON	PB8-3	20-Aug-57	39.79	5	HOLT	PB13-5	10-Sep-57	12.62	4
HENRY	UK11-2	5-Jun-53	3.85	2	HOLT	TS6-4	28-May-52	13.50	4
HENRY	TS1-3	3-Apr-52	4.01	2	HOWARD	TS5-1	7-May-52	3.87	2
HENRY	UK7-4	28-Apr-53	4.38	2	HOWARD	PB12-4	5-Sep-57	4.25	2
HENRY	UK7-3	27-Apr-53	4.70	2	HOWARD	UK9-2	20-May-53	4.97	2

INDIVIDUAL FALLOUT DAYS
MISSOURI

COUNTY	SHOT	DATE	µCi/SQ METER	INDEX	COUNTY	SHOT	DATE	µCi/SQ METER	INDEX
HOWARD	PB18-8	17-Jul-57	5.26	3	IRON	UK7-4	28-Apr-53	6.60	3
HOWARD	TS6-4	28-May-52	5.64	3	IRON	PB9-3	25-Aug-57	13.72	4
HOWARD	UK7-4	28-Apr-53	6.68	3	IRON	TP10-3	7-May-55	14.51	4
HOWARD	UK2-3	26-Mar-53	6.70	3	JACKSON	PB18-8	17-Jul-57	3.53	2
HOWARD	PB4-5	9-Jul-57	7.08	3	JACKSON	PB4-4	8-Jul-57	3.58	2
HOWARD	PB6-3	26-Jul-57	7.72	3	JACKSON	PB8-3	20-Aug-57	4.00	2
HOWARD	TP10-3	7-May-55	8.00	3	JACKSON	TS1-3	3-Apr-52	4.01	2
HOWARD	PB9-4	26-Aug-57	8.37	3	JACKSON	TP4-2	8-Mar-55	5.25	3
HOWARD	TS7-5	5-Jun-52	11.08	4	JACKSON	TP10-2	6-May-55	5.48	3
HOWARD	TS1-2	2-Apr-52	18.05	4	JACKSON	TP10-3	7-May-55	5.61	3
HOWARD	PB8-3	20-Aug-57	23.89	4	JACKSON	PB13-5	10-Sep-57	6.27	3
HOWELL	TS7-5	5-Jun-52	3.77	2	JACKSON	UK9-2	20-May-53	7.14	3
HOWELL	PB12-5	6-Sep-57	3.86	2	JACKSON	UK2-3	26-Mar-53	7.74	3
HOWELL	TS1-3	3-Apr-52	4.01	2	JACKSON	BJ2-2	31-Oct-51	8.76	3
HOWELL	UK2-3	26-Mar-53	4.22	2	JACKSON	PB4-5	9-Jul-57	10.65	4
HOWELL	UK7-3	27-Apr-53	4.47	2	JACKSON	PB12-4	5-Sep-57	14.46	4
HOWELL	PB12-4	5-Sep-57	4.73	2	JASPER	UK9-2	20-May-53	3.70	2
HOWELL	PB18-8	17-Jul-57	5.26	3	JASPER	PB8-3	20-Aug-57	4.00	2
HOWELL	TP11-6	20-May-55	5.59	3	JASPER	PB13-6	11-Sep-57	4.09	2
HOWELL	TS6-4	28-May-52	6.75	3	JASPER	BJ2-2	31-Oct-51	8.76	3
HOWELL	PB8-3	20-Aug-57	7.99	3	JASPER	TS6-4	28-May-52	9.64	3
HOWELL	UK7-4	28-Apr-53	11.73	4	JASPER	UK7-3	27-Apr-53	11.48	4
HOWELL	TS1-2	2-Apr-52	11.93	4	JASPER	PB12-4	5-Sep-57	16.01	4
HOWELL	UK2-7	30-Mar-53	12.19	4	JASPER	TS7-5	5-Jun-52	21.48	4
HOWELL	PB9-3	25-Aug-57	13.72	4	JASPER	TS1-3	3-Apr-52	24.86	4
HOWELL	UK2-8	31-Mar-53	3.50	1	JASPER	TP10-3	7-May-55	29.23	5
HOWELL	TP10-3	7-May-55	34.19	5	JEFFERSON	PB8-3	20-Aug-57	4.00	2
IRON	PB8-3	20-Aug-57	4.00	2	JEFFERSON	TS1-3	3-Apr-52	4.01	2
IRON	TS1-3	3-Apr-52	4.01	2	JEFFERSON	UK7-4	28-Apr-53	5.01	3
IRON	PB6-4	27-Jul-57	4.03	2	JEFFERSON	UK2-3	26-Mar-53	5.23	3
IRON	TS7-6	6-Jun-52	4.09	2	JEFFERSON	PB9-2	24-Aug-57	5.46	3
IRON	PB9-2	24-Aug-57	5.46	3	JEFFERSON	PB6-4	27-Jul-57	5.89	3
IRON	UK2-3	26-Mar-53	6.50	3	JEFFERSON	TS6-4	28-May-52	7.71	3

INDIVIDUAL FALLOUT DAYS
MISSOURI

COUNTY	SHOT	DATE	µCi/SQ METER	INDEX	COUNTY	SHOT	DATE	µCi/SQ METER	INDEX
JEFFERSON	TP10-3	7-May-55	12.55	4	LACLEDE	UK7-3	27-Apr-53	4.47	2
JEFFERSON	PB9-3	25-Aug-57	13.72	4	LACLEDE	PB12-5	6-Sep-57	5.64	3
JEFFERSON	TS7-3	3-Jun-52	42.04	5	LACLEDE	UK2-3	26-Mar-53	5.74	3
JOHNSON	UK7-4	28-Apr-53	3.52	2	LACLEDE	TS6-4	28-May-52	6.75	3
JOHNSON	TS1-3	3-Apr-52	4.01	2	LACLEDE	UK7-4	28-Apr-53	9.31	3
JOHNSON	UK7-3	27-Apr-53	4.01	2	LACLEDE	PB4-5	9-Jul-57	10.65	4
JOHNSON	TP3-3	3-Mar-55	5.17	3	LACLEDE	PB8-3	20-Aug-57	15.90	4
JOHNSON	TP4-2	8-Mar-55	5.25	3	LACLEDE	R1-2	29-Jan-51	18.93	4
JOHNSON	PB18-8	17-Jul-57	5.26	3	LACLEDE	TP10-3	7-May-55	59.74	6
JOHNSON	TP10-3	7-May-55	7.06	3	LAFAYETTE	TP10-2	6-May-55	3.62	2
JOHNSON	UK2-3	26-Mar-53	8.59	3	LAFAYETTE	TP4-2	8-Mar-55	5.25	3
JOHNSON	PB4-4	8-Jul-57	8.66	3	LAFAYETTE	PB18-8	17-Jul-57	5.26	3
JOHNSON	TS6-4	28-May-52	9.64	3	LAFAYETTE	PB4-5	9-Jul-57	7.08	3
JOHNSON	PB12-4	5-Sep-57	10.20	4	LAFAYETTE	PB9-4	26-Aug-57	8.37	3
JOHNSON	TS7-5	5-Jun-52	10.37	4	LAFAYETTE	UK2-3	26-Mar-53	8.71	3
JOHNSON	PB4-5	9-Jul-57	10.65	4	LAFAYETTE	TS7-5	5-Jun-52	9.50	3
JOHNSON	PB8-3	20-Aug-57	39.79	5	LAFAYETTE	PB12-4	5-Sep-57	9.86	3
KNOX	PB6-4	27-Jul-57	3.55	2	LAFAYETTE	TS1-2	2-Apr-52	11.93	4
KNOX	PB8-3	20-Aug-57	4.00	2	LAFAYETTE	TS6-4	28-May-52	17.36	4
KNOX	PB5-7	21-Jul-57	4.15	2	LAFAYETTE	TP10-3	7-May-55	21.04	4
KNOX	TP4-2	8-Mar-55	5.25	3	LAFAYETTE	PB8-3	20-Aug-57	39.79	5
KNOX	PB18-8	17-Jul-57	5.26	3	LAWRENCE	PB18-8	17-Jul-57	3.53	2
KNOX	TS6-4	28-May-52	5.79	3	LAWRENCE	PB4-5	9-Jul-57	3.57	2
KNOX	PB6-3	26-Jul-57	7.72	3	LAWRENCE	PB13-6	11-Sep-57	3.76	2
KNOX	PB9-4	26-Aug-57	8.37	3	LAWRENCE	PB8-3	20-Aug-57	4.00	2
KNOX	TS7-5	5-Jun-52	13.02	4	LAWRENCE	UK7-4	28-Apr-53	4.01	2
KNOX	UK9-2	20-May-53	13.46	4	LAWRENCE	UK3-5	4-Apr-53	4.10	2
KNOX	PB9-3	25-Aug-57	13.72	4	LAWRENCE	PB5-3	17-Jul-57	4.85	2
KNOX	TP10-3	7-May-55	20.54	4	LAWRENCE	UK7-3	27-Apr-53	5.43	3
KNOX	SE3	8-Jul-62	358.08	8	LAWRENCE	UK1-1	17-Mar-53	7.40	3
KNOX	TS7-3	3-Jun-52	220.42	8	LAWRENCE	TS6-4	28-May-52	8.68	3
LACLEDE	PB18-8	17-Jul-57	3.53	2	LAWRENCE	BJ2-2	31-Oct-51	8.76	3
LACLEDE	TS1-3	3-Apr-52	4.01	2	LAWRENCE	PB12-4	5-Sep-57	14.93	4

INDIVIDUAL FALLOUT DAYS
MISSOURI

COUNTY	SHOT	DATE	µCi/SQ METER	INDEX	COUNTY	SHOT	DATE	µCi/SQ METER	INDEX
LAWRENCE	TS1-3	3-Apr-52	24.86	4	LINN	UK2-3	26-Mar-53	5.25	3
LAWRENCE	TS7-5	5-Jun-52	27.25	5	LINN	PB18-8	17-Jul-57	5.26	3
LAWRENCE	TP10-3	7-May-55	36.07	5	LINN	TP10-3	7-May-55	7.25	3
LEWIS	PB18-8	17-Jul-57	3.98	2	LINN	TS7-5	5-Jun-52	9.37	3
LEWIS	TS5-2	8-May-52	4.80	2	LINN	TS1-2	2-Apr-52	11.93	4
LEWIS	TS6-4	28-May-52	5.79	3	LINN	PB9-4	26-Aug-57	16.67	4
LEWIS	PB8-3	20-Aug-57	7.99	3	LINN	UK9-2	20-May-53	17.00	4
LEWIS	TS7-5	5-Jun-52	8.84	3	LINN	PB8-3	20-Aug-57	23.89	4
LEWIS	PB9-3	25-Aug-57	13.72	4	LINN	SE3	8-Jul-62	99.74	6
LEWIS	UK9-2	20-May-53	15.48	4	LINN	TS7-3	3-Jun-52	48.04	5
LEWIS	PB9-4	26-Aug-57	16.67	4	LIVINGSTON	TP10-2	6-May-55	3.62	2
LEWIS	TP10-3	7-May-55	19.47	4	LIVINGSTON	TS6-4	28-May-52	4.03	2
LEWIS	PB6-4	27-Jul-57	3.51	1	LIVINGSTON	PB5-7	21-Jul-57	4.15	2
LEWIS	SE3	8-Jul-62	200.06	8	LIVINGSTON	UK7-4	28-Apr-53	4.33	2
LEWIS	TS7-3	3-Jun-52	205.59	8	LIVINGSTON	TS7-4	4-Jun-52	4.65	2
LINCOLN	TS5-1	7-May-52	3.99	2	LIVINGSTON	PB13-5	10-Sep-57	5.09	3
LINCOLN	PB8-3	20-Aug-57	4.00	2	LIVINGSTON	TP4-2	8-Mar-55	5.25	3
LINCOLN	TS5-2	8-May-52	4.17	2	LIVINGSTON	UK9-2	20-May-53	5.41	3
LINCOLN	UK2-3	26-Mar-53	4.84	2	LIVINGSTON	UK2-3	26-Mar-53	5.48	3
LINCOLN	PB6-4	27-Jul-57	5.60	3	LIVINGSTON	TS1-2	2-Apr-52	6.13	3
LINCOLN	TP10-3	7-May-55	5.68	3	LIVINGSTON	TS7-5	5-Jun-52	7.26	3
LINCOLN	TS6-4	28-May-52	6.75	3	LIVINGSTON	PB9-4	26-Aug-57	8.37	3
LINCOLN	TS7-5	5-Jun-52	7.96	3	LIVINGSTON	PB12-4	5-Sep-57	12.36	4
LINCOLN	PB9-4	26-Aug-57	8.37	3	LIVINGSTON	TP10-3	7-May-55	14.49	4
LINCOLN	PB9-3	25-Aug-57	13.72	4	LIVINGSTON	SE3	8-Jul-62	35.48	5
LINCOLN	TS7-3	3-Jun-52	54.94	6	LIVINGSTON	PB8-3	20-Aug-57	39.79	5
LINN	TP10-2	6-May-55	3.62	2	MACON	UK7-4	28-Apr-53	3.79	2
LINN	PB12-4	5-Sep-57	3.92	2	MACON	PB5-7	21-Jul-57	4.15	2
LINN	TS7-4	4-Jun-52	3.93	2	MACON	UK2-3	26-Mar-53	4.42	2
LINN	PB5-7	21-Jul-57	4.15	2	MACON	TP4-2	8-Mar-55	5.25	3
LINN	TP5-3	14-Mar-55	4.19	2	MACON	PB18-8	17-Jul-57	5.26	3
LINN	PB6-3	26-Jul-57	4.63	2	MACON	TP10-2	6-May-55	5.48	3
LINN	TP4-2	8-Mar-55	5.25	3	MACON	PB6-3	26-Jul-57	7.72	3

INDITVIDUAL FALLOUT DAYS
MISSOURI

COUNTY	SHOT	DATE	µCi/SQ METER	INDEX	COUNTY	SHOT	DATE	µCi/SQ METER	INDEX
MACON	UK9-2	20-May-53	7.86	3	MARION	PB6-3	26-Jul-57	4.63	2
MACON	PB9-4	26-Aug-57	8.37	3	MARION	PB6-4	27-Jul-57	5.66	3
MACON	TS7-5	5-Jun-52	8.79	3	MARION	UK9-2	20-May-53	5.78	3
MACON	TS6-4	28-May-52	11.57	4	MARION	TS6-4	28-May-52	5.79	3
MACON	TP10-3	7-May-55	22.30	4	MARION	TS1-2	2-Apr-52	6.13	3
MACON	PB8-3	20-Aug-57	23.89	4	MARION	TS7-5	5-Jun-52	8.63	3
MACON	SE4	9-Jul-62	46.20	5	MARION	PB18-8	17-Jul-57	8.80	3
MACON	TS7-3	3-Jun-52	123.69	7	MARION	TS7-4	4-Jun-52	12.64	4
MADISON	PB8-3	20-Aug-57	4.00	2	MARION	PB9-3	25-Aug-57	13.72	4
MADISON	PB6-4	27-Jul-57	4.08	2	MARION	TP10-3	7-May-55	14.37	4
MADISON	TP10-3	7-May-55	4.21	2	MARION	PB9-4	26-Aug-57	16.67	4
MADISON	UK2-3	26-Mar-53	5.60	3	MARION	SE3	8-Jul-62	76.52	6
MADISON	PB9-3	25-Aug-57	13.72	4	MARION	TS7-3	3-Jun-52	113.83	7
MADISON	TS1-3	3-Apr-52	15.04	4	MCDONALD	PB8-3	20-Aug-57	4.00	2
MARIES	PB4-5	9-Jul-57	3.57	2	MCDONALD	UK3-5	4-Apr-53	4.10	2
MARIES	TS1-3	3-Apr-52	4.01	2	MCDONALD	UK7-3	27-Apr-53	4.40	2
MARIES	UK7-4	28-Apr-53	4.37	2	MCDONALD	PB13-6	11-Sep-57	4.42	2
MARIES	PB18-8	17-Jul-57	5.26	3	MCDONALD	TP11-5	19-May-55	7.39	3
MARIES	TS6-4	28-May-52	6.75	3	MCDONALD	UK1-1	17-Mar-53	7.40	3
MARIES	UK2-3	26-Mar-53	6.77	3	MCDONALD	BJ2-2	31-Oct-51	8.76	3
MARIES	PB6-3	26-Jul-57	7.72	3	MCDONALD	PB12-4	5-Sep-57	15.68	4
MARIES	TP10-3	7-May-55	7.88	3	MCDONALD	TS6-4	28-May-52	16.39	4
MARIES	PB9-4	26-Aug-57	8.37	3	MCDONALD	TP10-3	7-May-55	28.56	5
MARIES	PB12-4	5-Sep-57	8.72	3	MCDONALD	TS7-5	5-Jun-52	28.95	5
MARIES	PB9-3	25-Aug-57	13.72	4	MCDONALD	TS1-3	3-Apr-52	41.51	5
MARIES	PB4-4	8-Jul-57	15.03	4	MERCER	UK7-4	28-Apr-53	4.22	2
MARIES	PB8-3	20-Aug-57	15.90	4	MERCER	TP4-2	8-Mar-55	5.25	3
MARIES	TS1-2	2-Apr-52	18.05	4	MERCER	TP10-3	7-May-55	5.36	3
MARIES	UK7-3	27-Apr-53	3.51	1	MERCER	TP10-2	6-May-55	5.48	3
MARION	TS5-1	7-May-52	3.74	2	MERCER	PB13-5	10-Sep-57	7.67	3
MARION	TS5-2	8-May-52	3.99	2	MERCER	PB9-4	26-Aug-57	8.37	3
MARION	PB8-3	20-Aug-57	4.00	2	MERCER	PB12-4	5-Sep-57	9.69	3
MARION	UK7-4	28-Apr-53	4.55	2	MERCER	TS7-4	4-Jun-52	19.13	4

INDIVIDUAL FALLOUT DAYS
MISSOURI

COUNTY	SHOT	DATE	µCi/SQ METER	INDEX	COUNTY	SHOT	DATE	µCi/SQ METER	INDEX
MERCER	UK9-2	20-May-53	23.03	4	MONITEAU	PB6-3	26-Jul-57	7.72	3
MERCER	PB8-3	20-Aug-57	39.79	5	MONITEAU	TP10-3	7-May-55	8.19	3
MILLER	UK7-3	27-Apr-53	3.78	2	MONITEAU	PB9-4	26-Aug-57	8.37	3
MILLER	TS1-3	3-Apr-52	4.01	2	MONITEAU	PB8-3	20-Aug-57	15.90	4
MILLER	PB6-3	26-Jul-57	4.63	2	MONITEAU	PB4-4	8-Jul-57	26.40	5
MILLER	PB18-8	17-Jul-57	5.26	3	MONROE	PB6-4	27-Jul-57	3.99	2
MILLER	TS1-2	2-Apr-52	6.13	3	MONROE	UK2-3	26-Mar-53	4.70	2
MILLER	PB12-4	5-Sep-57	6.42	3	MONROE	UK9-2	20-May-53	5.78	3
MILLER	TS6-4	28-May-52	6.75	3	MONROE	TS6-4	28-May-52	5.79	3
MILLER	UK2-3	26-Mar-53	6.77	3	MONROE	UK7-4	28-Apr-53	7.00	3
MILLER	PB9-4	26-Aug-57	8.37	3	MONROE	TS7-5	5-Jun-52	7.32	3
MILLER	UK7-4	28-Apr-53	9.56	3	MONROE	PB6-3	26-Jul-57	7.72	3
MILLER	PB4-5	9-Jul-57	10.65	4	MONROE	PB9-4	26-Aug-57	8.37	3
MILLER	PB4-4	8-Jul-57	13.50	4	MONROE	PB18-8	17-Jul-57	8.80	3
MILLER	PB8-3	20-Aug-57	23.89	4	MONROE	PB9-3	25-Aug-57	13.72	4
MILLER	TP10-3	7-May-55	42.31	5	MONROE	TP10-3	7-May-55	15.88	4
MISSISSIPPI	PB3-4	27-Jun-57	3.53	2	MONROE	PB8-3	20-Aug-57	15.90	4
MISSISSIPPI	UK9-3	21-May-53	3.57	2	MONROE	SE3	8-Jul-62	90.94	6
MISSISSIPPI	TS7-6	6-Jun-52	3.73	2	MONTGOMERY	TS5-1	7-May-52	3.99	2
MISSISSIPPI	UK1-3	19-Mar-53	5.03	3	MONTGOMERY	UK9-2	20-May-53	4.61	2
MISSISSIPPI	TS7-5	5-Jun-52	6.61	3	MONTGOMERY	PB18-8	17-Jul-57	5.26	3
MISSISSIPPI	TS1-3	3-Apr-52	9.02	3	MONTGOMERY	UK2-3	26-Mar-53	6.01	3
MISSISSIPPI	UK2-7	30-Mar-53	12.19	4	MONTGOMERY	TS1-2	2-Apr-52	6.13	3
MISSISSIPPI	TP10-3	7-May-55	16.53	4	MONTGOMERY	TP10-3	7-May-55	7.62	3
MISSISSIPPI	UK7-4	28-Apr-53	20.66	4	MONTGOMERY	PB6-3	26-Jul-57	7.72	3
MISSISSIPPI	UK2-8	31-Mar-53	3.50	1	MONTGOMERY	PB8-3	20-Aug-57	7.99	3
MONITEAU	UK9-2	20-May-53	3.70	2	MONTGOMERY	PB9-4	26-Aug-57	8.37	3
MONITEAU	TP10-2	6-May-55	3.94	2	MONTGOMERY	TS7-5	5-Jun-52	8.75	3
MONITEAU	PB18-8	17-Jul-57	5.26	3	MONTGOMERY	PB9-3	25-Aug-57	13.72	4
MONITEAU	TS7-5	5-Jun-52	5.63	3	MORGAN	UK7-3	27-Apr-53	3.85	2
MONITEAU	PB12-4	5-Sep-57	6.89	3	MORGAN	TS1-3	3-Apr-52	4.01	2
MONITEAU	PB4-5	9-Jul-57	7.08	3	MORGAN	TS5-1	7-May-52	4.20	2
MONITEAU	UK2-3	26-Mar-53	7.12	3	MORGAN	PB18-8	17-Jul-57	5.26	3

INDIVIDUAL FALLOUT DAYS
MISSOURI

COUNTY	SHOT	DATE	µCi/SQ METER	INDEX	COUNTY	SHOT	DATE	µCi/SQ METER	INDEX
MORGAN	UK7-4	28-Apr-53	6.90	3	NODAWAY	UK7-4	28-Apr-53	4.70	2
MORGAN	UK2-3	26-Mar-53	7.46	3	NODAWAY	TP4-2	8-Mar-55	5.25	3
MORGAN	TS7-5	5-Jun-52	7.88	3	NODAWAY	UK9-2	20-May-53	10.30	4
MORGAN	PB9-4	26-Aug-57	8.37	3	NODAWAY	TS7-4	4-Jun-52	11.11	4
MORGAN	PB4-5	9-Jul-57	10.65	4	NODAWAY	PB13-5	10-Sep-57	11.32	4
MORGAN	PB4-4	8-Jul-57	10.81	4	NODAWAY	PB12-4	5-Sep-57	12.09	4
MORGAN	PB12-4	5-Sep-57	11.22	4	NODAWAY	PB8-3	20-Aug-57	23.89	4
MORGAN	TS1-2	2-Apr-52	11.93	4	NODAWAY	PB9-4	26-Aug-57	33.34	5
MORGAN	PB8-3	20-Aug-57	23.89	4	OREGON	PB18-8	17-Jul-57	3.53	2
MORGAN	TP10-3	7-May-55	60.95	6	OREGON	UK8-3	10-May-53	3.68	2
NEW MADRID	UK8-3	10-May-53	3.68	2	OREGON	PB11-2	1-Sep-57	3.73	2
NEW MADRID	PB8-3	20-Aug-57	4.00	2	OREGON	PB8-3	20-Aug-57	4.00	2
NEW MADRID	UK1-3	19-Mar-53	4.43	2	OREGON	UK7-3	27-Apr-53	4.12	2
NEW MADRID	TS7-5	5-Jun-52	6.91	3	OREGON	TP11-6	20-May-55	5.12	3
NEW MADRID	UK2-8	31-Mar-53	7.04	3	OREGON	UK7-4	28-Apr-53	6.42	3
NEW MADRID	TS1-3	3-Apr-52	9.02	3	OREGON	PB12-6	7-Sep-57	6.69	3
NEW MADRID	UK2-7	30-Mar-53	12.19	4	OREGON	UK2-8	31-Mar-53	7.04	3
NEW MADRID	UK7-4	28-Apr-53	19.25	4	OREGON	UK2-3	26-Mar-53	9.33	3
NEW MADRID	TP10-3	7-May-55	25.10	5	OREGON	UK2-7	30-Mar-53	12.19	4
NEWTON	UK9-2	20-May-53	3.79	2	OREGON	PB9-3	25-Aug-57	13.72	4
NEWTON	TP11-5	19-May-55	3.81	2	OREGON	TS1-3	3-Apr-52	15.04	4
NEWTON	PB8-3	20-Aug-57	4.00	2	OREGON	TP10-3	7-May-55	43.96	5
NEWTON	PB13-6	11-Sep-57	4.30	2	OSAGE	PB3-6	29-Jun-57	3.73	2
NEWTON	UK7-3	27-Apr-53	5.16	3	OSAGE	TS7-5	5-Jun-52	3.80	2
NEWTON	UK3-5	4-Apr-53	6.83	3	OSAGE	PB6-4	27-Jul-57	3.93	2
NEWTON	UK1-1	17-Mar-53	7.40	3	OSAGE	TS1-3	3-Apr-52	4.01	2
NEWTON	BJ2-2	31-Oct-51	8.76	3	OSAGE	PB18-8	17-Jul-57	5.26	3
NEWTON	PB12-4	5-Sep-57	15.88	4	OSAGE	UK2-3	26-Mar-53	6.77	3
NEWTON	TS6-4	28-May-52	16.39	4	OSAGE	PB9-4	26-Aug-57	8.37	3
NEWTON	TS1-3	3-Apr-52	24.86	4	OSAGE	PB4-5	9-Jul-57	10.65	4
NEWTON	TS7-5	5-Jun-52	27.46	5	OSAGE	PB9-3	25-Aug-57	13.72	4
NEWTON	TP10-3	7-May-55	41.78	5	OSAGE	PB8-3	20-Aug-57	15.90	4
NODAWAY	TP10-3	7-May-55	4.10	2	OSAGE	TP10-3	7 May-55	59.59	6

INDIVIDUAL FALLOUT DAYS
MISSOURI

COUNTY	SHOT	DATE	µCi/SQ METER	INDEX	COUNTY	SHOT	DATE	µCi/SQ METER	INDEX
OSAGE	PB12-5	6-Sep-57	3.50	1	PETTIS	TP4-2	8-Mar-55	5.25	3
OSAGE	PB4-4	8-Jul-57	30.60	5	PETTIS	PB18-8	17-Jul-57	5.26	3
OZARK	PB4-5	9-Jul-57	3.57	2	PETTIS	PB4-5	9-Jul-57	7.08	3
OZARK	TP11-5	19-May-55	3.78	2	PETTIS	PB4-4	8-Jul-57	7.23	3
OZARK	PB12-5	6-Sep-57	3.82	2	PETTIS	PB9-4	26-Aug-57	8.37	3
OZARK	UK7-3	27-Apr-53	4.61	2	PETTIS	UK2-3	26-Mar-53	8.71	3
OZARK	PB18-8	17-Jul-57	5.26	3	PETTIS	PB12-4	5-Sep-57	9.26	3
OZARK	UK2-3	26-Mar-53	6.43	3	PETTIS	TS7-5	5-Jun-52	12.28	4
OZARK	PB12-4	5-Sep-57	6.62	3	PETTIS	TS6-4	28-May-52	14.46	4
OZARK	TS6-4	28-May-52	6.75	3	PETTIS	TP10-3	7-May-55	58.54	6
OZARK	PB8-3	20-Aug-57	7.99	3	PETTIS	PB8-3	20-Aug-57	39.79	5
OZARK	UK7-4	28-Apr-53	12.11	4	PHELPS	PB4-5	9-Jul-57	3.57	2
OZARK	UK2-7	30-Mar-53	12.19	4	PHELPS	PB12-5	6-Sep-57	3.58	2
OZARK	UK1-1	17-Mar-53	12.33	4	PHELPS	UK7-3	27-Apr-53	3.85	2
OZARK	TP10-3	7-May-55	53.28	6	PHELPS	TS1-3	3-Apr-52	4.01	2
PEMISCOT	UK8-3	10-May-53	3.68	2	PHELPS	PB4-4	8-Jul-57	5.08	3
PEMISCOT	UK7-4	28-Apr-53	3.84	2	PHELPS	PB18-8	17-Jul-57	5.26	3
PEMISCOT	PB8-3	20-Aug-57	4.00	2	PHELPS	UK2-3	26-Mar-53	6.57	3
PEMISCOT	TS7-6	6-Jun-52	4.59	2	PHELPS	PB8-3	20-Aug-57	7.99	3
PEMISCOT	UK1-3	19-Mar-53	5.08	3	PHELPS	TS6-4	28-May-52	13.50	4
PEMISCOT	TS1-3	3-Apr-52	9.02	3	PHELPS	PB9-3	25-Aug-57	13.72	4
PEMISCOT	UK2-7	30-Mar-53	12.19	4	PHELPS	R1-2	29-Jan-51	23.97	4
PEMISCOT	UK2-8	31-Mar-53	21.07	4	PHELPS	TP10-3	7-May-55	39.45	5
PEMISCOT	TP10-3	7-May-55	23.22	4	PIKE	UK7-4	28-Apr-53	4.01	2
PERRY	UK2-3	26-Mar-53	3.52	2	PIKE	PB6-3	26-Jul-57	4.63	2
PERRY	TP10-3	7-May-55	8.04	3	PIKE	PB6-4	27-Jul-57	4.65	2
PERRY	PB9-2	24-Aug-57	8.19	3	PIKE	UK2-3	26-Mar-53	4.70	2
PERRY	TS1-3	3-Apr-52	15.04	4	PIKE	TP10-3	7-May-55	5.78	3
PETTIS	UK9-2	20-May-53	3.61	2	PIKE	TS1-2	2-Apr-52	6.13	3
PETTIS	UK7-3	27-Apr-53	3.78	2	PIKE	TS5-1	7-May-52	7.94	3
PETTIS	TS1-3	3-Apr-52	4.01	2	PIKE	PB8-3	20-Aug-57	7.99	3
PETTIS	TS7-6	6-Jun-52	4.52	2	PIKE	TS7-5	5-Jun-52	8.13	3
PETTIS	TP3-3	3-Mar-55	5.17	3	PIKE	PB9-4	26-Aug-57	8.37	3

INDIVIDUAL FALLOUT DAYS
MISSOURI

COUNTY	SHOT	DATE	µCi/SQ METER	INDEX	COUNTY	SHOT	DATE	µCi/SQ METER	INDEX
PIKE	TS6-4	28-May-52	12.54	4	PULASKI	PB12-4	5-Sep-57	7.84	3
PIKE	PB9-3	25-Aug-57	13.72	4	PULASKI	PB4-4	8-Jul-57	9.59	3
PIKE	SE3	8-Jul-62	90.94	6	PULASKI	PB4-5	9-Jul-57	10.65	4
PIKE	R1-2	29-Jan-51	37.86	5	PULASKI	PB9-3	25-Aug-57	13.72	4
PIKE	TS7-3	3-Jun-52	123.69	7	PULASKI	PB8-3	20-Aug-57	23.89	4
PLATTE	PB5-7	21-Jul-57	4.15	2	PULASKI	TP10-3	7-May-55	40.81	5
PLATTE	TP10-3	7-May-55	4.79	2	PUTNAM	TP10-2	6-May-55	3.62	2
PLATTE	TP4-2	8-Mar-55	5.25	3	PUTNAM	PB13-5	10-Sep-57	3.65	2
PLATTE	UK2-3	26-Mar-53	5.47	3	PUTNAM	TP4-2	8-Mar-55	5.25	3
PLATTE	PB13-5	10-Sep-57	7.03	3	PUTNAM	TS7-4	4-Jun-52	5.53	3
PLATTE	UK9-2	20-May-53	8.13	3	PUTNAM	PB12-4	5-Sep-57	5.61	3
PLATTE	TP10-2	6-May-55	9.09	3	PUTNAM	TS6-4	28-May-52	5.79	3
PLATTE	PB12-4	5-Sep-57	14.26	4	PUTNAM	PB9-4	26-Aug-57	8.37	3
PLATTE	PB8-3	20-Aug-57	23.89	4	PUTNAM	PB8-3	20-Aug-57	23.89	4
POLK	PB18-8	17-Jul-57	3.53	2	PUTNAM	TS7-3	3-Jun-52	95.72	6
POLK	UK2-3	26-Mar-53	5.32	3	PUTNAM	UK9-2	20-May-53	32.05	5
POLK	UK7-3	27-Apr-53	5.36	3	PUTNAM	TP10-3	7-May-55	34.49	5
POLK	UK7-4	28-Apr-53	7.00	3	PUTNAM	SE3	8-Jul-62	200.06	8
POLK	TS1-2	2-Apr-52	11.93	4	RALLS	TS5-2	8-May-52	3.94	2
POLK	PB12-4	5-Sep-57	13.65	4	RALLS	UK2-3	26-Mar-53	4.22	2
POLK	TS7-5	5-Jun-52	14.32	4	RALLS	UK9-2	20-May-53	4.79	2
POLK	TS6-4	28-May-52	14.46	4	RALLS	PB18-8	17-Jul-57	5.26	3
POLK	TP10-3	7-May-55	16.26	4	RALLS	PB6-4	27-Jul-57	6.53	3
POLK	PB4-5	9-Jul-57	17.72	4	RALLS	PB8-3	20-Aug-57	7.99	3
POLK	PB8-3	20-Aug-57	39.79	5	RALLS	PB9-4	26-Aug-57	8.37	3
PULASKI	PB18-8	17-Jul-57	3.53	2	RALLS	TS6-4	28-May-52	11.57	4
PULASKI	PB12-5	6-Sep-57	3.54	2	RALLS	TS7-5	5-Jun-52	12.36	4
PULASKI	TS1-3	3-Apr-52	4.01	2	RALLS	PB9-3	25-Aug-57	13.72	4
PULASKI	UK7-3	27-Apr-53	4.12	2	RALLS	TP10-3	7-May-55	21.61	4
PULASKI	TS1-2	2-Apr-52	6.13	3	RALLS	R1-2	29-Jan-51	25.61	5
PULASKI	UK2-3	26-Mar-53	6.22	3	RALLS	TS7-3	3-Jun-52	128.91	7
PULASKI	UK7-4	28-Apr-53	6.74	3	RALLS	SE3	8-Jul-62	200.06	8
PULASKI	TS6-4	28-May-52	6.75	3	RANDOLPH	UK7-4	28-Apr-53	4.28	2

INDIVIDUAL FALLOUT DAYS
MISSOURI

COUNTY	SHOT	DATE	µCi/SQ METER	INDEX	COUNTY	SHOT	DATE	µCi/SQ METER	INDEX
RANDOLPH	PB18-8	17-Jul-57	5.26	3	REYNOLDS	TS1-3	3-Apr-52	4.01	2
RANDOLPH	UK2-3	26-Mar-53	5.53	3	REYNOLDS	TS7-6	6-Jun-52	4.09	2
RANDOLPH	TS6-4	28-May-52	5.79	3	REYNOLDS	UK2-3	26-Mar-53	6.22	3
RANDOLPH	PB12-4	5-Sep-57	6.01	3	REYNOLDS	PB9-3	25-Aug-57	13.72	4
RANDOLPH	UK9-2	20-May-53	6.05	3	REYNOLDS	TP10-3	7-May-55	30.74	5
RANDOLPH	PB6-3	26-Jul-57	7.72	3	RIPLEY	PB8-3	20-Aug-57	4.00	2
RANDOLPH	TS5-1	7-May-52	7.79	3	RIPLEY	TP11-6	20-May-55	4.62	2
RANDOLPH	TP10-3	7-May-55	7.81	3	RIPLEY	UK2-3	26-Mar-53	5.05	3
RANDOLPH	PB9-4	26-Aug-57	8.37	3	RIPLEY	UK2-8	31-Mar-53	7.04	3
RANDOLPH	TS7-5	5-Jun-52	10.56	4	RIPLEY	PB9-2	24-Aug-57	8.19	3
RANDOLPH	TS1-2	2-Apr-52	11.93	4	RIPLEY	TS1-3	3-Apr-52	9.02	3
RANDOLPH	PB8-3	20-Aug-57	23.89	4	RIPLEY	PB9-3	25-Aug-57	13.72	4
RANDOLPH	SE3	8-Jul-62	90.94	6	RIPLEY	TP10-3	7-May-55	14.74	4
RAY	PB4-5	9-Jul-57	3.57	2	RIPLEY	UK7-4	28-Apr-53	17.53	4
RAY	UK9-2	20-May-53	3.61	2	RIPLEY	UK2-7	30-Mar-53	18.26	4
RAY	TP10-2	6-May-55	3.62	2	SALINE	PB4-5	9-Jul-57	3.57	2
RAY	UK7-4	28-Apr-53	3.92	2	SALINE	PB4-4	8-Jul-57	4.01	2
RAY	PB5-7	21-Jul-57	4.15	2	SALINE	UK9-2	20-May-53	4.52	2
RAY	PB6-3	26-Jul-57	4.63	2	SALINE	PB6-3	26-Jul-57	4.63	2
RAY	TP4-2	8-Mar-55	5.25	3	SALINE	TP4-2	8-Mar-55	5.25	3
RAY	PB18-8	17-Jul-57	5.26	3	SALINE	PB18-8	17-Jul-57	5.26	3
RAY	PB13-5	10-Sep-57	5.77	3	SALINE	PB12-4	5-Sep-57	5.33	3
RAY	TP10-3	7-May-55	6.43	3	SALINE	UK7-4	28-Apr-53	5.51	3
RAY	UK2-3	26-Mar-53	7.05	3	SALINE	TP10-3	7-May-55	7.69	3
RAY	TS7-5	5-Jun-52	9.62	3	SALINE	TS6-4	28-May-52	7.71	3
RAY	PB12-4	5-Sep-57	13.58	4	SALINE	UK2-3	26-Mar-53	8.09	3
RAY	PB9-4	26-Aug-57	16.67	4	SALINE	PB9-4	26-Aug-57	8.37	3
RAY	TS1-2	2-Apr-52	18.05	4	SALINE	TS1-2	2-Apr-52	11.93	4
RAY	TS7-4	4-Jun-52	22.59	4	SALINE	TS7-5	5-Jun-52	15.76	4
RAY	PB8-3	20-Aug-57	23.89	4	SALINE	PB8-3	20-Aug-57	39.79	5
REYNOLDS	UK7-3	27-Apr-53	3.57	2	SCHUYLER	TP10-2	6-May-55	3.62	2
REYNOLDS	TP11-6	20-May-55	3.83	2	SCHUYLER	TS7-4	4-Jun-52	4.34	2
REYNOLDS	PB8-3	20-Aug-57	4.00	2	SCHUYLER	TP4-2	8-Mar-55	5.25	3

U.S. FALLOUT ATLAS: COUNTY COMPARISONS

INDIVIDUAL FALLOUT DAYS
MISSOURI

COUNTY	SHOT	DATE	µCi/SQ METER	INDEX	COUNTY	SHOT	DATE	µCi/SQ METER	INDEX
SCHUYLER	TS6-4	28-May-52	5.79	3	SHANNON	TP10-3	7-May-55	33.37	5
SCHUYLER	PB9-4	26-Aug-57	8.37	3	SHELBY	TS5-2	8-May-52	3.53	2
SCHUYLER	TP10-3	7-May-55	19.22	4	SHELBY	UK2-3	26-Mar-53	3.87	2
SCHUYLER	PB8-3	20-Aug-57	23.89	4	SHELBY	PB12-4	5-Sep-57	4.39	2
SCHUYLER	TS7-3	3-Jun-52	86.78	6	SHELBY	TS6-4	28-May-52	5.79	3
SCHUYLER	UK9-2	20-May-53	30.32	5	SHELBY	PB9-4	26-Aug-57	8.37	3
SCHUYLER	SE3	8-Jul-62	200.06	8	SHELBY	PB18-8	17-Jul-57	8.80	3
SCOTLAND	TP10-2	6-May-55	3.62	2	SHELBY	TS7-5	5-Jun-52	8.88	3
SCOTLAND	PB18-8	17-Jul-57	3.98	2	SHELBY	UK9-2	20-May-53	10.93	4
SCOTLAND	PB8-3	20-Aug-57	4.00	2	SHELBY	PB9-3	25-Aug-57	13.72	4
SCOTLAND	TS5-1	7-May-52	4.05	2	SHELBY	TP10-3	7-May-55	15.18	4
SCOTLAND	TS7-4	4-Jun-52	4.32	2	SHELBY	PB8-3	20-Aug-57	15.90	4
SCOTLAND	TP4-2	8-Mar-55	5.25	3	SHELBY	TS1-2	2-Apr-52	18.05	4
SCOTLAND	TP10-3	7-May-55	6.11	3	SHELBY	TS7-3	3-Jun-52	46.91	5
SCOTLAND	PB9-4	26-Aug-57	8.37	3	SHELBY	SE3	8-Jul-62	200.06	8
SCOTLAND	PB9-3	25-Aug-57	13.72	4	ST CHARLES	PB8-3	20-Aug-57	4.00	2
SCOTLAND	UK9-2	20-May-53	26.09	5	ST CHARLES	TS5-1	7-May-52	4.35	2
SCOTLAND	TS7-3	3-Jun-52	177.11	7	ST CHARLES	UK2-3	26-Mar-53	4.89	2
SCOTLAND	SE3	8-Jul-62	358.08	8	ST CHARLES	TS7-5	5-Jun-52	5.23	3
SCOTT	TS7-6	6-Jun-52	6.18	3	ST CHARLES	PB6-4	27-Jul-57	5.42	3
SCOTT	TS1-3	3-Apr-52	9.02	3	ST CHARLES	TS6-4	28-May-52	6.75	3
SCOTT	TP10-3	7-May-55	19.46	4	ST CHARLES	PB4-4	8-Jul-57	7.51	3
SHANNON	PB18-8	17-Jul-57	3.53	2	ST CHARLES	PB9-4	26-Aug-57	8.37	3
SHANNON	PB4-5	9-Jul-57	3.57	2	ST CHARLES	TP10-3	7-May-55	13.43	4
SHANNON	UK7-4	28-Apr-53	3.69	2	ST CHARLES	PB9-3	25-Aug-57	13.72	4
SHANNON	PB12-5	6-Sep-57	3.78	2	ST CLAIR	TP10-2	6-May-55	3.94	2
SHANNON	UK7-3	27-Apr-53	4.12	2	ST CLAIR	TP10-3	7-May-55	4.42	2
SHANNON	TS7-6	6-Jun-52	4.33	2	ST CLAIR	UK2-3	26-Mar-53	4.89	2
SHANNON	TP11-6	20-May-55	4.50	2	ST CLAIR	UK9-4	22-May-53	5.58	3
SHANNON	UK2-3	26-Mar-53	5.67	3	ST CLAIR	TS6-4	28-May-52	6.75	3
SHANNON	TS6-4	28-May-52	6.75	3	ST CLAIR	PB9-4	26-Aug-57	8.37	3
SHANNON	PB8-3	20-Aug-57	7.99	3	ST CLAIR	UK7-4	28-Apr-53	9.32	3
SHANNON	PB9-3	25-Aug-57	13.72	4	ST CLAIR	PB9-3	25-Aug-57	13.72	4

INDIVIDUAL FALLOUT DAYS
MISSOURI

COUNTY	SHOT	DATE	µCi/SQ METER	INDEX	COUNTY	SHOT	DATE	µCi/SQ METER	INDEX
ST CLAIR	TS1-2	2-Apr-52	18.05	4	STONE	UK7-3	27-Apr-53	4.67	2
ST FRANCOIS	PB8-3	20-Aug-57	4.00	2	STONE	PB18-8	17-Jul-57	5.26	3
ST FRANCOIS	TS1-3	3-Apr-52	4.01	2	STONE	PB12-5	6-Sep-57	5.52	3
ST FRANCOIS	UK2-3	26-Mar-53	5.42	3	STONE	UK7-4	28-Apr-53	5.67	3
ST FRANCOIS	TP10-3	7-May-55	9.72	3	STONE	TP11-6	20-May-55	6.43	3
ST FRANCOIS	UK7-4	28-Apr-53	10.00	3	STONE	TP10-3	7-May-55	7.31	3
ST FRANCOIS	TS1-2	2-Apr-52	11.93	4	STONE	UK1-1	17-Mar-53	7.40	3
ST FRANCOIS	PB9-3	25-Aug-57	13.72	4	STONE	TS6-4	28-May-52	7.71	3
ST LOUIS	TS1-3	3-Apr-52	4.01	2	STONE	PB8-3	20-Aug-57	7.99	3
ST LOUIS	UK2-3	26-Mar-53	4.45	2	STONE	BJ2-2	31-Oct-51	8.76	3
ST LOUIS	TS7-5	5-Jun-52	5.87	3	STONE	TS1-3	3-Apr-52	41.51	5
ST LOUIS	PB6-4	27-Jul-57	6.00	3	SULLIVAN	PB13-5	10-Sep-57	3.76	2
ST LOUIS	UK7-4	28-Apr-53	6.09	3	SULLIVAN	UK2-3	26-Mar-53	4.01	2
ST LOUIS	TS1-2	2-Apr-52	6.13	3	SULLIVAN	TS7-4	4-Jun-52	4.89	2
ST LOUIS	TS6-4	28-May-52	6.75	3	SULLIVAN	TP4-2	8-Mar-55	5.25	3
ST LOUIS	TS7-3	3-Jun-52	7.63	3	SULLIVAN	TS6-4	28-May-52	6.75	3
ST LOUIS	PB9-4	26-Aug-57	8.37	3	SULLIVAN	TP10-3	7-May-55	6.93	3
ST LOUIS	PB9-3	25-Aug-57	13.72	4	SULLIVAN	PB9-4	26-Aug-57	8.37	3
STE GENEVIEV	TS1-3	3-Apr-52	4.01	2	SULLIVAN	PB12-4	5-Sep-57	8.61	3
STE GENEVIEV	TP10-3	7-May-55	4.36	2	SULLIVAN	PB8-3	20-Aug-57	23.89	4
STE GENEVIEV	UK2-3	26-Mar-53	4.84	2	SULLIVAN	SE3	8-Jul-62	76.52	6
STE GENEVIEV	TS6-4	28-May-52	7.71	3	SULLIVAN	UK9-2	20-May-53	25.55	5
STE GENEVIEV	UK7-4	28-Apr-53	10.66	4	SULLIVAN	TS7-3	3-Jun-52	109.03	7
STE GENEVIEV	PB9-3	25-Aug-57	13.72	4	TANEY	TP11-6	20-May-55	3.69	2
STODDARD	TS7-6	6-Jun-52	3.61	2	TANEY	PB8-3	20-Aug-57	4.00	2
STODDARD	UK8-3	10-May-53	3.68	2	TANEY	UK3-5	4-Apr-53	4.10	2
STODDARD	PB8-3	20-Aug-57	4.00	2	TANEY	TS1-3	3-Apr-52	4.21	2
STODDARD	UK2-3	26-Mar-53	4.15	2	TANEY	UK7-3	27-Apr-53	4.61	2
STODDARD	PB9-2	24-Aug-57	5.46	3	TANEY	PB12-4	5-Sep-57	5.16	3
STODDARD	UK2-7	30-Mar-53	6.07	3	TANEY	PB12-5	6-Sep-57	5.17	3
STODDARD	TS1-3	3-Apr-52	9.02	3	TANEY	PB18-8	17-Jul-57	5.26	3
STODDARD	UK2-8	31-Mar-53	14.03	4	TANEY	TS6-4	28-May-52	6.75	3
STODDARD	TP10-3	7-May-55	20.44	4	TANEY	UK1-1	17-Mar-53	12.33	4

INDIVIDUAL FALLOUT DAYS
MISSOURI

COUNTY	SHOT	DATE	µCi/SQ METER	INDEX	COUNTY	SHOT	DATE	µCi/SQ METER	INDEX
TANEY	TP10-3	7-May-55	22.49	4	WARREN	UK2-3	26-Mar-53	5.59	3
TEXAS	TS1-3	3-Apr-52	4.01	2	WARREN	TP10-3	7-May-55	5.99	3
TEXAS	PB12-5	6-Sep-57	4.12	2	WARREN	TS5-1	7-May-52	7.49	3
TEXAS	UK7-3	27-Apr-53	4.40	2	WARREN	PB8-3	20-Aug-57	7.99	3
TEXAS	TP11-6	20-May-55	4.80	2	WARREN	PB9-4	26-Aug-57	8.37	3
TEXAS	PB18-8	17-Jul-57	5.26	3	WARREN	PB9-3	25-Aug-57	13.72	4
TEXAS	UK2-3	26-Mar-53	5.39	3	WASHINGTON	PB3-6	29-Jun-57	3.63	2
TEXAS	TS6-4	28-May-52	6.75	3	WASHINGTON	PB8-3	20-Aug-57	4.00	2
TEXAS	PB4-5	9-Jul-57	7.08	3	WASHINGTON	TS1-3	3-Apr-52	4.01	2
TEXAS	UK7-4	28-Apr-53	7.27	3	WASHINGTON	TS7-6	6-Jun-52	4.21	2
TEXAS	PB9-2	24-Aug-57	8.19	3	WASHINGTON	PB6-4	27-Jul-57	4.50	2
TEXAS	PB9-3	25-Aug-57	13.72	4	WASHINGTON	PB9-2	24-Aug-57	5.46	3
TEXAS	PB8-3	20-Aug-57	15.90	4	WASHINGTON	UK2-3	26-Mar-53	6.05	3
TEXAS	R1-2	29-Jan-51	16.71	4	WASHINGTON	UK7-4	28-Apr-53	6.20	3
TEXAS	TP10-3	7-May-55	37.65	5	WASHINGTON	PB9-3	25-Aug-57	13.72	4
VERNON	PB13-6	11-Sep-57	3.55	2	WASHINGTON	TP10-3	7-May-55	15.93	4
VERNON	PB8-3	20-Aug-57	4.00	2	WAYNE	TP11-6	20-May-55	3.71	2
VERNON	TS1-3	3-Apr-52	4.01	2	WAYNE	PB8-3	20-Aug-57	4.00	2
VERNON	PB14-7	20-Sep-57	4.04	2	WAYNE	UK2-3	26-Mar-53	5.39	3
VERNON	UK11-2	5-Jun-53	4.72	2	WAYNE	PB9-2	24-Aug-57	8.19	3
VERNON	UK2-3	26-Mar-53	5.05	3	WAYNE	PB9-3	25-Aug-57	13.72	4
VERNON	PB18-8	17-Jul-57	5.26	3	WAYNE	TS1-3	3-Apr-52	15.04	4
VERNON	TP10-3	7-May-55	5.73	3	WAYNE	TP10-3	7-May-55	25.10	5
VERNON	BJ2-2	31-Oct-51	5.84	3	WEBSTER	PB12-5	6-Sep-57	3.56	2
VERNON	UK7-3	27-Apr-53	6.02	3	WEBSTER	PB11-2	1-Sep-57	3.73	2
VERNON	PB4-5	9-Jul-57	10.65	4	WEBSTER	TS1-3	3-Apr-52	4.01	2
VERNON	TS1-2	2-Apr-52	18.05	4	WEBSTER	UK2-3	26-Mar-53	4.49	2
VERNON	PB12-4	5-Sep-57	21.82	4	WEBSTER	TP11-5	19-May-55	4.64	2
VERNON	TS7-5	5-Jun-52	27.79	5	WEBSTER	UK7-3	27-Apr-53	4.88	2
WARREN	TS1-3	3-Apr-52	4.01	2	WEBSTER	TS1-2	2-Apr-52	6.13	3
WARREN	PB6-3	26-Jul-57	4.63	2	WEBSTER	TS6-4	28-May-52	6.75	3
WARREN	PB4-4	8-Jul-57	5.30	3	WEBSTER	UK7-4	28-Apr-53	10.33	4
WARREN	PB6-4	27-Jul-57	5.52	3	WEBSTER	PB4-5	9-Jul-57	10.65	4

INDIVIDUAL FALLOUT DAYS
MISSOURI

COUNTY	SHOT	DATE	µCi/SQ METER	INDEX	COUNTY	SHOT	DATE	µCi/SQ METER	INDEX
WEBSTER	PB8-3	20-Aug-57	23.89	4	WRIGHT	PB12-5	6-Sep-57	4.04	2
WEBSTER	TP10-3	7-May-55	59.37	6	WRIGHT	UK7-3	27-Apr-53	4.54	2
WORTH	UK7-4	28-Apr-53	3.80	2	WRIGHT	TP11-6	20-May-55	4.88	2
WORTH	TP10-3	7-May-55	4.60	2	WRIGHT	UK2-3	26-Mar-53	4.98	2
WORTH	TP4-2	8-Mar-55	5.25	3	WRIGHT	PB18-8	17-Jul-57	5.26	3
WORTH	PB13-5	10-Sep-57	8.88	3	WRIGHT	PB12-4	5-Sep-57	6.01	3
WORTH	PB12-4	5-Sep-57	10.08	4	WRIGHT	TS6-4	28-May-52	6.75	3
WORTH	UK9-2	20-May-53	16.44	4	WRIGHT	PB8-3	20-Aug-57	7.99	3
WORTH	PB9-4	26-Aug-57	33.34	5	WRIGHT	UK7-4	28-Apr-53	10.27	4
WORTH	TS7-4	4-Jun-52	33.82	5	WRIGHT	PB9-3	25-Aug-57	13.72	4
WORTH	PB8-3	20-Aug-57	39.79	5	WRIGHT	R1-2	29-Jan-51	16.71	4
WORTH	SE3	8-Jul-62	200.06	8	WRIGHT	TP10-3	7-May-55	55.99	6
WRIGHT	PB4-5	9-Jul-57	3.57	2					
WRIGHT	TS1-3	3-Apr-52	4.01	2					

INDIVIDUAL FALLOUT DAYS
MISSISSIPPI

COUNTY	SHOT	DATE	µCi/SQ METER	INDEX	COUNTY	SHOT	DATE	µCi/SQ METER	INDEX
ADAMS	TP6-3	24-Mar-55	5.55	3	BOLIVAR	TS6-4	28-May-52	4.03	2
ADAMS	UK7-3	27-Apr-53	6.37	3	BOLIVAR	TS5-1	7-May-52	4.13	2
ADAMS	UK7-4	28-Apr-53	47.88	5	BOLIVAR	PB12-6	7-Sep-57	4.60	2
ADAMS	PB3-3	26-Jun-57	114.67	7	BOLIVAR	TP11-6	20-May-55	4.72	2
ALCORN	UK1-3	19-Mar-53	3.60	2	BOLIVAR	UK2-7	30-Mar-53	6.07	3
ALCORN	UK3-6	5-Apr-53	3.67	2	BOLIVAR	UK2-8	31-Mar-53	7.04	3
ALCORN	UK9-3	21-May-53	4.71	2	BOLIVAR	TS1-3	3-Apr-52	9.02	3
ALCORN	PB12-6	7-Sep-57	5.75	3	BOLIVAR	UK7-4	28-Apr-53	21.49	4
ALCORN	TS1-3	3-Apr-52	6.02	3	CALHOUN	UK7-4	28-Apr-53	3.66	2
ALCORN	UK2-7	30-Mar-53	6.07	3	CALHOUN	UK8-3	10-May-53	3.68	2
ALCORN	UK2-8	31-Mar-53	14.03	4	CALHOUN	UK9-3	21-May-53	3.81	2
AMITE	PB17-5	2-Oct-57	5.46	3	CALHOUN	UK2-3	26-Mar-53	3.87	2
AMITE	TP6-3	24-Mar-55	5.55	3	CALHOUN	PB2-5	22-Jun-57	4.64	2
AMITE	PB12-6	7-Sep-57	6.42	3	CALHOUN	UK2-7	30-Mar-53	6.07	3
AMITE	UK7-3	27-Apr-53	6.48	3	CALHOUN	PB12-6	7-Sep-57	7.44	3
AMITE	PB3-3	26-Jun-57	22.97	4	CALHOUN	PB17-5	2-Oct-57	8.03	3
AMITE	UK7-4	28-Apr-53	24.86	4	CALHOUN	TS1-3	3-Apr-52	9.02	3
ATTALA	UK7-4	28-Apr-53	3.64	2	CALHOUN	UK2-8	31-Mar-53	3.50	1
ATTALA	TP6-4	25-Mar-55	3.99	2	CARROLL	PB2-5	22-Jun-57	4.64	2
ATTALA	PB17-5	2-Oct-57	4.11	2	CARROLL	PB17-5	2-Oct-57	4.65	2
ATTALA	PB2-5	22-Jun-57	4.64	2	CARROLL	PB12-6	7-Sep-57	4.67	2
ATTALA	TP6-3	24-Mar-55	5.55	3	CARROLL	PB9-2	24-Aug-57	5.46	3
ATTALA	PB12-6	7-Sep-57	8.14	3	CARROLL	TS6-4	28-May-52	9.64	3
ATTALA	TS6-4	28-May-52	18.32	4	CARROLL	TP6-3	24-Mar-55	11.09	4
BENTON	UK3-6	5-Apr-53	3.67	2	CARROLL	UK7-4	28-Apr-53	26.62	5
BENTON	UK8-3	10-May-53	3.68	2	CHICKASAW	UK9-3	21-May-53	3.88	2
BENTON	PB8-3	20-Aug-57	4.00	2	CHICKASAW	PB2-5	22-Jun-57	4.64	2
BENTON	UK9-3	21-May-53	5.27	3	CHICKASAW	TS6-4	28-May-52	4.83	2
BENTON	UK2-3	26-Mar-53	6.84	3	CHICKASAW	TP11-6	20-May-55	5.38	3
BENTON	TS1-3	3-Apr-52	9.02	3	CHICKASAW	PB9-2	24-Aug-57	5.46	3
BENTON	UK2-8	31-Mar-53	21.07	4	CHICKASAW	TS1-3	3-Apr-52	6.02	3
BOLIVAR	UK8-3	10-May-53	3.68	2	CHICKASAW	UK2-7	30-Mar-53	6.07	3
BOLIVAR	UK7-3	27-Apr-53	3.84	2	CHICKASAW	PB12-6	7-Sep-57	6.56	3

INDIVIDUAL FALLOUT DAYS
MISSISSIPPI

COUNTY	SHOT	DATE	µCi/SQ METER	INDEX	COUNTY	SHOT	DATE	µCi/SQ METER	INDEX
CHICKASAW	UK2-8	31-Mar-53	14.03	4	COPIAH	UK7-3	27-Apr-53	5.30	3
CHICKASAW	UK7-4	28-Apr-53	14.15	4	COPIAH	TP6-3	24-Mar-55	5.55	3
CHICKASAW	PB17-5	2-Oct-57	14.72	4	COPIAH	TS6-4	28-May-52	8.68	3
CHOCTAW	PB17-5	2-Oct-57	3.65	2	COPIAH	UK7-4	28-Apr-53	9.39	3
CHOCTAW	PB2-5	22-Jun-57	4.64	2	COPIAH	PB3-3	26-Jun-57	45.85	5
CHOCTAW	PB9-2	24-Aug-57	5.46	3	COVINGTON	UK7-4	28-Apr-53	3.60	2
CHOCTAW	TP6-3	24-Mar-55	5.55	3	COVINGTON	TP6-3	24-Mar-55	5.55	3
CHOCTAW	PB12-6	7-Sep-57	7.33	3	COVINGTON	PB3-3	26-Jun-57	11.44	4
CLAIBORNE	TP6-3	24-Mar-55	5.55	3	COVINGTON	PB12-6	7-Sep-57	21.82	4
CLAIBORNE	UK7-3	27-Apr-53	6.88	3	DE SOTO	UK3-6	5-Apr-53	3.67	2
CLAIBORNE	PB3-3	26-Jun-57	45.85	5	DE SOTO	TP11-6	20-May-55	3.84	2
CLAIBORNE	UK7-4	28-Apr-53	46.46	5	DE SOTO	PB8-3	20-Aug-57	4.00	2
CLARKE	TP6-5	26-Mar-55	3.54	2	DE SOTO	UK9-3	21-May-53	4.32	2
CLARKE	PB12-6	7-Sep-57	3.65	2	DE SOTO	UK1-2	18-Mar-53	4.42	2
CLARKE	TP6-3	24-Mar-55	5.55	3	DE SOTO	PB2-5	22-Jun-57	4.64	2
CLARKE	PB3-3	26-Jun-57	45.85	5	DE SOTO	UK8-3	10-May-53	6.18	3
CLAY	TP6-4	25-Mar-55	3.99	2	DE SOTO	UK2-8	31-Mar-53	7.04	3
CLAY	PB2-5	22-Jun-57	4.64	2	DE SOTO	UK7-4	28-Apr-53	8.65	3
CLAY	TS5-1	7-May-52	4.94	2	DE SOTO	TS1-3	3-Apr-52	9.02	3
CLAY	TP6-3	24-Mar-55	5.55	3	DE SOTO	UK2-3	26-Mar-53	9.40	3
CLAY	PB17-5	2-Oct-57	6.57	3	DE SOTO	UK2-7	30-Mar-53	18.26	4
CLAY	PB12-6	7-Sep-57	13.50	4	FORREST	TP6-5	26-Mar-55	3.54	2
COAHOMA	UK2-3	26-Mar-53	3.66	2	FORREST	PB12-6	7-Sep-57	9.89	3
COAHOMA	UK3-6	5-Apr-53	3.67	2	FORREST	UK6-2	19-Apr-53	37.36	5
COAHOMA	PB12-6	7-Sep-57	4.70	2	FORREST	PB3-3	26-Jun-57	45.85	5
COAHOMA	TP11-6	20-May-55	4.75	2	FRANKLIN	TP6-3	24-Mar-55	5.55	3
COAHOMA	UK2-7	30-Mar-53	6.07	3	FRANKLIN	UK7-3	27-Apr-53	6.71	3
COAHOMA	UK8-3	10-May-53	6.18	3	FRANKLIN	UK7-4	28-Apr-53	20.31	4
COAHOMA	PB9-2	24-Aug-57	8.19	3	FRANKLIN	PB3-3	26-Jun-57	114.67	7
COAHOMA	TS1-3	3-Apr-52	9.02	3	GEORGE	TP6-5	26-Mar-55	3.54	2
COAHOMA	UK7-4	28-Apr-53	22.03	4	GEORGE	PB3-3	26-Jun-57	68.82	6
COAHOMA	UK2-8	31-Mar-53	3.50	1	GEORGE	UK6-2	19-Apr-53	37.36	5
COPIAH	PB17-5	2-Oct-57	5.15	3	GREENE	TP6-5	26-Mar-55	3.54	2

INDIVIDUAL FALLOUT DAYS
MISSISSIPPI

COUNTY	SHOT	DATE	µCi/SQ METER	INDEX	COUNTY	SHOT	DATE	µCi/SQ METER	INDEX
GREENE	UK6-2	19-Apr-53	37.36	5	ISSAQUENA	TP6-3	24-Mar-55	5.55	3
GREENE	PB3-3	26-Jun-57	45.85	5	ISSAQUENA	UK7-3	27-Apr-53	5.85	3
GRENADA	UK8-3	10-May-53	3.68	2	ISSAQUENA	TS6-4	28-May-52	16.39	4
GRENADA	PB2-5	22-Jun-57	4.64	2	ISSAQUENA	UK7-4	28-Apr-53	43.62	5
GRENADA	TS1-3	3-Apr-52	6.02	3	ITAWAMBA	UK9-3	21-May-53	4.55	2
GRENADA	UK2-8	31-Mar-53	7.04	3	ITAWAMBA	PB2-5	22-Jun-57	4.64	2
GRENADA	PB9-2	24-Aug-57	8.19	3	ITAWAMBA	TP11-6	20-May-55	5.09	3
GRENADA	PB12-6	7-Sep-57	8.31	3	ITAWAMBA	PB12-6	7-Sep-57	5.19	3
GRENADA	PB17-5	2-Oct-57	9.38	3	ITAWAMBA	PB17-5	2-Oct-57	5.77	3
GRENADA	UK7-4	28-Apr-53	15.08	4	ITAWAMBA	UK2-8	31-Mar-53	3.50	1
HANCOCK	TS6-4	28-May-52	15.43	4	JACKSON	TP6-5	26-Mar-55	3.54	2
HANCOCK	PB3-3	26-Jun-57	68.82	6	JACKSON	TP11-2	16-May-55	5.05	3
HANCOCK	UK6-2	19-Apr-53	37.36	5	JACKSON	UK6-2	19-Apr-53	37.36	5
HARRISON	TP6-5	26-Mar-55	3.54	2	JACKSON	PB3-3	26-Jun-57	45.85	5
HARRISON	UK6-2	19-Apr-53	37.36	5	JASPER	PB12-6	7-Sep-57	4.38	2
HARRISON	PB3-3	26-Jun-57	45.85	5	JASPER	TP6-3	24-Mar-55	5.55	3
HINDS	UK7-5	29-Apr-53	3.62	2	JASPER	PB17-5	2-Oct-57	8.38	3
HINDS	TP5-2	13-Mar-55	4.00	2	JASPER	PB3-3	26-Jun-57	22.97	4
HINDS	UK7-3	27-Apr-53	4.59	2	JEFFERSON	TP6-3	24-Mar-55	5.55	3
HINDS	PB17-5	2-Oct-57	5.23	3	JEFFERSON	UK7-3	27-Apr-53	6.82	3
HINDS	TS6-4	28-May-52	17.36	4	JEFFERSON	UK7-4	28-Apr-53	44.42	5
HINDS	PB3-3	26-Jun-57	68.82	6	JEFFERSON	PB3-3	26-Jun-57	45.85	5
HINDS	UK7-4	28-Apr-53	32.87	5	JEFFERSON DA	UK7-4	28-Apr-53	4.27	2
HOLMES	TP6-4	25-Mar-55	3.99	2	JEFFERSON DA	TP6-3	24-Mar-55	5.55	3
HOLMES	UK7-4	28-Apr-53	4.57	2	JEFFERSON DA	PB3-3	26-Jun-57	11.44	4
HOLMES	PB2-5	22-Jun-57	4.64	2	JONES	TP5-2	13-Mar-55	5.40	3
HOLMES	TP6-3	24-Mar-55	5.55	3	JONES	TP6-3	24-Mar-55	5.55	3
HOLMES	PB12-6	7-Sep-57	8.80	3	JONES	PB12-6	7-Sep-57	10.51	4
HUMPHREYS	UK7-3	27-Apr-53	4.59	2	JONES	PB3-3	26-Jun-57	11.44	4
HUMPHREYS	PB17-5	2-Oct-57	5.46	3	KEMPER	TP6-4	25-Mar-55	3.99	2
HUMPHREYS	PB12-6	7-Sep-57	8.91	3	KEMPER	TS5-1	7-May-52	4.20	2
HUMPHREYS	TP6-3	24-Mar-55	11.09	4	KEMPER	TP6-3	24-Mar-55	5.55	3
HUMPHREYS	UK7-4	28-Apr-53	24.70	4	KEMPER	TS6-4	28-May-52	10.61	4

INDITIONAL FALLOUT DAYS
MISSISSIPPI

COUNTY	SHOT	DATE	µCi/SQ METER	INDEX	COUNTY	SHOT	DATE	µCi/SQ METER	INDEX
KEMPER	UK7-4	28-Apr-53	15.37	4	LEE	TP11-6	20-May-55	5.24	3
LAFAYETTE	UK3-6	5-Apr-53	3.67	2	LEE	PB12-6	7-Sep-57	5.93	3
LAFAYETTE	UK8-3	10-May-53	3.68	2	LEE	TS1-3	3-Apr-52	6.02	3
LAFAYETTE	UK9-3	21-May-53	4.15	2	LEE	UK2-7	30-Mar-53	6.07	3
LAFAYETTE	PB2-5	22-Jun-57	4.64	2	LEE	UK2-8	31-Mar-53	7.04	3
LAFAYETTE	UK7-4	28-Apr-53	5.90	3	LEE	UK7-4	28-Apr-53	16.19	4
LAFAYETTE	UK2-7	30-Mar-53	6.07	3	LEFLORE	PB2-5	22-Jun-57	4.64	2
LAFAYETTE	TS1-3	3-Apr-52	9.02	3	LEFLORE	PB12-6	7-Sep-57	4.77	2
LAFAYETTE	UK2-8	31-Mar-53	14.03	4	LEFLORE	PB17-5	2-Oct-57	5.11	3
LAMAR	PB17-5	2-Oct-57	3.80	2	LEFLORE	TP6-3	24-Mar-55	5.55	3
LAMAR	TS1-3	3-Apr-52	4.01	2	LEFLORE	UK7-4	28-Apr-53	22.40	4
LAMAR	TP6-3	24-Mar-55	5.55	3	LINCOLN	UK7-3	27-Apr-53	4.92	2
LAMAR	PB12-6	7-Sep-57	10.80	4	LINCOLN	TP6-3	24-Mar-55	5.55	3
LAMAR	PB3-3	26-Jun-57	45.85	5	LINCOLN	PB12-6	7-Sep-57	6.21	3
LAUDERDALE	TP6-3	24-Mar-55	5.55	3	LINCOLN	PB3-3	26-Jun-57	11.44	4
LAUDERDALE	UK7-4	28-Apr-53	15.94	4	LINCOLN	UK7-4	28-Apr-53	17.21	4
LAUDERDALE	TS6-4	28-May-52	18.32	4	LOWNDES	PB2-5	22-Jun-57	4.64	2
LAUDERDALE	PB3-3	26-Jun-57	68.82	6	LOWNDES	TP6-3	24-Mar-55	5.55	3
LAWRENCE	UK7-3	27-Apr-53	3.72	2	LOWNDES	PB17-5	2-Oct-57	5.73	3
LAWRENCE	UK7-4	28-Apr-53	4.86	2	MADISON	UK7-5	29-Apr-53	3.77	2
LAWRENCE	TP6-3	24-Mar-55	5.55	3	MADISON	PB12-6	7-Sep-57	5.02	3
LAWRENCE	PB12-6	7-Sep-57	6.14	3	MADISON	TP6-3	24-Mar-55	5.55	3
LAWRENCE	PB3-3	26-Jun-57	11.44	4	MADISON	UK7-4	28-Apr-53	37.24	5
LAWRENCE	TS6-4	28-May-52	29.89	5	MARION	TS1-3	3-Apr-52	4.01	2
LEAKE	UK7-4	28-Apr-53	3.79	2	MARION	TP6-3	24-Mar-55	5.55	3
LEAKE	PB17-5	2-Oct-57	3.96	2	MARION	UK7-4	28-Apr-53	8.50	3
LEAKE	TP6-4	25-Mar-55	3.99	2	MARION	PB12-6	7-Sep-57	11.68	4
LEAKE	PB12-6	7-Sep-57	4.52	2	MARION	PB3-3	26-Jun-57	68.82	6
LEAKE	TP6-3	24-Mar-55	11.09	4	MARSHALL	PB12-6	7-Sep-57	3.65	2
LEAKE	TS6-4	28-May-52	18.32	4	MARSHALL	UK3-6	5-Apr-53	3.67	2
LEE	UK3-6	5-Apr-53	3.67	2	MARSHALL	UK8-3	10-May-53	3.68	2
LEE	PB2-5	22-Jun-57	4.64	2	MARSHALL	UK1-2	18-Mar-53	3.70	2
LEE	UK9-3	21-May-53	4.67	2	MARSHALL	UK7-4	28-Apr-53	3.79	2

INDIVIDUAL FALLOUT DAYS
MISSISSIPPI

COUNTY	SHOT	DATE	µCi/SQ METER	INDEX	COUNTY	SHOT	DATE	µCi/SQ METER	INDEX
MARSHALL	PB8-3	20-Aug-57	4.00	2	OKTIBBEHA	TS6-4	28-May-52	9.64	3
MARSHALL	UK9-3	21-May-53	5.27	3	OKTIBBEHA	UK7-4	28-Apr-53	22.00	4
MARSHALL	UK2-3	26-Mar-53	7.32	3	PANOLA	UK9-3	21-May-53	3.63	2
MARSHALL	TS1-3	3-Apr-52	9.02	3	PANOLA	UK3-6	5-Apr-53	3.67	2
MARSHALL	UK2-8	31-Mar-53	14.03	4	PANOLA	TP11-6	20-May-55	4.58	2
MARSHALL	UK2-7	30-Mar-53	18.26	4	PANOLA	PB2-5	22-Jun-57	4.64	2
MONROE	UK9-3	21-May-53	3.75	2	PANOLA	UK8-3	10-May-53	6.18	3
MONROE	TP11-6	20-May-55	5.24	3	PANOLA	TS1-3	3-Apr-52	9.02	3
MONROE	PB12-6	7-Sep-57	5.44	3	PANOLA	UK2-7	30-Mar-53	12.19	4
MONROE	PB17-5	2-Oct-57	5.92	3	PANOLA	UK2-8	31-Mar-53	14.03	4
MONROE	UK2-8	31-Mar-53	3.50	1	PANOLA	UK7-4	28-Apr-53	14.45	4
MONTGOMERY	PB17-5	2-Oct-57	4.19	2	PEARL RIVER	TS6-4	28-May-52	4.03	2
MONTGOMERY	PB3-4	27-Jun-57	4.26	2	PEARL RIVER	UK7-4	28-Apr-53	10.97	4
MONTGOMERY	PB12-6	7-Sep-57	8.03	3	PEARL RIVER	PB3-3	26-Jun-57	68.82	6
MONTGOMERY	PB9-2	24-Aug-57	8.19	3	PEARL RIVER	UK6-2	19-Apr-53	37.36	5
MONTGOMERY	TP6-3	24-Mar-55	22.18	4	PERRY	TP6-5	26-Mar-55	3.54	2
MONTGOMERY	UK7-4	28-Apr-53	23.04	4	PERRY	PB12-6	7-Sep-57	4.84	2
NESHOBA	TP6-4	25-Mar-55	3.99	2	PERRY	PB3-3	26-Jun-57	22.97	4
NESHOBA	TP10-5	9-May-55	4.81	2	PERRY	UK6-2	19-Apr-53	37.36	5
NESHOBA	TP6-3	24-Mar-55	5.55	3	PIKE	TS1-3	3-Apr-52	4.01	2
NEWTON	PB12-6	7-Sep-57	4.17	2	PIKE	TP6-3	24-Mar-55	5.55	3
NEWTON	TP6-3	24-Mar-55	5.55	3	PIKE	UK7-3	27-Apr-53	5.62	3
NEWTON	PB17-5	2-Oct-57	8.48	3	PIKE	TS6-4	28-May-52	15.43	4
NEWTON	TS6-4	28-May-52	10.61	4	PIKE	PB3-3	26-Jun-57	68.82	6
NEWTON	UK7-4	28-Apr-53	14.65	4	PIKE	UK7-4	28-Apr-53	31.54	5
NEWTON	PB3-3	26-Jun-57	22.97	4	PONTOTOC	UK3-6	5-Apr-53	3.67	2
NOXUBEE	TP6-3	24-Mar-55	5.55	3	PONTOTOC	UK9-3	21-May-53	4.74	2
NOXUBEE	PB17-5	2-Oct-57	5.88	3	PONTOTOC	TS1-3	3-Apr-52	6.02	3
OKTIBBEHA	UK2-3	26-Mar-53	4.37	2	PONTOTOC	TS5-1	7-May-52	6.44	3
OKTIBBEHA	PB2-5	22-Jun-57	4.64	2	PONTOTOC	PB12-6	7-Sep-57	6.80	3
OKTIBBEHA	TP6-3	24-Mar-55	5.55	3	PONTOTOC	PB17-5	2-Oct-57	7.26	3
OKTIBBEHA	PB12-6	7-Sep-57	6.42	3	PONTOTOC	UK2-7	30-Mar-53	12.19	4
OKTIBBEHA	PB17-5	2-Oct-57	6.73	3	PONTOTOC	UK2-8	31-Mar-53	14.03	4

INDIVIDUAL FALLOUT DAYS
MISSISSIPPI

COUNTY	SHOT	DATE	µCi/SQ METER	INDEX	COUNTY	SHOT	DATE	µCi/SQ METER	INDEX
PRENTISS	UK3-6	5-Apr-53	3.67	2	SIMPSON	PB3-3	26-Jun-57	11.44	4
PRENTISS	PB2-5	22-Jun-57	4.64	2	SMITH	UK7-4	28-Apr-53	3.79	2
PRENTISS	UK9-3	21-May-53	5.29	3	SMITH	PB17-5	2-Oct-57	3.84	2
PRENTISS	PB12-6	7-Sep-57	5.61	3	SMITH	TP6-3	24-Mar-55	5.55	3
PRENTISS	UK2-7	30-Mar-53	6.07	3	SMITH	PB3-3	26-Jun-57	22.97	4
PRENTISS	UK2-8	31-Mar-53	21.07	4	STONE	TP6-5	26-Mar-55	3.54	2
QUITMAN	UK3-6	5-Apr-53	3.67	2	STONE	TS6-4	28-May-52	15.43	4
QUITMAN	UK2-3	26-Mar-53	4.35	2	STONE	UK6-2	19-Apr-53	37.36	5
QUITMAN	TP11-6	20-May-55	4.62	2	STONE	PB3-3	26-Jun-57	45.85	5
QUITMAN	TP7-4	1-Apr-55	5.18	3	SUNFLOWER	UK7-3	27-Apr-53	3.84	2
QUITMAN	PB9-2	24-Aug-57	5.46	3	SUNFLOWER	PB2-5	22-Jun-57	4.64	2
QUITMAN	UK2-7	30-Mar-53	6.07	3	SUNFLOWER	PB12-6	7-Sep-57	4.74	2
QUITMAN	UK8-3	10-May-53	6.18	3	SUNFLOWER	PB17-5	2-Oct-57	5.53	3
QUITMAN	TS1-3	3-Apr-52	9.02	3	SUNFLOWER	TP6-3	24-Mar-55	5.55	3
QUITMAN	UK7-4	28-Apr-53	17.59	4	SUNFLOWER	UK7-4	28-Apr-53	22.51	4
QUITMAN	UK2-8	31-Mar-53	21.07	4	TALLAHATCHIE	UK3-6	5-Apr-53	3.67	2
RANKIN	UK7-4	28-Apr-53	4.50	2	TALLAHATCHIE	UK8-3	10-May-53	3.68	2
RANKIN	PB12-6	7-Sep-57	5.23	3	TALLAHATCHIE	TP11-6	20-May-55	4.62	2
RANKIN	TP6-3	24-Mar-55	5.55	3	TALLAHATCHIE	UK2-8	31-Mar-53	7.04	3
RANKIN	PB3-3	26-Jun-57	11.44	4	TALLAHATCHIE	PB9-2	24-Aug-57	8.19	3
SCOTT	UK7-4	28-Apr-53	3.97	2	TALLAHATCHIE	TS1-3	3-Apr-52	9.02	3
SCOTT	TP6-4	25-Mar-55	3.99	2	TALLAHATCHIE	UK2-7	30-Mar-53	12.19	4
SCOTT	TP6-3	24-Mar-55	5.55	3	TALLAHATCHIE	UK7-4	28-Apr-53	16.84	4
SCOTT	PB17-5	2-Oct-57	8.30	3	TATE	UK1-2	18-Mar-53	3.58	2
SCOTT	PB3-3	26-Jun-57	22.97	4	TATE	UK3-6	5-Apr-53	3.67	2
SHARKEY	PB11-2	1-Sep-57	4.26	2	TATE	UK9-3	21-May-53	3.76	2
SHARKEY	UK7-3	27-Apr-53	5.51	3	TATE	TS7-5	5-Jun-52	3.93	2
SHARKEY	TP6-3	24-Mar-55	5.55	3	TATE	PB8-3	20-Aug-57	4.00	2
SHARKEY	PB12-6	7-Sep-57	8.91	3	TATE	UK8-3	10-May-53	6.18	3
SHARKEY	UK7-4	28-Apr-53	33.73	5	TATE	TS1-3	3-Apr-52	9.02	3
SIMPSON	UK7-4	28-Apr-53	4.09	2	TATE	UK7-4	28-Apr-53	9.95	3
SIMPSON	PB17-5	2-Oct-57	4.42	2	TATE	UK2-7	30-Mar-53	12.19	4
SIMPSON	TP6-3	24-Mar-55	5.55	3	TATE	UK2-8	31-Mar-53	14.03	4

INDIVIDUAL FALLOUT DAYS
MISSISSIPPI

COUNTY	SHOT	DATE	µCi/SQ METER	INDEX	COUNTY	SHOT	DATE	µCi/SQ METER	INDEX
TIPPAH	UK3-6	5-Apr-53	3.67	2	WALTHALL	UK7-4	28-Apr-53	22.72	4
TIPPAH	UK8-3	10-May-53	3.68	2	WALTHALL	PB3-3	26-Jun-57	22.97	4
TIPPAH	UK9-3	21-May-53	4.91	2	WALTHALL	UK6-2	19-Apr-53	37.36	5
TIPPAH	UK2-3	26-Mar-53	5.05	3	WARREN	UK7-3	27-Apr-53	5.49	3
TIPPAH	PB12-6	7-Sep-57	6.52	3	WARREN	TP6-3	24-Mar-55	5.55	3
TIPPAH	TS1-3	3-Apr-52	9.02	3	WARREN	TS6-4	28-May-52	16.39	4
TIPPAH	UK2-7	30-Mar-53	12.19	4	WARREN	UK7-4	28-Apr-53	47.26	5
TIPPAH	UK2-8	31-Mar-53	21.07	4	WARREN	PB3-3	26-Jun-57	114.67	7
TISHOMINGO	UK3-6	5-Apr-53	3.67	2	WASHINGTON	PB12-6	7-Sep-57	4.63	2
TISHOMINGO	UK1-3	19-Mar-53	3.68	2	WASHINGTON	UK7-3	27-Apr-53	4.76	2
TISHOMINGO	TS5-1	7-May-52	4.35	2	WASHINGTON	TP6-3	24-Mar-55	5.55	3
TISHOMINGO	PB12-6	7-Sep-57	5.02	3	WASHINGTON	UK7-4	28-Apr-53	29.78	5
TISHOMINGO	UK9-3	21-May-53	5.17	3	WAYNE	TP6-5	26-Mar-55	3.54	2
TISHOMINGO	TS1-3	3-Apr-52	6.02	3	WAYNE	TP6-3	24-Mar-55	5.55	3
TISHOMINGO	UK2-8	31-Mar-53	21.07	4	WAYNE	PB3-3	26-Jun-57	45.85	5
TUNICA	UK3-6	5-Apr-53	3.67	2	WEBSTER	TP6-4	25-Mar-55	3.99	2
TUNICA	UK8-3	10-May-53	3.68	2	WEBSTER	PB2-5	22-Jun-57	4.64	2
TUNICA	PB8-3	20-Aug-57	4.00	2	WEBSTER	TS5-1	7-May-52	4.65	2
TUNICA	UK1-2	18-Mar-53	4.30	2	WEBSTER	TP6-3	24-Mar-55	5.55	3
TUNICA	TS7-6	6-Jun-52	5.42	3	WEBSTER	PB17-5	2-Oct-57	7.88	3
TUNICA	TP11-6	20-May-55	8.47	3	WEBSTER	PB12-6	7-Sep-57	16.10	4
TUNICA	TS1-3	3-Apr-52	9.02	3	WILKINSON	TS1-3	3-Apr-52	4.01	2
TUNICA	UK7-4	28-Apr-53	10.17	4	WILKINSON	TP6-3	24-Mar-55	5.55	3
TUNICA	UK2-7	30-Mar-53	12.19	4	WILKINSON	UK7-3	27-Apr-53	6.19	3
TUNICA	UK2-8	31-Mar-53	3.50	1	WILKINSON	UK7-4	28-Apr-53	29.72	5
UNION	UK3-6	5-Apr-53	3.67	2	WILKINSON	PB3-3	26-Jun-57	114.67	7
UNION	UK9-3	21-May-53	4.50	2	WINSTON	UK2-3	26-Mar-53	3.54	2
UNION	PB2-5	22-Jun-57	4.64	2	WINSTON	PB12-6	7-Sep-57	3.75	2
UNION	TS5-2	8-May-52	4.80	2	WINSTON	TP11-6	20-May-55	4.16	2
UNION	TS1-3	3-Apr-52	9.02	3	WINSTON	BJ2-4	2-Nov-51	4.38	2
UNION	UK2-7	30-Mar-53	12.19	4	WINSTON	TP6-3	24-Mar-55	5.55	3
UNION	UK2-8	31-Mar-53	14.03	4	WINSTON	TS6-4	28-May-52	18.32	4
WALTHALL	UK7-3	27-Apr-53	4.36	2	YALOBUSHA	PB17-5	2-Oct-57	3.58	2

INDIVIDUAL FALLOUT DAYS
MISSISSIPPI

COUNTY	SHOT	DATE	µCi/SQ METER	INDEX	COUNTY	SHOT	DATE	µCi/SQ METER	INDEX
YALOBUSHA	UK2-3	26-Mar-53	3.59	2	YALOBUSHA	UK7-4	28-Apr-53	14.92	4
YALOBUSHA	UK3-6	5-Apr-53	3.67	2	YAZOO	UK7-3	27-Apr-53	4.34	2
YALOBUSHA	UK8-3	10-May-53	3.68	2	YAZOO	TS6-4	28-May-52	4.83	2
YALOBUSHA	PB12-6	7-Sep-57	4.49	2	YAZOO	PB17-5	2-Oct-57	5.27	3
YALOBUSHA	PB2-5	22-Jun-57	4.64	2	YAZOO	PB12-6	7-Sep-57	9.19	3
YALOBUSHA	TS1-3	3-Apr-52	9.02	3	YAZOO	TP6-3	24-Mar-55	11.09	4
YALOBUSHA	UK2-7	30-Mar-53	12.19	4	YAZOO	UK7-4	28-Apr-53	29.48	5
YALOBUSHA	UK2-8	31-Mar-53	14.03	4					

U.S. FALLOUT ATLAS: COUNTY COMPARISONS

INDIVIDUAL FALLOUT DAYS
MONTANA

COUNTY	SHOT	DATE	µCi/SQ METER	INDEX	COUNTY	SHOT	DATE	µCi/SQ METER	INDEX
BEAVERHEAD	PB17-5	2-Oct-57	4.98	2	BLAINE	TS8-2	6-Jun-52	33.69	5
BEAVERHEAD	PB15-3	18-Sep-57	5.34	3	BLAINE	TS8-1	5-Jun-52	5850.58	10
BEAVERHEAD	UK8-2	9-May-53	5.46	3	BROADWATER	PB17-6	3-Oct-57	4.26	2
BEAVERHEAD	PB16-3	25-Sep-57	7.58	3	BROADWATER	PB6-2	25-Jul-57	7.94	3
BEAVERHEAD	TS5-1	7-May-52	11.32	4	BROADWATER	TS8-3	7-Jun-52	14.70	4
BEAVERHEAD	TS8-3	7-Jun-52	15.96	4	BROADWATER	PB6-3	26-Jul-57	24.56	4
BEAVERHEAD	PB6-2	25-Jul-57	21.00	4	BROADWATER	TS7-3	3-Jun-52	33.91	5
BEAVERHEAD	PB6-3	26-Jul-57	24.56	4	BROADWATER	TS8-2	6-Jun-52	113.84	7
BEAVERHEAD	TS8-2	6-Jun-52	137.67	7	BROADWATER	TS8-1	5-Jun-52	19771.47	10
BEAVERHEAD	TS8-1	5-Jun-52	23909.68	10	CARBON	PB9-3	25-Aug-57	4.49	2
BIG HORN	PB9-4	26-Aug-57	3.68	2	CARBON	PB6-4	27-Jul-57	4.76	2
BIG HORN	PB17-6	3-Oct-57	3.82	2	CARBON	TS8-3	7-Jun-52	4.85	2
BIG HORN	PB6-4	27-Jul-57	4.76	2	CARBON	UK8-3	10-May-53	5.26	3
BIG HORN	PB5-3	17-Jul-57	5.09	3	CARBON	TP11-2	16-May-55	8.69	3
BIG HORN	PB15-2	17-Sep-57	5.14	3	CARBON	TS5-1	7-May-52	10.47	4
BIG HORN	UK2-2	25-Mar-53	5.17	3	CARBON	PB6-2	25-Jul-57	11.91	4
BIG HORN	UK7-4	28-Apr-53	7.27	3	CARBON	UK8-2	9-May-53	16.38	4
BIG HORN	TS8-3	7-Jun-52	7.87	3	CARBON	TS8-2	6-Jun-52	16.43	4
BIG HORN	UK8-3	10-May-53	7.89	3	CARBON	PB17-6	3-Oct-57	3.50	1
BIG HORN	PB6-2	25-Jul-57	7.94	3	CARBON	PB8-2	19-Aug-57	29.82	5
BIG HORN	TP11-2	16-May-55	8.69	3	CARBON	TS8-1	5-Jun-52	2853.94	10
BIG HORN	TS5-1	7-May-52	13.79	4	CARTER	UK8-1	8-May-53	4.73	2
BIG HORN	UK8-2	9-May-53	32.75	5	CARTER	PB5-2	16-Jul-57	4.90	2
BIG HORN	TS8-1	5-Jun-52	332.35	8	CARTER	PB5-3	17-Jul-57	5.09	3
BLAINE	UK10-7	31-May-53	4.13	2	CARTER	PB9-4	26-Aug-57	5.22	3
BLAINE	TP11-2	16-May-55	4.34	2	CARTER	TS8-3	7-Jun-52	5.95	3
BLAINE	PB6-4	27-Jul-57	4.43	2	CARTER	PB11-2	1-Sep-57	6.81	3
BLAINE	PB15-2	17-Sep-57	5.14	3	CARTER	PB6-5	28-Jul-57	7.20	3
BLAINE	TS7-3	3-Jun-52	6.08	3	CARTER	PB8-4	21-Aug-57	8.05	3
BLAINE	TS8-3	7-Jun-52	6.44	3	CARTER	TS7-3	3-Jun-52	10.60	4
BLAINE	PB6-2	25-Jul-57	7.94	3	CARTER	UK7-4	28-Apr-53	15.30	4
BLAINE	PB8-2	19-Aug-57	29.82	5	CARTER	TS5-1	7-May-52	18.50	4
BLAINE	UK8-2	9-May-53	32.75	5	CARTER	TS8-1	5-Jun-52	66.47	6

INDIVIDUAL FALLOUT DAYS
MONTANA

COUNTY	SHOT	DATE	µCi/SQ METER	INDEX	COUNTY	SHOT	DATE	µCi/SQ METER	INDEX
CARTER	PB8-3	20-Aug-57	39.46	5	DANIELS	PB6-2	25-Jul-57	7.94	3
CARTER	UK2-2	25-Mar-53	45.45	5	DANIELS	UK8-1	8-May-53	17.76	4
CASCADE	PB17-5	2-Oct-57	3.79	2	DANIELS	PB8-3	20-Aug-57	19.73	4
CASCADE	PB15-2	17-Sep-57	5.14	3	DANIELS	UK2-2	25-Mar-53	61.09	6
CASCADE	TS8-3	7-Jun-52	8.78	3	DANIELS	TS8-1	5-Jun-52	332.35	8
CASCADE	PB6-2	25-Jul-57	11.91	4	DAWSON	PB15-2	17-Sep-57	5.14	3
CASCADE	PB6-3	26-Jul-57	24.56	4	DAWSON	UK8-2	9-May-53	5.46	3
CASCADE	TS8-2	6-Jun-52	45.60	5	DAWSON	TS8-3	7-Jun-52	9.00	3
CASCADE	TS8-1	5-Jun-52	7920.56	10	DAWSON	PB12-2	3-Sep-57	9.03	3
CHOUTEAU	TS8-4	8-Jun-52	4.21	2	DAWSON	UK7-4	28-Apr-53	11.99	4
CHOUTEAU	PB5-2	16-Jul-57	4.67	2	DAWSON	PB11-4	3-Sep-57	15.54	4
CHOUTEAU	PB17-6	3-Oct-57	4.76	2	DAWSON	PB5-2	16-Jul-57	19.36	4
CHOUTEAU	PB15-2	17-Sep-57	5.14	3	DAWSON	PB8-3	20-Aug-57	19.73	4
CHOUTEAU	PB12-2	3-Sep-57	6.02	3	DAWSON	UK8-1	8-May-53	53.66	6
CHOUTEAU	PB6-2	25-Jul-57	7.94	3	DAWSON	UK2-2	25-Mar-53	122.17	7
CHOUTEAU	TS8-3	7-Jun-52	11.90	4	DAWSON	TS8-1	5-Jun-52	279.17	8
CHOUTEAU	PB6-3	26-Jul-57	18.45	4	DEER LODGE	UK8-2	9-May-53	3.64	2
CHOUTEAU	TS8-2	6-Jun-52	145.15	7	DEER LODGE	TS8-7	11-Jun-52	5.07	3
CHOUTEAU	TS8-1	5-Jun-52	25209.81	10	DEER LODGE	TS5-1	7-May-52	6.11	3
CUSTER	UK8-2	9-May-53	5.46	3	DEER LODGE	PB16-3	25-Sep-57	7.58	3
CUSTER	PB12-2	3-Sep-57	6.02	3	DEER LODGE	TS8-3	7-Jun-52	7.76	3
CUSTER	PB9-4	26-Aug-57	7.36	3	DEER LODGE	PB17-5	2-Oct-57	9.12	3
CUSTER	PB6-2	25-Jul-57	7.94	3	DEER LODGE	PB6-3	26-Jul-57	12.28	4
CUSTER	TS8-3	7-Jun-52	11.56	4	DEER LODGE	PB6-2	25-Jul-57	21.00	4
CUSTER	UK7-4	28-Apr-53	14.09	4	DEER LODGE	TS8-2	6-Jun-52	221.29	8
CUSTER	TS5-1	7-May-52	15.21	4	DEER LODGE	TS8-1	5-Jun-52	38433.07	10
CUSTER	UK8-1	8-May-53	89.57	6	FALLON	PB8-5	22-Aug-57	3.78	2
CUSTER	UK2-2	25-Mar-53	122.17	7	FALLON	PB11-4	3-Sep-57	5.18	3
CUSTER	TS8-1	5-Jun-52	159.53	7	FALLON	UK8-2	9-May-53	5.46	3
DANIELS	PB11-4	3-Sep-57	5.18	3	FALLON	TS8-3	7-Jun-52	5.79	3
DANIELS	UK7-4	28-Apr-53	5.23	3	FALLON	TS5-1	7-May-52	9.52	3
DANIELS	UK8-2	9-May-53	5.46	3	FALLON	PB5-2	16-Jul-57	9.68	3
DANIELS	TS8-3	7-Jun-52	6.72	3	FALLON	PB5-3	17-Jul-57	10.10	4

INDIVIDUAL FALLOUT DAYS
MONTANA

COUNTY	SHOT	DATE	µCi/SQ METER	INDEX	COUNTY	SHOT	DATE	µCi/SQ METER	INDEX
FALLON	UK7-4	28-Apr-53	10.97	4	GARFIELD	PB9-4	26-Aug-57	3.68	2
FALLON	UK8-1	8-May-53	53.66	6	GARFIELD	TS8-2	6-Jun-52	4.67	2
FALLON	UK2-2	25-Mar-53	61.09	6	GARFIELD	PB6-4	27-Jul-57	4.96	2
FALLON	TS8-1	5-Jun-52	26.59	5	GARFIELD	PB15-2	17-Sep-57	5.14	3
FALLON	PB8-3	20-Aug-57	39.46	5	GARFIELD	UK2-2	25-Mar-53	5.17	3
FERGUS	PB9-2	24-Aug-57	3.60	2	GARFIELD	PB6-2	25-Jul-57	7.94	3
FERGUS	UK10-7	31-May-53	4.13	2	GARFIELD	UK10-7	31-May-53	8.26	3
FERGUS	TP11-2	16-May-55	4.34	2	GARFIELD	UK7-4	28-Apr-53	9.76	3
FERGUS	PB15-2	17-Sep-57	5.14	3	GARFIELD	TS8-3	7-Jun-52	10.02	4
FERGUS	UK8-3	10-May-53	5.26	3	GARFIELD	TP11-2	16-May-55	13.03	4
FERGUS	PB6-4	27-Jul-57	6.10	3	GARFIELD	UK8-2	9-May-53	49.13	5
FERGUS	PB6-2	25-Jul-57	15.87	4	GARFIELD	TS8-1	5-Jun-52	810.92	10
FERGUS	TS8-3	7-Jun-52	18.32	4	GLACIER	TS8-3	7-Jun-52	3.85	2
FERGUS	PB8-2	19-Aug-57	29.82	5	GLACIER	TS8-7	11-Jun-52	4.53	2
FERGUS	UK8-2	9-May-53	32.75	5	GLACIER	PB5-2	16-Jul-57	4.67	2
FERGUS	TS8-2	6-Jun-52	40.62	5	GLACIER	PB15-2	17-Sep-57	5.14	3
FERGUS	TS8-1	5-Jun-52	7055.58	10	GLACIER	PB6-2	25-Jul-57	7.94	3
FLATHEAD	PB17-5	2-Oct-57	3.85	2	GLACIER	PB6-3	26-Jul-57	12.28	4
FLATHEAD	TS8-3	7-Jun-52	3.96	2	GLACIER	TS8-2	6-Jun-52	20.28	4
FLATHEAD	PB16-3	25-Sep-57	7.58	3	GLACIER	TS8-1	5-Jun-52	3522.87	10
FLATHEAD	PB6-2	25-Jul-57	10.55	4	GOLDEN VALLE	TS8-2	6-Jun-52	3.83	2
FLATHEAD	PB6-3	26-Jul-57	12.28	4	GOLDEN VALLE	TP11-2	16-May-55	4.34	2
FLATHEAD	TS8-2	6-Jun-52	56.51	6	GOLDEN VALLE	PB2-3	20-Jun-57	4.44	2
FLATHEAD	TS8-1	5-Jun-52	9814.39	10	GOLDEN VALLE	UK8-3	10-May-53	5.26	3
GALLATIN	TS7-4	4-Jun-52	4.32	2	GOLDEN VALLE	PB17-6	3-Oct-57	5.92	3
GALLATIN	PB17-5	2-Oct-57	5.53	3	GOLDEN VALLE	PB6-4	27-Jul-57	6.18	3
GALLATIN	TS7-3	3-Jun-52	6.78	3	GOLDEN VALLE	TS8-3	7-Jun-52	6.38	3
GALLATIN	TS8-3	7-Jun-52	15.09	4	GOLDEN VALLE	TS5-1	7-May-52	14.39	4
GALLATIN	PB6-2	25-Jul-57	15.87	4	GOLDEN VALLE	PB6-2	25-Jul-57	15.87	4
GALLATIN	TS5-1	7-May-52	20.30	4	GOLDEN VALLE	UK8-2	9-May-53	16.38	4
GALLATIN	TS8-2	6-Jun-52	72.30	6	GOLDEN VALLE	PB8-2	19-Aug-57	29.82	5
GALLATIN	PB8-2	19-Aug-57	29.82	5	GOLDEN VALLE	TS8-1	5-Jun-52	664.69	9
GALLATIN	TS8-1	5-Jun-52	12557.34	10	GRANITE	UK8-2	9-May-53	3.64	2

INDIVIDUAL FALLOUT DAYS
MONTANA

COUNTY	SHOT	DATE	µCi/SQ METER	INDEX	COUNTY	SHOT	DATE	µCi/SQ METER	INDEX
GRANITE	PB15-3	18-Sep-57	5.34	3	LAKE	TS8-3	7-Jun-52	3.52	2
GRANITE	TS8-3	7-Jun-52	6.66	3	LAKE	PB17-5	2-Oct-57	4.62	2
GRANITE	PB16-3	25-Sep-57	7.58	3	LAKE	PB16-3	25-Sep-57	7.58	3
GRANITE	PB17-5	2-Oct-57	7.69	3	LAKE	PB6-3	26-Jul-57	12.28	4
GRANITE	TS5-1	7-May-52	9.43	3	LAKE	PB6-2	25-Jul-57	15.78	4
GRANITE	TS6-4	28-May-52	17.36	4	LAKE	TS8-2	6-Jun-52	38.81	5
GRANITE	PB6-2	25-Jul-57	21.00	4	LAKE	TS8-1	5-Jun-52	6739.98	10
GRANITE	PB6-3	26-Jul-57	24.56	4	LEWIS AND CL	PB17-5	2-Oct-57	3.52	2
GRANITE	TS8-2	6-Jun-52	40.34	5	LEWIS AND CL	TS8-4	8-Jun-52	3.95	2
GRANITE	TS8-1	5-Jun-52	7005.85	10	LEWIS AND CL	PB15-2	17-Sep-57	5.14	3
HILL	PB15-2	17-Sep-57	5.14	3	LEWIS AND CL	TS5-1	7-May-52	5.21	3
HILL	PB6-2	25-Jul-57	7.94	3	LEWIS AND CL	TS8-3	7-Jun-52	10.24	4
HILL	TS8-3	7-Jun-52	9.64	3	LEWIS AND CL	PB6-2	25-Jul-57	15.87	4
HILL	PB6-3	26-Jul-57	12.28	4	LEWIS AND CL	PB6-3	26-Jul-57	18.45	4
HILL	TS8-2	6-Jun-52	60.53	6	LEWIS AND CL	TS8-2	6-Jun-52	69.04	6
HILL	TS8-1	5-Jun-52	10512.02	10	LEWIS AND CL	TS8-1	5-Jun-52	11991.04	10
JEFFERSON	PB1-6	2-Jun-57	3.87	2	LIBERTY	TS8-4	8-Jun-52	4.12	2
JEFFERSON	PB17-5	2-Oct-57	4.10	2	LIBERTY	PB15-2	17-Sep-57	5.14	3
JEFFERSON	PB15-2	17-Sep-57	5.14	3	LIBERTY	PB12-2	3-Sep-57	6.02	3
JEFFERSON	TS5-1	7-May-52	6.29	3	LIBERTY	TS8-3	7-Jun-52	7.03	3
JEFFERSON	PB6-3	26-Jul-57	12.28	4	LIBERTY	PB6-2	25-Jul-57	7.94	3
JEFFERSON	TS8-3	7-Jun-52	15.31	4	LIBERTY	PB6-3	26-Jul-57	12.28	4
JEFFERSON	PB6-2	25-Jul-57	15.87	4	LIBERTY	TS8-2	6-Jun-52	45.16	5
JEFFERSON	TS7-3	3-Jun-52	27.06	5	LIBERTY	TS8-1	5-Jun-52	7843.37	10
JEFFERSON	TS8-2	6-Jun-52	124.25	7	LINCOLN	PB16-3	25-Sep-57	7.58	3
JEFFERSON	TS8-1	5-Jun-52	21578.97	10	LINCOLN	PB6-2	25-Jul-57	10.55	4
JUDITH BASIN	TS8-4	8-Jun-52	3.73	2	LINCOLN	PB6-3	26-Jul-57	12.28	4
JUDITH BASIN	PB6-4	27-Jul-57	4.12	2	LINCOLN	TS8-2	6-Jun-52	26.84	5
JUDITH BASIN	PB6-2	25-Jul-57	15.87	4	LINCOLN	TS8-1	5-Jun-52	4661.44	10
JUDITH BASIN	TS8-3	7-Jun-52	19.22	4	MADISON	UK8-2	9-May-53	3.64	2
JUDITH BASIN	PB8-2	19-Aug-57	44.80	5	MADISON	TS6-4	28-May-52	5.64	3
JUDITH BASIN	TS8-2	6-Jun-52	128.08	7	MADISON	TS5-1	7-May-52	12.57	4
JUDITH BASIN	TS8-1	5-Jun-52	22244.89	10	MADISON	TS7-3	3-Jun-52	13.78	4

INDIVIDUAL FALLOUT DAYS
MONTANA

COUNTY	SHOT	DATE	µCi/SQ METER	INDEX	COUNTY	SHOT	DATE	µCi/SQ METER	INDEX
MADISON	PB6-2	25-Jul-57	15.87	4	MISSOULA	TS5-1	7-May-52	4.71	2
MADISON	TS8-3	7-Jun-52	18.91	4	MISSOULA	PB17-5	2-Oct-57	5.71	3
MADISON	TS8-2	6-Jun-52	92.11	6	MISSOULA	PB16-3	25-Sep-57	7.58	3
MADISON	PB8-2	19-Aug-57	29.82	5	MISSOULA	PB6-3	26-Jul-57	12.28	4
MADISON	TS8-1	5-Jun-52	15997.93	10	MISSOULA	PB6-2	25-Jul-57	15.78	4
MCCONE	PB5-2	16-Jul-57	4.67	2	MISSOULA	TS8-2	6-Jun-52	101.06	7
MCCONE	PB15-2	17-Sep-57	5.14	3	MISSOULA	TS8-1	5-Jun-52	17551.74	10
MCCONE	PB12-2	3-Sep-57	6.02	3	MUSSELSHELL	PB9-4	26-Aug-57	3.68	2
MCCONE	UK8-2	9-May-53	9.10	3	MUSSELSHELL	UK7-4	28-Apr-53	4.50	2
MCCONE	UK7-4	28-Apr-53	10.90	4	MUSSELSHELL	TS8-3	7-Jun-52	4.97	2
MCCONE	TS8-3	7-Jun-52	11.34	4	MUSSELSHELL	UK2-2	25-Mar-53	5.17	3
MCCONE	PB6-2	25-Jul-57	15.87	4	MUSSELSHELL	UK8-3	10-May-53	5.26	3
MCCONE	PB8-3	20-Aug-57	19.73	4	MUSSELSHELL	PB6-4	27-Jul-57	7.32	3
MCCONE	UK8-1	8-May-53	53.66	6	MUSSELSHELL	PB6-2	25-Jul-57	7.94	3
MCCONE	UK2-2	25-Mar-53	61.09	6	MUSSELSHELL	TP11-2	16-May-55	8.69	3
MCCONE	TS8-1	5-Jun-52	172.82	7	MUSSELSHELL	TS5-1	7-May-52	11.54	4
MEAGHER	PB17-6	3-Oct-57	4.20	2	MUSSELSHELL	UK8-2	9-May-53	32.75	5
MEAGHER	TS5-1	7-May-52	8.54	3	MUSSELSHELL	TS8-1	5-Jun-52	398.82	8
MEAGHER	TS8-3	7-Jun-52	11.35	4	PARK	PB4-2	6-Jul-57	5.26	3
MEAGHER	PB6-2	25-Jul-57	15.87	4	PARK	PB17-5	2-Oct-57	5.90	3
MEAGHER	TS7-3	3-Jun-52	96.81	6	PARK	TS7-4	4-Jun-52	6.62	3
MEAGHER	TS8-2	6-Jun-52	98.78	6	PARK	TS8-3	7-Jun-52	10.15	4
MEAGHER	PB8-2	19-Aug-57	29.82	5	PARK	PB6-2	25-Jul-57	15.87	4
MEAGHER	TS8-1	5-Jun-52	17155.36	10	PARK	TS5-1	7-May-52	25.87	5
MINERAL	PB17-5	2-Oct-57	4.23	2	PARK	PB8-2	19-Aug-57	29.82	5
MINERAL	PB16-3	25-Sep-57	7.58	3	PARK	TS8-2	6-Jun-52	48.93	5
MINERAL	BJ5-3	21-Nov-51	9.82	3	PARK	TS8-1	5-Jun-52	8498.40	10
MINERAL	BJ5-2	20-Nov-51	9.86	3	PETROLEUM	PB15-2	17-Sep-57	5.14	3
MINERAL	PB6-2	25-Jul-57	10.55	4	PETROLEUM	UK8-3	10-May-53	5.26	3
MINERAL	PB6-3	26-Jul-57	12.28	4	PETROLEUM	UK7-4	28-Apr-53	5.74	3
MINERAL	TS8-2	6-Jun-52	73.95	6	PETROLEUM	PB12-2	3-Sep-57	6.02	3
MINERAL	TS8-1	5-Jun-52	12842.74	10	PETROLEUM	PB6-4	27-Jul-57	7.11	3
MISSOULA	TS8-3	7-Jun-52	4.68	2	PETROLEUM	PB9-4	26-Aug-57	7.36	3

INDIVIDUAL FALLOUT DAYS
MONTANA

COUNTY	SHOT	DATE	µCi/SQ METER	INDEX	COUNTY	SHOT	DATE	µCi/SQ METER	INDEX
PETROLEUM	PB6-2	25-Jul-57	7.94	3	POWDER RIVER	TS7-3	3-Jun-52	9.11	3
PETROLEUM	UK10-7	31-May-53	8.26	3	POWDER RIVER	UK7-4	28-Apr-53	13.45	4
PETROLEUM	TP11-2	16-May-55	8.69	3	POWDER RIVER	TP11-2	16-May-55	20.60	4
PETROLEUM	TS8-3	7-Jun-52	10.30	4	POWDER RIVER	TS5-1	7-May-52	22.81	4
PETROLEUM	TS8-2	6-Jun-52	10.49	4	POWDER RIVER	UK2-2	25-Mar-53	23.57	4
PETROLEUM	UK8-2	9-May-53	32.75	5	POWDER RIVER	TS8-1	5-Jun-52	39.88	5
PETROLEUM	TS8-1	5-Jun-52	1821.26	10	POWDER RIVER	UK2-1	24-Mar-53	170.07	7
PHILLIPS	UK7-4	28-Apr-53	3.89	2	POWELL	TS7-5	5-Jun-52	3.88	2
PHILLIPS	UK10-7	31-May-53	4.13	2	POWELL	TS5-1	7-May-52	3.95	2
PHILLIPS	TP11-2	16-May-55	4.34	2	POWELL	PB15-2	17-Sep-57	5.14	3
PHILLIPS	PB6-4	27-Jul-57	4.69	2	POWELL	UK8-2	9-May-53	7.28	3
PHILLIPS	PB15-2	17-Sep-57	5.14	3	POWELL	PB17-5	2-Oct-57	7.31	3
PHILLIPS	PB12-2	3-Sep-57	6.02	3	POWELL	TS8-3	7-Jun-52	11.23	4
PHILLIPS	PB6-2	25-Jul-57	7.94	3	POWELL	PB6-2	25-Jul-57	15.87	4
PHILLIPS	TS8-2	6-Jun-52	9.41	3	POWELL	PB6-3	26-Jul-57	24.56	4
PHILLIPS	TS8-3	7-Jun-52	11.69	4	POWELL	TS8-2	6-Jun-52	127.81	7
PHILLIPS	UK8-2	9-May-53	32.75	5	POWELL	TS8-1	5-Jun-52	22197.32	10
PHILLIPS	TS8-1	5-Jun-52	1635.14	10	PRAIRIE	TS5-1	7-May-52	4.85	2
PONDERA	TS8-4	8-Jun-52	4.21	2	PRAIRIE	PB15-2	17-Sep-57	5.14	3
PONDERA	PB5-2	16-Jul-57	4.67	2	PRAIRIE	UK8-2	9-May-53	5.46	3
PONDERA	PB15-2	17-Sep-57	5.14	3	PRAIRIE	PB6-2	25-Jul-57	7.94	3
PONDERA	TS8-3	7-Jun-52	6.11	3	PRAIRIE	UK7-4	28-Apr-53	13.45	4
PONDERA	PB6-2	25-Jul-57	7.94	3	PRAIRIE	TS8-3	7-Jun-52	13.66	4
PONDERA	PB6-3	26-Jul-57	12.28	4	PRAIRIE	PB8-3	20-Aug-57	19.73	4
PONDERA	TS8-2	6-Jun-52	31.54	5	PRAIRIE	UK8-1	8-May-53	53.66	6
PONDERA	TS8-1	5-Jun-52	5477.06	10	PRAIRIE	UK2-2	25-Mar-53	61.09	6
POWDER RIVER	UK11-2	5-Jun-53	3.70	2	PRAIRIE	TS8-1	5-Jun-52	172.82	7
POWDER RIVER	PB8-4	21-Aug-57	4.60	2	RAVALLI	UK8-2	9-May-53	3.64	2
POWDER RIVER	UK8-1	8-May-53	4.73	2	RAVALLI	TS8-3	7-Jun-52	5.45	3
POWDER RIVER	PB5-2	16-Jul-57	4.90	2	RAVALLI	PB17-5	2-Oct-57	6.13	3
POWDER RIVER	TS8-3	7-Jun-52	6.28	3	RAVALLI	PB16-3	25-Sep-57	7.58	3
POWDER RIVER	PB6-5	28-Jul-57	6.44	3	RAVALLI	TS5-1	7-May-52	10.07	4
POWDER RIVER	PB9-4	26-Aug-57	7.36	3	RAVALLI	PB6-3	26-Jul-57	12.28	4

INDIVIDUAL FALLOUT DAYS
MONTANA

COUNTY	SHOT	DATE	µCi/SQ METER	INDEX	COUNTY	SHOT	DATE	µCi/SQ METER	INDEX
RAVALLI	PB6-2	25-Jul-57	15.78	4	ROSEBUD	UK7-4	28-Apr-53	11.60	4
RAVALLI	TS8-2	6-Jun-52	48.99	5	ROSEBUD	TS5-1	7-May-52	12.39	4
RAVALLI	TS8-1	5-Jun-52	8508.06	10	ROSEBUD	TP11-2	16-May-55	13.03	4
RICHLAND	PB15-2	17-Sep-57	5.14	3	ROSEBUD	TS8-3	7-Jun-52	13.20	4
RICHLAND	PB9-4	26-Aug-57	5.22	3	ROSEBUD	UK8-2	9-May-53	32.75	5
RICHLAND	UK8-2	9-May-53	5.46	3	ROSEBUD	TS8-1	5-Jun-52	106.35	7
RICHLAND	UK7-4	28-Apr-53	7.91	3	SANDERS	PB16-3	25-Sep-57	7.58	3
RICHLAND	TS8-3	7-Jun-52	8.31	3	SANDERS	PB6-2	25-Jul-57	10.55	4
RICHLAND	PB12-2	3-Sep-57	9.03	3	SANDERS	PB6-3	26-Jul-57	12.28	4
RICHLAND	PB11-4	3-Sep-57	15.54	4	SANDERS	TS8-2	6-Jun-52	50.30	6
RICHLAND	PB5-2	16-Jul-57	19.36	4	SANDERS	TS8-1	5-Jun-52	8736.23	10
RICHLAND	PB8-3	20-Aug-57	19.73	4	SHERIDAN	UK7-4	28-Apr-53	3.74	2
RICHLAND	UK2-2	25-Mar-53	61.09	6	SHERIDAN	TS8-2	6-Jun-52	4.02	2
RICHLAND	TS8-1	5-Jun-52	66.47	6	SHERIDAN	PB6-5	28-Jul-57	4.64	2
RICHLAND	UK8-1	8-May-53	89.57	6	SHERIDAN	PB11-4	3-Sep-57	5.18	3
ROOSEVELT	TS8-2	6-Jun-52	4.47	2	SHERIDAN	UK8-2	9-May-53	5.46	3
ROOSEVELT	PB11-4	3-Sep-57	5.18	3	SHERIDAN	TS8-3	7-Jun-52	6.98	3
ROOSEVELT	UK8-2	9-May-53	5.46	3	SHERIDAN	PB5-2	16-Jul-57	9.68	3
ROOSEVELT	PB5-2	16-Jul-57	7.00	3	SHERIDAN	PB8-3	20-Aug-57	19.73	4
ROOSEVELT	PB6-2	25-Jul-57	7.94	3	SHERIDAN	UK8-1	8-May-53	53.66	6
ROOSEVELT	UK7-4	28-Apr-53	8.22	3	SHERIDAN	UK2-2	25-Mar-53	61.09	6
ROOSEVELT	TS8-3	7-Jun-52	9.33	3	SHERIDAN	TS8-1	5-Jun-52	697.63	9
ROOSEVELT	PB8-3	20-Aug-57	19.73	4	SILVER BOW	TS7-5	5-Jun-52	4.18	2
ROOSEVELT	UK8-1	8-May-53	53.66	6	SILVER BOW	PB15-2	17-Sep-57	5.14	3
ROOSEVELT	UK2-2	25-Mar-53	61.09	6	SILVER BOW	PB17-5	2-Oct-57	8.62	3
ROOSEVELT	TS8-1	5-Jun-52	776.91	9	SILVER BOW	TS8-3	7-Jun-52	10.02	4
ROSEBUD	PB9-4	26-Aug-57	3.68	2	SILVER BOW	TS5-1	7-May-52	11.14	4
ROSEBUD	PB6-4	27-Jul-57	4.82	2	SILVER BOW	PB6-3	26-Jul-57	12.28	4
ROSEBUD	PB15-2	17-Sep-57	5.14	3	SILVER BOW	PB6-2	25-Jul-57	15.87	4
ROSEBUD	UK2-2	25-Mar-53	5.17	3	SILVER BOW	TS8-2	6-Jun-52	129.36	7
ROSEBUD	UK8-3	10-May-53	5.26	3	SILVER BOW	TS8-1	5-Jun-52	22466.86	10
ROSEBUD	TS7-4	4-Jun-52	7.17	3	STILLWATER	PB17-6	3-Oct-57	3.75	2
ROSEBUD	PB6-2	25-Jul-57	7.94	3	STILLWATER	PB6-4	27-Jul-57	4.98	2

INDIVIDUAL FALLOUT DAYS
MONTANA

COUNTY	SHOT	DATE	µCi/SQ METER	INDEX	COUNTY	SHOT	DATE	µCi/SQ METER	INDEX
STILLWATER	TS8-2	6-Jun-52	5.13	3	TOOLE	PB15-2	17-Sep-57	5.14	3
STILLWATER	UK2-2	25-Mar-53	5.17	3	TOOLE	TS8-3	7-Jun-52	5.83	3
STILLWATER	UK8-3	10-May-53	5.26	3	TOOLE	PB12-2	3-Sep-57	6.02	3
STILLWATER	TS8-3	7-Jun-52	6.04	3	TOOLE	PB6-3	26-Jul-57	12.28	4
STILLWATER	TS5-1	7-May-52	14.83	4	TOOLE	PB6-2	25-Jul-57	15.87	4
STILLWATER	PB6-2	25-Jul-57	15.87	4	TOOLE	TS8-2	6-Jun-52	44.85	5
STILLWATER	UK8-2	9-May-53	16.38	4	TOOLE	TS8-1	5-Jun-52	7790.19	10
STILLWATER	PB8-2	19-Aug-57	29.82	5	TREASURE	PB2-3	20-Jun-57	4.44	2
STILLWATER	TS8-1	5-Jun-52	890.69	10	TREASURE	PB8-4	21-Aug-57	4.60	2
SWEET GRASS	PB2-3	20-Jun-57	4.44	2	TREASURE	TS8-3	7-Jun-52	4.73	2
SWEET GRASS	PB6-4	27-Jul-57	4.47	2	TREASURE	PB15-2	17-Sep-57	5.14	3
SWEET GRASS	TS8-2	6-Jun-52	4.67	2	TREASURE	UK2-2	25-Mar-53	5.17	3
SWEET GRASS	PB17-6	3-Oct-57	5.15	3	TREASURE	PB6-4	27-Jul-57	6.23	3
SWEET GRASS	UK2-2	25-Mar-53	5.17	3	TREASURE	UK8-3	10-May-53	7.89	3
SWEET GRASS	TS7-3	3-Jun-52	5.19	3	TREASURE	PB6-2	25-Jul-57	7.94	3
SWEET GRASS	UK8-2	9-May-53	8.29	3	TREASURE	UK7-4	28-Apr-53	8.55	3
SWEET GRASS	TS8-3	7-Jun-52	14.37	4	TREASURE	TP11-2	16-May-55	13.03	4
SWEET GRASS	PB6-2	25-Jul-57	15.87	4	TREASURE	TS5-1	7-May-52	13.29	4
SWEET GRASS	TS5-1	7-May-52	23.89	4	TREASURE	UK8-2	9-May-53	16.38	4
SWEET GRASS	PB8-2	19-Aug-57	29.82	5	TREASURE	TS8-1	5-Jun-52	146.23	7
SWEET GRASS	TS8-1	5-Jun-52	810.92	10	VALLEY	PB9-2	24-Aug-57	3.60	2
TETON	TS8-4	8-Jun-52	4.43	2	VALLEY	UK8-2	9-May-53	3.64	2
TETON	PB5-2	16-Jul-57	4.67	2	VALLEY	PB9-4	26-Aug-57	3.68	2
TETON	PB15-2	17-Sep-57	5.14	3	VALLEY	TS8-2	6-Jun-52	4.90	2
TETON	PB12-2	3-Sep-57	6.02	3	VALLEY	UK7-4	28-Apr-53	7.65	3
TETON	TS8-3	7-Jun-52	7.26	3	VALLEY	PB6-2	25-Jul-57	7.94	3
TETON	PB6-2	25-Jul-57	7.94	3	VALLEY	PB12-2	3-Sep-57	9.03	3
TETON	PB6-3	26-Jul-57	12.28	4	VALLEY	TS8-3	7-Jun-52	9.80	3
TETON	TS8-2	6-Jun-52	61.08	6	VALLEY	UK8-1	8-May-53	17.76	4
TETON	TS8-1	5-Jun-52	10608.48	10	VALLEY	UK2-2	25-Mar-53	61.09	6
TOOLE	PB9-2	24-Aug-57	3.60	2	VALLEY	TS8-1	5-Jun-52	850.81	10
TOOLE	TS8-4	8-Jun-52	4.08	2	WHEATLAND	PB17-5	2-Oct-57	3.73	2
TOOLE	PB5-2	16-Jul-57	4.67	2	WHEATLAND	PB2-3	20-Jun-57	4.44	2

INDIVIDUAL FALLOUT DAYS
MONTANA

COUNTY	SHOT	DATE	µCi/SQ METER	INDEX	COUNTY	SHOT	DATE	µCi/SQ METER	INDEX
WHEATLAND	PB6-4	27-Jul-57	5.22	3	WIBAUX	PB8-3	20-Aug-57	19.73	4
WHEATLAND	PB12-2	3-Sep-57	6.02	3	WIBAUX	UK8-1	8-May-53	53.66	6
WHEATLAND	TS8-3	7-Jun-52	7.81	3	WIBAUX	UK2-2	25-Mar-53	61.09	6
WHEATLAND	PB6-2	25-Jul-57	7.94	3	WIBAUX	PB11-4	3-Sep-57	25.90	5
WHEATLAND	UK10-7	31-May-53	8.26	3	WIBAUX	PB5-2	16-Jul-57	29.04	5
WHEATLAND	TS5-1	7-May-52	14.91	4	WIBAUX	TS8-1	5-Jun-52	39.88	5
WHEATLAND	UK8-2	9-May-53	16.38	4	YELLOWSTONE	TP11-2	16-May-55	3.61	2
WHEATLAND	TS8-2	6-Jun-52	83.62	6	YELLOWSTONE	PB9-4	26-Aug-57	3.68	2
WHEATLAND	PB8-2	19-Aug-57	29.82	5	YELLOWSTONE	PB17-6	3-Oct-57	3.76	2
WHEATLAND	TS8-1	5-Jun-52	14523.39	10	YELLOWSTONE	TS8-3	7-Jun-52	3.93	2
WIBAUX	PB6-5	28-Jul-57	3.85	2	YELLOWSTONE	UK7-4	28-Apr-53	4.57	2
WIBAUX	PB15-2	17-Sep-57	5.14	3	YELLOWSTONE	PB8-4	21-Aug-57	4.60	2
WIBAUX	TS8-3	7-Jun-52	5.33	3	YELLOWSTONE	PB6-4	27-Jul-57	5.65	3
WIBAUX	PB8-4	21-Aug-57	5.37	3	YELLOWSTONE	UK8-2	9-May-53	6.80	3
WIBAUX	UK8-2	9-May-53	5.46	3	YELLOWSTONE	TS5-1	7-May-52	9.85	3
WIBAUX	UK7-4	28-Apr-53	10.05	4	YELLOWSTONE	TS8-1	5-Jun-52	493.59	9
WIBAUX	PB12-2	3-Sep-57	15.05	4					

INDIVIDUAL FALLOUT DAYS
NORTH CAROLINA

COUNTY	SHOT	DATE	µCi/SQ METER	INDEX	COUNTY	SHOT	DATE	µCi/SQ METER	INDEX
ALAMANCE	UK9-4	22-May-53	4.71	2	AVERY	PB5-8	22-Jul-57	5.97	3
ALAMANCE	PB5-9	23-Jul-57	4.71	2	BEAUFORT	TS7-6	6-Jun-52	5.69	3
ALAMANCE	BJ2-2	31-Oct-51	6.42	3	BEAUFORT	TS3-4	25-Apr-52	6.78	3
ALAMANCE	PB5-8	22-Jul-57	8.96	3	BEAUFORT	BJ2-3	1-Nov-51	8.06	3
ALAMANCE	BJ2-3	1-Nov-51	10.30	4	BEAUFORT	BJ2-4	2-Nov-51	11.45	4
ALAMANCE	BJ2-4	2-Nov-51	12.69	4	BEAUFORT	BJ3-6	6-Nov-51	11.57	4
ALEXANDER	PB6-3	26-Jul-57	3.96	2	BEAUFORT	PB4-5	9-Jul-57	14.27	4
ALEXANDER	PB12-6	7-Sep-57	4.10	2	BEAUFORT	SE5	10-Jul-62	38.35	5
ALEXANDER	UK9-4	22-May-53	4.21	2	BERTIE	PB4-5	9-Jul-57	3.57	2
ALEXANDER	TS7-6	6-Jun-52	5.05	3	BERTIE	PB5-9	23-Jul-57	4.71	2
ALEXANDER	BJ2-3	1-Nov-51	5.25	3	BERTIE	BJ2-3	1-Nov-51	5.68	3
ALEXANDER	PB5-8	22-Jul-57	5.97	3	BERTIE	TS3-4	25-Apr-52	6.78	3
ALEXANDER	PB2-5	22-Jun-57	6.96	3	BERTIE	BJ2-4	2-Nov-51	9.85	3
ALLEGHANY	BJ2-2	31-Oct-51	3.89	2	BERTIE	BJ3-6	6-Nov-51	11.57	4
ALLEGHANY	BJ2-4	2-Nov-51	6.97	3	BLADEN	PB4-5	9-Jul-57	3.57	2
ALLEGHANY	SE4	9-Jul-62	17.11	4	BLADEN	PB5-9	23-Jul-57	4.71	2
ANSON	BJ2-3	1-Nov-51	8.47	3	BLADEN	BJ2-4	2-Nov-51	11.25	4
ANSON	BJ2-4	2-Nov-51	9.27	3	BLADEN	BJ2-3	1-Nov-51	11.77	4
ASHE	TP10-2	6-May-55	3.62	2	BRUNSWICK	PB4-5	9-Jul-57	3.57	2
ASHE	PB6-3	26-Jul-57	3.96	2	BRUNSWICK	BJ2-4	2-Nov-51	4.48	2
ASHE	BJ2-3	1-Nov-51	3.97	2	BRUNSWICK	TS5-1	7-May-52	8.35	3
ASHE	PB2-5	22-Jun-57	4.18	2	BRUNSWICK	BJ2-3	1-Nov-51	12.79	4
ASHE	PB4-5	9-Jul-57	5.24	3	BUNCOMBE	TP10-2	6-May-55	3.62	2
ASHE	PB5-8	22-Jul-57	5.97	3	BUNCOMBE	BJ2-2	31-Oct-51	3.89	2
ASHE	UK9-4	22-May-53	8.37	3	BUNCOMBE	PB6-3	26-Jul-57	3.96	2
ASHE	SE4	9-Jul-62	18.06	4	BUNCOMBE	PB2-5	22-Jun-57	4.18	2
AVERY	TP10-2	6-May-55	3.62	2	BUNCOMBE	TP6-4	25-Mar-55	4.32	2
AVERY	BJ2-2	31-Oct-51	3.89	2	BUNCOMBE	UK9-4	22-May-53	4.52	2
AVERY	UK9-4	22-May-53	3.90	2	BUNCOMBE	UK1-2	18-Mar-53	6.49	3
AVERY	PB6-3	26-Jul-57	3.96	2	BURKE	TP10-2	6-May-55	3.62	2
AVERY	TP6-4	25-Mar-55	4.32	2	BURKE	PB6-3	26-Jul-57	3.96	2
AVERY	UK1-2	18-Mar-53	4.55	2	BURKE	TS6-4	28-May-52	4.17	2
AVERY	TS5-2	8-May-52	5.36	3	BURKE	PB2-5	22-Jun-57	4.18	2

INDIVIDUAL FALLOUT DAYS
NORTH CAROLINA

COUNTY	SHOT	DATE	µCi/SQ METER	INDEX	COUNTY	SHOT	DATE	µCi/SQ METER	INDEX
BURKE	UK9-4	22-May-53	4.23	2	CATAWBA	PB2-5	22-Jun-57	4.18	2
BURKE	BJ2-3	1-Nov-51	4.61	2	CATAWBA	UK9-4	22-May-53	4.67	2
BURKE	TS7-6	6-Jun-52	4.82	2	CATAWBA	BJ2-3	1-Nov-51	5.88	3
BURKE	TS5-2	8-May-52	5.27	3	CATAWBA	BJ2-4	2-Nov-51	6.37	3
BURKE	PB5-8	22-Jul-57	5.97	3	CHATHAM	PB4-5	9-Jul-57	3.57	2
CABARRUS	UK9-5	23-May-53	4.07	2	CHATHAM	BJ2-2	31-Oct-51	3.89	2
CABARRUS	UK9-4	22-May-53	4.21	2	CHATHAM	PB5-9	23-Jul-57	4.71	2
CABARRUS	BJ2-4	2-Nov-51	4.93	2	CHATHAM	BJ2-3	1-Nov-51	10.20	4
CABARRUS	BJ2-3	1-Nov-51	7.72	3	CHATHAM	BJ2-4	2-Nov-51	11.21	4
CALDWELL	TP10-2	6-May-55	3.62	2	CHATHAM	SE4	9-Jul-62	43.75	5
CALDWELL	UK9-4	22-May-53	3.85	2	CHEROKEE	TP10-2	6-May-55	3.62	2
CALDWELL	BJ2-2	31-Oct-51	3.89	2	CHEROKEE	TP6-4	25-Mar-55	4.32	2
CALDWELL	PB6-3	26-Jul-57	3.96	2	CHEROKEE	TS7-6	6-Jun-52	4.85	2
CALDWELL	PB2-5	22-Jun-57	4.18	2	CHEROKEE	BJ3-6	6-Nov-51	8.10	3
CALDWELL	BJ2-3	1-Nov-51	4.35	2	CHEROKEE	UK1-2	18-Mar-53	10.40	4
CALDWELL	BJ2-4	2-Nov-51	6.57	3	CHEROKEE	PB17-3	30-Sep-57	14.98	4
CAMDEN	PB4-5	9-Jul-57	3.57	2	CHOWAN	PB4-5	9-Jul-57	3.57	2
CAMDEN	BJ2-3	1-Nov-51	3.58	2	CHOWAN	BJ2-3	1-Nov-51	4.61	2
CAMDEN	TS3-4	25-Apr-52	6.78	3	CHOWAN	TS3-4	25-Apr-52	6.78	3
CAMDEN	BJ2-4	2-Nov-51	7.03	3	CHOWAN	BJ2-4	2-Nov-51	9.27	3
CAMDEN	PB5-8	22-Jul-57	8.96	3	CHOWAN	BJ3-6	6-Nov-51	11.57	4
CAMDEN	BJ3-6	6-Nov-51	11.57	4	CHOWAN	PB5-8	22-Jul-57	14.93	4
CAMDEN	SE4	9-Jul-62	94.45	6	CHOWAN	SE5	10-Jul-62	38.35	5
CAMDEN	SE5	10-Jul-62	96.55	6	CHOWAN	SE4	9-Jul-62	45.80	5
CARTERET	TS3-4	25-Apr-52	4.52	2	CLAY	TP10-2	6-May-55	3.62	2
CARTERET	PB4-5	9-Jul-57	7.14	3	CLAY	UK9-4	22-May-53	3.64	2
CARTERET	BJ2-4	2-Nov-51	8.76	3	CLAY	PB2-5	22-Jun-57	4.18	2
CARTERET	BJ2-3	1-Nov-51	8.95	3	CLAY	TP10-8	12-May-55	4.27	2
CARTERET	BJ3-6	6-Nov-51	11.57	4	CLAY	TP6-4	25-Mar-55	4.32	2
CASWELL	BJ2-2	31-Oct-51	3.89	2	CLAY	TS7-6	6-Jun-52	7.33	3
CASWELL	BJ2-3	1-Nov-51	5.04	3	CLAY	UK1-2	18-Mar-53	12.47	4
CASWELL	BJ2-4	2-Nov-51	11.35	4	CLAY	PB17-3	30-Sep-57	22.47	4
CATAWBA	PB6-3	26-Jul-57	3.96	2	CLEVELAND	TP10-2	6-May-55	3.62	2

INDIVIDUAL FALLOUT DAYS
NORTH CAROLINA

COUNTY	SHOT	DATE	µCi/SQ METER	INDEX	COUNTY	SHOT	DATE	µCi/SQ METER	INDEX
CLEVELAND	PB6-3	26-Jul-57	3.96	2	DAVIE	BJ2-2	31-Oct-51	3.89	2
CLEVELAND	UK9-4	22-May-53	4.67	2	DAVIE	BJ2-4	2-Nov-51	6.97	3
CLEVELAND	BJ2-3	1-Nov-51	5.88	3	DAVIE	BJ2-3	1-Nov-51	7.80	3
CLEVELAND	BJ2-4	2-Nov-51	6.17	3	DUPLIN	PB4-5	9-Jul-57	3.57	2
COLUMBUS	PB4-5	9-Jul-57	3.57	2	DUPLIN	TS5-1	7-May-52	5.78	3
COLUMBUS	PB5-9	23-Jul-57	4.71	2	DUPLIN	TS3-4	25-Apr-52	6.78	3
COLUMBUS	BJ2-4	2-Nov-51	9.96	3	DUPLIN	BJ2-4	2-Nov-51	12.25	4
COLUMBUS	BJ2-3	1-Nov-51	13.18	4	DUPLIN	BJ2-3	1-Nov-51	12.41	4
CRAVEN	TS3-4	25-Apr-52	6.78	3	DURHAM	BJ2-2	31-Oct-51	3.89	2
CRAVEN	PB4-5	9-Jul-57	7.14	3	DURHAM	BJ2-4	2-Nov-51	4.69	2
CRAVEN	BJ2-3	1-Nov-51	8.44	3	DURHAM	PB5-8	22-Jul-57	8.96	3
CRAVEN	BJ2-4	2-Nov-51	22.00	4	DURHAM	BJ2-3	1-Nov-51	9.16	3
CUMBERLAND	PB5-9	23-Jul-57	4.71	2	DURHAM	SE4	9-Jul-62	21.81	4
CUMBERLAND	PB4-5	9-Jul-57	5.35	3	EDGECOMBE	PB4-5	9-Jul-57	3.57	2
CUMBERLAND	BJ2-4	2-Nov-51	9.61	3	EDGECOMBE	BJ2-3	1-Nov-51	6.08	3
CUMBERLAND	BJ2-3	1-Nov-51	12.23	4	EDGECOMBE	BJ2-4	2-Nov-51	11.02	4
CURRITUCK	PB4-5	9-Jul-57	3.57	2	FORSYTH	PB12-6	7-Sep-57	5.05	3
CURRITUCK	BJ2-3	1-Nov-51	4.50	2	FORSYTH	BJ2-2	31-Oct-51	6.42	3
CURRITUCK	TS3-4	25-Apr-52	6.78	3	FORSYTH	BJ2-4	2-Nov-51	7.67	3
CURRITUCK	BJ2-4	2-Nov-51	7.10	3	FORSYTH	BJ2-3	1-Nov-51	8.19	3
CURRITUCK	PB5-8	22-Jul-57	8.96	3	FRANKLIN	PB4-5	9-Jul-57	3.57	2
CURRITUCK	BJ3-6	6-Nov-51	11.57	4	FRANKLIN	PB5-9	23-Jul-57	4.71	2
CURRITUCK	SE4	9-Jul-62	94.45	6	FRANKLIN	BJ2-4	2-Nov-51	5.15	3
CURRITUCK	SE5	10-Jul-62	96.55	6	FRANKLIN	BJ2-3	1-Nov-51	10.20	4
DARE	BJ2-3	1-Nov-51	5.63	3	GASTON	UK9-4	22-May-53	5.19	3
DARE	TS3-4	25-Apr-52	6.78	3	GASTON	PB5-8	22-Jul-57	5.97	3
DARE	BJ2-4	2-Nov-51	10.55	4	GASTON	BJ2-3	1-Nov-51	7.80	3
DARE	BJ3-6	6-Nov-51	11.57	4	GATES	PB4-5	9-Jul-57	3.57	2
DARE	PB4-5	9-Jul-57	14.84	4	GATES	BJ2-3	1-Nov-51	4.21	2
DAVIDSON	BJ2-2	31-Oct-51	6.42	3	GATES	PB5-9	23-Jul-57	4.71	2
DAVIDSON	BJ2-4	2-Nov-51	6.77	3	GATES	TS3-4	25-Apr-52	6.78	3
DAVIDSON	BJ2-3	1-Nov-51	9.47	3	GATES	BJ2-4	2-Nov-51	7.45	3
DAVIDSON	TS5-2	8-May-52	18.99	4	GATES	BJ3-6	6-Nov-51	11.57	4

U.S. FALLOUT ATLAS: COUNTY COMPARISONS

INDIVIDUAL FALLOUT DAYS
NORTH CAROLINA

COUNTY	SHOT	DATE	µCi/SQ METER	INDEX	COUNTY	SHOT	DATE	µCi/SQ METER	INDEX
GRAHAM	TP10-2	6-May-55	3.62	2	HAYWOOD	UK1-2	18-Mar-53	10.20	4
GRAHAM	TP6-4	25-Mar-55	4.32	2	HAYWOOD	PB17-3	30-Sep-57	14.98	4
GRAHAM	TS7-6	6-Jun-52	5.76	3	HENDERSON	TP10-2	6-May-55	3.62	2
GRAHAM	PB17-3	30-Sep-57	7.49	3	HENDERSON	TS7-6	6-Jun-52	3.65	2
GRAHAM	BJ3-6	6-Nov-51	8.10	3	HENDERSON	UK1-2	18-Mar-53	3.71	2
GRAHAM	UK1-2	18-Mar-53	12.66	4	HENDERSON	TP10-8	12-May-55	3.72	2
GRANVILLE	BJ2-2	31-Oct-51	3.89	2	HENDERSON	BJ2-2	31-Oct-51	3.89	2
GRANVILLE	TS5-2	8-May-52	4.94	2	HENDERSON	PB6-3	26-Jul-57	3.96	2
GRANVILLE	BJ2-4	2-Nov-51	4.94	2	HENDERSON	BJ2-3	1-Nov-51	4.09	2
GRANVILLE	BJ2-3	1-Nov-51	8.68	3	HENDERSON	TP6-4	25-Mar-55	4.32	2
GRANVILLE	PB5-8	22-Jul-57	8.96	3	HENDERSON	PB4-5	9-Jul-57	5.24	3
GRANVILLE	SE4	9-Jul-62	50.92	6	HENDERSON	UK9-4	22-May-53	7.84	3
GREENE	PB4-5	9-Jul-57	3.57	2	HERTFORD	PB4-5	9-Jul-57	3.57	2
GREENE	BJ2-4	2-Nov-51	5.76	3	HERTFORD	PB5-9	23-Jul-57	4.71	2
GREENE	PB5-8	22-Jul-57	8.96	3	HERTFORD	BJ2-3	1-Nov-51	6.11	3
GREENE	BJ2-3	1-Nov-51	9.98	3	HERTFORD	TS3-4	25-Apr-52	6.78	3
GUILFORD	BJ2-2	31-Oct-51	3.89	2	HERTFORD	BJ2-4	2-Nov-51	8.01	3
GUILFORD	BJ2-4	2-Nov-51	6.18	3	HERTFORD	BJ3-6	6-Nov-51	11.57	4
GUILFORD	BJ2-3	1-Nov-51	8.58	3	HOKE	PB4-5	9-Jul-57	3.57	2
GUILFORD	SE4	9-Jul-62	18.06	4	HOKE	BJ2-2	31-Oct-51	3.89	2
HALIFAX	PB4-5	9-Jul-57	3.57	2	HOKE	PB5-9	23-Jul-57	4.71	2
HALIFAX	PB5-9	23-Jul-57	4.71	2	HOKE	BJ2-3	1-Nov-51	6.33	3
HALIFAX	BJ2-4	2-Nov-51	5.43	3	HOKE	BJ2-4	2-Nov-51	10.77	4
HALIFAX	TS3-4	25-Apr-52	6.78	3	HYDE	TS5-1	7-May-52	3.86	2
HALIFAX	BJ2-3	1-Nov-51	8.80	3	HYDE	BJ2-4	2-Nov-51	10.55	4
HARNETT	PB4-5	9-Jul-57	3.57	2	HYDE	TS3-4	25-Apr-52	11.30	4
HARNETT	BJ2-2	31-Oct-51	3.89	2	HYDE	BJ3-6	6-Nov-51	11.57	4
HARNETT	PB5-9	23-Jul-57	4.71	2	HYDE	PB4-5	9-Jul-57	21.46	4
HARNETT	BJ2-4	2-Nov-51	11.14	4	IREDELL	BJ2-2	31-Oct-51	3.89	2
HARNETT	BJ2-3	1-Nov-51	11.27	4	IREDELL	UK9-4	22-May-53	4.04	2
HAYWOOD	TP10-2	6-May-55	3.62	2	IREDELL	PB2-5	22-Jun-57	4.18	2
HAYWOOD	UK9-4	22-May-53	3.80	2	IREDELL	PB5-8	22-Jul-57	5.97	3
HAYWOOD	TP6-4	25-Mar-55	4.32	2	IREDELL	BJ2-3	1-Nov-51	7.16	3

INDIVIDUAL FALLOUT DAYS
NORTH CAROLINA

COUNTY	SHOT	DATE	µCi/SQ METER	INDEX	COUNTY	SHOT	DATE	µCi/SQ METER	INDEX
IREDELL	TS5-2	8-May-52	10.99	4	MACON	TP10-2	6-May-55	3.62	2
JACKSON	TP10-2	6-May-55	3.62	2	MACON	TS7-5	5-Jun-52	3.82	2
JACKSON	PB2-5	22-Jun-57	4.18	2	MACON	UK9-4	22-May-53	3.92	2
JACKSON	TP6-4	25-Mar-55	4.32	2	MACON	TP6-4	25-Mar-55	4.32	2
JACKSON	UK1-2	18-Mar-53	8.08	3	MACON	TP10-8	12-May-55	4.38	2
JACKSON	PB17-3	30-Sep-57	14.98	4	MACON	TS7-6	6-Jun-52	4.69	2
JACKSON	UK9-4	22-May-53	16.93	4	MACON	UK1-2	18-Mar-53	8.86	3
JOHNSTON	PB4-5	9-Jul-57	3.57	2	MACON	PB17-3	30-Sep-57	14.98	4
JOHNSTON	PB5-9	23-Jul-57	4.71	2	MADISON	TP10-2	6-May-55	3.62	2
JOHNSTON	BJ2-4	2-Nov-51	4.75	2	MADISON	BJ2-2	31-Oct-51	3.89	2
JOHNSTON	BJ2-3	1-Nov-51	11.27	4	MADISON	PB6-3	26-Jul-57	3.96	2
JONES	PB4-5	9-Jul-57	3.57	2	MADISON	UK9-4	22-May-53	4.18	2
JONES	TS5-1	7-May-52	4.93	2	MADISON	TP6-4	25-Mar-55	4.32	2
JONES	BJ2-3	1-Nov-51	9.34	3	MADISON	TP10-8	12-May-55	4.34	2
JONES	TS3-4	25-Apr-52	11.30	4	MADISON	PB17-3	30-Sep-57	7.49	3
JONES	BJ2-4	2-Nov-51	11.55	4	MADISON	UK1-2	18-Mar-53	12.41	4
JONES	TS5-2	8-May-52	3.50	1	MARTIN	PB4-5	9-Jul-57	3.57	2
JONES	SE5	10-Jul-62	27.88	5	MARTIN	BJ2-3	1-Nov-51	6.33	3
LEE	PB4-5	9-Jul-57	3.57	2	MARTIN	TS3-4	25-Apr-52	6.78	3
LEE	BJ2-2	31-Oct-51	3.89	2	MARTIN	BJ2-4	2-Nov-51	10.18	4
LEE	PB5-9	23-Jul-57	4.71	2	MARTIN	BJ3-6	6-Nov-51	11.57	4
LEE	BJ2-3	1-Nov-51	10.47	4	MARTIN	SE5	10-Jul-62	38.35	5
LEE	BJ2-4	2-Nov-51	10.93	4	MCDOWELL	TP10-2	6-May-55	3.62	2
LENOIR	TS5-2	8-May-52	6.50	3	MCDOWELL	BJ2-2	31-Oct-51	3.89	2
LENOIR	TS3-4	25-Apr-52	6.78	3	MCDOWELL	PB6-3	26-Jul-57	3.96	2
LENOIR	PB4-5	9-Jul-57	7.14	3	MCDOWELL	PB2-5	22-Jun-57	4.18	2
LENOIR	BJ2-3	1-Nov-51	10.36	4	MCDOWELL	UK9-4	22-May-53	4.43	2
LENOIR	BJ2-4	2-Nov-51	10.94	4	MCDOWELL	BJ2-3	1-Nov-51	4.48	2
LINCOLN	TP10-2	6-May-55	3.62	2	MCDOWELL	UK1-2	18-Mar-53	5.16	3
LINCOLN	PB6-3	26-Jul-57	3.96	2	MECKLENBURG	UK9-4	22-May-53	4.79	2
LINCOLN	TP6-4	25-Mar-55	4.32	2	MECKLENBURG	BJ2-3	1-Nov-51	7.40	3
LINCOLN	UK9-4	22-May-53	5.02	3	MECKLENBURG	PB5-8	22-Jul-57	8.96	3
LINCOLN	BJ2-3	1-Nov-51	7.04	3	MITCHELL	TP10-2	6-May-55	3.62	2

INDIVIDUAL FALLOUT DAYS
NORTH CAROLINA

COUNTY	SHOT	DATE	µCi/SQ METER	INDEX	COUNTY	SHOT	DATE	µCi/SQ METER	INDEX
MITCHELL	TP10-8	12-May-55	3.74	2	ONSLOW	TS5-2	8-May-52	4.00	2
MITCHELL	BJ2-2	31-Oct-51	3.89	2	ONSLOW	BJ2-3	1-Nov-51	7.08	3
MITCHELL	UK9-4	22-May-53	4.04	2	ONSLOW	BJ2-4	2-Nov-51	10.06	4
MITCHELL	TP6-4	25-Mar-55	4.32	2	ONSLOW	TS3-4	25-Apr-52	11.30	4
MITCHELL	UK1-2	18-Mar-53	4.64	2	ONSLOW	PB4-5	9-Jul-57	14.27	4
MITCHELL	TS7-6	6-Jun-52	5.25	3	ORANGE	BJ2-2	31-Oct-51	3.89	2
MITCHELL	PB6-3	26-Jul-57	7.85	3	ORANGE	PB5-9	23-Jul-57	4.71	2
MONTGOMERY	BJ2-2	31-Oct-51	3.89	2	ORANGE	BJ2-4	2-Nov-51	5.50	3
MONTGOMERY	TS5-2	8-May-52	6.68	3	ORANGE	BJ2-3	1-Nov-51	8.68	3
MONTGOMERY	BJ2-3	1-Nov-51	9.65	3	ORANGE	SE4	9-Jul-62	43.75	5
MOORE	PB4-5	9-Jul-57	3.57	2	PAMLICO	BJ3-5	5-Nov-51	3.83	2
MOORE	PB5-9	23-Jul-57	4.71	2	PAMLICO	TS5-1	7-May-52	4.28	2
MOORE	BJ2-3	1-Nov-51	11.26	4	PAMLICO	BJ2-4	2-Nov-51	5.28	3
MOORE	BJ2-4	2-Nov-51	11.52	4	PAMLICO	TS3-4	25-Apr-52	6.78	3
MOORE	TS5-2	8-May-52	16.63	4	PAMLICO	BJ3-6	6-Nov-51	6.94	3
NASH	PB4-5	9-Jul-57	3.57	2	PAMLICO	BJ2-3	1-Nov-51	8.32	3
NASH	BJ2-4	2-Nov-51	5.01	3	PAMLICO	PB4-5	9-Jul-57	14.27	4
NASH	TS3-4	25-Apr-52	6.78	3	PASQUOTANK	PB4-5	9-Jul-57	3.57	2
NASH	BJ2-3	1-Nov-51	9.13	3	PASQUOTANK	BJ2-3	1-Nov-51	3.76	2
NEW HANOVER	TS5-1	7-May-52	4.50	2	PASQUOTANK	TS3-4	25-Apr-52	6.78	3
NEW HANOVER	TS3-4	25-Apr-52	4.52	2	PASQUOTANK	BJ2-4	2-Nov-51	7.24	3
NEW HANOVER	PB5-9	23-Jul-57	4.71	2	PASQUOTANK	PB5-8	22-Jul-57	8.96	3
NEW HANOVER	BJ2-4	2-Nov-51	8.76	3	PASQUOTANK	BJ3-6	6-Nov-51	11.57	4
NEW HANOVER	BJ2-3	1-Nov-51	13.56	4	PASQUOTANK	SE4	9-Jul-62	94.45	6
NEW HANOVER	PB4-5	9-Jul-57	14.27	4	PASQUOTANK	SE5	10-Jul-62	96.55	6
NORTHAMPTON	PB4-5	9-Jul-57	3.57	2	PENDER	PB4-5	9-Jul-57	3.57	2
NORTHAMPTON	PB5-9	23-Jul-57	4.71	2	PENDER	UK9-4	22-May-53	4.90	2
NORTHAMPTON	BJ2-4	2-Nov-51	5.09	3	PENDER	TS5-1	7-May-52	6.64	3
NORTHAMPTON	TS3-4	25-Apr-52	6.78	3	PENDER	TS3-4	25-Apr-52	6.78	3
NORTHAMPTON	BJ2-3	1-Nov-51	7.62	3	PENDER	BJ2-4	2-Nov-51	9.96	3
NORTHAMPTON	PB5-8	22-Jul-57	8.96	3	PENDER	BJ2-3	1-Nov-51	13.30	4
NORTHAMPTON	BJ3-6	6-Nov-51	11.57	4	PERQUIMANS	PB4-5	9-Jul-57	3.57	2
NORTHAMPTON	SE4	9-Jul-62	57.04	6	PERQUIMANS	BJ2-3	1-Nov 51	4.83	2

INDIVIDUAL FALLOUT DAYS
NORTH CAROLINA

COUNTY	SHOT	DATE	µCi/SQ METER	INDEX	COUNTY	SHOT	DATE	µCi/SQ METER	INDEX
PERQUIMANS	TS3-4	25-Apr-52	6.78	3	ROBESON	BJ2-4	2-Nov-51	4.93	2
PERQUIMANS	BJ2-4	2-Nov-51	7.52	3	ROBESON	BJ2-3	1-Nov-51	13.18	4
PERQUIMANS	PB5-8	22-Jul-57	8.96	3	ROCKINGHAM	BJ2-2	31-Oct-51	3.89	2
PERQUIMANS	BJ3-6	6-Nov-51	11.57	4	ROCKINGHAM	BJ2-4	2-Nov-51	5.93	3
PERQUIMANS	SE4	9-Jul-62	94.45	6	ROCKINGHAM	BJ2-3	1-Nov-51	6.65	3
PERQUIMANS	SE5	10-Jul-62	96.55	6	ROWAN	BJ2-2	31-Oct-51	3.89	2
PERSON	BJ2-2	31-Oct-51	3.89	2	ROWAN	PB5-9	23-Jul-57	4.71	2
PERSON	PB5-9	23-Jul-57	4.71	2	ROWAN	BJ2-4	2-Nov-51	6.37	3
PERSON	BJ2-3	1-Nov-51	7.70	3	ROWAN	BJ2-3	1-Nov-51	8.70	3
PERSON	BJ2-4	2-Nov-51	9.54	3	RUTHERFORD	TP10-2	6-May-55	3.62	2
PERSON	SE4	9-Jul-62	73.06	6	RUTHERFORD	PB6-3	26-Jul-57	3.96	2
PITT	TS3-4	25-Apr-52	6.78	3	RUTHERFORD	UK9-4	22-May-53	4.76	2
PITT	PB4-5	9-Jul-57	7.14	3	RUTHERFORD	BJ2-3	1-Nov-51	5.50	3
PITT	BJ2-3	1-Nov-51	7.62	3	SAMPSON	TS5-2	8-May-52	3.55	2
PITT	BJ2-4	2-Nov-51	20.95	4	SAMPSON	PB4-5	9-Jul-57	3.57	2
POLK	TP10-2	6-May-55	3.62	2	SAMPSON	BJ2-4	2-Nov-51	5.68	3
POLK	BJ2-2	31-Oct-51	3.89	2	SAMPSON	BJ2-3	1-Nov-51	11.69	4
POLK	PB6-3	26-Jul-57	3.96	2	SCOTLAND	PB4-5	9-Jul-57	3.57	2
POLK	TP6-4	25-Mar-55	4.32	2	SCOTLAND	BJ2-2	31-Oct-51	3.89	2
POLK	UK9-4	22-May-53	4.91	2	SCOTLAND	PB5-9	23-Jul-57	4.71	2
POLK	BJ2-3	1-Nov-51	5.25	3	SCOTLAND	BJ2-3	1-Nov-51	6.01	3
POLK	PB2-5	22-Jun-57	6.96	3	SCOTLAND	BJ2-4	2-Nov-51	9.93	3
RANDOLPH	UK9-5	23-May-53	3.59	2	STANLY	TS5-2	8-May-52	7.17	3
RANDOLPH	BJ2-2	31-Oct-51	3.89	2	STANLY	BJ2-3	1-Nov-51	8.69	3
RANDOLPH	PB5-9	23-Jul-57	4.71	2	STANLY	PB5-8	22-Jul-57	8.96	3
RANDOLPH	BJ2-4	2-Nov-51	5.84	3	STOKES	BJ2-2	31-Oct-51	3.89	2
RANDOLPH	BJ2-3	1-Nov-51	9.44	3	STOKES	PB5-8	22-Jul-57	5.97	3
RANDOLPH	UK9-4	22-May-53	12.11	4	STOKES	BJ2-3	1-Nov-51	7.16	3
RICHMOND	PB4-5	9-Jul-57	3.57	2	STOKES	BJ2-4	2-Nov-51	7.97	3
RICHMOND	BJ2-4	2-Nov-51	5.09	3	SURRY	BJ2-3	1-Nov-51	5.12	3
RICHMOND	PB5-8	22-Jul-57	8.96	3	SURRY	BJ2-2	31-Oct-51	6.42	3
RICHMOND	BJ2-3	1-Nov-51	9.22	3	SURRY	BJ2-4	2-Nov-51	7.57	3
ROBESON	PB4-5	9-Jul-57	3.57	2	SURRY	SE4	9-Jul-62	15.20	4

INDIVIDUAL FALLOUT DAYS
NORTH CAROLINA

COUNTY	SHOT	DATE	µCi/SQ METER	INDEX	COUNTY	SHOT	DATE	µCi/SQ METER	INDEX
SWAIN	TP10-2	6-May-55	3.62	2	WARREN	BJ2-2	31-Oct-51	6.42	3
SWAIN	UK9-4	22-May-53	3.68	2	WARREN	TS3-4	25-Apr-52	6.78	3
SWAIN	TP6-4	25-Mar-55	4.32	2	WARREN	BJ2-3	1-Nov-51	7.61	3
SWAIN	BJ3-6	6-Nov-51	8.10	3	WARREN	PB5-8	22-Jul-57	8.96	3
SWAIN	PB17-3	30-Sep-57	14.98	4	WASHINGTON	PB4-5	9-Jul-57	3.57	2
SWAIN	UK1-2	18-Mar-53	15.13	4	WASHINGTON	TS7-5	5-Jun-52	4.33	2
TRANSYLVANIA	TP10-2	6-May-55	3.62	2	WASHINGTON	BJ2-3	1-Nov-51	5.88	3
TRANSYLVANIA	TP10-8	12-May-55	3.89	2	WASHINGTON	TS3-4	25-Apr-52	6.78	3
TRANSYLVANIA	PB2-5	22-Jun-57	4.18	2	WASHINGTON	BJ2-4	2-Nov-51	9.35	3
TRANSYLVANIA	TP6-4	25-Mar-55	4.32	2	WASHINGTON	BJ3-6	6-Nov-51	11.57	4
TRANSYLVANIA	UK9-4	22-May-53	4.95	2	WASHINGTON	SE4	9-Jul-62	94.45	6
TRANSYLVANIA	UK1-2	18-Mar-53	6.18	3	WATAUGA	UK9-4	22-May-53	3.61	2
TRANSYLVANIA	PB17-3	30-Sep-57	14.98	4	WATAUGA	TP10-2	6-May-55	3.62	2
TYRRELL	PB4-5	9-Jul-57	3.57	2	WATAUGA	UK1-2	18-Mar-53	3.69	2
TYRRELL	TS3-4	25-Apr-52	4.52	2	WATAUGA	BJ2-2	31-Oct-51	3.89	2
TYRRELL	BJ2-3	1-Nov-51	6.27	3	WATAUGA	PB6-3	26-Jul-57	3.96	2
TYRRELL	BJ2-4	2-Nov-51	9.02	3	WATAUGA	TP6-4	25-Mar-55	4.32	2
UNION	TS7-6	6-Jun-52	3.58	2	WATAUGA	SE4	9-Jul-62	18.06	4
UNION	UK9-4	22-May-53	3.99	2	WAYNE	PB4-5	9-Jul-57	3.57	2
UNION	BJ2-4	2-Nov-51	4.59	2	WAYNE	TS5-2	8-May-52	4.10	2
UNION	PB4-5	9-Jul-57	5.24	3	WAYNE	TS3-4	25-Apr-52	4.52	2
UNION	BJ2-3	1-Nov-51	7.83	3	WAYNE	PB5-9	23-Jul-57	4.71	2
VANCE	BJ2-4	2-Nov-51	4.81	2	WAYNE	BJ2-3	1-Nov-51	7.52	3
VANCE	BJ2-2	31-Oct-51	6.42	3	WAYNE	BJ2-4	2-Nov-51	12.10	4
VANCE	BJ2-3	1-Nov-51	8.23	3	WILKES	PB2-5	22-Jun-57	4.18	2
VANCE	SE4	9-Jul-62	73.06	6	WILKES	BJ2-3	1-Nov-51	5.12	3
WAKE	PB4-5	9-Jul-57	3.57	2	WILKES	PB5-8	22-Jul-57	8.96	3
WAKE	BJ2-4	2-Nov-51	4.21	2	WILKES	SE4	9-Jul-62	43.75	5
WAKE	PB5-9	23-Jul-57	4.71	2	WILSON	PB4-5	9-Jul-57	3.57	2
WAKE	PB5-8	22-Jul-57	5.97	3	WILSON	BJ2-4	2-Nov-51	5.08	3
WAKE	BJ2-3	1-Nov-51	9.65	3	WILSON	TS3-4	25-Apr-52	6.78	3
WAKE	SE4	9-Jul-62	21.81	4	WILSON	PB5-8	22-Jul-57	8.96	3
WARREN	BJ2-4	2-Nov-51	4.67	2	WILSON	BJ2-3	1-Nov-51	11.05	4

INDIVIDUAL FALLOUT DAYS
NORTH CAROLINA

COUNTY	SHOT	DATE	µCi/SQ METER	INDEX	COUNTY	SHOT	DATE	µCi/SQ METER	INDEX
YADKIN	BJ2-4	2-Nov-51	3.68	2	YANCEY	BJ2-2	31-Oct-51	3.89	2
YADKIN	BJ2-2	31-Oct-51	3.89	2	YANCEY	PB6-3	26-Jul-57	3.96	2
YADKIN	PB2-5	22-Jun-57	4.18	2	YANCEY	PB2-5	22-Jun-57	4.18	2
YADKIN	BJ2-3	1-Nov-51	7.55	3	YANCEY	UK9-4	22-May-53	4.18	2
YADKIN	TS5-2	8-May-52	10.99	4	YANCEY	TP6-4	25-Mar-55	7.15	3
YADKIN	UK9-4	22-May-53	13.90	4	YANCEY	UK1-2	18-Mar-53	7.62	3
YANCEY	TP10-2	6-May-55	3.62	2					

INDIVIDUAL FALLOUT DAYS
NORTH DAKOTA

COUNTY	SHOT	DATE	µCi/SQ METER	INDEX		COUNTY	SHOT	DATE	µCi/SQ METER	INDEX
ADAMS	TS8-3	7-Jun-52	4.29	2		BILLINGS	PB5-3	17-Jul-57	5.09	3
ADAMS	UK8-1	8-May-53	4.73	2		BILLINGS	UK8-2	9-May-53	5.46	3
ADAMS	PB11-4	3-Sep-57	5.18	3		BILLINGS	UK7-4	28-Apr-53	7.59	3
ADAMS	PB8-4	21-Aug-57	5.37	3		BILLINGS	TS8-3	7-Jun-52	8.76	3
ADAMS	TS5-1	7-May-52	5.57	3		BILLINGS	PB11-2	1-Sep-57	18.31	4
ADAMS	PB6-5	28-Jul-57	7.56	3		BILLINGS	PB5-2	16-Jul-57	19.36	4
ADAMS	PB5-3	17-Jul-57	10.10	4		BILLINGS	PB15-2	17-Sep-57	20.04	4
ADAMS	UK7-4	28-Apr-53	11.80	4		BILLINGS	UK8-1	8-May-53	53.66	6
ADAMS	PB11-2	1-Sep-57	18.31	4		BILLINGS	UK2-2	25-Mar-53	61.09	6
ADAMS	PB5-2	16-Jul-57	19.36	4		BILLINGS	TS8-1	5-Jun-52	26.59	5
ADAMS	PB8-3	20-Aug-57	19.73	4		BILLINGS	PB8-3	20-Aug-57	118.39	7
ADAMS	PB15-2	17-Sep-57	20.04	4		BOTTINEAU	UK8-2	9-May-53	3.64	2
ADAMS	TS8-1	5-Jun-52	66.47	6		BOTTINEAU	PB8-5	22-Aug-57	3.78	2
ADAMS	UK2-2	25-Mar-53	45.45	5		BOTTINEAU	PB15-2	17-Sep-57	6.68	3
BARNES	PB8-5	22-Aug-57	3.78	2		BOTTINEAU	PB11-2	1-Sep-57	9.15	3
BARNES	PB9-4	26-Aug-57	5.22	3		BOTTINEAU	PB2-3	20-Jun-57	15.08	4
BARNES	PB5-2	16-Jul-57	8.17	3		BOTTINEAU	PB8-3	20-Aug-57	19.73	4
BARNES	PB5-4	18-Jul-57	8.86	3		BOTTINEAU	TS8-1	5-Jun-52	26.59	5
BARNES	PB2-3	20-Jun-57	15.08	4		BOTTINEAU	UK8-1	8-May-53	35.91	5
BARNES	PB8-3	20-Aug-57	19.73	4		BOTTINEAU	UK2-2	25-Mar-53	122.17	7
BARNES	PB15-2	17-Sep-57	20.04	4		BOWMAN	PB6-5	28-Jul-57	4.14	2
BARNES	PB11-2	1-Sep-57	45.77	5		BOWMAN	TS8-3	7-Jun-52	5.14	3
BENSON	PB5-2	16-Jul-57	4.90	2		BOWMAN	PB11-4	3-Sep-57	5.18	3
BENSON	PB9-4	26-Aug-57	5.22	3		BOWMAN	PB8-4	21-Aug-57	8.05	3
BENSON	TP9-3	16-Apr-55	6.06	3		BOWMAN	TS5-1	7-May-52	8.08	3
BENSON	PB2-3	20-Jun-57	7.54	3		BOWMAN	PB5-2	16-Jul-57	9.68	3
BENSON	PB15-2	17-Sep-57	20.04	4		BOWMAN	PB5-3	17-Jul-57	10.10	4
BENSON	TS8-1	5-Jun-52	26.59	5		BOWMAN	UK7-4	28-Apr-53	12.82	4
BENSON	PB11-2	1-Sep-57	27.46	5		BOWMAN	PB11-2	1-Sep-57	18.31	4
BENSON	PB8-3	20-Aug-57	39.46	5		BOWMAN	PB8-3	20-Aug-57	19.73	4
BILLINGS	PB9-3	25-Aug-57	3.88	2		BOWMAN	PB15-2	17-Sep-57	20.04	4
BILLINGS	PB11-4	3-Sep-57	3.89	2		BOWMAN	TS8-1	5-Jun-52	26.59	5
BILLINGS	PB6-5	28-Jul-57	3.89	2		BOWMAN	UK2-2	25-Mar-53	45.45	5

INDIVIDUAL FALLOUT DAYS
NORTH DAKOTA

COUNTY	SHOT	DATE	µCi/SQ METER	INDEX	COUNTY	SHOT	DATE	µCi/SQ METER	INDEX
BURKE	PB9-3	25-Aug-57	3.88	2	CAVALIER	PB15-2	17-Sep-57	6.68	3
BURKE	PB9-4	26-Aug-57	5.22	3	CAVALIER	PB2-3	20-Jun-57	7.54	3
BURKE	UK8-2	9-May-53	5.46	3	CAVALIER	TP9-3	16-Apr-55	8.16	3
BURKE	PB15-2	17-Sep-57	6.68	3	CAVALIER	PB8-3	20-Aug-57	19.73	4
BURKE	PB11-2	1-Sep-57	9.15	3	CAVALIER	PB11-2	1-Sep-57	27.46	5
BURKE	PB5-2	16-Jul-57	9.68	3	CAVALIER	TS8-1	5-Jun-52	39.88	5
BURKE	UK8-1	8-May-53	53.66	6	DICKEY	UK2-2	25-Mar-53	3.97	2
BURKE	TS8-1	5-Jun-52	66.47	6	DICKEY	TS7-4	4-Jun-52	6.73	3
BURKE	UK2-2	25-Mar-53	91.63	6	DICKEY	PB8-5	22-Aug-57	7.56	3
BURKE	PB8-3	20-Aug-57	39.46	5	DICKEY	PB5-4	18-Jul-57	8.86	3
BURLEIGH	PB8-5	22-Aug-57	3.78	2	DICKEY	PB2-3	20-Jun-57	15.08	4
BURLEIGH	PB11-4	3-Sep-57	3.89	2	DICKEY	PB15-2	17-Sep-57	20.04	4
BURLEIGH	UK7-4	28-Apr-53	4.08	2	DICKEY	TS8-1	5-Jun-52	26.59	5
BURLEIGH	PB5-2	16-Jul-57	4.90	2	DICKEY	PB8-3	20-Aug-57	39.46	5
BURLEIGH	PB8-2	19-Aug-57	4.95	2	DICKEY	PB11-2	1-Sep-57	45.77	5
BURLEIGH	UK8-1	8-May-53	9.08	3	DIVIDE	PB11-2	1-Sep-57	4.58	2
BURLEIGH	PB11-2	1-Sep-57	9.15	3	DIVIDE	TS8-3	7-Jun-52	4.85	2
BURLEIGH	PB8-3	20-Aug-57	19.73	4	DIVIDE	PB11-4	3-Sep-57	5.18	3
BURLEIGH	PB15-2	17-Sep-57	20.04	4	DIVIDE	UK8-2	9-May-53	5.46	3
BURLEIGH	UK2-2	25-Mar-53	61.09	6	DIVIDE	PB15-2	17-Sep-57	6.68	3
BURLEIGH	TS8-1	5-Jun-52	26.59	5	DIVIDE	PB5-2	16-Jul-57	9.68	3
BURLEIGH	PB2-3	20-Jun-57	30.08	5	DIVIDE	UK8-1	8-May-53	53.66	6
CASS	PB5-2	16-Jul-57	4.90	2	DIVIDE	UK2-2	25-Mar-53	61.09	6
CASS	PB9-4	26-Aug-57	5.22	3	DIVIDE	PB8-3	20-Aug-57	78.93	6
CASS	PB5-4	18-Jul-57	5.89	3	DIVIDE	TS8-1	5-Jun-52	210.72	8
CASS	PB8-3	20-Aug-57	19.73	4	DUNN	PB6-5	28-Jul-57	3.60	2
CASS	PB15-2	17-Sep-57	20.04	4	DUNN	UK8-2	9-May-53	3.64	2
CASS	PB2-3	20-Jun-57	45.16	5	DUNN	PB8-5	22-Aug-57	3.78	2
CASS	PB11-2	1-Sep-57	45.77	5	DUNN	PB9-3	25-Aug-57	3.88	2
CAVALIER	PB8-5	22-Aug-57	3.78	2	DUNN	TS8-3	7-Jun-52	4.78	2
CAVALIER	PB5-3	17-Jul-57	3.88	2	DUNN	PB8-2	19-Aug-57	4.95	2
CAVALIER	PB11-4	3-Sep-57	3.89	2	DUNN	PB5-3	17-Jul-57	5.09	3
CAVALIER	PB9-4	26-Aug-57	5.22	3	DUNN	PB8-4	21-Aug-57	5.37	3

INDIVIDUAL FALLOUT DAYS
NORTH DAKOTA

COUNTY	SHOT	DATE	µCi/SQ METER	INDEX	COUNTY	SHOT	DATE	µCi/SQ METER	INDEX
DUNN	UK7-4	28-Apr-53	5.61	3	FOSTER	TS8-1	5-Jun-52	26.59	5
DUNN	PB8-3	20-Aug-57	19.73	4	FOSTER	PB11-2	1-Sep-57	27.46	5
DUNN	PB15-2	17-Sep-57	20.04	4	FOSTER	PB8-3	20-Aug-57	39.46	5
DUNN	TS8-1	5-Jun-52	53.18	6	FOSTER	PB2-3	20-Jun-57	45.16	5
DUNN	UK2-2	25-Mar-53	91.63	6	GOLDEN VALLE	PB8-5	22-Aug-57	3.78	2
DUNN	PB11-2	1-Sep-57	27.46	5	GOLDEN VALLE	PB5-3	17-Jul-57	3.80	2
DUNN	PB5-2	16-Jul-57	29.04	5	GOLDEN VALLE	PB9-3	25-Aug-57	3.88	2
DUNN	UK8-1	8-May-53	35.91	5	GOLDEN VALLE	TS7-4	4-Jun-52	5.15	3
EDDY	PB8-5	22-Aug-57	3.78	2	GOLDEN VALLE	UK8-2	9-May-53	5.46	3
EDDY	PB2-3	20-Jun-57	7.54	3	GOLDEN VALLE	PB6-5	28-Jul-57	6.65	3
EDDY	PB5-2	16-Jul-57	8.17	3	GOLDEN VALLE	UK7-4	28-Apr-53	7.11	3
EDDY	PB8-3	20-Aug-57	19.73	4	GOLDEN VALLE	TS8-3	7-Jun-52	9.91	3
EDDY	PB15-2	17-Sep-57	20.04	4	GOLDEN VALLE	PB11-4	3-Sep-57	10.36	4
EDDY	TS8-1	5-Jun-52	26.59	5	GOLDEN VALLE	PB11-2	1-Sep-57	18.31	4
EDDY	PB11-2	1-Sep-57	45.77	5	GOLDEN VALLE	PB8-3	20-Aug-57	19.73	4
EMMONS	PB8-5	22-Aug-57	3.78	2	GOLDEN VALLE	PB15-2	17-Sep-57	20.04	4
EMMONS	TS7-4	4-Jun-52	3.84	2	GOLDEN VALLE	UK8-1	8-May-53	53.66	6
EMMONS	PB9-3	25-Aug-57	3.88	2	GOLDEN VALLE	UK2-2	25-Mar-53	61.09	6
EMMONS	UK2-2	25-Mar-53	3.97	2	GOLDEN VALLE	PB5-2	16-Jul-57	29.04	5
EMMONS	PB8-2	19-Aug-57	4.95	2	GOLDEN VALLE	TS8-1	5-Jun-52	39.88	5
EMMONS	PB8-4	21-Aug-57	5.37	3	GRAND FORKS	PB5-2	16-Jul-57	8.17	3
EMMONS	UK7-4	28-Apr-53	6.44	3	GRAND FORKS	TP9-3	16-Apr-55	8.21	3
EMMONS	PB5-4	18-Jul-57	8.86	3	GRAND FORKS	PB2-3	20-Jun-57	15.08	4
EMMONS	PB15-2	17-Sep-57	20.04	4	GRAND FORKS	PB8-3	20-Aug-57	19.73	4
EMMONS	TS8-1	5-Jun-52	26.59	5	GRAND FORKS	PB15-2	17-Sep-57	20.04	4
EMMONS	PB11-2	1-Sep-57	27.46	5	GRAND FORKS	PB11-2	1-Sep-57	45.77	5
EMMONS	PB8-3	20-Aug-57	39.46	5	GRANT	PB8-5	22-Aug-57	3.78	2
EMMONS	PB2-3	20-Jun-57	45.16	5	GRANT	TS7-4	4-Jun-52	4.75	2
FOSTER	TS7-4	4-Jun-52	4.11	2	GRANT	PB11-4	3-Sep-57	5.18	3
FOSTER	TP9-3	16-Apr-55	4.56	2	GRANT	UK7-4	28-Apr-53	8.29	3
FOSTER	PB11-4	3-Sep-57	5.18	3	GRANT	PB11-2	1-Sep-57	9.15	3
FOSTER	PB5-2	16-Jul-57	8.17	3	GRANT	PB2-3	20-Jun-57	15.08	4
FOSTER	PB15-2	17-Sep-57	13.36	4	GRANT	UK8-1	8-May-53	17.76	4

INDIVIDUAL FALLOUT DAYS
NORTH DAKOTA

COUNTY	SHOT	DATE	µCi/SQ METER	INDEX	COUNTY	SHOT	DATE	µCi/SQ METER	INDEX
GRANT	PB8-3	20-Aug-57	19.73	4	LA MOURE	PB11-4	3-Sep-57	5.18	3
GRANT	PB15-2	17-Sep-57	20.04	4	LA MOURE	PB5-4	18-Jul-57	8.86	3
GRANT	UK2-2	25-Mar-53	61.09	6	LA MOURE	PB2-3	20-Jun-57	15.08	4
GRANT	TS8-1	5-Jun-52	26.59	5	LA MOURE	PB8-3	20-Aug-57	19.73	4
GRIGGS	TP9-3	16-Apr-55	5.47	3	LA MOURE	PB15-2	17-Sep-57	20.04	4
GRIGGS	PB5-4	18-Jul-57	5.89	3	LA MOURE	TS8-1	5-Jun-52	26.59	5
GRIGGS	PB2-3	20-Jun-57	7.54	3	LA MOURE	PB11-2	1-Sep-57	45.77	5
GRIGGS	PB5-2	16-Jul-57	8.17	3	LOGAN	UK2-2	25-Mar-53	3.97	2
GRIGGS	PB11-4	3-Sep-57	10.36	4	LOGAN	PB9-4	26-Aug-57	5.22	3
GRIGGS	PB8-3	20-Aug-57	19.73	4	LOGAN	PB5-2	16-Jul-57	8.17	3
GRIGGS	PB15-2	17-Sep-57	20.04	4	LOGAN	PB5-4	18-Jul-57	8.86	3
GRIGGS	PB11-2	1-Sep-57	45.77	5	LOGAN	PB8-3	20-Aug-57	19.73	4
HETTINGER	UK8-2	9-May-53	3.64	2	LOGAN	PB15-2	17-Sep-57	20.04	4
HETTINGER	TS5-1	7-May-52	4.13	2	LOGAN	TS8-1	5-Jun-52	26.59	5
HETTINGER	PB8-4	21-Aug-57	8.05	3	LOGAN	PB11-2	1-Sep-57	27.46	5
HETTINGER	PB5-2	16-Jul-57	9.68	3	LOGAN	PB2-3	20-Jun-57	30.08	5
HETTINGER	UK7-4	28-Apr-53	10.07	4	MCHENRY	PB15-2	17-Sep-57	6.68	3
HETTINGER	PB5-3	17-Jul-57	10.10	4	MCHENRY	PB11-2	1-Sep-57	9.15	3
HETTINGER	PB11-4	3-Sep-57	10.36	4	MCHENRY	UK8-1	8-May-53	17.76	4
HETTINGER	UK8-1	8-May-53	17.76	4	MCHENRY	PB8-3	20-Aug-57	19.73	4
HETTINGER	PB11-2	1-Sep-57	18.31	4	MCHENRY	TS8-1	5-Jun-52	53.18	6
HETTINGER	PB8-3	20-Aug-57	19.73	4	MCHENRY	PB2-3	20-Jun-57	30.08	5
HETTINGER	PB15-2	17-Sep-57	20.04	4	MCHENRY	UK2-2	25-Mar-53	122.17	7
HETTINGER	UK2-2	25-Mar-53	61.09	6	MCINTOSH	PB8-5	22-Aug-57	3.78	2
HETTINGER	TS8-1	5-Jun-52	26.59	5	MCINTOSH	UK2-2	25-Mar-53	3.97	2
KIDDER	PB5-2	16-Jul-57	8.17	3	MCINTOSH	UK7-4	28-Apr-53	5.16	3
KIDDER	PB2-3	20-Jun-57	15.08	4	MCINTOSH	PB11-4	3-Sep-57	5.18	3
KIDDER	PB8-3	20-Aug-57	19.73	4	MCINTOSH	PB9-4	26-Aug-57	5.22	3
KIDDER	PB15-2	17-Sep-57	20.04	4	MCINTOSH	PB5-4	18-Jul-57	8.86	3
KIDDER	TS8-1	5-Jun-52	26.59	5	MCINTOSH	TS7-4	4-Jun-52	9.74	3
KIDDER	PB11-2	1-Sep-57	27.46	5	MCINTOSH	PB15-2	17-Sep-57	13.36	4
LA MOURE	PB8-5	22-Aug-57	3.78	2	MCINTOSH	PB8-3	20-Aug-57	19.73	4
LA MOURE	PB5-2	16-Jul-57	4.90	2	MCINTOSH	TS8-1	5-Jun-52	26.59	5

INDIVIDUAL FALLOUT DAYS
NORTH DAKOTA

COUNTY	SHOT	DATE	µCi/SQ METER	INDEX	COUNTY	SHOT	DATE	µCi/SQ METER	INDEX
MCINTOSH	PB11-2	1-Sep-57	27.46	5	MERCER	UK2-2	25-Mar-53	61.09	6
MCINTOSH	PB2-3	20-Jun-57	30.08	5	MERCER	TS8-1	5-Jun-52	26.59	5
MCKENZIE	PB11-2	1-Sep-57	4.58	2	MERCER	PB2-3	20-Jun-57	45.16	5
MCKENZIE	UK7-4	28-Apr-53	4.64	2	MORTON	PB8-5	22-Aug-57	3.78	2
MCKENZIE	PB8-4	21-Aug-57	5.37	3	MORTON	PB5-3	17-Jul-57	3.88	2
MCKENZIE	UK8-2	9-May-53	5.46	3	MORTON	UK7-4	28-Apr-53	6.25	3
MCKENZIE	TS8-3	7-Jun-52	8.45	3	MORTON	PB11-2	1-Sep-57	9.15	3
MCKENZIE	PB5-2	16-Jul-57	9.68	3	MORTON	UK8-1	8-May-53	17.76	4
MCKENZIE	PB15-2	17-Sep-57	20.04	4	MORTON	PB8-3	20-Aug-57	19.73	4
MCKENZIE	UK8-1	8-May-53	53.66	6	MORTON	PB15-2	17-Sep-57	20.04	4
MCKENZIE	TS8-1	5-Jun-52	55.45	6	MORTON	UK2-2	25-Mar-53	61.09	6
MCKENZIE	UK2-2	25-Mar-53	91.63	6	MORTON	TS8-1	5-Jun-52	26.59	5
MCKENZIE	PB8-3	20-Aug-57	39.46	5	MORTON	PB2-3	20-Jun-57	30.08	5
MCLEAN	UK8-2	9-May-53	3.64	2	MOUNTRAIL	UK8-2	9-May-53	3.64	2
MCLEAN	TS8-3	7-Jun-52	3.74	2	MOUNTRAIL	PB9-3	25-Aug-57	3.88	2
MCLEAN	PB8-5	22-Aug-57	3.78	2	MOUNTRAIL	PB15-2	17-Sep-57	13.36	4
MCLEAN	PB5-3	17-Jul-57	3.88	2	MOUNTRAIL	PB11-2	1-Sep-57	18.31	4
MCLEAN	PB5-2	16-Jul-57	4.90	2	MOUNTRAIL	PB8-3	20-Aug-57	19.73	4
MCLEAN	PB9-4	26-Aug-57	5.22	3	MOUNTRAIL	UK8-1	8-May-53	53.66	6
MCLEAN	UK8-1	8-May-53	17.76	4	MOUNTRAIL	UK2-2	25-Mar-53	61.09	6
MCLEAN	PB11-2	1-Sep-57	18.31	4	MOUNTRAIL	PB5-2	16-Jul-57	29.04	5
MCLEAN	PB8-3	20-Aug-57	19.73	4	MOUNTRAIL	TS8-1	5-Jun-52	106.35	7
MCLEAN	PB15-2	17-Sep-57	20.04	4	NELSON	TP11-4	18-May-55	3.83	2
MCLEAN	UK2-2	25-Mar-53	61.09	6	NELSON	TS7-4	4-Jun-52	4.64	2
MCLEAN	PB2-3	20-Jun-57	30.08	5	NELSON	TP9-3	16-Apr-55	5.54	3
MCLEAN	TS8-1	5-Jun-52	301.25	8	NELSON	PB2-3	20-Jun-57	7.54	3
MERCER	PB8-5	22-Aug-57	3.78	2	NELSON	PB5-2	16-Jul-57	8.17	3
MERCER	TS8-3	7-Jun-52	5.06	3	NELSON	PB8-3	20-Aug-57	19.73	4
MERCER	UK7-4	28-Apr-53	5.10	3	NELSON	PB15-2	17-Sep-57	20.04	4
MERCER	PB11-2	1-Sep-57	9.15	3	NELSON	PB11-2	1-Sep-57	45.77	5
MERCER	PB8-3	20-Aug-57	19.73	4	OLIVER	PB5-2	16-Jul-57	4.90	2
MERCER	PB15-2	17-Sep-57	20.04	4	OLIVER	UK7-4	28-Apr-53	4.91	2
MERCER	UK8-1	8-May-53	53.66	6	OLIVER	PB11-2	1-Sep-57	9.15	3

INDIVIDUAL FALLOUT DAYS
NORTH DAKOTA

COUNTY	SHOT	DATE	µCi/SQ METER	INDEX	COUNTY	SHOT	DATE	µCi/SQ METER	INDEX
OLIVER	PB8-3	20-Aug-57	19.73	4	RANSOM	PB8-5	22-Aug-57	7.56	3
OLIVER	PB15-2	17-Sep-57	20.04	4	RANSOM	PB8-3	20-Aug-57	78.93	6
OLIVER	UK8-1	8-May-53	53.66	6	RANSOM	PB11-2	1-Sep-57	45.77	5
OLIVER	UK2-2	25-Mar-53	61.09	6	RENVILLE	PB9-3	25-Aug-57	3.88	2
OLIVER	PB2-3	20-Jun-57	45.16	5	RENVILLE	PB9-4	26-Aug-57	5.22	3
OLIVER	TS8-1	5-Jun-52	146.23	7	RENVILLE	UK8-2	9-May-53	5.46	3
PEMBINA	PB4-2	6-Jul-57	4.21	2	RENVILLE	PB15-2	17-Sep-57	6.68	3
PEMBINA	TS7-5	5-Jun-52	5.75	3	RENVILLE	PB2-3	20-Jun-57	7.54	3
PEMBINA	TP9-3	16-Apr-55	11.74	4	RENVILLE	PB11-2	1-Sep-57	18.31	4
PEMBINA	PB2-3	20-Jun-57	15.08	4	RENVILLE	UK8-1	8-May-53	53.66	6
PEMBINA	PB8-3	20-Aug-57	19.73	4	RENVILLE	UK2-2	25-Mar-53	61.09	6
PEMBINA	PB11-2	1-Sep-57	45.77	5	RENVILLE	TS8-1	5-Jun-52	26.59	5
PIERCE	TP9-3	16-Apr-55	3.58	2	RENVILLE	PB8-3	20-Aug-57	39.46	5
PIERCE	PB8-5	22-Aug-57	3.78	2	RICHLAND	PB5-2	16-Jul-57	4.90	2
PIERCE	PB5-3	17-Jul-57	3.88	2	RICHLAND	PB11-4	3-Sep-57	5.18	3
PIERCE	PB9-3	25-Aug-57	3.88	2	RICHLAND	PB8-5	22-Aug-57	7.56	3
PIERCE	PB15-2	17-Sep-57	6.68	3	RICHLAND	PB5-4	18-Jul-57	8.86	3
PIERCE	PB2-3	20-Jun-57	7.54	3	RICHLAND	PB15-2	17-Sep-57	20.04	4
PIERCE	PB11-2	1-Sep-57	18.31	4	RICHLAND	PB2-3	20-Jun-57	75.24	6
PIERCE	PB8-3	20-Aug-57	19.73	4	RICHLAND	PB8-3	20-Aug-57	39.46	5
PIERCE	TS8-1	5-Jun-52	26.59	5	RICHLAND	PB11-2	1-Sep-57	45.77	5
RAMSEY	TS7-4	4-Jun-52	3.98	2	ROLETTE	PB5-2	16-Jul-57	4.90	2
RAMSEY	PB2-3	20-Jun-57	7.54	3	ROLETTE	PB9-4	26-Aug-57	5.22	3
RAMSEY	TP9-3	16-Apr-55	7.77	3	ROLETTE	PB2-3	20-Jun-57	7.54	3
RAMSEY	PB15-2	17-Sep-57	13.36	4	ROLETTE	PB8-3	20-Aug-57	19.73	4
RAMSEY	PB8-3	20-Aug-57	19.73	4	ROLETTE	TS8-1	5-Jun-52	26.59	5
RAMSEY	TS8-1	5-Jun-52	39.88	5	ROLETTE	PB11-2	1-Sep-57	27.46	5
RAMSEY	PB11-2	1-Sep-57	45.77	5	SARGENT	PB5-2	16-Jul-57	4.90	2
RANSOM	PB5-2	16-Jul-57	4.90	2	SARGENT	TS7-4	4-Jun-52	5.57	3
RANSOM	PB11-4	3-Sep-57	5.18	3	SARGENT	PB8-5	22-Aug-57	7.56	3
RANSOM	PB5-4	18-Jul-57	5.89	3	SARGENT	PB5-4	18-Jul-57	8.86	3
RANSOM	PB15-2	17-Sep-57	6.68	3	SARGENT	PB8-3	20-Aug-57	19.73	4
RANSOM	PB2-3	20-Jun-57	7.54	3	SARGENT	PB15-2	17-Sep-57	20.04	4

INDIVIDUAL FALLOUT DAYS
NORTH DAKOTA

COUNTY	SHOT	DATE	µCi/SQ METER	INDEX	COUNTY	SHOT	DATE	µCi/SQ METER	INDEX
SARGENT	PB2-3	20-Jun-57	45.16	5	SLOPE	UK8-1	8-May-53	35.91	5
SARGENT	PB11-2	1-Sep-57	45.77	5	SLOPE	PB8-3	20-Aug-57	39.46	5
SHERIDAN	PB5-2	16-Jul-57	4.90	2	STARK	UK8-2	9-May-53	3.64	2
SHERIDAN	PB9-4	26-Aug-57	5.22	3	STARK	PB8-5	22-Aug-57	3.78	2
SHERIDAN	UK8-1	8-May-53	9.08	3	STARK	PB9-3	25-Aug-57	3.88	2
SHERIDAN	PB2-3	20-Jun-57	15.08	4	STARK	PB6-5	28-Jul-57	4.00	2
SHERIDAN	PB11-2	1-Sep-57	18.31	4	STARK	PB8-2	19-Aug-57	4.95	2
SHERIDAN	PB8-3	20-Aug-57	19.73	4	STARK	TS8-3	7-Jun-52	7.36	3
SHERIDAN	PB15-2	17-Sep-57	20.04	4	STARK	UK7-4	28-Apr-53	8.67	3
SHERIDAN	UK2-2	25-Mar-53	61.09	6	STARK	PB11-4	3-Sep-57	10.36	4
SHERIDAN	TS8-1	5-Jun-52	26.59	5	STARK	PB5-3	17-Jul-57	15.18	4
SIOUX	PB11-2	1-Sep-57	4.58	2	STARK	PB11-2	1-Sep-57	18.31	4
SIOUX	PB8-4	21-Aug-57	5.37	3	STARK	PB15-2	17-Sep-57	20.04	4
SIOUX	PB15-2	17-Sep-57	6.68	3	STARK	UK8-1	8-May-53	53.66	6
SIOUX	PB2-3	20-Jun-57	7.54	3	STARK	UK2-2	25-Mar-53	61.09	6
SIOUX	PB11-4	3-Sep-57	10.36	4	STARK	TS8-1	5-Jun-52	79.76	6
SIOUX	UK7-4	28-Apr-53	11.35	4	STARK	PB5-2	16-Jul-57	29.04	5
SIOUX	PB8-3	20-Aug-57	19.73	4	STARK	PB8-3	20-Aug-57	39.46	5
SIOUX	UK2-2	25-Mar-53	45.45	5	STEELE	PB8-5	22-Aug-57	3.78	2
SIOUX	TS8-1	5-Jun-52	132.94	7	STEELE	PB2-3	20-Jun-57	7.54	3
SLOPE	UK8-2	9-May-53	3.64	2	STEELE	PB5-2	16-Jul-57	8.17	3
SLOPE	PB8-5	22-Aug-57	3.78	2	STEELE	PB8-3	20-Aug-57	19.73	4
SLOPE	PB5-3	17-Jul-57	5.09	3	STEELE	PB15-2	17-Sep-57	20.04	4
SLOPE	PB11-4	3-Sep-57	5.18	3	STEELE	PB11-2	1-Sep-57	45.77	5
SLOPE	PB8-4	21-Aug-57	5.37	3	STUTSMAN	PB8-5	22-Aug-57	3.78	2
SLOPE	TS8-3	7-Jun-52	5.65	3	STUTSMAN	PB5-2	16-Jul-57	4.90	2
SLOPE	TS5-1	7-May-52	5.93	3	STUTSMAN	PB5-4	18-Jul-57	5.89	3
SLOPE	UK7-4	28-Apr-53	7.48	3	STUTSMAN	PB2-3	20-Jun-57	15.08	4
SLOPE	PB5-2	16-Jul-57	9.68	3	STUTSMAN	PB15-2	17-Sep-57	20.04	4
SLOPE	PB15-2	17-Sep-57	13.36	4	STUTSMAN	TS8-1	5-Jun-52	26.59	5
SLOPE	PB11-2	1-Sep-57	18.31	4	STUTSMAN	PB11-2	1-Sep-57	27.46	5
SLOPE	UK2-2	25-Mar-53	61.09	6	STUTSMAN	PB8-3	20-Aug-57	39.46	5
SLOPE	TS8-1	5-Jun-52	79.76	6	TOWNER	PB5-3	17-Jul-57	3.88	2

INDIVIDUAL FALLOUT DAYS
NORTH DAKOTA

COUNTY	SHOT	DATE	µCi/SQ METER	INDEX	COUNTY	SHOT	DATE	µCi/SQ METER	INDEX
TOWNER	PB9-4	26-Aug-57	5.22	3	WARD	UK8-1	8-May-53	53.66	6
TOWNER	PB15-2	17-Sep-57	6.68	3	WARD	UK2-2	25-Mar-53	91.63	6
TOWNER	PB2-3	20-Jun-57	7.54	3	WARD	TS8-1	5-Jun-52	26.59	5
TOWNER	PB8-3	20-Aug-57	19.73	4	WARD	PB2-3	20-Jun-57	30.08	5
TOWNER	TS8-1	5-Jun-52	26.59	5	WELLS	PB5-3	17-Jul-57	3.88	2
TOWNER	PB11-2	1-Sep-57	27.46	5	WELLS	PB5-2	16-Jul-57	4.90	2
TRAILL	PB5-2	16-Jul-57	4.90	2	WELLS	PB9-4	26-Aug-57	5.22	3
TRAILL	TP9-3	16-Apr-55	5.49	3	WELLS	PB15-2	17-Sep-57	13.36	4
TRAILL	PB8-3	20-Aug-57	19.73	4	WELLS	PB2-3	20-Jun-57	15.08	4
TRAILL	PB15-2	17-Sep-57	20.04	4	WELLS	PB11-2	1-Sep-57	18.31	4
TRAILL	PB2-3	20-Jun-57	30.08	5	WELLS	PB8-3	20-Aug-57	19.73	4
TRAILL	PB11-2	1-Sep-57	45.77	5	WELLS	TS8-1	5-Jun-52	26.59	5
WALSH	TS7-5	5-Jun-52	5.37	3	WILLIAMS	UK8-2	9-May-53	3.78	2
WALSH	TP9-3	16-Apr-55	7.62	3	WILLIAMS	TS8-3	7-Jun-52	4.54	2
WALSH	PB15-2	17-Sep-57	13.36	4	WILLIAMS	PB9-4	26-Aug-57	5.22	3
WALSH	PB8-3	20-Aug-57	19.73	4	WILLIAMS	PB11-2	1-Sep-57	6.92	3
WALSH	PB2-3	20-Jun-57	30.08	5	WILLIAMS	PB11-4	3-Sep-57	10.36	4
WALSH	PB11-2	1-Sep-57	45.77	5	WILLIAMS	PB15-2	17-Sep-57	13.36	4
WARD	PB9-4	26-Aug-57	5.22	3	WILLIAMS	PB5-2	16-Jul-57	19.36	4
WARD	UK8-2	9-May-53	5.46	3	WILLIAMS	PB8-3	20-Aug-57	19.73	4
WARD	PB11-2	1-Sep-57	9.15	3	WILLIAMS	UK8-1	8-May-53	22.29	4
WARD	PB15-2	17-Sep-57	13.36	4	WILLIAMS	UK2-2	25-Mar-53	25.37	5
WARD	PB8-3	20-Aug-57	19.73	4	WILLIAMS	TS8-1	5-Jun-52	131.11	7

INDIVIDUAL FALLOUT DAYS
NEBRASKA

COUNTY	SHOT	DATE	µCi/SQ METER	INDEX	COUNTY	SHOT	DATE	µCi/SQ METER	INDEX
ADAMS	PB13-4	9-Sep-57	3.55	2	ARTHUR	TS5-1	7-May-52	4.50	2
ADAMS	PB8-5	22-Aug-57	3.78	2	ARTHUR	PB18-3	12-Jul-57	4.73	2
ADAMS	TP9-2	15-Apr-55	4.09	2	ARTHUR	PB9-3	25-Aug-57	5.87	3
ADAMS	TS7-5	5-Jun-52	4.25	2	ARTHUR	TP4-2	8-Mar-55	5.97	3
ADAMS	UK10-2	26-May-53	4.38	2	ARTHUR	PB13-3	8-Sep-57	6.72	3
ADAMS	UK9-3	21-May-53	4.80	2	ARTHUR	PB5-4	18-Jul-57	7.28	3
ADAMS	PB5-4	18-Jul-57	5.89	3	ARTHUR	UK7-4	28-Apr-53	7.91	3
ADAMS	UK7-4	28-Apr-53	6.04	3	ARTHUR	TS1-2	2-Apr-52	8.70	3
ADAMS	TS7-4	4-Jun-52	7.53	3	ARTHUR	UK2-7	30-Mar-53	9.91	3
ADAMS	UK9-2	20-May-53	8.49	3	ARTHUR	TS8-1	5-Jun-52	13.29	4
ADAMS	TS6-3	27-May-52	11.56	4	ARTHUR	TP11-2	16-May-55	14.24	4
ADAMS	TP4-2	8-Mar-55	12.66	4	ARTHUR	TS6-3	27-May-52	18.62	4
ADAMS	PB13-3	8-Sep-57	12.75	4	ARTHUR	TS7-3	3-Jun-52	19.50	4
ADAMS	PB8-3	20-Aug-57	19.73	4	ARTHUR	PB8-3	20-Aug-57	19.73	4
ADAMS	SE3	8-Jul-62	76.52	6	BANNER	PB9-4	26-Aug-57	3.68	2
ADAMS	TS8-1	5-Jun-52	39.88	5	BANNER	UK9-1	19-May-53	3.88	2
ANTELOPE	PB8-5	22-Aug-57	3.78	2	BANNER	PB9-3	25-Aug-57	3.88	2
ANTELOPE	UK2-2	25-Mar-53	3.97	2	BANNER	TP3-2	2-Mar-55	4.00	2
ANTELOPE	PB15-3	18-Sep-57	4.13	2	BANNER	TP4-2	8-Mar-55	5.97	3
ANTELOPE	UK9-3	21-May-53	6.64	3	BANNER	PB8-3	20-Aug-57	6.85	3
ANTELOPE	PB15-2	17-Sep-57	6.68	3	BANNER	TS6-3	27-May-52	7.03	3
ANTELOPE	PB2-3	20-Jun-57	7.54	3	BANNER	PB2-3	20-Jun-57	7.04	3
ANTELOPE	TS7-4	4-Jun-52	7.67	3	BANNER	TS5-2	8-May-52	8.34	3
ANTELOPE	UK9-2	20-May-53	8.01	3	BANNER	TP11-2	16-May-55	8.58	3
ANTELOPE	UK7-4	28-Apr-53	13.39	4	BANNER	PB5-4	18-Jul-57	12.15	4
ANTELOPE	TS6-3	27-May-52	13.90	4	BANNER	TS5-1	7-May-52	31.67	5
ANTELOPE	PB8-3	20-Aug-57	19.73	4	BANNER	TS1-2	2-Apr-52	35.14	5
ANTELOPE	TS7-5	5-Jun-52	21.32	4	BLAINE	UK9-3	21-May-53	3.61	2
ANTELOPE	PB11-2	1-Sep-57	27.46	5	BLAINE	UK2-2	25-Mar-53	3.97	2
ANTELOPE	SE3	8-Jul-62	220.22	8	BLAINE	PB11-2	1-Sep-57	4.58	2
ARTHUR	PB2-3	20-Jun-57	3.52	2	BLAINE	TS5-1	7-May-52	6.11	3
ARTHUR	TP3-2	2-Mar-55	4.00	2	BLAINE	UK7-4	28-Apr-53	9.63	3
ARTHUR	TS5-2	8-May-52	4.45	2	BLAINE	TS7-4	4-Jun-52	10.29	4

INDIVIDUAL FALLOUT DAYS
NEBRASKA

COUNTY	SHOT	DATE	µCi/SQ METER	INDEX	COUNTY	SHOT	DATE	µCi/SQ METER	INDEX
BLAINE	PB8-5	22-Aug-57	11.33	4	BOYD	PB2-3	20-Jun-57	11.31	4
BLAINE	PB8-3	20-Aug-57	19.73	4	BOYD	PB15-2	17-Sep-57	13.36	4
BLAINE	TS8-1	5-Jun-52	26.59	5	BOYD	TS5-1	7-May-52	13.79	4
BLAINE	PB2-3	20-Jun-57	45.16	5	BOYD	UK7-4	28-Apr-53	17.41	4
BOONE	TS7-5	5-Jun-52	3.58	2	BOYD	PB8-3	20-Aug-57	19.73	4
BOONE	PB8-5	22-Aug-57	3.78	2	BOYD	TS8-1	5-Jun-52	26.59	5
BOONE	UK8-2	9-May-53	4.04	2	BOYD	TS7-4	4-Jun-52	30.36	5
BOONE	UK9-2	20-May-53	5.09	3	BROWN	TS5-2	8-May-52	3.90	2
BOONE	PB9-4	26-Aug-57	5.22	3	BROWN	UK2-2	25-Mar-53	3.97	2
BOONE	PB2-3	20-Jun-57	7.54	3	BROWN	PB11-2	1-Sep-57	4.58	2
BOONE	TS7-4	4-Jun-52	8.81	3	BROWN	PB18-3	12-Jul-57	4.73	2
BOONE	UK7-4	28-Apr-53	11.41	4	BROWN	UK9-3	21-May-53	5.68	3
BOONE	TP4-2	8-Mar-55	12.66	4	BROWN	TS6-4	28-May-52	7.25	3
BOONE	TS6-3	27-May-52	15.82	4	BROWN	PB8-5	22-Aug-57	7.56	3
BOONE	PB8-3	20-Aug-57	19.73	4	BROWN	TS7-4	4-Jun-52	9.25	3
BOONE	PB11-2	1-Sep-57	27.46	5	BROWN	TS7-3	3-Jun-52	9.75	3
BOX BUTTE	TP3-2	2-Mar-55	4.00	2	BROWN	TS5-1	7-May-52	12.03	4
BOX BUTTE	PB18-3	12-Jul-57	4.73	2	BROWN	UK7-4	28-Apr-53	14.03	4
BOX BUTTE	PB2-3	20-Jun-57	5.28	3	BROWN	PB8-3	20-Aug-57	19.73	4
BOX BUTTE	UK7-4	28-Apr-53	5.57	3	BROWN	TS8-1	5-Jun-52	26.59	5
BOX BUTTE	TP4-2	8-Mar-55	5.97	3	BROWN	PB2-3	20-Jun-57	45.16	5
BOX BUTTE	PB9-4	26-Aug-57	7.36	3	BUFFALO	UK7-3	27-Apr-53	3.71	2
BOX BUTTE	PB9-3	25-Aug-57	7.76	3	BUFFALO	PB8-5	22-Aug-57	3.78	2
BOX BUTTE	TS5-2	8-May-52	8.45	3	BUFFALO	UK8-2	9-May-53	4.04	2
BOX BUTTE	TP11-2	16-May-55	8.58	3	BUFFALO	UK9-3	21-May-53	4.37	2
BOX BUTTE	TP9-2	15-Apr-55	8.97	3	BUFFALO	PB13-4	9-Sep-57	5.36	3
BOX BUTTE	TS5-1	7-May-52	16.71	4	BUFFALO	UK9-2	20-May-53	5.78	3
BOX BUTTE	TS1-2	2-Apr-52	17.73	4	BUFFALO	TS7-4	4-Jun-52	6.95	3
BOYD	UK2-2	25-Mar-53	3.97	2	BUFFALO	UK7-4	28-Apr-53	8.48	3
BOYD	TS5-2	8-May-52	4.10	2	BUFFALO	TP4-2	8-Mar-55	12.66	4
BOYD	PB11-2	1-Sep-57	4.58	2	BUFFALO	PB8-3	20-Aug-57	19.73	4
BOYD	PB11-4	3-Sep-57	5.18	3	BUFFALO	TS6-3	27-May-52	22.27	4
BOYD	TS7-5	5-Jun-52	5.28	3	BUFFALO	SE3	8-Jul-62	76.52	6

INDIVIDUAL FALLOUT DAYS
NEBRASKA

COUNTY	SHOT	DATE	µCi/SQ METER	INDEX	COUNTY	SHOT	DATE	µCi/SQ METER	INDEX
BUFFALO	PB13-3	8-Sep-57	31.89	5	CASS	PB12-4	5-Sep-57	6.55	3
BUFFALO	TS8-1	5-Jun-52	39.88	5	CASS	TS7-4	4-Jun-52	7.99	3
BURT	UK9-5	23-May-53	3.97	2	CASS	TS6-3	27-May-52	9.01	3
BURT	TP10-3	7-May-55	3.97	2	CASS	TP4-2	8-Mar-55	12.66	4
BURT	UK7-5	29-Apr-53	4.18	2	CASS	UK9-2	20-May-53	16.02	4
BURT	UK9-3	21-May-53	4.28	2	CASS	SE3	8-Jul-62	146.81	7
BURT	PB12-4	5-Sep-57	4.46	2	CEDAR	UK2-2	25-Mar-53	3.97	2
BURT	PB5-5	19-Jul-57	6.09	3	CEDAR	PB15-3	18-Sep-57	4.13	2
BURT	UK9-2	20-May-53	7.68	3	CEDAR	UK9-3	21-May-53	4.87	2
BURT	PB2-3	20-Jun-57	8.04	3	CEDAR	PB11-4	3-Sep-57	5.18	3
BURT	UK7-4	28-Apr-53	8.48	3	CEDAR	PB9-4	26-Aug-57	5.22	3
BURT	TS7-3	3-Jun-52	9.37	3	CEDAR	TS5-1	7-May-52	5.24	3
BURT	TP4-2	8-Mar-55	12.66	4	CEDAR	UK9-2	20-May-53	6.06	3
BURT	TS6-3	27-May-52	15.04	4	CEDAR	TS7-5	5-Jun-52	6.84	3
BURT	TS7-4	4-Jun-52	16.35	4	CEDAR	PB2-3	20-Jun-57	7.54	3
BUTLER	UK10-2	26-May-53	4.13	2	CEDAR	UK7-4	28-Apr-53	11.16	4
BUTLER	TS7-5	5-Jun-52	4.45	2	CEDAR	TS6-3	27-May-52	12.79	4
BUTLER	UK9-2	20-May-53	6.05	3	CEDAR	PB11-2	1-Sep-57	18.31	4
BUTLER	PB13-3	8-Sep-57	6.38	3	CEDAR	PB8-3	20-Aug-57	19.73	4
BUTLER	UK7-4	28-Apr-53	7.84	3	CEDAR	SE4	9-Jul-62	24.53	4
BUTLER	PB13-4	9-Sep-57	8.92	3	CEDAR	TS7-4	4-Jun-52	33.43	5
BUTLER	TS7-4	4-Jun-52	10.96	4	CEDAR	SE2	7-Jul-62	145.87	7
BUTLER	TP4-2	8-Mar-55	12.66	4	CHASE	UK9-2	20-May-53	3.68	2
BUTLER	TS6-3	27-May-52	14.11	4	CHASE	UK7-3	27-Apr-53	3.96	2
BUTLER	PB5-4	18-Jul-57	14.75	4	CHASE	PB13-3	8-Sep-57	4.48	2
BUTLER	PB8-3	20-Aug-57	19.73	4	CHASE	PB5-4	18-Jul-57	4.87	2
BUTLER	SE3	8-Jul-62	139.13	7	CHASE	TS1-2	2-Apr-52	5.16	3
CASS	TS7-3	3-Jun-52	3.83	2	CHASE	PB2-3	20-Jun-57	5.28	3
CASS	PB8-3	20-Aug-57	4.00	2	CHASE	TP11-2	16-May-55	5.45	3
CASS	UK10-2	26-May-53	4.01	2	CHASE	TP9-2	15-Apr-55	6.94	3
CASS	PB9-3	25-Aug-57	4.14	2	CHASE	PB9-3	25-Aug-57	7.76	3
CASS	UK7-4	28-Apr-53	4.44	2	CHASE	TP3-2	2-Mar-55	7.78	3
CASS	PB13-5	10-Sep-57	6.45	3	CHASE	UK7-4	28-Apr-53	7.86	3

INDIVIDUAL FALLOUT DAYS
NEBRASKA

COUNTY	SHOT	DATE	µCi/SQ METER	INDEX	COUNTY	SHOT	DATE	µCi/SQ METER	INDEX
CHASE	PB9-4	26-Aug-57	11.05	4	CHEYENNE	TP11-2	16-May-55	8.58	3
CHASE	TS8-1	5-Jun-52	13.29	4	CHEYENNE	UK2-7	30-Mar-53	9.91	3
CHASE	TP4-2	8-Mar-55	51.16	6	CHEYENNE	PB5-4	18-Jul-57	12.15	4
CHASE	TS6-3	27-May-52	56.71	6	CHEYENNE	TS8-1	5-Jun-52	13.29	4
CHASE	TP10-2	6-May-55	33.30	5	CHEYENNE	PB9-3	25-Aug-57	15.53	4
CHERRY	PB18-3	12-Jul-57	3.55	2	CHEYENNE	TS1-2	2-Apr-52	17.73	4
CHERRY	TP11-5	19-May-55	3.58	2	CHEYENNE	TS6-3	27-May-52	27.87	5
CHERRY	PB9-3	25-Aug-57	3.88	2	CLAY	TP9-2	15-Apr-55	3.52	2
CHERRY	UK9-3	21-May-53	4.94	2	CLAY	PB13-4	9-Sep-57	3.55	2
CHERRY	PB8-4	21-Aug-57	5.37	3	CLAY	PB8-5	22-Aug-57	3.78	2
CHERRY	PB5-4	18-Jul-57	8.86	3	CLAY	UK9-3	21-May-53	3.94	2
CHERRY	TS5-2	8-May-52	8.97	3	CLAY	TS7-5	5-Jun-52	4.56	2
CHERRY	TS7-3	3-Jun-52	10.17	4	CLAY	TS7-3	3-Jun-52	4.77	2
CHERRY	TS8-1	5-Jun-52	13.29	4	CLAY	TS1-2	2-Apr-52	5.16	3
CHERRY	PB15-2	17-Sep-57	13.36	4	CLAY	UK10-2	26-May-53	5.51	3
CHERRY	UK7-4	28-Apr-53	13.58	4	CLAY	PB5-4	18-Jul-57	5.89	3
CHERRY	PB2-3	20-Jun-57	15.08	4	CLAY	PB13-3	8-Sep-57	6.38	3
CHERRY	TS5-1	7-May-52	15.45	4	CLAY	PB12-4	5-Sep-57	6.55	3
CHERRY	PB11-2	1-Sep-57	18.31	4	CLAY	UK7-4	28-Apr-53	7.32	3
CHERRY	PB8-3	20-Aug-57	78.93	6	CLAY	UK9-2	20-May-53	9.03	3
CHERRY	UK2-2	25-Mar-53	45.45	5	CLAY	TS6-3	27-May-52	9.12	3
CHEYENNE	PB18-3	12-Jul-57	3.55	2	CLAY	TS7-4	4-Jun-52	9.45	3
CHEYENNE	PB9-4	26-Aug-57	3.68	2	CLAY	TP4-2	8-Mar-55	12.66	4
CHEYENNE	UK7-4	28-Apr-53	3.97	2	CLAY	PB8-3	20-Aug-57	19.73	4
CHEYENNE	PB12-3	4-Sep-57	3.98	2	CLAY	SE3	8-Jul-62	99.74	6
CHEYENNE	TP3-2	2-Mar-55	4.00	2	COLFAX	UK9-3	21-May-53	3.63	2
CHEYENNE	UK11-2	5-Jun-53	4.10	2	COLFAX	TS7-5	5-Jun-52	3.72	2
CHEYENNE	TS5-2	8-May-52	5.09	3	COLFAX	UK9-5	23-May-53	5.21	3
CHEYENNE	TS5-1	7-May-52	5.24	3	COLFAX	PB5-4	18-Jul-57	5.89	3
CHEYENNE	TP4-2	8-Mar-55	5.97	3	COLFAX	TS7-4	4-Jun-52	8.97	3
CHEYENNE	PB11-2	1-Sep-57	6.81	3	COLFAX	UK7-4	28-Apr-53	10.97	4
CHEYENNE	PB2-3	20-Jun-57	7.04	3	COLFAX	UK9-2	20-May-53	11.15	4
CHEYENNE	TS6-4	28-May-52	7.25	3	COLFAX	TP4-2	8-Mar-55	12.66	4

INDIVIDUAL FALLOUT DAYS
NEBRASKA

COUNTY	SHOT	DATE	µCi/SQ METER	INDEX	COUNTY	SHOT	DATE	µCi/SQ METER	INDEX
COLFAX	TS6-3	27-May-52	15.52	4	DAKOTA	UK7-4	28-Apr-53	9.76	3
COLFAX	PB8-3	20-Aug-57	19.73	4	DAKOTA	TS6-3	27-May-52	16.75	4
COLFAX	SE3	8-Jul-62	172.89	7	DAKOTA	TS7-4	4-Jun-52	22.92	4
CUMING	UK7-5	29-Apr-53	3.51	2	DAKOTA	TS7-5	5-Jun-52	26.84	5
CUMING	PB12-4	5-Sep-57	4.39	2	DAKOTA	SE3	8-Jul-62	527.44	9
CUMING	UK7-4	28-Apr-53	6.95	3	DAWES	PB9-4	26-Aug-57	3.68	2
CUMING	UK9-2	20-May-53	10.18	4	DAWES	PB9-3	25-Aug-57	3.88	2
CUMING	TP4-2	8-Mar-55	12.66	4	DAWES	TP3-2	2-Mar-55	4.00	2
CUMING	TS6-3	27-May-52	15.88	4	DAWES	UK7-4	28-Apr-53	5.22	3
CUMING	PB8-3	20-Aug-57	19.73	4	DAWES	TP4-2	8-Mar-55	5.97	3
CUMING	TS7-4	4-Jun-52	50.69	6	DAWES	PB2-3	20-Jun-57	7.04	3
CUMING	SE3	8-Jul-62	208.70	8	DAWES	TP11-2	16-May-55	8.58	3
CUSTER	PB18-3	12-Jul-57	3.55	2	DAWES	TS5-2	8-May-52	13.20	4
CUSTER	PB8-5	22-Aug-57	3.78	2	DAWES	TS7-3	3-Jun-52	15.15	4
CUSTER	UK9-2	20-May-53	3.97	2	DAWES	TS5-1	7-May-52	54.99	6
CUSTER	UK9-3	21-May-53	4.42	2	DAWES	TS1-2	2-Apr-52	35.14	5
CUSTER	TS5-1	7-May-52	4.49	2	DAWSON	PB18-3	12-Jul-57	3.55	2
CUSTER	PB11-2	1-Sep-57	4.58	2	DAWSON	TP9-2	15-Apr-55	3.81	2
CUSTER	PB11-4	3-Sep-57	5.18	3	DAWSON	UK9-3	21-May-53	4.06	2
CUSTER	UK7-3	27-Apr-53	6.15	3	DAWSON	UK7-3	27-Apr-53	4.47	2
CUSTER	PB15-2	17-Sep-57	6.68	3	DAWSON	UK9-2	20-May-53	4.52	2
CUSTER	PB2-3	20-Jun-57	7.54	3	DAWSON	PB11-2	1-Sep-57	4.58	2
CUSTER	TS7-4	4-Jun-52	8.27	3	DAWSON	TS1-2	2-Apr-52	5.16	3
CUSTER	UK7-4	28-Apr-53	9.05	3	DAWSON	PB11-4	3-Sep-57	5.18	3
CUSTER	TP4-2	8-Mar-55	12.66	4	DAWSON	PB9-4	26-Aug-57	5.22	3
CUSTER	TS6-3	27-May-52	15.98	4	DAWSON	TP11-2	16-May-55	5.45	3
CUSTER	PB8-3	20-Aug-57	19.73	4	DAWSON	TS7-4	4-Jun-52	5.47	3
CUSTER	TS8-1	5-Jun-52	26.59	5	DAWSON	PB2-3	20-Jun-57	7.54	3
CUSTER	SE3	8-Jul-62	126.34	7	DAWSON	PB8-5	22-Aug-57	7.56	3
DAKOTA	UK2-2	25-Mar-53	3.97	2	DAWSON	TP3-2	2-Mar-55	7.78	3
DAKOTA	UK9-3	21-May-53	4.50	2	DAWSON	UK7-4	28-Apr-53	8.54	3
DAKOTA	UK7-5	29-Apr-53	4.99	2	DAWSON	TS6-3	27-May-52	12.84	4
DAKOTA	UK9-2	20-May-53	5.60	3	DAWSON	PB8-3	20-Aug-57	19.73	4

INDIVIDUAL FALLOUT DAYS
NEBRASKA

COUNTY	SHOT	DATE	µCi/SQ METER	INDEX	COUNTY	SHOT	DATE	µCi/SQ METER	INDEX
DAWSON	TP4-2	8-Mar-55	51.16	6	DODGE	TP10-3	7-May-55	4.35	2
DAWSON	TS8-1	5-Jun-52	26.59	5	DODGE	PB8-4	21-Aug-57	5.37	3
DAWSON	TP10-2	6-May-55	33.30	5	DODGE	UK7-4	28-Apr-53	8.16	3
DEUEL	PB2-3	20-Jun-57	3.52	2	DODGE	TS7-4	4-Jun-52	9.18	3
DEUEL	PB9-4	26-Aug-57	3.68	2	DODGE	TP4-2	8-Mar-55	12.66	4
DEUEL	TP3-2	2-Mar-55	4.00	2	DODGE	TS6-3	27-May-52	15.54	4
DEUEL	TS5-1	7-May-52	4.24	2	DODGE	UK9-2	20-May-53	16.79	4
DEUEL	TS5-2	8-May-52	4.24	2	DODGE	PB8-3	20-Aug-57	19.73	4
DEUEL	UK11-2	5-Jun-53	4.59	2	DOUGLAS	UK10-2	26-May-53	3.58	2
DEUEL	TP9-2	15-Apr-55	4.66	2	DOUGLAS	UK7-4	28-Apr-53	3.74	2
DEUEL	TP11-3	17-May-55	5.50	3	DOUGLAS	UK7-5	29-Apr-53	3.76	2
DEUEL	TP4-2	8-Mar-55	5.97	3	DOUGLAS	UK9-5	23-May-53	4.37	2
DEUEL	PB11-2	1-Sep-57	6.81	3	DOUGLAS	PB2-3	20-Jun-57	5.36	3
DEUEL	TS1-2	2-Apr-52	8.70	3	DOUGLAS	PB12-4	5-Sep-57	7.91	3
DEUEL	TS8-1	5-Jun-52	13.29	4	DOUGLAS	TS6-3	27-May-52	12.24	4
DEUEL	TP11-2	16-May-55	14.24	4	DOUGLAS	TP4-2	8-Mar-55	12.66	4
DEUEL	UK2-7	30-Mar-53	14.85	4	DOUGLAS	UK9-2	20-May-53	15.16	4
DEUEL	PB9-3	25-Aug-57	23.29	4	DOUGLAS	TS7-4	4-Jun-52	17.95	4
DEUEL	TS6-3	27-May-52	48.29	5	DOUGLAS	SE3	8-Jul-62	146.81	7
DIXON	UK7-5	29-Apr-53	3.67	2	DUNDY	TS5-1	7-May-52	3.75	2
DIXON	UK2-2	25-Mar-53	3.97	2	DUNDY	PB9-3	25-Aug-57	3.88	2
DIXON	UK9-2	20-May-53	4.11	2	DUNDY	PB12-4	5-Sep-57	4.08	2
DIXON	UK9-3	21-May-53	4.65	2	DUNDY	PB12-3	4-Sep-57	4.48	2
DIXON	PB2-3	20-Jun-57	5.36	3	DUNDY	PB18-3	12-Jul-57	4.73	2
DIXON	UK7-4	28-Apr-53	10.33	4	DUNDY	UK7-4	28-Apr-53	4.99	2
DIXON	TS7-5	5-Jun-52	11.39	4	DUNDY	TS1-2	2-Apr-52	5.16	3
DIXON	TS6-3	27-May-52	17.11	4	DUNDY	UK7-3	27-Apr-53	5.16	3
DIXON	PB8-3	20-Aug-57	19.73	4	DUNDY	TP11-2	16-May-55	5.45	3
DIXON	SE4	9-Jul-62	30.53	5	DUNDY	UK9-2	20-May-53	5.86	3
DIXON	TS7-4	4-Jun-52	41.33	5	DUNDY	TP9-2	15-Apr-55	6.98	3
DIXON	SE3	8-Jul-62	527.44	9	DUNDY	PB2-3	20-Jun-57	7.04	3
DODGE	TS7-5	5-Jun-52	4.00	2	DUNDY	PB9-4	26-Aug-57	7.36	3
DODGE	UK9-5	23-May-53	4.27	2	DUNDY	TP3-2	2-Mar-55	7.78	3

INDIVIDUAL FALLOUT DAYS
NEBRASKA

COUNTY	SHOT	DATE	µCi/SQ METER	INDEX	COUNTY	SHOT	DATE	µCi/SQ METER	INDEX
DUNDY	TS8-1	5-Jun-52	13.29	4	FRANKLIN	TS8-1	5-Jun-52	39.88	5
DUNDY	TP4-2	8-Mar-55	51.16	6	FRONTIER	PB18-3	12-Jul-57	3.55	2
DUNDY	TP10-2	6-May-55	33.30	5	FRONTIER	UK7-3	27-Apr-53	3.64	2
DUNDY	TS6-3	27-May-52	34.93	5	FRONTIER	TS7-4	4-Jun-52	4.05	2
FILLMORE	PB13-4	9-Sep-57	3.55	2	FRONTIER	PB5-4	18-Jul-57	4.87	2
FILLMORE	UK9-3	21-May-53	3.79	2	FRONTIER	TS1-2	2-Apr-52	5.16	3
FILLMORE	TS7-5	5-Jun-52	4.59	2	FRONTIER	TP11-2	16-May-55	5.45	3
FILLMORE	UK10-2	26-May-53	4.88	2	FRONTIER	UK9-2	20-May-53	5.78	3
FILLMORE	TS7-3	3-Jun-52	5.15	3	FRONTIER	TP9-2	15-Apr-55	6.09	3
FILLMORE	TS1-2	2-Apr-52	5.16	3	FRONTIER	UK7-4	28-Apr-53	6.25	3
FILLMORE	PB13-3	8-Sep-57	6.38	3	FRONTIER	PB13-3	8-Sep-57	6.72	3
FILLMORE	UK7-4	28-Apr-53	7.22	3	FRONTIER	PB2-3	20-Jun-57	7.04	3
FILLMORE	UK9-2	20-May-53	7.29	3	FRONTIER	TP3-2	2-Mar-55	7.78	3
FILLMORE	TS6-3	27-May-52	8.48	3	FRONTIER	TS6-3	27-May-52	18.70	4
FILLMORE	TS7-4	4-Jun-52	11.10	4	FRONTIER	PB8-3	20-Aug-57	19.73	4
FILLMORE	TP4-2	8-Mar-55	12.66	4	FRONTIER	TP4-2	8-Mar-55	51.16	6
FILLMORE	PB8-3	20-Aug-57	19.73	4	FRONTIER	TS8-1	5-Jun-52	26.59	5
FILLMORE	SE3	8-Jul-62	76.52	6	FRONTIER	TP10-2	6-May-55	33.30	5
FRANKLIN	TS7-5	5-Jun-52	3.76	2	FURNAS	UK9-3	21-May-53	4.12	2
FRANKLIN	PB8-5	22-Aug-57	3.78	2	FURNAS	UK7-3	27-Apr-53	4.40	2
FRANKLIN	PB8-2	19-Aug-57	4.95	2	FURNAS	TS1-2	2-Apr-52	5.16	3
FRANKLIN	UK7-4	28-Apr-53	5.03	3	FURNAS	PB13-4	9-Sep-57	5.36	3
FRANKLIN	UK9-3	21-May-53	5.04	3	FURNAS	TP9-2	15-Apr-55	6.94	3
FRANKLIN	TS1-2	2-Apr-52	5.16	3	FURNAS	UK9-2	20-May-53	7.77	3
FRANKLIN	PB13-4	9-Sep-57	5.36	3	FURNAS	TP3-2	2-Mar-55	7.78	3
FRANKLIN	TS7-4	4-Jun-52	6.35	3	FURNAS	UK7-4	28-Apr-53	7.97	3
FRANKLIN	TP9-2	15-Apr-55	6.75	3	FURNAS	TS6-4	28-May-52	8.86	3
FRANKLIN	TS6-3	27-May-52	7.31	3	FURNAS	PB8-3	20-Aug-57	19.73	4
FRANKLIN	UK9-2	20-May-53	10.75	4	FURNAS	TS6-3	27-May-52	22.10	4
FRANKLIN	TP4-2	8-Mar-55	12.66	4	FURNAS	TS7-4	4-Jun-52	24.68	4
FRANKLIN	PB13-3	8-Sep-57	12.75	4	FURNAS	TP4-2	8-Mar-55	51.16	6
FRANKLIN	PB8-3	20-Aug-57	19.73	4	FURNAS	TS8-1	5-Jun-52	26.59	5
FRANKLIN	UK7-3	27-Apr-53	3.51	1	FURNAS	TP10-2	6-May-55	33.30	5

INDIVIDUAL FALLOUT DAYS
NEBRASKA

COUNTY	SHOT	DATE	µCi/SQ METER	INDEX	COUNTY	SHOT	DATE	µCi/SQ METER	INDEX
GAGE	PB13-4	9-Sep-57	3.55	2	GARFIELD	UK7-3	27-Apr-53	4.26	2
GAGE	TS7-5	5-Jun-52	4.38	2	GARFIELD	PB11-2	1-Sep-57	4.58	2
GAGE	TS1-2	2-Apr-52	5.16	3	GARFIELD	PB5-4	18-Jul-57	5.89	3
GAGE	UK7-4	28-Apr-53	5.24	3	GARFIELD	TS6-3	27-May-52	7.82	3
GAGE	PB8-4	21-Aug-57	5.37	3	GARFIELD	UK7-4	28-Apr-53	12.69	4
GAGE	UK10-2	26-May-53	5.88	3	GARFIELD	TS7-4	4-Jun-52	14.18	4
GAGE	PB8-3	20-Aug-57	5.95	3	GARFIELD	PB2-3	20-Jun-57	15.08	4
GAGE	TS7-3	3-Jun-52	6.01	3	GARFIELD	PB8-3	20-Aug-57	19.73	4
GAGE	TS7-4	4-Jun-52	7.26	3	GARFIELD	TS8-1	5-Jun-52	26.59	5
GAGE	UK9-2	20-May-53	8.04	3	GARFIELD	PB15-2	17-Sep-57	33.40	5
GAGE	TP4-2	8-Mar-55	12.66	4	GARFIELD	SE3	8-Jul-62	220.22	8
GAGE	PB12-4	5-Sep-57	14.39	4	GOSPER	PB8-5	22-Aug-57	3.78	2
GAGE	PB13-5	10-Sep-57	16.00	4	GOSPER	UK8-2	9-May-53	4.04	2
GAGE	SE3	8-Jul-62	80.75	6	GOSPER	UK9-3	21-May-53	4.24	2
GARDEN	PB2-3	20-Jun-57	3.52	2	GOSPER	TS7-4	4-Jun-52	5.09	3
GARDEN	PB9-4	26-Aug-57	3.68	2	GOSPER	TS1-2	2-Apr-52	5.16	3
GARDEN	TP3-2	2-Mar-55	4.00	2	GOSPER	TP9-2	15-Apr-55	5.33	3
GARDEN	PB18-3	12-Jul-57	4.73	2	GOSPER	PB13-4	9-Sep-57	5.36	3
GARDEN	TS5-2	8-May-52	5.84	3	GOSPER	TP11-2	16-May-55	5.45	3
GARDEN	UK7-4	28-Apr-53	5.88	3	GOSPER	UK9-2	20-May-53	6.05	3
GARDEN	TP4-2	8-Mar-55	5.97	3	GOSPER	PB13-3	8-Sep-57	6.38	3
GARDEN	TS5-1	7-May-52	6.24	3	GOSPER	TP3-2	2-Mar-55	7.78	3
GARDEN	PB5-4	18-Jul-57	7.28	3	GOSPER	UK7-4	28-Apr-53	8.29	3
GARDEN	TP11-2	16-May-55	8.58	3	GOSPER	TS7-3	3-Jun-52	17.59	4
GARDEN	TS1-2	2-Apr-52	8.70	3	GOSPER	PB8-3	20-Aug-57	19.73	4
GARDEN	TS7-4	4-Jun-52	9.40	3	GOSPER	TS6-3	27-May-52	21.34	4
GARDEN	UK2-7	30-Mar-53	9.91	3	GOSPER	TP4-2	8-Mar-55	51.16	6
GARDEN	TS8-1	5-Jun-52	13.29	4	GOSPER	TS8-1	5-Jun-52	26.59	5
GARDEN	TS6-3	27-May-52	21.08	4	GOSPER	TP10-2	6-May-55	33.30	5
GARDEN	PB9-3	25-Aug-57	23.29	4	GRANT	TP3-2	2-Mar-55	4.00	2
GARFIELD	UK9-3	21-May-53	3.61	2	GRANT	TP4-2	8-Mar-55	5.97	3
GARFIELD	UK9-2	20-May-53	3.70	2	GRANT	PB2-3	20-Jun-57	7.04	3
GARFIELD	UK2-2	25-Mar-53	3.97	2	GRANT	PB8-4	21-Aug-57	8.05	3

INDIVIDUAL FALLOUT DAYS
NEBRASKA

COUNTY	SHOT	DATE	µCi/SQ METER	INDEX	COUNTY	SHOT	DATE	µCi/SQ METER	INDEX
GRANT	TS1-2	2-Apr-52	8.70	3	HALL	PB13-3	8-Sep-57	31.89	5
GRANT	TS5-2	8-May-52	8.90	3	HALL	TS8-1	5-Jun-52	39.88	5
GRANT	TS5-1	7-May-52	10.60	4	HAMILTON	PB12-4	5-Sep-57	3.68	2
GRANT	UK7-4	28-Apr-53	10.97	4	HAMILTON	PB8-5	22-Aug-57	3.78	2
GRANT	PB5-4	18-Jul-57	12.15	4	HAMILTON	TS7-3	3-Jun-52	3.89	2
GRANT	TS8-1	5-Jun-52	13.29	4	HAMILTON	UK9-3	21-May-53	4.06	2
GRANT	TP11-2	16-May-55	14.24	4	HAMILTON	TS7-5	5-Jun-52	4.49	2
GRANT	PB8-3	20-Aug-57	19.73	4	HAMILTON	UK10-2	26-May-53	4.88	2
GRANT	TP9-2	15-Apr-55	27.46	5	HAMILTON	UK7-4	28-Apr-53	5.88	3
GREELEY	TS7-5	5-Jun-52	3.83	2	HAMILTON	UK9-2	20-May-53	7.41	3
GREELEY	UK8-2	9-May-53	4.04	2	HAMILTON	PB13-4	9-Sep-57	8.92	3
GREELEY	UK9-2	20-May-53	4.16	2	HAMILTON	TS7-4	4-Jun-52	9.77	3
GREELEY	PB2-3	20-Jun-57	7.54	3	HAMILTON	TS6-3	27-May-52	11.48	4
GREELEY	UK7-4	28-Apr-53	8.61	3	HAMILTON	TP4-2	8-Mar-55	12.66	4
GREELEY	TS7-4	4-Jun-52	8.81	3	HAMILTON	PB8-3	20-Aug-57	19.73	4
GREELEY	PB11-2	1-Sep-57	9.15	3	HAMILTON	SE3	8-Jul-62	80.75	6
GREELEY	TP4-2	8-Mar-55	12.66	4	HARLAN	PB8-5	22-Aug-57	3.78	2
GREELEY	TS6-3	27-May-52	15.56	4	HARLAN	UK7-3	27-Apr-53	3.92	2
GREELEY	PB8-3	20-Aug-57	19.73	4	HARLAN	UK9-3	21-May-53	4.74	2
GREELEY	TS8-1	5-Jun-52	39.88	5	HARLAN	TS7-4	4-Jun-52	5.20	3
GREELEY	SE3	8-Jul-62	172.89	7	HARLAN	UK7-4	28-Apr-53	5.29	3
HALL	PB8-5	22-Aug-57	3.78	2	HARLAN	TP9-2	15-Apr-55	6.75	3
HALL	UK7-3	27-Apr-53	4.12	2	HARLAN	PB12-4	5-Sep-57	7.70	3
HALL	TS7-5	5-Jun-52	4.14	2	HARLAN	PB13-4	9-Sep-57	8.92	3
HALL	UK9-3	21-May-53	4.31	2	HARLAN	UK9-2	20-May-53	11.02	4
HALL	TS1-2	2-Apr-52	5.16	3	HARLAN	TP4-2	8-Mar-55	12.66	4
HALL	PB13-4	9-Sep-57	5.36	3	HARLAN	PB13-3	8-Sep-57	12.75	4
HALL	UK9-2	20-May-53	6.86	3	HARLAN	TS6-3	27-May-52	14.96	4
HALL	TS7-4	4-Jun-52	9.47	3	HARLAN	PB8-3	20-Aug-57	19.73	4
HALL	UK7-4	28-Apr-53	9.56	3	HARLAN	TS8-1	5-Jun-52	39.88	5
HALL	TP4-2	8-Mar-55	12.66	4	HAYES	PB2-3	20-Jun-57	3.52	2
HALL	TS6-3	27-May-52	13.60	4	HAYES	PB9-3	25-Aug-57	3.88	2
HALL	PB8-3	20-Aug-57	19.73	4	HAYES	UK7-3	27-Apr-53	4.33	2

INDIVIDUAL FALLOUT DAYS
NEBRASKA

COUNTY	SHOT	DATE	µCi/SQ METER	INDEX	COUNTY	SHOT	DATE	µCi/SQ METER	INDEX
HAYES	PB13-3	8-Sep-57	4.48	2	HOLT	UK9-3	21-May-53	5.16	3
HAYES	PB18-3	12-Jul-57	4.73	2	HOLT	PB11-4	3-Sep-57	5.18	3
HAYES	TS1-2	2-Apr-52	5.16	3	HOLT	PB15-2	17-Sep-57	6.68	3
HAYES	TP11-2	16-May-55	5.45	3	HOLT	TS5-1	7-May-52	7.04	3
HAYES	UK9-2	20-May-53	5.60	3	HOLT	PB2-3	20-Jun-57	7.54	3
HAYES	UK7-4	28-Apr-53	6.47	3	HOLT	TS6-3	27-May-52	9.01	3
HAYES	TP9-2	15-Apr-55	7.04	3	HOLT	UK7-4	28-Apr-53	15.24	4
HAYES	PB5-4	18-Jul-57	7.28	3	HOLT	PB8-3	20-Aug-57	19.73	4
HAYES	TP3-2	2-Mar-55	7.78	3	HOLT	TS8-1	5-Jun-52	26.59	5
HAYES	TP4-2	8-Mar-55	51.16	6	HOLT	TS7-4	4-Jun-52	34.21	5
HAYES	TS8-1	5-Jun-52	26.59	5	HOLT	SE2	7-Jul-62	145.87	7
HAYES	TP10-2	6-May-55	33.30	5	HOLT	SE3	8-Jul-62	252.68	8
HAYES	TS6-3	27-May-52	40.64	5	HOOKER	PB2-3	20-Jun-57	3.52	2
HITCHCOCK	PB2-3	20-Jun-57	3.52	2	HOOKER	PB9-3	25-Aug-57	3.88	2
HITCHCOCK	PB9-3	25-Aug-57	3.88	2	HOOKER	TP3-2	2-Mar-55	4.00	2
HITCHCOCK	UK7-3	27-Apr-53	4.76	2	HOOKER	TS5-2	8-May-52	4.45	2
HITCHCOCK	PB5-4	18-Jul-57	4.87	2	HOOKER	PB18-3	12-Jul-57	4.73	2
HITCHCOCK	TS1-2	2-Apr-52	5.16	3	HOOKER	PB8-2	19-Aug-57	4.95	2
HITCHCOCK	TP11-2	16-May-55	5.45	3	HOOKER	UK9-3	21-May-53	5.46	3
HITCHCOCK	UK7-4	28-Apr-53	6.20	3	HOOKER	TP4-2	8-Mar-55	5.97	3
HITCHCOCK	UK9-2	20-May-53	6.84	3	HOOKER	PB13-3	8-Sep-57	6.72	3
HITCHCOCK	TP3-2	2-Mar-55	7.78	3	HOOKER	PB5-4	18-Jul-57	7.28	3
HITCHCOCK	TP9-2	15-Apr-55	8.47	3	HOOKER	TS5-1	7-May-52	7.72	3
HITCHCOCK	PB5-2	16-Jul-57	9.10	3	HOOKER	TP11-2	16-May-55	8.58	3
HITCHCOCK	PB9-4	26-Aug-57	11.05	4	HOOKER	PB5-3	17-Jul-57	10.18	4
HITCHCOCK	TS6-3	27-May-52	15.33	4	HOOKER	UK7-4	28-Apr-53	11.41	4
HITCHCOCK	TP4-2	8-Mar-55	51.16	6	HOOKER	TS8-1	5-Jun-52	13.29	4
HITCHCOCK	TS8-1	5-Jun-52	26.59	5	HOOKER	TS1-2	2-Apr-52	17.73	4
HITCHCOCK	TP10-2	6-May-55	33.30	5	HOOKER	PB8-3	20-Aug-57	39.46	5
HOLT	PB8-5	22-Aug-57	3.78	2	HOWARD	PB8-5	22-Aug-57	3.78	2
HOLT	UK2-2	25-Mar-53	3.97	2	HOWARD	UK9-3	21-May-53	3.81	2
HOLT	PB15-3	18-Sep-57	4.13	2	HOWARD	TS7-5	5-Jun-52	4.00	2
HOLT	PB11-2	1-Sep-57	4.58	2	HOWARD	PB9-4	26-Aug-57	5.22	3

INDIVIDUAL FALLOUT DAYS
NEBRASKA

COUNTY	SHOT	DATE	µCi/SQ METER	INDEX	COUNTY	SHOT	DATE	µCi/SQ METER	INDEX
HOWARD	PB12-4	5-Sep-57	5.81	3	JOHNSON	PB13-5	10-Sep-57	14.34	4
HOWARD	UK9-2	20-May-53	7.23	3	JOHNSON	TS1-2	2-Apr-52	15.48	4
HOWARD	PB2-3	20-Jun-57	7.54	3	JOHNSON	SE3	8-Jul-62	80.75	6
HOWARD	TS7-4	4-Jun-52	9.31	3	KEARNEY	TS7-5	5-Jun-52	3.69	2
HOWARD	TP4-2	8-Mar-55	12.66	4	KEARNEY	TP9-2	15-Apr-55	4.66	2
HOWARD	PB11-2	1-Sep-57	18.31	4	KEARNEY	UK9-3	21-May-53	4.80	2
HOWARD	PB8-3	20-Aug-57	19.73	4	KEARNEY	PB13-4	9-Sep-57	5.36	3
HOWARD	TS6-3	27-May-52	23.46	4	KEARNEY	UK7-4	28-Apr-53	6.68	3
HOWARD	TS8-1	5-Jun-52	39.88	5	KEARNEY	TS7-4	4-Jun-52	7.06	3
HOWARD	SE3	8-Jul-62	345.56	8	KEARNEY	UK9-2	20-May-53	7.59	3
JEFFERSON	PB13-4	9-Sep-57	3.55	2	KEARNEY	TP4-2	8-Mar-55	12.66	4
JEFFERSON	UK9-3	21-May-53	3.89	2	KEARNEY	TS6-3	27-May-52	12.84	4
JEFFERSON	PB8-3	20-Aug-57	4.00	2	KEARNEY	PB8-3	20-Aug-57	19.73	4
JEFFERSON	PB12-4	5-Sep-57	4.36	2	KEARNEY	PB13-3	8-Sep-57	31.89	5
JEFFERSON	UK7-4	28-Apr-53	4.50	2	KEARNEY	TS8-1	5-Jun-52	39.88	5
JEFFERSON	UK10-2	26-May-53	5.64	3	KEITH	PB2-3	20-Jun-57	3.52	2
JEFFERSON	TS7-3	3-Jun-52	6.38	3	KEITH	TS5-2	8-May-52	3.55	2
JEFFERSON	TS7-5	5-Jun-52	8.39	3	KEITH	UK11-2	5-Jun-53	3.56	2
JEFFERSON	TS7-4	4-Jun-52	9.50	3	KEITH	PB9-4	26-Aug-57	3.68	2
JEFFERSON	PB13-5	10-Sep-57	9.83	3	KEITH	TP11-3	17-May-55	4.34	2
JEFFERSON	UK9-2	20-May-53	10.37	4	KEITH	TP9-2	15-Apr-55	4.38	2
JEFFERSON	TP4-2	8-Mar-55	12.66	4	KEITH	PB18-3	12-Jul-57	4.73	2
JEFFERSON	SE3	8-Jul-62	37.44	5	KEITH	PB5-4	18-Jul-57	4.87	2
JOHNSON	TS7-5	5-Jun-52	3.87	2	KEITH	TS1-2	2-Apr-52	5.16	3
JOHNSON	TS7-3	3-Jun-52	4.83	2	KEITH	PB5-3	17-Jul-57	6.78	3
JOHNSON	UK7-4	28-Apr-53	5.19	3	KEITH	UK7-4	28-Apr-53	7.59	3
JOHNSON	UK10-2	26-May-53	5.26	3	KEITH	TP3-2	2-Mar-55	7.78	3
JOHNSON	PB13-4	9-Sep-57	5.36	3	KEITH	TP11-2	16-May-55	9.09	3
JOHNSON	TS7-4	4-Jun-52	7.23	3	KEITH	TS8-1	5-Jun-52	13.29	4
JOHNSON	UK9-2	20-May-53	7.59	3	KEITH	PB9-3	25-Aug-57	23.29	4
JOHNSON	PB8-3	20-Aug-57	7.99	3	KEITH	TP4-2	8-Mar-55	51.16	6
JOHNSON	PB12-4	5-Sep-57	10.54	4	KEITH	TP10-2	6-May-55	33.30	5
JOHNSON	TP4-2	8-Mar-55	12.66	4	KEITH	TS6-3	27-May-52	37.83	5

INDIVIDUAL FALLOUT DAYS
NEBRASKA

COUNTY	SHOT	DATE	µCi/SQ METER	INDEX	COUNTY	SHOT	DATE	µCi/SQ METER	INDEX
KEYA PAHA	PB8-5	22-Aug-57	3.78	2	KNOX	PB15-2	17-Sep-57	5.01	3
KEYA PAHA	UK2-2	25-Mar-53	3.97	2	KNOX	PB2-3	20-Jun-57	7.54	3
KEYA PAHA	UK9-3	21-May-53	4.42	2	KNOX	PB11-2	1-Sep-57	9.15	3
KEYA PAHA	PB11-2	1-Sep-57	4.58	2	KNOX	TS6-3	27-May-52	10.12	4
KEYA PAHA	PB11-4	3-Sep-57	5.18	3	KNOX	PB11-4	3-Sep-57	10.36	4
KEYA PAHA	TS5-2	8-May-52	6.68	3	KNOX	UK7-4	28-Apr-53	11.99	4
KEYA PAHA	PB15-2	17-Sep-57	6.68	3	KNOX	TS5-1	7-May-52	12.14	4
KEYA PAHA	PB2-3	20-Jun-57	7.54	3	KNOX	TS7-4	4-Jun-52	13.97	4
KEYA PAHA	TS5-1	7-May-52	13.83	4	KNOX	PB8-3	20-Aug-57	19.73	4
KEYA PAHA	UK7-4	28-Apr-53	13.96	4	LANCASTER	PB13-4	9-Sep-57	3.55	2
KEYA PAHA	PB8-3	20-Aug-57	19.73	4	LANCASTER	PB8-3	20-Aug-57	4.00	2
KEYA PAHA	TS8-1	5-Jun-52	26.59	5	LANCASTER	PB13-5	10-Sep-57	4.10	2
KEYA PAHA	TS7-4	4-Jun-52	32.97	5	LANCASTER	TS7-5	5-Jun-52	4.25	2
KIMBALL	PB2-3	20-Jun-57	3.52	2	LANCASTER	TS7-3	3-Jun-52	4.89	2
KIMBALL	PB12-3	4-Sep-57	3.62	2	LANCASTER	UK7-4	28-Apr-53	5.83	3
KIMBALL	UK11-2	5-Jun-53	3.63	2	LANCASTER	UK10-2	26-May-53	5.88	3
KIMBALL	PB9-4	26-Aug-57	3.68	2	LANCASTER	PB13-3	8-Sep-57	6.38	3
KIMBALL	PB9-3	25-Aug-57	3.88	2	LANCASTER	PB12-4	5-Sep-57	6.42	3
KIMBALL	TP3-2	2-Mar-55	4.00	2	LANCASTER	UK9-2	20-May-53	8.22	3
KIMBALL	PB8-4	21-Aug-57	4.60	2	LANCASTER	TS7-4	4-Jun-52	8.68	3
KIMBALL	PB18-3	12-Jul-57	4.73	2	LANCASTER	TS6-3	27-May-52	9.95	3
KIMBALL	TP4-2	8-Mar-55	5.97	3	LANCASTER	TP4-2	8-Mar-55	12.66	4
KIMBALL	PB8-3	20-Aug-57	6.85	3	LANCASTER	SE3	8-Jul-62	76.52	6
KIMBALL	PB5-4	18-Jul-57	7.28	3	LINCOLN	PB2-3	20-Jun-57	3.52	2
KIMBALL	TS5-1	7-May-52	8.73	3	LINCOLN	TP9-2	15-Apr-55	4.47	2
KIMBALL	PB5-3	17-Jul-57	10.18	4	LINCOLN	PB13-3	8-Sep-57	4.48	2
KIMBALL	TS6-3	27-May-52	12.52	4	LINCOLN	PB18-3	12-Jul-57	4.73	2
KIMBALL	UK2-7	30-Mar-53	14.85	4	LINCOLN	UK7-3	27-Apr-53	5.02	3
KIMBALL	TS1-2	2-Apr-52	17.73	4	LINCOLN	TS1-2	2-Apr-52	5.16	3
KNOX	PB8-5	22-Aug-57	3.78	2	LINCOLN	PB11-2	1-Sep-57	6.81	3
KNOX	UK2-2	25-Mar-53	3.97	2	LINCOLN	PB5-4	18-Jul-57	7.28	3
KNOX	PB15-3	18-Sep-57	4.13	2	LINCOLN	TP3-2	2-Mar-55	7.78	3
KNOX	UK9-3	21-May-53	4.50	2	LINCOLN	UK7-4	28-Apr-53	8.29	3

INDIVIDUAL FALLOUT DAYS
NEBRASKA

COUNTY	SHOT	DATE	µCi/SQ METER	INDEX	COUNTY	SHOT	DATE	µCi/SQ METER	INDEX
LINCOLN	TP11-2	16-May-55	9.09	3	LOUP	PB8-3	20-Aug-57	19.73	4
LINCOLN	TS7-4	4-Jun-52	10.89	4	LOUP	TS8-1	5-Jun-52	26.59	5
LINCOLN	TS6-3	27-May-52	18.70	4	LOUP	SE3	8-Jul-62	436.50	9
LINCOLN	TP4-2	8-Mar-55	51.16	6	MADISON	PB8-5	22-Aug-57	3.78	2
LINCOLN	TS8-1	5-Jun-52	26.59	5	MADISON	UK9-3	21-May-53	4.24	2
LINCOLN	TP10-2	6-May-55	33.30	5	MADISON	PB5-4	18-Jul-57	5.89	3
LINCOLN	PB8-3	20-Aug-57	39.46	5	MADISON	PB15-2	17-Sep-57	6.68	3
LOGAN	UK9-3	21-May-53	3.61	2	MADISON	TS7-5	5-Jun-52	8.42	3
LOGAN	PB11-2	1-Sep-57	4.58	2	MADISON	TS7-4	4-Jun-52	10.16	4
LOGAN	TP11-2	16-May-55	5.45	3	MADISON	UK9-2	20-May-53	10.46	4
LOGAN	TS6-3	27-May-52	6.91	3	MADISON	UK7-4	28-Apr-53	12.24	4
LOGAN	PB2-3	20-Jun-57	7.54	3	MADISON	TP4-2	8-Mar-55	12.66	4
LOGAN	TP3-2	2-Mar-55	7.78	3	MADISON	PB2-3	20-Jun-57	15.08	4
LOGAN	PB5-4	18-Jul-57	8.86	3	MADISON	TS6-3	27-May-52	15.39	4
LOGAN	UK7-4	28-Apr-53	8.93	3	MADISON	PB11-2	1-Sep-57	27.46	5
LOGAN	TS1-2	2-Apr-52	9.99	3	MADISON	PB8-3	20-Aug-57	39.46	5
LOGAN	PB8-3	20-Aug-57	19.73	4	MADISON	SE3	8-Jul-62	208.70	8
LOGAN	PB15-2	17-Sep-57	20.04	4	MCPHERSON	PB2-3	20-Jun-57	3.52	2
LOGAN	TS7-4	4-Jun-52	21.09	4	MCPHERSON	TS5-2	8-May-52	3.69	2
LOGAN	TP4-2	8-Mar-55	51.16	6	MCPHERSON	PB13-3	8-Sep-57	4.48	2
LOGAN	TS8-1	5-Jun-52	26.59	5	MCPHERSON	PB5-4	18-Jul-57	4.87	2
LOGAN	TP10-2	6-May-55	33.30	5	MCPHERSON	TS1-2	2-Apr-52	5.16	3
LOUP	UK9-3	21-May-53	3.69	2	MCPHERSON	TP11-2	16-May-55	5.45	3
LOUP	UK2-2	25-Mar-53	3.97	2	MCPHERSON	TP3-2	2-Mar-55	7.78	3
LOUP	PB15-3	18-Sep-57	4.13	2	MCPHERSON	UK7-4	28-Apr-53	8.48	3
LOUP	PB11-2	1-Sep-57	4.58	2	MCPHERSON	TS8-1	5-Jun-52	13.29	4
LOUP	PB9-4	26-Aug-57	5.22	3	MCPHERSON	PB8-3	20-Aug-57	19.73	4
LOUP	TS7-4	4-Jun-52	5.69	3	MCPHERSON	TP4-2	8-Mar-55	51.16	6
LOUP	TS5-1	7-May-52	5.93	3	MCPHERSON	TP10-2	6-May-55	33.30	5
LOUP	TS6-3	27-May-52	7.31	3	MERRICK	UK9-3	21-May-53	3.63	2
LOUP	PB2-3	20-Jun-57	7.54	3	MERRICK	TS7-5	5-Jun-52	4.42	2
LOUP	UK7-4	28-Apr-53	12.69	4	MERRICK	UK10-2	26-May-53	5.23	3
LOUP	TS7-5	5-Jun-52	15.86	4	MERRICK	PB13-4	9-Sep-57	5.36	3

INDIVIDUAL FALLOUT DAYS
NEBRASKA

COUNTY	SHOT	DATE	µCi/SQ METER	INDEX	COUNTY	SHOT	DATE	µCi/SQ METER	INDEX
MERRICK	PB5-4	18-Jul-57	5.89	3	NANCE	PB13-3	8-Sep-57	19.13	4
MERRICK	UK9-2	20-May-53	6.14	3	NANCE	PB8-3	20-Aug-57	19.73	4
MERRICK	PB8-5	22-Aug-57	7.56	3	NANCE	TS7-4	4-Jun-52	20.46	4
MERRICK	PB12-4	5-Sep-57	7.91	3	NANCE	TS6-3	27-May-52	23.59	4
MERRICK	UK7-4	28-Apr-53	9.50	3	NANCE	SE3	8-Jul-62	139.13	7
MERRICK	TS7-4	4-Jun-52	9.64	3	NEMAHA	UK7-4	28-Apr-53	3.85	2
MERRICK	TP4-2	8-Mar-55	12.66	4	NEMAHA	TS7-5	5-Jun-52	3.90	2
MERRICK	PB13-3	8-Sep-57	19.13	4	NEMAHA	PB8-3	20-Aug-57	4.00	2
MERRICK	PB8-3	20-Aug-57	19.73	4	NEMAHA	UK10-2	26-May-53	4.63	2
MERRICK	TS6-3	27-May-52	20.96	4	NEMAHA	TS7-3	3-Jun-52	4.80	2
MERRICK	SE3	8-Jul-62	139.13	7	NEMAHA	TS1-3	3-Apr-52	4.81	2
MORRILL	PB2-3	20-Jun-57	3.52	2	NEMAHA	TS7-4	4-Jun-52	6.02	3
MORRILL	TS5-2	8-May-52	3.58	2	NEMAHA	PB12-4	5-Sep-57	11.08	4
MORRILL	PB9-4	26-Aug-57	3.68	2	NEMAHA	UK9-2	20-May-53	11.83	4
MORRILL	TP3-2	2-Mar-55	4.00	2	NEMAHA	TP4-2	8-Mar-55	12.66	4
MORRILL	UK7-4	28-Apr-53	4.01	2	NEMAHA	PB13-5	10-Sep-57	13.25	4
MORRILL	TP4-2	8-Mar-55	5.97	3	NEMAHA	SE3	8-Jul-62	80.75	6
MORRILL	TP11-2	16-May-55	8.58	3	NUCKOLLS	PB13-4	9-Sep-57	3.55	2
MORRILL	PB5-4	18-Jul-57	12.15	4	NUCKOLLS	TS7-5	5-Jun-52	3.89	2
MORRILL	TS8-1	5-Jun-52	13.29	4	NUCKOLLS	TP9-2	15-Apr-55	4.44	2
MORRILL	TS1-2	2-Apr-52	17.73	4	NUCKOLLS	UK9-3	21-May-53	4.50	2
MORRILL	PB9-3	25-Aug-57	23.29	4	NUCKOLLS	UK7-4	28-Apr-53	4.73	2
MORRILL	TS5-1	7-May-52	23.68	4	NUCKOLLS	TS7-3	3-Jun-52	4.76	2
MORRILL	TP9-2	15-Apr-55	26.06	5	NUCKOLLS	TS1-2	2-Apr-52	5.16	3
MORRILL	TS6-3	27-May-52	30.30	5	NUCKOLLS	UK10-2	26-May-53	5.33	3
NANCE	UK7-3	27-Apr-53	3.61	2	NUCKOLLS	PB13-5	10-Sep-57	5.59	3
NANCE	TS7-5	5-Jun-52	4.42	2	NUCKOLLS	TS6-3	27-May-52	6.99	3
NANCE	PB12-4	5-Sep-57	5.34	3	NUCKOLLS	TS7-4	4-Jun-52	7.56	3
NANCE	PB13-4	9-Sep-57	5.36	3	NUCKOLLS	UK9-2	20-May-53	9.10	3
NANCE	PB8-5	22-Aug-57	7.56	3	NUCKOLLS	PB12-4	5-Sep-57	9.80	3
NANCE	UK7-4	28-Apr-53	7.91	3	NUCKOLLS	TP4-2	8-Mar-55	12.66	4
NANCE	UK9-2	20-May-53	8.40	3	NUCKOLLS	SE3	8-Jul-62	37.44	5
NANCE	TP4-2	8-Mar-55	12.66	4	NUCKOLLS	PB8-3	20-Aug-57	39.46	5

INDIVIDUAL FALLOUT DAYS
NEBRASKA

COUNTY	SHOT	DATE	µCi/SQ METER	INDEX	COUNTY	SHOT	DATE	µCi/SQ METER	INDEX
OTOE	TS7-5	5-Jun-52	3.56	2	PERKINS	TS1-2	2-Apr-52	5.16	3
OTOE	UK10-2	26-May-53	3.88	2	PERKINS	TP9-2	15-Apr-55	5.71	3
OTOE	TS6-4	28-May-52	4.03	2	PERKINS	TP3-2	2-Mar-55	7.78	3
OTOE	TS7-3	3-Jun-52	4.30	2	PERKINS	TS5-1	7-May-52	7.90	3
OTOE	PB12-4	5-Sep-57	4.31	2	PERKINS	UK7-4	28-Apr-53	8.02	3
OTOE	TS6-3	27-May-52	4.51	2	PERKINS	TP11-2	16-May-55	9.09	3
OTOE	TS1-2	2-Apr-52	5.16	3	PERKINS	PB9-4	26-Aug-57	11.05	4
OTOE	UK7-4	28-Apr-53	5.40	3	PERKINS	TS8-1	5-Jun-52	13.29	4
OTOE	TP10-3	7-May-55	5.80	3	PERKINS	TS6-3	27-May-52	47.01	5
OTOE	PB13-5	10-Sep-57	7.17	3	PERKINS	TP4-2	8-Mar-55	51.16	6
OTOE	TS7-4	4-Jun-52	7.44	3	PERKINS	TP10-2	6-May-55	33.30	5
OTOE	PB8-3	20-Aug-57	7.99	3	PHELPS	TS7-5	5-Jun-52	3.53	2
OTOE	UK9-2	20-May-53	10.12	4	PHELPS	PB8-5	22-Aug-57	3.78	2
OTOE	TP4-2	8-Mar-55	12.66	4	PHELPS	TS1-2	2-Apr-52	3.87	2
OTOE	SE3	8-Jul-62	76.52	6	PHELPS	UK8-2	9-May-53	4.04	2
PAWNEE	PB13-4	9-Sep-57	3.55	2	PHELPS	UK9-3	21-May-53	4.61	2
PAWNEE	UK10-2	26-May-53	3.76	2	PHELPS	TP9-2	15-Apr-55	4.95	2
PAWNEE	TS7-5	5-Jun-52	3.94	2	PHELPS	TS7-4	4-Jun-52	5.69	3
PAWNEE	PB12-3	4-Sep-57	4.31	2	PHELPS	PB5-4	18-Jul-57	5.89	3
PAWNEE	TS7-3	3-Jun-52	4.71	2	PHELPS	UK9-2	20-May-53	6.50	3
PAWNEE	UK7-4	28-Apr-53	4.97	2	PHELPS	UK7-4	28-Apr-53	8.42	3
PAWNEE	TS7-4	4-Jun-52	6.08	3	PHELPS	PB13-4	9-Sep-57	8.92	3
PAWNEE	UK9-2	20-May-53	7.68	3	PHELPS	TP4-2	8-Mar-55	12.66	4
PAWNEE	PB8-3	20-Aug-57	7.99	3	PHELPS	PB13-3	8-Sep-57	19.13	4
PAWNEE	TS1-2	2-Apr-52	10.32	4	PHELPS	TS6-3	27-May-52	38.51	5
PAWNEE	PB12-4	5-Sep-57	11.42	4	PHELPS	SE3	8-Jul-62	38.93	5
PAWNEE	TP4-2	8-Mar-55	12.66	4	PHELPS	PB8-3	20-Aug-57	39.46	5
PAWNEE	PB13-5	10-Sep-57	15.64	4	PHELPS	TS8-1	5-Jun-52	39.88	5
PERKINS	PB2-3	20-Jun-57	3.52	2	PIERCE	TS7-5	5-Jun-52	3.69	2
PERKINS	UK7-3	27-Apr-53	3.64	2	PIERCE	UK9-2	20-May-53	3.79	2
PERKINS	PB9-3	25-Aug-57	3.88	2	PIERCE	UK2-2	25-Mar-53	3.97	2
PERKINS	UK11-2	5-Jun-53	4.15	2	PIERCE	PB15-3	18-Sep-57	4.13	2
PERKINS	PB5-4	18-Jul-57	4.87	2	PIERCE	PB15-2	17-Sep-57	5.01	3

INDIVIDUAL FALLOUT DAYS
NEBRASKA

COUNTY	SHOT	DATE	µCi/SQ METER	INDEX	COUNTY	SHOT	DATE	µCi/SQ METER	INDEX
PIERCE	TS5-1	7-May-52	5.11	3	RED WILLOW	TS5-1	7-May-52	3.59	2
PIERCE	PB11-4	3-Sep-57	5.18	3	RED WILLOW	TS7-4	4-Jun-52	3.61	2
PIERCE	PB9-4	26-Aug-57	5.22	3	RED WILLOW	UK7-3	27-Apr-53	4.95	2
PIERCE	UK9-3	21-May-53	6.12	3	RED WILLOW	UK7-4	28-Apr-53	4.97	2
PIERCE	PB2-3	20-Jun-57	7.54	3	RED WILLOW	TP11-2	16-May-55	5.45	3
PIERCE	UK7-4	28-Apr-53	13.58	4	RED WILLOW	PB13-3	8-Sep-57	6.72	3
PIERCE	PB11-2	1-Sep-57	18.31	4	RED WILLOW	TS1-2	2-Apr-52	7.42	3
PIERCE	TS7-4	4-Jun-52	18.64	4	RED WILLOW	TP9-2	15-Apr-55	7.61	3
PIERCE	PB8-3	20-Aug-57	19.73	4	RED WILLOW	TP3-2	2-Mar-55	7.78	3
PLATTE	PB13-4	9-Sep-57	3.55	2	RED WILLOW	UK9-2	20-May-53	7.95	3
PLATTE	TS7-5	5-Jun-52	3.89	2	RED WILLOW	PB8-3	20-Aug-57	19.73	4
PLATTE	PB13-5	10-Sep-57	6.18	3	RED WILLOW	TS8-1	5-Jun-52	26.59	5
PLATTE	TS7-4	4-Jun-52	8.82	3	RED WILLOW	TS6-3	27-May-52	30.86	5
PLATTE	PB5-4	18-Jul-57	8.86	3	RED WILLOW	TP10-2	6-May-55	33.30	5
PLATTE	UK9-2	20-May-53	10.83	4	RED WILLOW	TP4-2	8-Mar-55	51.16	6
PLATTE	UK7-4	28-Apr-53	11.16	4	RICHARDSON	TP10-3	7-May-55	3.65	2
PLATTE	TP4-2	8-Mar-55	12.66	4	RICHARDSON	TS7-5	5-Jun-52	3.82	2
PLATTE	TS6-3	27-May-52	24.50	4	RICHARDSON	PB8-3	20-Aug-57	4.00	2
PLATTE	PB8-3	20-Aug-57	39.46	5	RICHARDSON	UK10-2	26-May-53	4.26	2
PLATTE	SE3	8-Jul-62	139.13	7	RICHARDSON	TS7-3	3-Jun-52	4.45	2
POLK	UK10-2	26-May-53	3.76	2	RICHARDSON	UK7-4	28-Apr-53	4.70	2
POLK	TS7-5	5-Jun-52	4.52	2	RICHARDSON	TS7-4	4-Jun-52	4.93	2
POLK	PB12-4	5-Sep-57	5.41	3	RICHARDSON	UK7-3	27-Apr-53	7.95	3
POLK	UK9-2	20-May-53	6.14	3	RICHARDSON	UK9-2	20-May-53	11.47	4
POLK	UK7-4	28-Apr-53	7.78	3	RICHARDSON	PB12-4	5-Sep-57	12.03	4
POLK	PB13-4	9-Sep-57	8.92	3	RICHARDSON	TP4-2	8-Mar-55	12.66	4
POLK	TS7-4	4-Jun-52	10.78	4	RICHARDSON	PB13-5	10-Sep-57	13.93	4
POLK	TP4-2	8-Mar-55	12.66	4	RICHARDSON	TS1-2	2-Apr-52	15.48	4
POLK	PB13-3	8-Sep-57	12.75	4	ROCK	UK2-2	25-Mar-53	3.97	2
POLK	PB8-3	20-Aug-57	19.73	4	ROCK	PB11-2	1-Sep-57	4.58	2
POLK	TS6-3	27-May-52	22.24	4	ROCK	TS7-4	4-Jun-52	5.15	3
POLK	SE3	8-Jul-62	139.13	7	ROCK	TS5-2	8-May-52	5.15	3
RED WILLOW	PB2-3	20-Jun-57	3.52	2	ROCK	PB9-4	26-Aug-57	5.22	3

INDIVIDUAL FALLOUT DAYS
NEBRASKA

COUNTY	SHOT	DATE	µCi/SQ METER	INDEX	COUNTY	SHOT	DATE	µCi/SQ METER	INDEX
ROCK	UK9-3	21-May-53	5.60	3	SAUNDERS	UK10-2	26-May-53	5.08	3
ROCK	PB2-3	20-Jun-57	7.54	3	SAUNDERS	UK9-2	20-May-53	6.23	3
ROCK	TS5-1	7-May-52	12.21	4	SAUNDERS	UK7-4	28-Apr-53	7.59	3
ROCK	UK7-4	28-Apr-53	14.86	4	SAUNDERS	TS7-4	4-Jun-52	9.04	3
ROCK	PB8-3	20-Aug-57	19.73	4	SAUNDERS	TS6-3	27-May-52	12.12	4
ROCK	TS8-1	5-Jun-52	26.59	5	SAUNDERS	TP4-2	8-Mar-55	12.66	4
SALINE	PB13-4	9-Sep-57	3.55	2	SAUNDERS	PB8-3	20-Aug-57	19.73	4
SALINE	TS7-5	5-Jun-52	4.56	2	SAUNDERS	SE3	8-Jul-62	146.81	7
SALINE	PB13-5	10-Sep-57	4.78	2	SCOTTS BLUFF	PB18-3	12-Jul-57	3.55	2
SALINE	TS1-2	2-Apr-52	5.16	3	SCOTTS BLUFF	TS5-2	8-May-52	4.42	2
SALINE	TS7-3	3-Jun-52	5.35	3	SCOTTS BLUFF	PB5-4	18-Jul-57	5.05	3
SALINE	UK7-4	28-Apr-53	5.67	3	SCOTTS BLUFF	TP11-2	16-May-55	5.91	3
SALINE	UK10-2	26-May-53	6.39	3	SCOTTS BLUFF	TS7-3	3-Jun-52	5.95	3
SALINE	TS6-3	27-May-52	7.34	3	SCOTTS BLUFF	PB9-3	25-Aug-57	7.76	3
SALINE	UK9-2	20-May-53	8.13	3	SCOTTS BLUFF	TS6-3	27-May-52	12.24	4
SALINE	PB12-4	5-Sep-57	9.12	3	SCOTTS BLUFF	TS1-2	2-Apr-52	14.60	4
SALINE	TS7-4	4-Jun-52	10.41	4	SCOTTS BLUFF	TS5-1	7-May-52	19.49	4
SALINE	TP4-2	8-Mar-55	12.66	4	SEWARD	UK9-3	21-May-53	3.57	2
SALINE	PB8-3	20-Aug-57	39.46	5	SEWARD	UK9-5	23-May-53	3.71	2
SALINE	SE3	8-Jul-62	80.75	6	SEWARD	TS7-5	5-Jun-52	4.45	2
SARPY	UK11-3	6-Jun-53	3.51	2	SEWARD	TS7-3	3-Jun-52	5.01	3
SARPY	UK7-5	29-Apr-53	3.55	2	SEWARD	PB13-4	9-Sep-57	5.36	3
SARPY	PB8-3	20-Aug-57	4.00	2	SEWARD	UK10-2	26-May-53	5.88	3
SARPY	UK9-5	23-May-53	4.47	2	SEWARD	UK7-4	28-Apr-53	6.09	3
SARPY	UK7-4	28-Apr-53	7.08	3	SEWARD	UK9-2	20-May-53	7.05	3
SARPY	UK9-2	20-May-53	7.23	3	SEWARD	PB12-4	5-Sep-57	8.31	3
SARPY	PB2-3	20-Jun-57	8.04	3	SEWARD	TS6-3	27-May-52	10.26	4
SARPY	TS7-4	4-Jun-52	8.16	3	SEWARD	TS7-4	4-Jun-52	10.87	4
SARPY	TS6-3	27-May-52	10.54	4	SEWARD	TP4-2	8-Mar-55	12.66	4
SARPY	TP4-2	8-Mar-55	12.66	4	SEWARD	PB13-3	8-Sep-57	12.75	4
SARPY	TS7-3	3-Jun-52	16.21	4	SEWARD	PB8-3	20-Aug-57	19.73	4
SAUNDERS	TS7-3	3-Jun-52	3.54	2	SEWARD	SE3	8-Jul-62	76.52	6
SAUNDERS	TS7-5	5-Jun-52	4.07	2	SHERIDAN	TP3-2	2-Mar-55	4.00	2

INDIVIDUAL FALLOUT DAYS
NEBRASKA

COUNTY	SHOT	DATE	µCi/SQ METER	INDEX	COUNTY	SHOT	DATE	µCi/SQ METER	INDEX
SHERIDAN	TS7-3	3-Jun-52	4.42	2	SIOUX	PB9-4	26-Aug-57	11.05	4
SHERIDAN	TS7-4	4-Jun-52	4.71	2	SIOUX	TS5-2	8-May-52	13.49	4
SHERIDAN	PB18-3	12-Jul-57	4.73	2	SIOUX	PB2-3	20-Jun-57	14.08	4
SHERIDAN	TP4-2	8-Mar-55	5.97	3	SIOUX	TP11-2	16-May-55	14.24	4
SHERIDAN	PB2-3	20-Jun-57	7.04	3	SIOUX	TS1-2	2-Apr-52	35.14	5
SHERIDAN	PB5-4	18-Jul-57	7.28	3	SIOUX	TS5-1	7-May-52	64.60	6
SHERIDAN	TP11-2	16-May-55	8.58	3	SIOUX	TS7-3	3-Jun-52	78.77	6
SHERIDAN	UK7-4	28-Apr-53	9.19	3	STANTON	PB2-3	20-Jun-57	5.36	3
SHERIDAN	TS8-1	5-Jun-52	13.29	4	STANTON	UK9-3	21-May-53	5.38	3
SHERIDAN	TS5-2	8-May-52	13.43	4	STANTON	TS7-4	4-Jun-52	7.37	3
SHERIDAN	PB9-3	25-Aug-57	15.53	4	STANTON	UK7-4	28-Apr-53	9.31	3
SHERIDAN	TS1-2	2-Apr-52	17.73	4	STANTON	TS7-5	5-Jun-52	11.91	4
SHERIDAN	TS5-1	7-May-52	29.37	5	STANTON	TP4-2	8-Mar-55	12.66	4
SHERMAN	TS5-1	7-May-52	3.77	2	STANTON	UK9-2	20-May-53	12.91	4
SHERMAN	PB8-5	22-Aug-57	3.78	2	STANTON	TS6-3	27-May-52	16.28	4
SHERMAN	UK9-3	21-May-53	3.94	2	STANTON	PB8-3	20-Aug-57	19.73	4
SHERMAN	UK8-2	9-May-53	4.04	2	STANTON	SE3	8-Jul-62	527.44	9
SHERMAN	UK9-2	20-May-53	4.70	2	THAYER	PB13-4	9-Sep-57	3.55	2
SHERMAN	PB11-4	3-Sep-57	5.18	3	THAYER	TS7-5	5-Jun-52	3.98	2
SHERMAN	TS7-4	4-Jun-52	7.34	3	THAYER	UK9-3	21-May-53	4.45	2
SHERMAN	PB2-3	20-Jun-57	7.54	3	THAYER	UK7-4	28-Apr-53	4.55	2
SHERMAN	UK7-4	28-Apr-53	8.61	3	THAYER	UK10-2	26-May-53	6.06	3
SHERMAN	PB11-2	1-Sep-57	9.15	3	THAYER	TS7-3	3-Jun-52	6.72	3
SHERMAN	TP4-2	8-Mar-55	12.66	4	THAYER	UK9-2	20-May-53	8.64	3
SHERMAN	TS6-3	27-May-52	14.37	4	THAYER	TS7-4	4-Jun-52	9.23	3
SHERMAN	PB8-3	20-Aug-57	19.73	4	THAYER	PB12-4	5-Sep-57	9.66	3
SHERMAN	TS8-1	5-Jun-52	26.59	5	THAYER	PB13-5	10-Sep-57	10.01	4
SHERMAN	SE3	8-Jul-62	345.56	8	THAYER	TP4-2	8-Mar-55	12.66	4
SIOUX	PB9-3	25-Aug-57	3.88	2	THAYER	PB8-3	20-Aug-57	19.73	4
SIOUX	TP3-2	2-Mar-55	4.00	2	THAYER	SE3	8-Jul-62	37.44	5
SIOUX	UK7-4	28-Apr-53	4.24	2	THOMAS	TP11-2	16-May-55	3.64	2
SIOUX	TP4-2	8-Mar-55	5.97	3	THOMAS	PB8-5	22-Aug-57	3.78	2
SIOUX	TS7-4	4-Jun-52	8.49	3	THOMAS	UK9-3	21-May-53	3.81	2

INDIVIDUAL FALLOUT DAYS
NEBRASKA

COUNTY	SHOT	DATE	µCi/SQ METER	INDEX	COUNTY	SHOT	DATE	µCi/SQ METER	INDEX
THOMAS	PB9-3	25-Aug-57	3.88	2	VALLEY	PB11-2	1-Sep-57	9.15	3
THOMAS	PB11-2	1-Sep-57	4.58	2	VALLEY	TP4-2	8-Mar-55	12.66	4
THOMAS	TS1-2	2-Apr-52	5.16	3	VALLEY	TS6-3	27-May-52	13.69	4
THOMAS	PB9-4	26-Aug-57	5.22	3	VALLEY	TS7-4	4-Jun-52	15.11	4
THOMAS	PB5-4	18-Jul-57	5.89	3	VALLEY	PB8-3	20-Aug-57	19.73	4
THOMAS	TP3-2	2-Mar-55	7.78	3	VALLEY	TS8-1	5-Jun-52	26.59	5
THOMAS	PB8-2	19-Aug-57	8.25	3	VALLEY	UK9-3	21-May-53	3.51	1
THOMAS	UK7-4	28-Apr-53	11.92	4	VALLEY	SE3	8-Jul-62	139.13	7
THOMAS	PB2-3	20-Jun-57	15.08	4	WASHINGTON	UK7-4	28-Apr-53	3.96	2
THOMAS	PB8-3	20-Aug-57	19.73	4	WASHINGTON	UK7-5	29-Apr-53	3.97	2
THOMAS	TS8-1	5-Jun-52	26.59	5	WASHINGTON	UK9-5	23-May-53	4.22	2
THOMAS	TP10-2	6-May-55	33.30	5	WASHINGTON	PB5-5	19-Jul-57	6.09	3
THOMAS	TP4-2	8-Mar-55	51.16	6	WASHINGTON	PB12-4	5-Sep-57	7.16	3
THOMAS	TS7-4	4-Jun-52	3.50	1	WASHINGTON	UK9-2	20-May-53	7.80	3
THURSTON	UK2-2	25-Mar-53	3.97	2	WASHINGTON	TS7-4	4-Jun-52	8.87	3
THURSTON	UK7-5	29-Apr-53	4.12	2	WASHINGTON	TP4-2	8-Mar-55	12.66	4
THURSTON	UK9-5	23-May-53	4.43	2	WASHINGTON	TS6-3	27-May-52	14.71	4
THURSTON	UK9-3	21-May-53	4.87	2	WASHINGTON	SE3	8-Jul-62	345.56	8
THURSTON	PB2-3	20-Jun-57	5.36	3	WAYNE	UK2-2	25-Mar-53	3.97	2
THURSTON	UK9-2	20-May-53	6.23	3	WAYNE	PB12-4	5-Sep-57	3.99	2
THURSTON	UK7-4	28-Apr-53	9.25	3	WAYNE	UK9-3	21-May-53	5.53	3
THURSTON	TS7-5	5-Jun-52	10.98	4	WAYNE	TS7-5	5-Jun-52	7.62	3
THURSTON	TS6-3	27-May-52	17.25	4	WAYNE	UK9-2	20-May-53	8.01	3
THURSTON	TS7-4	4-Jun-52	43.03	5	WAYNE	UK7-4	28-Apr-53	9.88	3
THURSTON	SE3	8-Jul-62	527.44	9	WAYNE	TS6-3	27-May-52	18.02	4
VALLEY	PB8-5	22-Aug-57	3.78	2	WAYNE	PB8-3	20-Aug-57	19.73	4
VALLEY	UK7-3	27-Apr-53	4.18	2	WAYNE	TS7-4	4-Jun-52	24.25	4
VALLEY	UK9-2	20-May-53	4.33	2	WAYNE	SE3	8-Jul-62	208.70	8
VALLEY	TS5-1	7-May-52	4.85	2	WEBSTER	TS7-3	3-Jun-52	3.54	2
VALLEY	PB11-4	3-Sep-57	5.18	3	WEBSTER	PB13-4	9-Sep-57	3.55	2
VALLEY	PB15-2	17-Sep-57	6.68	3	WEBSTER	UK10-2	26-May-53	3.76	2
VALLEY	PB2-3	20-Jun-57	7.54	3	WEBSTER	TS7-5	5-Jun-52	4.32	2
VALLEY	UK7-4	28-Apr-53	9.05	3	WEBSTER	UK9-3	21-May-53	4.35	2

INDIVIDUAL FALLOUT DAYS
NEBRASKA

COUNTY	SHOT	DATE	µCi/SQ METER	INDEX	COUNTY	SHOT	DATE	µCi/SQ METER	INDEX
WEBSTER	UK7-4	28-Apr-53	4.65	2	WHEELER	PB2-3	20-Jun-57	7.54	3
WEBSTER	TS6-3	27-May-52	4.99	2	WHEELER	UK7-4	28-Apr-53	12.56	4
WEBSTER	TS1-2	2-Apr-52	5.16	3	WHEELER	PB8-3	20-Aug-57	19.73	4
WEBSTER	TP9-2	15-Apr-55	6.18	3	WHEELER	TS7-4	4-Jun-52	21.33	4
WEBSTER	TS7-4	4-Jun-52	6.85	3	WHEELER	TS6-3	27-May-52	22.27	4
WEBSTER	UK9-2	20-May-53	8.72	3	WHEELER	TS8-1	5-Jun-52	26.59	5
WEBSTER	PB12-4	5-Sep-57	10.07	4	YORK	TS7-3	3-Jun-52	3.87	2
WEBSTER	TP4-2	8-Mar-55	12.66	4	YORK	UK9-3	21-May-53	3.88	2
WEBSTER	PB8-3	20-Aug-57	19.73	4	YORK	TS7-5	5-Jun-52	4.52	2
WEBSTER	SE3	8-Jul-62	37.44	5	YORK	PB13-4	9-Sep-57	5.36	3
WEBSTER	TS8-1	5-Jun-52	39.88	5	YORK	UK10-2	26-May-53	5.63	3
WHEELER	TS7-5	5-Jun-52	3.56	2	YORK	PB12-4	5-Sep-57	5.88	3
WHEELER	PB8-5	22-Aug-57	3.78	2	YORK	UK7-4	28-Apr-53	5.93	3
WHEELER	PB9-3	25-Aug-57	3.88	2	YORK	UK9-2	20-May-53	7.32	3
WHEELER	UK9-2	20-May-53	3.90	2	YORK	TS7-4	4-Jun-52	10.96	4
WHEELER	UK2-2	25-Mar-53	3.97	2	YORK	TS6-3	27-May-52	11.26	4
WHEELER	PB15-3	18-Sep-57	4.13	2	YORK	TP4-2	8-Mar-55	12.66	4
WHEELER	PB11-2	1-Sep-57	4.58	2	YORK	PB13-3	8-Sep-57	12.75	4
WHEELER	UK9-3	21-May-53	6.64	3	YORK	PB8-3	20-Aug-57	19.73	4
WHEELER	PB15-2	17-Sep-57	6.68	3	YORK	SE3	8-Jul-62	76.52	6

INDIVIDUAL FALLOUT DAYS
NEW HAMPSHIRE

COUNTY	SHOT	DATE	µCi/SQ METER	INDEX	COUNTY	SHOT	DATE	µCi/SQ METER	INDEX
BELKNAP	BJ2-3	1-Nov-51	4.86	2	GRAFTON	R1-2	29-Jan-51	7.99	3
BELKNAP	PB5-8	22-Jul-57	5.97	3	GRAFTON	BJ2-4	2-Nov-51	10.26	4
BELKNAP	BJ2-2	31-Oct-51	7.98	3	GRAFTON	TS8-3	7-Jun-52	18.13	4
BELKNAP	TS8-3	7-Jun-52	9.60	3	HILLSBOROUGH	PB11-5	4-Sep-57	3.55	2
BELKNAP	BJ2-4	2-Nov-51	9.96	3	HILLSBOROUGH	UK4-4	9-Apr-53	3.98	2
BELKNAP	UK4-2	7-Apr-53	14.19	4	HILLSBOROUGH	BJ2-3	1-Nov-51	5.88	3
BELKNAP	R1-2	29-Jan-51	14.56	4	HILLSBOROUGH	PB5-8	22-Jul-57	5.97	3
CARROLL	UK4-4	9-Apr-53	3.98	2	HILLSBOROUGH	TS8-3	7-Jun-52	8.68	3
CARROLL	BJ2-2	31-Oct-51	12.07	4	HILLSBOROUGH	BJ2-4	2-Nov-51	11.45	4
CARROLL	TS8-3	7-Jun-52	12.17	4	HILLSBOROUGH	R1-2	29-Jan-51	14.56	4
CARROLL	BJ2-4	2-Nov-51	21.01	4	HILLSBOROUGH	UK4-2	7-Apr-53	24.87	4
CARROLL	R1-2	29-Jan-51	36.05	5	MERRIMACK	UK4-4	9-Apr-53	3.98	2
CHESHIRE	PB11-5	4-Sep-57	3.55	2	MERRIMACK	BJ2-3	1-Nov-51	5.37	3
CHESHIRE	UK4-4	9-Apr-53	3.98	2	MERRIMACK	BJ2-4	2-Nov-51	10.45	4
CHESHIRE	BJ2-3	1-Nov-51	5.26	3	MERRIMACK	TS8-3	7-Jun-52	13.93	4
CHESHIRE	PB5-8	22-Jul-57	5.97	3	MERRIMACK	R1-2	29-Jan-51	14.56	4
CHESHIRE	UK7-2	26-Apr-53	7.03	3	MERRIMACK	UK4-2	7-Apr-53	15.19	4
CHESHIRE	TS8-3	7-Jun-52	9.71	3	ROCKINGHAM	PB11-5	4-Sep-57	3.55	2
CHESHIRE	BJ2-4	2-Nov-51	12.77	4	ROCKINGHAM	UK4-4	9-Apr-53	3.98	2
CHESHIRE	UK4-2	7-Apr-53	15.36	4	ROCKINGHAM	TS8-3	7-Jun-52	7.23	3
CHESHIRE	R1-2	29-Jan-51	18.06	4	ROCKINGHAM	BJ2-4	2-Nov-51	9.26	3
COOS	BJ2-3	1-Nov-51	3.97	2	ROCKINGHAM	R1-2	29-Jan-51	36.05	5
COOS	UK4-4	9-Apr-53	3.98	2	ROCKINGHAM	UK4-2	7-Apr-53	44.91	5
COOS	UK7-3	27-Apr-53	4.10	2	STRAFFORD	TS8-3	7-Jun-52	5.97	3
COOS	BJ2-4	2-Nov-51	6.37	3	STRAFFORD	TS6-4	28-May-52	8.68	3
COOS	TS7-4	4-Jun-52	7.81	3	STRAFFORD	UK4-2	7-Apr-53	12.74	4
COOS	BJ2-2	31-Oct-51	7.98	3	STRAFFORD	BJ2-4	2-Nov-51	18.72	4
COOS	PB5-8	22-Jul-57	8.96	3	STRAFFORD	R1-2	29-Jan-51	36.05	5
COOS	TS8-3	7-Jun-52	13.73	4	SULLIVAN	PB12-6	7-Sep-57	3.56	2
GRAFTON	UK4-4	9-Apr-53	3.98	2	SULLIVAN	BJ2-3	1-Nov-51	6.27	3
GRAFTON	BJ2-3	1-Nov-51	4.61	2	SULLIVAN	UK7-2	26-Apr-53	8.72	3
GRAFTON	PB5-8	22-Jul-57	5.97	3	SULLIVAN	UK4-2	7-Apr-53	9.68	3
GRAFTON	BJ2-2	31-Oct-51	7.98	3	SULLIVAN	BJ2-4	2-Nov-51	10.77	4

INDIVIDUAL FALLOUT DAYS NEW HAMPSHIRE										
COUNTY	SHOT	DATE	µCi/SQ METER	INDEX		COUNTY	SHOT	DATE	µCi/SQ METER	INDEX
SULLIVAN	R1-2	29-Jan-51	14.56	4		SULLIVAN	TS8-3	7-Jun-52	15.20	4

INDIVIDUAL FALLOUT DAYS
NEW JERSEY

COUNTY	SHOT	DATE	μCi/SQ METER	INDEX	COUNTY	SHOT	DATE	μCi/SQ METER	INDEX
ATLANTIC	TS3-4	25-Apr-52	3.87	2	CAPE MAY	BJ2-4	2-Nov-51	13.85	4
ATLANTIC	BJ2-3	1-Nov-51	5.66	3	CAPE MAY	UK1-2	18-Mar-53	41.02	5
ATLANTIC	BJ2-4	2-Nov-51	7.65	3	CUMBERLAND	TS3-4	25-Apr-52	3.87	2
ATLANTIC	UK9-7	25-May-53	10.18	4	CUMBERLAND	BJ2-3	1-Nov-51	6.80	3
ATLANTIC	SE4	9-Jul-62	45.80	5	CUMBERLAND	BJ2-4	2-Nov-51	7.94	3
ATLANTIC	UK1-2	18-Mar-53	54.52	6	CUMBERLAND	UK9-7	25-May-53	10.18	4
BERGEN	TP11-8	22-May-55	3.61	2	CUMBERLAND	UK1-2	18-Mar-53	31.29	5
BERGEN	BJ2-3	1-Nov-51	5.37	3	ESSEX	BJ2-3	1-Nov-51	4.74	2
BERGEN	BJ2-4	2-Nov-51	6.38	3	ESSEX	TS7-5	5-Jun-52	4.80	2
BERGEN	TP11-9	23-May-55	10.65	4	ESSEX	TP11-9	23-May-55	7.10	3
BERGEN	TS1-4	4-Apr-52	19.67	4	ESSEX	BJ2-4	2-Nov-51	7.66	3
BERGEN	UK1-2	18-Mar-53	39.89	5	ESSEX	BJ3-7	7-Nov-51	11.62	4
BERGEN	R1-2	29-Jan-51	3.50	1	ESSEX	TS1-4	4-Apr-52	11.87	4
BURLINGTON	TS3-4	25-Apr-52	3.87	2	ESSEX	UK1-2	18-Mar-53	41.35	5
BURLINGTON	TS3-5	26-Apr-52	3.88	2	ESSEX	R1-2	29-Jan-51	3.50	1
BURLINGTON	TP6-4	25-Mar-55	4.32	2	GLOUCESTER	TS3-4	25-Apr-52	3.87	2
BURLINGTON	BJ2-3	1-Nov-51	5.91	3	GLOUCESTER	TS7-5	5-Jun-52	4.07	2
BURLINGTON	UK9-7	25-May-53	6.11	3	GLOUCESTER	BJ2-3	1-Nov-51	5.91	3
BURLINGTON	BJ2-4	2-Nov-51	8.50	3	GLOUCESTER	PB5-8	22-Jul-57	5.97	3
BURLINGTON	SE4	9-Jul-62	31.92	5	GLOUCESTER	BJ2-4	2-Nov-51	7.87	3
BURLINGTON	SE5	10-Jul-62	47.25	5	GLOUCESTER	UK9-7	25-May-53	10.18	4
BURLINGTON	UK1-2	18-Mar-53	51.84	6	GLOUCESTER	UK1-2	18-Mar-53	30.48	5
BURLINGTON	R1-2	29-Jan-51	3.50	1	HUDSON	TP11-8	22-May-55	3.61	2
CAMDEN	TS3-4	25-Apr-52	3.87	2	HUDSON	BJ2-3	1-Nov-51	4.91	2
CAMDEN	BJ2-3	1-Nov-51	6.53	3	HUDSON	BJ2-4	2-Nov-51	5.62	3
CAMDEN	BJ2-4	2-Nov-51	8.29	3	HUDSON	R1-2	29-Jan-51	9.14	3
CAMDEN	UK9-7	25-May-53	10.18	4	HUDSON	TP11-9	23-May-55	10.65	4
CAMDEN	UK1-2	18-Mar-53	36.92	5	HUDSON	TS1-4	4-Apr-52	19.67	4
CAPE MAY	TS7-5	5-Jun-52	3.83	2	HUDSON	UK1-2	18-Mar-53	45.22	5
CAPE MAY	PB12-6	7-Sep-57	4.03	2	HUNTERDON	TS3-4	25-Apr-52	3.87	2
CAPE MAY	BJ2-3	1-Nov-51	7.87	3	HUNTERDON	TP6-4	25-Mar-55	4.32	2
CAPE MAY	PB5-8	22-Jul-57	8.96	3	HUNTERDON	PB5-8	22-Jul-57	5.97	3
CAPE MAY	UK9-7	25-May-53	10.18	4	HUNTERDON	UK9-7	25-May-53	6.11	3

INDIVIDUAL FALLOUT DAYS
NEW JERSEY

COUNTY	SHOT	DATE	µCi/SQ METER	INDEX	COUNTY	SHOT	DATE	µCi/SQ METER	INDEX
HUNTERDON	BJ2-4	2-Nov-51	9.19	3	MORRIS	UK1-2	18-Mar-53	23.90	4
HUNTERDON	UK1-2	18-Mar-53	22.44	4	MORRIS	R1-2	29-Jan-51	3.50	1
HUNTERDON	R1-2	29-Jan-51	3.50	1	OCEAN	TS3-5	26-Apr-52	4.13	2
MERCER	TP6-4	25-Mar-55	4.32	2	OCEAN	TS7-5	5-Jun-52	5.39	3
MERCER	BJ2-3	1-Nov-51	5.55	3	OCEAN	PB5-8	22-Jul-57	5.97	3
MERCER	PB5-8	22-Jul-57	5.97	3	OCEAN	BJ2-4	2-Nov-51	6.49	3
MERCER	UK9-7	25-May-53	6.11	3	OCEAN	BJ2-3	1-Nov-51	6.98	3
MERCER	BJ2-4	2-Nov-51	8.29	3	OCEAN	TS1-4	4-Apr-52	14.05	4
MERCER	TS1-4	4-Apr-52	14.05	4	OCEAN	SE4	9-Jul-62	37.08	5
MERCER	UK1-2	18-Mar-53	42.30	5	OCEAN	UK1-2	18-Mar-53	62.16	6
MERCER	R1-2	29-Jan-51	3.50	1	OCEAN	R1-2	29-Jan-51	3.50	1
MIDDLESEX	BJ3-7	7-Nov-51	3.85	2	PASSAIC	TS7-5	5-Jun-52	3.94	2
MIDDLESEX	BJ2-3	1-Nov-51	4.03	2	PASSAIC	BJ2-3	1-Nov-51	4.12	2
MIDDLESEX	PB5-8	22-Jul-57	5.97	3	PASSAIC	TS3-4	25-Apr-52	5.70	3
MIDDLESEX	TS7-5	5-Jun-52	6.21	3	PASSAIC	BJ2-4	2-Nov-51	9.05	3
MIDDLESEX	BJ2-4	2-Nov-51	7.66	3	PASSAIC	BJ3-7	7-Nov-51	11.62	4
MIDDLESEX	TS1-4	4-Apr-52	14.05	4	PASSAIC	TS1-4	4-Apr-52	19.67	4
MIDDLESEX	UK1-2	18-Mar-53	48.32	5	PASSAIC	UK1-2	18-Mar-53	26.48	5
MIDDLESEX	R1-2	29-Jan-51	3.50	1	PASSAIC	R1-2	29-Jan-51	3.50	1
MONMOUTH	TS3-5	26-Apr-52	4.00	2	SALEM	TS3-4	25-Apr-52	3.87	2
MONMOUTH	BJ2-4	2-Nov-51	5.85	3	SALEM	BJ2-4	2-Nov-51	7.31	3
MONMOUTH	PB5-8	22-Jul-57	5.97	3	SALEM	BJ2-3	1-Nov-51	7.40	3
MONMOUTH	BJ2-3	1-Nov-51	6.53	3	SALEM	UK9-7	25-May-53	10.18	4
MONMOUTH	TS1-4	4-Apr-52	14.05	4	SALEM	UK1-2	18-Mar-53	23.21	4
MONMOUTH	SE6	11-Jul-62	20.31	4	SOMERSET	BJ3-7	7-Nov-51	3.85	2
MONMOUTH	UK1-2	18-Mar-53	63.79	6	SOMERSET	BJ2-4	2-Nov-51	4.32	2
MONMOUTH	R1-2	29-Jan-51	3.50	1	SOMERSET	BJ2-3	1-Nov-51	5.01	3
MORRIS	BJ2-3	1-Nov-51	3.94	2	SOMERSET	UK9-7	25-May-53	6.11	3
MORRIS	TS7-5	5-Jun-52	4.73	2	SOMERSET	TS1-4	4-Apr-52	11.87	4
MORRIS	BJ2-4	2-Nov-51	4.74	2	SOMERSET	UK1-2	18-Mar-53	33.36	5
MORRIS	TS3-4	25-Apr-52	5.70	3	SOMERSET	R1-2	29-Jan-51	3.50	1
MORRIS	BJ3-7	7-Nov-51	19.31	4	SUSSEX	BJ2-3	1-Nov-51	3.75	2
MORRIS	TS1-4	4-Apr-52	19.67	4	SUSSEX	PB5-8	22-Jul-57	5.97	3

INDICIDUAL FALLOUT DAYS
NEW JERSEY

COUNTY	SHOT	DATE	µCi/SQ METER	INDEX	COUNTY	SHOT	DATE	µCi/SQ METER	INDEX
SUSSEX	BJ3-7	7-Nov-51	7.70	3	UNION	R1-2	29-Jan-51	3.50	1
SUSSEX	BJ2-4	2-Nov-51	11.77	4	WARREN	TP6-4	25-Mar-55	4.32	2
SUSSEX	UK1-2	18-Mar-53	14.02	4	WARREN	UK9-4	22-May-53	4.62	2
SUSSEX	TS1-4	4-Apr-52	19.67	4	WARREN	TS3-4	25-Apr-52	5.70	3
SUSSEX	R1-2	29-Jan-51	3.50	1	WARREN	UK9-7	25-May-53	6.11	3
UNION	BJ3-7	7-Nov-51	3.85	2	WARREN	BJ2-4	2-Nov-51	10.86	4
UNION	BJ2-3	1-Nov-51	5.46	3	WARREN	UK1-2	18-Mar-53	11.52	4
UNION	TS7-5	5-Jun-52	6.73	3	WARREN	BJ3-7	7-Nov-51	11.62	4
UNION	TP11-9	23-May-55	7.10	3	WARREN	TS1-4	4-Apr-52	19.67	4
UNION	BJ2-4	2-Nov-51	7.59	3	WARREN	R1-2	29-Jan-51	3.50	1
UNION	TS1-4	4-Apr-52	11.87	4					
UNION	UK1-2	18-Mar-53	44.02	5					

INDIVIDUAL FALLOUT DAYS
NEW MEXICO

COUNTY	SHOT	DATE	µCi/SQ METER	INDEX	COUNTY	SHOT	DATE	µCi/SQ METER	INDEX
BERNALILLO	TP6-1	22-Mar-55	3.70	2	CHAVES	PB1-1	28-May-57	8.52	3
BERNALILLO	TS3-1	22-Apr-52	3.83	2	CHAVES	PB4-1	5-Jul-57	9.47	3
BERNALILLO	PB13-3	8-Sep-57	5.69	3	CHAVES	TP5-1	12-Mar-55	10.46	4
BERNALILLO	TP5-1	12-Mar-55	6.18	3	CHAVES	TP11-1	15-May-55	12.25	4
BERNALILLO	PB1-1	28-May-57	7.53	3	CHAVES	UK9-1	19-May-53	14.41	4
BERNALILLO	TP11-1	15-May-55	8.01	3	CHAVES	TP7-1	29-Mar-55	15.93	4
BERNALILLO	UK11-1	4-Jun-53	11.16	4	CHAVES	TS6-1	25-May-52	16.26	4
BERNALILLO	TP7-1	29-Mar-55	12.56	4	CHAVES	UK1-1	17-Mar-53	18.25	4
BERNALILLO	PB17-1	28-Sep-57	13.80	4	CHAVES	UK6-1	18-Apr-53	18.97	4
BERNALILLO	PB3-1	24-Jun-57	20.58	4	CHAVES	PB3-1	24-Jun-57	19.46	4
BERNALILLO	TS7-1	1-Jun-52	31.46	5	CHAVES	TS7-1	1-Jun-52	31.46	5
BERNALILLO	TS6-1	25-May-52	35.64	5	CHAVES	UK7-1	25-Apr-53	393.20	8
BERNALILLO	PB4-1	5-Jul-57	67.97	6	COLFAX	TP5-1	12-Mar-55	8.07	3
BERNALILLO	UK9-1	19-May-53	351.01	8	COLFAX	PB17-1	28-Sep-57	8.20	3
BERNALILLO	UK6-1	18-Apr-53	108.40	7	COLFAX	PB1-1	28-May-57	8.52	3
BERNALILLO	UK7-1	25-Apr-53	145.15	7	COLFAX	PB3-1	24-Jun-57	10.79	4
CATRON	TP6-1	22-Mar-55	4.08	2	COLFAX	TS7-1	1-Jun-52	17.80	4
CATRON	UK3-1	31-Mar-53	4.41	2	COLFAX	UK6-1	18-Apr-53	18.37	4
CATRON	UK11-1	4-Jun-53	5.15	3	COLFAX	TP7-1	29-Mar-55	19.20	4
CATRON	PB13-3	8-Sep-57	5.69	3	COLFAX	UK1-1	17-Mar-53	22.33	4
CATRON	PB17-1	28-Sep-57	8.20	3	COLFAX	TS6-1	25-May-52	25.20	5
CATRON	TP5-1	12-Mar-55	8.37	3	COLFAX	UK7-1	25-Apr-53	28.31	5
CATRON	PB1-1	28-May-57	8.52	3	COLFAX	TP10-1	5-May-55	57.87	6
CATRON	TP7-1	29-Mar-55	15.83	4	COLFAX	PB4-1	5-Jul-57	73.63	6
CATRON	PB4-1	5-Jul-57	17.73	4	COLFAX	UK9-1	19-May-53	112.06	7
CATRON	UK9-1	19-May-53	18.45	4	COLFAX	TP11-1	15-May-55	130.08	7
CATRON	PB3-1	24-Jun-57	18.75	4	CURRY	TP5-1	12-Mar-55	7.86	3
CATRON	TS6-1	25-May-52	32.38	5	CURRY	PB17-1	28-Sep-57	8.20	3
CATRON	TS7-1	1-Jun-52	35.60	5	CURRY	PB1-1	28-May-57	8.52	3
CATRON	UK7-1	25-Apr-53	43.22	5	CURRY	TP7-1	29-Mar-55	15.15	4
CATRON	UK6-1	18-Apr-53	104.94	7	CURRY	TS6-1	25-May-52	15.58	4
CHAVES	TP10-1	5-May-55	4.58	2	CURRY	TS7-1	1-Jun-52	17.80	4
CHAVES	PB17-1	28-Sep-57	8.20	3	CURRY	UK1-1	17-Mar-53	18.14	4

INDIVIDUAL FALLOUT DAYS
NEW MEXICO

COUNTY	SHOT	DATE	µCi/SQ METER	INDEX	COUNTY	SHOT	DATE	µCi/SQ METER	INDEX
CURRY	PB3-1	24-Jun-57	19.46	4	EDDY	UK9-1	19-May-53	8.94	3
CURRY	UK6-1	18-Apr-53	19.86	4	EDDY	UK1-1	17-Mar-53	9.12	3
CURRY	TP10-1	5-May-55	21.07	4	EDDY	PB4-1	5-Jul-57	9.34	3
CURRY	TP11-1	15-May-55	25.98	5	EDDY	UK6-1	18-Apr-53	9.87	3
CURRY	UK9-1	19-May-53	27.16	5	EDDY	TS6-1	25-May-52	14.59	4
CURRY	PB4-1	5-Jul-57	27.61	5	EDDY	PB3-1	24-Jun-57	19.46	4
CURRY	UK7-1	25-Apr-53	250.15	8	EDDY	TS7-1	1-Jun-52	35.60	5
DE BACA	TP10-1	5-May-55	6.99	3	EDDY	UK7-1	25-Apr-53	83.38	6
DE BACA	TP5-1	12-Mar-55	7.86	3	GRANT	TP6-1	22-Mar-55	4.08	2
DE BACA	PB17-1	28-Sep-57	8.20	3	GRANT	UK3-1	31-Mar-53	4.41	2
DE BACA	PB1-1	28-May-57	8.52	3	GRANT	PB17-1	28-Sep-57	8.20	3
DE BACA	TP7-1	29-Mar-55	15.34	4	GRANT	PB1-1	28-May-57	8.52	3
DE BACA	UK1-1	17-Mar-53	18.25	4	GRANT	UK6-1	18-Apr-53	10.38	4
DE BACA	TP11-1	15-May-55	19.53	4	GRANT	PB4-1	5-Jul-57	17.73	4
DE BACA	PB3-1	24-Jun-57	20.17	4	GRANT	PB3-1	24-Jun-57	18.04	4
DE BACA	UK6-1	18-Apr-53	20.25	4	GRANT	TS6-1	25-May-52	30.17	5
DE BACA	TS6-1	25-May-52	23.43	4	GRANT	TS7-1	1-Jun-52	35.60	5
DE BACA	PB4-1	5-Jul-57	27.61	5	GUADALUPE	TP10-1	5-May-55	7.09	3
DE BACA	TS7-1	1-Jun-52	35.60	5	GUADALUPE	TP5-1	12-Mar-55	7.86	3
DE BACA	UK9-1	19-May-53	45.26	5	GUADALUPE	PB17-1	28-Sep-57	8.20	3
DE BACA	UK7-1	25-Apr-53	250.15	8	GUADALUPE	PB1-1	28-May-57	8.52	3
DONA ANA	UK6-1	18-Apr-53	5.13	3	GUADALUPE	TP7-1	29-Mar-55	15.34	4
DONA ANA	PB17-1	28-Sep-57	8.20	3	GUADALUPE	UK1-1	17-Mar-53	18.25	4
DONA ANA	PB1-1	28-May-57	8.52	3	GUADALUPE	PB3-1	24-Jun-57	20.17	4
DONA ANA	PB4-1	5-Jul-57	9.34	3	GUADALUPE	TS6-1	25-May-52	24.31	4
DONA ANA	PB3-1	24-Jun-57	18.04	4	GUADALUPE	TP11-1	15-May-55	25.98	5
DONA ANA	TS6-1	25-May-52	29.06	5	GUADALUPE	TS7-1	1-Jun-52	35.60	5
DONA ANA	TS7-1	1-Jun-52	35.60	5	GUADALUPE	UK6-1	18-Apr-53	40.75	5
EDDY	TP5-1	12-Mar-55	3.93	2	GUADALUPE	PB4-1	5-Jul-57	54.82	6
EDDY	TP11-1	15-May-55	6.54	3	GUADALUPE	UK9-1	19-May-53	91.66	6
EDDY	TP7-1	29-Mar-55	7.72	3	GUADALUPE	UK7-1	25-Apr-53	250.15	8
EDDY	PB17-1	28-Sep-57	8.20	3	HARDING	TP5-1	12-Mar-55	7.86	3
EDDY	PB1-1	28-May-57	8.52	3	HARDING	PB17-1	28-Sep-57	8.20	3

INDIVIDUAL FALLOUT DAYS
NEW MEXICO

COUNTY	SHOT	DATE	µCi/SQ METER	INDEX	COUNTY	SHOT	DATE	µCi/SQ METER	INDEX
HARDING	PB1-1	28-May-57	8.52	3	LINCOLN	PB17-1	28-Sep-57	8.20	3
HARDING	PB3-1	24-Jun-57	10.51	4	LINCOLN	PB1-1	28-May-57	8.52	3
HARDING	TS7-1	1-Jun-52	17.80	4	LINCOLN	TP5-1	12-Mar-55	12.10	4
HARDING	UK1-1	17-Mar-53	18.14	4	LINCOLN	TP11-1	15-May-55	12.99	4
HARDING	UK6-1	18-Apr-53	19.86	4	LINCOLN	TP7-1	29-Mar-55	15.54	4
HARDING	TP7-1	29-Mar-55	22.68	4	LINCOLN	PB4-1	5-Jul-57	18.00	4
HARDING	TS6-1	25-May-52	24.31	4	LINCOLN	PB3-1	24-Jun-57	18.75	4
HARDING	TP10-1	5-May-55	50.59	6	LINCOLN	TS6-1	25-May-52	23.43	4
HARDING	PB4-1	5-Jul-57	73.63	6	LINCOLN	TS7-1	1-Jun-52	35.60	5
HARDING	TP11-1	15-May-55	78.03	6	LINCOLN	UK6-1	18-Apr-53	40.75	5
HARDING	UK7-1	25-Apr-53	83.38	6	LINCOLN	UK9-1	19-May-53	45.26	5
HARDING	UK9-1	19-May-53	91.32	6	LINCOLN	UK7-1	25-Apr-53	333.53	8
HIDALGO	TP6-1	22-Mar-55	4.08	2	LOS ALAMOS	PB17-1	28-Sep-57	8.20	3
HIDALGO	UK3-1	31-Mar-53	4.41	2	LOS ALAMOS	TP5-1	12-Mar-55	8.27	3
HIDALGO	PB17-1	28-Sep-57	8.20	3	LOS ALAMOS	PB1-1	28-May-57	8.52	3
HIDALGO	PB1-1	28-May-57	8.52	3	LOS ALAMOS	TP11-1	15-May-55	9.77	3
HIDALGO	PB4-1	5-Jul-57	17.73	4	LOS ALAMOS	PB3-1	24-Jun-57	11.22	4
HIDALGO	PB3-1	24-Jun-57	18.04	4	LOS ALAMOS	TP7-1	29-Mar-55	15.73	4
HIDALGO	TS6-1	25-May-52	29.06	5	LOS ALAMOS	UK11-1	4-Jun-53	16.28	4
HIDALGO	TS7-1	1-Jun-52	35.60	5	LOS ALAMOS	UK1-1	17-Mar-53	18.36	4
LEA	TP5-1	12-Mar-55	3.93	2	LOS ALAMOS	TS7-1	1-Jun-52	35.60	5
LEA	TP7-1	29-Mar-55	7.53	3	LOS ALAMOS	TS6-1	25-May-52	43.54	5
LEA	PB17-1	28-Sep-57	8.20	3	LOS ALAMOS	PB4-1	5-Jul-57	54.41	6
LEA	PB1-1	28-May-57	8.52	3	LOS ALAMOS	UK6-1	18-Apr-53	81.49	6
LEA	UK9-1	19-May-53	8.94	3	LOS ALAMOS	UK7-1	25-Apr-53	166.77	7
LEA	UK1-1	17-Mar-53	9.02	3	LOS ALAMOS	UK9-1	19-May-53	186.72	7
LEA	PB4-1	5-Jul-57	9.34	3	LUNA	UK3-1	31-Mar-53	3.56	2
LEA	UK6-1	18-Apr-53	9.87	3	LUNA	TP6-1	22-Mar-55	4.08	2
LEA	TP11-1	15-May-55	12.99	4	LUNA	UK6-1	18-Apr-53	5.13	3
LEA	TS6-1	25-May-52	14.59	4	LUNA	PB17-1	28-Sep-57	8.20	3
LEA	TS7-1	1-Jun-52	17.80	4	LUNA	PB1-1	28-May-57	8.52	3
LEA	PB3-1	24-Jun-57	19.46	4	LUNA	PB4-1	5-Jul-57	17.73	4
LEA	UK7-1	25-Apr-53	83.38	6	LUNA	PB3-1	24-Jun-57	18.04	4

INDIVIDUAL FALLOUT DAYS
NEW MEXICO

COUNTY	SHOT	DATE	µCi/SQ METER	INDEX		COUNTY	SHOT	DATE	µCi/SQ METER	INDEX
LUNA	TS6-1	25-May-52	29.06	5		MORA	UK9-1	19-May-53	92.00	6
LUNA	TS7-1	1-Jun-52	35.60	5		OTERO	TP5-1	12-Mar-55	4.03	2
MCKINLEY	TS4-1	1-May-52	4.43	2		OTERO	TP7-1	29-Mar-55	6.18	3
MCKINLEY	PB17-1	28-Sep-57	8.20	3		OTERO	TP11-1	15-May-55	6.54	3
MCKINLEY	TS3-1	22-Apr-52	8.29	3		OTERO	PB17-1	28-Sep-57	8.20	3
MCKINLEY	PB13-3	8-Sep-57	8.43	3		OTERO	PB1-1	28-May-57	8.52	3
MCKINLEY	PB1-1	28-May-57	8.52	3		OTERO	UK9-1	19-May-53	8.94	3
MCKINLEY	PB4-1	5-Jul-57	8.66	3		OTERO	PB4-1	5-Jul-57	9.34	3
MCKINLEY	UK1-1	17-Mar-53	9.23	3		OTERO	UK6-1	18-Apr-53	10.12	4
MCKINLEY	PB18-1	10-Jul-57	9.82	3		OTERO	PB3-1	24-Jun-57	18.75	4
MCKINLEY	TP11-1	15-May-55	15.82	4		OTERO	TS6-1	25-May-52	21.77	4
MCKINLEY	TP7-1	29-Mar-55	15.83	4		OTERO	TS7-1	1-Jun-52	35.60	5
MCKINLEY	TP5-1	12-Mar-55	17.24	4		QUAY	TP5-1	12-Mar-55	7.86	3
MCKINLEY	UK11-1	4-Jun-53	21.43	4		QUAY	PB17-1	28-Sep-57	8.20	3
MCKINLEY	PB3-1	24-Jun-57	33.80	5		QUAY	PB1-1	28-May-57	8.52	3
MCKINLEY	TS6-1	25-May-52	43.54	5		QUAY	TP7-1	29-Mar-55	15.15	4
MCKINLEY	TS7-1	1-Jun-52	44.50	5		QUAY	TS7-1	1-Jun-52	17.80	4
MCKINLEY	UK9-1	19-May-53	278.15	8		QUAY	UK1-1	17-Mar-53	18.14	4
MCKINLEY	UK6-1	18-Apr-53	211.30	8		QUAY	UK6-1	18-Apr-53	19.86	4
MCKINLEY	UK7-1	25-Apr-53	436.89	9		QUAY	PB3-1	24-Jun-57	20.17	4
MORA	TP5-1	12-Mar-55	8.07	3		QUAY	TS6-1	25-May-52	24.31	4
MORA	PB17-1	28-Sep-57	8.20	3		QUAY	TP10-1	5-May-55	35.63	5
MORA	PB1-1	28-May-57	8.52	3		QUAY	UK9-1	19-May-53	45.26	5
MORA	PB3-1	24-Jun-57	10.51	4		QUAY	TP11-1	15-May-55	52.05	6
MORA	UK1-1	17-Mar-53	18.25	4		QUAY	PB4-1	5-Jul-57	55.22	6
MORA	TP7-1	29-Mar-55	19.20	4		QUAY	UK7-1	25-Apr-53	208.52	8
MORA	TS6-1	25-May-52	25.20	5		RIO ARRIBA	PB17-1	28-Sep-57	8.20	3
MORA	TS7-1	1-Jun-52	35.60	5		RIO ARRIBA	TP5-1	12-Mar-55	8.27	3
MORA	UK6-1	18-Apr-53	39.59	5		RIO ARRIBA	PB1-1	28-May-57	8.52	3
MORA	TP10-1	5-May-55	43.40	5		RIO ARRIBA	PB4-1	5-Jul-57	8.66	3
MORA	PB4-1	5-Jul-57	73.09	6		RIO ARRIBA	TP11-1	15-May-55	9.77	3
MORA	TP11-1	15-May-55	78.03	6		RIO ARRIBA	PB3-1	24-Jun-57	11.22	4
MORA	UK7-1	25-Apr-53	83.38	6		RIO ARRIBA	TP7-1	29-Mar-55	15.73	4

INDIVIDUAL FALLOUT DAYS
NEW MEXICO

COUNTY	SHOT	DATE	µCi/SQ METER	INDEX	COUNTY	SHOT	DATE	µCi/SQ METER	INDEX
RIO ARRIBA	UK11-1	4-Jun-53	16.28	4	SAN JUAN	UK6-1	18-Apr-53	30.11	5
RIO ARRIBA	UK1-1	17-Mar-53	27.48	5	SAN JUAN	TS7-1	1-Jun-52	35.60	5
RIO ARRIBA	UK6-1	18-Apr-53	30.11	5	SAN JUAN	TS6-1	25-May-52	44.42	5
RIO ARRIBA	TS6-1	25-May-52	34.81	5	SAN JUAN	UK9-1	19-May-53	264.14	8
RIO ARRIBA	TS7-1	1-Jun-52	35.60	5	SAN JUAN	UK7-1	25-Apr-53	166.77	7
RIO ARRIBA	UK7-1	25-Apr-53	166.77	7	SAN MIGUEL	TP5-1	12-Mar-55	8.07	3
RIO ARRIBA	UK9-1	19-May-53	186.72	7	SAN MIGUEL	PB17-1	28-Sep-57	8.20	3
ROOSEVELT	TP5-1	12-Mar-55	7.86	3	SAN MIGUEL	PB1-1	28-May-57	8.52	3
ROOSEVELT	PB17-1	28-Sep-57	8.20	3	SAN MIGUEL	TP10-1	5-May-55	14.27	4
ROOSEVELT	PB1-1	28-May-57	8.52	3	SAN MIGUEL	TP7-1	29-Mar-55	15.34	4
ROOSEVELT	TP10-1	5-May-55	13.88	4	SAN MIGUEL	UK1-1	17-Mar-53	18.25	4
ROOSEVELT	TP7-1	29-Mar-55	15.15	4	SAN MIGUEL	PB3-1	24-Jun-57	20.88	4
ROOSEVELT	TS6-1	25-May-52	15.58	4	SAN MIGUEL	TS6-1	25-May-52	24.31	4
ROOSEVELT	TS7-1	1-Jun-52	17.80	4	SAN MIGUEL	TS7-1	1-Jun-52	35.60	5
ROOSEVELT	UK9-1	19-May-53	17.99	4	SAN MIGUEL	UK6-1	18-Apr-53	40.49	5
ROOSEVELT	UK1-1	17-Mar-53	18.14	4	SAN MIGUEL	TP11-1	15-May-55	52.05	6
ROOSEVELT	PB3-1	24-Jun-57	19.46	4	SAN MIGUEL	PB4-1	5-Jul-57	73.09	6
ROOSEVELT	TP11-1	15-May-55	19.53	4	SAN MIGUEL	UK9-1	19-May-53	92.00	6
ROOSEVELT	UK6-1	18-Apr-53	19.86	4	SAN MIGUEL	UK7-1	25-Apr-53	166.77	7
ROOSEVELT	PB4-1	5-Jul-57	27.34	5	SANDOVAL	TS3-1	22-Apr-52	4.06	2
ROOSEVELT	UK7-1	25-Apr-53	250.15	8	SANDOVAL	PB13-3	8-Sep-57	5.58	3
SAN JUAN	TS4-1	1-May-52	4.43	2	SANDOVAL	PB17-1	28-Sep-57	8.20	3
SAN JUAN	TS3-1	22-Apr-52	5.82	3	SANDOVAL	PB1-1	28-May-57	8.52	3
SAN JUAN	PB17-1	28-Sep-57	8.20	3	SANDOVAL	UK1-1	17-Mar-53	9.23	3
SAN JUAN	PB1-1	28-May-57	8.52	3	SANDOVAL	TP11-1	15-May-55	9.77	3
SAN JUAN	PB18-1	10-Jul-57	9.82	3	SANDOVAL	TP5-1	12-Mar-55	12.40	4
SAN JUAN	TP5-1	12-Mar-55	12.91	4	SANDOVAL	TP7-1	29-Mar-55	15.73	4
SAN JUAN	TP4-1	7-Mar-55	15.67	4	SANDOVAL	UK11-1	4-Jun-53	16.28	4
SAN JUAN	TP7-1	29-Mar-55	15.83	4	SANDOVAL	PB3-1	24-Jun-57	22.44	4
SAN JUAN	TP11-1	15-May-55	15.92	4	SANDOVAL	TS7-1	1-Jun-52	35.60	5
SAN JUAN	PB3-1	24-Jun-57	23.15	4	SANDOVAL	TS6-1	25-May-52	43.54	5
SAN JUAN	UK11-1	4-Jun-53	25.20	5	SANDOVAL	PB4-1	5-Jul-57	54.41	6
SAN JUAN	UK1-1	17-Mar-53	27.70	5	SANDOVAL	UK9-1	19-May-53	279.05	8

INDIVIDUAL FALLOUT DAYS
NEW MEXICO

COUNTY	SHOT	DATE	µCi/SQ METER	INDEX	COUNTY	SHOT	DATE	µCi/SQ METER	INDEX
SANDOVAL	UK7-1	25-Apr-53	338.39	8	SOCORRO	TP5-1	12-Mar-55	16.53	4
SANDOVAL	UK6-1	18-Apr-53	156.71	7	SOCORRO	PB4-1	5-Jul-57	17.87	4
SANTA FE	UK11-1	4-Jun-53	5.15	3	SOCORRO	PB3-1	24-Jun-57	18.75	4
SANTA FE	PB13-3	8-Sep-57	5.50	3	SOCORRO	TS6-1	25-May-52	32.38	5
SANTA FE	TP5-1	12-Mar-55	8.07	3	SOCORRO	TS7-1	1-Jun-52	35.60	5
SANTA FE	PB17-1	28-Sep-57	8.20	3	SOCORRO	UK7-1	25-Apr-53	42.31	5
SANTA FE	PB1-1	28-May-57	8.52	3	SOCORRO	UK9-1	19-May-53	91.32	6
SANTA FE	UK1-1	17-Mar-53	9.12	3	SOCORRO	UK6-1	18-Apr-53	103.41	7
SANTA FE	TP11-1	15-May-55	9.77	3	TAOS	TP10-1	5-May-55	3.69	2
SANTA FE	TP7-1	29-Mar-55	15.73	4	TAOS	UK11-1	4-Jun-53	6.82	3
SANTA FE	PB3-1	24-Jun-57	21.59	4	TAOS	PB17-1	28-Sep-57	8.20	3
SANTA FE	TS6-1	25-May-52	33.59	5	TAOS	TP5-1	12-Mar-55	8.27	3
SANTA FE	TS7-1	1-Jun-52	35.60	5	TAOS	PB1-1	28-May-57	8.52	3
SANTA FE	PB4-1	5-Jul-57	73.09	6	TAOS	TP11-1	15-May-55	9.77	3
SANTA FE	UK6-1	18-Apr-53	82.78	6	TAOS	PB3-1	24-Jun-57	10.79	4
SANTA FE	UK7-1	25-Apr-53	335.90	8	TAOS	TP7-1	29-Mar-55	15.73	4
SANTA FE	UK9-1	19-May-53	186.04	7	TAOS	UK6-1	18-Apr-53	19.86	4
SIERRA	TP7-1	29-Mar-55	7.82	3	TAOS	UK1-1	17-Mar-53	27.48	5
SIERRA	PB17-1	28-Sep-57	8.20	3	TAOS	TS6-1	25-May-52	34.04	5
SIERRA	TP5-1	12-Mar-55	8.27	3	TAOS	TS7-1	1-Jun-52	35.60	5
SIERRA	PB1-1	28-May-57	8.52	3	TAOS	PB4-1	5-Jul-57	55.22	6
SIERRA	UK9-1	19-May-53	9.05	3	TAOS	UK7-1	25-Apr-53	83.38	6
SIERRA	PB4-1	5-Jul-57	17.87	4	TAOS	UK9-1	19-May-53	185.36	7
SIERRA	PB3-1	24-Jun-57	18.04	4	TORRANCE	PB13-3	8-Sep-57	4.17	2
SIERRA	TS7-1	1-Jun-52	35.60	5	TORRANCE	UK11-1	4-Jun-53	5.01	3
SIERRA	UK6-1	18-Apr-53	40.75	5	TORRANCE	TP11-1	15-May-55	6.54	3
SIERRA	TS6-1	25-May-52	45.20	5	TORRANCE	TP5-1	12-Mar-55	8.07	3
SOCORRO	TP6-1	22-Mar-55	3.92	2	TORRANCE	PB17-1	28-Sep-57	8.20	3
SOCORRO	UK11-1	4-Jun-53	5.15	3	TORRANCE	PB1-1	28-May-57	8.52	3
SOCORRO	PB13-3	8-Sep-57	5.50	3	TORRANCE	UK1-1	17-Mar-53	9.12	3
SOCORRO	PB17-1	28-Sep-57	8.20	3	TORRANCE	TP7-1	29-Mar-55	15.54	4
SOCORRO	PB1-1	28-May-57	8.52	3	TORRANCE	PB3-1	24-Jun-57	20.17	4
SOCORRO	TP7-1	29-Mar-55	15.73	4	TORRANCE	TS6-1	25-May-52	24.31	4

INDIVIDUAL FALLOUT DAYS
NEW MEXICO

COUNTY	SHOT	DATE	µCi/SQ METER	INDEX	COUNTY	SHOT	DATE	µCi/SQ METER	INDEX
TORRANCE	TS7-1	1-Jun-52	35.60	5	VALENCIA	UK3-1	31-Mar-53	3.56	2
TORRANCE	PB4-1	5-Jul-57	72.55	6	VALENCIA	TP6-1	22-Mar-55	4.08	2
TORRANCE	UK6-1	18-Apr-53	82.78	6	VALENCIA	TS4-1	1-May-52	4.29	2
TORRANCE	UK7-1	25-Apr-53	251.96	8	VALENCIA	UK1-1	17-Mar-53	4.56	2
TORRANCE	UK9-1	19-May-53	275.09	8	VALENCIA	TS3-1	22-Apr-52	5.82	3
UNION	TP5-1	12-Mar-55	7.86	3	VALENCIA	PB17-1	28-Sep-57	8.20	3
UNION	PB17-1	28-Sep-57	8.20	3	VALENCIA	PB13-3	8-Sep-57	8.43	3
UNION	PB1-1	28-May-57	8.52	3	VALENCIA	PB1-1	28-May-57	8.52	3
UNION	TS7-1	1-Jun-52	8.90	3	VALENCIA	TP11-1	15-May-55	9.77	3
UNION	UK6-1	18-Apr-53	9.74	3	VALENCIA	UK11-1	4-Jun-53	11.13	4
UNION	PB3-1	24-Jun-57	10.51	4	VALENCIA	TP7-1	29-Mar-55	15.83	4
UNION	UK1-1	17-Mar-53	18.14	4	VALENCIA	TP5-1	12-Mar-55	16.84	4
UNION	TP7-1	29-Mar-55	22.68	4	VALENCIA	PB3-1	24-Jun-57	22.44	4
UNION	TS6-1	25-May-52	24.31	4	VALENCIA	TS7-1	1-Jun-52	35.60	5
UNION	UK7-1	25-Apr-53	49.99	5	VALENCIA	TS6-1	25-May-52	43.54	5
UNION	TP10-1	5-May-55	57.87	6	VALENCIA	PB4-1	5-Jul-57	53.60	6
UNION	PB4-1	5-Jul-57	73.63	6	VALENCIA	UK7-1	25-Apr-53	262.11	8
UNION	UK9-1	19-May-53	90.64	6	VALENCIA	UK6-1	18-Apr-53	211.30	8
UNION	TP11-1	15-May-55	130.08	7	VALENCIA	UK9-1	19-May-53	186.04	7

INDIVIDUAL FALLOUT DAYS
NEVADA

COUNTY	SHOT	DATE	µCi/SQ METER	INDEX	COUNTY	SHOT	DATE	µCi/SQ METER	INDEX
CARSON CITY	PB13-1	6-Sep-57	6.80	3	CLARK1	PB11-1	31-Aug-57	109.14	7
CARSON CITY	TS8-2	6-Jun-52	7.12	3	CLARK1	TP5-1	12-Mar-55	126.37	7
CARSON CITY	TP11-1	15-May-55	7.42	3	CLARK1	UK7-1	25-Apr-53	2185.05	10
CARSON CITY	TS7-1	1-Jun-52	8.90	3	CLARK2	UK11-1	4-Jun-53	19.07	4
CARSON CITY	UK6-1	18-Apr-53	8.97	3	CLARK2	TP11-1	15-May-55	27.29	5
CARSON CITY	TS3-1	22-Apr-52	9.53	3	CLARK2	TP6-1	22-Mar-55	48.05	5
CARSON CITY	TS6-1	25-May-52	14.15	4	CLARK2	TP2-1	22-Feb-55	85.77	6
CARSON CITY	UK10-1	25-May-53	18.52	4	CLARK2	UK6-1	18-Apr-53	255.63	8
CARSON CITY	PB14-1	14-Sep-57	39.80	5	CLARK3	UK6-1	18-Apr-53	57.72	6
CARSON CITY	PB6-1	24-Jul-57	43.57	5	CLARK3	TP6-1	22-Mar-55	104.23	7
CARSON CITY	PB16-1	23-Sep-57	45.88	5	DOUGLAS	TS8-2	6-Jun-52	3.54	2
CARSON CITY	PB1-1	28-May-57	234.66	8	DOUGLAS	PB13-1	6-Sep-57	6.80	3
CARSON CITY	TS8-1	5-Jun-52	1235.86	10	DOUGLAS	TP11-1	15-May-55	7.42	3
CHURCHILL	TS2-1	15-Apr-52	4.17	2	DOUGLAS	UK10-1	25-May-53	8.26	3
CHURCHILL	PB13-1	6-Sep-57	6.80	3	DOUGLAS	TS7-1	1-Jun-52	8.90	3
CHURCHILL	TS8-2	6-Jun-52	7.12	3	DOUGLAS	UK6-1	18-Apr-53	8.97	3
CHURCHILL	TP11-1	15-May-55	7.42	3	DOUGLAS	TS3-1	22-Apr-52	9.53	3
CHURCHILL	TS7-1	1-Jun-52	9.02	3	DOUGLAS	TS6-1	25-May-52	10.14	4
CHURCHILL	UK6-1	18-Apr-53	9.87	3	DOUGLAS	PB14-1	14-Sep-57	39.80	5
CHURCHILL	PB14-1	14-Sep-57	15.92	4	DOUGLAS	PB16-1	23-Sep-57	45.88	5
CHURCHILL	UK10-1	25-May-53	18.52	4	DOUGLAS	PB6-1	24-Jul-57	55.22	6
CHURCHILL	TS6-1	25-May-52	20.29	4	DOUGLAS	PB1-1	28-May-57	234.66	8
CHURCHILL	PB16-1	23-Sep-57	91.75	6	DOUGLAS	TS8-1	5-Jun-52	614.44	9
CHURCHILL	PB1-1	28-May-57	274.92	8	ELKO	PB5-1	15-Jul-57	4.29	2
CHURCHILL	PB6-1	24-Jul-57	121.94	7	ELKO	PB13-1	6-Sep-57	4.41	2
CHURCHILL	TS8-1	5-Jun-52	1235.86	10	ELKO	TP10-1	5-May-55	5.13	3
CLARK1	PB5-2	16-Jul-57	12.01	4	ELKO	PB9-1	23-Aug-57	5.23	3
CLARK1	TP6-2	23-Mar-55	26.74	5	ELKO	UK2-1	24-Mar-53	6.86	3
CLARK1	UK1-1	17-Mar-53	51.94	6	ELKO	UK10-1	25-May-53	7.12	3
CLARK1	UK11-1	4-Jun-53	87.97	6	ELKO	TS2-1	15-Apr-52	8.31	3
CLARK1	UK9-1	19-May-53	95.70	6	ELKO	BJ6-1	29-Nov-51	8.56	3
CLARK1	UK6-1	18-Apr-53	324.13	8	ELKO	PB12-1	2-Sep-57	10.27	4
CLARK1	TP11-1	15-May-55	387.19	8	ELKO	TS6-1	25-May-52	14.28	4

INDIVIDUAL FALLOUT DAYS
NEVADA

COUNTY	SHOT	DATE	µCi/SQ METER	INDEX	COUNTY	SHOT	DATE	µCi/SQ METER	INDEX
ELKO	TP11-1	15-May-55	15.04	4	EUREKA	BJ5 1	19-Nov-51	106.82	7
ELKO	PB6-2	25-Jul-57	15.18	4	EUREKA	PB8-1	18-Aug-57	482.83	9
ELKO	PB1-1	28-May-57	15.72	4	EUREKA	TS8-1	5-Jun-52	5867.23	10
ELKO	PB16-1	23-Sep-57	18.94	4	HUMBOLDT	PB13-1	6-Sep-57	4.41	2
ELKO	PB17-1	28-Sep-57	20.12	4	HUMBOLDT	TS6-1	25-May-52	4.75	2
ELKO	PB8-1	18-Aug-57	55.23	6	HUMBOLDT	TS7-1	1-Jun-52	8.45	3
ELKO	TS8-2	6-Jun-52	92.93	6	HUMBOLDT	PB6-1	24-Jul-57	9.38	3
ELKO	BJ5 1	19-Nov-51	105.23	7	HUMBOLDT	PB17-1	28-Sep-57	10.12	4
ELKO	TS7-1	1-Jun-52	184.19	7	HUMBOLDT	TP11-1	15-May-55	10.94	4
ELKO	TS8-1	5-Jun-52	16139.83	10	HUMBOLDT	PB1-1	28-May-57	15.55	4
ESMERALDA1	PB6-1	24-Jul-57	256.26	8	HUMBOLDT	PB8-1	18-Aug-57	16.85	4
ESMERALDA1	PB16-1	23-Sep-57	107.32	7	HUMBOLDT	UK10-1	25-May-53	17.47	4
ESMERALDA2	PB1-1	28-May-57	4.89	2	HUMBOLDT	BJ5 1	19-Nov-51	27.53	5
ESMERALDA2	PB13-1	6-Sep-57	14.05	4	HUMBOLDT	PB16-1	23-Sep-57	28.46	5
ESMERALDA2	TP4-1	7-Mar-55	41.77	5	HUMBOLDT	TS8-2	6-Jun-52	69.42	6
ESMERALDA2	PB16-1	23-Sep-57	274.35	8	HUMBOLDT	TS8-1	5-Jun-52	12057.13	10
ESMERALDA2	PB6-1	24-Jul-57	328.70	8	LANDER1	TS2-1	15-Apr-52	4.41	2
EUREKA	SE1	6-Jul-62	3.54	2	LANDER1	PB13-1	6-Sep-57	4.53	2
EUREKA	BJ6-1	29-Nov-51	4.65	2	LANDER1	PB17-1	28-Sep-57	5.24	3
EUREKA	UK6-1	18-Apr-53	5.00	2	LANDER1	TP11-1	15-May-55	7.42	3
EUREKA	PB17-1	28-Sep-57	5.24	3	LANDER1	UK10-1	25-May-53	9.69	3
EUREKA	UK10-1	25-May-53	5.27	3	LANDER1	TS7-1	1-Jun-52	10.07	4
EUREKA	TP11-1	15-May-55	7.42	3	LANDER1	TS6-1	25-May-52	10.14	4
EUREKA	UK2-1	24-Mar-53	9.18	3	LANDER1	PB8-1	18-Aug-57	16.28	4
EUREKA	PB6-2	25-Jul-57	15.08	4	LANDER1	PB6-1	24-Jul-57	18.86	4
EUREKA	TP4-1	7-Mar-55	15.23	4	LANDER1	PB16-1	23-Sep-57	36.74	5
EUREKA	TS6-1	25-May-52	20.41	4	LANDER1	PB1-1	28-May-57	39.85	5
EUREKA	TS2-1	15-Apr-52	22.96	4	LANDER1	BJ5 1	19-Nov-51	56.41	6
EUREKA	PB12-1	2-Sep-57	31.50	5	LANDER1	TS8-2	6-Jun-52	105.93	7
EUREKA	TS8-2	6-Jun-52	33.78	5	LANDER1	TS8-1	5-Jun-52	18398.33	10
EUREKA	TP10-1	5-May-55	43.77	5	LANDER2	UK6-1	18-Apr-53	5.00	2
EUREKA	PB1-1	28-May-57	70.83	6	LANDER2	PB17-1	28-Sep-57	5.24	3
EUREKA	TS7-1	1-Jun-52	231.27	8	LANDER2	PB13-1	6-Sep-57	6.68	3

INDIVIDUAL FALLOUT DAYS
NEVADA

COUNTY	SHOT	DATE	µCi/SQ METER	INDEX	COUNTY	SHOT	DATE	µCi/SQ METER	INDEX
LANDER2	TP11-1	15-May-55	7.42	3	LINCOLN2	UK7-1	25-Apr-53	6.28	3
LANDER2	BJ5 1	19-Nov-51	7.56	3	LINCOLN2	TS7-1	1-Jun-52	7.56	3
LANDER2	TS2-1	15-Apr-52	7.89	3	LINCOLN2	TP8-1	9-Apr-55	10.08	4
LANDER2	TP10-1	5-May-55	7.96	3	LINCOLN2	PB3-1	24-Jun-57	10.85	4
LANDER2	UK10-1	25-May-53	20.09	4	LINCOLN2	TP4-1	7-Mar-55	15.17	4
LANDER2	TS7-1	1-Jun-52	20.14	4	LINCOLN2	TP5-1	12-Mar-55	15.69	4
LANDER2	TS6-1	25-May-52	20.29	4	LINCOLN2	PB2-1	18-Jun-57	21.88	4
LANDER2	PB6-1	24-Jul-57	26.63	5	LINCOLN2	TP3-1	1-Mar-55	57.19	6
LANDER2	PB8-1	18-Aug-57	28.01	5	LINCOLN2	TS8-1	5-Jun-52	83.44	6
LANDER2	PB16-1	23-Sep-57	78.71	6	LINCOLN2	BJ6-1	29-Nov-51	85.19	6
LANDER2	TS8-2	6-Jun-52	89.25	6	LINCOLN2	UK9-1	19-May-53	321.44	8
LANDER2	PB1-1	28-May-57	278.84	8	LINCOLN2	TP7-1	29-Mar-55	333.26	8
LANDER2	TS8-1	5-Jun-52	15500.68	10	LINCOLN2	TP9-1	15-Apr-55	209.20	8
LINCOLN1	PB18-1	10-Jul-57	3.62	2	LINCOLN2	PB5-1	15-Jul-57	209.94	8
LINCOLN1	TP6-2	23-Mar-55	7.61	3	LINCOLN2	UK2-1	24-Mar-53	168.92	7
LINCOLN1	UK2-1	24-Mar-53	10.67	4	LINCOLN2	TS6-1	25-May-52	521.64	9
LINCOLN1	TP11-1	15-May-55	10.78	4	LYON	TS8-2	6-Jun-52	3.54	2
LINCOLN1	TP4-1	7-Mar-55	11.76	4	LYON	PB13-1	6-Sep-57	6.80	3
LINCOLN1	PB5-1	15-Jul-57	26.41	5	LYON	TP11-1	15-May-55	7.42	3
LINCOLN1	TP5-1	12-Mar-55	30.46	5	LYON	TS7-1	1-Jun-52	8.90	3
LINCOLN1	TP3-1	1-Mar-55	49.78	5	LYON	UK6-1	18-Apr-53	8.97	3
LINCOLN1	PB3-1	24-Jun-57	56.77	6	LYON	TS3-1	22-Apr-52	9.53	3
LINCOLN1	TP7-1	29-Mar-55	71.59	6	LYON	UK10-1	25-May-53	13.68	4
LINCOLN1	TS6-1	25-May-52	302.37	8	LYON	TS6-1	25-May-52	14.15	4
LINCOLN1	PB11-1	31-Aug-57	393.34	8	LYON	PB14-1	14-Sep-57	39.80	5
LINCOLN1	UK7-1	25-Apr-53	117.10	7	LYON	PB16-1	23-Sep-57	45.88	5
LINCOLN1	UK1-1	17-Mar-53	120.42	7	LYON	PB6-1	24-Jul-57	69.69	6
LINCOLN1	TP9-1	15-Apr-55	433.28	9	LYON	PB1-1	28-May-57	229.48	8
LINCOLN1	UK9-1	19-May-53	1716.20	10	LYON	TS8-1	5-Jun-52	614.44	9
LINCOLN2	BJ5 1	19-Nov-51	3.84	2	MINERAL	TP11-1	15-May-55	3.61	2
LINCOLN2	UK10-1	25-May-53	4.19	2	MINERAL	UK10-1	25-May-53	7.55	3
LINCOLN2	TS4-1	1-May-52	4.24	2	MINERAL	TS3-1	22-Apr-52	7.59	3
LINCOLN2	PB8-1	18-Aug-57	6.00	3	MINERAL	TS7-1	1-Jun-52	8.90	3

INDITVIDUAL FALLOUT DAYS
NEVADA

COUNTY	SHOT	DATE	µCi/SQ METER	INDEX	COUNTY	SHOT	DATE	µCi/SQ METER	INDEX
MINERAL	PB13-1	6-Sep-57	9.07	3	NYE3	PB13-2	7-Sep-57	6.29	3
MINERAL	TS6-1	25-May-52	10.14	4	NYE3	PB16-1	23-Sep-57	9.98	3
MINERAL	PB14-1	14-Sep-57	57.61	6	NYE3	PB2-1	18-Jun-57	20.33	4
MINERAL	PB16-1	23-Sep-57	86.53	6	NYE3	TP8-1	9-Apr-55	21.46	4
MINERAL	PB1-1	28-May-57	277.88	8	PERSHING	UK6-1	18-Apr-53	3.84	2
MINERAL	TS8-1	5-Jun-52	307.22	8	PERSHING	PB13-1	6-Sep-57	5.25	3
MINERAL	PB6-1	24-Jul-57	184.78	7	PERSHING	TP11-1	15-May-55	7.42	3
NYE1	PB6-1	24-Jul-57	7.00	3	PERSHING	TS6-1	25-May-52	8.14	3
NYE1	PB14-1	14-Sep-57	7.89	3	PERSHING	TS7-1	1-Jun-52	8.90	3
NYE1	TS8-2	6-Jun-52	9.53	3	PERSHING	TS8-2	6-Jun-52	10.57	4
NYE1	PB8-1	18-Aug-57	10.99	4	PERSHING	BJ5 1	19-Nov-51	18.62	4
NYE1	PB16-1	23-Sep-57	39.08	5	PERSHING	UK10-1	25-May-53	27.36	5
NYE1	PB1-1	28-May-57	511.88	9	PERSHING	PB6-1	24-Jul-57	37.35	5
NYE1	TS8-1	5-Jun-52	1656.00	10	PERSHING	PB16-1	23-Sep-57	54.49	6
NYE2	TS6-1	25-May-52	5.00	3	PERSHING	PB1-1	28-May-57	157.52	7
NYE2	PB14-1	14-Sep-57	12.09	4	PERSHING	TS8-1	5-Jun-52	1836.34	10
NYE2	PB4-1	5-Jul-57	12.54	4	STOREY	PB13-1	6-Sep-57	6.80	3
NYE2	PB16-1	23-Sep-57	14.06	4	STOREY	TS8-2	6-Jun-52	7.12	3
NYE2	PB6-2	25-Jul-57	17.91	4	STOREY	TP11-1	15-May-55	7.42	3
NYE2	UK10-1	25-May-53	26.05	5	STOREY	TS7-1	1-Jun-52	8.90	3
NYE2	BJ6-1	29-Nov-51	79.78	6	STOREY	UK6-1	18-Apr-53	8.97	3
NYE2	TS8-2	6-Jun-52	93.95	6	STOREY	TS3-1	22-Apr-52	9.53	3
NYE2	PB8-1	18-Aug-57	254.89	8	STOREY	TS6-1	25-May-52	14.15	4
NYE2	TP10-1	5-May-55	316.28	8	STOREY	UK10-1	25-May-53	18.52	4
NYE2	TP4-1	7-Mar-55	322.23	8	STOREY	PB6-1	24-Jul-57	36.99	5
NYE2	UK2-1	24-Mar-53	243.64	8	STOREY	PB14-1	14-Sep-57	39.80	5
NYE2	PB12-1	2-Sep-57	100.98	7	STOREY	PB16-1	23-Sep-57	45.88	5
NYE2	SE1	6-Jul-62	120.28	7	STOREY	PB1-1	28-May-57	233.81	8
NYE2	TS7-1	1-Jun-52	138.58	7	STOREY	TS8-1	5-Jun-52	1235.86	10
NYE2	BJ5 1	19-Nov-51	152.96	7	WASHOE	UK6-1	18-Apr-53	4.71	2
NYE2	PB5-1	15-Jul-57	544.73	9	WASHOE	TS8-2	6-Jun-52	6.64	3
NYE2	PB1-1	28-May-57	754.54	9	WASHOE	PB13-1	6-Sep-57	6.80	3
NYE2	TS8-1	5-Jun-52	16317.90	10	WASHOE	TP11-1	15-May-55	6.82	3

INDIVIDUAL FALLOUT DAYS
NEVADA

COUNTY	SHOT	DATE	µCi/SQ METER	INDEX	COUNTY	SHOT	DATE	µCi/SQ METER	INDEX
WASHOE	TS6-1	25-May-52	8.96	3	WHITE PINE1	PB5-1	15-Jul-57	105.36	7
WASHOE	TS3-1	22-Apr-52	8.99	3	WHITE PINE1	TS8-1	5-Jun-52	1235.86	10
WASHOE	TS7-1	1-Jun-52	15.94	4	WHITE PINE2	UK7-1	25-Apr-53	4.63	2
WASHOE	UK10-1	25-May-53	17.47	4	WHITE PINE2	PB15-1	16-Sep-57	5.93	3
WASHOE	PB6-1	24-Jul-57	37.35	5	WHITE PINE2	PB1-1	28-May-57	6.37	3
WASHOE	PB14-1	14-Sep-57	39.80	5	WHITE PINE2	TS3-1	22-Apr-52	6.53	3
WASHOE	PB16-1	23-Sep-57	45.88	5	WHITE PINE2	TP11-1	15-May-55	7.52	3
WASHOE	PB1-1	28-May-57	249.92	8	WHITE PINE2	UK10-1	25-May-53	8.69	3
WASHOE	TS8-1	5-Jun-52	1152.37	10	WHITE PINE2	PB4-1	5-Jul-57	9.81	3
WHITE PINE1	UK7-1	25-Apr-53	4.63	2	WHITE PINE2	UK6-1	18-Apr-53	9.87	3
WHITE PINE1	PB1-1	28-May-57	5.61	3	WHITE PINE2	TS7-1	1-Jun-52	9.95	3
WHITE PINE1	PB15-1	16-Sep-57	5.82	3	WHITE PINE2	UK9-1	19-May-53	10.07	4
WHITE PINE1	UK6-1	18-Apr-53	6.53	3	WHITE PINE2	PB17-1	28-Sep-57	10.37	4
WHITE PINE1	TS3-1	22-Apr-52	6.53	3	WHITE PINE2	TS8-2	6-Jun-52	10.73	4
WHITE PINE1	TP11-1	15-May-55	7.09	3	WHITE PINE2	TS1-1	1-Apr-52	19.81	4
WHITE PINE1	TS8-2	6-Jun-52	7.12	3	WHITE PINE2	TS6-1	25-May-52	20.52	4
WHITE PINE1	UK9-1	19-May-53	9.50	3	WHITE PINE2	PB6-2	25-Jul-57	21.87	4
WHITE PINE1	TS1-1	1-Apr-52	9.91	3	WHITE PINE2	TP8-1	9-Apr-55	29.00	5
WHITE PINE1	TS7-1	1-Jun-52	9.95	3	WHITE PINE2	TS2-1	15-Apr-52	33.67	5
WHITE PINE1	PB17-1	28-Sep-57	10.37	4	WHITE PINE2	BJ5 1	19-Nov-51	40.22	5
WHITE PINE1	PB6-2	25-Jul-57	12.22	4	WHITE PINE2	PB12-1	2-Sep-57	52.61	6
WHITE PINE1	TS2-1	15-Apr-52	16.83	4	WHITE PINE2	PB9-1	23-Aug-57	79.88	6
WHITE PINE1	TS6-1	25-May-52	20.52	4	WHITE PINE2	BJ6-1	29-Nov-51	88.82	6
WHITE PINE1	TP8-1	9-Apr-55	25.62	5	WHITE PINE2	PB5-1	15-Jul-57	283.40	8
WHITE PINE1	PB9-1	23-Aug-57	37.97	5	WHITE PINE2	PB8-1	18-Aug-57	335.38	8
WHITE PINE1	BJ5 1	19-Nov-51	40.01	5	WHITE PINE2	TP4-1	7-Mar-55	205.41	8
WHITE PINE1	BJ6-1	29-Nov-51	46.98	5	WHITE PINE2	UK2-1	24-Mar-53	122.36	7
WHITE PINE1	PB12-1	2-Sep-57	52.61	6	WHITE PINE2	SE1	6-Jul-62	143.84	7
WHITE PINE1	SE1	6-Jul-62	77.06	6	WHITE PINE2	TP10-1	5-May-55	430.02	9
WHITE PINE1	UK2-1	24-Mar-53	87.15	6	WHITE PINE2	TS8-1	5-Jun-52	1864.27	10
WHITE PINE1	TP4-1	7-Mar-55	95.05	6	WHITE PINE3	TP5-1	12-Mar-55	3.73	2
WHITE PINE1	TP10-1	5-May-55	238.09	8	WHITE PINE3	UK7-1	25-Apr-53	4.63	2
WHITE PINE1	PB8-1	18-Aug-57	249.74	8	WHITE PINE3	TS3-1	22-Apr-52	6.53	3

INDIVIDUAL FALLOUT DAYS
NEVADA

COUNTY	SHOT	DATE	µCi/SQ METER	INDEX	COUNTY	SHOT	DATE	µCi/SQ METER	INDEX
WHITE PINE3	TP11-1	15-May-55	7.52	3	WHITE PINE3	TS6-1	25-May-52	20.52	4
WHITE PINE3	PB9-1	23-Aug-57	8.79	3	WHITE PINE3	BJ6-1	29-Nov-51	28.14	5
WHITE PINE3	UK6-1	18-Apr-53	9.87	3	WHITE PINE3	UK10-1	25-May-53	35.05	5
WHITE PINE3	TS7-1	1-Jun-52	9.95	3	WHITE PINE3	BJ5 1	19-Nov-51	37.79	5
WHITE PINE3	UK9-1	19-May-53	10.07	4	WHITE PINE3	PB12-1	2-Sep-57	52.61	6
WHITE PINE3	PB15-1	16-Sep-57	10.13	4	WHITE PINE3	PB8-1	18-Aug-57	263.85	8
WHITE PINE3	PB17-1	28-Sep-57	10.37	4	WHITE PINE3	PB5-1	15-Jul-57	206.22	8
WHITE PINE3	PB6-2	25-Jul-57	15.26	4	WHITE PINE3	TP10-1	5-May-55	221.15	8
WHITE PINE3	TS2-1	15-Apr-52	16.83	4	WHITE PINE3	SE1	6-Jul-62	117.11	7
WHITE PINE3	TP8-1	9-Apr-55	18.09	4	WHITE PINE3	TP4-1	7-Mar-55	138.40	7
WHITE PINE3	PB4-1	5-Jul-57	19.61	4	WHITE PINE3	UK2-1	24-Mar-53	492.93	9
WHITE PINE3	TS1-1	1-Apr-52	19.81	4					

INDIVIDUAL FALLOUT DAYS
NEW YORK

COUNTY	SHOT	DATE	µCi/SQ METER	INDEX	COUNTY	SHOT	DATE	µCi/SQ METER	INDEX
ALBANY	TS1-4	4-Apr-52	4.28	2	CATTARAUGUS	BJ2-4	2-Nov-51	10.55	4
ALBANY	UK1-2	18-Mar-53	4.58	2	CATTARAUGUS	TS7-4	4-Jun-52	16.35	4
ALBANY	PB5-8	22-Jul-57	5.97	3	CATTARAUGUS	BJ3-6	6-Nov-51	16.67	4
ALBANY	R1-2	29-Jan-51	7.57	3	CAYUGA	PB5-7	21-Jul-57	4.10	2
ALBANY	BJ2-4	2-Nov-51	10.18	4	CAYUGA	BJ2-3	1-Nov-51	5.01	3
ALBANY	TS8-3	7-Jun-52	11.77	4	CAYUGA	TS7-4	4-Jun-52	5.46	3
ALBANY	UK7-2	26-Apr-53	182.51	7	CAYUGA	R1-2	29-Jan-51	6.99	3
ALLEGANY	TP4-4	10-Mar-55	3.75	2	CAYUGA	BJ2-4	2-Nov-51	27.51	5
ALLEGANY	BJ2-6	4-Nov-51	6.74	3	CHAUTAUQUA	PB5-8	22-Jul-57	5.97	3
ALLEGANY	R1-2	29-Jan-51	7.99	3	CHAUTAUQUA	BJ2-4	2-Nov-51	6.57	3
ALLEGANY	BJ3-7	7-Nov-51	8.40	3	CHAUTAUQUA	R1-2	29-Jan-51	7.99	3
ALLEGANY	BJ2-3	1-Nov-51	9.93	3	CHAUTAUQUA	BJ3-7	7-Nov-51	8.40	3
ALLEGANY	BJ2-4	2-Nov-51	13.02	4	CHAUTAUQUA	BJ2-3	1-Nov-51	8.47	3
ALLEGANY	PB5-8	22-Jul-57	14.93	4	CHAUTAUQUA	TP4-4	10-Mar-55	9.40	3
ALLEGANY	TS7-4	4-Jun-52	15.89	4	CHAUTAUQUA	TS7-4	4-Jun-52	14.37	4
ALLEGANY	BJ3-6	6-Nov-51	16.67	4	CHAUTAUQUA	BJ3-6	6-Nov-51	27.78	5
BRONX	BJ2-3	1-Nov-51	5.14	3	CHAUTAUQUA	TP9-2	15-Apr-55	34.72	5
BRONX	BJ2-4	2-Nov-51	5.39	3	CHEMUNG	BJ2-3	1-Nov-51	4.12	2
BRONX	TS7-5	5-Jun-52	5.77	3	CHEMUNG	BJ3-7	7-Nov-51	4.13	2
BRONX	BJ3-7	7-Nov-51	11.62	4	CHEMUNG	R1-2	29-Jan-51	7.57	3
BRONX	TS1-4	4-Apr-52	11.87	4	CHEMUNG	PB5-8	22-Jul-57	8.96	3
BRONX	UK1-2	18-Mar-53	41.14	5	CHEMUNG	BJ2-4	2-Nov-51	34.20	5
BRONX	R1-2	29-Jan-51	3.50	1	CHENANGO	PB11-5	4-Sep-57	4.48	2
BROOME	PB5-7	21-Jul-57	4.10	2	CHENANGO	UK7-2	26-Apr-53	4.48	2
BROOME	PB5-8	22-Jul-57	5.97	3	CHENANGO	BJ2-6	4-Nov-51	6.74	3
BROOME	R1-2	29-Jan-51	7.57	3	CHENANGO	R1-2	29-Jan-51	7.57	3
BROOME	BJ2-4	2-Nov-51	22.08	4	CHENANGO	PB5-8	22-Jul-57	8.96	3
CATTARAUGUS	BJ3-7	7-Nov-51	4.20	2	CHENANGO	BJ2-4	2-Nov-51	23.40	4
CATTARAUGUS	TP4-4	10-Mar-55	6.54	3	CLINTON	PB11-5	4-Sep-57	4.82	2
CATTARAUGUS	R1-2	29-Jan-51	7.99	3	CLINTON	PB5-6	20-Jul-57	5.40	3
CATTARAUGUS	TP9-2	15-Apr-55	8.65	3	CLINTON	BJ2-4	2-Nov-51	5.99	3
CATTARAUGUS	PB5-8	22-Jul-57	8.96	3	CLINTON	BJ2-2	31-Oct-51	7.98	3
CATTARAUGUS	BJ2-3	1-Nov-51	10.30	4	CLINTON	TS1-4	4-Apr-52	10.30	4

INDIVIDUAL FALLOUT DAYS
NEW YORK

COUNTY	SHOT	DATE	µCi/SQ METER	INDEX	COUNTY	SHOT	DATE	µCi/SQ METER	INDEX
CLINTON	TS8-3	7-Jun-52	11.36	4	DUTCHESS	UK1-2	18-Mar-53	14.01	4
CLINTON	TS7-4	4-Jun-52	27.10	5	DUTCHESS	TS1-4	4-Apr-52	17.17	4
CLINTON	UK7-2	26-Apr-53	35.61	5	ERIE	UK9-3	21-May-53	3.99	2
COLUMBIA	TS7-4	4-Jun-52	3.88	2	ERIE	BJ3-7	7-Nov-51	4.20	2
COLUMBIA	BJ2-3	1-Nov-51	4.18	2	ERIE	PB2-6	23-Jun-57	4.58	2
COLUMBIA	PB5-8	22-Jul-57	5.97	3	ERIE	BJ2-5	3-Nov-51	6.08	3
COLUMBIA	PB11-5	4-Sep-57	6.43	3	ERIE	TP4-4	10-Mar-55	7.11	3
COLUMBIA	UK1-2	18-Mar-53	7.31	3	ERIE	TS7-4	4-Jun-52	8.03	3
COLUMBIA	TS8-3	7-Jun-52	10.47	4	ERIE	PB5-8	22-Jul-57	8.96	3
COLUMBIA	R1-2	29-Jan-51	11.65	4	ERIE	BJ2-4	2-Nov-51	12.10	4
COLUMBIA	BJ2-4	2-Nov-51	16.53	4	ERIE	BJ2-6	4-Nov-51	20.21	4
COLUMBIA	TS1-4	4-Apr-52	17.17	4	ERIE	BJ2-3	1-Nov-51	20.85	4
COLUMBIA	UK7-2	26-Apr-53	173.71	7	ERIE	TP9-2	15-Apr-55	21.46	4
CORTLAND	PB5-7	21-Jul-57	4.10	2	ERIE	BJ3-6	6-Nov-51	27.78	5
CORTLAND	TS7-4	4-Jun-52	5.62	3	ESSEX	BJ2-3	1-Nov-51	3.97	2
CORTLAND	R1-2	29-Jan-51	7.57	3	ESSEX	PB5-8	22-Jul-57	5.97	3
CORTLAND	PB5-8	22-Jul-57	14.93	4	ESSEX	BJ2-2	31-Oct-51	7.98	3
CORTLAND	BJ2-4	2-Nov-51	27.16	5	ESSEX	TS1-4	4-Apr-52	10.30	4
DELAWARE	BJ3-7	7-Nov-51	4.13	2	ESSEX	TS8-3	7-Jun-52	10.63	4
DELAWARE	TS3-6	27-Apr-52	4.25	2	ESSEX	PB11-5	4-Sep-57	12.85	4
DELAWARE	PB11-5	4-Sep-57	4.48	2	ESSEX	TS7-4	4-Jun-52	13.08	4
DELAWARE	PB5-8	22-Jul-57	8.96	3	ESSEX	BJ2-4	2-Nov-51	16.51	4
DELAWARE	UK7-2	26-Apr-53	10.18	4	ESSEX	UK7-2	26-Apr-53	75.35	6
DELAWARE	TS1-4	4-Apr-52	10.30	4	FRANKLIN	PB11-5	4-Sep-57	6.43	3
DELAWARE	R1-2	29-Jan-51	19.29	4	FRANKLIN	TS1-4	4-Apr-52	6.87	3
DELAWARE	BJ2-4	2-Nov-51	32.39	5	FRANKLIN	BJ2-2	31-Oct-51	7.98	3
DUTCHESS	TS7-5	5-Jun-52	3.73	2	FRANKLIN	TS8-3	7-Jun-52	8.27	3
DUTCHESS	BJ2-3	1-Nov-51	4.61	2	FRANKLIN	UK7-2	26-Apr-53	21.20	4
DUTCHESS	PB5-8	22-Jul-57	5.97	3	FRANKLIN	TS7-4	4-Jun-52	21.51	4
DUTCHESS	TS8-3	7-Jun-52	7.12	3	FRANKLIN	BJ2-4	2-Nov-51	22.62	4
DUTCHESS	UK7-2	26-Apr-53	9.21	3	FULTON	BJ3-7	7-Nov-51	4.13	2
DUTCHESS	R1-2	29-Jan-51	11.65	4	FULTON	TS7-4	4-Jun-52	4.56	2
DUTCHESS	BJ2-4	2-Nov-51	11.91	4	FULTON	TS8-3	7-Jun-52	5.73	3

INDIVIDUAL FALLOUT DAYS
NEW YORK

COUNTY	SHOT	DATE	µCi/SQ METER	INDEX	COUNTY	SHOT	DATE	µCi/SQ METER	INDEX
FULTON	BJ2-6	4-Nov-51	6.74	3	HERKIMER	BJ2-3	1-Nov-51	3.71	2
FULTON	R1-2	29-Jan-51	7.57	3	HERKIMER	TS8-3	7-Jun-52	4.64	2
FULTON	TS1-4	4-Apr-52	10.30	4	HERKIMER	PB5-8	22-Jul-57	5.97	3
FULTON	PB11-5	4-Sep-57	12.85	4	HERKIMER	BJ2-6	4-Nov-51	6.74	3
FULTON	BJ2-4	2-Nov-51	13.27	4	HERKIMER	R1-2	29-Jan-51	7.57	3
FULTON	UK7-2	26-Apr-53	290.48	8	HERKIMER	TS7-4	4-Jun-52	8.40	3
GENESEE	TP4-4	10-Mar-55	3.67	2	HERKIMER	PB11-5	4-Sep-57	12.85	4
GENESEE	BJ2-6	4-Nov-51	6.74	3	HERKIMER	BJ2-4	2-Nov-51	17.28	4
GENESEE	TP9-2	15-Apr-55	8.17	3	HERKIMER	UK7-2	26-Apr-53	20.47	4
GENESEE	BJ2-5	3-Nov-51	8.75	3	JEFFERSON	BJ2-3	1-Nov-51	4.83	2
GENESEE	TS7-4	4-Jun-52	10.29	4	JEFFERSON	BJ3-7	7-Nov-51	8.40	3
GENESEE	PB5-8	22-Jul-57	14.93	4	JEFFERSON	BJ2-6	4-Nov-51	13.47	4
GENESEE	BJ2-4	2-Nov-51	18.04	4	JEFFERSON	BJ3-6	6-Nov-51	16.67	4
GENESEE	BJ2-3	1-Nov-51	23.09	4	JEFFERSON	TS7-4	4-Jun-52	18.06	4
GENESEE	BJ3-6	6-Nov-51	27.78	5	JEFFERSON	BJ2-4	2-Nov-51	27.28	5
GREENE	BJ3-7	7-Nov-51	3.71	2	JEFFERSON	TS7-6	6-Jun-52	3.50	1
GREENE	UK1-2	18-Mar-53	5.07	3	KINGS	TP11-9	23-May-55	3.55	2
GREENE	PB5-8	22-Jul-57	5.97	3	KINGS	R1-2	29-Jan-51	3.69	2
GREENE	PB11-5	4-Sep-57	6.43	3	KINGS	TS3-5	26-Apr-52	3.84	2
GREENE	TS8-3	7-Jun-52	9.55	3	KINGS	BJ2-4	2-Nov-51	4.93	2
GREENE	TS1-4	4-Apr-52	10.30	4	KINGS	BJ2-3	1-Nov-51	5.44	3
GREENE	BJ2-4	2-Nov-51	20.04	4	KINGS	TS1-4	4-Apr-52	23.42	4
GREENE	R1-2	29-Jan-51	28.94	5	KINGS	UK1-2	18-Mar-53	59.74	6
GREENE	UK7-2	26-Apr-53	62.99	6	LEWIS	UK7-2	26-Apr-53	4.12	2
HAMILTON	BJ2-3	1-Nov-51	3.97	2	LEWIS	PB11-5	4-Sep-57	4.48	2
HAMILTON	TS7-4	4-Jun-52	4.43	2	LEWIS	BJ2-3	1-Nov-51	4.73	2
HAMILTON	TS8-3	7-Jun-52	6.84	3	LEWIS	PB5-8	22-Jul-57	5.97	3
HAMILTON	BJ2-2	31-Oct-51	7.98	3	LEWIS	BJ2-6	4-Nov-51	6.74	3
HAMILTON	R1-2	29-Jan-51	7.99	3	LEWIS	TS7-4	4-Jun-52	11.74	4
HAMILTON	TS1-4	4-Apr-52	10.30	4	LEWIS	BJ2-4	2-Nov-51	24.19	4
HAMILTON	PB11-5	4-Sep-57	12.85	4	LIVINGSTON	PB2-6	23-Jun-57	4.58	2
HAMILTON	BJ2-4	2-Nov-51	27.38	5	LIVINGSTON	TP9-3	16-Apr-55	5.29	3
HAMILTON	UK7-2	26-Apr-53	55.12	6	LIVINGSTON	BJ2-6	4-Nov-51	6.74	3

INDIVIDUAL FALLOUT DAYS
NEW YORK

COUNTY	SHOT	DATE	µCi/SQ METER	INDEX	COUNTY	SHOT	DATE	µCi/SQ METER	INDEX
LIVINGSTON	R1-2	29-Jan-51	7.57	3	NEW YORK	BJ3-7	7-Nov-51	8.02	3
LIVINGSTON	PB5-8	22-Jul-57	8.96	3	NEW YORK	TS7-5	5-Jun-52	8.11	3
LIVINGSTON	BJ3-6	6-Nov-51	16.67	4	NEW YORK	TS1-4	4-Apr-52	11.87	4
LIVINGSTON	BJ2-4	2-Nov-51	19.78	4	NEW YORK	UK1-2	18-Mar-53	50.37	6
LIVINGSTON	BJ2-3	1-Nov-51	20.85	4	NEW YORK	R1-2	29-Jan-51	3.50	1
LIVINGSTON	TS7-4	4-Jun-52	23.41	4	NIAGARA	TP4-4	10-Mar-55	3.89	2
MADISON	UK7-2	26-Apr-53	3.76	2	NIAGARA	UK9-3	21-May-53	4.61	2
MADISON	PB5-8	22-Jul-57	5.97	3	NIAGARA	BJ2-6	4-Nov-51	6.74	3
MADISON	R1-2	29-Jan-51	7.99	3	NIAGARA	BJ2-5	3-Nov-51	6.77	3
MADISON	TS7-4	4-Jun-52	8.72	3	NIAGARA	TS7-4	4-Jun-52	10.00	4
MADISON	BJ2-4	2-Nov-51	27.30	5	NIAGARA	BJ3-7	7-Nov-51	12.59	4
MONROE	TS7-4	4-Jun-52	4.61	2	NIAGARA	TP9-2	15-Apr-55	13.41	4
MONROE	BJ3-8	8-Nov-51	4.69	2	NIAGARA	BJ2-4	2-Nov-51	14.69	4
MONROE	BJ2-4	2-Nov-51	20.97	4	NIAGARA	BJ2-3	1-Nov-51	17.81	4
MONROE	BJ2-3	1-Nov-51	23.77	4	NIAGARA	BJ3-6	6-Nov-51	27.78	5
MONTGOMERY	BJ3-7	7-Nov-51	4.13	2	ONEIDA	BJ2-6	4-Nov-51	5.05	3
MONTGOMERY	TS8-3	7-Jun-52	4.78	2	ONEIDA	TS7-4	4-Jun-52	5.74	3
MONTGOMERY	PB5-8	22-Jul-57	5.97	3	ONEIDA	UK7-2	26-Apr-53	5.94	3
MONTGOMERY	PB11-5	4-Sep-57	6.43	3	ONEIDA	PB5-8	22-Jul-57	5.97	3
MONTGOMERY	TS1-4	4-Apr-52	6.87	3	ONEIDA	R1-2	29-Jan-51	7.99	3
MONTGOMERY	R1-2	29-Jan-51	7.57	3	ONEIDA	BJ2-4	2-Nov-51	22.79	4
MONTGOMERY	BJ2-4	2-Nov-51	13.44	4	ONONDAGA	BJ2-3	1-Nov-51	4.29	2
MONTGOMERY	UK7-2	26-Apr-53	93.52	6	ONONDAGA	R1-2	29-Jan-51	7.57	3
NASSAU	BJ2-4	2-Nov-51	5.04	3	ONONDAGA	BJ2-4	2-Nov-51	26.40	5
NASSAU	BJ2-3	1-Nov-51	5.44	3	ONTARIO	PB5-7	21-Jul-57	4.10	2
NASSAU	BJ3-7	7-Nov-51	11.62	4	ONTARIO	PB2-6	23-Jun-57	4.58	2
NASSAU	TS1-4	4-Apr-52	14.05	4	ONTARIO	TP9-3	16-Apr-55	4.76	2
NASSAU	TS7-5	5-Jun-52	17.09	4	ONTARIO	R1-2	29-Jan-51	7.57	3
NASSAU	UK1-2	18-Mar-53	52.23	6	ONTARIO	BJ3-7	7-Nov-51	8.40	3
NASSAU	R1-2	29-Jan-51	3.50	1	ONTARIO	PB5-8	22-Jul-57	8.96	3
NEW YORK	BJ2-3	1-Nov-51	5.14	3	ONTARIO	BJ2-3	1-Nov-51	12.58	4
NEW YORK	BJ2-4	2-Nov-51	5.27	3	ONTARIO	TS7-4	4-Jun-52	14.44	4
NEW YORK	TP11-8	22-May-55	6.01	3	ONTARIO	BJ3-6	6-Nov-51	16.67	4

INDIVIDUAL FALLOUT DAYS
NEW YORK

COUNTY	SHOT	DATE	µCi/SQ METER	INDEX	COUNTY	SHOT	DATE	µCi/SQ METER	INDEX
ONTARIO	BJ2-4	2-Nov-51	26.33	5	PUTNAM	TS7-5	5-Jun-52	6.87	3
ORANGE	TP11-9	23-May-55	3.55	2	PUTNAM	R1-2	29-Jan-51	9.14	3
ORANGE	BJ3-7	7-Nov-51	3.85	2	PUTNAM	BJ2-4	2-Nov-51	9.89	3
ORANGE	BJ2-3	1-Nov-51	3.94	2	PUTNAM	BJ3-7	7-Nov-51	19.31	4
ORANGE	PB5-8	22-Jul-57	5.97	3	PUTNAM	TS1-4	4-Apr-52	19.67	4
ORANGE	R1-2	29-Jan-51	11.65	4	PUTNAM	UK1-2	18-Mar-53	19.77	4
ORANGE	BJ2-4	2-Nov-51	11.77	4	QUEENS	BJ2-4	2-Nov-51	3.83	2
ORANGE	UK1-2	18-Mar-53	14.10	4	QUEENS	TS3-5	26-Apr-52	4.27	2
ORANGE	TS1-4	4-Apr-52	19.67	4	QUEENS	BJ2-3	1-Nov-51	5.35	3
ORLEANS	BJ3-7	7-Nov-51	4.20	2	QUEENS	TP11-9	23-May-55	10.65	4
ORLEANS	TS7-4	4-Jun-52	4.45	2	QUEENS	TS1-4	4-Apr-52	23.42	4
ORLEANS	BJ2-5	3-Nov-51	4.54	2	QUEENS	UK1-2	18-Mar-53	55.60	6
ORLEANS	TP9-2	15-Apr-55	8.41	3	QUEENS	R1-2	29-Jan-51	3.50	1
ORLEANS	BJ2-3	1-Nov-51	17.87	4	RENSSELAER	UK1-2	18-Mar-53	3.79	2
ORLEANS	BJ2-4	2-Nov-51	19.64	4	RENSSELAER	BJ2-3	1-Nov-51	4.50	2
ORLEANS	BJ3-6	6-Nov-51	27.78	5	RENSSELAER	PB5-8	22-Jul-57	5.97	3
OSWEGO	TS8-3	7-Jun-52	3.52	2	RENSSELAER	PB11-5	4-Sep-57	6.43	3
OSWEGO	PB11-5	4-Sep-57	4.48	2	RENSSELAER	TS1-4	4-Apr-52	6.87	3
OSWEGO	BJ2-3	1-Nov-51	5.26	3	RENSSELAER	BJ2-4	2-Nov-51	8.85	3
OSWEGO	R1-2	29-Jan-51	7.57	3	RENSSELAER	TS8-3	7-Jun-52	10.70	4
OSWEGO	TS7-4	4-Jun-52	9.94	3	RENSSELAER	R1-2	29-Jan-51	28.94	5
OSWEGO	BJ2-4	2-Nov-51	55.93	6	RENSSELAER	UK7-2	26-Apr-53	484.47	9
OTSEGO	PB5-7	21-Jul-57	4.10	2	RICHMOND	BJ2-3	1-Nov-51	4.99	2
OTSEGO	PB11-5	4-Sep-57	4.48	2	RICHMOND	BJ2-4	2-Nov-51	5.68	3
OTSEGO	TS3-6	27-Apr-52	8.49	3	RICHMOND	TP11-9	23-May-55	7.10	3
OTSEGO	PB5-8	22-Jul-57	8.96	3	RICHMOND	TS1-4	4-Apr-52	14.05	4
OTSEGO	UK7-2	26-Apr-53	15.02	4	RICHMOND	UK1-2	18-Mar-53	47.72	5
OTSEGO	R1-2	29-Jan-51	19.29	4	RICHMOND	R1-2	29-Jan-51	3.50	1
OTSEGO	BJ2-4	2-Nov-51	37.23	5	ROCKLAND	TP11-9	23-May-55	3.55	2
PUTNAM	BJ2-3	1-Nov-51	4.38	2	ROCKLAND	BJ2-3	1-Nov-51	5.01	3
PUTNAM	UK4-2	7-Apr-53	4.84	2	ROCKLAND	BJ2-4	2-Nov-51	8.64	3
PUTNAM	TS8-3	7-Jun-52	5.19	3	ROCKLAND	TS1-4	4-Apr-52	19.67	4
PUTNAM	TS3-4	25-Apr-52	5.70	3	ROCKLAND	UK1-2	18-Mar 53	30.09	5

INDIVIDUAL FALLOUT DAYS
NEW YORK

COUNTY	SHOT	DATE	µCi/SQ METER	INDEX	COUNTY	SHOT	DATE	µCi/SQ METER	INDEX
ROCKLAND	R1-2	29-Jan-51	3.50	1	SENECA	TS7-4	4-Jun-52	11.51	4
SARATOGA	TS7-4	4-Jun-52	4.14	2	SENECA	BJ2-4	2-Nov-51	26.26	5
SARATOGA	PB11-5	4-Sep-57	6.43	3	ST LAWRENCE	BJ2-3	1-Nov-51	3.75	2
SARATOGA	R1-2	29-Jan-51	7.57	3	ST LAWRENCE	BJ2-2	31-Oct-51	4.09	2
SARATOGA	TS1-4	4-Apr-52	10.30	4	ST LAWRENCE	PB5-7	21-Jul-57	4.10	2
SARATOGA	BJ2-4	2-Nov-51	10.35	4	ST LAWRENCE	TS8-3	7-Jun-52	4.79	2
SARATOGA	TS8-3	7-Jun-52	11.62	4	ST LAWRENCE	TS7-6	6-Jun-52	5.32	3
SARATOGA	BJ2-2	31-Oct-51	12.07	4	ST LAWRENCE	PB11-5	4-Sep-57	6.43	3
SARATOGA	UK7-2	26-Apr-53	296.91	8	ST LAWRENCE	BJ2-4	2-Nov-51	19.71	4
SCHENECTADY	TS8-3	7-Jun-52	5.33	3	ST LAWRENCE	TS7-4	4-Jun-52	65.87	6
SCHENECTADY	PB11-5	4-Sep-57	6.43	3	STEUBEN	PB5-7	21-Jul-57	4.10	2
SCHENECTADY	R1-2	29-Jan-51	7.99	3	STEUBEN	BJ2-6	4-Nov-51	5.05	3
SCHENECTADY	BJ2-4	2-Nov-51	10.94	4	STEUBEN	R1-2	29-Jan-51	7.57	3
SCHENECTADY	TS1-4	4-Apr-52	17.17	4	STEUBEN	BJ3-7	7-Nov-51	8.40	3
SCHENECTADY	UK7-2	26-Apr-53	226.60	8	STEUBEN	BJ2-3	1-Nov-51	8.77	3
SCHOHARIE	BJ3-7	7-Nov-51	4.13	2	STEUBEN	TS7-4	4-Jun-52	12.51	4
SCHOHARIE	TS8-3	7-Jun-52	5.58	3	STEUBEN	PB5-8	22-Jul-57	14.93	4
SCHOHARIE	PB11-5	4-Sep-57	6.43	3	STEUBEN	BJ2-4	2-Nov-51	15.04	4
SCHOHARIE	R1-2	29-Jan-51	7.57	3	STEUBEN	BJ3-6	6-Nov-51	16.67	4
SCHOHARIE	PB5-8	22-Jul-57	8.96	3	SUFFOLK	TS8-3	7-Jun-52	5.39	3
SCHOHARIE	TS1-4	4-Apr-52	10.30	4	SUFFOLK	BJ2-3	1-Nov-51	6.08	3
SCHOHARIE	BJ2-4	2-Nov-51	12.94	4	SUFFOLK	BJ2-4	2-Nov-51	7.66	3
SCHOHARIE	UK7-2	26-Apr-53	69.53	6	SUFFOLK	TS7-5	5-Jun-52	9.50	3
SCHUYLER	BJ2-3	1-Nov-51	6.00	3	SUFFOLK	TS1-4	4-Apr-52	14.05	4
SCHUYLER	PB5-7	21-Jul-57	6.84	3	SUFFOLK	UK1-2	18-Mar-53	27.68	5
SCHUYLER	TS7-4	4-Jun-52	6.99	3	SUFFOLK	UK4-2	7-Apr-53	32.22	5
SCHUYLER	BJ2-4	2-Nov-51	20.68	4	SUFFOLK	R1-2	29-Jan-51	3.50	1
SENECA	PB2-6	23-Jun-57	6.87	3	SULLIVAN	UK1-2	18-Mar-53	4.43	2
SENECA	BJ2-3	1-Nov-51	7.25	3	SULLIVAN	UK7-2	26-Apr-53	4.72	2
SENECA	R1-2	29-Jan-51	7.57	3	SULLIVAN	BJ3-7	7-Nov-51	6.86	3
SENECA	BJ3-7	7-Nov-51	8.40	3	SULLIVAN	TS3-6	27-Apr-52	8.49	3
SENECA	PB5-8	22-Jul-57	8.96	3	SULLIVAN	PB5-8	22-Jul-57	8.96	3
SENECA	BJ3-6	6-Nov-51	11.11	4	SULLIVAN	TS1-4	4-Apr-52	11.87	4

INDIVIDUAL FALLOUT DAYS
NEW YORK

COUNTY	SHOT	DATE	µCi/SQ METER	INDEX	COUNTY	SHOT	DATE	µCi/SQ METER	INDEX
SULLIVAN	BJ2-4	2-Nov-51	22.21	4	WASHINGTON	BJ2-4	2-Nov-51	9.52	3
SULLIVAN	R1-2	29-Jan-51	28.94	5	WASHINGTON	TS1-4	4-Apr-52	10.30	4
TIOGA	R1-2	29-Jan-51	7.57	3	WASHINGTON	TS8-3	7-Jun-52	10.51	4
TIOGA	PB5-8	22-Jul-57	8.96	3	WASHINGTON	UK7-2	26-Apr-53	529.85	9
TIOGA	BJ2-4	2-Nov-51	19.13	4	WAYNE	BJ2-5	3-Nov-51	6.22	3
TOMPKINS	TS7-4	4-Jun-52	5.71	3	WAYNE	TP9-3	16-Apr-55	6.42	3
TOMPKINS	R1-2	29-Jan-51	7.57	3	WAYNE	R1-2	29-Jan-51	7.99	3
TOMPKINS	PB5-8	22-Jul-57	14.93	4	WAYNE	BJ3-7	7-Nov-51	8.40	3
TOMPKINS	BJ2-4	2-Nov-51	48.54	5	WAYNE	BJ2-3	1-Nov-51	9.38	3
ULSTER	BJ2-3	1-Nov-51	3.97	2	WAYNE	BJ3-6	6-Nov-51	16.67	4
ULSTER	TS8-3	7-Jun-52	4.92	2	WAYNE	TS7-4	4-Jun-52	17.82	4
ULSTER	PB5-8	22-Jul-57	5.97	3	WAYNE	BJ2-4	2-Nov-51	29.53	5
ULSTER	PB11-5	4-Sep-57	6.43	3	WESTCHESTER	TP11-9	23-May-55	3.55	2
ULSTER	UK1-2	18-Mar-53	6.45	3	WESTCHESTER	BJ2-3	1-Nov-51	5.46	3
ULSTER	UK7-2	26-Apr-53	13.57	4	WESTCHESTER	TS7-5	5-Jun-52	5.73	3
ULSTER	TS1-4	4-Apr-52	17.17	4	WESTCHESTER	BJ2-4	2-Nov-51	8.15	3
ULSTER	BJ2-4	2-Nov-51	18.37	4	WESTCHESTER	R1-2	29-Jan-51	9.14	3
ULSTER	BJ3-7	7-Nov-51	19.31	4	WESTCHESTER	BJ3-7	7-Nov-51	11.62	4
ULSTER	R1-2	29-Jan-51	28.94	5	WESTCHESTER	TS1-4	4-Apr-52	19.67	4
WARREN	BJ2-3	1-Nov-51	3.54	2	WESTCHESTER	UK1-2	18-Mar-53	34.82	5
WARREN	BJ2-2	31-Oct-51	7.98	3	WYOMING	TP4-4	10-Mar-55	3.99	2
WARREN	R1-2	29-Jan-51	7.99	3	WYOMING	TP9-3	16-Apr-55	4.46	2
WARREN	TS8-3	7-Jun-52	8.10	3	WYOMING	PB2-6	23-Jun-57	4.58	2
WARREN	TS7-4	4-Jun-52	10.59	4	WYOMING	TP9-2	15-Apr-55	5.08	3
WARREN	BJ2-4	2-Nov-51	11.02	4	WYOMING	R1-2	29-Jan-51	7.57	3
WARREN	TS1-4	4-Apr-52	17.17	4	WYOMING	BJ3-7	7-Nov-51	8.40	3
WARREN	UK7-2	26-Apr-53	503.93	9	WYOMING	PB5-8	22-Jul-57	8.96	3
WASHINGTON	BJ2-2	31-Oct-51	4.09	2	WYOMING	BJ2-6	4-Nov-51	13.47	4
WASHINGTON	BJ2-3	1-Nov-51	4.29	2	WYOMING	BJ2-3	1-Nov-51	16.46	4
WASHINGTON	TS7-4	4-Jun-52	4.79	2	WYOMING	BJ3-6	6-Nov-51	16.67	4
WASHINGTON	PB5-8	22-Jul-57	5.97	3	WYOMING	BJ2-4	2-Nov-51	17.20	4
WASHINGTON	PB11-5	4-Sep-57	6.43	3	WYOMING	TS7-4	4-Jun-52	25.71	5
WASHINGTON	R1-2	29-Jan-51	7.57	3	YATES	BJ3-7	7-Nov-51	4.20	2

INDIVIDUAL FALLOUT DAYS
NEW YORK

COUNTY	SHOT	DATE	µCi/SQ METER	INDEX	COUNTY	SHOT	DATE	µCi/SQ METER	INDEX
YATES	BJ2-3	1-Nov-51	7.89	3	YATES	BJ2-4	2-Nov-51	23.05	4
YATES	TS7-4	4-Jun-52	11.78	4					
YATES	BJ3-6	6-Nov-51	16.67	4					

INDIVIDUAL FALLOUT DAYS
OHIO

COUNTY	SHOT	DATE	µCi/SQ METER	INDEX	COUNTY	SHOT	DATE	µCi/SQ METER	INDEX
ADAMS	BJ2-4	2-Nov-51	4.34	2	ATHENS	SE3	8-Jul-62	43.89	5
ADAMS	R1-2	29-Jan-51	5.83	3	ATHENS	SE4	9-Jul-62	85.56	6
ADAMS	PB6-3	26-Jul-57	15.70	4	AUGLAIZE	PB6-3	26-Jul-57	3.96	2
ADAMS	SE4	9-Jul-62	208.78	8	AUGLAIZE	UK9-3	21-May-53	4.28	2
ALLEN	UK9-3	21-May-53	3.54	2	AUGLAIZE	UK2-8	31-Mar-53	6.34	3
ALLEN	TP4-4	10-Mar-55	3.57	2	AUGLAIZE	UK7-4	28-Apr-53	7.08	3
ALLEN	PB6-3	26-Jul-57	3.96	2	AUGLAIZE	UK9-4	22-May-53	8.60	3
ALLEN	UK9-4	22-May-53	4.15	2	AUGLAIZE	TS7-3	3-Jun-52	9.12	3
ALLEN	UK2-8	31-Mar-53	6.34	3	AUGLAIZE	SE4	9-Jul-62	85.56	6
ALLEN	R1-2	29-Jan-51	20.05	4	BELMONT	UK9-3	21-May-53	3.57	2
ALLEN	SE4	9-Jul-62	208.78	8	BELMONT	PB5-8	22-Jul-57	8.96	3
ASHLAND	UK9-4	22-May-53	3.63	2	BELMONT	R1-2	29-Jan-51	46.20	5
ASHLAND	TS7-4	4-Jun-52	4.27	2	BELMONT	SE4	9-Jul-62	90.29	6
ASHLAND	TP9-2	15-Apr-55	4.29	2	BROWN	PB6-4	27-Jul-57	4.54	2
ASHLAND	UK2-8	31-Mar-53	6.34	3	BROWN	TP5-3	14-Mar-55	4.71	2
ASHLAND	BJ2-2	31-Oct-51	7.20	3	BROWN	R1-2	29-Jan-51	15.23	4
ASHLAND	UK9-3	21-May-53	7.52	3	BROWN	PB6-3	26-Jul-57	15.70	4
ASHLAND	TP4-4	10-Mar-55	8.12	3	BROWN	SE3	8-Jul-62	43.89	5
ASHLAND	R1-2	29-Jan-51	19.06	4	BROWN	SE4	9-Jul-62	90.29	6
ASHLAND	SE4	9-Jul-62	103.59	7	BUTLER	TP10-3	7-May-55	4.16	2
ASHTABULA	BJ2-3	1-Nov-51	3.67	2	BUTLER	UK9-3	21-May-53	5.90	3
ASHTABULA	UK9-7	25-May-53	4.16	2	BUTLER	UK7-4	28-Apr-53	12.24	4
ASHTABULA	TP9-2	15-Apr-55	4.38	2	BUTLER	PB6-3	26-Jul-57	15.70	4
ASHTABULA	BJ2-2	31-Oct-51	7.20	3	BUTLER	R1-2	29-Jan-51	16.31	4
ASHTABULA	UK9-3	21-May-53	8.73	3	BUTLER	SE3	8-Jul-62	90.94	6
ASHTABULA	PB5-8	22-Jul-57	8.96	3	BUTLER	SE4	9-Jul-62	208.78	8
ASHTABULA	R1-2	29-Jan-51	9.22	3	CARROLL	UK9-4	22-May-53	4.62	2
ASHTABULA	TS7-4	4-Jun-52	10.23	4	CARROLL	TP4-4	10-Mar-55	5.92	3
ASHTABULA	TP4-4	10-Mar-55	12.03	4	CARROLL	BJ2-2	31-Oct-51	7.20	3
ATHENS	UK9-3	21-May-53	3.91	2	CARROLL	UK9-3	21-May-53	7.81	3
ATHENS	BJ2-2	31-Oct-51	7.20	3	CARROLL	PB5-8	22-Jul-57	8.96	3
ATHENS	PB5-8	22-Jul-57	14.93	4	CARROLL	R1-2	29-Jan-51	18.06	4
ATHENS	R1-2	29-Jan-51	37.06	5	CHAMPAIGN	TS1-3	3-Apr-52	3.61	2

INDIVIDUAL FALLOUT DAYS
OHIO

COUNTY	SHOT	DATE	μCi/SQ METER	INDEX	COUNTY	SHOT	DATE	μCi/SQ METER	INDEX
CHAMPAIGN	TP10-3	7-May-55	3.83	2	COLUMBIANA	UK9-3	21-May-53	10.27	4
CHAMPAIGN	PB6-3	26-Jul-57	3.96	2	COLUMBIANA	R1-2	29-Jan-51	22.27	4
CHAMPAIGN	UK9-3	21-May-53	4.87	2	COLUMBIANA	SE4	9-Jul-62	85.56	6
CHAMPAIGN	UK7-4	28-Apr-53	5.48	3	COSHOCTON	UK9-4	22-May-53	4.84	2
CHAMPAIGN	TS7-4	4-Jun-52	5.80	3	COSHOCTON	TP4-4	10-Mar-55	5.66	3
CHAMPAIGN	UK9-4	22-May-53	6.95	3	COSHOCTON	BJ2-2	31-Oct-51	7.20	3
CHAMPAIGN	TP9-2	15-Apr-55	12.03	4	COSHOCTON	UK9-3	21-May-53	7.37	3
CHAMPAIGN	R1-2	29-Jan-51	17.21	4	COSHOCTON	PB5-8	22-Jul-57	14.93	4
CHAMPAIGN	SE4	9-Jul-62	208.78	8	COSHOCTON	R1-2	29-Jan-51	19.06	4
CLARK	TS7-4	4-Jun-52	3.79	2	COSHOCTON	SE3	8-Jul-62	35.48	5
CLARK	UK7-4	28-Apr-53	3.90	2	COSHOCTON	SE4	9-Jul-62	85.56	6
CLARK	PB6-3	26-Jul-57	3.96	2	CRAWFORD	UK9-4	22-May-53	4.09	2
CLARK	UK9-3	21-May-53	6.95	3	CRAWFORD	TS7-4	4-Jun-52	4.76	2
CLARK	UK9-4	22-May-53	7.70	3	CRAWFORD	TP9-2	15-Apr-55	4.95	2
CLARK	R1-2	29-Jan-51	20.05	4	CRAWFORD	UK9-3	21-May-53	5.97	3
CLARK	SE3	8-Jul-62	37.44	5	CRAWFORD	UK2-8	31-Mar-53	6.34	3
CLARK	SE4	9-Jul-62	208.78	8	CRAWFORD	TP4-4	10-Mar-55	6.44	3
CLERMONT	PB6-4	27-Jul-57	4.90	2	CRAWFORD	BJ2-2	31-Oct-51	7.20	3
CLERMONT	UK9-3	21-May-53	5.53	3	CRAWFORD	SE4	9-Jul-62	90.29	6
CLERMONT	R1-2	29-Jan-51	15.23	4	CUYAHOGA	TP4-3	9-Mar-55	3.93	2
CLERMONT	PB6-3	26-Jul-57	23.55	4	CUYAHOGA	UK2-8	31-Mar-53	4.23	2
CLERMONT	SE3	8-Jul-62	35.48	5	CUYAHOGA	PB5-8	22-Jul-57	5.97	3
CLERMONT	SE4	9-Jul-62	85.56	6	CUYAHOGA	TS7-3	3-Jun-52	6.99	3
CLINTON	PB6-3	26-Jul-57	3.96	2	CUYAHOGA	UK9-3	21-May-53	9.51	3
CLINTON	TP10-3	7-May-55	4.43	2	CUYAHOGA	TP4-4	10-Mar-55	11.70	4
CLINTON	UK9-3	21-May-53	5.09	3	CUYAHOGA	R1-2	29-Jan-51	19.06	4
CLINTON	UK7-4	28-Apr-53	6.76	3	CUYAHOGA	TP9-2	15-Apr-55	74.67	6
CLINTON	R1-2	29-Jan-51	16.31	4	DARKE	TS1-3	3-Apr-52	3.61	2
CLINTON	SE3	8-Jul-62	37.44	5	DARKE	PB6-3	26-Jul-57	3.96	2
CLINTON	SE4	9-Jul-62	208.78	8	DARKE	PB3-4	27-Jun-57	4.43	2
COLUMBIANA	TP4-4	10-Mar-55	6.50	3	DARKE	TP10-3	7-May-55	4.88	2
COLUMBIANA	BJ2-2	31-Oct-51	7.20	3	DARKE	UK9-3	21-May-53	5.68	3
COLUMBIANA	PB5-8	22-Jul-57	8.96	3	DARKE	UK7-4	28-Apr-53	7.38	3

INDIVIDUAL FALLOUT DAYS
OHIO

COUNTY	SHOT	DATE	µCi/SQ METER	INDEX	COUNTY	SHOT	DATE	µCi/SQ METER	INDEX
DARKE	SE3	8-Jul-62	43.89	5	FRANKLIN	UK2-8	31-Mar-53	4.23	2
DARKE	SE4	9-Jul-62	85.56	6	FRANKLIN	UK9-4	22-May-53	5.09	3
DEFIANCE	UK7-4	28-Apr-53	3.79	2	FRANKLIN	UK9-3	21-May-53	5.16	3
DEFIANCE	PB6-3	26-Jul-57	3.96	2	FRANKLIN	SE3	8-Jul-62	35.48	5
DEFIANCE	TP4-4	10-Mar-55	4.22	2	FULTON	UK7-4	28-Apr-53	3.85	2
DEFIANCE	UK9-4	22-May-53	5.13	3	FULTON	PB9-5	27-Aug-57	4.52	2
DEFIANCE	UK2-8	31-Mar-53	6.34	3	FULTON	TP9-2	15-Apr-55	4.85	2
DELAWARE	UK9-4	22-May-53	3.57	2	FULTON	UK2-8	31-Mar-53	6.34	3
DELAWARE	TP4-4	10-Mar-55	3.94	2	FULTON	TS7-3	3-Jun-52	10.79	4
DELAWARE	UK2-8	31-Mar-53	4.23	2	FULTON	SE4	9-Jul-62	208.78	8
DELAWARE	UK9-3	21-May-53	4.57	2	GALLIA	BJ2-4	2-Nov-51	6.67	3
DELAWARE	BJ2-2	31-Oct-51	7.20	3	GALLIA	PB5-8	22-Jul-57	8.96	3
DELAWARE	R1-2	29-Jan-51	20.05	4	GALLIA	R1-2	29-Jan-51	15.23	4
DELAWARE	SE4	9-Jul-62	90.29	6	GALLIA	PB6-3	26-Jul-57	23.55	4
ERIE	BJ2-2	31-Oct-51	3.70	2	GALLIA	SE3	8-Jul-62	37.44	5
ERIE	UK9-3	21-May-53	6.15	3	GALLIA	SE4	9-Jul-62	85.56	6
ERIE	UK2-8	31-Mar-53	6.34	3	GEAUGA	BJ2-2	31-Oct-51	3.70	2
ERIE	TP4-4	10-Mar-55	9.28	3	GEAUGA	BJ3-5	5-Nov-51	4.21	2
ERIE	BJ3-5	5-Nov-51	10.53	4	GEAUGA	BJ2-3	1-Nov-51	4.30	2
ERIE	TS7-3	3-Jun-52	23.09	4	GEAUGA	PB5-8	22-Jul-57	5.97	3
ERIE	SE3	8-Jul-62	35.48	5	GEAUGA	TP4-4	10-Mar-55	11.49	4
ERIE	TP9-2	15-Apr-55	46.58	5	GEAUGA	UK9-3	21-May-53	11.65	4
FAIRFIELD	TP4-4	10-Mar-55	3.54	2	GEAUGA	R1-2	29-Jan-51	22.27	4
FAIRFIELD	PB6-3	26-Jul-57	5.90	3	GEAUGA	TP9-2	15-Apr-55	41.35	5
FAIRFIELD	R1-2	29-Jan-51	16.31	4	GREENE	PB6-4	27-Jul-57	3.62	2
FAIRFIELD	SE4	9-Jul-62	90.29	6	GREENE	PB6-3	26-Jul-57	3.96	2
FAYETTE	PB6-3	26-Jul-57	3.96	2	GREENE	TP10-3	7-May-55	3.98	2
FAYETTE	UK9-3	21-May-53	5.80	3	GREENE	TS7-4	4-Jun-52	4.41	2
FAYETTE	R1-2	29-Jan-51	16.31	4	GREENE	UK7-4	28-Apr-53	4.54	2
FAYETTE	SE4	9-Jul-62	90.29	6	GREENE	UK9-3	21-May-53	5.09	3
FRANKLIN	TS1-3	3-Apr-52	3.61	2	GREENE	SE3	8-Jul-62	90.94	6
FRANKLIN	TP4-4	10-Mar-55	3.65	2	GUERNSEY	TP4-4	10-Mar-55	4.08	2
FRANKLIN	PB6-3	26-Jul-57	3.96	2	GUERNSEY	BJ2-2	31-Oct-51	7.20	3

INDIVIDUAL FALLOUT DAYS
OHIO

COUNTY	SHOT	DATE	µCi/SQ METER	INDEX	COUNTY	SHOT	DATE	µCi/SQ METER	INDEX
GUERNSEY	PB5-8	22-Jul-57	8.96	3	HENRY	PB6-3	26-Jul-57	3.96	2
GUERNSEY	R1-2	29-Jan-51	46.20	5	HENRY	UK7-4	28-Apr-53	4.06	2
GUERNSEY	SE4	9-Jul-62	103.59	7	HENRY	PB9-5	27-Aug-57	4.52	2
HAMILTON	TS1-3	3-Apr-52	3.61	2	HENRY	UK2-8	31-Mar-53	6.34	3
HAMILTON	UK7-4	28-Apr-53	4.81	2	HENRY	TS7-3	3-Jun-52	11.04	4
HAMILTON	PB6-4	27-Jul-57	5.34	3	HENRY	R1-2	29-Jan-51	13.36	4
HAMILTON	UK9-3	21-May-53	6.12	3	HIGHLAND	UK7-4	28-Apr-53	3.69	2
HAMILTON	PB6-3	26-Jul-57	6.52	3	HIGHLAND	TP10-3	7-May-55	4.36	2
HAMILTON	R1-2	29-Jan-51	17.21	4	HIGHLAND	UK9-3	21-May-53	6.77	3
HAMILTON	SE3	8-Jul-62	35.48	5	HIGHLAND	R1-2	29-Jan-51	15.23	4
HAMILTON	SE4	9-Jul-62	72.20	6	HIGHLAND	PB6-3	26-Jul-57	23.55	4
HANCOCK	PB6-3	26-Jul-57	3.96	2	HIGHLAND	BJ2-4	2-Nov-51	3.51	1
HANCOCK	UK9-3	21-May-53	5.38	3	HIGHLAND	SE4	9-Jul-62	208.78	8
HANCOCK	UK2-8	31-Mar-53	6.34	3	HOCKING	TS1-3	3-Apr-52	3.61	2
HANCOCK	TP4-4	10-Mar-55	8.11	3	HOCKING	UK9-3	21-May-53	3.91	2
HANCOCK	TP9-2	15-Apr-55	11.32	4	HOCKING	PB6-3	26-Jul-57	3.96	2
HANCOCK	TS7-3	3-Jun-52	59.41	6	HOCKING	PB5-8	22-Jul-57	14.93	4
HANCOCK	SE3	8-Jul-62	157.12	7	HOCKING	R1-2	29-Jan-51	17.26	4
HARDIN	TP4-4	10-Mar-55	3.76	2	HOCKING	SE4	9-Jul-62	85.56	6
HARDIN	PB6-3	26-Jul-57	3.96	2	HOLMES	UK9-4	22-May-53	6.63	3
HARDIN	UK7-4	28-Apr-53	4.27	2	HOLMES	BJ2-2	31-Oct-51	7.20	3
HARDIN	UK9-3	21-May-53	5.53	3	HOLMES	UK9-3	21-May-53	7.96	3
HARDIN	TS7-4	4-Jun-52	5.94	3	HOLMES	PB5-8	22-Jul-57	8.96	3
HARDIN	UK2-8	31-Mar-53	6.34	3	HOLMES	TP4-4	10-Mar-55	10.71	4
HARDIN	SE3	8-Jul-62	37.44	5	HOLMES	R1-2	29-Jan-51	18.06	4
HARRISON	TP4-4	10-Mar-55	4.25	2	HURON	TS7-4	4-Jun-52	5.15	3
HARRISON	BJ2-2	31-Oct-51	7.20	3	HURON	BJ3-5	5-Nov-51	6.32	3
HARRISON	UK9-3	21-May-53	8.73	3	HURON	BJ2-2	31-Oct-51	7.20	3
HARRISON	PB5-8	22-Jul-57	8.96	3	HURON	TP4-4	10-Mar-55	8.35	3
HARRISON	R1-2	29-Jan-51	18.06	4	HURON	UK9-3	21-May-53	8.48	3
HARRISON	SE4	9-Jul-62	85.56	6	HURON	TP9-2	15-Apr-55	34.60	5
HENRY	UK9-3	21-May-53	3.69	2	HURON	SE3	8-Jul-62	35.48	5
HENRY	TP9-2	15-Apr-55	3.90	2	JACKSON	PB6-3	26-Jul-57	3.96	2

INDIVIDUAL FALLOUT DAYS
OHIO

COUNTY	SHOT	DATE	µCi/SQ METER	INDEX	COUNTY	SHOT	DATE	µCi/SQ METER	INDEX
JACKSON	UK9-3	21-May-53	5.45	3	LICKING	TP4-4	10-Mar-55	4.36	2
JACKSON	BJ2-4	2-Nov-51	7.17	3	LICKING	BJ2-2	31-Oct-51	7.20	3
JACKSON	PB5-8	22-Jul-57	8.96	3	LICKING	UK9-4	22-May-53	11.97	4
JACKSON	R1-2	29-Jan-51	15.23	4	LICKING	R1-2	29-Jan-51	19.06	4
JACKSON	SE4	9-Jul-62	208.78	8	LICKING	SE4	9-Jul-62	208.78	8
JEFFERSON	TP4-4	10-Mar-55	4.41	2	LOGAN	PB6-3	26-Jul-57	3.96	2
JEFFERSON	PB5-8	22-Jul-57	8.96	3	LOGAN	UK9-3	21-May-53	4.72	2
JEFFERSON	UK9-3	21-May-53	10.33	4	LOGAN	UK7-4	28-Apr-53	5.04	3
JEFFERSON	BJ2-2	31-Oct-51	10.90	4	LOGAN	UK9-4	22-May-53	5.19	3
KNOX	UK2-8	31-Mar-53	4.23	2	LOGAN	TS7-4	4-Jun-52	5.85	3
KNOX	UK9-4	22-May-53	5.02	3	LOGAN	UK2-8	31-Mar-53	6.34	3
KNOX	UK9-3	21-May-53	5.31	3	LOGAN	R1-2	29-Jan-51	13.97	4
KNOX	TP4-4	10-Mar-55	6.03	3	LOGAN	SE3	8-Jul-62	43.89	5
KNOX	BJ2-2	31-Oct-51	7.20	3	LOGAN	SE4	9-Jul-62	85.56	6
KNOX	R1-2	29-Jan-51	19.06	4	LORAIN	BJ3-5	5-Nov-51	4.21	2
KNOX	SE4	9-Jul-62	208.78	8	LORAIN	UK2-8	31-Mar-53	4.23	2
LAKE	BJ2-3	1-Nov-51	4.38	2	LORAIN	UK9-3	21-May-53	7.15	3
LAKE	PB5-8	22-Jul-57	5.97	3	LORAIN	BJ2-2	31-Oct-51	7.20	3
LAKE	BJ3-5	5-Nov-51	6.32	3	LORAIN	TP4-4	10-Mar-55	10.20	4
LAKE	TS7-4	4-Jun-52	7.50	3	LORAIN	TP9-2	15-Apr-55	32.43	5
LAKE	BJ2-2	31-Oct-51	10.90	4	LORAIN	SE3	8-Jul-62	37.44	5
LAKE	UK9-3	21-May-53	11.21	4	LUCAS	TP4-4	10-Mar-55	3.91	2
LAKE	TP4-4	10-Mar-55	12.55	4	LUCAS	UK2-8	31-Mar-53	4.23	2
LAKE	TP9-2	15-Apr-55	25.62	5	LUCAS	TP9-2	15-Apr-55	6.98	3
LAKE	SE4	9-Jul-62	72.20	6	LUCAS	SE3	8-Jul-62	37.44	5
LAWRENCE	TP10-2	6-May-55	3.62	2	LUCAS	SE4	9-Jul-62	85.56	6
LAWRENCE	BJ2-4	2-Nov-51	3.98	2	MADISON	PB6-3	26-Jul-57	3.96	2
LAWRENCE	PB5-8	22-Jul-57	5.97	3	MADISON	UK9-3	21-May-53	4.20	2
LAWRENCE	PB6-3	26-Jul-57	23.55	4	MADISON	UK2-8	31-Mar-53	4.23	2
LAWRENCE	SE4	9-Jul-62	85.56	6	MADISON	UK9-4	22-May-53	8.25	3
LAWRENCE	SE3	8-Jul-62	90.94	6	MADISON	R1-2	29-Jan-51	16.31	4
LICKING	BJ3-5	5-Nov-51	4.21	2	MADISON	SE3	8-Jul-62	43.89	5
LICKING	UK2-8	31-Mar-53	4.23	2	MADISON	SE4	9-Jul-62	103.59	7

INDIVIDUAL FALLOUT DAYS
OHIO

COUNTY	SHOT	DATE	µCi/SQ METER	INDEX	COUNTY	SHOT	DATE	µCi/SQ METER	INDEX
MAHONING	BJ2-2	31-Oct-51	3.70	2	MIAMI	PB6-3	26-Jul-57	3.96	2
MAHONING	TP11-8	22-May-55	3.82	2	MIAMI	UK7-4	28-Apr-53	5.56	3
MAHONING	TP11-9	23-May-55	4.62	2	MIAMI	TP10-3	7-May-55	5.71	3
MAHONING	PB5-8	22-Jul-57	5.97	3	MIAMI	UK9-3	21-May-53	5.75	3
MAHONING	TP4-4	10-Mar-55	8.08	3	MIAMI	UK9-4	22-May-53	6.60	3
MAHONING	UK9-3	21-May-53	13.53	4	MIAMI	R1-2	29-Jan-51	20.05	4
MAHONING	SE4	9-Jul-62	103.59	7	MIAMI	SE4	9-Jul-62	208.78	8
MARION	TP4-4	10-Mar-55	4.45	2	MONROE	PB5-8	22-Jul-57	8.96	3
MARION	UK9-3	21-May-53	4.50	2	MONROE	R1-2	29-Jan-51	21.83	4
MARION	UK2-8	31-Mar-53	6.34	3	MONROE	SE4	9-Jul-62	103.59	7
MARION	BJ2-2	31-Oct-51	7.20	3	MONTGOMERY	PB6-3	26-Jul-57	3.96	2
MARION	UK9-4	22-May-53	7.90	3	MONTGOMERY	TP10-3	7-May-55	5.03	3
MARION	R1-2	29-Jan-51	20.05	4	MONTGOMERY	UK9-3	21-May-53	5.23	3
MARION	SE4	9-Jul-62	85.56	6	MONTGOMERY	UK7-4	28-Apr-53	6.25	3
MEDINA	TS7-4	4-Jun-52	4.93	2	MONTGOMERY	R1-2	29-Jan-51	20.05	4
MEDINA	UK2-8	31-Mar-53	6.34	3	MONTGOMERY	SE3	8-Jul-62	35.48	5
MEDINA	BJ2-2	31-Oct-51	7.20	3	MONTGOMERY	TS7-3	3-Jun-52	36.01	5
MEDINA	UK9-3	21-May-53	8.92	3	MONTGOMERY	SE4	9-Jul-62	208.78	8
MEDINA	PB5-8	22-Jul-57	8.96	3	MORGAN	BJ2-2	31-Oct-51	7.20	3
MEDINA	TP4-4	10-Mar-55	16.74	4	MORGAN	PB5-8	22-Jul-57	8.96	3
MEDINA	TP9-2	15-Apr-55	80.47	6	MORGAN	R1-2	29-Jan-51	21.83	4
MEDINA	SE4	9-Jul-62	208.78	8	MORGAN	SE4	9-Jul-62	208.78	8
MEIGS	UK9-3	21-May-53	4.84	2	MORROW	TP4-4	10-Mar-55	5.56	3
MEIGS	UK9-4	22-May-53	8.11	3	MORROW	UK9-3	21-May-53	5.82	3
MEIGS	PB5-8	22-Jul-57	8.96	3	MORROW	BJ2-2	31-Oct-51	7.20	3
MEIGS	R1-2	29-Jan-51	15.23	4	MORROW	UK9-4	22-May-53	7.96	3
MEIGS	SE4	9-Jul-62	90.29	6	MORROW	R1-2	29-Jan-51	22.27	4
MERCER	PB6-3	26-Jul-57	3.96	2	MORROW	SE4	9-Jul-62	85.56	6
MERCER	UK9-3	21-May-53	4.13	2	MUSKINGUM	TP4-4	10-Mar-55	3.85	2
MERCER	PB3-4	27-Jun-57	4.21	2	MUSKINGUM	BJ3-5	5-Nov-51	4.21	2
MERCER	UK2-8	31-Mar-53	6.34	3	MUSKINGUM	BJ2-2	31-Oct-51	7.20	3
MERCER	UK7-4	28-Apr-53	10.14	4	MUSKINGUM	PB5-8	22-Jul-57	8.96	3
MERCER	SE3	8-Jul-62	35.48	5	MUSKINGUM	R1-2	29-Jan-51	18.06	4

INDIVIDUAL FALLOUT DAYS
OHIO

COUNTY	SHOT	DATE	µCi/SQ METER	INDEX	COUNTY	SHOT	DATE	µCi/SQ METER	INDEX
MUSKINGUM	SE3	8-Jul-62	35.48	5	PORTAGE	TP4-4	10-Mar-55	15.55	4
MUSKINGUM	SE4	9-Jul-62	90.29	6	PORTAGE	TP9-2	15-Apr-55	28.73	5
NOBLE	BJ2-2	31-Oct-51	7.20	3	PORTAGE	SE3	8-Jul-62	35.48	5
NOBLE	PB5-8	22-Jul-57	14.93	4	PORTAGE	SE4	9-Jul-62	85.56	6
NOBLE	SE4	9-Jul-62	85.56	6	PREBLE	UK9-4	22-May-53	3.52	2
OTTAWA	UK9-3	21-May-53	4.24	2	PREBLE	PB6-3	26-Jul-57	3.96	2
OTTAWA	TS7-4	4-Jun-52	4.75	2	PREBLE	UK9-3	21-May-53	5.53	3
OTTAWA	TP4-4	10-Mar-55	7.35	3	PREBLE	TP10-3	7-May-55	6.39	3
OTTAWA	TP9-2	15-Apr-55	10.00	3	PREBLE	UK7-4	28-Apr-53	8.13	3
OTTAWA	SE3	8-Jul-62	37.44	5	PREBLE	SE4	9-Jul-62	208.78	8
PAULDING	UK9-3	21-May-53	3.83	2	PUTNAM	PB6-3	26-Jul-57	3.96	2
PAULDING	PB6-3	26-Jul-57	3.96	2	PUTNAM	UK9-3	21-May-53	4.57	2
PAULDING	UK7-4	28-Apr-53	4.37	2	PUTNAM	UK2-8	31-Mar-53	6.34	3
PAULDING	TP4-4	10-Mar-55	6.17	3	PUTNAM	TP4-4	10-Mar-55	6.95	3
PAULDING	UK2-8	31-Mar-53	6.34	3	PUTNAM	TS7-3	3-Jun-52	71.28	6
PAULDING	TS7-3	3-Jun-52	22.51	4	RICHLAND	BJ2-2	31-Oct-51	3.70	2
PAULDING	SE3	8-Jul-62	43.89	5	RICHLAND	UK9-4	22-May-53	4.04	2
PAULDING	SE4	9-Jul-62	85.56	6	RICHLAND	TS7-4	4-Jun-52	4.27	2
PERRY	BJ3-5	5-Nov-51	6.32	3	RICHLAND	TP9-2	15-Apr-55	4.76	2
PERRY	BJ2-2	31-Oct-51	7.20	3	RICHLAND	BJ3-5	5-Nov-51	6.32	3
PERRY	PB5-8	22-Jul-57	8.96	3	RICHLAND	UK2-8	31-Mar-53	6.34	3
PERRY	R1-2	29-Jan-51	18.06	4	RICHLAND	TP4-4	10-Mar-55	6.65	3
PERRY	SE4	9-Jul-62	208.78	8	RICHLAND	UK9-3	21-May-53	8.04	3
PICKAWAY	PB6-3	26-Jul-57	3.96	2	RICHLAND	R1-2	29-Jan-51	22.27	4
PICKAWAY	UK9-3	21-May-53	4.06	2	RICHLAND	SE3	8-Jul-62	90.94	6
PICKAWAY	R1-2	29-Jan-51	16.31	4	RICHLAND	SE4	9-Jul-62	103.59	7
PIKE	UK9-3	21-May-53	5.01	3	ROSS	BJ2-4	2-Nov-51	5.93	3
PIKE	PB6-3	26-Jul-57	7.85	3	ROSS	UK9-3	21-May-53	6.33	3
PIKE	R1-2	29-Jan-51	15.23	4	ROSS	PB6-3	26-Jul-57	7.85	3
PIKE	SE4	9-Jul-62	208.78	8	ROSS	R1-2	29-Jan-51	17.26	4
PORTAGE	PB5-8	22-Jul-57	5.97	3	ROSS	SE4	9-Jul-62	90.29	6
PORTAGE	BJ2-2	31-Oct-51	7.20	3	SANDUSKY	UK9-3	21-May-53	4.12	2
PORTAGE	UK9-3	21-May-53	8.73	3	SANDUSKY	TS7-4	4-Jun-52	4.57	2

INDIVIDUAL FALLOUT DAYS
OHIO

COUNTY	SHOT	DATE	µCi/SQ METER	INDEX	COUNTY	SHOT	DATE	µCi/SQ METER	INDEX
SANDUSKY	TP4-4	10-Mar-55	6.61	3	SUMMIT	TP4-4	10-Mar-55	9.88	3
SANDUSKY	TP9-2	15-Apr-55	38.73	5	SUMMIT	UK9-3	21-May-53	11.58	4
SANDUSKY	SE4	9-Jul-62	90.29	6	SUMMIT	SE3	8-Jul-62	35.48	5
SCIOTO	PB6-3	26-Jul-57	3.96	2	TRUMBULL	BJ2-2	31-Oct-51	3.70	2
SCIOTO	BJ2-4	2-Nov-51	4.58	2	TRUMBULL	BJ3-5	5-Nov-51	4.21	2
SCIOTO	TS6-4	28-May-52	4.64	2	TRUMBULL	PB5-8	22-Jul-57	5.97	3
SCIOTO	R1-2	29-Jan-51	15.23	4	TRUMBULL	UK9-3	21-May-53	8.73	3
SCIOTO	SE4	9-Jul-62	359.52	8	TRUMBULL	TP4-4	10-Mar-55	10.02	4
SENECA	BJ2-2	31-Oct-51	3.70	2	TRUMBULL	R1-2	29-Jan-51	11.14	4
SENECA	UK9-3	21-May-53	4.87	2	TRUMBULL	TP9-2	15-Apr-55	24.73	4
SENECA	TP4-4	10-Mar-55	5.72	3	TRUMBULL	SE4	9-Jul-62	90.29	6
SENECA	UK9-4	22-May-53	5.77	3	TUSCARAWAS	UK9-4	22-May-53	4.04	2
SENECA	UK2-8	31-Mar-53	6.34	3	TUSCARAWAS	TP4-4	10-Mar-55	5.38	3
SENECA	R1-2	29-Jan-51	22.27	4	TUSCARAWAS	BJ2-2	31-Oct-51	7.20	3
SENECA	TP9-2	15-Apr-55	68.41	6	TUSCARAWAS	PB5-8	22-Jul-57	8.96	3
SENECA	SE4	9-Jul-62	208.78	8	TUSCARAWAS	UK9-3	21-May-53	9.29	3
SHELBY	PB6-3	26-Jul-57	3.96	2	TUSCARAWAS	R1-2	29-Jan-51	18.06	4
SHELBY	TP10-3	7-May-55	4.51	2	TUSCARAWAS	SE4	9-Jul-62	103.59	7
SHELBY	UK9-3	21-May-53	4.57	2	UNION	PB6-3	26-Jul-57	3.96	2
SHELBY	UK7-4	28-Apr-53	4.92	2	UNION	TS7-3	3-Jun-52	5.01	3
SHELBY	UK2-8	31-Mar-53	6.34	3	UNION	UK9-3	21-May-53	5.01	3
STARK	BJ2-2	31-Oct-51	3.70	2	UNION	UK2-8	31-Mar-53	6.34	3
STARK	UK9-4	22-May-53	5.02	3	UNION	R1-2	29-Jan-51	17.21	4
STARK	TP9-2	15-Apr-55	7.14	3	UNION	SE3	8-Jul-62	37.44	5
STARK	TP4-4	10-Mar-55	8.20	3	UNION	SE4	9-Jul-62	85.56	6
STARK	PB5-8	22-Jul-57	8.96	3	VAN WERT	UK9-3	21-May-53	3.61	2
STARK	UK9-3	21-May-53	10.25	4	VAN WERT	PB6-3	26-Jul-57	3.96	2
STARK	R1-2	29-Jan-51	18.06	4	VAN WERT	UK2-8	31-Mar-53	6.34	3
STARK	SE4	9-Jul-62	90.29	6	VAN WERT	UK7-4	28-Apr-53	8.80	3
SUMMIT	TP9-2	15-Apr-55	3.70	2	VAN WERT	SE3	8-Jul-62	90.94	6
SUMMIT	BJ3-5	5-Nov-51	6.32	3	VINTON	UK9-3	21-May-53	5.89	3
SUMMIT	BJ2-2	31-Oct-51	7.20	3	VINTON	R1-2	29-Jan-51	7.38	3
SUMMIT	PB5-8	22-Jul-57	8.96	3	VINTON	PB6-3	26-Jul-57	7.85	3

INDIVIDUAL FALLOUT DAYS
OHIO

COUNTY	SHOT	DATE	µCi/SQ METER	INDEX	COUNTY	SHOT	DATE	µCi/SQ METER	INDEX
VINTON	PB5-8	22-Jul-57	8.96	3	WAYNE	PB5-8	22-Jul-57	14.93	4
VINTON	SE4	9-Jul-62	85.56	6	WAYNE	R1-2	29-Jan-51	19.06	4
WARREN	TP10-3	7-May-55	5.56	3	WILLIAMS	UK7-4	28-Apr-53	3.75	2
WARREN	UK9-3	21-May-53	7.56	3	WILLIAMS	PB6-3	26-Jul-57	3.96	2
WARREN	PB6-3	26-Jul-57	7.85	3	WILLIAMS	TS7-3	3-Jun-52	10.10	4
WARREN	UK7-4	28-Apr-53	9.12	3	WOOD	UK9-3	21-May-53	3.75	2
WARREN	R1-2	29-Jan-51	16.31	4	WOOD	TP4-4	10-Mar-55	5.30	3
WARREN	SE3	8-Jul-62	37.44	5	WOOD	UK2-8	31-Mar-53	6.34	3
WARREN	SE4	9-Jul-62	208.78	8	WOOD	TP9-2	15-Apr-55	10.84	4
WASHINGTON	PB5-8	22-Jul-57	14.93	4	WOOD	SE3	8-Jul-62	37.44	5
WASHINGTON	R1-2	29-Jan-51	21.83	4	WOOD	SE4	9-Jul-62	85.56	6
WASHINGTON	SE4	9-Jul-62	90.29	6	WYANDOT	TP9-2	15-Apr-55	4.09	2
WAYNE	TP9-2	15-Apr-55	3.57	2	WYANDOT	TP4-4	10-Mar-55	5.05	3
WAYNE	BJ2-2	31-Oct-51	3.70	2	WYANDOT	UK9-3	21-May-53	6.12	3
WAYNE	UK9-4	22-May-53	5.53	3	WYANDOT	BJ3-5	5-Nov-51	6.32	3
WAYNE	UK9-3	21-May-53	8.63	3	WYANDOT	BJ2-2	31-Oct-51	7.20	3
WAYNE	TP4-4	10-Mar-55	8.78	3	WYANDOT	SE4	9-Jul-62	208.78	8

INDIVIDUAL FALLOUT DAYS
OKLAHOMA

COUNTY	SHOT	DATE	µCi/SQ METER	INDEX	COUNTY	SHOT	DATE	µCi/SQ METER	INDEX
ADAIR	PB8-3	20-Aug-57	4.00	2	ATOKA	PB13-6	11-Sep-57	5.33	3
ADAIR	UK3-5	4-Apr-53	4.10	2	ATOKA	UK1-2	18-Mar-53	5.67	3
ADAIR	UK9-2	20-May-53	4.13	2	ATOKA	UK9-2	20-May-53	5.78	3
ADAIR	PB13-9	14-Sep-57	4.15	2	ATOKA	TS7-6	6-Jun-52	6.58	3
ADAIR	TP11-6	20-May-55	4.26	2	ATOKA	TS7-5	5-Jun-52	10.54	4
ADAIR	TS7-6	6-Jun-52	4.62	2	ATOKA	TP6-2	23-Mar-55	13.77	4
ADAIR	TP11-5	19-May-55	6.39	3	ATOKA	TP11-5	19-May-55	13.82	4
ADAIR	PB13-6	11-Sep-57	6.53	3	ATOKA	TS1-3	3-Apr-52	24.86	4
ADAIR	UK1-1	17-Mar-53	7.40	3	ATOKA	TP10-3	7-May-55	28.41	5
ADAIR	PB12-4	5-Sep-57	15.14	4	ATOKA	UK7-3	27-Apr-53	34.27	5
ADAIR	TS6-4	28-May-52	16.39	4	BEAVER	UK9-1	19-May-53	4.09	2
ADAIR	TP10-3	7-May-55	18.03	4	BEAVER	UK6-3	20-Apr-53	4.23	2
ADAIR	TS1-3	3-Apr-52	24.86	4	BEAVER	TP11-3	17-May-55	4.54	2
ADAIR	TS7-5	5-Jun-52	29.58	5	BEAVER	TS6-3	27-May-52	4.93	2
ALFALFA	BJ5-6	24-Nov-51	3.70	2	BEAVER	TS6-4	28-May-52	5.64	3
ALFALFA	PB3-2	25-Jun-57	3.78	2	BEAVER	UK3-5	4-Apr-53	8.19	3
ALFALFA	PB12-4	5-Sep-57	3.88	2	BEAVER	TP10-3	7-May-55	8.76	3
ALFALFA	PB12-3	4-Sep-57	3.90	2	BEAVER	PB13-5	10-Sep-57	10.22	4
ALFALFA	PB8-3	20-Aug-57	4.00	2	BEAVER	UK9-2	20-May-53	10.75	4
ALFALFA	PB13-9	14-Sep-57	4.15	2	BEAVER	UK7-3	27-Apr-53	11.41	4
ALFALFA	TP10-3	7-May-55	4.16	2	BEAVER	TP7-2	30-Mar-55	26.42	5
ALFALFA	TP9-2	15-Apr-55	5.33	3	BEAVER	TP10-2	6-May-55	32.43	5
ALFALFA	PB13-5	10-Sep-57	9.06	3	BEAVER	TS8-1	5-Jun-52	132.94	7
ALFALFA	TS1-2	2-Apr-52	10.32	4	BECKHAM	UK9-5	23-May-53	3.56	2
ALFALFA	TS7-5	5-Jun-52	11.86	4	BECKHAM	UK7-3	27-Apr-53	3.71	2
ALFALFA	UK9-2	20-May-53	15.72	4	BECKHAM	UK6-3	20-Apr-53	4.23	2
ALFALFA	UK7-3	27-Apr-53	36.89	5	BECKHAM	TP10-3	7-May-55	4.54	2
ALFALFA	TS8-1	5-Jun-52	146.23	7	BECKHAM	UK9-2	20-May-53	4.88	2
ATOKA	PB8-3	20-Aug-57	4.00	2	BECKHAM	TS6-4	28-May-52	5.64	3
ATOKA	PB11-1	31-Aug-57	4.09	2	BECKHAM	UK8-2	9-May-53	6.06	3
ATOKA	PB13-9	14-Sep-57	4.15	2	BECKHAM	UK7-2	26-Apr-53	6.09	3
ATOKA	TS6-4	28-May-52	4.83	2	BECKHAM	UK9-4	22-May-53	10.15	4
ATOKA	TP11-6	20-May-55	4.86	2	BECKHAM	UK3-5	4-Apr-53	13.66	4

INDIVIDUAL FALLOUT DAYS
OKLAHOMA

COUNTY	SHOT	DATE	µCi/SQ METER	INDEX	COUNTY	SHOT	DATE	µCi/SQ METER	INDEX
BECKHAM	TP7-2	30-Mar-55	26.42	5	CANADIAN	PB8-3	20-Aug-57	4.00	2
BECKHAM	TP10-2	6-May-55	32.43	5	CANADIAN	PB14-7	20-Sep-57	4.04	2
BECKHAM	TS8-1	5-Jun-52	53.18	6	CANADIAN	PB13-9	14-Sep-57	4.15	2
BLAINE	BJ5-6	24-Nov-51	3.70	2	CANADIAN	TS1-3	3-Apr-52	5.61	3
BLAINE	PB8-3	20-Aug-57	4.00	2	CANADIAN	TP11-5	19-May-55	7.78	3
BLAINE	PB13-9	14-Sep-57	4.15	2	CANADIAN	UK7-3	27-Apr-53	8.66	3
BLAINE	TP11-5	19-May-55	6.40	3	CANADIAN	UK9-2	20-May-53	10.66	4
BLAINE	TS7-5	5-Jun-52	6.89	3	CANADIAN	TP10-3	7-May-55	25.25	5
BLAINE	TS6-4	28-May-52	8.06	3	CANADIAN	TS6-4	28-May-52	45.32	5
BLAINE	TP10-3	7-May-55	8.25	3	CARTER	PB12-5	6-Sep-57	3.65	2
BLAINE	UK7-3	27-Apr-53	11.14	4	CARTER	PB8-3	20-Aug-57	4.00	2
BLAINE	UK9-2	20-May-53	11.29	4	CARTER	UK9-2	20-May-53	6.14	3
BLAINE	TS8-1	5-Jun-52	79.76	6	CARTER	UK1-2	18-Mar-53	6.18	3
BRYAN	BJ5-6	24-Nov-51	3.70	2	CARTER	TP11-5	19-May-55	6.56	3
BRYAN	PB13-6	11-Sep-57	3.92	2	CARTER	TS1-3	3-Apr-52	11.23	4
BRYAN	PB8-3	20-Aug-57	4.00	2	CARTER	TP6-2	23-Mar-55	13.77	4
BRYAN	UK9-2	20-May-53	4.06	2	CARTER	TP10-3	7-May-55	16.01	4
BRYAN	PB12-4	5-Sep-57	6.62	3	CARTER	UK7-3	27-Apr-53	18.01	4
BRYAN	UK1-2	18-Mar-53	8.76	3	CARTER	TS6-4	28-May-52	28.93	5
BRYAN	TP6-2	23-Mar-55	13.77	4	CHEROKEE	BJ5-6	24-Nov-51	3.70	2
BRYAN	TP11-5	19-May-55	14.37	4	CHEROKEE	PB13-5	10-Sep-57	3.79	2
BRYAN	TS6-4	28-May-52	19.29	4	CHEROKEE	TP11-5	19-May-55	3.79	2
BRYAN	TS1-3	3-Apr-52	28.07	5	CHEROKEE	PB8-3	20-Aug-57	4.00	2
BRYAN	UK7-3	27-Apr-53	40.26	5	CHEROKEE	TS6-4	28-May-52	4.03	2
CADDO	PB8-3	20-Aug-57	4.00	2	CHEROKEE	PB14-7	20-Sep-57	4.04	2
CADDO	PB14-7	20-Sep-57	4.04	2	CHEROKEE	UK3-5	4-Apr-53	4.10	2
CADDO	UK7-3	27-Apr-53	6.32	3	CHEROKEE	PB13-9	14-Sep-57	4.15	2
CADDO	UK9-2	20-May-53	8.31	3	CHEROKEE	UK9-2	20-May-53	4.74	2
CADDO	TP11-5	19-May-55	9.25	3	CHEROKEE	PB13-6	11-Sep-57	5.08	3
CADDO	TP10-3	7-May-55	23.52	4	CHEROKEE	TP11-6	20-May-55	6.38	3
CADDO	TS6-4	28-May-52	50.14	6	CHEROKEE	UK1-1	17-Mar-53	12.33	4
CADDO	TS8-1	5-Jun-52	239.29	8	CHEROKEE	PB12-4	5-Sep-57	15.34	4
CANADIAN	BJ5-6	24-Nov-51	3.70	2	CHEROKEE	TP10-3	7-May-55	29.55	5

INDICATORVIDUAL FALLOUT DAYS
OKLAHOMA

COUNTY	SHOT	DATE	µCi/SQ METER	INDEX	COUNTY	SHOT	DATE	µCi/SQ METER	INDEX
CHEROKEE	TS7-5	5-Jun-52	34.47	5	CLEVELAND	PB8-3	20-Aug-57	4.00	2
CHEROKEE	TS1-3	3-Apr-52	41.51	5	CLEVELAND	PB13-9	14-Sep-57	4.15	2
CHOCTAW	UK9-2	20-May-53	3.61	2	CLEVELAND	TP11-5	19-May-55	5.28	3
CHOCTAW	PB12-5	6-Sep-57	3.73	2	CLEVELAND	TS1-3	3-Apr-52	5.61	3
CHOCTAW	UK5-4	14-Apr-53	3.91	2	CLEVELAND	UK7-3	27-Apr-53	7.77	3
CHOCTAW	PB8-3	20-Aug-57	4.00	2	CLEVELAND	UK9-2	20-May-53	9.48	3
CHOCTAW	PB13-6	11-Sep-57	4.01	2	CLEVELAND	TS7-5	5-Jun-52	9.79	3
CHOCTAW	PB13-9	14-Sep-57	4.15	2	CLEVELAND	TP6-2	23-Mar-55	13.77	4
CHOCTAW	TS7-6	6-Jun-52	5.42	3	CLEVELAND	TS6-4	28-May-52	34.72	5
CHOCTAW	TP11-6	20-May-55	5.73	3	COAL	TP10-3	7-May-55	3.97	2
CHOCTAW	UK1-2	18-Mar-53	7.94	3	COAL	PB8-3	20-Aug-57	4.00	2
CHOCTAW	TS6-4	28-May-52	8.68	3	COAL	PB13-9	14-Sep-57	4.15	2
CHOCTAW	TP6-2	23-Mar-55	13.77	4	COAL	TP11-6	20-May-55	4.24	2
CHOCTAW	TP11-5	19-May-55	13.79	4	COAL	UK1-2	18-Mar-53	4.43	2
CHOCTAW	UK7-3	27-Apr-53	14.78	4	COAL	PB13-6	11-Sep-57	6.28	3
CHOCTAW	TP10-3	7-May-55	21.93	4	COAL	UK7-3	27-Apr-53	6.46	3
CHOCTAW	TS1-3	3-Apr-52	41.51	5	COAL	UK9-2	20-May-53	6.59	3
CIMARRON	UK6-3	20-Apr-53	4.23	2	COAL	TP11-5	19-May-55	6.78	3
CIMARRON	TP11-4	18-May-55	4.58	2	COAL	TS7-6	6-Jun-52	10.31	4
CIMARRON	UK1-2	18-Mar-53	4.84	2	COAL	TS6-4	28-May-52	12.54	4
CIMARRON	UK8-2	9-May-53	6.06	3	COAL	TP6-2	23-Mar-55	13.77	4
CIMARRON	UK7-2	26-Apr-53	6.20	3	COAL	TS1-3	3-Apr-52	24.86	4
CIMARRON	TS6-4	28-May-52	6.45	3	COMANCHE	PB8-3	20-Aug-57	4.00	2
CIMARRON	TP11-3	17-May-55	7.01	3	COMANCHE	TS7-6	6-Jun-52	4.32	2
CIMARRON	TP10-3	7-May-55	7.88	3	COMANCHE	UK7-2	26-Apr-53	4.57	2
CIMARRON	UK9-2	20-May-53	12.92	4	COMANCHE	UK9-2	20-May-53	6.05	3
CIMARRON	UK7-3	27-Apr-53	21.10	4	COMANCHE	UK7-3	27-Apr-53	8.87	3
CIMARRON	TP10-2	6-May-55	32.43	5	COMANCHE	TP11-5	19-May-55	11.48	4
CIMARRON	TS8-1	5-Jun-52	39.88	5	COMANCHE	TP6-2	23-Mar-55	13.77	4
CIMARRON	TP7-2	30-Mar-55	52.84	6	COMANCHE	TP10-3	7-May-55	18.26	4
CIMARRON	UK9-1	19-May-53	71.31	6	COMANCHE	TS6-4	28-May-52	48.22	5
CLEVELAND	TP10-3	7-May-55	3.72	2	COMANCHE	TS8-1	5-Jun-52	475.66	9
CLEVELAND	TP10-5	9-May-55	3.90	2	COTTON	PB8-3	20-Aug-57	4.00	2

INDIVIDUAL FALLOUT DAYS
OKLAHOMA

COUNTY	SHOT	DATE	µCi/SQ METER	INDEX	COUNTY	SHOT	DATE	µCi/SQ METER	INDEX
COTTON	UK1-2	18-Mar-53	4.12	2	CREEK	TS6-4	28-May-52	14.46	4
COTTON	UK7-2	26-Apr-53	4.98	2	CREEK	TS1-3	3-Apr-52	24.86	4
COTTON	UK9-2	20-May-53	5.06	3	CREEK	TS7-5	5-Jun-52	36.01	5
COTTON	TP10-3	7-May-55	5.92	3	CREEK	UK7-3	27-Apr-53	47.39	5
COTTON	TP11-5	19-May-55	13.02	4	CUSTER	UK9-4	22-May-53	3.81	2
COTTON	TP6-2	23-Mar-55	13.77	4	CUSTER	TP11-5	19-May-55	4.01	2
COTTON	TS6-4	28-May-52	37.87	5	CUSTER	UK9-2	20-May-53	8.40	3
COTTON	TS8-1	5-Jun-52	146.23	7	CUSTER	UK7-3	27-Apr-53	8.87	3
CRAIG	PB8-3	20-Aug-57	4.00	2	CUSTER	TP10-3	7-May-55	13.86	4
CRAIG	PB13-6	11-Sep-57	4.87	2	CUSTER	TS8-1	5-Jun-52	146.23	7
CRAIG	PB13-5	10-Sep-57	5.59	3	DELAWARE	UK7-3	27-Apr-53	3.85	2
CRAIG	UK9-2	20-May-53	5.69	3	DELAWARE	PB8-3	20-Aug-57	4.00	2
CRAIG	TP11-5	19-May-55	6.56	3	DELAWARE	PB13-9	14-Sep-57	4.15	2
CRAIG	UK3-5	4-Apr-53	6.83	3	DELAWARE	UK9-2	20-May-53	4.21	2
CRAIG	UK1-1	17-Mar-53	7.40	3	DELAWARE	PB13-5	10-Sep-57	4.24	2
CRAIG	BJ2-2	31-Oct-51	8.76	3	DELAWARE	PB13-6	11-Sep-57	4.87	2
CRAIG	TS6-4	28-May-52	10.61	4	DELAWARE	TP10-5	9-May-55	5.19	3
CRAIG	PB12-4	5-Sep-57	16.28	4	DELAWARE	UK3-5	4-Apr-53	6.83	3
CRAIG	TS1-3	3-Apr-52	24.86	4	DELAWARE	UK1-1	17-Mar-53	7.40	3
CRAIG	UK7-3	27-Apr-53	32.06	5	DELAWARE	BJ2-2	31-Oct-51	8.76	3
CRAIG	TS7-5	5-Jun-52	33.68	5	DELAWARE	TP11-5	19-May-55	9.10	3
CRAIG	TP10-3	7-May-55	34.57	5	DELAWARE	TS6-4	28-May-52	9.64	3
CREEK	BJ5-6	24-Nov-51	3.70	2	DELAWARE	PB12-4	5-Sep-57	11.55	4
CREEK	PB8-3	20-Aug-57	4.00	2	DELAWARE	TP10-3	7-May-55	21.30	4
CREEK	UK3-5	4-Apr-53	4.10	2	DELAWARE	TS7-5	5-Jun-52	33.35	5
CREEK	PB13-9	14-Sep-57	4.15	2	DELAWARE	TS1-3	3-Apr-52	41.51	5
CREEK	PB13-6	11-Sep-57	5.10	3	DEWEY	PB13-5	10-Sep-57	3.54	2
CREEK	TP11-5	19-May-55	7.17	3	DEWEY	UK7-2	26-Apr-53	3.55	2
CREEK	UK1-1	17-Mar-53	7.40	3	DEWEY	BJ5-6	24-Nov-51	3.70	2
CREEK	PB13-5	10-Sep-57	7.48	3	DEWEY	TP10-3	7-May-55	5.23	3
CREEK	UK9-2	20-May-53	9.30	3	DEWEY	TP11-5	19-May-55	6.20	3
CREEK	TP10-3	7-May-55	9.96	3	DEWEY	UK9-2	20-May-53	9.94	3
CREEK	PB12-4	5-Sep-57	13.24	4	DEWEY	TS6-4	28-May-52	17.73	4

INDIVIDUAL FALLOUT DAYS
OKLAHOMA

COUNTY	SHOT	DATE	µCi/SQ METER	INDEX	COUNTY	SHOT	DATE	µCi/SQ METER	INDEX
DEWEY	UK7-3	27-Apr-53	24.27	4	GARVIN	TS1-3	3-Apr-52	11.23	4
DEWEY	TS8-1	5-Jun-52	53.18	6	GARVIN	TP6-2	23-Mar-55	13.77	4
ELLIS	UK7-2	26-Apr-53	3.76	2	GARVIN	TS6-4	28-May-52	57.86	6
ELLIS	TS6-4	28-May-52	4.03	2	GRADY	BJ5-6	24-Nov-51	3.70	2
ELLIS	UK6-3	20-Apr-53	4.23	2	GRADY	PB8-3	20-Aug-57	4.00	2
ELLIS	PB13-5	10-Sep-57	4.64	2	GRADY	TS7-5	5-Jun-52	4.65	2
ELLIS	UK3-5	4-Apr-53	8.19	3	GRADY	UK7-3	27-Apr-53	5.64	3
ELLIS	UK9-2	20-May-53	8.49	3	GRADY	UK9-2	20-May-53	8.58	3
ELLIS	UK9-4	22-May-53	12.34	4	GRADY	TP11-5	19-May-55	10.17	4
ELLIS	UK7-3	27-Apr-53	13.27	4	GRADY	TS1-3	3-Apr-52	11.23	4
ELLIS	TP10-3	7-May-55	14.55	4	GRADY	TP6-2	23-Mar-55	13.77	4
ELLIS	TP7-2	30-Mar-55	26.42	5	GRADY	TS6-4	28-May-52	24.11	4
ELLIS	TP10-2	6-May-55	32.43	5	GRANT	BJ5-6	24-Nov-51	3.70	2
ELLIS	TS8-1	5-Jun-52	53.18	6	GRANT	PB3-2	25-Jun-57	3.78	2
GARFIELD	PB3-2	25-Jun-57	3.78	2	GRANT	PB8-3	20-Aug-57	4.00	2
GARFIELD	PB13-6	11-Sep-57	3.79	2	GRANT	PB14-7	20-Sep-57	4.04	2
GARFIELD	TP11-5	19-May-55	3.92	2	GRANT	PB12-4	5-Sep-57	4.44	2
GARFIELD	PB8-3	20-Aug-57	4.00	2	GRANT	TP9-2	15-Apr-55	5.42	3
GARFIELD	PB13-9	14-Sep-57	4.15	2	GRANT	UK7-3	27-Apr-53	8.37	3
GARFIELD	PB13-5	10-Sep-57	5.66	3	GRANT	UK9-2	20-May-53	13.15	4
GARFIELD	BJ5-6	24-Nov-51	6.19	3	GRANT	TS1-2	2-Apr-52	15.48	4
GARFIELD	PB12-4	5-Sep-57	6.63	3	GRANT	PB13-5	10-Sep-57	17.26	4
GARFIELD	UK7-3	27-Apr-53	8.66	3	GRANT	TS7-5	5-Jun-52	31.94	5
GARFIELD	UK9-2	20-May-53	14.27	4	GREER	UK9-4	22-May-53	3.51	2
GARFIELD	TS7-5	5-Jun-52	17.13	4	GREER	UK9-2	20-May-53	4.06	2
GARFIELD	TP10-3	7-May-55	26.98	5	GREER	UK6-3	20-Apr-53	4.23	2
GARVIN	UK1-2	18-Mar-53	3.81	2	GREER	UK8-2	9-May-53	6.06	3
GARVIN	PB13-6	11-Sep-57	3.93	2	GREER	UK7-3	27-Apr-53	7.70	3
GARVIN	PB8-3	20-Aug-57	4.00	2	GREER	UK7-2	26-Apr-53	8.13	3
GARVIN	TP10-5	9-May-55	4.03	2	GREER	TP10-3	7-May-55	10.40	4
GARVIN	TP11-5	19-May-55	6.63	3	GREER	UK3-5	4-Apr-53	13.66	4
GARVIN	UK7-3	27-Apr-53	7.29	3	GREER	TP7-2	30-Mar-55	26.42	5
GARVIN	UK9-2	20-May-53	7.77	3	GREER	TP10-2	6-May-55	32.43	5

INDIVIDUAL FALLOUT DAYS
OKLAHOMA

COUNTY	SHOT	DATE	µCi/SQ METER	INDEX	COUNTY	SHOT	DATE	µCi/SQ METER	INDEX
GREER	TS8-1	5-Jun-52	239.29	8	HASKELL	TS1-3	3-Apr-52	41.51	5
HARMON	PB12-5	6-Sep-57	3.54	2	HUGHES	TP11-6	20-May-55	3.57	2
HARMON	TP11-4	18-May-55	3.59	2	HUGHES	PB8-3	20-Aug-57	4.00	2
HARMON	UK6-3	20-Apr-53	4.23	2	HUGHES	UK3-5	4-Apr-53	4.10	2
HARMON	UK8-2	9-May-53	6.06	3	HUGHES	PB13-9	14-Sep-57	4.15	2
HARMON	TP11-5	19-May-55	6.40	3	HUGHES	TP10-3	7-May-55	4.28	2
HARMON	TS6-4	28-May-52	8.86	3	HUGHES	PB13-6	11-Sep-57	4.65	2
HARMON	UK7-2	26-Apr-53	11.27	4	HUGHES	PB12-4	5-Sep-57	4.99	2
HARMON	UK3-5	4-Apr-53	13.66	4	HUGHES	UK1-1	17-Mar-53	7.40	3
HARMON	TP7-2	30-Mar-55	26.42	5	HUGHES	UK9-2	20-May-53	7.59	3
HARMON	TP10-2	6-May-55	32.43	5	HUGHES	TS7-6	6-Jun-52	9.35	3
HARMON	TS8-1	5-Jun-52	53.18	6	HUGHES	TS7-5	5-Jun-52	11.08	4
HARPER	UK9-4	22-May-53	3.51	2	HUGHES	TP11-5	19-May-55	11.22	4
HARPER	TP9-2	15-Apr-55	3.52	2	HUGHES	TP6-2	23-Mar-55	13.77	4
HARPER	TS6-4	28-May-52	4.03	2	HUGHES	TS1-3	3-Apr-52	24.86	4
HARPER	PB12-3	4-Sep-57	4.66	2	HUGHES	UK7-3	27-Apr-53	27.47	5
HARPER	TP10-3	7-May-55	7.43	3	JACKSON	UK9-2	20-May-53	3.61	2
HARPER	UK9-2	20-May-53	11.47	4	JACKSON	PB12-5	6-Sep-57	3.79	2
HARPER	UK7-3	27-Apr-53	16.98	4	JACKSON	TP10-3	7-May-55	5.10	3
HARPER	PB13-5	10-Sep-57	17.00	4	JACKSON	UK6-2	19-Apr-53	5.25	3
HARPER	TS8-1	5-Jun-52	39.88	5	JACKSON	TP11-5	19-May-55	12.25	4
HASKELL	TP10-3	7-May-55	3.73	2	JACKSON	UK7-2	26-Apr-53	20.52	4
HASKELL	PB8-3	20-Aug-57	4.00	2	JACKSON	TS6-4	28-May-52	29.89	5
HASKELL	PB12-5	6-Sep-57	4.01	2	JACKSON	TS8-1	5-Jun-52	53.18	6
HASKELL	PB13-9	14-Sep-57	4.15	2	JEFFERSON	PB12-5	6-Sep-57	3.69	2
HASKELL	TP11-5	19-May-55	4.17	2	JEFFERSON	TS7-6	6-Jun-52	3.78	2
HASKELL	PB13-6	11-Sep-57	4.67	2	JEFFERSON	PB8-3	20-Aug-57	4.00	2
HASKELL	TS7-6	6-Jun-52	4.69	2	JEFFERSON	UK7-2	26-Apr-53	4.06	2
HASKELL	UK9-2	20-May-53	4.74	2	JEFFERSON	UK7-3	27-Apr-53	4.47	2
HASKELL	UK1-1	17-Mar-53	12.33	4	JEFFERSON	UK9-2	20-May-53	5.33	3
HASKELL	TP6-2	23-Mar-55	13.77	4	JEFFERSON	UK1-2	18-Mar-53	5.87	3
HASKELL	TS7-5	5-Jun-52	23.40	4	JEFFERSON	TP11-5	19-May-55	6.40	3
HASKELL	TS6-4	28-May-52	30.86	5	JEFFERSON	TP6-2	23-Mar-55	13.77	4

INDIVIDUAL FALLOUT DAYS
OKLAHOMA

COUNTY	SHOT	DATE	µCi/SQ METER	INDEX	COUNTY	SHOT	DATE	µCi/SQ METER	INDEX
JEFFERSON	TP10-3	7-May-55	17.51	4	KINGFISHER	UK9-2	20-May-53	12.47	4
JEFFERSON	TS6-4	28-May-52	34.72	5	KINGFISHER	UK7-3	27-Apr-53	13.68	4
JOHNSTON	PB12-5	6-Sep-57	3.52	2	KINGFISHER	TP10-3	7-May-55	26.68	5
JOHNSTON	PB8-3	20-Aug-57	4.00	2	KIOWA	UK1-2	18-Mar-53	3.61	2
JOHNSTON	PB13-9	14-Sep-57	4.15	2	KIOWA	UK7-3	27-Apr-53	4.26	2
JOHNSTON	TP11-6	20-May-55	4.15	2	KIOWA	UK6-2	19-Apr-53	5.25	3
JOHNSTON	UK1-2	18-Mar-53	5.98	3	KIOWA	UK9-2	20-May-53	5.60	3
JOHNSTON	UK9-2	20-May-53	6.14	3	KIOWA	TP11-5	19-May-55	5.66	3
JOHNSTON	TS7-6	6-Jun-52	6.58	3	KIOWA	UK7-2	26-Apr-53	6.09	3
JOHNSTON	UK7-3	27-Apr-53	7.49	3	KIOWA	TP10-3	7-May-55	22.32	4
JOHNSTON	TP10-3	7-May-55	10.77	4	KIOWA	TS6-4	28-May-52	31.82	5
JOHNSTON	TS6-4	28-May-52	12.54	4	KIOWA	TS8-1	5-Jun-52	146.23	7
JOHNSTON	TP11-5	19-May-55	12.89	4	LATIMER	UK1-2	18-Mar-53	3.70	2
JOHNSTON	TP6-2	23-Mar-55	13.77	4	LATIMER	PB8-3	20-Aug-57	4.00	2
JOHNSTON	TS1-3	3-Apr-52	16.84	4	LATIMER	PB13-9	14-Sep-57	4.15	2
KAY	BJ5-6	24-Nov-51	3.70	2	LATIMER	PB12-5	6-Sep-57	4.58	2
KAY	PB3-2	25-Jun-57	3.78	2	LATIMER	UK9-2	20-May-53	4.59	2
KAY	PB13-6	11-Sep-57	3.83	2	LATIMER	TP11-5	19-May-55	4.76	2
KAY	PB8-3	20-Aug-57	4.00	2	LATIMER	TS7-6	6-Jun-52	4.95	2
KAY	TP9-2	15-Apr-55	4.00	2	LATIMER	PB13-6	11-Sep-57	5.82	3
KAY	PB12-4	5-Sep-57	7.18	3	LATIMER	UK1-1	17-Mar-53	12.33	4
KAY	PB13-5	10-Sep-57	7.92	3	LATIMER	TP6-2	23-Mar-55	13.77	4
KAY	UK7-3	27-Apr-53	9.86	3	LATIMER	TS7-5	5-Jun-52	21.57	4
KAY	TS1-2	2-Apr-52	10.32	4	LATIMER	TS1-3	3-Apr-52	24.86	4
KAY	PB12-3	4-Sep-57	10.61	4	LATIMER	TP10-3	7-May-55	26.72	5
KAY	UK9-2	20-May-53	11.20	4	LE FLORE	UK9-2	20-May-53	3.58	2
KAY	TP10-3	7-May-55	24.07	4	LE FLORE	UK1-2	18-Mar-53	3.79	2
KAY	TS7-5	5-Jun-52	41.65	5	LE FLORE	PB13-6	11-Sep-57	3.88	2
KINGFISHER	PB8-3	20-Aug-57	4.00	2	LE FLORE	PB8-3	20-Aug-57	4.00	2
KINGFISHER	PB13-5	10-Sep-57	4.07	2	LE FLORE	PB13-9	14-Sep-57	4.15	2
KINGFISHER	PB13-9	14-Sep-57	4.15	2	LE FLORE	TS7-6	6-Jun-52	4.18	2
KINGFISHER	TS6-4	28-May-52	12.09	4	LE FLORE	TP10-3	7-May-55	4.37	2
KINGFISHER	TS7-5	5-Jun-52	12.28	4	LE FLORE	PB12-5	6-Sep-57	4.68	2

　　　　U.S. FALLOUT ATLAS: COUNTY COMPARISONS

INDIVIDUAL FALLOUT DAYS
OKLAHOMA

COUNTY	SHOT	DATE	µCi/SQ METER	INDEX	COUNTY	SHOT	DATE	µCi/SQ METER	INDEX
LE FLORE	UK7-3	27-Apr-53	5.68	3	LOVE	PB8-3	20-Aug-57	4.00	2
LE FLORE	PB12-4	5-Sep-57	5.84	3	LOVE	PB11-1	31-Aug-57	4.09	2
LE FLORE	TP11-6	20-May-55	5.94	3	LOVE	UK7-2	26-Apr-53	4.37	2
LE FLORE	TP11-5	19-May-55	8.24	3	LOVE	UK9-2	20-May-53	5.15	3
LE FLORE	TS7-5	5-Jun-52	8.34	3	LOVE	UK1-9	25-Mar-53	6.00	3
LE FLORE	UK1-1	17-Mar-53	12.33	4	LOVE	PB12-5	6-Sep-57	6.47	3
LE FLORE	TP6-2	23-Mar-55	13.77	4	LOVE	UK7-3	27-Apr-53	6.53	3
LE FLORE	TS1-3	3-Apr-52	24.86	4	LOVE	UK1-2	18-Mar-53	8.35	3
LINCOLN	BJ5-6	24-Nov-51	3.70	2	LOVE	TP10-3	7-May-55	12.29	4
LINCOLN	PB8-3	20-Aug-57	4.00	2	LOVE	TP11-5	19-May-55	13.50	4
LINCOLN	PB14-7	20-Sep-57	4.04	2	LOVE	TP6-2	23-Mar-55	13.77	4
LINCOLN	PB13-9	14-Sep-57	4.15	2	LOVE	TS1-3	3-Apr-52	16.84	4
LINCOLN	TP10-5	9-May-55	4.23	2	LOVE	TS6-4	28-May-52	46.29	5
LINCOLN	TP10-3	7-May-55	4.41	2	MAJOR	PB8-3	20-Aug-57	4.00	2
LINCOLN	PB13-6	11-Sep-57	5.82	3	MAJOR	PB13-9	14-Sep-57	4.15	2
LINCOLN	PB12-4	5-Sep-57	8.18	3	MAJOR	TP10-3	7-May-55	4.47	2
LINCOLN	TP11-5	19-May-55	8.28	3	MAJOR	BJ5-6	24-Nov-51	6.19	3
LINCOLN	UK9-2	20-May-53	10.39	4	MAJOR	PB13-5	10-Sep-57	7.03	3
LINCOLN	TS1-2	2-Apr-52	15.48	4	MAJOR	UK9-2	20-May-53	13.28	4
LINCOLN	TS7-5	5-Jun-52	17.30	4	MAJOR	UK7-3	27-Apr-53	18.01	4
LINCOLN	UK7-3	27-Apr-53	17.32	4	MAJOR	TS8-1	5-Jun-52	53.18	6
LINCOLN	TS6-4	28-May-52	17.36	4	MARSHALL	PB8-3	20-Aug-57	4.00	2
LOGAN	BJ5-6	24-Nov-51	3.70	2	MARSHALL	TS7-6	6-Jun-52	4.13	2
LOGAN	PB3-2	25-Jun-57	3.78	2	MARSHALL	PB13-9	14-Sep-57	4.15	2
LOGAN	PB8-3	20-Aug-57	4.00	2	MARSHALL	TP11-6	20-May-55	4.39	2
LOGAN	PB13-9	14-Sep-57	4.15	2	MARSHALL	UK9-2	20-May-53	4.44	2
LOGAN	TS1-2	2-Apr-52	5.16	3	MARSHALL	UK7-3	27-Apr-53	6.31	3
LOGAN	PB13-6	11-Sep-57	6.37	3	MARSHALL	UK1-2	18-Mar-53	8.24	3
LOGAN	TP11-5	19-May-55	6.55	3	MARSHALL	TS6-4	28-May-52	12.54	4
LOGAN	UK7-3	27-Apr-53	8.52	3	MARSHALL	TP6-2	23-Mar-55	13.77	4
LOGAN	TP10-3	7-May-55	11.59	4	MARSHALL	TP11-5	19-May-55	13.85	4
LOGAN	UK9-2	20-May-53	12.10	4	MARSHALL	TS1-3	3-Apr-52	16.84	4
LOGAN	TS7-5	5-Jun-52	21.74	4	MAYES	BJ5-6	24-Nov-51	3.70	2

INDIGENOUS FALLOUT DAYS
OKLAHOMA

COUNTY	SHOT	DATE	µCi/SQ METER	INDEX	COUNTY	SHOT	DATE	µCi/SQ METER	INDEX
MAYES	PB8-3	20-Aug-57	4.00	2	MCCURTAIN	PB8-3	20-Aug-57	7.99	3
MAYES	PB13-9	14-Sep-57	4.15	2	MCCURTAIN	UK7-3	27-Apr-53	8.04	3
MAYES	UK7-3	27-Apr-53	4.33	2	MCCURTAIN	TP6-2	23-Mar-55	13.77	4
MAYES	PB13-5	10-Sep-57	4.73	2	MCCURTAIN	TP10-3	7-May-55	22.05	4
MAYES	TP11-5	19-May-55	4.85	2	MCCURTAIN	TS1-3	3-Apr-52	41.51	5
MAYES	UK9-2	20-May-53	5.04	3	MCINTOSH	UK2-10	2-Apr-53	3.70	2
MAYES	PB13-6	11-Sep-57	5.21	3	MCINTOSH	PB8-3	20-Aug-57	4.00	2
MAYES	UK3-5	4-Apr-53	6.83	3	MCINTOSH	TP10-5	9-May-55	4.09	2
MAYES	UK1-1	17-Mar-53	7.40	3	MCINTOSH	UK7-3	27-Apr-53	4.12	2
MAYES	PB12-4	5-Sep-57	15.74	4	MCINTOSH	PB13-9	14-Sep-57	4.15	2
MAYES	TS6-4	28-May-52	18.32	4	MCINTOSH	UK9-2	20-May-53	5.79	3
MAYES	TS1-3	3-Apr-52	24.86	4	MCINTOSH	TP11-5	19-May-55	6.72	3
MAYES	TP10-3	7-May-55	28.98	5	MCINTOSH	TP11-6	20-May-55	7.11	3
MAYES	TS7-5	5-Jun-52	34.10	5	MCINTOSH	PB13-6	11-Sep-57	7.31	3
MCCLAIN	TP10-5	9-May-55	3.82	2	MCINTOSH	TP10-3	7-May-55	7.73	3
MCCLAIN	PB8-3	20-Aug-57	4.00	2	MCINTOSH	TS6-4	28-May-52	10.61	4
MCCLAIN	PB13-9	14-Sep-57	4.15	2	MCINTOSH	UK1-1	17-Mar-53	12.33	4
MCCLAIN	TP11-5	19-May-55	5.74	3	MCINTOSH	PB12-4	5-Sep-57	13.51	4
MCCLAIN	UK7-3	27-Apr-53	7.22	3	MCINTOSH	TP6-2	23-Mar-55	13.77	4
MCCLAIN	UK9-2	20-May-53	8.76	3	MCINTOSH	TS1-3	3-Apr-52	24.86	4
MCCLAIN	TP6-2	23-Mar-55	13.77	4	MCINTOSH	TS7-5	5-Jun-52	25.80	5
MCCLAIN	TS1-3	3-Apr-52	16.84	4	MCINTOSH	UK3-3	2-Apr-53	3.51	1
MCCLAIN	TS6-4	28-May-52	63.64	6	MURRAY	PB8-3	20-Aug-57	4.00	2
MCCURTAIN	PB13-6	11-Sep-57	3.68	2	MURRAY	PB13-9	14-Sep-57	4.15	2
MCCURTAIN	PB12-4	5-Sep-57	3.68	2	MURRAY	PB12-5	6-Sep-57	4.60	2
MCCURTAIN	PB5-4	18-Jul-57	3.80	2	MURRAY	UK1-2	18-Mar-53	4.95	2
MCCURTAIN	PB12-5	6-Sep-57	3.90	2	MURRAY	UK9-2	20-May-53	6.86	3
MCCURTAIN	UK5-4	14-Apr-53	3.91	2	MURRAY	TP11-5	19-May-55	7.44	3
MCCURTAIN	TP11-6	20-May-55	5.38	3	MURRAY	UK7-3	27-Apr-53	7.56	3
MCCURTAIN	TS7-6	6-Jun-52	5.56	3	MURRAY	TS1-3	3-Apr-52	11.23	4
MCCURTAIN	PB11-1	31-Aug-57	6.14	3	MURRAY	TP6-2	23-Mar-55	13.77	4
MCCURTAIN	UK1-2	18-Mar-53	6.71	3	MURRAY	TS6-4	28-May-52	15.43	4
MCCURTAIN	TP11-5	19-May-55	6.75	3	MUSKOGEE	BJ5-6	24-Nov-51	3.70	2

INDIVIDUAL FALLOUT DAYS
OKLAHOMA

COUNTY	SHOT	DATE	µCi/SQ METER	INDEX	COUNTY	SHOT	DATE	µCi/SQ METER	INDEX
MUSKOGEE	PB8-3	20-Aug-57	4.00	2	NOWATA	UK9-2	20-May-53	6.77	3
MUSKOGEE	PB14-7	20-Sep-57	4.04	2	NOWATA	PB13-6	11-Sep-57	6.77	3
MUSKOGEE	UK3-5	4-Apr-53	4.10	2	NOWATA	UK3-5	4-Apr-53	6.83	3
MUSKOGEE	PB13-9	14-Sep-57	4.15	2	NOWATA	UK1-1	17-Mar-53	7.40	3
MUSKOGEE	TP10-5	9-May-55	4.40	2	NOWATA	BJ2-2	31-Oct-51	8.76	3
MUSKOGEE	UK9-2	20-May-53	5.41	3	NOWATA	PB12-4	5-Sep-57	16.28	4
MUSKOGEE	TP11-5	19-May-55	7.07	3	NOWATA	TS1-3	3-Apr-52	24.86	4
MUSKOGEE	PB13-6	11-Sep-57	7.23	3	NOWATA	TS7-5	5-Jun-52	51.19	6
MUSKOGEE	UK7-3	27-Apr-53	7.63	3	OKFUSKEE	PB8-3	20-Aug-57	4.00	2
MUSKOGEE	TP10-3	7-May-55	11.30	4	OKFUSKEE	PB14-7	20-Sep-57	4.04	2
MUSKOGEE	UK1-1	17-Mar-53	12.33	4	OKFUSKEE	UK3-5	4-Apr-53	4.10	2
MUSKOGEE	PB12-4	5-Sep-57	14.46	4	OKFUSKEE	PB13-9	14-Sep-57	4.15	2
MUSKOGEE	TS6-4	28-May-52	18.32	4	OKFUSKEE	TP10-3	7-May-55	4.54	2
MUSKOGEE	TS1-3	3-Apr-52	24.86	4	OKFUSKEE	PB13-6	11-Sep-57	5.10	3
MUSKOGEE	TS7-5	5-Jun-52	44.30	5	OKFUSKEE	PB12-4	5-Sep-57	5.33	3
NOBLE	BJ5-6	24-Nov-51	3.70	2	OKFUSKEE	UK7-3	27-Apr-53	6.94	3
NOBLE	PB8-3	20-Aug-57	4.00	2	OKFUSKEE	UK1-1	17-Mar-53	7.40	3
NOBLE	TP11-5	19-May-55	4.11	2	OKFUSKEE	TS7-6	6-Jun-52	8.26	3
NOBLE	PB13-9	14-Sep-57	4.15	2	OKFUSKEE	UK9-2	20-May-53	8.58	3
NOBLE	PB13-6	11-Sep-57	4.65	2	OKFUSKEE	TP11-5	19-May-55	9.22	3
NOBLE	TS6-4	28-May-52	4.83	2	OKFUSKEE	TS7-5	5-Jun-52	13.94	4
NOBLE	TS1-2	2-Apr-52	5.16	3	OKFUSKEE	TS1-3	3-Apr-52	24.86	4
NOBLE	PB13-5	10-Sep-57	5.45	3	OKLAHOMA	PB8-3	20-Aug-57	4.00	2
NOBLE	UK7-3	27-Apr-53	10.17	4	OKLAHOMA	PB14-7	20-Sep-57	4.04	2
NOBLE	PB12-4	5-Sep-57	10.48	4	OKLAHOMA	TS1-3	3-Apr-52	5.61	3
NOBLE	UK9-2	20-May-53	12.92	4	OKLAHOMA	TP10-3	7-May-55	7.94	3
NOBLE	TP10-3	7-May-55	20.59	4	OKLAHOMA	TP11-5	19-May-55	8.17	3
NOBLE	TS7-5	5-Jun-52	32.23	5	OKLAHOMA	TS7-5	5-Jun-52	8.21	3
NOWATA	PB13-5	10-Sep-57	3.79	2	OKLAHOMA	UK9-2	20-May-53	10.75	4
NOWATA	PB8-3	20-Aug-57	4.00	2	OKLAHOMA	UK7-3	27-Apr-53	11.07	4
NOWATA	TP10-3	7-May-55	4.79	2	OKLAHOMA	TS6-4	28-May-52	36.64	5
NOWATA	TP11-5	19-May-55	5.43	3	OKMULGEE	BJ5-6	24-Nov-51	3.70	2
NOWATA	UK7-3	27-Apr-53	6.60	3	OKMULGEE	PB8-3	20-Aug-57	4.00	2

INDIVIDUAL FALLOUT DAYS
OKLAHOMA

COUNTY	SHOT	DATE	µCi/SQ METER	INDEX	COUNTY	SHOT	DATE	µCi/SQ METER	INDEX
OKMULGEE	UK3-5	4-Apr-53	4.10	2	OTTAWA	TS6-4	28-May-52	9.64	3
OKMULGEE	PB13-9	14-Sep-57	4.15	2	OTTAWA	PB12-4	5-Sep-57	16.28	4
OKMULGEE	TP10-3	7-May-55	4.66	2	OTTAWA	UK7-3	27-Apr-53	21.73	4
OKMULGEE	TP10-5	9-May-55	5.09	3	OTTAWA	TS1-3	3-Apr-52	24.86	4
OKMULGEE	UK7-3	27-Apr-53	5.64	3	OTTAWA	TP10-3	7-May-55	25.40	5
OKMULGEE	PB12-4	5-Sep-57	5.84	3	OTTAWA	TS7-5	5-Jun-52	45.67	5
OKMULGEE	UK1-1	17-Mar-53	7.40	3	PAWNEE	BJ5-6	24-Nov-51	3.70	2
OKMULGEE	UK9-2	20-May-53	7.86	3	PAWNEE	PB8-3	20-Aug-57	4.00	2
OKMULGEE	PB13-6	11-Sep-57	7.89	3	PAWNEE	TS6-4	28-May-52	4.03	2
OKMULGEE	TS7-6	6-Jun-52	8.10	3	PAWNEE	PB13-9	14-Sep-57	4.15	2
OKMULGEE	TP11-5	19-May-55	9.74	3	PAWNEE	TP11-5	19-May-55	4.92	2
OKMULGEE	TS6-4	28-May-52	22.18	4	PAWNEE	TS1-2	2-Apr-52	5.16	3
OKMULGEE	TS1-3	3-Apr-52	24.86	4	PAWNEE	PB13-6	11-Sep-57	6.62	3
OKMULGEE	TS7-5	5-Jun-52	26.42	5	PAWNEE	UK9-2	20-May-53	10.93	4
OSAGE	BJ5-6	24-Nov-51	3.70	2	PAWNEE	PB12-4	5-Sep-57	13.65	4
OSAGE	PB12-3	4-Sep-57	3.76	2	PAWNEE	TP10-3	7-May-55	13.74	4
OSAGE	PB8-3	20-Aug-57	4.00	2	PAWNEE	UK7-3	27-Apr-53	13.82	4
OSAGE	TP11-5	19-May-55	4.40	2	PAWNEE	TS7-5	5-Jun-52	38.16	5
OSAGE	TS1-2	2-Apr-52	5.16	3	PAYNE	BJ5-6	24-Nov-51	3.70	2
OSAGE	PB13-6	11-Sep-57	6.00	3	PAYNE	PB8-3	20-Aug-57	4.00	2
OSAGE	PB13-5	10-Sep-57	6.73	3	PAYNE	PB13-9	14-Sep-57	4.15	2
OSAGE	PB12-4	5-Sep-57	9.18	3	PAYNE	TS1-2	2-Apr-52	5.16	3
OSAGE	UK9-2	20-May-53	10.03	4	PAYNE	TP11-5	19-May-55	5.37	3
OSAGE	UK7-3	27-Apr-53	15.54	4	PAYNE	PB13-6	11-Sep-57	7.34	3
OSAGE	TP10-3	7-May-55	24.65	4	PAYNE	TP10-3	7-May-55	9.01	3
OSAGE	TS7-5	5-Jun-52	46.96	5	PAYNE	UK7-3	27-Apr-53	9.76	3
OTTAWA	PB8-3	20-Aug-57	4.00	2	PAYNE	UK9-2	20-May-53	11.38	4
OTTAWA	UK3-5	4-Apr-53	4.10	2	PAYNE	PB12-4	5-Sep-57	12.16	4
OTTAWA	PB13-9	14-Sep-57	4.15	2	PAYNE	TS7-5	5-Jun-52	20.74	4
OTTAWA	UK9-2	20-May-53	4.79	2	PITTSBURG	PB5-4	18-Jul-57	3.80	2
OTTAWA	BJ2-2	31-Oct-51	5.84	3	PITTSBURG	PB8-3	20-Aug-57	4.00	2
OTTAWA	PB13-6	11-Sep-57	6.32	3	PITTSBURG	UK3-5	4-Apr-53	4.10	2
OTTAWA	UK1-1	17-Mar-53	7.40	3	PITTSBURG	PB13-9	14-Sep-57	4.15	2

INDIVIDUAL FALLOUT DAYS
OKLAHOMA

COUNTY	SHOT	DATE	µCi/SQ METER	INDEX	COUNTY	SHOT	DATE	µCi/SQ METER	INDEX
PITTSBURG	TP11-6	20-May-55	4.56	2	POTTAWATOMIE	UK7-3	27-Apr-53	15.95	4
PITTSBURG	PB13-6	11-Sep-57	4.79	2	POTTAWATOMIE	TS1-3	3-Apr-52	16.84	4
PITTSBURG	UK9-2	20-May-53	5.41	3	POTTAWATOMIE	TS6-4	28-May-52	54.00	6
PITTSBURG	TP11-5	19-May-55	7.36	3	PUSHMATAHA	PB12-4	5-Sep-57	3.80	2
PITTSBURG	UK1-1	17-Mar-53	12.33	4	PUSHMATAHA	PB5-4	18-Jul-57	3.80	2
PITTSBURG	PB12-4	5-Sep-57	12.36	4	PUSHMATAHA	PB8-3	20-Aug-57	4.00	2
PITTSBURG	TP6-2	23-Mar-55	13.77	4	PUSHMATAHA	UK9-2	20-May-53	4.06	2
PITTSBURG	TP10-3	7-May-55	18.15	4	PUSHMATAHA	PB13-9	14-Sep-57	4.15	2
PITTSBURG	TS7-5	5-Jun-52	19.16	4	PUSHMATAHA	TP11-6	20-May-55	4.82	2
PITTSBURG	TS6-4	28-May-52	19.29	4	PUSHMATAHA	PB13-6	11-Sep-57	4.87	2
PITTSBURG	TS1-3	3-Apr-52	24.86	4	PUSHMATAHA	UK1-2	18-Mar-53	5.07	3
PITTSBURG	UK7-3	27-Apr-53	26.07	5	PUSHMATAHA	TS7-5	5-Jun-52	5.73	3
PONTOTOC	UK1-2	18-Mar-53	3.81	2	PUSHMATAHA	PB11-1	31-Aug-57	6.14	3
PONTOTOC	PB8-3	20-Aug-57	4.00	2	PUSHMATAHA	TP11-5	19-May-55	8.07	3
PONTOTOC	PB13-9	14-Sep-57	4.15	2	PUSHMATAHA	TS7-6	6-Jun-52	8.67	3
PONTOTOC	PB13-6	11-Sep-57	4.27	2	PUSHMATAHA	UK1-1	17-Mar-53	12.33	4
PONTOTOC	TS7-6	6-Jun-52	6.10	3	PUSHMATAHA	TP6-2	23-Mar-55	13.77	4
PONTOTOC	UK9-2	20-May-53	7.41	3	PUSHMATAHA	TP10-3	7-May-55	24.32	4
PONTOTOC	UK7-3	27-Apr-53	7.56	3	PUSHMATAHA	TS1-3	3-Apr-52	24.86	4
PONTOTOC	TP6-2	23-Mar-55	13.77	4	ROGER MILLS	BJ5-6	24-Nov-51	3.70	2
PONTOTOC	TS1-3	3-Apr-52	16.84	4	ROGER MILLS	UK6-3	20-Apr-53	4.23	2
PONTOTOC	TP11-5	19-May-55	25.20	5	ROGER MILLS	TS6-7	31-May-52	4.27	2
PONTOTOC	TP10-3	7-May-55	29.38	5	ROGER MILLS	TP10-3	7-May-55	5.73	3
PONTOTOC	TP11-6	20-May-55	3.51	1	ROGER MILLS	UK8-2	9-May-53	6.06	3
POTTAWATOMIE	PB8-3	20-Aug-57	4.00	2	ROGER MILLS	UK9-2	20-May-53	6.32	3
POTTAWATOMIE	PB13-9	14-Sep-57	4.15	2	ROGER MILLS	UK7-3	27-Apr-53	13.13	4
POTTAWATOMIE	TP10-3	7-May-55	4.16	2	ROGER MILLS	UK3-5	4-Apr-53	13.66	4
POTTAWATOMIE	PB12-4	5-Sep-57	4.31	2	ROGER MILLS	UK7-2	26-Apr-53	17.93	4
POTTAWATOMIE	TP10-5	9-May-55	4.52	2	ROGER MILLS	UK9-4	22-May-53	20.41	4
POTTAWATOMIE	TS7-5	5-Jun-52	4.73	2	ROGER MILLS	TP7-2	30-Mar-55	26.42	5
POTTAWATOMIE	UK9-2	20-May-53	9.21	3	ROGER MILLS	TP10-2	6-May-55	32.43	5
POTTAWATOMIE	TP11-5	19-May-55	10.56	4	ROGER MILLS	TS8-1	5-Jun-52	53.18	6
POTTAWATOMIE	TP6-2	23-Mar-55	13.77	4	ROGERS	PB13-4	9-Sep-57	3.55	2

INDIVIDUAL FALLOUT DAYS
OKLAHOMA

COUNTY	SHOT	DATE	µCi/SQ METER	INDEX	COUNTY	SHOT	DATE	µCi/SQ METER	INDEX
ROGERS	BJ5-6	24-Nov-51	3.70	2	SEQUOYAH	TP10-3	7-May-55	14.48	4
ROGERS	TP11-5	19-May-55	3.92	2	SEQUOYAH	PB12-4	5-Sep-57	14.53	4
ROGERS	PB8-3	20-Aug-57	4.00	2	SEQUOYAH	TS1-3	3-Apr-52	41.51	5
ROGERS	TP10-3	7-May-55	4.73	2	SEQUOYAH	TS7-5	5-Jun-52	43.22	5
ROGERS	UK7-3	27-Apr-53	5.57	3	STEPHENS	PB8-3	20-Aug-57	4.00	2
ROGERS	UK3-5	4-Apr-53	6.83	3	STEPHENS	TS1-3	3-Apr-52	4.21	2
ROGERS	UK9-2	20-May-53	6.96	3	STEPHENS	UK1-2	18-Mar-53	4.33	2
ROGERS	UK1-1	17-Mar-53	7.40	3	STEPHENS	UK7-3	27-Apr-53	4.95	2
ROGERS	PB13-5	10-Sep-57	9.69	3	STEPHENS	UK9-2	20-May-53	6.59	3
ROGERS	PB12-4	5-Sep-57	21.62	4	STEPHENS	TP11-5	19-May-55	12.71	4
ROGERS	TS1-3	3-Apr-52	24.86	4	STEPHENS	TP6-2	23-Mar-55	13.77	4
ROGERS	TS7-5	5-Jun-52	49.86	5	STEPHENS	TP10-3	7-May-55	13.90	4
SEMINOLE	PB8-3	20-Aug-57	4.00	2	STEPHENS	TS6-4	28-May-52	68.47	6
SEMINOLE	UK3-5	4-Apr-53	4.10	2	TEXAS	TP11-3	17-May-55	3.58	2
SEMINOLE	PB13-9	14-Sep-57	4.15	2	TEXAS	TP11-4	18-May-55	4.03	2
SEMINOLE	PB13-6	11-Sep-57	5.17	3	TEXAS	PB12-4	5-Sep-57	4.08	2
SEMINOLE	TS6-4	28-May-52	7.25	3	TEXAS	UK6-3	20-Apr-53	4.23	2
SEMINOLE	UK1-1	17-Mar-53	7.40	3	TEXAS	TS6-4	28-May-52	7.25	3
SEMINOLE	UK9-2	20-May-53	8.58	3	TEXAS	UK3-5	4-Apr-53	8.19	3
SEMINOLE	TP11-5	19-May-55	11.56	4	TEXAS	UK9-2	20-May-53	12.74	4
SEMINOLE	TP10-3	7-May-55	12.98	4	TEXAS	UK7-3	27-Apr-53	16.43	4
SEMINOLE	TP6-2	23-Mar-55	13.77	4	TEXAS	UK9-1	19-May-53	19.39	4
SEMINOLE	TS7-5	5-Jun-52	14.27	4	TEXAS	TP10-3	7-May-55	20.92	4
SEMINOLE	TS1-3	3-Apr-52	16.64	4	TEXAS	TP10-2	6-May-55	32.43	5
SEMINOLE	UK7-3	27-Apr-53	20.21	4	TEXAS	TS8-1	5-Jun-52	39.88	5
SEQUOYAH	UK9-2	20-May-53	3.71	2	TEXAS	TP7-2	30-Mar-55	158.51	7
SEQUOYAH	PB12-5	6-Sep-57	3.85	2	TILLMAN	UK9-2	20-May-53	4.16	2
SEQUOYAH	TS7-6	6-Jun-52	3.87	2	TILLMAN	UK6-2	19-Apr-53	5.25	3
SEQUOYAH	PB8-3	20-Aug-57	4.00	2	TILLMAN	TP10-3	7-May-55	5.67	3
SEQUOYAH	PB13-9	14-Sep-57	4.15	2	TILLMAN	UK7-2	26-Apr-53	7.82	3
SEQUOYAH	TP11-6	20-May-55	5.23	3	TILLMAN	TP11-5	19-May-55	12.71	4
SEQUOYAH	PB13-6	11-Sep-57	6.32	3	TILLMAN	TS8-1	5-Jun-52	53.18	6
SEQUOYAH	UK1-1	17-Mar-53	12.33	4	TILLMAN	TS6-4	28-May-52	84.86	6

INDIVIDUAL FALLOUT DAYS
OKLAHOMA

COUNTY	SHOT	DATE	µCi/SQ METER	INDEX	COUNTY	SHOT	DATE	µCi/SQ METER	INDEX
TULSA	PB13-4	9-Sep-57	3.55	2	WASHINGTON	TS1-2	2-Apr-52	5.16	3
TULSA	PB12-3	4-Sep-57	3.79	2	WASHINGTON	PB13-5	10-Sep-57	5.98	3
TULSA	PB8-3	20-Aug-57	4.00	2	WASHINGTON	PB13-6	11-Sep-57	6.98	3
TULSA	PB13-5	10-Sep-57	4.44	2	WASHINGTON	UK9-2	20-May-53	7.86	3
TULSA	UK1-1	17-Mar-53	4.93	2	WASHINGTON	PB12-4	5-Sep-57	11.49	4
TULSA	PB13-6	11-Sep-57	5.66	3	WASHINGTON	UK7-3	27-Apr-53	14.37	4
TULSA	UK3-5	4-Apr-53	6.83	3	WASHINGTON	TP10-3	7-May-55	25.32	5
TULSA	TP11-5	19-May-55	7.46	3	WASHINGTON	TS7-5	5-Jun-52	51.10	6
TULSA	UK9-2	20-May-53	8.04	3	WASHITA	UK9-4	22-May-53	3.57	2
TULSA	TP10-3	7-May-55	14.55	4	WASHITA	TP10-3	7-May-55	3.84	2
TULSA	PB12-4	5-Sep-57	14.59	4	WASHITA	UK7-3	27-Apr-53	3.85	2
TULSA	TS6-4	28-May-52	22.18	4	WASHITA	PB14-7	20-Sep-57	4.04	2
TULSA	TS1-3	3-Apr-52	24.86	4	WASHITA	UK6-3	20-Apr-53	4.23	2
TULSA	UK7-3	27-Apr-53	38.29	5	WASHITA	UK7-2	26-Apr-53	4.27	2
TULSA	TS7-5	5-Jun-52	66.29	6	WASHITA	UK8-2	9-May-53	6.06	3
WAGONER	TP10-5	9-May-55	3.67	2	WASHITA	UK9-2	20-May-53	6.96	3
WAGONER	BJ5-6	24-Nov-51	3.70	2	WASHITA	UK3-5	4-Apr-53	13.66	4
WAGONER	PB8-3	20-Aug-57	4.00	2	WASHITA	TP7-2	30-Mar-55	26.42	5
WAGONER	UK3-5	4-Apr-53	4.10	2	WASHITA	TP10-2	6-May-55	32.43	5
WAGONER	PB13-9	14-Sep-57	4.15	2	WASHITA	TS8-1	5-Jun-52	239.29	8
WAGONER	UK7-3	27-Apr-53	4.40	2	WOODS	PB13-9	14-Sep-57	4.15	2
WAGONER	TP11-5	19-May-55	5.37	3	WOODS	PB12-3	4-Sep-57	5.09	3
WAGONER	UK9-2	20-May-53	5.71	3	WOODS	TP9-2	15-Apr-55	5.42	3
WAGONER	PB13-6	11-Sep-57	7.48	3	WOODS	TP10-3	7-May-55	5.54	3
WAGONER	TP10-3	7-May-55	11.67	4	WOODS	PB13-5	10-Sep-57	8.84	3
WAGONER	UK1-1	17-Mar-53	12.33	4	WOODS	UK9-2	20-May-53	14.00	4
WAGONER	PB12-4	5-Sep-57	20.68	4	WOODS	UK7-3	27-Apr-53	21.65	4
WAGONER	TS1-3	3-Apr-52	24.86	4	WOODS	TS8-1	5-Jun-52	132.94	7
WAGONER	TS6-4	28-May-52	34.72	5	WOODWARD	UK9-4	22-May-53	3.61	2
WAGONER	TS7-5	5-Jun-52	47.20	5	WOODWARD	BJ5-6	24-Nov-51	3.70	2
WASHINGTON	BJ5-6	24-Nov-51	3.70	2	WOODWARD	TP10-3	7-May-55	6.36	3
WASHINGTON	PB8-3	20-Aug-57	4.00	2	WOODWARD	UK7-3	27-Apr-53	7.01	3
WASHINGTON	TP11-5	19-May-55	5.05	3	WOODWARD	PB13-5	10-Sep-57	8.97	3

INDIVIDUAL FALLOUT DAYS
OKLAHOMA

COUNTY	SHOT	DATE	µCi/SQ METER	INDEX	COUNTY	SHOT	DATE	µCi/SQ METER	INDEX
WOODWARD	UK9-2	20-May-53	10.66	4	WOODWARD	TS8-1	5-Jun-52	53.18	6

INDIVIDUAL FALLOUT DAYS
OREGON

COUNTY	SHOT	DATE	µCi/SQ METER	INDEX	COUNTY	SHOT	DATE	µCi/SQ METER	INDEX
BAKER	TP8-1	9-Apr-55	3.77	2	HARNEY	UK10-1	25-May-53	8.83	3
BAKER	TS2-4	18-Apr-52	3.91	2	HARNEY	PB6-1	24-Jul-57	9.20	3
BAKER	UK10-2	26-May-53	4.01	2	HARNEY	PB16-1	23-Sep-57	17.37	4
BAKER	TP11-1	15-May-55	4.66	2	HARNEY	BJ5 1	19-Nov-51	18.28	4
BAKER	TP11-2	16-May-55	5.45	3	HARNEY	TP11-1	15-May-55	21.87	4
BAKER	PB16-3	25-Sep-57	7.58	3	HARNEY	TS8-1	5-Jun-52	600.48	9
BAKER	PB17-3	30-Sep-57	9.52	3	HOOD RIVER	TS8-1	5-Jun-52	13.29	4
BAKER	PB6-3	26-Jul-57	12.28	4	JACKSON	TS7-6	6-Jun-52	6.21	3
BAKER	PB6-2	25-Jul-57	21.00	4	JACKSON	TS8-1	5-Jun-52	9.23	3
BAKER	TS8-2	6-Jun-52	78.60	6	JEFFERSON	TS8-1	5-Jun-52	332.96	8
BAKER	TS8-1	5-Jun-52	13651.35	10	JOSEPHINE	UK7-2	26-Apr-53	3.51	2
CLACKAMAS	TS8-1	5-Jun-52	13.29	4	JOSEPHINE	TS7-6	6-Jun-52	5.32	3
CLATSOP	TS6-4	28-May-52	8.68	3	KLAMATH	TS3-3	24-Apr-52	6.67	3
COLUMBIA	UK7-2	26-Apr-53	5.69	3	KLAMATH	TS8-1	5-Jun-52	110.99	7
CROOK	TS8-2	6-Jun-52	5.29	3	LAKE	TS8-2	6-Jun-52	4.75	2
CROOK	TS8-1	5-Jun-52	919.60	10	LAKE	TS3-3	24-Apr-52	10.00	4
CURRY	UK7-2	26-Apr-53	3.51	2	LAKE	TS8-1	5-Jun-52	824.47	10
CURRY	UK9-1	19-May-53	3.60	2	LANE	UK7-2	26-Apr-53	3.51	2
DESCHUTES	TS8-1	5-Jun-52	190.26	7	LINCOLN	UK7-2	26-Apr-53	3.51	2
DOUGLAS	UK7-2	26-Apr-53	3.63	2	LINCOLN	TS6-4	28-May-52	4.03	2
GILLIAM	TS8-1	5-Jun-52	459.80	9	MALHEUR	PB1-1	28-May-57	3.82	2
GRANT	TP8-1	9-Apr-55	3.77	2	MALHEUR	TS2-1	15-Apr-52	3.94	2
GRANT	TS2-4	18-Apr-52	5.26	3	MALHEUR	TS8-2	6-Jun-52	7.00	3
GRANT	TP11-1	15-May-55	7.10	3	MALHEUR	TS7-1	1-Jun-52	8.34	3
GRANT	TP11-2	16-May-55	7.37	3	MALHEUR	PB17-1	28-Sep-57	8.66	3
GRANT	PB16-3	25-Sep-57	7.58	3	MALHEUR	UK10-1	25-May-53	8.83	3
GRANT	PB17-3	30-Sep-57	9.52	3	MALHEUR	PB16-1	23-Sep-57	17.37	4
GRANT	PB6-3	26-Jul-57	12.28	4	MALHEUR	BJ5 1	19-Nov-51	18.28	4
GRANT	PB6-2	25-Jul-57	21.00	4	MALHEUR	PB6-1	24-Jul-57	18.50	4
GRANT	TS8-2	6-Jun-52	27.84	5	MALHEUR	TP11-1	15-May-55	21.87	4
GRANT	TS8-1	5-Jun-52	4835.84	10	MALHEUR	TS8-1	5-Jun-52	1214.92	10
HARNEY	TS7-1	1-Jun-52	8.34	3	MARION	TS6-4	28-May-52	8.68	3
HARNEY	PB17-1	28-Sep-57	8.66	3	MORROW	TS8-2	6-Jun-52	5.29	3

INDIVIDUAL FALLOUT DAYS
OREGON

COUNTY	SHOT	DATE	µCi/SQ METER	INDEX	COUNTY	SHOT	DATE	µCi/SQ METER	INDEX
MORROW	TS8-1	5-Jun-52	919.60	10	UNION	PB6-3	26-Jul-57	12.28	4
SHERMAN	TS8-1	5-Jun-52	301.25	8	UNION	PB6-2	25-Jul-57	21.00	4
TILLAMOOK	UK9-1	19-May-53	3.85	2	UNION	TS8-2	6-Jun-52	36.06	5
TILLAMOOK	TS7-6	6-Jun-52	3.88	2	UNION	UK10-2	26-May-53	3.51	1
TILLAMOOK	TS6-4	28-May-52	4.03	2	UNION	TS8-1	5-Jun-52	6262.82	10
TILLAMOOK	TS8-1	5-Jun-52	31.71	5	WALLOWA	TS5-1	7-May-52	4.85	2
UMATILLA	UK10-2	26-May-53	4.13	2	WALLOWA	PB17-3	30-Sep-57	6.34	3
UMATILLA	PB16-4	26-Sep-57	5.16	3	WALLOWA	PB16-3	25-Sep-57	7.58	3
UMATILLA	PB16-3	25-Sep-57	7.58	3	WALLOWA	PB6-2	25-Jul-57	10.55	4
UMATILLA	PB17-3	30-Sep-57	9.52	3	WALLOWA	PB6-3	26-Jul-57	12.28	4
UMATILLA	PB6-2	25-Jul-57	10.55	4	WALLOWA	TS8-2	6-Jun-52	111.74	7
UMATILLA	PB6-3	26-Jul-57	12.28	4	WALLOWA	TS8-1	5-Jun-52	19406.80	10
UMATILLA	TS8-2	6-Jun-52	12.87	4	WASCO	TS8-1	5-Jun-52	190.26	7
UMATILLA	TS8-1	5-Jun-52	2235.59	10	WHEELER	TS8-2	6-Jun-52	4.11	2
UNION	PB16-3	25-Sep-57	7.58	3	WHEELER	TS8-1	5-Jun-52	713.49	9
UNION	PB17-3	30-Sep-57	9.52	3					

INDIVIDUAL FALLOUT DAYS
PENNSYLVANIA

COUNTY	SHOT	DATE	μCi/SQ METER	INDEX	COUNTY	SHOT	DATE	μCi/SQ METER	INDEX
ADAMS	BJ2-3	1-Nov-51	4.03	2	BERKS	TS3-4	25-Apr-52	3.87	2
ADAMS	BJ3-6	6-Nov-51	4.63	2	BERKS	BJ3-6	6-Nov-51	4.63	2
ADAMS	UK1-2	18-Mar-53	4.74	2	BERKS	TP11-9	23-May-55	5.63	3
ADAMS	TS3-4	25-Apr-52	6.03	3	BERKS	PB5-8	22-Jul-57	5.97	3
ADAMS	SE4	9-Jul-62	73.06	6	BERKS	BJ2-4	2-Nov-51	6.06	3
ADAMS	UK9-3	21-May-53	3.51	1	BERKS	UK1-2	18-Mar-53	6.29	3
ALLEGHENY	PB4-4	8-Jul-57	3.66	2	BERKS	UK9-7	25-May-53	10.18	4
ALLEGHENY	BJ2-3	1-Nov-51	3.71	2	BLAIR	PB4-4	8-Jul-57	3.94	2
ALLEGHENY	PB5-8	22-Jul-57	5.97	3	BLAIR	TS3-4	25-Apr-52	3.98	2
ALLEGHENY	UK9-3	21-May-53	10.14	4	BLAIR	UK9-7	25-May-53	4.16	2
ALLEGHENY	R1-2	29-Jan-51	21.83	4	BLAIR	BJ2-3	1-Nov-51	4.72	2
ALLEGHENY	SE4	9-Jul-62	72.20	6	BLAIR	UK9-3	21-May-53	4.92	2
ARMSTRONG	TP11-8	22-May-55	3.82	2	BLAIR	PB5-8	22-Jul-57	8.96	3
ARMSTRONG	UK9-7	25-May-53	4.16	2	BLAIR	R1-2	29-Jan-51	21.83	4
ARMSTRONG	TP11-9	23-May-55	4.62	2	BRADFORD	UK9-4	22-May-53	4.43	2
ARMSTRONG	PB4-4	8-Jul-57	4.87	2	BRADFORD	PB5-8	22-Jul-57	8.96	3
ARMSTRONG	PB5-8	22-Jul-57	8.96	3	BRADFORD	R1-2	29-Jan-51	9.22	3
ARMSTRONG	UK9-3	21-May-53	10.03	4	BRADFORD	BJ2-4	2-Nov-51	13.09	4
ARMSTRONG	R1-2	29-Jan-51	21.83	4	BUCKS	TS3-4	25-Apr-52	3.87	2
ARMSTRONG	SE4	9-Jul-62	90.29	6	BUCKS	TP6-4	25-Mar-55	4.32	2
BEAVER	TP4-4	10-Mar-55	4.02	2	BUCKS	BJ2-3	1-Nov-51	4.93	2
BEAVER	BJ2-2	31-Oct-51	7.20	3	BUCKS	PB5-8	22-Jul-57	5.97	3
BEAVER	UK9-3	21-May-53	8.55	3	BUCKS	UK9-7	25-May-53	6.11	3
BEAVER	PB5-8	22-Jul-57	8.96	3	BUCKS	BJ2-4	2-Nov-51	8.50	3
BEAVER	R1-2	29-Jan-51	21.83	4	BUCKS	UK1-2	18-Mar-53	20.82	4
BEAVER	SE4	9-Jul-62	103.59	7	BUCKS	R1-2	29-Jan-51	3.50	1
BEDFORD	TS3-4	25-Apr-52	3.98	2	BUTLER	TP11-8	22-May-55	3.82	2
BEDFORD	UK9-7	25-May-53	4.16	2	BUTLER	UK9-7	25-May-53	4.16	2
BEDFORD	BJ2-3	1-Nov-51	4.29	2	BUTLER	TP11-9	23-May-55	4.62	2
BEDFORD	UK9-3	21-May-53	5.29	3	BUTLER	BJ2-2	31-Oct-51	7.20	3
BEDFORD	PB5-8	22-Jul-57	8.96	3	BUTLER	UK9-3	21-May-53	8.55	3
BEDFORD	SE4	9-Jul-62	57.04	6	BUTLER	PB5-8	22-Jul-57	8.96	3
BERKS	BJ2-3	1-Nov-51	3.65	2	BUTLER	SE4	9-Jul-62	85.56	6

INDIVIDUAL FALLOUT DAYS
PENNSYLVANIA

COUNTY	SHOT	DATE	µCi/SQ METER	INDEX	COUNTY	SHOT	DATE	µCi/SQ METER	INDEX
CAMBRIA	BJ2-3	1-Nov-51	3.86	2	CHESTER	UK9-7	25-May-53	10.18	4
CAMBRIA	UK9-7	25-May-53	4.16	2	CHESTER	UK1-2	18-Mar-53	12.55	4
CAMBRIA	PB4-4	8-Jul-57	4.29	2	CHESTER	SE4	9-Jul-62	73.06	6
CAMBRIA	UK9-3	21-May-53	5.78	3	CLARION	TP11-8	22-May-55	3.82	2
CAMBRIA	PB5-8	22-Jul-57	5.97	3	CLARION	TP11-9	23-May-55	4.62	2
CAMBRIA	R1-2	29-Jan-51	21.83	4	CLARION	UK10-6	30-May-53	6.12	3
CAMBRIA	SE4	9-Jul-62	90.29	6	CLARION	TP9-2	15-Apr-55	6.37	3
CAMERON	TP9-3	16-Apr-55	4.84	2	CLARION	UK9-3	21-May-53	6.46	3
CAMERON	BJ2-4	2-Nov-51	6.27	3	CLARION	BJ2-3	1-Nov-51	6.52	3
CAMERON	BJ2-3	1-Nov-51	6.33	3	CLARION	UK9-7	25-May-53	6.94	3
CAMERON	PB5-8	22-Jul-57	8.96	3	CLARION	BJ2-2	31-Oct-51	7.20	3
CAMERON	R1-2	29-Jan-51	21.83	4	CLARION	R1-2	29-Jan-51	8.74	3
CAMERON	SE4	9-Jul-62	46.95	5	CLARION	PB5-8	22-Jul-57	8.96	3
CARBON	TS3-4	25-Apr-52	3.87	2	CLARION	SE4	9-Jul-62	85.56	6
CARBON	BJ3-7	7-Nov-51	4.13	2	CLEARFIELD	UK9-3	21-May-53	4.49	2
CARBON	UK9-4	22-May-53	4.86	2	CLEARFIELD	UK9-7	25-May-53	6.94	3
CARBON	TP11-9	23-May-55	5.63	3	CLEARFIELD	BJ2-3	1-Nov-51	7.42	3
CARBON	PB5-8	22-Jul-57	5.97	3	CLEARFIELD	PB5-8	22-Jul-57	8.96	3
CARBON	UK9-7	25-May-53	6.11	3	CLEARFIELD	R1-2	29-Jan-51	21.83	4
CARBON	BJ2-4	2-Nov-51	10.79	4	CLEARFIELD	SE4	9-Jul-62	103.59	7
CENTRE	UK9-3	21-May-53	3.57	2	CLINTON	TS3-4	25-Apr-52	3.98	2
CENTRE	TS3-4	25-Apr-52	3.98	2	CLINTON	TS7-6	6-Jun-52	4.45	2
CENTRE	BJ2-3	1-Nov-51	5.79	3	CLINTON	TP9-3	16-Apr-55	4.57	2
CENTRE	PB5-8	22-Jul-57	8.96	3	CLINTON	BJ2-4	2-Nov-51	4.59	2
CENTRE	R1-2	29-Jan-51	21.83	4	CLINTON	BJ2-3	1-Nov-51	6.11	3
CENTRE	SE4	9-Jul-62	57.04	6	CLINTON	R1-2	29-Jan-51	8.74	3
CHESTER	TP11-9	23-May-55	3.75	2	CLINTON	PB5-8	22-Jul-57	8.96	3
CHESTER	TP6-4	25-Mar-55	4.32	2	CLINTON	SE4	9-Jul-62	73.06	6
CHESTER	BJ3-6	6-Nov-51	4.63	2	COLUMBIA	UK9-4	22-May-53	3.70	2
CHESTER	PB5-8	22-Jul-57	5.97	3	COLUMBIA	PB5-8	22-Jul-57	5.97	3
CHESTER	BJ2-4	2-Nov-51	6.06	3	COLUMBIA	TS3-4	25-Apr-52	6.03	3
CHESTER	BJ2-3	1-Nov-51	6.11	3	COLUMBIA	BJ2-4	2-Nov-51	8.57	3
CHESTER	TS3-4	25-Apr-52	6.46	3	COLUMBIA	R1-2	29-Jan-51	8.74	3

U.S. FALLOUT ATLAS: COUNTY COMPARISONS

INDIVIDUAL FALLOUT DAYS
PENNSYLVANIA

COUNTY	SHOT	DATE	µCi/SQ METER	INDEX	COUNTY	SHOT	DATE	µCi/SQ METER	INDEX
CRAWFORD	BJ2-2	31-Oct-51	3.70	2	ERIE	BJ2-2	31-Oct-51	3.70	2
CRAWFORD	TP11-8	22-May-55	3.82	2	ERIE	UK9-3	21-May-53	4.55	2
CRAWFORD	BJ2-3	1-Nov-51	4.40	2	ERIE	BJ2-3	1-Nov-51	5.68	3
CRAWFORD	UK9-7	25-May-53	4.53	2	ERIE	PB5-8	22-Jul-57	5.97	3
CRAWFORD	TP11-9	23-May-55	4.62	2	ERIE	BJ3-5	5-Nov-51	6.32	3
CRAWFORD	PB5-8	22-Jul-57	5.97	3	ERIE	TS7-4	4-Jun-52	9.41	3
CRAWFORD	UK9-3	21-May-53	6.03	3	ERIE	TP4-4	10-Mar-55	10.36	4
CRAWFORD	R1-2	29-Jan-51	9.22	3	ERIE	R1-2	29-Jan-51	11.14	4
CRAWFORD	TP4-4	10-Mar-55	9.36	3	ERIE	SE4	9-Jul-62	21.07	4
CRAWFORD	TP9-2	15-Apr-55	19.22	4	ERIE	TP9-2	15-Apr-55	24.64	4
CRAWFORD	SE4	9-Jul-62	85.56	6	FAYETTE	PB4-4	8-Jul-57	5.73	3
CUMBERLAND	TS3-4	25-Apr-52	6.03	3	FAYETTE	UK9-3	21-May-53	6.45	3
CUMBERLAND	PB5-8	22-Jul-57	8.96	3	FAYETTE	PB5-8	22-Jul-57	8.96	3
DAUPHIN	BJ3-6	6-Nov-51	4.63	2	FAYETTE	R1-2	29-Jan-51	21.83	4
DAUPHIN	PB5-8	22-Jul-57	8.96	3	FAYETTE	SE5	10-Jul-62	32.93	5
DELAWARE	TS3-4	25-Apr-52	3.87	2	FAYETTE	SE4	9-Jul-62	85.56	6
DELAWARE	TP6-4	25-Mar-55	4.32	2	FOREST	BJ3-7	7-Nov-51	4.20	2
DELAWARE	PB5-8	22-Jul-57	5.97	3	FOREST	BJ2-3	1-Nov-51	4.29	2
DELAWARE	BJ2-3	1-Nov-51	6.01	3	FOREST	UK9-7	25-May-53	4.53	2
DELAWARE	BJ2-4	2-Nov-51	7.17	3	FOREST	UK9-3	21-May-53	4.67	2
DELAWARE	UK9-7	25-May-53	10.18	4	FOREST	PB5-8	22-Jul-57	5.97	3
DELAWARE	UK1-2	18-Mar-53	20.75	4	FOREST	TP11-8	22-May-55	6.36	3
DELAWARE	SE4	9-Jul-62	57.04	6	FOREST	TP11-9	23-May-55	7.70	3
ELK	BJ3-7	7-Nov-51	4.20	2	FOREST	R1-2	29-Jan-51	8.74	3
ELK	UK9-7	25-May-53	4.53	2	FOREST	TP4-4	10-Mar-55	9.28	3
ELK	TP9-2	15-Apr-55	5.22	3	FOREST	TP9-2	15-Apr-55	16.22	4
ELK	BJ2-3	1-Nov-51	6.86	3	FOREST	BJ3-6	6-Nov-51	16.67	4
ELK	PB5-8	22-Jul-57	8.96	3	FOREST	SE4	9-Jul-62	85.56	6
ELK	BJ3-6	6-Nov-51	16.67	4	FRANKLIN	UK1-2	18-Mar-53	3.61	2
ELK	R1-2	29-Jan-51	21.83	4	FRANKLIN	UK9-3	21-May-53	3.69	2
ELK	SE5	10-Jul-62	47.25	5	FRANKLIN	BJ3-6	6-Nov-51	4.63	2
ELK	SE4	9-Jul-62	85.56	6	FRANKLIN	BJ2-3	1-Nov-51	4.65	2
ERIE	UK10-6	30-May-53	3.57	2	FRANKLIN	PB5-8	22-Jul-57	5.97	3

INDIVIDUAL FALLOUT DAYS
PENNSYLVANIA

COUNTY	SHOT	DATE	µCi/SQ METER	INDEX	COUNTY	SHOT	DATE	µCi/SQ METER	INDEX
FRANKLIN	TS3-4	25-Apr-52	6.03	3	JEFFERSON	R1-2	29-Jan-51	9.22	3
FULTON	UK9-3	21-May-53	4.06	2	JEFFERSON	SE4	9-Jul-62	90.29	6
FULTON	BJ2-3	1-Nov-51	5.68	3	JUNIATA	TS3-4	25-Apr-52	6.03	3
FULTON	TS3-4	25-Apr-52	6.03	3	JUNIATA	R1-2	29-Jan-51	8.74	3
FULTON	PB5-8	22-Jul-57	8.96	3	JUNIATA	UK9-3	21-May-53	3.51	1
FULTON	SE4	9-Jul-62	149.13	7	LACKAWANNA	TP11-9	23-May-55	3.75	2
GREENE	PB5-9	23-Jul-57	4.71	2	LACKAWANNA	PB5-8	22-Jul-57	5.97	3
GREENE	PB5-8	22-Jul-57	8.96	3	LACKAWANNA	TS3-6	27-Apr-52	12.74	4
GREENE	R1-2	29-Jan-51	21.83	4	LACKAWANNA	R1-2	29-Jan-51	15.59	4
GREENE	SE4	9-Jul-62	85.56	6	LACKAWANNA	BJ2-4	2-Nov-51	20.27	4
HUNTINGDON	BJ2-3	1-Nov-51	4.29	2	LACKAWANNA	SE5	10-Jul-62	40.85	5
HUNTINGDON	UK9-3	21-May-53	4.37	2	LANCASTER	BJ2-4	2-Nov-51	3.97	2
HUNTINGDON	PB5-8	22-Jul-57	5.97	3	LANCASTER	BJ2-3	1-Nov-51	4.56	2
HUNTINGDON	UK10-6	30-May-53	6.02	3	LANCASTER	BJ3-6	6-Nov-51	4.63	2
HUNTINGDON	TS3-4	25-Apr-52	6.03	3	LANCASTER	UK1-2	18-Mar-53	6.02	3
HUNTINGDON	R1-2	29-Jan-51	21.83	4	LANCASTER	TS3-4	25-Apr-52	6.03	3
HUNTINGDON	SE4	9-Jul-62	57.04	6	LANCASTER	PB5-8	22-Jul-57	8.96	3
INDIANA	BJ2-3	1-Nov-51	4.08	2	LANCASTER	SE4	9-Jul-62	60.19	6
INDIANA	UK9-7	25-May-53	4.16	2	LAWRENCE	BJ2-2	31-Oct-51	3.70	2
INDIANA	BJ3-5	5-Nov-51	4.59	2	LAWRENCE	TP9-2	15-Apr-55	4.09	2
INDIANA	PB4-4	8-Jul-57	4.65	2	LAWRENCE	TP4-4	10-Mar-55	5.34	3
INDIANA	UK9-3	21-May-53	7.01	3	LAWRENCE	PB5-8	22-Jul-57	5.97	3
INDIANA	PB5-8	22-Jul-57	8.96	3	LAWRENCE	UK9-3	21-May-53	10.33	4
INDIANA	R1-2	29-Jan-51	21.83	4	LAWRENCE	SE4	9-Jul-62	103.59	7
INDIANA	SE4	9-Jul-62	90.29	6	LEBANON	UK7-2	26-Apr-53	3.63	2
JEFFERSON	TP4-4	10-Mar-55	3.60	2	LEBANON	UK1-2	18-Mar-53	3.81	2
JEFFERSON	TP11-8	22-May-55	3.82	2	LEBANON	BJ3-6	6-Nov-51	4.63	2
JEFFERSON	TP11-9	23-May-55	4.62	2	LEBANON	TS3-4	25-Apr-52	6.03	3
JEFFERSON	TP9-2	15-Apr-55	5.11	3	LEHIGH	UK9-4	22-May-53	4.14	2
JEFFERSON	UK9-3	21-May-53	5.41	3	LEHIGH	TP6-4	25-Mar-55	4.32	2
JEFFERSON	UK9-7	25-May-53	6.94	3	LEHIGH	BJ3-6	6-Nov-51	4.63	2
JEFFERSON	BJ2-3	1-Nov-51	7.16	3	LEHIGH	TP11-9	23-May-55	5.63	3
JEFFERSON	PB5-8	22-Jul-57	8.96	3	LEHIGH	PB5-8	22-Jul-57	5.97	3

INDIVIDUAL FALLOUT DAYS
PENNSYLVANIA

COUNTY	SHOT	DATE	µCi/SQ METER	INDEX	COUNTY	SHOT	DATE	µCi/SQ METER	INDEX
LEHIGH	UK9-7	25-May-53	6.11	3	MERCER	TP4-4	10-Mar-55	7.93	3
LEHIGH	TS3-4	25-Apr-52	6.46	3	MERCER	UK9-3	21-May-53	8.37	3
LEHIGH	UK1-2	18-Mar-53	6.62	3	MERCER	TP9-2	15-Apr-55	23.88	4
LEHIGH	BJ2-4	2-Nov-51	10.27	4	MERCER	SE4	9-Jul-62	85.56	6
LUZERNE	TP11-9	23-May-55	3.75	2	MIFFLIN	UK9-3	21-May-53	3.63	2
LUZERNE	BJ3-7	7-Nov-51	4.13	2	MIFFLIN	BJ2-3	1-Nov-51	3.67	2
LUZERNE	PB11-5	4-Sep-57	4.48	2	MIFFLIN	PB5-8	22-Jul-57	5.97	3
LUZERNE	PB5-8	22-Jul-57	8.96	3	MIFFLIN	TS3-4	25-Apr-52	6.03	3
LUZERNE	R1-2	29-Jan-51	9.22	3	MIFFLIN	R1-2	29-Jan-51	9.22	3
LUZERNE	TS3-6	27-Apr-52	12.74	4	MONROE	UK9-7	25-May-53	4.07	2
LUZERNE	BJ2-4	2-Nov-51	13.30	4	MONROE	BJ3-7	7-Nov-51	4.13	2
LUZERNE	SE4	9-Jul-62	16.72	4	MONROE	UK1-2	18-Mar-53	4.84	2
LYCOMING	TS3-4	25-Apr-52	3.98	2	MONROE	PB5-8	22-Jul-57	5.97	3
LYCOMING	BJ2-3	1-Nov-51	4.50	2	MONROE	R1-2	29-Jan-51	11.68	4
LYCOMING	BJ2-4	2-Nov-51	5.01	3	MONROE	TS3-6	27-Apr-52	12.74	4
LYCOMING	PB5-8	22-Jul-57	5.97	3	MONROE	BJ2-4	2-Nov-51	15.78	4
LYCOMING	R1-2	29-Jan-51	8.74	3	MONTGOMERY	TS3-4	25-Apr-52	3.87	2
MCKEAN	BJ2-5	3-Nov-51	3.57	2	MONTGOMERY	TP6-4	25-Mar-55	4.32	2
MCKEAN	BJ3-7	7-Nov-51	4.20	2	MONTGOMERY	BJ2-3	1-Nov-51	4.93	2
MCKEAN	UK9-7	25-May-53	4.53	2	MONTGOMERY	PB5-8	22-Jul-57	5.97	3
MCKEAN	TP4-4	10-Mar-55	4.68	2	MONTGOMERY	BJ2-4	2-Nov-51	7.66	3
MCKEAN	TP9-2	15-Apr-55	5.80	3	MONTGOMERY	UK9-7	25-May-53	10.18	4
MCKEAN	PB5-8	22-Jul-57	5.97	3	MONTGOMERY	UK1-2	18-Mar-53	16.74	4
MCKEAN	BJ2-4	2-Nov-51	7.87	3	MONTOUR	BJ2-4	2-Nov-51	3.55	2
MCKEAN	BJ2-3	1-Nov-51	8.90	3	MONTOUR	PB11-5	4-Sep-57	4.48	2
MCKEAN	R1-2	29-Jan-51	9.22	3	MONTOUR	TS3-4	25-Apr-52	6.03	3
MCKEAN	BJ3-6	6-Nov-51	16.67	4	MONTOUR	PB5-8	22-Jul-57	8.96	3
MERCER	BJ2-2	31-Oct-51	3.70	2	MONTOUR	R1-2	29-Jan-51	21.83	4
MERCER	TP11-8	22-May-55	3.82	2	NORTHAMPTON	BJ2-3	1-Nov-51	3.54	2
MERCER	BJ2-3	1-Nov-51	4.08	2	NORTHAMPTON	UK9-7	25-May-53	4.07	2
MERCER	TP11-9	23-May-55	4.62	2	NORTHAMPTON	BJ3-7	7-Nov-51	4.13	2
MERCER	PB5-8	22-Jul-57	5.97	3	NORTHAMPTON	UK9-4	22-May-53	4.57	2
MERCER	R1-2	29-Jan-51	7.76	3	NORTHAMPTON	R1-2	29-Jan-51	4.66	2

INDIVIDUAL FALLOUT DAYS
PENNSYLVANIA

COUNTY	SHOT	DATE	μCi/SQ METER	INDEX	COUNTY	SHOT	DATE	μCi/SQ METER	INDEX
NORTHAMPTON	PB5-8	22-Jul-57	5.97	3	SCHUYLKILL	BJ2-4	2-Nov-51	6.13	3
NORTHAMPTON	TS3-4	25-Apr-52	6.46	3	SCHUYLKILL	PB5-8	22-Jul-57	8.96	3
NORTHAMPTON	UK1-2	18-Mar-53	7.22	3	SNYDER	TS3-4	25-Apr-52	6.03	3
NORTHAMPTON	BJ2-4	2-Nov-51	12.27	4	SNYDER	PB5-8	22-Jul-57	8.96	3
NORTHUMBERLA	BJ2-4	2-Nov-51	5.01	3	SNYDER	R1-2	29-Jan-51	21.83	4
NORTHUMBERLA	TS3-4	25-Apr-52	6.03	3	SNYDER	SE4	9-Jul-62	149.13	7
NORTHUMBERLA	PB5-8	22-Jul-57	8.96	3	SOMERSET	UK9-7	25-May-53	4.16	2
NORTHUMBERLA	SE4	9-Jul-62	73.06	6	SOMERSET	UK9-3	21-May-53	6.70	3
PERRY	TS3-4	25-Apr-52	6.03	3	SOMERSET	PB5-8	22-Jul-57	8.96	3
PHILADELPHIA	TS3-4	25-Apr-52	3.87	2	SOMERSET	SE4	9-Jul-62	85.56	6
PHILADELPHIA	BJ2-4	2-Nov-51	4.04	2	SULLIVAN	BJ3-7	7-Nov-51	4.13	2
PHILADELPHIA	BJ2-3	1-Nov-51	5.73	3	SULLIVAN	PB5-8	22-Jul-57	5.97	3
PHILADELPHIA	UK1-2	18-Mar-53	28.16	5	SULLIVAN	BJ2-4	2-Nov-51	7.73	3
PIKE	UK1-2	18-Mar-53	4.23	2	SULLIVAN	R1-2	29-Jan-51	21.83	4
PIKE	UK7-2	26-Apr-53	5.09	3	SUSQUEHANNA	UK9-4	22-May-53	5.04	3
PIKE	PB5-8	22-Jul-57	5.97	3	SUSQUEHANNA	PB5-8	22-Jul-57	8.96	3
PIKE	BJ3-7	7-Nov-51	6.86	3	SUSQUEHANNA	BJ2-4	2-Nov-51	15.13	4
PIKE	BJ2-4	2-Nov-51	8.08	3	SUSQUEHANNA	R1-2	29-Jan-51	21.83	4
PIKE	TS3-6	27-Apr-52	12.74	4	TIOGA	TP9-3	16-Apr-55	4.89	2
PIKE	R1-2	29-Jan-51	14.48	4	TIOGA	BJ2-3	1-Nov-51	6.76	3
PIKE	TS1-4	4-Apr-52	19.67	4	TIOGA	PB5-8	22-Jul-57	8.96	3
POTTER	UK10-6	30-May-53	3.70	2	TIOGA	BJ2-4	2-Nov-51	10.44	4
POTTER	PB5-8	22-Jul-57	5.97	3	TIOGA	R1-2	29-Jan-51	21.83	4
POTTER	SE5	10-Jul-62	7.38	3	UNION	TS3-4	25-Apr-52	6.03	3
POTTER	BJ2-4	2-Nov-51	8.01	3	UNION	PB5-8	22-Jul-57	8.96	3
POTTER	BJ3-7	7-Nov-51	8.40	3	UNION	R1-2	29-Jan-51	21.83	4
POTTER	R1-2	29-Jan-51	8.74	3	VENANGO	BJ2-2	31-Oct-51	3.70	2
POTTER	BJ2-3	1-Nov-51	9.44	3	VENANGO	TP11-8	22-May-55	3.82	2
POTTER	BJ3-6	6-Nov-51	16.67	4	VENANGO	TP11-9	23-May-55	4.62	2
SCHUYLKILL	TP11-9	23-May-55	3.75	2	VENANGO	UK9-3	21-May-53	6.46	3
SCHUYLKILL	BJ3-6	6-Nov-51	4.63	2	VENANGO	UK9-7	25-May-53	6.94	3
SCHUYLKILL	TS3-4	25-Apr-52	6.03	3	VENANGO	PB5-8	22-Jul-57	8.96	3
SCHUYLKILL	UK9-7	25-May-53	6.11	3	VENANGO	R1-2	29-Jan-51	11.14	4

INDIVIDUAL FALLOUT DAYS
PENNSYLVANIA

COUNTY	SHOT	DATE	µCi/SQ METER	INDEX	COUNTY	SHOT	DATE	µCi/SQ METER	INDEX
VENANGO	TP4-4	10-Mar-55	11.29	4	WAYNE	UK7-2	26-Apr-53	8.12	3
VENANGO	TP9-2	15-Apr-55	17.79	4	WAYNE	SE5	10-Jul-62	8.99	3
VENANGO	SE4	9-Jul-62	208.78	8	WAYNE	TS3-6	27-Apr-52	12.74	4
WARREN	TS7-4	4-Jun-52	4.52	2	WAYNE	BJ2-4	2-Nov-51	23.68	4
WARREN	UK9-7	25-May-53	4.53	2	WAYNE	R1-2	29-Jan-51	30.97	5
WARREN	UK10-6	30-May-53	5.07	3	WESTMORELAND	UK9-3	21-May-53	7.93	3
WARREN	BJ2-4	2-Nov-51	5.28	3	WESTMORELAND	PB5-8	22-Jul-57	8.96	3
WARREN	TP4-4	10-Mar-55	7.15	3	WESTMORELAND	R1-2	29-Jan-51	21.83	4
WARREN	BJ2-3	1-Nov-51	7.19	3	WESTMORELAND	SE4	9-Jul-62	90.29	6
WARREN	BJ3-7	7-Nov-51	8.40	3	WYOMING	PB5-7	21-Jul-57	4.10	2
WARREN	R1-2	29-Jan-51	8.74	3	WYOMING	BJ3-7	7-Nov-51	4.13	2
WARREN	PB5-8	22-Jul-57	8.96	3	WYOMING	PB11-5	4-Sep-57	4.48	2
WARREN	TP9-2	15-Apr-55	11.89	4	WYOMING	PB5-8	22-Jul-57	8.96	3
WARREN	BJ3-6	6-Nov-51	16.67	4	WYOMING	R1-2	29-Jan-51	15.59	4
WARREN	SE4	9-Jul-62	21.07	4	WYOMING	SE5	10-Jul-62	16.19	4
WASHINGTON	PB5-8	22-Jul-57	8.96	3	WYOMING	BJ2-4	2-Nov-51	21.80	4
WASHINGTON	UK9-3	21-May-53	10.08	4	YORK	UK1-2	18-Mar-53	4.90	2
WASHINGTON	R1-2	29-Jan-51	21.83	4	YORK	TS3-4	25-Apr-52	6.03	3
WASHINGTON	SE4	9-Jul-62	85.56	6	YORK	PB5-8	22-Jul-57	8.96	3
WAYNE	BJ3-7	7-Nov-51	4.13	2	YORK	SE4	9-Jul-62	73.06	6
WAYNE	PB5-8	22-Jul-57	5.97	3	YORK	BJ2-3	1-Nov-51	3.50	1

INDIVIDUAL FALLOUT DAYS
RHODE ISLAND

COUNTY	SHOT	DATE	µCi/SQ METER	INDEX		COUNTY	SHOT	DATE	µCi/SQ METER	INDEX
BRISTOL	BJ2-3	1-Nov-51	5.88	3		NEWPORT	BJ2-4	2-Nov-51	10.06	4
BRISTOL	TS7-5	5-Jun-52	7.21	3		NEWPORT	UK4-2	7-Apr-53	65.44	6
BRISTOL	TS8-3	7-Jun-52	8.02	3		NEWPORT	R1-2	29-Jan-51	3.50	1
BRISTOL	BJ2-4	2-Nov-51	10.26	4		PROVIDENCE	TS7-5	5-Jun-52	5.37	3
BRISTOL	TS1-4	4-Apr-52	10.77	4		PROVIDENCE	BJ2-3	1-Nov-51	6.65	3
BRISTOL	UK4-2	7-Apr-53	99.38	6		PROVIDENCE	TS8-3	7-Jun-52	8.56	3
KENT	BJ3-7	7-Nov-51	3.71	2		PROVIDENCE	BJ2-4	2-Nov-51	12.35	4
KENT	PB5-8	22-Jul-57	5.97	3		PROVIDENCE	UK4-2	7-Apr-53	73.45	6
KENT	TS8-3	7-Jun-52	6.48	3		PROVIDENCE	R1-2	29-Jan-51	3.50	1
KENT	TS7-5	5-Jun-52	6.97	3		WASHINGTON	BJ3-7	7-Nov-51	3.71	2
KENT	TS1-4	4-Apr-52	7.18	3		WASHINGTON	TS8-3	7-Jun-52	5.81	3
KENT	BJ2-3	1-Nov-51	7.55	3		WASHINGTON	PB5-8	22-Jul-57	5.97	3
KENT	BJ2-4	2-Nov-51	12.35	4		WASHINGTON	TS1-4	4-Apr-52	7.18	3
KENT	UK4-2	7-Apr-53	82.45	6		WASHINGTON	TS7-5	5-Jun-52	7.21	3
KENT	R1-2	29-Jan-51	3.50	1		WASHINGTON	BJ2-3	1-Nov-51	7.55	3
NEWPORT	TS8-3	7-Jun-52	5.88	3		WASHINGTON	BJ2-4	2-Nov-51	12.45	4
NEWPORT	BJ2-3	1-Nov-51	6.65	3		WASHINGTON	UK4-2	7-Apr-53	99.17	6
NEWPORT	TS1-4	4-Apr-52	7.18	3		WASHINGTON	R1-2	29-Jan-51	3.50	1

INDIVIDUAL FALLOUT DAYS
SOUTH CAROLINA

COUNTY	SHOT	DATE	µCi/SQ METER	INDEX	COUNTY	SHOT	DATE	µCi/SQ METER	INDEX
ABBEVILLE	BJ2-4	2-Nov-51	3.76	2	CALHOUN	BJ2-3	1-Nov-51	6.89	3
ABBEVILLE	PB16-5	27-Sep-57	4.18	2	CALHOUN	TS5-2	8-May-52	7.76	3
ABBEVILLE	BJ2-3	1-Nov-51	4.61	2	CALHOUN	BJ2-4	2-Nov-51	7.87	3
ABBEVILLE	UK9-4	22-May-53	5.87	3	CALHOUN	TS3-4	25-Apr-52	8.50	3
AIKEN	PB16-5	27-Sep-57	3.62	2	CHARLESTON	TS7-6	6-Jun-52	3.61	2
AIKEN	UK9-4	22-May-53	6.06	3	CHARLESTON	PB5-9	23-Jul-57	4.71	2
AIKEN	BJ2-3	1-Nov-51	7.19	3	CHARLESTON	TS3-7	28-Apr-52	5.26	3
ALLENDALE	BJ2-3	1-Nov-51	5.04	3	CHARLESTON	TS5-1	7-May-52	5.39	3
ALLENDALE	UK9-4	22-May-53	5.77	3	CHARLESTON	TS3-4	25-Apr-52	8.50	3
ALLENDALE	BJ2-4	2-Nov-51	8.01	3	CHARLESTON	BJ2-3	1-Nov-51	8.70	3
ANDERSON	PB16-5	27-Sep-57	3.62	2	CHEROKEE	TP10-2	6-May-55	3.62	2
ANDERSON	BJ2-3	1-Nov-51	5.12	3	CHEROKEE	UK9-4	22-May-53	5.05	3
ANDERSON	UK9-4	22-May-53	5.63	3	CHEROKEE	BJ2-3	1-Nov-51	6.11	3
BAMBERG	TS3-4	25-Apr-52	4.20	2	CHESTER	BJ2-4	2-Nov-51	3.83	2
BAMBERG	BJ2-3	1-Nov-51	4.56	2	CHESTER	UK9-4	22-May-53	5.10	3
BAMBERG	UK9-4	22-May-53	4.80	2	CHESTER	BJ2-3	1-Nov-51	6.98	3
BAMBERG	TS5-2	8-May-52	4.81	2	CHESTERFIELD	UK9-4	22-May-53	3.90	2
BAMBERG	BJ2-4	2-Nov-51	8.52	3	CHESTERFIELD	TS7-6	6-Jun-52	4.18	2
BARNWELL	BJ2-3	1-Nov-51	5.47	3	CHESTERFIELD	BJ2-3	1-Nov-51	9.12	3
BARNWELL	UK9-4	22-May-53	5.92	3	CHESTERFIELD	BJ2-4	2-Nov-51	9.35	3
BARNWELL	BJ2-4	2-Nov-51	7.85	3	CLARENDON	UK9-4	22-May-53	4.08	2
BEAUFORT	PB16-5	27-Sep-57	3.52	2	CLARENDON	TS5-2	8-May-52	5.15	3
BEAUFORT	UK9-4	22-May-53	4.04	2	CLARENDON	TS3-7	28-Apr-52	7.89	3
BEAUFORT	BJ2-3	1-Nov-51	5.37	3	CLARENDON	BJ2-3	1-Nov-51	8.47	3
BEAUFORT	TS3-4	25-Apr-52	8.50	3	CLARENDON	BJ2-4	2-Nov-51	9.77	3
BEAUFORT	BJ2-4	2-Nov-51	8.76	3	CLARENDON	TS3-4	25-Apr-52	12.70	4
BERKELEY	TS5-2	8-May-52	3.76	2	COLLETON	TS7-6	6-Jun-52	4.15	2
BERKELEY	BJ2-3	1-Nov-51	5.90	3	COLLETON	UK9-4	22-May-53	4.48	2
BERKELEY	PB11-4	3-Sep-57	7.77	3	COLLETON	BJ2-3	1-Nov-51	7.80	3
BERKELEY	TS3-4	25-Apr-52	8.50	3	COLLETON	TS3-4	25-Apr-52	8.50	3
BERKELEY	BJ2-4	2-Nov-51	10.75	4	COLLETON	BJ2-4	2-Nov-51	10.45	4
CALHOUN	PB11-4	3-Sep-57	3.89	2	DARLINGTON	TS7-6	6-Jun-52	3.68	2
CALHOUN	UK9-4	22-May-53	5.53	3	DARLINGTON	UK9-4	22-May-53	3.94	2

INDIVIDUAL FALLOUT DAYS
SOUTH CAROLINA

COUNTY	SHOT	DATE	µCi/SQ METER	INDEX	COUNTY	SHOT	DATE	µCi/SQ METER	INDEX
DARLINGTON	BJ2-4	2-Nov-51	9.60	3	GREENWOOD	PB16-5	27-Sep-57	3.55	2
DARLINGTON	BJ2-3	1-Nov-51	10.62	4	GREENWOOD	BJ2-4	2-Nov-51	3.84	2
DILLON	PB4-5	9-Jul-57	3.57	2	GREENWOOD	TS6-6	30-May-52	4.20	2
DILLON	TS3-4	25-Apr-52	8.50	3	GREENWOOD	BJ2-3	1-Nov-51	5.15	3
DILLON	BJ2-3	1-Nov-51	8.69	3	GREENWOOD	UK9-4	22-May-53	5.92	3
DILLON	BJ2-4	2-Nov-51	9.10	3	HAMPTON	PB11-4	3-Sep-57	3.89	2
DORCHESTER	UK9-4	22-May-53	3.75	2	HAMPTON	PB16-5	27-Sep-57	4.19	2
DORCHESTER	BJ2-3	1-Nov-51	7.93	3	HAMPTON	UK9-4	22-May-53	4.64	2
DORCHESTER	BJ2-4	2-Nov-51	10.75	4	HAMPTON	BJ2-3	1-Nov-51	6.52	3
DORCHESTER	TS3-4	25-Apr-52	12.70	4	HAMPTON	BJ2-4	2-Nov-51	9.46	3
EDGEFIELD	BJ2-3	1-Nov-51	3.85	2	HORRY	PB4-5	9-Jul-57	3.57	2
EDGEFIELD	PB16-5	27-Sep-57	4.08	2	HORRY	TS3-4	25-Apr-52	8.50	3
EDGEFIELD	UK9-4	22-May-53	6.11	3	HORRY	BJ2-4	2-Nov-51	10.06	4
EDGEFIELD	BJ2-4	2-Nov-51	7.01	3	HORRY	BJ2-3	1-Nov-51	13.05	4
FAIRFIELD	BJ2-4	2-Nov-51	3.69	2	JASPER	PB16-5	27-Sep-57	4.15	2
FAIRFIELD	UK9-4	22-May-53	5.34	3	JASPER	UK9-4	22-May-53	4.28	2
FAIRFIELD	BJ2-3	1-Nov-51	6.80	3	JASPER	BJ2-3	1-Nov-51	6.65	3
FLORENCE	PB4-5	9-Jul-57	3.57	2	JASPER	BJ2-4	2-Nov-51	8.76	3
FLORENCE	UK9-4	22-May-53	3.90	2	JASPER	PB11-4	3-Sep-57	11.66	4
FLORENCE	TS3-7	28-Apr-52	5.26	3	JASPER	TS3-4	25-Apr-52	12.70	4
FLORENCE	BJ2-4	2-Nov-51	9.43	3	KERSHAW	BJ2-4	2-Nov-51	4.04	2
FLORENCE	BJ2-3	1-Nov-51	12.54	4	KERSHAW	UK9-4	22-May-53	4.76	2
FLORENCE	TS3-4	25-Apr-52	12.70	4	KERSHAW	SE6	11-Jul-62	7.67	3
FLORENCE	PB11-4	3-Sep-57	19.43	4	KERSHAW	BJ2-3	1-Nov-51	8.59	3
GEORGETOWN	PB4-5	9-Jul-57	3.57	2	LANCASTER	UK9-4	22-May-53	4.52	2
GEORGETOWN	BJ2-3	1-Nov-51	5.26	3	LANCASTER	BJ2-4	2-Nov-51	7.59	3
GEORGETOWN	BJ2-4	2-Nov-51	10.45	4	LANCASTER	BJ2-3	1-Nov-51	9.55	3
GREENVILLE	TP10-2	6-May-55	3.62	2	LAURENS	TP10-2	6-May-55	3.62	2
GREENVILLE	BJ2-2	31-Oct-51	3.89	2	LAURENS	PB16-5	27-Sep-57	3.72	2
GREENVILLE	PB2-5	22-Jun-57	4.18	2	LAURENS	UK9-4	22-May-53	5.68	3
GREENVILLE	TS6-6	30-May-52	4.26	2	LAURENS	BJ2-3	1-Nov-51	6.01	3
GREENVILLE	UK9-4	22-May-53	5.29	3	LEE	UK9-4	22-May-53	4.52	2
GREENVILLE	BJ2-3	1-Nov-51	5.76	3	LEE	BJ2-4	2-Nov-51	8.22	3

INDIVIDUAL FALLOUT DAYS
SOUTH CAROLINA

COUNTY	SHOT	DATE	µCi/SQ METER	INDEX	COUNTY	SHOT	DATE	µCi/SQ METER	INDEX
LEE	BJ2-3	1-Nov-51	10.40	4	PICKENS	PB2-5	22-Jun-57	4.18	2
LEE	TS3-4	25-Apr-52	21.20	4	PICKENS	TP6-4	25-Mar-55	4.32	2
LEXINGTON	BJ2-4	2-Nov-51	5.68	3	PICKENS	BJ2-3	1-Nov-51	4.61	2
LEXINGTON	UK9-4	22-May-53	5.82	3	PICKENS	BJ2-4	2-Nov-51	4.68	2
LEXINGTON	BJ2-3	1-Nov-51	6.03	3	PICKENS	UK9-4	22-May-53	5.29	3
MARION	PB4-5	9-Jul-57	3.57	2	PICKENS	UK1-2	18-Mar-53	5.65	3
MARION	TS3-4	25-Apr-52	8.50	3	RICHLAND	UK9-4	22-May-53	5.44	3
MARION	BJ2-4	2-Nov-51	10.75	4	RICHLAND	BJ2-3	1-Nov-51	8.27	3
MARION	BJ2-3	1-Nov-51	13.05	4	SALUDA	PB16-5	27-Sep-57	4.25	2
MARLBORO	PB4-5	9-Jul-57	3.57	2	SALUDA	UK9-4	22-May-53	5.96	3
MARLBORO	BJ2-4	2-Nov-51	4.76	2	SALUDA	BJ2-3	1-Nov-51	6.86	3
MARLBORO	BJ2-3	1-Nov-51	10.62	4	SPARTANBURG	TP10-2	6-May-55	3.62	2
MARLBORO	TS5-2	8-May-52	10.94	4	SPARTANBURG	BJ2-2	31-Oct-51	3.89	2
MCCORMICK	BJ2-3	1-Nov-51	4.61	2	SPARTANBURG	UK9-4	22-May-53	5.24	3
MCCORMICK	PB16-5	27-Sep-57	4.77	2	SPARTANBURG	BJ2-3	1-Nov-51	6.52	3
MCCORMICK	UK9-4	22-May-53	6.06	3	SUMTER	BJ2-4	2-Nov-51	4.25	2
MCCORMICK	BJ2-4	2-Nov-51	6.93	3	SUMTER	PB5-9	23-Jul-57	4.71	2
NEWBERRY	BJ2-3	1-Nov-51	5.46	3	SUMTER	UK9-4	22-May-53	4.95	2
NEWBERRY	UK9-4	22-May-53	5.77	3	SUMTER	TS3-7	28-Apr-52	5.26	3
OCONEE	TP10-2	6-May-55	3.62	2	SUMTER	BJ2-3	1-Nov-51	8.32	3
OCONEE	PB2-5	22-Jun-57	4.18	2	SUMTER	TS3-4	25-Apr-52	12.70	4
OCONEE	BJ2-3	1-Nov-51	4.35	2	UNION	BJ2-4	2-Nov-51	4.42	2
OCONEE	UK9-4	22-May-53	5.29	3	UNION	UK9-4	22-May-53	5.44	3
OCONEE	UK1-2	18-Mar-53	6.27	3	UNION	BJ2-3	1-Nov-51	6.86	3
OCONEE	PB17-3	30-Sep-57	22.47	4	WILLIAMSBURG	UK9-4	22-May-53	3.52	2
ORANGEBURG	PB11-4	3-Sep-57	3.89	2	WILLIAMSBURG	PB4-5	9-Jul-57	3.57	2
ORANGEBURG	UK9-4	22-May-53	4.68	2	WILLIAMSBURG	TS3-4	25-Apr-52	4.20	2
ORANGEBURG	BJ2-3	1-Nov-51	6.08	3	WILLIAMSBURG	TS5-2	8-May-52	5.38	3
ORANGEBURG	TS5-2	8-May-52	7.47	3	WILLIAMSBURG	BJ2-3	1-Nov-51	7.72	3
ORANGEBURG	BJ2-4	2-Nov-51	7.66	3	WILLIAMSBURG	BJ2-4	2-Nov-51	11.15	4
ORANGEBURG	TS3-4	25-Apr-52	8.50	3	YORK	TS7-6	6-Jun-52	3.65	2
PICKENS	TP10-2	6-May-55	3.62	2	YORK	UK9-4	22-May-53	4.76	2
PICKENS	BJ2-2	31-Oct-51	3.89	2	YORK	BJ2-4	2-Nov-51	4.93	2

INDIVIDUAL FALLOUT DAYS
SOUTH CAROLINA

COUNTY	SHOT	DATE	µCi/SQ METER	INDEX		COUNTY	SHOT	DATE	µCi/SQ METER	INDEX
YORK	BJ2-3	1-Nov-51	7.51	3						

INDIVIDUAL FALLOUT DAYS
SOUTH DAKOTA

COUNTY	SHOT	DATE	µCi/SQ METER	INDEX	COUNTY	SHOT	DATE	µCi/SQ METER	INDEX
AURORA	UK2-2	25-Mar-53	3.97	2	BENNETT	PB8-3	20-Aug-57	19.73	4
AURORA	TP9-3	16-Apr-55	5.82	3	BENNETT	TS5-1	7-May-52	22.09	4
AURORA	PB5-4	18-Jul-57	5.89	3	BENNETT	PB2-3	20-Jun-57	30.08	5
AURORA	TS5-1	7-May-52	10.79	4	BENNETT	UK2-2	25-Mar-53	45.45	5
AURORA	PB8-5	22-Aug-57	11.33	4	BON HOMME	UK2-2	25-Mar-53	3.97	2
AURORA	UK7-4	28-Apr-53	14.05	4	BON HOMME	PB15-3	18-Sep-57	4.13	2
AURORA	PB8-3	20-Aug-57	19.73	4	BON HOMME	PB11-2	1-Sep-57	4.58	2
AURORA	PB15-2	17-Sep-57	20.04	4	BON HOMME	PB2-3	20-Jun-57	7.54	3
AURORA	TS7-4	4-Jun-52	21.79	4	BON HOMME	UK7-4	28-Apr-53	11.01	4
AURORA	TS8-1	5-Jun-52	26.59	5	BON HOMME	TS7-4	4-Jun-52	11.74	4
AURORA	PB11-2	1-Sep-57	27.46	5	BON HOMME	TS5-1	7-May-52	13.79	4
AURORA	PB2-3	20-Jun-57	45.16	5	BON HOMME	PB8-3	20-Aug-57	19.73	4
BEADLE	PB9-3	25-Aug-57	3.88	2	BROOKINGS	TS6-3	27-May-52	3.66	2
BEADLE	TP9-3	16-Apr-55	3.93	2	BROOKINGS	UK2-2	25-Mar-53	3.97	2
BEADLE	PB9-4	26-Aug-57	5.22	3	BROOKINGS	TP9-3	16-Apr-55	3.97	2
BEADLE	PB5-4	18-Jul-57	5.89	3	BROOKINGS	UK7-5	29-Apr-53	4.51	2
BEADLE	PB8-5	22-Aug-57	7.56	3	BROOKINGS	PB11-2	1-Sep-57	4.58	2
BEADLE	UK7-4	28-Apr-53	8.87	3	BROOKINGS	TS5-1	7-May-52	5.93	3
BEADLE	PB11-2	1-Sep-57	9.15	3	BROOKINGS	TS7-5	5-Jun-52	6.83	3
BEADLE	TS7-4	4-Jun-52	18.36	4	BROOKINGS	UK7-4	28-Apr-53	8.77	3
BEADLE	PB8-3	20-Aug-57	19.73	4	BROOKINGS	PB8-5	22-Aug-57	11.33	4
BEADLE	PB15-2	17-Sep-57	20.04	4	BROOKINGS	PB2-3	20-Jun-57	15.08	4
BEADLE	TS8-1	5-Jun-52	26.59	5	BROOKINGS	TS7-4	4-Jun-52	23.37	4
BEADLE	PB2-3	20-Jun-57	45.16	5	BROOKINGS	PB8-3	20-Aug-57	78.93	6
BENNETT	PB8-5	22-Aug-57	3.78	2	BROOKINGS	SE3	8-Jul-62	181.88	7
BENNETT	PB11-2	1-Sep-57	4.58	2	BROWN	PB8-5	22-Aug-57	3.78	2
BENNETT	PB9-3	25-Aug-57	5.87	3	BROWN	UK2-2	25-Mar-53	3.97	2
BENNETT	PB5-4	18-Jul-57	8.86	3	BROWN	UK7-4	28-Apr-53	5.88	3
BENNETT	TS5-2	8-May-52	10.99	4	BROWN	PB15-2	17-Sep-57	13.36	4
BENNETT	UK7-4	28-Apr-53	12.18	4	BROWN	PB8-3	20-Aug-57	19.73	4
BENNETT	TS8-1	5-Jun-52	13.29	4	BROWN	TS8-1	5-Jun-52	26.59	5
BENNETT	PB15-2	17-Sep-57	13.36	4	BROWN	PB11-2	1-Sep-57	27.46	5
BENNETT	PB8-4	21-Aug-57	13.41	4	BROWN	PB2-3	20-Jun-57	30.08	5

INDIVIDUAL FALLOUT DAYS
SOUTH DAKOTA

COUNTY	SHOT	DATE	µCi/SQ METER	INDEX	COUNTY	SHOT	DATE	µCi/SQ METER	INDEX
BRULE	PB12-3	4-Sep-57	3.54	2	BUTTE	PB8-4	21-Aug-57	8.05	3
BRULE	PB9-3	25-Aug-57	3.88	2	BUTTE	PB5-2	16-Jul-57	9.68	3
BRULE	UK2-2	25-Mar-53	3.97	2	BUTTE	UK7-4	28-Apr-53	11.33	4
BRULE	TP9-3	16-Apr-55	4.02	2	BUTTE	TS8-1	5-Jun-52	13.29	4
BRULE	TS5-1	7-May-52	4.99	2	BUTTE	PB5-3	17-Jul-57	15.18	4
BRULE	TS5-2	8-May-52	6.19	3	BUTTE	PB8-3	20-Aug-57	19.73	4
BRULE	PB8-5	22-Aug-57	7.56	3	BUTTE	TS5-1	7-May-52	24.13	4
BRULE	TS7-3	3-Jun-52	12.47	4	BUTTE	UK2-2	25-Mar-53	45.45	5
BRULE	PB15-2	17-Sep-57	13.36	4	CAMPBELL	UK2-2	25-Mar-53	3.97	2
BRULE	UK7-4	28-Apr-53	14.54	4	CAMPBELL	PB8-4	21-Aug-57	5.37	3
BRULE	PB8-3	20-Aug-57	19.73	4	CAMPBELL	PB9-3	25-Aug-57	5.87	3
BRULE	TS8-1	5-Jun-52	26.59	5	CAMPBELL	PB5-4	18-Jul-57	8.86	3
BRULE	PB11-2	1-Sep-57	27.46	5	CAMPBELL	UK7-4	28-Apr-53	11.35	4
BRULE	TS7-4	4-Jun-52	27.64	5	CAMPBELL	PB11-2	1-Sep-57	18.31	4
BRULE	PB2-3	20-Jun-57	45.16	5	CAMPBELL	PB8-3	20-Aug-57	19.73	4
BUFFALO	PB12-3	4-Sep-57	3.71	2	CAMPBELL	PB15-2	17-Sep-57	20.04	4
BUFFALO	PB8-5	22-Aug-57	3.78	2	CAMPBELL	TS8-1	5-Jun-52	26.59	5
BUFFALO	TS5-2	8-May-52	3.90	2	CAMPBELL	PB2-3	20-Jun-57	45.16	5
BUFFALO	UK2-2	25-Mar-53	3.97	2	CHARLES MIX	TS7-5	5-Jun-52	3.56	2
BUFFALO	TS5-1	7-May-52	8.69	3	CHARLES MIX	PB8-5	22-Aug-57	3.78	2
BUFFALO	PB11-2	1-Sep-57	9.15	3	CHARLES MIX	UK2-2	25-Mar-53	3.97	2
BUFFALO	PB15-2	17-Sep-57	13.36	4	CHARLES MIX	TS5-2	8-May-52	4.45	2
BUFFALO	UK7-4	28-Apr-53	15.18	4	CHARLES MIX	PB8-4	21-Aug-57	5.37	3
BUFFALO	PB8-3	20-Aug-57	19.73	4	CHARLES MIX	TS7-3	3-Jun-52	8.12	3
BUFFALO	TS7-4	4-Jun-52	25.40	5	CHARLES MIX	PB11-2	1-Sep-57	9.15	3
BUFFALO	TS8-1	5-Jun-52	26.59	5	CHARLES MIX	PB15-2	17-Sep-57	13.36	4
BUFFALO	PB2-3	20-Jun-57	45.16	5	CHARLES MIX	PB2-3	20-Jun-57	15.08	4
BUTTE	PB6-4	27-Jul-57	3.68	2	CHARLES MIX	TS5-1	7-May-52	15.58	4
BUTTE	TS8-3	7-Jun-52	4.41	2	CHARLES MIX	UK7-4	28-Apr-53	15.61	4
BUTTE	PB9-4	26-Aug-57	5.22	3	CHARLES MIX	PB8-3	20-Aug-57	19.73	4
BUTTE	PB9-3	25-Aug-57	5.87	3	CHARLES MIX	TS7-4	4-Jun-52	24.47	4
BUTTE	TS7-3	3-Jun-52	6.72	3	CHARLES MIX	TS8-1	5-Jun-52	26.59	5
BUTTE	PB11-2	1-Sep-57	6.81	3	CLARK	UK2-2	25-Mar-53	3.97	2

INDIVIDUAL FALLOUT DAYS
SOUTH DAKOTA

COUNTY	SHOT	DATE	µCi/SQ METER	INDEX	COUNTY	SHOT	DATE	µCi/SQ METER	INDEX
CLARK	PB9-4	26-Aug-57	5.22	3	CORSON	PB6-5	28-Jul-57	3.93	2
CLARK	PB5-4	18-Jul-57	5.89	3	CORSON	TS5-1	7-May-52	4.05	2
CLARK	UK7-4	28-Apr-53	7.22	3	CORSON	TS7-4	4-Jun-52	4.66	2
CLARK	PB8-5	22-Aug-57	7.56	3	CORSON	PB8-4	21-Aug-57	5.37	3
CLARK	TS7-4	4-Jun-52	17.08	4	CORSON	PB8-5	22-Aug-57	7.56	3
CLARK	PB11-2	1-Sep-57	18.31	4	CORSON	PB11-2	1-Sep-57	9.15	3
CLARK	PB8-3	20-Aug-57	19.73	4	CORSON	UK7-4	28-Apr-53	14.54	4
CLARK	PB15-2	17-Sep-57	20.04	4	CORSON	PB8-3	20-Aug-57	19.73	4
CLARK	PB2-3	20-Jun-57	30.08	5	CORSON	PB15-2	17-Sep-57	20.04	4
CLAY	UK7-5	29-Apr-53	3.67	2	CORSON	TS8-1	5-Jun-52	26.59	5
CLAY	UK9-3	21-May-53	3.91	2	CORSON	PB2-3	20-Jun-57	30.08	5
CLAY	UK2-2	25-Mar-53	3.97	2	CORSON	UK2-2	25-Mar-53	45.45	5
CLAY	PB12-4	5-Sep-57	4.19	2	CUSTER	PB9-4	26-Aug-57	3.68	2
CLAY	PB9-4	26-Aug-57	5.22	3	CUSTER	PB5-2	16-Jul-57	4.90	2
CLAY	UK9-2	20-May-53	5.52	3	CUSTER	TS5-2	8-May-52	5.27	3
CLAY	TS6-3	27-May-52	7.77	3	CUSTER	PB11-2	1-Sep-57	6.81	3
CLAY	UK7-4	28-Apr-53	11.67	4	CUSTER	UK7-4	28-Apr-53	6.98	3
CLAY	TS7-4	4-Jun-52	19.13	4	CUSTER	PB9-3	25-Aug-57	7.76	3
CLAY	PB8-3	20-Aug-57	19.73	4	CUSTER	TS7-4	4-Jun-52	13.52	4
CLAY	SE3	8-Jul-62	208.70	8	CUSTER	UK2-2	25-Mar-53	45.45	5
CODINGTON	UK7-5	29-Apr-53	3.73	2	CUSTER	TS5-1	7-May-52	50.01	6
CODINGTON	PB9-3	25-Aug-57	3.88	2	CUSTER	TS7-3	3-Jun-52	150.62	7
CODINGTON	UK2-2	25-Mar-53	3.97	2	CUSTER	SE2	7-Jul-62	434.17	9
CODINGTON	PB11-2	1-Sep-57	4.58	2	DAVISON	UK2-2	25-Mar-53	3.97	2
CODINGTON	PB9-4	26-Aug-57	5.22	3	DAVISON	TS5-2	8-May-52	4.11	2
CODINGTON	PB8-4	21-Aug-57	5.37	3	DAVISON	PB15-2	17-Sep-57	6.68	3
CODINGTON	UK7-4	28-Apr-53	7.11	3	DAVISON	PB11-2	1-Sep-57	9.15	3
CODINGTON	PB8-5	22-Aug-57	7.56	3	DAVISON	TP9-3	16-Apr-55	10.00	4
CODINGTON	TS7-4	4-Jun-52	10.29	4	DAVISON	UK7-4	28-Apr-53	10.48	4
CODINGTON	PB8-3	20-Aug-57	19.73	4	DAVISON	PB2-3	20-Jun-57	15.08	4
CODINGTON	PB15-2	17-Sep-57	33.40	5	DAVISON	PB8-5	22-Aug-57	18.89	4
CODINGTON	PB2-3	20-Jun-57	45.16	5	DAVISON	PB8-3	20-Aug-57	19.73	4
CORSON	PB9-3	25-Aug-57	3.88	2	DAVISON	TS7-4	4-Jun-52	28.86	5

INDIVIDUAL FALLOUT DAYS
SOUTH DAKOTA

COUNTY	SHOT	DATE	µCi/SQ METER	INDEX	COUNTY	SHOT	DATE	µCi/SQ METER	INDEX
DAVISON	SE3	8-Jul-62	208.70	8	DOUGLAS	TS5-1	7-May-52	10.34	4
DAY	UK2-2	25-Mar-53	3.97	2	DOUGLAS	PB2-3	20-Jun-57	15.08	4
DAY	UK7-4	28-Apr-53	4.60	2	DOUGLAS	UK7-4	28-Apr-53	15.93	4
DAY	TP9-3	16-Apr-55	5.16	3	DOUGLAS	TS7-3	3-Jun-52	16.43	4
DAY	PB5-4	18-Jul-57	5.89	3	DOUGLAS	PB8-3	20-Aug-57	19.73	4
DAY	TS7-4	4-Jun-52	6.58	3	DOUGLAS	TS8-1	5-Jun-52	26.59	5
DAY	PB8-3	20-Aug-57	19.73	4	DOUGLAS	TS7-4	4-Jun-52	35.69	5
DAY	PB15-2	17-Sep-57	20.04	4	EDMUNDS	PB11-4	3-Sep-57	3.89	2
DAY	PB11-2	1-Sep-57	27.46	5	EDMUNDS	UK2-2	25-Mar-53	3.97	2
DAY	PB2-3	20-Jun-57	45.16	5	EDMUNDS	TS7-4	4-Jun-52	4.05	2
DEUEL	TS6-3	27-May-52	3.74	2	EDMUNDS	PB5-4	18-Jul-57	5.89	3
DEUEL	UK2-2	25-Mar-53	3.97	2	EDMUNDS	PB8-5	22-Aug-57	7.56	3
DEUEL	UK7-5	29-Apr-53	4.73	2	EDMUNDS	UK7-4	28-Apr-53	10.52	4
DEUEL	UK7-4	28-Apr-53	7.06	3	EDMUNDS	PB2-3	20-Jun-57	15.08	4
DEUEL	TS7-4	4-Jun-52	11.69	4	EDMUNDS	PB8-3	20-Aug-57	19.73	4
DEWEY	PB9-3	25-Aug-57	5.87	3	EDMUNDS	PB15-2	17-Sep-57	20.04	4
DEWEY	TS7-4	4-Jun-52	7.17	3	EDMUNDS	TS8-1	5-Jun-52	26.59	5
DEWEY	PB8-5	22-Aug-57	7.56	3	EDMUNDS	PB11-2	1-Sep-57	27.46	5
DEWEY	TS5-1	7-May-52	7.72	3	FALL RIVER	PB5-3	17-Jul-57	3.80	2
DEWEY	PB5-4	18-Jul-57	8.86	3	FALL RIVER	PB13-3	8-Sep-57	4.48	2
DEWEY	PB11-2	1-Sep-57	9.15	3	FALL RIVER	TS5-2	8-May-52	6.19	3
DEWEY	UK7-4	28-Apr-53	18.04	4	FALL RIVER	UK7-4	28-Apr-53	6.42	3
DEWEY	PB8-3	20-Aug-57	19.73	4	FALL RIVER	PB9-3	25-Aug-57	7.76	3
DEWEY	PB15-2	17-Sep-57	20.04	4	FALL RIVER	TS7-3	3-Jun-52	8.44	3
DEWEY	TS8-1	5-Jun-52	26.59	5	FALL RIVER	PB5-2	16-Jul-57	9.68	3
DEWEY	PB2-3	20-Jun-57	45.16	5	FALL RIVER	TS7-4	4-Jun-52	24.74	4
DEWEY	UK2-2	25-Mar-53	45.45	5	FALL RIVER	UK2-2	25-Mar-53	45.45	5
DOUGLAS	TS5-2	8-May-52	3.76	2	FALL RIVER	TS5-1	7-May-52	65.48	6
DOUGLAS	PB8-5	22-Aug-57	3.78	2	FALL RIVER	SE2	7-Jul-62	345.60	8
DOUGLAS	TP9-3	16-Apr-55	3.81	2	FAULK	PB8-5	22-Aug-57	3.78	2
DOUGLAS	UK2-2	25-Mar-53	3.97	2	FAULK	UK2-2	25-Mar-53	3.97	2
DOUGLAS	PB11-2	1-Sep-57	4.58	2	FAULK	TS5-1	7-May-52	4.65	2
DOUGLAS	PB5-4	18-Jul-57	5.89	3	FAULK	PB9-4	26-Aug-57	5.22	3

INDIVIDUAL FALLOUT DAYS
SOUTH DAKOTA

COUNTY	SHOT	DATE	µCi/SQ METER	INDEX	COUNTY	SHOT	DATE	µCi/SQ METER	INDEX
FAULK	UK7-4	28-Apr-53	11.01	4	HAAKON	PB15-2	17-Sep-57	20.04	4
FAULK	TS7-4	4-Jun-52	19.54	4	HAAKON	UK7-4	28-Apr-53	23.27	4
FAULK	PB15-2	17-Sep-57	20.04	4	HAAKON	TS7-4	4-Jun-52	25.27	5
FAULK	TS8-1	5-Jun-52	26.59	5	HAAKON	TS7-3	3-Jun-52	29.91	5
FAULK	PB11-2	1-Sep-57	27.46	5	HAAKON	PB2-3	20-Jun-57	30.08	5
FAULK	PB8-3	20-Aug-57	39.46	5	HAAKON	UK2-2	25-Mar-53	45.45	5
FAULK	PB2-3	20-Jun-57	45.16	5	HAMLIN	UK7-5	29-Apr-53	3.76	2
GRANT	UK2-2	25-Mar-53	3.97	2	HAMLIN	UK2-2	25-Mar-53	3.97	2
GRANT	UK7-5	29-Apr-53	4.39	2	HAMLIN	TP9-3	16-Apr-55	3.97	2
GRANT	UK7-4	28-Apr-53	4.49	2	HAMLIN	PB15-3	18-Sep-57	4.13	2
GRANT	TS6-3	27-May-52	4.93	2	HAMLIN	PB5-4	18-Jul-57	5.89	3
GRANT	TS7-5	5-Jun-52	10.00	3	HAMLIN	UK7-4	28-Apr-53	8.45	3
GREGORY	UK2-2	25-Mar-53	3.97	2	HAMLIN	PB11-2	1-Sep-57	9.15	3
GREGORY	PB11-2	1-Sep-57	4.58	2	HAMLIN	PB8-5	22-Aug-57	11.33	4
GREGORY	TS5-2	8-May-52	5.70	3	HAMLIN	TS7-4	4-Jun-52	18.12	4
GREGORY	PB8-5	22-Aug-57	7.56	3	HAMLIN	PB8-3	20-Aug-57	19.73	4
GREGORY	TS7-3	3-Jun-52	9.68	3	HAMLIN	PB15-2	17-Sep-57	20.04	4
GREGORY	PB15-2	17-Sep-57	13.36	4	HAMLIN	PB2-3	20-Jun-57	30.08	5
GREGORY	PB2-3	20-Jun-57	15.08	4	HAMLIN	SE3	8-Jul-62	90.43	6
GREGORY	TS5-1	7-May-52	16.52	4	HAMLIN	SE2	7-Jul-62	361.42	8
GREGORY	PB8-3	20-Aug-57	19.73	4	HAND	TS5-1	7-May-52	3.87	2
GREGORY	UK7-4	28-Apr-53	20.53	4	HAND	PB9-3	25-Aug-57	3.88	2
GREGORY	TS7-4	4-Jun-52	24.74	4	HAND	UK2-2	25-Mar-53	3.97	2
GREGORY	TS8-1	5-Jun-52	26.59	5	HAND	PB9-4	26-Aug-57	5.22	3
HAAKON	TS5-2	8-May-52	4.73	2	HAND	PB11-2	1-Sep-57	9.15	3
HAAKON	PB11-4	3-Sep-57	5.18	3	HAND	UK7-4	28-Apr-53	11.15	4
HAAKON	PB8-5	22-Aug-57	7.56	3	HAND	PB8-3	20-Aug-57	19.73	4
HAAKON	PB8-4	21-Aug-57	8.05	3	HAND	PB15-2	17-Sep-57	20.04	4
HAAKON	PB5-4	18-Jul-57	8.86	3	HAND	TS8-1	5-Jun-52	26.59	5
HAAKON	PB11-2	1-Sep-57	9.15	3	HAND	TS7-4	4-Jun-52	27.97	5
HAAKON	TS5-1	7-May-52	10.24	4	HAND	PB2-3	20-Jun-57	30.08	5
HAAKON	TS8-1	5-Jun-52	13.29	4	HANSON	UK2-2	25-Mar-53	3.97	2
HAAKON	PB8-3	20-Aug-57	19.73	4	HANSON	PB11-2	1-Sep-57	4.58	2

INDIVIDUAL FALLOUT DAYS
SOUTH DAKOTA

COUNTY	SHOT	DATE	µCi/SQ METER	INDEX	COUNTY	SHOT	DATE	µCi/SQ METER	INDEX
HANSON	TS5-1	7-May-52	4.99	2	HUGHES	TS8-1	5-Jun-52	26.59	5
HANSON	PB9-4	26-Aug-57	5.22	3	HUGHES	TS7-4	4-Jun-52	28.53	5
HANSON	TP9-3	16-Apr-55	6.85	3	HUTCHINSON	PB8-5	22-Aug-57	3.78	2
HANSON	UK7-4	28-Apr-53	10.03	4	HUTCHINSON	UK2-2	25-Mar-53	3.97	2
HANSON	PB2-3	20-Jun-57	15.08	4	HUTCHINSON	TS6-3	27-May-52	4.42	2
HANSON	PB8-5	22-Aug-57	18.89	4	HUTCHINSON	TP9-3	16-Apr-55	4.51	2
HANSON	PB8-3	20-Aug-57	19.73	4	HUTCHINSON	PB11-2	1-Sep-57	4.58	2
HANSON	TS7-4	4-Jun-52	34.32	5	HUTCHINSON	TS5-1	7-May-52	9.14	3
HANSON	SE3	8-Jul-62	220.22	8	HUTCHINSON	UK7-4	28-Apr-53	11.65	4
HARDING	PB8-5	22-Aug-57	3.78	2	HUTCHINSON	PB2-3	20-Jun-57	15.08	4
HARDING	PB9-3	25-Aug-57	3.88	2	HUTCHINSON	PB8-3	20-Aug-57	19.73	4
HARDING	PB11-4	3-Sep-57	5.18	3	HUTCHINSON	PB15-2	17-Sep-57	20.04	4
HARDING	PB8-4	21-Aug-57	5.37	3	HUTCHINSON	TS7-4	4-Jun-52	55.40	6
HARDING	PB6-5	28-Jul-57	5.87	3	HUTCHINSON	SE3	8-Jul-62	208.70	8
HARDING	PB5-2	16-Jul-57	9.68	3	HUTCHINSON	SE2	7-Jul-62	138.24	7
HARDING	PB5-3	17-Jul-57	10.10	4	HYDE	PB9-3	25-Aug-57	3.88	2
HARDING	UK7-4	28-Apr-53	12.14	4	HYDE	PB12-3	4-Sep-57	3.97	2
HARDING	PB11-2	1-Sep-57	18.31	4	HYDE	UK2-2	25-Mar-53	3.97	2
HARDING	PB15-2	17-Sep-57	20.04	4	HYDE	PB9-4	26-Aug-57	5.22	3
HARDING	TS5-1	7-May-52	22.09	4	HYDE	TS5-1	7-May-52	6.44	3
HARDING	PB8-3	20-Aug-57	39.46	5	HYDE	PB11-2	1-Sep-57	9.15	3
HARDING	UK2-2	25-Mar-53	45.45	5	HYDE	UK7-4	28-Apr-53	15.18	4
HARDING	TS8-1	5-Jun-52	53.18	6	HYDE	PB8-3	20-Aug-57	19.73	4
HUGHES	PB11-2	1-Sep-57	3.80	2	HYDE	PB15-2	17-Sep-57	20.04	4
HUGHES	TS5-2	8-May-52	3.97	2	HYDE	TS8-1	5-Jun-52	26.59	5
HUGHES	UK2-2	25-Mar-53	3.97	2	HYDE	TS7-4	4-Jun-52	31.79	5
HUGHES	PB12-3	4-Sep-57	4.48	2	HYDE	PB2-3	20-Jun-57	45.16	5
HUGHES	PB6-5	28-Jul-57	4.80	2	JACKSON	PB8-5	22-Aug-57	3.78	2
HUGHES	PB15-2	17-Sep-57	5.55	3	JACKSON	PB11-2	1-Sep-57	4.58	2
HUGHES	PB8-3	20-Aug-57	8.19	3	JACKSON	PB11-4	3-Sep-57	5.18	3
HUGHES	TS5-1	7-May-52	12.21	4	JACKSON	PB5-4	18-Jul-57	8.86	3
HUGHES	PB2-3	20-Jun-57	12.49	4	JACKSON	TS5-1	7-May-52	12.39	4
HUGHES	UK7-4	28-Apr-53	24.93	4	JACKSON	TS8-1	5-Jun-52	13.29	4

INDIVIDUAL FALLOUT DAYS
SOUTH DAKOTA

COUNTY	SHOT	DATE	µCi/SQ METER	INDEX	COUNTY	SHOT	DATE	µCi/SQ METER	INDEX
JACKSON	PB8-4	21-Aug-57	13.41	4	JONES	TS7-4	4-Jun-52	36.82	5
JACKSON	PB8-3	20-Aug-57	19.73	4	KINGSBURY	PB11-4	3-Sep-57	3.89	2
JACKSON	PB15-2	17-Sep-57	20.04	4	KINGSBURY	UK2-2	25-Mar-53	3.97	2
JACKSON	UK7-4	28-Apr-53	20.34	4	KINGSBURY	PB15-3	18-Sep-57	4.13	2
JACKSON	PB2-3	20-Jun-57	30.08	5	KINGSBURY	TP9-3	16-Apr-55	4.80	2
JACKSON	TS7-4	4-Jun-52	35.25	5	KINGSBURY	UK7-4	28-Apr-53	8.83	3
JACKSON	UK2-2	25-Mar-53	45.45	5	KINGSBURY	PB11-2	1-Sep-57	9.15	3
JERAULD	UK2-2	25-Mar-53	3.97	2	KINGSBURY	PB8-5	22-Aug-57	18.89	4
JERAULD	PB11-2	1-Sep-57	4.58	2	KINGSBURY	PB15-2	17-Sep-57	20.04	4
JERAULD	TS5-1	7-May-52	4.69	2	KINGSBURY	TS7-4	4-Jun-52	24.47	4
JERAULD	TS5-2	8-May-52	5.50	3	KINGSBURY	PB2-3	20-Jun-57	30.08	5
JERAULD	PB5-4	18-Jul-57	5.89	3	KINGSBURY	PB8-3	20-Aug-57	39.46	5
JERAULD	TP9-3	16-Apr-55	7.28	3	KINGSBURY	SE2	7-Jul-62	361.42	8
JERAULD	PB8-5	22-Aug-57	7.56	3	LAKE	UK7-5	29-Apr-53	3.79	2
JERAULD	PB15-2	17-Sep-57	13.36	4	LAKE	UK2-2	25-Mar-53	3.97	2
JERAULD	UK7-4	28-Apr-53	14.23	4	LAKE	TP9-3	16-Apr-55	4.40	2
JERAULD	PB8-3	20-Aug-57	19.73	4	LAKE	TS6-3	27-May-52	4.68	2
JERAULD	TS7-4	4-Jun-52	25.25	5	LAKE	UK7-4	28-Apr-53	10.85	4
JERAULD	TS8-1	5-Jun-52	26.59	5	LAKE	PB2-3	20-Jun-57	15.08	4
JERAULD	PB2-3	20-Jun-57	30.08	5	LAKE	PB11-2	1-Sep-57	18.31	4
JERAULD	SE2	7-Jul-62	145.87	7	LAKE	PB8-5	22-Aug-57	18.89	4
JONES	PB6-5	28-Jul-57	3.67	2	LAKE	PB8-3	20-Aug-57	19.73	4
JONES	UK2-2	25-Mar-53	3.97	2	LAKE	PB15-2	17-Sep-57	20.04	4
JONES	PB11-2	1-Sep-57	4.58	2	LAKE	TS7-4	4-Jun-52	39.03	5
JONES	TS5-2	8-May-52	4.87	2	LAKE	SE3	8-Jul-62	327.38	8
JONES	PB8-5	22-Aug-57	7.56	3	LAWRENCE	PB8-4	21-Aug-57	4.60	2
JONES	TS5-1	7-May-52	8.98	3	LAWRENCE	PB5-2	16-Jul-57	4.90	2
JONES	PB9-3	25-Aug-57	9.75	3	LAWRENCE	TS5-2	8-May-52	4.92	2
JONES	PB15-2	17-Sep-57	13.36	4	LAWRENCE	PB6-4	27-Jul-57	6.05	3
JONES	UK7-4	28-Apr-53	17.98	4	LAWRENCE	PB9-4	26-Aug-57	7.36	3
JONES	PB8-3	20-Aug-57	19.73	4	LAWRENCE	PB9-3	25-Aug-57	7.76	3
JONES	TS8-1	5-Jun-52	26.59	5	LAWRENCE	TS7-3	3-Jun-52	9.07	3
JONES	PB2-3	20-Jun-57	30.08	5	LAWRENCE	UK7-4	28-Apr-53	10.30	4

INDIVIDUAL FALLOUT DAYS
SOUTH DAKOTA

COUNTY	SHOT	DATE	µCi/SQ METER	INDEX	COUNTY	SHOT	DATE	µCi/SQ METER	INDEX
LAWRENCE	TS8-1	5-Jun-52	11.09	4	MARSHALL	PB2-3	20-Jun-57	30.08	5
LAWRENCE	PB5-3	17-Jul-57	15.18	4	MARSHALL	PB11-2	1-Sep-57	45.77	5
LAWRENCE	TS5-1	7-May-52	26.97	5	MCCOOK	UK2-2	25-Mar-53	3.97	2
LAWRENCE	UK2-2	25-Mar-53	45.45	5	MCCOOK	TS5-1	7-May-52	4.24	2
LINCOLN	UK9-2	20-May-53	3.70	2	MCCOOK	TP9-3	16-Apr-55	4.40	2
LINCOLN	UK2-2	25-Mar-53	3.97	2	MCCOOK	TS5-2	8-May-52	4.46	2
LINCOLN	UK7-5	29-Apr-53	4.27	2	MCCOOK	PB11-2	1-Sep-57	4.58	2
LINCOLN	PB12-4	5-Sep-57	4.86	2	MCCOOK	TS6-3	27-May-52	5.02	3
LINCOLN	PB9-4	26-Aug-57	5.22	3	MCCOOK	PB8-4	21-Aug-57	5.37	3
LINCOLN	TS6-3	27-May-52	7.48	3	MCCOOK	UK7-4	28-Apr-53	11.55	4
LINCOLN	UK7-4	28-Apr-53	12.18	4	MCCOOK	PB15-2	17-Sep-57	13.36	4
LINCOLN	PB8-3	20-Aug-57	19.73	4	MCCOOK	PB2-3	20-Jun-57	15.08	4
LINCOLN	TS7-4	4-Jun-52	47.59	5	MCCOOK	PB8-5	22-Aug-57	18.89	4
LINCOLN	SE3	8-Jul-62	208.70	8	MCCOOK	PB8-3	20-Aug-57	19.73	4
LYMAN	UK2-2	25-Mar-53	3.97	2	MCCOOK	TS7-4	4-Jun-52	33.28	5
LYMAN	PB12-3	4-Sep-57	4.14	2	MCCOOK	SE3	8-Jul-62	208.70	8
LYMAN	TS5-2	8-May-52	4.38	2	MCCOOK	SE2	7-Jul-62	138.24	7
LYMAN	PB9-4	26-Aug-57	5.22	3	MCPHERSON	TS7-4	4-Jun-52	3.72	2
LYMAN	PB9-3	25-Aug-57	5.87	3	MCPHERSON	PB9-3	25-Aug-57	3.88	2
LYMAN	TS5-1	7-May-52	9.16	3	MCPHERSON	UK2-2	25-Mar-53	3.97	2
LYMAN	PB8-5	22-Aug-57	11.33	4	MCPHERSON	PB9-4	26-Aug-57	5.22	3
LYMAN	PB15-2	17-Sep-57	13.36	4	MCPHERSON	PB5-4	18-Jul-57	5.89	3
LYMAN	TS7-3	3-Jun-52	13.48	4	MCPHERSON	PB8-5	22-Aug-57	7.56	3
LYMAN	PB11-2	1-Sep-57	18.31	4	MCPHERSON	UK7-4	28-Apr-53	8.03	3
LYMAN	UK7-4	28-Apr-53	19.19	4	MCPHERSON	PB2-3	20-Jun-57	15.08	4
LYMAN	PB8-3	20-Aug-57	19.73	4	MCPHERSON	PB8-3	20-Aug-57	19.73	4
LYMAN	TS8-1	5-Jun-52	26.59	5	MCPHERSON	PB15-2	17-Sep-57	20.04	4
LYMAN	TS7-4	4-Jun-52	38.52	5	MCPHERSON	TS8-1	5-Jun-52	26.59	5
LYMAN	PB2-3	20-Jun-57	45.16	5	MCPHERSON	PB11-2	1-Sep-57	27.46	5
MARSHALL	TS7-4	4-Jun-52	4.06	2	MEADE	TS5-2	8-May-52	3.71	2
MARSHALL	PB5-4	18-Jul-57	5.89	3	MEADE	PB9-3	25-Aug-57	3.88	2
MARSHALL	PB8-3	20-Aug-57	19.73	4	MEADE	PB5-2	16-Jul-57	4.90	2
MARSHALL	PB15-2	17-Sep-57	20.04	4	MEADE	PB5-3	17-Jul-57	5.09	3

INDIVIDUAL FALLOUT DAYS
SOUTH DAKOTA

COUNTY	SHOT	DATE	µCi/SQ METER	INDEX	COUNTY	SHOT	DATE	µCi/SQ METER	INDEX
MEADE	TS7-4	4-Jun-52	6.44	3	MINER	SE3	8-Jul-62	132.13	7
MEADE	PB11-2	1-Sep-57	6.92	3	MINER	SE2	7-Jul-62	177.44	7
MEADE	PB8-4	21-Aug-57	8.05	3	MINNEHAHA	TS7-3	3-Jun-52	3.60	2
MEADE	TS8-1	5-Jun-52	11.09	4	MINNEHAHA	UK2-2	25-Mar-53	3.97	2
MEADE	UK7-4	28-Apr-53	12.31	4	MINNEHAHA	UK7-5	29-Apr-53	4.36	2
MEADE	PB8-3	20-Aug-57	19.73	4	MINNEHAHA	PB11-2	1-Sep-57	4.58	2
MEADE	PB15-2	17-Sep-57	20.04	4	MINNEHAHA	PB9-4	26-Aug-57	5.22	3
MEADE	TS5-1	7-May-52	22.93	4	MINNEHAHA	PB8-5	22-Aug-57	7.56	3
MEADE	TS7-3	3-Jun-52	27.82	5	MINNEHAHA	UK7-4	28-Apr-53	10.53	4
MEADE	UK2-2	25-Mar-53	45.45	5	MINNEHAHA	PB8-4	21-Aug-57	13.41	4
MELLETTE	PB9-3	25-Aug-57	5.87	3	MINNEHAHA	PB2-3	20-Jun-57	15.08	4
MELLETTE	TS7-4	4-Jun-52	6.08	3	MINNEHAHA	PB8-3	20-Aug-57	19.73	4
MELLETTE	PB15-2	17-Sep-57	6.68	3	MINNEHAHA	PB15-2	17-Sep-57	20.04	4
MELLETTE	PB11-2	1-Sep-57	9.15	3	MINNEHAHA	TS7-4	4-Jun-52	37.67	5
MELLETTE	PB8-5	22-Aug-57	11.33	4	MINNEHAHA	SE2	7-Jul-62	138.24	7
MELLETTE	TS8-1	5-Jun-52	13.29	4	MOODY	UK2-2	25-Mar-53	3.97	2
MELLETTE	TS5-2	8-May-52	14.47	4	MOODY	PB15-2	17-Sep-57	4.11	2
MELLETTE	PB5-4	18-Jul-57	14.75	4	MOODY	UK7-5	29-Apr-53	4.76	2
MELLETTE	TS5-1	7-May-52	15.63	4	MOODY	TS6-3	27-May-52	7.57	3
MELLETTE	PB8-3	20-Aug-57	19.73	4	MOODY	UK7-4	28-Apr-53	9.68	3
MELLETTE	UK7-4	28-Apr-53	20.72	4	MOODY	TS7-4	4-Jun-52	29.05	5
MELLETTE	PB2-3	20-Jun-57	45.16	5	MOODY	SE2	7-Jul-62	361.42	8
MELLETTE	UK2-2	25-Mar-53	45.45	5	PENNINGTON	PB9-3	25-Aug-57	3.88	2
MINER	UK2-2	25-Mar-53	3.97	2	PENNINGTON	PB6-5	28-Jul-57	3.90	2
MINER	PB15-3	18-Sep-57	4.13	2	PENNINGTON	PB5-2	16-Jul-57	4.02	2
MINER	TP9-3	16-Apr-55	4.57	2	PENNINGTON	PB11-2	1-Sep-57	5.11	3
MINER	PB11-2	1-Sep-57	9.15	3	PENNINGTON	TS5-2	8-May-52	5.21	3
MINER	UK7-4	28-Apr-53	9.72	3	PENNINGTON	PB9-4	26-Aug-57	5.22	3
MINER	PB8-5	22-Aug-57	18.89	4	PENNINGTON	TS7-4	4-Jun-52	5.74	3
MINER	PB8-3	20-Aug-57	19.73	4	PENNINGTON	PB8-4	21-Aug-57	8.05	3
MINER	PB15-2	17-Sep-57	20.04	4	PENNINGTON	UK7-4	28-Apr-53	8.87	3
MINER	TS7-4	4-Jun-52	24.84	4	PENNINGTON	TS8-1	5-Jun-52	9.23	3
MINER	PB2-3	20-Jun-57	30.08	5	PENNINGTON	UK2-2	25-Mar-53	18.88	4

INDIVIDUAL FALLOUT DAYS
SOUTH DAKOTA

COUNTY	SHOT	DATE	µCi/SQ METER	INDEX	COUNTY	SHOT	DATE	µCi/SQ METER	INDEX
PENNINGTON	TS5-1	7-May-52	20.08	4	ROBERTS	PB8-3	20-Aug-57	19.73	4
PENNINGTON	PB8-3	20-Aug-57	29.60	5	ROBERTS	PB15-2	17-Sep-57	20.04	4
PENNINGTON	TS7-3	3-Jun-52	35.51	5	ROBERTS	PB11-2	1-Sep-57	27.46	5
PERKINS	PB5-2	16-Jul-57	4.90	2	ROBERTS	PB2-3	20-Jun-57	75.24	6
PERKINS	PB9-3	25-Aug-57	5.87	3	SANBORN	UK2-2	25-Mar-53	3.97	2
PERKINS	PB6-5	28-Jul-57	6.66	3	SANBORN	PB11-2	1-Sep-57	4.58	2
PERKINS	PB8-4	21-Aug-57	8.05	3	SANBORN	TS5-1	7-May-52	4.90	2
PERKINS	PB11-2	1-Sep-57	9.15	3	SANBORN	TS5-2	8-May-52	5.04	3
PERKINS	TS5-1	7-May-52	9.70	3	SANBORN	TP9-3	16-Apr-55	5.34	3
PERKINS	PB5-3	17-Jul-57	10.10	4	SANBORN	UK7-4	28-Apr-53	8.57	3
PERKINS	TS8-1	5-Jun-52	13.29	4	SANBORN	PB15-2	17-Sep-57	13.36	4
PERKINS	UK7-4	28-Apr-53	16.00	4	SANBORN	PB8-5	22-Aug-57	18.89	4
PERKINS	PB8-3	20-Aug-57	19.73	4	SANBORN	PB8-3	20-Aug-57	19.73	4
PERKINS	PB15-2	17-Sep-57	20.04	4	SANBORN	TS7-4	4-Jun-52	27.81	5
PERKINS	UK2-2	25-Mar-53	45.45	5	SANBORN	PB2-3	20-Jun-57	45.16	5
POTTER	PB8-5	22-Aug-57	3.78	2	SHANNON	PB9-3	25-Aug-57	3.88	2
POTTER	UK2-2	25-Mar-53	3.97	2	SHANNON	PB5-2	16-Jul-57	4.90	2
POTTER	PB6-5	28-Jul-57	4.08	2	SHANNON	TS5-2	8-May-52	6.66	3
POTTER	PB9-4	26-Aug-57	5.22	3	SHANNON	UK7-4	28-Apr-53	12.24	4
POTTER	PB5-4	18-Jul-57	5.89	3	SHANNON	TS8-1	5-Jun-52	13.29	4
POTTER	TS5-1	7-May-52	8.08	3	SHANNON	PB8-3	20-Aug-57	19.73	4
POTTER	TS7-4	4-Jun-52	12.15	4	SHANNON	UK2-2	25-Mar-53	45.45	5
POTTER	UK7-4	28-Apr-53	16.96	4	SHANNON	TS5-1	7-May-52	56.19	6
POTTER	PB8-3	20-Aug-57	19.73	4	SHANNON	SE2	7-Jul-62	345.60	8
POTTER	PB15-2	17-Sep-57	20.04	4	SPINK	PB8-5	22-Aug-57	3.78	2
POTTER	TS8-1	5-Jun-52	26.59	5	SPINK	UK2-2	25-Mar-53	3.97	2
POTTER	PB11-2	1-Sep-57	27.46	5	SPINK	PB9-4	26-Aug-57	5.22	3
POTTER	PB2-3	20-Jun-57	45.16	5	SPINK	UK7-4	28-Apr-53	10.26	4
ROBERTS	TS7-5	5-Jun-52	3.52	2	SPINK	PB8-3	20-Aug-57	19.73	4
ROBERTS	UK7-5	29-Apr-53	3.91	2	SPINK	PB15-2	17-Sep-57	20.04	4
ROBERTS	PB5-2	16-Jul-57	4.90	2	SPINK	TS7-4	4-Jun-52	21.83	4
ROBERTS	PB11-4	3-Sep-57	5.18	3	SPINK	TS8-1	5-Jun-52	26.59	5
ROBERTS	PB5-4	18-Jul-57	5.89	3	SPINK	PB11-2	1-Sep-57	27.46	5

INDIVIDUAL FALLOUT DAYS
SOUTH DAKOTA

COUNTY	SHOT	DATE	µCi/SQ METER	INDEX	COUNTY	SHOT	DATE	µCi/SQ METER	INDEX
SPINK	PB2-3	20-Jun-57	45.16	5	TODD	TS7-4	4-Jun-52	5.86	3
STANLEY	PB9-3	25-Aug-57	3.88	2	TODD	TS5-2	8-May-52	8.77	3
STANLEY	TS5-2	8-May-52	4.17	2	TODD	PB8-5	22-Aug-57	11.33	4
STANLEY	PB12-3	4-Sep-57	4.40	2	TODD	TS8-1	5-Jun-52	13.29	4
STANLEY	TS5-1	7-May-52	7.72	3	TODD	UK7-4	28-Apr-53	14.09	4
STANLEY	PB5-4	18-Jul-57	8.86	3	TODD	TS5-1	7-May-52	15.45	4
STANLEY	PB8-5	22-Aug-57	11.33	4	TODD	PB8-3	20-Aug-57	19.73	4
STANLEY	PB11-2	1-Sep-57	18.31	4	TODD	PB2-3	20-Jun-57	45.16	5
STANLEY	UK7-4	28-Apr-53	19.13	4	TODD	UK2-2	25-Mar-53	45.45	5
STANLEY	PB8-3	20-Aug-57	19.73	4	TRIPP	UK2-2	25-Mar-53	3.97	2
STANLEY	PB15-2	17-Sep-57	20.04	4	TRIPP	PB11-2	1-Sep-57	4.58	2
STANLEY	TS8-1	5-Jun-52	26.59	5	TRIPP	TS7-3	3-Jun-52	4.59	2
STANLEY	TS7-4	4-Jun-52	27.03	5	TRIPP	TS5-2	8-May-52	7.51	3
STANLEY	PB2-3	20-Jun-57	30.08	5	TRIPP	PB8-5	22-Aug-57	11.33	4
STANLEY	UK2-2	25-Mar-53	45.45	5	TRIPP	PB15-2	17-Sep-57	13.36	4
STANLEY	SE2	7-Jul-62	345.60	8	TRIPP	TS5-1	7-May-52	14.73	4
SULLY	PB9-3	25-Aug-57	3.88	2	TRIPP	TS7-4	4-Jun-52	19.13	4
SULLY	UK2-2	25-Mar-53	3.97	2	TRIPP	PB8-3	20-Aug-57	19.73	4
SULLY	PB9-4	26-Aug-57	5.22	3	TRIPP	UK7-4	28-Apr-53	21.42	4
SULLY	UK2-3	26-Mar-53	7.01	3	TRIPP	TS8-1	5-Jun-52	26.59	5
SULLY	PB8-5	22-Aug-57	7.56	3	TRIPP	PB2-3	20-Jun-57	30.08	5
SULLY	PB11-2	1-Sep-57	9.15	3	TURNER	UK7-5	29-Apr-53	3.58	2
SULLY	TS5-1	7-May-52	10.24	4	TURNER	PB12-4	5-Sep-57	3.65	2
SULLY	UK7-4	28-Apr-53	18.87	4	TURNER	TS5-1	7-May-52	3.74	2
SULLY	PB8-3	20-Aug-57	19.73	4	TURNER	PB8-5	22-Aug-57	3.78	2
SULLY	PB15-2	17-Sep-57	20.04	4	TURNER	UK2-2	25-Mar-53	3.97	2
SULLY	TS8-1	5-Jun-52	26.59	5	TURNER	PB11-2	1-Sep-57	4.58	2
SULLY	TS7-4	4-Jun-52	29.38	5	TURNER	PB15-2	17-Sep-57	6.68	3
SULLY	PB2-3	20-Jun-57	45.16	5	TURNER	PB2-3	20-Jun-57	7.54	3
TODD	PB9-3	25-Aug-57	3.88	2	TURNER	TS6-3	27-May-52	8.84	3
TODD	UK9-3	21-May-53	4.06	2	TURNER	UK7-4	28-Apr-53	10.96	4
TODD	PB11-2	1-Sep-57	4.58	2	TURNER	PB8-3	20-Aug-57	19.73	4
TODD	PB8-4	21-Aug-57	5.37	3	TURNER	TS7-4	4-Jun-52	57.70	6

INDIVIDUAL FALLOUT DAYS
SOUTH DAKOTA

COUNTY	SHOT	DATE	µCi/SQ METER	INDEX	COUNTY	SHOT	DATE	µCi/SQ METER	INDEX
TURNER	SE3	8-Jul-62	527.44	9	WASHABAUGH	PB2-3	20-Jun-57	15.08	4
UNION	UK2-2	25-Mar-53	3.97	2	WASHABAUGH	UK7-4	28-Apr-53	18.24	4
UNION	UK7-5	29-Apr-53	4.12	2	WASHABAUGH	PB8-3	20-Aug-57	19.73	4
UNION	UK9-2	20-May-53	4.97	2	WASHABAUGH	TS5-1	7-May-52	33.77	5
UNION	PB9-4	26-Aug-57	5.22	3	WASHABAUGH	UK2-2	25-Mar-53	45.45	5
UNION	PB12-4	5-Sep-57	5.81	3	WASHABAUGH	SE2	7-Jul-62	860.52	10
UNION	TS6-3	27-May-52	8.84	3	YANKTON	UK2-2	25-Mar-53	3.97	2
UNION	UK7-4	28-Apr-53	10.84	4	YANKTON	PB2-3	20-Jun-57	7.54	3
UNION	PB8-3	20-Aug-57	19.73	4	YANKTON	PB8-5	22-Aug-57	7.56	3
UNION	TS7-4	4-Jun-52	49.70	5	YANKTON	TS6-3	27-May-52	8.91	3
UNION	SE3	8-Jul-62	208.70	8	YANKTON	PB11-2	1-Sep-57	9.15	3
WALWORTH	TS5-1	7-May-52	3.59	2	YANKTON	TS7-4	4-Jun-52	12.06	4
WALWORTH	TS7-4	4-Jun-52	3.61	2	YANKTON	UK7-4	28-Apr-53	12.62	4
WALWORTH	PB8-5	22-Aug-57	3.78	2	YANKTON	PB8-3	20-Aug-57	19.73	4
WALWORTH	PB9-3	25-Aug-57	3.88	2	YANKTON	SE3	8-Jul-62	252.68	8
WALWORTH	UK2-2	25-Mar-53	3.97	2	ZIEBACH	PB8-5	22-Aug-57	3.78	2
WALWORTH	PB5-4	18-Jul-57	8.86	3	ZIEBACH	PB8-4	21-Aug-57	5.37	3
WALWORTH	UK7-4	28-Apr-53	14.22	4	ZIEBACH	PB9-3	25-Aug-57	5.87	3
WALWORTH	PB8-3	20-Aug-57	19.73	4	ZIEBACH	PB5-4	18-Jul-57	5.89	3
WALWORTH	PB15-2	17-Sep-57	20.04	4	ZIEBACH	TS7-4	4-Jun-52	6.35	3
WALWORTH	TS8-1	5-Jun-52	26.59	5	ZIEBACH	PB11-2	1-Sep-57	9.15	3
WALWORTH	PB11-2	1-Sep-57	27.46	5	ZIEBACH	TS5-1	7-May-52	11.14	4
WALWORTH	PB2-3	20-Jun-57	45.16	5	ZIEBACH	TS8-1	5-Jun-52	13.29	4
WASHABAUGH	PB11-2	1-Sep-57	4.58	2	ZIEBACH	UK7-4	28-Apr-53	19.13	4
WASHABAUGH	PB9-3	25-Aug-57	5.87	3	ZIEBACH	PB8-3	20-Aug-57	19.73	4
WASHABAUGH	PB8-4	21-Aug-57	8.05	3	ZIEBACH	PB15-2	17-Sep-57	20.04	4
WASHABAUGH	PB5-4	18-Jul-57	8.86	3	ZIEBACH	PB2-3	20-Jun-57	45.16	5
WASHABAUGH	TS5-2	8-May-52	10.37	4	ZIEBACH	UK2-2	25-Mar-53	45.45	5
WASHABAUGH	TS8-1	5-Jun-52	13.29	4					

INDIANA FALLOUT DAYS
TENNESSEE

COUNTY	SHOT	DATE	µCi/SQ METER	INDEX	COUNTY	SHOT	DATE	µCi/SQ METER	INDEX
ANDERSON	TP10-2	6-May-55	3.62	2	CAMPBELL	PB17-3	30-Sep-57	3.79	2
ANDERSON	TS7-5	5-Jun-52	3.80	2	CAMPBELL	TP6-4	25-Mar-55	4.32	2
ANDERSON	TP6-4	25-Mar-55	4.32	2	CAMPBELL	TP10-8	12-May-55	4.42	2
ANDERSON	BJ3-5	5-Nov-51	4.59	2	CAMPBELL	UK1-2	18-Mar-53	15.96	4
ANDERSON	TP10-8	12-May-55	5.03	3	CAMPBELL	SE4	9-Jul-62	43.75	5
ANDERSON	PB17-3	30-Sep-57	7.49	3	CANNON	TP10-2	6-May-55	3.62	2
ANDERSON	BJ3-6	6-Nov-51	8.10	3	CANNON	PB17-3	30-Sep-57	3.79	2
ANDERSON	UK1-2	18-Mar-53	18.35	4	CANNON	PB2-5	22-Jun-57	4.18	2
BEDFORD	TP10-2	6-May-55	3.62	2	CANNON	UK7-4	28-Apr-53	5.35	3
BEDFORD	UK1-3	19-Mar-53	4.92	2	CARROLL	PB3-4	27-Jun-57	3.63	2
BEDFORD	TS7-4	4-Jun-52	5.36	3	CARROLL	UK9-3	21-May-53	4.15	2
BEDFORD	PB17-3	30-Sep-57	14.98	4	CARROLL	TS7-6	6-Jun-52	4.65	2
BENTON	TS5-1	7-May-52	4.05	2	CARROLL	UK1-3	19-Mar-53	8.09	3
BENTON	TS1-3	3-Apr-52	6.02	3	CARROLL	TP10-3	7-May-55	8.27	3
BENTON	UK1-3	19-Mar-53	8.98	3	CARROLL	TS1-3	3-Apr-52	9.02	3
BLEDSOE	TP10-2	6-May-55	3.62	2	CARTER	TP10-2	6-May-55	3.62	2
BLEDSOE	TP6-4	25-Mar-55	4.32	2	CARTER	UK9-4	22-May-53	3.66	2
BLEDSOE	TS7-6	6-Jun-52	5.62	3	CARTER	BJ2-2	31-Oct-51	3.89	2
BLEDSOE	BJ3-6	6-Nov-51	8.10	3	CARTER	PB6-3	26-Jul-57	3.96	2
BLEDSOE	UK1-2	18-Mar-53	10.57	4	CARTER	TP6-4	25-Mar-55	4.32	2
BLEDSOE	PB17-3	30-Sep-57	14.98	4	CARTER	UK1-2	18-Mar-53	5.78	3
BLOUNT	TP10-2	6-May-55	3.62	2	CARTER	SE4	9-Jul-62	43.75	5
BLOUNT	TP6-4	25-Mar-55	4.32	2	CHEATHAM	UK7-5	29-Apr-53	3.87	2
BLOUNT	BJ3-6	6-Nov-51	4.86	2	CHEATHAM	TP5-3	14-Mar-55	3.93	2
BLOUNT	UK1-2	18-Mar-53	14.59	4	CHEATHAM	TP10-3	7-May-55	7.21	3
BLOUNT	PB17-3	30-Sep-57	14.98	4	CHEATHAM	UK1-3	19-Mar-53	8.34	3
BRADLEY	TP10-2	6-May-55	3.62	2	CHEATHAM	PB4-5	9-Jul-57	11.16	4
BRADLEY	TS7-6	6-Jun-52	4.52	2	CHESTER	UK3-6	5-Apr-53	3.67	2
BRADLEY	UK1-2	18-Mar-53	4.84	2	CHESTER	UK9-3	21-May-53	4.86	2
BRADLEY	TP6-4	25-Mar-55	7.15	3	CHESTER	TS1-3	3-Apr-52	6.02	3
BRADLEY	BJ3-6	6-Nov-51	8.10	3	CHESTER	UK1-3	19-Mar-53	6.20	3
BRADLEY	PB17-3	30-Sep-57	14.98	4	CHESTER	TS7-6	6-Jun-52	7.30	3
CAMPBELL	TP10-2	6-May-55	3.62	2	CHESTER	UK2-8	31-Mar-53	21.07	4

INDIVIDUAL FALLOUT DAYS
TENNESSEE

COUNTY	SHOT	DATE	µCi/SQ METER	INDEX	COUNTY	SHOT	DATE	µCi/SQ METER	INDEX
CLAIBORNE	TP10-2	6-May-55	3.62	2	CROCKETT	TS1-3	3-Apr-52	9.02	3
CLAIBORNE	PB17-3	30-Sep-57	3.79	2	CROCKETT	UK2-8	31-Mar-53	35.10	5
CLAIBORNE	TS7-5	5-Jun-52	4.31	2	CUMBERLAND	TP10-2	6-May-55	3.62	2
CLAIBORNE	TP6-4	25-Mar-55	4.32	2	CUMBERLAND	TS7-6	6-Jun-52	4.22	2
CLAIBORNE	PB4-5	9-Jul-57	5.24	3	CUMBERLAND	TP6-4	25-Mar-55	4.32	2
CLAIBORNE	UK1-2	18-Mar-53	14.95	4	CUMBERLAND	BJ3-6	6-Nov-51	8.10	3
CLAIBORNE	SE4	9-Jul-62	43.75	5	CUMBERLAND	UK1-2	18-Mar-53	8.25	3
CLAY	TP10-2	6-May-55	3.62	2	CUMBERLAND	PB17-3	30-Sep-57	14.98	4
CLAY	TP5-3	14-Mar-55	3.78	2	DAVIDSON	TP10-3	7-May-55	3.65	2
CLAY	PB2-5	22-Jun-57	4.18	2	DAVIDSON	UK7-5	29-Apr-53	3.74	2
CLAY	PB17-3	30-Sep-57	7.49	3	DAVIDSON	UK7-4	28-Apr-53	5.46	3
CLAY	PB4-5	9-Jul-57	7.83	3	DAVIDSON	UK1-3	19-Mar-53	8.03	3
CLAY	SE4	9-Jul-62	43.75	5	DAVIDSON	PB4-5	9-Jul-57	11.16	4
COCKE	TP10-2	6-May-55	3.62	2	DE KALB	TP10-2	6-May-55	3.62	2
COCKE	TS7-5	5-Jun-52	3.77	2	DE KALB	PB4-5	9-Jul-57	5.24	3
COCKE	PB6-3	26-Jul-57	3.96	2	DE KALB	UK7-4	28-Apr-53	5.40	3
COCKE	PB2-5	22-Jun-57	4.18	2	DE KALB	PB17-3	30-Sep-57	7.49	3
COCKE	TP6-4	25-Mar-55	4.32	2	DE KALB	UK1-2	18-Mar-53	3.50	1
COCKE	BJ3-6	6-Nov-51	4.86	2	DECATUR	UK9-3	21-May-53	3.94	2
COCKE	BJ2-4	2-Nov-51	5.18	3	DECATUR	TS1-3	3-Apr-52	6.02	3
COCKE	PB17-3	30-Sep-57	7.49	3	DECATUR	TS7-6	6-Jun-52	7.62	3
COCKE	UK1-2	18-Mar-53	16.80	4	DECATUR	UK1-3	19-Mar-53	7.80	3
COFFEE	UK1-3	19-Mar-53	3.60	2	DICKSON	TP5-3	14-Mar-55	3.78	2
COFFEE	TP10-2	6-May-55	3.62	2	DICKSON	TS5-1	7-May-52	4.05	2
COFFEE	PB2-5	22-Jun-57	4.18	2	DICKSON	PB17-5	2-Oct-57	4.57	2
COFFEE	BJ3-6	6-Nov-51	4.86	2	DICKSON	TS1-3	3-Apr-52	4.81	2
COFFEE	PB17-3	30-Sep-57	22.47	4	DICKSON	UK7-4	28-Apr-53	5.35	3
CROCKETT	UK8-3	10-May-53	3.68	2	DICKSON	UK1-3	19-Mar-53	9.69	3
CROCKETT	UK1-2	18-Mar-53	4.84	2	DICKSON	TP10-3	7-May-55	9.92	3
CROCKETT	UK9-3	21-May-53	4.91	2	DYER	UK1-2	18-Mar-53	3.81	2
CROCKETT	UK2-7	30-Mar-53	6.07	3	DYER	PB8-3	20-Aug-57	4.00	2
CROCKETT	TS7-6	6-Jun-52	6.86	3	DYER	UK9-3	21-May-53	4.30	2
CROCKETT	UK1-3	19-Mar-53	7.21	3	DYER	UK8-3	10-May-53	6.18	3

INDIVIDUAL FALLOUT DAYS
TENNESSEE

COUNTY	SHOT	DATE	µCi/SQ METER	INDEX	COUNTY	SHOT	DATE	µCi/SQ METER	INDEX
DYER	UK1-3	19-Mar-53	6.56	3	GIBSON	TS1-3	3-Apr-52	9.02	3
DYER	TS1-3	3-Apr-52	9.02	3	GIBSON	TP10-3	7-May-55	15.03	4
DYER	UK7-4	28-Apr-53	19.35	4	GIBSON	UK7-4	28-Apr-53	16.14	4
DYER	UK2-7	30-Mar-53	30.44	5	GIBSON	UK2-7	30-Mar-53	30.44	5
DYER	UK2-8	31-Mar-53	3.50	1	GIBSON	UK2-8	31-Mar-53	3.50	1
FAYETTE	UK1-2	18-Mar-53	3.79	2	GILES	PB12-6	7-Sep-57	3.74	2
FAYETTE	PB8-3	20-Aug-57	4.00	2	GILES	UK7-5	29-Apr-53	3.76	2
FAYETTE	UK1-3	19-Mar-53	4.13	2	GILES	TP11-6	20-May-55	3.89	2
FAYETTE	TS7-5	5-Jun-52	4.23	2	GILES	UK1-3	19-Mar-53	5.85	3
FAYETTE	UK9-3	21-May-53	4.88	2	GRAINGER	TP10-2	6-May-55	3.62	2
FAYETTE	UK8-3	10-May-53	6.18	3	GRAINGER	PB17-3	30-Sep-57	3.79	2
FAYETTE	TS1-3	3-Apr-52	9.02	3	GRAINGER	TP6-4	25-Mar-55	4.32	2
FAYETTE	UK2-7	30-Mar-53	18.26	4	GRAINGER	TP10-8	12-May-55	4.72	2
FAYETTE	UK7-4	28-Apr-53	19.36	4	GRAINGER	UK1-2	18-Mar-53	13.74	4
FAYETTE	UK2-8	31-Mar-53	3.50	1	GREENE	TP10-2	6-May-55	3.62	2
FAYETTE	PB12-6	7-Sep-57	3.50	1	GREENE	PB6-3	26-Jul-57	3.96	2
FENTRESS	TP10-2	6-May-55	3.62	2	GREENE	TP6-4	25-Mar-55	4.32	2
FENTRESS	PB17-5	2-Oct-57	4.13	2	GREENE	UK9-4	22-May-53	6.06	3
FENTRESS	PB2-5	22-Jun-57	4.18	2	GREENE	PB17-3	30-Sep-57	7.49	3
FENTRESS	TP6-4	25-Mar-55	4.32	2	GREENE	UK1-2	18-Mar-53	15.61	4
FENTRESS	BJ3-6	6-Nov-51	4.86	2	GRUNDY	TP10-2	6-May-55	3.62	2
FENTRESS	UK1-2	18-Mar-53	6.10	3	GRUNDY	PB17-5	2-Oct-57	3.69	2
FENTRESS	PB17-3	30-Sep-57	7.49	3	GRUNDY	PB2-5	22-Jun-57	4.18	2
FENTRESS	TS7-6	6-Jun-52	7.73	3	GRUNDY	TS7-6	6-Jun-52	4.22	2
FRANKLIN	TP6-4	25-Mar-55	3.99	2	GRUNDY	BJ3-5	5-Nov-51	4.59	2
FRANKLIN	BJ3-6	6-Nov-51	4.86	2	GRUNDY	BJ3-6	6-Nov-51	4.86	2
FRANKLIN	PB17-3	30-Sep-57	5.99	3	GRUNDY	PB17-3	30-Sep-57	14.98	4
GIBSON	UK8-3	10-May-53	3.68	2	HAMBLEN	TP10-2	6-May-55	3.62	2
GIBSON	PB3-4	27-Jun-57	3.79	2	HAMBLEN	PB6-3	26-Jul-57	3.96	2
GIBSON	TP11-6	20-May-55	3.80	2	HAMBLEN	TP6-4	25-Mar-55	4.32	2
GIBSON	UK9-3	21-May-53	4.56	2	HAMBLEN	PB17-3	30-Sep-57	7.49	3
GIBSON	TS7-5	5-Jun-52	5.42	3	HAMBLEN	UK1-2	18-Mar-53	12.64	4
GIBSON	UK1-3	19-Mar-53	7.44	3	HAMILTON	TP10-2	6-May-55	3.62	2

INDIVIDUAL FALLOUT DAYS
TENNESSEE

COUNTY	SHOT	DATE	µCi/SQ METER	INDEX	COUNTY	SHOT	DATE	µCi/SQ METER	INDEX
HAMILTON	PB2-5	22-Jun-57	4.18	2	HAYWOOD	TP11-6	20-May-55	3.72	2
HAMILTON	TP6-4	25-Mar-55	4.32	2	HAYWOOD	PB8-3	20-Aug-57	4.00	2
HAMILTON	UK1-2	18-Mar-53	4.95	2	HAYWOOD	UK1-2	18-Mar-53	4.99	2
HAMILTON	PB17-3	30-Sep-57	14.98	4	HAYWOOD	UK9-3	21-May-53	5.32	3
HANCOCK	TP10-2	6-May-55	3.62	2	HAYWOOD	UK1-3	19-Mar-53	5.51	3
HANCOCK	PB6-3	26-Jul-57	3.96	2	HAYWOOD	UK2-7	30-Mar-53	6.07	3
HANCOCK	TP6-4	25-Mar-55	4.32	2	HAYWOOD	TS7-6	6-Jun-52	6.73	3
HANCOCK	PB4-5	9-Jul-57	5.24	3	HAYWOOD	TS1-3	3-Apr-52	9.02	3
HANCOCK	PB17-3	30-Sep-57	7.49	3	HAYWOOD	UK2-8	31-Mar-53	35.10	5
HANCOCK	UK1-2	18-Mar-53	11.09	4	HENDERSON	TP10-3	7-May-55	3.97	2
HANCOCK	SE4	9-Jul-62	43.75	5	HENDERSON	UK9-3	21-May-53	4.40	2
HARDEMAN	UK3-6	5-Apr-53	3.67	2	HENDERSON	TS1-3	3-Apr-52	6.02	3
HARDEMAN	TP11-6	20-May-55	3.87	2	HENDERSON	UK1-3	19-Mar-53	7.44	3
HARDEMAN	PB8-3	20-Aug-57	4.00	2	HENRY	UK9-3	21-May-53	3.53	2
HARDEMAN	UK1-3	19-Mar-53	5.08	3	HENRY	TS7-6	6-Jun-52	5.74	3
HARDEMAN	UK9-3	21-May-53	5.37	3	HENRY	TS5-1	7-May-52	7.54	3
HARDEMAN	UK8-3	10-May-53	6.18	3	HENRY	UK1-3	19-Mar-53	7.74	3
HARDEMAN	PB12-6	7-Sep-57	6.66	3	HENRY	TS1-3	3-Apr-52	9.02	3
HARDEMAN	TS1-3	3-Apr-52	9.02	3	HENRY	TP10-3	7-May-55	9.39	3
HARDEMAN	UK7-4	28-Apr-53	17.70	4	HICKMAN	TS7-5	5-Jun-52	7.43	3
HARDEMAN	UK2-8	31-Mar-53	3.50	1	HICKMAN	UK1-3	19-Mar-53	8.90	3
HARDEMAN	UK1-2	18-Mar-53	3.50	1	HOUSTON	PB3-4	27-Jun-57	3.58	2
HARDIN	UK9-3	21-May-53	4.35	2	HOUSTON	TS1-3	3-Apr-52	9.02	3
HARDIN	PB12-6	7-Sep-57	4.91	2	HOUSTON	UK1-3	19-Mar-53	9.39	3
HARDIN	UK1-3	19-Mar-53	5.38	3	HUMPHREYS	TS7-6	6-Jun-52	3.51	2
HARDIN	UK7-4	28-Apr-53	7.38	3	HUMPHREYS	TS1-3	3-Apr-52	6.02	3
HAWKINS	TP10-2	6-May-55	3.62	2	HUMPHREYS	TP10-3	7-May-55	6.76	3
HAWKINS	PB17-3	30-Sep-57	3.79	2	HUMPHREYS	UK1-3	19-Mar-53	9.98	3
HAWKINS	PB6-3	26-Jul-57	3.96	2	JACKSON	TP10-2	6-May-55	3.62	2
HAWKINS	TP6-4	25-Mar-55	4.32	2	JACKSON	TP5-3	14-Mar-55	3.78	2
HAWKINS	UK1-2	18-Mar-53	11.85	4	JACKSON	PB2-5	22-Jun-57	4.18	2
HAWKINS	SE4	9-Jul-62	17.11	4	JACKSON	PB17-3	30-Sep-57	7.49	3
HAYWOOD	UK8-3	10-May-53	3.68	2	JACKSON	PB4-5	9-Jul-57	7.83	3

INDIVIDUAL FALLOUT DAYS
TENNESSEE

COUNTY	SHOT	DATE	µCi/SQ METER	INDEX	COUNTY	SHOT	DATE	µCi/SQ METER	INDEX
JEFFERSON	TP10-2	6-May-55	3.62	2	LAWRENCE	UK7-5	29-Apr-53	3.70	2
JEFFERSON	TP6-4	25-Mar-55	4.32	2	LAWRENCE	TP11-6	20-May-55	4.07	2
JEFFERSON	BJ3-6	6-Nov-51	4.86	2	LAWRENCE	UK1-3	19-Mar-53	6.14	3
JEFFERSON	PB17-3	30-Sep-57	7.49	3	LAWRENCE	TS5-1	7-May-52	7.04	3
JEFFERSON	UK1-2	18-Mar-53	10.52	4	LEWIS	TP11-6	20-May-55	3.77	2
JOHNSON	TP10-2	6-May-55	3.62	2	LEWIS	UK1-3	19-Mar-53	8.68	3
JOHNSON	UK1-2	18-Mar-53	3.69	2	LINCOLN	PB17-3	30-Sep-57	3.96	2
JOHNSON	PB6-3	26-Jul-57	3.96	2	LINCOLN	TP6-4	25-Mar-55	3.99	2
JOHNSON	TP6-4	25-Mar-55	4.32	2	LINCOLN	UK1-3	19-Mar-53	4.37	2
JOHNSON	SE4	9-Jul-62	17.11	4	LINCOLN	TS7-4	4-Jun-52	4.49	2
KNOX	TP10-8	12-May-55	6.32	3	LOUDON	TP10-2	6-May-55	3.62	2
KNOX	BJ3-6	6-Nov-51	8.10	3	LOUDON	TP6-4	25-Mar-55	4.32	2
KNOX	UK1-2	18-Mar-53	20.37	4	LOUDON	TP10-8	12-May-55	4.47	2
LAKE	UK9-3	21-May-53	3.53	2	LOUDON	PB17-3	30-Sep-57	7.49	3
LAKE	UK8-3	10-May-53	3.68	2	LOUDON	BJ3-6	6-Nov-51	8.10	3
LAKE	PB8-3	20-Aug-57	4.00	2	LOUDON	UK1-2	18-Mar-53	12.23	4
LAKE	UK1-3	19-Mar-53	5.55	3	MACON	PB4-5	9-Jul-57	5.58	3
LAKE	TS7-5	5-Jun-52	6.36	3	MADISON	UK1-2	18-Mar-53	3.61	2
LAKE	UK2-8	31-Mar-53	7.04	3	MADISON	TP10-3	7-May-55	4.85	2
LAKE	TS1-3	3-Apr-52	9.02	3	MADISON	UK9-3	21-May-53	5.02	3
LAKE	UK2-7	30-Mar-53	12.19	4	MADISON	TS1-3	3-Apr-52	6.02	3
LAKE	UK7-4	28-Apr-53	19.14	4	MADISON	UK1-3	19-Mar-53	6.91	3
LAKE	TP10-3	7-May-55	22.02	4	MADISON	UK7-4	28-Apr-53	12.46	4
LAUDERDALE	PB8-3	20-Aug-57	4.00	2	MADISON	UK2-7	30-Mar-53	18.26	4
LAUDERDALE	UK1-2	18-Mar-53	4.56	2	MADISON	UK2-8	31-Mar-53	21.07	4
LAUDERDALE	UK9-3	21-May-53	4.81	2	MARION	PB17-3	30-Sep-57	3.96	2
LAUDERDALE	UK1-3	19-Mar-53	5.26	3	MARION	TP6-4	25-Mar-55	3.99	2
LAUDERDALE	UK8-3	10-May-53	6.18	3	MARION	BJ3-6	6-Nov-51	8.10	3
LAUDERDALE	UK2-3	26-Mar-53	6.23	3	MARSHALL	TP10-2	6-May-55	3.62	2
LAUDERDALE	TP10-3	7-May-55	10.84	4	MARSHALL	TP6-4	25-Mar-55	4.32	2
LAUDERDALE	UK2-7	30-Mar-53	12.19	4	MARSHALL	TS7-4	4-Jun-52	4.48	2
LAUDERDALE	TS1-3	3-Apr-52	15.04	4	MARSHALL	UK1-3	19-Mar-53	6.19	3
LAUDERDALE	UK2-8	31-Mar-53	21.07	4	MARSHALL	PB17-3	30-Sep-57	14.98	4

INDIVIDUAL FALLOUT DAYS
TENNESSEE

COUNTY	SHOT	DATE	µCi/SQ METER	INDEX	COUNTY	SHOT	DATE	µCi/SQ METER	INDEX
MAURY	PB12-6	7-Sep-57	4.04	2	MOORE	PB17-5	2-Oct-57	3.80	2
MAURY	TS7-5	5-Jun-52	5.31	3	MOORE	TP6-4	25-Mar-55	3.99	2
MAURY	UK1-3	19-Mar-53	8.36	3	MOORE	UK1-3	19-Mar-53	4.31	2
MCMINN	TP10-2	6-May-55	3.62	2	MOORE	PB17-3	30-Sep-57	5.99	3
MCMINN	TP10-8	12-May-55	4.04	2	MORGAN	TP10-2	6-May-55	3.62	2
MCMINN	TP6-4	25-Mar-55	7.15	3	MORGAN	TP10-8	12-May-55	4.21	2
MCMINN	BJ3-6	6-Nov-51	8.10	3	MORGAN	TP6-4	25-Mar-55	4.32	2
MCMINN	UK1-2	18-Mar-53	11.09	4	MORGAN	PB17-3	30-Sep-57	7.49	3
MCMINN	PB17-3	30-Sep-57	14.98	4	MORGAN	BJ3-6	6-Nov-51	8.10	3
MCNAIRY	UK3-6	5-Apr-53	3.67	2	MORGAN	UK1-2	18-Mar-53	13.33	4
MCNAIRY	TS5-1	7-May-52	3.75	2	OBION	TP11-6	20-May-55	3.63	2
MCNAIRY	PB2-5	22-Jun-57	4.64	2	OBION	UK8-3	10-May-53	3.68	2
MCNAIRY	UK9-3	21-May-53	4.86	2	OBION	UK9-3	21-May-53	3.89	2
MCNAIRY	UK1-3	19-Mar-53	4.96	2	OBION	TS7-5	5-Jun-52	6.07	3
MCNAIRY	TS1-3	3-Apr-52	6.02	3	OBION	UK1-3	19-Mar-53	6.32	3
MCNAIRY	UK2-7	30-Mar-53	12.19	4	OBION	TS1-3	3-Apr-52	9.02	3
MCNAIRY	UK2-8	31-Mar-53	14.03	4	OBION	UK2-7	30-Mar-53	12.19	4
MEIGS	TP10-2	6-May-55	3.62	2	OBION	TP10-3	7-May-55	19.24	4
MEIGS	TP10-8	12-May-55	3.72	2	OBION	UK2-8	31-Mar-53	21.07	4
MEIGS	UK1-2	18-Mar-53	6.45	3	OVERTON	TP10-2	6-May-55	3.62	2
MEIGS	TP6-4	25-Mar-55	7.15	3	OVERTON	PB17-3	30-Sep-57	3.79	2
MEIGS	PB17-3	30-Sep-57	7.49	3	OVERTON	PB2-5	22-Jun-57	4.18	2
MEIGS	BJ3-6	6-Nov-51	8.10	3	OVERTON	UK1-2	18-Mar-53	4.84	2
MONROE	TP10-2	6-May-55	3.62	2	OVERTON	PB4-5	9-Jul-57	5.24	3
MONROE	TS7-6	6-Jun-52	3.78	2	OVERTON	BJ3-6	6-Nov-51	8.10	3
MONROE	BJ3-6	6-Nov-51	4.86	2	PERRY	UK1-3	19-Mar-53	8.51	3
MONROE	TP6-4	25-Mar-55	7.15	3	PICKETT	TP10-2	6-May-55	3.62	2
MONROE	PB17-3	30-Sep-57	7.49	3	PICKETT	PB17-3	30-Sep-57	3.79	2
MONROE	UK1-2	18-Mar-53	13.38	4	PICKETT	PB2-5	22-Jun-57	4.18	2
MONTGOMERY	UK1-3	19-Mar-53	6.83	3	PICKETT	TP6-4	25-Mar-55	4.32	2
MONTGOMERY	TP10-3	7-May-55	12.78	4	PICKETT	BJ3-5	5-Nov-51	4.59	2
MONTGOMERY	PB4-5	9-Jul-57	16.75	4	PICKETT	TS7-6	6-Jun-52	4.72	2
MOORE	TS7-5	5-Jun-52	3.65	2	PICKETT	BJ3-6	6-Nov-51	4.86	2

INDIGIDUAL FALLOUT DAYS
TENNESSEE

COUNTY	SHOT	DATE	µCi/SQ METER	INDEX	COUNTY	SHOT	DATE	µCi/SQ METER	INDEX
PICKETT	UK1-2	18-Mar-53	5.36	3	ROBERTSON	TP10-3	7-May-55	4.98	2
PICKETT	PB4-5	9-Jul-57	7.83	3	ROBERTSON	UK1-3	19-Mar-53	5.22	3
PICKETT	SE4	9-Jul-62	17.11	4	ROBERTSON	PB4-5	9-Jul-57	16.75	4
POLK	TP10-2	6-May-55	3.62	2	RUTHERFORD	PB17-2	29-Sep-57	5.07	3
POLK	TP6-4	25-Mar-55	4.32	2	RUTHERFORD	UK1-3	19-Mar-53	5.65	3
POLK	UK1-2	18-Mar-53	7.91	3	SCOTT	TP10-2	6-May-55	3.62	2
POLK	BJ3-6	6-Nov-51	8.10	3	SCOTT	PB17-3	30-Sep-57	3.79	2
POLK	PB17-3	30-Sep-57	14.98	4	SCOTT	BJ2-4	2-Nov-51	4.17	2
PUTNAM	TP10-2	6-May-55	3.62	2	SCOTT	TP6-4	25-Mar-55	4.32	2
PUTNAM	UK1-2	18-Mar-53	4.02	2	SCOTT	UK1-2	18-Mar-53	10.14	4
PUTNAM	TP6-4	25-Mar-55	4.32	2	SCOTT	SE4	9-Jul-62	43.75	5
PUTNAM	PB2-5	22-Jun-57	6.96	3	SEQUATCHIE	TP10-2	6-May-55	3.62	2
PUTNAM	PB17-3	30-Sep-57	7.49	3	SEQUATCHIE	TP6-4	25-Mar-55	4.32	2
PUTNAM	PB4-5	9-Jul-57	7.83	3	SEQUATCHIE	BJ3-5	5-Nov-51	4.59	2
PUTNAM	BJ3-6	6-Nov-51	8.10	3	SEQUATCHIE	BJ3-6	6-Nov-51	8.10	3
RHEA	TP10-2	6-May-55	3.62	2	SEQUATCHIE	PB17-3	30-Sep-57	14.98	4
RHEA	TS7-6	6-Jun-52	3.68	2	SEQUATCHIE	UK1-2	18-Mar-53	3.50	1
RHEA	PB2-5	22-Jun-57	4.18	2	SEVIER	TP10-2	6-May-55	3.62	2
RHEA	TP6-4	25-Mar-55	4.32	2	SEVIER	TP6-4	25-Mar-55	4.32	2
RHEA	UK1-2	18-Mar-53	7.11	3	SEVIER	BJ2-4	2-Nov-51	4.48	2
RHEA	BJ3-6	6-Nov-51	8.10	3	SEVIER	BJ3-6	6-Nov-51	4.86	2
RHEA	PB17-3	30-Sep-57	14.98	4	SEVIER	TP10-8	12-May-55	4.94	2
RHEA	TP10-8	12-May-55	3.50	1	SEVIER	TS7-6	6-Jun-52	6.35	3
ROANE	TP10-2	6-May-55	3.62	2	SEVIER	PB17-3	30-Sep-57	14.98	4
ROANE	TP10-8	12-May-55	3.97	2	SEVIER	UK1-2	18-Mar-53	17.46	4
ROANE	TS7-4	4-Jun-52	3.97	2	SHELBY	PB8-3	20-Aug-57	4.00	2
ROANE	TP6-4	25-Mar-55	4.32	2	SHELBY	UK9-3	21-May-53	4.49	2
ROANE	BJ3-5	5-Nov-51	4.59	2	SHELBY	UK2-3	26-Mar-53	5.81	3
ROANE	BJ3-6	6-Nov-51	4.86	2	SHELBY	UK1-2	18-Mar-53	6.82	3
ROANE	UK9-4	22-May-53	4.92	2	SHELBY	UK2-7	30-Mar-53	7.58	3
ROANE	UK1-2	18-Mar-53	11.59	4	SHELBY	UK2-8	31-Mar-53	8.75	3
ROANE	PB17-3	30-Sep-57	14.98	4	SHELBY	UK7-4	28-Apr-53	21.49	4
ROBERTSON	UK7-5	29-Apr-53	3.65	2	SMITH	TP5-3	14-Mar-55	3.93	2

INDIVIDUAL FALLOUT DAYS
TENNESSEE

COUNTY	SHOT	DATE	µCi/SQ METER	INDEX	COUNTY	SHOT	DATE	µCi/SQ METER	INDEX
SMITH	PB17-2	29-Sep-57	5.07	3	UNION	TP10-2	6-May-55	3.62	2
SMITH	PB4-5	9-Jul-57	16.75	4	UNION	PB17-3	30-Sep-57	3.79	2
STEWART	PB3-4	27-Jun-57	3.79	2	UNION	TP6-4	25-Mar-55	4.32	2
STEWART	UK1-3	19-Mar-53	7.62	3	UNION	TS7-5	5-Jun-52	5.56	3
STEWART	TS1-3	3-Apr-52	9.02	3	UNION	UK1-2	18-Mar-53	12.26	4
SULLIVAN	TP10-2	6-May-55	3.62	2	VAN BUREN	TP10-2	6-May-55	3.62	2
SULLIVAN	PB6-3	26-Jul-57	3.96	2	VAN BUREN	UK1-2	18-Mar-53	4.12	2
SULLIVAN	PB2-5	22-Jun-57	4.18	2	VAN BUREN	PB2-5	22-Jun-57	4.18	2
SULLIVAN	TP6-4	25-Mar-55	4.32	2	VAN BUREN	TP6-4	25-Mar-55	4.32	2
SULLIVAN	UK1-2	18-Mar-53	5.05	3	VAN BUREN	BJ3-6	6-Nov-51	8.10	3
SULLIVAN	SE4	9-Jul-62	17.11	4	VAN BUREN	PB17-3	30-Sep-57	14.98	4
SULLIVAN	UK9-4	22-May-53	27.50	5	WARREN	TP10-2	6-May-55	3.62	2
SUMNER	UK1-3	19-Mar-53	4.23	2	WARREN	BJ3-6	6-Nov-51	4.86	2
SUMNER	PB4-5	9-Jul-57	16.75	4	WARREN	PB2-5	22-Jun-57	6.96	3
TIPTON	PB8-3	20-Aug-57	4.00	2	WARREN	PB17-3	30-Sep-57	14.98	4
TIPTON	UK1-3	19-Mar-53	4.03	2	WARREN	UK1-2	18-Mar-53	3.50	1
TIPTON	UK9-3	21-May-53	4.58	2	WASHINGTON	TP10-2	6-May-55	3.62	2
TIPTON	UK1-2	18-Mar-53	5.15	3	WASHINGTON	PB6-3	26-Jul-57	3.96	2
TIPTON	UK2-3	26-Mar-53	6.05	3	WASHINGTON	TP6-4	25-Mar-55	4.32	2
TIPTON	UK8-3	10-May-53	6.18	3	WASHINGTON	UK9-4	22-May-53	5.92	3
TIPTON	TP10-3	7-May-55	8.57	3	WASHINGTON	PB17-3	30-Sep-57	7.49	3
TIPTON	UK2-7	30-Mar-53	12.19	4	WASHINGTON	UK1-2	18-Mar-53	9.71	3
TIPTON	TS1-3	3-Apr-52	15.04	4	WASHINGTON	SE4	9-Jul-62	77.90	6
TIPTON	UK2-8	31-Mar-53	21.07	4	WAYNE	UK9-3	21-May-53	3.63	2
TROUSDALE	PB4-5	9-Jul-57	5.58	3	WAYNE	PB12-6	7-Sep-57	4.21	2
UNICOI	TP10-2	6-May-55	3.62	2	WAYNE	UK1-3	19-Mar-53	6.08	3
UNICOI	BJ2-2	31-Oct-51	3.89	2	WEAKLEY	UK8-3	10-May-53	3.68	2
UNICOI	UK9-4	22-May-53	3.90	2	WEAKLEY	UK9-3	21-May-53	3.99	2
UNICOI	PB6-3	26-Jul-57	3.96	2	WEAKLEY	TS7-6	6-Jun-52	5.94	3
UNICOI	TP6-4	25-Mar-55	4.32	2	WEAKLEY	TS7-5	5-Jun-52	6.02	3
UNICOI	TP6-5	26-Mar-55	6.53	3	WEAKLEY	UK1-3	19-Mar-53	7.21	3
UNICOI	PB17-3	30-Sep-57	7.49	3	WEAKLEY	TS1-3	3-Apr-52	9.02	3
UNICOI	UK1-2	18-Mar-53	9.22	3	WEAKLEY	UK7-4	28-Apr-53	9.14	3

INDIVIDUAL FALLOUT DAYS
TENNESSEE

COUNTY	SHOT	DATE	µCi/SQ METER	INDEX	COUNTY	SHOT	DATE	µCi/SQ METER	INDEX
WEAKLEY	TP10-3	7-May-55	10.82	4	WHITE	PB17-3	30-Sep-57	7.49	3
WEAKLEY	UK2-7	30-Mar-53	12.19	4	WILLIAMSON	UK7-5	29-Apr-53	3.92	2
WEAKLEY	UK2-8	31-Mar-53	21.07	4	WILLIAMSON	PB17-2	29-Sep-57	5.07	3
WHITE	TP10-2	6-May-55	3.62	2	WILLIAMSON	UK1-3	19-Mar-53	8.67	3
WHITE	UK1-2	18-Mar-53	4.23	2	WILSON	UK1-3	19-Mar-53	4.52	2
WHITE	TP6-4	25-Mar-55	4.32	2	WILSON	PB17-2	29-Sep-57	5.07	3
WHITE	BJ3-6	6-Nov-51	4.86	2	WILSON	PB4-5	9-Jul-57	11.16	4
WHITE	PB2-5	22-Jun-57	6.96	3					

INDICIDUAL FALLOUT DAYS
TEXAS

COUNTY	SHOT	DATE	µCi/SQ METER	INDEX	COUNTY	SHOT	DATE	µCi/SQ METER	INDEX
ANDERSON	TP10-3	7-May-55	4.43	2	ARMSTRONG	TP11-5	19-May-55	4.98	2
ANDERSON	TS6-4	28-May-52	4.82	2	ARMSTRONG	UK7-3	27-Apr-53	5.82	3
ANDERSON	UK1-2	18-Mar-53	5.36	3	ARMSTRONG	TP10-3	7-May-55	5.86	3
ANDERSON	TP6-2	23-Mar-55	13.77	4	ARMSTRONG	TP11-4	18-May-55	12.48	4
ANDREWS	UK8-2	9-May-53	3.64	2	ARMSTRONG	UK3-5	4-Apr-53	13.66	4
ANDREWS	PB12-5	6-Sep-57	3.79	2	ARMSTRONG	UK9-1	19-May-53	14.00	4
ANDREWS	TP7-2	30-Mar-55	5.54	3	ARMSTRONG	UK7-2	26-Apr-53	25.70	5
ANDREWS	UK9-1	19-May-53	6.03	3	ARMSTRONG	TP7-2	30-Mar-55	26.42	5
ANDREWS	PB13-5	10-Sep-57	7.20	3	ARMSTRONG	TP10-2	6-May-55	32.43	5
ANDREWS	PB3-2	25-Jun-57	11.19	4	ARMSTRONG	TS8-1	5-Jun-52	53.18	6
ANDREWS	UK6-2	19-Apr-53	16.20	4	ARMSTRONG	TS6-4	28-May-52	61.72	6
ANDREWS	TP7-1	29-Mar-55	18.63	4	ATASCOSA	UK6-2	19-Apr-53	4.52	2
ANDREWS	TS6-4	28-May-52	26.04	5	ATASCOSA	TS6-4	28-May-52	13.50	4
ANDREWS	UK7-2	26-Apr-53	49.67	5	ATASCOSA	TS8-1	5-Jun-52	475.66	9
ANDREWS	TS8-1	5-Jun-52	53.18	6	AUSTIN	TP6-3	24-Mar-55	8.63	3
ANGELINA	UK7-4	28-Apr-53	3.85	2	AUSTIN	TP11-2	16-May-55	11.92	4
ANGELINA	PB12-4	5-Sep-57	3.92	2	AUSTIN	TS6-4	28-May-52	12.54	4
ANGELINA	TP6-3	24-Mar-55	8.63	3	AUSTIN	UK6-2	19-Apr-53	77.35	6
ANGELINA	UK7-3	27-Apr-53	18.69	4	BAILEY	UK6-3	20-Apr-53	4.23	2
ANGELINA	UK6-2	19-Apr-53	77.35	6	BAILEY	UK1-2	18-Mar-53	7.32	3
ARANSAS	UK6-2	19-Apr-53	4.52	2	BAILEY	PB12-5	6-Sep-57	8.01	3
ARANSAS	PB1-5	1-Jun-57	5.04	3	BAILEY	TP11-4	18-May-55	9.59	3
ARANSAS	TS6-4	28-May-52	23.14	4	BAILEY	UK7-3	27-Apr-53	9.86	3
ARCHER	TS7-6	6-Jun-52	3.76	2	BAILEY	PB13-4	9-Sep-57	9.99	3
ARCHER	PB12-5	6-Sep-57	4.48	2	BAILEY	PB3-2	25-Jun-57	11.19	4
ARCHER	UK1-2	18-Mar-53	4.53	2	BAILEY	TP7-2	30-Mar-55	26.42	5
ARCHER	UK6-2	19-Apr-53	5.25	3	BAILEY	TP10-2	6-May-55	32.43	5
ARCHER	TP11-5	19-May-55	6.46	3	BAILEY	UK9-1	19-May-53	36.84	5
ARCHER	UK7-2	26-Apr-53	6.50	3	BAILEY	TS6-4	28-May-52	48.22	5
ARCHER	TS6-4	28-May-52	46.74	5	BAILEY	TS8-1	5-Jun-52	53.18	6
ARCHER	TS8-1	5-Jun-52	475.66	9	BAILEY	UK7-2	26-Apr-53	72.82	6
ARMSTRONG	UK1-2	18-Mar-53	3.94	2	BANDERA	TS6-4	28-May-52	4.82	2
ARMSTRONG	UK6-3	20-Apr-53	4.23	2	BANDERA	PB1-5	1-Jun-57	5.04	3

INDIVIDUAL FALLOUT DAYS
TEXAS

COUNTY	SHOT	DATE	µCi/SQ METER	INDEX	COUNTY	SHOT	DATE	µCi/SQ METER	INDEX
BANDERA	TP6-2	23-Mar-55	6.49	3	BORDEN	TS8-1	5-Jun-52	53.18	6
BANDERA	TS8-2	6-Jun-52	7.39	3	BOSQUE	UK7-3	27-Apr-53	4.18	2
BANDERA	TS8-1	5-Jun-52	1284.27	10	BOSQUE	UK7-2	26-Apr-53	4.77	2
BASTROP	UK6-2	19-Apr-53	4.52	2	BOSQUE	UK1-2	18-Mar-53	5.26	3
BASTROP	TS6-4	28-May-52	13.50	4	BOSQUE	PB12-5	6-Sep-57	6.25	3
BAYLOR	TS7-6	6-Jun-52	3.57	2	BOSQUE	TS1-3	3-Apr-52	7.22	3
BAYLOR	UK1-2	18-Mar-53	3.81	2	BOSQUE	TS6-4	28-May-52	9.64	3
BAYLOR	UK6-2	19-Apr-53	5.25	3	BOSQUE	TP6-2	23-Mar-55	13.77	4
BAYLOR	TP11-5	19-May-55	6.49	3	BOWIE	TS7-4	4-Jun-52	3.53	2
BAYLOR	UK7-2	26-Apr-53	8.94	3	BOWIE	UK5-4	14-Apr-53	3.91	2
BAYLOR	TS6-4	28-May-52	48.22	5	BOWIE	PB8-3	20-Aug-57	4.00	2
BAYLOR	TS8-1	5-Jun-52	475.66	9	BOWIE	BJ3-5	5-Nov-51	4.02	2
BEE	UK6-2	19-Apr-53	4.52	2	BOWIE	TS7-6	6-Jun-52	4.32	2
BEE	PB1-5	1-Jun-57	8.42	3	BOWIE	TP11-5	19-May-55	4.43	2
BEE	TS6-4	28-May-52	21.21	4	BOWIE	UK1-2	18-Mar-53	5.37	3
BELL	TS1-3	3-Apr-52	3.61	2	BOWIE	TP11-6	20-May-55	5.50	3
BELL	PB12-5	6-Sep-57	4.37	2	BOWIE	PB12-5	6-Sep-57	5.57	3
BELL	TS6-4	28-May-52	9.27	3	BOWIE	TP6-2	23-Mar-55	13.77	4
BELL	TP6-2	23-Mar-55	13.77	4	BOWIE	TP10-3	7-May-55	19.24	4
BEXAR	TS8-2	6-Jun-52	4.47	2	BOWIE	TS1-3	3-Apr-52	24.86	4
BEXAR	UK6-2	19-Apr-53	4.52	2	BRAZORIA	TP11-2	16-May-55	7.17	3
BEXAR	TS6-4	28-May-52	6.75	3	BRAZORIA	TP6-3	24-Mar-55	8.63	3
BEXAR	TS8-1	5-Jun-52	776.91	9	BRAZORIA	TS6-4	28-May-52	10.61	4
BLANCO	TS8-2	6-Jun-52	4.47	2	BRAZORIA	UK6-2	19-Apr-53	77.35	6
BLANCO	PB1-5	1-Jun-57	5.04	3	BRAZOS	UK7-3	27-Apr-53	4.67	2
BLANCO	UK6-2	19-Apr-53	5.25	3	BRAZOS	TP6-2	23-Mar-55	13.77	4
BLANCO	TS6-4	28-May-52	10.61	4	BREWSTER	TS6-4	28-May-52	5.79	3
BLANCO	TS8-1	5-Jun-52	776.91	9	BREWSTER	TP6-2	23-Mar-55	6.49	3
BORDEN	PB12-5	6-Sep-57	4.41	2	BREWSTER	TS8-1	5-Jun-52	53.18	6
BORDEN	TP11-5	19-May-55	4.74	2	BRISCOE	TP11-5	19-May-55	3.63	2
BORDEN	UK6-2	19-Apr-53	5.25	3	BRISCOE	TP11-3	17-May-55	3.74	2
BORDEN	UK7-2	26-Apr-53	34.02	5	BRISCOE	UK7-3	27-Apr-53	4.07	2
					BRISCOE	TP10-3	7-May-55	4.10	2

INDIVIDUAL FALLOUT DAYS
TEXAS

COUNTY	SHOT	DATE	µCi/SQ METER	INDEX	COUNTY	SHOT	DATE	µCi/SQ METER	INDEX
BRISCOE	UK6-3	20-Apr-53	4.23	2	CAMERON	PB1-5	1-Jun-57	8.42	3
BRISCOE	TS7-6	6-Jun-52	4.25	2	CAMERON	TS6-4	28-May-52	34.76	5
BRISCOE	UK1-2	18-Mar-53	4.38	2	CAMP	PB12-5	6-Sep-57	3.73	2
BRISCOE	UK8-2	9-May-53	6.06	3	CAMP	BJ3-5	5-Nov-51	4.02	2
BRISCOE	TP11-4	18-May-55	6.55	3	CAMP	PB11-1	31-Aug-57	4.09	2
BRISCOE	UK9-1	19-May-53	7.54	3	CAMP	TP10-3	7-May-55	6.24	3
BRISCOE	UK3-5	4-Apr-53	8.19	3	CAMP	UK1-2	18-Mar-53	7.57	3
BRISCOE	UK9-4	22-May-53	23.29	4	CAMP	TP11-5	19-May-55	8.40	3
BRISCOE	UK7-2	26-Apr-53	31.69	5	CAMP	TP6-2	23-Mar-55	13.77	4
BRISCOE	TP10-2	6-May-55	32.43	5	CAMP	TS6-4	28-May-52	20.25	4
BRISCOE	TP7-2	30-Mar-55	52.84	6	CAMP	TS1-3	3-Apr-52	41.51	5
BRISCOE	TS8-1	5-Jun-52	475.66	9	CARSON	UK1-2	18-Mar-53	3.65	2
BROOKS	UK6-2	19-Apr-53	4.52	2	CARSON	UK6-3	20-Apr-53	4.23	2
BROOKS	PB1-5	1-Jun-57	8.42	3	CARSON	TP11-5	19-May-55	7.25	3
BROOKS	TS6-4	28-May-52	24.11	4	CARSON	TP10-3	7-May-55	7.66	3
BROWN	PB13-5	10-Sep-57	3.66	2	CARSON	UK7-3	27-Apr-53	7.87	3
BROWN	UK6-2	19-Apr-53	5.25	3	CARSON	TP11-4	18-May-55	11.17	4
BROWN	TS8-1	5-Jun-52	475.66	9	CARSON	UK3-5	4-Apr-53	13.66	4
BURLESON	TP6-2	23-Mar-55	13.77	4	CARSON	UK7-2	26-Apr-53	17.16	4
BURNET	UK6-2	19-Apr-53	5.25	3	CARSON	UK9-1	19-May-53	17.45	4
BURNET	TS6-4	28-May-52	6.75	3	CARSON	TP7-2	30-Mar-55	26.42	5
CALDWELL	UK6-2	19-Apr-53	4.52	2	CARSON	TP10-2	6-May-55	32.43	5
CALDWELL	PB1-5	1-Jun-57	5.04	3	CARSON	TS8-1	5-Jun-52	53.18	6
CALDWELL	TS6-4	28-May-52	13.50	4	CARSON	TS6-4	28-May-52	78.11	6
CALHOUN	UK6-2	19-Apr-53	4.52	2	CASS	PB11-1	31-Aug-57	4.09	2
CALHOUN	PB1-5	1-Jun-57	8.42	3	CASS	UK1-2	18-Mar-53	4.58	2
CALHOUN	TS6-4	28-May-52	19.29	4	CASS	PB12-5	6-Sep-57	5.26	3
CALLAHAN	TS7-6	6-Jun-52	4.23	2	CASS	TP11-5	19-May-55	5.89	3
CALLAHAN	TS8-2	6-Jun-52	4.47	2	CASS	TP11-6	20-May-55	8.60	3
CALLAHAN	PB12-5	6-Sep-57	5.90	3	CASS	TS6-4	28-May-52	11.57	4
CALLAHAN	UK6-2	19-Apr-53	21.02	4	CASS	TP6-2	23-Mar-55	13.77	4
CALLAHAN	TS8-1	5-Jun-52	776.91	9	CASS	TS1-3	3-Apr-52	41.51	5
CAMERON	UK6-2	19-Apr-53	4.52	2	CASTRO	PB12-5	6-Sep-57	3.72	2

INDIVIDUAL FALLOUT DAYS
TEXAS

COUNTY	SHOT	DATE	µCi/SQ METER	INDEX	COUNTY	SHOT	DATE	µCi/SQ METER	INDEX
CASTRO	TP10-3	7-May-55	3.94	2	CHILDRESS	TP7-2	30-Mar-55	26.42	5
CASTRO	UK6-3	20-Apr-53	4.23	2	CHILDRESS	TP10-2	6-May-55	32.43	5
CASTRO	UK1-2	18-Mar-53	6.28	3	CHILDRESS	UK7-2	26-Apr-53	32.70	5
CASTRO	TP11-5	19-May-55	7.42	3	CHILDRESS	TS8-1	5-Jun-52	53.18	6
CASTRO	UK3-5	4-Apr-53	8.19	3	CLAY	TS7-6	6-Jun-52	3.54	2
CASTRO	UK7-3	27-Apr-53	9.06	3	CLAY	UK9-2	20-May-53	3.97	2
CASTRO	TP11-4	18-May-55	9.59	3	CLAY	PB8-3	20-Aug-57	4.00	2
CASTRO	PB13-4	9-Sep-57	9.99	3	CLAY	UK7-2	26-Apr-53	5.48	3
CASTRO	PB3-2	25-Jun-57	11.19	4	CLAY	UK1-2	18-Mar-53	5.77	3
CASTRO	TP7-2	30-Mar-55	26.42	5	CLAY	UK7-3	27-Apr-53	6.46	3
CASTRO	TP10-2	6-May-55	32.43	5	CLAY	TP11-5	19-May-55	6.59	3
CASTRO	UK9-1	19-May-53	38.35	5	CLAY	PB12-5	6-Sep-57	6.92	3
CASTRO	UK7-2	26-Apr-53	47.43	5	CLAY	TP10-3	7-May-55	7.89	3
CASTRO	TS6-4	28-May-52	53.04	6	CLAY	TP6-2	23-Mar-55	13.77	4
CASTRO	TS8-1	5-Jun-52	53.18	6	CLAY	TS6-4	28-May-52	51.57	6
CHAMBERS	TS6-4	28-May-52	3.86	2	COCHRAN	UK8-2	9-May-53	3.64	2
CHAMBERS	TP11-2	16-May-55	7.17	3	COCHRAN	PB12-5	6-Sep-57	5.15	3
CHAMBERS	TP6-3	24-Mar-55	8.63	3	COCHRAN	TP7-2	30-Mar-55	5.54	3
CHAMBERS	PB11-1	31-Aug-57	9.32	3	COCHRAN	UK1-2	18-Mar-53	5.98	3
CHAMBERS	UK6-2	19-Apr-53	77.35	6	COCHRAN	TP11-5	19-May-55	6.04	3
CHEROKEE	PB12-5	6-Sep-57	3.54	2	COCHRAN	UK7-3	27-Apr-53	8.66	3
CHEROKEE	BJ3-5	5-Nov-51	4.02	2	COCHRAN	PB13-4	9-Sep-57	9.99	3
CHEROKEE	UK1-2	18-Mar-53	4.43	2	COCHRAN	PB3-2	25-Jun-57	11.19	4
CHEROKEE	PB12-4	5-Sep-57	4.66	2	COCHRAN	UK6-2	19-Apr-53	16.20	4
CHEROKEE	TS6-4	28-May-52	7.71	3	COCHRAN	TP7-1	29-Mar-55	18.63	4
CHEROKEE	UK7-3	27-Apr-53	10.17	4	COCHRAN	UK9-1	19-May-53	23.27	4
CHEROKEE	TP6-2	23-Mar-55	13.77	4	COCHRAN	TS8-1	5-Jun-52	53.18	6
CHEROKEE	TP11-5	19-May-55	3.51	1	COCHRAN	UK7-2	26-Apr-53	84.20	6
CHILDRESS	UK1-2	18-Mar-53	3.71	2	COKE	UK7-2	26-Apr-53	4.16	2
CHILDRESS	UK6-3	20-Apr-53	4.23	2	COKE	UK6-2	19-Apr-53	5.25	3
CHILDRESS	UK8-2	9-May-53	6.06	3	COKE	TS8-1	5-Jun-52	239.29	8
CHILDRESS	TP10-3	7-May-55	6.17	3	COLEMAN	UK6-2	19-Apr-53	5.25	3
CHILDRESS	UK3-5	4-Apr-53	8.19	3	COLEMAN	TS8-1	5-Jun-52	475.66	9

INDIVIDUAL FALLOUT DAYS
TEXAS

COUNTY	SHOT	DATE	µCi/SQ METER	INDEX	COUNTY	SHOT	DATE	µCi/SQ METER	INDEX
COLLIN	TS7-5	5-Jun-52	3.63	2	COMAL	TS6-4	28-May-52	6.75	3
COLLIN	TP10-3	7-May-55	3.98	2	COMAL	TS8-1	5-Jun-52	776.91	9
COLLIN	PB8-3	20-Aug-57	4.00	2	COMANCHE	TS6-4	28-May-52	3.86	2
COLLIN	PB11-1	31-Aug-57	4.09	2	COMANCHE	UK6-2	19-Apr-53	5.25	3
COLLIN	TS7-6	6-Jun-52	5.90	3	COMANCHE	PB12-5	6-Sep-57	5.52	3
COLLIN	TP11-5	19-May-55	7.33	3	COMANCHE	TS8-1	5-Jun-52	53.18	6
COLLIN	UK7-2	26-Apr-53	8.63	3	CONCHO	PB13-5	10-Sep-57	3.60	2
COLLIN	PB12-5	6-Sep-57	8.92	3	CONCHO	TP11-5	19-May-55	3.92	2
COLLIN	UK1-2	18-Mar-53	13.59	4	CONCHO	TS6-4	28-May-52	4.82	2
COLLIN	TP6-2	23-Mar-55	13.77	4	CONCHO	UK6-2	19-Apr-53	5.25	3
COLLIN	TS1-3	3-Apr-52	16.84	4	CONCHO	TS8-1	5-Jun-52	475.66	9
COLLIN	TS6-4	28-May-52	27.97	5	COOKE	PB8-3	20-Aug-57	4.00	2
COLLIN	UK7-3	27-Apr-53	36.07	5	COOKE	PB13-9	14-Sep-57	4.15	2
COLLINGSWORT	TP11-3	17-May-55	3.58	2	COOKE	TS1-3	3-Apr-52	5.61	3
COLLINGSWORT	UK1-2	18-Mar-53	3.61	2	COOKE	UK7-2	26-Apr-53	6.09	3
COLLINGSWORT	UK6-3	20-Apr-53	4.23	2	COOKE	PB12-5	6-Sep-57	7.86	3
COLLINGSWORT	TP10-3	7-May-55	4.54	2	COOKE	UK1-2	18-Mar-53	9.37	3
COLLINGSWORT	TP11-4	18-May-55	4.86	2	COOKE	TP6-2	23-Mar-55	13.77	4
COLLINGSWORT	UK8-2	9-May-53	6.06	3	COOKE	TP11-5	19-May-55	14.69	4
COLLINGSWORT	UK7-3	27-Apr-53	9.97	3	COOKE	TP10-3	7-May-55	16.13	4
COLLINGSWORT	UK7-2	26-Apr-53	12.09	4	COOKE	TS6-4	28-May-52	22.18	4
COLLINGSWORT	UK3-5	4-Apr-53	13.66	4	COOKE	UK7-3	27-Apr-53	32.03	5
COLLINGSWORT	UK9-4	22-May-53	15.39	4	CORYELL	PB12-5	6-Sep-57	5.20	3
COLLINGSWORT	TP7-2	30-Mar-55	26.42	5	CORYELL	TS6-4	28-May-52	7.71	3
COLLINGSWORT	TP10-2	6-May-55	32.43	5	CORYELL	TP6-2	23-Mar-55	13.77	4
COLLINGSWORT	TS8-1	5-Jun-52	53.18	6	COTTLE	UK1-2	18-Mar-53	3.71	2
COLORADO	UK6-2	19-Apr-53	4.52	2	COTTLE	UK6-2	19-Apr-53	5.25	3
COLORADO	PB11-1	31-Aug-57	6.37	3	COTTLE	TP11-4	18-May-55	6.16	3
COLORADO	PB1-5	1-Jun-57	8.42	3	COTTLE	TP11-5	19-May-55	6.52	3
COLORADO	TS6-4	28-May-52	24.11	4	COTTLE	UK7-2	26-Apr-53	21.84	4
COMAL	TS8-2	6-Jun-52	4.47	2	COTTLE	TS6-4	28-May-52	41.47	5
COMAL	UK6-2	19-Apr-53	4.52	2	COTTLE	TS8-1	5-Jun-52	53.18	6
COMAL	PB1-5	1-Jun-57	5.04	3	CRANE	TP6-2	23-Mar-55	6.49	3

INDIVIDUAL FALLOUT DAYS
TEXAS

COUNTY	SHOT	DATE	µCi/SQ METER	INDEX	COUNTY	SHOT	DATE	µCi/SQ METER	INDEX
CRANE	UK7-2	26-Apr-53	10.77	4	DALLAM	PB3-2	25-Jun-57	11.19	4
CRANE	TS6-4	28-May-52	15.06	4	DALLAM	TP10-3	7-May-55	14.09	4
CRANE	TS8-1	5-Jun-52	53.18	6	DALLAM	UK7-3	27-Apr-53	17.26	4
CROCKETT	TS6-4	28-May-52	4.82	2	DALLAM	TP10-2	6-May-55	32.43	5
CROCKETT	TP6-2	23-Mar-55	6.49	3	DALLAM	TS8-1	5-Jun-52	39.88	5
CROCKETT	UK7-2	26-Apr-53	7.27	3	DALLAM	R1-1	28-Jan-51	46.74	5
CROCKETT	TS8-1	5-Jun-52	53.18	6	DALLAM	UK9-1	19-May-53	87.04	6
CROSBY	TS7-5	5-Jun-52	3.68	2	DALLAM	TP7-2	30-Mar-55	105.67	7
CROSBY	UK1-2	18-Mar-53	4.23	2	DALLAS	TS1-3	3-Apr-52	5.61	3
CROSBY	UK6-3	20-Apr-53	4.23	2	DALLAS	TP10-3	7-May-55	6.18	3
CROSBY	TS6-4	28-May-52	19.29	4	DALLAS	TP11-5	19-May-55	6.79	3
CROSBY	TP7-2	30-Mar-55	26.42	5	DALLAS	UK7-2	26-Apr-53	9.21	3
CROSBY	TP10-2	6-May-55	32.43	5	DALLAS	PB12-5	6-Sep-57	9.96	3
CROSBY	UK7-2	26-Apr-53	42.25	5	DALLAS	TS6-4	28-May-52	13.50	4
CROSBY	TS8-1	5-Jun-52	53.18	6	DALLAS	TP6-2	23-Mar-55	13.77	4
CULBERSON	UK8-2	9-May-53	3.64	2	DALLAS	UK1-2	18-Mar-53	15.06	4
CULBERSON	UK9-1	19-May-53	4.09	2	DALLAS	UK7-3	27-Apr-53	45.34	5
CULBERSON	TP7-2	30-Mar-55	5.54	3	DAWSON	PB5-5	19-Jul-57	3.59	2
CULBERSON	PB3-2	25-Jun-57	11.19	4	DAWSON	UK9-1	19-May-53	4.09	2
CULBERSON	UK6-2	19-Apr-53	16.20	4	DAWSON	PB12-5	6-Sep-57	4.28	2
CULBERSON	TP7-1	29-Mar-55	18.63	4	DAWSON	UK6-2	19-Apr-53	5.25	3
CULBERSON	TS6-4	28-May-52	35.92	5	DAWSON	TS6-4	28-May-52	23.14	4
CULBERSON	UK7-2	26-Apr-53	47.03	5	DAWSON	UK7-2	26-Apr-53	47.74	5
CULBERSON	TS8-1	5-Jun-52	53.18	6	DAWSON	TS8-1	5-Jun-52	53.18	6
DALLAM	UK6-3	20-Apr-53	4.23	2	DE WITT	UK6-2	19-Apr-53	4.52	2
DALLAM	PB12-4	5-Sep-57	4.66	2	DE WITT	PB1-5	1-Jun-57	8.42	3
DALLAM	TP11-4	18-May-55	5.13	3	DE WITT	TS6-4	28-May-52	29.89	5
DALLAM	TP11-3	17-May-55	5.88	3	DEAF SMITH	UK6-3	20-Apr-53	4.23	2
DALLAM	TS6-4	28-May-52	6.45	3	DEAF SMITH	TP10-3	7-May-55	4.72	2
DALLAM	UK1-2	18-Mar-53	6.70	3	DEAF SMITH	UK1-2	18-Mar-53	7.22	3
DALLAM	UK7-2	26-Apr-53	7.41	3	DEAF SMITH	UK3-5	4-Apr-53	8.19	3
DALLAM	UK9-2	20-May-53	7.74	3	DEAF SMITH	TP11-4	18-May-55	9.43	3
DALLAM	PB13-4	9-Sep-57	9.99	3	DEAF SMITH	PB13-4	9-Sep-57	9.99	3

INDICES INDIVIDUAL FALLOUT DAYS
TEXAS

COUNTY	SHOT	DATE	µCi/SQ METER	INDEX	COUNTY	SHOT	DATE	µCi/SQ METER	INDEX
DEAF SMITH	PB3-2	25-Jun-57	11.19	4	DICKENS	UK7-2	26-Apr-53	31.89	5
DEAF SMITH	UK7-3	27-Apr-53	13.71	4	DICKENS	TS8-1	5-Jun-52	239.29	8
DEAF SMITH	TP7-2	30-Mar-55	26.42	5	DIMMIT	TS5-1	7-May-52	3.64	2
DEAF SMITH	TP10-2	6-May-55	32.43	5	DIMMIT	TS6-4	28-May-52	4.82	2
DEAF SMITH	UK7-2	26-Apr-53	42.05	5	DIMMIT	TP6-2	23-Mar-55	6.49	3
DEAF SMITH	TS8-1	5-Jun-52	53.18	6	DIMMIT	TS8-1	5-Jun-52	475.66	9
DEAF SMITH	TS6-4	28-May-52	67.50	6	DONLEY	PB12-4	5-Sep-57	3.58	2
DEAF SMITH	UK9-1	19-May-53	68.08	6	DONLEY	TS6-4	28-May-52	4.03	2
DELTA	PB8-3	20-Aug-57	4.00	2	DONLEY	UK6-3	20-Apr-53	4.23	2
DELTA	UK7-3	27-Apr-53	4.13	2	DONLEY	UK1-2	18-Mar-53	4.43	2
DELTA	TS7-6	6-Jun-52	6.06	3	DONLEY	UK7-3	27-Apr-53	4.59	2
DELTA	PB11-1	31-Aug-57	6.14	3	DONLEY	PB12-5	6-Sep-57	5.03	3
DELTA	TP11-5	19-May-55	6.43	3	DONLEY	TP10-3	7-May-55	5.05	3
DELTA	PB12-5	6-Sep-57	6.90	3	DONLEY	UK9-1	19-May-53	5.17	3
DELTA	TS6-4	28-May-52	7.71	3	DONLEY	TP11-5	19-May-55	5.43	3
DELTA	UK1-2	18-Mar-53	9.80	3	DONLEY	TP11-4	18-May-55	10.07	4
DELTA	TP6-2	23-Mar-55	13.77	4	DONLEY	UK3-5	4-Apr-53	13.66	4
DELTA	TS1-3	3-Apr-52	24.86	4	DONLEY	UK7-2	26-Apr-53	17.98	4
DENTON	PB8-3	20-Aug-57	4.00	2	DONLEY	TP7-2	30-Mar-55	26.42	5
DENTON	TP11-5	19-May-55	7.30	3	DONLEY	UK9-4	22-May-53	27.67	5
DENTON	TP10-3	7-May-55	8.46	3	DONLEY	TP10-2	6-May-55	32.43	5
DENTON	PB12-5	6-Sep-57	8.56	3	DONLEY	TS8-1	5-Jun-52	53.18	6
DENTON	UK7-2	26-Apr-53	10.16	4	DUVAL	UK6-2	19-Apr-53	4.52	2
DENTON	UK1-2	18-Mar-53	11.81	4	DUVAL	PB1-5	1-Jun-57	5.04	3
DENTON	TP6-2	23-Mar-55	13.77	4	DUVAL	TS6-4	28-May-52	10.61	4
DENTON	TS1-3	3-Apr-52	16.84	4	EASTLAND	TS1-3	3-Apr-52	3.61	2
DENTON	TS6-4	28-May-52	18.32	4	EASTLAND	TP11-5	19-May-55	5.21	3
DENTON	UK7-3	27-Apr-53	33.61	5	EASTLAND	UK6-2	19-Apr-53	5.25	3
DICKENS	UK1-2	18-Mar-53	3.61	2	EASTLAND	PB12-5	6-Sep-57	5.83	3
DICKENS	UK6-2	19-Apr-53	5.25	3	EASTLAND	TS8-1	5-Jun-52	475.66	9
DICKENS	PB12-5	6-Sep-57	5.28	3	ECTOR	UK8-2	9-May-53	3.64	2
DICKENS	TP11-5	19-May-55	7.17	3	ECTOR	UK9-1	19-May-53	4.09	2
DICKENS	TS6-4	28-May-52	16.39	4	ECTOR	TP7-2	30-Mar-55	5.54	3

INDIVIDUAL FALLOUT DAYS
TEXAS

COUNTY	SHOT	DATE	µCi/SQ METER	INDEX	COUNTY	SHOT	DATE	µCi/SQ METER	INDEX
ECTOR	UK6-2	19-Apr-53	16.20	4	FANNIN	TS7-5	5-Jun-52	4.23	2
ECTOR	TP7-1	29-Mar-55	18.63	4	FANNIN	UK1-9	25-Mar-53	6.00	3
ECTOR	UK7-2	26-Apr-53	25.29	5	FANNIN	PB11-1	31-Aug-57	6.14	3
ECTOR	TS8-1	5-Jun-52	53.18	6	FANNIN	PB12-5	6-Sep-57	7.51	3
EDWARDS	TP6-2	23-Mar-55	6.49	3	FANNIN	PB12-4	5-Sep-57	8.92	3
EDWARDS	TS8-1	5-Jun-52	53.18	6	FANNIN	UK1-2	18-Mar-53	9.89	3
EL PASO	UK8-2	9-May-53	3.64	2	FANNIN	TP6-2	23-Mar-55	13.77	4
EL PASO	TP7-1	30-Mar-55	5.54	3	FANNIN	TP11-5	19-May-55	14.27	4
EL PASO	UK6-3	20-Apr-53	6.04	3	FANNIN	TS1-3	3-Apr-52	16.84	4
EL PASO	PB3-2	25-Jun-57	11.19	4	FANNIN	TS6-4	28-May-52	28.93	5
EL PASO	UK6-2	19-Apr-53	16.20	4	FANNIN	UK7-3	27-Apr-53	54.77	6
EL PASO	TP7-1	29-Mar-55	18.63	4	FAYETTE	UK6-2	19-Apr-53	4.52	2
EL PASO	UK7-2	26-Apr-53	40.12	5	FAYETTE	PB1-5	1-Jun-57	5.04	3
EL PASO	TS6-4	28-May-52	45.32	5	FAYETTE	PB11-1	31-Aug-57	6.37	3
EL PASO	TS8-1	5-Jun-52	53.18	6	FAYETTE	TS6-4	28-May-52	13.50	4
EL PASO	TS7-3	3-Jun-52	62.27	6	FISHER	PB11-1	31-Aug-57	4.09	2
ELLIS	TS1-3	3-Apr-52	5.61	3	FISHER	PB12-5	6-Sep-57	4.97	2
ELLIS	PB12-5	6-Sep-57	8.82	3	FISHER	UK6-2	19-Apr-53	5.25	3
ELLIS	UK7-2	26-Apr-53	9.57	3	FISHER	TS1-3	3-Apr-52	7.22	3
ELLIS	TP11-5	19-May-55	10.22	4	FISHER	TS6-4	28-May-52	10.61	4
ELLIS	UK1-2	18-Mar-53	11.09	4	FISHER	UK7-2	26-Apr-53	11.58	4
ELLIS	TS6-4	28-May-52	11.57	4	FISHER	TP11-5	19-May-55	3.50	1
ELLIS	TP6-2	23-Mar-55	13.77	4	FISHER	TS8-1	5-Jun-52	475.66	9
ELLIS	UK7-3	27-Apr-53	19.84	4	FLOYD	PB12-5	6-Sep-57	3.54	2
ERATH	TS1-3	3-Apr-52	3.61	2	FLOYD	TP11-5	19-May-55	4.08	2
ERATH	UK7-2	26-Apr-53	4.37	2	FLOYD	UK6-3	20-Apr-53	4.23	2
ERATH	UK1-2	18-Mar-53	4.64	2	FLOYD	UK1-2	18-Mar-53	4.95	2
ERATH	PB12-5	6-Sep-57	6.97	3	FLOYD	UK9-1	19-May-53	5.60	3
ERATH	TP6-2	23-Mar-55	13.77	4	FLOYD	TP11-4	18-May-55	7.97	3
FALLS	TS1-3	3-Apr-52	7.22	3	FLOYD	TS6-4	28-May-52	8.06	3
FALLS	TP6-2	23-Mar-55	13.77	4	FLOYD	UK9-4	22-May-53	9.04	3
FANNIN	PB8-3	20-Aug-57	4.00	2	FLOYD	TS7-3	3-Jun-52	12.39	4
FANNIN	TS7-6	6-Jun-52	4.01	2	FLOYD	TP7-2	30-Mar-55	26.42	5

INDIVIDUAL FALLOUT DAYS
TEXAS

COUNTY	SHOT	DATE	µCi/SQ METER	INDEX	COUNTY	SHOT	DATE	µCi/SQ METER	INDEX
FLOYD	TP10-2	6-May-55	32.43	5					7
FLOYD	UK7-2	26-Apr-53	38.90	5	GAINES	UK8-2	9-May-53	3.64	2
FLOYD	TS8-1	5-Jun-52	53.18	6	GAINES	UK7-3	27-Apr-53	3.78	2
FOARD	PB12-5	6-Sep-57	4.16	2	GAINES	PB12-5	6-Sep-57	4.28	2
FOARD	TP11-4	18-May-55	4.22	2	GAINES	TP7-2	30-Mar-55	5.54	3
FOARD	UK6-2	19-Apr-53	5.25	3	GAINES	PB13-5	10-Sep-57	7.85	3
FOARD	TP11-5	19-May-55	14.33	4	GAINES	UK9-1	19-May-53	8.83	3
FOARD	UK7-2	26-Apr-53	15.64	4	GAINES	PB3-2	25-Jun-57	11.19	4
FOARD	TS6-4	28-May-52	35.68	5	GAINES	UK6-2	19-Apr-53	16.20	4
FOARD	TS8-1	5-Jun-52	53.18	6	GAINES	TP7-1	29-Mar-55	18.63	4
FOARD	UK1-2	18-Mar-53	3.50	1	GAINES	TS6-4	28-May-52	19.29	4
FORT BEND	PB1-5	1-Jun-57	5.04	3	GAINES	TS8-1	5-Jun-52	53.18	6
FORT BEND	TP6-3	24-Mar-55	8.63	3	GAINES	UK7-2	26-Apr-53	67.85	6
FORT BEND	TS6-4	28-May-52	11.57	4	GALVESTON	TS6-4	28-May-52	4.82	2
FORT BEND	UK6-2	19-Apr-53	77.35	6	GALVESTON	PB1-5	1-Jun-57	5.04	3
FRANKLIN	TS7-6	6-Jun-52	4.45	2	GALVESTON	TP6-3	24-Mar-55	8.63	3
FRANKLIN	TP11-5	19-May-55	4.85	2	GALVESTON	UK6-2	19-Apr-53	77.35	6
FRANKLIN	PB12-5	6-Sep-57	5.99	3	GARZA	UK6-2	19-Apr-53	5.25	3
FRANKLIN	PB11-1	31-Aug-57	6.14	3	GARZA	PB12-5	6-Sep-57	7.01	3
FRANKLIN	TS6-4	28-May-52	6.75	3	GARZA	UK7-2	26-Apr-53	39.81	5
FRANKLIN	UK1-2	18-Mar-53	8.77	3	GARZA	TS6-4	28-May-52	41.47	5
FRANKLIN	TP6-2	23-Mar-55	13.77	4	GARZA	TS8-1	5-Jun-52	53.18	6
FRANKLIN	TS1-3	3-Apr-52	16.64	4	GILLESPIE	TS8-2	6-Jun-52	4.47	2
FREESTONE	UK7-2	26-Apr-53	4.37	2	GILLESPIE	TS6-4	28-May-52	4.82	2
FREESTONE	UK1-2	18-Mar-53	5.67	3	GILLESPIE	PB1-5	1-Jun-57	5.04	3
FREESTONE	TS6-4	28-May-52	5.79	3	GILLESPIE	TP6-2	23-Mar-55	6.49	3
FREESTONE	PB12-5	6-Sep-57	5.90	3	GILLESPIE	TS8-1	5-Jun-52	776.91	9
FREESTONE	PB11-1	31-Aug-57	6.14	3	GLASSCOCK	UK6-2	19-Apr-53	5.25	3
FREESTONE	TP6-2	23-Mar-55	13.77	4	GLASSCOCK	UK7-2	26-Apr-53	10.56	4
FRIO	TS6-4	28-May-52	5.79	3	GLASSCOCK	TS8-1	5-Jun-52	53.18	6
FRIO	TP6-2	23-Mar-55	6.49	3	GOLIAD	UK6-2	19-Apr-53	4.52	2
FRIO	TS8-2	6-Jun-52	7.39	3	GOLIAD	TS6-4	28-May-52	20.25	4
FRIO	TS8-1	5-Jun-52	1284.2	10	GONZALES	UK6-2	19-Apr-53	4.52	2

INDIVIDUAL FALLOUT DAYS
TEXAS

COUNTY	SHOT	DATE	µCi/SQ METER	INDEX	COUNTY	SHOT	DATE	µCi/SQ METER	INDEX
GONZALES	BJ3-5	5-Nov-51	4.79	2	GREGG	TP11-5	19-May-55	5.05	3
GONZALES	PB1-5	1-Jun-57	5.04	3	GREGG	PB12-5	6-Sep-57	5.62	3
GONZALES	TS6-4	28-May-52	14.46	4	GREGG	UK1-2	18-Mar-53	6.29	3
GRAY	UK9-2	20-May-53	3.61	2	GREGG	PB11-1	31-Aug-57	10.23	4
GRAY	TP11-3	17-May-55	3.90	2	GREGG	TP6-2	23-Mar-55	13.77	4
GRAY	UK1-2	18-Mar-53	4.12	2	GRIMES	PB5-4	18-Jul-57	3.80	2
GRAY	UK6-3	20-Apr-53	4.23	2	GRIMES	UK7-3	27-Apr-53	4.67	2
GRAY	TS6-4	28-May-52	4.83	2	GRIMES	BJ3-5	5-Nov-51	4.79	2
GRAY	UK9-1	19-May-53	6.25	3	GRIMES	TP6-3	24-Mar-55	8.63	3
GRAY	UK7-3	27-Apr-53	6.42	3	GRIMES	UK6-2	19-Apr-53	77.35	6
GRAY	TP10-3	7-May-55	6.68	3	GUADALUPE	UK6-2	19-Apr-53	4.52	2
GRAY	UK3-5	4-Apr-53	8.19	3	GUADALUPE	TS6-4	28-May-52	6.75	3
GRAY	UK7-2	26-Apr-53	11.27	4	HALE	TP11-3	17-May-55	3.61	2
GRAY	TP11-4	18-May-55	12.36	4	HALE	UK7-3	27-Apr-53	4.01	2
GRAY	TP7-2	30-Mar-55	26.42	5	HALE	UK6-3	20-Apr-53	4.23	2
GRAY	TP10-2	6-May-55	32.43	5	HALE	TP11-5	19-May-55	4.40	2
GRAY	TS8-1	5-Jun-52	53.18	6	HALE	PB12-5	6-Sep-57	5.21	3
GRAYSON	BJ5-6	24-Nov-51	3.70	2	HALE	UK3-5	4-Apr-53	5.46	3
GRAYSON	TS7-6	6-Jun-52	3.97	2	HALE	UK1-2	18-Mar-53	5.87	3
GRAYSON	PB8-3	20-Aug-57	4.00	2	HALE	TS6-4	28-May-52	8.86	3
GRAYSON	TP10-3	7-May-55	5.26	3	HALE	PB13-4	9-Sep-57	9.99	3
GRAYSON	UK7-2	26-Apr-53	5.28	3	HALE	PB3-2	25-Jun-57	11.19	4
GRAYSON	UK1-9	25-Mar-53	6.00	3	HALE	TP11-4	18-May-55	12.91	4
GRAYSON	PB12-4	5-Sep-57	7.64	3	HALE	UK9-1	19-May-53	12.93	4
GRAYSON	PB12-5	6-Sep-57	8.29	3	HALE	TP7-2	30-Mar-55	26.42	5
GRAYSON	TP11-5	19-May-55	8.29	3	HALE	TP10-2	6-May-55	32.43	5
GRAYSON	UK1-2	18-Mar-53	10.57	4	HALE	UK7-2	26-Apr-53	48.55	5
GRAYSON	TS1-3	3-Apr-52	11.23	4	HALE	TS8-1	5-Jun-52	53.18	6
GRAYSON	TP6-2	23-Mar-55	13.77	4	HALL	PB12-5	6-Sep-57	3.60	2
GRAYSON	TS6-4	28-May-52	19.29	4	HALL	UK6-3	20-Apr-53	4.23	2
GRAYSON	UK7-3	27-Apr-53	54.72	6	HALL	TS8-2	6-Jun-52	4.56	2
GREGG	BJ3-5	5-Nov-51	4.02	2	HALL	UK1-2	18-Mar-53	5.67	3
GREGG	TS6-4	28-May-52	4.82	2	HALL	UK8-2	9-May-53	6.06	3

INDIVIDUAL FALLOUT DAYS
TEXAS

COUNTY	SHOT	DATE	µCi/SQ METER	INDEX	COUNTY	SHOT	DATE	µCi/SQ METER	INDEX
HALL	UK7-3	27-Apr-53	6.32	3	HARDEMAN	TS6-4	28-May-52	26.04	5
HALL	TP11-4	18-May-55	6.43	3	HARDEMAN	TS8-1	5-Jun-52	53.18	6
HALL	TS7-6	6-Jun-52	7.06	3	HARDEMAN	UK1-2	18-Mar-53	3.50	1
HALL	UK3-5	4-Apr-53	8.19	3	HARDIN	TS6-4	28-May-52	3.86	2
HALL	UK7-2	26-Apr-53	22.55	4	HARDIN	TP11-2	16-May-55	4.75	2
HALL	TP7-2	30-Mar-55	26.42	5	HARDIN	TP6-3	24-Mar-55	8.63	3
HALL	TP10-2	6-May-55	32.43	5	HARDIN	UK6-2	19-Apr-53	77.35	6
HALL	TS6-4	28-May-52	36.64	5	HARRIS	TP11-2	16-May-55	4.75	2
HALL	TS8-1	5-Jun-52	792.76	9	HARRIS	PB1-5	1-Jun-57	5.04	3
HAMILTON	PB12-5	6-Sep-57	5.62	3	HARRIS	TP6-3	24-Mar-55	8.63	3
HAMILTON	TS1-3	3-Apr-52	7.22	3	HARRIS	TS6-4	28-May-52	9.64	3
HAMILTON	TS6-4	28-May-52	7.71	3	HARRIS	UK6-2	19-Apr-53	77.35	6
HAMILTON	TP6-2	23-Mar-55	13.77	4	HARRISON	UK7-4	28-Apr-53	3.52	2
HANSFORD	UK6-3	20-Apr-53	4.23	2	HARRISON	PB12-4	5-Sep-57	3.74	2
HANSFORD	UK7-2	26-Apr-53	4.27	2	HARRISON	PB5-4	18-Jul-57	3.80	2
HANSFORD	TP11-3	17-May-55	5.08	3	HARRISON	TP11-5	19-May-55	3.93	2
HANSFORD	UK3-5	4-Apr-53	5.46	3	HARRISON	PB11-1	31-Aug-57	4.09	2
HANSFORD	PB12-4	5-Sep-57	5.68	3	HARRISON	UK1-2	18-Mar-53	4.21	2
HANSFORD	TP11-4	18-May-55	6.28	3	HARRISON	TS1-3	3-Apr-52	6.22	3
HANSFORD	TS6-4	28-May-52	7.25	3	HARRISON	TS6-4	28-May-52	9.64	3
HANSFORD	UK9-2	20-May-53	7.67	3	HARRISON	TP6-2	23-Mar-55	13.77	4
HANSFORD	TP10-3	7-May-55	9.15	3	HARTLEY	UK6-3	20-Apr-53	4.23	2
HANSFORD	UK7-3	27-Apr-53	12.50	4	HARTLEY	UK9-2	20-May-53	5.26	3
HANSFORD	UK9-1	19-May-53	18.10	4	HARTLEY	TP11-3	17-May-55	5.84	3
HANSFORD	TP10-2	6-May-55	32.43	5	HARTLEY	TS6-4	28-May-52	6.45	3
HANSFORD	TS8-1	5-Jun-52	53.18	6	HARTLEY	UK1-2	18-Mar-53	6.45	3
HANSFORD	TP7-2	30-Mar-55	105.67	7	HARTLEY	TP11-4	18-May-55	7.50	3
HARDEMAN	PB12-5	6-Sep-57	3.97	2	HARTLEY	PB13-4	9-Sep-57	9.99	3
HARDEMAN	UK6-2	19-Apr-53	5.25	3	HARTLEY	PB3-2	25-Jun-57	11.19	4
HARDEMAN	TP11-5	19-May-55	7.24	3	HARTLEY	UK7-2	26-Apr-53	15.24	4
HARDEMAN	UK7-3	27-Apr-53	10.33	4	HARTLEY	UK7-3	27-Apr-53	16.86	4
HARDEMAN	UK7-2	26-Apr-53	14.52	4	HARTLEY	TP10-3	7-May-55	21.13	4
HARDEMAN	TP10-3	7-May-55	14.65	4	HARTLEY	TP10-2	6-May-55	32.43	5

INDIVIDUAL FALLOUT DAYS
TEXAS

COUNTY	SHOT	DATE	µCi/SQ METER	INDEX	COUNTY	SHOT	DATE	µCi/SQ METER	INDEX
HARTLEY	TS8-1	5-Jun-52	39.88	5	HIDALGO	UK6-2	19-Apr-53	4.52	2
HARTLEY	TP7-2	30-Mar-55	52.84	6	HIDALGO	TS6-4	28-May-52	16.22	4
HARTLEY	UK9-1	19-May-53	89.63	6	HILL	TS1-3	3-Apr-52	5.61	3
HASKELL	UK6-2	19-Apr-53	5.25	3	HILL	TS6-4	28-May-52	5.79	3
HASKELL	PB12-5	6-Sep-57	6.27	3	HILL	UK1-2	18-Mar-53	6.79	3
HASKELL	TP11-5	19-May-55	6.52	3	HILL	UK7-2	26-Apr-53	7.21	3
HASKELL	UK7-2	26-Apr-53	9.34	3	HILL	PB12-5	6-Sep-57	11.33	4
HASKELL	TS6-4	28-May-52	27.00	5	HILL	TP6-2	23-Mar-55	13.77	4
HASKELL	TS8-1	5-Jun-52	475.66	9	HOCKLEY	PB11-1	31-Aug-57	3.87	2
HAYS	UK6-2	19-Apr-53	4.52	2	HOCKLEY	UK6-3	20-Apr-53	4.23	2
HAYS	PB1-5	1-Jun-57	5.04	3	HOCKLEY	UK7-3	27-Apr-53	5.22	3
HAYS	TS6-4	28-May-52	12.54	4	HOCKLEY	UK1-2	18-Mar-53	5.57	3
HEMPHILL	UK9-4	22-May-53	3.51	2	HOCKLEY	TP10-3	7-May-55	6.62	3
HEMPHILL	UK11-2	5-Jun-53	3.70	2	HOCKLEY	TP11-4	18-May-55	7.86	3
HEMPHILL	TP11-5	19-May-55	3.81	2	HOCKLEY	UK3-5	4-Apr-53	8.19	3
HEMPHILL	UK6-3	20-Apr-53	4.23	2	HOCKLEY	PB13-4	9-Sep-57	9.99	3
HEMPHILL	UK7-2	26-Apr-53	4.37	2	HOCKLEY	PB3-2	25-Jun-57	11.19	4
HEMPHILL	TP11-4	18-May-55	4.74	2	HOCKLEY	UK9-1	19-May-53	15.94	4
HEMPHILL	UK9-2	20-May-53	6.14	3	HOCKLEY	TP7-2	30-Mar-55	26.42	5
HEMPHILL	UK7-3	27-Apr-53	7.08	3	HOCKLEY	TP10-2	6-May-55	32.43	5
HEMPHILL	TP10-3	7-May-55	7.43	3	HOCKLEY	TS8-1	5-Jun-52	53.18	6
HEMPHILL	UK3-5	4-Apr-53	8.19	3	HOCKLEY	UK7-2	26-Apr-53	65.21	6
HEMPHILL	TS6-4	28-May-52	15.31	4	HOOD	TS1-3	3-Apr-52	5.61	3
HEMPHILL	TP7-2	30-Mar-55	26.42	5	HOOD	UK7-2	26-Apr-53	6.20	3
HEMPHILL	TP10-2	6-May-55	32.43	5	HOOD	UK1-2	18-Mar-53	6.28	3
HEMPHILL	TS8-1	5-Jun-52	53.18	6	HOOD	PB12-5	6-Sep-57	7.29	3
HENDERSON	TS7-6	6-Jun-52	3.93	2	HOOD	UK7-3	27-Apr-53	8.44	3
HENDERSON	UK7-2	26-Apr-53	4.06	2	HOOD	TS6-4	28-May-52	12.54	4
HENDERSON	PB12-5	6-Sep-57	4.78	2	HOOD	TP6-2	23-Mar-55	13.77	4
HENDERSON	UK7-3	27-Apr-53	6.25	3	HOPKINS	UK7-3	27-Apr-53	3.84	2
HENDERSON	TP11-5	19-May-55	6.65	3	HOPKINS	PB8-3	20-Aug-57	4.00	2
HENDERSON	UK1-2	18-Mar-53	8.00	3	HOPKINS	TS7-6	6-Jun-52	5.54	3
HENDERSON	TP6-2	23-Mar-55	13.77	4	HOPKINS	TS6-4	28-May-52	6.75	3

INDIVIDUAL FALLOUT DAYS
TEXAS

COUNTY	SHOT	DATE	µCi/SQ METER	INDEX	COUNTY	SHOT	DATE	µCi/SQ METER	INDEX
HOPKINS	PB12-5	6-Sep-57	6.90	3	HUTCHINSON	TP11-3	17-May-55	5.12	3
HOPKINS	UK1-2	18-Mar-53	10.06	4	HUTCHINSON	UK9-2	20-May-53	5.41	3
HOPKINS	TP11-5	19-May-55	10.45	4	HUTCHINSON	UK3-5	4-Apr-53	5.46	3
HOPKINS	TP6-2	23-Mar-55	13.77	4	HUTCHINSON	TP11-5	19-May-55	6.24	3
HOPKINS	TS1-3	3-Apr-52	41.51	5	HUTCHINSON	TS6-4	28-May-52	7.25	3
HOUSTON	UK7-4	28-Apr-53	3.57	2	HUTCHINSON	TP11-4	18-May-55	8.02	3
HOUSTON	TP6-2	23-Mar-55	13.77	4	HUTCHINSON	UK7-2	26-Apr-53	9.04	3
HOWARD	PB12-5	6-Sep-57	3.97	2	HUTCHINSON	PB12-4	5-Sep-57	9.19	3
HOWARD	UK6-2	19-Apr-53	5.25	3	HUTCHINSON	TP10-3	7-May-55	9.62	3
HOWARD	UK7-2	26-Apr-53	20.21	4	HUTCHINSON	UK7-3	27-Apr-53	11.30	4
HOWARD	TS8-1	5-Jun-52	53.18	6	HUTCHINSON	UK9-1	19-May-53	18.74	4
HUDSPETH	UK8-2	9-May-53	3.64	2	HUTCHINSON	TP10-2	6-May-55	32.43	5
HUDSPETH	TS6-4	28-May-52	4.82	2	HUTCHINSON	TS8-1	5-Jun-52	53.18	6
HUDSPETH	TP7-2	30-Mar-55	5.54	3	HUTCHINSON	TP7-2	30-Mar-55	105.67	7
HUDSPETH	PB3-2	25-Jun-57	11.19	4	IRION	UK6-2	19-Apr-53	5.25	3
HUDSPETH	UK6-2	19-Apr-53	16.20	4	IRION	TS6-4	28-May-52	5.79	3
HUDSPETH	TP7-1	29-Mar-55	18.63	4	IRION	TS8-1	5-Jun-52	475.66	9
HUDSPETH	TS7-3	3-Jun-52	26.20	5	JACK	TP11-5	19-May-55	3.63	2
HUDSPETH	UK7-2	26-Apr-53	48.85	5	JACK	PB8-3	20-Aug-57	4.00	2
HUDSPETH	TS8-1	5-Jun-52	53.18	6	JACK	UK7-3	27-Apr-53	4.40	2
HUNT	PB8-3	20-Aug-57	4.00	2	JACK	PB12-5	6-Sep-57	4.56	2
HUNT	PB11-1	31-Aug-57	4.09	2	JACK	TS1-3	3-Apr-52	5.61	3
HUNT	UK7-2	26-Apr-53	4.47	2	JACK	UK7-2	26-Apr-53	6.09	3
HUNT	UK7-3	27-Apr-53	4.68	2	JACK	UK1-2	18-Mar-53	6.70	3
HUNT	PB12-5	6-Sep-57	7.37	3	JACK	TP6-2	23-Mar-55	13.77	4
HUNT	TS6-4	28-May-52	7.71	3	JACK	TS6-4	28-May-52	21.21	4
HUNT	TS7-6	6-Jun-52	9.51	3	JACKSON	UK6-2	19-Apr-53	4.52	2
HUNT	UK1-2	18-Mar-53	12.90	4	JACKSON	PB1-5	1-Jun-57	8.42	3
HUNT	TP11-5	19-May-55	13.27	4	JACKSON	TS6-4	28-May-52	28.93	5
HUNT	TP6-2	23-Mar-55	13.77	4	JASPER	PB5-4	18-Jul-57	3.80	2
HUNT	TS1-3	3-Apr-52	16.84	4	JASPER	TS6-4	28-May-52	3.86	2
HUTCHINSON	UK1-2	18-Mar-53	3.61	2	JASPER	PB11-1	31-Aug-57	4.09	2
HUTCHINSON	UK6-3	20-Apr-53	4.23	2	JASPER	UK7-3	27-Apr-53	6.05	3

INDIVIDUAL FALLOUT DAYS
TEXAS

COUNTY	SHOT	DATE	µCi/SQ METER	INDEX	COUNTY	SHOT	DATE	µCi/SQ METER	INDEX
JASPER	TP11-2	16-May-55	7.17	3	KARNES	UK6-2	19-Apr-53	4.52	2
JASPER	UK7-4	28-Apr-53	8.07	3	KARNES	PB1-5	1-Jun-57	5.04	3
JASPER	TP6-3	24-Mar-55	8.63	3	KARNES	TS6-4	28-May-52	16.39	4
JASPER	UK6-2	19-Apr-53	77.35	6	KAUFMAN	UK7-3	27-Apr-53	4.53	2
JEFF DAVIS	PB5-5	19-Jul-57	3.59	2	KAUFMAN	TS7-6	6-Jun-52	4.89	2
JEFF DAVIS	UK8-2	9-May-53	3.64	2	KAUFMAN	TP6-2	23-Mar-55	5.72	3
JEFF DAVIS	PB4-5	9-Jul-57	4.60	2	KAUFMAN	PB12-5	6-Sep-57	8.45	3
JEFF DAVIS	TP7-2	30-Mar-55	5.54	3	KAUFMAN	UK1-2	18-Mar-53	12.02	4
JEFF DAVIS	UK7-2	26-Apr-53	9.24	3	KAUFMAN	UK7-2	26-Apr-53	16.35	4
JEFF DAVIS	UK6-2	19-Apr-53	16.20	4	KAUFMAN	TS1-3	3-Apr-52	16.84	4
JEFF DAVIS	TS7-3	3-Jun-52	16.26	4	KAUFMAN	TS6-4	28-May-52	26.65	5
JEFF DAVIS	TS6-4	28-May-52	17.38	4	KENDALL	TS6-4	28-May-52	5.79	3
JEFF DAVIS	TP7-1	29-Mar-55	18.63	4	KENDALL	TP6-2	23-Mar-55	6.49	3
JEFF DAVIS	PB3-2	25-Jun-57	22.38	4	KENDALL	PB1-5	1-Jun-57	8.42	3
JEFF DAVIS	TS8-1	5-Jun-52	53.18	6	KENDALL	TS8-1	5-Jun-52	475.66	9
JEFFERSON	TP6-3	24-Mar-55	3.58	2	KENEDY	UK6-2	19-Apr-53	4.52	2
JEFFERSON	UK6-2	19-Apr-53	32.12	5	KENEDY	PB1-5	1-Jun-57	5.04	3
JIM HOGG	UK6-2	19-Apr-53	4.52	2	KENEDY	TS6-4	28-May-52	27.97	5
JIM HOGG	PB1-5	1-Jun-57	8.42	3	KENT	TP11-5	19-May-55	3.82	2
JIM WELLS	UK6-2	19-Apr-53	4.52	2	KENT	TP11-4	18-May-55	4.03	2
JIM WELLS	PB1-5	1-Jun-57	8.42	3	KENT	PB12-5	6-Sep-57	5.03	3
JIM WELLS	TS6-4	28-May-52	13.50	4	KENT	UK6-2	19-Apr-53	5.25	3
JOHNSON	TS6-4	28-May-52	6.75	3	KENT	TS6-4	28-May-52	10.61	4
JOHNSON	UK7-2	26-Apr-53	8.84	3	KENT	UK7-2	26-Apr-53	27.22	5
JOHNSON	UK1-2	18-Mar-53	9.29	3	KENT	TS8-1	5-Jun-52	53.18	6
JOHNSON	PB12-5	6-Sep-57	10.91	4	KERR	TS8-2	6-Jun-52	4.47	2
JOHNSON	UK7-3	27-Apr-53	13.20	4	KERR	TP6-2	23-Mar-55	6.49	3
JOHNSON	TP6-2	23-Mar-55	13.77	4	KERR	TS6-4	28-May-52	7.71	3
JONES	UK7-2	26-Apr-53	5.08	3	KERR	TS8-1	5-Jun-52	776.91	9
JONES	UK6-2	19-Apr-53	5.25	3	KIMBLE	TS6-4	28-May-52	3.86	2
JONES	PB12-5	6-Sep-57	5.65	3	KIMBLE	TP6-2	23-Mar-55	6.49	3
JONES	TS6-4	28-May-52	7.25	3	KIMBLE	TS8-1	5-Jun-52	475.66	9
JONES	TS8-1	5-Jun-52	475.66	9	KING	TP11-4	18-May-55	3.63	2

INDIVIDUAL FALLOUT DAYS
TEXAS

COUNTY	SHOT	DATE	µCi/SQ METER	INDEX	COUNTY	SHOT	DATE	µCi/SQ METER	INDEX
KING	TP11-5	19-May-55	3.63	2	LAMB	UK6-3	20-Apr-53	4.23	2
KING	UK6-2	19-Apr-53	5.25	3	LAMB	TP11-5	19-May-55	4.63	2
KING	UK7-2	26-Apr-53	21.23	4	LAMB	PB12-5	6-Sep-57	5.28	3
KING	TS6-4	28-May-52	26.04	5	LAMB	UK7-3	27-Apr-53	6.54	3
KING	TS8-1	5-Jun-52	53.18	6	LAMB	UK1-2	18-Mar-53	6.70	3
KINNEY	TP6-2	23-Mar-55	6.49	3	LAMB	TP11-4	18-May-55	9.63	3
KINNEY	TS8-1	5-Jun-52	53.18	6	LAMB	PB13-4	9-Sep-57	9.99	3
KLEBERG	BJ3-2	2-Nov-51	4.34	2	LAMB	PB3-2	25-Jun-57	11.19	4
KLEBERG	UK6-2	19-Apr-53	4.52	2	LAMB	UK9-1	19-May-53	25.85	5
KLEBERG	PB1-5	1-Jun-57	5.04	3	LAMB	TP7-2	30-Mar-55	26.42	5
KLEBERG	TS6-4	28-May-52	16.39	4	LAMB	TP10-2	6-May-55	32.43	5
KNOX	TS7-6	6-Jun-52	4.15	2	LAMB	TS6-4	28-May-52	39.54	5
KNOX	PB12-5	6-Sep-57	4.28	2	LAMB	UK7-2	26-Apr-53	59.72	6
KNOX	UK6-2	19-Apr-53	5.25	3	LAMB	TS8-1	5-Jun-52	239.29	8
KNOX	TP11-5	19-May-55	12.34	4	LAMPASAS	TS1-3	3-Apr-52	3.61	2
KNOX	UK7-2	26-Apr-53	13.20	4	LAMPASAS	UK6-2	19-Apr-53	5.25	3
KNOX	TS6-4	28-May-52	25.07	5	LAMPASAS	TS6-4	28-May-52	12.54	4
KNOX	TS8-1	5-Jun-52	475.66	9	LAMPASAS	TS8-1	5-Jun-52	475.66	9
LA SALLE	UK6-2	19-Apr-53	4.52	2	LAVACA	UK6-2	19-Apr-53	4.52	2
LA SALLE	TS6-4	28-May-52	12.54	4	LAVACA	PB1-5	1-Jun-57	5.04	3
LAMAR	PB8-3	20-Aug-57	4.00	2	LAVACA	TS6-4	28-May-52	14.46	4
LAMAR	PB13-9	14-Sep-57	4.15	2	LEE	TS6-4	28-May-52	9.27	3
LAMAR	TS7-6	6-Jun-52	5.29	3	LEE	TP6-2	23-Mar-55	13.77	4
LAMAR	TP11-6	20-May-55	5.67	3	LEON	TS6-4	28-May-52	4.64	2
LAMAR	PB11-1	31-Aug-57	6.14	3	LEON	TP6-2	23-Mar-55	13.77	4
LAMAR	PB12-5	6-Sep-57	6.21	3	LIBERTY	PB11-1	31-Aug-57	4.09	2
LAMAR	TP11-5	19-May-55	6.78	3	LIBERTY	TP11-2	16-May-55	7.17	3
LAMAR	UK1-2	18-Mar-53	8.43	3	LIBERTY	TS6-4	28-May-52	7.71	3
LAMAR	TP10-3	7-May-55	13.48	4	LIBERTY	TP6-3	24-Mar-55	8.63	3
LAMAR	TP6-2	23-Mar-55	13.77	4	LIBERTY	UK6-2	19-Apr-53	77.35	6
LAMAR	TS6-4	28-May-52	15.43	4	LIMESTONE	UK1-2	18-Mar-53	4.64	2
LAMAR	UK7-3	27-Apr-53	26.56	5	LIMESTONE	UK7-2	26-Apr-53	4.67	2
LAMAR	TS1-3	3-Apr-52	41.51	5	LIMESTONE	TS1-3	3-Apr-52	5.61	3

INDIVIDUAL FALLOUT DAYS
TEXAS

COUNTY	SHOT	DATE	µCi/SQ METER	INDEX	COUNTY	SHOT	DATE	µCi/SQ METER	INDEX
LIMESTONE	PB12-5	6-Sep-57	5.69	3	LOVING	UK7-2	26-Apr-53	51.60	6
LIMESTONE	UK7-3	27-Apr-53	6.89	3	LOVING	TS8-1	5-Jun-52	53.18	6
LIMESTONE	TS6-4	28-May-52	10.43	4	LOVING	TS6-4	28-May-52	79.95	6
LIMESTONE	TP6-2	23-Mar-55	13.77	4	LUBBOCK	UK9-4	22-May-53	3.75	2
LIPSCOMB	TS6-7	31-May-52	3.81	2	LUBBOCK	UK6-3	20-Apr-53	4.23	2
LIPSCOMB	PB12-4	5-Sep-57	3.85	2	LUBBOCK	UK1-2	18-Mar-53	4.84	2
LIPSCOMB	TP11-3	17-May-55	4.09	2	LUBBOCK	TP11-4	18-May-55	5.33	3
LIPSCOMB	UK6-3	20-Apr-53	4.23	2	LUBBOCK	UK3-5	4-Apr-53	5.46	3
LIPSCOMB	TS6-4	28-May-52	4.83	2	LUBBOCK	TS6-4	28-May-52	6.45	3
LIPSCOMB	UK9-2	20-May-53	8.13	3	LUBBOCK	UK9-1	19-May-53	7.97	3
LIPSCOMB	UK3-5	4-Apr-53	8.19	3	LUBBOCK	PB13-4	9-Sep-57	9.99	3
LIPSCOMB	PB13-5	10-Sep-57	9.68	3	LUBBOCK	PB3-2	25-Jun-57	11.19	4
LIPSCOMB	UK9-4	22-May-53	16.14	4	LUBBOCK	TP7-2	30-Mar-55	26.42	5
LIPSCOMB	TP10-3	7-May-55	17.14	4	LUBBOCK	TP10-2	6-May-55	32.43	5
LIPSCOMB	UK7-3	27-Apr-53	23.44	4	LUBBOCK	UK7-2	26-Apr-53	51.49	6
LIPSCOMB	TP10-2	6-May-55	32.43	5	LUBBOCK	TS8-1	5-Jun-52	53.18	6
LIPSCOMB	TP7-2	30-Mar-55	52.84	6	LYNN	UK1-2	18-Mar-53	3.81	2
LIPSCOMB	TS8-1	5-Jun-52	53.18	6	LYNN	PB13-5	10-Sep-57	3.98	2
LIVE OAK	UK6-2	19-Apr-53	4.52	2	LYNN	UK6-3	20-Apr-53	4.23	2
LIVE OAK	TS6-4	28-May-52	19.29	4	LYNN	PB12-5	6-Sep-57	4.65	2
LLANO	TS1-3	3-Apr-52	3.61	2	LYNN	UK9-4	22-May-53	4.91	2
LLANO	TS8-2	6-Jun-52	4.47	2	LYNN	UK9-1	19-May-53	4.96	2
LLANO	UK6-2	19-Apr-53	5.25	3	LYNN	UK3-5	4-Apr-53	8.19	3
LLANO	TS6-4	28-May-52	9.64	3	LYNN	TS6-4	28-May-52	16.39	4
LLANO	TS8-1	5-Jun-52	776.91	9	LYNN	TP7-2	30-Mar-55	26.42	5
LOVING	UK8-2	9-May-53	3.64	2	LYNN	TP10-2	6-May-55	32.43	5
LOVING	UK7-3	27-Apr-53	3.99	2	LYNN	UK7-2	26-Apr-53	51.90	6
LOVING	PB13-5	10-Sep-57	4.46	2	LYNN	TS8-1	5-Jun-52	53.18	6
LOVING	TP7-2	30-Mar-55	5.54	3	MADISON	BJ3-5	5-Nov-51	4.02	2
LOVING	UK9-1	19-May-53	6.25	3	MADISON	UK7-3	27-Apr-53	11.07	4
LOVING	PB3-2	25-Jun-57	11.19	4	MADISON	TP6-2	23-Mar-55	13.77	4
LOVING	UK6-2	19-Apr-53	16.20	4	MADISON	UK7-2	26-Apr-53	32.10	5
LOVING	TP7-1	29-Mar-55	18.63	4	MARION	UK1-2	18-Mar-53	4.81	2

INDIVIDUAL FALLOUT DAYS
TEXAS

COUNTY	SHOT	DATE	µCi/SQ METER	INDEX	COUNTY	SHOT	DATE	µCi/SQ METER	INDEX
MARION	TP11-5	19-May-55	4.82	2	MCMULLEN	UK6-2	19-Apr-53	4.52	2
MARION	TP11-6	20-May-55	7.84	3	MCMULLEN	TS8-2	6-Jun-52	7.39	3
MARION	TS6-4	28-May-52	10.61	4	MCMULLEN	TS6-4	28-May-52	15.43	4
MARION	TP6-2	23-Mar-55	13.77	4	MCMULLEN	TS8-1	5-Jun-52	1284.27	10
MARION	TS1-3	3-Apr-52	16.64	4	MEDINA	PB1-5	1-Jun-57	5.04	3
MARTIN	PB12-5	6-Sep-57	3.85	2	MEDINA	TP6-2	23-Mar-55	6.49	3
MARTIN	UK6-2	19-Apr-53	5.25	3	MEDINA	TS8-2	6-Jun-52	7.39	3
MARTIN	PB13-5	10-Sep-57	6.13	3	MEDINA	TS6-4	28-May-52	9.64	3
MARTIN	TS6-4	28-May-52	16.39	4	MEDINA	TS8-1	5-Jun-52	1284.27	10
MARTIN	UK7-2	26-Apr-53	31.18	5	MENARD	TS1-3	3-Apr-52	3.61	2
MARTIN	TS8-1	5-Jun-52	53.18	6	MENARD	UK6-2	19-Apr-53	5.25	3
MASON	PB11-1	31-Aug-57	4.09	2	MENARD	TS6-4	28-May-52	7.71	3
MASON	TS8-2	6-Jun-52	4.47	2	MENARD	TS8-1	5-Jun-52	239.29	8
MASON	UK6-2	19-Apr-53	5.25	3	MIDLAND	UK6-2	19-Apr-53	5.25	3
MASON	TS6-4	28-May-52	8.68	3	MIDLAND	TS6-4	28-May-52	6.75	3
MASON	TS8-1	5-Jun-52	776.91	9	MIDLAND	UK7-2	26-Apr-53	16.45	4
MATAGORDA	UK6-2	19-Apr-53	4.52	2	MIDLAND	TS8-1	5-Jun-52	53.18	6
MATAGORDA	PB1-5	1-Jun-57	5.04	3	MILAM	PB12-5	6-Sep-57	3.80	2
MATAGORDA	PB11-1	31-Aug-57	6.37	3	MILAM	TP6-2	23-Mar-55	13.77	4
MATAGORDA	TS6-4	28-May-52	7.71	3	MILLS	UK6-2	19-Apr-53	5.25	3
MAVERICK	TP6-2	23-Mar-55	6.49	3	MILLS	TS6-4	28-May-52	6.75	3
MAVERICK	TS8-1	5-Jun-52	53.18	6	MILLS	TS8-1	5-Jun-52	239.29	8
MCCULLOCH	TS8-2	6-Jun-52	4.47	2	MITCHELL	UK6-2	19-Apr-53	5.25	3
MCCULLOCH	UK6-2	19-Apr-53	5.25	3	MITCHELL	UK7-2	26-Apr-53	12.39	4
MCCULLOCH	UK7-2	26-Apr-53	5.94	3	MITCHELL	TS8-1	5-Jun-52	53.18	6
MCCULLOCH	TS6-4	28-May-52	8.68	3	MONTAGUE	PB8-3	20-Aug-57	4.00	2
MCCULLOCH	TS8-1	5-Jun-52	776.91	9	MONTAGUE	PB12-5	6-Sep-57	4.65	2
MCLENNAN	UK1-2	18-Mar-53	4.12	2	MONTAGUE	PB12-4	5-Sep-57	5.54	3
MCLENNAN	UK7-2	26-Apr-53	4.37	2	MONTAGUE	UK7-2	26-Apr-53	5.59	3
MCLENNAN	PB12-5	6-Sep-57	5.60	3	MONTAGUE	UK1-9	25-Mar-53	6.00	3
MCLENNAN	TS6-4	28-May-52	10.43	4	MONTAGUE	TP11-5	19-May-55	7.14	3
MCLENNAN	TS1-3	3-Apr-52	11.23	4	MONTAGUE	UK1-2	18-Mar-53	8.45	3
MCLENNAN	TP6-2	23-Mar-55	13.77	4					

INDIVIDUAL FALLOUT DAYS
TEXAS

COUNTY	SHOT	DATE	µCi/SQ METER	INDEX	COUNTY	SHOT	DATE	µCi/SQ METER	INDEX
MONTAGUE	TP10-3	7-May-55	8.76	3	MOTLEY	TP11-4	18-May-55	6.04	3
MONTAGUE	UK7-3	27-Apr-53	10.79	4	MOTLEY	UK8-2	9-May-53	6.06	3
MONTAGUE	TP6-2	23-Mar-55	13.77	4	MOTLEY	TP10-3	7-May-55	11.87	4
MONTAGUE	TS6-4	28-May-52	27.00	5	MOTLEY	TS6-4	28-May-52	12.09	4
MONTGOMERY	TS6-4	28-May-52	5.79	3	MOTLEY	TP7-2	30-Mar-55	26.42	5
MONTGOMERY	TP6-3	24-Mar-55	8.63	3	MOTLEY	UK7-2	26-Apr-53	29.56	5
MONTGOMERY	UK6-2	19-Apr-53	77.35	6	MOTLEY	TP10-2	6-May-55	32.43	5
MOORE	UK1-2	18-Mar-53	3.86	2	MOTLEY	TS8-1	5-Jun-52	239.29	8
MOORE	UK6-3	20-Apr-53	4.23	2	NACOGDOCHES	TS6-4	28-May-52	3.86	2
MOORE	TP11-5	19-May-55	5.03	3	NACOGDOCHES	BJ3-5	5-Nov-51	4.02	2
MOORE	UK9-2	20-May-53	5.49	3	NACOGDOCHES	TP11-2	16-May-55	4.75	2
MOORE	TP10-3	7-May-55	8.36	3	NACOGDOCHES	UK7-4	28-Apr-53	5.19	3
MOORE	TP11-4	18-May-55	9.69	3	NACOGDOCHES	TP6-3	24-Mar-55	8.63	3
MOORE	PB13-4	9-Sep-57	9.99	3	NACOGDOCHES	PB11-1	31-Aug-57	10.23	4
MOORE	PB3-2	25-Jun-57	11.19	4	NAVARRO	PB12-5	6-Sep-57	5.56	3
MOORE	UK7-2	26-Apr-53	12.19	4	NAVARRO	UK7-2	26-Apr-53	7.11	3
MOORE	UK7-3	27-Apr-53	12.60	4	NAVARRO	UK1-2	18-Mar-53	8.34	3
MOORE	TS6-4	28-May-52	13.70	4	NAVARRO	TS1-3	3-Apr-52	11.23	4
MOORE	TP7-2	30-Mar-55	26.42	5	NAVARRO	TS6-4	28-May-52	12.75	4
MOORE	TP10-2	6-May-55	32.43	5	NAVARRO	TP6-2	23-Mar-55	13.77	4
MOORE	UK9-1	19-May-53	46.75	5	NEWTON	UK7-3	27-Apr-53	4.30	2
MOORE	TS8-1	5-Jun-52	53.18	6	NEWTON	TS6-4	28-May-52	4.82	2
MORRIS	BJ3-5	5-Nov-51	4.02	2	NEWTON	TP6-3	24-Mar-55	8.63	3
MORRIS	PB12-5	6-Sep-57	4.11	2	NEWTON	UK7-4	28-Apr-53	10.37	4
MORRIS	TP11-5	19-May-55	4.24	2	NEWTON	TP11-2	16-May-55	11.92	4
MORRIS	UK1-2	18-Mar-53	6.88	3	NEWTON	UK6-2	19-Apr-53	77.35	6
MORRIS	TS6-4	28-May-52	11.57	4	NOLAN	TS6-4	28-May-52	3.86	2
MORRIS	TP6-2	23-Mar-55	13.77	4	NOLAN	PB12-5	6-Sep-57	4.47	2
MORRIS	TS1-3	3-Apr-52	16.64	4	NOLAN	TS8-2	6-Jun-52	4.47	2
MOTLEY	TP11-5	19-May-55	3.70	2	NOLAN	TS7-6	6-Jun-52	5.05	3
MOTLEY	UK1-2	18-Mar-53	4.23	2	NOLAN	UK6-2	19-Apr-53	5.25	3
MOTLEY	UK6-3	20-Apr-53	4.23	2	NOLAN	UK7-2	26-Apr-53	6.40	3
MOTLEY	UK3-5	4-Apr-53	5.46	3	NOLAN	TS8-1	5-Jun-52	776.91	9

INDIVIDUAL FALLOUT DAYS
TEXAS

COUNTY	SHOT	DATE	µCi/SQ METER	INDEX	COUNTY	SHOT	DATE	µCi/SQ METER	INDEX
NUECES	PB11-1	31-Aug-57	6.52	3	ORANGE	PB3-3	26-Jun-57	114.67	7
NUECES	TS6-4	28-May-52	14.50	4	PALO PINTO	UK7-3	27-Apr-53	3.69	2
NUECES	PB1-5	1-Jun-57	3.50	1	PALO PINTO	PB8-3	20-Aug-57	4.00	2
OCHILTREE	PB12-4	5-Sep-57	3.68	2	PALO PINTO	UK1-2	18-Mar-53	4.56	2
OCHILTREE	UK6-3	20-Apr-53	4.23	2	PALO PINTO	UK6-2	19-Apr-53	5.25	3
OCHILTREE	TP11-3	17-May-55	5.10	3	PALO PINTO	UK7-2	26-Apr-53	5.38	3
OCHILTREE	PB13-5	10-Sep-57	5.32	3	PALO PINTO	TS1-3	3-Apr-52	5.61	3
OCHILTREE	UK3-5	4-Apr-53	5.46	3	PALO PINTO	PB12-5	6-Sep-57	7.60	3
OCHILTREE	TS6-4	28-May-52	6.45	3	PALO PINTO	TS8-1	5-Jun-52	146.23	7
OCHILTREE	UK9-1	19-May-53	7.33	3	PANOLA	UK1-2	18-Mar-53	3.61	2
OCHILTREE	UK9-2	20-May-53	8.40	3	PANOLA	BJ3-5	5-Nov-51	4.02	2
OCHILTREE	TP10-3	7-May-55	9.64	3	PANOLA	TP11-5	19-May-55	4.89	2
OCHILTREE	UK7-3	27-Apr-53	11.69	4	PANOLA	UK7-4	28-Apr-53	4.92	2
OCHILTREE	TP10-2	6-May-55	32.43	5	PANOLA	PB12-4	5-Sep-57	5.54	3
OCHILTREE	TP7-2	30-Mar-55	105.67	7	PANOLA	TP6-3	24-Mar-55	8.63	3
OCHILTREE	TS8-1	5-Jun-52	132.94	7	PANOLA	UK7-3	27-Apr-53	12.95	4
OLDHAM	UK6-3	20-Apr-53	4.23	2	PANOLA	TS6-4	28-May-52	14.46	4
OLDHAM	UK3-5	4-Apr-53	5.46	3	PARKER	PB8-3	20-Aug-57	4.00	2
OLDHAM	TP10-3	7-May-55	5.64	3	PARKER	TS6-4	28-May-52	4.03	2
OLDHAM	TS6-4	28-May-52	6.45	3	PARKER	TP10-3	7-May-55	4.22	2
OLDHAM	UK1-2	18-Mar-53	7.05	3	PARKER	UK7-2	26-Apr-53	7.21	3
OLDHAM	TP11-4	18-May-55	8.31	3	PARKER	UK1-2	18-Mar-53	7.65	3
OLDHAM	PB13-4	9-Sep-57	9.99	3	PARKER	PB12-5	6-Sep-57	11.55	4
OLDHAM	PB3-2	25-Jun-57	11.19	4	PARKER	TP6-2	23-Mar-55	13.77	4
OLDHAM	UK7-3	27-Apr-53	13.17	4	PARKER	TS1-3	3-Apr-52	16.84	4
OLDHAM	UK7-2	26-Apr-53	27.73	5	PARMER	UK6-3	20-Apr-53	4.23	2
OLDHAM	TP10-2	6-May-55	32.43	5	PARMER	TS6-4	28-May-52	4.83	2
OLDHAM	TS8-1	5-Jun-52	53.18	6	PARMER	UK1-2	18-Mar-53	7.05	3
OLDHAM	UK9-1	19-May-53	83.16	6	PARMER	PB13-4	9-Sep-57	9.99	3
OLDHAM	TP7-2	30-Mar-55	158.51	7	PARMER	TP11-4	18-May-55	10.70	4
ORANGE	TP11-2	16-May-55	4.75	2	PARMER	PB3-2	25-Jun-57	11.19	4
ORANGE	TP6-3	24-Mar-55	8.63	3	PARMER	TP10-3	7-May-55	11.51	4
ORANGE	UK6-2	19-Apr-53	77.35	6	PARMER	UK7-3	27-Apr-53	12.16	4

INDIVIDUAL FALLOUT DAYS
TEXAS

COUNTY	SHOT	DATE	µCi/SQ METER	INDEX	COUNTY	SHOT	DATE	µCi/SQ METER	INDEX
PARMER	UK3-5	4-Apr-53	13.66	4	PRESIDIO	TS8-1	5-Jun-52	53.18	6
PARMER	TP7-2	30-Mar-55	26.42	5	RAINS	UK7-3	27-Apr-53	4.42	2
PARMER	TP10-2	6-May-55	32.43	5	RAINS	TS7-6	6-Jun-52	5.14	3
PARMER	TS8-1	5-Jun-52	53.18	6	RAINS	PB12-5	6-Sep-57	5.34	3
PARMER	UK9-1	19-May-53	54.08	6	RAINS	PB11-1	31-Aug-57	6.14	3
PARMER	UK7-2	26-Apr-53	55.05	6	RAINS	TS1-4	4-Apr-52	9.37	3
PECOS	PB13-5	10-Sep-57	5.16	3	RAINS	UK1-2	18-Mar-53	11.26	4
PECOS	TP6-2	23-Mar-55	6.49	3	RAINS	TS6-4	28-May-52	12.54	4
PECOS	TS6-4	28-May-52	12.75	4	RAINS	TP6-2	23-Mar-55	13.77	4
PECOS	TS8-1	5-Jun-52	53.18	6	RAINS	TS1-3	3-Apr-52	41.51	5
POLK	UK7-4	28-Apr-53	3.64	2	RANDALL	UK1-2	18-Mar-53	4.01	2
POLK	PB5-4	18-Jul-57	3.80	2	RANDALL	TP10-3	7-May-55	5.92	3
POLK	BJ3-5	5-Nov-51	4.02	2	RANDALL	UK7-3	27-Apr-53	7.18	3
POLK	PB11-1	31-Aug-57	4.09	2	RANDALL	PB13-4	9-Sep-57	9.99	3
POLK	TP11-2	16-May-55	7.17	3	RANDALL	TP7-2	30-Mar-55	10.97	4
POLK	TP6-3	24-Mar-55	8.63	3	RANDALL	PB3-2	25-Jun-57	11.19	4
POLK	UK6-2	19-Apr-53	77.35	6	RANDALL	TP11-4	18-May-55	11.56	4
POTTER	UK1-2	18-Mar-53	3.77	2	RANDALL	TP10-2	6-May-55	13.47	4
POTTER	UK6-3	20-Apr-53	4.23	2	RANDALL	UK7-2	26-Apr-53	25.95	5
POTTER	UK3-5	4-Apr-53	5.46	3	RANDALL	UK9-1	19-May-53	36.84	5
POTTER	TS6-4	28-May-52	6.19	3	RANDALL	TS8-1	5-Jun-52	53.18	6
POTTER	TP10-3	7-May-55	7.79	3	RANDALL	TS6-4	28-May-52	69.43	6
POTTER	TP11-4	18-May-55	9.00	3	REAGAN	UK7-2	26-Apr-53	3.86	2
POTTER	UK7-3	27-Apr-53	9.37	3	REAGAN	TP6-2	23-Mar-55	6.49	3
POTTER	PB13-4	9-Sep-57	9.99	3	REAGAN	TS6-4	28-May-52	6.75	3
POTTER	PB3-2	25-Jun-57	11.19	4	REAGAN	TS8-1	5-Jun-52	475.66	9
POTTER	UK7-2	26-Apr-53	18.19	4	REAL	TP6-2	23-Mar-55	6.49	3
POTTER	TP10-2	6-May-55	32.43	5	REAL	TS6-4	28-May-52	6.75	3
POTTER	UK9-1	19-May-53	39.54	5	REAL	TS8-1	5-Jun-52	146.23	7
POTTER	TS8-1	5-Jun-52	53.18	6	RED RIVER	UK5-4	14-Apr-53	3.91	2
POTTER	TP7-2	30-Mar-55	158.51	7	RED RIVER	PB8-3	20-Aug-57	4.00	2
PRESIDIO	TP6-2	23-Mar-55	6.49	3	RED RIVER	TS7-6	6-Jun-52	5.22	3
PRESIDIO	PB3-2	25-Jun-57	11.19	4	RED RIVER	TP11-5	19-May-55	5.79	3

INDIVIDUAL FALLOUT DAYS
TEXAS

COUNTY	SHOT	DATE	µCi/SQ METER	INDEX	COUNTY	SHOT	DATE	µCi/SQ METER	INDEX
RED RIVER	TP11-6	20-May-55	5.85	3	ROBERTS	TP10-2	6-May-55	32.43	5
RED RIVER	UK1-2	18-Mar-53	8.00	3	ROBERTS	TS8-1	5-Jun-52	53.18	6
RED RIVER	TP10-3	7-May-55	8.82	3	ROBERTSON	PB12-5	6-Sep-57	4.53	2
RED RIVER	PB12-5	6-Sep-57	9.57	3	ROBERTSON	TS6-4	28-May-52	9.27	3
RED RIVER	TP6-2	23-Mar-55	13.77	4	ROBERTSON	TP6-2	23-Mar-55	13.77	4
RED RIVER	TS1-3	3-Apr-52	24.86	4	ROCKWALL	UK7-3	27-Apr-53	5.63	3
REEVES	UK8-2	9-May-53	3.64	2	ROCKWALL	UK10-4	28-May-53	6.04	3
REEVES	PB13-5	10-Sep-57	3.92	2	ROCKWALL	TP11-5	19-May-55	6.66	3
REEVES	UK9-1	19-May-53	4.31	2	ROCKWALL	UK7-2	26-Apr-53	7.80	3
REEVES	PB4-5	9-Jul-57	4.60	2	ROCKWALL	TS7-6	6-Jun-52	8.87	3
REEVES	TS6-4	28-May-52	4.82	2	ROCKWALL	PB12-5	6-Sep-57	9.28	3
REEVES	TP7-2	30-Mar-55	5.54	3	ROCKWALL	TS6-4	28-May-52	13.50	4
REEVES	PB3-2	25-Jun-57	11.19	4	ROCKWALL	TP6-2	23-Mar-55	13.77	4
REEVES	UK6-2	19-Apr-53	16.20	4	ROCKWALL	UK1-2	18-Mar-53	14.52	4
REEVES	TP7-1	29-Mar-55	18.63	4	ROCKWALL	TS1-3	3-Apr-52	16.84	4
REEVES	UK7-2	26-Apr-53	21.94	4	RUNNELS	UK6-2	19-Apr-53	5.25	3
REEVES	TS8-1	5-Jun-52	53.18	6	RUNNELS	TS8-1	5-Jun-52	475.66	9
REFUGIO	UK6-2	19-Apr-53	4.52	2	RUSK	UK7-4	28-Apr-53	3.64	2
REFUGIO	PB1-5	1-Jun-57	5.04	3	RUSK	PB5-4	18-Jul-57	3.80	2
REFUGIO	TS6-4	28-May-52	41.47	5	RUSK	UK1-2	18-Mar-53	4.53	2
REFUGIO	R2-2	3-Feb-51	1067.00	10	RUSK	PB12-4	5-Sep-57	7.43	3
ROBERTS	UK6-3	20-Apr-53	4.23	2	RUSK	TS6-4	28-May-52	8.68	3
ROBERTS	PB13-5	10-Sep-57	5.05	3	RUSK	TP6-2	23-Mar-55	13.77	4
ROBERTS	UK9-2	20-May-53	5.11	3	RUSK	UK7-3	27-Apr-53	19.18	4
ROBERTS	UK7-2	26-Apr-53	6.30	3	SABINE	BJ3-5	5-Nov-51	4.02	2
ROBERTS	TP11-4	18-May-55	6.83	3	SABINE	PB11-1	31-Aug-57	4.09	2
ROBERTS	UK9-1	19-May-53	7.11	3	SABINE	TS6-4	28-May-52	5.79	3
ROBERTS	TP10-3	7-May-55	7.73	3	SABINE	TP11-2	16-May-55	7.17	3
ROBERTS	UK3-5	4-Apr-53	8.19	3	SABINE	TP6-3	24-Mar-55	8.63	3
ROBERTS	UK7-3	27-Apr-53	9.83	3	SABINE	UK7-4	28-Apr-53	10.05	4
ROBERTS	TS6-4	28-May-52	19.34	4	SABINE	UK6-2	19-Apr-53	77.35	6
ROBERTS	TP7-2	30-Mar-55	26.42	5	SAN AUGUSTIN	BJ3-5	5-Nov-51	4.02	2
					SAN AUGUSTIN	TS6-4	28-May-52	5.79	3

INDIVIDUAL FALLOUT DAYS
TEXAS

COUNTY	SHOT	DATE	µCi/SQ METER	INDEX	COUNTY	SHOT	DATE	µCi/SQ METER	INDEX
SAN AUGUSTIN	UK7-4	28-Apr-53	7.70	3	SHERMAN	TS6-4	28-May-52	7.25	3
SAN AUGUSTIN	TP6-3	24-Mar-55	8.63	3	SHERMAN	TP11-4	18-May-55	7.38	3
SAN AUGUSTIN	TP11-2	16-May-55	11.92	4	SHERMAN	UK9-2	20-May-53	7.82	3
SAN AUGUSTIN	UK6-2	19-Apr-53	77.35	6	SHERMAN	TP10-3	7-May-55	8.99	3
SAN JACINTO	BJ3-5	5-Nov-51	4.02	2	SHERMAN	UK7-3	27-Apr-53	15.89	4
SAN JACINTO	TP6-3	24-Mar-55	8.63	3	SHERMAN	TP7-2	30-Mar-55	26.42	5
SAN JACINTO	UK6-2	19-Apr-53	77.35	6	SHERMAN	TP10-2	6-May-55	32.43	5
SAN PATRICIO	UK6-2	19-Apr-53	4.52	2	SHERMAN	TS8-1	5-Jun-52	39.88	5
SAN PATRICIO	PB1-5	1-Jun-57	5.04	3	SHERMAN	UK9-1	19-May-53	42.87	5
SAN PATRICIO	TS6-4	28-May-52	13.70	4	SMITH	TS7-6	6-Jun-52	3.65	2
SAN SABA	UK6-2	19-Apr-53	5.25	3	SMITH	TP11-5	19-May-55	5.30	3
SAN SABA	TS6-4	28-May-52	5.79	3	SMITH	PB12-4	5-Sep-57	5.47	3
SAN SABA	TS8-1	5-Jun-52	475.66	9	SMITH	PB12-5	6-Sep-57	5.51	3
SCHLEICHER	TP6-2	23-Mar-55	6.49	3	SMITH	UK1-2	18-Mar-53	7.73	3
SCHLEICHER	TS8-1	5-Jun-52	53.18	6	SMITH	TS6-4	28-May-52	9.64	3
SCURRY	TP11-5	19-May-55	3.73	2	SMITH	PB11-1	31-Aug-57	10.23	4
SCURRY	PB12-5	6-Sep-57	4.59	2	SMITH	TP6-2	23-Mar-55	13.77	4
SCURRY	UK6-2	19-Apr-53	5.25	3	SMITH	UK7-3	27-Apr-53	19.35	4
SCURRY	TS6-4	28-May-52	13.50	4	SOMERVELL	UK1-2	18-Mar-53	5.59	3
SCURRY	UK7-2	26-Apr-53	21.53	4	SOMERVELL	TS1-3	3-Apr-52	5.61	3
SCURRY	TS8-1	5-Jun-52	53.18	6	SOMERVELL	UK7-2	26-Apr-53	5.69	3
SHACKELFORD	UK7-2	26-Apr-53	4.57	2	SOMERVELL	TS6-4	28-May-52	5.79	3
SHACKELFORD	UK6-2	19-Apr-53	5.25	3	SOMERVELL	PB12-5	6-Sep-57	6.95	3
SHACKELFORD	PB12-5	6-Sep-57	9.56	3	SOMERVELL	TP6-2	23-Mar-55	13.77	4
SHACKELFORD	TS8-1	5-Jun-52	475.66	9	STARR	TS6-4	28-May-52	3.86	2
SHELBY	TS6-4	28-May-52	6.75	3	STARR	UK6-2	19-Apr-53	4.52	2
SHELBY	TP11-2	16-May-55	7.17	3	STARR	PB1-5	1-Jun-57	5.04	3
SHELBY	UK7-4	28-Apr-53	7.81	3	STEPHENS	UK7-2	26-Apr-53	4.47	2
SHELBY	TP6-3	24-Mar-55	8.63	3	STEPHENS	UK6-2	19-Apr-53	5.25	3
SHERMAN	UK1-2	18-Mar-53	3.70	2	STEPHENS	TP11-5	19-May-55	5.95	3
SHERMAN	UK6-3	20-Apr-53	4.23	2	STEPHENS	PB12-5	6-Sep-57	6.40	3
SHERMAN	UK3-5	4-Apr-53	5.46	3	STEPHENS	PB13-5	10-Sep-57	7.96	3
SHERMAN	UK7-2	26-Apr-53	5.48	3	STEPHENS	TS8-1	5-Jun-52	146.23	7

INDIVIDUAL FALLOUT DAYS
TEXAS

COUNTY	SHOT	DATE	µCi/SQ METER	INDEX	COUNTY	SHOT	DATE	µCi/SQ METER	INDEX
STERLING	PB13-5	10-Sep-57	4.73	2	TARRANT	TS1-3	3-Apr-52	5.61	3
STERLING	UK6-2	19-Apr-53	5.25	3	TARRANT	UK1-2	18-Mar-53	11.09	4
STERLING	PB11-1	31-Aug-57	6.14	3	TARRANT	UK7-2	26-Apr-53	11.38	4
STERLING	UK7-2	26-Apr-53	6.40	3	TARRANT	TP11-5	19-May-55	12.54	4
STERLING	TS8-1	5-Jun-52	53.18	6	TARRANT	PB12-5	6-Sep-57	12.72	4
STONEWALL	TS7-6	6-Jun-52	3.78	2	TARRANT	TP6-2	23-Mar-55	13.77	4
STONEWALL	PB12-5	6-Sep-57	3.79	2	TARRANT	TS6-4	28-May-52	14.46	4
STONEWALL	UK6-2	19-Apr-53	5.25	3	TARRANT	UK7-3	27-Apr-53	22.55	4
STONEWALL	TP10-3	7-May-55	5.56	3	TAYLOR	PB13-5	10-Sep-57	4.52	2
STONEWALL	TP11-5	19-May-55	6.78	3	TAYLOR	TS8-1	5-Jun-52	146.23	7
STONEWALL	TS6-4	28-May-52	8.68	3	TERRELL	TP6-2	23-Mar-55	6.49	3
STONEWALL	UK7-2	26-Apr-53	15.54	4	TERRELL	TS8-1	5-Jun-52	53.18	6
STONEWALL	TS8-1	5-Jun-52	475.66	9	TERRY	UK7-3	27-Apr-53	3.71	2
SUTTON	TS6-4	28-May-52	3.86	2	TERRY	TP10-3	7-May-55	4.10	2
SUTTON	TP6-2	23-Mar-55	6.49	3	TERRY	UK6-3	20-Apr-53	4.23	2
SUTTON	TS8-1	5-Jun-52	146.23	7	TERRY	UK1-2	18-Mar-53	4.33	2
SWISHER	PB12-5	6-Sep-57	3.60	2	TERRY	TP11-4	18-May-55	6.32	3
SWISHER	TP10-3	7-May-55	4.16	2	TERRY	UK9-4	22-May-53	8.13	3
SWISHER	UK6-3	20-Apr-53	4.23	2	TERRY	UK3-5	4-Apr-53	8.19	3
SWISHER	UK7-3	27-Apr-53	5.20	3	TERRY	UK9-1	19-May-53	10.13	4
SWISHER	PB2-1	18-Jun-57	5.29	3	TERRY	PB3-2	25-Jun-57	11.19	4
SWISHER	UK1-2	18-Mar-53	5.42	3	TERRY	TS6-4	28-May-52	21.21	4
SWISHER	TP11-5	19-May-55	7.36	3	TERRY	TP7-2	30-Mar-55	26.42	5
SWISHER	TP11-4	18-May-55	9.53	3	TERRY	TP10-2	6-May-55	32.43	5
SWISHER	PB13-4	9-Sep-57	9.99	3	TERRY	TS8-1	5-Jun-52	53.18	6
SWISHER	PB3-2	25-Jun-57	11.19	4	TERRY	UK7-2	26-Apr-53	64.70	6
SWISHER	UK9-1	19-May-53	19.61	4	THROCKMORTON	PB12-5	6-Sep-57	4.06	2
SWISHER	TS6-4	28-May-52	23.37	4	THROCKMORTON	TS8-2	6-Jun-52	4.47	2
SWISHER	TP7-2	30-Mar-55	26.42	5	THROCKMORTON	UK6-2	19-Apr-53	5.25	3
SWISHER	TP10-2	6-May-55	32.43	5	THROCKMORTON	TS7-6	6-Jun-52	5.32	3
SWISHER	UK7-2	26-Apr-53	41.13	5	THROCKMORTON	UK7-2	26-Apr-53	6.60	3
SWISHER	TS8-1	5-Jun-52	53.18	6	THROCKMORTON	TS6-4	28-May-52	16.39	4
TARRANT	PB8-3	20-Aug-57	4.00	2	THROCKMORTON	TS8-1	5-Jun-52	776.91	9

INDIVIDUAL FALLOUT DAYS
TEXAS

COUNTY	SHOT	DATE	µCi/SQ METER	INDEX	COUNTY	SHOT	DATE	µCi/SQ METER	INDEX
TITUS	TS7-6	6-Jun-52	4.52	2	UPTON	TP6-2	23-Mar-55	6.49	3
TITUS	PB12-5	6-Sep-57	5.47	3	UPTON	TS6-4	28-May-52	9.64	3
TITUS	TP10-3	7-May-55	7.18	3	UPTON	TS8-1	5-Jun-52	53.18	6
TITUS	UK1-2	18-Mar-53	7.91	3	UVALDE	PB1-5	1-Jun-57	5.04	3
TITUS	TP11-5	19-May-55	8.16	3	UVALDE	TP6-2	23-Mar-55	6.49	3
TITUS	TP6-2	23-Mar-55	13.77	4	UVALDE	TS6-4	28-May-52	7.71	3
TITUS	TS6-4	28-May-52	22.18	4	UVALDE	TS8-1	5-Jun-52	146.23	7
TITUS	TS1-3	3-Apr-52	24.86	4	VAL VERDE	TS8-1	5-Jun-52	53.18	6
TOM GREEN	PB13-5	10-Sep-57	3.92	2	VAN ZANDT	UK7-2	26-Apr-53	3.96	2
TOM GREEN	UK6-2	19-Apr-53	5.25	3	VAN ZANDT	TS7-6	6-Jun-52	4.61	2
TOM GREEN	TS8-1	5-Jun-52	79.76	6	VAN ZANDT	TP11-5	19-May-55	4.69	2
TRAVIS	UK6-2	19-Apr-53	4.52	2	VAN ZANDT	PB12-5	6-Sep-57	7.77	3
TRAVIS	PB1-5	1-Jun-57	5.04	3	VAN ZANDT	UK1-2	18-Mar-53	10.49	4
TRAVIS	TS6-4	28-May-52	6.75	3	VAN ZANDT	TP6-2	23-Mar-55	13.77	4
TRINITY	UK7-4	28-Apr-53	3.83	2	VAN ZANDT	TS1-3	3-Apr-52	16.84	4
TRINITY	UK7-3	27-Apr-53	5.74	3	VAN ZANDT	TS6-4	28-May-52	20.25	4
TRINITY	TP6-3	24-Mar-55	8.63	3	VAN ZANDT	UK7-3	27-Apr-53	24.88	4
TRINITY	UK6-2	19-Apr-53	77.35	6	VICTORIA	UK6-2	19-Apr-53	4.52	2
TYLER	TS6-4	28-May-52	4.82	2	VICTORIA	TS6-4	28-May-52	9.64	3
TYLER	UK7-4	28-Apr-53	5.61	3	WALKER	BJ3-5	5-Nov-51	4.02	2
TYLER	UK7-3	27-Apr-53	5.99	3	WALKER	TS6-4	28-May-52	5.79	3
TYLER	TP6-3	24-Mar-55	8.63	3	WALKER	PB11-1	31-Aug-57	6.14	3
TYLER	UK6-2	19-Apr-53	77.35	6	WALKER	TP11-2	16-May-55	7.17	3
UPSHUR	TP10-3	7-May-55	3.65	2	WALKER	TP6-3	24-Mar-55	8.63	3
UPSHUR	UK5-4	14-Apr-53	3.91	2	WALKER	UK6-2	19-Apr-53	77.35	6
UPSHUR	TS1-3	3-Apr-52	4.21	2	WALLER	BJ3-5	5-Nov-51	4.79	2
UPSHUR	PB12-4	5-Sep-57	6.35	3	WALLER	TS6-4	28-May-52	6.75	3
UPSHUR	UK1-2	18-Mar-53	6.71	3	WALLER	PB1-5	1-Jun-57	8.42	3
UPSHUR	TP11-5	19-May-55	6.82	3	WALLER	TP6-3	24-Mar-55	8.63	3
UPSHUR	TP6-2	23-Mar-55	13.77	4	WALLER	UK6-2	19-Apr-53	77.35	6
UPSHUR	UK7-3	27-Apr-53	16.81	4	WARD	UK8-2	9-May-53	3.64	2
UPSHUR	TS6-4	28-May-52	18.32	4	WARD	UK9-1	19-May-53	4.31	2
UPTON	UK7-2	26-Apr-53	5.99	3	WARD	TP7-2	30-Mar-55	5.54	3

INDIVIDUAL FALLOUT DAYS
TEXAS

COUNTY	SHOT	DATE	µCi/SQ METER	INDEX	COUNTY	SHOT	DATE	µCi/SQ METER	INDEX
WARD	PB3-2	25-Jun-57	11.19	4	WICHITA	UK1-2	18-Mar-53	4.12	2
WARD	UK6-2	19-Apr-53	16.20	4	WICHITA	UK6-2	19-Apr-53	5.25	3
WARD	TP7-1	29-Mar-55	18.63	4	WICHITA	UK7-2	26-Apr-53	6.80	3
WARD	UK7-2	26-Apr-53	21.02	4	WICHITA	TP11-5	19-May-55	7.40	3
WARD	TS8-1	5-Jun-52	53.18	6	WICHITA	TS6-4	28-May-52	35.46	5
WASHINGTON	BJ3-5	5-Nov-51	4.79	2	WICHITA	TS8-1	5-Jun-52	475.66	9
WASHINGTON	TP6-3	24-Mar-55	8.63	3	WILBARGER	UK1-2	18-Mar-53	3.61	2
WASHINGTON	TS6-4	28-May-52	15.06	4	WILBARGER	UK6-2	19-Apr-53	5.25	3
WASHINGTON	UK6-2	19-Apr-53	77.35	6	WILBARGER	UK7-3	27-Apr-53	5.82	3
WEBB	UK6-2	19-Apr-53	4.52	2	WILBARGER	UK7-2	26-Apr-53	10.36	4
WHARTON	BJ3-2	2-Nov-51	4.34	2	WILBARGER	TS6-4	28-May-52	39.54	5
WHARTON	UK6-2	19-Apr-53	4.52	2	WILBARGER	TS8-1	5-Jun-52	53.18	6
WHARTON	PB1-5	1-Jun-57	8.42	3	WILLACY	UK6-2	19-Apr-53	4.52	2
WHARTON	TS6-4	28-May-52	24.11	4	WILLACY	PB1-5	1-Jun-57	5.04	3
WHEELER	BJ5-6	24-Nov-51	3.70	2	WILLACY	TS6-4	28-May-52	33.60	5
WHEELER	UK9-4	22-May-53	3.75	2	WILLIAMSON	TS1-3	3-Apr-52	7.22	3
WHEELER	UK8-2	9-May-53	4.04	2	WILLIAMSON	TP6-2	23-Mar-55	13.77	4
WHEELER	TP11-5	19-May-55	4.15	2	WILLIAMSON	TS6-4	28-May-52	16.22	4
WHEELER	UK6-3	20-Apr-53	4.23	2	WILSON	UK6-2	19-Apr-53	4.52	2
WHEELER	TP11-4	18-May-55	4.26	2	WINKLER	UK8-2	9-May-53	3.64	2
WHEELER	UK9-2	20-May-53	4.52	2	WINKLER	UK9-1	19-May-53	5.39	3
WHEELER	UK9-5	23-May-53	5.42	3	WINKLER	TP7-2	30-Mar-55	5.54	3
WHEELER	TP10-3	7-May-55	6.11	3	WINKLER	PB3-2	25-Jun-57	11.19	4
WHEELER	UK7-2	26-Apr-53	7.62	3	WINKLER	UK6-2	19-Apr-53	16.20	4
WHEELER	UK3-5	4-Apr-53	13.66	4	WINKLER	TP7-1	29-Mar-55	18.63	4
WHEELER	TS6-4	28-May-52	13.70	4	WINKLER	UK7-2	26-Apr-53	36.36	5
WHEELER	UK7-3	27-Apr-53	14.09	4	WINKLER	TS8-1	5-Jun-52	53.18	6
WHEELER	TP10-2	6-May-55	32.43	5	WISE	TP10-3	7-May-55	3.99	2
WHEELER	TP7-2	30-Mar-55	52.84	6	WISE	PB8-3	20-Aug-57	4.00	2
WHEELER	TS8-1	5-Jun-52	53.18	6	WISE	UK7-3	27-Apr-53	5.56	3
WICHITA	UK9-2	20-May-53	3.70	2	WISE	UK1-9	25-Mar-53	6.00	3
WICHITA	PB8-3	20-Aug-57	4.00	2	WISE	UK7-2	26-Apr-53	7.41	3
WICHITA	TS7-6	6-Jun-52	4.07	2	WISE	PB12-5	6-Sep-57	8.16	3

INDIVIDUAL FALLOUT DAYS
TEXAS

COUNTY	SHOT	DATE	µCi/SQ METER	INDEX	COUNTY	SHOT	DATE	µCi/SQ METER	INDEX
WISE	UK1-2	18-Mar-53	9.11	3	YOAKUM	UK7-3	27-Apr-53	6.26	3
WISE	TS1-3	3-Apr-52	11.23	4	YOAKUM	PB3-2	25-Jun-57	11.19	4
WISE	TP6-2	23-Mar-55	13.77	4	YOAKUM	UK9-1	19-May-53	14.87	4
WISE	TP11-5	19-May-55	14.08	4	YOAKUM	UK6-2	19-Apr-53	16.20	4
WISE	TS6-4	28-May-52	20.25	4	YOAKUM	TP7-1	29-Mar-55	18.63	4
WOOD	TP10-3	7-May-55	3.97	2	YOAKUM	TS6-4	28-May-52	28.93	5
WOOD	TP11-5	19-May-55	4.15	2	YOAKUM	TS8-1	5-Jun-52	53.18	6
WOOD	PB12-5	6-Sep-57	4.34	2	YOAKUM	UK7-2	26-Apr-53	82.68	6
WOOD	TS7-6	6-Jun-52	4.57	2	YOUNG	UK1-2	18-Mar-53	4.53	2
WOOD	PB12-4	5-Sep-57	6.08	3	YOUNG	UK6-2	19-Apr-53	5.25	3
WOOD	UK7-3	27-Apr-53	8.49	3	YOUNG	UK7-2	26-Apr-53	5.79	3
WOOD	UK1-2	18-Mar-53	8.77	3	YOUNG	PB12-5	6-Sep-57	6.82	3
WOOD	PB11-1	31-Aug-57	10.23	4	YOUNG	TS8-1	5-Jun-52	239.29	8
WOOD	TP6-2	23-Mar-55	13.77	4	ZAPATA	TS7-6	6-Jun-52	3.64	2
WOOD	TS6-4	28-May-52	20.25	4	ZAPATA	UK6-2	19-Apr-53	4.52	2
WOOD	TS1-3	3-Apr-52	24.86	4	ZAVALA	TS6-4	28-May-52	4.82	2
YOAKUM	UK8-2	9-May-53	3.64	2	ZAVALA	TP6-2	23-Mar-55	6.49	3
YOAKUM	UK1-2	18-Mar-53	4.64	2	ZAVALA	TS8-1	5-Jun-52	475.66	9
YOAKUM	TP7-2	30-Mar-55	5.54	3					

INDIVIDUAL FALLOUT DAYS
UTAH

COUNTY	SHOT	DATE	µCi/SQ METER	INDEX	COUNTY	SHOT	DATE	µCi/SQ METER	INDEX
BEAVER	PB3-1	24-Jun-57	4.89	2	BOX ELDER1	TP11-1	15-May-55	7.71	3
BEAVER	PB4-1	5-Jul-57	5.20	3	BOX ELDER1	TP10-1	5-May-55	7.86	3
BEAVER	UK5-1	11-Apr-53	5.51	3	BOX ELDER1	PB5-1	15-Jul-57	8.47	3
BEAVER	TP5-1	12-Mar-55	5.61	3	BOX ELDER1	PB12-1	2-Sep-57	8.67	3
BEAVER	TS4-1	1-May-52	5.86	3	BOX ELDER1	TS6-1	25-May-52	8.73	3
BEAVER	PB11-1	31-Aug-57	6.23	3	BOX ELDER1	BJ5 1	19-Nov-51	9.14	3
BEAVER	TS2-1	15-Apr-52	7.19	3	BOX ELDER1	PB9-1	23-Aug-57	10.33	4
BEAVER	PB17-1	28-Sep-57	7.93	3	BOX ELDER1	PB6-2	25-Jul-57	11.04	4
BEAVER	PB12-1	2-Sep-57	8.99	3	BOX ELDER1	PB15-1	16-Sep-57	11.30	4
BEAVER	TP10-1	5-May-55	9.07	3	BOX ELDER1	PB17-1	28-Sep-57	23.90	4
BEAVER	TP8-1	9-Apr-55	11.44	4	BOX ELDER1	TP4-1	7-Mar-55	37.39	5
BEAVER	PB15-1	16-Sep-57	11.52	4	BOX ELDER1	PB8-1	18-Aug-57	40.59	5
BEAVER	PB18-1	10-Jul-57	14.62	4	BOX ELDER1	TS8-2	6-Jun-52	52.58	6
BEAVER	TP3-1	1-Mar-55	15.25	4	BOX ELDER1	UK2-1	24-Mar-53	88.82	6
BEAVER	UK10-1	25-May-53	17.07	4	BOX ELDER1	TS7-1	1-Jun-52	138.47	7
BEAVER	TS7-1	1-Jun-52	17.77	4	BOX ELDER1	TS8-1	5-Jun-52	9132.83	10
BEAVER	UK6-1	18-Apr-53	19.09	4	BOX ELDER2	PB4-1	5-Jul-57	4.06	2
BEAVER	PB2-1	18-Jun-57	20.88	4	BOX ELDER2	UK7-1	25-Apr-53	4.17	2
BEAVER	TP7-1	29-Mar-55	23.12	4	BOX ELDER2	PB16-1	23-Sep-57	4.37	2
BEAVER	TP4-1	7-Mar-55	36.30	5	BOX ELDER2	PB13-1	6-Sep-57	4.41	2
BEAVER	TS8-1	5-Jun-52	55.86	6	BOX ELDER2	UK6-1	18-Apr-53	4.48	2
BEAVER	TS1-1	1-Apr-52	56.63	6	BOX ELDER2	BJ5 1	19-Nov-51	4.63	2
BEAVER	TP11-1	15-May-55	66.21	6	BOX ELDER2	TP9-1	15-Apr-55	6.85	3
BEAVER	UK7-1	25-Apr-53	93.64	6	BOX ELDER2	TS8-2	6-Jun-52	7.00	3
BEAVER	TS6-1	25-May-52	119.90	7	BOX ELDER2	TP10-1	5-May-55	7.86	3
BEAVER	UK9-1	19-May-53	189.43	7	BOX ELDER2	UK9-1	19-May-53	8.26	3
BEAVER	TP9-1	15-Apr-55	406.51	9	BOX ELDER2	PB5-1	15-Jul-57	8.47	3
BOX ELDER1	PB4-1	5-Jul-57	4.06	2	BOX ELDER2	TS1-1	1-Apr-52	9.04	3
BOX ELDER1	TP9-1	15-Apr-55	4.13	2	BOX ELDER2	UK10-1	25-May-53	10.69	4
BOX ELDER1	TP8-1	9-Apr-55	4.17	2	BOX ELDER2	PB6-2	25-Jul-57	11.04	4
BOX ELDER1	UK10-1	25-May-53	5.70	3	BOX ELDER2	SE1	6-Jul-62	11.17	4
BOX ELDER1	PB16-1	23-Sep-57	6.05	3	BOX ELDER2	PB15-1	16-Sep-57	11.30	4
BOX ELDER1	TS2-1	15-Apr-52	6.96	3	BOX ELDER2	TP8-1	9-Apr-55	16.58	4

INDIVIDUAL FALLOUT DAYS
UTAH

COUNTY	SHOT	DATE	µCi/SQ METER	INDEX	COUNTY	SHOT	DATE	µCi/SQ METER	INDEX
BOX ELDER2	TS6-1	25-May-52	17.46	4	CARBON	PB15-1	16-Sep-57	6.60	3
BOX ELDER2	TP11-1	15-May-55	23.24	4	CARBON	PB17-1	28-Sep-57	7.93	3
BOX ELDER2	PB17-1	28-Sep-57	23.90	4	CARBON	PB8-1	18-Aug-57	7.93	3
BOX ELDER2	PB12-1	2-Sep-57	25.91	5	CARBON	TP9-1	15-Apr-55	7.96	3
BOX ELDER2	TS7-1	1-Jun-52	36.98	5	CARBON	PB4-1	5-Jul-57	8.37	3
BOX ELDER2	TP4-1	7-Mar-55	37.39	5	CARBON	PB12-1	2-Sep-57	8.81	3
BOX ELDER2	PB8-1	18-Aug-57	40.59	5	CARBON	PB2-1	18-Jun-57	10.48	4
BOX ELDER2	PB9-1	23-Aug-57	43.10	5	CARBON	UK11-1	4-Jun-53	11.55	4
BOX ELDER2	UK2-1	24-Mar-53	443.88	9	CARBON	PB1-1	28-May-57	12.24	4
BOX ELDER2	TS8-1	5-Jun-52	1214.92	10	CARBON	PB5-1	15-Jul-57	16.62	4
CACHE	UK6-1	18-Apr-53	4.48	2	CARBON	UK7-1	25-Apr-53	16.70	4
CACHE	PB4-1	5-Jul-57	4.82	2	CARBON	TP8-1	9-Apr-55	16.76	4
CACHE	PB16-1	23-Sep-57	5.27	3	CARBON	TP11-1	15-May-55	24.41	4
CACHE	TP10-1	5-May-55	6.21	3	CARBON	TP10-1	5-May-55	24.98	4
CACHE	TP9-1	15-Apr-55	6.85	3	CARBON	PB9-1	23-Aug-57	31.24	5
CACHE	UK9-1	19-May-53	8.37	3	CARBON	UK10-1	25-May-53	32.77	5
CACHE	TS6-1	25-May-52	8.73	3	CARBON	TS1-1	1-Apr-52	37.36	5
CACHE	TS1-1	1-Apr-52	8.80	3	CARBON	TP4-1	7-Mar-55	37.49	5
CACHE	TS8-2	6-Jun-52	10.37	4	CARBON	TS7-1	1-Jun-52	37.71	5
CACHE	UK10-1	25-May-53	10.54	4	CARBON	PB11-1	31-Aug-57	41.90	5
CACHE	PB6-2	25-Jul-57	10.91	4	CARBON	TS6-1	25-May-52	72.49	6
CACHE	PB15-1	16-Sep-57	11.30	4	CARBON	UK9-1	19-May-53	374.79	8
CACHE	PB5-1	15-Jul-57	12.44	4	CARBON	TS8-1	5-Jun-52	118.70	7
CACHE	PB12-1	2-Sep-57	18.51	4	DAGGETT	PB6-2	25-Jul-57	3.62	2
CACHE	TP11-1	15-May-55	20.80	4	DAGGETT	TP7-1	29-Mar-55	4.22	2
CACHE	PB17-1	28-Sep-57	23.90	4	DAGGETT	UK6-1	18-Apr-53	5.51	3
CACHE	PB9-1	23-Aug-57	31.50	5	DAGGETT	PB1-1	28-May-57	6.17	3
CACHE	PB8-1	18-Aug-57	31.82	5	DAGGETT	PB15-1	16-Sep-57	6.49	3
CACHE	TP4-1	7-Mar-55	37.12	5	DAGGETT	TP9-1	15-Apr-55	6.95	3
CACHE	TS7-1	1-Jun-52	46.52	5	DAGGETT	TS1-1	1-Apr-52	7.61	3
CACHE	UK2-1	24-Mar-53	536.50	9	DAGGETT	PB17-1	28-Sep-57	7.93	3
CACHE	TS8-1	5-Jun-52	1801.43	10	DAGGETT	UK7-1	25-Apr-53	8.35	3
CARBON	UK6-1	18-Apr-53	4.48	2	DAGGETT	TS7-1	1-Jun-52	9.33	3

INDIVIDUAL FALLOUT DAYS
UTAH

COUNTY	SHOT	DATE	µCi/SQ METER	INDEX	COUNTY	SHOT	DATE	µCi/SQ METER	INDEX
DAGGETT	PB2-1	18-Jun-57	9.43	3	DAVIS	PB17-1	28-Sep-57	23.90	4
DAGGETT	PB4-1	5-Jul-57	10.53	4	DAVIS	TP8-1	9-Apr-55	31.07	5
DAGGETT	PB5-1	15-Jul-57	16.41	4	DAVIS	PB8-1	18-Aug-57	32.56	5
DAGGETT	TP8-1	9-Apr-55	16.49	4	DAVIS	PB12-1	2-Sep-57	34.59	5
DAGGETT	TP11-1	15-May-55	21.29	4	DAVIS	PB9-1	23-Aug-57	49.94	5
DAGGETT	UK10-1	25-May-53	21.94	4	DAVIS	TP4-1	7-Mar-55	75.34	6
DAGGETT	PB8-1	18-Aug-57	23.36	4	DAVIS	TP10-1	5-May-55	118.26	7
DAGGETT	PB12-1	2-Sep-57	26.53	5	DAVIS	UK2-1	24-Mar-53	723.10	9
DAGGETT	UK9-1	19-May-53	32.59	5	DAVIS	TS8-1	5-Jun-52	900.71	10
DAGGETT	TS6-1	25-May-52	36.14	5	DUCHESNE	UK6-1	18-Apr-53	4.48	2
DAGGETT	PB9-1	23-Aug-57	42.21	5	DUCHESNE	PB4-1	5-Jul-57	4.95	2
DAGGETT	TP4-1	7-Mar-55	73.70	6	DUCHESNE	PB15-1	16-Sep-57	7.38	3
DAGGETT	TS8-1	5-Jun-52	230.42	8	DUCHESNE	TP9-1	15-Apr-55	7.56	3
DAGGETT	PB11-1	31-Aug-57	232.42	8	DUCHESNE	PB17-1	28-Sep-57	7.93	3
DAGGETT	TP10-1	5-May-55	233.13	8	DUCHESNE	TS1-1	1-Apr-52	8.80	3
DAVIS	TS3-1	22-Apr-52	4.06	2	DUCHESNE	PB2-1	18-Jun-57	9.66	3
DAVIS	UK6-1	18-Apr-53	4.48	2	DUCHESNE	PB8-1	18-Aug-57	15.96	4
DAVIS	PB16-1	23-Sep-57	4.93	2	DUCHESNE	UK7-1	25-Apr-53	16.70	4
DAVIS	TS8-2	6-Jun-52	5.19	3	DUCHESNE	PB1-1	28-May-57	18.41	4
DAVIS	PB4-1	5-Jul-57	8.24	3	DUCHESNE	TS7-1	1-Jun-52	18.85	4
DAVIS	UK7-1	25-Apr-53	8.35	3	DUCHESNE	TP11-1	15-May-55	22.56	4
DAVIS	UK9-1	19-May-53	8.49	3	DUCHESNE	TP8-1	9-Apr-55	24.92	4
DAVIS	TS7-1	1-Jun-52	9.33	3	DUCHESNE	PB12-1	2-Sep-57	26.53	5
DAVIS	UK10-1	25-May-53	10.69	4	DUCHESNE	PB5-1	15-Jul-57	32.40	5
DAVIS	PB6-2	25-Jul-57	11.04	4	DUCHESNE	UK10-1	25-May-53	32.92	5
DAVIS	SE1	6-Jul-62	11.17	4	DUCHESNE	UK9-1	19-May-53	37.12	5
DAVIS	PB15-1	16-Sep-57	11.30	4	DUCHESNE	PB11-1	31-Aug-57	38.85	5
DAVIS	TP9-1	15-Apr-55	13.91	4	DUCHESNE	TS6-1	25-May-52	45.31	5
DAVIS	TS1-1	1-Apr-52	14.04	4	DUCHESNE	TP4-1	7-Mar-55	52.17	6
DAVIS	PB5-1	15-Jul-57	16.93	4	DUCHESNE	PB9-1	23-Aug-57	52.28	6
DAVIS	TS6-1	25-May-52	18.23	4	DUCHESNE	TP10-1	5-May-55	235.65	8
DAVIS	TP11-1	15-May-55	21.09	4	DUCHESNE	TS8-1	5-Jun-52	237.40	8
DAVIS	PB1-1	28-May-57	22.94	4	EMERY	UK5-1	11-Apr-53	4.01	2

INDIVIDUAL FALLOUT DAYS
UTAH

COUNTY	SHOT	DATE	µCi/SQ METER	INDEX	COUNTY	SHOT	DATE	µCi/SQ METER	INDEX
EMERY	PB18-1	10-Jul-57	5.09	3	GARFIELD	TP5-1	12-Mar-55	16.94	4
EMERY	UK6-1	18-Apr-53	5.51	3	GARFIELD	TP4-1	7-Mar-55	22.62	4
EMERY	PB15-1	16-Sep-57	6.49	3	GARFIELD	PB3-1	24-Jun-57	26.86	5
EMERY	PB17-1	28-Sep-57	7.93	3	GARFIELD	UK6-1	18-Apr-53	31.01	5
EMERY	TP8-1	9-Apr-55	8.60	3	GARFIELD	UK11-1	4-Jun-53	33.82	5
EMERY	PB12-1	2-Sep-57	8.81	3	GARFIELD	TP3-1	1-Mar-55	38.02	5
EMERY	TP3-1	1-Mar-55	9.41	3	GARFIELD	TP11-1	15-May-55	41.11	5
EMERY	PB4-1	5-Jul-57	10.91	4	GARFIELD	UK7-1	25-Apr-53	44.12	5
EMERY	PB1-1	28-May-57	12.24	4	GARFIELD	TS8-1	5-Jun-52	55.86	6
EMERY	PB5-1	15-Jul-57	12.44	4	GARFIELD	TS6-1	25-May-52	69.51	6
EMERY	PB2-1	18-Jun-57	12.92	4	GARFIELD	TP7-1	29-Mar-55	72.85	6
EMERY	TP7-1	29-Mar-55	15.92	4	GARFIELD	UK9-1	19-May-53	568.41	9
EMERY	UK11-1	4-Jun-53	22.13	4	GARFIELD	PB11-1	31-Aug-57	1238.11	10
EMERY	UK10-1	25-May-53	22.66	4	GRAND	PB13-1	6-Sep-57	3.70	2
EMERY	TP11-1	15-May-55	24.51	4	GRAND	UK5-1	11-Apr-53	3.86	2
EMERY	TS1-1	1-Apr-52	27.13	5	GRAND	UK6-1	18-Apr-53	4.48	2
EMERY	TP4-1	7-Mar-55	30.01	5	GRAND	PB15-1	16-Sep-57	5.59	3
EMERY	UK7-1	25-Apr-53	42.43	5	GRAND	PB1-1	28-May-57	6.17	3
EMERY	TS8-1	5-Jun-52	55.86	6	GRAND	TP7-1	29-Mar-55	7.91	3
EMERY	TS7-1	1-Jun-52	55.98	6	GRAND	PB17-1	28-Sep-57	7.93	3
EMERY	PB11-1	31-Aug-57	79.41	6	GRAND	PB2-1	18-Jun-57	8.03	3
EMERY	TS6-1	25-May-52	91.50	6	GRAND	TP8-1	9-Apr-55	8.51	3
EMERY	UK9-1	19-May-53	281.09	8	GRAND	PB12-1	2-Sep-57	8.81	3
EMERY	TP9-1	15-Apr-55	325.27	8	GRAND	TP3-1	1-Mar-55	9.31	3
GARFIELD	UK5-1	11-Apr-53	5.05	3	GRAND	PB5-1	15-Jul-57	11.71	4
GARFIELD	PB17-1	28-Sep-57	7.93	3	GRAND	TS1-1	1-Apr-52	12.61	4
GARFIELD	TP9-1	15-Apr-55	8.06	3	GRAND	PB4-1	5-Jul-57	20.80	4
GARFIELD	TP8-1	9-Apr-55	8.69	3	GRAND	UK11-1	4-Jun-53	21.85	4
GARFIELD	PB18-1	10-Jul-57	10.18	4	GRAND	UK10-1	25-May-53	22.37	4
GARFIELD	UK10-1	25-May-53	10.97	4	GRAND	PB11-1	31-Aug-57	23.83	4
GARFIELD	PB1-1	28-May-57	12.24	4	GRAND	TP11-1	15-May-55	24.32	4
GARFIELD	TS7-1	1-Jun-52	13.82	4	GRAND	TS8-1	5-Jun-52	55.86	6
GARFIELD	PB2-1	18-Jun-57	14.67	4	GRAND	TP4-1	7-Mar-55	59.56	6

INDIVIDUAL FALLOUT DAYS
UTAH

COUNTY	SHOT	DATE	µCi/SQ METER	INDEX	COUNTY	SHOT	DATE	µCi/SQ METER	INDEX
GRAND	UK7-1	25-Apr-53	66.68	6	IRON2	UK10-1	25-May-53	9.55	3
GRAND	TS7-1	1-Jun-52	73.31	6	IRON2	TS1-1	1-Apr-52	9.91	3
GRAND	TS6-1	25-May-52	82.11	6	IRON2	TS7-1	1-Jun-52	13.28	4
GRAND	UK9-1	19-May-53	280.07	8	IRON2	PB18-1	10-Jul-57	15.50	4
GRAND	TP9-1	15-Apr-55	325.27	8	IRON2	TP9-1	15-Apr-55	16.23	4
IRON1	UK5-1	11-Apr-53	6.53	3	IRON2	TP5-1	12-Mar-55	17.24	4
IRON1	UK10-1	25-May-53	6.54	3	IRON2	PB2-1	18-Jun-57	21.00	4
IRON1	TP4-1	7-Mar-55	7.66	3	IRON2	TP4-1	7-Mar-55	22.80	4
IRON1	PB17-1	28-Sep-57	7.93	3	IRON2	PB3-1	24-Jun-57	22.87	4
IRON1	TP11-1	15-May-55	8.30	3	IRON2	TP3-1	1-Mar-55	29.00	5
IRON1	TP8-1	9-Apr-55	8.96	3	IRON2	PB11-1	31-Aug-57	31.07	5
IRON1	TS7-1	1-Jun-52	13.28	4	IRON2	UK6-1	18-Apr-53	32.69	5
IRON1	TS4-1	1-May-52	13.73	4	IRON2	UK7-1	25-Apr-53	45.13	5
IRON1	TS2-1	15-Apr-52	14.38	4	IRON2	TS8-1	5-Jun-52	55.86	6
IRON1	PB18-1	10-Jul-57	21.54	4	IRON2	TP7-1	29-Mar-55	65.52	6
IRON1	TP5-1	12-Mar-55	26.11	5	IRON2	TS6-1	25-May-52	130.90	7
IRON1	TP3-1	1-Mar-55	29.48	5	IRON2	UK9-1	19-May-53	266.15	8
IRON1	PB2-1	18-Jun-57	43.12	5	IRON2	TP11-1	15-May-55	413.43	9
IRON1	PB11-1	31-Aug-57	45.43	5	IRON3	TS2-1	15-Apr-52	4.17	2
IRON1	UK6-1	18-Apr-53	55.53	6	IRON3	UK1-1	17-Mar-53	4.78	2
IRON1	TS8-1	5-Jun-52	55.86	6	IRON3	TS4-1	1-May-52	4.86	2
IRON1	PB3-1	24-Jun-57	59.51	6	IRON3	UK5-1	11-Apr-53	6.23	3
IRON1	TP7-1	29-Mar-55	69.71	6	IRON3	UK10-1	25-May-53	6.54	3
IRON1	TP9-1	15-Apr-55	84.89	6	IRON3	PB17-1	28-Sep-57	7.93	3
IRON1	UK7-1	25-Apr-53	85.77	6	IRON3	TP9-1	15-Apr-55	8.16	3
IRON1	UK9-1	19-May-53	296.90	8	IRON3	TP8-1	9-Apr-55	8.96	3
IRON1	TS6-1	25-May-52	509.73	9	IRON3	UK11-1	4-Jun-53	11.83	4
IRON2	UK5-1	11-Apr-53	5.20	3	IRON3	TS7-1	1-Jun-52	13.28	4
IRON2	UK11-1	4-Jun-53	5.79	3	IRON3	TP4-1	7-Mar-55	15.23	4
IRON2	TS2-1	15-Apr-52	6.26	3	IRON3	PB18-1	10-Jul-57	15.50	4
IRON2	PB17-1	28-Sep-57	7.93	3	IRON3	TP5-1	12-Mar-55	17.34	4
IRON2	TS4-1	1-May-52	8.39	3	IRON3	PB3-1	24-Jun-57	23.08	4
IRON2	TP8-1	9-Apr-55	8.96	3	IRON3	PB2-1	18-Jun-57	32.43	5

INDIVIDUAL FALLOUT DAYS
UTAH

COUNTY	SHOT	DATE	µCi/SQ METER	INDEX	COUNTY	SHOT	DATE	µCi/SQ METER	INDEX
IRON3	UK6-1	18-Apr-53	33.10	5	JUAB	TP10-1	5-May-55	158.85	7
IRON3	TP3-1	1-Mar-55	36.62	5	JUAB	TS8-1	5-Jun-52	181.54	7
IRON3	UK7-1	25-Apr-53	45.13	5	JUAB	UK9-1	19-May-53	281.09	8
IRON3	TS6-1	25-May-52	52.32	6	KANE1	TP4-1	7-Mar-55	3.74	2
IRON3	TS8-1	5-Jun-52	55.86	6	KANE1	TP8-1	9-Apr-55	4.35	2
IRON3	TP7-1	29-Mar-55	92.64	6	KANE1	UK5-1	11-Apr-53	5.05	3
IRON3	PB11-1	31-Aug-57	162.62	7	KANE1	PB18-1	10-Jul-57	5.09	3
IRON3	TP11-1	15-May-55	180.05	7	KANE1	UK3-1	31-Mar-53	5.12	3
IRON3	UK9-1	19-May-53	502.13	9	KANE1	TS3-1	22-Apr-52	5.82	3
JUAB	BJ6-1	29-Nov-51	3.63	2	KANE1	TS2-1	15-Apr-52	6.68	3
JUAB	PB4-1	5-Jul-57	5.07	3	KANE1	PB3-1	24-Jun-57	7.28	3
JUAB	TS3-1	22-Apr-52	5.82	3	KANE1	PB17-1	28-Sep-57	7.93	3
JUAB	PB1-1	28-May-57	6.17	3	KANE1	TP11-1	15-May-55	8.20	3
JUAB	UK6-1	18-Apr-53	6.66	3	KANE1	UK1-1	17-Mar-53	9.34	3
JUAB	PB17-1	28-Sep-57	7.93	3	KANE1	PB1-1	28-May-57	12.24	4
JUAB	TP7-1	29-Mar-55	8.65	3	KANE1	TS7-1	1-Jun-52	13.58	4
JUAB	TS1-1	1-Apr-52	9.04	3	KANE1	PB11-1	31-Aug-57	16.32	4
JUAB	UK2-1	24-Mar-53	9.18	3	KANE1	UK6-1	18-Apr-53	21.40	4
JUAB	TS7-1	1-Jun-52	9.44	3	KANE1	TP6-1	22-Mar-55	28.08	5
JUAB	TP8-1	9-Apr-55	12.95	4	KANE1	TP7-1	29-Mar-55	32.62	5
JUAB	TS2-1	15-Apr-52	14.38	4	KANE1	TP5-1	12-Mar-55	34.28	5
JUAB	UK7-1	25-Apr-53	16.92	4	KANE1	UK11-1	4-Jun-53	47.69	5
JUAB	BJ5 1	19-Nov-51	18.73	4	KANE1	TS6-1	25-May-52	55.70	6
JUAB	PB15-1	16-Sep-57	21.81	4	KANE1	TS8-1	5-Jun-52	55.86	6
JUAB	TP9-1	15-Apr-55	24.19	4	KANE1	TP3-1	1-Mar-55	64.42	6
JUAB	PB12-1	2-Sep-57	27.08	5	KANE1	UK7-1	25-Apr-53	90.27	6
JUAB	UK10-1	25-May-53	33.20	5	KANE1	UK9-1	19-May-53	2334.06	10
JUAB	PB8-1	18-Aug-57	33.93	5	KANE2	TP8-1	9-Apr-55	4.35	2
JUAB	TP11-1	15-May-55	43.26	5	KANE2	UK5-1	11-Apr-53	5.05	3
JUAB	PB9-1	23-Aug-57	54.07	6	KANE2	UK10-1	25-May-53	5.98	3
JUAB	TS6-1	25-May-52	55.70	6	KANE2	TS2-1	15-Apr-52	6.26	3
JUAB	PB5-1	15-Jul-57	69.19	6	KANE2	TP4-1	7-Mar-55	7.57	3
JUAB	TP4-1	7-Mar-55	114.19	7	KANE2	PB17-1	28-Sep-57	7.93	3

INDIVIDUAL FALLOUT DAYS
UTAH

COUNTY	SHOT	DATE	µCi/SQ METER	INDEX	COUNTY	SHOT	DATE	µCi/SQ METER	INDEX
KANE2	TP11-1	15-May-55	8.20	3	MILLARD	TP9-1	15-Apr-55	32.46	5
KANE2	PB18-1	10-Jul-57	9.49	3	MILLARD	UK10-1	25-May-53	33.91	5
KANE2	PB1-1	28-May-57	12.24	4	MILLARD	PB5-1	15-Jul-57	43.27	5
KANE2	TS7-1	1-Jun-52	13.58	4	MILLARD	PB12-1	2-Sep-57	45.16	5
KANE2	TP6-1	22-Mar-55	14.12	4	MILLARD	UK7-1	25-Apr-53	53.37	6
KANE2	TP5-1	12-Mar-55	17.14	4	MILLARD	TS8-1	5-Jun-52	55.86	6
KANE2	PB11-1	31-Aug-57	30.32	5	MILLARD	TP10-1	5-May-55	80.30	6
KANE2	UK6-1	18-Apr-53	31.91	5	MILLARD	TP11-1	15-May-55	87.66	6
KANE2	UK11-1	4-Jun-53	36.40	5	MILLARD	TP4-1	7-Mar-55	115.01	7
KANE2	TP7-1	29-Mar-55	46.14	5	MILLARD	TS6-1	25-May-52	120.23	7
KANE2	TS6-1	25-May-52	55.70	6	MILLARD	UK9-1	19-May-53	376.15	8
KANE2	TS8-1	5-Jun-52	55.86	6	MORGAN	PB2-1	18-Jun-57	3.61	2
KANE2	PB3-1	24-Jun-57	67.77	6	MORGAN	TS3-1	22-Apr-52	4.06	2
KANE2	UK7-1	25-Apr-53	90.27	6	MORGAN	PB16-1	23-Sep-57	4.09	2
KANE2	TP3-1	1-Mar-55	91.68	6	MORGAN	UK6-1	18-Apr-53	4.48	2
KANE2	UK1-1	17-Mar-53	213.70	8	MORGAN	TS8-2	6-Jun-52	4.50	2
KANE2	UK9-1	19-May-53	2334.06	10	MORGAN	PB6-2	25-Jul-57	7.33	3
MILLARD	TS3-1	22-Apr-52	4.06	2	MORGAN	PB4-1	5-Jul-57	8.12	3
MILLARD	TP3-1	1-Mar-55	4.45	2	MORGAN	UK7-1	25-Apr-53	8.35	3
MILLARD	TS4-1	1-May-52	4.86	2	MORGAN	UK9-1	19-May-53	8.49	3
MILLARD	PB2-1	18-Jun-57	4.89	2	MORGAN	TS1-1	1-Apr-52	8.80	3
MILLARD	PB1-1	28-May-57	6.17	3	MORGAN	TS7-1	1-Jun-52	9.33	3
MILLARD	PB17-1	28-Sep-57	7.93	3	MORGAN	UK10-1	25-May-53	10.69	4
MILLARD	TP7-1	29-Mar-55	8.11	3	MORGAN	SE1	6-Jul-62	11.17	4
MILLARD	UK6-1	18-Apr-53	9.87	3	MORGAN	PB15-1	16-Sep-57	11.30	4
MILLARD	PB4-1	5-Jul-57	11.16	4	MORGAN	TP9-1	15-Apr-55	13.91	4
MILLARD	PB15-1	16-Sep-57	11.52	4	MORGAN	PB5-1	15-Jul-57	16.62	4
MILLARD	TS2-1	15-Apr-52	14.38	4	MORGAN	TS6-1	25-May-52	18.23	4
MILLARD	PB8-1	18-Aug-57	17.23	4	MORGAN	TP11-1	15-May-55	21.09	4
MILLARD	TS1-1	1-Apr-52	18.32	4	MORGAN	PB1-1	28-May-57	22.94	4
MILLARD	PB9-1	23-Aug-57	21.55	4	MORGAN	PB17-1	28-Sep-57	23.90	4
MILLARD	TP8-1	9-Apr-55	26.16	5	MORGAN	PB8-1	18-Aug-57	32.56	5
MILLARD	TS7-1	1-Jun-52	28.53	5	MORGAN	TP8-1	9-Apr-55	33.17	5

U.S. FALLOUT ATLAS: COUNTY COMPARISONS

INDIVIDUAL FALLOUT DAYS
UTAH

COUNTY	SHOT	DATE	μCi/SQ METER	INDEX	COUNTY	SHOT	DATE	μCi/SQ METER	INDEX
MORGAN	PB12-1	2-Sep-57	36.92	5	RICH	UK6-1	18-Apr-53	4.48	2
MORGAN	PB9-1	23-Aug-57	40.14	5	RICH	TS8-2	6-Jun-52	5.11	3
MORGAN	TP4-1	7-Mar-55	97.59	6	RICH	PB16-1	23-Sep-57	5.27	3
MORGAN	TP10-1	5-May-55	117.39	7	RICH	UK7-1	25-Apr-53	5.87	3
MORGAN	UK2-1	24-Mar-53	725.74	9	RICH	TP10-1	5-May-55	6.21	3
MORGAN	TS8-1	5-Jun-52	782.02	9	RICH	PB4-1	5-Jul-57	6.47	3
PIUTE	TS4-1	1-May-52	3.57	2	RICH	TP9-1	15-Apr-55	6.85	3
PIUTE	PB3-1	24-Jun-57	4.26	2	RICH	UK9-1	19-May-53	8.26	3
PIUTE	TP5-1	12-Mar-55	5.04	3	RICH	TS1-1	1-Apr-52	8.80	3
PIUTE	UK5-1	11-Apr-53	5.05	3	RICH	TS6-1	25-May-52	8.95	3
PIUTE	PB4-1	5-Jul-57	5.07	3	RICH	UK10-1	25-May-53	10.54	4
PIUTE	PB1-1	28-May-57	6.17	3	RICH	PB6-2	25-Jul-57	10.91	4
PIUTE	UK11-1	4-Jun-53	7.10	3	RICH	PB15-1	16-Sep-57	11.30	4
PIUTE	PB17-1	28-Sep-57	7.93	3	RICH	PB5-1	15-Jul-57	12.44	4
PIUTE	PB15-1	16-Sep-57	8.50	3	RICH	PB12-1	2-Sep-57	18.51	4
PIUTE	TP8-1	9-Apr-55	8.69	3	RICH	TP11-1	15-May-55	20.80	4
PIUTE	PB12-1	2-Sep-57	8.81	3	RICH	PB8-1	18-Aug-57	23.89	4
PIUTE	PB18-1	10-Jul-57	10.18	4	RICH	PB17-1	28-Sep-57	23.90	4
PIUTE	UK10-1	25-May-53	10.97	4	RICH	TS7-1	1-Jun-52	27.87	5
PIUTE	TP3-1	1-Mar-55	19.01	4	RICH	PB9-1	23-Aug-57	31.50	5
PIUTE	PB2-1	18-Jun-57	24.45	4	RICH	TP4-1	7-Mar-55	37.03	5
PIUTE	UK6-1	18-Apr-53	28.45	5	RICH	UK2-1	24-Mar-53	623.63	9
PIUTE	TS7-1	1-Jun-52	28.58	5	RICH	TS8-1	5-Jun-52	886.75	10
PIUTE	TP4-1	7-Mar-55	30.28	5	SALT LAKE	TP7-1	29-Mar-55	3.73	2
PIUTE	TS1-1	1-Apr-52	37.84	5	SALT LAKE	TS3-1	22-Apr-52	3.83	2
PIUTE	PB11-1	31-Aug-57	40.06	5	SALT LAKE	PB16-1	23-Sep-57	3.86	2
PIUTE	TP7-1	29-Mar-55	40.24	5	SALT LAKE	PB6-2	25-Jul-57	4.18	2
PIUTE	UK7-1	25-Apr-53	44.12	5	SALT LAKE	TS7-1	1-Jun-52	4.45	2
PIUTE	TS8-1	5-Jun-52	55.86	6	SALT LAKE	TS8-2	6-Jun-52	4.89	2
PIUTE	TP11-1	15-May-55	82.13	6	SALT LAKE	UK6-1	18-Apr-53	5.20	3
PIUTE	TS6-1	25-May-52	92.16	6	SALT LAKE	UK9-1	19-May-53	8.00	3
PIUTE	UK9-1	19-May-53	188.75	7	SALT LAKE	PB4-1	5-Jul-57	10.05	4
PIUTE	TP9-1	15-Apr-55	325.27	8	SALT LAKE	UK7-1	25-Apr-53	11.07	4

INDIVIDUAL FALLOUT DAYS
UTAH

COUNTY	SHOT	DATE	µCi/SQ METER	INDEX	COUNTY	SHOT	DATE	µCi/SQ METER	INDEX
SALT LAKE	SE1	6-Jul-62	11.17	4	SAN JUAN	TP3-1	1-Mar-55	28.13	5
SALT LAKE	TP9-1	15-Apr-55	13.12	4	SAN JUAN	UK11-1	4-Jun-53	32.99	5
SALT LAKE	PB15-1	16-Sep-57	13.29	4	SAN JUAN	TS6-1	25-May-52	54.48	6
SALT LAKE	TS1-1	1-Apr-52	16.83	4	SAN JUAN	TS8-1	5-Jun-52	55.86	6
SALT LAKE	TS6-1	25-May-52	19.91	4	SAN JUAN	UK1-1	17-Mar-53	65.17	6
SALT LAKE	TP11-1	15-May-55	20.08	4	SAN JUAN	UK7-1	25-Apr-53	127.39	7
SALT LAKE	UK10-1	25-May-53	20.96	4	SAN JUAN	UK9-1	19-May-53	470.30	9
SALT LAKE	PB1-1	28-May-57	21.63	4	SANPETE	UK11-1	4-Jun-53	3.62	2
SALT LAKE	PB17-1	28-Sep-57	24.38	4	SANPETE	TS4-1	1-May-52	3.86	2
SALT LAKE	PB8-1	18-Aug-57	30.71	5	SANPETE	UK6-1	18-Apr-53	5.64	3
SALT LAKE	PB12-1	2-Sep-57	32.62	5	SANPETE	PB1-1	28-May-57	6.17	3
SALT LAKE	TP8-1	9-Apr-55	36.91	5	SANPETE	TS2-1	15-Apr-52	7.19	3
SALT LAKE	PB5-1	15-Jul-57	42.33	5	SANPETE	PB17-1	28-Sep-57	7.93	3
SALT LAKE	PB9-1	23-Aug-57	47.10	5	SANPETE	TP7-1	29-Mar-55	8.01	3
SALT LAKE	TP4-1	7-Mar-55	114.06	7	SANPETE	TP9-1	15-Apr-55	8.06	3
SALT LAKE	TP10-1	5-May-55	119.41	7	SANPETE	PB8-1	18-Aug-57	8.14	3
SALT LAKE	UK2-1	24-Mar-53	598.89	9	SANPETE	PB4-1	5-Jul-57	8.50	3
SALT LAKE	TS8-1	5-Jun-52	849.46	10	SANPETE	PB15-1	16-Sep-57	8.50	3
SAN JUAN	UK10-1	25-May-53	4.13	2	SANPETE	TP8-1	9-Apr-55	8.51	3
SAN JUAN	TP8-1	9-Apr-55	4.26	2	SANPETE	PB12-1	2-Sep-57	9.03	3
SAN JUAN	TP6-1	22-Mar-55	6.74	3	SANPETE	PB2-1	18-Jun-57	9.78	3
SAN JUAN	PB17-1	28-Sep-57	7.93	3	SANPETE	PB11-1	31-Aug-57	15.92	4
SAN JUAN	TP5-1	12-Mar-55	8.57	3	SANPETE	TP10-1	5-May-55	25.08	5
SAN JUAN	PB12-1	2-Sep-57	8.81	3	SANPETE	UK7-1	25-Apr-53	25.16	5
SAN JUAN	PB2-1	18-Jun-57	9.66	3	SANPETE	UK10-1	25-May-53	33.63	5
SAN JUAN	PB18-1	10-Jul-57	9.94	3	SANPETE	TP4-1	7-Mar-55	37.76	5
SAN JUAN	UK6-1	18-Apr-53	10.25	4	SANPETE	TS1-1	1-Apr-52	37.84	5
SAN JUAN	PB1-1	28-May-57	12.24	4	SANPETE	TS7-1	1-Jun-52	38.06	5
SAN JUAN	TS7-1	1-Jun-52	13.58	4	SANPETE	PB5-1	15-Jul-57	42.33	5
SAN JUAN	TP11-1	15-May-55	16.21	4	SANPETE	PB9-1	23-Aug-57	43.10	5
SAN JUAN	TP7-1	29-Mar-55	16.79	4	SANPETE	TP11-1	15-May-55	53.79	6
SAN JUAN	PB3-1	24-Jun-57	21.96	4	SANPETE	TS8-1	5-Jun-52	55.86	6
SAN JUAN	TP4-1	7-Mar-55	22.25	4	SANPETE	TS6-1	25-May-52	64.31	6

INDIVIDUAL FALLOUT DAYS
UTAH

COUNTY	SHOT	DATE	µCi/SQ METER	INDEX	COUNTY	SHOT	DATE	µCi/SQ METER	INDEX
SANPETE	UK9-1	19-May-53	376.15	8	SUMMIT	TP9-1	15-Apr-55	6.95	3
SEVIER	UK11-1	4-Jun-53	3.62	2	SUMMIT	UK6-1	18-Apr-53	7.30	3
SEVIER	TS4-1	1-May-52	3.86	2	SUMMIT	PB6-2	25-Jul-57	7.33	3
SEVIER	TS2-1	15-Apr-52	4.17	2	SUMMIT	UK7-1	25-Apr-53	8.35	3
SEVIER	TP5-1	12-Mar-55	4.23	2	SUMMIT	PB4-1	5-Jul-57	10.53	4
SEVIER	UK5-1	11-Apr-53	5.05	3	SUMMIT	PB15-1	16-Sep-57	11.30	4
SEVIER	PB18-1	10-Jul-57	5.09	3	SUMMIT	TS1-1	1-Apr-52	12.61	4
SEVIER	PB1-1	28-May-57	6.17	3	SUMMIT	PB17-1	28-Sep-57	15.85	4
SEVIER	TP7-1	29-Mar-55	7.55	3	SUMMIT	UK10-1	25-May-53	16.39	4
SEVIER	TP10-1	5-May-55	7.77	3	SUMMIT	UK9-1	19-May-53	16.52	4
SEVIER	PB17-1	28-Sep-57	7.93	3	SUMMIT	PB1-1	28-May-57	18.41	4
SEVIER	PB5-1	15-Jul-57	8.47	3	SUMMIT	TP11-1	15-May-55	21.29	4
SEVIER	UK6-1	18-Apr-53	8.59	3	SUMMIT	PB8-1	18-Aug-57	24.42	4
SEVIER	TP8-1	9-Apr-55	8.69	3	SUMMIT	TS7-1	1-Jun-52	27.98	5
SEVIER	PB12-1	2-Sep-57	9.03	3	SUMMIT	TP8-1	9-Apr-55	31.24	5
SEVIER	PB15-1	16-Sep-57	9.40	3	SUMMIT	PB12-1	2-Sep-57	33.84	5
SEVIER	PB9-1	23-Aug-57	10.20	4	SUMMIT	TS6-1	25-May-52	36.36	5
SEVIER	PB4-1	5-Jul-57	11.03	4	SUMMIT	PB9-1	23-Aug-57	40.14	5
SEVIER	TP3-1	1-Mar-55	14.26	4	SUMMIT	PB5-1	15-Jul-57	41.39	5
SEVIER	PB2-1	18-Jun-57	14.67	4	SUMMIT	TP10-1	5-May-55	110.40	7
SEVIER	PB11-1	31-Aug-57	23.83	4	SUMMIT	TP4-1	7-Mar-55	112.55	7
SEVIER	UK10-1	25-May-53	33.63	5	SUMMIT	UK2-1	24-Mar-53	451.90	9
SEVIER	TP4-1	7-Mar-55	35.61	5	SUMMIT	TS8-1	5-Jun-52	712.19	9
SEVIER	TS1-1	1-Apr-52	37.84	5	TOOELE1	UK9-1	19-May-53	4.19	2
SEVIER	TS7-1	1-Jun-52	38.06	5	TOOELE1	PB13-1	6-Sep-57	4.41	2
SEVIER	UK7-1	25-Apr-53	43.67	5	TOOELE1	UK6-1	18-Apr-53	4.48	2
SEVIER	TS8-1	5-Jun-52	55.86	6	TOOELE1	PB4-1	5-Jul-57	5.07	3
SEVIER	TP11-1	15-May-55	57.32	6	TOOELE1	UK10-1	25-May-53	5.84	3
SEVIER	TS6-1	25-May-52	92.16	6	TOOELE1	BJ6-1	29-Nov-51	5.89	3
SEVIER	UK9-1	19-May-53	188.07	7	TOOELE1	PB1-1	28-May-57	6.17	3
SEVIER	TP9-1	15-Apr-55	243.92	8	TOOELE1	TP9-1	15-Apr-55	6.95	3
SUMMIT	TS8-2	6-Jun-52	4.10	2	TOOELE1	TS2-1	15-Apr-52	6.96	3
SUMMIT	PB2-1	18-Jun-57	4.31	2	TOOELE1	TP8-1	9-Apr-55	8.51	3

INDIVIDUAL FALLOUT DAYS
UTAH

COUNTY	SHOT	DATE	µCi/SQ METER	INDEX	COUNTY	SHOT	DATE	µCi/SQ METER	INDEX
TOOELE1	BJ5 1	19-Nov-51	8.72	3	TOOELE2	SE1	6-Jul-62	22.33	4
TOOELE1	PB16-1	23-Sep-57	8.74	3	TOOELE2	TP11-1	15-May-55	23.66	4
TOOELE1	TS8-2	6-Jun-52	13.99	4	TOOELE2	PB17-1	28-Sep-57	23.90	4
TOOELE1	TP11-1	15-May-55	15.84	4	TOOELE2	PB12-1	2-Sep-57	34.59	5
TOOELE1	TS6-1	25-May-52	18.23	4	TOOELE2	TP8-1	9-Apr-55	39.13	5
TOOELE1	TS7-1	1-Jun-52	18.65	4	TOOELE2	PB5-1	15-Jul-57	42.33	5
TOOELE1	PB17-1	28-Sep-57	23.90	4	TOOELE2	PB8-1	18-Aug-57	42.39	5
TOOELE1	TP10-1	5-May-55	29.76	5	TOOELE2	PB9-1	23-Aug-57	53.43	6
TOOELE1	PB9-1	23-Aug-57	32.13	5	TOOELE2	TP4-1	7-Mar-55	60.65	6
TOOELE1	PB12-1	2-Sep-57	36.17	5	TOOELE2	TP10-1	5-May-55	78.84	6
TOOELE1	PB6-1	24-Jul-57	36.99	5	TOOELE2	UK2-1	24-Mar-53	635.02	9
TOOELE1	PB5-1	15-Jul-57	42.33	5	TOOELE2	TS8-1	5-Jun-52	1214.92	10
TOOELE1	TP4-1	7-Mar-55	60.65	6	UINTAH	UK6-1	18-Apr-53	3.59	2
TOOELE1	PB8-1	18-Aug-57	84.89	6	UINTAH	PB13-1	6-Sep-57	3.70	2
TOOELE1	UK2-1	24-Mar-53	119.78	7	UINTAH	TP7-1	29-Mar-55	4.22	2
TOOELE1	TS8-1	5-Jun-52	2429.84	10	UINTAH	PB15-1	16-Sep-57	6.49	3
TOOELE2	PB13-1	6-Sep-57	3.58	2	UINTAH	TS1-1	1-Apr-52	7.61	3
TOOELE2	TP6-1	22-Mar-55	3.61	2	UINTAH	PB17-1	28-Sep-57	7.93	3
TOOELE2	TS2-1	15-Apr-52	3.94	2	UINTAH	TP9-1	15-Apr-55	7.96	3
TOOELE2	PB16-1	23-Sep-57	4.37	2	UINTAH	PB2-1	18-Jun-57	9.55	3
TOOELE2	UK6-1	18-Apr-53	4.48	2	UINTAH	PB1-1	28-May-57	12.24	4
TOOELE2	PB4-1	5-Jul-57	5.07	3	UINTAH	PB8-1	18-Aug-57	15.54	4
TOOELE2	PB1-1	28-May-57	6.17	3	UINTAH	PB4-1	5-Jul-57	16.36	4
TOOELE2	TS8-2	6-Jun-52	7.00	3	UINTAH	UK7-1	25-Apr-53	16.70	4
TOOELE2	UK9-1	19-May-53	8.49	3	UINTAH	PB12-1	2-Sep-57	17.72	4
TOOELE2	TS7-1	1-Jun-52	9.33	3	UINTAH	TS7-1	1-Jun-52	18.50	4
TOOELE2	UK10-1	25-May-53	10.69	4	UINTAH	UK10-1	25-May-53	21.94	4
TOOELE2	PB15-1	16-Sep-57	11.30	4	UINTAH	TP11-1	15-May-55	23.73	4
TOOELE2	UK7-1	25-Apr-53	12.30	4	UINTAH	PB5-1	15-Jul-57	24.35	4
TOOELE2	TP9-1	15-Apr-55	13.91	4	UINTAH	TP8-1	9-Apr-55	24.74	4
TOOELE2	TS1-1	1-Apr-52	17.85	4	UINTAH	UK9-1	19-May-53	46.51	5
TOOELE2	TS6-1	25-May-52	18.23	4	UINTAH	PB9-1	23-Aug-57	51.90	6
TOOELE2	PB6-1	24-Jul-57	18.50	4	UINTAH	TS6-1	25-May-52	63.21	6

INDIVIDUAL FALLOUT DAYS
UTAH

COUNTY	SHOT	DATE	µCi/SQ METER	INDEX	COUNTY	SHOT	DATE	µCi/SQ METER	INDEX
UINTAH	TP4-1	7-Mar-55	73.97	6	WASATCH	TS7-1	1-Jun-52	9.60	3
UINTAH	TS8-1	5-Jun-52	230.42	8	WASATCH	PB2-1	18-Jun-57	9.66	3
UINTAH	TP10-1	5-May-55	233.13	8	WASATCH	PB4-1	5-Jul-57	10.78	4
UINTAH	PB11-1	31-Aug-57	235.72	8	WASATCH	PB15-1	16-Sep-57	11.30	4
UTAH	UK11-1	4-Jun-53	4.31	2	WASATCH	UK7-1	25-Apr-53	12.52	4
UTAH	UK6-1	18-Apr-53	6.41	3	WASATCH	PB17-1	28-Sep-57	15.85	4
UTAH	TP7-1	29-Mar-55	8.55	3	WASATCH	PB8-1	18-Aug-57	16.28	4
UTAH	TS7-1	1-Jun-52	9.72	3	WASATCH	PB1-1	28-May-57	18.41	4
UTAH	PB2-1	18-Jun-57	9.78	3	WASATCH	TS1-1	1-Apr-52	21.65	4
UTAH	PB15-1	16-Sep-57	11.30	4	WASATCH	TP11-1	15-May-55	21.87	4
UTAH	UK7-1	25-Apr-53	12.52	4	WASATCH	UK10-1	25-May-53	22.37	4
UTAH	PB4-1	5-Jul-57	12.55	4	WASATCH	TP8-1	9-Apr-55	33.43	5
UTAH	TP9-1	15-Apr-55	14.11	4	WASATCH	PB12-1	2-Sep-57	36.13	5
UTAH	TS2-1	15-Apr-52	15.35	4	WASATCH	TS6-1	25-May-52	36.36	5
UTAH	PB17-1	28-Sep-57	15.85	4	WASATCH	UK2-1	24-Mar-53	47.74	5
UTAH	PB1-1	28-May-57	24.49	4	WASATCH	PB5-1	15-Jul-57	66.27	6
UTAH	TS1-1	1-Apr-52	27.13	5	WASATCH	PB9-1	23-Aug-57	74.47	6
UTAH	TP8-1	9-Apr-55	29.44	5	WASATCH	TP4-1	7-Mar-55	113.01	7
UTAH	UK10-1	25-May-53	33.20	5	WASATCH	UK9-1	19-May-53	280.07	8
UTAH	TP11-1	15-May-55	35.45	5	WASATCH	TS8-1	5-Jun-52	237.40	8
UTAH	PB8-1	18-Aug-57	40.59	5	WASATCH	TP10-1	5-May-55	237.40	8
UTAH	PB12-1	2-Sep-57	46.17	5	WASHINGTON1	TP3-1	1-Mar-55	16.54	4
UTAH	TS6-1	25-May-52	46.41	5	WASHINGTON1	TS6-1	25-May-52	18.49	4
UTAH	PB5-1	15-Jul-57	84.66	6	WASHINGTON1	PB18-1	10-Jul-57	20.12	4
UTAH	UK2-1	24-Mar-53	96.49	6	WASHINGTON1	TP11-1	15-May-55	60.67	6
UTAH	PB9-1	23-Aug-57	103.16	7	WASHINGTON1	UK7-1	25-Apr-53	64.00	6
UTAH	TP4-1	7-Mar-55	151.68	7	WASHINGTON1	TP7-1	29-Mar-55	89.86	6
UTAH	UK9-1	19-May-53	280.07	8	WASHINGTON1	PB3-1	24-Jun-57	188.87	7
UTAH	TS8-1	5-Jun-52	237.40	8	WASHINGTON1	PB11-1	31-Aug-57	318.50	8
UTAH	TP10-1	5-May-55	238.18	8	WASHINGTON1	UK9-1	19-May-53	2758.95	10
WASATCH	UK6-1	18-Apr-53	4.48	2	WASHINGTON2	PB3-1	24-Jun-57	27.52	5
WASATCH	TP9-1	15-Apr-55	6.95	3	WASHINGTON2	UK7-1	25-Apr-53	69.39	6
WASATCH	PB11-1	31-Aug-57	7.81	3	WASHINGTON2	TP11-1	15-May-55	104.21	7

INDIVIDUAL FALLOUT DAYS
UTAH

COUNTY	SHOT	DATE	µCi/SQ METER	INDEX	COUNTY	SHOT	DATE	µCi/SQ METER	INDEX
WASHINGTON2	TP3-1	1-Mar-55	254.31	8	WAYNE	TS7-1	1-Jun-52	46.14	5
WASHINGTON2	PB11-1	31-Aug-57	641.04	9	WAYNE	TS8-1	5-Jun-52	55.86	6
WASHINGTON2	UK1-1	17-Mar-53	1303.21	10	WAYNE	TP9-1	15-Apr-55	80.94	6
WASHINGTON2	UK9-1	19-May-53	4392.12	10	WAYNE	TS6-1	25-May-52	82.99	6
WASHINGTON3	TP7-1	29-Mar-55	8.97	3	WAYNE	PB11-1	31-Aug-57	85.40	6
WASHINGTON3	UK7-1	25-Apr-53	10.64	4	WAYNE	UK9-1	19-May-53	282.11	8
WASHINGTON3	PB18-1	10-Jul-57	15.36	4	WEBER	TS3-1	22-Apr-52	4.06	2
WASHINGTON3	PB3-1	24-Jun-57	52.16	6	WEBER	UK6-1	18-Apr-53	4.48	2
WASHINGTON3	TP11-1	15-May-55	62.19	6	WEBER	PB16-1	23-Sep-57	4.93	2
WASHINGTON3	TP3-1	1-Mar-55	68.79	6	WEBER	TS8-2	6-Jun-52	5.19	3
WASHINGTON3	PB11-1	31-Aug-57	500.51	9	WEBER	UK7-1	25-Apr-53	5.87	3
WASHINGTON3	UK1-1	17-Mar-53	596.14	9	WEBER	PB4-1	5-Jul-57	6.47	3
WASHINGTON3	UK9-1	19-May-53	3642.40	10	WEBER	TP9-1	15-Apr-55	6.95	3
WAYNE	TP5-1	12-Mar-55	4.13	2	WEBER	UK9-1	19-May-53	8.49	3
WAYNE	UK5-1	11-Apr-53	5.05	3	WEBER	TS1-1	1-Apr-52	8.80	3
WAYNE	PB4-1	5-Jul-57	5.07	3	WEBER	TS7-1	1-Jun-52	9.33	3
WAYNE	PB15-1	16-Sep-57	5.59	3	WEBER	UK10-1	25-May-53	10.69	4
WAYNE	PB17-1	28-Sep-57	7.93	3	WEBER	PB6-2	25-Jul-57	11.04	4
WAYNE	PB3-1	24-Jun-57	8.52	3	WEBER	SE1	6-Jul-62	11.17	4
WAYNE	TP8-1	9-Apr-55	8.60	3	WEBER	PB15-1	16-Sep-57	11.30	4
WAYNE	PB12-1	2-Sep-57	8.81	3	WEBER	PB5-1	15-Jul-57	12.44	4
WAYNE	TP3-1	1-Mar-55	9.41	3	WEBER	TS6-1	25-May-52	18.23	4
WAYNE	PB18-1	10-Jul-57	10.18	4	WEBER	TP11-1	15-May-55	21.00	4
WAYNE	UK10-1	25-May-53	10.97	4	WEBER	PB1-1	28-May-57	22.94	4
WAYNE	PB1-1	28-May-57	12.24	4	WEBER	PB17-1	28-Sep-57	23.90	4
WAYNE	TP11-1	15-May-55	16.41	4	WEBER	TP8-1	9-Apr-55	24.92	4
WAYNE	TS1-1	1-Apr-52	18.08	4	WEBER	PB12-1	2-Sep-57	27.66	5
WAYNE	PB2-1	18-Jun-57	19.44	4	WEBER	PB8-1	18-Aug-57	32.56	5
WAYNE	UK6-1	18-Apr-53	19.86	4	WEBER	PB9-1	23-Aug-57	40.14	5
WAYNE	UK11-1	4-Jun-53	20.87	4	WEBER	TP4-1	7-Mar-55	60.29	6
WAYNE	TP4-1	7-Mar-55	22.53	4	WEBER	TP10-1	5-May-55	117.39	7
WAYNE	TP7-1	29-Mar-55	23.93	4	WEBER	UK2-1	24-Mar-53	679.47	9
WAYNE	UK7-1	25-Apr-53	42.88	5	WEBER	TS8-1	5-Jun-52	900.71	10

INDIVIDUAL FALLOUT DAYS
VIRGINIA

COUNTY	SHOT	DATE	µCi/SQ METER	INDEX	COUNTY	SHOT	DATE	µCi/SQ METER	INDEX
ACCOMACK	PB5-9	23-Jul-57	4.71	2	AUGUSTA	BJ3-5	5-Nov-51	4.59	2
ACCOMACK	BJ2-3	1-Nov-51	5.10	3	AUGUSTA	PB5-8	22-Jul-57	8.96	3
ACCOMACK	UK1-2	18-Mar-53	7.52	3	AUGUSTA	SE4	9-Jul-62	60.19	6
ACCOMACK	BJ2-4	2-Nov-51	7.76	3	BATH	PB5-8	22-Jul-57	8.96	3
ACCOMACK	BJ3-6	6-Nov-51	11.57	4	BATH	SE4	9-Jul-62	208.78	8
ACCOMACK	SE4	9-Jul-62	37.08	5	BEDFORD	BJ2-4	2-Nov-51	3.67	2
ACCOMACK	SE6	11-Jul-62	66.88	6	BEDFORD	TS5-2	8-May-52	4.11	2
ALBEMARLE	BJ2-3	1-Nov-51	4.61	2	BEDFORD	BJ2-3	1-Nov-51	4.72	2
ALBEMARLE	BJ2-4	2-Nov-51	5.51	3	BEDFORD	PB5-8	22-Jul-57	8.96	3
ALLEGHANY	PB12-6	7-Sep-57	3.53	2	BEDFORD	BJ3-5	5-Nov-51	9.19	3
ALLEGHANY	SE4	9-Jul-62	85.56	6	BEDFORD	SE4	9-Jul-62	60.19	6
AMELIA	BJ2-2	31-Oct-51	3.89	2	BLAND	PB4-5	9-Jul-57	7.83	3
AMELIA	BJ2-4	2-Nov-51	4.17	2	BOTETOURT	PB12-6	7-Sep-57	6.31	3
AMELIA	PB12-6	7-Sep-57	5.89	3	BOTETOURT	BJ2-4	2-Nov-51	3.51	1
AMELIA	TS3-4	25-Apr-52	6.78	3	BOTETOURT	SE4	9-Jul-62	208.78	8
AMELIA	BJ2-3	1-Nov-51	8.69	3	BRUNSWICK	BJ2-4	2-Nov-51	4.93	2
AMELIA	PB5-8	22-Jul-57	8.96	3	BRUNSWICK	BJ2-2	31-Oct-51	6.42	3
AMELIA	SE4	9-Jul-62	149.13	7	BRUNSWICK	BJ2-3	1-Nov-51	7.83	3
AMHERST	BJ2-3	1-Nov-51	3.54	2	BRUNSWICK	PB5-8	22-Jul-57	8.96	3
AMHERST	BJ2-4	2-Nov-51	5.84	3	BRUNSWICK	TS3-4	25-Apr-52	11.30	4
AMHERST	SE4	9-Jul-62	73.06	6	BUCHANAN	TP10-2	6-May-55	3.62	2
APPOMATTOX	BJ2-4	2-Nov-51	3.59	2	BUCHANAN	PB6-3	26-Jul-57	3.96	2
APPOMATTOX	BJ2-3	1-Nov-51	6.11	3	BUCHANAN	PB5-8	22-Jul-57	5.97	3
APPOMATTOX	BJ2-2	31-Oct-51	6.42	3	BUCHANAN	UK9-4	22-May-53	12.05	4
APPOMATTOX	UK9-4	22-May-53	7.98	3	BUCHANAN	SE4	9-Jul-62	149.13	7
APPOMATTOX	SE4	9-Jul-62	60.19	6	BUCKINGHAM	PB5-8	22-Jul-57	5.97	3
ARLINGTON	TS3-5	26-Apr-52	3.72	2	BUCKINGHAM	BJ2-2	31-Oct-51	6.42	3
ARLINGTON	TS3-4	25-Apr-52	3.87	2	BUCKINGHAM	BJ2-3	1-Nov-51	6.54	3
ARLINGTON	PB5-8	22-Jul-57	5.97	3	CAMPBELL	BJ2-4	2-Nov-51	3.76	2
ARLINGTON	UK1-2	18-Mar-53	6.87	3	CAMPBELL	PB5-8	22-Jul-57	5.97	3
ARLINGTON	BJ2-4	2-Nov-51	7.56	3	CAMPBELL	BJ2-3	1-Nov-51	6.33	3
ARLINGTON	BJ2-3	1-Nov-51	21.07	4	CAMPBELL	BJ2-2	31-Oct-51	6.42	3
AUGUSTA	BJ2-3	1-Nov-51	3.75	2	CAMPBELL	SE4	9-Jul-62	57.04	6

INDIVIDUAL FALLOUT DAYS
VIRGINIA

COUNTY	SHOT	DATE	µCi/SQ METER	INDEX	COUNTY	SHOT	DATE	µCi/SQ METER	INDEX
CAROLINE	UK1-2	18-Mar-53	5.98	3	CUMBERLAND	PB5-8	22-Jul-57	5.97	3
CAROLINE	TS3-4	25-Apr-52	6.78	3	CUMBERLAND	BJ2-2	31-Oct-51	6.42	3
CAROLINE	BJ2-4	2-Nov-51	7.45	3	CUMBERLAND	TS3-4	25-Apr-52	6.78	3
CAROLINE	BJ2-3	1-Nov-51	8.50	3	CUMBERLAND	BJ2-3	1-Nov-51	7.29	3
CAROLINE	SE4	9-Jul-62	57.04	6	DICKENSON	TP10-2	6-May-55	3.62	2
CARROLL	BJ2-4	2-Nov-51	3.98	2	DICKENSON	UK1-2	18-Mar-53	3.71	2
CARROLL	PB4-5	9-Jul-57	5.24	3	DICKENSON	PB17-3	30-Sep-57	3.79	2
CARROLL	BJ2-2	31-Oct-51	6.42	3	DICKENSON	PB6-3	26-Jul-57	3.96	2
CARROLL	PB5-8	22-Jul-57	8.96	3	DICKENSON	BJ2-4	2-Nov-51	7.37	3
CARROLL	SE4	9-Jul-62	94.45	6	DICKENSON	SE4	9-Jul-62	94.45	6
CHARLES CITY	BJ2-4	2-Nov-51	3.62	2	DINWIDDIE	BJ2-4	2-Nov-51	4.59	2
CHARLES CITY	BJ2-3	1-Nov-51	5.82	3	DINWIDDIE	BJ3-6	6-Nov-51	6.94	3
CHARLES CITY	TS3-4	25-Apr-52	11.30	4	DINWIDDIE	BJ2-3	1-Nov-51	7.40	3
CHARLES CITY	BJ3-6	6-Nov-51	11.57	4	DINWIDDIE	PB5-8	22-Jul-57	8.96	3
CHARLES CITY	SE4	9-Jul-62	60.19	6	DINWIDDIE	TS3-4	25-Apr-52	11.30	4
CHARLOTTE	PB12-8	9-Sep-57	3.66	2	ESSEX	BJ2-4	2-Nov-51	3.90	2
CHARLOTTE	BJ2-2	31-Oct-51	6.42	3	ESSEX	UK1-2	18-Mar-53	5.36	3
CHARLOTTE	BJ2-3	1-Nov-51	7.40	3	ESSEX	TS3-4	25-Apr-52	6.78	3
CHARLOTTE	BJ2-4	2-Nov-51	8.52	3	ESSEX	BJ2-3	1-Nov-51	10.11	4
CHESTERFIELD	BJ2-4	2-Nov-51	4.34	2	FAIRFAX	TS3-4	25-Apr-52	3.87	2
CHESTERFIELD	TS3-4	25-Apr-52	4.69	2	FAIRFAX	UK1-2	18-Mar-53	5.01	3
CHESTERFIELD	BJ3-6	6-Nov-51	6.94	3	FAIRFAX	PB5-8	22-Jul-57	5.97	3
CHESTERFIELD	BJ2-3	1-Nov-51	8.80	3	FAIRFAX	BJ2-4	2-Nov-51	7.59	3
CHESTERFIELD	SE4	9-Jul-62	149.13	7	FAIRFAX	BJ2-3	1-Nov-51	16.23	4
CLARKE	BJ2-3	1-Nov-51	5.26	3	FAIRFAX	SE4	9-Jul-62	60.19	6
CLARKE	PB5-8	22-Jul-57	8.96	3	FAUQUIER	UK1-2	18-Mar-53	6.08	3
CRAIG	SE4	9-Jul-62	90.29	6	FAUQUIER	BJ2-4	2-Nov-51	6.20	3
CULPEPER	BJ2-4	2-Nov-51	7.01	3	FAUQUIER	BJ2-3	1-Nov-51	7.43	3
CULPEPER	PB5-8	22-Jul-57	8.96	3	FAUQUIER	TS3-4	25-Apr-52	11.30	4
CULPEPER	TS6-4	28-May-52	11.11	4	FAUQUIER	SE4	9-Jul-62	57.04	6
CULPEPER	TS3-4	25-Apr-52	11.30	4	FLOYD	BJ2-4	2-Nov-51	3.68	2
CULPEPER	BJ2-3	1-Nov-51	12.12	4	FLOYD	BJ2-3	1-Nov-51	4.35	2
CUMBERLAND	BJ2-4	2-Nov-51	3.67	2	FLOYD	TS5-2	8-May-52	5.84	3

INDIVIDUAL FALLOUT DAYS
VIRGINIA

COUNTY	SHOT	DATE	µCi/SQ METER	INDEX	COUNTY	SHOT	DATE	µCi/SQ METER	INDEX
FLOYD	PB5-8	22-Jul-57	8.96	3	GREENSVILLE	PB5-9	23-Jul-57	4.71	2
FLOYD	BJ3-5	5-Nov-51	9.19	3	GREENSVILLE	BJ2-4	2-Nov-51	5.01	3
FLOYD	SE4	9-Jul-62	60.19	6	GREENSVILLE	BJ2-3	1-Nov-51	7.94	3
FLUVANNA	BJ2-3	1-Nov-51	4.40	2	GREENSVILLE	TS3-4	25-Apr-52	11.30	4
FLUVANNA	PB5-8	22-Jul-57	5.97	3	GREENSVILLE	BJ3-6	6-Nov-51	11.57	4
FLUVANNA	BJ2-4	2-Nov-51	6.60	3	HALIFAX	BJ2-2	31-Oct-51	3.89	2
FLUVANNA	TS3-4	25-Apr-52	6.78	3	HALIFAX	PB5-9	23-Jul-57	4.71	2
FRANKLIN	PB11-3	2-Sep-57	3.91	2	HALIFAX	BJ2-4	2-Nov-51	4.84	2
FRANKLIN	PB5-9	23-Jul-57	4.71	2	HALIFAX	TS5-2	8-May-52	4.92	2
FRANKLIN	BJ2-3	1-Nov-51	5.88	3	HALIFAX	BJ2-3	1-Nov-51	8.58	3
FRANKLIN	BJ2-4	2-Nov-51	6.07	3	HALIFAX	TS7-4	4-Jun-52	8.76	3
FRANKLIN	BJ2-2	31-Oct-51	6.42	3	HAMPTON	TS3-4	25-Apr-52	4.52	2
FRANKLIN	SE4	9-Jul-62	149.13	7	HAMPTON	BJ2-4	2-Nov-51	4.98	2
FREDERICK	UK1-2	18-Mar-53	4.23	2	HAMPTON	PB5-8	22-Jul-57	8.96	3
FREDERICK	BJ2-3	1-Nov-51	4.65	2	HAMPTON	UK10-2	26-May-53	9.11	3
FREDERICK	SE4	9-Jul-62	57.04	6	HAMPTON	BJ3-6	6-Nov-51	11.57	4
GILES	SE4	9-Jul-62	57.04	6	HANOVER	BJ2-4	2-Nov-51	4.34	2
GLOUCESTER	UK1-2	18-Mar-53	4.43	2	HANOVER	PB5-8	22-Jul-57	8.96	3
GLOUCESTER	BJ2-3	1-Nov-51	5.10	3	HANOVER	BJ2-3	1-Nov-51	10.40	4
GLOUCESTER	PB5-8	22-Jul-57	5.97	3	HANOVER	TS3-4	25-Apr-52	11.30	4
GLOUCESTER	TS3-4	25-Apr-52	6.78	3	HANOVER	SE4	9-Jul-62	149.13	7
GLOUCESTER	BJ3-6	6-Nov-51	11.57	4	HENRICO	BJ2-4	2-Nov-51	4.34	2
GOOCHLAND	PB5-8	22-Jul-57	5.97	3	HENRICO	BJ3-6	6-Nov-51	6.94	3
GOOCHLAND	BJ2-4	2-Nov-51	7.68	3	HENRICO	PB5-8	22-Jul-57	8.96	3
GOOCHLAND	BJ2-3	1-Nov-51	8.26	3	HENRICO	BJ2-3	1-Nov-51	9.33	3
GOOCHLAND	TS3-4	25-Apr-52	11.30	4	HENRICO	TS3-4	25-Apr-52	11.30	4
GOOCHLAND	UK1-2	18-Mar-53	3.50	1	HENRY	TS7-4	4-Jun-52	4.96	2
GOOCHLAND	SE4	9-Jul-62	149.13	7	HENRY	BJ2-2	31-Oct-51	6.42	3
GRAYSON	PB4-5	9-Jul-57	5.24	3	HENRY	BJ2-4	2-Nov-51	6.87	3
GRAYSON	TS6-4	28-May-52	5.56	3	HENRY	BJ2-3	1-Nov-51	7.16	3
GRAYSON	SE4	9-Jul-62	43.75	5	HIGHLAND	PB12-6	7-Sep-57	3.70	2
GREENE	BJ2-3	1-Nov-51	5.36	3	HIGHLAND	PB5-9	23-Jul-57	4.71	2
GREENE	SE4	9-Jul-62	60.19	6	HIGHLAND	SE4	9-Jul-62	85.56	6

INDICES INDIVIDUAL FALLOUT DAYS
VIRGINIA

COUNTY	SHOT	DATE	μCi/SQ METER	INDEX	COUNTY	SHOT	DATE	μCi/SQ METER	INDEX
ISLE OF WIGH	BJ2-3	1-Nov-51	4.30	2	LANCASTER	BJ3-6	6-Nov-51	11.57	4
ISLE OF WIGH	PB5-9	23-Jul-57	4.71	2	LEE	BJ2-4	2-Nov-51	3.58	2
ISLE OF WIGH	BJ2-4	2-Nov-51	5.56	3	LEE	TP10-2	6-May-55	3.62	2
ISLE OF WIGH	TS3-4	25-Apr-52	6.78	3	LEE	PB17-3	30-Sep-57	3.79	2
ISLE OF WIGH	PB5-8	22-Jul-57	8.96	3	LEE	PB6-3	26-Jul-57	3.96	2
ISLE OF WIGH	BJ3-6	6-Nov-51	11.57	4	LEE	PB2-5	22-Jun-57	4.18	2
JAMES CITY	BJ2-3	1-Nov-51	5.01	3	LEE	TP6-4	25-Mar-55	4.32	2
JAMES CITY	TS3-4	25-Apr-52	6.78	3	LEE	UK1-2	18-Mar-53	10.72	4
JAMES CITY	BJ2-4	2-Nov-51	6.83	3	LEE	SE4	9-Jul-62	43.75	5
JAMES CITY	BJ3-6	6-Nov-51	11.57	4	LOUDOUN	UK1-2	18-Mar-53	4.81	2
KING AND QUE	UK1-2	18-Mar-53	3.71	2	LOUDOUN	BJ2-4	2-Nov-51	5.99	3
KING AND QUE	BJ2-4	2-Nov-51	3.76	2	LOUDOUN	PB5-8	22-Jul-57	8.96	3
KING AND QUE	BJ2-5	3-Nov-51	4.31	2	LOUDOUN	BJ2-3	1-Nov-51	9.04	3
KING AND QUE	BJ3-6	6-Nov-51	6.94	3	LOUDOUN	SE4	9-Jul-62	60.19	6
KING AND QUE	BJ2-3	1-Nov-51	7.34	3	LOUISA	BJ2-4	2-Nov-51	3.67	2
KING AND QUE	PB5-8	22-Jul-57	8.96	3	LOUISA	TS3-4	25-Apr-52	6.78	3
KING AND QUE	TS3-4	25-Apr-52	11.30	4	LOUISA	PB5-8	22-Jul-57	8.96	3
KING AND QUE	SE4	9-Jul-62	57.04	6	LOUISA	BJ2-3	1-Nov-51	9.65	3
KING GEORGE	BJ2-4	2-Nov-51	4.25	2	LUNENBURG	BJ2-4	2-Nov-51	4.59	2
KING GEORGE	UK1-2	18-Mar-53	7.63	3	LUNENBURG	PB5-9	23-Jul-57	4.71	2
KING GEORGE	TS3-4	25-Apr-52	11.30	4	LUNENBURG	BJ2-2	31-Oct-51	6.42	3
KING GEORGE	BJ2-3	1-Nov-51	15.57	4	LUNENBURG	TS3-4	25-Apr-52	6.78	3
KING WILLIAM	BJ2-4	2-Nov-51	3.76	2	LUNENBURG	BJ2-3	1-Nov-51	7.94	3
KING WILLIAM	BJ2-5	3-Nov-51	4.12	2	LUNENBURG	SE4	9-Jul-62	57.04	6
KING WILLIAM	BJ3-6	6-Nov-51	6.94	3	MADISON	BJ2-3	1-Nov-51	5.19	3
KING WILLIAM	BJ2-3	1-Nov-51	8.90	3	MADISON	TS3-4	25-Apr-52	6.78	3
KING WILLIAM	PB5-8	22-Jul-57	8.96	3	MADISON	PB5-8	22-Jul-57	8.96	3
KING WILLIAM	TS3-4	25-Apr-52	11.30	4	MADISON	SE4	9-Jul-62	60.19	6
KING WILLIAM	SE4	9-Jul-62	57.04	6	MATHEWS	BJ2-3	1-Nov-51	3.57	2
LANCASTER	BJ2-4	2-Nov-51	3.55	2	MATHEWS	PB5-8	22-Jul-57	5.97	3
LANCASTER	UK1-2	18-Mar-53	5.57	3	MATHEWS	BJ2-4	2-Nov-51	6.48	3
LANCASTER	TS3-4	25-Apr-52	6.78	3	MATHEWS	TS3-4	25-Apr-52	6.78	3
LANCASTER	BJ2-3	1-Nov-51	6.80	3	MATHEWS	BJ3-6	6-Nov-51	11.57	4

INDIVIDUAL FALLOUT DAYS
VIRGINIA

COUNTY	SHOT	DATE	µCi/SQ METER	INDEX	COUNTY	SHOT	DATE	µCi/SQ METER	INDEX
MECKLENBURG	PB5-8	22-Jul-57	5.97	3	NORFOLK/CHES	BJ3-6	6-Nov-51	11.57	4
MECKLENBURG	BJ2-2	31-Oct-51	6.42	3	NORTHAMPTON	UK1-2	18-Mar-53	5.36	3
MECKLENBURG	BJ2-3	1-Nov-51	8.69	3	NORTHAMPTON	PB5-8	22-Jul-57	5.97	3
MECKLENBURG	BJ2-4	2-Nov-51	10.02	4	NORTHAMPTON	BJ2-4	2-Nov-51	6.20	3
MECKLENBURG	SE4	9-Jul-62	57.04	6	NORTHAMPTON	TS3-4	25-Apr-52	6.78	3
MIDDLESEX	BJ2-4	2-Nov-51	3.55	2	NORTHAMPTON	BJ3-6	6-Nov-51	11.57	4
MIDDLESEX	PB5-9	23-Jul-57	4.71	2	NORTHUMBERLA	BJ2-4	2-Nov-51	3.62	2
MIDDLESEX	UK1-2	18-Mar-53	5.05	3	NORTHUMBERLA	UK10-2	26-May-53	4.07	2
MIDDLESEX	BJ2-3	1-Nov-51	6.26	3	NORTHUMBERLA	UK1-2	18-Mar-53	4.64	2
MIDDLESEX	TS3-4	25-Apr-52	6.78	3	NORTHUMBERLA	TS3-4	25-Apr-52	6.78	3
MIDDLESEX	BJ3-6	6-Nov-51	11.57	4	NORTHUMBERLA	BJ2-3	1-Nov-51	7.70	3
MONTGOMERY	TS5-2	8-May-52	5.29	3	NORTHUMBERLA	BJ3-6	6-Nov-51	11.57	4
MONTGOMERY	SE4	9-Jul-62	60.19	6	NOTTOWAY	BJ2-2	31-Oct-51	3.89	2
NELSON	BJ2-3	1-Nov-51	5.47	3	NOTTOWAY	BJ2-4	2-Nov-51	4.34	2
NELSON	PB5-8	22-Jul-57	5.97	3	NOTTOWAY	PB12-6	7-Sep-57	5.63	3
NELSON	SE4	9-Jul-62	60.19	6	NOTTOWAY	TS3-4	25-Apr-52	6.78	3
NEW KENT	BJ2-4	2-Nov-51	3.62	2	NOTTOWAY	BJ2-3	1-Nov-51	8.69	3
NEW KENT	BJ2-5	3-Nov-51	5.01	3	NOTTOWAY	PB5-8	22-Jul-57	8.96	3
NEW KENT	BJ2-3	1-Nov-51	6.26	3	ORANGE	UK1-2	18-Mar-53	4.64	2
NEW KENT	BJ3-6	6-Nov-51	6.94	3	ORANGE	BJ2-3	1-Nov-51	6.53	3
NEW KENT	TS3-4	25-Apr-52	11.30	4	ORANGE	TS3-4	25-Apr-52	6.78	3
NEW KENT	SE4	9-Jul-62	60.19	6	ORANGE	BJ2-4	2-Nov-51	6.93	3
NEWPORT NEWS	PB4-5	9-Jul-57	3.57	2	ORANGE	SE4	9-Jul-62	60.19	6
NEWPORT NEWS	TS3-4	25-Apr-52	4.52	2	PAGE	PB12-6	7-Sep-57	3.91	2
NEWPORT NEWS	PB5-9	23-Jul-57	4.71	2	PAGE	BJ2-3	1-Nov-51	4.12	2
NEWPORT NEWS	BJ2-4	2-Nov-51	5.04	3	PAGE	PB5-8	22-Jul-57	8.96	3
NEWPORT NEWS	PB5-8	22-Jul-57	8.96	3	PATRICK	PB4-5	9-Jul-57	5.24	3
NEWPORT NEWS	UK10-2	26-May-53	9.11	3	PATRICK	BJ2-3	1-Nov-51	5.88	3
NEWPORT NEWS	BJ3-6	6-Nov-51	11.57	4	PATRICK	PB5-8	22-Jul-57	5.97	3
NORFOLK/CHES	PB4-5	9-Jul-57	3.57	2	PATRICK	BJ2-2	31-Oct-51	6.42	3
NORFOLK/CHES	PB5-9	23-Jul-57	4.71	2	PATRICK	BJ2-4	2-Nov-51	7.67	3
NORFOLK/CHES	BJ2-4	2-Nov-51	5.27	3	PATRICK	SE4	9-Jul-62	37.08	5
NORFOLK/CHES	PB5-8	22-Jul-57	8.96	3	PITTSYLVANIA	BJ2-2	31-Oct-51	3.89	2

INDIVIDUAL FALLOUT DAYS
VIRGINIA

COUNTY	SHOT	DATE	µCi/SQ METER	INDEX	COUNTY	SHOT	DATE	µCi/SQ METER	INDEX
PITTSYLVANIA	BJ2-4	2-Nov-51	4.76	2	RICHMOND	TS3-4	25-Apr-52	6.78	3
PITTSYLVANIA	PB5-8	22-Jul-57	5.97	3	RICHMOND	BJ2-3	1-Nov-51	9.93	3
PITTSYLVANIA	BJ2-3	1-Nov-51	6.97	3	ROANOKE	TS5-2	8-May-52	4.34	2
PITTSYLVANIA	SE4	9-Jul-62	60.19	6	ROANOKE	BJ2-3	1-Nov-51	4.48	2
POWHATAN	TS3-4	25-Apr-52	6.78	3	ROANOKE	PB5-8	22-Jul-57	5.97	3
POWHATAN	BJ2-4	2-Nov-51	7.93	3	ROANOKE	BJ3-5	5-Nov-51	9.19	3
POWHATAN	BJ2-3	1-Nov-51	8.04	3	ROANOKE	SE4	9-Jul-62	60.19	6
POWHATAN	PB5-8	22-Jul-57	14.93	4	ROCKBRIDGE	PB12-6	7-Sep-57	3.57	2
POWHATAN	SE4	9-Jul-62	149.13	7	ROCKBRIDGE	PB5-8	22-Jul-57	5.97	3
PRINCE EDWAR	BJ2-4	2-Nov-51	4.01	2	ROCKBRIDGE	SE4	9-Jul-62	57.04	6
PRINCE EDWAR	BJ2-2	31-Oct-51	6.42	3	ROCKINGHAM	BJ2-3	1-Nov-51	3.65	2
PRINCE EDWAR	BJ2-3	1-Nov-51	8.15	3	ROCKINGHAM	PB5-8	22-Jul-57	8.96	3
PRINCE EDWAR	PB5-8	22-Jul-57	8.96	3	ROCKINGHAM	SE6	11-Jul-62	25.03	5
PRINCE EDWAR	SE4	9-Jul-62	60.19	6	ROCKINGHAM	SE4	9-Jul-62	57.04	6
PRINCE GEORG	BJ2-4	2-Nov-51	3.69	2	RUSSELL	TP10-2	6-May-55	3.62	2
PRINCE GEORG	BJ2-3	1-Nov-51	6.76	3	RUSSELL	PB6-3	26-Jul-57	3.96	2
PRINCE GEORG	PB5-8	22-Jul-57	8.96	3	RUSSELL	TP6-4	25-Mar-55	4.32	2
PRINCE GEORG	TS3-4	25-Apr-52	11.30	4	RUSSELL	PB4-5	9-Jul-57	5.24	3
PRINCE GEORG	BJ3-6	6-Nov-51	11.57	4	RUSSELL	TS6-4	28-May-52	5.56	3
PRINCE WILLI	BJ2-4	2-Nov-51	7.87	3	RUSSELL	SE4	9-Jul-62	43.75	5
PRINCE WILLI	PB5-8	22-Jul-57	8.96	3	SCOTT	TP10-2	6-May-55	3.62	2
PRINCE WILLI	BJ2-3	1-Nov-51	13.24	4	SCOTT	PB6-3	26-Jul-57	3.96	2
PULASKI	BJ3-5	5-Nov-51	4.59	2	SCOTT	TP6-4	25-Mar-55	4.32	2
PULASKI	TS6-4	28-May-52	5.56	3	SCOTT	UK1-2	18-Mar-53	6.90	3
PULASKI	PB4-5	9-Jul-57	7.83	3	SCOTT	PB17-3	30-Sep-57	7.49	3
PULASKI	SE4	9-Jul-62	57.04	6	SCOTT	SE4	9-Jul-62	43.75	5
RAPPAHANNOCK	UK1-2	18-Mar-53	4.64	2	SHENANDOAH	BJ2-3	1-Nov-51	3.86	2
RAPPAHANNOCK	BJ2-3	1-Nov-51	4.83	2	SHENANDOAH	SE4	9-Jul-62	57.04	6
RAPPAHANNOCK	PB5-8	22-Jul-57	5.97	3	SMYTH	PB6-3	26-Jul-57	3.96	2
RAPPAHANNOCK	TS3-4	25-Apr-52	6.78	3	SMYTH	PB4-5	9-Jul-57	7.83	3
RAPPAHANNOCK	SE4	9-Jul-62	57.04	6	SMYTH	SE4	9-Jul-62	77.90	6
RICHMOND	BJ2-4	2-Nov-51	3.90	2	SOUTHAMPTON	PB4-5	9-Jul-57	3.57	2
RICHMOND	UK1-2	18-Mar-53	5.87	3	SOUTHAMPTON	BJ2-3	1-Nov-51	5.37	3

INDIVIDUAL FALLOUT DAYS
VIRGINIA

COUNTY	SHOT	DATE	µCi/SQ METER	INDEX	COUNTY	SHOT	DATE	µCi/SQ METER	INDEX
SOUTHAMPTON	TS3-4	25-Apr-52	6.78	3	TAZEWELL	SE4	9-Jul-62	60.19	6
SOUTHAMPTON	BJ2-4	2-Nov-51	7.66	3	VIRGINIA BEA	PB4-5	9-Jul-57	3.57	2
SOUTHAMPTON	BJ3-6	6-Nov-51	11.57	4	VIRGINIA BEA	BJ3-6	6-Nov-51	4.81	2
SPOTSYLVANIA	UK1-2	18-Mar-53	5.26	3	VIRGINIA BEA	BJ2-4	2-Nov-51	5.16	3
SPOTSYLVANIA	TS3-4	25-Apr-52	6.78	3	VIRGINIA BEA	PB5-8	22-Jul-57	8.96	3
SPOTSYLVANIA	BJ2-4	2-Nov-51	6.89	3	VIRGINIA BEA	SE5	10-Jul-62	40.47	5
SPOTSYLVANIA	BJ2-3	1-Nov-51	8.23	3	WARREN	UK1-2	18-Mar-53	3.92	2
SPOTSYLVANIA	SE4	9-Jul-62	57.04	6	WARREN	TS3-4	25-Apr-52	6.78	3
STAFFORD	UK1-2	18-Mar-53	3.71	2	WARREN	BJ2-3	1-Nov-51	7.19	3
STAFFORD	BJ2-4	2-Nov-51	3.97	2	WARREN	SE4	9-Jul-62	73.06	6
STAFFORD	TS3-4	25-Apr-52	6.78	3	WASHINGTON	TP10-2	6-May-55	3.62	2
STAFFORD	PB5-8	22-Jul-57	8.96	3	WASHINGTON	TP6-4	25-Mar-55	4.32	2
STAFFORD	BJ2-3	1-Nov-51	15.12	4	WASHINGTON	PB6-3	26-Jul-57	5.90	3
SUFFOLK/NANS	PB4-5	9-Jul-57	3.57	2	WASHINGTON	UK9-4	22-May-53	12.84	4
SUFFOLK/NANS	BJ2-3	1-Nov-51	3.94	2	WASHINGTON	SE4	9-Jul-62	17.11	4
SUFFOLK/NANS	PB5-9	23-Jul-57	4.71	2	WESTMORELAND	BJ2-4	2-Nov-51	4.11	2
SUFFOLK/NANS	BJ2-4	2-Nov-51	5.74	3	WESTMORELAND	UK1-2	18-Mar-53	6.29	3
SUFFOLK/NANS	PB5-8	22-Jul-57	5.97	3	WESTMORELAND	TS3-4	25-Apr-52	6.78	3
SUFFOLK/NANS	TS3-4	25-Apr-52	6.78	3	WESTMORELAND	BJ2-3	1-Nov-51	11.90	4
SUFFOLK/NANS	BJ3-6	6-Nov-51	11.57	4	WISE	TP10-2	6-May-55	3.62	2
SUFFOLK/NANS	SE5	10-Jul-62	40.47	5	WISE	BJ2-4	2-Nov-51	3.78	2
SURRY	BJ2-3	1-Nov-51	4.74	2	WISE	PB6-3	26-Jul-57	3.96	2
SURRY	TS3-4	25-Apr-52	6.78	3	WISE	TP6-4	25-Mar-55	4.32	2
SURRY	BJ2-4	2-Nov-51	6.83	3	WISE	PB5-8	22-Jul-57	5.97	3
SURRY	PB5-8	22-Jul-57	8.96	3	WISE	PB17-3	30-Sep-57	7.49	3
SURRY	BJ3-6	6-Nov-51	11.57	4	WISE	UK1-2	18-Mar-53	7.99	3
SUSSEX	TS3-4	25-Apr-52	6.78	3	WISE	SE4	9-Jul-62	17.11	4
SUSSEX	BJ2-3	1-Nov-51	7.08	3	WYTHE	PB4-5	9-Jul-57	7.83	3
SUSSEX	BJ2-4	2-Nov-51	7.52	3	YORK	PB5-9	23-Jul-57	4.71	2
SUSSEX	BJ3-6	6-Nov-51	11.57	4	YORK	TS3-4	25-Apr-52	6.78	3
TAZEWELL	PB5-8	22-Jul-57	5.97	3	YORK	BJ3-6	6-Nov-51	11.57	4
TAZEWELL	PB4-5	9-Jul-57	7.83	3					
TAZEWELL	PB6-3	26-Jul-57	15.70	4					

INDIVIDUAL FALLOUT DAYS
VERMONT

COUNTY	SHOT	DATE	µCi/SQ METER	INDEX	COUNTY	SHOT	DATE	µCi/SQ METER	INDEX
ADDISON	PB5-8	22-Jul-57	5.97	3	CHITTENDEN	UK7-2	26-Apr-53	97.27	6
ADDISON	BJ2-4	2-Nov-51	5.99	3	ESSEX	BJ2-3	1-Nov-51	3.58	2
ADDISON	BJ2-2	31-Oct-51	7.98	3	ESSEX	UK7-3	27-Apr-53	3.94	2
ADDISON	R1-2	29-Jan-51	7.99	3	ESSEX	BJ2-4	2-Nov-51	5.48	3
ADDISON	TS1-4	4-Apr-52	10.30	4	ESSEX	TS7-4	4-Jun-52	7.81	3
ADDISON	PB11-5	4-Sep-57	12.85	4	ESSEX	BJ2-2	31-Oct-51	7.98	3
ADDISON	TS7-4	4-Jun-52	13.14	4	ESSEX	PB5-6	20-Jul-57	8.08	3
ADDISON	TS8-3	7-Jun-52	14.70	4	ESSEX	TS8-3	7-Jun-52	14.84	4
ADDISON	UK7-2	26-Apr-53	171.29	7	ESSEX	PB5-8	22-Jul-57	14.93	4
BENNINGTON	BJ2-3	1-Nov-51	4.93	2	FRANKLIN	UK7-3	27-Apr-53	4.67	2
BENNINGTON	PB11-5	4-Sep-57	6.43	3	FRANKLIN	TS1-4	4-Apr-52	6.87	3
BENNINGTON	PB5-8	22-Jul-57	8.96	3	FRANKLIN	BJ2-4	2-Nov-51	7.24	3
BENNINGTON	TS1-4	4-Apr-52	10.30	4	FRANKLIN	BJ2-2	31-Oct-51	12.07	4
BENNINGTON	TS8-3	7-Jun-52	15.57	4	FRANKLIN	TS8-3	7-Jun-52	15.63	4
BENNINGTON	BJ2-4	2-Nov-51	16.86	4	FRANKLIN	UK7-2	26-Apr-53	16.11	4
BENNINGTON	R1-2	29-Jan-51	19.29	4	FRANKLIN	TS7-4	4-Jun-52	36.69	5
BENNINGTON	UK7-2	26-Apr-53	249.42	8	GRAND ISLE	UK8-4	11-May-53	3.55	2
CALEDONIA	UK7-3	27-Apr-53	3.61	2	GRAND ISLE	BJ2-4	2-Nov-51	7.53	3
CALEDONIA	BJ2-3	1-Nov-51	4.48	2	GRAND ISLE	PB5-6	20-Jul-57	8.08	3
CALEDONIA	BJ2-4	2-Nov-51	5.18	3	GRAND ISLE	TS1-4	4-Apr-52	10.30	4
CALEDONIA	UK7-2	26-Apr-53	5.45	3	GRAND ISLE	TS8-3	7-Jun-52	11.10	4
CALEDONIA	BJ2-2	31-Oct-51	7.98	3	GRAND ISLE	BJ2-2	31-Oct-51	12.07	4
CALEDONIA	TS7-4	4-Jun-52	8.13	3	GRAND ISLE	UK7-2	26-Apr-53	24.78	4
CALEDONIA	PB5-8	22-Jul-57	8.96	3	GRAND ISLE	TS7-4	4-Jun-52	41.07	5
CALEDONIA	TS8-3	7-Jun-52	16.48	4	LAMOILLE	UK7-3	27-Apr-53	3.53	2
CHITTENDEN	BJ2-4	2-Nov-51	3.88	2	LAMOILLE	BJ2-4	2-Nov-51	3.62	2
CHITTENDEN	BJ2-2	31-Oct-51	5.01	3	LAMOILLE	BJ2-3	1-Nov-51	3.65	2
CHITTENDEN	PB5-6	20-Jul-57	5.40	3	LAMOILLE	PB11-5	4-Sep-57	5.35	3
CHITTENDEN	TS1-4	4-Apr-52	6.87	3	LAMOILLE	PB5-6	20-Jul-57	5.40	3
CHITTENDEN	PB5-8	22-Jul-57	8.96	3	LAMOILLE	PB5-8	22-Jul-57	5.97	3
CHITTENDEN	TS7-4	4-Jun-52	11.99	4	LAMOILLE	BJ2-2	31-Oct-51	7.98	3
CHITTENDEN	TS8-3	7-Jun-52	13.20	4	LAMOILLE	TS1-4	4-Apr-52	10.30	4
CHITTENDEN	PB11-5	4-Sep-57	19.28	4	LAMOILLE	UK7-2	26-Apr-53	14.05	4

U.S. FALLOUT ATLAS: COUNTY COMPARISONS

INDIVIDUAL FALLOUT DAYS
VERMONT

COUNTY	SHOT	DATE	µCi/SQ METER	INDEX	COUNTY	SHOT	DATE	µCi/SQ METER	INDEX
LAMOILLE	TS8-3	7-Jun-52	15.56	4	RUTLAND	UK7-2	26-Apr-53	77.89	6
LAMOILLE	TS7-4	4-Jun-52	15.66	4	WASHINGTON	BJ2-4	2-Nov-51	3.90	2
ORANGE	BJ2-2	31-Oct-51	4.09	2	WASHINGTON	BJ2-3	1-Nov-51	4.08	2
ORANGE	BJ2-4	2-Nov-51	4.67	2	WASHINGTON	PB5-6	20-Jul-57	5.40	3
ORANGE	BJ2-3	1-Nov-51	5.25	3	WASHINGTON	BJ2-2	31-Oct-51	7.98	3
ORANGE	PB5-6	20-Jul-57	5.40	3	WASHINGTON	PB5-8	22-Jul-57	8.96	3
ORANGE	TS7-4	4-Jun-52	6.44	3	WASHINGTON	TS1-4	4-Apr-52	10.30	4
ORANGE	R1-2	29-Jan-51	7.57	3	WASHINGTON	TS7-4	4-Jun-52	11.88	4
ORANGE	PB5-8	22-Jul-57	8.96	3	WASHINGTON	TS8-3	7-Jun-52	17.21	4
ORANGE	TS1-4	4-Apr-52	10.30	4	WASHINGTON	UK7-2	26-Apr-53	17.69	4
ORANGE	UK7-2	26-Apr-53	12.23	4	WINDHAM	BJ3-7	7-Nov-51	3.71	2
ORANGE	TS8-3	7-Jun-52	16.35	4	WINDHAM	UK4-2	7-Apr-53	5.18	3
ORLEANS	UK7-2	26-Apr-53	5.45	3	WINDHAM	BJ2-3	1-Nov-51	5.47	3
ORLEANS	TS1-4	4-Apr-52	6.87	3	WINDHAM	TS1-4	4-Apr-52	6.87	3
ORLEANS	PB5-6	20-Jul-57	8.08	3	WINDHAM	PB5-8	22-Jul-57	8.96	3
ORLEANS	BJ2-4	2-Nov-51	8.26	3	WINDHAM	PB11-5	4-Sep-57	12.85	4
ORLEANS	TS8-3	7-Jun-52	9.53	3	WINDHAM	TS8-3	7-Jun-52	14.52	4
ORLEANS	BJ2-2	31-Oct-51	12.07	4	WINDHAM	BJ2-4	2-Nov-51	15.28	4
ORLEANS	TS7-4	4-Jun-52	25.14	5	WINDHAM	UK7-2	26-Apr-53	28.71	5
RUTLAND	BJ2-3	1-Nov-51	4.08	2	WINDHAM	R1-2	29-Jan-51	45.69	5
RUTLAND	TS7-4	4-Jun-52	4.57	2	WINDSOR	BJ2-3	1-Nov-51	4.93	2
RUTLAND	PB11-5	4-Sep-57	4.82	2	WINDSOR	R1-2	29-Jan-51	7.57	3
RUTLAND	PB5-8	22-Jul-57	5.97	3	WINDSOR	BJ2-2	31-Oct-51	7.98	3
RUTLAND	BJ2-4	2-Nov-51	6.69	3	WINDSOR	TS1-4	4-Apr-52	10.30	4
RUTLAND	R1-2	29-Jan-51	7.57	3	WINDSOR	BJ2-4	2-Nov-51	11.94	4
RUTLAND	BJ2-2	31-Oct-51	7.98	3	WINDSOR	TS8-3	7-Jun-52	17.18	4
RUTLAND	TS1-4	4-Apr-52	10.30	4	WINDSOR	UK7-2	26-Apr-53	24.23	4
RUTLAND	TS8-3	7-Jun-52	15.64	4					

INDIVIDUAL FALLOUT DAYS
WASHINGTON

COUNTY	SHOT	DATE	µCi/SQ METER	INDEX	COUNTY	SHOT	DATE	µCi/SQ METER	INDEX
ADAMS	UK10-2	26-May-53	6.79	3	GRANT	UK10-2	26-May-53	6.01	3
ADAMS	TS8-1	5-Jun-52	478.58	9	GRANT	TS8-1	5-Jun-52	119.64	7
ASOTIN	PB16-3	25-Sep-57	7.58	3	GRAYS HARBOR	UK7-2	26-Apr-53	5.69	3
ASOTIN	PB17-3	30-Sep-57	9.52	3	KING	UK10-2	26-May-53	4.07	2
ASOTIN	PB6-2	25-Jul-57	10.55	4	KING	TS8-1	5-Jun-52	26.59	5
ASOTIN	PB6-3	26-Jul-57	12.28	4	KITTITAS	UK10-2	26-May-53	7.17	3
ASOTIN	TS8-2	6-Jun-52	37.52	5	KITTITAS	TS8-1	5-Jun-52	26.59	5
ASOTIN	TS8-1	5-Jun-52	6516.50	10	KLICKITAT	TS8-1	5-Jun-52	119.64	7
BENTON	UK10-2	26-May-53	4.63	2	LEWIS	TS8-1	5-Jun-52	13.29	4
BENTON	TS8-1	5-Jun-52	332.35	8	LINCOLN	UK10-2	26-May-53	9.40	3
CHELAN	UK10-2	26-May-53	10.30	4	LINCOLN	TS8-1	5-Jun-52	226.00	8
CHELAN	TS8-1	5-Jun-52	13.29	4	OKANOGAN	UK10-2	26-May-53	23.15	4
COLUMBIA	UK10-2	26-May-53	3.76	2	OKANOGAN	TS8-1	5-Jun-52	39.88	5
COLUMBIA	PB16-3	25-Sep-57	7.58	3	PEND OREILLE	PB16-4	26-Sep-57	5.16	3
COLUMBIA	PB16-4	26-Sep-57	7.74	3	PEND OREILLE	TS8-2	6-Jun-52	6.30	3
COLUMBIA	PB17-3	30-Sep-57	9.52	3	PEND OREILLE	PB17-3	30-Sep-57	6.34	3
COLUMBIA	PB6-2	25-Jul-57	10.55	4	PEND OREILLE	PB16-3	25-Sep-57	7.58	3
COLUMBIA	PB6-3	26-Jul-57	12.28	4	PEND OREILLE	PB6-2	25-Jul-57	10.55	4
COLUMBIA	TS8-2	6-Jun-52	16.98	4	PEND OREILLE	PB6-3	26-Jul-57	12.28	4
COLUMBIA	TS8-1	5-Jun-52	2949.07	10	PEND OREILLE	UK10-2	26-May-53	28.42	5
COWLITZ	TS8-1	5-Jun-52	13.29	4	PEND OREILLE	TS8-1	5-Jun-52	1094.01	10
DOUGLAS	UK10-2	26-May-53	13.89	4	PIERCE	UK10-2	26-May-53	4.81	2
DOUGLAS	TS8-1	5-Jun-52	53.18	6	PIERCE	TS8-1	5-Jun-52	39.88	5
FERRY	UK10-2	26-May-53	34.05	5	SAN JUAN	TS6-4	28-May-52	11.11	4
FERRY	TS8-1	5-Jun-52	146.23	7	SKAGIT	UK9-1	19-May-53	3.85	2
FRANKLIN	TS8-1	5-Jun-52	292.46	8	SKAMANIA	UK7-2	26-Apr-53	5.57	3
GARFIELD	PB17-3	30-Sep-57	6.34	3	SNOHOMISH	UK9-1	19-May-53	4.11	2
GARFIELD	PB16-3	25-Sep-57	7.58	3	SNOHOMISH	UK10-2	26-May-53	5.12	3
GARFIELD	PB6-2	25-Jul-57	10.55	4	SNOHOMISH	TS8-1	5-Jun-52	26.59	5
GARFIELD	PB6-3	26-Jul-57	12.28	4	SPOKANE	PB17-3	30-Sep-57	6.34	3
GARFIELD	UK10-2	26-May-53	12.52	4	SPOKANE	PB16-3	25-Sep-57	7.58	3
GARFIELD	TS8-2	6-Jun-52	58.06	6	SPOKANE	PB16-4	26-Sep-57	7.74	3
GARFIELD	TS8-1	5-Jun-52	10083.93	10	SPOKANE	UK10-2	26-May-53	8.50	3

INDIVIDUAL FALLOUT DAYS
WASHINGTON

COUNTY	SHOT	DATE	µCi/SQ METER	INDEX	COUNTY	SHOT	DATE	µCi/SQ METER	INDEX
SPOKANE	PB6-2	25-Jul-57	10.55	4	WALLA WALLA	PB6-2	25-Jul-57	10.55	4
SPOKANE	PB6-3	26-Jul-57	12.28	4	WALLA WALLA	PB6-3	26-Jul-57	12.28	4
SPOKANE	TS8-1	5-Jun-52	154.25	7	WALLA WALLA	TS8-1	5-Jun-52	917.28	10
STEVENS	UK10-2	26-May-53	24.54	4	WHATCOM	UK10-2	26-May-53	3.63	2
STEVENS	TS8-1	5-Jun-52	385.52	8	WHITMAN	PB17-3	30-Sep-57	6.34	3
THURSTON	TS8-1	5-Jun-52	13.29	4	WHITMAN	TS8-2	6-Jun-52	7.27	3
WAHKIAKUM	UK9-1	19-May-53	3.85	2	WHITMAN	PB16-3	25-Sep-57	7.58	3
WAHKIAKUM	UK7-2	26-Apr-53	5.69	3	WHITMAN	UK10-2	26-May-53	9.04	3
WALLA WALLA	UK10-2	26-May-53	5.26	3	WHITMAN	PB6-2	25-Jul-57	10.55	4
WALLA WALLA	TS8-2	6-Jun-52	5.28	3	WHITMAN	PB6-3	26-Jul-57	12.28	4
WALLA WALLA	PB16-3	25-Sep-57	7.58	3	WHITMAN	TS8-1	5-Jun-52	1262.91	10
WALLA WALLA	PB16-4	26-Sep-57	7.74	3	YAKIMA	UK10-2	26-May-53	4.93	2
WALLA WALLA	PB17-3	30-Sep-57	9.52	3	YAKIMA	TS8-1	5-Jun-52	66.47	6

INDIVIDUAL FALLOUT DAYS
WISCONSIN

COUNTY	SHOT	DATE	µCi/SQ METER	INDEX	COUNTY	SHOT	DATE	µCi/SQ METER	INDEX
ADAMS	TS7-3	3-Jun-52	3.54	2	BURNETT	PB11-3	2-Sep-57	3.98	2
ADAMS	PB9-4	26-Aug-57	8.37	3	BURNETT	UK9-1	19-May-53	4.88	2
ADAMS	PB9-3	25-Aug-57	13.72	4	BURNETT	TP10-2	6-May-55	7.01	3
ADAMS	TP10-2	6-May-55	28.92	5	BURNETT	PB5-5	19-Jul-57	10.11	4
ADAMS	UK9-2	20-May-53	35.19	5	BURNETT	TS6-3	27-May-52	21.08	4
ASHLAND	PB11-3	2-Sep-57	3.98	2	BURNETT	UK9-2	20-May-53	39.74	5
ASHLAND	PB5-5	19-Jul-57	10.11	4	CALUMET	TS7-5	5-Jun-52	3.59	2
ASHLAND	TS6-3	27-May-52	11.48	4	CALUMET	TS7-3	3-Jun-52	5.48	3
ASHLAND	TP10-2	6-May-55	14.02	4	CALUMET	PB9-4	26-Aug-57	8.37	3
ASHLAND	UK9-2	20-May-53	55.14	6	CALUMET	TP10-2	6-May-55	9.64	3
BARRON	PB11-3	2-Sep-57	3.98	2	CALUMET	UK9-2	20-May-53	12.78	4
BARRON	PB5-5	19-Jul-57	10.11	4	CALUMET	PB9-3	25-Aug-57	13.72	4
BARRON	TS6-3	27-May-52	15.73	4	CALUMET	TS6-4	28-May-52	44.32	5
BARRON	UK9-2	20-May-53	60.96	6	CHIPPEWA	PB11-3	2-Sep-57	3.98	2
BARRON	TP10-2	6-May-55	3.51	1	CHIPPEWA	TP10-2	6-May-55	7.01	3
BAYFIELD	PB5-5	19-Jul-57	6.09	3	CHIPPEWA	TS6-3	27-May-52	9.95	3
BAYFIELD	PB11-3	2-Sep-57	6.62	3	CHIPPEWA	UK9-2	20-May-53	64.64	6
BAYFIELD	TP10-2	6-May-55	7.01	3	CLARK	TS7-5	5-Jun-52	3.69	2
BAYFIELD	TS6-3	27-May-52	14.79	4	CLARK	TS7-3	3-Jun-52	5.22	3
BAYFIELD	UK9-2	20-May-53	51.91	6	CLARK	TP10-2	6-May-55	19.28	4
BROWN	TP10-2	6-May-55	4.00	2	CLARK	TS6-4	28-May-52	22.18	4
BROWN	PB9-4	26-Aug-57	8.37	3	CLARK	UK9-2	20-May-53	49.16	5
BROWN	UK9-2	20-May-53	10.43	4	COLUMBIA	PB18-8	17-Jul-57	3.98	2
BROWN	PB9-3	25-Aug-57	13.72	4	COLUMBIA	UK7-4	28-Apr-53	4.28	2
BUFFALO	PB5-5	19-Jul-57	4.02	2	COLUMBIA	TS7-3	3-Jun-52	4.31	2
BUFFALO	TS5-1	7-May-52	4.80	2	COLUMBIA	TS7-5	5-Jun-52	6.06	3
BUFFALO	TP10-2	6-May-55	5.26	3	COLUMBIA	TP10-2	6-May-55	13.36	4
BUFFALO	UK7-4	28-Apr-53	5.93	3	COLUMBIA	PB9-3	25-Aug-57	13.72	4
BUFFALO	TS7-5	5-Jun-52	7.18	3	COLUMBIA	PB9-4	26-Aug-57	16.67	4
BUFFALO	TS6-3	27-May-52	8.27	3	COLUMBIA	TS6-4	28-May-52	23.14	4
BUFFALO	TS6-4	28-May-52	20.25	4	COLUMBIA	UK9-2	20-May-53	27.61	5
BUFFALO	UK9-2	20-May-53	61.61	6	CRAWFORD	PB18-8	17-Jul-57	3.98	2
BUFFALO	SE3	8-Jul-62	325.19	8	CRAWFORD	TS5-1	7-May-52	4.67	2

INDIVIDUAL FALLOUT DAYS
WISCONSIN

COUNTY	SHOT	DATE	µCi/SQ METER	INDEX	COUNTY	SHOT	DATE	µCi/SQ METER	INDEX
CRAWFORD	UK7-4	28-Apr-53	5.99	3	DUNN	TS5-1	7-May-52	3.90	2
CRAWFORD	TS7-5	5-Jun-52	12.86	4	DUNN	PB11-3	2-Sep-57	3.98	2
CRAWFORD	PB9-3	25-Aug-57	13.72	4	DUNN	PB5-5	19-Jul-57	6.09	3
CRAWFORD	TS6-4	28-May-52	15.43	4	DUNN	TP10-2	6-May-55	7.01	3
CRAWFORD	PB9-4	26-Aug-57	16.67	4	DUNN	TS6-3	27-May-52	14.03	4
CRAWFORD	TP10-2	6-May-55	21.03	4	DUNN	TS6-4	28-May-52	24.11	4
CRAWFORD	UK9-2	20-May-53	51.43	6	DUNN	UK9-2	20-May-53	67.78	6
CRAWFORD	SE3	8-Jul-62	56.35	6	EAU CLAIRE	TS7-5	5-Jun-52	3.97	2
DANE	UK7-4	28-Apr-53	3.88	2	EAU CLAIRE	TS7-3	3-Jun-52	4.80	2
DANE	PB18-8	17-Jul-57	3.98	2	EAU CLAIRE	TP10-2	6-May-55	7.01	3
DANE	TP10-2	6-May-55	5.04	3	EAU CLAIRE	TS6-3	27-May-52	8.42	3
DANE	TS7-5	5-Jun-52	9.29	3	EAU CLAIRE	TS6-4	28-May-52	22.18	4
DANE	PB9-3	25-Aug-57	13.72	4	EAU CLAIRE	UK9-2	20-May-53	58.36	6
DANE	UK9-2	20-May-53	23.28	4	FLORENCE	TS6-4	28-May-52	4.83	2
DANE	PB9-4	26-Aug-57	33.34	5	FLORENCE	PB5-5	19-Jul-57	10.11	4
DANE	SE3	8-Jul-62	70.48	6	FLORENCE	UK9-2	20-May-53	31.71	5
DODGE	TS7-5	5-Jun-52	3.73	2	FOND DU LAC	PB9-4	26-Aug-57	8.37	3
DODGE	TS7-3	3-Jun-52	4.36	2	FOND DU LAC	TP10-2	6-May-55	13.36	4
DODGE	UK7-4	28-Apr-53	5.17	3	FOND DU LAC	PB9-3	25-Aug-57	13.72	4
DODGE	TP10-2	6-May-55	6.68	3	FOND DU LAC	UK9-2	20-May-53	15.81	4
DODGE	PB9-4	26-Aug-57	8.37	3	FOREST	TS6-3	27-May-52	4.00	2
DODGE	PB9-3	25-Aug-57	13.72	4	FOREST	TP10-2	6-May-55	19.28	4
DODGE	UK9-2	20-May-53	16.17	4	FOREST	UK9-2	20-May-53	29.27	5
DOOR	UK9-2	20-May-53	11.88	4	GRANT	PB18-8	17-Jul-57	3.98	2
DOOR	TS6-4	28-May-52	27.00	5	GRANT	PB5-7	21-Jul-57	4.15	2
DOOR	TP10-2	6-May-55	28.92	5	GRANT	UK7-4	28-Apr-53	4.49	2
DOUGLAS	PB11-3	2-Sep-57	3.98	2	GRANT	TS5-1	7-May-52	4.85	2
DOUGLAS	TP11-5	19-May-55	5.01	3	GRANT	TP10-2	6-May-55	13.36	4
DOUGLAS	TP10-2	6-May-55	7.01	3	GRANT	TS7-5	5-Jun-52	13.67	4
DOUGLAS	TS6-4	28-May-52	8.68	3	GRANT	PB9-3	25-Aug-57	13.72	4
DOUGLAS	PB5-5	19-Jul-57	10.11	4	GRANT	TS6-4	28-May-52	14.46	4
DOUGLAS	TS6-3	27-May-52	18.96	4	GRANT	PB9-4	26-Aug-57	33.34	5
DOUGLAS	UK9-2	20-May-53	50.23	6	GRANT	UK9-2	20-May-53	44.28	5

INDIVIDUAL FALLOUT DAYS
WISCONSIN

COUNTY	SHOT	DATE	µCi/SQ METER	INDEX	COUNTY	SHOT	DATE	µCi/SQ METER	INDEX
GRANT	SE3	8-Jul-62	172.89	7	JACKSON	TS6-4	28-May-52	9.67	3
GREEN	TS5-1	7-May-52	3.60	2	JACKSON	TP10-2	6-May-55	21.03	4
GREEN	TS7-5	5-Jun-52	3.66	2	JACKSON	UK9-2	20-May-53	52.51	6
GREEN	UK7-4	28-Apr-53	5.83	3	JEFFERSON	UK7-4	28-Apr-53	5.98	3
GREEN	TS7-3	3-Jun-52	7.06	3	JEFFERSON	TP10-2	6-May-55	6.68	3
GREEN	PB9-4	26-Aug-57	8.37	3	JEFFERSON	TS7-5	5-Jun-52	7.22	3
GREEN	PB9-3	25-Aug-57	13.72	4	JEFFERSON	PB9-4	26-Aug-57	8.37	3
GREEN	UK9-2	20-May-53	27.07	5	JEFFERSON	TS6-4	28-May-52	10.48	4
GREEN	SE3	8-Jul-62	120.50	7	JEFFERSON	PB9-3	25-Aug-57	13.72	4
GREEN LAKE	UK7-4	28-Apr-53	3.80	2	JEFFERSON	UK9-2	20-May-53	15.54	4
GREEN LAKE	PB18-8	17-Jul-57	3.98	2	JEFFERSON	SE3	8-Jul-62	70.48	6
GREEN LAKE	TP10-2	6-May-55	4.82	2	JUNEAU	UK7-4	28-Apr-53	3.57	2
GREEN LAKE	TS7-5	5-Jun-52	5.52	3	JUNEAU	TS7-5	5-Jun-52	4.69	2
GREEN LAKE	PB9-4	26-Aug-57	8.37	3	JUNEAU	TS6-4	28-May-52	5.64	3
GREEN LAKE	PB9-3	25-Aug-57	13.72	4	JUNEAU	TS7-3	3-Jun-52	7.75	3
GREEN LAKE	UK9-2	20-May-53	18.52	4	JUNEAU	PB9-4	26-Aug-57	8.37	3
GREEN LAKE	TS6-4	28-May-52	45.32	5	JUNEAU	PB9-3	25-Aug-57	13.72	4
IOWA	PB18-8	17-Jul-57	3.98	2	JUNEAU	TP10-2	6-May-55	28.92	5
IOWA	UK7-4	28-Apr-53	4.44	2	JUNEAU	UK9-2	20-May-53	40.82	5
IOWA	TS7-5	5-Jun-52	12.08	4	KENOSHA	TP5-3	14-Mar-55	3.78	2
IOWA	TP10-2	6-May-55	13.36	4	KENOSHA	TS7-5	5-Jun-52	4.62	2
IOWA	PB9-3	25-Aug-57	13.72	4	KENOSHA	UK7-4	28-Apr-53	6.09	3
IOWA	PB9-4	26-Aug-57	16.67	4	KENOSHA	UK9-2	20-May-53	11.50	4
IOWA	UK9-2	20-May-53	36.92	5	KENOSHA	TS7-3	3-Jun-52	13.67	4
IOWA	SE3	8-Jul-62	345.56	8	KENOSHA	TS6-4	28-May-52	37.61	5
IRON	PB11-3	2-Sep-57	3.98	2	KEWAUNEE	UK9-2	20-May-53	7.29	3
IRON	PB5-5	19-Jul-57	6.09	3	KEWAUNEE	PB9-4	26-Aug-57	8.37	3
IRON	TS6-3	27-May-52	9.86	3	KEWAUNEE	PB9-3	25-Aug-57	13.72	4
IRON	TS6-4	28-May-52	13.50	4	KEWAUNEE	TP10-2	6-May-55	19.28	4
IRON	TP10-2	6-May-55	19.28	4	LA CROSSE	PB18-8	17-Jul-57	3.98	2
IRON	UK9-2	20-May-53	52.17	6	LA CROSSE	TS7-5	5-Jun-52	4.04	2
JACKSON	TS7-3	3-Jun-52	5.73	3	LA CROSSE	UK7-4	28-Apr-53	5.74	3
JACKSON	TS7-5	5-Jun-52	9.00	3	LA CROSSE	PB9-3	25-Aug-57	13.72	4

INDIVIDUAL FALLOUT DAYS
WISCONSIN

COUNTY	SHOT	DATE	µCi/SQ METER	INDEX	COUNTY	SHOT	DATE	µCi/SQ METER	INDEX
LA CROSSE	PB9-4	26-Aug-57	16.67	4	MARINETTE	PB9-4	26-Aug-57	8.37	3
LA CROSSE	TS6-4	28-May-52	18.32	4	MARINETTE	TP10-2	6-May-55	9.64	3
LA CROSSE	UK9-2	20-May-53	57.49	6	MARINETTE	TS6-4	28-May-52	10.48	4
LA CROSSE	TP10-2	6-May-55	3.51	1	MARINETTE	PB9-3	25-Aug-57	13.72	4
LAFAYETTE	PB18-8	17-Jul-57	3.98	2	MARINETTE	UK9-2	20-May-53	27.01	5
LAFAYETTE	PB5-7	21-Jul-57	4.15	2	MARQUETTE	UK7-4	28-Apr-53	3.85	2
LAFAYETTE	TS5-1	7-May-52	4.85	2	MARQUETTE	PB18-8	17-Jul-57	3.98	2
LAFAYETTE	UK7-4	28-Apr-53	5.24	3	MARQUETTE	PB9-4	26-Aug-57	8.37	3
LAFAYETTE	TS7-5	5-Jun-52	6.72	3	MARQUETTE	PB9-3	25-Aug-57	13.72	4
LAFAYETTE	PB9-4	26-Aug-57	8.37	3	MARQUETTE	TP10-2	6-May-55	28.92	5
LAFAYETTE	PB9-3	25-Aug-57	13.72	4	MARQUETTE	UK9-2	20-May-53	29.23	5
LAFAYETTE	TS6-4	28-May-52	16.39	4	MENOMINEE	TP5-3	14-Mar-55	3.65	2
LAFAYETTE	UK9-2	20-May-53	33.89	5	MENOMINEE	PB9-4	26-Aug-57	8.37	3
LAFAYETTE	SE3	8-Jul-62	146.81	7	MENOMINEE	TP10-2	6-May-55	9.64	3
LANGLADE	PB11-4	3-Sep-57	4.24	2	MENOMINEE	TS6-4	28-May-52	12.09	4
LANGLADE	TP10-2	6-May-55	9.64	3	MENOMINEE	PB9-3	25-Aug-57	13.72	4
LANGLADE	TS6-4	28-May-52	11.28	4	MENOMINEE	UK9-2	20-May-53	24.12	4
LANGLADE	UK9-2	20-May-53	31.83	5	MILWAUKEE	TS7-5	5-Jun-52	4.24	2
LINCOLN	PB11-3	2-Sep-57	3.98	2	MILWAUKEE	UK7-4	28-Apr-53	8.50	3
LINCOLN	TP10-2	6-May-55	19.28	4	MILWAUKEE	UK9-2	20-May-53	10.93	4
LINCOLN	UK9-2	20-May-53	36.60	5	MILWAUKEE	TS6-4	28-May-52	11.01	4
LINCOLN	TS6-4	28-May-52	41.47	5	MONROE	TS5-1	7-May-52	3.59	2
MANITOWOC	PB9-4	26-Aug-57	8.37	3	MONROE	TS7-5	5-Jun-52	3.94	2
MANITOWOC	UK9-2	20-May-53	8.79	3	MONROE	TP10-2	6-May-55	4.82	2
MANITOWOC	TP10-2	6-May-55	9.64	3	MONROE	UK7-4	28-Apr-53	5.04	3
MANITOWOC	TS6-4	28-May-52	11.70	4	MONROE	PB9-4	26-Aug-57	8.37	3
MANITOWOC	PB9-3	25-Aug-57	13.72	4	MONROE	PB9-3	25-Aug-57	13.72	4
MARATHON	PB11-3	2-Sep-57	3.98	2	MONROE	TS7-3	3-Jun-52	15.42	4
MARATHON	PB5-5	19-Jul-57	6.09	3	MONROE	UK9-2	20-May-53	42.34	5
MARATHON	TP10-2	6-May-55	9.64	3	OCONTO	PB9-4	26-Aug-57	8.37	3
MARATHON	TS6-4	28-May-52	24.11	4	OCONTO	PB9-3	25-Aug-57	13.72	4
MARATHON	UK9-2	20-May-53	36.49	5	OCONTO	TP10-2	6-May-55	19.28	4
MARINETTE	TP5-3	14-Mar-55	3.57	2	OCONTO	UK9-2	20-May-53	22.33	4

INDIVIDUAL FALLOUT DAYS
WISCONSIN

COUNTY	SHOT	DATE	µCi/SQ METER	INDEX	COUNTY	SHOT	DATE	µCi/SQ METER	INDEX
ONEIDA	PB11-3	2-Sep-57	3.98	2	POLK	UK9-2	20-May-53	44.26	5
ONEIDA	TS7-3	3-Jun-52	4.38	2	POLK	TP10-2	6-May-55	3.51	1
ONEIDA	TS6-3	27-May-52	5.87	3	PORTAGE	PB9-4	26-Aug-57	8.37	3
ONEIDA	TP10-2	6-May-55	19.28	4	PORTAGE	PB9-3	25-Aug-57	13.72	4
ONEIDA	TS6-4	28-May-52	23.14	4	PORTAGE	TP10-2	6-May-55	19.28	4
ONEIDA	UK9-2	20-May-53	35.30	5	PORTAGE	UK9-2	20-May-53	27.50	5
OUTAGAMIE	TP10-2	6-May-55	4.82	2	PRICE	PB11-3	2-Sep-57	3.98	2
OUTAGAMIE	PB9-4	26-Aug-57	8.37	3	PRICE	PB5-5	19-Jul-57	4.02	2
OUTAGAMIE	PB9-3	25-Aug-57	13.72	4	PRICE	TP10-2	6-May-55	7.23	3
OUTAGAMIE	UK9-2	20-May-53	13.98	4	PRICE	TS6-3	27-May-52	7.91	3
OZAUKEE	TS7-5	5-Jun-52	3.89	2	PRICE	UK9-2	20-May-53	59.40	6
OZAUKEE	UK7-4	28-Apr-53	4.27	2	RACINE	TS7-3	3-Jun-52	4.02	2
OZAUKEE	PB9-4	26-Aug-57	8.37	3	RACINE	UK7-4	28-Apr-53	5.12	3
OZAUKEE	UK9-2	20-May-53	11.80	4	RACINE	TP10-2	6-May-55	6.68	3
OZAUKEE	PB9-3	25-Aug-57	13.72	4	RACINE	UK9-2	20-May-53	12.18	4
PEPIN	PB11-3	2-Sep-57	3.98	2	RACINE	TS6-4	28-May-52	19.34	4
PEPIN	UK7-4	28-Apr-53	4.12	2	RICHLAND	PB18-8	17-Jul-57	3.98	2
PEPIN	TS5-1	7-May-52	4.80	2	RICHLAND	UK7-4	28-Apr-53	7.01	3
PEPIN	PB5-5	19-Jul-57	10.11	4	RICHLAND	TS7-5	5-Jun-52	13.43	4
PEPIN	TS6-3	27-May-52	10.98	4	RICHLAND	PB9-3	25-Aug-57	13.72	4
PEPIN	TS7-5	5-Jun-52	12.07	4	RICHLAND	PB9-4	26-Aug-57	16.67	4
PEPIN	TP10-2	6-May-55	21.03	4	RICHLAND	TP10-2	6-May-55	20.05	4
PEPIN	TS6-4	28-May-52	22.18	4	RICHLAND	UK9-2	20-May-53	43.96	5
PEPIN	UK9-2	20-May-53	60.31	6	RICHLAND	SE3	8-Jul-62	56.35	6
PIERCE	PB11-3	2-Sep-57	3.98	2	ROCK	UK7-4	28-Apr-53	5.44	3
PIERCE	UK9-3	21-May-53	4.18	2	ROCK	TP10-2	6-May-55	6.68	3
PIERCE	PB5-5	19-Jul-57	10.11	4	ROCK	TS7-3	3-Jun-52	8.19	3
PIERCE	TS6-3	27-May-52	14.76	4	ROCK	PB9-3	25-Aug-57	13.72	4
PIERCE	UK9-2	20-May-53	48.05	5	ROCK	PB9-4	26-Aug-57	16.67	4
PIERCE	TP10-2	6-May-55	3.51	1	ROCK	UK9-2	20-May-53	18.25	4
POLK	PB11-3	2-Sep-57	3.98	2	ROCK	TS6-4	28-May-52	20.25	4
POLK	PB5-5	19-Jul-57	10.11	4	ROCK	SE3	8-Jul-62	139.13	7
POLK	TS6-3	27-May-52	20.49	4	RUSK	TS3-8	29-Apr-52	3.95	2

INDIVIDUAL FALLOUT DAYS
WISCONSIN

COUNTY	SHOT	DATE	µCi/SQ METER	INDEX	COUNTY	SHOT	DATE	µCi/SQ METER	INDEX
RUSK	PB11-3	2-Sep-57	3.98	2	ST CROIX	PB5-5	19-Jul-57	10.11	4
RUSK	PB5-5	19-Jul-57	10.11	4	ST CROIX	TS6-3	27-May-52	16.04	4
RUSK	TS6-3	27-May-52	10.80	4	ST CROIX	UK9-2	20-May-53	51.76	6
RUSK	UK9-2	20-May-53	69.48	6	ST CROIX	TP10-2	6-May-55	3.51	1
RUSK	TP10-2	6-May-55	3.51	1	TAYLOR	PB11-3	2-Sep-57	3.98	2
SAUK	PB18-8	17-Jul-57	3.98	2	TAYLOR	TS6-3	27-May-52	6.63	3
SAUK	UK7-4	28-Apr-53	6.76	3	TAYLOR	TP10-2	6-May-55	9.64	3
SAUK	TS6-4	28-May-52	9.67	3	TAYLOR	TS6-4	28-May-52	27.81	5
SAUK	TS7-3	3-Jun-52	10.78	4	TAYLOR	UK9-2	20-May-53	55.40	6
SAUK	TS7-5	5-Jun-52	11.59	4	TREMPEALEAU	TS5-1	7-May-52	4.05	2
SAUK	PB9-3	25-Aug-57	13.72	4	TREMPEALEAU	UK7-4	28-Apr-53	5.16	3
SAUK	PB9-4	26-Aug-57	33.34	5	TREMPEALEAU	TS7-5	5-Jun-52	6.42	3
SAUK	UK9-2	20-May-53	36.60	5	TREMPEALEAU	TP10-2	6-May-55	21.03	4
SAUK	SE3	8-Jul-62	59.46	6	TREMPEALEAU	TS6-4	28-May-52	35.68	5
SAWYER	PB11-3	2-Sep-57	3.98	2	TREMPEALEAU	UK9-2	20-May-53	70.05	6
SAWYER	PB5-5	19-Jul-57	6.09	3	VERNON	PB18-8	17-Jul-57	3.98	2
SAWYER	TS6-3	27-May-52	12.50	4	VERNON	PB5-7	21-Jul-57	4.15	2
SAWYER	TP10-2	6-May-55	14.02	4	VERNON	TS5-1	7-May-52	4.31	2
SAWYER	TS6-4	28-May-52	30.13	5	VERNON	UK7-4	28-Apr-53	6.50	3
SAWYER	UK9-2	20-May-53	72.96	6	VERNON	PB9-4	26-Aug-57	8.37	3
SHAWANO	TP5-3	14-Mar-55	3.91	2	VERNON	TS7-3	3-Jun-52	8.43	3
SHAWANO	PB9-4	26-Aug-57	8.37	3	VERNON	TS7-5	5-Jun-52	13.02	4
SHAWANO	TP10-2	6-May-55	9.64	3	VERNON	PB9-3	25-Aug-57	13.72	4
SHAWANO	TS6-4	28-May-52	12.09	4	VERNON	TP10-2	6-May-55	14.02	4
SHAWANO	PB9-3	25-Aug-57	13.72	4	VERNON	TS6-4	28-May-52	17.36	4
SHAWANO	UK9-2	20-May-53	23.03	4	VERNON	UK9-2	20-May-53	51.86	6
SHEBOYGAN	TS7-3	3-Jun-52	4.48	2	VERNON	SE3	8-Jul-62	139.44	7
SHEBOYGAN	PB9-4	26-Aug-57	8.37	3	VILAS	PB11-3	2-Sep-57	3.98	2
SHEBOYGAN	UK9-2	20-May-53	8.67	3	VILAS	PB5-5	19-Jul-57	4.02	2
SHEBOYGAN	TP10-2	6-May-55	13.36	4	VILAS	TS7-3	3-Jun-52	4.38	2
SHEBOYGAN	PB9-3	25-Aug-57	13.72	4	VILAS	TS6-3	27-May-52	7.14	3
SHEBOYGAN	TS6-4	28-May-52	43.51	5	VILAS	TP10-2	6-May-55	9.64	3
ST CROIX	PB11-3	2-Sep-57	3.98	2	VILAS	TS6-4	28-May-52	26.65	5

INDIVIDUAL FALLOUT DAYS
WISCONSIN

COUNTY	SHOT	DATE	µCi/SQ METER	INDEX	COUNTY	SHOT	DATE	µCi/SQ METER	INDEX
VILAS	UK9-2	20-May-53	41.14	5	WAUKESHA	UK7-4	28-Apr-53	8.13	3
WALWORTH	UK7-4	28-Apr-53	5.16	3	WAUKESHA	PB9-4	26-Aug-57	8.37	3
WALWORTH	TP10-2	6-May-55	6.68	3	WAUKESHA	UK9-2	20-May-53	13.61	4
WALWORTH	TS7-5	5-Jun-52	6.73	3	WAUKESHA	PB9-3	25-Aug-57	13.72	4
WALWORTH	TS7-3	3-Jun-52	9.31	3	WAUPACA	PB9-4	26-Aug-57	8.37	3
WALWORTH	PB9-3	25-Aug-57	13.72	4	WAUPACA	TP10-2	6-May-55	19.28	4
WALWORTH	UK9-2	20-May-53	15.72	4	WAUPACA	PB9-3	25-Aug-57	20.62	4
WALWORTH	PB9-4	26-Aug-57	16.67	4	WAUPACA	UK9-2	20-May-53	22.31	4
WALWORTH	TS6-4	28-May-52	21.21	4	WAUSHARA	PB9-4	26-Aug-57	8.37	3
WALWORTH	SE3	8-Jul-62	172.89	7	WAUSHARA	PB9-3	25-Aug-57	13.72	4
WASHBURN	PB11-3	2-Sep-57	3.98	2	WAUSHARA	UK9-2	20-May-53	28.04	5
WASHBURN	PB5-5	19-Jul-57	10.11	4	WAUSHARA	TP10-2	6-May-55	28.92	5
WASHBURN	TS6-3	27-May-52	16.92	4	WINNEBAGO	TS7-5	5-Jun-52	3.87	2
WASHBURN	UK9-2	20-May-53	73.09	6	WINNEBAGO	TS6-4	28-May-52	4.03	2
WASHBURN	TP10-2	6-May-55	3.51	1	WINNEBAGO	PB9-4	26-Aug-57	8.37	3
WASHINGTON	UK7-4	28-Apr-53	4.12	2	WINNEBAGO	TP10-2	6-May-55	9.64	3
WASHINGTON	TS6-4	28-May-52	6.19	3	WINNEBAGO	PB9-3	25-Aug-57	13.72	4
WASHINGTON	PB9-4	26-Aug-57	8.37	3	WINNEBAGO	UK9-2	20-May-53	16.71	4
WASHINGTON	UK9-2	20-May-53	12.25	4	WOOD	TS7-5	5-Jun-52	4.31	2
WASHINGTON	TP10-2	6-May-55	13.36	4	WOOD	TS6-4	28-May-52	5.64	3
WASHINGTON	PB9-3	25-Aug-57	13.72	4	WOOD	PB9-4	26-Aug-57	12.52	4
WAUKESHA	TP10-2	6-May-55	6.68	3	WOOD	PB9-3	25-Aug-57	13.72	4
WAUKESHA	TS7-3	3-Jun-52	7.21	3	WOOD	TP10-2	6-May-55	19.28	4
WAUKESHA	TS7-5	5-Jun-52	7.21	3	WOOD	UK9-2	20-May-53	40.60	5

INDIVIDUAL FALLOUT DAYS
WEST VIRGINIA

COUNTY	SHOT	DATE	µCi/SQ METER	INDEX	COUNTY	SHOT	DATE	µCi/SQ METER	INDEX
BARBOUR	UK9-3	21-May-53	4.37	2	GILMER	SE4	9-Jul-62	103.59	7
BARBOUR	UK9-4	22-May-53	5.10	3	GRANT	UK9-3	21-May-53	3.75	2
BARBOUR	PB5-8	22-Jul-57	5.97	3	GRANT	PB5-8	22-Jul-57	5.97	3
BERKELEY	TS3-4	25-Apr-52	6.03	3	GRANT	SE4	9-Jul-62	85.56	6
BERKELEY	BJ2-3	1-Nov-51	7.08	3	GREENBRIER	TS5-2	8-May-52	3.55	2
BERKELEY	PB5-8	22-Jul-57	8.96	3	GREENBRIER	UK9-4	22-May-53	4.67	2
BOONE	UK9-4	22-May-53	3.99	2	GREENBRIER	PB5-8	22-Jul-57	5.97	3
BOONE	BJ2-4	2-Nov-51	6.57	3	GREENBRIER	SE4	9-Jul-62	103.59	7
BOONE	SE4	9-Jul-62	359.52	8	HAMPSHIRE	TS3-4	25-Apr-52	6.03	3
BRAXTON	PB5-8	22-Jul-57	5.97	3	HAMPSHIRE	PB5-8	22-Jul-57	8.96	3
BRAXTON	UK9-4	22-May-53	10.55	4	HANCOCK	TP11-8	22-May-55	3.82	2
BRAXTON	SE4	9-Jul-62	85.56	6	HANCOCK	TP4-4	10-Mar-55	3.89	2
BROOKE	TP4-4	10-Mar-55	3.64	2	HANCOCK	TP11-9	23-May-55	4.62	2
BROOKE	R1-2	29-Jan-51	8.74	3	HANCOCK	BJ2-2	31-Oct-51	7.20	3
BROOKE	PB5-8	22-Jul-57	8.96	3	HANCOCK	R1-2	29-Jan-51	8.74	3
BROOKE	UK9-3	21-May-53	10.89	4	HANCOCK	PB5-8	22-Jul-57	8.96	3
BROOKE	SE4	9-Jul-62	85.56	6	HANCOCK	UK9-3	21-May-53	11.32	4
CABELL	TP10-2	6-May-55	3.62	2	HARDY	PB5-8	22-Jul-57	8.96	3
CABELL	BJ2-4	2-Nov-51	6.97	3	HARDY	SE4	9-Jul-62	57.04	6
CABELL	PB5-8	22-Jul-57	8.96	3	HARRISON	UK9-3	21-May-53	4.92	2
CABELL	PB6-3	26-Jul-57	23.55	4	HARRISON	PB5-8	22-Jul-57	8.96	3
CALHOUN	UK9-3	21-May-53	3.54	2	HARRISON	SE4	9-Jul-62	103.59	7
CALHOUN	PB5-8	22-Jul-57	8.96	3	JACKSON	UK9-3	21-May-53	3.76	2
CALHOUN	SE4	9-Jul-62	103.59	7	JACKSON	TP11-8	22-May-55	3.82	2
CLAY	UK9-4	22-May-53	8.30	3	JACKSON	TP11-9	23-May-55	4.62	2
CLAY	SE4	9-Jul-62	90.29	6	JACKSON	UK9-4	22-May-53	7.50	3
DODDRIDGE	UK9-3	21-May-53	6.49	3	JACKSON	PB5-8	22-Jul-57	8.96	3
DODDRIDGE	PB5-8	22-Jul-57	8.96	3	JEFFERSON	TS3-4	25-Apr-52	3.87	2
FAYETTE	PB5-9	23-Jul-57	4.71	2	JEFFERSON	UK1-2	18-Mar-53	4.53	2
FAYETTE	SE6	11-Jul-62	6.62	3	JEFFERSON	BJ2-3	1-Nov-51	6.53	3
FAYETTE	SE4	9-Jul-62	85.56	6	JEFFERSON	PB5-8	22-Jul-57	8.96	3
GILMER	UK9-3	21-May-53	4.72	2	KANAWHA	UK9-4	22-May-53	5.15	3
GILMER	PB5-8	22-Jul-57	8.96	3	KANAWHA	PB5-8	22-Jul-57	5.97	3

INDIVIDUAL FALLOUT DAYS
WEST VIRGINIA

COUNTY	SHOT	DATE	µCi/SQ METER	INDEX	COUNTY	SHOT	DATE	µCi/SQ METER	INDEX
KANAWHA	SE4	9-Jul-62	208.78	8	MCDOWELL	PB4-5	9-Jul-57	13.06	4
LEWIS	UK9-4	22-May-53	5.02	3	MCDOWELL	UK9-4	22-May-53	33.76	5
LEWIS	UK9-3	21-May-53	5.31	3	MCDOWELL	SE4	9-Jul-62	149.13	7
LEWIS	PB5-8	22-Jul-57	8.96	3	MERCER	BJ2-4	2-Nov-51	3.58	2
LEWIS	SE4	9-Jul-62	85.56	6	MERCER	TS5-2	8-May-52	3.76	2
LINCOLN	TP10-2	6-May-55	3.62	2	MERCER	BJ3-5	5-Nov-51	4.59	2
LINCOLN	PB5-8	22-Jul-57	5.97	3	MERCER	UK9-4	22-May-53	4.76	2
LINCOLN	BJ2-4	2-Nov-51	6.77	3	MERCER	PB5-8	22-Jul-57	5.97	3
LINCOLN	UK9-4	22-May-53	7.44	3	MERCER	PB4-5	9-Jul-57	7.83	3
LINCOLN	PB6-3	26-Jul-57	15.70	4	MERCER	SE4	9-Jul-62	149.13	7
LINCOLN	SE4	9-Jul-62	208.78	8	MINERAL	UK1-2	18-Mar-53	3.81	2
LOGAN	TP10-2	6-May-55	3.62	2	MINERAL	PB5-8	22-Jul-57	5.97	3
LOGAN	PB6-3	26-Jul-57	3.96	2	MINGO	BJ2-4	2-Nov-51	3.58	2
LOGAN	BJ2-4	2-Nov-51	6.77	3	MINGO	TP10-2	6-May-55	3.62	2
LOGAN	PB4-5	9-Jul-57	13.06	4	MINGO	PB6-3	26-Jul-57	3.96	2
LOGAN	SE4	9-Jul-62	359.52	8	MINGO	PB17-3	30-Sep-57	7.49	3
MARION	TP11-8	22-May-55	3.82	2	MINGO	PB4-5	9-Jul-57	7.83	3
MARION	UK9-3	21-May-53	4.30	2	MINGO	UK9-4	22-May-53	9.57	3
MARION	TP11-9	23-May-55	4.62	2	MINGO	SE4	9-Jul-62	149.13	7
MARION	PB5-8	22-Jul-57	14.93	4	MONONGALIA	PB5-8	22-Jul-57	8.96	3
MARION	SE4	9-Jul-62	72.20	6	MONONGALIA	SE4	9-Jul-62	85.56	6
MARSHALL	PB5-8	22-Jul-57	8.96	3	MONROE	TS5-2	8-May-52	7.17	3
MARSHALL	R1-2	29-Jan-51	21.83	4	MONROE	SE4	9-Jul-62	208.78	8
MARSHALL	SE4	9-Jul-62	103.59	7	MORGAN	UK1-2	18-Mar-53	3.93	2
MASON	UK9-3	21-May-53	3.52	2	MORGAN	UK10-6	30-May-53	5.39	3
MASON	TP11-8	22-May-55	3.82	2	MORGAN	BJ2-3	1-Nov-51	5.68	3
MASON	TP11-9	23-May-55	4.62	2	MORGAN	TS3-4	25-Apr-52	6.03	3
MASON	PB5-8	22-Jul-57	5.97	3	MORGAN	PB5-8	22-Jul-57	8.96	3
MASON	PB6-3	26-Jul-57	23.55	4	NICHOLAS	UK9-4	22-May-53	4.33	2
MASON	SE4	9-Jul-62	208.78	8	NICHOLAS	PB5-8	22-Jul-57	5.97	3
MCDOWELL	PB6-3	26-Jul-57	3.96	2	NICHOLAS	SE4	9-Jul-62	85.56	6
MCDOWELL	PB2-5	22-Jun-57	4.18	2	OHIO	BJ3-5	5-Nov-51	4.59	2
MCDOWELL	TS3-6	27-Apr-52	5.50	3	OHIO	PB5-8	22-Jul-57	8.96	3

INDIVIDUAL FALLOUT DAYS
WEST VIRGINIA

COUNTY	SHOT	DATE	µCi/SQ METER	INDEX	COUNTY	SHOT	DATE	µCi/SQ METER	INDEX
OHIO	UK9-3	21-May-53	9.96	3	TUCKER	SE4	9-Jul-62	85.56	6
OHIO	R1-2	29-Jan-51	46.20	5	TYLER	UK9-3	21-May-53	4.31	2
PENDLETON	SE4	9-Jul-62	208.78	8	TYLER	BJ3-5	5-Nov-51	4.59	2
PLEASANTS	UK9-3	21-May-53	5.23	3	TYLER	PB5-8	22-Jul-57	14.93	4
PLEASANTS	PB5-8	22-Jul-57	8.96	3	TYLER	R1-2	29-Jan-51	21.83	4
PLEASANTS	R1-2	29-Jan-51	39.78	5	TYLER	SE4	9-Jul-62	90.29	6
POCAHONTAS	PB5-8	22-Jul-57	8.96	3	UPSHUR	TP11-8	22-May-55	3.82	2
POCAHONTAS	SE4	9-Jul-62	90.29	6	UPSHUR	TP11-9	23-May-55	4.62	2
PRESTON	UK9-4	22-May-53	3.66	2	UPSHUR	UK9-4	22-May-53	4.79	2
PRESTON	PB5-9	23-Jul-57	4.71	2	UPSHUR	UK9-3	21-May-53	5.01	3
PRESTON	PB5-8	22-Jul-57	8.96	3	UPSHUR	PB5-8	22-Jul-57	8.96	3
PUTNAM	PB6-3	26-Jul-57	3.96	2	UPSHUR	SE4	9-Jul-62	103.59	7
PUTNAM	BJ2-4	2-Nov-51	6.17	3	WAYNE	TP10-2	6-May-55	3.62	2
PUTNAM	SE4	9-Jul-62	85.56	6	WAYNE	PB4-4	8-Jul-57	3.94	2
RALEIGH	SE4	9-Jul-62	208.78	8	WAYNE	PB6-3	26-Jul-57	3.96	2
RANDOLPH	UK9-3	21-May-53	4.42	2	WAYNE	TP6-4	25-Mar-55	4.32	2
RANDOLPH	PB5-8	22-Jul-57	5.97	3	WAYNE	UK9-4	22-May-53	4.67	2
RANDOLPH	UK9-4	22-May-53	7.15	3	WAYNE	BJ2-4	2-Nov-51	7.97	3
RANDOLPH	SE4	9-Jul-62	85.56	6	WAYNE	PB5-8	22-Jul-57	8.96	3
RITCHIE	UK9-3	21-May-53	5.53	3	WAYNE	SE4	9-Jul-62	208.78	8
RITCHIE	PB5-8	22-Jul-57	8.96	3	WEBSTER	PB5-9	23-Jul-57	4.71	2
ROANE	PB5-8	22-Jul-57	8.96	3	WEBSTER	SE4	9-Jul-62	90.29	6
SUMMERS	BJ3-5	5-Nov-51	4.59	2	WETZEL	UK9-3	21-May-53	4.30	2
SUMMERS	TS5-2	8-May-52	6.12	3	WETZEL	R1-2	29-Jan-51	8.74	3
SUMMERS	PB5-8	22-Jul-57	8.96	3	WETZEL	PB5-8	22-Jul-57	14.93	4
SUMMERS	SE4	9-Jul-62	208.78	8	WETZEL	SE4	9-Jul-62	85.56	6
TAYLOR	UK9-7	25-May-53	4.16	2	WIRT	TP11-8	22-May-55	3.82	2
TAYLOR	UK9-3	21-May-53	5.29	3	WIRT	TP11-9	23-May-55	4.62	2
TAYLOR	PB5-8	22-Jul-57	8.96	3	WIRT	UK9-3	21-May-53	5.23	3
TUCKER	UK9-4	22-May-53	4.23	2	WIRT	PB5-8	22-Jul-57	5.97	3
TUCKER	PB5-9	23-Jul-57	4.71	2	WIRT	UK9-4	22-May-53	6.28	3
TUCKER	UK9-3	21-May-53	4.86	2	WIRT	SE6	11-Jul-62	8.10	3
TUCKER	PB5-8	22-Jul-57	5.97	3	WIRT	SE4	9-Jul-62	85.56	6

INDIVIDUAL FALLOUT DAYS
WEST VIRGINIA

COUNTY	SHOT	DATE	µCi/SQ METER	INDEX		COUNTY	SHOT	DATE	µCi/SQ METER	INDEX
WOOD	BJ3-5	5-Nov-51	4.59	2		WYOMING	PB5-9	23-Jul-57	4.71	2
WOOD	UK9-3	21-May-53	4.87	2		WYOMING	TS3-6	27-Apr-52	5.50	3
WOOD	PB5-8	22-Jul-57	8.96	3		WYOMING	PB4-5	9-Jul-57	13.06	4
WOOD	R1-2	29-Jan-51	19.29	4		WYOMING	SE4	9-Jul-62	149.13	7
WOOD	SE4	9-Jul-62	85.56	6						

INDIVIDUAL FALLOUT DAYS
WYOMING

COUNTY	SHOT	DATE	µCi/SQ METER	INDEX	COUNTY	SHOT	DATE	µCi/SQ METER	INDEX
ALBANY	UK9-3	21-May-53	3.58	2	CAMPBELL	PB5-2	16-Jul-57	4.90	2
ALBANY	PB9-4	26-Aug-57	3.68	2	CAMPBELL	PB11-2	1-Sep-57	6.81	3
ALBANY	PB2-3	20-Jun-57	4.36	2	CAMPBELL	PB9-4	26-Aug-57	7.36	3
ALBANY	TS6-2	26-May-52	4.83	2	CAMPBELL	PB9-3	25-Aug-57	7.76	3
ALBANY	TP4-2	8-Mar-55	4.84	2	CAMPBELL	UK7-4	28-Apr-53	8.02	3
ALBANY	TS7-3	3-Jun-52	5.86	3	CAMPBELL	PB5-3	17-Jul-57	10.10	4
ALBANY	PB9-3	25-Aug-57	5.87	3	CAMPBELL	TP11-2	16-May-55	20.60	4
ALBANY	UK9-4	22-May-53	5.87	3	CAMPBELL	UK2-2	25-Mar-53	23.57	4
ALBANY	SE1	6-Jul-62	5.91	3	CAMPBELL	TS5-1	7-May-52	24.97	4
ALBANY	TS7-4	4-Jun-52	5.94	3	CAMPBELL	TS8-1	5-Jun-52	39.88	5
ALBANY	PB2-2	19-Jun-57	7.29	3	CAMPBELL	UK2-1	24-Mar-53	170.07	7
ALBANY	UK11-2	5-Jun-53	9.53	3	CARBON	UK6-1	18-Apr-53	3.59	2
ALBANY	TP11-2	16-May-55	11.61	4	CARBON	PB18-1	10-Jul-57	4.02	2
ALBANY	TS5-1	7-May-52	17.68	4	CARBON	PB1-1	28-May-57	5.17	3
ALBANY	TS1-2	2-Apr-52	17.73	4	CARBON	PB15-1	16-Sep-57	5.37	3
ALBANY	UK7-3	27-Apr-53	25.43	5	CARBON	PB6-2	25-Jul-57	5.41	3
ALBANY	TP10-2	6-May-55	25.63	5	CARBON	TS1-1	1-Apr-52	8.57	3
ALBANY	TS8-1	5-Jun-52	39.88	5	CARBON	PB2-1	18-Jun-57	13.27	4
ALBANY	TP10-1	5-May-55	84.89	6	CARBON	PB4-1	5-Jul-57	14.58	4
ALBANY	TP7-1	29-Mar-55	3.51	1	CARBON	PB17-1	28-Sep-57	15.24	4
BIG HORN	PB9-4	26-Aug-57	3.68	2	CARBON	TP9-1	15-Apr-55	15.52	4
BIG HORN	TP11-2	16-May-55	4.34	2	CARBON	PB8-1	18-Aug-57	15.54	4
BIG HORN	TS8-3	7-Jun-52	5.01	3	CARBON	TS7-1	1-Jun-52	15.58	4
BIG HORN	UK11-2	5-Jun-53	5.59	3	CARBON	TP8-1	9-Apr-55	16.49	4
BIG HORN	PB6-2	25-Jul-57	7.94	3	CARBON	UK7-1	25-Apr-53	16.92	4
BIG HORN	UK8-2	9-May-53	16.38	4	CARBON	PB12-1	2-Sep-57	17.72	4
BIG HORN	TS5-1	7-May-52	34.49	5	CARBON	UK9-1	19-May-53	19.46	4
BIG HORN	PB6-4	27-Jul-57	3.51	1	CARBON	UK11-1	4-Jun-53	21.02	4
BIG HORN	TS8-1	5-Jun-52	412.11	9	CARBON	PB9-1	23-Aug-57	30.35	5
CAMPBELL	TP11-5	19-May-55	3.66	2	CARBON	UK10-1	25-May-53	31.06	5
CAMPBELL	TP11-3	17-May-55	4.19	2	CARBON	PB5-1	15-Jul-57	40.55	5
CAMPBELL	TS7-3	3-Jun-52	4.38	2	CARBON	TP4-1	7-Mar-55	43.14	5
CAMPBELL	UK8-1	8-May-53	4.73	2	CARBON	TP11-1	15-May-55	43.75	5

INDIVIDUAL FALLOUT DAYS
WYOMING

COUNTY	SHOT	DATE	µCi/SQ METER	INDEX	COUNTY	SHOT	DATE	µCi/SQ METER	INDEX
CARBON	TS6-1	25-May-52	62.22	6	FREMONT	PB16-1	23-Sep-57	4.03	2
CARBON	PB11-1	31-Aug-57	151.11	7	FREMONT	PB15-1	16-Sep-57	6.26	3
CARBON	TP10-1	5-May-55	154.87	7	FREMONT	TP4-1	7-Mar-55	7.21	3
CARBON	TS8-1	5-Jun-52	391.01	8	FREMONT	TS1-1	1-Apr-52	7.38	3
CONVERSE	UK11-2	5-Jun-53	3.79	2	FREMONT	PB8-1	18-Aug-57	7.82	3
CONVERSE	SE2	7-Jul-62	4.66	2	FREMONT	PB2-1	18-Jun-57	8.50	3
CONVERSE	TS5-2	8-May-52	5.22	3	FREMONT	PB12-1	2-Sep-57	8.81	3
CONVERSE	PB9-3	25-Aug-57	7.76	3	FREMONT	TS6-1	25-May-52	8.95	3
CONVERSE	TS7-4	4-Jun-52	9.92	3	FREMONT	TS8-2	6-Jun-52	9.69	3
CONVERSE	PB9-4	26-Aug-57	11.05	4	FREMONT	PB9-1	23-Aug-57	9.82	3
CONVERSE	PB2-3	20-Jun-57	13.07	4	FREMONT	PB6-2	25-Jul-57	10.78	4
CONVERSE	TS8-1	5-Jun-52	13.29	4	FREMONT	UK11-1	4-Jun-53	10.86	4
CONVERSE	TP11-2	16-May-55	13.73	4	FREMONT	TP11-1	15-May-55	14.16	4
CONVERSE	PB2-2	19-Jun-57	14.59	4	FREMONT	PB17-1	28-Sep-57	15.24	4
CONVERSE	TS1-2	2-Apr-52	17.73	4	FREMONT	UK9-1	19-May-53	15.28	4
CONVERSE	UK2-2	25-Mar-53	23.57	4	FREMONT	TP10-1	5-May-55	15.44	4
CONVERSE	TS5-1	7-May-52	38.08	5	FREMONT	TP9-1	15-Apr-55	15.62	4
CONVERSE	TS7-3	3-Jun-52	84.51	6	FREMONT	TP8-1	9-Apr-55	16.49	4
CONVERSE	UK2-1	24-Mar-53	170.07	7	FREMONT	UK7-1	25-Apr-53	16.70	4
CROOK	PB6-4	27-Jul-57	3.99	2	FREMONT	UK10-1	25-May-53	20.95	4
CROOK	PB8-3	20-Aug-57	4.57	2	FREMONT	TS7-1	1-Jun-52	36.10	5
CROOK	PB8-4	21-Aug-57	4.60	2	FREMONT	PB5-1	15-Jul-57	40.55	5
CROOK	PB11-2	1-Sep-57	6.81	3	FREMONT	PB11-1	31-Aug-57	228.21	8
CROOK	PB9-4	26-Aug-57	7.36	3	FREMONT	UK2-1	24-Mar-53	564.43	9
CROOK	PB5-2	16-Jul-57	9.68	3	FREMONT	TS8-1	5-Jun-52	1682.73	10
CROOK	PB5-3	17-Jul-57	10.10	4	GOSHEN	PB9-4	26-Aug-57	3.68	2
CROOK	UK7-4	28-Apr-53	11.60	4	GOSHEN	UK2-7	30-Mar-53	3.71	2
CROOK	TS8-1	5-Jun-52	13.29	4	GOSHEN	PB9-3	25-Aug-57	3.88	2
CROOK	PB9-3	25-Aug-57	15.53	4	GOSHEN	TP3-2	2-Mar-55	4.00	2
CROOK	TS7-3	3-Jun-52	19.36	4	GOSHEN	UK11-2	5-Jun-53	4.15	2
CROOK	TS5-1	7-May-52	24.43	4	GOSHEN	PB5-4	18-Jul-57	4.87	2
CROOK	UK2-2	25-Mar-53	45.45	5	GOSHEN	TP4-2	8-Mar-55	5.97	3
FREMONT	UK6-1	18-Apr-53	3.59	2	GOSHEN	TS5-2	8-May-52	6.60	3

INDIVIDUAL FALLOUT DAYS
WYOMING

COUNTY	SHOT	DATE	µCi/SQ METER	INDEX	COUNTY	SHOT	DATE	µCi/SQ METER	INDEX
GOSHEN	PB8-3	20-Aug-57	6.85	3	LARAMIE	TP11-3	17-May-55	5.68	3
GOSHEN	PB2-3	20-Jun-57	7.04	3	LARAMIE	TS6-2	26-May-52	6.19	3
GOSHEN	UK9-4	22-May-53	8.22	3	LARAMIE	TP5-2	13-Mar-55	7.86	3
GOSHEN	TP11-2	16-May-55	8.58	3	LARAMIE	TS6-3	27-May-52	7.91	3
GOSHEN	TS6-3	27-May-52	8.91	3	LARAMIE	TP11-2	16-May-55	9.60	3
GOSHEN	PB5-3	17-Jul-57	10.18	4	LARAMIE	TP10-2	6-May-55	10.65	4
GOSHEN	TS1-2	2-Apr-52	17.73	4	LARAMIE	TS5-1	7-May-52	15.09	4
GOSHEN	TS5-1	7-May-52	46.00	5	LARAMIE	TS1-2	2-Apr-52	17.73	4
HOT SPRINGS	PB9-2	24-Aug-57	3.60	2	LARAMIE	TP10-1	5-May-55	35.26	5
HOT SPRINGS	PB9-4	26-Aug-57	3.68	2	LINCOLN	TS1-1	1-Apr-52	3.57	2
HOT SPRINGS	SE1	6-Jul-62	4.73	2	LINCOLN	TP6-1	22-Mar-55	3.61	2
HOT SPRINGS	UK7-3	27-Apr-53	6.48	3	LINCOLN	TS8-2	6-Jun-52	3.74	2
HOT SPRINGS	PB6-2	25-Jul-57	7.94	3	LINCOLN	UK7-1	25-Apr-53	4.29	2
HOT SPRINGS	UK8-2	9-May-53	16.38	4	LINCOLN	PB4-1	5-Jul-57	4.69	2
HOT SPRINGS	TS5-1	7-May-52	89.81	6	LINCOLN	PB16-1	23-Sep-57	4.82	2
HOT SPRINGS	TS8-1	5-Jun-52	159.53	7	LINCOLN	TP10-1	5-May-55	5.44	3
JOHNSON	PB9-4	26-Aug-57	3.68	2	LINCOLN	SE1	6-Jul-62	5.45	3
JOHNSON	PB8-3	20-Aug-57	4.57	2	LINCOLN	PB15-1	16-Sep-57	7.16	3
JOHNSON	SE1	6-Jul-62	4.73	2	LINCOLN	PB6-2	25-Jul-57	7.20	3
JOHNSON	PB5-3	17-Jul-57	5.09	3	LINCOLN	TP4-1	7-Mar-55	7.39	3
JOHNSON	UK7-4	28-Apr-53	6.20	3	LINCOLN	TP8-1	9-Apr-55	8.34	3
JOHNSON	UK11-2	5-Jun-53	7.33	3	LINCOLN	UK10-1	25-May-53	10.26	4
JOHNSON	PB6-2	25-Jul-57	7.94	3	LINCOLN	PB5-1	15-Jul-57	12.12	4
JOHNSON	TP11-2	16-May-55	13.73	4	LINCOLN	TP11-1	15-May-55	13.87	4
JOHNSON	UK2-2	25-Mar-53	23.57	4	LINCOLN	PB8-1	18-Aug-57	15.54	4
JOHNSON	TS8-1	5-Jun-52	26.59	5	LINCOLN	UK9-1	19-May-53	16.30	4
JOHNSON	TS5-1	7-May-52	51.19	6	LINCOLN	PB12-1	2-Sep-57	17.72	4
JOHNSON	UK2-1	24-Mar-53	170.07	7	LINCOLN	PB17-1	28-Sep-57	19.02	4
LARAMIE	PB18-3	12-Jul-57	3.55	2	LINCOLN	PB9-1	23-Aug-57	20.78	4
LARAMIE	UK7-3	27-Apr-53	3.99	2	LINCOLN	TS7-1	1-Jun-52	36.98	5
LARAMIE	TS6-4	28-May-52	4.03	2	LINCOLN	PB11-1	31-Aug-57	60.68	6
LARAMIE	PB12-3	4-Sep-57	4.32	2	LINCOLN	UK2-1	24-Mar-53	568.59	9
LARAMIE	UK11-2	5-Jun-53	5.26	3	LINCOLN	TS8-1	5-Jun-52	649.35	9

INDIVIDUAL FALLOUT DAYS
WYOMING

COUNTY	SHOT	DATE	µCi/SQ METER	INDEX	COUNTY	SHOT	DATE	µCi/SQ METER	INDEX
NATRONA	PB15-1	16-Sep-57	4.06	2	PARK	PB9-3	25-Aug-57	4.49	2
NATRONA	UK7-4	28-Apr-53	4.50	2	PARK	TS8-3	7-Jun-52	5.79	3
NATRONA	TS7-3	3-Jun-52	4.52	2	PARK	PB6-2	25-Jul-57	11.91	4
NATRONA	SE1	6-Jul-62	4.73	2	PARK	UK8-2	9-May-53	12.33	4
NATRONA	TP8-2	10-Apr-55	5.32	3	PARK	TS5-1	7-May-52	40.41	5
NATRONA	UK11-2	5-Jun-53	5.91	3	PARK	PB8-2	19-Aug-57	44.80	5
NATRONA	PB9-4	26-Aug-57	7.36	3	PARK	TS8-1	5-Jun-52	558.34	9
NATRONA	PB9-3	25-Aug-57	7.76	3	PLATTE	PB9-3	25-Aug-57	3.88	2
NATRONA	PB2-3	20-Jun-57	8.71	3	PLATTE	PB2-3	20-Jun-57	4.36	2
NATRONA	UK7-3	27-Apr-53	8.83	3	PLATTE	TP4-2	8-Mar-55	4.84	2
NATRONA	TS7-4	4-Jun-52	9.34	3	PLATTE	UK9-4	22-May-53	5.68	3
NATRONA	UK2-2	25-Mar-53	9.79	3	PLATTE	TS5-2	8-May-52	5.70	3
NATRONA	TS8-1	5-Jun-52	13.29	4	PLATTE	UK11-2	5-Jun-53	6.32	3
NATRONA	PB2-2	19-Jun-57	29.18	5	PLATTE	TS7-3	3-Jun-52	6.36	3
NATRONA	UK2-1	24-Mar-53	70.63	6	PLATTE	PB2-2	19-Jun-57	7.29	3
NATRONA	TS5-1	7-May-52	76.16	6	PLATTE	PB9-4	26-Aug-57	7.36	3
NIOBRARA	PB9-3	25-Aug-57	3.88	2	PLATTE	TS1-2	2-Apr-52	8.70	3
NIOBRARA	TP3-2	2-Mar-55	4.00	2	PLATTE	TS6-3	27-May-52	9.69	3
NIOBRARA	PB5-4	18-Jul-57	4.87	2	PLATTE	TP10-2	6-May-55	25.63	5
NIOBRARA	TP4-2	8-Mar-55	5.97	3	PLATTE	TP11-2	16-May-55	34.74	5
NIOBRARA	UK7-4	28-Apr-53	6.31	3	PLATTE	TS5-1	7-May-52	44.37	5
NIOBRARA	TS5-2	8-May-52	8.42	3	PLATTE	TP10-1	5-May-55	84.89	6
NIOBRARA	PB5-3	17-Jul-57	10.18	4	SHERIDAN	TS8-3	7-Jun-52	3.77	2
NIOBRARA	PB9-4	26-Aug-57	11.05	4	SHERIDAN	UK2-2	25-Mar-53	3.85	2
NIOBRARA	TP11-2	16-May-55	14.24	4	SHERIDAN	PB9-3	25-Aug-57	4.49	2
NIOBRARA	TS7-4	4-Jun-52	16.13	4	SHERIDAN	UK8-3	10-May-53	5.26	3
NIOBRARA	TS1-2	2-Apr-52	17.73	4	SHERIDAN	UK11-2	5-Jun-53	5.84	3
NIOBRARA	PB2-3	20-Jun-57	21.11	4	SHERIDAN	UK7-4	28-Apr-53	5.99	3
NIOBRARA	TS8-1	5-Jun-52	26.59	5	SHERIDAN	PB9-4	26-Aug-57	7.36	3
NIOBRARA	TS5-1	7-May-52	66.23	6	SHERIDAN	PB6-2	25-Jul-57	7.94	3
NIOBRARA	TS7-3	3-Jun-52	191.18	7	SHERIDAN	TP11-2	16-May-55	8.69	3
PARK	UK10-7	31-May-53	4.13	2	SHERIDAN	TS5-1	7-May-52	23.71	4
PARK	TP11-2	16-May-55	4.34	2	SHERIDAN	UK8-2	9-May-53	32.75	5

U.S. FALLOUT ATLAS: COUNTY COMPARISONS

INDIVIDUAL FALLOUT DAYS
WYOMING

COUNTY	SHOT	DATE	µCi/SQ METER	INDEX	COUNTY	SHOT	DATE	µCi/SQ METER	INDEX
SHERIDAN	TS8-1	5-Jun-52	53.18	6	SWEETWATER	PB2-1	18-Jun-57	8.85	3
SUBLETTE	TS6-1	25-May-52	3.54	2	SWEETWATER	TP9-1	15-Apr-55	11.39	4
SUBLETTE	PB4-1	5-Jul-57	3.93	2	SWEETWATER	TP11-1	15-May-55	14.16	4
SUBLETTE	PB16-1	23-Sep-57	4.03	2	SWEETWATER	UK11-1	4-Jun-53	14.44	4
SUBLETTE	UK7-1	25-Apr-53	4.17	2	SWEETWATER	TS7-1	1-Jun-52	14.90	4
SUBLETTE	TP10-1	5-May-55	4.66	2	SWEETWATER	PB4-1	5-Jul-57	19.91	4
SUBLETTE	TS1-1	1-Apr-52	5.00	2	SWEETWATER	PB17-1	28-Sep-57	22.80	4
SUBLETTE	TP11-1	15-May-55	7.03	3	SWEETWATER	PB8-1	18-Aug-57	23.89	4
SUBLETTE	PB6-2	25-Jul-57	7.20	3	SWEETWATER	UK10-1	25-May-53	24.06	4
SUBLETTE	UK9-1	19-May-53	7.92	3	SWEETWATER	TP8-1	9-Apr-55	24.74	4
SUBLETTE	PB15-1	16-Sep-57	8.05	3	SWEETWATER	UK9-1	19-May-53	25.61	5
SUBLETTE	TP8-1	9-Apr-55	8.25	3	SWEETWATER	PB12-1	2-Sep-57	26.53	5
SUBLETTE	TS8-2	6-Jun-52	9.89	3	SWEETWATER	PB9-1	23-Aug-57	30.99	5
SUBLETTE	PB9-1	23-Aug-57	9.95	3	SWEETWATER	PB5-1	15-Jul-57	40.55	5
SUBLETTE	UK10-1	25-May-53	10.26	4	SWEETWATER	TP4-1	7-Mar-55	58.37	6
SUBLETTE	TP4-1	7-Mar-55	14.68	4	SWEETWATER	TP10-1	5-May-55	116.61	7
SUBLETTE	PB17-1	28-Sep-57	15.24	4	SWEETWATER	PB11-1	31-Aug-57	384.53	8
SUBLETTE	PB8-1	18-Aug-57	15.54	4	SWEETWATER	TS8-1	5-Jun-52	539.97	9
SUBLETTE	PB12-1	2-Sep-57	17.72	4	TETON	TS8-2	6-Jun-52	4.98	2
SUBLETTE	PB5-1	15-Jul-57	24.35	4	TETON	TP7-1	29-Mar-55	5.26	3
SUBLETTE	TS7-1	1-Jun-52	36.54	5	TETON	TS8-3	7-Jun-52	5.70	3
SUBLETTE	PB11-1	31-Aug-57	76.10	6	TETON	PB9-3	25-Aug-57	6.73	3
SUBLETTE	UK2-1	24-Mar-53	564.43	9	TETON	PB6-2	25-Jul-57	7.94	3
SUBLETTE	TS8-1	5-Jun-52	1717.64	10	TETON	UK2-1	24-Mar-53	8.38	3
SWEETWATER	UK2-1	24-Mar-53	3.83	2	TETON	PB17-5	2-Oct-57	10.96	4
SWEETWATER	PB16-1	23-Sep-57	4.03	2	TETON	PB8-2	19-Aug-57	29.82	5
SWEETWATER	UK6-1	18-Apr-53	4.23	2	TETON	TS5-1	7-May-52	62.33	6
SWEETWATER	TS1-1	1-Apr-52	4.71	2	TETON	TS8-1	5-Jun-52	864.10	10
SWEETWATER	TS6-1	25-May-52	5.11	3	UINTA	TS8-2	6-Jun-52	3.74	2
SWEETWATER	PB1-1	28-May-57	5.17	3	UINTA	PB16-1	23-Sep-57	4.03	2
SWEETWATER	PB6-2	25-Jul-57	5.41	3	UINTA	PB2-1	18-Jun-57	4.42	2
SWEETWATER	PB15-1	16-Sep-57	7.16	3	UINTA	UK6-1	18-Apr-53	4.48	2
SWEETWATER	UK7-1	25-Apr-53	7.98	3	UINTA	UK11-1	4-Jun-53	5.15	3

INDIVIDUAL FALLOUT DAYS
WYOMING

COUNTY	SHOT	DATE	µCi/SQ METER	INDEX	COUNTY	SHOT	DATE	µCi/SQ METER	INDEX
UINTA	TP9-1	15-Apr-55	6.75	3	WASHAKIE	PB9-2	24-Aug-57	3.60	2
UINTA	PB6-2	25-Jul-57	7.20	3	WASHAKIE	PB9-4	26-Aug-57	3.68	2
UINTA	PB15-1	16-Sep-57	8.05	3	WASHAKIE	UK7-4	28-Apr-53	3.69	2
UINTA	TS7-1	1-Jun-52	8.12	3	WASHAKIE	PB8-4	21-Aug-57	4.60	2
UINTA	UK7-1	25-Apr-53	8.46	3	WASHAKIE	SE1	6-Jul-62	4.73	2
UINTA	PB4-1	5-Jul-57	10.40	4	WASHAKIE	UK8-1	8-May-53	4.73	2
UINTA	TS1-1	1-Apr-52	12.37	4	WASHAKIE	PB6-2	25-Jul-57	7.94	3
UINTA	TS6-1	25-May-52	13.59	4	WASHAKIE	UK2-2	25-Mar-53	23.57	4
UINTA	UK9-1	19-May-53	16.30	4	WASHAKIE	TS8-1	5-Jun-52	39.88	5
UINTA	TP11-1	15-May-55	21.00	4	WASHAKIE	TS5-1	7-May-52	47.42	5
UINTA	UK10-1	25-May-53	21.94	4	WASHAKIE	UK2-1	24-Mar-53	170.07	7
UINTA	PB17-1	28-Sep-57	22.80	4	WESTON	PB9-4	26-Aug-57	3.68	2
UINTA	TP10-1	5-May-55	23.50	4	WESTON	TS7-3	3-Jun-52	4.17	2
UINTA	PB8-1	18-Aug-57	23.89	4	WESTON	TS7-4	4-Jun-52	6.62	3
UINTA	PB12-1	2-Sep-57	26.53	5	WESTON	PB9-3	25-Aug-57	7.76	3
UINTA	TP8-1	9-Apr-55	28.82	5	WESTON	UK7-4	28-Apr-53	8.98	3
UINTA	PB9-1	23-Aug-57	31.24	5	WESTON	PB5-2	16-Jul-57	9.68	3
UINTA	PB11-1	31-Aug-57	38.15	5	WESTON	TS8-1	5-Jun-52	13.29	4
UINTA	PB5-1	15-Jul-57	41.39	5	WESTON	PB5-3	17-Jul-57	15.18	4
UINTA	TP4-1	7-Mar-55	73.42	6	WESTON	TS5-1	7-May-52	31.62	5
UINTA	UK2-1	24-Mar-53	286.32	8	WESTON	UK2-2	25-Mar-53	45.45	5
UINTA	TS8-1	5-Jun-52	649.35	9					

SECTION 2

U.S. COUNTY RANKS
FOR
SIGNIFICANT FALLOUT EVENTS

1951-1962

NATIONAL RANKING AMONG U.S. COUNTIES BY FALLOUT DATE

STATE	COUNTY	SHOT	DATE	RANK FOR DATE	NUMBER OF TIMES IN TOP 10
AL	AUTAUGA	TS2-2	16-Apr-52	8	3
AL	AUTAUGA	TP6-5	26-Mar-55	2	3
AL	AUTAUGA	PB13-2	07-Sep-57	2	3
AL	BALDWIN	TS2-2	16-Apr-52	9	3
AL	BALDWIN	TP6-5	26-Mar-55	3	3
AL	BALDWIN	PB13-2	07-Sep-57	3	3
AL	BARBOUR	TS2-2	16-Apr-52	10	2
AL	BARBOUR	PB13-2	07-Sep-57	4	2
AL	BIBB	TS7-8	08-Jun-52	1	4
AL	BIBB	TP6-5	26-Mar-55	4	4
AL	BIBB	PB13-2	07-Sep-57	5	4
AL	BIBB	PB13-10	15-Sep-57	1	4
AL	BLOUNT	PB13-2	07-Sep-57	6	2
AL	BLOUNT	PB13-10	15-Sep-57	2	2
AL	BULLOCK	PB13-2	07-Sep-57	7	1
AL	BUTLER	TS5-4	10-May-52	8	3
AL	BUTLER	TP6-5	26-Mar-55	5	3
AL	BUTLER	PB13-2	07-Sep-57	8	3
AL	CALHOUN	BJ3-5	05-Nov-51	5	3
AL	CALHOUN	PB13-2	07-Sep-57	9	3
AL	CALHOUN	PB13-10	15-Sep-57	3	3
AL	CHAMBERS	PB13-2	07-Sep-57	10	1
AL	CHILTON	TP10-4	08-May-55	10	1
AL	CHOCTAW	TP6-5	26-Mar-55	6	1
AL	CLARKE	TP6-5	26-Mar-55	7	1
AL	COFFEE	TP6-5	26-Mar-55	8	1
AL	COLBERT	TP5-9	20-Mar-55	1	1
AL	CONECUH	TS3-3	24-Apr-52	1	2
AL	CONECUH	TP6-5	26-Mar-55	9	2
AL	COOSA	TP10-4	08-May-55	4	2
AL	COOSA	PB13-10	15-Sep-57	4	2
AL	COVINGTON	UK5-5	15-Apr-53	7	3
AL	COVINGTON	TP6-5	26-Mar-55	10	3
AL	COVINGTON	PB18-10	16-Oct-57	6	3
AL	DALLAS	PB2-4	21-Jun-57	4	1
AL	ELMORE	PB12-8	09-Sep-57	8	1

NATIONAL RANKING AMONG U.S. COUNTIES BY FALLOUT DATE

STATE	COUNTY	SHOT	DATE	RANK FOR DATE	NUMBER OF TIMES IN TOP 10
AL	ESCAMBIA	TP8-5	13-Apr-55	3	1
AL	ETOWAH	UK2-5	28-Mar-53	7	2
AL	ETOWAH	PB13-10	15-Sep-57	5	2
AL	FAYETTE	TP5-9	20-Mar-55	2	1
AL	FRANKLIN	TP5-9	20-Mar-55	3	1
AL	GENEVA	TS3-3	24-Apr-52	2	1
AL	GREENE	TS3-3	24-Apr-52	3	1
AL	HOUSTON	TS3-7	28-Apr-52	2	1
AL	JEFFERSON	PB13-10	15-Sep-57	6	2
AL	JEFFERSON	PB18-10	16-Oct-57	7	2
AL	LAMAR	PB2-4	21-Jun-57	1	1
AL	LAUDERDALE	TP5-9	20-Mar-55	4	2
AL	LAUDERDALE	PB16-9	01-Oct-57	3	2
AL	LAWRENCE	TP5-9	20-Mar-55	5	1
AL	LEE	UK5-5	15-Apr-53	8	2
AL	LEE	PB17-6	03-Oct-57	10	2
AL	LIMESTONE	TS4-6	06-May-52	4	2
AL	LIMESTONE	PB2-4	21-Jun-57	5	2
AL	LOWNDES	TS3-3	24-Apr-52	4	1
AL	MADISON	TS4-6	06-May-52	5	1
AL	MARENGO	TP6-4	25-Mar-55	6	1
AL	MARION	TP5-9	20-Mar-55	6	2
AL	MARION	PB2-5	22-Jun-57	9	2
AL	MARSHALL	PB13-10	15-Sep-57	7	1
AL	MOBILE	PB6-8	31-Jul-57	10	1
AL	MONROE	TP8-5	13-Apr-55	4	1
AL	MONTGOMERY	TP10-4	08-May-55	2	1
AL	MORGAN	PB2-4	21-Jun-57	6	1
AL	PERRY	TS7-8	08-Jun-52	2	3
AL	PERRY	PB13-10	15-Sep-57	8	3
AL	PERRY	PB18-10	16-Oct-57	8	3
AL	RANDOLPH	BJ1-2	29-Oct-51	7	1
AL	ST CLAIR	PB13-10	15-Sep-57	9	1
AL	SUMTER	PB2-5	22-Jun-57	10	2
AL	SUMTER	PB16-9	01-Oct-57	1	2
AL	TALLAPOOSA	TP10-4	08-May-55	7	1

NATIONAL RANKING AMONG U.S. COUNTIES BY FALLOUT DATE

STATE	COUNTY	SHOT	DATE	RANK FOR DATE	NUMBER OF TIMES IN TOP 10
AL	TUSCALOOSA	TP6-3	24-Mar-55	2	3
AL	TUSCALOOSA	PB13-10	15-Sep-57	10	3
AL	TUSCALOOSA	PB16-9	01-Oct-57	4	3
AL	WALKER	TS7-8	08-Jun-52	3	1
AL	WILCOX	TS3-3	24-Apr-52	5	1
AL	WINSTON	TP5-9	20-Mar-55	7	1
AR	ARKANSAS	UK3-6	05-Apr-53	1	3
AR	ARKANSAS	UK8-3	10-May-53	3	3
AR	ARKANSAS	TP5-9	20-Mar-55	8	3
AR	BAXTER	UK2-7	30-Mar-53	3	2
AR	BAXTER	UK9-9	27-May-53	2	2
AR	BENTON	UK2-10	02-Apr-53	2	3
AR	BENTON	UK3-3	02-Apr-53	2	3
AR	BENTON	UK9-9	27-May-53	3	3
AR	BOONE	UK9-9	27-May-53	4	1
AR	BRADLEY	UK5-4	14-Apr-53	1	1
AR	CALHOUN	UK5-4	14-Apr-53	2	2
AR	CALHOUN	PB1-6	02-Jun-57	5	2
AR	CARROLL	UK9-9	27-May-53	5	1
AR	CLARK	UK5-4	14-Apr-53	3	1
AR	CLAY	TP5-9	20-Mar-55	9	1
AR	CLEBURNE	UK2-8	31-Mar-53	4	6
AR	CLEBURNE	UK3-6	05-Apr-53	2	6
AR	CLEBURNE	UK8-3	10-May-53	4	6
AR	CLEBURNE	TP5-9	20-Mar-55	10	6
AR	CLEBURNE	PB6-6	29-Jul-57	6	6
AR	CLEBURNE	PB9-2	24-Aug-57	6	6
AR	CLEVELAND	UK5-4	14-Apr-53	4	1
AR	COLUMBIA	UK5-4	14-Apr-53	5	1
AR	CONWAY	UK9-9	27-May-53	6	1
AR	CRAIGHEAD	UK2-3	26-Mar-53	3	4
AR	CRAIGHEAD	UK2-7	30-Mar-53	4	4
AR	CRAIGHEAD	UK2-8	31-Mar-53	5	4
AR	CRAIGHEAD	UK8-3	10-May-53	5	4
AR	CRAWFORD	UK2-10	02-Apr-53	3	4
AR	CRAWFORD	UK3-3	02-Apr-53	3	4

NATIONAL RANKING AMONG U.S. COUNTIES BY FALLOUT DATE

STATE	COUNTY	SHOT	DATE	RANK FOR DATE	NUMBER OF TIMES IN TOP 10
AR	CRAWFORD	UK9-9	27-May-53	7	4
AR	CRAWFORD	PB13-9	14-Sep-57	1	4
AR	CRITTENDEN	uk1 5	21-Mar-53	2	6
AR	CRITTENDEN	UK2-3	26-Mar-53	9	6
AR	CRITTENDEN	UK2-8	31-Mar-53	6	6
AR	CRITTENDEN	UK3-6	05-Apr-53	3	6
AR	CRITTENDEN	UK8-3	10-May-53	6	6
AR	CRITTENDEN	TP7-4	01-Apr-55	3	6
AR	CROSS	uk1 5	21-Mar-53	4	6
AR	CROSS	UK2-3	26-Mar-53	8	6
AR	CROSS	UK2-7	30-Mar-53	5	6
AR	CROSS	UK8-3	10-May-53	7	6
AR	CROSS	UK8-5	12-May-53	4	6
AR	CROSS	TP7-4	01-Apr-55	7	6
AR	DALLAS	UK5-4	14-Apr-53	6	2
AR	DALLAS	PB6-6	29-Jul-57	4	2
AR	DESHA	UK3-6	05-Apr-53	4	1
AR	DREW	UK7-4	28-Apr-53	10	2
AR	DREW	PB1-6	02-Jun-57	8	2
AR	FAULKNER	UK2-7	30-Mar-53	6	3
AR	FAULKNER	UK9-9	27-May-53	8	3
AR	FAULKNER	PB6-6	29-Jul-57	3	3
AR	FRANKLIN	ts1 3	03-Apr-52	1	3
AR	FRANKLIN	UK9-9	27-May-53	9	3
AR	FRANKLIN	TP11-6	20-May-55	5	3
AR	FULTON	UK2-3	26-Mar-53	1	2
AR	FULTON	UK2-7	30-Mar-53	7	2
AR	GARLAND	UK5-4	14-Apr-53	7	1
AR	GRANT	UK5-4	14-Apr-53	8	2
AR	GRANT	PB1-8	04-Jun-57	1	2
AR	GREENE	UK2-7	30-Mar-53	8	1
AR	HEMPSTEAD	UK5-4	14-Apr-53	9	2
AR	HEMPSTEAD	TP6-2	23-Mar-55	2	2
AR	HOT SPRING	UK5-4	14-Apr-53	10	1
AR	HOWARD	TP6-2	23-Mar-55	3	3
AR	HOWARD	PB1-6	02-Jun-57	6	3

STATE	COUNTY	SHOT	DATE	RANK FOR DATE	NUMBER OF TIMES IN TOP 10
		NATIONAL RANKING AMONG U.S. COUNTIES BY FALLOUT DATE			
AR	HOWARD	PB1-8	04-Jun-57	2	3
AR	INDEPENDENCE	uk1 4	20-Mar-53	9	4
AR	INDEPENDENCE	UK2-7	30-Mar-53	9	4
AR	INDEPENDENCE	UK8-3	10-May-53	8	4
AR	INDEPENDENCE	PB9-2	24-Aug-57	7	4
AR	IZARD	PB9-2	24-Aug-57	8	1
AR	JACKSON	UK2-3	26-Mar-53	7	4
AR	JACKSON	UK2-7	30-Mar-53	10	4
AR	JACKSON	UK3-6	05-Apr-53	5	4
AR	JACKSON	UK8-3	10-May-53	9	4
AR	JEFFERSON	uk1 4	20-Mar-53	3	4
AR	JEFFERSON	UK3-6	05-Apr-53	6	4
AR	JEFFERSON	UK8-3	10-May-53	10	4
AR	JEFFERSON	PB6-6	29-Jul-57	5	4
AR	JOHNSON	ts1 3	03-Apr-52	2	2
AR	JOHNSON	UK9-9	27-May-53	10	2
AR	LAFAYETTE	TP6-2	23-Mar-55	4	1
AR	LEE	UK2-8	31-Mar-53	7	3
AR	LEE	UK3-6	05-Apr-53	7	3
AR	LEE	PB16-9	01-Oct-57	5	3
AR	LINCOLN	UK3-6	05-Apr-53	8	2
AR	LINCOLN	PB6-6	29-Jul-57	8	2
AR	LITTLE RIVER	TP6-2	23-Mar-55	5	3
AR	LITTLE RIVER	PB1-8	04-Jun-57	5	3
AR	LITTLE RIVER	PB18-7	13-Oct-57	1	3
AR	LOGAN	TP11-6	20-May-55	4	1
AR	LONOKE	UK3-6	05-Apr-53	9	2
AR	LONOKE	PB6-6	29-Jul-57	10	2
AR	MADISON	UK2-10	02-Apr-53	4	2
AR	MADISON	UK3-3	02-Apr-53	4	2
AR	MILLER	TP6-2	23-Mar-55	6	2
AR	MILLER	PB18-7	13-Oct-57	2	2
AR	MONROE	UK2-8	31-Mar-53	8	3
AR	MONROE	UK3-6	05-Apr-53	10	3
AR	MONROE	TP10-7	11-May-55	10	3
AR	MONTGOMERY	ts1 3	03-Apr-52	3	3

NATIONAL RANKING AMONG U.S. COUNTIES BY FALLOUT DATE

STATE	COUNTY	SHOT	DATE	RANK FOR DATE	NUMBER OF TIMES IN TOP 10
AR	MONTGOMERY	TP6-2	23-Mar-55	7	3
AR	MONTGOMERY	TP11-6	20-May-55	6	3
AR	NEVADA	PB1-8	04-Jun-57	6	1
AR	NEWTON	ts1 3	03-Apr-52	4	3
AR	NEWTON	UK4-1	06-Apr-53	8	3
AR	NEWTON	TP11-6	20-May-55	9	3
AR	OUACHITA	PB1-6	02-Jun-57	3	2
AR	OUACHITA	PB12-6	07-Sep-57	10	2
AR	PERRY	ts1 3	03-Apr-52	5	2
AR	PERRY	TP10-3	07-May-55	7	2
AR	PIKE	TP6-2	23-Mar-55	8	3
AR	PIKE	TP11-6	20-May-55	2	3
AR	PIKE	PB1-8	04-Jun-57	9	3
AR	POINSETT	uk1 5	21-Mar-53	5	5
AR	POINSETT	UK2-3	26-Mar-53	4	5
AR	POINSETT	UK2-8	31-Mar-53	9	5
AR	POINSETT	UK9-6	24-May-53	9	5
AR	POINSETT	TP7-4	01-Apr-55	9	5
AR	POLK	TP6-2	23-Mar-55	9	1
AR	POPE	ts1 3	03-Apr-52	6	1
AR	PRAIRIE	UK2-8	31-Mar-53	1	3
AR	PRAIRIE	PB6-6	29-Jul-57	1	3
AR	PRAIRIE	PB9-2	24-Aug-57	1	3
AR	PULASKI	uk1 4	20-Mar-53	2	2
AR	PULASKI	PB6-6	29-Jul-57	9	2
AR	RANDOLPH	uk1 5	21-Mar-53	6	3
AR	RANDOLPH	TP10-7	11-May-55	5	3
AR	RANDOLPH	PB9-2	24-Aug-57	9	3
AR	SCOTT	TP6-2	23-Mar-55	10	2
AR	SCOTT	PB13-9	14-Sep-57	2	2
AR	SEARCY	UK4-1	06-Apr-53	9	2
AR	SEARCY	PB9-2	24-Aug-57	10	2
AR	SEBASTIAN	UK4-1	06-Apr-53	10	3
AR	SEBASTIAN	TP11-6	20-May-55	7	3
AR	SEBASTIAN	PB13-9	14-Sep-57	3	3
AR	SHARP	TP11-6	20-May-55	3	1

STATE	COUNTY	SHOT	DATE	RANK FOR DATE	NUMBER OF TIMES IN TOP 10
NATIONAL RANKING AMONG U.S. COUNTIES BY FALLOUT DATE					
AR	ST FRANCIS	uk1 5	21-Mar-53	7	2
AR	ST FRANCIS	UK2-8	31-Mar-53	10	2
AR	VAN BUREN	UK8-5	12-May-53	5	3
AR	VAN BUREN	TP11-6	20-May-55	10	3
AR	VAN BUREN	PB6-6	29-Jul-57	7	3
AR	WASHINGTON	UK2-10	02-Apr-53	5	2
AR	WASHINGTON	UK3-3	02-Apr-53	5	2
AR	WHITE	PB6-6	29-Jul-57	2	1
AR	WOODRUFF	TP11-6	20-May-55	1	1
AR	YELL	ts1 3	03-Apr-52	7	2
AR	YELL	TP11-6	20-May-55	8	2
AZ	APACHE	TS3-1	22-Apr-52	10	7
AZ	APACHE	UK1-1	17-Mar-53	9	7
AZ	APACHE	UK6-1	18-Apr-53	4	7
AZ	APACHE	UK7-1	25-Apr-53	3	7
AZ	APACHE	UK11-1	04-Jun-53	9	7
AZ	APACHE	TP5-1	12-Mar-55	10	7
AZ	APACHE	PB3-1	24-Jun-57	7	7
AZ	COCONINO1	TS4-1	01-May-52	9	6
AZ	COCONINO1	UK9-1	19-May-53	9	6
AZ	COCONINO1	UK11-1	04-Jun-53	4	6
AZ	COCONINO1	TP5-1	12-Mar-55	4	6
AZ	COCONINO1	TP6-1	22-Mar-55	5	6
AZ	COCONINO1	TP7-1	29-Mar-55	10	6
AZ	COCONINO2	TS3-1	22-Apr-52	7	8
AZ	COCONINO2	TS4-1	01-May-52	7	8
AZ	COCONINO2	UK3-1	31-Mar-53	9	8
AZ	COCONINO2	UK6-1	18-Apr-53	1	8
AZ	COCONINO2	UK7-1	25-Apr-53	2	8
AZ	COCONINO2	UK11-1	04-Jun-53	1	8
AZ	COCONINO2	TP5-1	12-Mar-55	2	8
AZ	COCONINO2	PB13-3	08-Sep-57	4	8
AZ	COCONINO3	TS3-1	22-Apr-52	2	4
AZ	COCONINO3	UK3-1	31-Mar-53	10	4
AZ	COCONINO3	TP5-1	12-Mar-55	5	4
AZ	COCONINO3	PB13-3	08-Sep-57	5	4

NATIONAL RANKING AMONG U.S. COUNTIES BY FALLOUT DATE

STATE	COUNTY	SHOT	DATE	RANK FOR DATE	NUMBER OF TIMES IN TOP 10
AZ	GILA	UK3-1	31-Mar-53	2	1
AZ	MARICOPA	UK3-1	31-Mar-53	1	2
AZ	MARICOPA	TP6-1	22-Mar-55	10	2
AZ	MOHAVE1	TS4-1	01-May-52	5	4
AZ	MOHAVE1	TP3-1	01-Mar-55	10	4
AZ	MOHAVE1	TP5-1	12-Mar-55	3	4
AZ	MOHAVE1	TP6-1	22-Mar-55	3	4
AZ	MOHAVE2	TS3-1	22-Apr-52	1	9
AZ	MOHAVE2	TS4-1	01-May-52	6	9
AZ	MOHAVE2	UK3-1	31-Mar-53	3	9
AZ	MOHAVE2	UK9-1	19-May-53	6	9
AZ	MOHAVE2	UK11-1	04-Jun-53	7	9
AZ	MOHAVE2	TP3-1	01-Mar-55	9	9
AZ	MOHAVE2	TP6-1	22-Mar-55	2	9
AZ	MOHAVE2	TP11-1	15-May-55	3	9
AZ	MOHAVE2	PB11-1	31-Aug-57	10	9
AZ	MOHAVE3	TS2-1	15-Apr-52	2	6
AZ	MOHAVE3	TS4-1	01-May-52	3	6
AZ	MOHAVE3	UK3-1	31-Mar-53	6	6
AZ	MOHAVE3	UK5-1	11-Apr-53	3	6
AZ	MOHAVE3	TP6-1	22-Mar-55	8	6
AZ	MOHAVE3	TP11-1	15-May-55	8	6
AZ	MOHAVE4	TS2-1	15-Apr-52	3	6
AZ	MOHAVE4	TS4-1	01-May-52	4	6
AZ	MOHAVE4	UK3-1	31-Mar-53	7	6
AZ	MOHAVE4	UK5-1	11-Apr-53	4	6
AZ	MOHAVE4	TP6-1	22-Mar-55	9	6
AZ	MOHAVE4	TP11-1	15-May-55	9	6
AZ	NAVAJO	TS3-1	22-Apr-52	9	5
AZ	NAVAJO	UK6-1	18-Apr-53	3	5
AZ	NAVAJO	UK7-1	25-Apr-53	6	5
AZ	NAVAJO	UK11-1	04-Jun-53	5	5
AZ	NAVAJO	TP5-1	12-Mar-55	6	5
AZ	PIMA	TP1-1	18-Feb-55	4	2
AZ	PIMA	PB4-1	05-Jul-57	1	2
AZ	PINAL	UK3-1	31-Mar-53	5	1

NATIONAL RANKING AMONG U.S. COUNTIES BY FALLOUT DATE

STATE	COUNTY	SHOT	DATE	RANK FOR DATE	NUMBER OF TIMES IN TOP 10
AZ	SANTA CRUZ	TP1-1	18-Feb-55	3	2
AZ	SANTA CRUZ	PB4-1	05-Jul-57	2	2
AZ	YAVAPAI	TS2-1	15-Apr-52	5	5
AZ	YAVAPAI	TS3-1	22-Apr-52	8	5
AZ	YAVAPAI	UK3-1	31-Mar-53	4	5
AZ	YAVAPAI	UK5-1	11-Apr-53	7	5
AZ	YAVAPAI	TP6-1	22-Mar-55	7	5
AZ	YUMA	UK5-1	11-Apr-53	1	2
AZ	YUMA	TP1-1	18-Feb-55	2	2
CA	ALPINE	TS3-3	24-Apr-52	7	2
CA	ALPINE	TS7-2	02-Jun-52	9	2
CA	AMADOR	TS3-3	24-Apr-52	8	1
CA	BUTTE	TS3-3	24-Apr-52	9	1
CA	CALAVERAS	TS3-3	24-Apr-52	10	1
CA	COLUSA	UK2-5	28-Mar-53	9	1
CA	DEL NORTE	PB14-3	16-Sep-57	9	1
CA	EL DORADO	TS7-2	02-Jun-52	10	2
CA	EL DORADO	TP6-6	27-Mar-55	1	2
CA	FRESNO	BJ01 BAKER 1	28-Oct-51	1	3
CA	FRESNO	BJ-2 1	30-Oct-51	3	3
CA	FRESNO	BJ4-3	07-Nov-51	1	3
CA	GLENN	TS3-4	25-Apr-52	1	2
CA	GLENN	UK2-5	28-Mar-53	10	2
CA	HUMBOLDT	PB14-3	16-Sep-57	10	1
CA	IMPERIAL	BJ4-3	07-Nov-51	2	4
CA	IMPERIAL	TS2-2	16-Apr-52	6	4
CA	IMPERIAL	TS2-3	17-Apr-52	1	4
CA	IMPERIAL	TS2-5	19-Apr-52	1	4
CA	INYO1	TS3-1	22-Apr-52	3	3
CA	INYO1	PB2-1	18-Jun-57	3	3
CA	INYO1	PB6-1	24-Jul-57	5	3
CA	INYO2	TS3-1	22-Apr-52	4	3
CA	INYO2	PB2-1	18-Jun-57	4	3
CA	INYO2	PB6-1	24-Jul-57	6	3
CA	INYO3	BJ-2 1	30-Oct-51	1	7
CA	INYO3	TS2-1	15-Apr-52	1	7

NATIONAL RANKING AMONG U.S. COUNTIES BY FALLOUT DATE

STATE	COUNTY	SHOT	DATE	RANK FOR DATE	NUMBER OF TIMES IN TOP 10
CA	INYO3	TS3-1	22-Apr-52	5	7
CA	INYO3	TS7-1	01-Jun-52	6	7
CA	INYO3	UK5-1	11-Apr-53	9	7
CA	INYO3	TP4-1	07-Mar-55	1	7
CA	INYO3	PB11-1	31-Aug-57	2	7
CA	KERN	BJ01 BAKER 1	28-Oct-51	2	8
CA	KERN	BJ-2 1	30-Oct-51	4	8
CA	KERN	BJ4-3	07-Nov-51	3	8
CA	KERN	TS2-2	16-Apr-52	1	8
CA	KERN	TS2-4	18-Apr-52	9	8
CA	KERN	TS2-5	19-Apr-52	5	8
CA	KERN	TS2-8	22-Apr-52	2	8
CA	KERN	TS3-2	23-Apr-52	2	8
CA	KINGS	BJ01 BAKER 1	28-Oct-51	3	3
CA	KINGS	BJ-2 1	30-Oct-51	5	3
CA	KINGS	BJ4-3	07-Nov-51	4	3
CA	LASSEN	PB14-3	16-Sep-57	1	1
CA	LOS ANGELES	BJ-2 1	30-Oct-51	2	2
CA	LOS ANGELES	TS2-1	15-Apr-52	7	2
CA	MODOC	PB14-3	16-Sep-57	2	1
CA	MONO	TS3-1	22-Apr-52	6	5
CA	MONO	PB6-1	24-Jul-57	9	5
CA	MONO	PB13-1	06-Sep-57	2	5
CA	MONO	PB14-1	14-Sep-57	7	5
CA	MONO	PB16-1	23-Sep-57	7	5
CA	MONTEREY	BJ01 BAKER 1	28-Oct-51	4	3
CA	MONTEREY	BJ-2 1	30-Oct-51	6	3
CA	MONTEREY	BJ4-3	07-Nov-51	5	3
CA	NEVADA	TP6-6	27-Mar-55	2	1
CA	ORANGE	BJ4-3	07-Nov-51	6	6
CA	ORANGE	TS2-2	16-Apr-52	2	6
CA	ORANGE	TS2-4	18-Apr-52	2	6
CA	ORANGE	TS2-5	19-Apr-52	3	6
CA	ORANGE	TS2-8	22-Apr-52	3	6
CA	ORANGE	TS3-2	23-Apr-52	3	6
CA	PLACER	TP6-6	27-Mar-55	3	1

STATE	COUNTY	SHOT	DATE	RANK FOR DATE	NUMBER OF TIMES IN TOP 10
CA	PLUMAS	TP6-6	27-Mar-55	4	1
CA	RIVERSIDE	BJ4-3	07-Nov-51	7	5
CA	RIVERSIDE	TS2-2	16-Apr-52	7	5
CA	RIVERSIDE	TS2-3	17-Apr-52	2	5
CA	RIVERSIDE	TS2-5	19-Apr-52	2	5
CA	RIVERSIDE	TS2-6	20-Apr-52	1	5
CA	SAN BENITO	BJ01 BAKER 1	28-Oct-51	5	3
CA	SAN BENITO	BJ-2 1	30-Oct-51	7	3
CA	SAN BENITO	BJ4-3	07-Nov-51	8	3
CA	SAN BERNADIN	TS2-1	15-Apr-52	4	4
CA	SAN BERNADIN	UK3-1	31-Mar-53	8	4
CA	SAN BERNADIN	UK5-1	11-Apr-53	2	4
CA	SAN BERNADIN	TP1-1	18-Feb-55	1	4
CA	SAN DIEGO	TS2-2	16-Apr-52	3	5
CA	SAN DIEGO	TS2-4	18-Apr-52	3	5
CA	SAN DIEGO	TS2-5	19-Apr-52	4	5
CA	SAN DIEGO	TS2-8	22-Apr-52	4	5
CA	SAN DIEGO	TS3-2	23-Apr-52	1	5
CA	SAN LUIS OBI	BJ01 BAKER 1	28-Oct-51	6	3
CA	SAN LUIS OBI	BJ-2 1	30-Oct-51	8	3
CA	SAN LUIS OBI	BJ4-3	07-Nov-51	9	3
CA	SANTA BARBAR	BJ01 BAKER 1	28-Oct-51	9	5
CA	SANTA BARBAR	TS2-2	16-Apr-52	4	5
CA	SANTA BARBAR	TS2-5	19-Apr-52	6	5
CA	SANTA BARBAR	TS2-8	22-Apr-52	5	5
CA	SANTA BARBAR	TS3-2	23-Apr-52	4	5
CA	SHASTA	TP6-6	27-Mar-55	8	2
CA	SHASTA	PB14-3	16-Sep-57	7	2
CA	SIERRA	TP6-6	27-Mar-55	5	1
CA	SISKIYOU	PB14-3	16-Sep-57	3	1
CA	SONOMA	TS3-4	25-Apr-52	2	1
CA	TEHAMA	TS3-4	25-Apr-52	3	3
CA	TEHAMA	TP6-6	27-Mar-55	6	3
CA	TEHAMA	PB14-3	16-Sep-57	4	3
CA	TULARE	BJ01 BAKER 1	28-Oct-51	7	3
CA	TULARE	BJ-2 1	30-Oct-51	9	3

NATIONAL RANKING AMONG U.S. COUNTIES BY FALLOUT DATE

NATIONAL RANKING AMONG U.S. COUNTIES BY FALLOUT DATE

STATE	COUNTY	SHOT	DATE	RANK FOR DATE	NUMBER OF TIMES IN TOP 10
CA	TULARE	BJ4-3	07-Nov-51	10	3
CA	VENTURA	BJ01 BAKER 1	28-Oct-51	8	7
CA	VENTURA	BJ-2 1	30-Oct-51	10	7
CA	VENTURA	TS2-2	16-Apr-52	5	7
CA	VENTURA	TS2-4	18-Apr-52	4	7
CA	VENTURA	TS2-5	19-Apr-52	7	7
CA	VENTURA	TS2-8	22-Apr-52	6	7
CA	VENTURA	TS3-2	23-Apr-52	5	7
CA	YUBA	TP6-6	27-Mar-55	7	1
CO	ADAMS	TS6-5	29-May-52	10	8
CO	ADAMS	TP3-2	02-Mar-55	1	8
CO	ADAMS	TP3-3	03-Mar-55	1	8
CO	ADAMS	TP4-2	08-Mar-55	1	8
CO	ADAMS	PB1-10	06-Jun-57	6	8
CO	ADAMS	PB4-7	11-Jul-57	4	8
CO	ADAMS	PB4-8	12-Jul-57	4	8
CO	ADAMS	PB12-3	04-Sep-57	8	8
CO	ALAMOSA	TS2-7	21-Apr-52	4	4
CO	ALAMOSA	TS2-8	22-Apr-52	7	4
CO	ALAMOSA	TP10-2	06-May-55	3	4
CO	ALAMOSA	TP11-3	17-May-55	8	4
CO	ARAPAHOE	TP3-2	02-Mar-55	2	8
CO	ARAPAHOE	TP3-3	03-Mar-55	4	8
CO	ARAPAHOE	TP4-2	08-Mar-55	2	8
CO	ARAPAHOE	PB1-10	06-Jun-57	7	8
CO	ARAPAHOE	PB4-8	12-Jul-57	5	8
CO	ARAPAHOE	PB8-4	21-Aug-57	5	8
CO	ARAPAHOE	PB13-8	13-Sep-57	3	8
CO	ARAPAHOE	PB18-2	08-Oct-57	2	8
CO	ARCHULETA	R1-1	28-Jan-51	3	15
CO	ARCHULETA	TS2-7	21-Apr-52	1	15
CO	ARCHULETA	TS2-8	22-Apr-52	8	15
CO	ARCHULETA	TS6-2	26-May-52	5	15
CO	ARCHULETA	TS6-4	28-May-52	1	15
CO	ARCHULETA	UK3-2	01-Apr-53	1	15
CO	ARCHULETA	UK3-4	03-Apr-53	3	15

NATIONAL RANKING AMONG U.S. COUNTIES BY FALLOUT DATE

STATE	COUNTY	SHOT	DATE	RANK FOR DATE	NUMBER OF TIMES IN TOP 10
CO	ARCHULETA	UK4-1	06-Apr-53	6	15
CO	ARCHULETA	UK6-1	18-Apr-53	8	15
CO	ARCHULETA	UK6-5	22-Apr-53	1	15
CO	ARCHULETA	UK7-3	27-Apr-53	2	15
CO	ARCHULETA	UK11-6	09-Jun-53	9	15
CO	ARCHULETA	UK11-7	10-Jun-53	3	15
CO	ARCHULETA	PB3-2	25-Jun-57	2	15
CO	ARCHULETA	PB13-4	09-Sep-57	1	15
CO	BACA	TS4-3	03-May-52	1	4
CO	BACA	PB1-10	06-Jun-57	8	4
CO	BACA	PB18-2	08-Oct-57	3	4
CO	BACA	PB18-3	09-Oct-57	1	4
CO	BENT	TS4-3	03-May-52	2	3
CO	BENT	TP10-2	06-May-55	4	3
CO	BENT	PB1-10	06-Jun-57	2	3
CO	BOULDER	TP3-2	02-Mar-55	3	9
CO	BOULDER	TP3-3	03-Mar-55	5	9
CO	BOULDER	TP4-2	08-Mar-55	3	9
CO	BOULDER	TP11-2	16-May-55	7	9
CO	BOULDER	TP11-3	17-May-55	6	9
CO	BOULDER	PB1-10	06-Jun-57	9	9
CO	BOULDER	PB4-8	12-Jul-57	6	9
CO	BOULDER	PB13-8	13-Sep-57	4	9
CO	BOULDER	PB18-2	08-Oct-57	4	9
CO	CHAFFEE	TS6-2	26-May-52	9	2
CO	CHAFFEE	TP11-3	17-May-55	9	2
CO	CHEYENNE	TS2-6	20-Apr-52	3	4
CO	CHEYENNE	TS4-3	03-May-52	3	4
CO	CHEYENNE	PB18-3	09-Oct-57	2	4
CO	CHEYENNE	PB18-4	10-Oct-57	1	4
CO	CLEAR CREEK	TP3-2	02-Mar-55	4	7
CO	CLEAR CREEK	TP3-3	03-Mar-55	6	7
CO	CLEAR CREEK	TP4-2	08-Mar-55	4	7
CO	CLEAR CREEK	TP11-2	16-May-55	8	7
CO	CLEAR CREEK	PB4-7	11-Jul-57	3	7
CO	CLEAR CREEK	PB4-9	13-Jul-57	3	7

NATIONAL RANKING AMONG U.S. COUNTIES BY FALLOUT DATE

STATE	COUNTY	SHOT	DATE	RANK FOR DATE	NUMBER OF TIMES IN TOP 10
CO	CLEAR CREEK	PB13-8	13-Sep-57	5	7
CO	CONEJOS	R1-1	28-Jan-51	4	7
CO	CONEJOS	TS2-7	21-Apr-52	5	7
CO	CONEJOS	TS2-8	22-Apr-52	9	7
CO	CONEJOS	UK9-1	19-May-53	10	7
CO	CONEJOS	TP10-2	06-May-55	2	7
CO	CONEJOS	PB3-2	25-Jun-57	3	7
CO	CONEJOS	PB13-4	09-Sep-57	2	7
CO	COSTILLA	TS2-7	21-Apr-52	3	5
CO	COSTILLA	TS2-8	22-Apr-52	10	5
CO	COSTILLA	TP10-2	06-May-55	1	5
CO	COSTILLA	PB3-2	25-Jun-57	4	5
CO	COSTILLA	PB13-4	09-Sep-57	3	5
CO	CROWLEY	TS2-6	20-Apr-52	4	5
CO	CROWLEY	TS4-3	03-May-52	4	5
CO	CROWLEY	TP10-2	06-May-55	5	5
CO	CROWLEY	PB1-10	06-Jun-57	1	5
CO	CROWLEY	PB13-8	13-Sep-57	6	5
CO	CUSTER	TS2-7	21-Apr-52	6	6
CO	CUSTER	TS6-2	26-May-52	10	6
CO	CUSTER	TP10-2	06-May-55	6	6
CO	CUSTER	TP11-3	17-May-55	2	6
CO	CUSTER	PB4-10	14-Jul-57	2	6
CO	CUSTER	PB18-2	08-Oct-57	5	6
CO	DELTA	UK10-1	25-May-53	7	2
CO	DELTA	TP9-1	15-Apr-55	7	2
CO	DENVER	PB12-3	04-Sep-57	3	1
CO	DOUGLAS	TP3-2	02-Mar-55	5	8
CO	DOUGLAS	TP3-3	03-Mar-55	7	8
CO	DOUGLAS	TP4-2	08-Mar-55	5	8
CO	DOUGLAS	TP11-3	17-May-55	7	8
CO	DOUGLAS	PB4-8	12-Jul-57	7	8
CO	DOUGLAS	PB4-9	13-Jul-57	2	8
CO	DOUGLAS	PB12-3	04-Sep-57	7	8
CO	DOUGLAS	PB13-8	13-Sep-57	7	8
CO	EAGLE	TP3-2	02-Mar-55	6	6

NATIONAL RANKING AMONG U.S. COUNTIES BY FALLOUT DATE

STATE	COUNTY	SHOT	DATE	RANK FOR DATE	NUMBER OF TIMES IN TOP 10
CO	EAGLE	TP3-3	03-Mar-55	8	6
CO	EAGLE	TP4-2	08-Mar-55	6	6
CO	EAGLE	TP11-2	16-May-55	9	6
CO	EAGLE	PB4-2	06-Jul-57	2	6
CO	EAGLE	PB15-4	19-Sep-57	1	6
CO	EL PASO	TS2-6	20-Apr-52	5	7
CO	EL PASO	TS4-3	03-May-52	5	7
CO	EL PASO	PB1-10	06-Jun-57	10	7
CO	EL PASO	PB12-3	04-Sep-57	4	7
CO	EL PASO	PB13-8	13-Sep-57	8	7
CO	EL PASO	PB18-2	08-Oct-57	1	7
CO	EL PASO	PB18-3	09-Oct-57	3	7
CO	ELBERT	TS4-3	03-May-52	6	3
CO	ELBERT	PB8-4	21-Aug-57	6	3
CO	ELBERT	PB13-8	13-Sep-57	9	3
CO	FREMONT	TP11-3	17-May-55	5	4
CO	FREMONT	PB1-10	06-Jun-57	3	4
CO	FREMONT	PB4-10	14-Jul-57	1	4
CO	FREMONT	PB18-2	08-Oct-57	6	4
CO	GARFIELD	TP9-1	15-Apr-55	8	2
CO	GARFIELD	PB4-1	05-Jul-57	3	2
CO	GILPIN	TP3-2	02-Mar-55	7	6
CO	GILPIN	TP3-3	03-Mar-55	9	6
CO	GILPIN	TP4-2	08-Mar-55	7	6
CO	GILPIN	TP11-2	16-May-55	10	6
CO	GILPIN	PB4-9	13-Jul-57	10	6
CO	GILPIN	PB13-8	13-Sep-57	10	6
CO	GRAND	UK11-2	05-Jun-53	5	7
CO	GRAND	TP3-2	02-Mar-55	8	7
CO	GRAND	TP3-3	03-Mar-55	10	7
CO	GRAND	TP4-2	08-Mar-55	8	7
CO	GRAND	TP4-5	11-Mar-55	9	7
CO	GRAND	TP11-2	16-May-55	3	7
CO	GRAND	PB8-4	21-Aug-57	7	7
CO	GUNNISON	TS6-2	26-May-52	2	12
CO	GUNNISON	UK5-3	13-Apr-53	3	12

NATIONAL RANKING AMONG U.S. COUNTIES BY FALLOUT DATE

STATE	COUNTY	SHOT	DATE	RANK FOR DATE	NUMBER OF TIMES IN TOP 10
CO	GUNNISON	UK9-1	19-May-53	8	12
CO	GUNNISON	UK9-3	21-May-53	6	12
CO	GUNNISON	UK11-6	09-Jun-53	4	12
CO	GUNNISON	UK11-7	10-Jun-53	1	12
CO	GUNNISON	UK11-8	11-Jun-53	3	12
CO	GUNNISON	TP4-3	09-Mar-55	9	12
CO	GUNNISON	TP8-2	10-Apr-55	8	12
CO	GUNNISON	TP10-10	14-May-55	1	12
CO	GUNNISON	PB5-3	17-Jul-57	5	12
CO	GUNNISON	PB15-4	19-Sep-57	4	12
CO	HINSDALE	TS6-2	26-May-52	1	12
CO	HINSDALE	TS6-3	27-May-52	2	12
CO	HINSDALE	UK4-1	06-Apr-53	5	12
CO	HINSDALE	UK5-3	13-Apr-53	5	12
CO	HINSDALE	UK9-3	21-May-53	2	12
CO	HINSDALE	UK10-3	27-May-53	2	12
CO	HINSDALE	UK11-6	09-Jun-53	5	12
CO	HINSDALE	UK11-7	10-Jun-53	4	12
CO	HINSDALE	UK11-8	11-Jun-53	4	12
CO	HINSDALE	TP10-10	14-May-55	2	12
CO	HINSDALE	TP11-3	17-May-55	3	12
CO	HINSDALE	PB15-4	19-Sep-57	5	12
CO	HUERFANO	TS2-7	21-Apr-52	7	5
CO	HUERFANO	TS6-2	26-May-52	8	5
CO	HUERFANO	TS6-5	29-May-52	7	5
CO	HUERFANO	TP10-2	06-May-55	7	5
CO	HUERFANO	PB18-2	08-Oct-57	7	5
CO	JACKSON	UK11-2	05-Jun-53	2	3
CO	JACKSON	TP8-2	10-Apr-55	1	3
CO	JACKSON	PB2-2	19-Jun-57	4	3
CO	JEFFERSON	UK11-2	05-Jun-53	10	7
CO	JEFFERSON	TP3-2	02-Mar-55	9	7
CO	JEFFERSON	TP4-2	08-Mar-55	9	7
CO	JEFFERSON	TP11-3	17-May-55	4	7
CO	JEFFERSON	PB4-8	12-Jul-57	8	7
CO	JEFFERSON	PB12-3	04-Sep-57	10	7

STATE	COUNTY	SHOT	DATE	RANK FOR DATE	NUMBER OF TIMES IN TOP 10
		NATIONAL RANKING AMONG U.S. COUNTIES BY FALLOUT DATE			
CO	JEFFERSON	PB18-5	11-Oct-57	10	7
CO	KIOWA	TS4-3	03-May-52	7	3
CO	KIOWA	UK6-4	21-Apr-53	5	3
CO	KIOWA	UK7-3	27-Apr-53	1	3
CO	KIT CARSON	TS4-3	03-May-52	8	3
CO	KIT CARSON	PB18-3	09-Oct-57	4	3
CO	KIT CARSON	PB18-4	10-Oct-57	7	3
CO	LA PLATA	R1-1	28-Jan-51	1	4
CO	LA PLATA	TS7-1	01-Jun-52	10	4
CO	LA PLATA	UK1-1	17-Mar-53	8	4
CO	LA PLATA	PB18-1	07-Oct-57	10	4
CO	LAKE	TS5-9	15-May-52	10	5
CO	LAKE	TP3-2	02-Mar-55	10	5
CO	LAKE	TP4-2	08-Mar-55	10	5
CO	LAKE	TP4-3	09-Mar-55	3	5
CO	LAKE	PB15-4	19-Sep-57	6	5
CO	LARIMER	UK11-2	05-Jun-53	3	4
CO	LARIMER	UK11-8	11-Jun-53	6	4
CO	LARIMER	TP11-2	16-May-55	4	4
CO	LARIMER	PB2-2	19-Jun-57	5	4
CO	LAS ANIMAS	TS4-4	04-May-52	1	2
CO	LAS ANIMAS	TP10-2	06-May-55	8	2
CO	LINCOLN	TS4-3	03-May-52	9	6
CO	LINCOLN	TP10-2	06-May-55	9	6
CO	LINCOLN	PB1-9	05-Jun-57	9	6
CO	LINCOLN	PB4-9	13-Jul-57	9	6
CO	LINCOLN	PB8-4	21-Aug-57	8	6
CO	LINCOLN	PB18-2	08-Oct-57	8	6
CO	LOGAN	TS5-9	15-May-52	1	7
CO	LOGAN	TS6-3	27-May-52	4	7
CO	LOGAN	UK3-2	01-Apr-53	5	7
CO	LOGAN	TP3-6	06-Mar-55	5	7
CO	LOGAN	PB4-7	11-Jul-57	5	7
CO	LOGAN	PB4-8	12-Jul-57	9	7
CO	LOGAN	PB18-3	09-Oct-57	5	7
CO	MESA	TP9-1	15-Apr-55	3	1

NATIONAL RANKING AMONG U.S. COUNTIES BY FALLOUT DATE

STATE	COUNTY	SHOT	DATE	RANK FOR DATE	NUMBER OF TIMES IN TOP 10
CO	MINERAL	TS6-2	26-May-52	3	8
CO	MINERAL	UK4-1	06-Apr-53	7	8
CO	MINERAL	UK5-3	13-Apr-53	4	8
CO	MINERAL	UK7-3	27-Apr-53	9	8
CO	MINERAL	UK11-6	09-Jun-53	6	8
CO	MINERAL	UK11-7	10-Jun-53	5	8
CO	MINERAL	UK11-8	11-Jun-53	1	8
CO	MINERAL	TP10-10	14-May-55	3	8
CO	MOFFAT	TP10-1	05-May-55	7	1
CO	MONTEZUMA	UK1-1	17-Mar-53	7	1
CO	MONTROSE	TS7-1	01-Jun-52	5	1
CO	MORGAN	TP11-2	16-May-55	1	3
CO	MORGAN	PB4-8	12-Jul-57	10	3
CO	MORGAN	PB8-4	21-Aug-57	1	3
CO	OTERO	TS4-3	03-May-52	10	3
CO	OTERO	TP10-2	06-May-55	10	3
CO	OTERO	PB1-9	05-Jun-57	10	3
CO	PHILLIPS	TS6-3	27-May-52	1	4
CO	PHILLIPS	PB9-3	25-Aug-57	10	4
CO	PHILLIPS	PB9-6	28-Aug-57	2	4
CO	PHILLIPS	PB18-3	09-Oct-57	6	4
CO	PITKIN	TS1-2	02-Apr-52	5	14
CO	PITKIN	TS6-2	26-May-52	7	14
CO	PITKIN	UK5-3	13-Apr-53	1	14
CO	PITKIN	UK7-3	27-Apr-53	8	14
CO	PITKIN	UK9-3	21-May-53	9	14
CO	PITKIN	UK11-6	09-Jun-53	7	14
CO	PITKIN	UK11-7	10-Jun-53	6	14
CO	PITKIN	UK11-8	11-Jun-53	5	14
CO	PITKIN	TP4-3	09-Mar-55	5	14
CO	PITKIN	TP8-2	10-Apr-55	3	14
CO	PITKIN	TP8-3	11-Apr-55	3	14
CO	PITKIN	TP10-10	14-May-55	4	14
CO	PITKIN	TP11-3	17-May-55	1	14
CO	PITKIN	PB15-4	19-Sep-57	2	14
CO	PROWERS	TP10-4	08-May-55	9	1

NATIONAL RANKING AMONG U.S. COUNTIES BY FALLOUT DATE

STATE	COUNTY	SHOT	DATE	RANK FOR DATE	NUMBER OF TIMES IN TOP 10
CO	PUEBLO	TS2-6	20-Apr-52	6	2
CO	PUEBLO	PB18-2	08-Oct-57	9	2
CO	RIO BLANCO	TP10-1	05-May-55	10	2
CO	RIO BLANCO	PB4-1	05-Jul-57	4	2
CO	RIO GRANDE	TS2-7	21-Apr-52	8	5
CO	RIO GRANDE	TS2-8	22-Apr-52	1	5
CO	RIO GRANDE	TS6-2	26-May-52	6	5
CO	RIO GRANDE	PB3-2	25-Jun-57	5	5
CO	RIO GRANDE	PB13-4	09-Sep-57	4	5
CO	ROUTT	UK5-3	13-Apr-53	2	9
CO	ROUTT	UK11-2	05-Jun-53	1	9
CO	ROUTT	UK11-6	09-Jun-53	8	9
CO	ROUTT	UK11-7	10-Jun-53	2	9
CO	ROUTT	UK11-8	11-Jun-53	2	9
CO	ROUTT	TP8-2	10-Apr-55	6	9
CO	ROUTT	TP10-10	14-May-55	5	9
CO	ROUTT	PB4-2	06-Jul-57	6	9
CO	ROUTT	PB15-4	19-Sep-57	3	9
CO	SAGUACHE	TS6-2	26-May-52	4	4
CO	SAGUACHE	TP11-3	17-May-55	10	4
CO	SAGUACHE	PB4-2	06-Jul-57	3	4
CO	SAGUACHE	PB8-4	21-Aug-57	9	4
CO	SEDGWICK	TS5-8	14-May-52	3	4
CO	SEDGWICK	TS5-9	15-May-52	2	4
CO	SEDGWICK	TP3-6	06-Mar-55	6	4
CO	SEDGWICK	PB18-3	09-Oct-57	7	4
CO	SUMMIT	TP4-3	09-Mar-55	6	2
CO	SUMMIT	TP8-2	10-Apr-55	5	2
CO	WASHINGTON	PB1-10	06-Jun-57	4	4
CO	WASHINGTON	PB4-2	06-Jul-57	4	4
CO	WASHINGTON	PB8-4	21-Aug-57	10	4
CO	WASHINGTON	PB18-2	08-Oct-57	10	4
CO	WELD	PB2-2	19-Jun-57	2	2
CO	WELD	PB9-6	28-Aug-57	3	2
CO	YUMA	TS6-3	27-May-52	8	2
CO	YUMA	PB18-3	09-Oct-57	8	2

NATIONAL RANKING AMONG U.S. COUNTIES BY FALLOUT DATE

STATE	COUNTY	SHOT	DATE	RANK FOR DATE	NUMBER OF TIMES IN TOP 10
CT	FAIRFIELD	BJ3-7	07-Nov-51	5	6
CT	FAIRFIELD	ts1 4	04-Apr-52	3	6
CT	FAIRFIELD	ts1 5	05-Apr-52	9	6
CT	FAIRFIELD	TS5-5	11-May-52	5	6
CT	FAIRFIELD	UK4-7	12-Apr-53	2	6
CT	FAIRFIELD	TP9-7	20-Apr-55	1	6
CT	HARTFORD	TS4-7	07-May-52	8	6
CT	HARTFORD	TS5-5	11-May-52	6	6
CT	HARTFORD	UK4-7	12-Apr-53	3	6
CT	HARTFORD	TP7-6	03-Apr-55	7	6
CT	HARTFORD	TP9-7	20-Apr-55	2	6
CT	HARTFORD	PB11-5	04-Sep-57	9	6
CT	LITCHFIELD	ts1 5	05-Apr-52	10	5
CT	LITCHFIELD	TS5-5	11-May-52	7	5
CT	LITCHFIELD	UK4-7	12-Apr-53	4	5
CT	LITCHFIELD	TP9-7	20-Apr-55	3	5
CT	LITCHFIELD	PB11-5	04-Sep-57	10	5
CT	MIDDLESEX	TS4-7	07-May-52	9	4
CT	MIDDLESEX	TS5-5	11-May-52	8	4
CT	MIDDLESEX	UK4-2	07-Apr-53	8	4
CT	MIDDLESEX	UK4-7	12-Apr-53	5	4
CT	NEW HAVEN	TS5-5	11-May-52	9	1
CT	NEW LONDON	TS4-7	07-May-52	10	6
CT	NEW LONDON	TS5-5	11-May-52	10	6
CT	NEW LONDON	UK1-10	26-Mar-53	4	6
CT	NEW LONDON	UK5-5	15-Apr-53	9	6
CT	NEW LONDON	UK5-9	19-Apr-53	3	6
CT	NEW LONDON	TP9-7	20-Apr-55	4	6
CT	TOLLAND	R2-6	07-Feb-51	2	3
CT	TOLLAND	UK4-7	12-Apr-53	6	3
CT	TOLLAND	TP9-7	20-Apr-55	5	3
CT	WINDHAM	UK1-10	26-Mar-53	5	5
CT	WINDHAM	UK5-5	15-Apr-53	10	5
CT	WINDHAM	UK5-9	19-Apr-53	1	5
CT	WINDHAM	UK7-6	30-Apr-53	7	5
CT	WINDHAM	TP9-7	20-Apr-55	6	5

NATIONAL RANKING AMONG U.S. COUNTIES BY FALLOUT DATE

STATE	COUNTY	SHOT	DATE	RANK FOR DATE	NUMBER OF TIMES IN TOP 10
DC	WASHINGTON	BJ-2 3	01-Nov-51	7	2
DC	WASHINGTON	TS3-5	26-Apr-52	9	2
DE	KENT	BJ4-6	10-Nov-51	1	2
DE	KENT	UK9-7	25-May-53	1	2
DE	NEW CASTLE	BJ4-6	10-Nov-51	2	3
DE	NEW CASTLE	uk3 7	06-Apr-53	3	3
DE	NEW CASTLE	UK9-7	25-May-53	2	3
DE	SUSSEX	BJ4-6	10-Nov-51	3	2
DE	SUSSEX	uk3 7	06-Apr-53	4	2
FL	ALACHUA	R2-3	04-Feb-51	1	5
FL	ALACHUA	TS3-8	29-Apr-52	4	5
FL	ALACHUA	UK4-3	08-Apr-53	10	5
FL	ALACHUA	TP6-7	28-Mar-55	1	5
FL	ALACHUA	PB2-4	21-Jun-57	7	5
FL	BAKER	R2-3	04-Feb-51	2	4
FL	BAKER	TS3-8	29-Apr-52	5	4
FL	BAKER	TP6-7	28-Mar-55	2	4
FL	BAKER	TP10-10	14-May-55	6	4
FL	BAY	R2-3	04-Feb-51	3	2
FL	BAY	TS3-7	28-Apr-52	3	2
FL	BRADFORD	TS3-8	29-Apr-52	6	1
FL	BREVARD	TS3-8	29-Apr-52	7	4
FL	BREVARD	TP6-7	28-Mar-55	3	4
FL	BREVARD	PB8-6	23-Aug-57	6	4
FL	BREVARD	PB11-4	03-Sep-57	2	4
FL	BROWARD	R2-4	05-Feb-51	2	4
FL	BROWARD	TS3-8	29-Apr-52	8	4
FL	BROWARD	UK9-8	26-May-53	3	4
FL	BROWARD	PB8-6	23-Aug-57	7	4
FL	CALHOUN	TS3-7	28-Apr-52	4	2
FL	CALHOUN	PB12-8	09-Sep-57	3	2
FL	CHARLOTTE	TS3-8	29-Apr-52	9	3
FL	CHARLOTTE	UK9-8	26-May-53	4	3
FL	CHARLOTTE	PB2-4	21-Jun-57	8	3
FL	CITRUS	R2-5	06-Feb-51	8	3
FL	CITRUS	TS3-8	29-Apr-52	10	3

NATIONAL RANKING AMONG U.S. COUNTIES BY FALLOUT DATE

STATE	COUNTY	SHOT	DATE	RANK FOR DATE	NUMBER OF TIMES IN TOP 10
FL	CITRUS	PB2-4	21-Jun-57	9	3
FL	CLAY	TS7-8	08-Jun-52	5	2
FL	CLAY	TP6-7	28-Mar-55	4	2
FL	COLLIER	R2-4	05-Feb-51	3	4
FL	COLLIER	UK9-8	26-May-53	5	4
FL	COLLIER	PB2-4	21-Jun-57	10	4
FL	COLLIER	PB8-6	23-Aug-57	8	4
FL	DADE	R2-4	05-Feb-51	1	1
FL	DE SOTO	R2-5	06-Feb-51	9	3
FL	DE SOTO	UK9-8	26-May-53	6	3
FL	DE SOTO	PB8-6	23-Aug-57	9	3
FL	DIXIE	TS3-7	28-Apr-52	5	3
FL	DIXIE	UK4-3	08-Apr-53	2	3
FL	DIXIE	TP10-10	14-May-55	7	3
FL	FLAGLER	PB11-4	03-Sep-57	3	1
FL	FRANKLIN	R2-5	06-Feb-51	3	3
FL	FRANKLIN	TS3-7	28-Apr-52	6	3
FL	FRANKLIN	PB12-7	08-Sep-57	1	3
FL	GADSDEN	TS3-7	28-Apr-52	7	2
FL	GADSDEN	TS7-7	07-Jun-52	7	2
FL	GILCHRIST	UK4-3	08-Apr-53	3	2
FL	GILCHRIST	TP10-10	14-May-55	8	2
FL	GLADES	UK9-8	26-May-53	7	2
FL	GLADES	PB2-10	27-Jun-57	7	2
FL	GULF	TS3-7	28-Apr-52	8	2
FL	GULF	PB12-7	08-Sep-57	2	2
FL	HAMILTON	UK4-3	08-Apr-53	4	1
FL	HARDEE	UK9-8	26-May-53	8	1
FL	HENDRY	UK9-8	26-May-53	9	2
FL	HENDRY	PB2-10	27-Jun-57	8	2
FL	HERNANDO	PB11-4	03-Sep-57	4	1
FL	HIGHLANDS	UK9-8	26-May-53	10	1
FL	HILLSBOROUGH	R2-5	06-Feb-51	1	3
FL	HILLSBOROUGH	TS3-8	29-Apr-52	1	3
FL	HILLSBOROUGH	PB2-10	27-Jun-57	9	3
FL	HOLMES	TS3-3	24-Apr-52	6	1

STATE	COUNTY	SHOT	DATE	RANK FOR DATE	NUMBER OF TIMES IN TOP 10
FL	INDIAN RIVER	PB2-10	27-Jun-57	4	1
FL	JACKSON	TS3-7	28-Apr-52	9	1
FL	JEFFERSON	R2-5	06-Feb-51	10	3
FL	JEFFERSON	TS3-7	28-Apr-52	10	3
FL	JEFFERSON	TP10-10	14-May-55	9	3
FL	LAKE	R2-5	06-Feb-51	2	4
FL	LAKE	TP6-7	28-Mar-55	5	4
FL	LAKE	PB2-10	27-Jun-57	10	4
FL	LAKE	PB11-4	03-Sep-57	5	4
FL	LEON	UK4-3	08-Apr-53	1	2
FL	LEON	PB12-7	08-Sep-57	3	2
FL	LIBERTY	R2-5	06-Feb-51	4	3
FL	LIBERTY	TP6-7	28-Mar-55	6	3
FL	LIBERTY	PB12-8	09-Sep-57	4	3
FL	MADISON	UK4-3	08-Apr-53	5	1
FL	MANATEE	PB2-4	21-Jun-57	2	1
FL	MARION	TP6-7	28-Mar-55	7	2
FL	MARION	TP10-6	10-May-55	2	2
FL	MONROE	UK9-8	26-May-53	2	1
FL	OKEECHOBEE	PB2-10	27-Jun-57	5	1
FL	ORANGE	TP6-7	28-Mar-55	8	1
FL	OSCEOLA	TP6-7	28-Mar-55	9	2
FL	OSCEOLA	PB2-4	21-Jun-57	3	2
FL	PALM BEACH	R2-4	05-Feb-51	4	3
FL	PALM BEACH	UK9-8	26-May-53	1	3
FL	PALM BEACH	PB2-10	27-Jun-57	6	3
FL	PINELLAS	TP6-7	28-Mar-55	10	1
FL	SEMINOLE	TP10-6	10-May-55	1	1
FL	ST JOHNS	PB5-9	23-Jul-57	1	2
FL	ST JOHNS	PB11-4	03-Sep-57	6	2
FL	SUMTER	UK2-3	26-Mar-53	2	1
FL	TAYLOR	TS6-10	03-Jun-52	5	1
FL	VOLUSIA	R2-5	06-Feb-51	5	2
FL	VOLUSIA	PB11-4	03-Sep-57	7	2
FL	WAKULLA	PB12-7	08-Sep-57	4	1
FL	WALTON	TS7-8	08-Jun-52	4	2

NATIONAL RANKING AMONG U.S. COUNTIES BY FALLOUT DATE

NATIONAL RANKING AMONG U.S. COUNTIES BY FALLOUT DATE

STATE	COUNTY	SHOT	DATE	RANK FOR DATE	NUMBER OF TIMES IN TOP 10
FL	WALTON	PB1-9	05-Jun-57	1	2
GA	APPLING	TP10-10	14-May-55	10	1
GA	BACON	UK4-3	08-Apr-53	6	2
GA	BACON	PB17-4	01-Oct-57	5	2
GA	BALDWIN	BJ1-2	29-Oct-51	8	1
GA	BARROW	TS5-4	10-May-52	4	1
GA	BIBB	PB16-5	27-Sep-57	9	1
GA	BRYAN	TS3-4	25-Apr-52	7	3
GA	BRYAN	TS6-6	30-May-52	9	3
GA	BRYAN	TP7-10	07-Apr-55	8	3
GA	BULLOCH	TS3-4	25-Apr-52	8	3
GA	BULLOCH	TP7-9	06-Apr-55	6	3
GA	BULLOCH	TP7-10	07-Apr-55	1	3
GA	BURKE	TP7-9	06-Apr-55	7	3
GA	BURKE	TP7-10	07-Apr-55	3	3
GA	BURKE	PB16-6	28-Sep-57	5	3
GA	CHATHAM	TP7-10	07-Apr-55	9	1
GA	CLARKE	BJ1-2	29-Oct-51	9	1
GA	CLAYTON	PB16-5	27-Sep-57	2	2
GA	CLAYTON	PB17-6	03-Oct-57	6	2
GA	COFFEE	PB12-7	08-Sep-57	5	1
GA	COLUMBIA	PB2-8	25-Jun-57	2	3
GA	COLUMBIA	PB16-6	28-Sep-57	2	3
GA	COLUMBIA	PB16-8	30-Sep-57	2	3
GA	CRAWFORD	PB16-5	27-Sep-57	8	2
GA	CRAWFORD	PB17-6	03-Oct-57	8	2
GA	DAWSON	BJ1-2	29-Oct-51	10	1
GA	DE KALB	PB16-5	27-Sep-57	4	1
GA	DOUGHERTY	R2-5	06-Feb-51	6	1
GA	DOUGLAS	PB16-5	27-Sep-57	6	2
GA	DOUGLAS	PB17-6	03-Oct-57	3	2
GA	EARLY	PB12-7	08-Sep-57	6	1
GA	EFFINGHAM	TS3-4	25-Apr-52	9	2
GA	EFFINGHAM	TP7-9	06-Apr-55	8	2
GA	ELBERT	TS5-4	10-May-52	3	1
GA	FANNIN	TS5-4	10-May-52	9	1

NATIONAL RANKING AMONG U.S. COUNTIES BY FALLOUT DATE

STATE	COUNTY	SHOT	DATE	RANK FOR DATE	NUMBER OF TIMES IN TOP 10
GA	FAYETTE	PB16-5	27-Sep-57	1	2
GA	FAYETTE	PB17-6	03-Oct-57	2	2
GA	FULTON	PB16-5	27-Sep-57	3	1
GA	GLASCOCK	TS6-10	03-Jun-52	6	2
GA	GLASCOCK	PB16-6	28-Sep-57	1	2
GA	GWINNETT	PB16-5	27-Sep-57	7	1
GA	JEFF DAVIS	UK4-3	08-Apr-53	7	2
GA	JEFF DAVIS	PB17-4	01-Oct-57	6	2
GA	JENKINS	TP7-9	06-Apr-55	9	1
GA	LIBERTY	TS3-4	25-Apr-52	10	2
GA	LIBERTY	PB11-4	03-Sep-57	8	2
GA	LINCOLN	BJ-2 5	03-Nov-51	9	4
GA	LINCOLN	PB2-8	25-Jun-57	3	4
GA	LINCOLN	PB16-6	28-Sep-57	7	4
GA	LINCOLN	PB16-8	30-Sep-57	3	4
GA	LONG	PB11-4	03-Sep-57	9	1
GA	LUMPKIN	R2-5	06-Feb-51	7	1
GA	MACON	PB17-4	01-Oct-57	7	1
GA	MARION	PB17-4	01-Oct-57	8	1
GA	MCDUFFIE	TS6-10	03-Jun-52	7	1
GA	MCINTOSH	PB16-6	28-Sep-57	10	1
GA	MERIWETHER	BJ1-2	29-Oct-51	1	1
GA	MONROE	PB16-5	27-Sep-57	5	1
GA	MONTGOMERY	TS3-4	25-Apr-52	4	1
GA	OGLETHORPE	PB17-6	03-Oct-57	1	1
GA	PAULDING	PB17-6	03-Oct-57	5	1
GA	PIKE	BJ1-2	29-Oct-51	2	1
GA	RABUN	TP6-4	25-Mar-55	7	3
GA	RABUN	PB2-5	22-Jun-57	1	3
GA	RABUN	PB17-3	30-Sep-57	4	3
GA	RANDOLPH	PB12-7	08-Sep-57	7	1
GA	RICHMOND	TP7-9	06-Apr-55	10	1
GA	SCHLEY	PB16-5	27-Sep-57	10	2
GA	SCHLEY	PB17-4	01-Oct-57	9	2
GA	SCREVEN	TP7-10	07-Apr-55	2	1
GA	TALIAFERRO	TS6-10	03-Jun-52	8	1

NATIONAL RANKING AMONG U.S. COUNTIES BY FALLOUT DATE

STATE	COUNTY	SHOT	DATE	RANK FOR DATE	NUMBER OF TIMES IN TOP 10
GA	TATTNALL	PB17-4	01-Oct-57	10	1
GA	TOWNS	UK5-2	12-Apr-53	5	3
GA	TOWNS	TP6-4	25-Mar-55	8	3
GA	TOWNS	PB17-3	30-Sep-57	5	3
GA	WARREN	TS6-10	03-Jun-52	9	1
GA	WAYNE	PB11-4	03-Sep-57	10	1
GA	WHEELER	TS3-4	25-Apr-52	5	1
IA	ADAIR	TP10-4	08-May-55	8	3
IA	ADAIR	PB9-4	26-Aug-57	1	3
IA	ADAIR	PB16-2	24-Sep-57	8	3
IA	ADAMS	TS7-4	04-Jun-52	6	3
IA	ADAMS	PB4-10	14-Jul-57	5	3
IA	ADAMS	PB16-2	24-Sep-57	9	3
IA	ALLAMAKEE	PB6-9	01-Aug-57	4	1
IA	APPANOOSE	TS7-3	03-Jun-52	4	2
IA	APPANOOSE	PB16-2	24-Sep-57	10	2
IA	AUDUBON	uk1 4	20-Mar-53	7	5
IA	AUDUBON	UK2-3	26-Mar-53	6	5
IA	AUDUBON	UK9-5	23-May-53	1	5
IA	AUDUBON	TP7-6	03-Apr-55	9	5
IA	AUDUBON	PB9-4	26-Aug-57	2	5
IA	BENTON	PB9-3	25-Aug-57	5	1
IA	BLACK HAWK	PB9-3	25-Aug-57	6	1
IA	BOONE	TP7-6	03-Apr-55	1	2
IA	BOONE	PB9-4	26-Aug-57	3	2
IA	BREMER	PB6-8	31-Jul-57	1	2
IA	BREMER	PB9-3	25-Aug-57	7	2
IA	BUENA VISTA	TS3-10	01-May-52	9	3
IA	BUENA VISTA	TS8-10	14-Jun-52	3	3
IA	BUENA VISTA	UK7-5	29-Apr-53	6	3
IA	CARROLL	TS7-4	04-Jun-52	10	3
IA	CARROLL	PB4-10	14-Jul-57	6	3
IA	CARROLL	PB9-4	26-Aug-57	4	3
IA	CASS	TS3-10	01-May-52	10	3
IA	CASS	TS7-4	04-Jun-52	5	3
IA	CASS	PB9-4	26-Aug-57	5	3

NATIONAL RANKING AMONG U.S. COUNTIES BY FALLOUT DATE

STATE	COUNTY	SHOT	DATE	RANK FOR DATE	NUMBER OF TIMES IN TOP 10
IA	CEDAR	PB4-3	07-Jul-57	6	2
IA	CEDAR	PB18-8	14-Oct-57	6	2
IA	CHICKASAW	PB6-8	31-Jul-57	2	1
IA	CLARKE	TS7-4	04-Jun-52	9	1
IA	CLAY	TS8-10	14-Jun-52	4	2
IA	CLAY	UK7-5	29-Apr-53	4	2
IA	CLAYTON	PB6-8	31-Jul-57	3	1
IA	CRAWFORD	TS3-10	01-May-52	2	1
IA	DALLAS	UK2-3	26-Mar-53	10	2
IA	DALLAS	PB9-4	26-Aug-57	6	2
IA	DAVIS	PB9-4	26-Aug-57	7	1
IA	DECATUR	UK11-3	06-Jun-53	4	5
IA	DECATUR	TP7-5	02-Apr-55	4	5
IA	DECATUR	PB4-10	14-Jul-57	7	5
IA	DECATUR	PB5-7	21-Jul-57	2	5
IA	DECATUR	PB8-3	20-Aug-57	6	5
IA	DELAWARE	UK9-2	20-May-53	8	3
IA	DELAWARE	TP8-5	13-Apr-55	8	3
IA	DELAWARE	PB6-8	31-Jul-57	4	3
IA	DES MOINES	PB5-7	21-Jul-57	3	1
IA	DICKINSON	UK7-5	29-Apr-53	3	2
IA	DICKINSON	PB4-3	07-Jul-57	7	2
IA	DUBUQUE	PB6-8	31-Jul-57	5	1
IA	EMMET	UK7-5	29-Apr-53	9	1
IA	FAYETTE	PB6-8	31-Jul-57	6	1
IA	FRANKLIN	PB9-4	26-Aug-57	8	1
IA	FREMONT	UK11-5	08-Jun-53	5	1
IA	GREENE	PB4-9	13-Jul-57	4	1
IA	GRUNDY	PB2-2	19-Jun-57	10	2
IA	GRUNDY	PB5-7	21-Jul-57	4	2
IA	GUTHRIE	UK9-5	23-May-53	5	1
IA	HARRISON	PB4-10	14-Jul-57	8	1
IA	HENRY	PB5-7	21-Jul-57	5	2
IA	HENRY	PB18-8	14-Oct-57	7	2
IA	HOWARD	SE3	08-Jul-62	1	1
IA	HUMBOLDT	PB4-3	07-Jul-57	2	1

STATE	COUNTY	SHOT	DATE	RANK FOR DATE	NUMBER OF TIMES IN TOP 10
IA	IDA	TP7-6	03-Apr-55	3	1
IA	JASPER	PB4-9	13-Jul-57	1	2
IA	JASPER	PB9-4	26-Aug-57	9	2
IA	JEFFERSON	TS8-10	14-Jun-52	5	2
IA	JEFFERSON	SE3	08-Jul-62	4	2
IA	JOHNSON	TS8-10	14-Jun-52	6	2
IA	JOHNSON	PB4-3	07-Jul-57	8	2
IA	KEOKUK	TS8-10	14-Jun-52	1	1
IA	KOSSUTH	TS8-10	14-Jun-52	7	1
IA	LEE	PB4-9	13-Jul-57	6	4
IA	LEE	PB5-7	21-Jul-57	6	4
IA	LEE	PB18-8	14-Oct-57	8	4
IA	LEE	SE3	08-Jul-62	5	4
IA	LINN	TS8-10	14-Jun-52	8	1
IA	LOUISA	PB5-7	21-Jul-57	7	2
IA	LOUISA	PB18-8	14-Oct-57	9	2
IA	MADISON	UK2-3	26-Mar-53	5	2
IA	MADISON	PB9-4	26-Aug-57	10	2
IA	MARSHALL	TS8-10	14-Jun-52	9	4
IA	MARSHALL	UK9-2	20-May-53	9	4
IA	MARSHALL	PB4-9	13-Jul-57	7	4
IA	MARSHALL	PB5-7	21-Jul-57	8	4
IA	MITCHELL	UK9-2	20-May-53	4	3
IA	MITCHELL	PB6-9	01-Aug-57	10	3
IA	MITCHELL	SE3	08-Jul-62	2	3
IA	MONONA	TS3-10	01-May-52	3	2
IA	MONONA	TS4-6	06-May-52	6	2
IA	MONROE	TS7-3	03-Jun-52	6	2
IA	MONROE	TP8-5	13-Apr-55	9	2
IA	OSCEOLA	UK7-5	29-Apr-53	7	1
IA	PLYMOUTH	TS3-10	01-May-52	4	1
IA	POLK	TP7-5	02-Apr-55	1	2
IA	POLK	PB17-9	06-Oct-57	3	2
IA	POWESHIEK	PB9-3	25-Aug-57	1	1
IA	RINGGOLD	TS7-4	04-Jun-52	1	5
IA	RINGGOLD	TP8-5	13-Apr-55	10	5

NATIONAL RANKING AMONG U.S. COUNTIES BY FALLOUT DATE

STATE	COUNTY	SHOT	DATE	RANK FOR DATE	NUMBER OF TIMES IN TOP 10
IA	RINGGOLD	TP10-4	08-May-55	3	5
IA	RINGGOLD	PB4-10	14-Jul-57	9	5
IA	RINGGOLD	PB8-3	20-Aug-57	7	5
IA	SHELBY	TS7-4	04-Jun-52	3	2
IA	SHELBY	UK9-5	23-May-53	2	2
IA	SIOUX	TP7-5	02-Apr-55	9	1
IA	STORY	PB5-7	21-Jul-57	9	1
IA	TAMA	PB4-9	13-Jul-57	5	2
IA	TAMA	PB9-3	25-Aug-57	2	2
IA	TAYLOR	PB8-3	20-Aug-57	8	1
IA	UNION	TS7-4	04-Jun-52	8	1
IA	VAN BUREN	PB9-3	25-Aug-57	8	3
IA	VAN BUREN	PB18-8	14-Oct-57	10	3
IA	VAN BUREN	SE3	08-Jul-62	6	3
IA	WAPELLO	PB9-3	25-Aug-57	3	1
IA	WARREN	PB17-9	06-Oct-57	10	1
IA	WASHINGTON	SE3	08-Jul-62	7	1
IA	WEBSTER	PB4-3	07-Jul-57	1	1
IA	WINNESHIEK	PB6-9	01-Aug-57	5	1
IA	WOODBURY	TS3-10	01-May-52	5	1
IA	WORTH	SE3	08-Jul-62	3	1
IA	WRIGHT	TS8-10	14-Jun-52	2	1
ID	ADA	BJ5 1	19-Nov-51	5	1
ID	ADAMS	BJ5-2	20-Nov-51	1	12
ID	ADAMS	BJ5 3	21-Nov-51	6	12
ID	ADAMS	BJ5 4	22-Nov-51	1	12
ID	ADAMS	BJ5 5	23-Nov-51	1	12
ID	ADAMS	BJ5 7	25-Nov-51	2	12
ID	ADAMS	BJ5 8	26-Nov-51	1	12
ID	ADAMS	TS2-4	18-Apr-52	5	12
ID	ADAMS	TS8-5	09-Jun-52	1	12
ID	ADAMS	TS8-6	10-Jun-52	6	12
ID	ADAMS	TS8-9	13-Jun-52	2	12
ID	ADAMS	PB16-3	25-Sep-57	1	12
ID	ADAMS	PB17-4	01-Oct-57	1	12
ID	BENEWAH	PB1-9	05-Jun-57	5	2

NATIONAL RANKING AMONG U.S. COUNTIES BY FALLOUT DATE

STATE	COUNTY	SHOT	DATE	RANK FOR DATE	NUMBER OF TIMES IN TOP 10
ID	BENEWAH	PB16-3	25-Sep-57	2	2
ID	BLAINE	TS5-8	14-May-52	4	5
ID	BLAINE	TS8-1	05-Jun-52	3	5
ID	BLAINE	TS8-2	06-Jun-52	3	5
ID	BLAINE	PB16-3	25-Sep-57	3	5
ID	BLAINE	PB17-5	02-Oct-57	4	5
ID	BOISE	BJ5-2	20-Nov-51	3	10
ID	BOISE	BJ5 3	21-Nov-51	4	10
ID	BOISE	BJ5 4	22-Nov-51	2	10
ID	BOISE	BJ5 5	23-Nov-51	2	10
ID	BOISE	BJ5 7	25-Nov-51	6	10
ID	BOISE	BJ5 8	26-Nov-51	2	10
ID	BOISE	TS2-4	18-Apr-52	6	10
ID	BOISE	TS8-6	10-Jun-52	9	10
ID	BOISE	TS8-9	13-Jun-52	4	10
ID	BOISE	PB16-3	25-Sep-57	4	10
ID	BONNER	UK10-2	26-May-53	5	3
ID	BONNER	PB16-3	25-Sep-57	5	3
ID	BONNER	PB16-4	26-Sep-57	7	3
ID	BOUNDARY	UK10-2	26-May-53	9	3
ID	BOUNDARY	PB16-3	25-Sep-57	6	3
ID	BOUNDARY	PB16-4	26-Sep-57	8	3
ID	BUTTE	TS5-6	12-May-52	9	5
ID	BUTTE	TS5-8	14-May-52	5	5
ID	BUTTE	TS7-2	02-Jun-52	2	5
ID	BUTTE	TS8-7	11-Jun-52	9	5
ID	BUTTE	PB16-3	25-Sep-57	7	5
ID	CAMAS	BJ5-2	20-Nov-51	7	9
ID	CAMAS	BJ5 3	21-Nov-51	7	9
ID	CAMAS	BJ5 4	22-Nov-51	3	9
ID	CAMAS	BJ5 5	23-Nov-51	3	9
ID	CAMAS	BJ5 7	25-Nov-51	7	9
ID	CAMAS	BJ5 8	26-Nov-51	3	9
ID	CAMAS	TS8-1	05-Jun-52	8	9
ID	CAMAS	TS8-2	06-Jun-52	8	9
ID	CAMAS	PB16-3	25-Sep-57	8	9

NATIONAL RANKING AMONG U.S. COUNTIES BY FALLOUT DATE

STATE	COUNTY	SHOT	DATE	RANK FOR DATE	NUMBER OF TIMES IN TOP 10
ID	CANYON	BJ5 1	19-Nov-51	8	1
ID	CASSIA	TS7-1	01-Jun-52	7	1
ID	CLARK	TS5-6	12-May-52	1	7
ID	CLARK	TS5-8	14-May-52	6	7
ID	CLARK	UK10-8	01-Jun-53	6	7
ID	CLARK	PB2-2	19-Jun-57	8	7
ID	CLARK	PB8-2	19-Aug-57	3	7
ID	CLARK	PB9-2	24-Aug-57	2	7
ID	CLARK	PB16-2	24-Sep-57	1	7
ID	CLEARWATER	BJ5 3	21-Nov-51	1	8
ID	CLEARWATER	BJ5 4	22-Nov-51	4	8
ID	CLEARWATER	BJ5 5	23-Nov-51	4	8
ID	CLEARWATER	BJ5 7	25-Nov-51	3	8
ID	CLEARWATER	BJ5 8	26-Nov-51	9	8
ID	CLEARWATER	TS8-8	12-Jun-52	5	8
ID	CLEARWATER	PB1-9	05-Jun-57	6	8
ID	CLEARWATER	PB16-3	25-Sep-57	9	8
ID	CUSTER	BJ5-2	20-Nov-51	8	10
ID	CUSTER	BJ5 3	21-Nov-51	5	10
ID	CUSTER	BJ5 4	22-Nov-51	5	10
ID	CUSTER	BJ5 5	23-Nov-51	5	10
ID	CUSTER	BJ5 7	25-Nov-51	8	10
ID	CUSTER	BJ5 8	26-Nov-51	4	10
ID	CUSTER	TS8-1	05-Jun-52	2	10
ID	CUSTER	TS8-2	06-Jun-52	2	10
ID	CUSTER	PB6-2	25-Jul-57	2	10
ID	CUSTER	PB16-3	25-Sep-57	10	10
ID	ELMORE	BJ5 1	19-Nov-51	7	1
ID	FREMONT	TS5-6	12-May-52	10	4
ID	FREMONT	TS5-8	14-May-52	7	4
ID	FREMONT	PB8-2	19-Aug-57	4	4
ID	FREMONT	PB17-5	02-Oct-57	1	4
ID	GEM	BJ5-2	20-Nov-51	2	10
ID	GEM	BJ5 3	21-Nov-51	8	10
ID	GEM	BJ5 4	22-Nov-51	6	10
ID	GEM	BJ5 5	23-Nov-51	6	10

NATIONAL RANKING AMONG U.S. COUNTIES BY FALLOUT DATE

STATE	COUNTY	SHOT	DATE	RANK FOR DATE	NUMBER OF TIMES IN TOP 10
ID	GEM	BJ5 7	25-Nov-51	9	10
ID	GEM	BJ5 8	26-Nov-51	5	10
ID	GEM	TS8-1	05-Jun-52	1	10
ID	GEM	TS8-2	06-Jun-52	1	10
ID	GEM	TS8-6	10-Jun-52	2	10
ID	GEM	TS8-9	13-Jun-52	5	10
ID	GOODING	TS8-1	05-Jun-52	10	2
ID	GOODING	TS8-2	06-Jun-52	10	2
ID	IDAHO	BJ5-2	20-Nov-51	4	13
ID	IDAHO	BJ5 3	21-Nov-51	2	13
ID	IDAHO	BJ5 4	22-Nov-51	7	13
ID	IDAHO	BJ5 5	23-Nov-51	7	13
ID	IDAHO	BJ5 7	25-Nov-51	4	13
ID	IDAHO	BJ5 8	26-Nov-51	10	13
ID	IDAHO	TS2-4	18-Apr-52	1	13
ID	IDAHO	TS8-1	05-Jun-52	7	13
ID	IDAHO	TS8-2	06-Jun-52	7	13
ID	IDAHO	TS8-6	10-Jun-52	5	13
ID	IDAHO	TS8-7	11-Jun-52	6	13
ID	IDAHO	TS8-8	12-Jun-52	1	13
ID	IDAHO	TS8-9	13-Jun-52	1	13
ID	JEFFERSON	TS5-6	12-May-52	4	5
ID	JEFFERSON	TS7-2	02-Jun-52	1	5
ID	JEFFERSON	PB8-2	19-Aug-57	5	5
ID	JEFFERSON	PB9-2	24-Aug-57	3	5
ID	JEFFERSON	PB16-2	24-Sep-57	2	5
ID	KOOTENAI	UK10-2	26-May-53	7	1
ID	LATAH	UK10-2	26-May-53	8	2
ID	LATAH	PB6-2	25-Jul-57	3	2
ID	LEMHI	TS5-7	13-May-52	3	7
ID	LEMHI	TS5-8	14-May-52	1	7
ID	LEMHI	TS8-1	05-Jun-52	4	7
ID	LEMHI	TS8-2	06-Jun-52	4	7
ID	LEMHI	PB1-6	02-Jun-57	2	7
ID	LEMHI	PB6-2	25-Jul-57	4	7
ID	LEMHI	PB15-3	18-Sep-57	1	7

NATIONAL RANKING AMONG U.S. COUNTIES BY FALLOUT DATE

STATE	COUNTY	SHOT	DATE	RANK FOR DATE	NUMBER OF TIMES IN TOP 10
ID	LEWIS	TS8-6	10-Jun-52	8	1
ID	MADISON	TS5-6	12-May-52	5	5
ID	MADISON	TS7-2	02-Jun-52	5	5
ID	MADISON	PB8-2	19-Aug-57	6	5
ID	MADISON	PB9-2	24-Aug-57	4	5
ID	MADISON	PB16-2	24-Sep-57	3	5
ID	NEZ PERCE	PB16-4	26-Sep-57	4	1
ID	ONEIDA	TS7-1	01-Jun-52	8	1
ID	OWYHEE	BJ5 1	19-Nov-51	4	1
ID	PAYETTE	BJ5-2	20-Nov-51	5	7
ID	PAYETTE	BJ5 3	21-Nov-51	9	7
ID	PAYETTE	BJ5 4	22-Nov-51	8	7
ID	PAYETTE	BJ5 5	23-Nov-51	8	7
ID	PAYETTE	BJ5 7	25-Nov-51	10	7
ID	PAYETTE	TS8-6	10-Jun-52	1	7
ID	PAYETTE	PB17-4	01-Oct-57	2	7
ID	SHOSHONE	PB16-4	26-Sep-57	9	1
ID	TETON	TS5-1	07-May-52	9	6
ID	TETON	TS5-6	12-May-52	6	6
ID	TETON	PB5-2	16-Jul-57	6	6
ID	TETON	PB8-2	19-Aug-57	7	6
ID	TETON	PB9-2	24-Aug-57	5	6
ID	TETON	PB16-2	24-Sep-57	4	6
ID	TWIN FALLS	TS7-1	01-Jun-52	9	1
ID	VALLEY	BJ5-2	20-Nov-51	6	14
ID	VALLEY	BJ5 3	21-Nov-51	3	14
ID	VALLEY	BJ5 4	22-Nov-51	9	14
ID	VALLEY	BJ5 5	23-Nov-51	9	14
ID	VALLEY	BJ5 7	25-Nov-51	5	14
ID	VALLEY	BJ5 8	26-Nov-51	6	14
ID	VALLEY	TS2-4	18-Apr-52	7	14
ID	VALLEY	TS8-1	05-Jun-52	6	14
ID	VALLEY	TS8-2	06-Jun-52	6	14
ID	VALLEY	TS8-6	10-Jun-52	3	14
ID	VALLEY	TS8-9	13-Jun-52	6	14
ID	VALLEY	PB6-2	25-Jul-57	5	14

NATIONAL RANKING AMONG U.S. COUNTIES BY FALLOUT DATE

STATE	COUNTY	SHOT	DATE	RANK FOR DATE	NUMBER OF TIMES IN TOP 10
ID	VALLEY	PB15-3	18-Sep-57	2	14
ID	VALLEY	PB17-4	01-Oct-57	4	14
ID	WASHINGTON	BJ5-2	20-Nov-51	9	7
ID	WASHINGTON	BJ5 3	21-Nov-51	10	7
ID	WASHINGTON	BJ5 4	22-Nov-51	10	7
ID	WASHINGTON	BJ5 5	23-Nov-51	10	7
ID	WASHINGTON	BJ5 7	25-Nov-51	1	7
ID	WASHINGTON	BJ5 8	26-Nov-51	7	7
ID	WASHINGTON	TS8-9	13-Jun-52	3	7
IL	ADAMS	TP9-9	22-Apr-55	1	1
IL	ALEXANDER	uk1 5	21-Mar-53	8	2
IL	ALEXANDER	TP5-8	19-Mar-55	1	2
IL	BOND	TP9-9	22-Apr-55	2	1
IL	BOONE	TS8-8	12-Jun-52	6	1
IL	BROWN	TS8-5	09-Jun-52	7	3
IL	BROWN	TP9-9	22-Apr-55	3	3
IL	BROWN	PB18-9	15-Oct-57	1	3
IL	BUREAU	TS8-9	13-Jun-52	8	2
IL	BUREAU	TP7-7	04-Apr-55	8	2
IL	CARROLL	TS8-10	14-Jun-52	10	2
IL	CARROLL	PB5-7	21-Jul-57	10	2
IL	CASS	TP7-7	04-Apr-55	3	1
IL	CHAMPAIGN	PB18-9	15-Oct-57	2	1
IL	CHRISTIAN	PB18-9	15-Oct-57	3	1
IL	CLARK	PB9-5	27-Aug-57	5	1
IL	COLES	PB18-9	15-Oct-57	4	1
IL	COOK	PB9-5	27-Aug-57	6	1
IL	CRAWFORD	PB9-5	27-Aug-57	7	1
IL	CUMBERLAND	TP4-3	09-Mar-55	2	2
IL	CUMBERLAND	PB18-9	15-Oct-57	5	2
IL	DE KALB	TS8-8	12-Jun-52	8	1
IL	DE WITT	PB18-9	15-Oct-57	6	1
IL	DOUGLAS	PB18-9	15-Oct-57	7	1
IL	EDWARDS	TP5-8	19-Mar-55	2	2
IL	EDWARDS	PB18-9	15-Oct-57	8	2
IL	EFFINGHAM	PB18-9	15-Oct-57	9	1

STATE	COUNTY	SHOT	DATE	RANK FOR DATE	NUMBER OF TIMES IN TOP 10
				NATIONAL RANKING AMONG U.S. COUNTIES BY FALLOUT DATE	
IL	FAYETTE	TS8-5	09-Jun-52	8	2
IL	FAYETTE	PB18-9	15-Oct-57	10	2
IL	FRANKLIN	uk1 5	21-Mar-53	9	2
IL	FRANKLIN	TP5-8	19-Mar-55	3	2
IL	FULTON	TS8-5	09-Jun-52	4	3
IL	FULTON	TP4-3	09-Mar-55	7	3
IL	FULTON	TP9-9	22-Apr-55	4	3
IL	GREENE	UK2-6	29-Mar-53	7	2
IL	GREENE	PB4-4	08-Jul-57	5	2
IL	GRUNDY	TS8-9	13-Jun-52	9	1
IL	HAMILTON	TP5-8	19-Mar-55	4	1
IL	HANCOCK	TP9-9	22-Apr-55	5	2
IL	HANCOCK	SE3	08-Jul-62	8	2
IL	HARDIN	TP5-8	19-Mar-55	5	1
IL	HENDERSON	TP9-9	22-Apr-55	6	1
IL	IROQUOIS	TP3-4	04-Mar-55	6	1
IL	JACKSON	TP5-8	19-Mar-55	6	2
IL	JACKSON	PB15-7	22-Sep-57	4	2
IL	JO DAVIESS	PB4-3	07-Jul-57	9	1
IL	JOHNSON	TP5-8	19-Mar-55	7	1
IL	KANKAKEE	TP3-4	04-Mar-55	7	1
IL	KENDALL	TS8-9	13-Jun-52	10	1
IL	KNOX	TP7-7	04-Apr-55	9	2
IL	KNOX	TP9-9	22-Apr-55	7	2
IL	LIVINGSTON	TS8-5	09-Jun-52	5	1
IL	LOGAN	TS8-5	09-Jun-52	9	1
IL	MACOUPIN	PB12-7	08-Sep-57	8	1
IL	MADISON	TP7-7	04-Apr-55	2	1
IL	MCDONOUGH	TP7-7	04-Apr-55	10	2
IL	MCDONOUGH	TP9-9	22-Apr-55	8	2
IL	MCLEAN	TS8-5	09-Jun-52	3	1
IL	MENARD	TP7-7	04-Apr-55	4	2
IL	MENARD	PB6-8	31-Jul-57	7	2
IL	MERCER	TP9-9	22-Apr-55	9	1
IL	MONTGOMERY	TP7-7	04-Apr-55	5	1
IL	PEORIA	TP4-3	09-Mar-55	8	2

NATIONAL RANKING AMONG U.S. COUNTIES BY FALLOUT DATE

STATE	COUNTY	SHOT	DATE	RANK FOR DATE	NUMBER OF TIMES IN TOP 10
IL	PEORIA	TP9-9	22-Apr-55	10	2
IL	PERRY	TP5-5	16-Mar-55	3	2
IL	PERRY	TP5-8	19-Mar-55	8	2
IL	PIKE	TP7-7	04-Apr-55	6	2
IL	PIKE	PB9-3	25-Aug-57	9	2
IL	POPE	PB1-9	05-Jun-57	2	1
IL	PULASKI	uk1 5	21-Mar-53	10	3
IL	PULASKI	TP5-5	16-Mar-55	1	3
IL	PULASKI	TP5-8	19-Mar-55	9	3
IL	PUTNAM	TS8-5	09-Jun-52	6	1
IL	RICHLAND	TP5-8	19-Mar-55	10	1
IL	SANGAMON	TP4-3	09-Mar-55	4	1
IL	ST CLAIR	TP5-5	16-Mar-55	4	1
IL	TAZEWELL	TP4-3	09-Mar-55	1	1
IL	UNION	TS8-5	09-Jun-52	10	1
IL	VERMILION	PB9-5	27-Aug-57	8	1
IL	WILLIAMSON	TP5-5	16-Mar-55	5	1
IL	WINNEBAGO	TS8-8	12-Jun-52	4	1
IL	WOODFORD	TS8-5	09-Jun-52	2	1
IN	ADAMS	PB11-6	05-Sep-57	4	2
IN	ADAMS	PB18-10	16-Oct-57	9	2
IN	ALLEN	PB11-6	05-Sep-57	1	2
IN	ALLEN	SE4	09-Jul-62	9	2
IN	BARTHOLOMEW	PB9-5	27-Aug-57	1	1
IN	BLACKFORD	UK11-4	07-Jun-53	5	2
IN	BLACKFORD	PB11-6	05-Sep-57	5	2
IN	BOONE	UK11-4	07-Jun-53	6	3
IN	BOONE	PB3-4	27-Jun-57	1	3
IN	BOONE	PB9-5	27-Aug-57	9	3
IN	CARROLL	TS4-5	05-May-52	1	1
IN	CASS	TP3-4	04-Mar-55	8	2
IN	CASS	PB12-10	11-Sep-57	1	2
IN	CLARK	UK5-7	17-Apr-53	1	2
IN	CLARK	TP5-3	14-Mar-55	9	2
IN	CLINTON	TS4-5	05-May-52	2	3
IN	CLINTON	UK11-4	07-Jun-53	9	3

NATIONAL RANKING AMONG U.S. COUNTIES BY FALLOUT DATE

STATE	COUNTY	SHOT	DATE	RANK FOR DATE	NUMBER OF TIMES IN TOP 10
IN	CLINTON	PB8-6	23-Aug-57	1	3
IN	CRAWFORD	UK4-6	11-Apr-53	2	1
IN	DAVIESS	UK4-6	11-Apr-53	3	2
IN	DAVIESS	TP5-3	14-Mar-55	4	2
IN	DEARBORN	PB6-3	26-Jul-57	1	4
IN	DEARBORN	PB11-6	05-Sep-57	6	4
IN	DEARBORN	PB12-10	11-Sep-57	2	4
IN	DEARBORN	PB16-10	02-Oct-57	3	4
IN	DECATUR	PB6-3	26-Jul-57	9	4
IN	DECATUR	PB9-5	27-Aug-57	10	4
IN	DECATUR	PB11-6	05-Sep-57	7	4
IN	DECATUR	PB18-10	16-Oct-57	1	4
IN	DELAWARE	UK11-4	07-Jun-53	8	3
IN	DELAWARE	PB11-6	05-Sep-57	8	3
IN	DELAWARE	PB18-10	16-Oct-57	10	3
IN	DUBOIS	UK5-7	17-Apr-53	2	2
IN	DUBOIS	TP5-3	14-Mar-55	3	2
IN	ELKHART	PB15-6	21-Sep-57	5	1
IN	FAYETTE	PB11-6	05-Sep-57	9	2
IN	FAYETTE	PB16-10	02-Oct-57	4	2
IN	FLOYD	UK4-6	11-Apr-53	4	2
IN	FLOYD	PB17-2	29-Sep-57	5	2
IN	FRANKLIN	PB6-3	26-Jul-57	10	3
IN	FRANKLIN	PB11-6	05-Sep-57	10	3
IN	FRANKLIN	PB16-10	02-Oct-57	5	3
IN	FULTON	TP3-4	04-Mar-55	9	1
IN	GIBSON	UK4-6	11-Apr-53	5	1
IN	GRANT	SE4	09-Jul-62	10	1
IN	GREENE	UK4-6	11-Apr-53	6	1
IN	HAMILTON	UK11-4	07-Jun-53	1	3
IN	HAMILTON	PB3-4	27-Jun-57	4	3
IN	HAMILTON	PB18-10	16-Oct-57	2	3
IN	HANCOCK	UK11-4	07-Jun-53	2	2
IN	HANCOCK	PB9-5	27-Aug-57	2	2
IN	HARRISON	UK4-6	11-Apr-53	7	2
IN	HARRISON	PB17-2	29-Sep-57	6	2

NATIONAL RANKING AMONG U.S. COUNTIES BY FALLOUT DATE

STATE	COUNTY	SHOT	DATE	RANK FOR DATE	NUMBER OF TIMES IN TOP 10
IN	HENDRICKS	PB3-4	27-Jun-57	3	1
IN	HENRY	PB9-5	27-Aug-57	3	1
IN	HOWARD	TS4-5	05-May-52	4	1
IN	JACKSON	UK4-6	11-Apr-53	8	2
IN	JACKSON	TP5-3	14-Mar-55	8	2
IN	JEFFERSON	UK5-7	17-Apr-53	3	1
IN	JENNINGS	UK4-6	11-Apr-53	9	1
IN	JOHNSON	UK4-6	11-Apr-53	10	2
IN	JOHNSON	PB6-10	02-Aug-57	1	2
IN	KOSCIUSKO	TP3-4	04-Mar-55	10	1
IN	LA PORTE	UK9-6	24-May-53	3	1
IN	LAGRANGE	R1-3	30-Jan-51	1	2
IN	LAGRANGE	PB15-6	21-Sep-57	2	2
IN	LAWRENCE	TP5-3	14-Mar-55	1	1
IN	MADISON	UK11-4	07-Jun-53	7	2
IN	MADISON	PB3-4	27-Jun-57	5	2
IN	MARION	UK11-4	07-Jun-53	3	2
IN	MARION	PB3-4	27-Jun-57	10	2
IN	MARSHALL	PB12-10	11-Sep-57	3	1
IN	MARTIN	TP5-3	14-Mar-55	2	1
IN	MONTGOMERY	PB3-4	27-Jun-57	6	1
IN	NEWTON	UK7-7	01-May-53	10	1
IN	OHIO	UK5-7	17-Apr-53	4	4
IN	OHIO	PB12-10	11-Sep-57	4	4
IN	OHIO	PB13-7	12-Sep-57	1	4
IN	OHIO	PB16-10	02-Oct-57	6	4
IN	ORANGE	TP5-3	14-Mar-55	6	1
IN	PARKE	PB3-4	27-Jun-57	7	1
IN	PIKE	TP5-3	14-Mar-55	7	1
IN	POSEY	UK6-5	22-Apr-53	6	1
IN	PUTNAM	PB3-4	27-Jun-57	2	1
IN	RANDOLPH	UK11-4	07-Jun-53	10	2
IN	RANDOLPH	PB16-10	02-Oct-57	7	2
IN	RIPLEY	TS4-5	05-May-52	6	5
IN	RIPLEY	PB6-3	26-Jul-57	2	5
IN	RIPLEY	PB12-10	11-Sep-57	5	5

STATE	COUNTY	SHOT	DATE	RANK FOR DATE	NUMBER OF TIMES IN TOP 10
				NATIONAL RANKING AMONG U.S. COUNTIES BY FALLOUT DATE	
IN	RIPLEY	PB16-10	02-Oct-57	8	5
IN	RIPLEY	PB18-10	16-Oct-57	3	5
IN	RUSH	TS6-10	03-Jun-52	1	1
IN	SCOTT	TP5-3	14-Mar-55	10	1
IN	ST JOSEPH	PB9-5	27-Aug-57	4	1
IN	STARKE	PB12-10	11-Sep-57	6	1
IN	STEUBEN	PB15-6	21-Sep-57	3	1
IN	SULLIVAN	PB3-4	27-Jun-57	8	1
IN	SWITZERLAND	PB16-10	02-Oct-57	9	1
IN	TIPPECANOE	TS4-5	05-May-52	3	1
IN	TIPTON	TS4-5	05-May-52	5	4
IN	TIPTON	UK11-4	07-Jun-53	4	4
IN	TIPTON	PB8-6	23-Aug-57	2	4
IN	TIPTON	PB18-10	16-Oct-57	4	4
IN	UNION	TS4-5	05-May-52	7	3
IN	UNION	PB16-10	02-Oct-57	10	3
IN	UNION	PB18-10	16-Oct-57	5	3
IN	VANDERBURGH	UK5-7	17-Apr-53	5	2
IN	VANDERBURGH	UK6-5	22-Apr-53	7	2
IN	VERMILLION	TP4-3	09-Mar-55	10	1
IN	VIGO	PB3-4	27-Jun-57	9	1
IN	WARREN	PB6-10	02-Aug-57	2	1
IN	WARRICK	UK5-7	17-Apr-53	6	1
IN	WASHINGTON	UK5-7	17-Apr-53	7	2
IN	WASHINGTON	TP5-3	14-Mar-55	5	2
IN	WAYNE	TS4-5	05-May-52	8	2
IN	WAYNE	PB12-10	11-Sep-57	7	2
IN	WHITLEY	PB12-10	11-Sep-57	8	1
KS	ALLEN	PB14 7		1	1
KS	ANDERSON	UK11-2	05-Jun-53	8	2
KS	ANDERSON	PB14 7		2	2
KS	ATCHISON	TP4-6	12-Mar-55	2	2
KS	ATCHISON	PB12-4	05-Sep-57	10	2
KS	BARBER	TS6-7	31-May-52	7	3
KS	BARBER	PB14-6	19-Sep-57	1	3
KS	BARBER	PB17-10	07-Oct-57	9	3

NATIONAL RANKING AMONG U.S. COUNTIES BY FALLOUT DATE

STATE	COUNTY	SHOT	DATE	RANK FOR DATE	NUMBER OF TIMES IN TOP 10
KS	BARTON	TS3-9	30-Apr-52	1	4
KS	BARTON	TS6-7	31-May-52	10	4
KS	BARTON	TP4-6	12-Mar-55	3	4
KS	BARTON	PB13-5	10-Sep-57	6	4
KS	BOURBON	PB14 7		3	1
KS	BROWN	TP4-6	12-Mar-55	4	1
KS	BUTLER	PB14-6	19-Sep-57	2	2
KS	BUTLER	PB14 7		4	2
KS	CHASE	TS7-5	05-Jun-52	3	3
KS	CHASE	PB14-6	19-Sep-57	3	3
KS	CHASE	PB14 7		5	3
KS	CHAUTAUQUA	TS7-5	05-Jun-52	6	2
KS	CHAUTAUQUA	TP10-4	08-May-55	6	2
KS	CHEROKEE	UK2-10	02-Apr-53	6	2
KS	CHEROKEE	UK3-3	02-Apr-53	6	2
KS	CHEYENNE	TS6-3	27-May-52	5	2
KS	CHEYENNE	TP8-3	11-Apr-55	2	2
KS	CLAY	TS6-7	31-May-52	6	3
KS	CLAY	TP4-6	12-Mar-55	5	3
KS	CLAY	PB13-5	10-Sep-57	10	3
KS	CLOUD	TP8-4	12-Apr-55	8	1
KS	COFFEY	PB14 7		6	1
KS	COMANCHE	TS6-7	31-May-52	1	2
KS	COMANCHE	UK9-5	23-May-53	7	2
KS	COWLEY	BJ5 6	24-Nov-51	3	3
KS	COWLEY	TS7-5	05-Jun-52	2	3
KS	COWLEY	PB14 7		7	3
KS	CRAWFORD	ts1 3	03-Apr-52	8	2
KS	CRAWFORD	PB12-4	05-Sep-57	2	2
KS	DECATUR	PB4-10	14-Jul-57	3	1
KS	DICKINSON	TP4-6	12-Mar-55	6	3
KS	DICKINSON	TP8-4	12-Apr-55	3	3
KS	DICKINSON	PB13-5	10-Sep-57	9	3
KS	DONIPHAN	UK11-3	06-Jun-53	2	1
KS	DOUGLAS	PB14 7		8	1
KS	EDWARDS	TS6-7	31-May-52	8	1

NATIONAL RANKING AMONG U.S. COUNTIES BY FALLOUT DATE

STATE	COUNTY	SHOT	DATE	RANK FOR DATE	NUMBER OF TIMES IN TOP 10
KS	ELK	TS7-5	05-Jun-52	5	2
KS	ELK	PB14 7		9	2
KS	ELLIS	TS3-9	30-Apr-52	2	4
KS	ELLIS	TP4-6	12-Mar-55	7	4
KS	ELLIS	TP7-3	31-Mar-55	2	4
KS	ELLIS	TP8-4	12-Apr-55	9	4
KS	ELLSWORTH	TS3-9	30-Apr-52	10	4
KS	ELLSWORTH	TP4-6	12-Mar-55	8	4
KS	ELLSWORTH	TP8-4	12-Apr-55	4	4
KS	ELLSWORTH	PB13-5	10-Sep-57	8	4
KS	FRANKLIN	PB14-6	19-Sep-57	4	2
KS	FRANKLIN	PB14 7		10	2
KS	GEARY	TP4-6	12-Mar-55	9	2
KS	GEARY	TP8-4	12-Apr-55	5	2
KS	GOVE	TP7-3	31-Mar-55	8	1
KS	GRANT	TS1-2	02-Apr-52	6	3
KS	GRANT	TP7-3	31-Mar-55	7	3
KS	GRANT	TP8-3	11-Apr-55	10	3
KS	GREELEY	TS2-6	20-Apr-52	7	1
KS	GREENWOOD	TS7-5	05-Jun-52	4	1
KS	HAMILTON	TS2-6	20-Apr-52	8	2
KS	HAMILTON	PB9-6	28-Aug-57	7	2
KS	HARPER	PB13-9	14-Sep-57	4	2
KS	HARPER	PB17-10	07-Oct-57	5	2
KS	HARVEY	PB14-6	19-Sep-57	5	1
KS	HODGEMAN	TS1-2	02-Apr-52	7	1
KS	JACKSON	TP4-6	12-Mar-55	10	1
KS	JEFFERSON	UK11-2	05-Jun-53	9	3
KS	JEFFERSON	PB12-4	05-Sep-57	9	3
KS	JEFFERSON	PB14-6	19-Sep-57	6	3
KS	JOHNSON	PB4-5	09-Jul-57	3	2
KS	JOHNSON	PB15-5	20-Sep-57	1	2
KS	KINGMAN	PB12-3	04-Sep-57	9	4
KS	KINGMAN	PB13-9	14-Sep-57	5	4
KS	KINGMAN	PB14-6	19-Sep-57	7	4
KS	KINGMAN	PB17-10	07-Oct-57	7	4

NATIONAL RANKING AMONG U.S. COUNTIES BY FALLOUT DATE

STATE	COUNTY	SHOT	DATE	RANK FOR DATE	NUMBER OF TIMES IN TOP 10
KS	LANE	TP7-3	31-Mar-55	10	1
KS	LEAVENWORTH	UK2-6	29-Mar-53	8	5
KS	LEAVENWORTH	UK7-9	03-May-53	6	5
KS	LEAVENWORTH	UK11-3	06-Jun-53	3	5
KS	LEAVENWORTH	PB12-4	05-Sep-57	8	5
KS	LEAVENWORTH	PB14-6	19-Sep-57	8	5
KS	LINCOLN	TP7-3	31-Mar-55	5	2
KS	LINCOLN	PB13-5	10-Sep-57	5	2
KS	LYON	PB14-6	19-Sep-57	9	1
KS	MARION	TS6-7	31-May-52	5	3
KS	MARION	TS7-5	05-Jun-52	10	3
KS	MARION	TP9-5	18-Apr-55	7	3
KS	MCPHERSON	TP8-4	12-Apr-55	6	3
KS	MCPHERSON	PB12-3	04-Sep-57	5	3
KS	MCPHERSON	PB13-5	10-Sep-57	1	3
KS	MEADE	TS4-4	04-May-52	2	3
KS	MEADE	UK6-3	20-Apr-53	2	3
KS	MEADE	PB5-10	24-Jul-57	7	3
KS	MIAMI	UK2-6	29-Mar-53	2	2
KS	MIAMI	UK11-2	05-Jun-53	6	2
KS	MITCHELL	TS3-9	30-Apr-52	3	2
KS	MITCHELL	PB13-3	08-Sep-57	9	2
KS	MONTGOMERY	TP10-4	08-May-55	5	1
KS	MORRIS	PB14-6	19-Sep-57	10	1
KS	MORTON	TS2-7	21-Apr-52	9	5
KS	MORTON	TS4-4	04-May-52	3	5
KS	MORTON	UK6-3	20-Apr-53	3	5
KS	MORTON	PB9-6	28-Aug-57	8	5
KS	MORTON	PB13-8	13-Sep-57	1	5
KS	NEOSHO	UK7-9	03-May-53	7	1
KS	NESS	TP7-3	31-Mar-55	1	2
KS	NESS	PB4-10	14-Jul-57	4	2
KS	OSBORNE	TS3-9	30-Apr-52	4	2
KS	OSBORNE	TP7-3	31-Mar-55	3	2
KS	OTTAWA	TS6-7	31-May-52	4	4
KS	OTTAWA	TP7-3	31-Mar-55	9	4

NATIONAL RANKING AMONG U.S. COUNTIES BY FALLOUT DATE

STATE	COUNTY	SHOT	DATE	RANK FOR DATE	NUMBER OF TIMES IN TOP 10
KS	OTTAWA	TP8-4	12-Apr-55	2	4
KS	OTTAWA	PB13-5	10-Sep-57	2	4
KS	PHILLIPS	TS3-9	30-Apr-52	5	1
KS	RENO	UK7-3	27-Apr-53	7	2
KS	RENO	PB12-3	04-Sep-57	6	2
KS	RICE	TP8-4	12-Apr-55	10	2
KS	RICE	PB13-5	10-Sep-57	4	2
KS	RILEY	TS3-10	01-May-52	8	1
KS	ROOKS	TS3-9	30-Apr-52	6	1
KS	RUSH	TS3-9	30-Apr-52	7	2
KS	RUSH	TP7-3	31-Mar-55	4	2
KS	RUSSELL	TS3-9	30-Apr-52	8	1
KS	SALINE	TP8-4	12-Apr-55	1	2
KS	SALINE	PB13-5	10-Sep-57	7	2
KS	SCOTT	PB13-8	13-Sep-57	2	1
KS	SEDGWICK	TS8-4	08-Jun-52	2	2
KS	SEDGWICK	PB12-3	04-Sep-57	2	2
KS	SEWARD	TS4-4	04-May-52	4	2
KS	SEWARD	UK6-3	20-Apr-53	4	2
KS	SHAWNEE	UK7-9	03-May-53	8	2
KS	SHAWNEE	PB12-4	05-Sep-57	6	2
KS	STAFFORD	TS6-7	31-May-52	2	2
KS	STAFFORD	PB13-5	10-Sep-57	3	2
KS	STANTON	TS2-6	20-Apr-52	9	2
KS	STANTON	TP8-3	11-Apr-55	1	2
KS	STEVENS	TS2-7	21-Apr-52	10	5
KS	STEVENS	TS4-4	04-May-52	5	5
KS	STEVENS	UK6-3	20-Apr-53	5	5
KS	STEVENS	TP7-2	30-Mar-55	1	5
KS	STEVENS	PB13-7	12-Sep-57	2	5
KS	SUMNER	BJ5 6	24-Nov-51	4	3
KS	SUMNER	PB12-3	04-Sep-57	1	3
KS	SUMNER	PB13-9	14-Sep-57	6	3
KS	WICHITA	PB9-6	28-Aug-57	9	1
KS	WILSON	TS7-5	05-Jun-52	7	2
KS	WILSON	PB12-4	05-Sep-57	1	2

NATIONAL RANKING AMONG U.S. COUNTIES BY FALLOUT DATE

STATE	COUNTY	SHOT	DATE	RANK FOR DATE	NUMBER OF TIMES IN TOP 10
KS	WYANDOTTE	TS1-2	02-Apr-52	8	4
KS	WYANDOTTE	UK7-9	03-May-53	9	4
KS	WYANDOTTE	UK11-3	06-Jun-53	5	4
KS	WYANDOTTE	PB15-5	20-Sep-57	2	4
KY	ADAIR	TP10-6	10-May-55	4	2
KY	ADAIR	PB4-5	09-Jul-57	7	2
KY	BATH	PB12-10	11-Sep-57	9	1
KY	BELL	TP6-4	25-Mar-55	9	1
KY	BOYD	TS2-5	19-Apr-52	9	2
KY	BOYD	PB13-7	12-Sep-57	3	2
KY	BOYLE	PB4-5	09-Jul-57	8	2
KY	BOYLE	PB17-2	29-Sep-57	7	2
KY	CALLOWAY	TP4-5	11-Mar-55	5	1
KY	CAMPBELL	PB6-4	27-Jul-57	1	1
KY	CARLISLE	TP4-5	11-Mar-55	1	1
KY	CARTER	TS2-5	19-Apr-52	10	3
KY	CARTER	uk1 8	24-Mar-53	1	3
KY	CARTER	PB13-7	12-Sep-57	4	3
KY	CASEY	PB17-2	29-Sep-57	8	1
KY	CHRISTIAN	PB4-5	09-Jul-57	9	1
KY	CLARK	PB12-10	11-Sep-57	10	1
KY	CLAY	TP6-4	25-Mar-55	10	1
KY	CUMBERLAND	PB4-5	09-Jul-57	1	1
KY	ELLIOTT	PB6-7	30-Jul-57	3	2
KY	ELLIOTT	PB13-7	12-Sep-57	5	2
KY	ESTILL	PB13-7	12-Sep-57	6	2
KY	ESTILL	PB16-10	02-Oct-57	1	2
KY	FLOYD	uk1 8	24-Mar-53	2	4
KY	FLOYD	UK9-4	22-May-53	6	4
KY	FLOYD	PB2-5	22-Jun-57	2	4
KY	FLOYD	PB17-3	30-Sep-57	6	4
KY	GARRARD	PB4-5	09-Jul-57	10	1
KY	GRANT	PB15-7	22-Sep-57	2	1
KY	GRAVES	TP4-5	11-Mar-55	6	1
KY	GREENUP	SE4	09-Jul-62	1	1
KY	HARLAN	UK5-2	12-Apr-53	6	1

NATIONAL RANKING AMONG U.S. COUNTIES BY FALLOUT DATE

STATE	COUNTY	SHOT	DATE	RANK FOR DATE	NUMBER OF TIMES IN TOP 10
KY	HICKMAN	TP4-5	11-Mar-55	7	1
KY	JOHNSON	PB13-7	12-Sep-57	7	2
KY	JOHNSON	PB16-8	30-Sep-57	1	2
KY	KENTON	PB6-4	27-Jul-57	6	1
KY	KNOTT	TS3-6	27-Apr-52	8	2
KY	KNOTT	uk1 8	24-Mar-53	3	2
KY	LAUREL	PB2-5	22-Jun-57	3	1
KY	LAWRENCE	PB13-7	12-Sep-57	8	2
KY	LAWRENCE	SE4	09-Jul-62	2	2
KY	LEE	uk1 8	24-Mar-53	4	1
KY	LESLIE	PB5-8	22-Jul-57	1	2
KY	LESLIE	SE5	10-Jul-62	5	2
KY	LETCHER	uk1 8	24-Mar-53	5	1
KY	LEWIS	TP5-4	15-Mar-55	1	3
KY	LEWIS	PB15-7	22-Sep-57	3	3
KY	LEWIS	SE4	09-Jul-62	3	3
KY	LOGAN	TP5-7	18-Mar-55	1	1
KY	MADISON	PB13-7	12-Sep-57	9	1
KY	MARTIN	uk1 8	24-Mar-53	6	2
KY	MARTIN	PB5-8	22-Jul-57	2	2
KY	MCCRACKEN	TP5-5	16-Mar-55	6	2
KY	MCCRACKEN	TP7-8	05-Apr-55	3	2
KY	MCCREARY	uk1 8	24-Mar-53	7	1
KY	MEADE	UK5-7	17-Apr-53	8	1
KY	MENIFEE	PB6-3	26-Jul-57	3	2
KY	MENIFEE	PB13-7	12-Sep-57	10	2
KY	METCALFE	TS7-6	06-Jun-52	10	1
KY	MONROE	PB17-2	29-Sep-57	9	1
KY	MORGAN	PB6-7	30-Jul-57	4	1
KY	MUHLENBERG	TP10-7	11-May-55	4	1
KY	NELSON	UK5-7	17-Apr-53	9	1
KY	OWSLEY	uk1 8	24-Mar-53	8	1
KY	PENDLETON	PB6-4	27-Jul-57	2	1
KY	PERRY	UK9-4	22-May-53	7	1
KY	POWELL	PB16-10	02-Oct-57	2	2
KY	POWELL	SE4	09-Jul-62	8	2

NATIONAL RANKING AMONG U.S. COUNTIES BY FALLOUT DATE

STATE	COUNTY	SHOT	DATE	RANK FOR DATE	NUMBER OF TIMES IN TOP 10
KY	SIMPSON	uk1 6	22-Mar-53	9	1
KY	TAYLOR	UK5-7	17-Apr-53	10	1
KY	TRIMBLE	SE4	09-Jul-62	4	1
KY	WARREN	TP10-6	10-May-55	8	1
KY	WASHINGTON	TP10-6	10-May-55	6	1
KY	WOODFORD	PB17-2	29-Sep-57	10	1
LA	ACADIA	TS4-8	08-May-52	3	6
LA	ACADIA	UK6-2	19-Apr-53	1	6
LA	ACADIA	UK6-7	24-Apr-53	1	6
LA	ACADIA	UK8-5	12-May-53	6	6
LA	ACADIA	TP6-3	24-Mar-55	7	6
LA	ACADIA	PB3-3	26-Jun-57	1	6
LA	ALLEN	TS4-8	08-May-52	4	5
LA	ALLEN	UK6-2	19-Apr-53	2	5
LA	ALLEN	UK6-7	24-Apr-53	2	5
LA	ALLEN	UK8-5	12-May-53	7	5
LA	ALLEN	TP6-3	24-Mar-55	8	5
LA	ASSUMPTION	PB3-3	26-Jun-57	2	1
LA	AVOYELLES	PB3-3	26-Jun-57	3	1
LA	BEAUREGARD	TS4-8	08-May-52	5	6
LA	BEAUREGARD	TS4-9	09-May-52	6	6
LA	BEAUREGARD	UK6-2	19-Apr-53	3	6
LA	BEAUREGARD	TP6-3	24-Mar-55	9	6
LA	BEAUREGARD	PB1-7	03-Jun-57	6	6
LA	BEAUREGARD	PB3-3	26-Jun-57	4	6
LA	BIENVILLE	TP6-3	24-Mar-55	10	2
LA	BIENVILLE	PB1-8	04-Jun-57	8	2
LA	BOSSIER	PB1-8	04-Jun-57	7	1
LA	CALCASIEU	TS4-8	08-May-52	6	5
LA	CALCASIEU	UK6-2	19-Apr-53	4	5
LA	CALCASIEU	UK6-7	24-Apr-53	3	5
LA	CALCASIEU	UK8-5	12-May-53	8	5
LA	CALCASIEU	PB3-3	26-Jun-57	5	5
LA	CALDWELL	PB1-8	04-Jun-57	10	1
LA	CAMERON	TS4-8	08-May-52	7	5
LA	CAMERON	UK6-2	19-Apr-53	5	5

NATIONAL RANKING AMONG U.S. COUNTIES BY FALLOUT DATE					
STATE	COUNTY	SHOT	DATE	RANK FOR DATE	NUMBER OF TIMES IN TOP 10
LA	CAMERON	UK6-7	24-Apr-53	4	5
LA	CAMERON	UK8-5	12-May-53	9	5
LA	CAMERON	PB3-3	26-Jun-57	6	5
LA	CLAIBORNE	PB1-8	04-Jun-57	3	1
LA	EAST BATON R	PB3-3	26-Jun-57	7	1
LA	EVANGELINE	TS4-8	08-May-52	8	5
LA	EVANGELINE	UK6-2	19-Apr-53	6	5
LA	EVANGELINE	UK6-7	24-Apr-53	5	5
LA	EVANGELINE	UK8-5	12-May-53	10	5
LA	EVANGELINE	PB3-3	26-Jun-57	8	5
LA	GRANT	TS4-8	08-May-52	9	5
LA	GRANT	TS4-9	09-May-52	1	5
LA	GRANT	UK6-2	19-Apr-53	7	5
LA	GRANT	TP8-3	11-Apr-55	5	5
LA	GRANT	PB3-3	26-Jun-57	9	5
LA	IBERIA	TP10-7	11-May-55	1	3
LA	IBERIA	PB3-3	26-Jun-57	10	3
LA	IBERIA	PB12-9	10-Sep-57	3	3
LA	JEFFERSON DA	TS4-8	08-May-52	10	2
LA	JEFFERSON DA	UK6-2	19-Apr-53	8	2
LA	LA SALLE	UK7-4	28-Apr-53	8	3
LA	LA SALLE	TP5-2	13-Mar-55	2	3
LA	LA SALLE	TP8-3	11-Apr-55	7	3
LA	LAFAYETTE	UK6-2	19-Apr-53	9	3
LA	LAFAYETTE	TP10-7	11-May-55	6	3
LA	LAFAYETTE	PB12-9	10-Sep-57	5	3
LA	LAFOURCHE	PB12-6	07-Sep-57	1	1
LA	LIVINGSTON	TS6-5	29-May-52	4	1
LA	MADISON	UK7-4	28-Apr-53	6	3
LA	MADISON	TP5-2	13-Mar-55	10	3
LA	MADISON	PB12-6	07-Sep-57	8	3
LA	ORLEANS	PB12-9	10-Sep-57	2	1
LA	RAPIDES	UK6-2	19-Apr-53	10	2
LA	RAPIDES	UK6-7	24-Apr-53	6	2
LA	SABINE	UK6-7	24-Apr-53	7	2
LA	SABINE	PB1-7	03-Jun-57	8	2

NATIONAL RANKING AMONG U.S. COUNTIES BY FALLOUT DATE

STATE	COUNTY	SHOT	DATE	RANK FOR DATE	NUMBER OF TIMES IN TOP 10
LA	ST CHARLES	PB12-6	07-Sep-57	2	1
LA	ST HELENA	PB12-9	10-Sep-57	4	1
LA	ST JAMES	PB1-7	03-Jun-57	7	1
LA	ST JOHN THE	PB1-7	03-Jun-57	5	1
LA	TANGIPAHOA	UK6-6	23-Apr-53	2	2
LA	TANGIPAHOA	PB12-9	10-Sep-57	1	2
LA	TENSAS	UK7-4	28-Apr-53	7	1
LA	TERREBONNE	PB1-7	03-Jun-57	2	1
LA	VERMILION	UK4-1	06-Apr-53	2	2
LA	VERMILION	UK6-7	24-Apr-53	8	2
LA	VERNON	TS4-9	09-May-52	2	2
LA	VERNON	UK6-7	24-Apr-53	9	2
LA	WASHINGTON	TP8-5	13-Apr-55	1	1
LA	WEBSTER	PB1-8	04-Jun-57	4	1
MA	BARNS	UK4-2	07-Apr-53	10	2
MA	BARNS	UK4-5	10-Apr-53	9	2
MA	BARNSTABLE	UK4-7	12-Apr-53	10	1
MA	BERKSHIRE	UK7-6	30-Apr-53	6	3
MA	BERKSHIRE	UK7-8	02-May-53	1	3
MA	BERKSHIRE	TP7-6	03-Apr-55	2	3
MA	BRISTOL	UK4-2	07-Apr-53	3	2
MA	BRISTOL	UK5-9	19-Apr-53	4	2
MA	DUKES	UK1-10	26-Mar-53	7	3
MA	DUKES	UK4-2	07-Apr-53	9	3
MA	DUKES	UK5-9	19-Apr-53	5	3
MA	ESSEX	R1-2	29-Jan-51	9	7
MA	ESSEX	TS8-4	08-Jun-52	10	7
MA	ESSEX	UK4-3	08-Apr-53	8	7
MA	ESSEX	UK4-4	09-Apr-53	3	7
MA	ESSEX	UK4-5	10-Apr-53	10	7
MA	ESSEX	UK5-3	13-Apr-53	6	7
MA	ESSEX	UK5-6	16-Apr-53	4	7
MA	FRANKLIN	UK7-8	02-May-53	2	1
MA	HAMPDEN	UK4-7	12-Apr-53	7	3
MA	HAMPDEN	TP9-7	20-Apr-55	7	3
MA	HAMPDEN	PB5-6	20-Jul-57	9	3

NATIONAL RANKING AMONG U.S. COUNTIES BY FALLOUT DATE

STATE	COUNTY	SHOT	DATE	RANK FOR DATE	NUMBER OF TIMES IN TOP 10
MA	HAMPSHIRE	UK4-7	12-Apr-53	8	3
MA	HAMPSHIRE	TP4-6	12-Mar-55	1	3
MA	HAMPSHIRE	PB11-5	04-Sep-57	1	3
MA	MIDDLESEX	R1-2	29-Jan-51	10	7
MA	MIDDLESEX	R2-6	07-Feb-51	4	7
MA	MIDDLESEX	UK4-2	07-Apr-53	5	7
MA	MIDDLESEX	UK4-4	09-Apr-53	1	7
MA	MIDDLESEX	UK4-5	10-Apr-53	1	7
MA	MIDDLESEX	UK5-3	13-Apr-53	7	7
MA	MIDDLESEX	UK5-6	16-Apr-53	5	7
MA	NANTUCKET	UK4-4	09-Apr-53	2	4
MA	NANTUCKET	UK4-6	11-Apr-53	1	4
MA	NANTUCKET	UK4-7	12-Apr-53	1	4
MA	NANTUCKET	UK5-5	15-Apr-53	1	4
MA	NORFOLK	TS5-5	11-May-52	1	6
MA	NORFOLK	UK4-2	07-Apr-53	2	6
MA	NORFOLK	UK4-3	08-Apr-53	9	6
MA	NORFOLK	UK4-4	09-Apr-53	4	6
MA	NORFOLK	UK5-3	13-Apr-53	8	6
MA	NORFOLK	UK5-6	16-Apr-53	6	6
MA	PLYMOUTH	UK4-2	07-Apr-53	1	3
MA	PLYMOUTH	UK5-3	13-Apr-53	9	3
MA	PLYMOUTH	UK5-6	16-Apr-53	7	3
MA	SUFFOLK	TS5-5	11-May-52	2	2
MA	SUFFOLK	UK4-2	07-Apr-53	4	2
MA	WORCESTER	UK1-10	26-Mar-53	6	2
MA	WORCESTER	UK5-9	19-Apr-53	2	2
MD	ANNE ARUNDEL	TS3-5	26-Apr-52	6	3
MD	ANNE ARUNDEL	PB8-7	24-Aug-57	1	3
MD	ANNE ARUNDEL	PB12-8	09-Sep-57	10	3
MD	CALVERT	TS3-5	26-Apr-52	10	3
MD	CALVERT	TP9-10	23-Apr-55	1	3
MD	CALVERT	PB8-7	24-Aug-57	2	3
MD	CAROLINE	UK2-9	01-Apr-53	2	1
MD	CHARLES	BJ-2 3	01-Nov-51	6	3
MD	CHARLES	TP9-10	23-Apr-55	3	3

NATIONAL RANKING AMONG U.S. COUNTIES BY FALLOUT DATE

STATE	COUNTY	SHOT	DATE	RANK FOR DATE	NUMBER OF TIMES IN TOP 10
MD	CHARLES	PB8-7	24-Aug-57	3	3
MD	GARRETT	UK2-9	01-Apr-53	3	1
MD	HARFORD	UK10-6	30-May-53	1	1
MD	HOWARD	PB8-7	24-Aug-57	4	1
MD	KENT	TP9-7	20-Apr-55	8	1
MD	MONTGOMERY	PB12-8	09-Sep-57	9	1
MD	PRINCE GEORG	R2-6	07-Feb-51	1	3
MD	PRINCE GEORG	BJ-2 3	01-Nov-51	8	3
MD	PRINCE GEORG	TS3-5	26-Apr-52	2	3
MD	QUEEN ANNES	PB15-8	23-Sep-57	2	1
MD	SOMERSET	BJ4-7	11-Nov-51	1	1
MD	ST MARYS	TS3-5	26-Apr-52	4	2
MD	ST MARYS	PB8-7	24-Aug-57	5	2
MD	TALBOT	TS3-5	26-Apr-52	5	2
MD	TALBOT	UK2-9	01-Apr-53	4	2
MD	WASHINGTON	R2-6	07-Feb-51	5	2
MD	WASHINGTON	uk3 8	07-Apr-53	3	2
MD	WICOMICO	UK2-9	01-Apr-53	5	1
MD	WORCESTER	BJ4-6	10-Nov-51	4	2
MD	WORCESTER	PB5-8	22-Jul-57	3	2
ME	ANDROSCOGGIN	UK1-10	26-Mar-53	10	9
ME	ANDROSCOGGIN	UK4-4	09-Apr-53	5	9
ME	ANDROSCOGGIN	UK5-5	15-Apr-53	2	9
ME	ANDROSCOGGIN	UK5-6	16-Apr-53	8	9
ME	ANDROSCOGGIN	UK6-8	25-Apr-53	1	9
ME	ANDROSCOGGIN	TP8-7	15-Apr-55	10	9
ME	ANDROSCOGGIN	TP8-8	16-Apr-55	9	9
ME	ANDROSCOGGIN	PB5-6	20-Jul-57	10	9
ME	ANDROSCOGGIN	PB16-8	30-Sep-57	4	9
ME	AROOSTOOK	R1-4	31-Jan-51	5	5
ME	AROOSTOOK	BJ-2 4	02-Nov-51	1	5
ME	AROOSTOOK	TS6-9	02-Jun-52	4	5
ME	AROOSTOOK	UK2-4	27-Mar-53	1	5
ME	AROOSTOOK	PB16-8	30-Sep-57	5	5
ME	CUMBERLAND	BJ2-2	31-Oct-51	1	7
ME	CUMBERLAND	UK4-4	09-Apr-53	6	7

NATIONAL RANKING AMONG U.S. COUNTIES BY FALLOUT DATE

STATE	COUNTY	SHOT	DATE	RANK FOR DATE	NUMBER OF TIMES IN TOP 10
ME	CUMBERLAND	UK5-3	13-Apr-53	10	7
ME	CUMBERLAND	UK5-5	15-Apr-53	3	7
ME	CUMBERLAND	UK5-6	16-Apr-53	9	7
ME	CUMBERLAND	UK6-8	25-Apr-53	2	7
ME	CUMBERLAND	TP8-8	16-Apr-55	1	7
ME	FRANKLIN	R1-4	31-Jan-51	7	5
ME	FRANKLIN	UK2-4	27-Mar-53	7	5
ME	FRANKLIN	UK5-6	16-Apr-53	10	5
ME	FRANKLIN	UK6-8	25-Apr-53	3	5
ME	FRANKLIN	TP8-8	16-Apr-55	10	5
ME	HANCOCK	ts1 5	05-Apr-52	6	5
ME	HANCOCK	TS6-9	02-Jun-52	2	5
ME	HANCOCK	UK1-10	26-Mar-53	3	5
ME	HANCOCK	UK2-4	27-Mar-53	5	5
ME	HANCOCK	UK7-7	01-May-53	4	5
ME	KENNEBEC	R1-3	30-Jan-51	2	5
ME	KENNEBEC	TS6-9	02-Jun-52	10	5
ME	KENNEBEC	UK5-6	16-Apr-53	1	5
ME	KENNEBEC	UK6-8	25-Apr-53	4	5
ME	KENNEBEC	TP8-8	16-Apr-55	2	5
ME	KNOX	R1-3	30-Jan-51	3	6
ME	KNOX	ts1 5	05-Apr-52	7	6
ME	KNOX	TS6-9	02-Jun-52	8	6
ME	KNOX	UK1-10	26-Mar-53	1	6
ME	KNOX	UK2-4	27-Mar-53	9	6
ME	KNOX	TP8-8	16-Apr-55	3	6
ME	LINCOLN	R1-3	30-Jan-51	4	5
ME	LINCOLN	TS6-9	02-Jun-52	9	5
ME	LINCOLN	UK5-6	16-Apr-53	2	5
ME	LINCOLN	UK6-8	25-Apr-53	5	5
ME	LINCOLN	TP8-7	15-Apr-55	2	5
ME	OXFORD	R1-4	31-Jan-51	8	6
ME	OXFORD	BJ2-2	31-Oct-51	2	6
ME	OXFORD	UK4-4	09-Apr-53	7	6
ME	OXFORD	UK5-5	15-Apr-53	4	6
ME	OXFORD	UK6-8	25-Apr-53	6	6

NATIONAL RANKING AMONG U.S. COUNTIES BY FALLOUT DATE

STATE	COUNTY	SHOT	DATE	RANK FOR DATE	NUMBER OF TIMES IN TOP 10
ME	OXFORD	PB16-8	30-Sep-57	6	6
ME	PENOBSCOT	R1-4	31-Jan-51	9	7
ME	PENOBSCOT	R2-6	07-Feb-51	3	7
ME	PENOBSCOT	BJ-2 4	02-Nov-51	4	7
ME	PENOBSCOT	ts1 5	05-Apr-52	1	7
ME	PENOBSCOT	UK2-4	27-Mar-53	3	7
ME	PENOBSCOT	UK7-7	01-May-53	5	7
ME	PENOBSCOT	PB16-8	30-Sep-57	7	7
ME	PISCATAQUIS	R1-4	31-Jan-51	10	8
ME	PISCATAQUIS	BJ-2 4	02-Nov-51	5	8
ME	PISCATAQUIS	ts1 5	05-Apr-52	2	8
ME	PISCATAQUIS	TS4-8	08-May-52	1	8
ME	PISCATAQUIS	TS6-9	02-Jun-52	5	8
ME	PISCATAQUIS	UK2-4	27-Mar-53	4	8
ME	PISCATAQUIS	UK11-5	08-Jun-53	3	8
ME	PISCATAQUIS	PB16-8	30-Sep-57	8	8
ME	SAGADAHOC	BJ2-2	31-Oct-51	3	5
ME	SAGADAHOC	UK4-4	09-Apr-53	8	5
ME	SAGADAHOC	UK5-6	16-Apr-53	3	5
ME	SAGADAHOC	UK6-8	25-Apr-53	7	5
ME	SAGADAHOC	TP8-8	16-Apr-55	4	5
ME	SOMERSET	ts1 5	05-Apr-52	3	5
ME	SOMERSET	UK2-4	27-Mar-53	6	5
ME	SOMERSET	UK7-7	01-May-53	7	5
ME	SOMERSET	TP8-7	15-Apr-55	3	5
ME	SOMERSET	PB16-8	30-Sep-57	9	5
ME	WALDO	R1-3	30-Jan-51	5	7
ME	WALDO	ts1 5	05-Apr-52	8	7
ME	WALDO	TS6-9	02-Jun-52	6	7
ME	WALDO	UK1-10	26-Mar-53	2	7
ME	WALDO	UK2-4	27-Mar-53	8	7
ME	WALDO	UK11-5	08-Jun-53	4	7
ME	WALDO	TP8-8	16-Apr-55	5	7
ME	WASHINGTON	R1-3	30-Jan-51	6	5
ME	WASHINGTON	BJ-2 4	02-Nov-51	6	5
ME	WASHINGTON	TS6-9	02-Jun-52	1	5

NATIONAL RANKING AMONG U.S. COUNTIES BY FALLOUT DATE

STATE	COUNTY	SHOT	DATE	RANK FOR DATE	NUMBER OF TIMES IN TOP 10
ME	WASHINGTON	UK2-4	27-Mar-53	2	5
ME	WASHINGTON	UK7-7	01-May-53	1	5
ME	YORK	UK6-8	25-Apr-53	8	1
MI	ALCONA	UK10-5	29-May-53	8	2
MI	ALCONA	UK10-10	03-Jun-53	1	2
MI	ALGER	TP9-4	17-Apr-55	1	1
MI	ALLEGAN	PB15-6	21-Sep-57	6	1
MI	ALPENA	UK10-5	29-May-53	7	1
MI	ANTRIM	UK10-10	03-Jun-53	2	1
MI	ARENAC	UK10-10	03-Jun-53	3	1
MI	BARAGA	UK10-4	28-May-53	3	1
MI	BAY	UK10-10	03-Jun-53	4	1
MI	BERRIEN	PB8-6	23-Aug-57	3	1
MI	CASS	PB8-6	23-Aug-57	4	2
MI	CASS	PB15-6	21-Sep-57	7	2
MI	CHARLEVOIX	UK10-10	03-Jun-53	5	1
MI	CHEBOYGAN	UK10-10	03-Jun-53	6	1
MI	CHIPPEWA	TS8-4	08-Jun-52	1	3
MI	CHIPPEWA	UK10-5	29-May-53	6	3
MI	CHIPPEWA	PB15-6	21-Sep-57	8	3
MI	CRAWFORD	UK10-10	03-Jun-53	7	1
MI	EATON	TP9-2	15-Apr-55	10	1
MI	EMMET	TP8-5	13-Apr-55	2	2
MI	EMMET	TP9-4	17-Apr-55	9	2
MI	GLADWIN	UK10-10	03-Jun-53	8	1
MI	GOGEBIC	PB11-3	02-Sep-57	7	1
MI	GRAND TRAVER	UK9-6	24-May-53	5	1
MI	HILLSDALE	PB15-6	21-Sep-57	9	1
MI	HOUGHTON	PB11-3	02-Sep-57	8	1
MI	HURON	BJ4-5	09-Nov-51	3	5
MI	HURON	BJ4-8	12-Nov-51	10	5
MI	HURON	UK10-6	30-May-53	9	5
MI	HURON	UK10-10	03-Jun-53	9	5
MI	HURON	TP9-2	15-Apr-55	7	5
MI	IOSCO	UK10-10	03-Jun-53	10	1
MI	IRON	PB16-2	24-Sep-57	5	1

STATE	COUNTY	SHOT	DATE	RANK FOR DATE	NUMBER OF TIMES IN TOP 10
MI	ISABELLA	UK9-6	24-May-53	6	2
MI	ISABELLA	PB15-6	21-Sep-57	10	2
MI	LAKE	UK9-6	24-May-53	1	1
MI	LAPEER	BJ4-5	09-Nov-51	4	2
MI	LAPEER	TP9-4	17-Apr-55	5	2
MI	LEELANAU	TP9-4	17-Apr-55	6	1
MI	LUCE	TS8-4	08-Jun-52	4	2
MI	LUCE	UK10-6	30-May-53	10	2
MI	MACKINAC	TS8-4	08-Jun-52	5	2
MI	MACKINAC	TP9-4	17-Apr-55	7	2
MI	MACOMB	BJ3-5	05-Nov-51	6	3
MI	MACOMB	BJ4-5	09-Nov-51	5	3
MI	MACOMB	TP9-2	15-Apr-55	5	3
MI	MANISTEE	UK9-6	24-May-53	2	1
MI	MENOMINEE	UK10-4	28-May-53	2	1
MI	MONROE	TP5-4	15-Mar-55	5	1
MI	MONTMORENCY	TP9-4	17-Apr-55	2	1
MI	MUSKEGON	UK9-6	24-May-53	4	1
MI	OAKLAND	BJ4-5	09-Nov-51	6	2
MI	OAKLAND	TP5-4	15-Mar-55	6	2
MI	OCEANA	UK9-6	24-May-53	7	1
MI	OGEMAW	TP9-4	17-Apr-55	10	1
MI	ONTONAGON	PB11-3	02-Sep-57	9	1
MI	PRESQUE ISLE	UK10-5	29-May-53	3	1
MI	SANILAC	BJ4-5	09-Nov-51	7	2
MI	SANILAC	TP9-4	17-Apr-55	3	2
MI	ST CLAIR	BJ4-5	09-Nov-51	8	2
MI	ST CLAIR	TP9-4	17-Apr-55	4	2
MI	ST JOSEPH	PB8-6	23-Aug-57	5	1
MI	TUSCOLA	TP9-4	17-Apr-55	8	1
MI	WAYNE	BJ3-5	05-Nov-51	7	6
MI	WAYNE	BJ4-5	09-Nov-51	9	6
MI	WAYNE	BJ4-8	12-Nov-51	1	6
MI	WAYNE	TP5-4	15-Mar-55	8	6
MI	WAYNE	TP9-2	15-Apr-55	1	6
MI	WAYNE	PB4-3	07-Jul-57	10	6

NATIONAL RANKING AMONG U.S. COUNTIES BY FALLOUT DATE

STATE	COUNTY	SHOT	DATE	RANK FOR DATE	NUMBER OF TIMES IN TOP 10
MI	WEXFORD	UK9-6	24-May-53	8	1
MN	AITKIN	UK10-4	28-May-53	5	4
MN	AITKIN	PB4-7	11-Jul-57	6	4
MN	AITKIN	PB5-5	19-Jul-57	1	4
MN	AITKIN	PB11-3	02-Sep-57	10	4
MN	ANOKA	UK10-4	28-May-53	4	2
MN	ANOKA	PB5-5	19-Jul-57	2	2
MN	BECKER	PB6-10	02-Aug-57	3	1
MN	BENTON	PB5-5	19-Jul-57	3	1
MN	BIG STONE	PB6-10	02-Aug-57	4	1
MN	BROWN	UK7-5	29-Apr-53	8	1
MN	CARLTON	UK10-4	28-May-53	7	4
MN	CARLTON	PB4-7	11-Jul-57	7	4
MN	CARLTON	PB5-5	19-Jul-57	4	4
MN	CARLTON	PB11-3	02-Sep-57	1	4
MN	CARVER	PB5-5	19-Jul-57	5	2
MN	CARVER	PB6-9	01-Aug-57	1	2
MN	CHIPPEWA	PB6-9	01-Aug-57	2	2
MN	CHIPPEWA	PB6-10	02-Aug-57	5	2
MN	CHISAGO	UK10-4	28-May-53	9	2
MN	CHISAGO	PB4-7	11-Jul-57	9	2
MN	COTTONWOOD	UK7-5	29-Apr-53	2	1
MN	DAKOTA	PB5-5	19-Jul-57	6	2
MN	DAKOTA	PB6-10	02-Aug-57	6	2
MN	DODGE	TS3-8	29-Apr-52	2	1
MN	DOUGLAS	PB6-9	01-Aug-57	3	1
MN	FARIBAULT	SE3	08-Jul-62	9	1
MN	FREEBORN	PB5-5	19-Jul-57	7	1
MN	GOODHUE	PB4-3	07-Jul-57	3	2
MN	GOODHUE	PB5-5	19-Jul-57	8	2
MN	GRANT	PB6-10	02-Aug-57	7	1
MN	ISANTI	UK10-4	28-May-53	10	3
MN	ISANTI	PB4-7	11-Jul-57	10	3
MN	ISANTI	PB6-9	01-Aug-57	6	3
MN	ITASCA	PB5-5	19-Jul-57	9	1
MN	JACKSON	UK7-5	29-Apr-53	1	1

NATIONAL RANKING AMONG U.S. COUNTIES BY FALLOUT DATE

STATE	COUNTY	SHOT	DATE	RANK FOR DATE	NUMBER OF TIMES IN TOP 10
MN	KANDIYOHI	PB6-7	30-Jul-57	5	2
MN	KANDIYOHI	PB6-10	02-Aug-57	8	2
MN	KITTSON	TP9-3	16-Apr-55	2	2
MN	KITTSON	PB6-9	01-Aug-57	7	2
MN	LAKE	PB11-3	02-Sep-57	2	1
MN	LE SUEUR	PB4-3	07-Jul-57	4	3
MN	LE SUEUR	PB5-5	19-Jul-57	10	3
MN	LE SUEUR	PB6-10	02-Aug-57	9	3
MN	MAHNOMEN	PB11-3	02-Sep-57	3	1
MN	MARTIN	PB6-7	30-Jul-57	6	1
MN	MCLEOD	PB6-10	02-Aug-57	10	1
MN	MEEKER	PB6-7	30-Jul-57	7	1
MN	MOWER	TS3-8	29-Apr-52	3	2
MN	MOWER	SE3	08-Jul-62	10	2
MN	POPE	PB6-9	01-Aug-57	8	1
MN	REDWOOD	UK7-5	29-Apr-53	5	1
MN	ROSEAU	TP9-3	16-Apr-55	4	1
MN	SCOTT	PB6-7	30-Jul-57	8	1
MN	TODD	uk1 4	20-Mar-53	6	2
MN	TODD	PB11-3	02-Sep-57	4	2
MN	WADENA	PB11-3	02-Sep-57	5	1
MN	WASECA	PB4-3	07-Jul-57	5	1
MN	WATONWAN	UK7-5	29-Apr-53	10	2
MN	WATONWAN	UK10-4	28-May-53	6	2
MO	ADAIR	PB4-10	14-Jul-57	10	2
MO	ADAIR	PB18-8	14-Oct-57	1	2
MO	ANDREW	UK2-5	28-Mar-53	6	4
MO	ANDREW	UK2-6	29-Mar-53	9	4
MO	ANDREW	UK7-9	03-May-53	10	4
MO	ANDREW	UK11-3	06-Jun-53	6	4
MO	ATCHISON	UK11-5	08-Jun-53	6	1
MO	AUDRAIN	R1-2	29-Jan-51	6	2
MO	AUDRAIN	TS7-3	03-Jun-52	9	2
MO	BARRY	ts1 3	03-Apr-52	9	3
MO	BARRY	UK2-10	02-Apr-53	7	3
MO	BARRY	UK3-3	02-Apr-53	7	3

NATIONAL RANKING AMONG U.S. COUNTIES BY FALLOUT DATE					
STATE	COUNTY	SHOT	DATE	RANK FOR DATE	NUMBER OF TIMES IN TOP 10
MO	BATES	TS1-2	02-Apr-52	9	2
MO	BATES	PB4-5	09-Jul-57	4	2
MO	BENTON	PB15-5	20-Sep-57	3	1
MO	BOLLINGER	PB15-7	22-Sep-57	5	1
MO	BUCHANAN	UK2-5	28-Mar-53	4	4
MO	BUCHANAN	UK2-6	29-Mar-53	4	4
MO	BUCHANAN	UK7-9	03-May-53	2	4
MO	BUCHANAN	UK11-3	06-Jun-53	1	4
MO	CALDWELL	UK7-9	03-May-53	1	2
MO	CALDWELL	PB8-3	20-Aug-57	9	2
MO	CALLAWAY	PB3-6	29-Jun-57	4	2
MO	CALLAWAY	PB4-4	08-Jul-57	4	2
MO	CAMDEN	TP5-5	16-Mar-55	7	3
MO	CAMDEN	TP10-3	07-May-55	1	3
MO	CAMDEN	PB15-5	20-Sep-57	4	3
MO	CARROLL	UK11-5	08-Jun-53	7	3
MO	CARROLL	PB15-5	20-Sep-57	5	3
MO	CARROLL	PB18-8	14-Oct-57	2	3
MO	CARTER	TP5-5	16-Mar-55	8	1
MO	CASS	UK2-6	29-Mar-53	1	2
MO	CASS	PB15-5	20-Sep-57	6	2
MO	CEDAR	TS1-2	02-Apr-52	10	2
MO	CEDAR	PB12-4	05-Sep-57	5	2
MO	CHARITON	PB15-5	20-Sep-57	7	1
MO	CHRISTIAN	ts1 3	03-Apr-52	10	1
MO	CLARK	PB9-3	25-Aug-57	4	1
MO	CLAY	TS1-2	02-Apr-52	4	3
MO	CLAY	UK2-6	29-Mar-53	3	3
MO	CLAY	UK7-9	03-May-53	3	3
MO	CLINTON	UK2-5	28-Mar-53	1	2
MO	CLINTON	PB15-4	19-Sep-57	7	2
MO	COLE	PB4-4	08-Jul-57	2	2
MO	COLE	PB4-6	10-Jul-57	3	2
MO	COOPER	PB4-4	08-Jul-57	9	3
MO	COOPER	PB4-6	10-Jul-57	1	3
MO	COOPER	PB15-5	20-Sep-57	8	3

NATIONAL RANKING AMONG U.S. COUNTIES BY FALLOUT DATE

STATE	COUNTY	SHOT	DATE	RANK FOR DATE	NUMBER OF TIMES IN TOP 10
MO	DALLAS	PB3-6	29-Jun-57	7	3
MO	DALLAS	PB4-5	09-Jul-57	5	3
MO	DALLAS	PB4-6	10-Jul-57	4	3
MO	DAVIESS	UK2-6	29-Mar-53	10	4
MO	DAVIESS	UK11-5	08-Jun-53	8	4
MO	DAVIESS	PB8-3	20-Aug-57	10	4
MO	DAVIESS	PB15-4	19-Sep-57	8	4
MO	DE KALB	UK11-5	08-Jun-53	1	1
MO	DOUGLAS	TP10-3	07-May-55	9	1
MO	DUNKLIN	uk1 4	20-Mar-53	1	2
MO	DUNKLIN	TP10-7	11-May-55	3	2
MO	FRANKLIN	PB3-6	29-Jun-57	1	1
MO	GASCONADE	PB3-5	28-Jun-57	1	2
MO	GASCONADE	PB4-4	08-Jul-57	8	2
MO	GENTRY	UK11-5	08-Jun-53	2	2
MO	GENTRY	PB15-4	19-Sep-57	9	2
MO	HENRY	TP10-3	07-May-55	10	2
MO	HENRY	PB15-5	20-Sep-57	9	2
MO	HICKORY	PB4-6	10-Jul-57	6	2
MO	HICKORY	PB15-5	20-Sep-57	10	2
MO	HOWARD	UK2-5	28-Mar-53	8	1
MO	IRON	PB3-6	29-Jun-57	5	2
MO	IRON	PB15-7	22-Sep-57	6	2
MO	JOHNSON	UK2-6	29-Mar-53	5	2
MO	JOHNSON	TP3-3	03-Mar-55	2	2
MO	KNOX	TS7-3	03-Jun-52	1	1
MO	LACLEDE	TP10-3	07-May-55	3	2
MO	LACLEDE	PB4-6	10-Jul-57	2	2
MO	LEWIS	TS7-3	03-Jun-52	2	1
MO	LINCOLN	TP7-7	04-Apr-55	7	1
MO	LIVINGSTON	PB15-4	19-Sep-57	10	1
MO	MACON	TS7-3	03-Jun-52	10	2
MO	MACON	uk1 4	20-Mar-53	10	2
MO	MARIES	uk1 4	20-Mar-53	5	3
MO	MARIES	TP5-5	16-Mar-55	9	3
MO	MARIES	PB4-4	08-Jul-57	6	3

NATIONAL RANKING AMONG U.S. COUNTIES BY FALLOUT DATE

STATE	COUNTY	SHOT	DATE	RANK FOR DATE	NUMBER OF TIMES IN TOP 10
MO	MARION	PB18-8	14-Oct-57	3	1
MO	MCDONALD	UK2-10	02-Apr-53	8	2
MO	MCDONALD	UK3-3	02-Apr-53	8	2
MO	MILLER	PB4-4	08-Jul-57	7	2
MO	MILLER	PB4-6	10-Jul-57	5	2
MO	MONITEAU	PB4-4	08-Jul-57	3	1
MO	MONROE	PB18-8	14-Oct-57	4	1
MO	MORGAN	TP10-3	07-May-55	2	4
MO	MORGAN	PB3-6	29-Jun-57	8	4
MO	MORGAN	PB4-4	08-Jul-57	10	4
MO	MORGAN	PB4-6	10-Jul-57	9	4
MO	NEW MADRID	TP4-5	11-Mar-55	8	1
MO	NEWTON	UK2-10	02-Apr-53	9	2
MO	NEWTON	UK3-3	02-Apr-53	9	2
MO	NODAWAY	UK11-5	08-Jun-53	9	1
MO	OSAGE	TP10-3	07-May-55	4	4
MO	OSAGE	PB3-6	29-Jun-57	2	4
MO	OSAGE	PB4-4	08-Jul-57	1	4
MO	OSAGE	PB4-6	10-Jul-57	7	4
MO	OZARK	uk1 4	20-Mar-53	8	1
MO	PETTIS	TP3-3	03-Mar-55	3	2
MO	PETTIS	TP10-3	07-May-55	6	2
MO	PHELPS	PB3-6	29-Jun-57	6	1
MO	PIKE	R1-2	29-Jan-51	7	2
MO	PIKE	TP7-7	04-Apr-55	1	2
MO	PLATTE	UK2-6	29-Mar-53	6	2
MO	PLATTE	UK7-9	03-May-53	4	2
MO	POLK	PB4-5	09-Jul-57	6	1
MO	PULASKI	TP5-5	16-Mar-55	10	1
MO	RALLS	TS7-3	03-Jun-52	8	2
MO	RALLS	PB6-4	27-Jul-57	5	2
MO	RAY	UK2-5	28-Mar-53	2	1
MO	SCOTLAND	TS7-3	03-Jun-52	5	1
MO	SCOTT	TP10-7	11-May-55	8	1
MO	SHANNON	TP7-8	05-Apr-55	4	1
MO	SHELBY	PB18-8	14-Oct-57	5	1

NATIONAL RANKING AMONG U.S. COUNTIES BY FALLOUT DATE

STATE	COUNTY	SHOT	DATE	RANK FOR DATE	NUMBER OF TIMES IN TOP 10
MO	ST CHARLES	TP9-7	20-Apr-55	9	1
MO	ST FRANCOIS	PB3-5	28-Jun-57	8	2
MO	ST FRANCOIS	PB3-6	29-Jun-57	9	2
MO	ST LOUIS	TP9-7	20-Apr-55	10	1
MO	STONE	UK9-9	27-May-53	1	1
MO	TANEY	uk1 4	20-Mar-53	4	1
MO	TEXAS	TP5-5	16-Mar-55	2	2
MO	TEXAS	PB4-6	10-Jul-57	10	2
MO	VERNON	PB12-4	05-Sep-57	3	1
MO	WARREN	PB3-6	29-Jun-57	10	1
MO	WASHINGTON	PB3-6	29-Jun-57	3	2
MO	WASHINGTON	PB15-7	22-Sep-57	7	2
MO	WAYNE	PB15-7	22-Sep-57	8	1
MO	WEBSTER	TP10-3	07-May-55	5	1
MO	WORTH	UK2-5	28-Mar-53	3	1
MO	WRIGHT	TP10-3	07-May-55	8	2
MO	WRIGHT	PB4-6	10-Jul-57	8	2
MS	ADAMS	UK7-4	28-Apr-53	1	2
MS	ADAMS	PB12-9	10-Sep-57	8	2
MS	CARROLL	TP6-3	24-Mar-55	3	2
MS	CARROLL	PB16-9	01-Oct-57	6	2
MS	CHICKASAW	PB17-5	02-Oct-57	2	1
MS	CHOCTAW	TS5-4	10-May-52	2	1
MS	CLAIBORNE	UK7-4	28-Apr-53	3	2
MS	CLAIBORNE	TP5-2	13-Mar-55	9	2
MS	CLAY	PB12-6	07-Sep-57	5	1
MS	COAHOMA	TP7-4	01-Apr-55	2	1
MS	COVINGTON	PB12-6	07-Sep-57	3	1
MS	DE SOTO	TP7-4	01-Apr-55	4	1
MS	FORREST	TS6-5	29-May-52	5	1
MS	FRANKLIN	UK4-1	06-Apr-53	3	1
MS	GEORGE	TP8-5	13-Apr-55	5	1
MS	GREENE	TP8-5	13-Apr-55	6	1
MS	GRENADA	PB17-5	02-Oct-57	5	1
MS	HANCOCK	TP10-7	11-May-55	7	1
MS	HINDS	TP5-2	13-Mar-55	4	2

	NATIONAL RANKING AMONG U.S. COUNTIES BY FALLOUT DATE				
STATE	COUNTY	SHOT	DATE	RANK FOR DATE	NUMBER OF TIMES IN TOP 10
MS	HINDS	TP10-4	08-May-55	1	2
MS	HUMPHREYS	TP6-3	24-Mar-55	4	1
MS	ISSAQUENA	UK7-4	28-Apr-53	5	1
MS	JASPER	PB17-5	02-Oct-57	9	1
MS	JEFFERSON	UK7-4	28-Apr-53	4	1
MS	JONES	TS5-4	10-May-52	6	3
MS	JONES	TP5-2	13-Mar-55	3	3
MS	JONES	PB12-6	07-Sep-57	9	3
MS	LAFAYETTE	PB16-9	01-Oct-57	7	1
MS	LAMAR	UK5-5	15-Apr-53	5	2
MS	LAMAR	PB12-6	07-Sep-57	7	2
MS	LAWRENCE	UK5-5	15-Apr-53	6	1
MS	LEAKE	TP6-3	24-Mar-55	5	2
MS	LEAKE	PB16-9	01-Oct-57	8	2
MS	LEE	PB16-9	01-Oct-57	9	1
MS	LINCOLN	UK4-1	06-Apr-53	4	2
MS	LINCOLN	TP8-4	12-Apr-55	7	2
MS	MADISON	UK7-4	28-Apr-53	9	1
MS	MARION	PB12-6	07-Sep-57	6	1
MS	MONROE	BJ01 BAKER 1	28-Oct-51	10	2
MS	MONROE	UK2-4	27-Mar-53	10	2
MS	MONTGOMERY	TP6-3	24-Mar-55	1	1
MS	NESHOBA	TP10-5	09-May-55	3	1
MS	NEWTON	PB17-5	02-Oct-57	8	1
MS	PIKE	TP8-3	11-Apr-55	9	1
MS	QUITMAN	TP7-4	01-Apr-55	1	1
MS	SCOTT	TS5-4	10-May-52	5	2
MS	SCOTT	PB17-5	02-Oct-57	10	2
MS	STONE	TP8-5	13-Apr-55	7	1
MS	SUNFLOWER	TP7-4	01-Apr-55	6	1
MS	TALLAHATCHIE	TP7-4	01-Apr-55	5	1
MS	TATE	TP7-4	01-Apr-55	10	1
MS	TUNICA	TP7-4	01-Apr-55	8	1
MS	UNION	PB16-9	01-Oct-57	2	1
MS	WARREN	UK7-4	28-Apr-53	2	1
MS	WEBSTER	PB12-6	07-Sep-57	4	1

NATIONAL RANKING AMONG U.S. COUNTIES BY FALLOUT DATE

STATE	COUNTY	SHOT	DATE	RANK FOR DATE	NUMBER OF TIMES IN TOP 10
MS	YAZOO	TS5-4	10-May-52	7	2
MS	YAZOO	TP6-3	24-Mar-55	6	2
MT	BEAVERHEAD	TS5-6	12-May-52	2	7
MT	BEAVERHEAD	TS5-7	13-May-52	1	7
MT	BEAVERHEAD	TS5-8	14-May-52	2	7
MT	BEAVERHEAD	TS8-3	07-Jun-52	9	7
MT	BEAVERHEAD	PB6-2	25-Jul-57	6	7
MT	BEAVERHEAD	PB6-3	26-Jul-57	4	7
MT	BEAVERHEAD	PB15-3	18-Sep-57	3	7
MT	BIG HORN	UK8-2	09-May-53	2	3
MT	BIG HORN	UK8-3	10-May-53	1	3
MT	BIG HORN	UK10-7	31-May-53	8	3
MT	BLAINE	TS4-2	02-May-52	2	4
MT	BLAINE	UK8-2	09-May-53	3	4
MT	BLAINE	UK10-7	31-May-53	4	4
MT	BLAINE	PB8-2	19-Aug-57	8	4
MT	BROADWATER	PB6-3	26-Jul-57	5	1
MT	CARBON	TS2-6	20-Apr-52	2	4
MT	CARBON	UK8-2	09-May-53	10	4
MT	CARBON	UK10-7	31-May-53	9	4
MT	CARBON	PB8-2	19-Aug-57	9	4
MT	CARTER	PB6-5	28-Jul-57	2	1
MT	CASCADE	PB6-3	26-Jul-57	6	1
MT	CHOUTEAU	TS4-2	02-May-52	3	6
MT	CHOUTEAU	TS8-1	05-Jun-52	9	6
MT	CHOUTEAU	TS8-2	06-Jun-52	9	6
MT	CHOUTEAU	TS8-4	08-Jun-52	6	6
MT	CHOUTEAU	PB12-2	03-Sep-57	5	6
MT	CHOUTEAU	PB17-6	03-Oct-57	9	6
MT	CUSTER	UK2-2	25-Mar-53	1	5
MT	CUSTER	UK8-1	08-May-53	1	5
MT	CUSTER	UK10-9	02-Jun-53	10	5
MT	CUSTER	PB4-2	06-Jul-57	7	5
MT	CUSTER	PB12-2	03-Sep-57	6	5
MT	DANIELS	UK2-2	25-Mar-53	9	2
MT	DANIELS	UK10-9	02-Jun-53	1	2

NATIONAL RANKING AMONG U.S. COUNTIES BY FALLOUT DATE

STATE	COUNTY	SHOT	DATE	RANK FOR DATE	NUMBER OF TIMES IN TOP 10
MT	DAWSON	UK2-2	25-Mar-53	2	4
MT	DAWSON	UK8-1	08-May-53	3	4
MT	DAWSON	PB5-2	16-Jul-57	7	4
MT	DAWSON	PB12-2	03-Sep-57	2	4
MT	DEER LODGE	TS4-2	02-May-52	4	7
MT	DEER LODGE	TS8-1	05-Jun-52	5	7
MT	DEER LODGE	TS8-2	06-Jun-52	5	7
MT	DEER LODGE	TS8-7	11-Jun-52	1	7
MT	DEER LODGE	PB1-7	03-Jun-57	1	7
MT	DEER LODGE	PB6-2	25-Jul-57	7	7
MT	DEER LODGE	PB17-5	02-Oct-57	6	7
MT	FALLON	UK2-2	25-Mar-53	10	3
MT	FALLON	UK8-1	08-May-53	4	3
MT	FALLON	PB5-3	17-Jul-57	10	3
MT	FERGUS	TS2-5	19-Apr-52	8	7
MT	FERGUS	TS8-3	07-Jun-52	3	7
MT	FERGUS	UK8-2	09-May-53	4	7
MT	FERGUS	UK10-7	31-May-53	5	7
MT	FERGUS	PB4-2	06-Jul-57	8	7
MT	FERGUS	PB6-4	27-Jul-57	9	7
MT	FERGUS	PB8-2	19-Aug-57	10	7
MT	FLATHEAD	TS4-2	02-May-52	5	3
MT	FLATHEAD	TS8-7	11-Jun-52	5	3
MT	FLATHEAD	TS8-8	12-Jun-52	7	3
MT	GALLATIN	TS4-2	02-May-52	6	5
MT	GALLATIN	TS4-7	07-May-52	1	5
MT	GALLATIN	TS5-6	12-May-52	3	5
MT	GALLATIN	TS8-7	11-Jun-52	7	5
MT	GALLATIN	PB1-6	02-Jun-57	9	5
MT	GARFIELD	UK8-2	09-May-53	1	4
MT	GARFIELD	UK10-3	27-May-53	6	4
MT	GARFIELD	UK10-7	31-May-53	1	4
MT	GARFIELD	UK10-8	01-Jun-53	1	4
MT	GLACIER	TS8-7	11-Jun-52	2	2
MT	GLACIER	TS8-8	12-Jun-52	9	2
MT	GOLDEN VALLE	UK10-7	31-May-53	10	3

NATIONAL RANKING AMONG U.S. COUNTIES BY FALLOUT DATE

STATE	COUNTY	SHOT	DATE	RANK FOR DATE	NUMBER OF TIMES IN TOP 10
MT	GOLDEN VALLE	PB6-4	27-Jul-57	8	3
MT	GOLDEN VALLE	PB17-6	03-Oct-57	4	3
MT	GRANITE	TS4-7	07-May-52	2	4
MT	GRANITE	PB6-2	25-Jul-57	8	4
MT	GRANITE	PB6-3	26-Jul-57	7	4
MT	GRANITE	PB15-3	18-Sep-57	4	4
MT	HILL	TS4-2	02-May-52	7	1
MT	JEFFERSON	TS4-2	02-May-52	8	2
MT	JEFFERSON	PB1-6	02-Jun-57	1	2
MT	JUDITH BASIN	TS4-2	02-May-52	1	3
MT	JUDITH BASIN	TS8-3	07-Jun-52	1	3
MT	JUDITH BASIN	PB8-2	19-Aug-57	1	3
MT	LAKE	TS4-2	02-May-52	9	4
MT	LAKE	TS8-6	10-Jun-52	7	4
MT	LAKE	TS8-7	11-Jun-52	3	4
MT	LAKE	TS8-8	12-Jun-52	2	4
MT	LEWIS AND CL	TS4-2	02-May-52	10	2
MT	LEWIS AND CL	TS4-7	07-May-52	3	2
MT	LIBERTY	TS8-4	08-Jun-52	8	2
MT	LIBERTY	PB12-2	03-Sep-57	7	2
MT	MADISON	TS5-6	12-May-52	7	4
MT	MADISON	TS8-3	07-Jun-52	2	4
MT	MADISON	PB1-6	02-Jun-57	7	4
MT	MADISON	PB4-2	06-Jul-57	9	4
MT	MCCONE	UK8-1	08-May-53	5	2
MT	MCCONE	PB12-2	03-Sep-57	8	2
MT	MEAGHER	TS4-7	07-May-52	4	1
MT	MINERAL	BJ5-2	20-Nov-51	10	4
MT	MINERAL	BJ5 8	26-Nov-51	8	4
MT	MINERAL	TS8-7	11-Jun-52	10	4
MT	MINERAL	PB1-9	05-Jun-57	7	4
MT	MISSOULA	TS8-8	12-Jun-52	10	1
MT	MUSSELSHELL	UK8-2	09-May-53	5	3
MT	MUSSELSHELL	UK10-3	27-May-53	4	3
MT	MUSSELSHELL	PB6-4	27-Jul-57	3	3
MT	PARK	PB4-2	06-Jul-57	1	1

STATE	COUNTY	SHOT	DATE	RANK FOR DATE	NUMBER OF TIMES IN TOP 10
MT	PETROLEUM	UK8-2	09-May-53	6	4
MT	PETROLEUM	UK10-7	31-May-53	2	4
MT	PETROLEUM	PB6-4	27-Jul-57	4	4
MT	PETROLEUM	PB12-2	03-Sep-57	9	4
MT	PHILLIPS	TS8-7	11-Jun-52	8	5
MT	PHILLIPS	UK8-2	09-May-53	7	5
MT	PHILLIPS	UK10-7	31-May-53	6	5
MT	PHILLIPS	UK10-8	01-Jun-53	2	5
MT	PHILLIPS	PB12-2	03-Sep-57	10	5
MT	PONDERA	TS8-4	08-Jun-52	7	3
MT	PONDERA	TS8-7	11-Jun-52	4	3
MT	PONDERA	UK10-8	01-Jun-53	7	3
MT	POWDER RIVER	UK10-8	01-Jun-53	4	3
MT	POWDER RIVER	TP11-2	16-May-55	5	3
MT	POWDER RIVER	PB6-5	28-Jul-57	5	3
MT	POWELL	TS8-6	10-Jun-52	4	4
MT	POWELL	PB1-6	02-Jun-57	10	4
MT	POWELL	PB4-2	06-Jul-57	10	4
MT	POWELL	PB6-3	26-Jul-57	8	4
MT	PRAIRIE	UK8-1	08-May-53	6	1
MT	RAVALLI	TS4-7	07-May-52	5	1
MT	RICHLAND	UK8-1	08-May-53	2	4
MT	RICHLAND	UK10-9	02-Jun-53	2	4
MT	RICHLAND	PB5-2	16-Jul-57	8	4
MT	RICHLAND	PB12-2	03-Sep-57	3	4
MT	ROOSEVELT	UK8-1	08-May-53	7	2
MT	ROOSEVELT	UK10-9	02-Jun-53	3	2
MT	ROSEBUD	UK8-2	09-May-53	8	2
MT	ROSEBUD	UK10-8	01-Jun-53	3	2
MT	SANDERS	PB1-9	05-Jun-57	8	1
MT	SHERIDAN	UK8-1	08-May-53	8	3
MT	SHERIDAN	UK10-9	02-Jun-53	4	3
MT	SHERIDAN	PB6-5	28-Jul-57	8	3
MT	SILVER BOW	TS4-7	07-May-52	6	2
MT	SILVER BOW	PB17-5	02-Oct-57	7	2
MT	SWEET GRASS	PB17-6	03-Oct-57	7	1

STATE	COUNTY	SHOT	DATE	RANK FOR DATE	NUMBER OF TIMES IN TOP 10
MT	TETON	TS8-4	08-Jun-52	3	2
MT	TETON	UK10-8	01-Jun-53	8	2
MT	TOOLE	TS8-4	08-Jun-52	9	1
MT	TREASURE	UK8-3	10-May-53	2	2
MT	TREASURE	PB6-4	27-Jul-57	7	2
MT	VALLEY	PB12-2	03-Sep-57	4	1
MT	WHEATLAND	UK10-7	31-May-53	3	1
MT	WIBAUX	UK8-1	08-May-53	9	4
MT	WIBAUX	PB5-2	16-Jul-57	1	4
MT	WIBAUX	PB11-4	03-Sep-57	1	4
MT	WIBAUX	PB12-2	03-Sep-57	1	4
NC	ALAMANCE	PB5-9	23-Jul-57	2	2
NC	ALAMANCE	PB8-7	24-Aug-57	6	2
NC	ALEXANDER	PB2-5	22-Jun-57	4	2
NC	ALEXANDER	PB2-8	25-Jun-57	4	2
NC	ANSON	PB2-9	26-Jun-57	2	2
NC	ANSON	PB8-7	24-Aug-57	7	2
NC	ASHE	PB2-9	26-Jun-57	3	1
NC	AVERY	UK5-2	12-Apr-53	7	2
NC	AVERY	PB2-9	26-Jun-57	4	2
NC	BEAUFORT	BJ4-7	11-Nov-51	2	2
NC	BEAUFORT	PB16-7	29-Sep-57	8	2
NC	BERTIE	BJ4-7	11-Nov-51	3	4
NC	BERTIE	UK5-8	18-Apr-53	1	4
NC	BERTIE	TP5-6	17-Mar-55	10	4
NC	BERTIE	PB5-9	23-Jul-57	3	4
NC	BLADEN	TP7-8	05-Apr-55	5	2
NC	BLADEN	PB5-9	23-Jul-57	4	2
NC	BRUNSWICK	TP7-9	06-Apr-55	1	3
NC	BRUNSWICK	PB2-8	25-Jun-57	5	3
NC	BRUNSWICK	PB2-9	26-Jun-57	5	3
NC	BUNCOMBE	UK5-2	12-Apr-53	8	1
NC	CALDWELL	PB2-9	26-Jun-57	6	1
NC	CAMDEN	BJ4-7	11-Nov-51	4	3
NC	CAMDEN	PB16-8	30-Sep-57	10	3
NC	CAMDEN	SE5	10-Jul-62	1	3

NATIONAL RANKING AMONG U.S. COUNTIES BY FALLOUT DATE

STATE	COUNTY	SHOT	DATE	RANK FOR DATE	NUMBER OF TIMES IN TOP 10
NC	CARTERET	BJ4-7	11-Nov-51	5	3
NC	CARTERET	UK5-8	18-Apr-53	2	3
NC	CARTERET	PB16-7	29-Sep-57	1	3
NC	CASWELL	R2-6	07-Feb-51	6	2
NC	CASWELL	PB8-7	24-Aug-57	8	2
NC	CATAWBA	PB2-9	26-Jun-57	7	1
NC	CHATHAM	PB5-9	23-Jul-57	5	2
NC	CHATHAM	PB8-7	24-Aug-57	9	2
NC	CHEROKEE	UK5-2	12-Apr-53	9	2
NC	CHEROKEE	PB17-3	30-Sep-57	7	2
NC	CHOWAN	BJ4-7	11-Nov-51	6	2
NC	CHOWAN	PB5-8	22-Jul-57	4	2
NC	CLAY	UK5-2	12-Apr-53	1	3
NC	CLAY	TP10-8	12-May-55	9	3
NC	CLAY	PB17-3	30-Sep-57	1	3
NC	COLUMBUS	TS7-7	07-Jun-52	8	2
NC	COLUMBUS	PB5-9	23-Jul-57	6	2
NC	CRAVEN	PB2-8	25-Jun-57	10	2
NC	CRAVEN	PB16-7	29-Sep-57	7	2
NC	CUMBERLAND	PB5-9	23-Jul-57	7	2
NC	CUMBERLAND	PB8-7	24-Aug-57	10	2
NC	CURRITUCK	R2-6	07-Feb-51	7	3
NC	CURRITUCK	BJ4-7	11-Nov-51	7	3
NC	CURRITUCK	SE5	10-Jul-62	2	3
NC	DARE	BJ4-7	11-Nov-51	8	3
NC	DARE	uk3 7	06-Apr-53	2	3
NC	DARE	PB16-7	29-Sep-57	6	3
NC	DAVIDSON	TS5-2	08-May-52	1	1
NC	DAVIE	TS5-3	09-May-52	8	2
NC	DAVIE	PB2-8	25-Jun-57	6	2
NC	FRANKLIN	PB2-9	26-Jun-57	8	2
NC	FRANKLIN	PB5-9	23-Jul-57	8	2
NC	GASTON	TP7-8	05-Apr-55	6	1
NC	GATES	BJ4-7	11-Nov-51	9	3
NC	GATES	uk3 8	07-Apr-53	2	3
NC	GATES	PB5-9	23-Jul-57	9	3

NATIONAL RANKING AMONG U.S. COUNTIES BY FALLOUT DATE

STATE	COUNTY	SHOT	DATE	RANK FOR DATE	NUMBER OF TIMES IN TOP 10
NC	GRAHAM	UK5-2	12-Apr-53	2	1
NC	GREENE	UK5-8	18-Apr-53	3	1
NC	HALIFAX	PB5-9	23-Jul-57	10	1
NC	HAYWOOD	UK5-2	12-Apr-53	10	2
NC	HAYWOOD	PB17-3	30-Sep-57	8	2
NC	HENDERSON	TS6-6	30-May-52	10	2
NC	HENDERSON	TP10-9	13-May-55	3	2
NC	HERTFORD	BJ4-7	11-Nov-51	10	2
NC	HERTFORD	TS5-3	09-May-52	9	2
NC	HOKE	TP7-8	05-Apr-55	7	1
NC	HYDE	UK5-8	18-Apr-53	4	3
NC	HYDE	PB4-5	09-Jul-57	2	3
NC	HYDE	PB16-7	29-Sep-57	5	3
NC	IREDELL	TS5-2	08-May-52	7	1
NC	JACKSON	UK9-4	22-May-53	8	2
NC	JACKSON	PB17-3	30-Sep-57	9	2
NC	JONES	PB16-7	29-Sep-57	3	1
NC	LENOIR	UK5-8	18-Apr-53	5	2
NC	LENOIR	PB16-7	29-Sep-57	2	2
NC	MACON	TP10-8	12-May-55	7	2
NC	MACON	PB17-3	30-Sep-57	10	2
NC	MADISON	TP10-8	12-May-55	8	2
NC	MADISON	TP10-9	13-May-55	10	2
NC	MECKLENBURG	TP7-8	05-Apr-55	8	1
NC	MITCHELL	PB2-9	26-Jun-57	1	1
NC	MOORE	TS5-2	08-May-52	2	1
NC	NEW HANOVER	uk3 7	06-Apr-53	1	1
NC	ONSLOW	PB16-7	29-Sep-57	4	1
NC	ORANGE	UK2-9	01-Apr-53	1	1
NC	PAMLICO	PB16-7	29-Sep-57	9	1
NC	PASQUOTANK	SE5	10-Jul-62	3	1
NC	PERQUIMANS	SE5	10-Jul-62	4	1
NC	POLK	TS6-6	30-May-52	3	2
NC	POLK	PB2-5	22-Jun-57	5	2
NC	RICHMOND	TP7-8	05-Apr-55	9	1
NC	ROBESON	TS7-7	07-Jun-52	5	1

NATIONAL RANKING AMONG U.S. COUNTIES BY FALLOUT DATE

STATE	COUNTY	SHOT	DATE	RANK FOR DATE	NUMBER OF TIMES IN TOP 10
NC	SCOTLAND	TS7-7	07-Jun-52	9	2
NC	SCOTLAND	TP7-8	05-Apr-55	10	2
NC	SWAIN	TP10-9	13-May-55	8	1
NC	TYRRELL	uk3 8	07-Apr-53	1	2
NC	TYRRELL	TP5-6	17-Mar-55	3	2
NC	WASHINGTON	UK5-8	18-Apr-53	6	2
NC	WASHINGTON	PB16-7	29-Sep-57	10	2
NC	WATAUGA	PB2-9	26-Jun-57	9	1
NC	WAYNE	TS5-3	09-May-52	10	1
NC	WILKES	PB2-9	26-Jun-57	10	1
NC	WILSON	UK5-8	18-Apr-53	7	1
NC	YADKIN	TS5-2	08-May-52	8	1
NC	YANCEY	TP6-4	25-Mar-55	1	1
ND	ADAMS	PB5-2	16-Jul-57	9	3
ND	ADAMS	PB6-5	28-Jul-57	1	3
ND	ADAMS	PB15-2	17-Sep-57	3	3
ND	BARNES	PB5-4	18-Jul-57	7	3
ND	BARNES	PB11-2	01-Sep-57	1	3
ND	BARNES	PB15-2	17-Sep-57	4	3
ND	BENSON	PB15-2	17-Sep-57	5	2
ND	BENSON	PB17-7	04-Oct-57	2	2
ND	BILLINGS	UK8-1	08-May-53	10	4
ND	BILLINGS	PB5-2	16-Jul-57	10	4
ND	BILLINGS	PB8-3	20-Aug-57	1	4
ND	BILLINGS	PB15-2	17-Sep-57	6	4
ND	BOTTINEAU	UK2-2	25-Mar-53	3	1
ND	BOWMAN	UK10-3	27-May-53	9	3
ND	BOWMAN	PB6-5	28-Jul-57	9	3
ND	BOWMAN	PB15-2	17-Sep-57	7	3
ND	BURKE	UK2-2	25-Mar-53	5	3
ND	BURKE	UK10-9	02-Jun-53	5	3
ND	BURKE	TP9-5	18-Apr-55	6	3
ND	BURLEIGH	PB15-2	17-Sep-57	8	1
ND	CASS	PB2-3	20-Jun-57	3	3
ND	CASS	PB11-2	01-Sep-57	2	3
ND	CASS	PB15-2	17-Sep-57	9	3

NATIONAL RANKING AMONG U.S. COUNTIES BY FALLOUT DATE

STATE	COUNTY	SHOT	DATE	RANK FOR DATE	NUMBER OF TIMES IN TOP 10
ND	CAVALIER	TP9-3	16-Apr-55	6	1
ND	DICKEY	PB5-4	18-Jul-57	8	3
ND	DICKEY	PB11-2	01-Sep-57	3	3
ND	DICKEY	PB15-2	17-Sep-57	10	3
ND	DIVIDE	UK10-9	02-Jun-53	6	2
ND	DIVIDE	PB8-3	20-Aug-57	2	2
ND	DUNN	UK2-2	25-Mar-53	6	3
ND	DUNN	UK10-9	02-Jun-53	7	3
ND	DUNN	PB5-2	16-Jul-57	2	3
ND	EDDY	PB11-2	01-Sep-57	4	2
ND	EDDY	PB17-7	04-Oct-57	1	2
ND	EMMONS	PB2-3	20-Jun-57	4	2
ND	EMMONS	PB5-4	18-Jul-57	9	2
ND	FOSTER	PB2-3	20-Jun-57	5	1
ND	GOLDEN VALLE	PB5-2	16-Jul-57	3	2
ND	GOLDEN VALLE	PB6-5	28-Jul-57	4	2
ND	GRAND FORKS	TP9-3	16-Apr-55	5	2
ND	GRAND FORKS	PB11-2	01-Sep-57	5	2
ND	GRIGGS	PB11-2	01-Sep-57	6	1
ND	LA MOURE	PB5-4	18-Jul-57	10	2
ND	LA MOURE	PB11-2	01-Sep-57	7	2
ND	LOGAN	PB17-7	04-Oct-57	8	1
ND	MCHENRY	UK2-2	25-Mar-53	4	2
ND	MCHENRY	UK10-3	27-May-53	7	2
ND	MCINTOSH	PB17-7	04-Oct-57	9	1
ND	MCKENZIE	UK2-2	25-Mar-53	7	1
ND	MERCER	PB2-3	20-Jun-57	6	1
ND	MOUNTRAIL	UK10-9	02-Jun-53	8	2
ND	MOUNTRAIL	PB5-2	16-Jul-57	4	2
ND	NELSON	PB11-2	01-Sep-57	8	1
ND	OLIVER	PB2-3	20-Jun-57	7	1
ND	PEMBINA	TS3-9	30-Apr-52	9	4
ND	PEMBINA	TP9-3	16-Apr-55	1	4
ND	PEMBINA	PB4-2	06-Jul-57	5	4
ND	PEMBINA	PB11-2	01-Sep-57	9	4
ND	PIERCE	PB17-7	04-Oct-57	3	1

NATIONAL RANKING AMONG U.S. COUNTIES BY FALLOUT DATE

STATE	COUNTY	SHOT	DATE	RANK FOR DATE	NUMBER OF TIMES IN TOP 10
ND	RAMSEY	TP9-3	16-Apr-55	7	3
ND	RAMSEY	PB11-2	01-Sep-57	10	3
ND	RAMSEY	PB17-7	04-Oct-57	4	3
ND	RANSOM	PB8-3	20-Aug-57	3	1
ND	RENVILLE	UK10-9	02-Jun-53	9	1
ND	RICHLAND	PB2-3	20-Jun-57	1	1
ND	ROLETTE	UK10-3	27-May-53	3	1
ND	SARGENT	PB2-3	20-Jun-57	8	1
ND	SLOPE	UK10-3	27-May-53	8	1
ND	STARK	PB5-2	16-Jul-57	5	2
ND	STARK	PB5-3	17-Jul-57	1	2
ND	WALSH	TP9-3	16-Apr-55	8	1
ND	WARD	UK2-2	25-Mar-53	8	2
ND	WARD	UK10-3	27-May-53	10	2
NE	ADAMS	PB13-3	08-Sep-57	10	1
NE	ANTELOPE	PB15-3	18-Sep-57	5	1
NE	ARTHUR	TS5-7	13-May-52	5	5
NE	ARTHUR	TS5-9	15-May-52	3	5
NE	ARTHUR	TP3-6	06-Mar-55	7	5
NE	ARTHUR	PB1-10	06-Jun-57	5	5
NE	ARTHUR	PB18-3	09-Oct-57	9	5
NE	BANNER	TS1-2	02-Apr-52	1	5
NE	BANNER	TP3-6	06-Mar-55	8	5
NE	BANNER	PB4-8	12-Jul-57	3	5
NE	BANNER	PB5-4	18-Jul-57	3	5
NE	BANNER	PB9-6	28-Aug-57	4	5
NE	BLAINE	PB2-3	20-Jun-57	9	2
NE	BLAINE	PB8-5	22-Aug-57	8	2
NE	BOX BUTTE	TP3-6	06-Mar-55	9	2
NE	BOX BUTTE	PB18-3	09-Oct-57	10	2
NE	BROWN	PB2-3	20-Jun-57	10	1
NE	BUFFALO	PB13-3	08-Sep-57	1	1
NE	BURT	TS4-6	06-May-52	7	3
NE	BURT	UK11-3	06-Jun-53	8	3
NE	BURT	TP9-8	21-Apr-55	8	3
NE	BUTLER	TP9-8	21-Apr-55	9	2

	NATIONAL RANKING AMONG U.S. COUNTIES BY FALLOUT DATE				
STATE	COUNTY	SHOT	DATE	RANK FOR DATE	NUMBER OF TIMES IN TOP 10
NE	BUTLER	PB5-4	18-Jul-57	1	2
NE	CASS	TP9-8	21-Apr-55	10	1
NE	CEDAR	TS4-6	06-May-52	8	3
NE	CEDAR	PB15-3	18-Sep-57	6	3
NE	CEDAR	SE2	07-Jul-62	10	3
NE	CHASE	TS6-3	27-May-52	3	1
NE	CHERRY	PB8-3	20-Aug-57	4	1
NE	CHEYENNE	TS5-9	15-May-52	4	6
NE	CHEYENNE	UK10-8	01-Jun-53	9	6
NE	CHEYENNE	TP3-6	06-Mar-55	10	6
NE	CHEYENNE	PB4-7	11-Jul-57	8	6
NE	CHEYENNE	PB5-4	18-Jul-57	4	6
NE	CHEYENNE	PB18-4	10-Oct-57	8	6
NE	COLFAX	UK9-5	23-May-53	4	1
NE	CUMING	TS4-6	06-May-52	9	1
NE	CUSTER	PB18-4	10-Oct-57	2	1
NE	DAKOTA	TP7-5	02-Apr-55	5	1
NE	DAWES	TS1-2	02-Apr-52	2	3
NE	DAWES	TS5-1	07-May-52	8	3
NE	DAWES	TS5-2	08-May-52	6	3
NE	DEUEL	TS5-9	15-May-52	5	3
NE	DEUEL	TS6-3	27-May-52	6	3
NE	DEUEL	PB4-7	11-Jul-57	1	3
NE	DODGE	UK9-5	23-May-53	10	1
NE	DOUGLAS	UK9-5	23-May-53	9	1
NE	DUNDY	TP8-3	11-Apr-55	4	1
NE	GARDEN	TS5-9	15-May-52	6	1
NE	GARFIELD	PB15-2	17-Sep-57	1	1
NE	GRANT	TS5-9	15-May-52	7	2
NE	GRANT	PB5-4	18-Jul-57	5	2
NE	HALL	PB13-3	08-Sep-57	2	1
NE	HAYES	TS6-3	27-May-52	9	1
NE	HITCHCOCK	TS2-6	20-Apr-52	10	1
NE	HOLT	PB15-3	18-Sep-57	7	1
NE	HOOKER	TS5-9	15-May-52	8	2
NE	HOOKER	PB5-3	17-Jul-57	6	2

NATIONAL RANKING AMONG U.S. COUNTIES BY FALLOUT DATE

STATE	COUNTY	SHOT	DATE	RANK FOR DATE	NUMBER OF TIMES IN TOP 10
NE	KEARNEY	UK10-5	29-May-53	2	2
NE	KEARNEY	PB13-3	08-Sep-57	3	2
NE	KEITH	PB9-6	28-Aug-57	5	1
NE	KEYA PAHA	PB17-10	07-Oct-57	3	1
NE	KIMBALL	TS5-9	15-May-52	9	5
NE	KIMBALL	UK10-8	01-Jun-53	10	5
NE	KIMBALL	PB4-7	11-Jul-57	2	5
NE	KIMBALL	PB4-8	12-Jul-57	2	5
NE	KIMBALL	PB5-3	17-Jul-57	7	5
NE	KNOX	PB15-3	18-Sep-57	8	1
NE	LINCOLN	PB18-4	10-Oct-57	3	1
NE	LOGAN	PB18-4	10-Oct-57	4	1
NE	LOUP	PB15-3	18-Sep-57	9	1
NE	MERRICK	UK11-3	06-Jun-53	9	2
NE	MERRICK	PB13-3	08-Sep-57	6	2
NE	MORRILL	PB5-4	18-Jul-57	6	2
NE	MORRILL	PB9-6	28-Aug-57	1	2
NE	NANCE	PB13-3	08-Sep-57	7	1
NE	NEMAHA	UK7-9	03-May-53	5	1
NE	PERKINS	TS6-3	27-May-52	7	1
NE	PHELPS	TS6-3	27-May-52	10	3
NE	PHELPS	PB13-3	08-Sep-57	8	3
NE	PHELPS	PB18-4	10-Oct-57	5	3
NE	PIERCE	UK11-3	06-Jun-53	10	3
NE	PIERCE	TP7-5	02-Apr-55	7	3
NE	PIERCE	PB15-3	18-Sep-57	10	3
NE	SARPY	UK9-5	23-May-53	6	3
NE	SARPY	UK11-3	06-Jun-53	7	3
NE	SARPY	TP9-8	21-Apr-55	3	3
NE	SAUNDERS	TP9-8	21-Apr-55	4	1
NE	SCOTTS BLUFF	UK3-2	01-Apr-53	7	4
NE	SCOTTS BLUFF	PB4-8	12-Jul-57	1	4
NE	SCOTTS BLUFF	PB9-6	28-Aug-57	6	4
NE	SCOTTS BLUFF	PB18-4	10-Oct-57	9	4
NE	SHERIDAN	TS5-2	08-May-52	5	2
NE	SHERIDAN	UK3-2	01-Apr-53	2	2

NATIONAL RANKING AMONG U.S. COUNTIES BY FALLOUT DATE

STATE	COUNTY	SHOT	DATE	RANK FOR DATE	NUMBER OF TIMES IN TOP 10
NE	SIOUX	TS1-2	02-Apr-52	3	4
NE	SIOUX	TS5-1	07-May-52	5	4
NE	SIOUX	TS5-2	08-May-52	4	4
NE	SIOUX	UK3-2	01-Apr-53	3	4
NE	STANTON	TS4-6	06-May-52	10	1
NE	THURSTON	UK9-5	23-May-53	8	2
NE	THURSTON	TP7-5	02-Apr-55	10	2
NH	BELKNAP	UK4-5	10-Apr-53	2	1
NH	CARROLL	BJ2-2	31-Oct-51	4	2
NH	CARROLL	UK4-4	09-Apr-53	9	2
NH	CHESHIRE	UK4-4	09-Apr-53	10	2
NH	CHESHIRE	UK4-5	10-Apr-53	3	2
NH	COOS	R1-4	31-Jan-51	3	3
NH	COOS	UK6-8	25-Apr-53	9	3
NH	COOS	TP8-7	15-Apr-55	8	3
NH	GRAFTON	TS8-3	07-Jun-52	4	3
NH	GRAFTON	UK6-8	25-Apr-53	10	3
NH	GRAFTON	TP8-8	16-Apr-55	8	3
NH	HILLSBOROUGH	UK4-5	10-Apr-53	4	1
NH	MERRIMACK	UK4-5	10-Apr-53	5	1
NH	ROCKINGHAM	UK4-5	10-Apr-53	6	1
NH	STRAFFORD	UK4-5	10-Apr-53	7	1
NH	SULLIVAN	R1-3	30-Jan-51	7	2
NH	SULLIVAN	UK4-5	10-Apr-53	8	2
NJ	ATLANTIC	UK1-2	18-Mar-53	5	2
NJ	ATLANTIC	UK9-7	25-May-53	3	2
NJ	BERGEN	BJ4-9	13-Nov-51	1	6
NJ	BERGEN	ts1 4	04-Apr-52	4	6
NJ	BERGEN	TP5-10	21-Mar-55	1	6
NJ	BERGEN	TP11-9	23-May-55	1	6
NJ	BERGEN	PB2-10	27-Jun-57	2	6
NJ	BERGEN	PB15-9	24-Sep-57	1	6
NJ	BURLINGTON	BJ4-6	10-Nov-51	5	4
NJ	BURLINGTON	TS3-5	26-Apr-52	8	4
NJ	BURLINGTON	UK1-2	18-Mar-53	7	4
NJ	BURLINGTON	SE5	10-Jul-62	6	4

NATIONAL RANKING AMONG U.S. COUNTIES BY FALLOUT DATE

STATE	COUNTY	SHOT	DATE	RANK FOR DATE	NUMBER OF TIMES IN TOP 10
NJ	CAMDEN	BJ4-6	10-Nov-51	6	2
NJ	CAMDEN	UK9-7	25-May-53	4	2
NJ	CAPE MAY	BJ4-6	10-Nov-51	7	3
NJ	CAPE MAY	uk3 7	06-Apr-53	5	3
NJ	CAPE MAY	UK9-7	25-May-53	5	3
NJ	CUMBERLAND	BJ4-6	10-Nov-51	8	2
NJ	CUMBERLAND	UK9-7	25-May-53	6	2
NJ	ESSEX	BJ3-7	07-Nov-51	6	5
NJ	ESSEX	TP5-10	21-Mar-55	2	5
NJ	ESSEX	TP11-9	23-May-55	5	5
NJ	ESSEX	PB12-9	10-Sep-57	9	5
NJ	ESSEX	PB15-9	24-Sep-57	2	5
NJ	GLOUCESTER	BJ4-6	10-Nov-51	9	3
NJ	GLOUCESTER	uk3 7	06-Apr-53	6	3
NJ	GLOUCESTER	UK9-7	25-May-53	7	3
NJ	HUDSON	BJ4-9	13-Nov-51	2	6
NJ	HUDSON	ts1 4	04-Apr-52	5	6
NJ	HUDSON	TS6-8	01-Jun-52	4	6
NJ	HUDSON	TP5-10	21-Mar-55	3	6
NJ	HUDSON	TP11-9	23-May-55	2	6
NJ	HUDSON	PB15-9	24-Sep-57	3	6
NJ	HUNTERDON	BJ4-9	13-Nov-51	3	3
NJ	HUNTERDON	uk3 7	06-Apr-53	7	3
NJ	HUNTERDON	TP5-10	21-Mar-55	4	3
NJ	MERCER	BJ4-6	10-Nov-51	10	3
NJ	MERCER	uk1 7	23-Mar-53	1	3
NJ	MERCER	uk3 7	06-Apr-53	8	3
NJ	MIDDLESEX	UK1-2	18-Mar-53	9	3
NJ	MIDDLESEX	PB12-9	10-Sep-57	10	3
NJ	MIDDLESEX	PB15-9	24-Sep-57	4	3
NJ	MONMOUTH	BJ4-9	13-Nov-51	4	5
NJ	MONMOUTH	TS3-5	26-Apr-52	7	5
NJ	MONMOUTH	UK1-2	18-Mar-53	1	5
NJ	MONMOUTH	PB15-9	24-Sep-57	5	5
NJ	MONMOUTH	SE6	11-Jul-62	3	5
NJ	MORRIS	BJ3-7	07-Nov-51	1	3

NATIONAL RANKING AMONG U.S. COUNTIES BY FALLOUT DATE

STATE	COUNTY	SHOT	DATE	RANK FOR DATE	NUMBER OF TIMES IN TOP 10
NJ	MORRIS	ts1 4	04-Apr-52	6	3
NJ	MORRIS	PB15-9	24-Sep-57	6	3
NJ	OCEAN	TS3-5	26-Apr-52	3	3
NJ	OCEAN	UK1-2	18-Mar-53	2	3
NJ	OCEAN	TP7-8	05-Apr-55	2	3
NJ	PASSAIC	BJ3-7	07-Nov-51	7	4
NJ	PASSAIC	ts1 4	04-Apr-52	7	4
NJ	PASSAIC	PB2-10	27-Jun-57	3	4
NJ	PASSAIC	PB15-9	24-Sep-57	7	4
NJ	SALEM	uk3 7	06-Apr-53	9	2
NJ	SALEM	UK9-7	25-May-53	8	2
NJ	SOMERSET	BJ4-9	13-Nov-51	5	5
NJ	SOMERSET	uk3 7	06-Apr-53	10	5
NJ	SOMERSET	TP5-10	21-Mar-55	5	5
NJ	SOMERSET	PB15-8	23-Sep-57	3	5
NJ	SOMERSET	PB15-9	24-Sep-57	8	5
NJ	SUSSEX	BJ4-9	13-Nov-51	6	5
NJ	SUSSEX	ts1 4	04-Apr-52	8	5
NJ	SUSSEX	TP5-10	21-Mar-55	6	5
NJ	SUSSEX	PB2-10	27-Jun-57	1	5
NJ	SUSSEX	PB15-9	24-Sep-57	9	5
NJ	UNION	BJ4-9	13-Nov-51	7	6
NJ	UNION	TS6-8	01-Jun-52	5	6
NJ	UNION	TP5-10	21-Mar-55	7	6
NJ	UNION	TP11-9	23-May-55	6	6
NJ	UNION	PB12-9	10-Sep-57	7	6
NJ	UNION	PB15-9	24-Sep-57	10	6
NJ	WARREN	BJ3-7	07-Nov-51	8	2
NJ	WARREN	ts1 4	04-Apr-52	9	2
NM	BERNALILLO	UK6-1	18-Apr-53	10	1
NM	CHAVES	UK7-1	25-Apr-53	5	1
NM	COLFAX	TP11-1	15-May-55	5	2
NM	COLFAX	PB4-1	05-Jul-57	5	2
NM	HARDING	PB4-1	05-Jul-57	6	1
NM	LINCOLN	UK7-1	25-Apr-53	9	1
NM	MCKINLEY	UK6-1	18-Apr-53	6	3

NATIONAL RANKING AMONG U.S. COUNTIES BY FALLOUT DATE

STATE	COUNTY	SHOT	DATE	RANK FOR DATE	NUMBER OF TIMES IN TOP 10
NM	MCKINLEY	UK7-1	25-Apr-53	4	3
NM	MCKINLEY	PB3-1	24-Jun-57	6	3
NM	MORA	PB4-1	05-Jul-57	8	1
NM	SAN JUAN	UK1-1	17-Mar-53	10	2
NM	SAN JUAN	PB3-1	24-Jun-57	10	2
NM	SAN MIGUEL	PB4-1	05-Jul-57	9	1
NM	SANDOVAL	UK6-1	18-Apr-53	9	2
NM	SANDOVAL	UK7-1	25-Apr-53	7	2
NM	SANTA FE	UK7-1	25-Apr-53	8	2
NM	SANTA FE	PB4-1	05-Jul-57	10	2
NM	UNION	TP11-1	15-May-55	6	2
NM	UNION	PB4-1	05-Jul-57	7	2
NM	VALENCIA	UK6-1	18-Apr-53	7	2
NM	VALENCIA	UK7-1	25-Apr-53	10	2
NV	CARSON CITY	PB1-1	28-May-57	7	5
NV	CARSON CITY	PB6-1	24-Jul-57	10	5
NV	CARSON CITY	PB13-1	06-Sep-57	4	5
NV	CARSON CITY	PB14-1	14-Sep-57	2	5
NV	CARSON CITY	PB16-1	23-Sep-57	8	5
NV	CHURCHILL	PB1-1	28-May-57	5	5
NV	CHURCHILL	PB6-1	24-Jul-57	4	5
NV	CHURCHILL	PB13-1	06-Sep-57	5	5
NV	CHURCHILL	PB14-1	14-Sep-57	8	5
NV	CHURCHILL	PB16-1	23-Sep-57	3	5
NV	CLARK1	UK1-1	17-Mar-53	6	8
NV	CLARK1	UK6-1	18-Apr-53	2	8
NV	CLARK1	UK7-1	25-Apr-53	1	8
NV	CLARK1	UK11-1	04-Jun-53	2	8
NV	CLARK1	TP2-1	22-Feb-55	2	8
NV	CLARK1	TP5-1	12-Mar-55	1	8
NV	CLARK1	TP6-2	23-Mar-55	1	8
NV	CLARK1	TP11-1	15-May-55	2	8
NV	CLARK2	UK6-1	18-Apr-53	5	3
NV	CLARK2	TP2-1	22-Feb-55	1	3
NV	CLARK2	TP6-1	22-Mar-55	4	3
NV	CLARK3	TP6-1	22-Mar-55	1	1

STATE	COUNTY	SHOT	DATE	RANK FOR DATE	NUMBER OF TIMES IN TOP 10
NV	DOUGLAS	PB1-1	28-May-57	8	5
NV	DOUGLAS	PB6-1	24-Jul-57	8	5
NV	DOUGLAS	PB13-1	06-Sep-57	6	5
NV	DOUGLAS	PB14-1	14-Sep-57	3	5
NV	DOUGLAS	PB16-1	23-Sep-57	9	5
NV	ELKO	BJ5 1	19-Nov-51	3	4
NV	ELKO	BJ6-1	29-Nov-51	6	4
NV	ELKO	TS7-1	01-Jun-52	2	4
NV	ELKO	PB8-1	18-Aug-57	7	4
NV	ESMERALDA1	PB6-1	24-Jul-57	2	2
NV	ESMERALDA1	PB16-1	23-Sep-57	2	2
NV	ESMERALDA2	PB6-1	24-Jul-57	1	3
NV	ESMERALDA2	PB13-1	06-Sep-57	1	3
NV	ESMERALDA2	PB16-1	23-Sep-57	1	3
NV	EUREKA	BJ5 1	19-Nov-51	2	5
NV	EUREKA	BJ6-1	29-Nov-51	8	5
NV	EUREKA	TS2-1	15-Apr-52	8	5
NV	EUREKA	TS7-1	01-Jun-52	1	5
NV	EUREKA	PB8-1	18-Aug-57	1	5
NV	LANDER1	BJ5 1	19-Nov-51	6	1
NV	LANDER2	PB1-1	28-May-57	3	3
NV	LANDER2	PB13-1	06-Sep-57	10	3
NV	LANDER2	PB16-1	23-Sep-57	5	3
NV	LINCOLN1	TS6-1	25-May-52	3	9
NV	LINCOLN1	UK1-1	17-Mar-53	4	9
NV	LINCOLN1	UK9-1	19-May-53	7	9
NV	LINCOLN1	TP3-1	01-Mar-55	6	9
NV	LINCOLN1	TP5-1	12-Mar-55	8	9
NV	LINCOLN1	TP7-1	29-Mar-55	5	9
NV	LINCOLN1	TP9-1	15-Apr-55	1	9
NV	LINCOLN1	PB3-1	24-Jun-57	4	9
NV	LINCOLN1	PB11-1	31-Aug-57	5	9
NV	LINCOLN2	BJ6-1	29-Nov-51	2	7
NV	LINCOLN2	TS6-1	25-May-52	1	7
NV	LINCOLN2	TP3-1	01-Mar-55	5	7
NV	LINCOLN2	TP7-1	29-Mar-55	1	7

NATIONAL RANKING AMONG U.S. COUNTIES BY FALLOUT DATE

STATE	COUNTY	SHOT	DATE	RANK FOR DATE	NUMBER OF TIMES IN TOP 10
NV	LINCOLN2	TP9-1	15-Apr-55	10	7
NV	LINCOLN2	PB2-1	18-Jun-57	6	7
NV	LINCOLN2	PB5-1	15-Jul-57	3	7
NV	LYON	PB1-1	28-May-57	10	5
NV	LYON	PB6-1	24-Jul-57	7	5
NV	LYON	PB13-1	06-Sep-57	7	5
NV	LYON	PB14-1	14-Sep-57	4	5
NV	LYON	PB16-1	23-Sep-57	10	5
NV	MINERAL	PB1-1	28-May-57	4	5
NV	MINERAL	PB6-1	24-Jul-57	3	5
NV	MINERAL	PB13-1	06-Sep-57	3	5
NV	MINERAL	PB14-1	14-Sep-57	1	5
NV	MINERAL	PB16-1	23-Sep-57	4	5
NV	NYE1	PB1-1	28-May-57	2	2
NV	NYE1	PB14-1	14-Sep-57	10	2
NV	NYE2	BJ5 1	19-Nov-51	1	11
NV	NYE2	BJ6-1	29-Nov-51	3	11
NV	NYE2	TS7-1	01-Jun-52	3	11
NV	NYE2	TP4-1	07-Mar-55	2	11
NV	NYE2	TP10-1	05-May-55	2	11
NV	NYE2	PB1-1	28-May-57	1	11
NV	NYE2	PB5-1	15-Jul-57	1	11
NV	NYE2	PB8-1	18-Aug-57	4	11
NV	NYE2	PB12-1	02-Sep-57	1	11
NV	NYE2	PB14-1	14-Sep-57	9	11
NV	NYE2	SE1	06-Jul-62	2	11
NV	NYE3	PB2-1	18-Jun-57	9	2
NV	NYE3	PB13-2	07-Sep-57	1	2
NV	PERSHING	PB16-1	23-Sep-57	6	1
NV	STOREY	PB1-1	28-May-57	9	3
NV	STOREY	PB13-1	06-Sep-57	8	3
NV	STOREY	PB14-1	14-Sep-57	5	3
NV	WASHOE	PB1-1	28-May-57	6	3
NV	WASHOE	PB13-1	06-Sep-57	9	3
NV	WASHOE	PB14-1	14-Sep-57	6	3
NV	WHITE PINE1	BJ5 1	19-Nov-51	10	8

NATIONAL RANKING AMONG U.S. COUNTIES BY FALLOUT DATE

STATE	COUNTY	SHOT	DATE	RANK FOR DATE	NUMBER OF TIMES IN TOP 10
NV	WHITE PINE1	BJ6-1	29-Nov-51	4	8
NV	WHITE PINE1	TS2-1	15-Apr-52	9	8
NV	WHITE PINE1	TP10-1	05-May-55	4	8
NV	WHITE PINE1	PB5-1	15-Jul-57	5	8
NV	WHITE PINE1	PB8-1	18-Aug-57	5	8
NV	WHITE PINE1	PB12-1	02-Sep-57	2	8
NV	WHITE PINE1	SE1	06-Jul-62	4	8
NV	WHITE PINE2	BJ5 1	19-Nov-51	9	13
NV	WHITE PINE2	BJ6-1	29-Nov-51	1	13
NV	WHITE PINE2	TS1-1	01-Apr-52	9	13
NV	WHITE PINE2	TS2-1	15-Apr-52	6	13
NV	WHITE PINE2	TP4-1	07-Mar-55	3	13
NV	WHITE PINE2	TP8-1	09-Apr-55	8	13
NV	WHITE PINE2	TP10-1	05-May-55	1	13
NV	WHITE PINE2	PB5-1	15-Jul-57	2	13
NV	WHITE PINE2	PB6-2	25-Jul-57	1	13
NV	WHITE PINE2	PB8-1	18-Aug-57	2	13
NV	WHITE PINE2	PB9-1	23-Aug-57	2	13
NV	WHITE PINE2	PB12-1	02-Sep-57	3	13
NV	WHITE PINE2	SE1	06-Jul-62	1	13
NV	WHITE PINE3	BJ6-1	29-Nov-51	5	9
NV	WHITE PINE3	TS1-1	01-Apr-52	10	9
NV	WHITE PINE3	TS2-1	15-Apr-52	10	9
NV	WHITE PINE3	UK10-1	25-May-53	1	9
NV	WHITE PINE3	TP4-1	07-Mar-55	5	9
NV	WHITE PINE3	PB5-1	15-Jul-57	4	9
NV	WHITE PINE3	PB8-1	18-Aug-57	3	9
NV	WHITE PINE3	PB12-1	02-Sep-57	4	9
NV	WHITE PINE3	SE1	06-Jul-62	3	9
NY	ALBANY	UK7-2	26-Apr-53	8	3
NY	ALBANY	UK7-6	30-Apr-53	8	3
NY	ALBANY	UK7-7	01-May-53	8	3
NY	ALLEGANY	BJ-2 6	04-Nov-51	4	9
NY	ALLEGANY	BJ3-6	06-Nov-51	6	9
NY	ALLEGANY	BJ3-8	08-Nov-51	2	9
NY	ALLEGANY	BJ3-9	09-Nov-51	1	9

NATIONAL RANKING AMONG U.S. COUNTIES BY FALLOUT DATE

STATE	COUNTY	SHOT	DATE	RANK FOR DATE	NUMBER OF TIMES IN TOP 10
NY	ALLEGANY	BJ3-10	10-Nov-51	2	9
NY	ALLEGANY	TP3-4	04-Mar-55	3	9
NY	ALLEGANY	PB3-5	28-Jun-57	5	9
NY	ALLEGANY	PB5-8	22-Jul-57	5	9
NY	ALLEGANY	PB15-7	22-Sep-57	9	9
NY	BRONX	BJ3-7	07-Nov-51	9	4
NY	BRONX	TS6-8	01-Jun-52	9	4
NY	BRONX	TP5-10	21-Mar-55	8	4
NY	BRONX	PB12-9	10-Sep-57	6	4
NY	BROOME	TP3-5	05-Mar-55	3	1
NY	CATTARAUGUS	BJ3-6	06-Nov-51	7	10
NY	CATTARAUGUS	BJ3-8	08-Nov-51	3	10
NY	CATTARAUGUS	BJ3-9	09-Nov-51	2	10
NY	CATTARAUGUS	BJ3-10	10-Nov-51	3	10
NY	CATTARAUGUS	UK10-5	29-May-53	1	10
NY	CATTARAUGUS	TP5-4	15-Mar-55	2	10
NY	CATTARAUGUS	PB2-6	23-Jun-57	6	10
NY	CATTARAUGUS	PB3-5	28-Jun-57	3	10
NY	CATTARAUGUS	PB15-7	22-Sep-57	10	10
NY	CATTARAUGUS	PB15-8	23-Sep-57	4	10
NY	CAYUGA	R1-3	30-Jan-51	8	2
NY	CAYUGA	BJ4-10	14-Nov-51	10	2
NY	CHAUTAUQUA	R1-3	30-Jan-51	9	6
NY	CHAUTAUQUA	BJ3-6	06-Nov-51	1	6
NY	CHAUTAUQUA	BJ3-8	08-Nov-51	4	6
NY	CHAUTAUQUA	BJ3-9	09-Nov-51	3	6
NY	CHAUTAUQUA	BJ3-10	10-Nov-51	4	6
NY	CHAUTAUQUA	TP5-4	15-Mar-55	4	6
NY	CHEMUNG	R1-3	30-Jan-51	10	2
NY	CHEMUNG	BJ-2 4	02-Nov-51	8	2
NY	CHENANGO	BJ-2 6	04-Nov-51	5	1
NY	CLINTON	PB5-6	20-Jul-57	4	1
NY	COLUMBIA	UK7-2	26-Apr-53	9	3
NY	COLUMBIA	UK7-6	30-Apr-53	9	3
NY	COLUMBIA	TP7-6	03-Apr-55	4	3
NY	CORTLAND	BJ4-10	14-Nov-51	1	3

NATIONAL RANKING AMONG U.S. COUNTIES BY FALLOUT DATE

STATE	COUNTY	SHOT	DATE	RANK FOR DATE	NUMBER OF TIMES IN TOP 10
NY	CORTLAND	TP3-4	04-Mar-55	2	3
NY	CORTLAND	PB5-8	22-Jul-57	6	3
NY	DELAWARE	BJ-2 4	02-Nov-51	9	2
NY	DELAWARE	BJ4-10	14-Nov-51	2	2
NY	ERIE	BJ-2 3	01-Nov-51	4	12
NY	ERIE	BJ-2 5	03-Nov-51	4	12
NY	ERIE	BJ-2 6	04-Nov-51	1	12
NY	ERIE	BJ3-6	06-Nov-51	2	12
NY	ERIE	BJ3-8	08-Nov-51	5	12
NY	ERIE	BJ3-9	09-Nov-51	4	12
NY	ERIE	BJ3-10	10-Nov-51	5	12
NY	ERIE	UK10-5	29-May-53	4	12
NY	ERIE	TP5-4	15-Mar-55	3	12
NY	ERIE	TP8-7	15-Apr-55	9	12
NY	ERIE	PB2-6	23-Jun-57	2	12
NY	ERIE	PB3-5	28-Jun-57	2	12
NY	ESSEX	UK7-8	02-May-53	3	2
NY	ESSEX	PB11-5	04-Sep-57	3	2
NY	FRANKLIN	UK6-5	22-Apr-53	9	2
NY	FRANKLIN	TP3-5	05-Mar-55	4	2
NY	FULTON	BJ-2 6	04-Nov-51	6	7
NY	FULTON	BJ4-10	14-Nov-51	3	7
NY	FULTON	UK7-2	26-Apr-53	5	7
NY	FULTON	UK7-8	02-May-53	4	7
NY	FULTON	TP3-5	05-Mar-55	5	7
NY	FULTON	PB11-5	04-Sep-57	4	7
NY	FULTON	PB11-6	05-Sep-57	2	7
NY	GENESEE	BJ-2 3	01-Nov-51	2	11
NY	GENESEE	BJ-2 5	03-Nov-51	1	11
NY	GENESEE	BJ-2 6	04-Nov-51	7	11
NY	GENESEE	BJ3-6	06-Nov-51	3	11
NY	GENESEE	BJ3-9	09-Nov-51	5	11
NY	GENESEE	BJ3-10	10-Nov-51	6	11
NY	GENESEE	TP9-6	19-Apr-55	5	11
NY	GENESEE	PB2-6	23-Jun-57	7	11
NY	GENESEE	PB3-5	28-Jun-57	6	11

NATIONAL RANKING AMONG U.S. COUNTIES BY FALLOUT DATE					
STATE	COUNTY	SHOT	DATE	RANK FOR DATE	NUMBER OF TIMES IN TOP 10
NY	GENESEE	PB5-8	22-Jul-57	7	11
NY	GENESEE	PB15-8	23-Sep-57	5	11
NY	HAMILTON	UK7-8	02-May-53	5	3
NY	HAMILTON	TP3-5	05-Mar-55	6	3
NY	HAMILTON	PB11-5	04-Sep-57	5	3
NY	HERKIMER	BJ-2 6	04-Nov-51	8	4
NY	HERKIMER	BJ4-10	14-Nov-51	4	4
NY	HERKIMER	TP3-5	05-Mar-55	7	4
NY	HERKIMER	PB11-5	04-Sep-57	6	4
NY	JEFFERSON	BJ-2 6	04-Nov-51	2	8
NY	JEFFERSON	BJ3-6	06-Nov-51	8	8
NY	JEFFERSON	BJ3-8	08-Nov-51	6	8
NY	JEFFERSON	BJ3-9	09-Nov-51	6	8
NY	JEFFERSON	BJ3-10	10-Nov-51	1	8
NY	JEFFERSON	TP3-5	05-Mar-55	8	8
NY	JEFFERSON	PB2-6	23-Jun-57	8	8
NY	JEFFERSON	PB15-8	23-Sep-57	6	8
NY	KINGS	BJ4-9	13-Nov-51	8	4
NY	KINGS	ts1 4	04-Apr-52	1	4
NY	KINGS	TS6-8	01-Jun-52	2	4
NY	KINGS	UK1-2	18-Mar-53	3	4
NY	LEWIS	BJ-2 6	04-Nov-51	9	2
NY	LEWIS	PB11-6	05-Sep-57	3	2
NY	LIVINGSTON	BJ-2 3	01-Nov-51	5	7
NY	LIVINGSTON	BJ-2 6	04-Nov-51	10	7
NY	LIVINGSTON	BJ3-6	06-Nov-51	9	7
NY	LIVINGSTON	BJ3-9	09-Nov-51	7	7
NY	LIVINGSTON	BJ3-10	10-Nov-51	7	7
NY	LIVINGSTON	PB2-6	23-Jun-57	3	7
NY	LIVINGSTON	PB3-5	28-Jun-57	10	7
NY	MONROE	BJ-2 3	01-Nov-51	1	3
NY	MONROE	BJ3-8	08-Nov-51	1	3
NY	MONROE	TP9-6	19-Apr-55	3	3
NY	MONTGOMERY	UK7-8	02-May-53	6	2
NY	MONTGOMERY	TP3-5	05-Mar-55	9	2
NY	NASSAU	BJ3-7	07-Nov-51	10	4

STATE	COUNTY	SHOT	DATE	RANK FOR DATE	NUMBER OF TIMES IN TOP 10
NY	NASSAU	TS6-8	01-Jun-52	3	4
NY	NASSAU	UK1-2	18-Mar-53	6	4
NY	NASSAU	UK11-5	08-Jun-53	10	4
NY	NEW YORK	TS6-8	01-Jun-52	6	4
NY	NEW YORK	UK1-2	18-Mar-53	8	4
NY	NEW YORK	TP5-10	21-Mar-55	9	4
NY	NEW YORK	TP11-8	22-May-55	2	4
NY	NIAGARA	BJ-2 3	01-Nov-51	10	10
NY	NIAGARA	BJ-2 5	03-Nov-51	2	10
NY	NIAGARA	BJ3-6	06-Nov-51	4	10
NY	NIAGARA	BJ3-7	07-Nov-51	4	10
NY	NIAGARA	BJ3-9	09-Nov-51	8	10
NY	NIAGARA	BJ3-10	10-Nov-51	8	10
NY	NIAGARA	UK10-5	29-May-53	5	10
NY	NIAGARA	TP9-6	19-Apr-55	4	10
NY	NIAGARA	PB3-5	28-Jun-57	4	10
NY	NIAGARA	PB15-8	23-Sep-57	7	10
NY	ONEIDA	BJ4-10	14-Nov-51	5	2
NY	ONEIDA	TP3-5	05-Mar-55	10	2
NY	ONTARIO	BJ3-6	06-Nov-51	10	6
NY	ONTARIO	BJ3-8	08-Nov-51	7	6
NY	ONTARIO	BJ3-9	09-Nov-51	9	6
NY	ONTARIO	BJ3-10	10-Nov-51	9	6
NY	ONTARIO	TP3-4	04-Mar-55	4	6
NY	ONTARIO	PB2-6	23-Jun-57	4	6
NY	ORANGE	BJ4-9	13-Nov-51	9	4
NY	ORANGE	ts1 4	04-Apr-52	10	4
NY	ORANGE	TS6-8	01-Jun-52	7	4
NY	ORANGE	TP5-10	21-Mar-55	10	4
NY	ORLEANS	BJ-2 3	01-Nov-51	9	7
NY	ORLEANS	BJ-2 5	03-Nov-51	6	7
NY	ORLEANS	BJ3-6	06-Nov-51	5	7
NY	ORLEANS	BJ3-9	09-Nov-51	10	7
NY	ORLEANS	BJ3-10	10-Nov-51	10	7
NY	ORLEANS	UK10-5	29-May-53	9	7
NY	ORLEANS	TP9-6	19-Apr-55	1	7

NATIONAL RANKING AMONG U.S. COUNTIES BY FALLOUT DATE

STATE	COUNTY	SHOT	DATE	RANK FOR DATE	NUMBER OF TIMES IN TOP 10
NY	OSWEGO	BJ-2 4	02-Nov-51	2	1
NY	OTSEGO	BJ-2 4	02-Nov-51	7	2
NY	OTSEGO	TS3-6	27-Apr-52	6	2
NY	PUTNAM	BJ3-7	07-Nov-51	2	2
NY	PUTNAM	ts1 5	05-Apr-52	4	2
NY	QUEENS	BJ4-9	13-Nov-51	10	6
NY	QUEENS	ts1 4	04-Apr-52	2	6
NY	QUEENS	TS3-5	26-Apr-52	1	6
NY	QUEENS	TS6-8	01-Jun-52	1	6
NY	QUEENS	UK1-2	18-Mar-53	4	6
NY	QUEENS	TP11-9	23-May-55	3	6
NY	RENSSELAER	UK7-2	26-Apr-53	3	4
NY	RENSSELAER	UK7-6	30-Apr-53	2	4
NY	RENSSELAER	UK7-7	01-May-53	6	4
NY	RENSSELAER	TP7-6	03-Apr-55	6	4
NY	RICHMOND	TS6-8	01-Jun-52	10	3
NY	RICHMOND	UK1-2	18-Mar-53	10	3
NY	RICHMOND	TP11-9	23-May-55	7	3
NY	ROCKLAND	TS6-8	01-Jun-52	8	1
NY	SARATOGA	BJ2-2	31-Oct-51	5	6
NY	SARATOGA	UK7-2	26-Apr-53	4	6
NY	SARATOGA	UK7-6	30-Apr-53	1	6
NY	SARATOGA	UK7-7	01-May-53	2	6
NY	SARATOGA	UK7-8	02-May-53	7	6
NY	SARATOGA	TP7-6	03-Apr-55	5	6
NY	SCHENECTADY	UK7-2	26-Apr-53	7	3
NY	SCHENECTADY	UK7-6	30-Apr-53	3	3
NY	SCHENECTADY	UK7-7	01-May-53	3	3
NY	SCHUYLER	PB5-7	21-Jul-57	1	1
NY	SENECA	PB2-6	23-Jun-57	1	1
NY	ST LAWRENCE	TS7-4	04-Jun-52	2	1
NY	STEUBEN	TP3-4	04-Mar-55	5	2
NY	STEUBEN	PB5-8	22-Jul-57	8	2
NY	SUFFOLK	UK4-7	12-Apr-53	9	1
NY	SULLIVAN	BJ4-10	14-Nov-51	6	2
NY	SULLIVAN	TS3-6	27-Apr-52	7	2

NATIONAL RANKING AMONG U.S. COUNTIES BY FALLOUT DATE

STATE	COUNTY	SHOT	DATE	RANK FOR DATE	NUMBER OF TIMES IN TOP 10
NY	TOMPKINS	BJ-2 4	02-Nov-51	3	2
NY	TOMPKINS	PB5-8	22-Jul-57	9	2
NY	ULSTER	BJ3-7	07-Nov-51	3	1
NY	WARREN	UK7-2	26-Apr-53	2	3
NY	WARREN	UK7-8	02-May-53	8	3
NY	WARREN	PB6-7	30-Jul-57	2	3
NY	WASHINGTON	UK7-2	26-Apr-53	1	3
NY	WASHINGTON	UK7-7	01-May-53	9	3
NY	WASHINGTON	UK7-8	02-May-53	9	3
NY	WAYNE	BJ-2 4	02-Nov-51	10	3
NY	WAYNE	BJ-2 5	03-Nov-51	3	3
NY	WAYNE	PB2-6	23-Jun-57	9	3
NY	WESTCHESTER	ts1 5	05-Apr-52	5	1
NY	WYOMING	BJ-2 6	04-Nov-51	3	7
NY	WYOMING	TP5-4	15-Mar-55	7	7
NY	WYOMING	TP8-7	15-Apr-55	1	7
NY	WYOMING	TP9-6	19-Apr-55	8	7
NY	WYOMING	PB2-6	23-Jun-57	5	7
NY	WYOMING	PB3-5	28-Jun-57	7	7
NY	WYOMING	PB15-8	23-Sep-57	8	7
OH	ASHLAND	BJ4-5	09-Nov-51	10	3
OH	ASHLAND	TP8-6	14-Apr-55	1	3
OH	ASHLAND	TP9-6	19-Apr-55	7	3
OH	ASHTABULA	TP4-4	10-Mar-55	4	2
OH	ASHTABULA	TP8-6	14-Apr-55	2	2
OH	ATHENS	R1-2	29-Jan-51	8	3
OH	ATHENS	UK2-9	01-Apr-53	6	3
OH	ATHENS	PB5-8	22-Jul-57	10	3
OH	AUGLAIZE	TS6-10	03-Jun-52	2	1
OH	BELMONT	R1-2	29-Jan-51	1	3
OH	BELMONT	UK2-9	01-Apr-53	7	3
OH	BELMONT	TP11-7	21-May-55	2	3
OH	CARROLL	TP8-6	14-Apr-55	3	2
OH	CARROLL	TP8-7	15-Apr-55	5	2
OH	CHAMPAIGN	TP9-8	21-Apr-55	1	1
OH	COLUMBIANA	PB6-7	30-Jul-57	10	1

NATIONAL RANKING AMONG U.S. COUNTIES BY FALLOUT DATE

STATE	COUNTY	SHOT	DATE	RANK FOR DATE	NUMBER OF TIMES IN TOP 10
OH	COSHOCTON	TP9-8	21-Apr-55	6	1
OH	CUYAHOGA	TP4-4	10-Mar-55	5	2
OH	CUYAHOGA	TP9-2	15-Apr-55	3	2
OH	DARKE	TS4-5	05-May-52	9	1
OH	ERIE	BJ3-5	05-Nov-51	1	4
OH	ERIE	BJ4-8	12-Nov-51	2	4
OH	ERIE	TP3-6	06-Mar-55	1	4
OH	ERIE	TP9-2	15-Apr-55	6	4
OH	FRANKLIN	TS4-5	05-May-52	10	1
OH	GEAUGA	UK9-3	21-May-53	3	7
OH	GEAUGA	TP3-6	06-Mar-55	2	7
OH	GEAUGA	TP4-4	10-Mar-55	6	7
OH	GEAUGA	TP8-6	14-Apr-55	4	7
OH	GEAUGA	TP9-2	15-Apr-55	8	7
OH	GEAUGA	TP9-5	18-Apr-55	2	7
OH	GEAUGA	TP9-10	23-Apr-55	9	7
OH	GUERNSEY	R1-2	29-Jan-51	2	3
OH	GUERNSEY	TP8-6	14-Apr-55	5	3
OH	GUERNSEY	TP9-8	21-Apr-55	2	3
OH	HARRISON	TP11-10	24-May-55	3	1
OH	HOLMES	TP4-4	10-Mar-55	8	3
OH	HOLMES	TP8-6	14-Apr-55	6	3
OH	HOLMES	TP9-6	19-Apr-55	9	3
OH	HURON	BJ3-5	05-Nov-51	8	3
OH	HURON	BJ4-8	12-Nov-51	3	3
OH	HURON	TP8-6	14-Apr-55	7	3
OH	JACKSON	TP8-6	14-Apr-55	8	1
OH	JEFFERSON	BJ2-2	31-Oct-51	9	2
OH	JEFFERSON	UK9-3	21-May-53	10	2
OH	KNOX	TP9-6	19-Apr-55	10	1
OH	LAKE	BJ2-2	31-Oct-51	10	6
OH	LAKE	BJ3-5	05-Nov-51	9	6
OH	LAKE	BJ4-8	12-Nov-51	4	6
OH	LAKE	UK9-3	21-May-53	7	6
OH	LAKE	TP4-4	10-Mar-55	3	6
OH	LAKE	TP9-5	18-Apr-55	3	6

NATIONAL RANKING AMONG U.S. COUNTIES BY FALLOUT DATE

STATE	COUNTY	SHOT	DATE	RANK FOR DATE	NUMBER OF TIMES IN TOP 10
OH	LICKING	TS6-10	03-Jun-52	4	3
OH	LICKING	TP8-6	14-Apr-55	9	3
OH	LICKING	TP9-8	21-Apr-55	7	3
OH	LORAIN	BJ4-8	12-Nov-51	5	3
OH	LORAIN	TP4-4	10-Mar-55	10	3
OH	LORAIN	TP8-6	14-Apr-55	10	3
OH	MAHONING	UK9-3	21-May-53	1	3
OH	MAHONING	TP9-5	18-Apr-55	9	3
OH	MAHONING	TP11-8	22-May-55	3	3
OH	MEDINA	TP4-4	10-Mar-55	1	4
OH	MEDINA	TP9-2	15-Apr-55	2	4
OH	MEDINA	TP9-5	18-Apr-55	1	4
OH	MEDINA	TP9-6	19-Apr-55	2	4
OH	MONROE	TP11-10	24-May-55	4	1
OH	MORROW	TP3-6	06-Mar-55	3	2
OH	MORROW	PB15-6	21-Sep-57	1	2
OH	NOBLE	UK2-9	01-Apr-53	8	1
OH	OTTAWA	BJ4-8	12-Nov-51	6	1
OH	PERRY	BJ3-5	05-Nov-51	10	2
OH	PERRY	UK2-9	01-Apr-53	9	2
OH	PORTAGE	TP4-4	10-Mar-55	2	3
OH	PORTAGE	TP8-7	15-Apr-55	6	3
OH	PORTAGE	TP9-5	18-Apr-55	4	3
OH	RICHLAND	BJ4-8	12-Nov-51	7	1
OH	SANDUSKY	BJ4-8	12-Nov-51	8	2
OH	SANDUSKY	TP9-2	15-Apr-55	9	2
OH	SCIOTO	TP5-4	15-Mar-55	10	2
OH	SCIOTO	SE4	09-Jul-62	5	2
OH	SENECA	TP9-2	15-Apr-55	4	1
OH	SHELBY	TP9-8	21-Apr-55	5	1
OH	STARK	TP9-5	18-Apr-55	5	1
OH	SUMMIT	UK9-3	21-May-53	4	2
OH	SUMMIT	TP9-5	18-Apr-55	10	2
OH	TRUMBULL	TP8-7	15-Apr-55	7	2
OH	TRUMBULL	TP9-5	18-Apr-55	8	2
OH	UNION	TS6-10	03-Jun-52	3	1

STATE	COUNTY	SHOT	DATE	RANK FOR DATE	NUMBER OF TIMES IN TOP 10
		NATIONAL RANKING AMONG U.S. COUNTIES BY FALLOUT DATE			
OH	WAYNE	TP9-6	19-Apr-55	6	1
OH	WILLIAMS	PB15-6	21-Sep-57	4	1
OH	WYANDOT	BJ4-8	12-Nov-51	9	1
OK	ADAIR	UK2-10	02-Apr-53	10	4
OK	ADAIR	UK3-3	02-Apr-53	10	4
OK	ADAIR	PB13-6	11-Sep-57	9	4
OK	ADAIR	PB13-9	14-Sep-57	7	4
OK	ALFALFA	BJ5 6	24-Nov-51	5	3
OK	ALFALFA	PB13-9	14-Sep-57	8	3
OK	ALFALFA	PB17-10	07-Oct-57	8	3
OK	ATOKA	uk1 7	23-Mar-53	6	9
OK	ATOKA	UK1-9	25-Mar-53	7	9
OK	ATOKA	UK6-6	23-Apr-53	4	9
OK	ATOKA	UK8-4	11-May-53	2	9
OK	ATOKA	TP11-5	19-May-55	8	9
OK	ATOKA	PB5-10	24-Jul-57	8	9
OK	ATOKA	PB13-9	14-Sep-57	9	9
OK	ATOKA	PB14-8	21-Sep-57	1	9
OK	ATOKA	PB18-7	13-Oct-57	3	9
OK	BEAVER	TS4-4	04-May-52	6	3
OK	BEAVER	UK6-3	20-Apr-53	6	3
OK	BEAVER	PB5-10	24-Jul-57	9	3
OK	BECKHAM	UK3-5	04-Apr-53	1	4
OK	BECKHAM	UK6-3	20-Apr-53	7	4
OK	BECKHAM	TP5-6	17-Mar-55	4	4
OK	BECKHAM	PB18-6	12-Oct-57	1	4
OK	BLAINE	BJ5 6	24-Nov-51	6	2
OK	BLAINE	PB13-9	14-Sep-57	10	2
OK	BRYAN	BJ5 6	24-Nov-51	7	7
OK	BRYAN	uk1 7	23-Mar-53	7	7
OK	BRYAN	UK1-9	25-Mar-53	8	7
OK	BRYAN	UK7-3	27-Apr-53	10	7
OK	BRYAN	TP11-5	19-May-55	3	7
OK	BRYAN	PB14-8	21-Sep-57	2	7
OK	BRYAN	PB18-7	13-Oct-57	4	7
OK	CADDO	PB18-6	12-Oct-57	2	1

STATE	COUNTY	SHOT	DATE	RANK FOR DATE	NUMBER OF TIMES IN TOP 10
OK	CANADIAN	BJ5 6	24-Nov-51	8	2
OK	CANADIAN	PB18-6	12-Oct-57	3	2
OK	CARTER	uk1 7	23-Mar-53	8	2
OK	CARTER	UK1-9	25-Mar-53	9	2
OK	CHEROKEE	BJ5 6	24-Nov-51	9	1
OK	CHOCTAW	TP11-5	19-May-55	9	3
OK	CHOCTAW	PB14-8	21-Sep-57	3	3
OK	CHOCTAW	PB18-7	13-Oct-57	5	3
OK	CIMARRON	TS4-4	04-May-52	7	5
OK	CIMARRON	TS4-6	06-May-52	1	5
OK	CIMARRON	UK6-3	20-Apr-53	8	5
OK	CIMARRON	TP7-2	30-Mar-55	9	5
OK	CIMARRON	PB18-5	11-Oct-57	3	5
OK	CLEVELAND	uk1 7	23-Mar-53	9	3
OK	CLEVELAND	UK1-9	25-Mar-53	10	3
OK	CLEVELAND	TP10-5	09-May-55	9	3
OK	COAL	TS7-6	06-Jun-52	1	4
OK	COAL	uk1 7	23-Mar-53	10	4
OK	COAL	UK6-6	23-Apr-53	5	4
OK	COAL	PB14-8	21-Sep-57	4	4
OK	COMANCHE	PB18-6	12-Oct-57	4	1
OK	COTTON	PB18-6	12-Oct-57	5	1
OK	CREEK	BJ5 6	24-Nov-51	10	2
OK	CREEK	UK7-3	27-Apr-53	5	2
OK	DELAWARE	TP10-5	09-May-55	1	1
OK	ELLIS	TS4-4	04-May-52	8	2
OK	ELLIS	UK6-3	20-Apr-53	9	2
OK	GARFIELD	BJ5 6	24-Nov-51	1	1
OK	GARVIN	TS6-4	28-May-52	10	3
OK	GARVIN	TP10-5	09-May-55	8	3
OK	GARVIN	PB5-10	24-Jul-57	1	3
OK	GRADY	PB18-6	12-Oct-57	6	1
OK	GREER	UK3-5	04-Apr-53	2	5
OK	GREER	UK6-3	20-Apr-53	10	5
OK	GREER	TP5-6	17-Mar-55	5	5
OK	GREER	PB17-10	07-Oct-57	10	5

NATIONAL RANKING AMONG U.S. COUNTIES BY FALLOUT DATE

STATE	COUNTY	SHOT	DATE	RANK FOR DATE	NUMBER OF TIMES IN TOP 10
OK	GREER	PB18-6	12-Oct-57	7	5
OK	HARMON	UK3-5	04-Apr-53	3	1
OK	HUGHES	TS7-6	06-Jun-52	3	1
OK	JACKSON	UK6-4	21-Apr-53	6	3
OK	JACKSON	UK6-5	22-Apr-53	10	3
OK	JACKSON	PB18-6	12-Oct-57	8	3
OK	JEFFERSON	PB14-8	21-Sep-57	5	2
OK	JEFFERSON	PB18-6	12-Oct-57	9	2
OK	JOHNSTON	PB14-8	21-Sep-57	6	1
OK	KINGFISHER	PB18-6	12-Oct-57	10	1
OK	KIOWA	PB17-10	07-Oct-57	6	1
OK	LATIMER	PB14-8	21-Sep-57	7	1
OK	LINCOLN	TP10-5	09-May-55	6	1
OK	LOGAN	PB13-6	11-Sep-57	10	1
OK	LOVE	UK1-9	25-Mar-53	1	4
OK	LOVE	TP11-5	19-May-55	10	4
OK	LOVE	PB14-8	21-Sep-57	8	4
OK	LOVE	PB18-7	13-Oct-57	6	4
OK	MAJOR	BJ5 6	24-Nov-51	2	1
OK	MARSHALL	TP11-5	19-May-55	7	2
OK	MARSHALL	PB14-8	21-Sep-57	9	2
OK	MCCLAIN	TS6-4	28-May-52	8	2
OK	MCCLAIN	TP10-5	09-May-55	10	2
OK	MCCURTAIN	PB14-8	21-Sep-57	10	1
OK	MCINTOSH	UK2-10	02-Apr-53	1	4
OK	MCINTOSH	UK3-3	02-Apr-53	1	4
OK	MCINTOSH	TP10-5	09-May-55	7	4
OK	MCINTOSH	PB13-6	11-Sep-57	4	4
OK	MURRAY	UK8-4	11-May-53	3	1
OK	MUSKOGEE	TP10-5	09-May-55	5	2
OK	MUSKOGEE	PB13-6	11-Sep-57	5	2
OK	NOWATA	TS7-5	05-Jun-52	8	2
OK	NOWATA	PB13-6	11-Sep-57	7	2
OK	OKFUSKEE	TS7-6	06-Jun-52	6	1
OK	OKMULGEE	TS7-6	06-Jun-52	7	3
OK	OKMULGEE	TP10-5	09-May-55	2	3

NATIONAL RANKING AMONG U.S. COUNTIES BY FALLOUT DATE

STATE	COUNTY	SHOT	DATE	RANK FOR DATE	NUMBER OF TIMES IN TOP 10
OK	OKMULGEE	PB13-6	11-Sep-57	1	3
OK	PAWNEE	PB13-6	11-Sep-57	8	1
OK	PAYNE	PB13-6	11-Sep-57	3	1
OK	PONTOTOC	UK8-4	11-May-53	4	2
OK	PONTOTOC	TP11-5	19-May-55	1	2
OK	POTTAWATOMIE	TP10-5	09-May-55	4	1
OK	PUSHMATAHA	TS7-6	06-Jun-52	5	2
OK	PUSHMATAHA	PB18-7	13-Oct-57	7	2
OK	ROGER MILLS	TS6-7	31-May-52	3	4
OK	ROGER MILLS	UK3-5	04-Apr-53	4	4
OK	ROGER MILLS	UK9-4	22-May-53	5	4
OK	ROGER MILLS	TP5-6	17-Mar-55	6	4
OK	ROGERS	PB12-4	05-Sep-57	4	1
OK	STEPHENS	TS6-4	28-May-52	6	1
OK	TEXAS	TS4-4	04-May-52	9	2
OK	TEXAS	TP7-2	30-Mar-55	2	2
OK	TILLMAN	TS6-4	28-May-52	2	2
OK	TILLMAN	PB5-10	24-Jul-57	2	2
OK	TULSA	TS7-5	05-Jun-52	1	1
OK	WAGONER	PB12-4	05-Sep-57	7	2
OK	WAGONER	PB13-6	11-Sep-57	2	2
OK	WASHINGTON	TS7-5	05-Jun-52	9	2
OK	WASHINGTON	PB13-6	11-Sep-57	6	2
OK	WASHITA	UK3-5	04-Apr-53	5	3
OK	WASHITA	TP5-6	17-Mar-55	1	3
OK	WASHITA	PB17-10	07-Oct-57	2	3
OR	BAKER	TS2-4	18-Apr-52	10	4
OR	BAKER	TS8-9	13-Jun-52	7	4
OR	BAKER	PB6-2	25-Jul-57	9	4
OR	BAKER	PB17-4	01-Oct-57	3	4
OR	COOS	TP6-6	27-Mar-55	9	1
OR	CROOK	PB14-3	16-Sep-57	5	1
OR	CURRY	TP6-6	27-Mar-55	10	1
OR	GILLIAM	PB14-4	17-Sep-57	1	1
OR	GRANT	TS2-4	18-Apr-52	8	3
OR	GRANT	PB6-2	25-Jul-57	10	3

STATE	COUNTY	SHOT	DATE	RANK FOR DATE	NUMBER OF TIMES IN TOP 10
			NATIONAL RANKING AMONG U.S. COUNTIES BY FALLOUT DATE		
OR	GRANT	PB16-4	26-Sep-57	10	3
OR	LAKE	PB14-3	16-Sep-57	6	1
OR	LINCOLN	PB14-3	16-Sep-57	8	1
OR	MORROW	PB14-4	17-Sep-57	2	1
OR	SHERMAN	PB14-4	17-Sep-57	3	1
OR	TILLAMOOK	PB14-4	17-Sep-57	5	1
OR	UMATILLA	PB16-4	26-Sep-57	5	1
OR	WALLOWA	TS8-6	10-Jun-52	10	1
PA	ARMSTRONG	UK2-9	01-Apr-53	10	3
PA	ARMSTRONG	TP11-8	22-May-55	4	3
PA	ARMSTRONG	TP11-10	24-May-55	5	3
PA	BEAVER	TP11-10	24-May-55	6	2
PA	BEAVER	PB2-7	24-Jun-57	1	2
PA	BERKS	uk1 7	23-Mar-53	2	3
PA	BERKS	UK9-7	25-May-53	9	3
PA	BERKS	TP11-9	23-May-55	8	3
PA	BLAIR	TP11-10	24-May-55	7	1
PA	BUTLER	TP11-8	22-May-55	5	2
PA	BUTLER	TP11-10	24-May-55	8	2
PA	CAMBRIA	TP11-10	24-May-55	1	2
PA	CAMBRIA	PB2-7	24-Jun-57	2	2
PA	CAMERON	PB15-7	22-Sep-57	1	1
PA	CARBON	uk1 7	23-Mar-53	3	2
PA	CARBON	TP11-9	23-May-55	9	2
PA	CHESTER	UK9-7	25-May-53	10	1
PA	CLARION	UK10-6	30-May-53	2	4
PA	CLARION	TP11-8	22-May-55	6	4
PA	CLARION	TP11-10	24-May-55	9	4
PA	CLARION	PB2-7	24-Jun-57	3	4
PA	CLEARFIELD	PB2-7	24-Jun-57	4	1
PA	CLINTON	TP3-5	05-Mar-55	1	1
PA	CRAWFORD	TP11-8	22-May-55	7	2
PA	CRAWFORD	PB2-7	24-Jun-57	5	2
PA	ELK	BJ3-8	08-Nov-51	8	3
PA	ELK	PB2-7	24-Jun-57	6	3
PA	ELK	SE5	10-Jul-62	7	3

NATIONAL RANKING AMONG U.S. COUNTIES BY FALLOUT DATE

STATE	COUNTY	SHOT	DATE	RANK FOR DATE	NUMBER OF TIMES IN TOP 10
PA	ERIE	TS4-4	04-May-52	10	3
PA	ERIE	UK10-6	30-May-53	7	3
PA	ERIE	TP4-4	10-Mar-55	9	3
PA	FOREST	BJ3-8	08-Nov-51	9	4
PA	FOREST	TP11-8	22-May-55	1	4
PA	FOREST	TP11-9	23-May-55	4	4
PA	FOREST	PB2-7	24-Jun-57	7	4
PA	FRANKLIN	uk3 8	07-Apr-53	4	1
PA	FULTON	TP9-10	23-Apr-55	4	1
PA	HUNTINGDON	UK10-6	30-May-53	3	1
PA	INDIANA	PB2-7	24-Jun-57	8	1
PA	JEFFERSON	TP11-7	21-May-55	3	2
PA	JEFFERSON	TP11-8	22-May-55	8	2
PA	LACKAWANNA	R1-4	31-Jan-51	1	3
PA	LACKAWANNA	TS3-6	27-Apr-52	1	3
PA	LACKAWANNA	SE5	10-Jul-62	8	3
PA	LEHIGH	TP11-9	23-May-55	10	1
PA	LUZERNE	TS3-6	27-Apr-52	2	1
PA	MCKEAN	BJ-2 5	03-Nov-51	10	5
PA	MCKEAN	BJ3-8	08-Nov-51	10	5
PA	MCKEAN	UK10-5	29-May-53	10	5
PA	MCKEAN	TP5-4	15-Mar-55	9	5
PA	MCKEAN	PB3-5	28-Jun-57	9	5
PA	MERCER	TP11-8	22-May-55	9	1
PA	MONROE	BJ4-10	14-Nov-51	7	3
PA	MONROE	TS3-6	27-Apr-52	3	3
PA	MONROE	uk1 7	23-Mar-53	4	3
PA	PIKE	BJ4-10	14-Nov-51	8	2
PA	PIKE	TS3-6	27-Apr-52	4	2
PA	POTTER	UK10-6	30-May-53	6	4
PA	POTTER	TP3-4	04-Mar-55	1	4
PA	POTTER	TP3-5	05-Mar-55	2	4
PA	POTTER	PB2-6	23-Jun-57	10	4
PA	SCHUYLKILL	uk1 7	23-Mar-53	5	1
PA	SULLIVAN	BJ4-10	14-Nov-51	9	1
PA	TIOGA	UK10-6	30-May-53	8	1

NATIONAL RANKING AMONG U.S. COUNTIES BY FALLOUT DATE

STATE	COUNTY	SHOT	DATE	RANK FOR DATE	NUMBER OF TIMES IN TOP 10
PA	VENANGO	TP4-4	10-Mar-55	7	3
PA	VENANGO	TP11-8	22-May-55	10	3
PA	VENANGO	PB2-7	24-Jun-57	9	3
PA	WARREN	UK10-6	30-May-53	5	2
PA	WARREN	PB2-7	24-Jun-57	10	2
PA	WAYNE	TS3-6	27-Apr-52	5	1
PA	WYOMING	R1-4	31-Jan-51	2	1
RI	BRISTOL	TS5-5	11-May-52	3	4
RI	BRISTOL	UK4-2	07-Apr-53	6	4
RI	BRISTOL	UK5-9	19-Apr-53	6	4
RI	BRISTOL	UK7-6	30-Apr-53	10	4
RI	KENT	UK1-10	26-Mar-53	8	3
RI	KENT	UK5-9	19-Apr-53	8	3
RI	KENT	UK7-6	30-Apr-53	4	3
RI	NEWPORT	UK5-9	19-Apr-53	9	1
RI	PROVIDENCE	TS5-5	11-May-52	4	3
RI	PROVIDENCE	UK5-9	19-Apr-53	7	3
RI	PROVIDENCE	UK7-6	30-Apr-53	5	3
RI	WASHINGTON	UK1-10	26-Mar-53	9	3
RI	WASHINGTON	UK4-2	07-Apr-53	7	3
RI	WASHINGTON	UK5-9	19-Apr-53	10	3
SC	ABBEVILLE	TS6-6	30-May-52	8	2
SC	ABBEVILLE	PB16-6	28-Sep-57	8	2
SC	ALLENDALE	TP7-10	07-Apr-55	4	1
SC	BAMBERG	TS6-6	30-May-52	7	2
SC	BAMBERG	TP7-10	07-Apr-55	10	2
SC	BARNWELL	TP7-10	07-Apr-55	5	2
SC	BARNWELL	PB16-6	28-Sep-57	6	2
SC	BEAUFORT	TP7-10	07-Apr-55	6	1
SC	CHARLESTON	PB2-8	25-Jun-57	7	1
SC	CHESTER	TP7-8	05-Apr-55	1	1
SC	CHESTERFIELD	TP7-9	06-Apr-55	2	1
SC	CLARENDON	TS3-7	28-Apr-52	1	1
SC	COLLETON	PB2-8	25-Jun-57	8	1
SC	DARLINGTON	BJ4-5	09-Nov-51	2	1
SC	DILLON	TS7-7	07-Jun-52	2	2

STATE	COUNTY	SHOT	DATE	RANK FOR DATE	NUMBER OF TIMES IN TOP 10
SC	DILLON	TP7-9	06-Apr-55	3	2
SC	DORCHESTER	TP7-10	07-Apr-55	7	1
SC	EDGEFIELD	TS6-10	03-Jun-52	10	1
SC	FLORENCE	TS7-7	07-Jun-52	4	1
SC	GREENVILLE	TS6-6	30-May-52	1	2
SC	GREENVILLE	PB18-5	11-Oct-57	1	2
SC	GREENWOOD	TS6-6	30-May-52	2	2
SC	GREENWOOD	PB16-6	28-Sep-57	3	2
SC	HORRY	TS7-7	07-Jun-52	3	1
SC	KERSHAW	SE6	11-Jul-62	5	1
SC	LAURENS	PB2-8	25-Jun-57	9	1
SC	LEE	TS3-4	25-Apr-52	6	1
SC	MARION	TS7-7	07-Jun-52	1	2
SC	MARION	TP7-9	06-Apr-55	4	2
SC	MARLBORO	TS5-2	08-May-52	10	2
SC	MARLBORO	TS7-7	07-Jun-52	6	2
SC	MCCORMICK	TS5-4	10-May-52	10	3
SC	MCCORMICK	TS6-6	30-May-52	6	3
SC	MCCORMICK	PB16-6	28-Sep-57	4	3
SC	OCONEE	TP10-9	13-May-55	4	2
SC	OCONEE	PB17-3	30-Sep-57	2	2
SC	PICKENS	TS6-6	30-May-52	4	2
SC	PICKENS	PB18-5	11-Oct-57	2	2
SC	SPARTANBURG	TS6-6	30-May-52	5	2
SC	SPARTANBURG	PB16-6	28-Sep-57	9	2
SC	WILLIAMSBURG	TS7-7	07-Jun-52	10	1
SC	YORK	TP7-9	06-Apr-55	5	1
SD	AURORA	TP7-5	02-Apr-55	3	2
SD	AURORA	PB8-5	22-Aug-57	9	2
SD	BEADLE	TS6-9	02-Jun-52	3	2
SD	BEADLE	TS7-2	02-Jun-52	3	2
SD	BENNETT	TS5-2	08-May-52	9	2
SD	BENNETT	PB8-4	21-Aug-57	2	2
SD	BROOKINGS	PB8-3	20-Aug-57	5	2
SD	BROOKINGS	PB8-5	22-Aug-57	10	2
SD	BUFFALO	PB17-9	06-Oct-57	9	2

NATIONAL RANKING AMONG U.S. COUNTIES BY FALLOUT DATE

STATE	COUNTY	SHOT	DATE	RANK FOR DATE	NUMBER OF TIMES IN TOP 10
SD	BUFFALO	PB17-10	07-Oct-57	1	2
SD	BUTTE	PB5-3	17-Jul-57	2	2
SD	BUTTE	PB18-4	10-Oct-57	10	2
SD	CLAY	TS3-10	01-May-52	6	1
SD	CODINGTON	PB15-2	17-Sep-57	2	1
SD	CUSTER	TS7-3	03-Jun-52	7	3
SD	CUSTER	PB18-4	10-Oct-57	6	3
SD	CUSTER	SE2	07-Jul-62	2	3
SD	DAVISON	TP7-5	02-Apr-55	2	3
SD	DAVISON	TP9-3	16-Apr-55	3	3
SD	DAVISON	PB8-5	22-Aug-57	1	3
SD	EDMUNDS	PB17-7	04-Oct-57	7	1
SD	FALL RIVER	TS5-1	07-May-52	4	2
SD	FALL RIVER	SE2	07-Jul-62	6	2
SD	GRANT	PB6-7	30-Jul-57	9	1
SD	HAAKON	PB6-8	31-Jul-57	9	1
SD	HAMLIN	SE2	07-Jul-62	3	1
SD	HAND	TS7-2	02-Jun-52	8	1
SD	HANSON	TP9-3	16-Apr-55	10	2
SD	HANSON	PB8-5	22-Aug-57	2	2
SD	HARDING	PB6-5	28-Jul-57	6	1
SD	HUGHES	PB6-5	28-Jul-57	7	2
SD	HUGHES	PB17-9	06-Oct-57	1	2
SD	HUTCHINSON	TS7-4	04-Jun-52	7	2
SD	HUTCHINSON	TP7-5	02-Apr-55	8	2
SD	HYDE	PB17-9	06-Oct-57	6	1
SD	JACKSON	PB8-4	21-Aug-57	3	1
SD	JERAULD	TS7-2	02-Jun-52	6	3
SD	JERAULD	TP7-5	02-Apr-55	6	3
SD	JERAULD	TP9-3	16-Apr-55	9	3
SD	JONES	PB17-9	06-Oct-57	4	1
SD	KINGSBURY	PB8-5	22-Aug-57	3	2
SD	KINGSBURY	SE2	07-Jul-62	4	2
SD	LAKE	PB8-5	22-Aug-57	4	1
SD	LAWRENCE	PB4-9	13-Jul-57	8	3
SD	LAWRENCE	PB5-3	17-Jul-57	3	3

NATIONAL RANKING AMONG U.S. COUNTIES BY FALLOUT DATE

STATE	COUNTY	SHOT	DATE	RANK FOR DATE	NUMBER OF TIMES IN TOP 10
SD	LAWRENCE	PB6-4	27-Jul-57	10	3
SD	MCCOOK	PB8-5	22-Aug-57	5	1
SD	MCPHERSON	PB17-7	04-Oct-57	10	1
SD	MELLETTE	TS5-2	08-May-52	3	3
SD	MELLETTE	PB5-4	18-Jul-57	2	3
SD	MELLETTE	PB17-9	06-Oct-57	7	3
SD	MINER	PB8-5	22-Aug-57	6	2
SD	MINER	SE2	07-Jul-62	9	2
SD	MINNEHAHA	PB8-4	21-Aug-57	4	1
SD	MOODY	SE2	07-Jul-62	5	1
SD	PERKINS	PB6-5	28-Jul-57	3	1
SD	POTTER	PB6-5	28-Jul-57	10	1
SD	ROBERTS	PB2-3	20-Jun-57	2	1
SD	SANBORN	TS7-2	02-Jun-52	4	2
SD	SANBORN	PB8-5	22-Aug-57	7	2
SD	SHANNON	TS5-1	07-May-52	7	2
SD	SHANNON	SE2	07-Jul-62	7	2
SD	SPINK	TS7-2	02-Jun-52	7	1
SD	STANLEY	PB17-7	04-Oct-57	5	3
SD	STANLEY	PB17-9	06-Oct-57	2	3
SD	STANLEY	SE2	07-Jul-62	8	3
SD	SULLY	PB17-7	04-Oct-57	6	2
SD	SULLY	PB17-9	06-Oct-57	5	2
SD	TRIPP	PB17-9	06-Oct-57	8	1
SD	TURNER	TS3-10	01-May-52	7	2
SD	TURNER	TS7-4	04-Jun-52	4	2
SD	UNION	TP7-6	03-Apr-55	10	1
SD	WASHABAUGH	SE2	07-Jul-62	1	1
TN	ANDERSON	TP10-8	12-May-55	2	2
TN	ANDERSON	TP10-9	13-May-55	9	2
TN	BENTON	uk1 3	19-Mar-53	4	2
TN	BENTON	PB1-9	05-Jun-57	3	2
TN	BLOUNT	TP10-9	13-May-55	2	1
TN	BRADLEY	TP6-4	25-Mar-55	2	1
TN	CAMPBELL	TP10-8	12-May-55	6	1
TN	CARTER	BJ4-5	09-Nov-51	1	1

U.S. FALLOUT ATLAS : COUNTY COMPARISIONS

NATIONAL RANKING AMONG U.S. COUNTIES BY FALLOUT DATE

STATE	COUNTY	SHOT	DATE	RANK FOR DATE	NUMBER OF TIMES IN TOP 10
TN	CHEATHAM	TS6-5	29-May-52	2	4
TN	CHEATHAM	uk1 3	19-Mar-53	10	4
TN	CHEATHAM	uk1 6	22-Mar-53	2	4
TN	CHEATHAM	TP5-7	18-Mar-55	2	4
TN	CHESTER	PB16-9	01-Oct-57	10	1
TN	COCKE	UK5-2	12-Apr-53	3	1
TN	COFFEE	PB17-3	30-Sep-57	3	1
TN	CROCKETT	UK2-8	31-Mar-53	2	1
TN	DAVIDSON	TS6-5	29-May-52	1	3
TN	DAVIDSON	uk1 6	22-Mar-53	1	3
TN	DAVIDSON	TP5-7	18-Mar-55	3	3
TN	DECATUR	TS7-6	06-Jun-52	9	1
TN	DICKSON	uk1 3	19-Mar-53	2	4
TN	DICKSON	uk1 6	22-Mar-53	7	4
TN	DICKSON	TP5-7	18-Mar-55	4	4
TN	DICKSON	TP10-7	11-May-55	9	4
TN	DYER	UK2-7	30-Mar-53	1	1
TN	FAYETTE	uk1 5	21-Mar-53	3	1
TN	FENTRESS	TS7-6	06-Jun-52	8	1
TN	GIBSON	UK2-7	30-Mar-53	2	2
TN	GIBSON	TP10-7	11-May-55	2	2
TN	GRAINGER	uk1 8	24-Mar-53	9	2
TN	GRAINGER	TP10-8	12-May-55	4	2
TN	HAYWOOD	UK2-8	31-Mar-53	3	1
TN	HENRY	TP4-5	11-Mar-55	2	1
TN	HICKMAN	uk1 3	19-Mar-53	5	1
TN	HOUSTON	uk1 3	19-Mar-53	3	1
TN	HUMPHREYS	uk1 3	19-Mar-53	1	1
TN	JEFFERSON	TP10-9	13-May-55	6	1
TN	KNOX	TP10-8	12-May-55	1	2
TN	KNOX	TP10-9	13-May-55	1	2
TN	LEWIS	TS6-5	29-May-52	3	2
TN	LEWIS	uk1 3	19-Mar-53	6	2
TN	LOUDON	TP10-8	12-May-55	5	1
TN	MAURY	uk1 3	19-Mar-53	9	3
TN	MAURY	uk1 6	22-Mar-53	6	3

NATIONAL RANKING AMONG U.S. COUNTIES BY FALLOUT DATE

STATE	COUNTY	SHOT	DATE	RANK FOR DATE	NUMBER OF TIMES IN TOP 10
TN	MAURY	TP5-7	18-Mar-55	5	3
TN	MCMINN	TP6-4	25-Mar-55	3	1
TN	MEIGS	TP6-4	25-Mar-55	4	1
TN	MONROE	TP6-4	25-Mar-55	5	1
TN	MONTGOMERY	uk1 6	22-Mar-53	8	2
TN	MONTGOMERY	TP5-7	18-Mar-55	6	2
TN	MORGAN	TP10-8	12-May-55	10	1
TN	OBION	TP4-5	11-Mar-55	3	1
TN	PERRY	TS6-5	29-May-52	6	2
TN	PERRY	uk1 3	19-Mar-53	8	2
TN	PUTNAM	PB2-5	22-Jun-57	6	1
TN	ROBERTSON	uk1 6	22-Mar-53	4	1
TN	RUTHERFORD	TP5-7	18-Mar-55	7	2
TN	RUTHERFORD	PB17-2	29-Sep-57	1	2
TN	SEVIER	UK5-2	12-Apr-53	4	3
TN	SEVIER	TP10-8	12-May-55	3	3
TN	SEVIER	TP10-9	13-May-55	5	3
TN	SHELBY	uk1 5	21-Mar-53	1	1
TN	SMITH	TP5-7	18-Mar-55	8	2
TN	SMITH	PB17-2	29-Sep-57	2	2
TN	STEWART	PB1-9	05-Jun-57	4	1
TN	SULLIVAN	UK9-4	22-May-53	3	1
TN	SUMNER	uk1 6	22-Mar-53	5	1
TN	TROUSDALE	TP5-7	18-Mar-55	9	1
TN	UNICOI	TP6-5	26-Mar-55	1	1
TN	UNION	TP10-9	13-May-55	7	1
TN	WARREN	PB2-5	22-Jun-57	7	1
TN	WEAKLEY	TP4-5	11-Mar-55	4	1
TN	WHITE	PB2-5	22-Jun-57	8	1
TN	WILLIAMSON	TS6-5	29-May-52	8	5
TN	WILLIAMSON	uk1 3	19-Mar-53	7	5
TN	WILLIAMSON	uk1 6	22-Mar-53	3	5
TN	WILLIAMSON	TP5-7	18-Mar-55	10	5
TN	WILLIAMSON	PB17-2	29-Sep-57	3	5
TN	WILSON	TS6-5	29-May-52	9	3
TN	WILSON	uk1 6	22-Mar-53	10	3

U.S. FALLOUT ATLAS : COUNTY COMPARISIONS

				RANK FOR	NUMBER OF
STATE	COUNTY	SHOT	DATE	DATE	TIMES IN TOP 10

NATIONAL RANKING AMONG U.S. COUNTIES BY FALLOUT DATE

STATE	COUNTY	SHOT	DATE	RANK FOR DATE	NUMBER OF TIMES IN TOP 10
TN	WILSON	PB17-2	29-Sep-57	4	3
TX	ANDERSON	BJ3-4	04-Nov-51	1	3
TX	ANDERSON	UK8-4	11-May-53	5	3
TX	ANDERSON	PB18-7	13-Oct-57	8	3
TX	ANDREWS	BJ3-4	04-Nov-51	2	7
TX	ANDREWS	TS2-7	21-Apr-52	2	7
TX	ANDREWS	TS5-10	16-May-52	1	7
TX	ANDREWS	TS7-9	09-Jun-52	1	7
TX	ANDREWS	UK3-4	03-Apr-53	4	7
TX	ANDREWS	UK11-6	09-Jun-53	10	7
TX	ANDREWS	PB3-2	25-Jun-57	6	7
TX	ANGELINA	BJ3-4	04-Nov-51	3	3
TX	ANGELINA	TS4-9	09-May-52	3	3
TX	ANGELINA	PB18-7	13-Oct-57	9	3
TX	ARANSAS	BJ3-2	02-Nov-51	6	2
TX	ARANSAS	BJ3-4	04-Nov-51	4	2
TX	ARCHER	BJ3-4	04-Nov-51	5	1
TX	ARMSTRONG	BJ3-4	04-Nov-51	6	5
TX	ARMSTRONG	TS6-4	28-May-52	9	5
TX	ARMSTRONG	UK3-5	04-Apr-53	6	5
TX	ARMSTRONG	TP11-4	18-May-55	2	5
TX	ARMSTRONG	PB9-6	28-Aug-57	10	5
TX	ATASCOSA	BJ3-2	02-Nov-51	7	2
TX	ATASCOSA	BJ3-4	04-Nov-51	7	2
TX	AUSTIN	BJ3-2	02-Nov-51	8	2
TX	AUSTIN	BJ3-4	04-Nov-51	8	2
TX	BAILEY	BJ3-4	04-Nov-51	9	4
TX	BAILEY	TP5-2	13-Mar-55	7	4
TX	BAILEY	PB3-2	25-Jun-57	7	4
TX	BAILEY	PB13-4	09-Sep-57	5	4
TX	BANDERA	BJ3-3	03-Nov-51	4	2
TX	BANDERA	BJ3-4	04-Nov-51	10	2
TX	BASTROP	BJ3-2	02-Nov-51	9	1
TX	BAYLOR	UK6-6	23-Apr-53	6	1
TX	BEE	BJ3-2	02-Nov-51	10	2
TX	BEE	PB1-5	01-Jun-57	1	2

NATIONAL RANKING AMONG U.S. COUNTIES BY FALLOUT DATE

STATE	COUNTY	SHOT	DATE	RANK FOR DATE	NUMBER OF TIMES IN TOP 10
TX	BELL	UK8-4	11-May-53	6	2
TX	BELL	PB18-7	13-Oct-57	10	2
TX	BOSQUE	UK8-4	11-May-53	7	1
TX	BRAZOS	UK8-4	11-May-53	8	2
TX	BRAZOS	PB14-9	22-Sep-57	1	2
TX	BREWSTER	BJ3-3	03-Nov-51	5	1
TX	BRISCOE	UK9-4	22-May-53	4	2
TX	BRISCOE	TP7-2	30-Mar-55	10	2
TX	BROOKS	PB1-5	01-Jun-57	2	1
TX	BURLESON	PB14-9	22-Sep-57	2	1
TX	BURNET	UK6-5	22-Apr-53	2	2
TX	BURNET	UK8-4	11-May-53	9	2
TX	CALHOUN	PB1-5	01-Jun-57	3	1
TX	CALLAHAN	UK6-4	21-Apr-53	7	2
TX	CALLAHAN	UK6-6	23-Apr-53	10	2
TX	CAMERON	BJ3-2	02-Nov-51	5	3
TX	CAMERON	TS7-8	08-Jun-52	6	3
TX	CAMERON	PB1-5	01-Jun-57	4	3
TX	CARSON	TS6-4	28-May-52	4	3
TX	CARSON	UK3-5	04-Apr-53	7	3
TX	CARSON	TP11-4	18-May-55	5	3
TX	CASTRO	TP11-4	18-May-55	10	4
TX	CASTRO	PB3-2	25-Jun-57	8	4
TX	CASTRO	PB13-4	09-Sep-57	6	4
TX	CASTRO	PB18-5	11-Oct-57	4	4
TX	CHAMBERS	BJ3-2	02-Nov-51	3	1
TX	CHEROKEE	UK8-4	11-May-53	10	1
TX	CLAY	UK6-6	23-Apr-53	7	1
TX	COCHRAN	TS7-9	09-Jun-52	2	4
TX	COCHRAN	UK3-4	03-Apr-53	5	4
TX	COCHRAN	PB3-2	25-Jun-57	9	4
TX	COCHRAN	PB13-4	09-Sep-57	7	4
TX	COLEMAN	UK6-4	21-Apr-53	8	1
TX	COLLIN	TP10-6	10-May-55	9	2
TX	COLLIN	PB12-5	06-Sep-57	9	2
TX	COLLINGSWORT	UK3-5	04-Apr-53	8	2

NATIONAL RANKING AMONG U.S. COUNTIES BY FALLOUT DATE

STATE	COUNTY	SHOT	DATE	RANK FOR DATE	NUMBER OF TIMES IN TOP 10
TX	COLLINGSWORT	UK9-4	22-May-53	10	2
TX	COLORADO	PB1-5	01-Jun-57	5	1
TX	CONCHO	UK6-4	21-Apr-53	1	1
TX	COOKE	TP11-5	19-May-55	2	1
TX	CORYELL	PB14-9	22-Sep-57	3	1
TX	CRANE	BJ3-3	03-Nov-51	6	1
TX	CROCKETT	BJ3-3	03-Nov-51	7	1
TX	CROSBY	TP5-6	17-Mar-55	7	1
TX	CULBERSON	BJ3-3	03-Nov-51	8	5
TX	CULBERSON	TS7-9	09-Jun-52	3	5
TX	CULBERSON	UK3-4	03-Apr-53	6	5
TX	CULBERSON	UK11-6	09-Jun-53	1	5
TX	CULBERSON	PB3-2	25-Jun-57	10	5
TX	DALLAM	R1-1	28-Jan-51	2	4
TX	DALLAM	TP7-2	30-Mar-55	5	4
TX	DALLAM	PB13-4	09-Sep-57	8	4
TX	DALLAM	PB18-5	11-Oct-57	5	4
TX	DALLAS	UK7-3	27-Apr-53	6	3
TX	DALLAS	TP10-6	10-May-55	3	3
TX	DALLAS	PB12-5	06-Sep-57	5	3
TX	DE WITT	PB1-5	01-Jun-57	6	1
TX	DEAF SMITH	TS5-10	16-May-52	9	4
TX	DEAF SMITH	TS6-4	28-May-52	7	4
TX	DEAF SMITH	TP5-2	13-Mar-55	5	4
TX	DEAF SMITH	PB13-4	09-Sep-57	9	4
TX	DELTA	PB5-10	24-Jul-57	3	1
TX	DIMMIT	BJ3-3	03-Nov-51	9	2
TX	DIMMIT	TS4-7	07-May-52	7	2
TX	DONLEY	UK3-5	04-Apr-53	9	3
TX	DONLEY	UK9-4	22-May-53	2	3
TX	DONLEY	TP11-4	18-May-55	7	3
TX	EASTLAND	UK6-6	23-Apr-53	3	1
TX	ECTOR	TS7-9	09-Jun-52	4	2
TX	ECTOR	UK3-4	03-Apr-53	1	2
TX	EDWARDS	BJ3-3	03-Nov-51	10	1
TX	EL PASO	BJ3-3	03-Nov-51	1	6

NATIONAL RANKING AMONG U.S. COUNTIES BY FALLOUT DATE

STATE	COUNTY	SHOT	DATE	RANK FOR DATE	NUMBER OF TIMES IN TOP 10
TX	EL PASO	TS5-10	16-May-52	10	6
TX	EL PASO	TS7-9	09-Jun-52	5	6
TX	EL PASO	UK3-4	03-Apr-53	7	6
TX	EL PASO	UK6-3	20-Apr-53	1	6
TX	EL PASO	UK11-6	09-Jun-53	2	6
TX	ELLIS	TP8-3	11-Apr-55	6	3
TX	ELLIS	TP10-6	10-May-55	10	3
TX	ELLIS	PB12-5	06-Sep-57	10	3
TX	FANNIN	UK1-9	25-Mar-53	2	3
TX	FANNIN	UK7-3	27-Apr-53	3	3
TX	FANNIN	TP11-5	19-May-55	5	3
TX	FISHER	TP7-3	31-Mar-55	6	1
TX	FOARD	TP11-5	19-May-55	4	2
TX	FOARD	PB5-10	24-Jul-57	4	2
TX	GAINES	TS7-9	09-Jun-52	6	3
TX	GAINES	UK3-4	03-Apr-53	8	3
TX	GAINES	UK8-5	12-May-53	1	3
TX	GRAY	TP11-4	18-May-55	3	1
TX	GRAYSON	UK1-9	25-Mar-53	3	2
TX	GRAYSON	UK7-3	27-Apr-53	4	2
TX	GREGG	PB1-6	02-Jun-57	4	1
TX	HALE	TP11-4	18-May-55	1	2
TX	HALE	PB13-4	09-Sep-57	10	2
TX	HANSFORD	TP7-2	30-Mar-55	6	1
TX	HARDIN	UK6-7	24-Apr-53	10	2
TX	HARDIN	PB14-9	22-Sep-57	4	2
TX	HARTLEY	TS5-10	16-May-52	5	2
TX	HARTLEY	PB18-5	11-Oct-57	6	2
TX	HEMPHILL	PB5-10	24-Jul-57	5	1
TX	HIDALGO	BJ3-2	02-Nov-51	4	1
TX	HILL	PB12-5	06-Sep-57	3	1
TX	HOCKLEY	TS5-10	16-May-52	2	1
TX	HOUSTON	TS4-9	09-May-52	4	2
TX	HOUSTON	PB1-7	03-Jun-57	10	2
TX	HUDSPETH	TS7-9	09-Jun-52	7	3
TX	HUDSPETH	UK3-4	03-Apr-53	9	3

NATIONAL RANKING AMONG U.S. COUNTIES BY FALLOUT DATE

STATE	COUNTY	SHOT	DATE	RANK FOR DATE	NUMBER OF TIMES IN TOP 10
TX	HUDSPETH	UK6-4	21-Apr-53	9	3
TX	HUNT	TS7-6	06-Jun-52	2	1
TX	HUTCHINSON	TP7-2	30-Mar-55	7	1
TX	IRION	UK6-4	21-Apr-53	10	1
TX	JACKSON	TS7-8	08-Jun-52	7	2
TX	JACKSON	PB1-5	01-Jun-57	7	2
TX	JASPER	TS4-9	09-May-52	7	2
TX	JASPER	PB14-9	22-Sep-57	5	2
TX	JEFF DAVIS	TS7-9	09-Jun-52	8	4
TX	JEFF DAVIS	UK3-4	03-Apr-53	10	4
TX	JEFF DAVIS	UK11-6	09-Jun-53	3	4
TX	JEFF DAVIS	PB3-2	25-Jun-57	1	4
TX	JEFFERSON	PB14-9	22-Sep-57	6	1
TX	JIM HOGG	PB1-5	01-Jun-57	8	1
TX	JIM WELLS	TS7-8	08-Jun-52	8	2
TX	JIM WELLS	PB1-5	01-Jun-57	9	2
TX	JOHNSON	TP8-3	11-Apr-55	8	2
TX	JOHNSON	PB12-5	06-Sep-57	4	2
TX	KAUFMAN	TP10-6	10-May-55	7	1
TX	KENDALL	PB1-5	01-Jun-57	10	1
TX	KING	UK6-6	23-Apr-53	8	1
TX	KLEBERG	BJ3-2	02-Nov-51	1	1
TX	LAMAR	PB1-7	03-Jun-57	3	2
TX	LAMAR	PB5-10	24-Jul-57	6	2
TX	LAMB	TS5-10	16-May-52	6	3
TX	LAMB	TP5-6	17-Mar-55	8	3
TX	LAMB	TP11-4	18-May-55	9	3
TX	LAMPASAS	UK6-4	21-Apr-53	2	1
TX	LEE	PB14-9	22-Sep-57	7	1
TX	LEON	TS4-9	09-May-52	8	2
TX	LEON	UK1-9	25-Mar-53	6	2
TX	LIBERTY	PB14-9	22-Sep-57	8	1
TX	LIMESTONE	PB1-7	03-Jun-57	4	1
TX	LIPSCOMB	TS6-7	31-May-52	9	2
TX	LIPSCOMB	UK9-4	22-May-53	9	2
TX	LOVING	TS6-4	28-May-52	3	2

NATIONAL RANKING AMONG U.S. COUNTIES BY FALLOUT DATE

STATE	COUNTY	SHOT	DATE	RANK FOR DATE	NUMBER OF TIMES IN TOP 10
TX	LOVING	TS7-9	09-Jun-52	9	2
TX	LUBBOCK	PB18-5	11-Oct-57	7	1
TX	LYNN	TP5-6	17-Mar-55	2	1
TX	MIDLAND	UK6-4	21-Apr-53	3	1
TX	MILAM	PB14-9	22-Sep-57	9	1
TX	MITCHELL	UK6-5	22-Apr-53	3	1
TX	MONTAGUE	UK1-9	25-Mar-53	4	1
TX	MONTGOMERY	TS4-9	09-May-52	9	2
TX	MONTGOMERY	PB14-9	22-Sep-57	10	2
TX	MOORE	TS4-6	06-May-52	2	2
TX	MOORE	TP11-4	18-May-55	8	2
TX	MOTLEY	TP5-6	17-Mar-55	9	1
TX	NEWTON	TS4-8	08-May-52	2	2
TX	NEWTON	TS4-9	09-May-52	10	2
TX	OCHILTREE	TP7-2	30-Mar-55	8	1
TX	OLDHAM	TS5-10	16-May-52	7	4
TX	OLDHAM	TP5-2	13-Mar-55	6	4
TX	OLDHAM	TP7-2	30-Mar-55	3	4
TX	OLDHAM	PB18-5	11-Oct-57	8	4
TX	PALO PINTO	UK6-6	23-Apr-53	9	1
TX	PARKER	UK6-6	23-Apr-53	1	2
TX	PARKER	PB12-5	06-Sep-57	2	2
TX	PARMER	TS5-10	16-May-52	8	4
TX	PARMER	UK3-5	04-Apr-53	10	4
TX	PARMER	TP5-2	13-Mar-55	8	4
TX	PARMER	TP11-4	18-May-55	6	4
TX	POTTER	TP7-2	30-Mar-55	4	2
TX	POTTER	PB18-5	11-Oct-57	9	2
TX	RANDALL	TS6-4	28-May-52	5	2
TX	RANDALL	TP11-4	18-May-55	4	2
TX	REAL	BJ3-3	03-Nov-51	2	1
TX	RED RIVER	PB12-5	06-Sep-57	6	1
TX	REEVES	TS7-9	09-Jun-52	10	1
TX	REFUGIO	R2-2	03-Feb-51	1	1
TX	ROCKWALL	TS7-6	06-Jun-52	4	4
TX	ROCKWALL	UK10-4	28-May-53	1	4

NATIONAL RANKING AMONG U.S. COUNTIES BY FALLOUT DATE

STATE	COUNTY	SHOT	DATE	RANK FOR DATE	NUMBER OF TIMES IN TOP 10
TX	ROCKWALL	TP10-6	10-May-55	5	4
TX	ROCKWALL	PB12-5	06-Sep-57	8	4
TX	SCURRY	UK6-5	22-Apr-53	4	1
TX	SHACKELFORD	PB12-5	06-Sep-57	7	1
TX	SHERMAN	TS4-6	06-May-52	3	1
TX	SMITH	PB1-7	03-Jun-57	9	1
TX	STARR	TS7-8	08-Jun-52	9	1
TX	STERLING	UK6-4	21-Apr-53	4	1
TX	STONEWALL	PB17-10	07-Oct-57	4	1
TX	SUTTON	UK6-5	22-Apr-53	8	1
TX	SWISHER	TS6-9	02-Jun-52	7	1
TX	TARRANT	PB12-5	06-Sep-57	1	1
TX	TERRY	TS5-10	16-May-52	3	1
TX	TRINITY	TS4-9	09-May-52	5	1
TX	UVALDE	BJ3-3	03-Nov-51	3	1
TX	WHARTON	BJ3-2	02-Nov-51	2	1
TX	WHEELER	UK9-5	23-May-53	3	1
TX	WILBARGER	UK6-5	22-Apr-53	5	1
TX	WILLACY	TS7-8	08-Jun-52	10	1
TX	WINKLER	UK3-4	03-Apr-53	2	2
TX	WINKLER	UK8-5	12-May-53	2	2
TX	WISE	UK1-9	25-Mar-53	5	2
TX	WISE	TP11-5	19-May-55	6	2
TX	YOAKUM	TS5-10	16-May-52	4	2
TX	YOAKUM	UK8-5	12-May-53	3	2
UT	BEAVER	TS1-1	01-Apr-52	1	8
UT	BEAVER	TS4-1	01-May-52	8	8
UT	BEAVER	TS6-1	25-May-52	6	8
UT	BEAVER	UK5-1	11-Apr-53	8	8
UT	BEAVER	TP9-1	15-Apr-55	2	8
UT	BEAVER	PB2-1	18-Jun-57	8	8
UT	BEAVER	PB15-1	16-Sep-57	3	8
UT	BEAVER	PB18-1	07-Oct-57	6	8
UT	BOX ELDER1	BJ6-1	29-Nov-51	10	5
UT	BOX ELDER1	TS7-1	01-Jun-52	4	5
UT	BOX ELDER1	PB8-1	18-Aug-57	9	5

NATIONAL RANKING AMONG U.S. COUNTIES BY FALLOUT DATE

STATE	COUNTY	SHOT	DATE	RANK FOR DATE	NUMBER OF TIMES IN TOP 10
UT	BOX ELDER1	PB15-1	16-Sep-57	5	5
UT	BOX ELDER1	PB17-1	28-Sep-57	2	5
UT	BOX ELDER2	PB8-1	18-Aug-57	10	5
UT	BOX ELDER2	PB9-1	23-Aug-57	10	5
UT	BOX ELDER2	PB15-1	16-Sep-57	6	5
UT	BOX ELDER2	PB17-1	28-Sep-57	3	5
UT	BOX ELDER2	SE1	06-Jul-62	6	5
UT	CACHE	UK2-1	24-Mar-53	10	3
UT	CACHE	PB15-1	16-Sep-57	7	3
UT	CACHE	PB17-1	28-Sep-57	4	3
UT	CARBON	TS1-1	01-Apr-52	5	2
UT	CARBON	UK10-1	25-May-53	9	2
UT	DAGGETT	TP10-1	05-May-55	8	2
UT	DAGGETT	PB11-1	31-Aug-57	9	2
UT	DAVIS	UK2-1	24-Mar-53	2	7
UT	DAVIS	TP8-1	09-Apr-55	6	7
UT	DAVIS	PB9-1	23-Aug-57	8	7
UT	DAVIS	PB12-1	02-Sep-57	10	7
UT	DAVIS	PB15-1	16-Sep-57	8	7
UT	DAVIS	PB17-1	28-Sep-57	5	7
UT	DAVIS	SE1	06-Jul-62	7	7
UT	DUCHESNE	UK10-1	25-May-53	8	3
UT	DUCHESNE	TP10-1	05-May-55	6	3
UT	DUCHESNE	PB9-1	23-Aug-57	6	3
UT	EMERY	TS1-1	01-Apr-52	6	3
UT	EMERY	TS6-1	25-May-52	9	3
UT	EMERY	TP9-1	15-Apr-55	4	3
UT	GARFIELD	UK11-1	04-Jun-53	8	6
UT	GARFIELD	TP3-1	01-Mar-55	7	6
UT	GARFIELD	TP7-1	29-Mar-55	4	6
UT	GARFIELD	PB3-1	24-Jun-57	9	6
UT	GARFIELD	PB11-1	31-Aug-57	1	6
UT	GARFIELD	PB18-1	07-Oct-57	7	6
UT	GRAND	TP9-1	15-Apr-55	5	1
UT	IRON1	TS4-1	01-May-52	1	8
UT	IRON1	TS6-1	25-May-52	2	8

NATIONAL RANKING AMONG U.S. COUNTIES BY FALLOUT DATE

STATE	COUNTY	SHOT	DATE	RANK FOR DATE	NUMBER OF TIMES IN TOP 10
UT	IRON1	UK5-1	11-Apr-53	5	8
UT	IRON1	TP5-1	12-Mar-55	9	8
UT	IRON1	TP7-1	29-Mar-55	6	8
UT	IRON1	PB2-1	18-Jun-57	1	8
UT	IRON1	PB3-1	24-Jun-57	3	8
UT	IRON1	PB18-1	07-Oct-57	1	8
UT	IRON2	TS4-1	01-May-52	2	7
UT	IRON2	TS6-1	25-May-52	4	7
UT	IRON2	UK5-1	11-Apr-53	10	7
UT	IRON2	TP7-1	29-Mar-55	7	7
UT	IRON2	TP11-1	15-May-55	1	7
UT	IRON2	PB2-1	18-Jun-57	7	7
UT	IRON2	PB18-1	07-Oct-57	3	7
UT	IRON3	TS4-1	01-May-52	10	7
UT	IRON3	UK5-1	11-Apr-53	6	7
UT	IRON3	TP3-1	01-Mar-55	8	7
UT	IRON3	TP7-1	29-Mar-55	2	7
UT	IRON3	TP11-1	15-May-55	4	7
UT	IRON3	PB2-1	18-Jun-57	2	7
UT	IRON3	PB18-1	07-Oct-57	4	7
UT	JUAB	BJ6-1	29-Nov-51	9	6
UT	JUAB	UK10-1	25-May-53	5	6
UT	JUAB	TP4-1	07-Mar-55	7	6
UT	JUAB	PB5-1	15-Jul-57	7	6
UT	JUAB	PB9-1	23-Aug-57	4	6
UT	JUAB	PB15-1	16-Sep-57	1	6
UT	KANE1	UK9-1	19-May-53	4	5
UT	KANE1	UK11-1	04-Jun-53	3	5
UT	KANE1	TP3-1	01-Mar-55	4	5
UT	KANE1	TP5-1	12-Mar-55	7	5
UT	KANE1	TP6-1	22-Mar-55	6	5
UT	KANE2	UK1-1	17-Mar-53	3	6
UT	KANE2	UK9-1	19-May-53	5	6
UT	KANE2	UK11-1	04-Jun-53	6	6
UT	KANE2	TP3-1	01-Mar-55	2	6
UT	KANE2	TP7-1	29-Mar-55	8	6

NATIONAL RANKING AMONG U.S. COUNTIES BY FALLOUT DATE

STATE	COUNTY	SHOT	DATE	RANK FOR DATE	NUMBER OF TIMES IN TOP 10
UT	KANE2	PB3-1	24-Jun-57	2	6
UT	MILLARD	TS6-1	25-May-52	5	8
UT	MILLARD	UK10-1	25-May-53	2	8
UT	MILLARD	TP4-1	07-Mar-55	6	8
UT	MILLARD	TP8-1	09-Apr-55	10	8
UT	MILLARD	TP11-1	15-May-55	10	8
UT	MILLARD	PB5-1	15-Jul-57	9	8
UT	MILLARD	PB12-1	02-Sep-57	6	8
UT	MILLARD	PB15-1	16-Sep-57	4	8
UT	MORGAN	UK2-1	24-Mar-53	1	6
UT	MORGAN	TP8-1	09-Apr-55	4	6
UT	MORGAN	PB12-1	02-Sep-57	7	6
UT	MORGAN	PB15-1	16-Sep-57	9	6
UT	MORGAN	PB17-1	28-Sep-57	6	6
UT	MORGAN	SE1	06-Jul-62	8	6
UT	PIUTE	TS1-1	01-Apr-52	2	6
UT	PIUTE	TS6-1	25-May-52	7	6
UT	PIUTE	TP7-1	29-Mar-55	9	6
UT	PIUTE	TP9-1	15-Apr-55	6	6
UT	PIUTE	PB2-1	18-Jun-57	5	6
UT	PIUTE	PB18-1	07-Oct-57	8	6
UT	RICH	UK2-1	24-Mar-53	5	3
UT	RICH	PB15-1	16-Sep-57	10	3
UT	RICH	PB17-1	28-Sep-57	7	3
UT	SALT LAKE	UK2-1	24-Mar-53	6	8
UT	SALT LAKE	TP4-1	07-Mar-55	8	8
UT	SALT LAKE	TP8-1	09-Apr-55	2	8
UT	SALT LAKE	PB5-1	15-Jul-57	10	8
UT	SALT LAKE	PB9-1	23-Aug-57	9	8
UT	SALT LAKE	PB15-1	16-Sep-57	2	8
UT	SALT LAKE	PB17-1	28-Sep-57	1	8
UT	SALT LAKE	SE1	06-Jul-62	9	8
UT	SAN JUAN	UK1-1	17-Mar-53	5	2
UT	SAN JUAN	UK11-1	04-Jun-53	10	2
UT	SANPETE	TS1-1	01-Apr-52	3	2
UT	SANPETE	UK10-1	25-May-53	3	2

NATIONAL RANKING AMONG U.S. COUNTIES BY FALLOUT DATE

STATE	COUNTY	SHOT	DATE	RANK FOR DATE	NUMBER OF TIMES IN TOP 10
UT	SEVIER	TS1-1	01-Apr-52	4	4
UT	SEVIER	TS6-1	25-May-52	8	4
UT	SEVIER	UK10-1	25-May-53	4	4
UT	SEVIER	TP9-1	15-Apr-55	9	4
UT	SUMMIT	TP4-1	07-Mar-55	10	2
UT	SUMMIT	TP8-1	09-Apr-55	5	2
UT	TOOELE1	BJ6-1	29-Nov-51	7	4
UT	TOOELE1	PB8-1	18-Aug-57	6	4
UT	TOOELE1	PB12-1	02-Sep-57	8	4
UT	TOOELE1	PB17-1	28-Sep-57	8	4
UT	TOOELE2	UK2-1	24-Mar-53	4	6
UT	TOOELE2	TP8-1	09-Apr-55	1	6
UT	TOOELE2	PB8-1	18-Aug-57	8	6
UT	TOOELE2	PB9-1	23-Aug-57	5	6
UT	TOOELE2	PB17-1	28-Sep-57	9	6
UT	TOOELE2	SE1	06-Jul-62	5	6
UT	UINTAH	TP10-1	05-May-55	9	3
UT	UINTAH	PB9-1	23-Aug-57	7	3
UT	UINTAH	PB11-1	31-Aug-57	8	3
UT	UTAH	TS1-1	01-Apr-52	7	8
UT	UTAH	UK10-1	25-May-53	6	8
UT	UTAH	TP4-1	07-Mar-55	4	8
UT	UTAH	TP8-1	09-Apr-55	7	8
UT	UTAH	TP10-1	05-May-55	3	8
UT	UTAH	PB5-1	15-Jul-57	6	8
UT	UTAH	PB9-1	23-Aug-57	1	8
UT	UTAH	PB12-1	02-Sep-57	5	8
UT	WASATCH	TS1-1	01-Apr-52	8	7
UT	WASATCH	TP4-1	07-Mar-55	9	7
UT	WASATCH	TP8-1	09-Apr-55	3	7
UT	WASATCH	TP10-1	05-May-55	5	7
UT	WASATCH	PB5-1	15-Jul-57	8	7
UT	WASATCH	PB9-1	23-Aug-57	3	7
UT	WASATCH	PB12-1	02-Sep-57	9	7
UT	WASHINGTON1	UK9-1	19-May-53	3	5
UT	WASHINGTON1	TP7-1	29-Mar-55	3	5

STATE	COUNTY	SHOT	DATE	RANK FOR DATE	NUMBER OF TIMES IN TOP 10
			NATIONAL RANKING AMONG U.S. COUNTIES BY FALLOUT DATE		
UT	WASHINGTON1	PB3-1	24-Jun-57	1	5
UT	WASHINGTON1	PB11-1	31-Aug-57	7	5
UT	WASHINGTON1	PB18-1	07-Oct-57	2	5
UT	WASHINGTON2	UK1-1	17-Mar-53	1	7
UT	WASHINGTON2	UK4-1	06-Apr-53	1	7
UT	WASHINGTON2	UK9-1	19-May-53	1	7
UT	WASHINGTON2	TP3-1	01-Mar-55	1	7
UT	WASHINGTON2	TP11-1	15-May-55	7	7
UT	WASHINGTON2	PB3-1	24-Jun-57	8	7
UT	WASHINGTON2	PB11-1	31-Aug-57	3	7
UT	WASHINGTON3	UK1-1	17-Mar-53	2	6
UT	WASHINGTON3	UK9-1	19-May-53	2	6
UT	WASHINGTON3	TP3-1	01-Mar-55	3	6
UT	WASHINGTON3	PB3-1	24-Jun-57	5	6
UT	WASHINGTON3	PB11-1	31-Aug-57	4	6
UT	WASHINGTON3	PB18-1	07-Oct-57	5	6
UT	WAYNE	TS6-1	25-May-52	10	3
UT	WAYNE	PB2-1	18-Jun-57	10	3
UT	WAYNE	PB18-1	07-Oct-57	9	3
UT	WEBER	UK2-1	24-Mar-53	3	3
UT	WEBER	PB17-1	28-Sep-57	10	3
UT	WEBER	SE1	06-Jul-62	10	3
VA	ACCOMACK	SE6	11-Jul-62	1	1
VA	ALLEGHANY	UK8-6	13-May-53	7	1
VA	AMHERST	PB15-8	23-Sep-57	9	1
VA	APPOMATTOX	TS5-3	09-May-52	2	1
VA	ARLINGTON	BJ-2 3	01-Nov-51	3	2
VA	ARLINGTON	uk3 8	07-Apr-53	5	2
VA	AUGUSTA	UK5-8	18-Apr-53	8	3
VA	AUGUSTA	UK8-6	13-May-53	8	3
VA	AUGUSTA	PB15-8	23-Sep-57	10	3
VA	BEDFORD	BJ3-5	05-Nov-51	2	2
VA	BEDFORD	TS5-3	09-May-52	7	2
VA	BRUNSWICK	TS5-3	09-May-52	3	1
VA	BUCHANAN	uk1 8	24-Mar-53	10	1
VA	CAROLINE	uk3 8	07-Apr-53	6	1

NATIONAL RANKING AMONG U.S. COUNTIES BY FALLOUT DATE

STATE	COUNTY	SHOT	DATE	RANK FOR DATE	NUMBER OF TIMES IN TOP 10
VA	CHARLOTTE	PB12-7	08-Sep-57	9	2
VA	CHARLOTTE	PB12-8	09-Sep-57	1	2
VA	CHESTERFIELD	PB17-8	05-Oct-57	1	1
VA	CLARKE	TP9-10	23-Apr-55	10	1
VA	CRAIG	TP11-7	21-May-55	4	1
VA	DINWIDDIE	TS5-3	09-May-52	1	1
VA	ESSEX	R2-6	07-Feb-51	8	1
VA	FAIRFAX	uk3 8	07-Apr-53	7	1
VA	FAUQUIER	uk3 8	07-Apr-53	8	1
VA	FLOYD	BJ3-5	05-Nov-51	3	3
VA	FLOYD	UK8-6	13-May-53	9	3
VA	FLOYD	TP11-7	21-May-55	5	3
VA	FLUVANNA	PB2-8	25-Jun-57	1	1
VA	GLOUCESTER	PB17-8	05-Oct-57	6	1
VA	GRAYSON	BJ1-2	29-Oct-51	3	1
VA	GREENE	TS5-3	09-May-52	4	2
VA	GREENE	PB12-8	09-Sep-57	6	2
VA	GREENSVILLE	TS5-3	09-May-52	5	1
VA	HANOVER	TP9-10	23-Apr-55	2	2
VA	HANOVER	PB17-8	05-Oct-57	3	2
VA	HENRICO	TP9-10	23-Apr-55	5	2
VA	HENRICO	PB17-8	05-Oct-57	2	2
VA	HENRY	R2-6	07-Feb-51	9	1
VA	JAMES CITY	PB12-8	09-Sep-57	2	1
VA	KING AND QUE	BJ-2 5	03-Nov-51	7	2
VA	KING AND QUE	PB17-8	05-Oct-57	8	2
VA	KING WILLIAM	BJ-2 5	03-Nov-51	8	3
VA	KING WILLIAM	TP9-10	23-Apr-55	6	3
VA	KING WILLIAM	PB17-8	05-Oct-57	4	3
VA	LANCASTER	R2-6	07-Feb-51	10	2
VA	LANCASTER	PB17-8	05-Oct-57	9	2
VA	LOUDOUN	uk3 8	07-Apr-53	9	2
VA	LOUDOUN	PB12-8	09-Sep-57	7	2
VA	LOUISA	PB17-8	05-Oct-57	5	1
VA	MADISON	TS5-3	09-May-52	6	2
VA	MADISON	UK8-6	13-May-53	1	2

NATIONAL RANKING AMONG U.S. COUNTIES BY FALLOUT DATE

STATE	COUNTY	SHOT	DATE	RANK FOR DATE	NUMBER OF TIMES IN TOP 10
VA	MATHEWS	PB17-8	05-Oct-57	10	1
VA	MIDDLESEX	PB17-8	05-Oct-57	7	1
VA	MONTGOMERY	TP11-7	21-May-55	6	1
VA	NELSON	PB15-8	23-Sep-57	1	1
VA	NEW KENT	BJ-2 5	03-Nov-51	5	1
VA	NORFOLK/CHES	PB12-7	08-Sep-57	10	1
VA	ORANGE	uk3 8	07-Apr-53	10	1
VA	PAGE	UK8-6	13-May-53	2	1
VA	PRINCE WILLI	TS5-4	10-May-52	1	1
VA	RAPPAHANNOCK	UK8-6	13-May-53	3	1
VA	ROANOKE	BJ3-5	05-Nov-51	4	2
VA	ROANOKE	TP11-7	21-May-55	1	2
VA	ROCKBRIDGE	TP11-7	21-May-55	7	1
VA	ROCKINGHAM	UK8-6	13-May-53	4	2
VA	ROCKINGHAM	SE6	11-Jul-62	2	2
VA	SHENANDOAH	UK8-6	13-May-53	5	1
VA	SMYTH	UK5-8	18-Apr-53	9	1
VA	STAFFORD	TP9-10	23-Apr-55	7	1
VA	SUFFOLK/NANS	SE5	10-Jul-62	9	1
VA	VIRGINIA BEA	SE5	10-Jul-62	10	1
VA	WESTMORELAND	TP9-10	23-Apr-55	8	1
VA	WYTHE	UK5-8	18-Apr-53	10	1
VA	YORK	PB12-8	09-Sep-57	5	1
VT	ADDISON	UK7-2	26-Apr-53	10	2
VT	ADDISON	PB11-5	04-Sep-57	7	2
VT	BENNINGTON	UK7-2	26-Apr-53	6	2
VT	BENNINGTON	UK7-8	02-May-53	10	2
VT	CALEDONIA	R1-4	31-Jan-51	6	3
VT	CALEDONIA	TS8-3	07-Jun-52	7	3
VT	CALEDONIA	TP8-7	15-Apr-55	4	3
VT	CHITTENDEN	PB5-6	20-Jul-57	5	2
VT	CHITTENDEN	PB11-5	04-Sep-57	2	2
VT	ESSEX	PB5-6	20-Jul-57	1	1
VT	FRANKLIN	BJ2-2	31-Oct-51	6	1
VT	GRAND ISLE	BJ2-2	31-Oct-51	7	4
VT	GRAND ISLE	UK8-4	11-May-53	1	4

NATIONAL RANKING AMONG U.S. COUNTIES BY FALLOUT DATE

STATE	COUNTY	SHOT	DATE	RANK FOR DATE	NUMBER OF TIMES IN TOP 10
VT	GRAND ISLE	TP8-8	16-Apr-55	6	4
VT	GRAND ISLE	PB5-6	20-Jul-57	2	4
VT	LAMOILLE	TP8-8	16-Apr-55	7	2
VT	LAMOILLE	PB5-6	20-Jul-57	6	2
VT	ORANGE	TS8-3	07-Jun-52	8	2
VT	ORANGE	PB5-6	20-Jul-57	7	2
VT	ORLEANS	BJ2-2	31-Oct-51	8	2
VT	ORLEANS	PB5-6	20-Jul-57	3	2
VT	RUTLAND	TS8-3	07-Jun-52	10	1
VT	WASHINGTON	R1-4	31-Jan-51	4	3
VT	WASHINGTON	TS8-3	07-Jun-52	5	3
VT	WASHINGTON	PB5-6	20-Jul-57	8	3
VT	WINDHAM	R1-2	29-Jan-51	4	3
VT	WINDHAM	TP7-6	03-Apr-55	8	3
VT	WINDHAM	PB11-5	04-Sep-57	8	3
VT	WINDSOR	TS8-3	07-Jun-52	6	1
WA	BENTON	PB14-4	17-Sep-57	6	1
WA	CHELAN	PB14-4	17-Sep-57	7	1
WA	COLUMBIA	PB16-4	26-Sep-57	1	1
WA	DOUGLAS	UK10-2	26-May-53	6	1
WA	FERRY	UK10-2	26-May-53	1	1
WA	GARFIELD	UK10-2	26-May-53	10	1
WA	KLICKITAT	PB14-4	17-Sep-57	8	1
WA	LEWIS	PB14-4	17-Sep-57	9	1
WA	LINCOLN	PB14-4	17-Sep-57	10	1
WA	OKANOGAN	UK10-2	26-May-53	4	1
WA	PEND OREILLE	UK10-2	26-May-53	2	2
WA	PEND OREILLE	PB16-4	26-Sep-57	6	2
WA	PIERCE	PB14-4	17-Sep-57	4	1
WA	SPOKANE	PB16-4	26-Sep-57	2	1
WA	STEVENS	UK10-2	26-May-53	3	1
WA	WAHKIAKUM	UK2-5	28-Mar-53	5	1
WA	WALLA WALLA	PB16-4	26-Sep-57	3	1
WI	ADAMS	TS5-7	13-May-52	6	1
WI	BAYFIELD	PB11-3	02-Sep-57	6	1
WI	BUFFALO	UK9-2	20-May-53	10	1

NATIONAL RANKING AMONG U.S. COUNTIES BY FALLOUT DATE

STATE	COUNTY	SHOT	DATE	RANK FOR DATE	NUMBER OF TIMES IN TOP 10
WI	CALUMET	TS5-8	14-May-52	9	1
WI	CHIPPEWA	UK9-2	20-May-53	7	1
WI	CRAWFORD	PB6-9	01-Aug-57	9	1
WI	DOOR	TS5-7	13-May-52	7	1
WI	DOUGLAS	UK10-4	28-May-53	8	1
WI	DUNN	UK9-2	20-May-53	6	1
WI	FLORENCE	PB16-2	24-Sep-57	6	1
WI	FOREST	TS5-7	13-May-52	8	2
WI	FOREST	PB16-2	24-Sep-57	7	2
WI	GREEN	TS8-8	12-Jun-52	3	1
WI	GREEN LAKE	TS5-8	14-May-52	10	1
WI	JUNEAU	TS5-7	13-May-52	9	1
WI	KEWAUNEE	TS5-7	13-May-52	10	1
WI	RICHLAND	PB6-8	31-Jul-57	8	1
WI	RUSK	UK9-2	20-May-53	5	1
WI	SAUK	TS3-10	01-May-52	1	1
WI	SAWYER	UK9-2	20-May-53	2	1
WI	TREMPEALEAU	UK9-2	20-May-53	3	1
WI	WASHBURN	UK9-2	20-May-53	1	1
WV	BOONE	SE4	09-Jul-62	6	1
WV	BROOKE	UK9-3	21-May-53	8	2
WV	BROOKE	TP11-7	21-May-55	8	2
WV	FAYETTE	TP11-7	21-May-55	9	2
WV	FAYETTE	SE6	11-Jul-62	6	2
WV	HANCOCK	UK9-3	21-May-53	5	1
WV	HARDY	UK8-6	13-May-53	10	1
WV	LOGAN	PB6-7	30-Jul-57	1	2
WV	LOGAN	SE4	09-Jul-62	7	2
WV	MARSHALL	TP11-10	24-May-55	2	1
WV	MCDOWELL	TS3-6	27-Apr-52	9	2
WV	MCDOWELL	UK9-4	22-May-53	1	2
WV	MORGAN	UK10-6	30-May-53	4	1
WV	OHIO	R1-2	29-Jan-51	3	1
WV	PENDLETON	UK8-6	13-May-53	6	1
WV	PLEASANTS	R1-2	29-Jan-51	5	2
WV	PLEASANTS	TP11-7	21-May-55	10	2

NATIONAL RANKING AMONG U.S. COUNTIES BY FALLOUT DATE

STATE	COUNTY	SHOT	DATE	RANK FOR DATE	NUMBER OF TIMES IN TOP 10
WV	PUTNAM	BJ1-2	29-Oct-51	4	1
WV	RALEIGH	BJ1-2	29-Oct-51	5	1
WV	SUMMERS	BJ1-2	29-Oct-51	6	1
WV	WIRT	SE6	11-Jul-62	4	1
WV	WYOMING	TS3-6	27-Apr-52	10	1
WY	ALBANY	UK11-2	05-Jun-53	4	4
WY	ALBANY	UK11-8	11-Jun-53	7	4
WY	ALBANY	TP8-2	10-Apr-55	9	4
WY	ALBANY	PB2-2	19-Jun-57	6	4
WY	CAMPBELL	TP8-2	10-Apr-55	10	2
WY	CAMPBELL	TP11-2	16-May-55	6	2
WY	CARBON	UK10-1	25-May-53	10	1
WY	CONVERSE	TP8-2	10-Apr-55	4	2
WY	CONVERSE	PB2-2	19-Jun-57	3	2
WY	FREMONT	UK2-1	24-Mar-53	8	1
WY	GOSHEN	UK3-2	01-Apr-53	6	3
WY	GOSHEN	TP3-6	06-Mar-55	4	3
WY	GOSHEN	PB5-3	17-Jul-57	8	3
WY	HOT SPRINGS	TS5-1	07-May-52	1	1
WY	JOHNSON	TS5-1	07-May-52	10	4
WY	JOHNSON	UK10-3	27-May-53	5	4
WY	JOHNSON	UK10-8	01-Jun-53	5	4
WY	JOHNSON	UK11-2	05-Jun-53	7	4
WY	LARAMIE	UK11-8	11-Jun-53	8	4
WY	LARAMIE	TP5-2	13-Mar-55	1	4
WY	LARAMIE	TP8-2	10-Apr-55	7	4
WY	LARAMIE	PB2-2	19-Jun-57	9	4
WY	LINCOLN	UK2-1	24-Mar-53	7	1
WY	NATRONA	TS5-1	07-May-52	2	5
WY	NATRONA	TS5-7	13-May-52	2	5
WY	NATRONA	UK10-3	27-May-53	1	5
WY	NATRONA	TP8-2	10-Apr-55	2	5
WY	NATRONA	PB2-2	19-Jun-57	1	5
WY	NIOBRARA	TS5-1	07-May-52	3	4
WY	NIOBRARA	TS7-3	03-Jun-52	3	4
WY	NIOBRARA	UK3-2	01-Apr-53	4	4

STATE	COUNTY	SHOT	DATE	RANK FOR DATE	NUMBER OF TIMES IN TOP 10
WY	NIOBRARA	PB5-3	17-Jul-57	9	4
WY	PARK	UK10-7	31-May-53	7	2
WY	PARK	PB8-2	19-Aug-57	2	2
WY	PLATTE	TP11-2	16-May-55	2	2
WY	PLATTE	PB2-2	19-Jun-57	7	2
WY	SHERIDAN	TS5-6	12-May-52	8	2
WY	SHERIDAN	UK8-2	09-May-53	9	2
WY	SUBLETTE	UK2-1	24-Mar-53	9	1
WY	SWEETWATER	PB11-1	31-Aug-57	6	1
WY	TETON	TS5-1	07-May-52	6	4
WY	TETON	TS5-7	13-May-52	4	4
WY	TETON	TS5-8	14-May-52	8	4
WY	TETON	PB17-5	02-Oct-57	3	4
WY	UINTA	TP8-1	09-Apr-55	9	1
WY	WESTON	PB5-3	17-Jul-57	4	1

NATIONAL RANKING AMONG U.S. COUNTIES BY FALLOUT DATE

SECTION 3

TOP 500 SHOT DAYS
HIGHEST AVERAGE
TOTAL FALLOUT BY DATE

1951-1962

	TOP 500 SHOT DAYS: HIGHEST AVERAGE TOTAL FALLOUT BY DATE				
STATE	COUNTY	SHOT DAY	DATE	uCi/ SQ METER	RANK
UT	WASHINGTON2	UK9-1	19-May-53	4392.12	1
UT	WASHINGTON3	UK9-1	19-May-53	3642.40	2
UT	WASHINGTON1	UK9-1	19-May-53	2758.95	3
UT	KANE1	UK9-1	19-May-53	2334.06	4
UT	KANE2	UK9-1	19-May-53	2334.06	5
NV	CLARK1	UK7-1	25-Apr-53	2185.05	6
AZ	MOHAVE2	UK9-1	19-May-53	1986.84	7
NV	LINCOLN1	UK9-1	19-May-53	1716.20	8
CO	GUNNISON	UK9-1	19-May-53	1570.05	9
AZ	COCONINO1	UK9-1	19-May-53	1522.26	10
CO	CONEJOS	UK9-1	19-May-53	1437.92	11
UT	GARFIELD	PB11-1	31-Aug-57	1238.11	12
TX	REFUGIO	R2-2	03-Feb-51	1067.00	13
AZ	MOHAVE1	UK9-1	19-May-53	1045.83	14
IA	HOWARD	SE3	08-Jul-62	950.00	15
IA	MITCHELL	SE3	08-Jul-62	950.00	16
IA	WORTH	SE3	08-Jul-62	950.00	17
AZ	COCONINO2	UK7-1	25-Apr-53	912.14	18
CO	ARCHULETA	UK9-1	19-May-53	910.28	19
CA	INYO3	PB11-1	31-Aug-57	898.04	20
SD	WASHABAUGH	SE2	07-Jul-62	860.52	21
CO	MINERAL	UK9-1	19-May-53	755.80	22
NV	NYE2	PB1-1	28-May-57	754.54	23
CO	HINSDALE	UK9-1	19-May-53	747.40	24
UT	MORGAN	UK2-1	24-Mar-53	725.74	25
UT	DAVIS	UK2-1	24-Mar-53	723.10	26
UT	WEBER	UK2-1	24-Mar-53	679.47	27
CO	RIO GRANDE	UK9-1	19-May-53	643.77	28
UT	WASHINGTON2	PB11-1	31-Aug-57	641.04	29
UT	TOOELE2	UK2-1	24-Mar-53	635.02	30
UT	RICH	UK2-1	24-Mar-53	623.63	31
IA	JEFFERSON	SE3	08-Jul-62	621.15	32
IA	LEE	SE3	08-Jul-62	621.15	33
IA	VAN BUREN	SE3	08-Jul-62	621.15	34
IA	WASHINGTON	SE3	08-Jul-62	621.15	35

STATE	COUNTY	SHOT DAY	DATE	uCi/ SQ METER	RANK
		TOP 500 SHOT DAYS: HIGHEST AVERAGE TOTAL FALLOUT BY DATE			
IL	HANCOCK	SE3	08-Jul-62	621.15	36
CO	PITKIN	UK9-1	19-May-53	611.57	37
UT	SALT LAKE	UK2-1	24-Mar-53	598.89	38
MN	FARIBAULT	SE3	08-Jul-62	584.61	39
MN	MOWER	SE3	08-Jul-62	584.61	40
MN	WATONWAN	SE3	08-Jul-62	584.61	41
WY	LINCOLN	UK2-1	24-Mar-53	568.59	42
UT	GARFIELD	UK9-1	19-May-53	568.41	43
WY	FREMONT	UK2-1	24-Mar-53	564.43	44
WY	SUBLETTE	UK2-1	24-Mar-53	564.43	45
NV	NYE2	PB5-1	15-Jul-57	544.73	46
AZ	APACHE	UK7-1	25-Apr-53	537.54	47
UT	CACHE	UK2-1	24-Mar-53	536.50	48
NY	WASHINGTON	UK7-2	26-Apr-53	529.85	49
IA	BENTON	SE3	08-Jul-62	527.44	50
IA	BOONE	SE3	08-Jul-62	527.44	51
IA	BUENA VISTA	SE3	08-Jul-62	527.44	52
IA	CALHOUN	SE3	08-Jul-62	527.44	53
IA	CARROLL	SE3	08-Jul-62	527.44	54
IA	CHEROKEE	SE3	08-Jul-62	527.44	55
IA	CLAY	SE3	08-Jul-62	527.44	56
IA	CRAWFORD	SE3	08-Jul-62	527.44	57
IA	DICKINSON	SE3	08-Jul-62	527.44	58
IA	EMMET	SE3	08-Jul-62	527.44	59
IA	FLOYD	SE3	08-Jul-62	527.44	60
IA	GREENE	SE3	08-Jul-62	527.44	61
IA	HAMILTON	SE3	08-Jul-62	527.44	62
IA	HANCOCK	SE3	08-Jul-62	527.44	63
IA	HUMBOLDT	SE3	08-Jul-62	527.44	64
IA	IDA	SE3	08-Jul-62	527.44	65
IA	IOWA	SE3	08-Jul-62	527.44	66
IA	JASPER	SE3	08-Jul-62	527.44	67
IA	KOSSUTH	SE3	08-Jul-62	527.44	68
IA	LYON	SE3	08-Jul-62	527.44	69
IA	MARSHALL	SE3	08-Jul-62	527.44	70

STATE	COUNTY	SHOT DAY	DATE	uCi/ SQ METER	RANK
IA	MONONA	SE3	08-Jul-62	527.44	71
IA	O BRIEN	SE3	08-Jul-62	527.44	72
IA	OSCEOLA	SE3	08-Jul-62	527.44	73
IA	PALO ALTO	SE3	08-Jul-62	527.44	74
IA	PLYMOUTH	SE3	08-Jul-62	527.44	75
IA	POCAHONTAS	SE3	08-Jul-62	527.44	76
IA	SAC	SE3	08-Jul-62	527.44	77
IA	SIOUX	SE3	08-Jul-62	527.44	78
IA	STORY	SE3	08-Jul-62	527.44	79
IA	WINNEBAGO	SE3	08-Jul-62	527.44	80
IA	WINNESHIEK	SE3	08-Jul-62	527.44	81
IA	WOODBURY	SE3	08-Jul-62	527.44	82
MN	ROCK	SE3	08-Jul-62	527.44	83
NE	DAKOTA	SE3	08-Jul-62	527.44	84
NE	DIXON	SE3	08-Jul-62	527.44	85
NE	STANTON	SE3	08-Jul-62	527.44	86
NE	THURSTON	SE3	08-Jul-62	527.44	87
SD	TURNER	SE3	08-Jul-62	527.44	88
NV	NYE1	PB1-1	28-May-57	511.88	89
NY	WARREN	UK7-2	26-Apr-53	503.93	90
UT	IRON3	UK9-1	19-May-53	502.13	91
UT	WASHINGTON3	PB11-1	31-Aug-57	500.51	92
NV	WHITE PINE3	UK2-1	24-Mar-53	492.93	93
NY	RENSSELAER	UK7-2	26-Apr-53	484.47	94
NV	EUREKA	PB8-1	18-Aug-57	482.83	95
UT	SAN JUAN	UK9-1	19-May-53	470.30	96
CO	DOLORES	UK9-1	19-May-53	466.90	97
CO	LA PLATA	UK9-1	19-May-53	466.90	98
CO	OURAY	UK9-1	19-May-53	466.90	99
CO	SAN JUAN	UK9-1	19-May-53	466.90	100
CO	SAN MIGUEL	UK9-1	19-May-53	466.90	101
CO	MONTROSE	UK9-1	19-May-53	463.51	102
UT	SUMMIT	UK2-1	24-Mar-53	451.90	103
ID	BEAR LAKE	UK2-1	24-Mar-53	443.88	104
UT	BOX ELDER2	UK2-1	24-Mar-53	443.88	105

TOP 500 SHOT DAYS: HIGHEST AVERAGE TOTAL FALLOUT BY DATE

STATE	COUNTY	SHOT DAY	DATE	uCi/ SQ METER	RANK
CO	ALAMOSA	UK9-1	19-May-53	441.46	106
NM	MCKINLEY	UK7-1	25-Apr-53	436.89	107
NE	LOUP	SE3	08-Jul-62	436.50	108
SD	CUSTER	SE2	07-Jul-62	434.17	109
NV	LINCOLN1	TP9-1	15-Apr-55	433.28	110
NV	WHITE PINE2	TP10-1	05-May-55	430.02	111
UT	IRON2	TP11-1	15-May-55	413.43	112
UT	BEAVER	TP9-1	15-Apr-55	406.51	113
NV	LINCOLN1	PB11-1	31-Aug-57	393.34	114
NM	CHAVES	UK7-1	25-Apr-53	393.20	115
CO	SAGUACHE	UK9-1	19-May-53	391.91	116
NV	CLARK1	TP11-1	15-May-55	387.19	117
WY	SWEETWATER	PB11-1	31-Aug-57	384.53	118
CO	MESA	TP9-1	15-Apr-55	382.05	119
UT	MILLARD	UK9-1	19-May-53	376.15	120
UT	SANPETE	UK9-1	19-May-53	376.15	121
CO	MONTEZUMA	UK9-1	19-May-53	374.79	122
UT	CARBON	UK9-1	19-May-53	374.79	123
CO	MESA	UK9-1	19-May-53	365.84	124
CO	COSTILLA	UK9-1	19-May-53	363.68	125
AZ	NAVAJO	UK7-1	25-Apr-53	363.55	126
SD	HAMLIN	SE2	07-Jul-62	361.42	127
SD	KINGSBURY	SE2	07-Jul-62	361.42	128
SD	MOODY	SE2	07-Jul-62	361.42	129
KY	GREENUP	SE4	09-Jul-62	359.52	130
KY	LAWRENCE	SE4	09-Jul-62	359.52	131
KY	LEWIS	SE4	09-Jul-62	359.52	132
KY	TRIMBLE	SE4	09-Jul-62	359.52	133
OH	SCIOTO	SE4	09-Jul-62	359.52	134
WV	BOONE	SE4	09-Jul-62	359.52	135
WV	LOGAN	SE4	09-Jul-62	359.52	136
MO	CLARK	SE3	08-Jul-62	358.08	137
MO	KNOX	SE3	08-Jul-62	358.08	138
MO	SCOTLAND	SE3	08-Jul-62	358.08	139
NM	BERNALILLO	UK9-1	19-May-53	351.01	140

				uCi/	
STATE	**COUNTY**	**SHOT DAY**	**DATE**	**SQ METER**	**RANK**
SD	FALL RIVER	SE2	07-Jul-62	345.60	141
SD	SHANNON	SE2	07-Jul-62	345.60	142
SD	STANLEY	SE2	07-Jul-62	345.60	143
IA	ADAIR	SE3	08-Jul-62	345.56	144
IA	ADAMS	SE3	08-Jul-62	345.56	145
IA	APPANOOSE	SE3	08-Jul-62	345.56	146
IA	AUDUBON	SE3	08-Jul-62	345.56	147
IA	CASS	SE3	08-Jul-62	345.56	148
IA	CLARKE	SE3	08-Jul-62	345.56	149
IA	DAVIS	SE3	08-Jul-62	345.56	150
IA	DECATUR	SE3	08-Jul-62	345.56	151
IA	DELAWARE	SE3	08-Jul-62	345.56	152
IA	GUTHRIE	SE3	08-Jul-62	345.56	153
IA	HENRY	SE3	08-Jul-62	345.56	154
IA	JOHNSON	SE3	08-Jul-62	345.56	155
IA	KEOKUK	SE3	08-Jul-62	345.56	156
IA	LOUISA	SE3	08-Jul-62	345.56	157
IA	MADISON	SE3	08-Jul-62	345.56	158
IA	MAHASKA	SE3	08-Jul-62	345.56	159
IA	MARION	SE3	08-Jul-62	345.56	160
IA	MONROE	SE3	08-Jul-62	345.56	161
IA	RINGGOLD	SE3	08-Jul-62	345.56	162
IA	SHELBY	SE3	08-Jul-62	345.56	163
IA	UNION	SE3	08-Jul-62	345.56	164
IA	WAPELLO	SE3	08-Jul-62	345.56	165
IA	WAYNE	SE3	08-Jul-62	345.56	166
IL	FULTON	SE3	08-Jul-62	345.56	167
IL	MCDONOUGH	SE3	08-Jul-62	345.56	168
IL	WARREN	SE3	08-Jul-62	345.56	169
NE	HOWARD	SE3	08-Jul-62	345.56	170
NE	SHERMAN	SE3	08-Jul-62	345.56	171
NE	WASHINGTON	SE3	08-Jul-62	345.56	172
WI	IOWA	SE3	08-Jul-62	345.56	173
CA	INYO3	TP4-1	07-Mar-55	341.80	174
CO	LAKE	UK9-1	19-May-53	341.50	175

TOP 500 SHOT DAYS: HIGHEST AVERAGE
TOTAL FALLOUT BY DATE

				uCi/	
STATE	COUNTY	SHOT DAY	DATE	SQ METER	RANK
NM	SANDOVAL	UK7-1	25-Apr-53	338.39	176
NM	SANTA FE	UK7-1	25-Apr-53	335.90	177
NV	WHITE PINE2	PB8-1	18-Aug-57	335.38	178
NM	LINCOLN	UK7-1	25-Apr-53	333.53	179
NV	LINCOLN2	TP7-1	29-Mar-55	333.26	180
NV	ESMERALDA2	PB6-1	24-Jul-57	328.70	181
AZ	COCONINO2	UK6-1	18-Apr-53	328.54	182
MN	FILLMORE	SE3	08-Jul-62	327.38	183
MN	MARTIN	SE3	08-Jul-62	327.38	184
MN	MURRAY	SE3	08-Jul-62	327.38	185
MN	PIPESTONE	SE3	08-Jul-62	327.38	186
SD	LAKE	SE3	08-Jul-62	327.38	187
UT	EMERY	TP9-1	15-Apr-55	325.27	188
UT	GRAND	TP9-1	15-Apr-55	325.27	189
UT	PIUTE	TP9-1	15-Apr-55	325.27	190
MN	BLUE EARTH	SE3	08-Jul-62	325.19	191
MN	BROWN	SE3	08-Jul-62	325.19	192
MN	LE SUEUR	SE3	08-Jul-62	325.19	193
MN	NICOLLET	SE3	08-Jul-62	325.19	194
MN	RICE	SE3	08-Jul-62	325.19	195
MN	WABASHA	SE3	08-Jul-62	325.19	196
MN	WASECA	SE3	08-Jul-62	325.19	197
WI	BUFFALO	SE3	08-Jul-62	325.19	198
NV	CLARK1	UK6-1	18-Apr-53	324.13	199
CO	DELTA	UK9-1	19-May-53	323.30	200
CO	DELTA	TP9-1	15-Apr-55	322.85	201
CO	GARFIELD	TP9-1	15-Apr-55	322.85	202
NV	NYE2	TP4-1	07-Mar-55	322.23	203
AZ	NAVAJO	UK6-1	18-Apr-53	321.49	204
NV	LINCOLN2	UK9-1	19-May-53	321.44	205
AZ	APACHE	UK6-1	18-Apr-53	319.19	206
UT	WASHINGTON1	PB11-1	31-Aug-57	318.50	207
NV	NYE2	TP10-1	05-May-55	316.28	208
NY	SARATOGA	UK7-2	26-Apr-53	296.91	209
UT	IRON1	UK9-1	19-May-53	296.90	210

				uCi/	
STATE	COUNTY	SHOT DAY	DATE	SQ METER	RANK

TOP 500 SHOT DAYS: HIGHEST AVERAGE TOTAL FALLOUT BY DATE

STATE	COUNTY	SHOT DAY	DATE	uCi/ SQ METER	RANK
NY	FULTON	UK7-2	26-Apr-53	290.48	211
WY	UINTA	UK2-1	24-Mar-53	286.32	212
NV	WHITE PINE2	PB5-1	15-Jul-57	283.40	213
UT	WAYNE	UK9-1	19-May-53	282.11	214
AZ	APACHE	UK9-1	19-May-53	281.09	215
UT	EMERY	UK9-1	19-May-53	281.09	216
UT	JUAB	UK9-1	19-May-53	281.09	217
UT	GRAND	UK9-1	19-May-53	280.07	218
UT	UTAH	UK9-1	19-May-53	280.07	219
UT	WASATCH	UK9-1	19-May-53	280.07	220
NM	SANDOVAL	UK9-1	19-May-53	279.05	221
NV	LANDER2	PB1-1	28-May-57	278.84	222
CO	GARFIELD	UK9-1	19-May-53	278.15	223
NM	MCKINLEY	UK9-1	19-May-53	278.15	224
NV	MINERAL	PB1-1	28-May-57	277.88	225
NM	TORRANCE	UK9-1	19-May-53	275.09	226
NV	CHURCHILL	PB1-1	28-May-57	274.92	227
NV	ESMERALDA2	PB16-1	23-Sep-57	274.35	228
NV	ESMERALDA2	PB16-1	23-Sep-57	274.35	229
UT	IRON2	UK9-1	19-May-53	266.15	230
NM	SAN JUAN	UK9-1	19-May-53	264.14	231
NV	WHITE PINE3	PB8-1	18-Aug-57	263.85	232
KY	POWELL	SE4	09-Jul-62	263.65	233
ID	FRANKLIN	UK2-1	24-Mar-53	263.50	234
NM	VALENCIA	UK7-1	25-Apr-53	262.11	235
NV	ESMERALDA1	PB6-1	24-Jul-57	256.26	236
NV	CLARK2	UK6-1	18-Apr-53	255.63	237
NV	NYE2	PB8-1	18-Aug-57	254.89	238
UT	WASHINGTON2	TP3-1	01-Mar-55	254.31	239
IA	BLACK HAWK	SE3	08-Jul-62	252.68	240
IA	BLACK HAWK	SE3	08-Jul-62	252.68	241
NE	HOLT	SE3	08-Jul-62	252.68	242
SD	YANKTON	SE3	08-Jul-62	252.68	243
NM	TORRANCE	UK7-1	25-Apr-53	251.96	244
NM	CURRY	UK7-1	25-Apr-53	250.15	245

				uCi/	
				TOP 500 SHOT DAYS: HIGHEST AVERAGE TOTAL FALLOUT BY DATE	
STATE	**COUNTY**	**SHOT DAY**	**DATE**	**SQ METER**	**RANK**
NM	DE BACA	UK7-1	25-Apr-53	250.15	246
NM	GUADALUPE	UK7-1	25-Apr-53	250.15	247
NM	ROOSEVELT	UK7-1	25-Apr-53	250.15	248
NV	WASHOE	PB1-1	28-May-57	249.92	249
NV	WHITE PINE1	PB8-1	18-Aug-57	249.74	250
VT	BENNINGTON	UK7-2	26-Apr-53	249.42	251
UT	SEVIER	TP9-1	15-Apr-55	243.92	252
NV	NYE2	UK2-1	24-Mar-53	243.64	253
UT	UTAH	TP10-1	05-May-55	238.18	254
NV	WHITE PINE1	TP10-1	05-May-55	238.09	255
UT	WASATCH	TP10-1	05-May-55	237.40	256
UT	UINTAH	PB11-1	31-Aug-57	235.72	257
UT	DUCHESNE	TP10-1	05-May-55	235.65	258
NV	CARSON CITY	PB1-1	28-May-57	234.66	259
NV	DOUGLAS	PB1-1	28-May-57	234.66	260
NV	STOREY	PB1-1	28-May-57	233.81	261
CO	MOFFAT	TP10-1	05-May-55	233.13	262
UT	DAGGETT	TP10-1	05-May-55	233.13	263
UT	UINTAH	TP10-1	05-May-55	233.13	264
UT	DAGGETT	PB11-1	31-Aug-57	232.42	265
CO	RIO BLANCO	TP10-1	05-May-55	232.25	266
AZ	MOHAVE2	PB11-1	31-Aug-57	230.98	267
NV	LYON	PB1-1	28-May-57	229.48	268
WY	FREMONT	PB11-1	31-Aug-57	228.21	269
NY	SCHENECTADY	UK7-2	26-Apr-53	226.60	270
CO	EAGLE	UK9-1	19-May-53	225.10	271
NV	WHITE PINE3	TP10-1	05-May-55	221.15	272
IA	BREMER	SE3	08-Jul-62	220.22	273
IA	BUCHANAN	SE3	08-Jul-62	220.22	274
NE	ANTELOPE	SE3	08-Jul-62	220.22	275
NE	GARFIELD	SE3	08-Jul-62	220.22	276
SD	HANSON	SE3	08-Jul-62	220.22	277
NM	MCKINLEY	UK6-1	18-Apr-53	211.30	278
NM	VALENCIA	UK6-1	18-Apr-53	211.30	279
NV	LINCOLN2	PB5-1	15-Jul-57	209.94	280

STATE	COUNTY	SHOT DAY	DATE	uCi/ SQ METER	RANK
TOP 500 SHOT DAYS: HIGHEST AVERAGE TOTAL FALLOUT BY DATE					
IN	ALLEN	SE4	09-Jul-62	208.78	281
IN	GRANT	SE4	09-Jul-62	208.78	282
IN	HAMILTON	SE4	09-Jul-62	208.78	283
IN	HOWARD	SE4	09-Jul-62	208.78	284
IN	TIPTON	SE4	09-Jul-62	208.78	285
IN	WAYNE	SE4	09-Jul-62	208.78	286
IN	WELLS	SE4	09-Jul-62	208.78	287
KY	BATH	SE4	09-Jul-62	208.78	288
KY	BOYD	SE4	09-Jul-62	208.78	289
KY	CAMPBELL	SE4	09-Jul-62	208.78	290
KY	CARROLL	SE4	09-Jul-62	208.78	291
KY	CARTER	SE4	09-Jul-62	208.78	292
KY	ELLIOTT	SE4	09-Jul-62	208.78	293
KY	FLEMING	SE4	09-Jul-62	208.78	294
KY	GALLATIN	SE4	09-Jul-62	208.78	295
KY	HARRISON	SE4	09-Jul-62	208.78	296
KY	HENRY	SE4	09-Jul-62	208.78	297
KY	KENTON	SE4	09-Jul-62	208.78	298
KY	MASON	SE4	09-Jul-62	208.78	299
KY	NICHOLAS	SE4	09-Jul-62	208.78	300
KY	OWEN	SE4	09-Jul-62	208.78	301
KY	ROBERTSON	SE4	09-Jul-62	208.78	302
KY	ROWAN	SE4	09-Jul-62	208.78	303
OH	ADAMS	SE4	09-Jul-62	208.78	304
OH	ALLEN	SE4	09-Jul-62	208.78	305
OH	BUTLER	SE4	09-Jul-62	208.78	306
OH	BUTLER	SE4	09-Jul-62	208.78	307
OH	CHAMPAIGN	SE4	09-Jul-62	208.78	308
OH	CLARK	SE4	09-Jul-62	208.78	309
OH	CLINTON	SE4	09-Jul-62	208.78	310
OH	FULTON	SE4	09-Jul-62	208.78	311
OH	HIGHLAND	SE4	09-Jul-62	208.78	312
OH	JACKSON	SE4	09-Jul-62	208.78	313
OH	KNOX	SE4	09-Jul-62	208.78	314
OH	LICKING	SE4	09-Jul-62	208.78	315

STATE	COUNTY	SHOT DAY	DATE	uCi/ SQ METER	RANK
OH	MEDINA	SE4	09-Jul-62	208.78	316
OH	MIAMI	SE4	09-Jul-62	208.78	317
OH	MONTGOMERY	SE4	09-Jul-62	208.78	318
OH	MORGAN	SE4	09-Jul-62	208.78	319
OH	PERRY	SE4	09-Jul-62	208.78	320
OH	PIKE	SE4	09-Jul-62	208.78	321
OH	PREBLE	SE4	09-Jul-62	208.78	322
OH	SENECA	SE4	09-Jul-62	208.78	323
OH	WARREN	SE4	09-Jul-62	208.78	324
OH	WYANDOT	SE4	09-Jul-62	208.78	325
PA	VENANGO	SE4	09-Jul-62	208.78	326
VA	BATH	SE4	09-Jul-62	208.78	327
VA	BOTETOURT	SE4	09-Jul-62	208.78	328
WV	KANAWHA	SE4	09-Jul-62	208.78	329
WV	LINCOLN	SE4	09-Jul-62	208.78	330
WV	MASON	SE4	09-Jul-62	208.78	331
WV	MONROE	SE4	09-Jul-62	208.78	332
WV	PENDLETON	SE4	09-Jul-62	208.78	333
WV	RALEIGH	SE4	09-Jul-62	208.78	334
WV	SUMMERS	SE4	09-Jul-62	208.78	335
WV	WAYNE	SE4	09-Jul-62	208.78	336
IA	BUTLER	SE3	08-Jul-62	208.70	337
IA	CERRO GORDO	SE3	08-Jul-62	208.70	338
IA	FAYETTE	SE3	08-Jul-62	208.70	339
IA	FRANKLIN	SE3	08-Jul-62	208.70	340
IA	HARDIN	SE3	08-Jul-62	208.70	341
IA	POWESHIEK	SE3	08-Jul-62	208.70	342
IA	TAMA	SE3	08-Jul-62	208.70	343
IA	WEBSTER	SE3	08-Jul-62	208.70	344
IA	WRIGHT	SE3	08-Jul-62	208.70	345
MN	NOBLES	SE3	08-Jul-62	208.70	346
NE	CUMING	SE3	08-Jul-62	208.70	347
NE	MADISON	SE3	08-Jul-62	208.70	348
NE	WAYNE	SE3	08-Jul-62	208.70	349
SD	CLAY	SE3	08-Jul-62	208.70	350

				uCi/	
STATE	COUNTY	SHOT DAY	DATE	SQ METER	RANK
SD	DAVISON	SE3	08-Jul-62	208.70	351
SD	HUTCHINSON	SE3	08-Jul-62	208.70	352
SD	LINCOLN	SE3	08-Jul-62	208.70	353
SD	MCCOOK	SE3	08-Jul-62	208.70	354
SD	UNION	SE3	08-Jul-62	208.70	355
NM	QUAY	UK7-1	25-Apr-53	208.52	356
AZ	MOHAVE2	TP11-1	15-May-55	207.52	357
NV	WHITE PINE3	PB5-1	15-Jul-57	206.22	358
MA	PLYMOUTH	UK4-2	07-Apr-53	205.84	359
NV	WHITE PINE2	TP4-1	07-Mar-55	205.41	360
IA	PAGE	SE3	08-Jul-62	200.06	361
IA	TAYLOR	SE3	08-Jul-62	200.06	362
IL	ADAMS	SE3	08-Jul-62	200.06	363
IL	BROWN	SE3	08-Jul-62	200.06	364
IL	CASS	SE3	08-Jul-62	200.06	365
IL	GREENE	SE3	08-Jul-62	200.06	366
IL	MACOUPIN	SE3	08-Jul-62	200.06	367
IL	MONTGOMERY	SE3	08-Jul-62	200.06	368
IL	MOULTRIE	SE3	08-Jul-62	200.06	369
IL	PIKE	SE3	08-Jul-62	200.06	370
IL	SANGAMON	SE3	08-Jul-62	200.06	371
IL	SCHUYLER	SE3	08-Jul-62	200.06	372
IL	SHELBY	SE3	08-Jul-62	200.06	373
MO	DAVIESS	SE3	08-Jul-62	200.06	374
MO	LEWIS	SE3	08-Jul-62	200.06	375
MO	PUTNAM	SE3	08-Jul-62	200.06	376
MO	RALLS	SE3	08-Jul-62	200.06	377
MO	SCHUYLER	SE3	08-Jul-62	200.06	378
MO	SHELBY	SE3	08-Jul-62	200.06	379
MO	WORTH	SE3	08-Jul-62	200.06	380
CO	ARCHULETA	UK6-1	18-Apr-53	193.20	381
UT	BEAVER	UK9-1	19-May-53	189.43	382
UT	WASHINGTON1	PB3-1	24-Jun-57	188.87	383
UT	PIUTE	UK9-1	19-May-53	188.75	384
UT	SEVIER	UK9-1	19-May-53	188.07	385

| | | | | TOP 500 SHOT DAYS: HIGHEST AVERAGE TOTAL FALLOUT BY DATE | | |
| | | | | | | |

STATE	COUNTY	SHOT DAY	DATE	uCi/ SQ METER	RANK
NM	LOS ALAMOS	UK9-1	19-May-53	186.72	386
NM	RIO ARRIBA	UK9-1	19-May-53	186.72	387
NM	SANTA FE	UK9-1	19-May-53	186.04	388
NM	VALENCIA	UK9-1	19-May-53	186.04	389
NM	TAOS	UK9-1	19-May-53	185.36	390
NV	MINERAL	PB6-1	24-Jul-57	184.78	391
NY	ALBANY	UK7-2	26-Apr-53	182.51	392
MN	DODGE	SE3	08-Jul-62	181.88	393
MN	GOODHUE	SE3	08-Jul-62	181.88	394
MN	LINCOLN	SE3	08-Jul-62	181.88	395
MN	LYON	SE3	08-Jul-62	181.88	396
MN	SIBLEY	SE3	08-Jul-62	181.88	397
MN	STEELE	SE3	08-Jul-62	181.88	398
MN	WINONA	SE3	08-Jul-62	181.88	399
SD	BROOKINGS	SE3	08-Jul-62	181.88	400
MA	NORFOLK	UK4-2	07-Apr-53	181.58	401
UT	IRON3	TP11-1	15-May-55	180.05	402
CO	LA PLATA	R1-1	29-Jan-51	179.46	403
SD	MINER	SE2	07-Jul-62	177.44	404
ID	CARIBOU	UK2-1	24-Mar-53	176.27	405
MN	JACKSON	SE3	08-Jul-62	173.92	406
NY	COLUMBIA	UK7-2	26-Apr-53	173.71	407
IA	CLINTON	SE3	08-Jul-62	172.89	408
IA	DUBUQUE	SE3	08-Jul-62	172.89	409
IA	JACKSON	SE3	08-Jul-62	172.89	410
IA	MILLS	SE3	08-Jul-62	172.89	411
IA	MONTGOMERY	SE3	08-Jul-62	172.89	412
IL	MARSHALL	SE3	08-Jul-62	172.89	413
IL	WOODFORD	SE3	08-Jul-62	172.89	414
NE	COLFAX	SE3	08-Jul-62	172.89	415
NE	GREELEY	SE3	08-Jul-62	172.89	416
WI	GRANT	SE3	08-Jul-62	172.89	417
WI	WALWORTH	SE3	08-Jul-62	172.89	418
AZ	COCONINO3	UK7-1	25-Apr-53	172.07	419
VT	ADDISON	UK7-2	26-Apr-53	171.29	420

	TOP 500 SHOT DAYS: HIGHEST AVERAGE TOTAL FALLOUT BY DATE				
STATE	COUNTY	SHOT DAY	DATE	uCi/ SQ METER	RANK
MT	POWDER RIVER	UK2-1	24-Mar-53	170.07	421
WY	CAMPBELL	UK2-1	24-Mar-53	170.07	422
WY	CONVERSE	UK2-1	24-Mar-53	170.07	423
WY	JOHNSON	UK2-1	24-Mar-53	170.07	424
WY	WASHAKIE	UK2-1	24-Mar-53	170.07	425
NV	LINCOLN2	UK2-1	24-Mar-53	168.92	426
NM	LOS ALAMOS	UK7-1	25-Apr-53	166.77	427
NM	RIO ARRIBA	UK7-1	25-Apr-53	166.77	428
NM	SAN JUAN	UK7-1	25-Apr-53	166.77	429
NM	SAN MIGUEL	UK7-1	25-Apr-53	166.77	430
CO	DOLORES	UK7-1	25-Apr-53	165.53	431
KY	BREATHITT	SE4	09-Jul-62	164.78	432
KY	JACKSON	SE4	09-Jul-62	164.78	433
KY	OWSLEY	SE4	09-Jul-62	164.78	434
UT	IRON3	PB11-1	31-Aug-57	162.62	435
CO	RIO BLANCO	TP9-1	15-Apr-55	159.66	436
UT	JUAB	TP10-1	05-May-55	158.85	437
KS	STEVENS	TP7-2	30-Mar-55	158.51	438
OK	TEXAS	TP7-2	30-Mar-55	158.51	439
TX	OLDHAM	TP7-2	30-Mar-55	158.51	440
TX	POTTER	TP7-2	30-Mar-55	158.51	441
NV	PERSHING	PB1-1	28-May-57	157.52	442
IN	CRAWFORD	SE3	08-Jul-62	157.12	443
IN	JEFFERSON	SE3	08-Jul-62	157.12	444
IN	SWITZERLAND	SE3	08-Jul-62	157.12	445
KY	ANDERSON	SE3	08-Jul-62	157.12	446
KY	MONTGOMERY	SE3	08-Jul-62	157.12	447
KY	OLDHAM	SE3	08-Jul-62	157.12	448
OH	HANCOCK	SE3	08-Jul-62	157.12	449
NM	SANDOVAL	UK6-1	18-Apr-53	156.71	450
AZ	MOHAVE1	UK7-1	25-Apr-53	156.16	451
CO	ADAMS	TP4-2	08-Mar-55	155.94	452
CO	ARAPAHOE	TP4-2	08-Mar-55	155.94	453
CO	BOULDER	TP4-2	08-Mar-55	155.94	454
CO	CLEAR CREEK	TP4-2	08-Mar-55	155.94	455

				uCi/	
STATE	COUNTY	SHOT DAY	DATE	SQ METER	RANK
CO	DOUGLAS	TP4-2	08-Mar-55	155.94	456
CO	EAGLE	TP4-2	08-Mar-55	155.94	457
CO	GILPIN	TP4-2	08-Mar-55	155.94	458
CO	GRAND	TP4-2	08-Mar-55	155.94	459
CO	JEFFERSON	TP4-2	08-Mar-55	155.94	460
CO	LAKE	TP4-2	08-Mar-55	155.94	461
CO	MORGAN	TP4-2	08-Mar-55	155.94	462
CO	SUMMIT	TP4-2	08-Mar-55	155.94	463
AZ	COCONINO1	UK7-1	25-Apr-53	155.03	464
WY	CARBON	TP10-1	05-May-55	154.87	465
MA	BRISTOL	UK4-2	07-Apr-53	153.92	466
UT	UTAH	TP4-1	07-Mar-55	151.68	467
WY	CARBON	PB11-1	31-Aug-57	151.11	468
CO	CUSTER	UK9-1	19-May-53	151.03	469
KY	CLARK	SE4	09-Jul-62	149.13	470
KY	FLOYD	SE4	09-Jul-62	149.13	471
KY	FRANKLIN	SE4	09-Jul-62	149.13	472
KY	JOHNSON	SE4	09-Jul-62	149.13	473
KY	MAGOFFIN	SE4	09-Jul-62	149.13	474
KY	MENIFEE	SE4	09-Jul-62	149.13	475
KY	MORGAN	SE4	09-Jul-62	149.13	476
KY	PIKE	SE4	09-Jul-62	149.13	477
KY	SCOTT	SE4	09-Jul-62	149.13	478
KY	SHELBY	SE4	09-Jul-62	149.13	479
KY	WOLFE	SE4	09-Jul-62	149.13	480
KY	WOODFORD	SE4	09-Jul-62	149.13	481
PA	FULTON	SE4	09-Jul-62	149.13	482
PA	SNYDER	SE4	09-Jul-62	149.13	483
VA	AMELIA	SE4	09-Jul-62	149.13	484
VA	BUCHANAN	SE4	09-Jul-62	149.13	485
VA	CHESTERFIELD	SE4	09-Jul-62	149.13	486
VA	FRANKLIN	SE4	09-Jul-62	149.13	487
VA	GOOCHLAND	SE4	09-Jul-62	149.13	488
VA	HANOVER	SE4	09-Jul-62	149.13	489
VA	POWHATAN	SE4	09-Jul-62	149.13	490

Table title: TOP 500 SHOT DAYS: HIGHEST AVERAGE TOTAL FALLOUT BY DATE

	TOP 500 SHOT DAYS: HIGHEST AVERAGE TOTAL FALLOUT BY DATE				
STATE	COUNTY	SHOT DAY	DATE	uCi/ SQ METER	RANK
WV	MCDOWELL	SE4	09-Jul-62	149.13	491
WV	MERCER	SE4	09-Jul-62	149.13	492
WV	MINGO	SE4	09-Jul-62	149.13	493
WV	WYOMING	SE4	09-Jul-62	149.13	494
AZ	PIMA	PB4-1	05-Jul-57	148.41	495
IA	CEDAR	SE3	08-Jul-62	146.81	496
IA	POTTAWATTAMI	SE3	08-Jul-62	146.81	497
IL	BOONE	SE3	08-Jul-62	146.81	498
IL	MCLEAN	SE3	08-Jul-62	146.81	499
IL	PEORIA	SE3	08-Jul-62	146.81	500

SECTION 4

COUNTIES RANKED
BY
AMOUNT OF NUCLEAR FALLOUT
DEPOSITED ON A SINGLE DAY

1951-1962

COUNTIES RANKED BY
AMOUNT OF NUCLEAR FALLOUT DEPOSITED ON SINGLE FALLOUT DAY

SHOT	DATE	No. 1 HIGHEST LEVEL OF FALLOUT IN U.S	No. 2 SECOND-HIGHEST LEVEL OF FALLOUT IN U.S.	No. 3 THIRD HIGHEST LEVEL OF FALLOUT IN U.S.	No. 4 FOURTH HIGHEST LEVEL OF FALLOUT IN U.S.	No. 5 FIFTH HIGHEST LEVEL OF FALLOUT IN U.S.
R1-1	28-Jan-51	LA PLATA CO	DALLAM TX	ARCHULETA CO	CONEJOS CO	0
R1-2	29-Jan-51	BELMONT OH	GUERNSEY OH	OHIO WV	WINDHAM VT	PLEASANTS WV
R1-3	30-Jan-51	LAGRANGE IN	KENNEBEC ME	KNOX ME	LINCOLN ME	WALDO ME
R1-4	31-Jan-51	LACKAWANNA PA	WYOMING PA	COOS NH	WASHINGTON VT	AROOSTOOK ME
R1-5	1-Feb-51	0	0	0	0	0
R2-1	2-Feb-51	0	0	0	0	0
R2-2	3-Feb-51	REFUGIO TX	0	0	0	0
R2-3	4-Feb-51	ALACHUA FL	BAKER FL	BAY FL	0	0
R2-4	5-Feb-51	DADE FL	BROWARD FL	COLLIER FL	PALM BEACH FL	0
R2-5	6-Feb-51	HILLSBOROUGH FL	LAKE FL	FRANKLIN FL	LIBERTY FL	VOLUSIA FL
R2-6	7-Feb-51	PRINCE GEORG MD	TOLLAND CT	PENOBSCOT ME	MIDDLESEX MA	WASHINGTON MD
R2-7	8-Feb-51	0	0	0	0	0
BJ01 BAKER 1	28-Oct-51	FRESNO CA	KERN CA	KINGS CA	MONTEREY CA	SAN BENITO CA
BJ1-2	29-Oct-51	MERIWETHER GA	PIKE GA	GRAYSON VA	PUTNAM WV	RALEIGH WV
BJ-2 1	30-Oct-51	INYO3 CA	LOS ANGELES CA	FRESNO CA	KERN CA	KINGS CA
BJ2-2	31-Oct-51	CUMBERLAND ME	OXFORD ME	SAGADAHOC ME	CARROLL NH	SARATOGA NY

U.S. FALLOUT ATLAS : COUNTY COMPARISONS

COUNTIES RANKED BY
AMOUNT OF NUCLEAR FALLOUT DEPOSITED ON SINGLE FALLOUT DAY

SHOT	DATE	No. 1 HIGHEST LEVEL OF FALLOUT IN U.S	No. 2 SECOND-HIGHEST LEVEL OF FALLOUT IN U.S.	No. 3 THIRD HIGHEST LEVEL OF FALLOUT IN U.S.	No. 4 FOURTH HIGHEST LEVEL OF FALLOUT IN U.S.	No. 5 FIFTH HIGHEST LEVEL OF FALLOUT IN U.S.
BJ-2 3	1-Nov-51	MONROE NY	GENESEE NY	ARLINGTON VA	ERIE NY	LIVINGSTON NY
BJ-2 4	2-Nov-51	AROOSTOOK ME	OSWEGO NY	TOMPKINS NY	PENOBSCOT ME	PISCATAQUIS ME
BJ-2 5	3-Nov-51	GENESEE NY	NIAGARA NY	WAYNE NY	ERIE NY	NEW KENT VA
BJ-2 6	4-Nov-51	ERIE NY	JEFFERSON NY	WYOMING NY	ALLEGANY NY	CHENANGO NY
BJ3-2	2-Nov-51	KLEBERG TX	WHARTON TX	CHAMBERS TX	HIDALGO TX	CAMERON TX
BJ3-3	3-Nov-51	EL PASO TX	REAL TX	UVALDE TX	BANDERA TX	BREWSTER TX
BJ3-4	4-Nov-51	ANDERSON TX	ANDREWS TX	ANGELINA TX	ARANSAS TX	ARCHER TX
BJ3-5	5-Nov-51	ERIE OH	BEDFORD VA	FLOYD VA	ROANOKE VA	CALHOUN AL
BJ3-6	6-Nov-51	CHAUTAUQUA NY	ERIE NY	GENESEE NY	NIAGARA NY	ORLEANS NY
BJ3-7	7-Nov-51	MORRIS NJ	PUTNAM NY	ULSTER NY	NIAGARA NY	FAIRFIELD CT
BJ3-8	8-Nov-51	MONROE NY	ALLEGANY NY	CATTARAUGUS NY	CHAUTAUQUA NY	ERIE NY
BJ3-9	9-Nov-51	ALLEGANY NY	CATTARAUGUS NY	CHAUTAUQUA NY	ERIE NY	GENESEE NY
BJ3-10	10-Nov-51	JEFFERSON NY	ALLEGANY NY	CATTARAUGUS NY	CHAUTAUQUA NY	ERIE NY
BJ4-3	7-Nov-51	FRESNO CA	IMPERIAL CA	KERN CA	KINGS CA	MONTEREY CA
BJ4-4	8-Nov-51	0	0	0	0	0
BJ4-5	9-Nov-51	CARTER TN	DARLINGTON SC	HURON MI	LAPEER MI	MACOMB MI

COUNTIES RANKED BY
AMOUNT OF NUCLEAR FALLOUT DEPOSITED ON SINGLE FALLOUT DAY

SHOT	DATE	No. 1 HIGHEST LEVEL OF FALLOUT IN U.S.	No. 2 SECOND-HIGHEST LEVEL OF FALLOUT IN U.S.	No. 3 THIRD HIGHEST LEVEL OF FALLOUT IN U.S.	No. 4 FOURTH HIGHEST LEVEL OF FALLOUT IN U.S.	No. 5 FIFTH HIGHEST LEVEL OF FALLOUT IN U.S.
BJ4-6	10-Nov-51	KENT DE	NEW CASTLE DE	SUSSEX DE	WORCESTER MD	BURLINGTON NJ
BJ4-7	11-Nov-51	SOMERSET MD	BEAUFORT NC	BERTIE NC	CAMDEN NC	CARTERET NC
BJ4-8	12-Nov-51	WAYNE MI	ERIE OH	HURON OH	LAKE OH	LORAIN OH
BJ4-9	13-Nov-51	BERGEN NJ	HUDSON NJ	HUNTERDON NJ	MONMOUTH NJ	SOMERSET NJ
BJ4-10	14-Nov-51	CORTLAND NY	DELAWARE NY	FULTON NY	HERKIMER NY	ONEIDA NY
BJ5 1	19-Nov-51	NYE2 NV	EUREKA NV	ELKO NV	OWYHEE ID	ADA ID
BJ5-2	20-Nov-51	ADAMS ID	GEM ID	BOISE ID	IDAHO ID	PAYETTE ID
BJ5 3	21-Nov-51	CLEARWATER ID	IDAHO ID	VALLEY ID	BOISE ID	CUSTER ID
BJ5 4	22-Nov-51	ADAMS ID	BOISE ID	CAMAS ID	CLEARWATER ID	CUSTER ID
BJ5 5	23-Nov-51	ADAMS ID	BOISE ID	CAMAS ID	CLEARWATER ID	CUSTER ID
BJ5 6	24-Nov-51	GARFIELD OK	MAJOR OK	COWLEY KS	SUMNER KS	ALFALFA OK
BJ5 7	25-Nov-51	WASHINGTON ID	ADAMS ID	CLEARWATER ID	IDAHO ID	VALLEY ID
BJ5 8	26-Nov-51	ADAMS ID	BOISE ID	CAMAS ID	CUSTER ID	GEM ID
BJ6-1	29-Nov-51	WHITE PINE2 NV	LINCOLN2 NV	NYE2 NV	WHITE PINE1 NV	WHITE PINE3 NV
TS1-1	1-Apr-52	BEAVER UT	PIUTE UT	SANPETE UT	SEVIER UT	CARBON UT
TS1-2	2-Apr-52	BANNER NE	DAWES NE	SIOUX NE	CLAY MO	PITKIN CO

U.S. FALLOUT ATLAS : COUNTY COMPARISONS

COUNTIES RANKED BY
AMOUNT OF NUCLEAR FALLOUT DEPOSITED ON SINGLE FALLOUT DAY

SHOT	DATE	No. 1 HIGHEST LEVEL OF FALLOUT IN U.S	No. 2 SECOND-HIGHEST LEVEL OF FALLOUT IN U.S.	No. 3 THIRD HIGHEST LEVEL OF FALLOUT IN U.S.	No. 4 FOURTH HIGHEST LEVEL OF FALLOUT IN U.S.	No. 5 FIFTH HIGHEST LEVEL OF FALLOUT IN U.S.
ts1 3	3-Apr-52	FRANKLIN AR	JOHNSON AR	MONTGOMERY AR	NEWTON AR	PERRY AR
ts1 4	4-Apr-52	KINGS NY	QUEENS NY	FAIRFIELD CT	BERGEN NJ	HUDSON NJ
ts1 5	5-Apr-52	PENOBSCOT ME	PISCATAQUIS ME	SOMERSET ME	PUTNAM NY	WESTCHESTER NY
TS2-1	15-Apr-52	INYO3 CA	MOHAVE3 AZ	MOHAVE4 AZ	SAN BERNADIN CA	YAVAPAI AZ
TS2-2	16-Apr-52	KERN CA	ORANGE CA	SAN DIEGO CA	SANTA BARBARA CA	VENTURA CA
TS2-3	17-Apr-52	IMPERIAL CA	RIVERSIDE CA	0	0	0
TS2-4	18-Apr-52	IDAHO ID	ORANGE CA	SAN DIEGO CA	VENTURA CA	ADAMS ID
TS2-5	19-Apr-52	IMPERIAL CA	RIVERSIDE CA	ORANGE CA	SAN DIEGO CA	KERN CA
TS2-6	20-Apr-52	RIVERSIDE CA	CARBON MT	CHEYENNE CO	CROWLEY CO	EL PASO CO
TS2-7	21-Apr-52	ARCHULETA CO	ANDREWS TX	COSTILLA CO	ALAMOSA CO	CONEJOS CO
TS2-8	22-Apr-52	RIO GRANDE CO	KERN CA	ORANGE CA	SAN DIEGO CA	SANTA BARBAR CA
TS3-1	22-Apr-52	MOHAVE2 AZ	COCONINO3 AZ	INYO1 CA	INYO2 CA	INYO3 CA
TS3-2	23-Apr-52	SAN DIEGO CA	KERN CA	ORANGE CA	SANTA BARBARA CA	VENTURA CA
TS3-3	24-Apr-52	CONECUH AL	GENEVA AL	GREENE AL	LOWNDES AL	WILCOX AL
TS3-4	25-Apr-52	GLENN CA	SONOMA CA	TEHAMA CA	MONTGOMERY GA	WHEELER GA
TS3-5	26-Apr-52	QUEENS NY	PRINCE GEORG MD	OCEAN NJ	ST MARYS MD	TALBOT MD

COUNTIES RANKED BY
AMOUNT OF NUCLEAR FALLOUT DEPOSITED ON SINGLE FALLOUT DAY

SHOT	DATE	No. 1 HIGHEST LEVEL OF FALLOUT IN U.S.	No. 2 SECOND-HIGHEST LEVEL OF FALLOUT IN U.S.	No. 3 THIRD HIGHEST LEVEL OF FALLOUT IN U.S.	No. 4 FOURTH HIGHEST LEVEL OF FALLOUT IN U.S.	No. 5 FIFTH HIGHEST LEVEL OF FALLOUT IN U.S.
TS3-6	27-Apr-52	LACKAWANNA PA	LUZERNE PA	MONROE PA	PIKE PA	WAYNE PA
TS3-7	28-Apr-52	CLARENDON SC	HOUSTON AL	BAY FL	CALHOUN FL	DIXIE FL
TS3-8	29-Apr-52	HILLSBOROUGH FL	DODGE MN	MOWER MN	ALACHUA FL	BAKER FL
TS3-9	30-Apr-52	BARTON KS	ELLIS KS	MITCHELL KS	OSBORNE KS	PHILLIPS KS
TS3-10	1-May-52	SAUK WI	CRAWFORD IA	MONONA IA	PLYMOUTH IA	WOODBURY IA
TS4-1	1-May-52	IRON1 UT	IRON2 UT	MOHAVE3 AZ	MOHAVE4 AZ	MOHAVE1 AZ
TS4-2	2-May-52	JUDITH BASIN MT	BLAINE MT	CHOUTEAU MT	DEER LODGE MT	FLATHEAD MT
TS4-3	3-May-52	BACA CO	BENT CO	CHEYENNE CO	CROWLEY CO	EL PASO CO
TS4-4	4-May-52	LAS ANIMAS CO	MEADE KS	MORTON KS	SEWARD KS	STEVENS KS
TS4-5	5-May-52	CARROLL IN	CLINTON IN	TIPPECANOE IN	HOWARD IN	TIPTON IN
TS4-6	6-May-52	CIMARRON OK	MOORE TX	SHERMAN TX	LIMESTONE AL	MADISON AL
TS4-7	7-May-52	GALLATIN MT	GRANITE MT	LEWIS AND CL MT	MEAGHER MT	RAVALLI MT
TS4-8	8-May-52	PISCATAQUIS ME	NEWTON TX	ACADIA LA	ALLEN LA	BEAUREGARD LA
TS4-9	9-May-52	GRANT LA	VERNON LA	ANGELINA TX	HOUSTON TX	TRINITY TX
TS5-1	7-May-52	HOT SPRINGS WY	NATRONA WY	NIOBRARA WY	FALL RIVER SD	SIOUX NE
TS5-2	8-May-52	DAVIDSON NC	MOORE NC	MELLETTE SD	SIOUX NE	SHERIDAN NE

COUNTIES RANKED BY
AMOUNT OF NUCLEAR FALLOUT DEPOSITED ON SINGLE FALLOUT DAY

SHOT	DATE	No. 1 HIGHEST LEVEL OF FALLOUT IN U.S	No. 2 SECOND-HIGHEST LEVEL OF FALLOUT IN U.S.	No. 3 THIRD HIGHEST LEVEL OF FALLOUT IN U.S.	No. 4 FOURTH HIGHEST LEVEL OF FALLOUT IN U.S.	No. 5 FIFTH HIGHEST LEVEL OF FALLOUT IN U.S.
TS5-3	9-May-52	DINWIDDIE VA	APPOMATTOX VA	BRUNSWICK VA	GREENE VA	GREENSVILLE VA
TS5-4	10-May-52	PRINCE WILLI VA	CHOCTAW MS	ELBERT GA	BARROW GA	SCOTT MS
TS5-5	11-May-52	NORFOLK MA	SUFFOLK MA	BRISTOL RI	PROVIDENCE RI	FAIRFIELD CT
TS5-6	12-May-52	CLARK ID	BEAVERHEAD MT	GALLATIN MT	JEFFERSON ID	MADISON ID
TS5-7	13-May-52	BEAVERHEAD MT	NATRONA WY	LEMHI ID	TETON WY	ARTHUR NE
TS5-8	14-May-52	LEMHI ID	BEAVERHEAD MT	SEDGWICK CO	BLAINE ID	BUTTE ID
TS5-9	15-May-52	LOGAN CO	SEDGWICK CO	ARTHUR NE	CHEYENNE NE	DEUEL NE
TS5-10	16-May-52	ANDREWS TX	HOCKLEY TX	TERRY TX	YOAKUM TX	HARTLEY TX
TS6-1	25-May-52	LINCOLN2 NV	IRON1 UT	LINCOLN1 NV	IRON2 UT	MILLARD UT
TS6-2	26-May-52	HINSDALE CO	GUNNISON CO	MINERAL CO	SAGUACHE CO	ARCHULETA CO
TS6-3	27-May-52	PHILLIPS CO	HINSDALE CO	CHASE NE	LOGAN CO	CHEYENNE KS
TS6-4	28-May-52	ARCHULETA CO	TILLMAN OK	LOVING TX	CARSON TX	RANDALL TX
TS6-5	29-May-52	DAVIDSON TN	CHEATHAM TN	LEWIS TN	LIVINGSTON LA	FORREST MS
TS6-6	30-May-52	GREENVILLE SC	GREENWOOD SC	POLK NC	PICKENS SC	SPARTANBURG SC
TS6-7	31-May-52	COMANCHE KS	STAFFORD KS	ROGER MILLS OK	OTTAWA KS	MARION KS
TS6-8	1-Jun-52	QUEENS NY	KINGS NY	NASSAU NY	HUDSON NJ	UNION NJ

U.S. FALLOUT ATLAS : COUNTY COMPARISONS

COUNTIES RANKED BY
AMOUNT OF NUCLEAR FALLOUT DEPOSITED ON SINGLE FALLOUT DAY

SHOT	DATE	No. 1 HIGHEST LEVEL OF FALLOUT IN U.S	No. 2 SECOND-HIGHEST LEVEL OF FALLOUT IN U.S.	No. 3 THIRD HIGHEST LEVEL OF FALLOUT IN U.S.	No. 4 FOURTH HIGHEST LEVEL OF FALLOUT IN U.S.	No. 5 FIFTH HIGHEST LEVEL OF FALLOUT IN U.S.
TS6-9	2-Jun-52	WASHINGTON ME	HANCOCK ME	BEADLE SD	AROOSTOOK ME	PISCATAQUIS ME
TS6-10	3-Jun-52	RUSH IN	AUGLAIZE OH	UNION OH	LICKING OH	TAYLOR FL
TS7-1	1-Jun-52	EUREKA NV	ELKO NV	NYE2 NV	BOX ELDER1 UT	MONTROSE CO
TS7-2	2-Jun-52	JEFFERSON ID	BUTTE ID	BEADLE SD	SANBORN SD	MADISON ID
TS7-3	3-Jun-52	KNOX MO	LEWIS MO	NIOBRARA WY	APPANOOSE IA	SCOTLAND MO
TS7-4	4-Jun-52	RINGGOLD IA	ST LAWRENCE NY	SHELBY IA	TURNER SD	CASS IA
TS7-5	5-Jun-52	TULSA OK	COWLEY KS	CHASE KS	GREENWOOD KS	ELK KS
TS7-6	6-Jun-52	COAL OK	HUNT TX	HUGHES OK	ROCKWALL TX	PUSHMATAHA OK
TS7-7	7-Jun-52	MARION SC	DILLON SC	HORRY SC	FLORENCE SC	ROBESON NC
TS7-8	8-Jun-52	BIBB AL	PERRY AL	WALKER AL	WALTON FL	CLAY FL
TS7-9	9-Jun-52	ANDREWS TX	COCHRAN TX	CULBERSON TX	ECTOR TX	EL PASO TX
TS8-1	5-Jun-52	GEM ID	CUSTER ID	BLAINE ID	LEMHI ID	DEER LODGE MT
TS8-2	6-Jun-52	GEM ID	CUSTER ID	BLAINE ID	LEMHI ID	DEER LODGE MT
TS8-3	7-Jun-52	JUDITH BASIN MT	MADISON MT	FERGUS MT	GRAFTON NH	WASHINGTON VT
TS8-4	8-Jun-52	CHIPPEWA MI	SEDGWICK KS	TETON MT	LUCE MI	MACKINAC MI
TS8-5	9-Jun-52	ADAMS ID	WOODFORD IL	MCLEAN IL	FULTON IL	LIVINGSTON IL

U.S. FALLOUT ATLAS : COUNTY COMPARISONS

COUNTIES RANKED BY
AMOUNT OF NUCLEAR FALLOUT DEPOSITED ON SINGLE FALLOUT DAY

SHOT	DATE	No. 1 HIGHEST LEVEL OF FALLOUT IN U.S	No. 2 SECOND-HIGHEST LEVEL OF FALLOUT IN U.S.	No. 3 THIRD HIGHEST LEVEL OF FALLOUT IN U.S.	No. 4 FOURTH HIGHEST LEVEL OF FALLOUT IN U.S.	No. 5 FIFTH HIGHEST LEVEL OF FALLOUT IN U.S.
TS8-6	10-Jun-52	PAYETTE ID	GEM ID	VALLEY ID	POWELL MT	IDAHO ID
TS8-7	11-Jun-52	DEER LODGE MT	GLACIER MT	LAKE MT	PONDERA MT	FLATHEAD MT
TS8-8	12-Jun-52	IDAHO ID	LAKE MT	GREEN WI	WINNEBAGO IL	CLEARWATER ID
TS8-9	13-Jun-52	IDAHO ID	ADAMS ID	WASHINGTON ID	BOISE ID	GEM ID
TS8-10	14-Jun-52	KEOKUK IA	WRIGHT IA	BUENA VISTA IA	CLAY IA	JEFFERSON IA
UK1-1	17-Mar-53	WASHINGTON2 UT	WASHINGTON3 UT	KANE2 UT	LINCOLN1 NV	SAN JUAN UT
UK1-2	18-Mar-53	MONMOUTH NJ	OCEAN NJ	KINGS NY	QUEENS NY	ATLANTIC NJ
uk1 3	19-Mar-53	HUMPHREYS TN	DICKSON TN	HOUSTON TN	BENTON TN	HICKMAN TN
uk1 4	20-Mar-53	DUNKLIN MO	PULASKI AR	JEFFERSON AR	TANEY MO	MARIES MO
uk1 5	21-Mar-53	SHELBY TN	CRITTENDEN AR	FAYETTE TN	CROSS AR	POINSETT AR
uk1 6	22-Mar-53	DAVIDSON TN	CHEATHAM TN	WILLIAMSON TN	ROBERTSON TN	SUMNER TN
uk1 7	23-Mar-53	MERCER NJ	BERKS PA	CARBON PA	MONROE PA	SCHUYLKILL PA
uk1 8	24-Mar-53	CARTER KY	FLOYD KY	KNOTT KY	LEE KY	LETCHER KY
UK1-9	25-Mar-53	LOVE OK	FANNIN TX	GRAYSON TX	MONTAGUE TX	WISE TX
UK1-10	26-Mar-53	KNOX ME	WALDO ME	HANCOCK ME	NEW LONDON CT	WINDHAM CT
UK2-1	24-Mar-53	MORGAN UT	DAVIS UT	WEBER UT	TOOELE2 UT	RICH UT

U.S. FALLOUT ATLAS : COUNTY COMPARISONS

COUNTIES RANKED BY
AMOUNT OF NUCLEAR FALLOUT DEPOSITED ON SINGLE FALLOUT DAY

SHOT	DATE	No. 1 HIGHEST LEVEL OF FALLOUT IN U.S	No. 2 SECOND-HIGHEST LEVEL OF FALLOUT IN U.S.	No. 3 THIRD HIGHEST LEVEL OF FALLOUT IN U.S.	No. 4 FOURTH HIGHEST LEVEL OF FALLOUT IN U.S.	No. 5 FIFTH HIGHEST LEVEL OF FALLOUT IN U.S.
UK2-2	25-Mar-53	CUSTER MT	DAWSON MT	BOTTINEAU ND	MCHENRY ND	BURKE ND
UK2-3	26-Mar-53	FULTON AR	SUMTER FL	CRAIGHEAD AR	POINSETT AR	MADISON IA
UK2-4	27-Mar-53	AROOSTOOK ME	WASHINGTON ME	PENOBSCOT ME	PISCATAQUIS ME	HANCOCK ME
UK2-5	28-Mar-53	CLINTON MO	RAY MO	WORTH MO	BUCHANAN MO	WAHKIAKUM WA
UK2-6	29-Mar-53	CASS MO	MIAMI KS	CLAY MO	BUCHANAN MO	JOHNSON MO
UK2-7	30-Mar-53	DYER TN	GIBSON TN	BAXTER AR	CRAIGHEAD AR	CROSS AR
UK2-8	31-Mar-53	PRAIRIE AR	CROCKETT TN	HAYWOOD TN	CLEBURNE AR	CRAIGHEAD AR
UK2-9	1-Apr-53	ORANGE NC	CAROLINE MD	GARRETT MD	TALBOT MD	WICOMICO MD
UK2-10	2-Apr-53	MCINTOSH OK	BENTON AR	CRAWFORD AR	MADISON AR	WASHINGTON AR
UK3-1	31-Mar-53	MARICOPA AZ	GILA AZ	MOHAVE2 AZ	YAVAPAI AZ	PINAL AZ
UK3-2	1-Apr-53	ARCHULETA CO	SHERIDAN NE	SIOUX NE	NIOBRARA WY	LOGAN CO
UK3-3	2-Apr-53	MCINTOSH OK	BENTON AR	CRAWFORD AR	MADISON AR	WASHINGTON AR
UK3-4	3-Apr-53	ECTOR TX	WINKLER TX	ARCHULETA CO	ANDREWS TX	COCHRAN TX
UK3-5	4-Apr-53	BECKHAM OK	GREER OK	HARMON OK	ROGER MILLS OK	WASHITA OK
UK3-6	5-Apr-53	ARKANSAS AR	CLEBURNE AR	CRITTENDEN AR	DESHA AR	JACKSON AR
uk3 7	6-Apr-53	NEW HANOVER NC	DARE NC	NEW CASTLE DE	SUSSEX DE	CAPE MAY NJ

U.S. FALLOUT ATLAS : COUNTY COMPARISONS

COUNTIES RANKED BY
AMOUNT OF NUCLEAR FALLOUT DEPOSITED ON SINGLE FALLOUT DAY

SHOT	DATE	No. 1 HIGHEST LEVEL OF FALLOUT IN U.S.	No. 2 SECOND-HIGHEST LEVEL OF FALLOUT IN U.S.	No. 3 THIRD HIGHEST LEVEL OF FALLOUT IN U.S.	No. 4 FOURTH HIGHEST LEVEL OF FALLOUT IN U.S.	No. 5 FIFTH HIGHEST LEVEL OF FALLOUT IN U.S.
uk3 8	7-Apr-53	TYRRELL NC	GATES NC	WASHINGTON MD	FRANKLIN PA	ARLINGTON VA
UK4-1	6-Apr-53	WASHINGTON2 UT	VERMILION LA	FRANKLIN MS	LINCOLN MS	HINSDALE CO
UK4-2	7-Apr-53	PLYMOUTH MA	NORFOLK MA	BRISTOL MA	SUFFOLK MA	MIDDLESEX MA
UK4-3	8-Apr-53	LEON FL	DIXIE FL	GILCHRIST FL	HAMILTON FL	MADISON FL
UK4-4	9-Apr-53	MIDDLESEX MA	NANTUCKET MA	ESSEX MA	NORFOLK MA	ANDROSCOGGIN ME
UK4-5	10-Apr-53	MIDDLESEX MA	BELKNAP NH	CHESHIRE NH	HILLSBOROUGH NH	MERRIMACK NH
UK4-6	11-Apr-53	NANTUCKET MA	CRAWFORD IN	DAVIESS IN	FLOYD IN	GIBSON IN
UK4-7	12-Apr-53	NANTUCKET MA	FAIRFIELD CT	HARTFORD CT	LITCHFIELD CT	MIDDLESEX CT
UK5-1	11-Apr-53	YUMA AZ	SAN BERNADIN CA	MOHAVE3 AZ	MOHAVE4 AZ	IRON1 UT
UK5-2	12-Apr-53	CLAY NC	GRAHAM NC	COCKE TN	SEVIER TN	TOWNS GA
UK5-3	13-Apr-53	PITKIN CO	ROUTT CO	GUNNISON CO	MINERAL CO	HINSDALE CO
UK5-4	14-Apr-53	BRADLEY AR	CALHOUN AR	CLARK AR	CLEVELAND AR	COLUMBIA AR
UK5-5	15-Apr-53	NANTUCKET MA	ANDROSCOGGIN ME	CUMBERLAND ME	OXFORD ME	LAMAR MS
UK5-6	16-Apr-53	KENNEBEC ME	LINCOLN ME	SAGADAHOC ME	ESSEX MA	MIDDLESEX MA
UK5-7	17-Apr-53	CLARK IN	DUBOIS IN	JEFFERSON IN	OHIO IN	VANDERBURGH IN
UK5-8	18-Apr-53	BERTIE NC	CARTERET NC	GREENE NC	HYDE NC	LENOIR NC

U.S. FALLOUT ATLAS : COUNTY COMPARISONS

COUNTIES RANKED BY
AMOUNT OF NUCLEAR FALLOUT DEPOSITED ON SINGLE FALLOUT DAY

SHOT	DATE	No. 1 HIGHEST LEVEL OF FALLOUT IN U.S.	No. 2 SECOND-HIGHEST LEVEL OF FALLOUT IN U.S.	No. 3 THIRD HIGHEST LEVEL OF FALLOUT IN U.S.	No. 4 FOURTH HIGHEST LEVEL OF FALLOUT IN U.S.	No. 5 FIFTH HIGHEST LEVEL OF FALLOUT IN U.S.
UK5-9	19-Apr-53	WINDHAM CT	WORCESTER MA	NEW LONDON CT	BRISTOL MA	DUKES MA
UK6-1	18-Apr-53	COCONINO2 AZ	CLARK1 NV	NAVAJO AZ	APACHE AZ	CLARK2 NV
UK6-2	19-Apr-53	ACADIA LA	ALLEN LA	BEAUREGARD LA	CALCASIEU LA	CAMERON LA
UK6-3	20-Apr-53	EL PASO TX	MEADE KS	MORTON KS	SEWARD KS	STEVENS KS
UK6-4	21-Apr-53	CONCHO TX	LAMPASAS TX	MIDLAND TX	STERLING TX	KIOWA CO
UK6-5	22-Apr-53	ARCHULETA CO	BURNET TX	MITCHELL TX	SCURRY TX	WILBARGER TX
UK6-6	23-Apr-53	PARKER TX	TANGIPAHOA LA	EASTLAND TX	ATOKA OK	COAL OK
UK6-7	24-Apr-53	ACADIA LA	ALLEN LA	CALCASIEU LA	CAMERON LA	EVANGELINE LA
UK6-8	25-Apr-53	ANDROSCOGGIN ME	CUMBERLAND ME	FRANKLIN ME	KENNEBEC ME	LINCOLN ME
UK7-1	25-Apr-53	CLARK1 NV	COCONINO2 AZ	APACHE AZ	MCKINLEY NM	CHAVES NM
UK7-2	26-Apr-53	WASHINGTON NY	WARREN NY	RENSSELAER NY	SARATOGA NY	FULTON NY
UK7-3	27-Apr-53	KIOWA CO	ARCHULETA CO	FANNIN TX	GRAYSON TX	CREEK OK
UK7-4	28-Apr-53	ADAMS MS	WARREN MS	CLAIBORNE MS	JEFFERSON MS	ISSAQUENA MS
UK7-5	29-Apr-53	JACKSON MN	COTTONWOOD MN	DICKINSON IA	CLAY IA	REDWOOD MN
UK7-6	30-Apr-53	SARATOGA NY	RENSSELAER NY	SCHENECTADY NY	KENT RI	PROVIDENCE RI
UK7-7	1-May-53	WASHINGTON ME	SARATOGA NY	SCHENECTADY NY	HANCOCK ME	PENOBSCOT ME

U.S. FALLOUT ATLAS :: COUNTY COMPARISONS

COUNTIES RANKED BY
AMOUNT OF NUCLEAR FALLOUT DEPOSITED ON SINGLE FALLOUT DAY

SHOT	DATE	No. 1 HIGHEST LEVEL OF FALLOUT IN U.S	No. 2 SECOND-HIGHEST LEVEL OF FALLOUT IN U.S.	No. 3 THIRD HIGHEST LEVEL OF FALLOUT IN U.S.	No. 4 FOURTH HIGHEST LEVEL OF FALLOUT IN U.S.	No. 5 FIFTH HIGHEST LEVEL OF FALLOUT IN U.S.
UK7-8	2-May-53	BERKSHIRE MA	FRANKLIN MA	ESSEX NY	FULTON NY	HAMILTON NY
UK7-9	3-May-53	CALDWELL MO	BUCHANAN MO	CLAY MO	PLATTE MO	NEMAHA NE
UK8-1	8-May-53	CUSTER MT	RICHLAND MT	DAWSON MT	FALLON MT	MCCONE MT
UK8-2	9-May-53	GARFIELD MT	BIG HORN MT	BLAINE MT	FERGUS MT	MUSSELSHELL MT
UK8-3	10-May-53	BIG HORN MT	TREASURE MT	ARKANSAS AR	CLEBURNE AR	CRAIGHEAD AR
UK8-4	11-May-53	GRAND ISLE VT	ATOKA OK	MURRAY OK	PONTOTOC OK	ANDERSON TX
UK8-5	12-May-53	GAINES TX	WINKLER TX	YOAKUM TX	CROSS AR	VAN BUREN AR
UK8-6	13-May-53	MADISON VA	PAGE VA	RAPPAHANNOCK VA	ROCKINGHAM VA	SHENANDOAH VA
UK9-1	19-May-53	WASHINGTON2 UT	WASHINGTON3 UT	WASHINGTON1 UT	KANE1 UT	KANE2 UT
UK9-2	20-May-53	WASHBURN WI	SAWYER WI	TREMPEALEAU WI	MITCHELL IA	RUSK WI
UK9-3	21-May-53	MAHONING OH	HINSDALE CO	GEAUGA OH	SUMMIT OH	HANCOCK WV
UK9-4	22-May-53	MCDOWELL WV	DONLEY TX	SULLIVAN TN	BRISCOE TX	ROGER MILLS OK
UK9-5	23-May-53	AUDUBON IA	SHELBY IA	WHEELER TX	COLFAX NE	GUTHRIE IA
UK9-6	24-May-53	LAKE MI	MANISTEE MI	LA PORTE IN	MUSKEGON MI	GRAND TRAVER MI
UK9-7	25-May-53	KENT DE	NEW CASTLE DE	ATLANTIC NJ	CAMDEN NJ	CAPE MAY NJ
UK9-8	26-May-53	PALM BEACH FL	MONROE FL	BROWARD FL	CHARLOTTE FL	COLLIER FL

U.S. FALLOUT ATLAS : COUNTY COMPARISONS

COUNTIES RANKED BY
AMOUNT OF NUCLEAR FALLOUT DEPOSITED ON SINGLE FALLOUT DAY

SHOT	DATE	No. 1 HIGHEST LEVEL OF FALLOUT IN U.S	No. 2 SECOND-HIGHEST LEVEL OF FALLOUT IN U.S.	No. 3 THIRD HIGHEST LEVEL OF FALLOUT IN U.S.	No. 4 FOURTH HIGHEST LEVEL OF FALLOUT IN U.S.	No. 5 FIFTH HIGHEST LEVEL OF FALLOUT IN U.S.
UK9-9	27-May-53	STONE MO	BAXTER AR	BENTON AR	BOONE AR	CARROLL AR
UK10-1	25-May-53	WHITE PINE3 NV	MILLARD UT	SANPETE UT	SEVIER UT	JUAB UT
UK10-2	26-May-53	FERRY WA	PEND OREILLE WA	STEVENS WA	OKANOGAN WA	BONNER ID
UK10-3	27-May-53	NATRONA WY	HINSDALE CO	ROLETTE ND	MUSSELSHELL MT	JOHNSON WY
UK10-4	28-May-53	ROCKWALL TX	MENOMINEE MI	BARAGA MI	ANOKA MN	AITKIN MN
UK10-5	29-May-53	CATTARAUGUS NY	KEARNEY NE	PRESQUE ISLE MI	ERIE NY	NIAGARA NY
UK10-6	30-May-53	HARFORD MD	CLARION PA	HUNTINGDON PA	MORGAN WV	WARREN PA
UK10-7	31-May-53	GARFIELD MT	PETROLEUM MT	WHEATLAND MT	BLAINE MT	FERGUS MT
UK10-8	1-Jun-53	GARFIELD MT	PHILLIPS MT	ROSEBUD MT	POWDER RIVER MT	JOHNSON WY
UK10-9	2-Jun-53	DANIELS MT	RICHLAND MT	ROOSEVELT MT	SHERIDAN MT	BURKE ND
UK10-10	3-Jun-53	ALCONA MI	ANTRIM MI	ARENAC MI	BAY MI	CHARLEVOIX MI
UK11-1	4-Jun-53	COCONINO2 AZ	CLARK1 NV	KANE1 UT	COCONINO1 AZ	NAVAJO AZ
UK11-2	5-Jun-53	ROUTT CO	JACKSON CO	LARIMER CO	ALBANY WY	GRAND CO
UK11-3	6-Jun-53	BUCHANAN MO	DONIPHAN KS	LEAVENWORTH KS	DECATUR IA	WYANDOTTE KS
UK11-4	7-Jun-53	HAMILTON IN	HANCOCK IN	MARION IN	TIPTON IN	BLACKFORD IN
UK11-5	8-Jun-53	DE KALB MO	GENTRY MO	PISCATAQUIS ME	WALDO ME	FREMONT IA

U.S. FALLOUT ATLAS : COUNTY COMPARISONS

COUNTIES RANKED BY
AMOUNT OF NUCLEAR FALLOUT DEPOSITED ON SINGLE FALLOUT DAY

SHOT	DATE	No. 1 HIGHEST LEVEL OF FALLOUT IN U.S.	No. 2 SECOND-HIGHEST LEVEL OF FALLOUT IN U.S.	No. 3 THIRD HIGHEST LEVEL OF FALLOUT IN U.S.	No. 4 FOURTH HIGHEST LEVEL OF FALLOUT IN U.S.	No. 5 FIFTH HIGHEST LEVEL OF FALLOUT IN U.S.
UK11-6	9-Jun-53	CULBERSON TX	EL PASO TX	JEFF DAVIS TX	GUNNISON CO	HINSDALE CO
UK11-7	10-Jun-53	GUNNISON CO	ROUTT CO	ARCHULETA CO	HINSDALE CO	MINERAL CO
UK11-8	11-Jun-53	MINERAL CO	ROUTT CO	GUNNISON CO	HINSDALE CO	PITKIN CO
TP1-1	18-Feb-55	SAN BERNADIN CA	YUMA AZ	SANTA CRUZ AZ	PIMA AZ	0
TP2-1	22-Feb-55	CLARK2 NV	CLARK1 NV	0	0	0
TP3-1	1-Mar-55	WASHINGTON2 UT	KANE2 UT	WASHINGTON3 UT	KANE1 UT	LINCOLN2 NV
TP3-2	2-Mar-55	ADAMS CO	ARAPAHOE CO	BOULDER CO	CLEAR CREEK CO	DOUGLAS CO
TP3-3	3-Mar-55	ADAMS CO	JOHNSON MO	PETTIS MO	ARAPAHOE CO	BOULDER CO
TP3-4	4-Mar-55	POTTER PA	CORTLAND NY	ALLEGANY NY	ONTARIO NY	STEUBEN NY
TP3-5	5-Mar-55	CLINTON PA	POTTER PA	BROOME NY	FRANKLIN NY	FULTON NY
TP3-6	6-Mar-55	ERIE OH	GEAUGA OH	MORROW OH	GOSHEN WY	LOGAN CO
TP4-1	7-Mar-55	INYO3 CA	NYE2 NV	WHITE PINE2 NV	UTAH UT	WHITE PINE3 NV
TP4-2	8-Mar-55	ADAMS CO	ARAPAHOE CO	BOULDER CO	CLEAR CREEK CO	DOUGLAS CO
TP4-3	9-Mar-55	TAZEWELL IL	CUMBERLAND IL	LAKE CO	SANGAMON IL	PITKIN CO
TP4-4	10-Mar-55	MEDINA OH	PORTAGE OH	LAKE OH	ASHTABULA OH	CUYAHOGA OH
TP4-5	11-Mar-55	CARLISLE KY	HENRY TN	OBION TN	WEAKLEY TN	CALLOWAY KY

U.S. FALLOUT ATLAS : COUNTY COMPARISONS

COUNTIES RANKED BY
AMOUNT OF NUCLEAR FALLOUT DEPOSITED ON SINGLE FALLOUT DAY

SHOT	DATE	No. 1 HIGHEST LEVEL OF FALLOUT IN U.S	No. 2 SECOND-HIGHEST LEVEL OF FALLOUT IN U.S.	No. 3 THIRD HIGHEST LEVEL OF FALLOUT IN U.S.	No. 4 FOURTH HIGHEST LEVEL OF FALLOUT IN U.S.	No. 5 FIFTH HIGHEST LEVEL OF FALLOUT IN U.S.
TP4-6	12-Mar-55	HAMPSHIRE MA	ATCHISON KS	BARTON KS	BROWN KS	CLAY KS
TP5-1	12-Mar-55	CLARK1 NV	COCONINO2 AZ	MOHAVE1 AZ	COCONINO1 AZ	COCONINO3 AZ
TP5-2	13-Mar-55	LARAMIE WY	LA SALLE LA	JONES MS	HINDS MS	DEAF SMITH TX
TP5-3	14-Mar-55	LAWRENCE IN	MARTIN IN	DUBOIS IN	DAVIESS IN	WASHINGTON IN
TP5-4	15-Mar-55	LEWIS KY	CATTARAUGUS NY	ERIE NY	CHAUTAUQUA NY	MONROE MI
TP5-5	16-Mar-55	PULASKI IL	TEXAS MO	PERRY IL	ST CLAIR IL	WILLIAMSON IL
TP5-6	17-Mar-55	WASHITA OK	LYNN TX	TYRRELL NC	BECKHAM OK	GREER OK
TP5-7	18-Mar-55	LOGAN KY	CHEATHAM TN	DAVIDSON TN	DICKSON TN	MAURY TN
TP5-8	19-Mar-55	ALEXANDER IL	EDWARDS IL	FRANKLIN IL	HAMILTON IL	HARDIN IL
TP5-9	20-Mar-55	COLBERT AL	FAYETTE AL	FRANKLIN AL	LAUDERDALE AL	LAWRENCE AL
TP5-10	21-Mar-55	BERGEN NJ	ESSEX NJ	HUDSON NJ	HUNTERDON NJ	SOMERSET NJ
TP6-1	22-Mar-55	CLARK3 NV	MOHAVE2 AZ	MOHAVE1 AZ	CLARK2 NV	COCONINO1 AZ
TP6-2	23-Mar-55	CLARK1 NV	HEMPSTEAD AR	HOWARD AR	LAFAYETTE AR	LITTLE RIVER AR
TP6-3	24-Mar-55	MONTGOMERY MS	TUSCALOOSA AL	CARROLL MS	HUMPHREYS MS	LEAKE MS
TP6-4	25-Mar-55	YANCEY NC	BRADLEY TN	MCMINN TN	MEIGS TN	MONROE TN
TP6-5	26-Mar-55	UNICOI TN	AUTAUGA AL	BALDWIN AL	BIBB AL	BUTLER AL

U.S. FALLOUT ATLAS : COUNTY COMPARISONS

COUNTIES RANKED BY
AMOUNT OF NUCLEAR FALLOUT DEPOSITED ON SINGLE FALLOUT DAY

SHOT	DATE	No. 1 HIGHEST LEVEL OF FALLOUT IN U.S	No. 2 SECOND-HIGHEST LEVEL OF FALLOUT IN U.S.	No. 3 THIRD HIGHEST LEVEL OF FALLOUT IN U.S.	No. 4 FOURTH HIGHEST LEVEL OF FALLOUT IN U.S.	No. 5 FIFTH HIGHEST LEVEL OF FALLOUT IN U.S.
TP6-6	27-Mar-55	EL DORADO CA	NEVADA CA	PLACER CA	PLUMAS CA	SIERRA CA
TP6-7	28-Mar-55	ALACHUA FL	BAKER FL	BREVARD FL	CLAY FL	LAKE FL
TP6-8	29-Mar-55	0	0	0	0	0
TP7-1	29-Mar-55	LINCOLN2 NV	IRON3 UT	WASHINGTON1 UT	GARFIELD UT	LINCOLN1 NV
TP7-2	30-Mar-55	STEVENS KS	TEXAS OK	OLDHAM TX	POTTER TX	DALLAM TX
TP7-3	31-Mar-55	NESS KS	ELLIS KS	OSBORNE KS	RUSH KS	LINCOLN KS
TP7-4	1-Apr-55	QUITMAN MS	COAHOMA MS	CRITTENDEN AR	DE SOTO MS	TALLAHATCHIE MS
TP7-5	2-Apr-55	POLK IA	DAVISON SD	AURORA SD	DECATUR IA	DAKOTA NE
TP7-6	3-Apr-55	BOONE IA	BERKSHIRE MA	IDA IA	COLUMBIA NY	SARATOGA NY
TP7-7	4-Apr-55	PIKE MO	MADISON IL	CASS IL	MENARD IL	MONTGOMERY IL
TP7-8	5-Apr-55	CHESTER SC	OCEAN NJ	MCCRACKEN KY	SHANNON MO	BLADEN NC
TP7-9	6-Apr-55	BRUNSWICK NC	CHESTERFIELD SC	DILLON SC	MARION SC	YORK SC
TP7-10	7-Apr-55	BULLOCH GA	SCREVEN GA	BURKE GA	ALLENDALE SC	BARNWELL SC
TP8-1	9-Apr-55	TOOELE2 UT	SALT LAKE UT	WASATCH UT	MORGAN UT	SUMMIT UT
TP8-2	10-Apr-55	JACKSON CO	NATRONA WY	PITKIN CO	CONVERSE WY	SUMMIT CO
TP8-3	11-Apr-55	STANTON KS	CHEYENNE KS	PITKIN CO	DUNDY NE	GRANT LA

COUNTIES RANKED BY
AMOUNT OF NUCLEAR FALLOUT DEPOSITED ON SINGLE FALLOUT DAY

SHOT	DATE	No. 1 HIGHEST LEVEL OF FALLOUT IN U.S.	No. 2 SECOND-HIGHEST LEVEL OF FALLOUT IN U.S.	No. 3 THIRD HIGHEST LEVEL OF FALLOUT IN U.S.	No. 4 FOURTH HIGHEST LEVEL OF FALLOUT IN U.S.	No. 5 FIFTH HIGHEST LEVEL OF FALLOUT IN U.S.
TP8-4	12-Apr-55	SALINE KS	OTTAWA KS	DICKINSON KS	ELLSWORTH KS	GEARY KS
TP8-5	13-Apr-55	WASHINGTON LA	EMMET MI	ESCAMBIA AL	MONROE AL	GEORGE MS
TP8-6	14-Apr-55	ASHLAND OH	ASHTABULA OH	CARROLL OH	GEAUGA OH	GUERNSEY OH
TP8-7	15-Apr-55	WYOMING NY	LINCOLN ME	SOMERSET ME	CALEDONIA VT	CARROLL OH
TP8-8	16-Apr-55	CUMBERLAND ME	KENNEBEC ME	KNOX ME	SAGADAHOC ME	WALDO ME
TP9-1	15-Apr-55	LINCOLN1 NV	BEAVER UT	MESA CO	EMERY UT	GRAND UT
TP9-2	15-Apr-55	WAYNE MI	MEDINA OH	CUYAHOGA OH	SENECA OH	MACOMB MI
TP9-3	16-Apr-55	PEMBINA ND	KITTSON MN	DAVISON SD	ROSEAU MN	GRAND FORKS ND
TP9-4	17-Apr-55	ALGER MI	MONTMORENCY MI	SANILAC MI	ST CLAIR MI	LAPEER MI
TP9-5	18-Apr-55	MEDINA OH	GEAUGA OH	LAKE OH	PORTAGE OH	STARK OH
TP9-6	19-Apr-55	ORLEANS NY	MEDINA OH	MONROE NY	NIAGARA NY	GENESEE NY
TP9-7	20-Apr-55	FAIRFIELD CT	HARTFORD CT	LITCHFIELD CT	NEW LONDON CT	TOLLAND CT
TP9-8	21-Apr-55	CHAMPAIGN OH	GUERNSEY OH	SARPY NE	SAUNDERS NE	SHELBY OH
TP9-9	22-Apr-55	ADAMS IL	BOND IL	BROWN IL	FULTON IL	HANCOCK IL
TP9-10	23-Apr-55	CALVERT MD	HANOVER VA	CHARLES MD	FULTON PA	HENRICO VA
TP10-1	5-May-55	WHITE PINE2 NV	NYE2 NV	UTAH UT	WHITE PINE1 NV	WASATCH UT

U.S. FALLOUT ATLAS : COUNTY COMPARISONS

COUNTIES RANKED BY
AMOUNT OF NUCLEAR FALLOUT DEPOSITED ON SINGLE FALLOUT DAY

SHOT	DATE	No. 1 HIGHEST LEVEL OF FALLOUT IN U.S	No. 2 SECOND-HIGHEST LEVEL OF FALLOUT IN U.S.	No. 3 THIRD HIGHEST LEVEL OF FALLOUT IN U.S.	No. 4 FOURTH HIGHEST LEVEL OF FALLOUT IN U.S.	No. 5 FIFTH HIGHEST LEVEL OF FALLOUT IN U.S.
TP10-2	6-May-55	COSTILLA CO	CONEJOS CO	ALAMOSA CO	BENT CO	CROWLEY CO
TP10-3	7-May-55	CAMDEN MO	MORGAN MO	LACLEDE MO	OSAGE MO	WEBSTER MO
TP10-4	8-May-55	HINDS MS	MONTGOMERY AL	RINGGOLD IA	COOSA AL	MONTGOMERY KS
TP10-5	9-May-55	DELAWARE OK	OKMULGEE OK	NESHOBA MS	POTTAWATOMIE OK	MUSKOGEE OK
TP10-6	10-May-55	SEMINOLE FL	MARION FL	DALLAS TX	ADAIR KY	ROCKWALL TX
TP10-7	11-May-55	IBERIA LA	GIBSON TN	DUNKLIN MO	MUHLENBERG KY	RANDOLPH AR
TP10-8	12-May-55	KNOX TN	ANDERSON TN	SEVIER TN	GRAINGER TN	LOUDON TN
TP10-9	13-May-55	KNOX TN	BLOUNT TN	HENDERSON NC	OCONEE SC	SEVIER TN
TP10-10	14-May-55	GUNNISON CO	HINSDALE CO	MINERAL CO	PITKIN CO	ROUTT CO
TP11-1	15-May-55	IRON2 UT	CLARK1 NV	MOHAVE2 AZ	IRON3 UT	COLFAX NM
TP11-2	16-May-55	MORGAN CO	PLATTE WY	GRAND CO	LARIMER CO	POWDER RIVER MT
TP11-3	17-May-55	PITKIN CO	CUSTER CO	HINSDALE CO	JEFFERSON CO	FREMONT CO
TP11-4	18-May-55	HALE TX	ARMSTRONG TX	GRAY TX	RANDALL TX	CARSON TX
TP11-5	19-May-55	PONTOTOC OK	COOKE TX	BRYAN OK	FOARD TX	FANNIN TX
TP11-6	20-May-55	WOODRUFF AR	PIKE AR	SHARP AR	LOGAN AR	FRANKLIN AR
TP11-7	21-May-55	ROANOKE VA	BELMONT OH	JEFFERSON PA	CRAIG VA	FLOYD VA

U.S. FALLOUT ATLAS : COUNTY COMPARISONS

COUNTIES RANKED BY
AMOUNT OF NUCLEAR FALLOUT DEPOSITED ON SINGLE FALLOUT DAY

SHOT	DATE	No. 1 HIGHEST LEVEL OF FALLOUT IN U.S	No. 2 SECOND-HIGHEST LEVEL OF FALLOUT IN U.S.	No. 3 THIRD HIGHEST LEVEL OF FALLOUT IN U.S.	No. 4 FOURTH HIGHEST LEVEL OF FALLOUT IN U.S.	No. 5 FIFTH HIGHEST LEVEL OF FALLOUT IN U.S.
TP11-8	22-May-55	FOREST PA	NEW YORK NY	MAHONING OH	ARMSTRONG PA	BUTLER PA
TP11-9	23-May-55	BERGEN NJ	HUDSON NJ	QUEENS NY	FOREST PA	ESSEX NJ
TP11-10	24-May-55	CAMBRIA PA	MARSHALL WV	HARRISON OH	MONROE OH	ARMSTRONG PA
PB1-1	28-May-57	NYE2 NV	NYE1 NV	LANDER2 NV	MINERAL NV	CHURCHILL NV
PB1-2	29-May-57	0	0	0	0	0
PB1-3	30-May-57	0	0	0	0	0
PB1-4	31-May-57	0	0	0	0	0
PB1-5	1-Jun-57	BEE TX	BROOKS TX	CALHOUN TX	CAMERON TX	COLORADO TX
PB1-6	2-Jun-57	JEFFERSON MT	LEMHI ID	OUACHITA AR	GREGG TX	CALHOUN AR
PB1-7	3-Jun-57	DEER LODGE MT	TERREBONNE LA	LAMAR TX	LIMESTONE TX	ST JOHN THE LA
PB1-8	4-Jun-57	GRANT AR	HOWARD AR	CLAIBORNE LA	WEBSTER LA	LITTLE RIVER AR
PB1-9	5-Jun-57	WALTON FL	POPE IL	BENTON TN	STEWART TN	BENEWAH ID
PB1-10	6-Jun-57	CROWLEY CO	BENT CO	FREMONT CO	WASHINGTON CO	ARTHUR NE
PB2-1	18-Jun-57	IRON1 UT	IRON3 UT	INYO1 CA	INYO2 CA	PIUTE UT
PB2-2	19-Jun-57	NATRONA WY	WELD CO	CONVERSE WY	JACKSON CO	LARIMER CO
PB2-3	20-Jun-57	RICHLAND ND	ROBERTS SD	CASS ND	EMMONS ND	FOSTER ND

U.S. FALLOUT ATLAS : COUNTY COMPARISONS

4-21

COUNTIES RANKED BY
AMOUNT OF NUCLEAR FALLOUT DEPOSITED ON SINGLE FALLOUT DAY

SHOT	DATE	No. 1 HIGHEST LEVEL OF FALLOUT IN U.S	No. 2 SECOND-HIGHEST LEVEL OF FALLOUT IN U.S.	No. 3 THIRD HIGHEST LEVEL OF FALLOUT IN U.S.	No. 4 FOURTH HIGHEST LEVEL OF FALLOUT IN U.S.	No. 5 FIFTH HIGHEST LEVEL OF FALLOUT IN U.S.
PB2-4	21-Jun-57	LAMAR AL	MANATEE FL	OSCEOLA FL	DALLAS AL	LIMESTONE AL
PB2-5	22-Jun-57	RABUN GA	FLOYD KY	LAUREL KY	ALEXANDER NC	POLK NC
PB2-6	23-Jun-57	SENECA NY	ERIE NY	LIVINGSTON NY	ONTARIO NY	WYOMING NY
PB2-7	24-Jun-57	BEAVER PA	CAMBRIA PA	CLARION PA	CLEARFIELD PA	CRAWFORD PA
PB2-8	25-Jun-57	FLUVANNA VA	COLUMBIA GA	LINCOLN GA	ALEXANDER NC	BRUNSWICK NC
PB2-9	26-Jun-57	MITCHELL NC	ANSON NC	ASHE NC	AVERY NC	BRUNSWICK NC
PB2-10	27-Jun-57	SUSSEX NJ	BERGEN NJ	PASSAIC NJ	INDIAN RIVER FL	OKEECHOBEE FL
PB3-1	24-Jun-57	WASHINGTON1 UT	KANE2 UT	IRON1 UT	LINCOLN1 NV	WASHINGTON3 UT
PB3-2	25-Jun-57	JEFF DAVIS TX	ARCHULETA CO	CONEJOS CO	COSTILLA CO	RIO GRANDE CO
PB3-3	26-Jun-57	ACADIA LA	ASSUMPTION LA	AVOYELLES LA	BEAUREGARD LA	CALCASIEU LA
PB3-4	27-Jun-57	BOONE IN	PUTNAM IN	HENDRICKS IN	HAMILTON IN	MADISON IN
PB3-5	28-Jun-57	GASCONADE MO	ERIE NY	CATTARAUGUS NY	NIAGARA NY	ALLEGANY NY
PB3-6	29-Jun-57	FRANKLIN MO	OSAGE MO	WASHINGTON MO	CALLAWAY MO	IRON MO
PB4-1	5-Jul-57	PIMA AZ	SANTA CRUZ AZ	GARFIELD CO	RIO BLANCO CO	COLFAX NM
PB4-2	6-Jul-57	PARK MT	EAGLE CO	SAGUACHE CO	WASHINGTON CO	PEMBINA ND
PB4-3	7-Jul-57	WEBSTER IA	HUMBOLDT IA	GOODHUE MN	LE SUEUR MN	WASECA MN

U.S. FALLOUT ATLAS : COUNTY COMPARISONS

COUNTIES RANKED BY
AMOUNT OF NUCLEAR FALLOUT DEPOSITED ON SINGLE FALLOUT DAY

SHOT	DATE	No. 1 HIGHEST LEVEL OF FALLOUT IN U.S	No. 2 SECOND-HIGHEST LEVEL OF FALLOUT IN U.S.	No. 3 THIRD HIGHEST LEVEL OF FALLOUT IN U.S.	No. 4 FOURTH HIGHEST LEVEL OF FALLOUT IN U.S.	No. 5 FIFTH HIGHEST LEVEL OF FALLOUT IN U.S.
PB4-4	8-Jul-57	OSAGE MO	COLE MO	MONITEAU MO	CALLAWAY MO	GREENE IL
PB4-5	9-Jul-57	CUMBERLAND KY	HYDE NC	JOHNSON KS	BATES MO	DALLAS MO
PB4-6	10-Jul-57	COOPER MO	LACLEDE MO	COLE MO	DALLAS MO	MILLER MO
PB4-7	11-Jul-57	DEUEL NE	KIMBALL NE	CLEAR CREEK CO	ADAMS CO	LOGAN CO
PB4-8	12-Jul-57	SCOTTS BLUFF NE	KIMBALL NE	BANNER NE	ADAMS CO	ARAPAHOE CO
PB4-9	13-Jul-57	JASPER IA	DOUGLAS CO	CLEAR CREEK CO	GREENE IA	TAMA IA
PB4-10	14-Jul-57	FREMONT CO	CUSTER CO	DECATUR KS	NESS KS	ADAMS IA
PB5-1	15-Jul-57	NYE2 NV	WHITE PINE2 NV	LINCOLN2 NV	WHITE PINE3 NV	WHITE PINE1 NV
PB5-2	16-Jul-57	WIBAUX MT	DUNN ND	GOLDEN VALLE ND	MOUNTRAIL ND	STARK ND
PB5-3	17-Jul-57	STARK ND	BUTTE SD	LAWRENCE SD	WESTON WY	GUNNISON CO
PB5-4	18-Jul-57	BUTLER NE	MELLETTE SD	BANNER NE	CHEYENNE NE	GRANT NE
PB5-5	19-Jul-57	AITKIN MN	ANOKA MN	BENTON MN	CARLTON MN	CARVER MN
PB5-6	20-Jul-57	ESSEX VT	GRAND ISLE VT	ORLEANS VT	CLINTON NY	CHITTENDEN VT
PB5-7	21-Jul-57	SCHUYLER NY	DECATUR IA	DES MOINES IA	GRUNDY IA	HENRY IA
PB5-8	22-Jul-57	LESLIE KY	MARTIN KY	WORCESTER MD	CHOWAN NC	ALLEGANY NY
PB5-9	23-Jul-57	ST JOHNS FL	ALAMANCE NC	BERTIE NC	BLADEN NC	CHATHAM NC

U.S. FALLOUT ATLAS : COUNTY COMPARISONS

COUNTIES RANKED BY
AMOUNT OF NUCLEAR FALLOUT DEPOSITED ON SINGLE FALLOUT DAY

SHOT	DATE	No. 1 HIGHEST LEVEL OF FALLOUT IN U.S	No. 2 SECOND-HIGHEST LEVEL OF FALLOUT IN U.S.	No. 3 THIRD HIGHEST LEVEL OF FALLOUT IN U.S.	No. 4 FOURTH HIGHEST LEVEL OF FALLOUT IN U.S.	No. 5 FIFTH HIGHEST LEVEL OF FALLOUT IN U.S.
PB5-10	24-Jul-57	GARVIN OK	TILLMAN OK	DELTA TX	FOARD TX	HEMPHILL TX
PB6-1	24-Jul-57	ESMERALDA2 NV	ESMERALDA1 NV	MINERAL NV	CHURCHILL NV	INYO1 CA
PB6-2	25-Jul-57	WHITE PINE2 NV	CUSTER ID	LATAH ID	LEMHI ID	VALLEY ID
PB6-3	26-Jul-57	DEARBORN IN	RIPLEY IN	MENIFEE KY	BEAVERHEAD MT	BROADWATER MT
PB6-4	27-Jul-57	CAMPBELL KY	PENDLETON KY	MUSSELSHELL MT	PETROLEUM MT	RALLS MO
PB6-5	28-Jul-57	ADAMS ND	CARTER MT	PERKINS SD	GOLDEN VALLE ND	POWDER RIVER MT
PB6-6	29-Jul-57	PRAIRIE AR	WHITE AR	FAULKNER AR	DALLAS AR	JEFFERSON AR
PB6-7	30-Jul-57	LOGAN WV	WARREN NY	ELLIOTT KY	MORGAN KY	KANDIYOHI MN
PB6-8	31-Jul-57	BREMER IA	CHICKASAW IA	CLAYTON IA	DELAWARE IA	DUBUQUE IA
PB6-9	1-Aug-57	CARVER MN	CHIPPEWA MN	DOUGLAS MN	ALLAMAKEE IA	WINNESHIEK IA
PB6-10	2-Aug-57	JOHNSON IN	WARREN IN	BECKER MN	BIG STONE MN	CHIPPEWA MN
PB8-1	18-Aug-57	EUREKA NV	WHITE PINE2 NV	WHITE PINE3 NV	NYE2 NV	WHITE PINE1 NV
PB8-2	19-Aug-57	JUDITH BASIN MT	PARK WY	CLARK ID	FREMONT ID	JEFFERSON ID
PB8-3	20-Aug-57	BILLINGS ND	DIVIDE ND	RANSOM ND	CHERRY NE	BROOKINGS SD
PB8-4	21-Aug-57	MORGAN CO	BENNETT SD	JACKSON SD	MINNEHAHA SD	ARAPAHOE CO
PB8-5	22-Aug-57	DAVISON SD	HANSON SD	KINGSBURY SD	LAKE SD	MCCOOK SD

U.S. FALLOUT ATLAS : COUNTY COMPARISONS

COUNTIES RANKED BY
AMOUNT OF NUCLEAR FALLOUT DEPOSITED ON SINGLE FALLOUT DAY

SHOT	DATE	No. 1 HIGHEST LEVEL OF FALLOUT IN U.S.	No. 2 SECOND-HIGHEST LEVEL OF FALLOUT IN U.S.	No. 3 THIRD HIGHEST LEVEL OF FALLOUT IN U.S.	No. 4 FOURTH HIGHEST LEVEL OF FALLOUT IN U.S.	No. 5 FIFTH HIGHEST LEVEL OF FALLOUT IN U.S.
PB8-6	23-Aug-57	CLINTON IN	TIPTON IN	BERRIEN MI	CASS MI	ST JOSEPH MI
PB8-7	24-Aug-57	ANNE ARUNDEL MD	CALVERT MD	CHARLES MD	HOWARD MD	ST MARYS MD
PB9-1	23-Aug-57	UTAH UT	WHITE PINE2 NV	WASATCH UT	JUAB UT	TOOELE2 UT
PB9-2	24-Aug-57	PRAIRIE AR	CLARK ID	JEFFERSON ID	MADISON ID	TETON ID
PB9-3	25-Aug-57	POWESHIEK IA	TAMA IA	WAPELLO IA	CLARK MO	BENTON IA
PB9-4	26-Aug-57	ADAIR IA	AUDUBON IA	BOONE IA	CARROLL IA	CASS IA
PB9-5	27-Aug-57	BARTHOLOMEW IN	HANCOCK IN	HENRY IN	ST JOSEPH IN	CLARK IL
PB9-6	28-Aug-57	MORRILL NE	PHILLIPS CO	WELD CO	BANNER NE	KEITH NE
PB11-1	31-Aug-57	GARFIELD UT	INYO3 CA	WASHINGTON2 UT	WASHINGTON3 UT	LINCOLN1 NV
PB11-2	1-Sep-57	BARNES ND	CASS ND	DICKEY ND	EDDY ND	GRAND FORKS ND
PB11-3	2-Sep-57	CARLTON MN	LAKE MN	MAHNOMEN MN	TODD MN	WADENA MN
PB11-4	3-Sep-57	WIBAUX MT	BREVARD FL	FLAGLER FL	HERNANDO FL	LAKE FL
PB11-5	4-Sep-57	HAMPSHIRE MA	CHITTENDEN VT	ESSEX NY	FULTON NY	HAMILTON NY
PB11-6	5-Sep-57	ALLEN IN	FULTON NY	LEWIS NY	ADAMS IN	BLACKFORD IN
PB12-1	2-Sep-57	NYE2 NV	WHITE PINE1 NV	WHITE PINE2 NV	WHITE PINE3 NV	UTAH UT
PB12-2	3-Sep-57	WIBAUX MT	DAWSON MT	RICHLAND MT	VALLEY MT	CHOUTEAU MT

U.S. FALLOUT ATLAS : COUNTY COMPARISONS

COUNTIES RANKED BY
AMOUNT OF NUCLEAR FALLOUT DEPOSITED ON SINGLE FALLOUT DAY

SHOT	DATE	No. 1 HIGHEST LEVEL OF FALLOUT IN U.S.	No. 2 SECOND-HIGHEST LEVEL OF FALLOUT IN U.S.	No. 3 THIRD HIGHEST LEVEL OF FALLOUT IN U.S.	No. 4 FOURTH HIGHEST LEVEL OF FALLOUT IN U.S.	No. 5 FIFTH HIGHEST LEVEL OF FALLOUT IN U.S.
PB12-3	4-Sep-57	SUMNER KS	SEDGWICK KS	DENVER CO	EL PASO CO	MCPHERSON KS
PB12-4	5-Sep-57	WILSON KS	CRAWFORD KS	VERNON MO	ROGERS OK	CEDAR MO
PB12-5	6-Sep-57	TARRANT TX	PARKER TX	HILL TX	JOHNSON TX	DALLAS TX
PB12-6	7-Sep-57	LAFOURCHE LA	ST CHARLES LA	COVINGTON MS	WEBSTER MS	CLAY MS
PB12-7	8-Sep-57	FRANKLIN FL	GULF FL	LEON FL	WAKULLA FL	COFFEE GA
PB12-8	9-Sep-57	CHARLOTTE VA	JAMES CITY VA	CALHOUN FL	LIBERTY FL	YORK VA
PB12-9	10-Sep-57	TANGIPAHOA LA	ORLEANS LA	IBERIA LA	ST HELENA LA	LAFAYETTE LA
PB12-10	11-Sep-57	CASS IN	DEARBORN IN	MARSHALL IN	OHIO IN	RIPLEY IN
PB13-1	6-Sep-57	ESMERALDA2 NV	MONO CA	MINERAL NV	CARSON CITY NV	CHURCHILL NV
PB13-2	7-Sep-57	NYE3 NV	AUTAUGA AL	BALDWIN AL	BARBOUR AL	BIBB AL
PB13-3	8-Sep-57	BUFFALO NE	HALL NE	KEARNEY NE	COCONINO2 AZ	COCONINO3 AZ
PB13-4	9-Sep-57	ARCHULETA CO	CONEJOS CO	COSTILLA CO	RIO GRANDE CO	BAILEY TX
PB13-5	10-Sep-57	MCPHERSON KS	OTTAWA KS	STAFFORD KS	RICE KS	LINCOLN KS
PB13-6	11-Sep-57	OKMULGEE OK	WAGONER OK	PAYNE OK	MCINTOSH OK	MUSKOGEE OK
PB13-7	12-Sep-57	OHIO IN	STEVENS KS	BOYD KY	CARTER KY	ELLIOTT KY
PB13-8	13-Sep-57	MORTON KS	SCOTT KS	ARAPAHOE CO	BOULDER CO	CLEAR CREEK CO

U.S. FALLOUT ATLAS : COUNTY COMPARISONS

COUNTIES RANKED BY
AMOUNT OF NUCLEAR FALLOUT DEPOSITED ON SINGLE FALLOUT DAY

SHOT	DATE	No. 1 HIGHEST LEVEL OF FALLOUT IN U.S	No. 2 SECOND-HIGHEST LEVEL OF FALLOUT IN U.S.	No. 3 THIRD HIGHEST LEVEL OF FALLOUT IN U.S.	No. 4 FOURTH HIGHEST LEVEL OF FALLOUT IN U.S.	No. 5 FIFTH HIGHEST LEVEL OF FALLOUT IN U.S.
PB13-9	14-Sep-57	CRAWFORD AR	SCOTT AR	SEBASTIAN AR	HARPER KS	KINGMAN KS
PB13-10	15-Sep-57	BIBB AL	BLOUNT AL	CALHOUN AL	COOSA AL	ETOWAH AL
PB14-1	14-Sep-57	MINERAL NV	CARSON CITY NV	DOUGLAS NV	LYON NV	STOREY NV
PB14-2	15-Sep-57	0	0	0	0	0
PB14-3	16-Sep-57	LASSEN CA	MODOC CA	SISKIYOU CA	TEHAMA CA	CROOK OR
PB14-4	17-Sep-57	GILLIAM OR	MORROW OR	SHERMAN OR	PIERCE WA	TILLAMOOK OR
PB14-5	18-Sep-57	0	0	0	0	0
PB14-6	19-Sep-57	BARBER KS	BUTLER KS	CHASE KS	FRANKLIN KS	HARVEY KS
PB14 7		ALLEN KS	ANDERSON KS	BOURBON KS	BUTLER KS	CHASE KS
PB14-8	21-Sep-57	ATOKA OK	BRYAN OK	CHOCTAW OK	COAL OK	JEFFERSON OK
PB14-9	22-Sep-57	BRAZOS TX	BURLESON TX	CORYELL TX	HARDIN TX	JASPER TX
PB15-1	16-Sep-57	JUAB UT	SALT LAKE UT	BEAVER UT	MILLARD UT	BOX ELDER1 UT
PB15-2	17-Sep-57	GARFIELD NE	CODINGTON SD	ADAMS ND	BARNES ND	BENSON ND
PB15-3	18-Sep-57	LEMHI ID	VALLEY ID	BEAVERHEAD MT	GRANITE MT	ANTELOPE NE
PB15-4	19-Sep-57	EAGLE CO	PITKIN CO	ROUTT CO	GUNNISON CO	HINSDALE CO
PB15-5	20-Sep-57	JOHNSON KS	WYANDOTTE KS	BENTON MO	CAMDEN MO	CARROLL MO

COUNTIES RANKED BY
AMOUNT OF NUCLEAR FALLOUT DEPOSITED ON SINGLE FALLOUT DAY

SHOT	DATE	No. 1 HIGHEST LEVEL OF FALLOUT IN U.S	No. 2 SECOND-HIGHEST LEVEL OF FALLOUT IN U.S.	No. 3 THIRD HIGHEST LEVEL OF FALLOUT IN U.S.	No. 4 FOURTH HIGHEST LEVEL OF FALLOUT IN U.S.	No. 5 FIFTH HIGHEST LEVEL OF FALLOUT IN U.S.
PB15-6	21-Sep-57	MORROW OH	LAGRANGE IN	STEUBEN IN	WILLIAMS OH	ELKHART IN
PB15-7	22-Sep-57	CAMERON PA	GRANT KY	LEWIS KY	JACKSON IL	BOLLINGER MO
PB15-8	23-Sep-57	NELSON VA	QUEEN ANNES MD	SOMERSET NJ	CATTARAUGUS NY	GENESEE NY
PB15-9	24-Sep-57	BERGEN NJ	ESSEX NJ	HUDSON NJ	MIDDLESEX NJ	MONMOUTH NJ
PB16-1	23-Sep-57	ESMERALDA2 NV	ESMERALDA1 NV	CHURCHILL NV	MINERAL NV	LANDER2 NV
PB16-2	24-Sep-57	CLARK ID	JEFFERSON ID	MADISON ID	TETON ID	IRON MI
PB16-3	25-Sep-57	ADAMS ID	BENEWAH ID	BLAINE ID	BOISE ID	BONNER ID
PB16-4	26-Sep-57	COLUMBIA WA	SPOKANE WA	WALLA WALLA WA	NEZ PERCE ID	UMATILLA OR
PB16-5	27-Sep-57	FAYETTE GA	CLAYTON GA	FULTON GA	DE KALB GA	MONROE GA
PB16-6	28-Sep-57	GLASCOCK GA	COLUMBIA GA	GREENWOOD SC	MCCORMICK SC	BURKE GA
PB16-7	29-Sep-57	CARTERET NC	LENOIR NC	JONES NC	ONSLOW NC	HYDE NC
PB16-8	30-Sep-57	JOHNSON KY	COLUMBIA GA	LINCOLN GA	ANDROSCOGGIN ME	AROOSTOOK ME
PB16-9	1-Oct-57	SUMTER AL	UNION MS	LAUDERDALE AL	TUSCALOOSA AL	LEE AR
PB16-10	2-Oct-57	ESTILL KY	POWELL KY	DEARBORN IN	FAYETTE IN	FRANKLIN IN
PB17-1	28-Sep-57	SALT LAKE UT	BOX ELDER1 UT	BOX ELDER2 UT	CACHE UT	DAVIS UT
PB17-2	29-Sep-57	RUTHERFORD TN	SMITH TN	WILLIAMSON TN	WILSON TN	FLOYD IN

U.S. FALLOUT ATLAS : COUNTY COMPARISONS

COUNTIES RANKED BY
AMOUNT OF NUCLEAR FALLOUT DEPOSITED ON SINGLE FALLOUT DAY

SHOT	DATE	No. 1 HIGHEST LEVEL OF FALLOUT IN U.S	No. 2 SECOND-HIGHEST LEVEL OF FALLOUT IN U.S.	No. 3 THIRD HIGHEST LEVEL OF FALLOUT IN U.S.	No. 4 FOURTH HIGHEST LEVEL OF FALLOUT IN U.S.	No. 5 FIFTH HIGHEST LEVEL OF FALLOUT IN U.S.
PB17-3	30-Sep-57	CLAY NC	OCONEE SC	COFFEE TN	RABUN GA	TOWNS GA
PB17-4	1-Oct-57	ADAMS ID	PAYETTE ID	BAKER OR	VALLEY ID	BACON GA
PB17-5	2-Oct-57	FREMONT ID	CHICKASAW MS	TETON WY	BLAINE ID	GRENADA MS
PB17-6	3-Oct-57	OGLETHORPE GA	FAYETTE GA	DOUGLAS GA	GOLDEN VALLE MT	PAULDING GA
PB17-7	4-Oct-57	EDDY ND	BENSON ND	PIERCE ND	RAMSEY ND	STANLEY SD
PB17-8	5-Oct-57	CHESTERFIELD VA	HENRICO VA	HANOVER VA	KING WILLIAM VA	LOUISA VA
PB17-9	6-Oct-57	HUGHES SD	STANLEY SD	POLK IA	JONES SD	SULLY SD
PB17-10	7-Oct-57	BUFFALO SD	WASHITA OK	KEYA PAHA NE	STONEWALL TX	HARPER KS
PB18-1	7-Oct-57	IRON1 UT	WASHINGTON1 UT	IRON2 UT	IRON3 UT	WASHINGTON3 UT
PB18-2	8-Oct-57	EL PASO CO	ARAPAHOE CO	BACA CO	BOULDER CO	CUSTER CO
PB18-3	9-Oct-57	BACA CO	CHEYENNE CO	EL PASO CO	KIT CARSON CO	LOGAN CO
PB18-4	10-Oct-57	CHEYENNE CO	CUSTER NE	LINCOLN NE	LOGAN NE	PHELPS NE
PB18-5	11-Oct-57	GREENVILLE SC	PICKENS SC	CIMARRON OK	CASTRO TX	DALLAM TX
PB18-6	12-Oct-57	BECKHAM OK	CADDO OK	CANADIAN OK	COMANCHE OK	COTTON OK
PB18-7	13-Oct-57	LITTLE RIVER AR	MILLER AR	ATOKA OK	BRYAN OK	CHOCTAW OK
PB18-8	14-Oct-57	ADAIR MO	CARROLL MO	MARION MO	MONROE MO	SHELBY MO

U.S. FALLOUT ATLAS : COUNTY COMPARISONS

4-29

COUNTIES RANKED BY
AMOUNT OF NUCLEAR FALLOUT DEPOSITED ON SINGLE FALLOUT DAY

SHOT	DATE	No. 1 HIGHEST LEVEL OF FALLOUT IN U.S	No. 2 SECOND-HIGHEST LEVEL OF FALLOUT IN U.S.	No. 3 THIRD HIGHEST LEVEL OF FALLOUT IN U.S.	No. 4 FOURTH HIGHEST LEVEL OF FALLOUT IN U.S.	No. 5 FIFTH HIGHEST LEVEL OF FALLOUT IN U.S.
PB18-9	15-Oct-57	BROWN IL	CHAMPAIGN IL	CHRISTIAN IL	COLES IL	CUMBERLAND IL
PB18-10	16-Oct-57	DECATUR IN	HAMILTON IN	RIPLEY IN	TIPTON IN	UNION IN
SE1	6-Jul-62	WHITE PINE2 NV	NYE2 NV	WHITE PINE3 NV	WHITE PINE1 NV	TOOELE2 UT
SE2	7-Jul-62	WASHABAUGH SD	CUSTER SD	HAMLIN SD	KINGSBURY SD	MOODY SD
SE3	8-Jul-62	HOWARD IA	MITCHELL IA	WORTH IA	JEFFERSON IA	LEE IA
SE4	9-Jul-62	GREENUP KY	LAWRENCE KY	LEWIS KY	TRIMBLE KY	SCIOTO OH
SE5	10-Jul-62	CAMDEN NC	CURRITUCK NC	PASQUOTANK NC	PERQUIMANS NC	LESLIE KY
SE6	11-Jul-62	ACCOMACK VA	ROCKINGHAM VA	MONMOUTH NJ	WIRT WV	KERSHAW SC
SE7	12-Jul-62	0	0	0	0	0

SECTION 5

COUNTIES RECEIVING MOST FALLOUT NATIONWIDE FOR A SINGLE FALLOUT DAY

1951-1962

U.S. FALLOUT ATLAS : COUNTY COMPARISIONS

COUNTIES RECEIVING MOST FALLOUT NATIONWIDE FOR A SINGLE FALLOUT DAY			
COUNTY	NUMBER OF TIMES No. 1	DATE	SHOT
ADAMS ID	7	20-Nov-51	BJ5-2
ADAMS ID	7	22-Nov-51	BJ5 4
ADAMS ID	7	23-Nov-51	BJ5 5
ADAMS ID	7	26-Nov-51	BJ5 8
ADAMS ID	7	9-Jun-52	TS8-5
ADAMS ID	7	25-Sep-57	PB16-3
ADAMS ID	7	1-Oct-57	PB17-4
ARCHULETA CO	5	21-Apr-52	TS2-7
ARCHULETA CO	5	28-May-52	TS6-4
ARCHULETA CO	5	1-Apr-53	UK3-2
ARCHULETA CO	5	22-Apr-53	UK6-5
ARCHULETA CO	5	9-Sep-57	PB13-4
BERGEN NJ	4	13-Nov-51	BJ4-9
BERGEN NJ	4	21-Mar-55	TP5-10
BERGEN NJ	4	23-May-55	TP11-9
BERGEN NJ	4	24-Sep-57	PB15-9
NYE2 NV	4	19-Nov-51	BJ5 1
NYE2 NV	4	28-May-57	PB1-1
NYE2 NV	4	15-Jul-57	PB5-1
NYE2 NV	4	2-Sep-57	PB12-1
WASHINGTON2 UT	4	17-Mar-53	UK1-1
WASHINGTON2 UT	4	6-Apr-53	UK4-1
WASHINGTON2 UT	4	19-May-53	UK9-1
WASHINGTON2 UT	4	1-Mar-55	TP3-1
WHITE PINE2 NV	4	29-Nov-51	BJ6-1
WHITE PINE2 NV	4	5-May-55	TP10-1
WHITE PINE2 NV	4	25-Jul-57	PB6-2
WHITE PINE2 NV	4	6-Jul-62	SE1
ACADIA LA	3	19-Apr-53	UK6-2
ACADIA LA	3	24-Apr-53	UK6-7
ACADIA LA	3	26-Jun-57	PB3-3
ADAMS CO	3	2-Mar-55	TP3-2
ADAMS CO	3	3-Mar-55	TP3-3

COUNTIES RECEIVING MOST FALLOUT NATIONWIDE FOR A SINGLE FALLOUT DAY

COUNTY	NUMBER OF TIMES No. 1	DATE	SHOT
ADAMS CO	3	8-Mar-55	TP4-2
CLARK1 NV	3	25-Apr-53	UK7-1
CLARK1 NV	3	12-Mar-55	TP5-1
CLARK1 NV	3	23-Mar-55	TP6-2
ESMERALDA2 NV	3	24-Jul-57	PB6-1
ESMERALDA2 NV	3	6-Sep-57	PB13-1
ESMERALDA2 NV	3	23-Sep-57	PB16-1
GARFIELD MT	3	9-May-53	UK8-2
GARFIELD MT	3	31-May-53	UK10-7
GARFIELD MT	3	1-Jun-53	UK10-8
IDAHO ID	3	18-Apr-52	TS2-4
IDAHO ID	3	12-Jun-52	TS8-8
IDAHO ID	3	13-Jun-52	TS8-9
INYO3 CA	3	30-Oct-51	BJ-2 1
INYO3 CA	3	15-Apr-52	TS2-1
INYO3 CA	3	7-Mar-55	TP4-1
IRON1 UT	3	1-May-52	TS4-1
IRON1 UT	3	18-Jun-57	PB2-1
IRON1 UT	3	7-Oct-57	PB18-1
JUDITH BASIN MT	3	2-May-52	TS4-2
JUDITH BASIN MT	3	7-Jun-52	TS8-3
JUDITH BASIN MT	3	19-Aug-57	PB8-2
NANTUCKET MA	3	11-Apr-53	UK4-6
NANTUCKET MA	3	12-Apr-53	UK4-7
NANTUCKET MA	3	15-Apr-53	UK5-5
PRAIRIE AR	3	31-Mar-53	UK2-8
PRAIRIE AR	3	29-Jul-57	PB6-6
PRAIRIE AR	3	24-Aug-57	PB9-2
WIBAUX MT	3	16-Jul-57	PB5-2
WIBAUX MT	3	3-Sep-57	PB11-4
WIBAUX MT	3	3-Sep-57	PB12-2
ALACHUA FL	2	4-Feb-51	R2-3
ALACHUA FL	2	28-Mar-55	TP6-7

COUNTIES RECEIVING MOST FALLOUT NATIONWIDE FOR A SINGLE FALLOUT DAY

COUNTY	NUMBER OF TIMES No. 1	DATE	SHOT
ANDREWS TX	2	16-May-52	TS5-10
ANDREWS TX	2	9-Jun-52	TS7-9
AROOSTOOK ME	2	2-Nov-51	BJ-2 4
AROOSTOOK ME	2	27-Mar-53	UK2-4
BACA CO	2	3-May-52	TS4-3
BACA CO	2	9-Oct-57	PB18-3
BECKHAM OK	2	4-Apr-53	UK3-5
BECKHAM OK	2	12-Oct-57	PB18-6
BIBB AL	2	8-Jun-52	TS7-8
BIBB AL	2	15-Sep-57	PB13-10
CLARK ID	2	12-May-52	TS5-6
CLARK ID	2	24-Sep-57	PB16-2
CLAY NC	2	12-Apr-53	UK5-2
CLAY NC	2	30-Sep-57	PB17-3
COCONINO2 AZ	2	18-Apr-53	UK6-1
COCONINO2 AZ	2	4-Jun-53	UK11-1
CUMBERLAND ME	2	31-Oct-51	BJ2-2
CUMBERLAND ME	2	16-Apr-55	TP8-8
CUSTER MT	2	25-Mar-53	UK2-2
CUSTER MT	2	8-May-53	UK8-1
DEER LODGE MT	2	11-Jun-52	TS8-7
DEER LODGE MT	2	3-Jun-57	PB1-7
EL PASO TX	2	3-Nov-51	BJ3-3
EL PASO TX	2	20-Apr-53	UK6-3
ERIE OH	2	5-Nov-51	BJ3-5
ERIE OH	2	6-Mar-55	TP3-6
EUREKA NV	2	18-Aug-57	PB8-1
FAIRFIELD CT	2	20-Apr-55	TP9-7
FRESNO CA	2	28-Oct-51	BJ01 BAKER 1
FRESNO CA	2	7-Nov-51	BJ4-3
GEM ID	2	5-Jun-52	TS8-1
GEM ID	2	6-Jun-52	TS8-2
GREENVILLE SC	2	30-May-52	TS6-6

COUNTIES RECEIVING MOST FALLOUT NATIONWIDE FOR A SINGLE FALLOUT DAY

COUNTY	NUMBER OF TIMES No. 1	DATE	SHOT
GREENVILLE SC	2	11-Oct-57	PB18-5
GUNNISON CO	2	10-Jun-53	UK11-7
GUNNISON CO	2	14-May-55	TP10-10
HAMPSHIRE MA	2	4-Sep-57	PB11-5
HARFORD MD	2	30-May-53	UK10-6
HILLSBOROUGH FL	2	6-Feb-51	R2-5
HILLSBOROUGH FL	2	29-Apr-52	TS3-8
IMPERIAL CA	2	17-Apr-52	TS2-3
IMPERIAL CA	2	19-Apr-52	TS2-5
KENT DE	2	10-Nov-51	BJ4-6
KENT DE	2	25-May-53	UK9-7
KNOX TN	2	12-May-55	TP10-8
KNOX TN	2	13-May-55	TP10-9
LACKAWANNA PA	2	31-Jan-51	R1-4
LACKAWANNA PA	2	27-Apr-52	TS3-6
LEMHI ID	2	14-May-52	TS5-8
LEMHI ID	2	18-Sep-57	PB15-3
LINCOLN2 NV	2	25-May-52	TS6-1
LINCOLN2 NV	2	29-Mar-55	TP7-1
MCINTOSH OK	2	2-Apr-53	UK2-10
MCINTOSH OK	2	2-Apr-53	UK3-3
MEDINA OH	2	10-Mar-55	TP4-4
MEDINA OH	2	18-Apr-55	TP9-5
MIDDLESEX MA	2	9-Apr-53	UK4-4
MIDDLESEX MA	2	10-Apr-53	UK4-5
MONROE NY	2	1-Nov-51	BJ-2 3
MONROE NY	2	8-Nov-51	BJ3-8
MORGAN CO	2	16-May-55	TP11-2
MORGAN CO	2	21-Aug-57	PB8-4
NATRONA WY	2	27-May-53	UK10-3
NATRONA WY	2	19-Jun-57	PB2-2
PITKIN CO	2	13-Apr-53	UK5-3
PITKIN CO	2	17-May-55	TP11-3

COUNTIES RECEIVING MOST FALLOUT NATIONWIDE FOR A SINGLE FALLOUT DAY

COUNTY	NUMBER OF TIMES No. 1	DATE	SHOT
QUEENS NY	2	26-Apr-52	TS3-5
QUEENS NY	2	1-Jun-52	TS6-8
WASHINGTON ME	2	2-Jun-52	TS6-9
WASHINGTON ME	2	1-May-53	UK7-7
WAYNE MI	2	12-Nov-51	BJ4-8
WAYNE MI	2	15-Apr-55	TP9-2
ACCOMACK VA	1	11-Jul-62	SE6
ADAIR IA	1	26-Aug-57	PB9-4
ADAIR MO	1	14-Oct-57	PB18-8
ADAMS IL	1	22-Apr-55	TP9-9
ADAMS MS	1	28-Apr-53	UK7-4
ADAMS ND	1	28-Jul-57	PB6-5
AITKIN MN	1	19-Jul-57	PB5-5
ALCONA MI	1	3-Jun-53	UK10-10
ALEXANDER IL	1	19-Mar-55	TP5-8
ALGER MI	1	17-Apr-55	TP9-4
ALLEGANY NY	1	9-Nov-51	BJ3-9
ALLEN IN	1	5-Sep-57	PB11-6
ALLEN KS	1		PB14 7
ANDERSON TX	1	4-Nov-51	BJ3-4
ANDROSCOGGIN ME	1	25-Apr-53	UK6-8
ANNE ARUNDEL MD	1	24-Aug-57	PB8-7
ARKANSAS AR	1	5-Apr-53	UK3-6
ASHLAND OH	1	14-Apr-55	TP8-6
ATOKA OK	1	21-Sep-57	PB14-8
AUDUBON IA	1	23-May-53	UK9-5
BANNER NE	1	2-Apr-52	TS1-2
BARBER KS	1	19-Sep-57	PB14-6
BARNES ND	1	1-Sep-57	PB11-2
BARTHOLOMEW IN	1	27-Aug-57	PB9-5
BARTON KS	1	30-Apr-52	TS3-9
BEAVER PA	1	24-Jun-57	PB2-7
BEAVER UT	1	1-Apr-52	TS1-1

COUNTIES RECEIVING MOST FALLOUT NATIONWIDE FOR A SINGLE FALLOUT DAY

COUNTY	NUMBER OF TIMES No. 1	DATE	SHOT
BEAVERHEAD MT	1	13-May-52	TS5-7
BEE TX	1	1-Jun-57	PB1-5
BELMONT OH	1	29-Jan-51	R1-2
BERKSHIRE MA	1	2-May-53	UK7-8
BERTIE NC	1	18-Apr-53	UK5-8
BIG HORN MT	1	10-May-53	UK8-3
BILLINGS ND	1	20-Aug-57	PB8-3
BOONE IA	1	3-Apr-55	TP7-6
BOONE IN	1	27-Jun-57	PB3-4
BRADLEY AR	1	14-Apr-53	UK5-4
BRAZOS TX	1	22-Sep-57	PB14-9
BREMER IA	1	31-Jul-57	PB6-8
BROWN IL	1	15-Oct-57	PB18-9
BRUNSWICK NC	1	6-Apr-55	TP7-9
BUCHANAN MO	1	6-Jun-53	UK11-3
BUFFALO NE	1	8-Sep-57	PB13-3
BUFFALO SD	1	7-Oct-57	PB17-10
BULLOCH GA	1	7-Apr-55	TP7-10
BUTLER NE	1	18-Jul-57	PB5-4
CALDWELL MO	1	3-May-53	UK7-9
CALVERT MD	1	23-Apr-55	TP9-10
CAMBRIA PA	1	24-May-55	TP11-10
CAMDEN MO	1	7-May-55	TP10-3
CAMDEN NC	1	10-Jul-62	SE5
CAMERON PA	1	22-Sep-57	PB15-7
CAMPBELL KY	1	27-Jul-57	PB6-4
CARLISLE KY	1	11-Mar-55	TP4-5
CARLTON MN	1	2-Sep-57	PB11-3
CARROLL IN	1	5-May-52	TS4-5
CARTER KY	1	24-Mar-53	uk1 8
CARTER TN	1	9-Nov-51	BJ4-5
CARTERET NC	1	29-Sep-57	PB16-7
CARVER MN	1	1-Aug-57	PB6-9

COUNTIES RECEIVING MOST FALLOUT NATIONWIDE FOR A SINGLE FALLOUT DAY

COUNTY	NUMBER OF TIMES No. 1	DATE	SHOT
CASS IN	1	11-Sep-57	PB12-10
CASS MO	1	29-Mar-53	UK2-6
CATTARAUGUS NY	1	29-May-53	UK10-5
CHAMPAIGN OH	1	21-Apr-55	TP9-8
CHARLOTTE VA	1	9-Sep-57	PB12-8
CHAUTAUQUA NY	1	6-Nov-51	BJ3-6
CHESTER SC	1	5-Apr-55	TP7-8
CHESTERFIELD VA	1	5-Oct-57	PB17-8
CHEYENNE CO	1	10-Oct-57	PB18-4
CHIPPEWA MI	1	8-Jun-52	TS8-4
CIMARRON OK	1	6-May-52	TS4-6
CLARENDON SC	1	28-Apr-52	TS3-7
CLARK IN	1	17-Apr-53	UK5-7
CLARK2 NV	1	22-Feb-55	TP2-1
CLARK3 NV	1	22-Mar-55	TP6-1
CLEARWATER ID	1	21-Nov-51	BJ5 3
CLINTON IN	1	23-Aug-57	PB8-6
CLINTON MO	1	28-Mar-53	UK2-5
CLINTON PA	1	5-Mar-55	TP3-5
COAL OK	1	6-Jun-52	TS7-6
COLBERT AL	1	20-Mar-55	TP5-9
COLUMBIA WA	1	26-Sep-57	PB16-4
COMANCHE KS	1	31-May-52	TS6-7
CONCHO TX	1	21-Apr-53	UK6-4
CONECUH AL	1	24-Apr-52	TS3-3
COOPER MO	1	10-Jul-57	PB4-6
CORTLAND NY	1	14-Nov-51	BJ4-10
COSTILLA CO	1	6-May-55	TP10-2
CRAWFORD AR	1	14-Sep-57	PB13-9
CROWLEY CO	1	6-Jun-57	PB1-10
CULBERSON TX	1	9-Jun-53	UK11-6
CUMBERLAND KY	1	9-Jul-57	PB4-5
DADE FL	1	5-Feb-51	R2-4

COUNTIES RECEIVING MOST FALLOUT NATIONWIDE FOR A SINGLE FALLOUT DAY

COUNTY	NUMBER OF TIMES No. 1	DATE	SHOT
DANIELS MT	1	2-Jun-53	UK10-9
DAVIDSON NC	1	8-May-52	TS5-2
DAVIDSON TN	1	29-May-52	TS6-5
DAVIDSON TN	1	22-Mar-53	uk1 6
DAVISON SD	1	22-Aug-57	PB8-5
DE KALB MO	1	8-Jun-53	UK11-5
DEARBORN IN	1	26-Jul-57	PB6-3
DECATUR IN	1	16-Oct-57	PB18-10
DELAWARE OK	1	9-May-55	TP10-5
DEUEL NE	1	11-Jul-57	PB4-7
DINWIDDIE VA	1	9-May-52	TS5-3
DUNKLIN MO	1	20-Mar-53	uk1 4
DYER TN	1	30-Mar-53	UK2-7
EAGLE CO	1	19-Sep-57	PB15-4
ECTOR TX	1	3-Apr-53	UK3-4
EDDY ND	1	4-Oct-57	PB17-7
EL DORADO CA	1	27-Mar-55	TP6-6
EL PASO CO	1	8-Oct-57	PB18-2
ERIE NY	1	4-Nov-51	BJ-2 6
ESSEX VT	1	20-Jul-57	PB5-6
ESTILL KY	1	2-Oct-57	PB16-10
EUREKA NV	1	1-Jun-52	TS7-1
FAYETTE GA	1	27-Sep-57	PB16-5
FERRY WA	1	26-May-53	UK10-2
FLUVANNA VA	1	25-Jun-57	PB2-8
FOREST PA	1	22-May-55	TP11-8
FRANKLIN AR	1	3-Apr-52	ts1 3
FRANKLIN FL	1	8-Sep-57	PB12-7
FRANKLIN MO	1	29-Jun-57	PB3-6
FREMONT CO	1	14-Jul-57	PB4-10
FREMONT ID	1	2-Oct-57	PB17-5
FULTON AR	1	26-Mar-53	UK2-3
GAINES TX	1	12-May-53	UK8-5

COUNTIES RECEIVING MOST FALLOUT NATIONWIDE FOR A SINGLE FALLOUT DAY

COUNTY	NUMBER OF TIMES No. 1	DATE	SHOT
GALLATIN MT	1	7-May-52	TS4-7
GARFIELD NE	1	17-Sep-57	PB15-2
GARFIELD OK	1	24-Nov-51	BJ5 6
GARFIELD UT	1	31-Aug-57	PB11-1
GARVIN OK	1	24-Jul-57	PB5-10
GASCONADE MO	1	28-Jun-57	PB3-5
GENESEE NY	1	3-Nov-51	BJ-2 5
GILLIAM OR	1	17-Sep-57	PB14-4
GLASCOCK GA	1	28-Sep-57	PB16-6
GLENN CA	1	25-Apr-52	TS3-4
GRAND ISLE VT	1	11-May-53	UK8-4
GRANT AR	1	4-Jun-57	PB1-8
GRANT LA	1	9-May-52	TS4-9
GREENUP KY	1	9-Jul-62	SE4
HALE TX	1	18-May-55	TP11-4
HAMILTON IN	1	7-Jun-53	UK11-4
HAMPSHIRE MA	1	12-Mar-55	TP4-6
HINDS MS	1	8-May-55	TP10-4
HINSDALE CO	1	26-May-52	TS6-2
HOT SPRINGS WY	1	7-May-52	TS5-1
HOWARD IA	1	8-Jul-62	SE3
HUGHES SD	1	6-Oct-57	PB17-9
HUMPHREYS TN	1	19-Mar-53	uk1 3
IBERIA LA	1	11-May-55	TP10-7
IRON2 UT	1	15-May-55	TP11-1
JACKSON CO	1	10-Apr-55	TP8-2
JACKSON MN	1	29-Apr-53	UK7-5
JASPER IA	1	13-Jul-57	PB4-9
JEFF DAVIS TX	1	25-Jun-57	PB3-2
JEFFERSON ID	1	2-Jun-52	TS7-2
JEFFERSON MT	1	2-Jun-57	PB1-6
JEFFERSON NY	1	10-Nov-51	BJ3-10
JOHNSON IN	1	2-Aug-57	PB6-10

COUNTIES RECEIVING MOST FALLOUT NATIONWIDE FOR A SINGLE FALLOUT DAY

COUNTY	NUMBER OF TIMES No. 1	DATE	SHOT
JOHNSON KS	1	20-Sep-57	PB15-5
JOHNSON KY	1	30-Sep-57	PB16-8
JUAB UT	1	16-Sep-57	PB15-1
KENNEBEC ME	1	16-Apr-53	UK5-6
KEOKUK IA	1	14-Jun-52	TS8-10
KERN CA	1	16-Apr-52	TS2-2
KINGS NY	1	4-Apr-52	ts1 4
KIOWA CO	1	27-Apr-53	UK7-3
KLEBERG TX	1	2-Nov-51	BJ3-2
KNOX ME	1	26-Mar-53	UK1-10
KNOX MO	1	3-Jun-52	TS7-3
LA PLATA CO	1	28-Jan-51	R1-1
LAFOURCHE LA	1	7-Sep-57	PB12-6
LAGRANGE IN	1	30-Jan-51	R1-3
LAKE MI	1	24-May-53	UK9-6
LAMAR AL	1	21-Jun-57	PB2-4
LARAMIE WY	1	13-Mar-55	TP5-2
LAS ANIMAS CO	1	4-May-52	TS4-4
LASSEN CA	1	16-Sep-57	PB14-3
LAWRENCE IN	1	14-Mar-55	TP5-3
LEON FL	1	8-Apr-53	UK4-3
LESLIE KY	1	22-Jul-57	PB5-8
LEWIS KY	1	15-Mar-55	TP5-4
LINCOLN1 NV	1	15-Apr-55	TP9-1
LITTLE RIVER AR	1	13-Oct-57	PB18-7
LOGAN CO	1	15-May-52	TS5-9
LOGAN KY	1	18-Mar-55	TP5-7
LOGAN WV	1	30-Jul-57	PB6-7
LOVE OK	1	25-Mar-53	UK1-9
MADISON VA	1	13-May-53	UK8-6
MAHONING OH	1	21-May-53	UK9-3
MARICOPA AZ	1	31-Mar-53	UK3-1
MARION SC	1	7-Jun-52	TS7-7

COUNTIES RECEIVING MOST FALLOUT NATIONWIDE FOR A SINGLE FALLOUT DAY

COUNTY	NUMBER OF TIMES No. 1	DATE	SHOT
MCDOWELL WV	1	22-May-53	UK9-4
MCPHERSON KS	1	10-Sep-57	PB13-5
MERCER NJ	1	23-Mar-53	uk1 7
MERIWETHER GA	1	29-Oct-51	BJ1-2
MINERAL CO	1	11-Jun-53	UK11-8
MINERAL NV	1	14-Sep-57	PB14-1
MITCHELL NC	1	26-Jun-57	PB2-9
MOHAVE2 AZ	1	22-Apr-52	TS3-1
MONMOUTH NJ	1	18-Mar-53	UK1-2
MONTGOMERY MS	1	24-Mar-55	TP6-3
MORGAN UT	1	24-Mar-53	UK2-1
MORRILL NE	1	28-Aug-57	PB9-6
MORRIS NJ	1	7-Nov-51	BJ3-7
MORROW OH	1	21-Sep-57	PB15-6
MORTON KS	1	13-Sep-57	PB13-8
NELSON VA	1	23-Sep-57	PB15-8
NESS KS	1	31-Mar-55	TP7-3
NEW HANOVER NC	1	6-Apr-53	uk3 7
NORFOLK MA	1	11-May-52	TS5-5
NYE3 NV	1	7-Sep-57	PB13-2
OGLETHORPE GA	1	3-Oct-57	PB17-6
OHIO IN	1	12-Sep-57	PB13-7
OKMULGEE OK	1	11-Sep-57	PB13-6
ORANGE NC	1	1-Apr-53	UK2-9
ORLEANS NY	1	19-Apr-55	TP9-6
OSAGE MO	1	8-Jul-57	PB4-4
PALM BEACH FL	1	26-May-53	UK9-8
PARK MT	1	6-Jul-57	PB4-2
PARKER TX	1	23-Apr-53	UK6-6
PAYETTE ID	1	10-Jun-52	TS8-6
PEMBINA ND	1	16-Apr-55	TP9-3
PENOBSCOT ME	1	5-Apr-52	ts1 5
PHILLIPS CO	1	27-May-52	TS6-3

COUNTIES RECEIVING MOST FALLOUT NATIONWIDE FOR A SINGLE FALLOUT DAY

COUNTY	NUMBER OF TIMES No. 1	DATE	SHOT
PIKE MO	1	4-Apr-55	TP7-7
PIMA AZ	1	5-Jul-57	PB4-1
PISCATAQUIS ME	1	8-May-52	TS4-8
PLYMOUTH MA	1	7-Apr-53	UK4-2
POLK IA	1	2-Apr-55	TP7-5
PONTOTOC OK	1	19-May-55	TP11-5
POTTER PA	1	4-Mar-55	TP3-4
POWESHIEK IA	1	25-Aug-57	PB9-3
PRINCE GEORG MD	1	7-Feb-51	R2-6
PRINCE WILLI VA	1	10-May-52	TS5-4
PULASKI IL	1	16-Mar-55	TP5-5
QUITMAN MS	1	1-Apr-55	TP7-4
RABUN GA	1	22-Jun-57	PB2-5
REFUGIO TX	1	3-Feb-51	R2-2
RICHLAND ND	1	20-Jun-57	PB2-3
RINGGOLD IA	1	4-Jun-52	TS7-4
RIO GRANDE CO	1	22-Apr-52	TS2-8
RIVERSIDE CA	1	20-Apr-52	TS2-6
ROANOKE VA	1	21-May-55	TP11-7
ROCKWALL TX	1	28-May-53	UK10-4
ROUTT CO	1	5-Jun-53	UK11-2
RUSH IN	1	3-Jun-52	TS6-10
RUTHERFORD TN	1	29-Sep-57	PB17-2
SALINE KS	1	12-Apr-55	TP8-4
SALT LAKE UT	1	28-Sep-57	PB17-1
SAN BERNADIN CA	1	18-Feb-55	TP1-1
SAN DIEGO CA	1	23-Apr-52	TS3-2
SARATOGA NY	1	30-Apr-53	UK7-6
SAUK WI	1	1-May-52	TS3-10
SCHUYLER NY	1	21-Jul-57	PB5-7
SCOTTS BLUFF NE	1	12-Jul-57	PB4-8
SEMINOLE FL	1	10-May-55	TP10-6
SENECA NY	1	23-Jun-57	PB2-6

COUNTIES RECEIVING MOST FALLOUT NATIONWIDE FOR A SINGLE FALLOUT DAY

COUNTY	NUMBER OF TIMES No. 1	DATE	SHOT
SHELBY TN	1	21-Mar-53	uk1 5
SOMERSET MD	1	11-Nov-51	BJ4-7
ST JOHNS FL	1	23-Jul-57	PB5-9
STANTON KS	1	11-Apr-55	TP8-3
STARK ND	1	17-Jul-57	PB5-3
STEVENS KS	1	30-Mar-55	TP7-2
STONE MO	1	27-May-53	UK9-9
SUMNER KS	1	4-Sep-57	PB12-3
SUMTER AL	1	1-Oct-57	PB16-9
SUSSEX NJ	1	27-Jun-57	PB2-10
TANGIPAHOA LA	1	10-Sep-57	PB12-9
TARRANT TX	1	6-Sep-57	PB12-5
TAZEWELL IL	1	9-Mar-55	TP4-3
TOOELE2 UT	1	9-Apr-55	TP8-1
TULSA OK	1	5-Jun-52	TS7-5
TYRRELL NC	1	7-Apr-53	uk3 8
UNICOI TN	1	26-Mar-55	TP6-5
UTAH UT	1	23-Aug-57	PB9-1
WALTON FL	1	5-Jun-57	PB1-9
WASHABAUGH SD	1	7-Jul-62	SE2
WASHBURN WI	1	20-May-53	UK9-2
WASHINGTON ID	1	25-Nov-51	BJ5 7
WASHINGTON LA	1	13-Apr-55	TP8-5
WASHINGTON NY	1	26-Apr-53	UK7-2
WASHINGTON1 UT	1	24-Jun-57	PB3-1
WASHITA OK	1	17-Mar-55	TP5-6
WEBSTER IA	1	7-Jul-57	PB4-3
WHITE PINE3 NV	1	25-May-53	UK10-1
WILSON KS	1	5-Sep-57	PB12-4
WINDHAM CT	1	19-Apr-53	UK5-9
WOODRUFF AR	1	20-May-55	TP11-6
WYOMING NY	1	15-Apr-55	TP8-7
YANCEY NC	1	25-Mar-55	TP6-4

COUNTIES RECEIVING MOST FALLOUT NATIONWIDE FOR A SINGLE FALLOUT DAY			
COUNTY	NUMBER OF TIMES No. 1	DATE	SHOT
YUMA AZ	1	11-Apr-53	UK5-1

SECTION 6

FALLOUT PATTERN ANALYSIS

1951-1995

FALLOUT PATTERNS: DAYS 1 THROUGH 10

Fallout from a nuclear detonation produces the most radiation during the first few days post shot. By separating the fallout data into days 1 through 10 post shot, we are able to determine which counties were exposed to the more active fallout.

COUNTIES EXPOSED TO DAY 1 FALLOUT

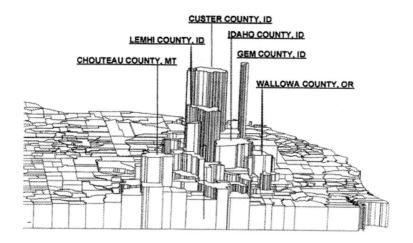

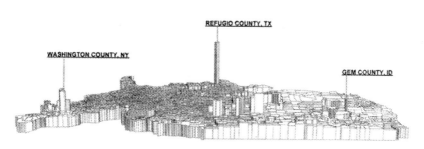

COUNTIES EXPOSED TO DAY 2 FALLOUT

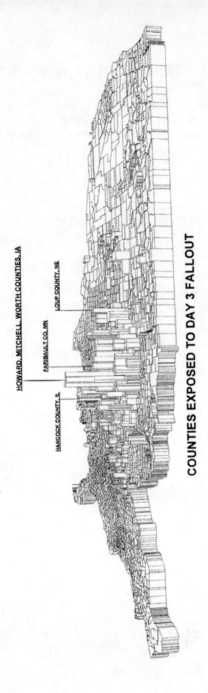

COUNTIES EXPOSED TO DAY 3 FALLOUT

HOWARD, MITCHELL, WORTH COUNTIES, IA

FARIBAULT CO, MN

LOUP COUNTY, NE

HANCOCK COUNTY, IL

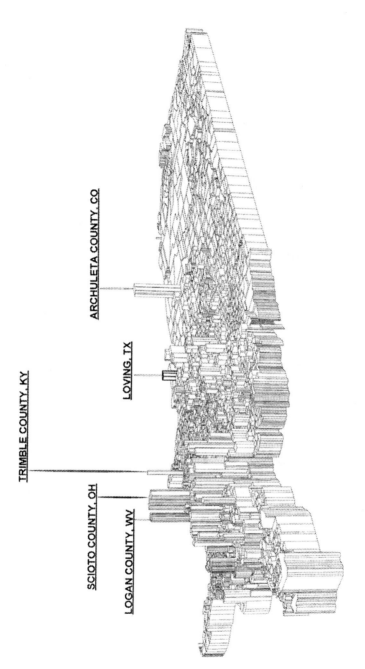

COUNTIES EXPOSED TO DAY 4 FALLOUT

ARCHULETA COUNTY, CO

LOVING, TX

TRIMBLE COUNTY, KY

SCIOTO COUNTY, OH

LOGAN COUNTY, WV

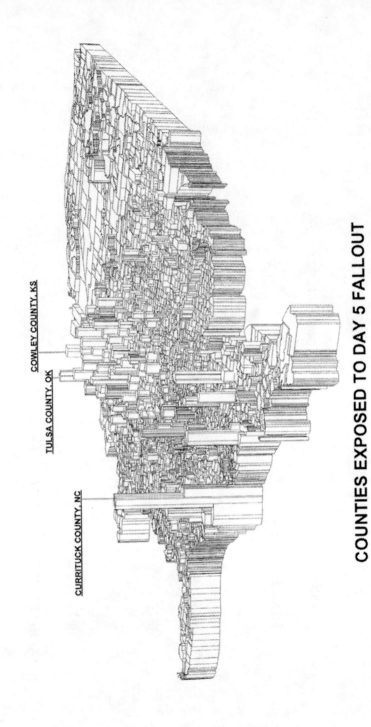

COUNTIES EXPOSED TO DAY 5 FALLOUT

COWLEY COUNTY, KS.

TULSA COUNTY, OK

CURRITUCK COUNTY, NC

US. FALLOUT ATLAS : COUNTY COMPARISIONS

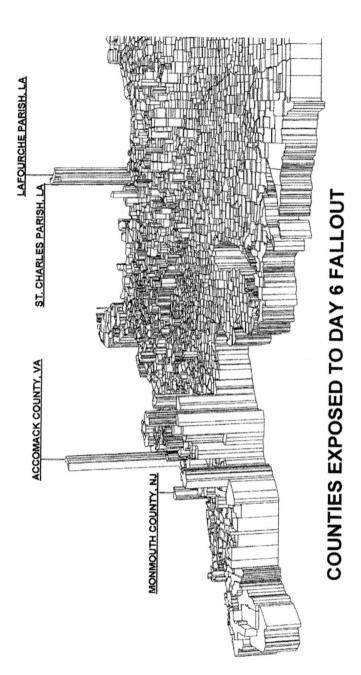

COUNTIES EXPOSED TO DAY 6 FALLOUT

Labels on image: LAFOURCHE PARISH, LA; ST. CHARLES PARISH, LA; ACCOMACK COUNTY, VA; MONMOUTH COUNTY, NJ

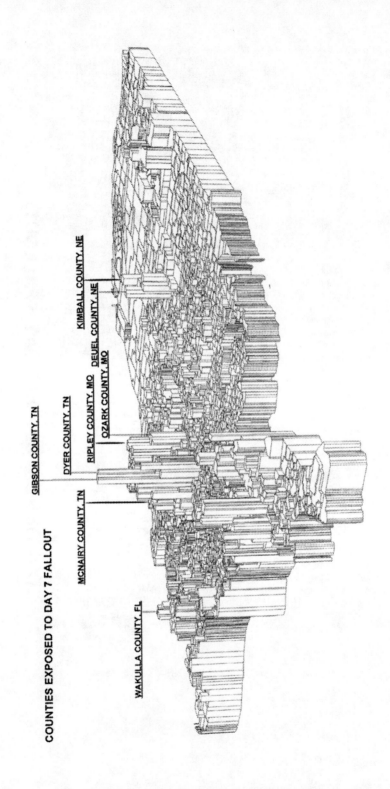

COUNTIES EXPOSED TO DAY 7 FALLOUT

GIBSON COUNTY, TN
DYER COUNTY, TN
MCNAIRY COUNTY, TN
RIPLEY COUNTY, MO
OZARK COUNTY, MO
DEUEL COUNTY, NE
KIMBALL COUNTY, NE
WAKULLA COUNTY, FL

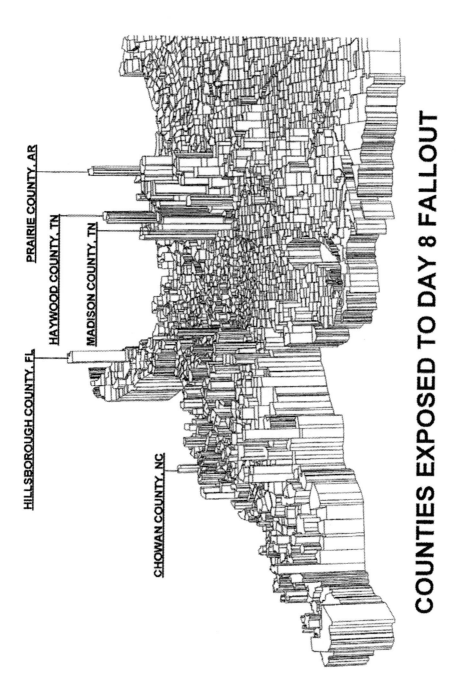

COUNTIES EXPOSED TO DAY 8 FALLOUT

PRAIRIE COUNTY, AR

HAYWOOD COUNTY, TN

MADISON COUNTY, TN

HILLSBOROUGH COUNTY, FL

CHOWAN COUNTY, NC

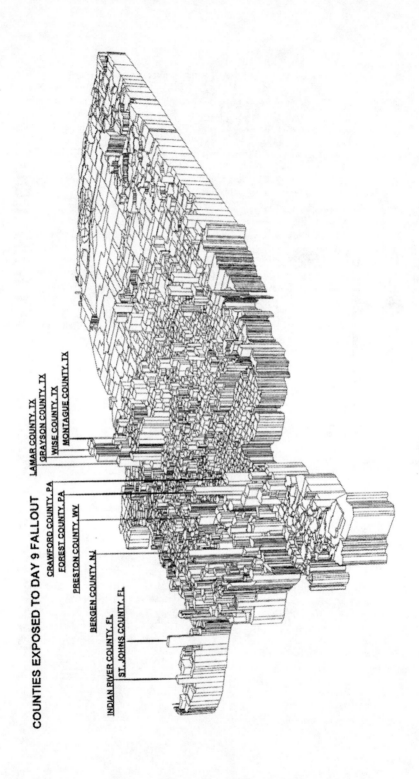

COUNTIES EXPOSED TO DAY 9 FALLOUT

LAMAR COUNTY, TX
GRAYSON COUNTY, TX
WISE COUNTY, TX
MONTAGUE COUNTY, TX

CRAWFORD COUNTY, PA
FOREST COUNTY, PA
PRESTON COUNTY, WV

BERGEN COUNTY, NJ

INDIAN RIVER COUNTY, FL
ST. JOHNS COUNTY, FL

US. FALLOUT ATLAS : COUNTY COMPARISIONS

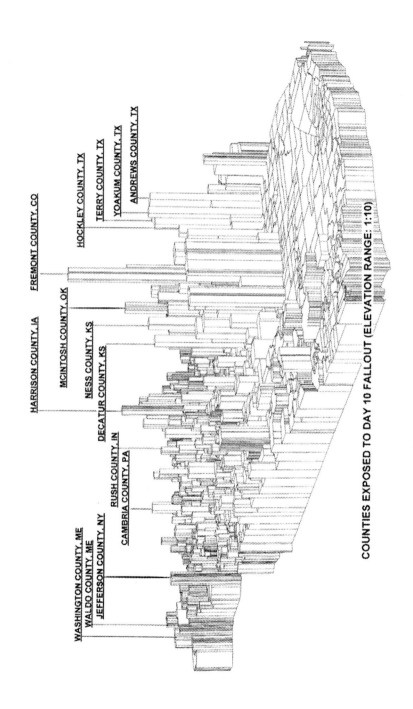

COUNTIES EXPOSED TO DAY 10 FALLOUT (ELEVATION RANGE: 1:10)

WASHINGTON COUNTY, ME
WALDO COUNTY, ME
JEFFERSON COUNTY, NY
CAMBRIA COUNTY, PA
RUSH COUNTY, IN
DECATUR COUNTY, KS
NESS COUNTY, KS
MCINTOSH COUNTY, OK
HARRISON COUNTY, IA
FREMONT COUNTY, CO
HOCKLEY COUNTY, TX
TERRY COUNTY, TX
YOAKUM COUNTY, TX
ANDREWS COUNTY, TX

US. FALLOUT ATLAS : COUNTY COMPARISIONS

INITIAL PATH OF TUMBLER-SNAPPER HOW (TS8)

Shot Tumbler-Snapper How resulted in the highest estimated thyroid doses of Iodine-131 of any shot during the test series (Gem County, ID, June, 1952). The fallout path first moves northeast and then, by day 10 settles in the Midwest.

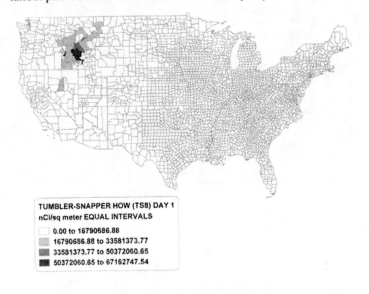

TUMBLER-SNAPPER HOW (TS8) DAY 1
nCi/sq meter EQUAL INTERVALS

☐ 0.00 to 16790686.88
▨ 16790686.88 to 33581373.77
▨ 33581373.77 to 50372060.65
■ 50372060.65 to 67162747.54

FALLOUT PATH: TUMBLER-SNAPPER HOW (TS8) DAY 1
5 JUNE, 1952

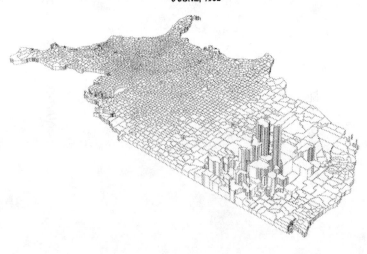

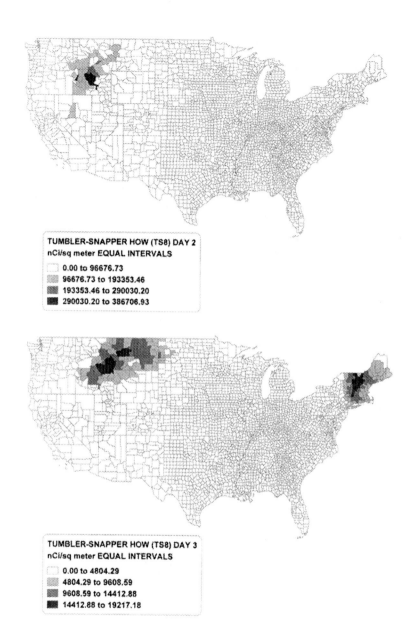

TUMBLER-SNAPPER HOW (TS8) DAY 2
nCi/sq meter EQUAL INTERVALS

- 0.00 to 96676.73
- 96676.73 to 193353.46
- 193353.46 to 290030.20
- 290030.20 to 386706.93

TUMBLER-SNAPPER HOW (TS8) DAY 3
nCi/sq meter EQUAL INTERVALS

- 0.00 to 4804.29
- 4804.29 to 9608.59
- 9608.59 to 14412.88
- 14412.88 to 19217.18

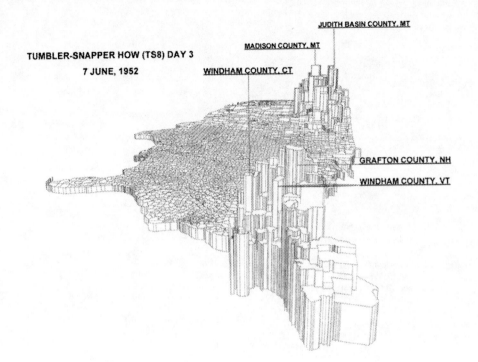

TUMBLER-SNAPPER HOW (TS8) DAY 3
7 JUNE, 1952

JUDITH BASIN COUNTY, MT

MADISON COUNTY, MT

WINDHAM COUNTY, CT

GRAFTON COUNTY, NH

WINDHAM COUNTY, VT

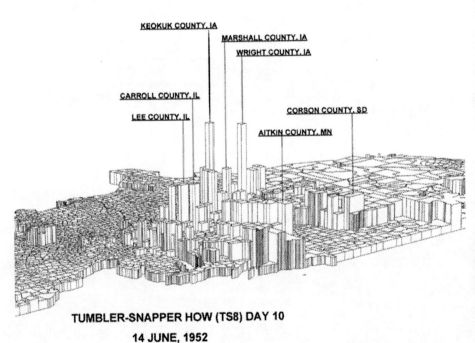

KEOKUK COUNTY, IA

MARSHALL COUNTY, IA

WRIGHT COUNTY, IA

CARROLL COUNTY, IL

CORSON COUNTY, SD

LEE COUNTY, IL

AITKIN COUNTY, MN

TUMBLER-SNAPPER HOW (TS8) DAY 10
14 JUNE, 1952

By ranking counties by fallout days, adding up the ranks one through ten, then reversing the ranks, one can determine counties which, overall, are associated with the lowest relative shot days and thus, the highest overall fallout activity.

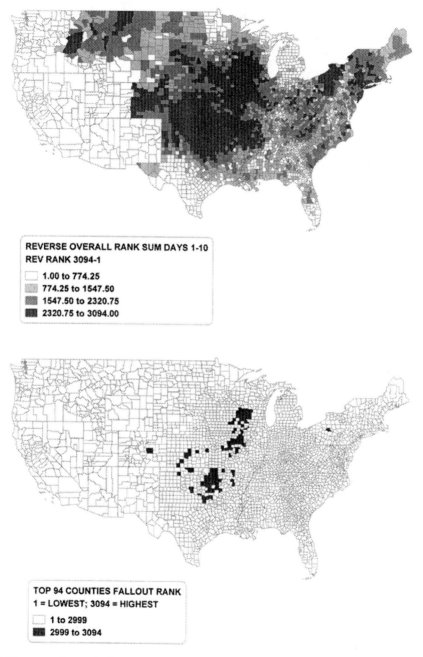

Using mapping techniques we can then isolate the top 94 counties in this group.

INDIVIDUAL FALLOUT EVENTS AND CANCER

Earlier volumes in the series included limited statistical investigations into possible associations between fallout and cancer. Volume I included statistical analysis of total fallout while Volume II included an examination of individual radionuclides and cancer.

Since this volume deals with individual fallout events, the "shot days," the statistical evaluation will concentrate on cancer rates in conjunction with these particular fallout events.

The first step in the evaluation involved comparing the pattern of deposition values for each day of fallout for every county in the United Sates with the latest National Cancer Institute county rate data (NCI 2000 Cancer Atlas) for the following cancers designations: All Cancers, Brain, Colon, Esophageal, Kidney, Leukemia, Liver, Lung, Oral, Non-Hodgkin's Lymphoma, Pancreatic, Rectal, Stomach, and Thyroid for the time periods 1950-69 and 1970-95 for both male and female, and Breast and Cervical for the same time periods for female.

Then, a data subset consisting of 513 Midwest counties were evaluated against male and female cancer rate data found in the NCI's 1983 Cancer Atlas for 1950-59, 60-69, 70-79; and the Centers for Disease Control's WONDER data set for the time period 1979-1995, 1996. All rates were age and population adjusted to 1970 as the standard year. Cancers in this group included: all cancers, brain, breast (female only), bone, eye cancer (male only) leukemia, lymphosarcoma (ICD 200.0-200.1) multiple myeloma, and uterine for 1950s, 60s, 70s and 79-95. An additional group of cancers were evaluated for the 1979-1995, 1996 time frame. They were: connective and soft tissue neoplasms (ICD 171.0), lymphosarcoma cell leukemia (ICD 207.8) nodular lymphoma (ICD 202.0), leukemic reticuloendotheliosis (ICD 202.4), and malignant histiocytosis (202.3). Except for connective and soft tissue neoplasms, this last group combined the incidence rates for male and female.

Spearman correlations were determined for each shot day with each of the above cancer parameters. In addition to the Spearman correlation, T-scores and probability levels were generated.

The second step in the evaluation involved simply summing the R values and associated T-Scores for each Cancer type as well as each shot day. Positive correlations result in positive rho values, and the lower the probability level, the higher the associated T-score. Thus, the third step in the process involved simply sorting the data to isolate sets of variables producing the highest r-values and T-scores. The Bonferroni correction resulted in "moving" the critical value for an α of 0.05 from 1.96 to approximately 4.0. Note that some pairwise comparisons resulted in T scores in excess of 6.0, which is normally associated with a p value of 1×10^{-9}.

A number of cancers were highly correlated with fallout days, and many were highly correlated with specific shot days. That data is presented in tables that follow. While a high Spearman correlation value between two variables does not prove causation, there is a strong indication that an association exists between certain cancers, such as female colon cancer 1979-1995 and individual fallout events taking place years before.

ERRATA

The initial (2001) edition of the County Comparisons Volume listed the NCI Atlas cancer rates as 1970-95. This is incorrect. The rates are from 1970 through 1994. Also, some Centers for Disease Control WONDER rates for the Midwest (MW) are listed for the years 1979-96. This is incorrect. These rates actually cover the years 1979-1995.

TABLE: SUM OF SPEARMAN R AND T SCORES FOR CANCER RATES AGAINST FALLOUT DAYS 1-10. FOR EACH ABOVEGROUND NUCLEAR TEST 1951-1962.

VARIABLE	SUM R	SUM T		VARIABLE	SUM R	SUM T
COLWF7	1.243325	71.0148		PROWM5	0.109446	6.1064
COLWM7	1.047388	59.423		BLWM50	0.076042	4.2497
COLWF5	0.99851	56.7407		LVWM5	0.074251	4.1375
COLWM5	0.749269	42.4553		ORAWM5	0.043044	2.3736
LNGWM7	0.483942	29.0376		ORAWM7	0.041536	2.2709
LEUWM7	0.51134	28.5404		BRNWF5	0.040297	2.2425
LEUWF5	0.507701	28.3262		ESOWF5	0.02117	1.0835
ALLWM7	0.452581	26.0962		ALL_WM5	-0.00195	-0.132
KIDWM7	0.459805	25.6381		OTHWM5	-0.00774	-0.3238
ALLWF5	0.440854	24.9174		CRVWF5	-0.00322	-0.4705
LEUWM5	0.4089	22.9048		OTHWF5	-0.06722	-3.7507
RECWM7	0.393994	22.1161		BLWF70	-0.07434	-4.2354
RECWF7	0.387549	21.676		LVWM7	-0.07725	-4.3006
RECWM5	0.383699	21.638		PANWM7	-0.0875	-4.8622
OVWF5	0.370618	20.8144		ORAWF5	-0.10463	-6.017
BSTWF5	0.366122	20.7374		ESOWM5	-0.10791	-6.0574
LVWF5	0.345738	19.4572		ALLWF7	-0.12357	-7.0667
RECWF5	0.34417	19.2902		ESOWM7	-0.19412	-10.9186
CRVWF7	0.33845	19.0084		STOWF5	-0.23448	-13.268
BRNWM7	0.338359	18.8806		PANWF5	-0.28259	-15.7433
KIDWM5	0.311686	17.5203		STOWM7	-0.30355	-17.0054
NHLWM7	0.306793	17.1014		LNGWM5	-0.30686	-17.2607
NHLWF5	0.287717	16.1066		STOWF7	-0.32675	-18.2247
BSTWF7	0.282404	15.8162		PROWM7	-0.36375	-20.3687
OVWF7	0.280757	15.7165		LNGWF5	-0.39582	-22.0925
NHLWM5	0.27587	15.4085		PANWM5	-0.40866	-22.7604
KIDWF7	0.26087	14.5852		OTHWM7	-0.42384	-24.1408
BLWF50	0.259423	14.4524		ORAWF7	-0.44257	-24.9513
BRNWM5	0.256575	14.2868		STOWM5	-0.43363	-24.9536
KIDWF5	0.232519	13.0123		PANWF7	-0.48858	-27.2697
NHLWF7	0.221355	12.3844		ESOWF7	-0.6262	-35.0416
LEUWF7	0.218051	12.1325		OTHWF7	-0.65485	-36.9286
BLWM7	0.182774	10.1627		LNGWF7	-0.70632	-40.1004
BRNWF7	0.162953	9.0698				
LVWF7	0.135749	7.5699				

COMPARISON OF MAXIMUM SPEARMAN CORRELATIONS BETWEEN FALLOUT DEPOSITION RATES AND CANCER RATES, USA (N:3094) AND MIDWEST (IA,IL,KS, MO,NE (N:513)

REGION	Pair	DATE	Variables	R	t(N-2)	p-level
MW	BJ_2_4	02-Nov-51	FTHYR5	0.21	4.74	0.000003
MW	BJ_2_4	02-Nov-51	MTHYR95	0.15	3.53	0.000457
USA	BJ_2_5	03-Nov-51	ESOWF5	0.16	8.97	0
MW	PB1_6	02-Jun-57	LNGWM7	0.63	18.50	0
MW	PB1_6	02-Jun-57	LNGWM5	0.40	9.78	0
USA	PB12_7	08-Sep-57	CRVWF5	0.35	20.94	0
MW	PB13_10	15-Sep-57	FSTO5	0.17	3.85	0.000133
MW	PB13_5	10-Sep-57	FBRAN7	0.13	3.03	0.002608
MW	PB13_7	12-Sep-57	FLEU7	0.15	3.32	0.000966
USA	PB15_2	17-Sep-57	STOWF5	0.21	11.76	0
USA	PB15_4	19-Sep-57	PROWM5	0.20	11.44	0
MW	PB15_6	21-Sep-57	FSTO6	0.17	3.89	0.000114
MW	PB15_7	22-Sep-57	B_MALHIS95	0.12	2.68	0.007573
USA	PB15_7	22-Sep-57	LVWF7	0.17	9.31	0
MW	PB15_8	23-Sep-57	BSTWF7	0.25	5.86	0
MW	PB16_3	25-Sep-57	FMM5	0.22	5.00	0.000001
MW	PB17_3	30-Sep-57	FKD95	0.16	3.73	0.000212
MW	PB17_8	05-Oct-57	MLS7	0.13	2.90	0.003866
MW	PB17_9	06-Oct-57	LEUWM5	0.17	3.86	0.000126
MW	PB18_10	16-Oct-57	BLR79_95	0.20	4.65	0.000004
MW	PB18_10	16-Oct-57	FLS5	0.19	4.38	0.000015
MW	PB18_10	16-Oct-57	MKD6	0.14	3.20	0.001443
MW	PB18_9	15-Oct-57	MBO95	0.26	6.03	0
MW	PB18_9	15-Oct-57	MBO6	0.20	4.64	0.000004
MW	PB18_9	15-Oct-57	MTHYR7	0.19	4.25	0.000025
MW	PB18_9	15-Oct-57	MKD7	0.12	2.69	0.007368
MW	PB2_8	25-Jun-57	MKD5	0.16	3.63	0.000314
MW	PB3_2	25-Jun-57	LEUWF5	0.12	2.69	0.00744
MW	PB4_3	07-Jul-57	UT95	0.23	5.29	0
MW	PB4_3	07-Jul-57	NHLWF5	0.21	4.83	0.000002
MW	PB4_3	07-Jul-57	FLS6	0.19	4.43	0.000012
MW	PB4_3	07-Jul-57	MBRAN95	0.18	4.22	0.000029
USA	PB4_3	07-Jul-57	COLWM5	0.36	21.38	0

REGION	Pair	DATE	Variables	R	t(N-2)	p-level
USA	PB4_4	08-Jul-57	COLWF7	0.37	22.36	0
MW	PB4_9	13-Jul-57	COLWM5	0.30	7.03	0
MW	PB4_9	13-Jul-57	COLWF5	0.29	6.83	0
MW	PB4_9	13-Jul-57	FCLN5	0.24	5.55	0
MW	PB5_6	20-Jul-57	FCONSAR95	0.12	2.61	0.009223
USA	PB5_6	20-Jul-57	KIDWM7	0.14	7.79	0
MW	PB5_7	21-Jul-57	FLEU5	0.14	3.12	0.001932
MW	PB5_8	22-Jul-57	MCONSAR95	0.15	3.46	0.000585
USA	PB5_8	22-Jul-57	OTHWM5	0.19	11.00	0
MW	PB5_9	23-Jul-57	FBRAN5	0.14	3.13	0.001833
MW	PB6_10	02-Aug-57	FKD7	0.16	3.69	0.000248
USA	PB6_10	02-Aug-57	BRNWF7	0.13	7.30	0
MW	PB6_8	31-Jul-57	NHLWM5	0.18	4.07	0.000054
MW	PB6_8	31-Jul-57	MLS5	0.16	3.74	0.000204
MW	PB8_2	19-Aug-57	MLEU7	0.18	4.14	0.000041
MW	PB8_6	23-Aug-57	FTHYR95	0.29	6.75	0
MW	PB8_6	23-Aug-57	MBO7	0.24	5.47	0
MW	PB8_6	23-Aug-57	FTHYR7	0.22	5.17	0
MW	PB8_6	23-Aug-57	FBO5	0.21	4.77	0.000002
MW	PB8_6	23-Aug-57	UT7	0.12	2.72	0.006833
USA	PB9_2	24-Aug-57	PANWM7	0.11	6.25	0
USA	PB9_5	27-Aug-57	LVWF5	0.28	16.50	0
MW	SE3	08-Jul-62	NHLWM7	0.17	3.91	0.000103
MW	TP10_4	08-May-55	FCLN95	0.46	11.73	0
MW	TP10_8	12-May-55	UT5	0.31	7.28	0
USA	TP10_8	12-May-55	CRVWF7	0.27	15.53	0
USA	TP10_9	13-May-55	ORAWF5	0.25	14.51	0
MW	TP11_6	20-May-55	MLS95	0.18	4.20	0.000031
MW	TP11_6	20-May-55	MKD95	0.17	3.86	0.00013
USA	TP3_4	04-Mar-55	COLWF5	0.38	23.18	0
USA	TP6_2	23-Mar-55	PANWM5	0.09	5.30	0
USA	TP6_4	25-Mar-55	OTHWM7	0.25	14.54	0
MW	TP7_4	01-Apr-55	FLEU95	0.12	2.72	0.006669

COMPARISON OF MAXIMUM SPEARMAN CORRELATIONS BETWEEN FALLOUT DEPOSITION RATES AND CANCER RATES, USA (N:3094) AND MIDWEST (IA,IL,KS, MO,NE (N:513)

REGION	Pair	DATE	Variables	R	t(N-2)	p-level
		COMPARISON OF MAXIMUM SPEARMAN CORRELATIONS BETWEEN FALLOUT DEPOSITION RATES AND CANCER RATES, USA (N:3094) AND MIDWEST (IA,IL,KS, MO,NE (N:513)				
MW	TP7_7	04-Apr-55	FBO95	0.26	6.02	0
MW	TP7_7	04-Apr-55	FBO7	0.22	5.04	0.000001
MW	TP7_7	04-Apr-55	FTHYR6	0.19	4.38	0.000015
MW	TP7_7	04-Apr-55	MTHYR6	0.18	4.12	0.000043
MW	TP8_5	13-Apr-55	FBO6	0.16	3.71	0.000232
MW	TP9_1	15-Apr-55	MBRAN7	0.14	3.29	0.001086
USA	TP9_1	15-Apr-55	LEUWM5	0.17	9.80	0
USA	TP9_2	15-Apr-55	LEUWF7	0.10	5.40	0
USA	TP9_3	16-Apr-55	PANWF5	0.09	4.77	0.000002
MW	TP9_9	22-Apr-55	FCLN6	0.22	5.09	0.000001
MW	TS1_3	03-Apr-52	UT6	0.16	3.55	0.000426
USA	TS1_4	04-Apr-52	LNGWF5	0.13	7.42	0
MW	TS3_5	26-Apr-52	MBRAN5	0.14	3.23	0.001311
MW	TS3_8	29-Apr-52	FLEU6	0.13	2.90	0.003924
MW	TS3_9	30-Apr-52	FKD5	0.12	2.81	0.005128
MW	TS4_4	04-May-52	LEUWF7	0.12	2.79	0.005505
MW	TS4_6	06-May-52	FMM95	0.19	4.30	0.000021
MW	TS4_6	06-May-52	MBRAN6	0.13	2.95	0.003279
USA	TS5_4	10-May-52	ORAWF7	0.19	10.67	0
MW	TS6_9	02-Jun-52	FBRST7	0.27	6.22	0
MW	TS7_4	04-Jun-52	FMM7	0.11	2.59	0.009764
USA	TS7_8	08-Jun-52	LVWM7	0.22	12.62	0
MW	TS8_10	14-Jun-52	FBRAN95	0.39	9.63	0
MW	TS8_10	14-Jun-52	COLWF7	0.35	8.53	0
MW	TS8_10	14-Jun-52	MCLN7	0.27	6.30	0
MW	TS8_10	14-Jun-52	FCLN7	0.24	5.54	0
MW	TS8_10	14-Jun-52	MTHYR5	0.19	4.43	0.000012
MW	TS8_10	14-Jun-52	MEYE95	0.11	2.56	0.010785
MW	TS8_2	06-Jun-52	MLEU6	0.12	2.65	0.008311
MW	TS8_3	07-Jun-52	MSTO5	0.30	7.00	0
MW	TS8_3	07-Jun-52	MSTO6	0.25	5.82	0
MW	TS8_3	07-Jun-52	FBRST95	0.19	4.39	0.000014
USA	TS8_3	07-Jun-52	RECWM5	0.40	24.49	0

COMPARISON OF MAXIMUM SPEARMAN CORRELATIONS BETWEEN FALLOUT DEPOSITION RATES AND CANCER RATES, USA (N:3094) AND MIDWEST (IA,IL,KS, MO,NE (N:513)

REGION	Pair	DATE	Variables	R	t(N-2)	p-level
MW	TS8_4	08-Jun-52	MLEU5	0.17	3.94	0.000094
USA	TS8_4	08-Jun-52	OVWF5	0.25	14.37	0
USA	TS8_5	09-Jun-52	COLWM7	0.34	19.88	0
MW	TS8_8	12-Jun-52	FBRST5	0.37	8.97	0
MW	TS8_8	12-Jun-52	BSTWF5	0.36	8.82	0
MW	TS8_8	12-Jun-52	MCLN5	0.25	5.88	0
MW	TS8_8	12-Jun-52	FBRST6	0.20	4.69	0.000003
MW	TS8_8	12-Jun-52	MEYE6	0.20	4.57	0.000006
MW	TS8_8	12-Jun-52	MSTO7	0.19	4.42	0.000012
MW	TS8_8	12-Jun-52	MSTO96	0.15	3.49	0.000522
MW	TS8_9	13-Jun-52	LEUWM7	0.15	3.40	0.000723
MW	UK1_4	20-Mar-53	MEYE5	0.21	4.83	0.000002
USA	UK1_4	20-Mar-53	BRNWM7	0.15	8.33	0
MW	UK1_6	22-Mar-53	BNODLYM95	0.21	4.85	0.000002
MW	UK10_2	26-May-53	MLS6	0.16	3.69	0.000253
MW	UK10_4	28-May-53	MLEU95	0.16	3.63	0.000311
MW	UK11_4	07-Jun-53	FLS7	0.26	6.12	0
MW	UK11_4	07-Jun-53	MMM6	0.24	5.57	0
MW	UK11_4	07-Jun-53	NHLWF7	0.19	4.43	0.000012
MW	UK11_4	07-Jun-53	FMM6	0.18	4.20	0.000031
MW	UK2_8	31-Mar-53	MEYE7	0.16	3.67	0.000267
MW	UK2_8	31-Mar-53	MBO5	0.12	2.81	0.005143
MW	UK4_4	09-Apr-53	MTHYM95	0.18	4.02	0.000067
USA	UK6_7	24-Apr-53	BRNWM5	0.09	5.30	0
USA	UK6_8	25-Apr-53	OTHWF5	0.14	8.02	0
MW	UK7_2	26-Apr-53	COLWM7	0.27	6.32	0
MW	UK7_2	26-Apr-53	MCLN6	0.25	5.92	0
USA	UK7_4	28-Apr-53	LEUWM7	0.14	8.08	0
MW	UK7_5	29-Apr-53	FLS95	0.31	7.47	0
MW	UK7_5	29-Apr-53	MCLN95	0.28	6.47	0
MW	UK7_5	29-Apr-53	MMM5	0.23	5.24	0
MW	UK7_5	29-Apr-53	MMM7	0.19	4.43	0.000012
MW	UK7_5	29-Apr-53	FKD6	0.16	3.72	0.000223

COMPARISON OF MAXIMUM SPEARMAN CORRELATIONS BETWEEN FALLOUT DEPOSITION RATES AND CANCER RATES, USA (N:3094) AND MIDWEST (IA,IL,KS, MO,NE (N:513)

REGION	Pair	DATE	Variables	R	t(N-2)	p-level
MW	UK7_5	29-Apr-53	FBRAN6	0.12	2.77	0.005748
MW	UK7_7	01-May-53	LNGWF7	0.46	11.73	0
MW	UK7_7	01-May-53	FTHYM95	0.20	4.51	0.000008
MW	UK8_2	09-May-53	FSTO7	0.14	3.13	0.001825
USA	UK8_5	12-May-53	LVWM5	0.19	10.69	0
MW	UK9_2	20-May-53	MMM9	0.22	5.03	0.000001
MW	UK9_5	23-May-53	FSTO95	0.18	4.14	0.000041

TOP 120 SHOT DAYS: SUMS OF SPEARMAN R AND T RANKED IN ORDER OF HIGHEST ASSOCIATION WITH SELECTED CANCER RATES (NCI CANCER ATLAS 2000)
3094 COUNTIES
120 OUT OF 429 SHOT DAYS
1951-1962

RANK	SHOTDAY	SUM R	SUM T	MAX R	MAX T
1	TS8_3	6.18	14.18	0.40	24.49
2	UK7_6	5.98	5.57	0.34	20.23
3	PB15_7	5.88	6.37	0.32	19.01
4	R1_2	5.82	6.02	0.32	18.50
5	PB11_5	5.29	3.18	0.31	18.04
6	TP9_4	5.22	6.54	0.32	18.79
7	TP9_3	5.14	12.02	0.38	22.75
8	TP11_10	5.07	9.14	0.25	14.42
9	TS8_5	4.88	-0.27	0.35	20.73
10	BJ4_8	4.78	5.95	0.26	14.99
11	UK7_7	4.77	-0.22	0.30	17.42
12	TP4_4	4.65	0.32	0.36	21.19
13	R1_3	4.52	4.10	0.23	13.37
14	UK6_8	4.50	2.48	0.29	17.10
15	PB12_9	4.49	3.45	0.28	16.37
16	TS5_8	4.44	8.17	0.32	18.56
17	UK5_6	4.35	6.82	0.18	10.13
18	TS5_5	4.28	8.04	0.23	13.10
19	PB4_4	4.23	-2.18	0.37	22.36
20	UK5_5	4.21	1.40	0.31	17.95
21	TS6_9	4.17	2.39	0.22	12.76
22	UK1_10	4.15	5.59	0.17	9.62
23	PB5_6	4.06	4.63	0.27	15.61
24	PB4_3	4.05	6.56	0.38	22.82
25	BJ_2_5	4.05	-1.00	0.25	14.47
26	BJ4_9	3.98	5.05	0.22	12.43
27	BJ3_9	3.88	5.33	0.22	12.81
28	PB16_4	3.81	6.70	0.24	13.92
29	PB2_6	3.79	0.97	0.27	15.34
30	UK4_7	3.74	6.05	0.16	9.15
31	TS1_4	3.69	-0.76	0.29	17.09

TOP 120 SHOT DAYS: SUMS OF SPEARMAN R AND T RANKED IN ORDER OF HIGHEST ASSOCIATION WITH SELECTED CANCER RATES (NCI CANCER ATLAS 2000)
3094 COUNTIES
120 OUT OF 429 SHOT DAYS
1951-1962

RANK	SHOTDAY	SUM R	SUM T	MAX R	MAX T
32	TP9_7	3.66	3.44	0.20	11.42
33	PB12_10	3.58	0.70	0.17	9.70
34	UK2_5	3.47	3.07	0.16	9.16
35	TP11_8	3.45	6.31	0.19	10.92
36	UK4_4	3.44	5.31	0.18	10.36
37	TP11_9	3.43	6.27	0.19	10.90
38	TS6_8	3.42	2.23	0.18	10.18
39	TP8_7	3.38	2.07	0.16	9.10
40	UK10_6	3.38	1.67	0.20	11.46
41	TP5_5	3.37	-1.46	0.27	15.82
42	TP3_4	3.33	-4.38	0.38	23.18
43	PB16_3	3.29	3.87	0.23	12.84
44	TP5_4	3.27	0.09	0.21	11.78
45	UK7_2	3.22	5.46	0.23	13.34
46	TP5_10	3.18	3.27	0.15	8.54
47	TP4_3	3.14	-2.81	0.24	13.62
48	BJ3_10	3.09	2.74	0.17	9.52
49	TP9_2	3.08	1.02	0.29	16.57
50	UK4_6	3.08	-0.03	0.21	12.06
51	BJ_2_4	3.06	2.59	0.27	15.45
52	TP9_10	3.05	3.61	0.20	11.12
53	UK2_9	3.04	3.97	0.17	9.77
54	PB2_7	2.95	2.80	0.17	9.78
55	TS8_4	2.93	5.99	0.37	22.30
56	PB9_5	2.91	2.79	0.31	17.87
57	UK4_2	2.80	3.54	0.18	10.11
58	PB16_10	2.79	1.71	0.18	10.06
59	TP3_5	2.79	-0.20	0.26	15.16
60	UK5_7	2.76	-0.84	0.23	13.24
61	BJ3_7	2.76	3.69	0.18	10.03
62	TP3_3	2.71	-1.59	0.34	19.80

TOP 120 SHOT DAYS: SUMS OF SPEARMAN R AND T RANKED IN ORDER OF HIGHEST ASSOCIATION WITH SELECTED CANCER RATES (NCI CANCER ATLAS 2000)
3094 COUNTIES
120 OUT OF 429 SHOT DAYS
1951-1962

RANK	SHOTDAY	SUM R	SUM T	MAX R	MAX T
63	PB16_9	2.71	4.98	0.14	7.87
64	UK7_8	2.71	-1.94	0.18	10.29
65	PB11_6	2.68	1.02	0.20	11.62
66	BJ4_7	2.66	2.88	0.18	10.39
67	UK4_3	2.63	0.84	0.18	10.11
68	R2_6	2.60	2.83	0.12	6.65
69	UK2_6	2.60	-0.73	0.16	8.98
70	PB6_7	2.59	4.25	0.19	11.05
71	PB11_4	2.57	5.15	0.22	12.36
72	TS3_10	2.57	0.38	0.22	12.68
73	TP8_8	2.57	1.44	0.11	6.30
74	PB2_9	2.56	3.80	0.16	9.01
75	UK11_4	2.47	1.84	0.26	14.72
76	PB2_8	2.44	2.34	0.19	10.84
77	TS8_7	2.40	5.25	0.24	13.62
78	TS6_10	2.36	1.83	0.13	7.11
79	PB17_9	2.34	5.60	0.21	11.70
80	TP9_5	2.32	1.97	0.25	14.43
81	BJ4_10	2.31	5.03	0.15	8.23
82	PB3_5	2.29	-5.22	0.26	14.83
83	UK6_7	2.24	3.29	0.14	8.12
84	PB11_3	2.22	5.91	0.19	10.93
85	TS3_9	2.19	3.82	0.26	14.80
86	UK8_5	2.17	1.14	0.25	14.22
87	PB18_9	2.14	1.36	0.21	12.05
88	PB15_8	2.12	1.30	0.17	9.34
89	BJ_2_6	2.12	-2.51	0.21	12.12
90	SE3	2.10	-0.81	0.27	15.63
91	R1_4	2.05	2.17	0.10	5.56
92	UK5_9	2.03	3.77	0.09	4.90
93	TS7_5	2.01	2.73	0.26	14.69

TOP 120 SHOT DAYS: SUMS OF SPEARMAN R AND T RANKED IN ORDER OF HIGHEST ASSOCIATION WITH SELECTED CANCER RATES (NCI CANCER ATLAS 2000)
3094 COUNTIES
120 OUT OF 429 SHOT DAYS
1951-1962

RANK	SHOTDAY	SUM R	SUM T	MAX R	MAX T
94	PB5_8	1.99	0.33	0.28	16.28
95	UK1_5	1.98	-3.49	0.26	14.77
96	BJ3_8	1.97	1.66	0.13	7.26
97	TS1_5	1.96	-0.70	0.17	9.72
98	PB15_6	1.94	6.62	0.24	13.59
99	TP4_6	1.93	0.99	0.14	7.94
100	TP3_6	1.89	-1.42	0.22	12.62
101	PB16_2	1.88	3.64	0.19	11.04
102	TS8_8	1.86	-0.15	0.16	9.01
103	PB4_9	1.78	1.25	0.24	13.58
104	TP7_8	1.72	-4.57	0.35	20.84
105	TP8_6	1.67	0.14	0.13	7.17
106	TP6_5	1.66	0.66	0.22	12.29
107	PB1_10	1.65	2.07	0.18	9.96
108	UK2_8	1.64	-1.74	0.18	10.20
109	TS7_6	1.61	-4.70	0.17	9.53
110	UK9_3	1.60	-4.70	0.26	15.26
111	BJ4_6	1.60	0.15	0.16	9.13
112	PB2_10	1.60	3.15	0.16	8.75
113	PB13_7	1.58	-7.99	0.38	22.82
114	UK11_5	1.57	2.44	0.14	7.96
115	BJ_2_3	1.54	-5.50	0.45	27.93
116	PB12_7	1.54	-7.54	0.50	32.00
117	SE4	1.52	2.38	0.19	10.80
118	TS6_7	1.49	2.95	0.19	10.98
119	TS4_4	1.46	3.53	0.15	8.55
120	UK9_7	1.46	-8.91	0.36	21.26

INTERNATIONAL CLASSIFICATION OF DISEASES CODES USED IN U.S. ATLAS OF NUCLEAR FALLOUT 1951-1962 (TABLE I)

ABBREV	VARIABLE	GENDER	DATES	ICD	ICD PUBLICATION NUMBER
ALLWM5	All Cancer	WM	1950-69	140.0-205, 207	6,7,8
ALLWF5	All Cancers	WF	1950-69	140.0-208.0	6,7,8
ALLWF7	All Cancers	WF	1970-94	140.0-208.0	8,9
ALLWM7	All Cancers	WM	1970-94	140.0-208.0	8,9
BLCL95	Lymphosarcoma Cell Leukemia	WF	1979-95	207.8-207.8	9
BLWF50	Bladder Cancer	WF	1950-69	181	6,7,8
BLWF70	Bladder Cancer	WF	1970-94	188, 189.3-189.9	8,9
BLWM50	Bladder Cancer	WM	1950-69	181	6,7,8
BLWM70	Bladder Cancer	WM	1970-94	188, 189.3-189.9	8,9
BMHST95	Malignant Histiocytosis	WF	1979-95	202.3-202.3	9
BNOD95	Nodular Lymphoma	WF	1979-95	202.0-202.0	9
BOTHLR95	Leukemic Reticuloendotheliosis	WF	1979-95	202.4-202.4	9
BRNWF5	Brain Cancer	WF	1950-69	193	6,7,8
BRNWF7	Brain Cancer	WF	1970-94	191, 192	8,9
BRNWM5	Brain Cancer	WM	1950-69	191, 192	6,7,8
BRNWM7	Brain Cancer	WM	1970-94	191.0-191.9	8,9
BSTWF5	Breast Cancer	WF	1950-69	170	6,7,8
BSTWF7	Breast Cancer	WF	1970-94	174, 175	8,9
COLWF5	Colon Cancer	WF	1950-69	153.0-153.9	6,7,8

INTERNATIONAL CLASSIFICATION OF DISEASES CODES USED IN U.S. ATLAS OF NUCLEAR FALLOUT 1951-1962 (TABLE I)

ABBREV	VARIABLE	GENDER	DATES	ICD	ICD PUBLICATION NUMBER
COLWF7	Colon Cancer	WF	1970-94	153, 159.0	8,9
COLWM5	Colon Cancer	WM	1950-69	153.0-153.9	6,7,8
COLWM7	Colon Cancer	WM	1970-94	153, 159.0	8,9
CONGEN	Congenital Anomalies	WF, WM	1979-95	740.0-759.9	9
CRVWF5	Cervical Cancer	WF	1950-69	180.0-180.9	6,7,8
CRVWF7	Cervical Cancer	WF	1970-94	180.0-180.9	8,9
ESOWF5	Cancer of Esophagus	WF	1950-69	150.0-150.9	6,7,8
ESOWF7	Cancer of Esophagus	WF	1970-94	150.0-150.9	8,9
ESOWM5	Cancer of Esophagus	WM	1950-69	150.0-150.9	6,7,8
ESOWM7	Cancer of Esophagus	WM	1970-94	150.0-150.9	8,9
FALL5	All Cancer	WF	1950-59	140.0-205.0	6,7
FALL60	All Cancer	WF	1960-69	140.0-205, 207	6,7,8
FALL70	All Cancer	WF	1970-79	140.0-208.0	8,9
FALL95	All Cancers	WF	1979-95	140.0-208.0	9
FBONE50	Bone Cancer	WF	1950-59	170.0-170.9	6,7
FBONE60	Bone Cancer	WF	1960-69	170.0-170.9	7,8
FBONE70	Bone Cancer	WF	1970-79	170.0-170.9	8,9
FBONE95	Bone Cancer	WF	1979-95	170.0-170.9	9
FBRAIN50	Brain Cancer	WF	1950-59	191.0-191.9	6,7
FBRAIN60	Brain Cancer	WF	1960-69	191.0-191.9	7,8

U.S. FALLOUT ATLAS : COUNTY COMPARISONS

INTERNATIONAL CLASSIFICATION OF DISEASES CODES USED IN U.S. ATLAS OF NUCLEAR FALLOUT 1951-1962 (TABLE I)

ABBREV	VARIABLE	GENDER	DATES	ICD	ICD PUBLICATION NUMBER
FBRAIN70	Brain Cancer	WF	1970-79	191.0-191.9	8,9
FBRAIN95	Brain Cancer	WF	1979-95	191.0-191.9	9
FBRST50	Breast Cancer	WF	1950-59	174	6,7
FBRST60	Breast Cancer	WF	1960-69	174.0-174.9	7,8
FBRST70	Breast Cancer	WF	1970-79	174.0-174.9	8,9
FBRST95	Breast Cancer	WF	1979-95	174.0-174.9	9
FCLN50	Colon Cancer	WF	1950-59	153.0-153.9	6,7
FCLN60	Colon Cancer	WF	1960-69	153.0-153.9	7,8
FCLN70	Colon Cancer	WF	1970-79	153.0-153.9	8,9
FCLN95	Colon Cancer	WF	1979-95	153, 159.0	9
FCONSAR9	Connective and Soft Tissue Neoplasms	WF	1979-95	171.0-171.0	9
FKDNY50	Kidney Cancer	WF	1950-59	180	6,7
FKDNY60	Kidney Cancer	WF	1960-69	189.0-189.1	7,8
FKDNY70	Kidney Cancer	WF	1970-79	189.0-189.1	8,9
FKDNY95	Kidney Cancer	WF	1979-95	189.0-189.1	9
FLEUK50	Leukemia	WF	1950-59	204.0-208.9	6,7
FLEUK60	Leukemia	WF	1960-69	204.0-208.9	7,8
FLEUK70	Leukemia	WF	1970-79	204.0-208.9	8,9
FLEUK95	Leukemia	WF	1979-95	204.0-208.9	9
FLS50	Lymphosarcoma	WF	1950-59	200.0-200.1	6,7

U.S. FALLOUT ATLAS : COUNTY COMPARISONS

INTERNATIONAL CLASSIFICATION OF DISEASES CODES USED IN U.S. ATLAS OF NUCLEAR FALLOUT 1951-1962 (TABLE I)

ABBREV	VARIABLE	GENDER	DATES	ICD	ICD PUBLICATION NUMBER
FLS60	Lymphosarcoma	WF	1960-69	200.0-200.1	7,8
FLS70	Lymphosarsoma	WF	1970-79	200.0-200.1	8,9
FLS95	Lymphosarsoma	WF	1979-95	200.0-200.1	9
FMM50	Multiple Myeloma	WF	1950-59	203.0-203.9	6,7
FMM60	Multiple Myeloma	WF	1960-69	203.0-203.9	7,8
FMM70	Multiple Myeloma	WF	1970-79	203.0-203.9	8,9
FMM95	Multiple Myeloma	WF	1979-95	203.0-203.9	9
FPAN95	Pancreatic Cancer	WF	1979-95	157.0-157.9	9
FSTOM50	Stomach Cancer	WF	1950-59	151.0-151.9	6,7
FSTOM60	Stomach Cancer	WF	1960-69	151.0-151.9	7,8
FSTOM70	Stomach Cancer	WF	1970-79	151.0-151.9	8,9
FSTOM95	Stomach Cancer	WF	1979-95	151.0-151.9	9
FTHYM95	Thymus Cancer	WF	1979-95	164.0-164.0	9
FTHYR50	Thyroid Cancer	WF	1950-59	193.0-193.9	6,7
FTHYR60	Thyroid Cancer	WF	1960-69	193.0-193.9	7,8
FTHYR70	Thyroid Cancer	WF	1970-79	193.0-193.9	8,9
FTHYR95	Thyroid Cancer	WF	1979-95	193.0-193.9	9
KIDWF5	Kidney Cancer	WF	1950-69	189.0-189.1	6,7,8
KIDWF7	Kidney Cancer	WF	1970-94	189.0-189.2	8,9
KIDWM5	Kidney Cancer	WM	1950-69	189.0-189.1	6,7,8

U.S. FALLOUT ATLAS : COUNTY COMPARISONS

INTERNATIONAL CLASSIFICATION OF DISEASES CODES USED IN U.S. ATLAS OF NUCLEAR FALLOUT 1951-1962 (TABLE I)

ABBREV	VARIABLE	GENDER	DATES	ICD	ICD PUBLICATION NUMBER
KIDWM7	Kidney Cancer	WM	1970-94	189.0-189.1	8,9
LEUWF5	Leukemia	WF	1950-69	204.0-208.9	6,7,8
LEUWF7	Leukemia	WF	1970-94	204.0-208.9	8,9
LEUWF7	Leukemia	WF	1970-94	204.0-208.9	8,9
LEUWM7	Leukemia	WM	1970-94	204.0-208.9	8,9
LNGWF5	Lung Cancer	WF	1950-69	162.0-162.9	6,7,8
LNGWF7	Lung Cancer	WF	1970-94	162.0-162.9	8,9
LNGWM5	Lung Cancer	WM	1950-69	162, 163	6,7,8
LNGWM7	Lung Cancer	WM	1970-94	162, 163	8,9
LVWF5	Liver Cancer	WF	1950-69	155.0-1, 197.8	6,7,8
LVWF7	Liver Cancer	WF	1970-94	155.0-1, 155.2	8,9
LVWM5	Liver Cancer	WM	1950-69	155.0-1, 197.8	6,7,8
LVWM7	Liver Cancer	WM	1970-94	155.0-1, 155.2	8,9
MALL50	All Cancer	WM	1950-59	140.0-205.0	6,7
MALL60	All Cancers	WM	1960-69	140.0-208.0	7,8
MALL70	All Cancer	WM	1970-79	140.0-208.0	8,9
MALL95	All Cancers	WM	1979-95	140.0-208.0	9
MBONE50	Bone Cancer	WM	1950-59	170.0-170.9	6,7
MBONE60	Bone Cancer	WM	1960-69	170.0-170.9	7,8
MBONE70	Bone Cancer	WM	1970-79	170.0-170.9	8,9

U.S. FALLOUT ATLAS : COUNTY COMPARISONS

INTERNATIONAL CLASSIFICATION OF DISEASES CODES USED IN U.S. ATLAS OF NUCLEAR FALLOUT 1951-1962 (TABLE I)

ABBREV	VARIABLE	GENDER	DATES	ICD	ICD PUBLICATION NUMBER
MBONE95	Bone Cancer	WM	1979-95	170.0-170.9	9
MBRAIN50	Brain Cancer	WM	1950-59	193	6,7
MBRAIN60	Brain Cancer	WM	1960-69	191.0-191.9	7,8
MBRAIN70	Brain Cancer	WM	1970-79	191.0-191.9	8,9
MBRAIN95	Brain Cancer	WM	1979-95	191.0-191.9	9
MCLN50	Colon Cancer	WM	1950-59	153.0-153.9	6,7
MCLN60	Colon Cancer	WM	1960-69	153.0-153.9	7,8
MCLN70	Colon Cancer	WM	1970-79	153.0-153.9	8,9
MCLN95	Colon Cancer	WM	1979-95	153.0-153.9	9
MCONSAR9	Connective and Soft Tissue Neoplasms	WM	1979-95	171.0-171.0	9
MEYE50	Eye Cancer	WM	1950-59	190.0-190.9	6,7
MEYE60	Eye Cancer	WM	1960-69	190.0-190.9	7,8
MEYE70	Eye Cancer	WM	1970-79	190.0-190.9	8,9
MEYE95	Eye Cancer	WM	1979-95	190.0-190.9	9
MKDNY50	Kidney Cancer	WM	1950-59	189.0-189.1	6,7
MKDNY60	Kidney Cancer	WM	1960-69	189.0-189.1	7,8
MKDNY70	Kidney Cancer	WM	1970-79	189.0-189.1	8,9
MKDNY95	Kidney Cancer	WM	1979-95	189.0-189.1	9
MLEUK50	Leukemia	WM	1950-59	204.0-208.9	6,7
MLEUK60	Leukemia	WM	1960-69	204.0-208.9	7,8

INTERNATIONAL CLASSIFICATION OF DISEASES CODES USED IN U.S. ATLAS OF NUCLEAR FALLOUT 1951-1962 (TABLE I)

ABBREV	VARIABLE	GENDER	DATES	ICD	ICD PUBLICATION NUMBER
MLEUK70	Leukemia	WM	1970-79	204.0-208.9	8,9
MLEUK95	Leukemia	WM	1979-95	204.0-208.9	9
MLIV95	Liver Cancer	WM	1979-95	155.0-155.1	9
MLS50	Lymphosarcoma	WM	1950-59	200.0-200.1	6,7
MLS60	Lymphosarcoma	WM	1960-69	200.0-200.1	7,8
MLS70	Lymphosarcoma	WM	1970-79	200.0-200.1	8,9
MLS95	Lymphosarcoma	WM	1979-95	200.0-200.1	9
MMM50	Multiple Myeloma	WM	1950-59	203.0-203.9	6,7
MMM60	Multiple Myeloma	WM	1960-69	203.0-203.9	7,8
MMM70	Multiple Myeloma	WM	1970-79	203.0-203.9	8,9
MMM95	Multiple Myeloma	WM	1979-95	203.0-203.9	9
MPAN95	Pancreatic Cancer	WM	1979-95	157.0-157.9	9
MSTOM50	Stomach Cancer	WM	1950-69	151.0-151.9	6,7,8
MSTOM60	Stomach Cancer	WM	1960-69	151.0-151.9	7,8
MSTOM70	Stomach Cancer	WM	1970-79	151.0-151.9	8,9
MSTOM95	Stomach Cancer	WM	1979-95	151.0-151.9	9
MTHYM95	Thymus,	WM	1979-95	164.0-164.0	9
MTHYR50	Thyroid Cancer	WM	1950-69	193.0-193.9	6,7,8
MTHYR60	Thyroid Cancer	WM	1960-69	193.0-193.9	7,8
MTHYR70	Thyroid Cancer	WM	1970-79	193.0-193.9	8,9

U.S. FALLOUT ATLAS : COUNTY COMPARISONS

INTERNATIONAL CLASSIFICATION OF DISEASES CODES USED IN U.S. ATLAS OF NUCLEAR FALLOUT 1951-1962 (TABLE I)

ABBREV	VARIABLE	GENDER	DATES	ICD	ICD PUBLICATION NUMBER
MTHYR95	Thyroid Cancer	WM	1979-95	193.0-193.9	9
NHLWF5	Non-Hodgkins Lymphoma	WF	1950-69	200, 202, 205	6,7,8
NHLWF7	Non-Hodgkins Lymphoma	WF	1970-94	200, 205	8,9
NHLWM5	NonHodgkins Lymphoma	WM	1950-69	200, 202, 205	6,7,8
NHLWM7	Non-Hodgkin's Lymphoma	WM	1970-94	200, 205	8,9
ORAWF5	Oral Cancer	WF	1950-69	141, 143-5, 147-8	6,7,8
ORAWF7	Oral Cancer	WF	1970-94	141, 143-6, 148-9	8,9
ORAWM5	Oral Cancer	WM	1950-69	141, 143-5, 147-8	6,7,8
ORAWM7	Oral Cancer	WM	1970-94	141, 143-6, 148-9	8,9
OTHWF5	Other and Unspecified Cancer	WF	1950-69	152, 156.2, 158-9, 164, 165, 176, 79, 198-9	6,7,8
OTHWF7	Other and Unspecified Cancer	WF	1970-94	152, 158, 159.2-9, 164.2-.9, 165, 184.8-.9, 187.5-.9, 195-9	8,9
OTHWM5	Other and Nonspecified Cancers	WM	1950-69	199.0-199.1	6,7,8
OTHWM7	Other and Nonspecified Cancers	WM	1970-94	199.0-199.1	8,9
OVWF5	Ovarian Cancer	WF	1950-69	183.0-183.9	6,7,8
OVWF7	Ovarian Cancer	WF	1970-94	183.0-183.9	8,9
PANWF5	Pancreatic Cancer	WF	1950-69	157.0-157.9	6,7,8

INTERNATIONAL CLASSIFICATION OF DISEASES CODES USED IN U.S. ATLAS OF NUCLEAR FALLOUT 1951-1962 (TABLE I)

ABBREV	VARIABLE	GENDER	DATES	ICD	ICD PUBLICATION NUMBER
PANWF7	Pancreatic Cancer	WF	1970-94	157.0-157.9	8,9
PANWM5	Pancreatic Cancer	WM	1950-69	157.0-157.9	6,7,8
PANWM7	Pancreatic Cancer	WM	1970-94	157.0-157.9	8,9
PROWM5	Prostate Cancer	WM	1950-69	177, 185	6,7,8
PROWM7	Prostate Cancer	WM	1970-94	185	9
RECWF5	Cancer of Rectum	WF	1950-69	154.0-154.9	6,7,8
RECWF7	Cancer of Rectum	WF	1970-94	154.0-154.9	8,9
RECWM5	Cancer of Rectum	WM	1950-69	154.0-154.9	6,7,8
RECWM7	Cancer of Rectum	WM	1970-94	154.0-154.9	8,9
STOWF5	Stomach Cancer	WF	1950-69	151.0-151.9	6,7,8
STOWF7	Stomach Cancer	WF	1970-94	151.0-151.9	8,9
STOWM5	Stomach Cancer	WM	1950-69	151.0-151.9	6,7,8
STOWM7	Stomach Cancer	WM	1970-94	151.0-151.9	8,9
UT50	Uterine Cancer	WF	1950-59	182.0-182.0	6,7
UT60	Uterine Cancer	WF	1960-69	182.0-182.0	7,8
UT70	Uterine Cancer	WF	1970-79	182.0-182.0	8,9
UT95	Uterine Cancer	WF	1979-95	182.0-182.0	9
WFLIV95	Liver Cancer	WF	1979-95	155.0-155.1	9

ABOUT THE AUTHOR

Richard L. Miller is an industrial health specialist with field experience in onsite coordination of more than 500 safety and health investigations primarily in petrochemical and energy-related industries.. His major areas of focus have included retrospective event and exposure reconstruction, and event cluster evaluation In 1979 Miller directed epidemiological field investigations on the relationship between rare brain cancers and chemical workplace exposures, and for this work received an OSHA Special Incentive Award and letter of commendation from the director of NIOSH for "findings of national impact and importance."

Miller has testified as an expert in federal cases involving toxic exposure and has performed onsite risk evaluations of industrial sites in such diverse places as Mexico, Soviet Latvia, Estonia, the Russian Federation (Tataria) and the Arabian Gulf. He has also performed extensive research on the nuclear test program and is the author of the 1986 book *Under The Cloud: the Decades of Nuclear Testing*, chosen by the *Library Journal* as one of the top science-technical books of 1986. Miller is a member of the American Statistical Association and is currently completing a technical book on calculating industrial exposures.

CPSIA information can be obtained at www.ICGtesting.com
Printed in the USA
LVOW080606200412

278403LV00001B/284/A